Studies in the Scriptures 1923-24

Volume 2 of 17 Volume Set

Studies in the Scriptures 1923 -24

Volume 2
of
17 Volume Set

Arthur W. Pink

Sovereign Grace Publishers, Inc.
P.O. Box 4998
Lafayette, IN 47903
2001

A. W. Pink's Studies in the Scriptures, Volume 2 - 1923 - 1924
Paperback Edition

Volume 2 = ISBN 1-58960-231-5

Printed In the United States of America
By Lightning Source, Inc.

Studies in the Scriptures -- 1924
Index

Studies In The Scriptures -- 1925
Index

VOL. III. JANUARY, 1924 NO. 1

STUDIES in the SCRIPTURES

"Search the Scriptures" John 5:39.

A PERIODICAL (MONTHLY "IF THE LORD WILL") DEVOTED TO BIBLE STUDIES and EXPOSITIONS

Arthur W. Pink, Publisher & Editor,
1128 South 47th. St., Philadelphia, Pa.

Price: 10 cents per copy; $1.00 per year. Foreign $1.00 per year.

My dear Friends:

A happy new year to you all. A happy year, like a happy day or a happy hour, can only come by being in fellowship with God. Material things cannot minister to the soul. Circumstances and surroundings may furnish ease and pleasure to the flesh, but they cannot give peace and satisfaction to the heart. Only in the presence of the Lord is there fulness of joy. There are some of our readers whose present circumstances are trying and painful and whose surroundings are uncongenial. But thank God it is possible, by grace, to rise above them. Paul and Silas sang songs even in the Philippian gaol. The light of God's countenance may be enjoyed even in a prison dungeon!

The greatest need of each of us is to maintain daily communion with God. For this we have to frequent the Throne of Grace, for there and there only, can we find that grace and mercy to help in time of need. Form the habit of making God your Confidant. He is not unmindful of your trials, but He delights to be inquired of. Cast *all* your care upon Him, for He careth for you. He may not remove the trial, but He is ready to impart spiritual strength which will enable you to endure it. He may not smooth the rugged road, but He is able to sustain you in it. Yea, what is more blessed, He *accompanies* you along it—"My presence shall go with thee" (Ex. 33:14) is His promise. Ask Him to *manifest* His presence. Ask Him to make you *conscious* that He is *with* you.

Fellowship with God can be maintained only as we make His written Word the subject of our daily study and meditation. It is in the Sanctuary of the Scriptures that the voice of God is to be heard. It is from the promises and precepts of the Holy Bible that consolation is to be drawn. Said the Psalmist, "This is my comfort in my affliction, *for* Thy Word hath quickened me." (Ps. 119:50). Faith is strengthened, fears are removed, joy is increased, as we feed upon the Bread of life. Let this new year mark a new era, when we shall give the Bible a larger place in our daily lives.

This issue commences the third year in the life of "Studies in the Scriptures", and this year the whole burden of editing and publishing will fall upon the writer. How thankful we are for that precious promise, "Cast thy burden upon the Lord, and He shall sustain thee" (Ps. 55:22). Mr. Herendeen has resigned from the co-editorship. Will subscribers therefore please address all communications direct to me at my new address. I need your intercessions more than ever now, that our Father will supply every need and use this magazine to His own glory and the blessing of His dear people. Counting on your prayerful support, I am, by grace.

Your brother in Christ,

Arthur W. Pink.

IMPORTANT NOTICES

All new subscriptions will be dated back to January, 1924.

Set of twelve issues for **1922,** unbound, **$1.00.** Bound, **$1.50.**

Set of twelve issues for **1923,** unbound, **$1.00.** Bound **$1.50.**

Note: We cannot break a set or now supply any **single** 1923 issues.

Subscription Price: **$1.00** per year to any address in the world. Single copies **10 cents.**

Change of Address: Please notify me promptly of any change of address, and be certain to give both old and new addresses.

Non-Subscribers receiving this Magazine regularly will understand their subscription has been entered by a friend.

Copies lost in the mail duplicated only if we are notified promptly.

Entered as second-class matter December 15th, 1923, at the post office at Philadelphia, Pa., under Act of March 3rd, 1879.

CONTENTS

JOHN'S GOSPEL

25. CHRIST AND THE FEAST OF TABERNACLES: John 7:1-13.

Below we give a rough Analysis of the passage which is to be before us:—

1. Jesus walking in Galilee: v. 1.
2. Time: immediately before the Feast of Tabernacles: v. 2.
3. The request of Christ's brethren: vv. 3-5.
4. Christ's reply to them: vv. 6-8.
5. Christ still in Galilee: v. 9.
6. Christ goes up to the Feast: v. 10.
7. The attitude of men toward Christ: vv. 11-13.

John 7 begins a new section of this fourth Gospel. Our Lord's ministry in Galilee was now over, though He still remained there, because the Judeans sought to kill Him. The annual Feast of Tabernacles was at hand, and His brethren were anxious for Christ to go up to Jerusalem, and there give a public display of His miraculous powers. To this request the Saviour made a reply which at first glance appears enigmatical. He bids His brethren go up to the Feast, but excuses Himself on the ground that *His* time was not yet fully come. After their departure, He abode still in Galilee. But very shortly after, He, too, goes up to the Feast; as it were in secret. The Jews who wished to kill Him, sought but were unable to discover Him. Among the people He formed the principal subject of discussion, some of whom considered Him a good man, others regarding Him as a deceiver. And then, in v. 14 we are told, "Now about the midst of the Feast Jesus went up into the temple, and taught". Such is a brief summary of the passage which is to be before us.

That our passage will present a number of real difficulties to the cursory reader is not to be denied, and perhaps the more diligent student may not be able to clear up all of them. The simplest and often the most effective way of studying a portion of God's Word is to draw up a list of questions upon it. This will insure a more definite approach: it will save us from mere generalizations: it will reveal the particular points upon which we need to seek God's help.

Who are meant by "His brethren"? (v. 3)—brethren who did not "believe in Him" (v. 5). To what did Christ refer when He said, "My time is not yet come" (v. 6)? Why did Christ refuse to go up to the Feast with His brethren (v. 8)? And why, after saying that His time was not yet come, did He go to the Feast at all (v. 10)? What is meant by "He went not openly, but as it were in secret" (v. 10)? If He went up to the Feast "as it were in secret", why did He, about the midst of the Feast, go into the temple, and teach (v. 14)? These are some of the more pertinent and important questions which will naturally occur to the inquiring mind.

It should be obvious that the central item in our passage is the Feast itself*, and in the scriptural meaning and significance of this Feast of Tabernacles must be sought the solution of most of our difficulties here. It will be necessary, then, to compare carefully the leading scriptures which treat of this Feast, and then shall we be the better able to understand what is to be before us. Having made these prelimi-

* Note there is a *sevenfold* reference to the "Feast" in John 7.

nary remarks we shall now turn to our passage and offer an exposition of it according to the measure of light which God has been pleased to grant us upon it.

"After these things Jesus walked in Galilee" (v. 1). The first three words intimate that a new section of the Gospel commences here—cf 6:1 and our comments thereon. "After *these* things" probably has a double reference. In its more general significance, it points back to the whole of His Galilean ministry, now ended. There is a peculiar and significant arrangement of the contents of the first seven chapters of John: a strange alternating between Judea and Galilee. In John 1 the scene is laid in Judea (see v. 28); but in 2:1-12 Christ is seen in Galilee. In 2:13 we are told that "Jesus went up to Jerusalem," and He remained in its vicinity till we reach 4:3, where we are told, "He left Judea, and departed again into Galilee." Then, in 5:1, we read, "Jesus went up to Jerusalem", and He is viewed there to the end of the chapter. But in 6:1 we are told, "After these things Jesus went over the sea of Galilee". And now in John 7 we are to see Him once more in Jerusalem.

But *why* this strange and repeated alternation? In the light of Matt. 4:15—"Galilee *of the Gentiles*"—we would suggest two answers: First, this fourth Gospel, in a special manner, concerns the *family* of God, which is made up of Jew *and* Gentile; hence the emphasis here by our attention being directed, again and again, to *both* Judea and Galilee. But note that Judea always comes before Galilee: "To the Jew first" being the lesson taught. In the second place, if our references above be studied carefully, it will be seen that the passages treating of Galilee and what happened there, come in *parenthetically;* inasmuch as Jerusalem is both the geographical and moral center of the Gospel. This hints at the *place* occupied by this present interval of grace, during which God is taking out of *the Gentiles* "a people for His name". It is indeed a parenthetical period, inasmuch as it comes in during the break between God's past and future dealings with Israel. And this is the more noticeable here, because in each of the later instances the Holy Spirit has been careful to show us that the occasion of Christ's going to "Galilee" was the opposition He encountered in Judea!

"After *these* things", then, points back to the conclusion of His Galilean ministry: 2:1-11; 4:43-54; 6:1-71. But we also regard these words as having a more restricted and specific reference to what is recorded at the close of chapter 6, particularly v. 66. "After *these* things" would thus point, more directly, to the forsaking of Christ by many of His Galilean disciples, following the miracles they had witnessed and the teaching they had heard.

"After these things Jesus *walked* (literally, "was walking") in Galilee" (v. 1). It appears as though the Lord was reluctant to leave Galilee, for it seems that He never returned there any more. It was useless to work any further miracles, and His teaching had been despised, nevertheless, His *person* He would still keep before them a little longer. Jesus walking in Galilee, rather than dwelling in privacy, suggests the thought of the continued public manifestation of Himself: let the reader compare John 1:36; 6:19; 10:23 and 11:54 for the other references in this Gospel to Jesus "walking", and he will find confirmation of what we have just said. Again; if John 7:1 be linked with 6:66 (as the "after *these* things" suggests) the marvelous grace of the Saviour will be evidenced. Many of His disciples went back and *walked no more* "with Him". Notwithstanding, *He* continued to "walk", and that too, "in *Galilee*"!

"After these things Jesus walked in Galilee: for He would not walk in Jewry, because *the Jews* sought to kill Him" (v. 1). Let the reader turn back and consult our remarks on 5:15 concerning "the Jews". It is indeed solemn to trace right through this fourth Gospel what is said about them. "The Jews" are not only to be distinguished from the Galileans, as being of Judea, but also from the common people of Judea. Note how in our present passage "the people" are distinguished from "the Jews": see vv. 11, 12, 13. "The Jews" were evidently the leaders, the religious leaders. Notice how in 8:48 it is **"the Jews"** who say to Christ "Thou art a Samaritan, and hast a demon". It was "the Jews" who cast out of the synagogue the man born blind, whose eyes Christ had opened (9:22, 34). It was "the Jews" who took up stones to stone Christ (10:31). It was "the officers of *the Jews*" who, "took Jesus, and bound Him" (18:12). And it was through "fear of the Jews" that Joseph of Arimathaea came secretly to Pilate and begged the body of the Saviour (19:38). And so here: it was because of *the Jews,* who sought to kill Him, that Jesus would not walk in Judea, but remained in Galilee. Christ here left us a perfect example. By His actions, He teaches us not to court danger, and unnecessarily expose ourselves before our enemies. This will be the more evident if we link this verse with 11:53, 54: "From that day forth they took counsel together for to put Him to death. Jesus *therefore* walked no more openly among the Jews; but went thence unto a country near to the wilderness", etc. It will thus appear that our Lord used prudence and care to avoid persecution and danger till His time was fully come; so it is our duty to endeavor by all wise means and precautions to protect and preserve ourselves, that we may have opportunities for further service.

"Now the Jews' Feast of Tabernacles was at hand" (v. 2). By comparing this verse with 6:4 it will be seen that upwards of six months is spanned by John 6 to 7:1. John 6:4 says the Passover was nigh, and from Lev. 23:5 we learn that this Feast was kept in the first month of the Jewish year; whereas Lev. 23:34 tells us that the Feast of Tabernacles was celebrated in the seventh month. How evident it is then that John was something more than an historian. Surely it is plain that the Holy Spirit has recorded what He has in this fourth Gospel (as in the others) according to a principle of selection, and in consonance with a definite design.

"Now the Jews' Feast of Tabernacles was at hand". As already intimated, it will be necessary for us to give careful attention to the leading scriptures of the Old Testament on the Feast of Tabernacles, that we may ascertain its historical, typical and dispensational significance, and thus be the better prepared to understand the details of the passage now before us.

Lev. 23 reveals the fact that there were seven Feasts in Israel's religious calendar, but there were three of these which were singled out as of special importance. This we gather from Deut. 16:16, where it is recorded that Jehovah said to Israel, "Three times in a year shall all thy males appear before the Lord thy God in the place which He shall choose (i. e. in the Tabernacle, and afterwards the Temple); in the Feast of Unleavened-bread (inseparably connected with the Passover), and in the Feast of Weeks (i. e. Pentecost), and in the Feast of Tabernacles". We reserve a brief comment on the first two of these, until we have considered the third.

The first time the Feast of Tabernacles is mentioned by name is in Lev. 23, namely, in vv. 34-36 and 39-44. As this passage is too long for us to quote here in full, we would request the reader to turn and read it through carefully before going farther. We give now a brief summary of its prominent features. First, the Feast began on the fifteenth day of the seventh month (v. 34). Second, it lasted for eight days (v. 39). Third, it was a "holy convocation", when Israel was to offer "an offering made by fire unto the Lord" (v. 36). Fourth, those who celebrated this Feast were to take "boughs of goodly trees" (v. 40). Fifth, they were to "rejoice before the Lord their God seven days" (v. 40). Sixth, they were to "dwell in booths" (v. 42). Seventh, the purpose of this was to memorialize the fact that "Jehovah made their fathers to dwell in booths, when He brought them out of the land of Egypt" (v. 43). In Num. 29:12-40 we have a detailed record of the ritual or sacrificial requirements connected with this Feast.

Though Lev. 23 is the first time the Feast of Tabernacles is mentioned by name, there is one earlier reference to it, namely, in Ex. 23:16, where it is termed the Feast of Ingathering*, "which is the end of the year (i. e. of the sacred calendar of Feasts), when thou hast gathered in thy labors out of the field". The Feast of Tabernacles, then, was the grand Harvest Festival, when the Lord of the harvest was praised for all His temporal mercies. This one was the most joyous Feast of the year. It was not observed by Israel till after they had entered and settled in Canaan: their dwelling in booths at this Feast memorialized their wanderings in the wilderness.

This last of Israel's Feasts, like their first, the Passover, looked forward as well as backward. The Feast of Tabernacles had a typical and dispensational significance as well as an historical. Its position in the sacred calendar hints at the time to which it pointed forward. As the *last* of their Feasts, it speaks plainly of the Millennium, and everything connected with it is in full accord with this. If the reader will refer to Lev. 23:27 he will find that

* That this is the same Feast appears by a comparison of Deut. 16:16 with Ex. 23:14-17.

the Feast which immediately preceded the Tabernacles was that of Atonement, which fell on the tenth day of the seventh month; the Feast of Tabernacles coming five days later, and lasting eight days. All of these numerals are marvelously significant. The fact that the Feast of Tabernacles was observed in the seventh month, foreshadowed the Millennium which will be the *seventh* and last of earth's great "days"—i. e. after six thousand years of Satan's activities. That it began on the *fifteenth* day of the month tells us that not until the Millennium will the *grace* of God be fully manifested to Israel: the factors of fifteen are 3 and 5; and in Scripture 3 signifies full manifestation and 5 is the number for grace. That this Feast had an *eighth* day, tells of a *new beginning,* which is in keeping with the fact that in the Millennium Israel will be under the *new* covenant. That the Feast of Tabernacles came *five* days after the great Day of Atonement, hints at the present *interval* of *grace* (of which 5 speaks), which comes in between the Cross and the Millennium!

When we come to examine the details connected with the observance of this Feast we find that they, too, typified millennial conditions. For example, Israel was commanded to take "boughs of goodly trees, boughs of palm trees", etc. How this reminds us of what we read of in Matt. 21:8, when the Jews "cut down branches from the trees, and strawed them in the way", as they cried, "Hosanna to the Son of David: blessed is He that cometh in the name of the Lord", all of which was anticipatory of the yet future and real Triumphal Entry of Israel's King into Jerusalem. So, too, the Feast of Tabernacles was a time of great *rejoicing,* as the Millennium will be for Israel. Their dwelling in "booths" as a memorial of their wilderness experiences, and which witnessed to the fact that they were once strangers and pilgrims, but were so no longer, now they were settled in Canaan; will have a far deeper meaning for Israel in the Millennium, as they look back over their world-wanderings during the past two thousand years! Finally, Zech. 14:16-20 furnishes us with a most conclusive proof that the Tabernacles is distinctively and peculiarly the Feast which pointed forward to the Millennium: "And it shall come to pass, that every one that is left of all the nations which came against Jerusalem shall even go up from year to year to worship *the King,* the Lord of hosts, and to keep *the Feast of Tabernacles*", etc.

The Old Testament records but two occasions when this Feast was ever observed by Israel in the past, and they are most significant as foreshadowing millennial times. The first of these is found in 1 Kings 8, see vv. 2, 11, 13, 62-66, and note particularly the "seventh month" in v. 2 and the "eighth day" in v. 66. This was in the days of Solomon (who foreshadowed the millennial reign of Christ), at the completion and dedication of the Temple. In like manner, the antitypical Feast of Tabernacles, the Millennium, will not be ushered in till the completion of the spiritual "temple", which God is now building (Eph. 2:22; 1 Pet. 2:5). The second account of Israel's past celebration of this Feast is recorded in Neh. 8:13-18. The occasion was the settlement of the Jewish remnant in Palestine, after they had come up out of captivity. So, the Millennium will follow the re-gathering of the Jews to their own land after their present dispersion.

We cannot offer here anything more than a very brief word on Deut. 16:16. The three great Feasts which God required every male Israelite to observe annually in Jerusalem, were those of Unleavened-bread (inseparably connected with the Passover), of Weeks (or Pentecost), and Tabernacles. The first has already received its antitypical accomplishment at the Cross. The second began to receive its fulfillment on the day of Pentecost (Acts 2), but was interrupted by the failure of the Nation to repent (see Acts 3:19-21). The third looks forward to the future, the Millennium.

"Now the Jews' Feast of Tabernacles was at hand" (v. 2). Someone has pointed out that in John 5, 6, and 7 there is a striking order followed in the typical suggestiveness of the contents of these chapters. In John 5 Israel may be seen, typically, as being delivered from the bondage *of Egypt:* this was adumbrated in the deliverance of the impotent man from lifelong suffering. In John 6 there is repeated reference made to Israel *in the wilderness,* eating the manna. While here in John 7 Israel is viewed *in the land,* keeping the Feast of Tabernacles.

"His brethren therefore said unto Him, Depart hence, and go into Judea, that Thy disciples also may see the works that Thou doest" (v. 3). These "brethren" were the brothers of Christ according to the flesh: that is, they were sons of Mary too. That they were completely blind to His Divine glory is evident from the fact they here told *Him* what to do. Blind to His glory, they were therefore devoid of all spiritual discernment, and hence their reasoning was according to the carnal mind. But what did they mean by "Go into Judea, that Thy *disciples* also may see the works that Thou doest"? The answer is to be found in the "also" and the "therefore" at the beginning of the verse—"His brethren *therefore* said unto Him", etc. The "therefore", of course, looks back to something previous. What this is, we find in the closing verses of John 6. In the first part of that chapter we have recorded a wonderful "work" performed by the Lord. But in v. 66 we are told, "From that time many of His *disciples* went back, and walked no more with Him". Now, said these brethren according to the flesh, don't waste any further efforts or time here, but go to Judea. They were evidently piqued at the reception which Christ had met with in Galilee. His work there seemed to amount to very little, why not, then, try Jerusalem, the headquarters of Judaism! Moreover, now was an opportune time: the Feast of Tabernacles was at hand, and Jerusalem would be full.

"For there is no man that doeth anything in secret, and he himself seeketh to be known openly. If Thou do these things, show Thyself to the world" (v. 4). Note the "if" here. There was evidently a slightly veiled taunt in these words. We take it that these brethren were really challenging Christ, and that the substance of their challenge was this: If these works of yours are genuine miracles, why confine yourself to villages and small country-towns in Galilee, where the illiterate and unsophisticated habituate. Go up to the Capital, where people are better qualified to judge. Go up to the Feast, and there display your powers, and if they will stand the test of the public scrutiny of the leaders, why, your disciples will gather around you, and your claims will be settled once for all. No doubt, these "brethren" really hoped that He *would* establish His claims, and in that event, as His near kinsmen, *they* would share the honors which would be heaped upon Him. But how insulting to our blessed Lord all this was! What indignities He suffered from those who were blind to His glory!

"If Thou do these things, show Thyself to the world". How these words betrayed their hearts! They were men of the world: consequently, they adopted its ways, spoke its language, and employed its logic. "Show thyself to the world" meant, Accompany us to Jerusalem, work some startling miracle before the great crowds who will be assembled there; and thus, not only make yourself the center of attraction, but convince everybody you *are* the Messiah. Ah, how ignorant they were of the mind of God and the purpose of His Son's mission! It was "the pride of life" (1 John 2:16) displaying itself. And how much of this same "pride of life" we see today, even among those who profess to be followers of that One whom the world crucified! What are the modern methods of Evangelistic Campaigns and Bible Conferences—the devices resorted to to draw the crowds, the parading of the preacher's photo, the self-advertising by the speakers —what are these, but the present-day expressions of *"Show thyself* to the world"!

"If Thou do these things, show thyself to *the world"*. One other comment, an exegetical one, should be made on this before we pass on to the next verse. Here is a case in point where "the world" does not always signify the whole human race. When these brethren of Christ said, "Go show Thyself to *the world",* it is evident that they did not mean, Display yourself before all mankind. No, here, as frequently in this Gospel, "the world" is merely a *general* term, signifying *all classes* of men.

"For neither did His brethren believe in Him" (v. 5). How this illustrates the desperate hardness and depravity of human nature. Holy and perfect as Christ was, faultless and flawless as were His character and conduct, yet, even those who had been brought up with Him in the same house believed not in Him! It was bad enough that the Nation at large believed not on Him, but the case of these "kinsmen" (Mark 3:21, margin) was even more excuseless. How this demonstrates the imperative need of God's almighty regenerating grace! And how this exemplifies Christ's own teaching that "No man can come to Me except the Father which hath sent Me draw Him"! And how striking to note that the unbelief of His "brethren" was the fulfillment of Old Testament prophecy: "I am become a stranger unto My brethren, and an alien unto *My mother's children*" (Psa. 69:8).

"Then Jesus said unto them, My time is not yet come: but your time is alway ready" (v. 6). These words of Christ must be interpreted in the light of the immediate context. His brethren had said, "Go *show* Thyself to the world". But His time to do this had not then come, nor has it yet arrived. Not then would He vindicate Himself by openly displaying His glory. This was the time of His humiliation. But how plainly His words here imply that *there is* a time coming when He will publicly reveal His majesty and glory. To this He referred when He said, "And they shall *see* the Son of man coming in the clouds of heaven with power and great glory" (Matt. 24:30). And what will be the effect of this on "the world"? Rev. 1:7 tells us: "Behold, He cometh with clouds; and every eye shall *see* Him, and they also which pierced Him: and all kindreds of the earth shall *wail* because of Him". And solemn will be the accompaniments of this showing of Himself to the world. Then shall He say, "But those Mine enemies, which would not that I should reign over them, bring hither, and slay them before Me" (Luke 19:27); see, too, the last half of Rev. 19. How little, then, did these brethren realize the import of their request! Had He openly manifested Himself then—before the Cross—it would have involved the perdition of the whole human race, for then there had been no atoning-blood under which sinners might shelter! Thankful must we ever be that He did not do what they asked. And how often *we* ask Him for things, which He in His Divine wisdom and grace denies us! How true it is that "we know not what we should pray for as we ought" (Rom. 8:26)!

"Then Jesus said unto them, My time is not yet come: but your time is alway ready" (v. 6). There was *no* "pride of life" in Christ. He demonstrated this in the great Temptation. All the kingdoms of the world and the glory of them, could not tempt Him. Instead of seeking to *show Himself* before the world, instead of advertising Himself, instead of endeavoring to attract attention, He frequently drew a veil over His works and sought to hide Himself: see Mark 1:36-38; 7:17; 7:36; 8:26, etc., etc. After He had been transfigured on the holy mount and His glory had appeared before the eyes of the three apostles, He bade them "that they should tell no man what things they had seen" (Mark 9:9). How truly did He make Himself of "no reputation"! But how different with these brethren. "Your time is alway ready", He said. *They* were ever willing and wanting to win the applause of men, and make themselves popular with the world.

"The world cannot hate you; but Me it hateth, because I testify of it, that the works thereof are evil" (v. 7). How this helps us to fix the meaning of the last clause of the previous verse. "Your time is alway ready" meant, as we have said, Your time to display yourself before the world, in order to court its smiles, is ever to hand. But how solemn is the *reason* Christ here gives for this! It was because they had not cast in their lot with this One who was "despised and rejected of men". Becauses of this, the world would not hate *them*. And why? Because they were *of* the world. Contrariwise, the world *did* hate Christ. It hated Christ because He testified *of it* (*not* "against" it!), that its works were evil. The holiness of *His* life condemned the worldliness of theirs. And right here is a solemn and searching test for those who profess to be His followers today. Dear reader, if you are *popular* with the world, that is indeed a solemn sign, an evil omen. The world has not changed. It still *hates* those whose lives condemn theirs. Listen to the words of Christ to His apostles, "If ye were of the world, the world would love his own. But because ye are not of the world, but I have chosen you out of the world, therefore the world hateth you" (John 15:19). Here our Lord tells us plainly that the world hates those who are truly His. This, then, is a searching test: does the world "hate" *you?*

"Go ye up unto this Feast: I go not up yet unto this Feast; for My time is not yet full come. When He had said these words unto them, He abode still in Galilee" (vv. 8, 9). The meaning of these verses is really very simple. Christ plainly qualified Himself. He did not say that He *would not* go up to the Feast; what He said was, He would not go *then*—His time to go had not *"yet* come." "My time" must not be confounded with "Mine hour" which He used when referring to His approaching death. The simple force, then, of these verses is that Christ declined to go up to the Feast *with His brethren.*

"But when His brethren were gone up, then went He also up unto the Feast" (v. 10). How tragic is this. How it reveals the hearts of these "brethren". They *left* Christ for the Feast! They preferred a religious festival for fellowship with the Christ of God. And how often we witness the same thing today. What zeal there is for religious performances, for forms and ceremonies, and how little heart for Christ Himself.

"But when His brethren were gone up, then went He also up unto the Feast, not openly, but as it were in secret" (v. 10). The first part of this verse supplies another reason why He would not accompany His brethren to the Feast, as well as explains the somewhat ambiguous "as it were in secret". The general method of travel in those days, and especially at festival seasons, was to form caravans, and join together in considerable companies (cf Luke 2:44). And when such a company reached Jerusalem, naturally it became known generally. It was, therefore, to avoid such publicity that our Lord waited till His brethren had gone, and then He went up to the Feast, "not openly, (R. V. "publicly"), but as it were in secret", i. e., in private. "But *when* His brethren were gone up, *then* went He also up unto the Feast". The words we have placed in italics are not so much a time-mark as a word of explanation. The "when" has the force of *because* as in 4:1; 6:12; 6:16, etc.

"Then went *He also* up to the Feast" (v. 10). This simple sentence gives us a striking revelation of our Lord's perfections. In order to appreciate what we have here it is necessary to go back to the first verse of the chapter, where we are told, "Jesus walked in Galilee, for He would not walk in Jewry, because the Jews *sought to kill Him*". Why is it that the Holy Spirit has begun the chapter thus? The central incident in John 7 is Christ in Jerusalem at the Feast of Tabernacles. Why, then, *introduce* the incident in this peculiar way? Ah, the Holy Spirit ever had the glory of Christ in view. Because the Jews "sought to kill Him" He "walked in Galilee". And therein, as pointed out, He left us an example not to needlessly expose ourselves to danger. But now in v. 10 we find that He *did* go to Judea, yes to Jerusalem itself. Why was this? We have to turn back to Deut. 16:16 for our answer. There we read, "Three times in a year shall all *thy* males appear before the Lord thy God in the place which He shall choose; in the feast of unleavened bread, and in the feast of weeks, and in *the feast of tabernacles.*" According to the flesh Christ was an Israelite, and "made under the Law" (Gal. 4:4). Therefore, did He, in perfect submission to the will of His Father, go up to Jerusalem to keep the feast. In the volume of the book it was "written of Him", and even though the Jews "sought to kill Him", He promptly *obeyed* the written Word! And here, too, He has left us an example. On the one hand, danger should not be courted by us; on the other, when the Word of God plainly bids us follow a certain line of conduct, we are to do so, no matter what the consequences.

"Then the Jews sought Him at the Feast, and said, Where is He? And there was much murmuring among the people concerning Him: for some said, He is a good man: others said, Nay; but He deceiveth the people. Howbeit no man spake openly of Him for fear of the Jews" (vv. 11-13). Mark what a strange variety of opinions there were concerning Christ even at the beginning! In the light of this passage the differences and divergencies of religious beliefs today ought not to surprise us. As said the late Bishop Ryle, "They are but the modern symptoms of an ancient disease". Christ Himself distinctly affirmed, "Think not that I am come to send peace". Whenever God's truth is faithfully proclaimed, opposition will be encountered and strife stirred up. The fault is not in God's truth, but in human nature. As the sun shines on the swamp it will call forth malaria: but the fault is not in the sun, but in the ground. The very same rays call forth fertility from the grainfields. So the truth of God will yield spiritual fruit from a believing heart, but from the carnal mind it will evoke endless cavil and blasphemy. Some thought Christ a good man; others regarded Him as a deceiver: sufficient for the disciple to be as his Master.

"Some said, He is a good man: others said, Nay; but He deceiveth the people" (v. 12). "The Lord might bring blessing out of it, but they were *reasoning* and *discussing.* In another place He asks His disciples, 'Whom do men say that I the Son of man am?' They tell Him, 'Some say that Thou art John the Baptist; some Elias; and others, one of the prophets'. It was all *discussion*. But when Peter replies, 'Thou art the Christ, the Son of the living God', He tells him, 'Blessed art thou Simon Bar-jona: for flesh and blood hath not revealed it unto thee, but My Father which is in heaven'. There was *personal recognition of Himself,* and where there is that, there is no *discussion*. Discussing Him as subject-matter in their minds, they had not submitted to the righteousness of God. Where people's minds are at work discussing the right and the wrong, there is not the mind of the new-born babe; they are not receiving, but judging" (J. N.D.)

"Howbeit no man spake openly of Him for fear of the Jews" (v. 13). What a solemn warning to us is this! What an awful thing is the fear of man! How often it has silenced faithful witness for Christ! It is written, "The fear of man bringeth a snare" (Prov. 29:25). This is still true. Let us pray then for holy boldness that we may testify faithfully for an absent Saviour before a world that cast Him out.

Briefly, we call attention to another striking dispensational picture. We confine ourself to the first nine verses of John 7. It is not until we reach v. 10 that Christ goes up "unto the Feast". This Feast, as we have seen, anticipates Millennial conditions; hence, what is found in the preceding nine verses refers (typically) to that which comes before the Millennium is reached. John 7:1-9 supplies us, then, with a view of this present interval. We shall just point out the various lines in the picture without commenting on them:

1. "Jesus walked *in Galilee*" (v. 1 and cf v. 9): this intimates that during the present dispensation Christ is dealing in grace with *Gentiles*. 2. "He would not walk in Jewry" (v. 1). This announces that during the present interval Israel is "Lo-ammi" (Hos. 1:9). 3. "The Jews sought to kill Him" (v. 1), tells of their present hatred of the Saviour. 4. "Jews' Feast of Tabernacles was at hand" (v. 2). This announces that Jewish enmity against Christ will continue until the very dawning of the Millennium. 5. "Neither did His brethren believe in Him" (v. 5) tells of the unbelief of Israel as a Nation prior to the Millennium. 6. The world's hatred of Christ (v. 7) shows that even among the Gentiles the work of grace is an elective one. 7. "I go not up yet unto this Feast; for My time is not yet full come" (v. 8). This, in the light of the context, tells us that the time for Christ to publicly manifest His glory is not during this present interval. The whole picture thus gives us a most solemn portrayal of the attitude of Israel and of the world toward Christ during this interval of grace!

The following questions on our next portion may help the student:—

1. Wherein is v. 15 being repeated today?
2. Why did Christ speak of His "doctrine" rather than doctrines, v. 16?
3. What is the relation of v. 17 to the context?
4. Wherein does v. 18 help us to carry out 1 John 4:1?
5. What is the difference between "the law of Moses" (vs. 23) and "the law of God" (Rom. 7:22, 25).
6. To what did the speakers refer in the second half of v. 27—cf v. 42?
7. What comforting truth is illustrated in v. 30?

—Arthur W. Pink.

GLEANINGS IN EXODUS

I. Introduction.

In commencing the *study* of any book in the Bible it is well to remind ourselves that each separate book has some prominent and dominant theme which, as such, is peculiar to itself, around which everything is made to center, and of which all the details are but the amplification. What that leading subject may be, we should make it our business to prayerfully and diligently ascertain. This can best be discovered by reading and re-reading the book under review. If other students before us have published the results of their labors, it is our duty to carefully examine their findings in the light of God's Word, and either verify or disprove. Yet, concerning this there are two extremes to guard against, two dangers to avoid. The first, and perhaps the one which ensnares the most, is the assumption that other students have done their work so well, it is needless for *us* to go over the same ground. But that is laziness and unbelief: God may be pleased to reveal to you something which He did not to them; remember that there are depths in His Word which no human sounding-line has fathomed. The second danger is the craze for orginality and the egotistical belief that *we* shall search more diligently than they who went before, and that therefore the results of *our* labors will be an improvement over all who have preceded us. This is unwarrantable conceit, from which may Divine grace deliver us all.

With some books of the Bible we can more readily discover the central theme than in others. This is noticeably the case with the first few books in the Old Testament. It is as though God had made it easier at the beginning so as to encourage us and prepare the way for some of the more complex books that follow—complex so far as their leading subjects are concerned. Historically considered, the book of Genesis is the book of *beginnings;* but viewed doctrinally, it is seen to be the book which treats of *election:*—God choosing Shem from the three sons of Noah to be the channel from which should issue, ultimately, the Saviour; God singling out Abraham to be the father of the chosen Nation; God passing by Ishmael and choosing Isaac; God passing by Esau and choosing Jacob; God appointing Joseph from all the twelve sons of his father to be the honored instrument for making provision against the famine, and being raised to the second place in all Egypt; finally, in the passing by of the elder of Joseph's sons and the bestowal of the firstborn's portion on Ephraim (48:13-20) we behold another illustration of the same principle. Yes, *election* is clearly the characteristic doctrine of Genesis. And this is exactly what we might expect. "God hath *from the beginning* chosen you unto salvation" (2 Thess. 2:13), hence this truth is illustrated again and again in this book which *begins* the Scriptures. Just as surely may we anticipate—in the light of the New Testament—the dominant theme of Exodus.

Historically, the book of Exodus treats of the deliverance of Israel from Egypt; but viewed doctrinally, it deals with *redemption.* Just as the first book of the Bible teaches that God elects unto salvation, so the second instructs us *how* God saves, namely, by redemption. Redemption, then, is the dominant subject of Exodus. Following this, we are shown what we are redeemed for—*worship,* and this characterizes Leviticus, where we learn of the holy requirements of God and the gracious provisions He has made to meet these. In Numbers we have *the walk and warfare of the wilderness,* where we have a typical representation of our experiences as we pass through this scene of sin and trial—our repeated and excuseless failures, and God's long-sufferance and faithfulness. And so we might continue.

But to return to Exodus. This we have pointed out (as others before us have done) treats of redemption. To the writer it appears that its contents fall into five divisions, which we may summarize as follows:— First, we see the *need* for redemption—pictured by a people enslaved: chapters 1 to 6. Second, we are shown the *might* of the Redeemer—displayed in the plagues on Egypt: chapters 7 to 11. Third, we behold the *character* of redemption—purchased by blood, emancipated by power: chapters 12 to 18. Fourth, we are taught the *duty* of the redeemed—obedience to the Lord: chapters 19 to 24. Fifth, we have revealed the *provisions made* for the failures of the redeemed—seen in the tabernacle and its services: chapters 25 to 40. In proof of what we have just said we would refer the reader to Ex. 15:13, which we regard as the key verse to the book, "Thou in Thy mercy hast led forth the people which Thou hast redeemed: Thou hast guided them in Thy strength unto Thy holy habitation". Note that here we have the *need* for redemption implied—God's "mercy"; the *power* of the Redeemer is referred to—His "strength"; the *character* of redemption is described—"led forth the people"; the *responsibilities* of the redeemed and their *privileges* are signified in a reference to the tabernacle—"unto Thy holy habitation".

Another thing which is a great help in the study of Exodus is to note its numerical position in the Sacred Canon. Exodus is the *second* book of the Bible, and it will be found that the character of its contents fully accords with this. The number two, in its scriptural significations, treats of *difference* or *division*. Proof of this is found in its first occurrence in the Bible: the *second* day of Gen. 1 was when God *divided* the waters. Hence, two is the number of *witness*, for if the testimony of two *different* men agree, the truth is established. Two is therefore the number of *opposition*. One is the number of unity, but two brings in another, who is either in accord with the first or opposed to him. Hence, two is also the number of *contrast*, consequently, whenever we find two men coupled together in Scripture it is, with rare exceptions, for the purpose of bringing out the *difference* there is between them: for example, Cain and Abel, Jacob and Esau, Moses and Aaron, David and Solomon, etc.

Let us now see how these slightly varied meanings of the number two are traceable in the character and contents of this second book of Scripture. Two is the number of *division*. In the first chapter of Exodus we find Pharaoh ordering a division to be made among the babies of the Israelites: if a son was born he should be killed, if a daughter she should be spared. In the plagues, the Lord made a division between His people and the Egyptians: "And I will *sever* in that day the land of Goshen, in which My people dwell, that no swarms of flies shall be there; to the end thou mayest know that I am the Lord in the midst of the earth. And I will put *a division* between My people and thy people; tomorrow shall this sign be" (Ex. 8:22, 23). So, too, He divided between their cattle: "And the Lord shall *sever* between the cattle of Israel and the cattle of Egypt: and there shall nothing die of all that is the children's of Israel" (Ex. 9:4). When Israel came to the Red Sea we are told, "And Moses stretched out his hand over the sea; and the Lord caused the Sea to go back by a strong east wind all that night, and made the sea dry land, and the waters were *divided*" (14:21). Again; it is only in Exodus (26:33) that we read of the veil which was to "*divide* between the holy place and the most holy".

Two is also the number of *witness*, and mark how this note is sounded throughout the book. The sufferings and groanings of the Hebrews witnessed to their need of deliverance. The plagues bore witness to the power and wrath of God, and it is noteworthy that God employed *two* witnesses, Moses and Aaron, in announcing these to Pharaoh. The Passover-night witnessed to the value and sufficiency of the blood. The wilderness experiences of Israel witnessed to the faithfulness and tender love of God. The giving of the law witnessed to the righteousness government of Jehovah. The tabernacle bore typical witness to the manifold perfections of Christ.

Again; two is the number of *opposition*. This is something which is prominently marked in Exodus. The antagonism of the Enemy is very manifest throughout. First, we behold it in the determined and cruel effort made to prevent the increase of the Hebrews. Then we see the children of Israel oppressed by merciless taskmasters. Next, when Moses goes in and performs his miraculous signs before the king, Pharaoh's magicians "withstood" him: and it is striking to observe that only *two* of their names have been preserved in Holy Writ (2 Tim. 3:8). In connection with Israel's exodus from Egypt, Pharaoh opposed every step of the way. Even after Israel left Egypt and crossed the Red Sea, we see the Amalakites opposing them in the wilderness (17:8)—note it was not the Israelites who attacked the Amalakites, but the enemy who came to fight against the people of God.

Finally, two is the number of *contrast*. Even a casual reading will reveal the marked differences between the first two books of Scripture: let us note a few of them. In the book of Genesis we have the history of a family, in Exodus the history of a nation. In Genesis the descendants of Abraham are seen few in number, in Exodus they are to be numbered by the million. In the former we see the Hebrews welcomed and honored in Egypt, in the latter they are viewed as feared and hated. In the former there is a Pharaoh who says to Joseph, "God hath showed thee all this" (41:39); in the latter there is a Pharaoh who says to Moses, "I know not the Lord" (5:2). In Genesis there is a "lamb" promised (22:8); in Exodus the "lamb" is slain (chap. 12). In the one we see the entry of Israel into Egypt; in the other we behold their exodus. In the one we see the patriarchs in the land "which flowed with milk and honey"; in the other we behold their descendants in the wilderness. Genesis ends with Joseph in a coffin; while

Exodus closes with the glory of the Lord filling the tabernacle. A series of more vivid contrasts could scarcely be imagined.

The central doctrine of the book of Exodus is redemption, but this is not formally expounded, rather is it strikingly illustrated. In earliest times, God, it would seem, did not communicate to His people an explicit and systematic form of doctrine; instead, He instructed them, mainly, through His providential dealings and by means of types and symbols. Once this is clearly grasped by us it gives new interest to the Old Testament scriptures. The opening books of the Bible contain very much more than an inspired history of events that happened thousands of years ago: they are filled with adumbrations and illustrations of the great doctrines of our faith which are set forth categorically in the New Testament epistles. Thus "whatsoever things were written aforetime were written for our learning" (Rom. 15:4), and we lose much if we neglect to study the historical portions of the Old Testament with this fact before us.

The deliverance of Israel from Egypt furnishes a remarkably full and accurate typification of our redemption by Christ. The details of this will come before us, God willing, in our later studies. Here, we can only call attention to the broad outlines of the picture. Israel in Egypt illustrates the place we were in before Divine grace saved us. Egypt symbolizes the world, according to the course of which we all walked in time past. Pharaoh, who knew not the Lord, who defied Him, who was the inveterate enemy of God's people, but who at the end was overthrown by God, shadows forth the great adversary, the Devil. The cruel bondage of the enslaved Hebrews pictures the tyrannical dominion of sin over its captives. The groaning of the Israelites under their burdens speaks of the painful exercises of conscience and heart when convicted of our lost condition. The deliverer raised up by God in the person of Moses, points to the greater Deliverer, even our Lord Jesus Christ. The passover-night tells of the security of the believer beneath the sheltering blood of God's Lamb. The exodus from Egypt announces our deliverance from the yoke of bondage and our judicial separation from the world. The crossing of the Red Sea depicts our union with Christ in His death and resurrection. The journey through the wilderness—its trials and testings, with God's provision to meet every need—represent the experiences of our pilgrim course. The giving of the law to Israel teaches us the obedient submission which we owe to our new Master. The tabernacle with its beautiful fittings and furnishings, shows us the varied excellencies and glories of Christ. Thus it will be found that almost everything in this second book of the Bible has a spiritual message and application to us.

It is also to be remarked that there is much in the book of Exodus that looks forward to and anticipates the future. The historical portions of this second book of Scripture have a dispensational as well as doctrinal value, a prophetic as well as a moral and spiritual signification. There is not a little in it that will minister instruction and comfort to the people of God in a coming day, as well as to us now. History repeats itself, and what is recorded in Exodus will be found to foreshadow a later chapter in the vicissitudes of Abraham's descendants. The lot of Israel in the Tribulation period will be even worse than it was in the days of Moses. A greater tyrant than Pharaoh will yet be "raised up" by God to chastise them. A more determined effort than that of old will be made to cut them off from being a nation. Groanings and cryings more intense and piteous will yet ascend to heaven. Plagues even more fearful than those sent upon the land of Pharaoh will yet be poured out upon the world from the vials of God's wrath. God shall again send forth two witnesses, empowered by Him to show forth mighty signs and wonders, but their testimony shall be rejected as was that of Moses and Aaron of old. Emissaries of Satan, supernaturally endowed, will perform greater prodigies than did the magicians of Egypt. A remnant of Israel shall again be found in the wilderness, there to be sustained by God. And at the end shall come forth the great Deliverer, who will vanquish the enemies of His people by a sorer judgment than that which overtook the Egyptians at the Red Sea. Finally, there shall yet be an even greater exodus than that from Egypt, when the Lord shall gather to Palestine the outcasts of Israel from "the uttermost part of the earth to the uttermost part of heaven".

In addition to the illustrations of the

various parts and aspects of the doctrine of redemption and the prophetic forecast of Israel's lot in the day to come, there are in the book of Exodus quite a number of precious types of the person and work of our Lord Jesus Christ. In many respects there is a remarkable correspondency between Moses and Christ, and if the Lord permits us to complete this series of articles, we shall, at the close, systematize these correspondencies, and show them to be as numerous and striking as those which engaged our attention when Joseph was before us. In addition to the personal type of Moses we shall consider how the burning bush, the passover lamb, the crossing of the Red Sea, the manna, the smitten rock, the tabernacle as a whole, and everything in it, looked at separately, each and all tell forth in symbolic but unmistakeable language the manifold glories of Christ. A rich feast is before us; may God the Holy Spirit sharpen our appetites so that we may feed upon them in faith, and be so nourished thereby that we shall grow in grace and in the knowledge of our Lord and Saviour Jesus Christ.

As the title of these papers intimates, we shall not attempt a complete verse by verse exposition of the book of Exodus, rather shall we continue the course followed by us in our articles on Genesis. Our endeavor will be to stimulate the people of God to a more careful and systematic study of the Old Testament scriptures, by calling attention to some of the hidden wonders which escape the notice of the careless reader, but which cause the reverent student to say with one of old, "I rejoice at Thy word as one that findeth great spoil" (Psa. 119:162). While we shall not ignore the practical application of the message to our own lives, and shall seek to profit from the many salutary lessons to be found for us in Exodus, nevertheless, our chief concern will be the study of those typical pictures which meet us at every turn. The next article will be devoted to Ex. 1, and in the meantime we would urge the interested reader to make a careful study of its contents. May the God of all grace anoint our eyes, and may the Spirit of Truth constantly guide our thoughts as we pass from chapter to chapter. —Arthur W. Pink.

THE SAINTS OF ALL AGES FELLOW-HEIRS

The weakness of our nature is seen in a very humbling light in the use, or rather the abuse, of truth discovered, as well as in the constant tendency to obscure or corrupt it. For when, to meet the need of any age or place, God has been pleased to give a testimony to some aspect of truth that had been lost sight of, or in opposition to some error that had prevailed, there is always danger that it may be made what, for want of a better word, may be called "a hobby", and that it may be carried to an extreme which involves the neglect or denial of some other aspect of the truth. The human mind in this respect has frequently been compared to a pendulum which, in its oscillations, is ever passing and repassing beyond the perpendicular line. This is, to a great extent, the history of error in successive generations. The correction of error passes over to its opposite.

This tendency too frequently appears in the case of those who are honored to bear the testimony. But, more especially, it is seen in those who receive the testimony; a large portion of whom receive it on the authority of the witness, and so become his partisans. In contrast with them we would place those on whose account Paul gave thanks without ceasing, "because, when ye received the Word of God which ye heard of us, ye received it, *not as the word of man,* but as it is in truth, the Word of God, which effectually worketh also in you that believe". His thankfulness on their behalf implies that there was danger of receiving it on his authority or persuasion, instead of going past the messenger to Him who sent the message; and, in that case, as his words imply, it would not have worked effectually in them. Instead of proving the means of their edification and comfort, it would have been only a party distinction, and they would have made his name a party rallying word, saying, as some at Corinth did, "I am of Paul".

In the case of those who receive the truth on human authority in our own time, though they may have learned to disclaim the name of a teacher as a party name, their partisanship is none the less apparent in their appeals to his authority as disciples, and to his teaching as defining the limits of legitimate inquiry. In the case of the teachers themselves, a tendency to give undue prominence to one aspect of truth or to carry it to the opposite extreme of the error against which they testify, is commonly increased by the opposition which they encounter, and the controversies in which they become engaged. The subject occupies their thoughts; everything is made tributary to its defense; personal feeling and the pride of position come in to give intensity to what they regard as zeal for the truth, and they become committed to strong statements which in calmer moments they would have avoided. In the case of their adherents, the conceit of superior enlightenment is gradually inflated till they make adherence to their favorite views terms of communion on earth, and, finally, conditions of salvation.

Perhaps, since we hold that blessed hope, we may with least offense take an illustration of this from the abuse of the testimony which God has given to our own age regarding the speedy and glorious coming of our Lord. Even where it has not been made the ground of a formal party division, there are not wanting those who, receiving the expositions of it from men, have more than hinted that salvation depends on the reception of the same. They put emphasis on such expressions as, "*To them that look for Him* shall He appear the second time without sin unto salvation", and demand on what grounds any others can be supposed to share the blessed results of His coming. Or if they shrink from so sweeping a conclusion, in face of the abundant assurances in the Word of God to all who are the children of God by faith in Christ Jesus, they still seek to find some distinction beyond the present privilege for those who hold their favorite views, by perverting such passages of Scripture as the parable of the wise and foolish virgins. In their view, both classes represent believers; the wise virgins representing those who adopt their views, and the foolish virgins representing those who reject them. Both classes, they tell us, will ultimately be saved, but there will be a distinction, which is represented in the parable by the former being admitted to the marriage, while the latter are, for the time being, shut out.

They forget that all these virgins alike went out to meet the bridegroom, all alike slumbered and slept, and all alike were aroused by the midnight cry, and that the ground of the exclusion of the foolish virgins is to be found in something which preceded their going out to meet Him. It may be observed that they did not suppose that they had oil in their vessels, and only found when it was too late that they were mistaken. Theirs was the willful error of the man who came to the feast not having a wedding garment; they took no oil in their vessels, and did not choose to do so. "Verily I say unto you, I know you not", would be strange language for the Lord to address to believers whom He had loved with an everlasting love, whom He had redeemed by His own blood, and who were members of His body.

Happy are they who receive any testimony to the truth without becoming partisans of those who are honored of God to bear it; who go past men to God; who are led to the Word of God, and not away from it, by all that exposes prevailing error; and who neither rest their faith on human authority, nor bound their views by any human expositions of God's truth. The Scriptures will never make a sectarian; and *there,* no aspect of truth overshadows the rest. Everything is in its place, and all is in due proportions; while in the Spirit's application of the truth the need of every soul is always precisely met. When the truth is learned there, instead of being inflated by the thought of our superior enlightenment, we are constantly humbled by a sense of our ignorance. Many men, going no further than Newton's works, have been elated with the thought of having mastered them; while Newton, going to God's works, saw himself but as a child on the sea-shore, who had picked up here and there a pebble, while the ocean lay before him all unexplored.

In noticing this tendency of the human mind, and in referring to the conceits which illustrate it, we have designed to open the way to the consideration of opposing views on a subject of deep interest and importance. . . .

. . . . Do the Scriptures teach that the saints of all ages will be fellow-heirs? It was as true before the incarnation as it is now, that men are by nature children of wrath, dead in trespasses and sins. The carnal mind was then, as now, enmity against God. The Lord announced no novel truth, nor one peculiar to the period **of this dispensation,** when He said to Nicodemus, "That which is born of the flesh is flesh; and that which is born of the Spirit is spirit", and consequently, "Except a man be born of water and of the Spirit, he cannot enter the kingdom of God". Nicodemus, a master in Israel, might as justly be rebuked for not knowing this as any teacher of the Church. The mission of the Spirit as the Comforter, to abide with the Church, "builded together as a habitation of God through the Spirit", and as "the Spirit of adoption whereby we cry, Abba, Father", was consequent on the exaltation of Jesus to the right hand of the Father. So far there is a distinction in the earthly privileges of those who lived before, and those who have lived subsequent to that event. But the day of Pentecost did not witness the first action of the Spirit of God upon the souls of men. From the fall of man there has been but one way of salvation, one Saviour in whom faith rested, and one Spirit who quickened unto spiritual and everlasting life; and all who thus have eternal life were born of the Spirit. Faith was not then, any more than it is now, indigenous to the heart of man; and, faith had the same object then as now. It is not necessary that we should here prove that Abraham not only believed *the promise* of a Saviour, but believed in *the Saviour* promised; or prove that, though the saints of old could by no means anticipate the wonderful particulars of the way by which the incarnate Word accomplished our redemption, they offered their typical sacrifices in faith, looking to that which they signified, and so, by anticipation, received the remission of sins in His blood. It was so from the first; for *"by faith* Abel offered unto God a more excellent sacrifice than Cain"—faith, which owning the need of a sacrifice for sin, presented to God that which prefigured it—"and by *it* he being dead yet speaketh"; it tells that no sinner ever has found, and no sinner ever can find pardon, peace, and eternal life, save in believing on Him, "whom God has set forth to be a propitiation through faith in His blood". Nothing short of this could ever justify the ungodly—nothing short of this could appease the awakened conscience.

But the question may still be raised, Shall those who, under previous dispensations, resting in the same Saviour, being quickened by the same Spirit, *also have the same glory* with believers of the present dispensation? The majority of our readers may think it strange that such a question could be raised; but what has been said may satisfy them that it is not well to take it for granted, and that we are called to know what answer the Word of God gives to the question. It will be understood that those who exclude them from the inheritance of the Church do not question that they will have *a* glory, but assert that their glory, whatever it may be, will not be that which the Lord has given to the Church. We need not, therefore, refer to the passages in which their future blessedness is revealed, but only to those which show that they and we shall be *united* in glory.

There seems to be something of the Gentile boasting which needs to be reminded of the apostle's words, "Thou bearest not the root, but the root thee", in these strange conceits of superiority to Abraham, Isaac, and Jacob. As the subject presents itself in the New Testament, the question in the minds of men was not, Shall the Old Testament saints share the blessedness of the Church? but, Shall we be admitted to a participation of the blessedness of these fathers? The Lord speaks of many who shall "come from the East and West, and shall sit down with Abraham, and Isaac, and Jacob, in the kingdom of heaven", or, as Luke has it, "The kingdom of God". One might suppose that there could be no difference of opinion as to the "many" who are described as coming from the East and West, or as to what is implied in this association with Abraham, Isaac and Jacob, in the kingdom of heaven. But if the application of the description to believers of this dispensation should be disputed, the passage would still conclusively show that the saints of previous dispensations shall inherit that to which we look forward as our inheritance —the kingdom of heaven when it is manifested in glory.

But the most satisfactory answer to the question will be found in the Epistles addressed to the Churches where there can be no dispute as to the persons intended.

And it is not unworthy of notice that, as it is in the Gospel of Matthew, which the teachers to whom we have referred would hand over to the Jewish remnant, that we find the only formal mention of the Church, so it is in the Epistles of Paul, the Apostle of the Gentiles, that we find the most explicit revelation of the glorious destiny of the Old Testament saints.

In the Epistle to the Romans, chapter three, the only ground of justification is shown to be in Him "whom God has set forth to be a propitiation through faith in His blood, to declare His righteousness for *the remission of sins that are past,* through the forbearance of God; to declare at this time His righteousness, that He might be just, and the justifier of him which believeth in Jesus". Then in chapter four, it is shown that the only way of justification is by faith. No other ground or way of justification has ever been known, and the example of this is found in the case of Abraham, to whom faith was reckoned for righteousness. But observe, this took place while he was yet uncircumcised, "that he might be the father of all them that believe, though they be not circumcised, that righteousness might be imputed to them also". This relationship has reference to the promise of an inheritance which "is of faith, that it might be by grace; to the end the promise might be sure to all the seed; not to that which is of the law, but to that also which is of the faith of Abraham; who is *the father of us all*". It is in view of this common justification, and with reference to this common inheritance in which Abraham is regarded, not as our inferior, but our father, that the argument is followed out to the conclusion, "for if by one man's offense death reigned by one; much more, they which receive abundance of grace and of the gift of righteousness *shall reign in life by one,* Jesus Christ". Whatever may be justly said of the difference in respect of life and privilege between believers of different dispensations, we behold them at last united to "reign in life by one, Jesus Christ", and thus, *without distinction* it is testified that "whom He did foreknow, them He also did predestinate to be conformed to the image of His Son, that He might be the first-born among many brethren. Moreover whom He did predestinate them He also called: and whom He called them He also justified; and whom He justified, them He also glorified". The concatenation is so complete that, if a man is found included in one of its terms, all the rest necessarily are affirmed of him; if, for example, we find Abraham among the justified, we may trace his justification back to the Divine foreknowledge, and find that he also was predestinated to be conformed to the image of God's Son; or, looking in the other direction, we see it resulting in his being glorified. And what higher destiny and prospect can there be for any of the justified?

Without following out the subject in the remaining portion of this Epistle, we turn to the Epistle of the Corinthians. We have already seen that Abraham was predestinated to be conformed to the image of the Son of God, and it is added, "that He (the Son) might be the firstborn among many brethren". In harmony with this we read in 1 Cor. 15:20, "But now is Christ risen from the dead, and become the firstfruits of them that slept". The verb is in the perfect tense, "them that *have fallen asleep*", which surely includes Abraham; and then we find that it is "in Christ" that they are raised, "at His coming", and that those who shall be raised at His coming are "Christ's". And again we ask, What more can be affirmed of the Church or of believers in this age? Abraham, as well as Paul, having borne the image of the earthly, shall also bear the image of the heavenly.

The most decisive proof of the union of the saints of the past dispensations with those of the present in glory, is found in the Epistle to the Galatians. It is so full that we can only glance at the outline of it. And here it is most evident that the error with which the apostle had to deal was the reverse of that which is now before us. These churches in Galatia, having received the Gospel, had been taught that there was yet some higher place of favor and future glory in association with Abraham and his seed; and that, in order to secure a participation in these, it was necessary for them, as Christians, to be circumcised. Now, if, as has been taught in our day, the position and prospects, the calling and glory of believers in this dispensation be superior to, or different from, those of Abraham, this was the place to affirm it. But the apostle is content to show that we have a common inheritance with him. In chapter three we find the statement, similar to that in the Epistle to the Romans, of the way in which Abraham and all believers are justified; and then this is shown to be introductory to a common blessing, "They which be of faith are blessed with faithful Abraham". This is shown to be altogether independent of the law, which could not affect a covenant confirmed of God, *in Christ,* four hundred and thirty years before the law was given. The seed in whom the promise was confirmed was Christ, and consequently, all who are in Him are heirs of it. But let it be observed, that the conclusion, "if ye be Christ's, then are ye Abraham's seed, and heirs according to the promise", follows the statement, "ye are all the children of God by faith in Christ Jesus". Was Abraham less a son and heir of God? If a more definite answer was needed to this question than the argument in chapter three supplies, we have it in the commencement of chapter four. There, while the sonship of all believers is affirmed, the difference between the condition of believers under the present dispensation, and that of believers under the dispensation which preceded it, is very strikingly illustrated by the condition of a son and heir before and after he has attained his majority. "The heir, as long as he is a child, differeth nothing from a servant, though he be lord of all". The difference is not in relationship, but in outward condition; they are equally the sons of God, and equally heirs—heirs of God, joint heirs with Christ. The fact that we now are not in the servant's place, but in the enjoyment of the Spirit of adoption, is surely an unspeakable privilege; but then it is only a step toward the consummation, when all the sons will be manifested, and introduced into the common inheritance. "When He shall appear, *we* shall be like Him; for we shall see Him as He is". But this is as true regarding all whom God hath predestinated to be conformed to the image of His Son, though during their earthly pilgrimage they were, as minors, under tutors and governors.

Even in the Epistle to the Ephesians, which contains the fullest exposition of the calling and glory of the Church, and especially of its present standing and privileges, the ultimate *community of blessing* is plainly intimated in the contrast between the original condition of these Ephesians, "being aliens from the commonwealth of Israel, and strangers from the covenants of promise", and their condition under grace, as "no longer strangers and foreigners, but fellow citizens with the saints, and of the household of God". Under this dispensation there is indeed a great difference in the privileges of believers, whether Jews or Gentiles, inasmuch as they "both have access by one Spirit unto the Father", and as they are "builded together as an habitation of God through the Spirit"; but this does not affect the common relationship and the common hope of fellow citizens and members of the household of God into which these Gentiles had now been introduced by the blood of Christ.

Without mentioning the other Epistles, the bearing of the whole of the Epistle to the Hebrews upon the question before us, would require a separate article. We can only refer to one or two passages in chapter eleven. In the enumeration of illustrious examples from among the elders, of "faith which is the substance of things hoped for, the evidence of things not seen", it is remarkable how many particulars are mentioned which have been represented as peculiar to a later revelation of the grace of God. Surely it is not without significance that, from the antediluvian era, we have, in Enoch, an instance of what the apostle shows as a mystery, "We shall not all sleep". Abraham, Isaac, and Jacob are represented as voluntarily occupying the place of strangers and pilgrims on the earth, the place which *all* the sons of God must occupy here; and that, too, as declaring plainly that they seek a country. In willing separation from this world with its lying hopes, they are pressing on to a better, that is, an *heavenly.* "Wherefore God is not ashamed to be called their God: for He hath prepared for them a city". Not only has He prepared for them a city, but they look for it, and the description of it leaves us in no doubt as to what city they looked for, and which God hath prepared for them, "a city which hath foundations, whose builder and maker is God"; nay, but in the Greek it is more explicit still, *"the* city which hath foundations", there is but one city, "the city of the living God, the heavenly Jerusalem," in which our hopes will find their full fruition, into which all who have washed their robes have right of entrance, where the redeemed of all ages shall together share the fulness of the love of Christ, their common Saviour. Surely it is not without meaning that, if the names of the twelve apostles —apostles of the Lamb—are on the twelve foundations of the walls of the city, the names of the twelve tribes of the children of Israel are inscribed on its twelve gates. These, indeed, all died in faith, not having received the promise, "God having provided some better thing for us, that they without us should not be made perfect". We cannot object to the exaltation of the grace of God in view of the better things God has provided for us, as now, through the Spirit, walking in conscious oneness with the risen Christ, whose promised coming they only saw afar off. But does not the intimation that they could not be made perfect without us, most emphatically intimate that we and they shall be perfected together in Him whose coming to suffer for sin, and whose resurrection from the dead, must needs precede the perfecting of either?—*James Inglis, Waymarks, 1868.*

FORGIVENESS OF SINS

In going to the Cross we went with all our guilt, to deposit it where alone it is lawful so to do; to bury it in a grave, out of which there can be no resurrection for it forever. We gave our burden to God, and He took it from us most lovingly and without a grudge. We "laid both our hands upon the head" of the great Surety, "confessing over him" all our iniquities and putting upon Him all our transgressions (Lev. 16:21), and we then, "coming into the tabernacle" as accepted worshippers (Lev. 16:23), nay, going into the holiest of all, through the veil that has been rent, to present our worship in "a cloud of incense that covers the mercy-seat that is upon the testimony" (Lev. 16: 13).

Having heard the voice that spoke of the great burnt Sacrifice, the Lamb of God who taketh away the sin of the world, we looked to it, went to it, and laid our sins upon it. That which we then beheld was not anything about ourselves save our sin and need; God's testimony to the slain Lamb was the one thing on which our faith rested. We read that "The Lord hath laid on Him the iniquity of us all" (that is, hath inflicted on Him our punishment); that the "chastisement of our peace was upon Him" (Isa. 53:5); that "the Lord was well-pleased for His righteousness' sake" (Isa. 42:21); and upon believing the report we realized the transfer—our sin passing over to Him, and His righteousness passing over to us. This was the exchange we made when we believed. In God's purpose, no doubt, all this was a certainty from eternal ages; and when Christ "carried up our sins in His own body to the tree" (1 Pet. 2:24, see Greek), this purpose began visibly to unfold itself. But this is only the *Divine,* not the *human* side, of the great question. In the eternal purpose we see God pre-arranging to do certain things when the time for doing them should come; and in the Cross we see the righteous provisions made for carrying these pre-arrangements into effect. But the human side is that which takes up events as they emerge, and individuals as they come into being and action. Hence the personal transference took place *upon our believing, not before;* and we might as well speak of eternal conversion and eternal forgiveness as of eternal justification. Both are equally true in one aspect; both are equally untrue in another. The *purpose* to convert and justify belong to the eternal past; the *carrying out of* that purpose is an act of time, a fragment of personal human history.

From the moment we believed, we could count ourselves forgiven men, and God began to deal with us as such. We had learned from the Epistle to the Romans our justification in law before God, and we learned from the Epistle to the Hebrews our justification *in conscience;* that is, our conscience was "purged from dead works to serve the living God", so that we being "once purged, had no more conscience of sins" (Heb. 10:2). Neither of these things, however, could mean that *our future sins* were *actually* pardoned, in the same sense as our past, and at the same time. A sin cannot be *pardoned* till it has been *committed.* If it can be pardoned before being committed, it must be pardoned before it be repented of, or it must be repented of before it is committed, or else repentance and confession are mockeries; and they who speak of all sins, past, present, and to come, being forgiven at once upon believing, are losing sight of the real meaning of words and things, and might as well affirm that we were converted before we were born, or that our disease was cured before we were sick, and that the one act of faith put forth at our conversion is enough for us, without our having recourse to such a life time's continuous believing, as is indicated in our Lord's expression, "He that believeth (not has believed) hath everlasting life". To say that from the day we believed, God regarded us as forgiven men, men not under wrath but under grace, is one thing; but to say that all our sins are actually pardoned before being committed is quite another. The apostle certainly did not think that all our future sins were actually pardoned at once, when he said, "If we confess our sins, He is faithful and just to forgive us our sins, and to cleanse us from all unrighteousness" (1 John 1:9); nor did the Lord think so when He taught us to pray, "Forgive us our debts as we forgive our debtors", making daily pardon as needful as daily bread (Matt. 6:11, 12). —Andrew Bonar in "God's Way of Holiness".

ASSURANCE

To say that assurance of one's salvation is of the essence of faith, and that it is the *first* part of the Gospel, is to depart from Scripture as much as from common sense. For to believe that I am saved, or to be sure that I am pardoned in order to be pardoned; is a contradiction such as only incoherency could announce. To say that assurance of salvation is the immediate and necessary *result* of faith, is to follow the teaching of the apostles, and to give the true interpretation to their Gospel. For if the belief of that Gospel does not forthwith assure me of my own acceptance, it must make me thoroughly miserable. The more that its blessings are apprehended, the more wretched must I become, if it can bring me no *present* certainty as to my share in these; if the result of my believing is to land me in an interval of *doubt*, from which I can only extricate myself by years of effort. To keep a prisoner waiting for twenty years before assuring him of the royal pardon, would not be half so cruel as to keep the accepted sinner for a day uncertain as to the pardon of his sin. Every hour's uncertainty would be a foretaste of hell. Yet this uncertainty is all the good news which many preach. They proclaim a gospel which merely sets the sinner a working for salvation, a *trying* to believe. They tell him that if he will only go on thus, doing his best and trying to believe, for twenty or thirty years, God will take pity upon his laborious endeavors, and show favor to his earnestness. They call on him to sum up his good feelings at certain seasons, and on that summation to build his hopes of becoming by degrees at least an accepted man. But all the while what is the poor soul to do with an awakened conscience, and terrors of doom, and thoughts of the possibility of being lost after all? This surely is not the Gospel of Christ and His apostles. It is not the Gospel which brought *immediate* joy, as soon as believed, to the sinners of Jerusalem, Antioch and Phillippi. It contains no good news, because no certainty of pardon to the sinner; no present purging of the conscience through the blood.

The want of assurance has frequently been defended from the Psalms. On this point we suggest the following thoughts:—

There are two extremes of interpretation in the case of the Psalms. The first almost sets aside Christ from them, and understands the expressions on bitterness and grief as merely David's utterances; as ofttimes the utterances of doubt, and unbelief, and want of assurance. That they were truly the utterances of David's feelings in the circumstances in which they were composed, is most true, and ought to be taken as the basis of all interpretations; but that they were not meant by the Holy Spirit for a greater than David, is a serious error; that they are the utterances of doubt, or unbelief, or non-assurance, or want of trust, is even more serious error; for not only does it make the Holy Spirit put words of distrust into a believer's lips (nay, we should say, into Messiah's lips), but it overlooks this notable fact, that even those Psalms which are darkest throughout, and read most like doubting, begin with "My God", or similar words of assurance; nay, that the very bitterness expressed is occasioned by the thought that this God, about whose relationship to them no doubt is entertained, is giving them over to the will of their enemies.

The second interpretation exhibits Christ in them as the true speaker, though the voice and the pen at first were David's. But though this seems to us, speaking generally, the correct view, we should not like to see it supersede the use of the Psalms by Christians, as in many parts expressive of New Testament sentiments as truly as of Old. To speak of Jewish saints as occupying lower ground and inheriting a lower kingdom than we do, or as liable to an experience of conflict from which we have been delivered, is to exhibit a one-sidedness of view and an ignorance of the Christian's warfare hardly to be expected in men who have studied the whole Word of God. To tear away the Psalms from us as obsolete, and to deny them to be the proper utterance of Christian worship because of the sorrow which breathes through so many of them, is to deprive us of the means of identifying ourselves with Old Testament saints, and to shut us out from the use of language which best embodies the feeling of one wrestling, not with flesh and blood, but with principalities, and powers; of one who "groans, being burdened" (2 Cor. 5:4); is in "heaviness, through manifold temptations" (1 Pet. 1:6); oppressed with "infirmities", pierced with "thorns in the flesh", and buffeted by messengers of Satan" (2 Cor. 12:7, 10); troubled on every side, fightings without and fears within (2 Cor. 7:5). Let those who have soared above Paul and David, who call conflict bondage, and treat the cries of Old Testament saints as something which it would be sin for us to listen to, reject the Psalms and their experiences; but those who know something of the warfare, will welcome them as suitable and precious above measure,—the breathings, not of spirit-bondage, but of liberty and adoption.

A. Bonar. Extract from "The Way of Holiness".

HOME AND THE HOUSEHOLD

Men who look no further than the temporal happiness of individuals and the welfare of existing society, are not insensible to the importance of our domestic relations, which the strongest affections of nature secure, and which even our wants and weaknesses cement. We can form no conception of the social virtue or enjoyment, or, we might say, no conception of human society itself, which has not its spring and fountain in the family. No matter how excellent the constitution and laws of a country may be, or what its resources and its means of power and prosperity, unless a sure foundation for social order, and public as well as private virtue be laid in the healthy regulation and wise discipline of its families. "A nation," it has been remarked, "is but a shorter name for the individuals who compose it, and when these are good fathers, good sons, good brothers and good husbands, it is superfluous to say they will be good citizens."

There are not a few who have become convinced that defective views of the family relationship, and the relaxation of family government, threaten the stability and prosperity of this country far more seriously than domestic treason or foreign hostility. The scriptural view of the relative duties of the members of the Christian household, presents the prevailing defects in an alarming aspect, as dishonoring to God, disastrous to the spiritual condition of the churches, and as throwing the most serious obstructions in the way of evangelical progress. Professing Christians are largely responsible for the general disregard of domestic obligations. At least, they will confess that it is from the churches alone that a healthful influence can ever be shed abroad upon the homes of the land. They, therefore, may, with propriety, be summoned to a serious and prayerful consideration of the revealed will of God on a subject as interesting as it is momentous.

Home! How much that word conveys to the heart of every man who is not utterly hardened in vice! Christianity aside, we regard a man as lost to society to whom home has lost its charm. But when, to all its natural attractions, are added the hallowed associations which gather round a Christian home, there is little wonder if, in our common forms of speech, the word should have been transferred from a terrestrial to a heavenly resting-place of our hopes and affections; as God has been pleased to employ its relations as symbols of the most exalted relations which subsist between Himself and His creatures.

It is a common saying that, in order to know a man you must see him at home; not because he is to be regarded as a hypocrite or an impostor, who only lays aside his mask when he can do it with safety; but because men learn to be guarded, both in action and expression, in the ordinary intercourse of life. In spite of themselves, their best as well as their worst characteristics are under restraint while they are surrounded by those with whom they are not perfectly familiar, or in whose friendship they have not perfect confidence. The reality and extent of a work of grace in the heart of a Christian are also revealed in the unguarded confidence and amid the multiplied petty trials of home. Here the husband, wife, parent, child, brother, and sister show whether they have a mere form of godliness or own its power. Here their consistency is most severely tested, and here the influence of each, for good or evil, finds it most energetic exercise. This is especially true of the head of the house, who cannot fail to stamp it with his own character. An accurate observer of wide experience says, "I never can form a correct judgment of a man from seeing him or hearing him in a religious meeting. He may seem a very spiritual person, and teach very beautiful and very true things, but let me go home with him, and then I learn the actual state of the case. He may speak like an angel from heaven, but if his house be not ordered according to the mind of God, he cannot be a true witness for Christ."

The character of those who appear most prominently on the page of Scripture is frequently subjected to this test. The curtain of the patriarch's tent is raised, the door of the saint's abode is opened, and we are permitted to see him within the sanctuary of home. We not only see himself there, but we see his household laid under a responsibility and made sharers of a blessing in proportion to his fidelity. Thus, when God was about to destroy the old world, He said to Noah, "Come thou and all thy house into the ark, for thee have I seen righteous before Me in this generation." We have no definite information, indeed, of the manner in which Noah discharged his obligations as the head of that family, but, so far as it goes, the record shows how God regards a man's household as identified with himself. It shows both the responsibility and the blessedness of such a connection. The members of his family were saved from the flood, because they formed the household of one who, in the language of Paul, had become heir of the righteousness which is by faith.

In addition to all that physiologists may tell us of hereditary influences on character, and in addition to all that a moralist may tell us of the far-reaching influence of parental instruction and example, we find throughout the Scriptures abundant proof of a peculiarity both of responsibility and blessing, resting upon the households of the children of God. Numerous examples are recorded of the favor with which God crowns the faithfulness of believers in their relations to their children. For example, God gave this as a reason for admitting Abraham into His confidence, "For I know him that he will command his children and his household after him, and they shall keep the way of the Lord to do justice and judgment." Nor is the lesson less impressive in the record of the disastrous consequences of a man's inconsistency and unfaithfulness in these relations. Two examples will occur to almost every reader—the bitter consequences to Lot's family, of his separation from Abraham to sojourn in Sodom, and the wreck of Eli's family because "his sons made themselves vile, and he restrained them not."

The principle involved in the numerous examples which might be cited from the Old Testament, must not be regarded as peculiar to a former dispensation. Although grace is not hereditary, the New Testament is not without its encouraging instances of a household joined with its head in the enjoyment of spiritual blessings. Prominent among these stands the case of the jailor at Philippi, who "rejoiced, believing with all his house;" and the house of Onesiphorus is joined with him in the apostolic benediction, "because," says Paul, "he oft refreshed me, and was not ashamed of my chain." There is a noticeable example of making the state of a man's house the test of his character, when we are taught that a bishop must be "one that ruleth well his own house," and that he shall have faithful or believing children as though the fact that his children were unbelievers would bring suspicion upon his fidelity and consistency, and must, therefore, invalidate his testimony to the truth.

Without multiplying proofs, it will readily be admitted that we have the sanction of Scripture when we say that a man's house furnishes the proper test of his character, and that the household of a believer enjoys important advantages, and is laid under corresponding responsibility by the very fact of its connection with him. A Christian, consequently, lies under peculiar responsibility for the manner in which he occupies his place as its head. His authority is sustained by a Divine ordinance, and he has the implied assurance of the Divine blessing in exercising it faithfully. In a certain sense, he represents God in that position, and is called to occupy it for God. Since he is not his own, but bought with a price, he must aim at the glory of God in every relation of life, and do everything in the name of the Lord Jesus, giving thanks unto God, even the Father, by Him. If in everything and in every place he is to show that he is Christ's, then, surely, next to the church of God, his own house will be the sphere of his most manifest devotedness. The love of God ruling in his heart will pervade his home, all its arrangements will bear the stamp of his heavenly vocation. As he occupies the place of its head by Divine appointment, we should find in everything an acknowledgment of the presence, the providence, the grace, and the authority of God. All its affairs should be so conducted as to leave on the mind of every spectator the impression, "God is here."

This influence will not be confined to the household, it will reach to the house itself, which, with all its furniture, will bespeak a heart dead to the world. On the one hand, there will be an absence of all that savors of the world's empty display and enslaving luxury, but, on the other hand, however humble his roof, and however poor its equipments, it will not be dishonored by filth and disorder. The charge that is given to us regarding the house of God, "let all things be done decently and in order," will be carried out in the house of the man of God. The admonition, "provide things honest in the sight of all men," which extends to all our social relations, as well as our personal deportment, will have its most accurate application to that sphere of our more immediate control. It would be difficult to tell which is the most unseemly in the dwelling of a Christian, ostentation and vanity, or slovenliness and confusion; but it is certain that either indicates something wrong in the state of a man's heart, and must mar his Christian influence.

Nothing can be more flagrantly absurd than to hear a man speak of being dead with Christ and of living in the expectation of a coming Saviour, while his home and his style of living plainly show that he is engaged in the carnal rivalries of the worldly, who know no other than an earthly home, no glory but to outshine their neighbors, no delights but such as minister to the lusts of the flesh, the lust of the eye, and the pride of life. Such a man may profess what he pleases, he may excuse or defend himself as he chooses, but the worldly, with whom he vies in fashion and display, are quick to discern the palpable contradiction of his profession. Little wonder if our public warnings and persuasions fall dead and ineffectual, when there is so much in the homes and households of those who bear the Christian name, which must carry to the world the irresistible conviction of our insincerity. The standard of life cannot, surely, be lower among those who profess to be crucified with Christ than it was among the ancient people of God amid the promised temporal blessings of their own land. Yet, when we listen to the woe pronounced upon those who were at ease in Zion, it requires but a slight change of terms to make the description of luxury which called down the Divine judgments on them, an accurate picture of many a so-called Christian home, where "they put far away the evil day, and lie upon beds of ivory, and stretch themselves on their couches, and eat the lambs of the flock and the calves out of the midst of the stall, and chant to the sound of the viol, and invent to themselves instruments of music like David, and drink wine in bowls, and anoint themselves with the chief ointments, but they are not grieved for the afflictions of Joseph" (Amos 6:3-6).

Familiarity reconciles us to the most unseemly and revolting sights, but it will doubtless appear in the record of history as a most heartless enormity, that fashionable display, luxury, and extravagance, instead of being arrested, should have received a new impulse amidst the calamities which threaten, not the prosperity alone, but the existence of a nation; nay, which threaten the overthrow of all that is dearest and most promising in the temporal hopes of mankind; to say nothing of the untold woes which have been inflicted on so many thousands of our fellow-citizens. Nothing more is necessary to expose the tendency of fashion and luxury and the character of those whose hearts are enslaved by them. But there is something even more monstrous than this, when we find those who profess to be watching, because they know not what a day nor an hour may bring forth, and to have their affections set on the things which are above, the foremost in the race of worldliness,—when we find the most flagrant display of fashions which outrage good taste and Christian propriety in the families of professing Christians, and in the assemblies of professed worshipers, as though they would defy God to His face. Do they forget Him who hath said, "The Lord will take away the bravery of their tinkling ornaments, and their curls, and their round tires like the moon, the chains, and the bracelets, and the mufflers, the bonnets, and the ornaments of the legs, and the head-bands, and the tablets and the ear-rings, and the rings and nose jewels, the changeable suits of apparel, and the mantles and the wimples, and the crisping-pin, the glasses and the fine linen, and the hood and the veil"? These things were not unnoticed by the All-seeing eye, and the enumeration of them stands in the Scriptures of truth. They are not, therefore, beneath our notice. Very vanity indeed they are in themselves; but not trivial is the sin which gives them a place in the hearts of men, and which displays them where sackcloth and ashes would best become the wearers.

The evil of which we speak is not confined to those who are the recognized votaries of fashion, and who attract general notice by their extravagance. The evil does not consist in the amount of money expended on it. The heart and home of many whose means of display are very limited are all overrun with the plague; and it may manifest itself only in the envy with which the poor look upon a splendor which they cannot emulate. Those who would be faithful in this, as in other matters, must go beyond the outward appearance, on which man looks, to the heart, upon which God looks, and must search themselves as in His sight. Instead of comparing their home, dress, and style of living with those of their wealthier neighbors, they should enquire whether the bent and aspirations of their hearts would not lead them to rival the excesses of the wealthy, and whether they are not going as far in that direction as their means and opportunities enable them. They should enquire whether they are not sacrificing opportunities of laying up treasures in heaven, for the sake of idle and hurtful display; and if they are not, after all, somewhat discontented with the circumstances of the lot which render that display so limited.

They must rest assured that just such things are taken by all, except themselves, as an index of their true character. Men judge of us not by the doctrines we profess, but the lives we lead. They do not follow us to religious meetings to hear how loudly we exhort, or how fervently we pray, but they look at our homes, and our households, and our mode of living, and if these bear the stamp of worldliness, then, though we speak with the tongues of men and of angels, we are become as sounding brass and a tinkling cymbal in the estimation of our children, friends, and neighbors. The state of things in the homes of Christians goes far to explain the want of spiritual power in our churches, and the want of apparent success in the preaching of the Gospel. Such power and success, it is true, depend directly on the agency of the Holy Spirit. But God, though sovereign, is not capricious or arbitrary in the bestowment of spiritual blessings. The Spirit, though quenched and grieved, has not been withdrawn. It becomes us, therefore, to search ourselves unsparingly for the hindrance of His manifested power. Let us not occupy ourselves with other churches, or the households of our neighbors, nor exhaust our zeal in vague lamentations over the condition of the country or the world; but let us begin in our own hearts and our own homes, each asking, "Lord, is it I?" After such an inquiry mayhap none of us will think ourselves entitled to cast the first stone, or, at least, we may find a beam to be cast out of our own eye, that we may see clearly to take the mote out of our brother's eye. But when we are thus led to take our place in genuine contrition at the feet of Christ, we may thence set out on a new course of service, and the fulness of blessing may be restored.

If a Christian's home contradicts his profession of being crucified with Christ, it is not surprising if his children go forth from it more settled in ungodliness, and less accessible to Christian influences, than children who go from homes where the pursuit of the world is undisguised. The tone of worldliness pervading a Christian's home reacts also powerfully upon himself. A worldly man finds in a home which is regulated on principles of worldly prudence, where the love of wife and children always wait to welcome him, not only a relaxation from toil and care, but an antidote to the more hardening and corrupting influence of his association with the outer world. The Christian surely ought to find, in a home regulated upon Christian principles, where all is purified and enhanced by the fear of the Lord, a powerful influence to counteract the secularizing tendencies of every-day life, if not an escape from the world itself. When he enters it he shuts the door upon the world, and there the tastes and affections of the new man might be expected to find unfettered scope. Everything speaks to him of another home, the light of which is reflected in this, and so recalls his distracted thoughts to their proper centre. An ungodly man said, "I never was so near heaven, and probably never shall be again, as when I spent a day in the home of Ebenezer Brown." Alas, that such homes are so rare. On the other hand, if the home to which the Christian ought to retire from the world, only presents the world to him in more inviting aspects, it must prove the most dangerous of all snares. His influence must chill every remaining affection of spirituality, and paralyze all his spiritual energies. Ultimately it must silence his testimony for Christ, or, at least, it will render his testimony a lifeless form, which were better abandoned.

The Christian head of a house does not stand alone in his responsibility there. His influence for good or evil is not complete in itself; he cannot dispense with the cooperation of his wife. In fact, so far as carrying out Christian principles, in their application to the details of family government is concerned, almost everything depends upon her. For, while he is occupied with the business of the day, which requires his absence, the business of her day lies in the discharge of many little duties in the household, which together they are to mould and control. Such a home as we have pictured that of a Christian to be, can only be found where they are dwelling together as heirs of the grace of life. No affliction throws a deeper shadow across an earthly lot than when the godly aims of the one party are thwarted by the worldliness of the other; and, in that case, a Christian can only be counselled to wrestle in prayer with God, to whom all things are possible. But when they profess a common faith, they should make the condition of their home a matter of joint-examination. They ought to deal with the errors and inconsistencies which exist there in the mutual confidence of those who are no more twain but one flesh, and who, moreover, are one in the Lord. They must act in concert in the removal of discovered errors; and with united voice, they must cry to God, whose name has been dishonored by these things. The fruits of such a course and the answer of such prayers will speedily be seen, not only in our homes, but in the Church of God, and God's name will be glorified where it is now blasphemed.

The Lord does not leave His people in this world for their personal salvation. That is secured forever when they believe on Him, and He would at once deliver them from the conflicts and sorrows of earth, were it not that He designs them to be His witnesses here, and to glorify the Father by bringing forth much fruit in a world that hates Him.

It is a solemn thought that a day is coming when, from many of our homes, "one shall be taken and another left." Eternal separations will take place among those who have been united in the closest affinities of earth—husbands and wives, parents and children, brothers and sisters. Reader, if that day were now to come, how would it be in your home? Is it ordered as you would desire to have it when the Master comes? Are those you love all ready and loving His appearing? —From "Waymarks in the Wilderness".

VOL. III FEBRUARY, 1924 NO. 2

STUDIES in the SCRIPTURES

"Search the Scriptures" John 5:39.

A PERIODICAL (MONTHLY "IF THE LORD WILL") DEVOTED TO BIBLE STUDIES and EXPOSITIONS

Arthur W. Pink, Publisher & Editor,
227 N. Creighton St., Philadelphia, Pa.

Price: 10 cents per copy; $1.00 per year. Foreign $1.00 per year.

OUR LORD'S HUMANITY.

"God was manifest in flesh" (1 Tim. 3:16).

The attentive reader will observe that our quotation above of this well-known text differs from the rendering given in the A.V. There we read, "God was manifest in *the* flesh". The definite article is also used in the R. V. But there is *no* article in the original. The Greek reads, "Theos ephanerothe en sarki", and herein we may discover the marvelous minute accuracy of Holy Writ.

"God was manifest in flesh" has reference to the Divine incarnation, and our text is strictly parallel with John 1:14—"The Word became flesh". The *absence* of the definite article in the Greek calls attention to the *uniqueness* of our Lord's humanity, and, indirectly, testifies to His "virgin birth". When God the Son "became flesh" He did not take upon Him corrupt flesh, but flesh that was sinless and holy. The passage where this is brought out the clearest is Luke 1:35: there we read that the angel said to Mary, "The Holy Ghost shall come upon thee, and the power of the Highest shall overshadow thee: *therefore* also that *holy thing* which shall be born of thee shall be called the Son of God". "That holy *thing*" is an abstract expression, referring to the character of our Lord's humanity. Its force is the more apparent if we contrast a sentence in Isa. 64:6: "But *we* all as an *unclean thing*". This is how the Holy Spirit describes our *depraved* human nature. It is an *unclean* "thing". But in marked contrast, the humanity of Christ is denominated that *holy* "thing"! "God was manifest in *the* flesh" is erroneous, horribly erroneous. It falsely declares that Christ partook of *our* fallen and corrupt human nature.* But "God was manifest in flesh" *distinguishes* His humanity from ours. Compare 1 John 5:2, 3; 2 John 7, where the article is also absent in the Greek.

It is indeed striking to note the sedulous care taken by the Holy Spirit to guard the glory of the God-man, and to prevent us arriving at false conclusions. God *did not* send His Son here in "sinful flesh", but *"in the likeness of* sinful flesh" (Rom. 8:3). Hence, in the meal offering, which typified the humanity of Christ, God expressly enjoined, "*No* meat offering, which ye shall bring unto the Lord, shall be made with *leaven*" (Lev. 2:11). And hence, too, the sacrificial lamb which pointed to the person of the Redeemer must be *"without* blemish" (Ex. 12:5). The holy "body" of the Saviour was intrinsically, essentially, radically, absolutely *different* from our bodies. Said He to His Father, "A *body* hast *Thou* prepared Me" (Heb. 10:5).

When referring to the person of "the Lord of glory" the greatest possible care must be taken in the selection of our language. Here, supremely, do we need to "hold fast the form of *sound* words" (2 Tim. 1:13), and that means, to employ the very words "which the Holy Ghost teacheth" (1 Cor. 2:13). Urgently do we need to seek wisdom from on high so that we shall not be found interpreting "in *all things* it behooved Him to be made like unto His brethren" (Heb. 2:17), in a way that will clash with "in *all things* He might have *the pre-eminence*" (Col. 1:18). May Divine wisdom and grace be given us so that we shall ever think and speak and write of the person of the God-man in a manner suited to His uniqueness, dignity, and glory. —Arthur W. Pink.

* In the New Testament "the flesh" has a clearly defined meaning and refers to depraved human nature, see John 3:6; Rom. 8:5, 13; Gal. 5:16, 17, etc.

IMPORTANT NOTICES

All new subscriptions will be dated back to January, 1924.
Set of twelve issues for **1922**, unbound, **$1.00.** Bound, **$1.50.**
Set of twelve issues for **1923**, unbound, **$1.00.** Bound **$1.50.**
Note: We cannot break a set or now supply any **single** 1923 issues.
Subscription Price: **$1.00** per year to any address in the world. Single copies **10 cents.**
Change of Address: Please notify me promptly of any change of address, and be certain to give both old and new addresses.
Non-subscribers receiving this Magazine regularly will understand their subscription has been entered by a friend.
Copies lost in the mail duplicated only if we are notified promptly.
Entered as second-class matter December 15th, 1923, at the post office at Philadelphia, Pa., under Act of March 3rd, 1879.

CONTENTS

JOHN'S GOSPEL

26. CHRIST TEACHING IN THE TEMPLE: John 7:14-31.

Below is an outline Analysis of the passage which is to be before us:—

1. Christ in the Temple, teaching: v. 14.
2. The Jews marvelling and Christ's answer: vv. 15-19.
3. The people's question and Christ's response: vv. 20-24.
4. The inquiry of those of Jerusalem: vv. 25-27.
5. The response of Christ: vv. 28, 29.
6. The futile attempt to apprehend Christ: v. 30.
7. The attitude of the common people: v. 31.

In our last lesson we discussed the first thirteen verses of John 7, from which we learned that notwithstanding "the Jews" (Judean leaders) sought to kill Him (v. 1), Christ, nevertheless, went up to Jerusalem to the Feast of Tabernacles (v. 10). We pointed out how this manifested the perfections of the Lord Jesus, inasmuch as it demonstrated His submission to the will and His obedience to the word of His father. Our present lesson records an important incident which transpired during the midst of the Feast. The Saviour entered the Temple, and, refusing to be intimidated by those who sought His life, boldly taught those who were there assembled.

"Now about the midst of the Feast Jesus went up into the temple, and taught" (v. 14). Twice previously has "the temple" been mentioned in this Gospel. In John 2 we behold Christ as the Vindicator of the Father's House, cleansing the Temple. In 5:14 we read how Christ found in the Temple the impotent man whom He had healed. But here in John 7, for the first time, we find our Lord *teaching* in the Temple. This was in beautiful accord with the dispensational character of the Feast. Christ teaching in the Temple gave a blessed foreshadowment of the antitypical fulfillment of this Feast in millennial times. If the last six verses of the prophecy of Zechariah be read, it will be found that in the Kingdom age, not only Israelites but Gentiles will go up to Jerusalem to "worship the King, the Lord of Hosts, and to keep the Feast of Tabernacles". This intimates that He will then be found in the newly-erected Temple (see Zech. 6:13), the place of worship. Note the double reference to "the Lord's House" in the last two verses of Zech. 14. In harmony with this, we read in Isa. 2:2, 3, "And it shall come to pass in the last days, that the mountain of the Lord's House shall be established in the top of the mountains, and shall be exalted above the hills; and all nations shall flow unto it. And many people shall go up and say, Come ye, and let us go up to the mountain of the Lord, to the House of the God of Jacob; and He will *teach* us of His ways, and we will walk in His paths: for out of Zion shall go forth the Law, and the Word of the Lord from Jerusalem." Thus we are enabled to perceive the deeper significance, the typical suggestiveness of what we are told here in John 7:14.

The Holy Spirit has not seen well to record the details of *what* it was that our

Lord "taught" on this significant occasion, but He intimates that the Saviour must have delivered a discourse of unusual weight. For in the very next verse we learn that even His enemies, "the Jews", *marvelled* at it. In keeping with His usual custom, we doubt not that He took advantage of the occasion to speak at length upon the different aspects and relations of the Feast itself. Most probably He linked together the various Old Testament scriptures which treat of the Feast, and brought out of them things which His hearers had never suspected were in them. And then there would be a searching application of the Word made to the consciences and hearts of those who listened.

"And the Jews marvelled, saying, How knoweth this man letters, having never learned?" (v. 15). "These words undoubtedly refer to our Lord's great acquaintance with the Scriptures, and the judicious and masterly manner in which He taught the people out of them, with far greater majesty and nobler eloquence than the scribes could attain by a learned education." (Dr. Philip Doddridge). But how their very speech betrayed these Jews! How this exclamation of theirs exposed the state of their hearts! It was not their consciences which were exercised, but their curiosity that was aroused. It was not the claims of God they were occupied with, but the schools of men. It was not the discourse itself they were pondering, but the manner of its delivery that engaged their attention.

"How knoweth this man letters, having never learned?" (v. 15). How like the spirit which is abroad today! How many there are in the educational and religious worlds who suppose it is impossible for a man to expound the Scriptures gracefully and to the edification of his hearers unless, forsooth, he has first been trained in some college or seminary! Education is an altar which is now thronged by a multitude of idolatrous worshippers. That, no doubt, is one reason why God's curse has fallen on almost all our seats of learning. He is jealous of His glory, and anything which enters into competition with Himself He blights and withers. An unholy valuation of human learning, which supplants humble dependence upon the Holy Spirit is, perhaps, the chief reason why God's presence and blessing have long since departed from the vast majority of our centers of Christian education. And in the judgment of the writer, there is an immediate and grave danger that we may shortly witness the same tragedy in connection with our Bible Schools and Bible Institutes.

If young men are taught, even though indirectly and by way of implication, that they *cannot* and must not expect to become able ministers of God's Word, unless they first take a course in one of the Bible Institutes, then the sooner all such institutions are shut down the better both for them and the cause of God. If such views are disseminated, if a course in some Bible School is advocated in preference to personal waiting upon God and the daily searching of the Scriptures *in private,* then God will blast these schools as surely as He did the seminaries and universities. And such an event is not so far beyond the bounds of probability as some may suppose. Already there are not wanting signs to show that "Ichabod" has been written over some of them. One of the principal Bible training schools in England closed down some years ago; and the fact that one of the leading Institutes in this country is constantly sending out urgent appeals for financial help is conclusive evidence that it is now being run in the energy of the flesh.

"Jesus answered them, and said, My doctrine is not Mine, but His that sent Me" (v. 16). Let every young man who reads these lines ponder carefully this sentence from Christ. If he is fully assured that he has received a call from God to devote his life to the Lord's service, and is now exercised as to *how* he may become equipped for such service, let him prayerfully meditate upon these words of the Saviour. Let him remember that Christ is here speaking not from the standpoint of His essential glories, not as a member of the Godhead, but as the Son of God *incarnate,* that is, as the *Servant* of Jehovah. Let him turn to John 8:28 and compare its closing sentence: "As *My Father* hath *taught* Me, I speak these things". It was in no human schools He had learned to teach so that men marvelled. This discourse He had delivered originated not in His own mind. His doctrine came from the One who sent Him.

It was the same with the apostle Paul. Hear him, as he says to the Galatians, "But I certify you, brethren that the Gospel which was preached of me is not after man. For I neither received it of man, neither was I taught it, but by the revelation of Jesus Christ" (1:11, 12). And these things, dear brethren, are recorded for our learning. No one *has to* take a course in any Bible School in order to gain a knowledge and insight of the Scriptures. The man most used of God last century—Mr. C. H. Spurgeon—was a graduate of no Bible Institute! We do not say that God has not used the Bible schools to help many who have gone there; we do not say there may not be such which He is so using today. But what we *do* say is, that such schools are not an *imperative* necessity. You have the same Bible to hand that they have; and you have the same Holy Spirit to guide you into all truth. God may be pleased to use human instruments in instructing and enlightening you, or He may give you the far greater honor and privilege of teaching you *directly*. That is for *you* to ascertain. Your first duty is to humbly and diligently look to HIM, *wait* on Him for guidance, *seek* His will, and the sure promise is, "The meek will He *guide* in judgment: and the meek will He *teach His way*" (Psa. 25:9).

"My doctrine is not Mine, but His that sent Me" (v. 16). These words were spoken by Christ to *correct* the Jews, who were unable to account for the wondrous words which fell from His lips. He would assure them that His "doctrine" had been taught Him by no man, nor had He invented it. "My doctrine is not Mine, *but His that sent Me*". How zealous He was for the Father's honor! How jealously He guarded the Father's glory! Let every servant of God learn from this blessed One who was "meek and lowly in heart" Whenever people praise *you* for some message of help, fail not to disclaim *all* credit, and remind your God-dishonoring admirers that the "doctrine" is not yours, but His that sent you.

"My doctrine is not Mine". Observe that Christ does not say "My doctrine*s* are not Mine", but "My doctrine". The word "doctrine" means "teaching", and the teaching (truth) of God, is one correlated and complete whole. In writing to Timothy, Paul said, "Take heed unto thyself, and unto the *doctrine*" (not doctrine*s*—1 Tim. 4:6). And again he wrote, "All Scripture is given by inspiration of God and is profitable for *doctrine*" (2 Tim. 3:16). In striking contrast from this, Scripture speaks of "the doctrine*s* of men" (Col. 2:22); "strange doctrine*s*" (Heb. 13:9); and "doctrine*s* of demons" (1 Tim. 4:1). Here the word is pluralized, because there is no unity or harmony about the teachings of men or the teachings of demons. *They* are diverse and conflicting. But God's truth is indivisible and harmonious.

"If any man will do His will, he shall know of the doctrine, whether it be of God, or whether I speak of Myself" (v. 17). The wording of this verse in the A. V. leaves something to be desired; we give, therefore, the translation found in Bagster's Interlinear*: "If any one desire His will to practise, he shall know concerning the teaching whether from God it is, or I from Myself speak". The Greek word here rendered "desire" signifies no fleeting impression or impulse, but a deeply rooted determination. The connection between this verse and the one preceding is as follows: 'What you have just heard from My lips is no invention of Mine, but instead, it proceedeth from Him that sent Me. Now if you really wish to test this and prove it for yourselves you must take care to preserve an honest mind and cultivate a heart that yields itself unquestioningly to God's truth'.

"If any man will do His will, he shall know of the doctrine, whether it be of God, or whether I speak of Myself" (v. 17). In this declaration our Lord laid down a principle of supreme practical importance. He informs us how *certainty* may be arrived at in connection with the things of God. He tells us how spiritual discernment and assurance are to be obtained. The fundamental condition for obtaining spiritual *knowledge* is a genuine heart-desire to carry out the revealed will of God in our lives. Wherever the heart is right God gives the capacity to apprehend His truth. If the heart be not right, wherein would be the value of knowing God's truth? God will not grant light on His Word unless we are truly anxious to walk according to that light. If the motive of the investigator be pure, than he will obtain an assurance that the teaching of Scripture *is* "of God" that will be far

* This is a work we strongly recommend to those who desire to be *students* of the Word. It gives the original Greek and immediately beneath, a literal, word for word, English translation. Obtainable from the Editor.

more convincing and conclusive than a hundred logical arguments.

"If any man will do His will, he shall know of the doctrine, whether it be of God, or whether I speak of Myself". How this word *rebuked*, again, these worldly-minded Jews; and how it reverses the judgment of many of our moderns! One does not have to enter a seminary or a Bible Institute and take a course in Christian Apologetics in order to obtain assurance that the Bible is inspired, or in order to learn how to interpret it. Spiritual intelligence comes not through the intellect, but via the heart: it is acquired not by force of reasoning, but by the exercise of faith. In Heb. 11:3 we read, "Through faith we *understand*", and faith cometh not by schooling but by *hearing*, and hearing by the Word of God! Thousands of years ago one of Israel's prophets was moved by the Holy Spirit to write, "Then shall we *know*, if we *follow on* to know THE LORD" (Hos. 6:3).

"He that speaketh of himself seeketh His own glory: but He that seeketh His glory that sent Him, the same is true, and no unrighteousness is in Him" (v. 18). Christ here appealed to the manner and purpose of His teaching, to show that He was no impostor. He that speaketh of, or better *from*, himself, means, he whose message originates with himself, rather than God. Such an one seeketh *his own* glory. That is to say, he attracts attention to himself: he aims at his own honor and aggrandizement. On the other hand, the one who seeks the glory of Him that sent him, the same is "true" or genuine (cf "true" in 6:32 and 15:1), i. e. a genuine servant of God. And of such, Christ added, "and no unrighteousness is in him". Interpreting this in the light of the context (namely, vv. 12 and 15), its evident meaning is, The one who seeks God's glory is no impostor.

"He that speaketh of himself seeketh his own glory: but he that seeketh His glory that sent him, the same is true, and no unrighteousness is in him" (v. 18). What a searching word is this for every servant of God today! How it condemns that spirit of self-exaltation which at times, alas, is found (we fear) in all of us. The Pharisees sought "the praise of men", and they have had many successors. But how different was it with the apostle Paul, who wrote, "I am the least of the apostles, that am not meet to be called an apostle" (1 Cor. 15:9). And again, "Unto me, who am less than the least of all saints" (Eph. 3:8). And what an important word does this eighteenth verse of John 7 contain for those who sit under the ministry of the profest servants of God. Here is one test by which we may discover whether the preacher has been called of God to the ministry, or **whether he ran without being** sent. Does he magnify himself or his Lord? Does he seek his own glory, or the glory of God? Does he speak about himself or about Christ? Can he truthfully say with the apostle, "We preach not ourselves, but Christ Jesus the Lord" (2 Cor. 4:5). Is the general trend of his ministry, Behold me, or Behold the church, or Behold the Lamb of God?

"Did not Moses give you the Law, and yet none of you keepeth the Law? Why go ye about to kill Me?" (v. 19). Here Christ completely turns the tables upon them. They were saying that He was unlettered, and now He charges *them* with having the letter of the Law, but failing to render obedience to it. They professed to be the disciples of Moses, and yet there they were with murder in their hearts, because He had healed the man on the Sabbath. He had just declared there was no unrighteousness in Himself; now He uncovered the unrighteousness which was in *them*, for they stood ready to break the sixth commandment in the Decalogue. His question, "Why go ye about to kill Me?" is very solemn. It was a word of more than local application. Where there is no heart *for* the truth, there is always an heart *against* it. And where there is enmity against the truth itself there is hatred of those who faithfully proclaim it. No one who is in anywise acquainted with the history of the last two thousand years can doubt that. And it is due alone to God's grace and restraining power that His servants do not now share the experiences of Stephen, and Paul, and thousands of the saints who were "faithful unto death" during the Middle Ages. Nor will it be long before the Divine restraint, which now holds Satan in leash and which is curbing the passions of God's enemies, shall be removed. Read through the prophecies of the Revelation and mark the awful sufferings which godly Jews will yet endure. Moreover, who can say how soon what is now transpiring in Russia may not become general and universal!

"The people answered and said, Thou hast a devil: who goeth about to kill Thee?" (v. 20). "The people" evidently refers to the miscellaneous company of Israelites in the Temple courts. At that season they came from all parts of Palestine up to Jerusalem to observe the Feast. Many of them were ignorant of the fact that the Judean leaders had designs upon the life of Christ; and when He said to the Jews (of v. 15) "Why go ye about to kill Me?" (v. 19, and cf v. 1), these "people" deemed our Lord insane, and said "Thou hast a demon", for insanity is often one of the marks of demonaical possession. This fearful blasphemy not only exposed their blindness to the glory of Christ, but also demonstrated the desperate evil of their hearts. To what awful indignities and insults did our blessed Lord submit in becoming incarnate! "Thou hast a demon": is such an aspersion ever cast on thee, fellow-christian? Then remember that thy Lord before thee was similarly reviled: sufficient for the disciple to be as his Master.

"Jesus answered and said unto them, I have done one work, and ye all marvel" (v. 21). Christ ignored the horrible charge of "the people", and continued to address Himself to "the Jews". And herein He has left us a blessed example. It is to be noted that in the passage where we are told, "Christ also suffered for us, leaving us an example, that we should follow His steps", the Holy Spirit has immediately followed this with, "Who did no sin, neither was guile found in His mouth: who, when He was reviled, reviled not again" (1 Pet. 2:22, 23). What a beautiful illustration John 7 gives of this! When He was reviled, *He* "reviled not again". He made no answer to their blasphemous declamation. O that Divine grace may enable us to "follow His steps". When Christ said to the Jews, "I have done one work, and ye all marvel", He was referring to what is recorded in John 5:1-16.

"Moses therefore gave unto you circumcision; (not because it is of Moses, but of the fathers;) and ye on the Sabbath day circumcise a man. If a man on the Sabbath day receive circumcision, that the Law of Moses should not be broken; are ye angry at Me, because I have made a man every whit whole on the Sabbath day?" (vv. 22, 23). Our Lord continued to point out how unreasonable was their criticism of Himself for healing the impotent man on the Sabbath day. He reminds them that circumcision was performed on the Sabbath; why then should they complain because He had made a poor sufferer whole on that day! By this argument Christ teaches us that works of necessity and works of mercy may be legitimately performed on the Sabbath. Circumcision was a work of necessity if the Law of Moses was to be observed, for if the infant reached its eighth day on the Sabbath, it was then he must be circumcised. The healing of the impotent man was a work of mercy. Thus are we permitted to engage in both works of necessity and works of mercy on the holy Sabbath.

It is to be observed that Christ here refers to circumcision as belonging to "the Law *of Moses*". For a right understanding of the teaching of Scripture concerning the Law it is of first importance that we distinguish sharply between "the Law of God" and "the Law of Moses". The Law of God is found in the Ten Commandments which Jehovah Himself wrote on the two tables of stone, thereby intimating that they were of lasting duration. This is what has been rightly termed the moral Law, inasmuch as the Decalogue (the Ten Commandments) enunciates a rule of conduct. The moral Law has no dispensational limitations, but is lastingly binding on every member of the human race. It was given not as a means of salvation, but as expressing the obligations of every human creature to the great Creator. The "Law of Moses" consists of the moral, social, and ceremonial laws which God gave to Moses *after* the Ten Commandments. The Law of Moses *included* the Ten Commandments as we learn from Deut. 5.

In one sense the Law of Moses is wider than "the Law of God", inasmuch as it contains far more than the Ten Commandments. In another sense, it is narrower, inasmuch as "the Law of Moses" is binding only upon Israelites and Gentile proselytes; whereas "the Law of God" is binding on Jews and Gentiles alike*. Christ clearly observes this distinction by referring to circumcision as belonging not to "the Law of God", but as being an es-

* See the author's booklet "The Saint and Law" for a fuller discussion of this subject.

sential part of "the Law of Moses" which related only to Israel.

"Judge not according to the appearance, but judge righteous judgment" (v. 24). The connection between this verse and the preceding ones is clear. Christ had been vindicating His act of healing the impotent man on the Sabbath day. To His superficial critics it might have seemed a breach of the Sabbatic law; but in reality it was not so. Their judgment was hasty and partial. They were looking for something they might condemn, and so seized upon this. But their verdict, as is usually the case when hurried and prejudiced, was altogether erroneous. Therefore, did our Lord bid them, "Judge not according to the appearance, but judge righteous judgment". He exhorted them to be fair; to take into account all the circumstances; to weigh *all* that God's Word revealed about the Sabbath. "In it thou shalt not do *any* work", was not to be taken absolutely: other scriptures plainly modified it. The ministrations of the priests in the Temple on the Sabbath, and the circumcising of the child on that day, when the Law required it, were cases in point. But the Jews had overlooked or ignored these. They had judged by appearances. They had not considered the incident according to its merits, nor in the light of the general tenor of Scripture. Hence, their judgment was *un*-righteous, because unfair and false.

"Judge not according to the appearance, but judge righteous judgment". This is a word which each of us much need to take to heart. Most of us fail at this point; fail in one of two directions. Some are prone to form too good an opinion of people. They are easily deceived by an air of piety. The mere fact that a man professes to be a Christian, does not prove that he is one. That he is sound in his morals and a regular attender of religious services, is no sure index to the state of his heart. Remember that all is not gold that glitters. On the other hand, some are too critical and harsh in their judgment. We must not make a man an offender for a word. In many things we *all* offend. There is not a just man on earth that doeth good and sinneth not (Ecc. 7:20). The evil nature, inherited from Adam, remains in every Christian to the end of his earthly course. And too, God bestows more grace on one than He does on another. There is real danger to some of us lest, forgetting the frailties and infirmities of our fellows, we regard certain Christians as unbelievers. Even a nugget of gold has been known to be covered with dust. It is highly probable that all of us who reach heaven will receive surprises there. Some whom we expected to meet will be absent, and some we never expected to see will be there. Let us seek grace to heed this timely word of our Lord's: "Judge not according to the appearance, but judge righteous judgment".

"Then said some of them of Jerusalem, Is not this He, whom they seek to kill? But, lo, He speaketh boldly, and they say nothing unto Him. Do the rulers know indeed that this is the very Christ?" (vv. 25, 26). In this chapter one party after another stand exposed. The Light was shining and it revealed the hidden things of darkness. First, the "brethren" of Christ (vv. 3-5) are exhibited as men of the world, unbelievers. Next, "the Jews" (the Judean leaders) display their carnality (v. 15). Then, the miscellaneous crowd, "the people" (v. 20) make manifest their hearts. Now the regular inhabitants of Jerusalem come before us. They, too, make bare their spiritual condition. In sheltering behind "the rulers" they showed what little anxiety they had to discover for themselves whether or not Christ was preaching the truth of God. Verily, "there is no difference, for *all* have sinned, and come short of the glory of God". The common people were no better than the rulers; the Lord's brethren no more believed on Him than did the Jews; the inhabitants of Jerusalem had no more heart for Christ than they of the provinces. How plain it was, then, that *no man* would come to Christ except he had been drawn of the Father! It is so still. One class is just as much opposed to the Gospel as any other. Human nature is the same the world over. It is nothing but the distinguishing grace of God that ever makes one to differ from another.

"Howbeit we know this man whence He is: but when Christ cometh, no man knoweth whence He is" (v. 27). What pride of heart these words evidence! These men of Jerusalem deemed themselves wiser than their credulous rulers. The religious leaders might stand in some doubt, but *they* knew whence Christ was. Evidently they were well acquainted with His early life in Nazareth. Supposing that

Joseph was His father, they were satisfied that He was merely a man: "We know *this man*" indicates plainly the trend of their thoughts.

"But when Christ cometh, no man knoweth whence He is" (v. 27). This sentence needs to be pondered with v. 42 before us. From Matt. 2:4, 5 it is also plain that it was well known at the time that the Messiah should first appear in Bethlehem. What, then, did these people mean when they said, "When Christ cometh, no man knoweth *whence* He is"? With Dr. Doddridge, we regard this statement as an expression of the Jewish belief that the Messiah would be *supernaturally born*, i. e. of a virgin, as Isa. 7:14 declared.

"Then cried Jesus in the Temple as He taught, saying, Ye both know Me, and ye know whence I am: and I am not come of Myself, but He that sent Me is true, whom ye know not" (v. 28). It appears to the writer that in the first part of this utterance the Lord was speaking ironically. Some of them who lived in Jerusalem had declared, "We know this man whence He is." Here Christ takes up their words and refutes them. "Ye both know Me, and ye know whence I am", such was their idle boast; but, continues the Saviour, "I am not come of Myself, but He that sent Me is true, whom ye *know not*". So they did not know whence He was. When Christ here declared of the Father, "He that sent Me is *true*", He looked back, no doubt, to the Old Testament Scriptures. God had been "true" to His promises and predictions, many of which had already been fulfilled, and others were even then in course of fulfillment; yea, *their* very rejection of His Son evidenced the Father's veracity.

"But I know Him: for I am from Him, and He hath sent Me" (v. 29). It was because Christ knew the Father, and was from Him, that He could reveal Him; for it is by the Son, and by Him alone, that the Father is made known. "No man knoweth the Son but the Father; neither knoweth any man the Father, save the Son, and he to whomsoever the Son will reveal him" (Matt. 11:27). None cometh unto the Father but by Christ; and none knoweth the Father but by Him.

"Then they thought to take Him: but no man laid hands on Him, because His hour had not yet come" (v. 30). This verse sets forth a truth which should be of great comfort to God's people, and indeed it is so, when received by unquestioning faith. We find here a striking example of the restraining hand of God upon His enemies. *Their* purpose was to apprehend Christ. They *sought* to take Him, yet not a hand was laid upon Him! They thirsted for His blood, and were determined to kill Him; yet by an invisible restraint from above, they were powerless to do so. How blessed, then, to know that everything is under the immediate control of God. Not a hair of our heads can be touched without His permission. The demon-possessed Saul might hurl his javelin at David, but hurling it and killing him were two different things. Daniel might be cast into the den of lions, but as his time to die had not then come, their mouths were mysteriously sealed. The three Hebrews were cast into the fiery furnace, but of what avail were the flames against those protected by Jehovah!

"Then they sought to take Him: but no man laid hands on Him, because His hour was not yet come" (v. 30). How this evidences the invincibility of God's eternal decrees! "There is no wisdom nor understanding nor counsel against the Lord" (Prov. 21:30). God had decreed that the Saviour should be betrayed by a familiar friend, and sold for thirty pieces of silver. How, then, was it possible for these men to seize Him? They could no more arrest Christ than they could stop the sun from shining. "There are many devices in a man's heart; nevertheless the counsel of the Lord, that shall stand" (Prov. 19:21). What an illustration of this is furnished by the incident before us!

"No man laid hands on Him, *because* His hour was not yet come". Not until the sixty-ninth "week" of Dan. 9:24 had run its course could Messiah the Prince be "cut off". All the hatred of men and all the enmity of Satan and his hosts could not hasten Christ's appointed death. Until God's foreordained hour struck, and the incarnate Son bowed to His Father's good pleasure, He was immortal. And blessed be God, it is our privilege to be assured that the hand of death *cannot* strike *us* down before God's predestined "hour" arrives for us to go hence. The enemy may war against us, and he may be permitted to strike our bodies; but shorten our lives he cannot, anymore than he could Job's. A frightful epidemic of disease may visit the neighborhood in which I live, but

I am immune till *God* suffers me to be affected. Unless it is *His* will for *me* to be sick or to die, no matter how the epidemic may rage, nor how many of those around me may fall victims to it, it cannot harm me. "I will say of the Lord, He is *my* refuge and *my* fortress: my God, in Him will I trust". His re-assuring voice answers me: "Thou shalt not be afraid for the terror by night; nor for the arrow that flieth by day; nor for the pestilence that walketh in darkness; nor for the destruction that wasteth at noonday. A thousand shall fall at thy side, and ten thousand at thy right hand; but *it shall not come nigh thee*" (Psa. 91:2, 6, 7). Should any be inclined to think we have expressed ourselves too strongly, we ask them to ponder the following scriptures: "Is there not an appointed time for man upon earth? are not his days also like the days of an hireling?"—that is, strictly numbered (Job 7:1). "Seeing his days *are determined*, the number of his months are with Thee, Thou *hast appointed* his bounds that he cannot pass. .... If a man die, shall he live again? all the days of my *appointed time* will I wait, till my change come" (Job 14:5, 14).

"No man laid hands on Him, because His hour was not yet come". How this brings out the fact that all of Christ's sufferings were undergone *voluntarily*. He did not go to the Cross because He was unable to escape it; nor did He die because He could not prevent it. Far, far from it. Had He so pleased, He could have smitten down these men with a single word from His mouth. But even that was not necessary. They were prevented from touching Him without so much as a single word being spoken!

"And many of the people believed on Him, and said, When Christ cometh, will He do more miracles than these which this man hath done?" (v. 31). Whether or not this was a saving faith it is rather difficult to ascertain. Personally, we do not think it was. Rather do we regard this verse as parallel with John 2:23: "Now when He was in Jerusalem at the Passover, in the feast day, many believed in His name, when they saw the miracles which He did". But that theirs was *not* a saving faith is evident from what follows: "But Jesus did not commit Himself unto *them*, because He knew all". So here, the remainder of v. 31 seems to argue against a saving faith. "When Christ cometh", intimates that they did not really regard the Lord Jesus as the Messiah Himself. And their closing words, "Will He do more miracles than these which *this* (fellow) hath done?" shows what a derogatory conception they had of the incarnate Son of God.

The following questions bear upon our next lesson: John 7:32-53:—

1. What is there in v. 34 which unmistakeably brings out the Deity of Christ?
2. What does v. 35 go to prove?
3. Does v. 38 describe *your* spiritual experience? If not, why?
4. What solemn warning is conveyed by vv. 41, 42?
5. What do vv. 50, 51 go to show?
6. Were the Pharisees correct in v. 52?
7. What is there is this passage which magnifies Christ as "the Word"?

—Arthur W. Pink.

GLEANINGS IN EXODUS.

2. Israel in Bondage: Ex. 1.

The opening verse of Exodus carries us back to what is recorded in the closing chapters of Genesis, where we read of Jacob and his family settling in the land of the Pharaohs. On their entry they were accorded a hearty welcome, for Goshen, which was "the best of the land" of Egypt, (Gen. 47:6), was allotted to their use. But not for long were they suffered to dwell there in peace and comfort. It would seem that about thirty years after their entrance into Egypt a spirit of enmity began to be manifested toward them, engendered at first, perhaps, from the fact that they were shepherds (see Gen. 46:34); and which terminated in their being subjected to hard bondage in the days of the new king which "knew not Joseph". That their peace was disturbed thirty years after their settlement in Goshen seems clear from a comparison of Acts 7:6 and Ex. 12:40: in the former we are told they were "evilly entreated four hundred years", in the latter we are informed that "the sojourning of the children of Israel, who dwelt in Egypt" was "four hundred and thirty years".

Several questions naturally suggest themselves at this point. What was God's reason for allowing Israel to spend so long a time in Egypt? Why did He suffer them to be so cruelly treated? The purpose of God was that the descendants of Abraham should occupy the land of Canaan, which He had given to their father. But why should an interval of more than four hundred years elapse before this purpose was realized? To this I think a twofold answer may be returned. First, to prepare Israel for their inheritance. The rough schooling they had in Egypt served to develop their muscles and toughen their sinews. Also, their bitter lot in Egypt and their trials in the wilderness were calculated to make the land that flowed with milk and honey the more appreciated when it became theirs. Moreover, the land of Canaan was too large for a single family or tribe, and the lengthy sojourn in Egypt gave time for them to develop into a nation that must have numbered fully two millions.

The second answer is suggested by Gen. 15:16: "But in the fourth generation they shall come hither again: *for* the iniquity of the Amorites is not yet full." God had told Abraham that his seed should sojourn in a strange land for four hundred years, but in the fourth generation they should return to Canaan, and then the iniquity of the Amorites would be filled up. The time for God to deal in judgment with the Amorites was not fully ripe in the days of Abraham: their iniquities had not reached the bound God had appointed. Thus God ordered it that by the time the iniquities of the Amorites were "filled up" (cf Matt. 23:32 and 1 Thess. 2:16) Israel was ready, as a nation, to be His instrument to destroy them. "Whatever the actings of men in wickedness and high-handed rebellion, they are made subservient to the establishment of the Divine counsels of grace and love. . . . Even the wrath of man is yoked to the chariot wheel of God's decrees" (Ed. Dennett).

But why did God allow the descendants of Abraham to suffer such indignities and trials at the hands of the Egyptians? Ah, does not the book of Genesis again supply the answer! Was the wicked treatment of Joseph by his brethren to pass unpunished? No, that could not be. They, like all others, must reap what they had sown; reap the bitter harvest not only themselves but in their offspring too, for the sins of the fathers are visited upon the children unto the third and fourth generation. So it proved here, for it was the *"fourth* generation" (Gen. 13:15) which came out of Egypt. Four generations, then, reaped the harvest, and reaped precisely "whatsoever" had been sown; for just as Joseph was sold into *slavery,* and carried down into *Egypt,* so *in Egyptian slavery* his brethren and their children suffered!! And what a foreshadowing was this of the bitter experiences of Israel during these nineteen centuries past, for their wicked treatment of that blessed One whom Joseph so strikingly typified! They, too, have reaped what they sowed. Israel delivered up Christ into the hands of the Gentiles, and so into *their* hands they also have been delivered. Christ was shamefully treated by the Romans, and the *same* people were employed by God to punish the Jews. Christ was "cut off" out of the land of the living, and from A. D. 70 Israel, too, has been "cut off" from the land of their fathers. Thus we see again how inexorable is the outworking of this law of sowing and reaping.

In our last article we intimated that the deliverance of Israel from Egyptian bondage foreshadowed the redemption of sinners by Christ. The land occupied by the enslaved Hebrews fitly portrays the place where the unregenerate are. Egypt symbolizes the world, the world as a system, away from God and opposed to Him. Concerning this we cannot do better than quote from the excellent comments of the late Mr. F. W. Grant:

"The land of Egypt is a remarkable land in this way, that it is a little strip of country along the great river which makes it what it is, and which is in perpetual conflict with the desert as to it. This desert runs on both sides, and a little strip through which the river flows alone is Egypt. The desert on each side hems it in, blowing in its sands in all directions, and the river is as constantly overflowing its banks and leaving its mud upon the sand, and renewing the soil. The Scripture name is indeed not Egypt but Mizraim; and Mizraim means 'double straitness'. This doubtless refers to the two strips, one on each side of the river.

"The land is a very remarkable one, looking at it as the scene of perpetual conflict between life and death. The mercy of God, feeding that land by the rain of a far country, no rain coming down there. It is another remarkable feature that rain seldom falls in Egypt. The rain falls far off. The people know nothing about it. It comes rolling down in the shape of a mighty river, and that perpetual stream ministers unfailing plenty to the land. They are, so to speak, independent of heaven. Of course, I do not mean really; but as to their thoughts, they are not on the clouds. They do not look up, but down. It is the very thing God points out in contrasting the land of Canaan with the land of Egypt, that Canaan, Israel's portion, drinks in the water and rain of heaven. Canaan is a land of dependence. Egypt is a land of independence.

"And that is the serious character of our natural condition, alas! what is natural to us now—that we are independent of God! God indeed supplies the streams of plenteous blessing, and none else than He; but they come so regularly, so constantly, we speak wisely (?) of natural laws, and shut God out. Just as they have been sending men for long, long years to explore the sources of that river in Egypt, so men have been constantly seeking to explore the sources of natural supply, and they have hardly succeeded yet.

"Egypt worshipped her river. The river came to her so constantly that she was practically independent of heaven; yet heaven was the source of her supply. She did not see the blue hills which shed down upon them what themselves received. And they worshipped but the river. It is our state of nature away from God. God was far off to us. We did not realize the blessed hand from which all things came, and we took the blessings in wilful ignorance of the hand upon which both they and we in reality depended.

"But this Egypt was remarkable in other ways. It was remarkable, as you know, as the abode of science and civilization. To that very wonderful country people go now to study her monuments and admirable architecture. Egypt built as if she had eternity before her to enjoy it in. Her buildings were made to outlast by ages the people of the day who builded them; they could not make the people last, yet they tried their best at that. They embalmed their dead; and sent their dead down to the generations yet to come, side by side with what their hands had made, as if solemnly saying: 'Here are the mighty works of those over whom a mightier has triumphed'. What a comment upon all her grandeur! Her main literary memorial is a 'book of the dead'. In her monuments death is stereotyped. The desert, after all, has vanquished the river. The land of science and art is a land of death, and not of life.

"And that is the history of the world itself. Death is what is stamped upon it everywhere. It is the stamp of 'vanity' upon a fallen creation. It is more; it is the stamp of Divine reprobation. For 'in His favor is life'. Could He repent and unmake, unless we had given Him cause for repentance? Surely He could not. What a solemn thing that we should have given Him a reason! When God is able to rest in His love, as He will bye and bye, that will necessitate the eternity of the condition in which He can rest. All that, in view of which He can rest, will be stamped as eternal.

"The religion of Egypt was very remarkable. They had a religion in which were embalmed the relics of another religion, the dead tradition of a life that had been. There is no doubt about that. It is very remarkable in fact, according to what they say, that the very expression which God employs to Moses when He tells Moses His name, 'I am that I am,' you find attributed to God in the monuments of Egypt. And yet, with all that, what did Egypt everywhere worship? Emphatically and universally, the creature and not the Creator. Egypt which testified of the true God took up everything which was His total opposite, and deified a hundred beastial objects, the images, in fact, of their own lusts, and debased themselves by the service of these. Their worship was a deification,—as all heathen worship is—of their own lusts and passions. And that is everywhere what controls men naturally as his god. You remember in the garden of Eden, Satan says to the woman, 'Ye shall be as gods'. It was the *bait* he presented to her: and man has found that true in an awful way. As the apostle says of some, even professing Christians, their "god is their belly". That is, there is a craving in man's heart for something that will satisfy; and not being able to find satisfaction in God, and not being able to trust God's love and care, lust and care devour him. He worships himself, in a way continually more and more brutalizing and degrading."

And how did the descendants of Abraham first get into Egypt? Let the chapter before us make answer, and note its typical significance: "Every man and his household came with Jacob" (v. 1). They came into the land of bondage with *their father* Jacob: he was the one who brought them there. Mark, too, the name here given to him—"Jacob", which speaks of the natural man, the "supplanter"; not "Israel" which was his new name, given in sovereign grace. How clearly this speaks to us. We, too, entered the place of spiritual bondage with *our father,* Adam. This was not the place he first occupied: in Eden he was free to eat of all the trees of the garden, with but a single restriction; but alas! he sinned, and this caused him to be driven from the garden, and it was *outside* Eden that all his children were born. They came into the place of bondage with him!

"And the children of Israel were fruitful, and increased abundantly, and multiplied, and waxed exceeding mighty; and the land was filled with them" (v. 7). This was the fulfillment of God's promise to Jacob, made as the patriarch was journeying from Canaan to Egypt—"And he said, I am God, the God of thy father: fear not to go down into Egypt; for I will *there* make of thee a *great* nation". And this was but a repetition of what God had declared to Abraham long years before (see Gen. 12:2). How comforting is this to the children of God today. Unto us are given "exceeding great and precious promises", and these are the promises of Him who can not lie. Rest, then, with implicit confidence on the sure Word—forever settled in heaven—of the Lord our God.

"Now there arose up a new king over Egypt, which knew not Joseph" (v. 8). To understand this we need to turn the light of other scriptures upon it. This "new" king belonged not merely to a new dynasty, but was of a different nationality: he was by birth an Assyrian, not an Egyptian. In Acts 7:18 we read, "Till another king arose, which knew not Joseph". As one has pointed out there are in the Greek two different words for "another"; allos, which means "another of the same kind"; heteros, which signifies "another of a different kind". It is the latter word which is used in Acts 7:18. By turning back to Isa. 52:4 we learn what this other kind (in this case, another nationality) actually was. There we read, "For thus saith the Lord God, My people went down aforetime into Egypt to sojourn there; and *the Assyrian* oppressed them without cause". Our purpose in calling attention to this is to remind the reader of the great importance of comparing scripture with scripture, and to show how scripture is self-interpreting.

"And he said unto his people, Behold, the people of the children of Israel are more and mightier than we" (v. 9). The light afforded by the scriptures we have just looked at should remove what has long been a difficulty in this verse. That the children of Israel (who probably numbered about two millions all told, at this time) should be more numerous than the Egyptians seems unthinkable. But this is not what v. 9 states at all. Mark attentively its wording. "And he (the "new" king) said to *his* people", not "*the* people". His people would be the Assyrians who had conquered Egypt, and particularly those in that land policing the country. Note the repetition of "*his* people" in v. 22.

"And he said unto his people, Behold, the people of the children of Israel are more and mightier than we: Come on, let us deal wisely with them; lest they multiply, and it come to pass, that, when there falleth out any war, they join also unto our enemies (that is, lest the Hebrews should unite forces with the Egyptians against the Assyrian invaders), and fight against us and so get them up out of the land. Therefore they did set over them taskmasters to afflict them with their burdens" (vv. 9-11). This was the proud reasoning of the carnal mind, which is enmity against God. It was the finite pitting itself against the Infinite. In thus oppressing and afflicting the children of Israel we have an illustration of the world's hatred for the people of God (John 15:18, 19). How true it is that "the tender mercies of the wicked are cruel" (Prov. 12:10)! How much, then, dear reader, do we owe to the restraining power of God, which holds in check the evil passions of men, and thus allows us to live a quiet and peaceable life! Let the withholding hand of God be withdrawn for a short season, and even now,

His people would be sorely "afflicted" too.

"But the more they afflicted them, the more they multiplied and grew" (v. 12). This proves how thoroughly vain it is to fight against the purpose of Him who hath sworn, "My counsel shall stand, and I will do all My pleasure" (Isa. 64:10). Pharaoh might purpose to "deal wisely", but "the wisdom of this world is foolishness with God" (1 Cor. 3:19). God hath declared, "I will destroy the wisdom of the wise, and will bring to nothing the understanding of the prudent" (1 Cor. 1:19). So it proved here—"the more they afflicted them the more they grew". This also illustrates a principle which has been exemplified again and again in the history of Christendom. Times of severest trial have always been seasons of blessing to the people of God. The more fiercely have burned the fires of persecution the stronger has faith waxed. So, too, it should be, and often has been, in individual lives. Opposition should cast us back more and more upon God. Persecution results in separating us from the world. Suffering ought to refine. The experience of the Psalmist was, "Before I was afflicted I went astray: but now have I kept Thy Word" (Psa. 119:67). May it prove true of writer and reader that "the more we are afflicted" the more shall we "grow" in grace and in the knowledge of the Lord.

"And the king of Egypt spake to the Hebrew midwives, of which the name of the one was Shiphrah, and the name of the other Puah: And he said, when you do the office of a midwive to the Hebrew women, and see them upon the stools; if it be a son, then ye shall kill him; but if it be a daughter, then she shall live" (vv. 15, 16). It is not difficult to peer behind the scenes and behold one who was seeking to use Pharaoh as an instrument with which to accomplish his fiendish design. Surely we can discover here an outbreaking of the Serpent's enmity against the Seed of the woman. Suppose this effort had succeeded, what then? Why, *the channel* through which the promised Redeemer was to come had been destroyed. If all the male children of the Hebrews were destroyed there had been no David, and if no David, no David's Son. Just as Rev. 12:4 gives us to behold Satan working behind and through the wicked edict of Herod, so we may discern him here working behind and through Pharaoh.

But once more Egypt's king was foiled, and again was Satan's attacks repulsed: "but the midwives feared God, and did not as the king of Egypt commanded them, but saved the men children alive" (v. 17). Better might a worm withstand the tread of an elephant than the puny creature resist the Almighty. "There is no wisdom, nor understanding, nor counsel against the Lord" (Prov. 21:30). What comfort and confidence should this impart to the believer! If God be for us, it matters not who are against us.

"Therefore God dealt well with the midwives: and the people multiplied, and waxed very mighty. And it came to pass, because the midwives feared God, that He made them houses" (vv. 20, 21). Here we have one more illustration of the law of sowing and reaping. These Hebrew midwives, who through fear of God had overcome the fear of Pharaoh, dealt kindly with the male children of the Israelites, and they were rewarded accordingly—"God dealt well" with them. God is not unrighteous to forget any work and labor of love which is shòwed toward His name or ministered to His people (Heb. 6:10). His promise is "For them that honor Me, I will honor" (1 Sam. 2:30). They "saved the men children alive", and God "made them houses", which, in the light of 2 Sam. 7:11, 1 Kings 2:24, etc., must mean that He, in turn, gave them husbands and blessed them with children.

"And Pharaoh charged all his people, saying, Every son that is born ye shall cast into the river, and every daughter ye shall save alive" (v. 22). We do not have to look far beneath the surface in order to discover here the malignity of one more vile than Pharaoh. Just as the twelfth of Revelation shows us that it was the Dragon himself who moved Herod to attempt the death of the Christ Child, so here he was employing the king of Egypt to destroy the channel through which He was to come. At the beginning, God declared He would put "enmity" between the woman and her Seed (Gen. 3:15), and in the light of subsequent scriptures it is abundantly clear that "the woman" is Israel—the one who was to bear the Messiah. Here in the passage before us we have a forceful illustration of the Serpent's "enmity". Had his effort succeeded, had all the *male* children of the Hebrews been slain, the channel through which the Saviour was to come had been destroyed.

"And Pharaoh charged all his people, saying, every son that is born ye shall cast into the river, and every daughter ye shall save alive" (v. 22). How this reminds us of the words of Eccl. 8:11: "Because sentence against an evil work is not executed speedily, therefore the heart of the sons of men is fully set in them to do evil". God bears with ***much long-suffering*** the vessels of wrath fitted to destruction. Every opportunity is given them to repent; the day of mercy is graciously prolonged for them; and if in the end they die in their sins, then is their blood, unmistakeably, on their own heads. How God frustrated this last move of Pharaoh we shall see in our next paper.

—Arthur W. Pink.

SUFFERING WITH CHRIST A CONDITION OF GLORY WITH CHRIST.

"Joint-heirs with Christ, if so be that we suffer with Him, that we may be also glorified together" (Rom. 8:17).

In the former part of this verse the Apostle tells us that in order to be heirs of God we must become sons through and joint-heirs with Christ. He seems at first sight to add to these words of our text another condition to those already specified, namely, that of suffering with Christ.

Now, of course, whatever may be the operation of suffering in fitting for the possession of the Christian inheritance, either here or in another world, the sonship and the sorrows do not stand on the same level in regard to it. The one is the indispensable condition of all; the other is but a means for the operation of the condition. The one,—being sons, "joint-heirs with Christ", is the root of the whole matter; the other,—the "suffering with Him", is but the various process by which from the root there come "the blade, and the ear, and the full corn in the ear". Given the sonship,—if it is to be worked out into power and beauty,—there must be suffering with Christ. But unless there be sonship, there is no possibility of inheriting God; discipline and suffering will be of no use at all.

The chief lesson which I wish to gather from this text now is that all God's sons must suffer with Christ, and in addition to this principle, we may complete our considerations by adding briefly, that the inheritance must be won by suffering, and that if we suffer with Him, we certainly shall receive the inheritance.

First, then, *Sonship with Christ necessarily involves suffering with Him.* I think that we entirely misapprehend the force of this passage before us, if we suppose it to refer principally or merely to the outward calamities, what you call trials and afflictions, which befall people; and see in it only the teaching, that the sorrows of daily life may have in them a sign of our being children of God, and some power to prepare us for the glory that is to come. There is a great deal more in the thought than that, brethren. This is not merely a text for people that are in affliction, but for all of us. It does not merely contain a law for a certain part of life, but it contains a law for the whole of life. It is not merely a promise that "in all our afflictions Christ shall be afflicted", but it is a solemn injunction that we seek to know "the fellowship of His sufferings, and be made conformable to His death", if we expect to be "found in the likeness of His resurrection", and to have any share in the community of His glory. In other words, the foundation of it is not that Christ shares in our suffering; but that we, as Christians, in a deep and real sense do necessarily share and participate in Christ's. We "suffer with Him"; *not,* He suffers with us.

Now, do not let us misunderstand each other, or the apostle's teaching. Do not suppose that I am forgetting, or wishing you to account as of small importance, the awful sense in which Christ's suffering stands as a thing by itself and unapproachable, a solitary pillar rising up, above the waste of time. The sufferings of Christ—of His life and of His death—both because of the nature which bore them, and of the aspect which they wore in regard to us, are in their source, in their intensity, in their character, and consequences, unapproachable, incapable of repetition, and needing no repetition whilst the world shall stand. But then, do not let us forget that the very books and writers in the New Testament that preach most broadly Christ's sole, all-sufficient, eternal redemption for the world, by His sufferings and death, turn round and say to us to, " 'Be planted together in the likeness of His death:' you are 'crucified to the world' by the cross of Christ; you are to 'fill up that which is behind of the sufferings of Christ' ". He Himself speaks of our drinking of the cup that He drank of, and being baptized with the baptism that He was baptized with, if we desire to sit yonder on His throne, and share with Him in glory. Now what do the apostles, and what does Christ Himself, in the passage that I have quoted, mean, by such solemn words as these? Some people shrink from them, and say that it is trenching upon the central doctrines of the Gospel, when we speak about drinking of the cup which Christ drank of. They ask, Can it be? Yes, it can be, if you will think thus:—If a Christian has the spirit and life of Christ in Him, his career will be moulded, imperfectly but really, by the same spirit that dwelt in His Lord; and similar causes will produce corresponding effects. Were the sufferings of the Lord only the sufferings that were wrought upon Calvary? Were the sufferings of the Lord only the sufferings which came from the "contradiction of sinners against Himself"? Were the sufferings of the Lord only the sufferings which were connected with the bodily afflictions and pain, precious and priceless as they were, and operative causes of our redemption as they were? Oh no. Conceive of that perfect, sinless, really human life, in the midst of a system of things that is all full of corruption and sin; coming ever and anon against misery, and wrong-doing, and rebellion; and ask yourselves whether part of His sufferings did not spring from the contact of the sinless Son of Man with a sinful world. If there had been nothing more than that, Christ's suffering as the Son of God in the midst of sinful men would have been deep and real. "O faithless generation, how long shall I be with you? how long shall I suffer you?" was wrung from Him by the painful sense of want of sympathy between His aims and theirs. "O that I had wings like a dove, for then would I fly away and be at rest", must often be the language of those who are like Him in spirit, and in consequent sufferings.

And then again, another branch of the "sufferings of Christ" is to be found in that deep and mysterious fact on which I durst not venture to speak beyond what the actual words of Scripture put into my lips—the fact that Christ wrought out His perfect obedience as a man, *through temptation and by suffering.* There was no sin *within* Him, no tendency to sin, no yielding to the evil that assailed. "The Prince of this world cometh, and hath nothing in Me". But yet, when that dark Power stood by His side, and said, "If Thou be the Son of God, cast Thyself down", it was a real temptation and not a sham one. No wish to do it, no faltering for a moment, no hesitation. There was no rising up in that calm will, of even a moment's impulse to do that thing which was presented;—but yet it was presented, and, when Christ triumphed, and the tempter departed for a season, there had been a temptation and there had been a conflict. And though obedience be a joy, and the doing of His Father's will was His delight, as it must needs be in pure and in purified hearts; yet obedience which is sustained in the face of temptation, and which never fails, though its path leads to bodily pains, and the "contradiction of sinners", may well be called suffering. There was no place in Christ's obedience for that casting out of sinful self, which makes our submission a surrender joined with suffering. But He knew temptation. Flesh, and sense, and the world, and the Prince of the world presented it to Him; and therefore His obedience too was suffering, even though to do the will of His Father were His meat, and His drink, His sustenance, and His refreshment.

Let me remind you still further, that not only does the life of Christ, as sinless in the midst of sinful men; and the life of Christ, as sinless whilst yet there was temptation presented to it—assumed the aspect of being a life of suffering, and become, in that respect, a model for us; but that also the death of Christ, besides its aspect as an atonement and sacrifice for sin, the power by which transgression is put away, and God's love flows out from our souls, has another power given to it in the teaching of the New Testament. The death of Christ is a type of the Christian's life, which is to be one long, protracted, and daily dying to sin, to self, and to the world. The crucifixion of the old manhood is to be the life's work of every Christian, through the power of faith in that cross by which "the world is crucified unto me, and I unto the world". That thought comes over and over again in all forms of earnest presentation in the apostle's teaching. Do not slur it over as if it were a mere fanciful metaphor. The truth is, that, if a Christian, you have a double life. There is Christ, with His power, with His Spirit, giving you a nature which is pure and sinless, incapable of transgression, like His own. The new man, that which is born of God, sinneth not, cannot sin. But side by side with it, working through it, working in it, indistinguishable from it to your consciousness by anything but this, that the one works righteousness, and the other works transgression; the latter is the "old man", "the flesh", your own godless, independent, selfish, proud being. And the one is to slay the other! Ah, let me tell you, these words —crucifying, putting off the old man, plucking out the right eye, maiming self of the right hand, mortifying the deeds of the body,—they are something very much deeper and more awful than poetical symbols and metaphors. They teach us this—there is no growth without sore sorrow. Conflict not progress is the word that defines man's path from darkness into light. In long lingering agony often, with the blood of the heart pouring out at every quivering vein, you are to cut right through the life and being of that sinful self; to do what the Word does, pierce to the dividing asunder of the thoughts and intents of the heart, and get rid by crucifying and slaying—a long process, a painful process —your own sinful self. And not until you can stand up, and say, "I live, yet not I, but Christ liveth in me", have you accomplished that to which you are consecrated and vowed by your sonship—"Being conformed unto the likeness of His death", and "knowing the fellowship of His sufferings".

It is this process, the inward strife and conflict in getting rid of evil, which the apostle designates here with the name of "suffering with Christ, that we may be also glorified together". On this high level and not upon the lower one of the consideration that Christ will help us to bear outward infirmities and afflictions, do we find the true meaning of all that scripture teaching that says indeed, "Yes, our sufferings are *His;*" but lays the foundation of it in this "His sufferings are *ours*". It begins by telling us that Christ has done a work and borne a sorrow that no second can ever do. Then it tells us that Christ's life of obedience—which, because it *was* a life of obedience, was a life of suffering, and brought Him into a condition of hostility to the men around Him—is to be repeated in us. It sets before us the Cross of Calvary, and the sorrows and pains which were felt there;—and it says to us, Christian men and women, if you want the power to holy living, have fellowship in that atoning death; and if you want the pattern of holy living, look at the Cross and know, "I am crucified to the world by it; and, the life that I live in the flesh, I live by the faith of the Son of God".

Such considerations as these, however, do not necessarily exclude the other (which we may just mention and dwell on for a moment), namely, that where there is this spiritual participation in the sufferings of Christ, and where His death is reproduced and perpetuated, as it were, in our daily mortifying ourselves in the present evil world,—there *Christ is with us in our afflictions.* God forbid that I should try to strike away any word of consolation which has come, as these words of my text have come, to so many sorrowing hearts in all generations, like music in the night and like cold waters to a thirsty soul. We need not hold that there is no reference here to that comforting tnought, "In all our affliction He is afflicted". Brethren, you and I have, each of us—one in one way, and one in another, all in some way, all in the right way, none in too severe a way, none in too slight a way—to tread in the path of sorrow; and is it not a blessed thing, as we go along through that dark valley of the shadow of death down into which the sunniest paths go sometimes, to come, amidst the twilight and the gathering clouds, upon tokens that Jesus has been on the road before us? They tell us that in some trackless lands, when one friend passes through the pathless forests, he breaks a twig ever and anon as he goes, that those who come after may see the traces of his having been there, and may know that they are not out of the road. Oh, when we are journeying through the murky night, and the dark woods of affliction and sorrow, it is something to find here and there a spray broken, or a leafy stem bent down with the tread of His foot and the brush of His hand as He passed; and to remember that the path He trod He hath hallowed, and thus to find lingering fragrances and hidden strengths in the remembrance of Him as "in all points tempted like as we are", bearing grief *for* us, bearing grief *with* us, bearing grief *like* us. O do not, do not, my brethren, keep these sacred thoughts of Christ's companionship in sorrow, for the larger trials of life. If the moat in the eye be large enough to annoy you, it is large enough to bring out His sympathy; and if the grief be too small for Him to compassionate and share, it is too small for you to be troubled by it. If you are ashamed to apply that Divine thought, "Christ bears this grief with me", to those petty molehills that you magnify into mountains sometimes, think to yourselves then it is a shame for you to be stumbling over them. But on the other-hand, never fear to be irreverent or too familiar in the thought, that Christ is willing to bear and help me to bear, the pettiest, the minutest, and most insignificant of the daily annoyances that can come to ruffle me. Whether it be a poison from one serpent's sting, or whether it be poison from a million of buzzing tiny mosquitoes; if there be a smart, go to Him, and He will help you to bear it. He will do more, He will bear it with you, for if so be that we suffer with Him, He suffers with us, and our oneness with Christ brings about a community of possessions whereby it becomes true of each trusting soul in its relations to Him, that "all mine (joys and sorrows alike) are Thine, and all Thine are mine".

There remains some other considerations which may be briefly stated, in order to complete the lessons of this text. In the second place, *This community of suffering is a necessary preparation for the community of glory.*

I name this principally of putting in a caution. The apostle does not mean to tell us, of course, that if there were such a case as that of a man becoming a son of God, and having no occasion or opportunity afterwards, by brevity of life or other causes, for passing through the discipline of sorrow, his inheritance would be forfeited. We must always take such passages as this,—which seem to make the discipline of the world an essential part of the preparing of us for glory—in conjunction with the other undeniable truth which completes them, that when a man has the love of God in his heart, however feebly, however newly, there and then he is fit for the inheritance. I think that Christian people make vast mistakes sometimes in talking about "being made meet for the inheritance of the saints in light", about being "ripe for glory", and the like. One thing at any rate is very certain, it is not the discipline that fits. That which fits goes before the discipline, and the discipline only develops the fitness. "God *hath made* us meet for the inheritance of the saints in light", says the apostle. That is a past act. The preparedness for heaven comes at the moment,—if it be a momentary act,—when a man turns to Christ. You may take the lowest and most abandoned form of human character, and in one moment (it is possible, and it is often the case) the entrance into that soul of the feeble germ of that new affection, shall at once change the whole moral habitude of that man. Though it *be* true, then, that heaven is only open to those who are capable,—by holy aspirations and Divine desires,—of entering into it, it is equally true that such aspirations and desires may be the work of an instant, and may be superinduced in a moment in a heart the most debased and the most degraded. "This day shalt thou be with Me in Paradise",—*fit* for the inheritance!

And, therefore, let us not misunderstand such words as this text, and fancy that the necessary discipline, which we have to go through before we are ready for heaven, is necessary in anything like the same sense in which it is necessary that a man should have faith in Christ in order to be saved. The one may be dispensed with, the other can not. A Christian at any period of his Christian experience, if it please God to take him, is fit for the kingdom. The life *is* life, whether it be the budding beauty and feebleness of childhood, or the strength of manhood, or the maturity and calm peace of old age. But "add to your faith", that "an entrance may be ministered unto you *abundantly*". Remember that though the root of the matter, the seed of the kingdom, may be in you; and that though therefore, you have a right to feel that, at any period of your Christian experience, if it please God to take you out of this world, you are fit for heaven,—yet in His mercy He is leaving you here, training you, disciplining you, cleansing you, making you to be polished shafts in His quiver; and that all the glowing furnaces of fiery trial and all the cold waters of affliction, are but the preparation through which the rough iron is to be passed before it becomes tempered steel, a shaft in the Master's hand. And so learn to look upon all trial as being at once the seal of your sonship, and the means by which God puts it within your power to win a higher place, a loftier throne, a nobler crown, a closer fellowship with Him "who hath suffered, being tempted", and who will receive into His own blessedness and rest them that are tempted. "The child, though he be an heir, differeth nothing from a servant, though he be lord of all; but is under tutors and governors". God puts us to the school of sorrow under that stern tutor and governor here, and gives us the opportunity of "suffering with Christ", that by the daily crucifixion of our old nature, by the lessons and blessings of outward calamities and change, there may grow up in us a still nobler and purer and perfecter Divine life; and that we may so be made capable—more capable, and capable of more—of that inheritance for which the only necessary thing is the death of Christ, and the only fitness is faith in His name.

Finally, *that inheritance is the necessary result of the suffering* that has gone before. The suffering results from our union with Christ. That union must needs culminate in glory. It is not only because the joy hereafter seems required in order to vindicate God's love to His children, who here reap sorrow from their sonship, that the discipline of life cannot but end in blessedness. *That* ground of mere compensation is a low one on which to rest the certainty of future bliss. But the inheritance is sure to all who here suffer with Christ, because the one cause—union with the Lord—produces both the present result of fellowship in His sorrow, and the future result of joy in His joy, of possession in His possessions. The inheritance is sure because Christ possesses it now. The inheritance is sure because earth's sorrows not merely require to be repaid by its peace, but because they have an evident design to fit us for it, and it would be destructive to all faith in God's wisdom, and God's knowledge of His own purposes, not to believe, that what He has wrought for us will be given to us. Trials have no meaning, unless they are means to an end. The end is the inheritance—and sorrows here, as well as the Spirit's work here, are the earnest of the inheritance. Measure the greatness of the glory by what has preceded it. God takes all these years of life, and all the sore trials and afflictions that belong inevitably to an earthly career and works them in, into that blessedness that *shall* come. If a fair measure of the greatness of any result of productive power be the length of time that was taken for getting it ready, we can dimly conceive what that joy must be for which seventy years of strife, and pain, and sorrow, are but a momentary preparation; and what must be the weight of that glory which is the counterpoise and consequence to the afflictions of this lower world. The further the pendulum swings on the one side, the further it goes up on the other. The deeper God plunges the comet into the darkness, out yonder, the closer does it come to the sun at its nearest distance, and the longer does it stand basking and glowing in the full blaze of the glory from the central orb. So in *our* revolution, the measure of the distance from the farthest point of our darkest earthly sorrow *to* the throne, may help us to the measure of the closeness of the bright, perfect, perpetual glory above, when we are *on* the throne: for if so be that we are sons, we *must* suffer with Him; if so be that we suffer, we *must* be glorified together! —Alexander McLaren

---

THE SABBATH.

To understand the progressive walk and sanctification of the believer, we need to remember that obedience is submission to authority, and that authority implies law. There is a very dangerous doctrine, working like a subtle leaven to corrupt even disciples, which is nothing less than *Antinomianism,* and which affirms that, because we are no longer "under the Law but under grace," therefore *all law is abrogated;* and this position finds a very plausible justification in sundry statements of the New Testament that the law imposed a yoke of bondage which neither our fathers nor we were able to bear, but that yoke is now broken and we are introduced into the liberty of the sons of God; and hence it is argued that even such a law as that of Sabbath rest is no longer in force.

Such views of obligation betray equally false exegesis of Scripture, and misleading notions of legal obligations. Law is not the ground of the sinner's *justification,* for "by the deeds of the law shall no flesh living be justified". But Law is none the less the *rule of duty.* It is the expression of God's will and our guide as to what pleases Him; and we are expressly told that "what the Law could not do, in that it was weak through the flesh, God sending His own Son in the likeness of sinful flesh, and for sin, condemned sin in the flesh, that the righteousness of the Law might be fulfilled in us, who walk not after the flesh, but after the spirit" (Rom. 8:3, 4).

The Law of the Old Testament is both *ceremonial* and *moral*—the former part having to do with typical ritual, that foreshadowed a coming dispensation; the other, with immutable principles of ethics. One was temporary and transient—the shadow of things to come; the other was eternal and permanent, the embodiment in commandment of the moral will of God. Hence a portion of the law, known as the "Ten Words" of Jehovah, was twice graven on tablets of stone by the very finger of God—separated from all minor injunctions, as a distinct and permanent code.

In the Creation account in Genesis will be found Ten Creative Fiats. "And God said" is the key-note to the narrative, the burden ten times repeated. Here are certain immutable laws for the government of the material creation, such as universal motion and rotation, evaporation and condensation, cohesion, gravitation, revolution, affinity, growth and multiplication. There has not been a moment since when such natural laws have not been in operation.

In Exodus, we meet the *moral* Tenfold Code. He who before spoke as Creator, here speaks as Governor, and His commands are equally changeless. As the material universe would fall into ruin if natural laws should cease to control, so the moral order is dependent on these commands of the Decalogue.

This moral code constitutes an *organic body* of itself, every command of which is a member of the body, necessary to the completeness of the whole. Four commands relate to *God:* the first puts Him as the supreme *Head* of all authority; the second defines the mode of His worship as a Spirit; the third forbids all careless trifling with His name, which expresses His nature; the fourth forbids trespassing on the time He sanctifies unto Himself. Similarly the remaining six prescribe duties to man, putting the parent at the head as God's representative in the family—then guarding all human interests—life, chastity, property, reputation, and finally forbidding all wrong desire as to what is another's.

It is plain that here is a complete code for man's guidance. There is only one way for it to pass away—when the perfect love that works no ill to God or one's neighbor so rules intelligent beings, as that there can be nothing in conduct or even character that could mar the new creation; then and not till then will the "Ten Words" pass away, because all will be fulfilled.

Yet by some it is said that all *Law is abrogated,* and that, among the abrogated things, Paul mentions to the Colossians, "The *Sabbaths*" (2:16). But the Sabbaths he refers to are not the weekly rest-days commanded in the Moral Code, but the festival Sabbaths of the *Ceremonial*—which therefore are in the same category with ceremonial meats and drinks and new moons and other festival days. The plural "Sabbaths" is commonly used in the Bible in this sense.

Few modern laxities work worse results on the whole social order, family, church, and State, than the rapidly increasing and flagrant disregard of all Sabbatic Law.

Undoubtedly this law of rest, one day in seven, has undergone some modification, but its essential principle survives. In Isa. 58:13, 14, curiously about midway between Moses and Christ, and in connection with significant blessings pronounced upon the "Repairer of the breach, the Restorer of paths to dwell in"—that is, one who rebuilds what is broken down and restores wanderers to forsaken ways of duty—we read, "If thou turn away thy foot from the Sabbath, from doing thy pleasure on My holy day,—and call the Sabbath a delight, the holy of the Lord, honorable; and shalt honor Him, not doing thine own ways, nor finding thine own pleasure, nor speaking thine own words: Then shalt thou delight thyself in the Lord; and I will cause thee to ride upon the high places of the earth, and feed thee with the heritage of Jacob thy father: for the mouth of the Lord hath spoken it."

It is most noticeable that while here all features of Sabbath observance that were merely external and ceremonial are eliminated, the substantial law of the Sabbath is not only preserved but lifted to a more sacred plane. The Sabbath observance is modified and glorified—a new principle is enunciated, in accordance with which the day is to be regarded, not primarily as a Rest Day from labor, but as God's Holy Day—it is the difference between man's holiday and God's holy day—and in it man is to abstain from "doing his own ways, finding his own pleasure", or even "speaking his own words". Before, it was a day fenced in as one to be kept for physical rest; but now it is to be a day of mental repose, and spiritual refreshment. Even the tongue is to be under control, and selfish pleasure to be curbed. In seems to be a sort of forecast on the permanent features of the weekly Rest Day. Certain it is that wherever the day is thus kept every richest blessing comes to a community. The fact is, however, that, on pretext of freedom from legal restraints, Sunday is fast becoming the day of self seeking and pleasure seeking, when even disciples find their own pleasure and speak their own words freely. It is getting to be the day pre-eminently of recreation, everything but the Holy of the Lord, kept as entitled to special honor. The enemy of God and man must rejoice over such desecration of what the Lord has consecrated. Voltaire more than a century ago declared, "There is no hope of destroying Christianity so long as Sunday is kept as a holy-day". Robert Ingersoll, discerning in the Sabbath a strong defence and bulwark of the whole Christian system, petulantly cried out: "Sunday is a pest! It must be taken out of the way!" The oracles of Infidelity all agree in a like verdict. Wherever the desecration of the Lord's Day prevails, it weakens all the line of Christian life and witness before the inrush of Atheism and Materialism. Finally to abandon this sacred observance would be preliminary to a sure defeat of the church of God, in all the campaigns for righteousness and peace, imperilling all the highest interests of man, both temporal and eternal.

If the Sabbath of weekly rest is abrogated as part of a Law no more in force, what of other commands of the Decalogue? Are we under no obligation not to use graven images in worship, not to take God's name in vain? And are the six commands of the Second Table abrogated? is there no longer an obligation on the believer to honor parents, to guard another's life, chastity, property, etc.? This would be not Antinomianism only, but Anarchy, sanctioned by Christianity.

But it is said the Sabbath is a *Mosaic* Institution—far from it, it is *Edenic.* It antedates not only Sinai but *Sin,* and is the only surviving relic of man's innocence, except marriage. God saw, even before man sinned, that he needed a sacred season of time once in seven days. This is one of two institutions that come down from a sinless Edenic life—thus joined together by God—the Sabbath rest and the marriage tie—is it surprising that man cannot put them asunder without weakening both! Whenever the Sabbath is desecrated the family purity is diminished, if not lost.

Moreover, our Lord declared the eternal principle: "The Sabbath was made for man". It meets a need which will continue so long as man's earthly conditions continue. The weekly rest is needful to keep a normal balance between body and spirit. The night's sleep does not fully recuperate the exhaustings of anxiety and activity, and the weekly recurrence of a rest day is restorative and complimentary. One of the greatest of British physicians warns his fellow countrymen of the rapid increase of insanity, and says that if this goes on, as now, it will not be long before the bulk of the race will be mentally unhinged; and it has been found that this insanity is largely due to the push and drive of modern life, for which the Sabbath is God's corrective.

The change of day, from the seventh to the first, does not affect the principle; for it is not any particular twenty-four hours that is essential, but one day in seven. In fact, the whole human race cannot keep the same exact time, because the rotation of the earth makes the day different in different parts of the earth. So long, therefore, as the same proportion is preserved, with uniformity in each locality, all essential principles are conserved.

The historical argument is overwhelming. The logic of events is conclusive, that God brands Sabbath desecration with His displeasure. Who of us that are old enough to remember the days, not so long ago, when there were no public vehicles running on Sunday, no newspapers hawked in the streets, no shops or public places of amusement open, no railroad and steamboat excursions, very little travelling, or private visiting and entertaining; and can recall the quiet of the hours, the full churches, the devout household habits, the general observance of the rest day, and contrast all these conditions with those now prevailing—can doubt that so far as man has trampled on God's decree of the Sabbath, he has worked harm to all individual, domestic and social life, as well as ecclesiastical. The tradition in ancient Troy was that, if ever the statute of Pallas in Minerva's Temple were removed, the city itself would be destroyed. The Sabbath is the Palladium in the Temple of our Christian civilization, and if it falls in ruin, it means widespread disaster to church and State, and Satan knows it.

History warns us that the Sabbath was made for man; for the preservation of his physical, mental, moral and spiritual balance. The tendency of crowding all seven days with secular work is to crowd out even the thought of God, and paralyze the very powers by which we commune with the unseen and eternal. The effect of consecrating one day in seven is to give man time to recover from the secularizing influence of the rest of the week, or better still prevent the business of this world from dragging down his spiritual life. God's weekly rest recurs often enough to prevent the hallowing influence of one sacred day from being lost before the influence of another is felt, reminding us of the telegraph poles that are placed near enough together to prevent the wires, however they sag between, from touching the earth. Sabbath observance is a help to fellowship with God.

A few conspicuous witnesses might be heard on this great question in these perilous times.

"Quite apart from the religious aspect of the question, on social and economic grounds", says Dr. McLaren of Manchester, England, "the seventh day of rest is of the greatest importance to the well-being of the nation. The present tendency is to break down the day of rest, and is, therefore, I think, disastrous. The habit of attending public worship is decreasing in proportion to population. The old-fashioned habit of rigorously attending service twice a day is dead, the change being chiefly because of the indifference of parents. It was customary years ago for children, certainly on Sunday evening, to get Christian teaching at home from their parents. The child was taught Gospel truths at its mother's knee; fitted for public worship. To some extent, no doubt, the custom still obtains; but not to the extent it obtained in my boyhood. Sunday School teaching is, of course, of the greatest value; but I look upon *the Christian teaching of parents as infinitely better.*"

The echos are still heard of Hon. Andrew D. White's recent utterance regarding the Sabbath, the occasion for which arose in the action of Bishop Luden, of the Roman Catholic Diocese of Syracuse, in refusing Christian burial to persons who died by accident on Sunday while culpably violating the duties and obligations of that day. In a letter to the Bishop, heartily commending the stand he had taken, Dr. White said:

"I have, for some time past, watched with ever-increasing regret the tendencies in our large cities, and, indeed, to some extent in the country districts, toward a complete paganizing of American life as regards the first day of the week. The extremes to which our communities have gone of late in appointing every sort of game and amusement through the morning hours, and of making Sunday resorts less and less decent, are such as to create just alarm among all thinking citizens. It was under this conviction that I observed the very bold and noble stand which you have taken."

This is the view, not of an extremist nor a fanatic, but of a liberal, broad-minded man, who sees, as all must see who are clear-eyed, sound-minded, and morally-erect, that the increasing Sunday desecration should be checked, not only in the interests of religion, but of law, order and public morality. The open, flagrant, defiant violations of the Sunday laws and of long-established and honored Sabbath customs and usages are a sure symptom of a spirit of irreverance for all laws and indifference to all moral obligation—a spirit fatal to the well-being of the family, the home, the State, and of every other institution which men hold sacred and dear.

All Antinomianism is unscriptural, unspiritual, unchristian. Moral law can never be abrogated, as a rule of conduct, or guide to character. The fact that we are not under law as a means of justification does not imply that we are not under law to Christ (1 Cor. 9:21) as to the regulation of life. This is to displace lawfulness by lawlessness, and obedience by apostasy. Abrogation of law can take place, even under a system of grace, only so far as the habit of voluntary and cheerful obedience makes all law unnecessary. Holy love can withhold nothing due to God or man, and this fulfilling of law is Love's way of abrogating it. Habits of obedience imply law, for otherwise what is it which is obeyed, and what is the standard of obedience? Law transferred *within* by love, from the tables of stone to the fleshly tablets of the hearts; this is the sublime method of doing away with legal bondage (Psa. 40:8).

It is sometimes said that obedience is impossible, because the standard of law is impracticable, ideal, beyond reach. Does God then command impossibilities? Yes, in a sense, and partly to show that, to the natural man, obedience *is* impossible, and so to teach that a true obedience is spiritual, and belongs not to the natural but supernatural; and so again to reveal the omnipotence of Grace as the corrective of human impotence—how Christ strengthening me I can do all things. Obedience is possible therefore only so far as fellowship with God is maintained.

Dr. Arthur T. Pierson.

LUTHER AND ERASMUS

If, my Erasmus, you consider these paradoxes (as you term them) to be no more than the inventions of men, why are you so extravagantly heated on the occasion? In that case, your arguments affect not me: for there is no person now living in the world who is a more avowed enemy to the doctrines of men than myself. But, if you believe the doctrines in debate between us to be (as indeed they are) the doctrines of God, you must have bid adieu to all sense of shame and decency thus to oppose them. I will not ask, Whither is the modesty of Erasmus fled? But, which is much more important, Where, alas! are your fear and reverence of the Deity when you roundly declare that this branch of truth, which He has revealed from heaven, is, at best, useless and unnecessary to be known? What! shall the glorious Creator be taught by you His creature what is fit to be preached, and what to be suppressed? Is the adorable God so very defective in wisdom and prudence as not to know, till you instruct Him, what would be useful and what pernicious? Or could not He, whose understanding is infinite, foresee previous to His revelation of this doctrine, what would be the consequences of His revealing it until those consequences were pointed out by you? You cannot, you dare not, say this. If, then, it was the Divine pleasure to make known these things in His Word, and to bid His messengers publish them abroad, and leave the consequences of their so doing to the wisdom and providence of Him in whose name they speak, and whose message they declare; who art thou, O Erasmus, that thou shouldest reply against God, and say to the Almighty, What doest Thou? St. Paul, discoursing of God, declares peremptorarily, Whom He will He hardeneth: and again, God, willing to show His wrath, etc. And the apostle did not write this to have it stifled among a few persons, and buried in a corner, but wrote it to the Christians at Rome: which was in effect bringing this doctrine upon the stage of the whole world; stamping an universal imprimature upon it; and publishing it to believers at large throughout the earth.—What can sound harsher in the uncircumcised ears of carnal men than those words of Christ, Many are called but few chosen? and elsewhere, I know whom I have chosen? Now these and similar assertions of Christ and His apostles are the very positions which you, O Erasmus, brand as useless and hurtful. You object, if these things are so, who will endeavor to amend his life? I answer; Without the Holy Ghost, no man can amend his life to purpose. Reformation is but varnished hypocrisy, unless it proceed from grace. The elect and truly pious are amended by the Spirit of God; and those of mankind who are not amended by Him will perish.

You ask, moreover, Who will dare to believe himself a favorite of heaven? I answer; It is not in man's own power to believe himself such upon just grounds until he is enabled from above. But the elect shall be so enabled: they shall believe themselves to be what indeed they are. As for the rest, who are not endued with faith, they shall perish; raging and blaspheming as you now do. But, say you, these doctrines open a door to ungodliness. I answer; Whatever door they may open to the impious and profane, yet they open a door of righteousness to the elect and holy, and show them the way to heaven, and the path of access unto God. Yet you would have us abstain from the mention of these grand doctrines, and leave our people in the dark as to their election of God: the consequence of which would be that every man would bolster himself up with a delusive hope of a share in that salvation which is supposed to lie open to all; and thus genuine humility, and the practical fear of God, would be kicked out of doors. This would be a pretty way indeed of stopping up the gap Erasmus complains of! Instead of closing up the door of licentiousness, as is falsely pretended, it would be, in fact, opening a gulf into the nethermost hell.

Still, you urge, Where is either the necessity or utility of preaching predestination? God Himself preaches it, and commands us to preach it: and that is answer enough. We are not to arraign the Deity, and bring the motives of His will to the test of human scrutiny, but simply to revere both Him and it. He who alone is all-wise and all-just can in reality (however things appear to us) do wrong to no man; neither can He do anything unwisely or rashly. And this consideration will suffice to silence all the objections of truly religious persons. However, let us, for argument's sake, go a step farther. I will venture to assign, over and above, two very important reasons why these doctrines should be publicly taught.

1. For the humiliation of our pride, and the manifestation of Divine grace. God hath assuredly promised His favor to the truly humble. By truly humble I mean those who are endued with repentance, and despair of saving themselves: for a man can never be said to be really penitent and humble until he is made to know that his salvation is not suspended in any measure whatever on his own strength, endeavors, free-will or works; but entirely depends on the free pleasure, purpose, determination, and efficiency of another; even of God alone. Whilst a man is persuaded that he has it in his power to contribute anything, be it ever so little, to his own salvation, he remains in carnal confidence; he is not a self-despairer, and therefore he is not duly humbled before God: so far from it, he hopes some favorable juncture or opportunity will offer, when he may be able to lend a helping hand to the business of his salvation. On the contrary, whoever is truly convinced that the whole work depends singly and absolutely on the will of God, who alone is the Author and Finisher of salvation; such a person despairs of all self-assistance: he renounces his own will and his own strength: he waits and prays for the operation of God: nor waits and prays in vain. For the elect's sake, these doctrines are to be preached: that the chosen of God being humbled by the knowledge of His truth's, self-emptied, and sunk as it were into nothing in His presence, may be saved in Christ with eternal glory. This, then, is one inducement to the publication of the doctrine; that the penitent may be made acquainted with the promise of grace, plead it in prayer to God, and receive it as their own.

2. The nature of the Christian faith requires it. Faith has to do with things not seen. And this is one of the highest degrees of faith, steadfastly to believe that God is infinitely merciful, though He saves (comparatively) but few, and condemns so many; and that He is strictly just, though of His own will He makes such numbers of mankind necessarily liable to damnation. Now, these are some of the unseen things whereof faith is the evidence. Whereas, was it in my power to comprehend them, or clearly to make out how God is both invincibly just and infinitely merciful, notwithstanding the display of wrath and seeming inequality in His dispensations respecting the reprobates, faith would have little or nothing to do. But now since these matters cannot be adequately comprehended by us in the present state of imperfection, there *is* room for the exercise of faith. The truths, therefore, respecting predestination in all its branches should be taught and published:

they, no less than the other mysteries of Christian doctrine, being proper objects of faith on the part of God's people.

—Luther on "The Bondage of the Will", 1530 A. D.

N. B. Let the reader note how closely the present-day objections made against the doctrine of God's sovereignty correspond to those refuted by Luther four hundred years ago. A. W. P.

I cannot pray, but I sin: I cannot preach, but I sin: I cannot administer, nor receive the holy sacrament, but I sin. My very repentance needs to be repented of: and the tears I shed want washing in the blood of Christ.—Bishop Beveridge, 1670.

Christ hath said, Ye shall then be free, when the Son makes you free: from whence it follows, that so long as men are unregenerated, they cannot, with truth, be pronounced free. Besides, the tyranny of Satan is such, that he detains men in captivity, till they are rescued by Christ: for our Lord has declared, that the strong man armed keeps peaceable possession of his palace, and continues master of the spoils; till One stronger than he, arrives, and dispossesses him by force. Likewise, in the second Epistle to Timothy, the apostle affirms, that such as oppose the truth are kept prisoners by Satan at his will. And it is a well-known illustration, that the will of man resembles a horse, which sometimes has grace for his rider, and sometimes the Devil. Now, perhaps, it is set in motion by the former: anon, it is whipp'd and spurr'd by the latter. Human liberty, therefore, is cut short by manifold slavery. And, seeing the freedom of the will is so exceedingly small, during the present state of things, it is wonderful to me, that men do not, with Luther, rather term the will a slave and a bond-woman, than free. If a man was shut up in prison, manacled and fettered; could he justly call himself free, only because he were able to move his head and lift up his eyelids?

—Peter Martyr, 1547.

In pursuance of God's will, the teeming earth produces, at the proper season, abundant provision both for men, and for wild beasts, and for all the animals which are upon it; without varying from, and without altering, ought of those things which were decreed by Him. By the word of His majesty He hath constituted all things; and He is able, by a word, to overturn them. Who shall say unto Him, What hast Thou done? or who shall resist the might of His power? He hath done all things at what season He pleased, and in what manner He pleased: and not one of the things which have been decreed by Him shall pass away. All things are open to His view, nor hath anything absconded from His will and pleasure.

—From Clement's Epistle to the Corinthians, A. D. 65.

Grace is that good pleasure of God, whereby He willeth to give us what we have not deserved, in order to our benefit, not to His. It is manifest, therefore, that all the good which is within us, whether it be natural, or freely conferred afterwards, proceeds from the grace of God: for there is no good thing of which His will is not the author; and what He wills is done. He Himself averts our will from evil, and converts our will to good, and makes our will to persevere in that good.—A will to good, whereby man becomes conformed to the will of God, is a grace freely given: for the divine will is grace. And grace is then said to be infused, when the divine will begins to operate on our will.

—Robert Grosthead, Bishop of Lincoln, 1235, A.D.

The Editor's address is now 227 N. Creighton St., Philadelphia, Pa.

Foreign subscribers please send *only* International Money Orders.

All orders for the Editor's books & booklets please send to him personally.

The 12 numbers for 1922 & 1923, *bound*—$1.50 each

VOL. III MARCH, 1924 No. 3

STUDIES in the SCRIPTURES

"Search the Scriptures" John 5:39.

A PERIODICAL (MONTHLY "IF THE LORD WILL") DEVOTED TO BIBLE STUDIES and EXPOSITIONS

Arthur W. Pink, Publisher & Editor,
227 N. Creighton St., Philadelphia, Pa.

Price: 10 cents per copy; $1.00 per year. Foreign $1.00 per year.

TO OUR SCRIPTURE STUDY FAMILY

Several letters have recently come to hand from China, Africa, and Australia, from servants of God to whom "Studies in the Scriptures," is sent out free. These Missionaries write to say how much they have been helped and blest by this little Magazine. The receipt of such letters fills us with praise to God who is pleased, in His sovereign grace, to use such an unworthy and unprofitable instrument. It also makes us long to increase the number upon our free list. There are many other Missionaries, laboring faithfully in the lonely and difficult places of the earth, who would value highly that which furnished food for the soul. We know of no ministry more needed, more blessed and yet more neglected, than this.

Probably there are some of our subscribers who are sometimes puzzled to know "*where* to place their gifts unto the Lord, or to place them to best advantage. Here is a call which surely must speak to every regenerate heart. Servants of God, thousands of miles away from home, deprived of all opportunity to hear the Word ministered by others. How they would welcome a monthly visit from a Magazine devoted solely to the exposition of Holy Writ! For every five dollars received, the Editor will send out "Studies in the Scriptures" to five preachers of the Gospel in foreign lands. The extra postage he will gladly pay out of his own pocket.

This Magazine is already going forth to over two hundred in distant lands and if the Lord's stewards will respond to this appeal and co-operate in this service for God and His ministers, we would greatly like to double this number. If any of our subscribers know the names and addresses of servants of God whom they feel *sure* would value this Magazine, please send them in to me, whether accompanied by a gift or not. The names and addresses of any servants or saints of God *in this country* who are too poor to pay for the Magazine for themselves will also be welcomed.

Opportunities for such service will soon be over forever. "The coming of the Lord draweth nigh". The "night" is far spent, the "day" is at hand. Then let us redeem the time. Let us "spend and be spent" in the "little while" we are yet privileged to witness for an absent Saviour.

Yours in His glad service,
Arthur W. Pink.

IMPORTANT NOTICES

All new subscriptions will be dated back to January, 1924.
Set of twelve issues for **1922**, unbound, **$1.00**. Bound, **$1.50**.
Set of twelve issues for **1923**, unbound, **$1.00**. Bound **$1.50**.
Note: We cannot break a set or now supply any **single** 1923 issues.
Subscription Price: **$1.00** per year to any address in the world. Single copies **10 cents**.
Change of Address: Please notify me promptly of any change of address, and be certain to give both old and new addresses.
Non-subscribers receiving this Magazine regularly will understand their subscription has been entered by a friend.
Copies lost in the mail duplicated only if we are notified promptly.

Entered as second-class matter December 15th, 1923, at the post office at Philadelphia, Pa., under Act of March 3rd, 1879.

CONTENTS

JOHN'S GOSPEL.

27. CHRIST IN THE TEMPLE (Concluded): John 7:32-53.

The following is a general Outline of the passage which is to be before us:—

1. The Pharisees' attempt to apprehend Christ: v. 32.
2. Christ's words to their officers: vv. 33, 34.
3. The mystification of the Jews: vv. 35, 36.
4. Christ's words on the last day of the Feast: vv. 37-39.
5. The divided opinion of the common people: vv. 40-44.
6. The confession of the officers: vv. 45, 46.
7. The conference of the Pharisees broken up by Nicodemus: vv. 47-53.

The passage for our present consideration continues and completes the one that was before us in our last lesson. It views our Lord still in the Temple, and supplies additional evidences of His absolute Deity. It also affords further proofs of the desperate wickedness of the human heart. There is a strange mingling of the lights and the shadows. First, the Pharisees send officers to arrest Christ, and then we find these returning to their masters and confessing that never man spake as He did. On the one hand, we hear of Christ ministering blessing to the thirsty souls who come unto Him and drink; on the other, we learn of there being a division among the people because of Him. The Sanhedrim sit in judgment upon Christ, and yet one of their own number, Nicodemus, is found rebuking them.

Before examining in detail the closing verses of John 7 this will be the best place, perhaps, to call attention (though very briefly) to the significant *order* of truth found in John 5, 6, and 7. This may be seen in two different directions: First, concerning Christ Himself; second, concerning His people. In John 5 Christ is seen disclosing His Divine attributes, His essential perfections. In John 6 He is viewed in His humiliation, as the One come down from heaven, and who was to "give His life" for the world. But here in John 7, He says, "Yet a little while am I with you, and then *I go* unto Him that sent Me" (v. 33), and speaks of the gift of the Holy Spirit, which was subsequent upon His glorification (v. 39). So, too, there is a similar progressive unfolding of truth in connection with the believer. In John 5 he is viewed as "quickened" (v. 21). In John 6 we see the result of this: he comes to Christ and is saved. Now, in John 7, we hear of "rivers of living water" flowing from him to others!

"The Pharisees heard that the people murmured such things concerning Him; and the Pharisees and the chief priests sent officers to take Him" (v. 32). Things began to move swiftly. An interval of but six months divides between the time contemplated in our lesson and the actual crucifixion of Christ. The shadows commence to fall more thickly and darkly across His path. The opposition of His enemies is more definite and relentless. The religious leaders were incensed: their intelligence had been called into question (v. 26), and they were losing their hold over many of the people (v. 31). When these tidings reached the ears of the Pharisees and chief priests, they sent out officers to arrest the Saviour.

"Then said Jesus unto them, Yet a little while am I with you, and then I go unto Him that sent Me" (v. 33). This was tantamount to saying, My presence here is a source of annoyance to your masters, but not for long will this be continued. But our Lord did not forget to remind these officers that *He* was complete master of the situation. None could remove Him until His work was finished: "Yet a little while *am* I with you". True that little while spanned only six months, but until these had run their course He *would be* with them, and no power on earth could prevent it; no power either human or satanic could shorten that little while by so much as a single day or hour. And when that little while had expired He would "go". He would return to His Father in heaven. Equally powerless would they be to prevent this. Of His own self He would lay down His life, and of His own self would He take it again.

"Then said Jesus unto them, Yet a little while am I with you, and then I go unto Him that sent Me" (v. 33). How solemnly these words apply to our own age! Christ is now here in the Person of the Holy Spirit. But not forever is the Holy Spirit to remain in the world. When the fulness of the Gentiles be come in, then shall the Holy Spirit return to the One that sent Him. And how many indications there are that this is not far distant! Verily, we are justified in saying to sinners, *"Yet a little while"* will the Holy Spirit be "with you" and then He will "go unto Him" that sent Him. Then resist Him no longer: "Today if ye will hear His voice, harden not your hearts."

"Ye shall seek Me, and shall not find Me: and where I am, thither ye cannot come" (v. 34). This, no doubt, received its first fulfillment immediately after our Lord had risen from the dead. When "some of the watch" came to Jerusalem and made known to the chief priests that Christ had risen, that the sepulchre was empty, we may be sure that a diligent search was made for Him. But never again did any of them set eyes upon Him—the next time they shall behold Him will be at the Great White Throne. Whither He had gone they could not come, for "Except a man be born again he *cannot* enter the kingdom of God". And how tragicly have these words of Christ received a continual verification in connection with Israel all through the centuries. In vain have the Jews sought their Messiah: in vain, because there is a veil over their hearts even as they read their own Scriptures (2 Cor. 3:15).

"Ye shall seek Me, and shall not find Me: and where I am, thither ye cannot come" (v. 34). These words also have a solemn message for unsaved Gentiles living today. In applying the previous verse to our own times we pointed out how that the words, "Yet a little while am I with you, and then I go unto Him that sent Me" find their fulfillment in the presence of the Spirit of Christ in the world today, a presence so soon to be removed. And once He *is* removed, once the Spirit of Christ returns to heaven, He will be sought in vain. In the Tribulation period there will be no salvation of Gentiles, at least of none of them who have received but have despised God's truth in the present interval. "Ye shall seek Me, and shall not find Me" will receive a most solemn verification in a soon-coming day. This is very clear from Prov. 1:24-28: "Because I have called, and ye refused; I have stretched out My hand, and no man regarded; But ye have set at nought all My counsel and would none of My reproof: I also will laugh at your calamity; I will mock when your fear cometh; When your fear cometh as desolation, and your destruction cometh as a whirlwind; when distress and anguish cometh upon you. Then shall they call upon Me, *but I will not answer;* they shall seek Me early, *but they shall not find Me.*" Nor does this solemn passage stand alone: "Strive to enter in at the strait gate, for many, I say unto you, will seek to enter in, *and shall not be able* when once the Master of the house is risen up, and hath shut to the door" (Luke 13:24, 25). In view of these solemn warnings let every unsaved reader heed promptly that imperative word in Isa. 55:6: "Seek ye the Lord *while He may be found,* call ye upon Him *while He is near.*"

"And where I am, thither ye cannot come" (v. 34). How this brings out the Deity of Christ. Mark He does not say, "Where I shall be," or "Where I *then* am, ye cannot come"; but, though still on earth, He declared, "Where *I am*, thither ye cannot come". In the previous verse He had said, "I *go* unto Him that sent Me." These two statements refer severally, to His distinct natures. "Where I *am*" intimated His perpetual presence in heaven by virtue of His Divine nature; His *going* there was yet a future thing for His human nature!

"Then said the Jews among themselves, Whither will He go, that we shall not find Him? Will He go unto the dispersed among the Gentiles, and teach the Gentiles" (v. 35)? How true it is that "the natural man receiveth not the things of the Spirit of God: for they are foolishness unto him, neither can he know them, because they are spiritually discerned" (1 Cor. 2:14). Devoid of any spiritual discernment, these Jews were unable to understand Christ's reference to His return to heaven. When they asked, "Will He go to the dispersed among the Gentiles?" they were referring to those Jews who lived away from Palestine. The Greek word is "diaspora" and signifies the Dispersion. It is found only here and in Jas. 1:1 where it is rendered "The twelve tribes *which are scattered abroad*", literally, "in the Dispersion", and in 1 Pet. 1:1, "sojourners of the Dispersion". Further, these Jews asked, "Will He teach the Gentiles?". What an evidence is this that unbelief will think about anything but God! God not being in their thoughts, it never occurred to them that the Lord Jesus might be referring to His Father in heaven; hence their minds turned to the Dispersion and the Gentiles. It is thus even with a Christian when he is under the control of unbelief: **the last one he will** think of is *God*. Solemn and humbling commentary is this on the corruption of our natural heart.

"What manner of saying is this that He said, Ye shall seek Me, and shall not find Me: and where I am, thither ye cannot come?" (v. 36). And mark it, these were not illiterate men who thus mused, but men of education and religious training. But no amount of culture or religious instruction can impart spiritual understanding to the intellect. A man must be Divinely illumined before he can perceive the meaning and value of the things of God. The truth is that the most illiterate babe in Christ has a capacity to understand spiritual things which an unregenerate university-graduate does not possess. The plainest and simplest word from God is far above the reach of the natural faculties.

"In the last day, that great day of the Feast, Jesus stood and cried, saying, If any man thirst, let him come unto Me, and drink" (v. 37). Their celebration of this Feast of Tabernacles was drawing to a close. The "last" or eighth day had now arrived. It is here termed "the last *great* day of the Feast"; in John 19:31 the same word is rendered *"high* day". It was so called because on this closing day there was a general and solemn convocation of the worshippers (see Lev. 23:36). On this eighth day, when the temple-courts would be thronged with unusually large crowds, Jesus "stood and cried". What a contrast this pointed between Himself and those who hated Him: they desired to rid the world of Him; He to minister unto needy souls.

"Jesus stood and cried, saying, If any man thirst, let Him **come unto Me, and** drink" (v. 37). Here is the Gospel in a single short sentence. Three words in it stand out and call for special **emphasis**—"thirst", "come", "drink". The first tells of a recognized need. Thirst, like hunger, is something of which we are acutely conscious. It is a craving for that which is not in our actual possession. There is a soul thirst as well as a bodily. The pathetic thing is that so many thirst for that which cannot slake them. Their thirst is for the things of the world: pleasure, money, fame, ease, self-indulgence; and over all of these Christ has written in imperishable letters, "Whosoever drinketh of this water shall thirst again."

But in our text Christ is referring to a thirst for something infinitely nobler and grander, even for Himself. He speaks of that intense longing for Himself which only the Spirit of God can create in the soul. If a poor sinner is convicted of his pollution and desires cleansing, if he is weighted down with the awful burden of concious guilt and desires pardon, if he is fully aware of his weakness and impotency and longs for strength and deliverance, if he is filled with fears and distrust and craves for peace and rest,—then, says Christ, let him "come unto Me." Happy the one who *so* thirsts after Christ that he can say, "As the hart panteth after the waterbrooks, so panteth my soul after Thee, O God" (Psa. 42:1).

"Let him *come* unto Me." "Come" is one of the simplest words in the English language. It signifies our *approach* to an object or person. It expresses action, and implies that the will is operative. To come to Christ means, that you do with your heart and will what you would do with your feet were He standing in bodily form before you and saying, "Come unto Me". It is an act of faith. It intimates that you have turned your back upon the world, and have abandoned all confidence in everything about yourself, and now cast yourself empty-handed, at the feet of incarnate Grace and Truth. But make sure that nothing whatever is substituted for *Christ.* It is not come to the Lord's table, or come to the waters of baptism, or come to the priest or minister, or come and join the church; but come to *Christ Himself,* and to none other.

"And *drink.*" It is here that so many seem to fail. There are numbers who give evidence of an awakened conscience, of heart-exercise, of a conscious need of Christ; and there are numbers who appear to be seeking Him, and yet stop short at that. But Christ not only said, "Come unto Me", but He added, "and *drink*". A river flowing through a country where people were dying of thirst, would avail them nothing unless they drank of it. The blood of the slain lamb availed the Israelite household nothing, unless the head had *applied* it to the door. So Christ saves none who do not receive Him by faith. "Drinking" is here a figurative expression, and signifies *making Christ your own.* In all ages God's saints have been those who saw their deep need, who came to the Lord, and *appropriated* the provision of grace.

"If any man thirst, let him come unto Me, and drink". Let us not forget *where* these words were first uttered. The Speaker was not in a penitentiary, but in the Temple. Christ was not addressing a company of profligates, but a religious crowd who were observing a Divinely-instituted Feast! What an example for each of His servants! Brother preacher, take nothing for granted. Do not suppose that because those you address are respectable people and punctual in their religious exercises that they are necessarily saved. Heed that word of your Master's, and "preach the Gospel to *every* creature", cultured as well as illiterate, the respectable as well as the profligate, the religious man as well as the irreligious.

"He that believeth on Me, as the Scripture hath said, out of his belly shall flow rivers of living water" (v. 38). The language used by our Lord really implies that He had some definite passage in mind. We believe that He referred to Isa. 58:11, "And thou shalt be like a watered garden, and like *a spring of water,* whose waters fail not." The prophet is referring to Israel in the Millennium, but our Lord applies the promise to believers of the present dispensation. The believer should not be like a sponge—taking in but not giving out—but like a spring, ever fresh and giving forth. Twice before had Christ employed "water" as a figure, and it is striking to observe the progressive order. In John 3:5 He had spoken of a man being born "of *water* and of the Spirit": here the "water" comes down *from God*—cf 3:3 margin, "born from above". In John 4:14 He says, "The *water* that I shall give him shall be in him a well of *water* springing up into everlasting life:" here the "water" springs up *to God,* reaching out to the Source from whence it came. But in John 7:38 He says, "Out of his belly shall flow rivers of *living water":* here the "water" flows forth *for God* in blessing to others.

"He that believeth on Me, as the Scripture hath said, out of his belly shall flow rivers of living water" (v. 38). This verse describes the normal Christian, and yet, how many of us would say that its contents are receiving a practical exemplification in our daily lives? How many of us would make so bold as to affirm that out of *our* innermost part *are* flowing "rivers of living water"? Few indeed, if we were honest and truthful. What, then, is wrong? Let us examine the verse a little more attentively.

"Out of his belly shall flow". What is the "belly"? It is that part of man which *constantly craves.* It is that part which, in his fallen condition, is the natural man's *god*—"Whose god is their belly" (Phil. 3:19), said the apostle: styled their "god" because it receives the most care and attention. The "belly" is that part of man which is never really *satisfied,* for it is constantly crying for something else to appease its cravings. Now the remarkable thing, yea, the *blessed* thing, is, that not only is the believer himself satisfied, but he *overflows with that* which satisfies—out of his innermost parts "flow (forth) rivers of living water". The thought indeed is a striking one. It is not merely "from him" shall flow, but *"out of his belly* shall flow"; that is, from that very part of our constitution which, in the natural man, is never satisfied, there shall be a constant overflow.

Now *how* is the believer satisfied? The answer is, By "coming" to Christ and *drinking;* which mean *receiving* from Him: by having his emptiness ministered to from His fulness. But does this refer only to *a single act?* Is this something that is done once for all? Such seems to be the common idea. Many appear to imagine that grace is a sort of thing which God puts into the soul like a seed, and that it will grow and develop into more. Not that we deny that the believer grows, but the believer grows *in grace;* it is not the grace in him which grows! O dear Christian reader, we are to *continue* as we began. Where was it that you found rest and peace? It was in Christ. And *how* did you obtain these? It was from a consciousness of your need (thirsting), and your coming to Christ to have this met, and by appropriating from Him. But why stop there? This ought to be a *daily* experience. And it is our failure at this very point which is the reason why John 7:38 does not describe *our* spiritual history.

A vessel will not *overflow* until it is full, and to be full it has to be filled! How simple; and yet how searching! The order of Christ in the scripture before us has never changed. I must first come to Him and "drink" *before* the rivers of living water will flow forth from my satisfied soul. What the Lord most wants from us is *receptiveness,* that is, the capacity to receive, to receive from Him. I *must* receive *from* Him, before I can give out *for* Him. The apostles came to Christ for the bread before they distributed to the hungry multitude. Here is the secret of all *real* service. When my own belly has been filled, that is, when my own needy heart has been *satisfied* by Christ, then no effort will be required, but out from me *shall* flow "rivers of living water". O may Divine grace teach us daily to first come *to* Christ before we attempt anything *for* Him.

"But this spake He of the Spirit, which they that believe on Him should receive: for the Holy Ghost was not yet given: because that Jesus was not yet glorified" (v. 39). This intimates a further reason why we are told in v. 37 that the words there recorded were uttered by Christ on "the *last*" day, that is the eighth day of the Feast. In Scripture eight ever refers to a *new beginning,* and for this reason, like the numeral three, eight is also the number of *resurrection:* Christ arose on the eighth day, "in the end of the Sabbath, as it began to dawn toward the first of the week" (Matt. 28:1). And, doctrinally considered, Christ was here speaking as from resurrection ground. He was referring to that which could not receive its accomplishment till after He had risen from the dead. When he said "The Holy Spirit was not yet", John meant that He was not yet publicly *manifested* on earth. His manifestation was subsequent to the glorification of Christ.

"Many of the people therefore, when they heard this saying, said, Of a truth this is the Prophet" (v. 40). The line of thought found in this verse and the twelve that follow it might be termed, The testing of men by the truth, and their failure to receive it. The first class brought before us here is the common people. Many of them were impressed by the gracious words which proceeded out of the mouth of Christ. They said, "Of a truth this is the Prophet." Their language was identical with that of the Galileans, recorded in 6:14. But observe they merely *said,* "This is the Prophet". We are not told that they received Him as such. Words are cheap, and worth little unless supported by action. It is significant, however, that John was the only one of the evangelists that records these sayings of the people, for they were in harmony with his special theme. As its first verse intimates, the fourth Gospel presents Christ as "the Word," that is, the Speech, the Revealer, of God. A "prophet" is God's spokesman!

"Others said, This is the Christ. But some said, Shall Christ come out of Galilee? Hath not the Scriptures said, That Christ cometh of the seed of David, and out of the town of Bethlehem, where David was?" (vv. 41, 42). Here is another illustration of an acquaintance with the letter of the Word which failed to regulate the walk. These people could quote prophecy while they rejected Christ! How vain is an intellectual knowledge of spiritual things when unaccompanied by grace in the heart! These men knew where Christ was to be born. They referred to the Scriptures as though familiar with their contents. And yet the eyes of their understanding were not enlightened. The Messiah Himself stood before them, but they knew Him not. What a solemn warning is there here for us! A knowledge of the letter of Scripture is not to be despised, far from it: would that all the Lord's people today were as familiar with the Word as probably these Jews were. It is a cause for deep thankfulness if we were taught to read and memorize Scripture from our earliest childhood. But while a knowledge of the letter of Scripture is to be prized, it ought not to be overestimated. It is not sufficient that we are versed in the historical facts of the Bible, nor that we have a clear grasp, intellectually, of the doctrines of Christianity. Unless our hearts are affected and our lives moulded by God's Word, we are no better off than a starving man with a cookery book in his hand.

"Others said, This is the Christ. But some said, Shall Christ come out of Galilee? Hath not the Scripture said, that Christ cometh of the seed of David, and out of the town of Bethlehem, where David was?" (vv. 41, 42). These words are recorded for our learning. We must not pass them over hurriedly as though they contained no message for us. They should lead us to solemnly and seriously examine ourselves. There are many today who, like these men of old, can quote the Scriptures readily and accurately, and yet who give no evidence that they have been born again. An experimental acquaintance with Christ is the one thing needful. A heart knowledge of God's truth is the vital thing, and it is that which no schooling or seminary training can confer. If you have discovered the plague of your own heart; if you have seen yourself as a lost sinner, and have received as yours the sinner's Saviour; if you have tasted for yourself that the Lord is gracious; if you are now, not only a hearer but a doer of the Word; then, abundant cause have you to thank God for thus enlightening you. You may be altogether ignorant of Hebrew and Greek, but if you know *Him*, whom to know is life eternal, and if you sit daily at *His* feet to be taught of Him, then have you that which is above the price of rubies. But O make quite sure on the point, dear reader. You cannot afford to remain in uncertainty. Rest not, until by Divine grace you can say, "One thing I know, that, whereas I was blind, now I see". And if your eyes have been opened, pray God daily to give you a better *heart-knowledge* of His Word.

"So there was a division among the people because of Him" (v. 43). How this fulfilled His own predicted word. Near the beginning of His public ministry (cf Matt. 10:34, 35) He said, "Suppose ye that I am come to give peace on earth? I tell you, Nay; but rather *division*. For from henceforth there shall be five in one house *divided*, three against two, and two against three", etc. (Luke 12:51, 52). So it proved then, and so it has been ever since. *Why* we do not know. God's ways are ever different from ours. There will be another *"division"* among the people of the earth when the Lord Jesus leaves the Father's throne and descends into the air; yea, a *"division"* also among the people in the graves. Only the "dead in Christ" shall then be raised, and only the living ones who have been saved by Him will be "caught up together to meet the Lord in the air". The rest will be left behind. What a "division" that will be! In which company would *you* be, dear reader, were Christ to come today? There will be another "division" at the beginning of the Millennium, for before Him shall be gathered all nations, and "He shall *separate* them one from another, as a shepherd *divideth* his sheep from the goats" (Matt. 25:32).

"So there was a division among the people because of Him" (v. 43). If this was the case when Christ was upon earth, then we must not be surprised if those who faithfully serve Him occasion a "division" during His absence. Scripture says, "Woe unto you when *all* men speak well of you." Read through the book of Acts and note what "divisions" the preaching of the apostles caused. Mark that solemn but explicit word in 1 Cor. 11:19, "For there *must be* also *factions* among you, that they that are approved may be made manifest among you" (R. V.). How senseless, then, is all this modern talk about the union of Christendom. Fellow-preacher, if you are faithfully declaring all the counsel of God, be not surprised, nor be dismayed, if there is a "division" because of *you*. Regard it as an ominous sign if it be otherwise.

"And some of them would have taken Him; but no man laid hands on Him" (v. 44). This is similar to what was before us in v. 30. Again and again is this noted in John's Gospel: cf 5:16, 18; 17:1; 8:20; 10:39, etc. But they were powerless before the decrees of God. "Some of them *would have* taken Him." The Greek word means they "desired" to do so. They had a will to, but not the ability. Ah, men may boast of their will-power and of their "free will", but after all, what does it amount to? Pilate said, "Knowest thou not that *I have power* to crucify Thee, and have power to release Thee" (John 19:10). So he boasted, and so he really believed. But what was our Lord's rejoinder? "Jesus answered, Thou couldest have *no* power at all against Me, *except it were given thee from above*". It was so here: these men *desired* to arrest Christ, but they were not given power from above to do so. Verily, we may say with the prophet of old, "O Lord, I know that the way of man is not in himself: it is not in man that walketh to direct his steps" (Jer. 10:23)!

"Then came the officers to the chief priests and Pharisees; and they said unto them, Why have you not brought Him?" (v. 45). Well might they ask such a question, for they were totally ignorant of the real answer. Well might Pharaoh now ask, Why did I fail in destroying the Hebrews? Or Nero, Why did I not succeed in exterminating all the Christians? Or the king of Spain, Why did my "invincible Armada" fail to reach the English ports and destroy the British navy? Or the Kaiser, Why did my legions not succeed in taking Paris? In each case the answer would be, Because *God* did not allow you to! Like these other infamous characters, the Pharisees had reckoned without God. They sent their officers to arrest Christ: they might as well have ordered them to stop the sun from shining. Not all the hosts of earth and hell could have arrested Him one moment before God's predestined hour had arrived. Ah, dear reader, the God of the Bible is no mere figure-head. He is Supreme in fact as well as in name. When *He* gets ready to act none can hinder; and until He *is* ready, none can speed Him. This is a hateful thought for His enemies, but one full of comfort to His people. If you, my reader, are fighting against Him, be it known that the great God laughs at your consummate folly, and will one day ere long deal with you in His fury. On the other hand, if you are, by sovereign grace, one of His children, then He is *for* you, and if *God be for you,* who can be against you? Who, indeed!

"The officers answered, Never man spake like this man." (v. 46). What a testimony was this from unbelievers! Instead of arresting Him, they had been arrested by what they had heard. Mark again how this magnifies Christ as *"the Word"!* It was not His miracles which had so deeply impressed them, but His speech! "Never man *spake* as this man". True indeed was their witness, for the One they had listened to was *more* than "man"—"the Word was God"! No man ever spake like Christ because *His* words were spirit and life (John 6:63). What sayest *thou* of Christ, my reader? Do you own that "never man spake as this man"? Have His words come *to you* with a force that none other's ever did? Have they pierced you through to "the dividing asunder of soul and spirit"? Have they brought life to your soul, joy to your heart, rest to your conscience, peace to your mind? Ah, if *you* have heard *Him* say "Come unto Me, all ye that labor and are heavy laden, and I will give you rest", and you have responded to His voice, then can you say indeed, "Never man spake like *this* man".

"Then answered them the Pharisees, Are ye also deceived? Have any of the rulers or of the Pharisees believed on Him?" (vv. 47, 48). The "rulers" were men of official rank; the "Pharisees", the religious formalists of that day. Few "rulers" or men of eminent standing, few "scribes" or men of erudition, few "Pharisees" or men of strict morality, were numbered among the followers of the Lamb. They were too well satisfied with themselves to see any need of a Saviour. The sneering criticism of these Pharisees has been repeated in every age, and the very fact that it *is* made only supplies another evidence of the veracity of God's Word. Said the apostle Paul, *"Not many* wise men after the flesh, *not many* mighty, *not many* noble, are called: but God hath chosen the foolish things of the world to confound the wise; and God hath chosen the weak things of the world to confound the things which are mighty; and base things of the world, and things which are despised, hath God chosen, yea, and things which are not, to bring to naught things which are" (1 Cor. 1:26-28). And why—"that no flesh *should glory* in His presence"!

"But this people who knoweth not the law are cursed" (v. 49). "This people" was a term of contempt. It has been rendered by some scholars, "This rabble—this mob—this riff raff". Nothing was more mortifying to these proud Pharisees, and nothing is more humiliating to their modern descendants than to find harlots and publicans entering the kingdom while they are left outside.

"Nicodemus saith unto them, (he that came to Jesus by night, being one of them,) Doth our law judge any man, before it hear him, and know what he doeth?" (vv. 50, 51). Have *any* of the Pharisees believed on Christ, they asked? Not many had, but at least one had, as Nicodemus gave evidence. Here is the one ray of light which relieves this dark picture. Sovereign grace had singled out one of these very Pharisees, and gave him courage to rebuke his unrighteous fellows. It is true that Nicodemus does not appear to have said much on this occasion, but he said sufficient to break up their conference. Not yet did he come out boldly on the Lord's side; but he was no longer one of His enemies. The work of grace proceeds slowly in some hearts, as in the case of Nicodemus; for eighteen months had elapsed since what is recorded in John 3. With others the work of grace acts more swiftly, as in the case of Saul of Tarsus. Here, as everywhere, God acts according to His own sovereign pleasure. Later, if the Lord wills, Nicodemus will come before us again, and then we shall behold the full corn in the ear. John's Gospel depicts three stages in the spiritual career of Nicodemus. In John 3 it is midnight: here in John 7 it is twilight: in John 19 it is daylight in his soul.

"They answered and said unto him, Art thou also of Galilee? Search, and look: for out of Galilee ariseth no prophet" (v. 52). But they were wrong. Their own Scriptures refuted them. Jonah was a "prophet", and he arose from *Galilee:* see 2 Kings 14:25. So, most probably, did one or two other of their prophets. When they asked Nicodemus, "Art thou also of Galilee", they evidently meant, Art thou also a Galilean, that is, one of His party?

"And every man went unto his own house" (v. 53). The reference here is to "every man" mentioned throughout this chapter. The Feast was now over. The temporary "booths" would be taken down; and all would now retire to their regular dwellings. Every man *went* unto his own house", is very solemn. *Away* from Christ they went. Him they left! They desired His company no longer. And there the curtain falls.

The following questions are designed to prepare the student for the next lesson on John 8:1-11:—

1. Wherein does this passage supply a further proof of the awful condition of Israel?
2. What is the force and significance of "He *sat down*" (v. 2)?—contrast "Jesus *stood*" in 7:37.
3. Wherein lay the "temptation": v. 6?
4. What was the significance of Christ writing with His finger on the ground: v. 6?
5. Why did He "again" write on the ground: v. 8?
6. According to which of the Divine attributes was Christ acting in v. 11?
7. What dispensational picture can you discover in this passage? Ponder carefully the first two verses.

—Arthur W. Pink.

GLEANINGS IN EXODUS.

3. The Early Days of Moses: Ex. 2.

From Adam to Christ there is none greater than Moses. He is one of the few characters of Scripture whose course is sketched from his infancy to his death. The fierce light of criticism has been turned upon him for generations, but he is still the most commanding figure of the ancient world. In character, in faith, in the unique position assigned him as the mediator of the old covenant, and in achievements, he stands first among the heroes of the Old Testament. All of God's early dealings with Israel were transacted through Moses. He was a prophet, priest, and king in one person, and so united all the great and important functions which later were distributed among a plurality of persons. The history of such an one is worthy of the strictest attention, and his remarkable life deserves the closest study.

"The life of Moses presents a series of striking antitheses. He was the child of a slave, and the son of a queen. He was born in a hut, and lived in a palace. He inherited poverty, and enjoyed unlimited wealth. He was the leader of armies, and the keeper of flocks. He was the mightiest of warriors, and the meekest of men. He was educated in the court, and dwelt in the desert. He had the wisdom of Egypt, and the faith of a child. He was fitted for the city, and wandered in the wilderness. He was tempted with the pleasures of sin, and endured the hardships of virtue. He was backward in speech, and talked with God. He had the rod of a shepherd, and the power of the Infinite. He was a fugitive from Pharaoh, and an ambassador from heaven. He was the giver of the Law, and the forerunner of grace. He died alone on Mount Moab, and appeared with Christ in Judea. No man assisted at his funeral, yet God buried him." (Dr. I. M. Haldeman).

Exodus 2 furnishes us with a brief account of the infancy of Moses. The king of Egypt was determined to check the rapid growth of the Hebrew people. First, he had them placed under taskmasters, who were given orders to "afflict them with their burdens". But this measure failed entirely: "The more they afflicted them, the more they multiplied and grew". Next, the king gave orders to the Hebrew midwives that whenever a male Israelite was born, he should be killed. But once more the evil designs of Pharaoh came to nought. The mid-wives feared God, "and did not as the king of Egypt commanded them, but saved the men children alive". Finally, we are told, "And Pharaoh charged all his people, saying, every son that is born ye shall cast into the river, and every daughter ye shall save alive" (1:22). It was during this time and under such conditions that the future deliverer of Abraham's descendants was born.

"And there went a man of the house of Levi, and took to wife a daughter of Levi. And the woman conceived, and bare a son: and when she saw him that he was a goodly child, she hid him three months. And when she could not longer hide him, she took for him an ark of bulrushes, and daubed it with slime and with pitch, and put the child therein; and she laid it in the flags by the river's brink" (Ex. 2:1-3). Much of a sentimental nature has been written on these verses. Commentators have reasoned that it was mother-love and the beauty of the child which caused Jochebed to act as she did. But this will not stand the test of Holy Writ. Scripture informs us that it was neither affection nor infatuation but *faith* which was the mainspring of action. Heb. 11:23 declares, "By *faith* Moses, when he was born, was hid three months of his parents, because they saw he was a proper child; and they were not afraid of the king's commandment." Faith "cometh by *hearing*" (Rom. 10:17): the parents of Moses must, therefore, have received a direct communication from God, informing them of what should happen and instructing them what to do. And they believed what God had told them and acted accordingly.

It was faith which saw that the child was "goodly" (in the sight of God), as it was faith which made them defy "the king's commandment"—first by hiding the child, later in placing him in the ark of bulrushes. It is true that in this instance grace did not run counter to natural affection; nevertheless, it was not by feelings but "by faith" they acted. When commanded to do so, we are to obey God against our natural affections. Thus it was with Abraham when called to go out from the land of his birth and leave all his kindred behind; and so later, when called upon to offer up Isaac.

Should it be asked, Wherein is the faith of Moses' parents to be seen? The answer is: In overcoming the fear of the king and in trusting God's protection for the preservation of the child. And is not the strength of their faith evidenced by the selection of the place where the young child was put, after he could be no longer hid in the home? Surely the parents of Moses took him to the very last spot which carnal reasoning would have suggested. The mother laid him "in the flags by the river's brink"! But that was the very place where the babies were drowned! Ah, is not *that* the last location we had chosen? Would not *we* have carried him as far away from the river as possible? It is to be noted that in Heb. 11:23 the faith of both parents is spoken of, while that of the mother's is singled out here in Ex. 2, but his father receives particular mention by Stephen in Acts 7:20. It is blessed to see this concurrence between them. Husband and wife should go hand in hand to the throne of grace and act together in every good work.

Ere passing from our notice of the faith of Amram and Jochebed there are two other points which deserve notice. Though faith vanquished fear, yet *lawful means were used* to overcome danger: the mother "hid" the child, and later, had recourse to the ark. It is not faith but fanaticism which deliberately courts danger. Faith never tempts God. Even Christ, though He knew full well of the Father's will to preserve Him, yet withdrew from those who sought His life (Luke 4:30; John 8:59). It is not lack of faith to avoid danger by legitimate precautions. It is no want of trust to employ means, even when assured by God of the event (Acts 27:31). Christ never supplied by a miracle when ordinary means were to hand (Mk. 5:43).

Another important truth which here receives illustration and exemplification is, that civil authorities are to be defied when their decrees are contrary to the expressed mind of God. The Word of God requires us to obey the laws of the land in which we live and exhorts us to be "subject unto the powers that be" (Rom. 13), and this, no matter how wise and just, or how foolish and unjust those laws appear to us. Yet, our obedience and submission to human authorities is plainly qualified. If a human government enacts a law and compliance with it by a saint would compel him to disobey some command or precept of God, then the human must be rejected for the Divine. The cases of Moses' parents, of Daniel (6:7-11) and of the apostles (Acts 5:29), establishes this unequivocally. But if such rejection of human authority be necessitated, let it be performed not in the spirit of carnal defiance, but in the fear of God, and then the issue may safely be left with Him. It was "by *faith*" the parents of Moses "were not afraid of the king's commandment". May Divine grace work in us "like precious faith" which overcomes all fear of man.

In the opening verses of our chapter we have a lovely picture of salvation. The infant Moses was placed on the brink of the river, the place of death—the last spot we had selected. It is so in salvation. Death is the wages of sin, and from this there can be no escape. Having flagrantly broken God's holy law, justice demands the execution of its penalty. But is not this to close the door of hope against us, and seal our doom? Ah, it is just at this point that the Gospel announces God's gracious provision and tells us (what we had never conceived for ourselves) that life comes to us through death.

Though Moses was brought to the place of death, he was made secure *in the ark*. And this speaks to us of Christ* who went down into death for us. The righteousness of God made imperative the payment of sin's awful wages, and so his spotless Son "died the just for the unjust that He might bring us to God" (1 Pet. 3:15). Thus, *in Christ* our Substitute, we too *have been* in the place of death as was the infant Moses. And note that as it was *"faith"* which placed him there, it is faith which identifies us with Christ. Again; just as Moses was brought out of the place of death, so when Christ rose again, we rose with Him (Eph. 2:5, 6). The typical picture may be followed still farther. In the merciful provision which the providence of God arranged for the infant Moses (Ex. 2:4) we have illustrated the tender care of our heavenly Father for every babe in Christ. And, later, in the entrance of Moses into the household and palace of Pharaoh, we have foreshadowed the "mansions" on high, which are now being prepared for us!

"And the daughter of Pharaoh came down to wash herself at the river; and her maidens walked along by the river's side; and when she saw the ark among the flags, she sent her maid to fetch it. And when she had opened it, she saw the child: and, behold, the babe wept. And she had compassion on him, and said, This is one of the Hebrews' children. Then said his sister to Pharaoh's daughter, Shall I go and call to thee a nurse of the Hebrew women, that she may nurse the child for thee? And Pharaoh's daughter said to her, Go. And the maid went and called the

*It is significant that the Hebrew word is used only here and in connection with the ark of Noah, which so clearly typified Christ.

child's mother. And Pharaoh's daughter said unto her, Take this child away, and nurse it for me, and I will give thee thy wages. And the woman took the child and nursed it" (Ex. 2:5-9). It was neither by chance nor accident that Pharaoh's daughter went down to the river that day, for there are no accidents nor chance happenings in a world presided over by the living God. Whatsover happens in time is but the outworking of His eternal decrees—"for Whom are all things, and *by* Whom are all things" (Heb. 2:10). God is behind the scenes, ordering everything for His own glory; hence our smallest actions are controlled by Him. "O Lord, I know that the way of man *is not in himself:* it is not in man that walketh to direct his steps" (Jer. 10:23). It is because that whatsoever happens in time is the outworking of God's eternal decrees, that "all things are working together (the verb is in the present tense) for good to them that love God, who are the called according to His purpose." Big doors often swing on small hinges. God not only directs the rise and fall of empires, but also rules the fall of a sparrow. It was *God* who put it into the heart of this Egyptian princess to go to the river to bathe, and to that particular spot where the ark lay amid the flags; as it was He who caused her to be moved with compassion (rather than with indignation at the defiance of her father's authority) when she beheld the weeping child. And it was God who caused this daughter of the haughty monarch to yield submissively to the suggestion of Miriam, and made the princess willing for its own mother to care for the little child. Only here can the mind repose in unruffled peace. What a haven of rest is this—to know that "of Him, and through Him, and to Him, *are all things:* to whom be glory for ever" (Rom. 11:36).

"And Pharaoh's daughter said unto her, Take this child away, and nurse it for me, and I will give thee thy wages. And the woman took the child, and nursed it" (v. 9). This whole incident of the Divine safeguarding of the infant life of Moses supplies a striking and blessed illustration of God's preservation of His elect during their unregeneracy—a fact that few believers are as thankful over as they should be. We believe it is this which explains a point that has been a sore puzzle to many commentators in Jude 1: "Jude, the servant of Jesus Christ, and brother of James, to them that are sanctified by God the Father, and preserved in Jesus Christ, and called". The *order* of the verbs here is most significant. The "sanctification" by the Father manifestly speaks of our eternal election, when before the foundation of the world God, in His counsels, *separated* us from the mass of our fallen race, and appointed us to salvation. The "calling" evidently refers to that inward and invincible call which comes to each of God's elect at the hour of their regeneration (Rom. 8:30), when the dead hear the voice of the Son of God and live (John 5:25). But observe that in Jude 1 it is said they are "preserved" in Jesus Christ, and "called." Clearly the reference is to *temporal preservation prior to salvation.* As the writer looks back to his unregenerate days he recalls with a shudder a number of occasions when he was in imminent peril, brought face to face with death. But even then, even while in his sins, he was (because in Christ by eternal election) miraculously preserved. What cause for gratitude and praise is this! Doubtless, each Christian reader will recall similar deliverances out of danger. It is this which Ex. 2:6-9 so beautifully illustrates. Even in his unregenerate days, as a babe, the Angel of the Lord encamped round about the infant Moses and delivered him!

"And the child grew, and she brought him unto Pharaoh's daughter, and he became her son. And she called his name Moses: and she said, Because I drew him out of the water". (v. 10) This is a striking illustration of Job 5:13—"He taketh the wise in their own craftiness: and the counsel of the froward is carried headlong". Pharaoh proposed to "deal wisely" with the Israelites, and this, in order that they might not "get them up out of the land" (1:10); and yet, in the end, God compels him to give board, lodging, and education, to the very man which accomplished the very thing that Pharaoh was trying to prevent! Thus was Pharaoh's wisdom turned to foolishness, and Satan's devices defeated.

There are two passages in the New Testament which throw light on the interval passed over between verses 10 and 11 in Ex. 2. In Acts 7:22 we read, "And Moses was learned in all the wisdom of the Egyptians, and was mighty in words and in deeds". But his heart was not in these things. There was something which had a more powerful attraction for him than the honors and comforts of Egypt's court. Doubtless his believing parents had acquainted him with the promises of Jehovah to his forefathers. That the time was not far distant when the Hebrews were to be delivered from their bondage and should journey to the land given to Abraham, Moses had heard, and hearing he believed. The result of his faith is described in Heb. 11:24-26: "By faith Moses, when he was come to years, refused to be called the son of Pharaoh's daughter; Choosing rather to suffer affliction with the people of God, than to enjoy the pleasures of sin for a season; esteeming the reproach of Christ greater riches than the treasures in Egypt: for he had respect unto the recompense of the reward". Upon the character of his faith and this remarkable renunciation we can only comment briefly.

The first thing to be observed is *the nature of his renunciation:* he "refused to be called the son of Pharaoh's daughter". Josephus tells us that Pharaoh had no other children, and that his daughter, Thermutis, had no children of her own. So, most probably Moses would have succeeded to the throne. That some *offer* was made to Moses, after he had reached manhood, is clearly implied by the words "he *refused*". What he refused then was wealth, honors, power, and, most likely, a throne. Had he accepted, he could readily have mitigated the sufferings of His own people, and lightened their heavy burdens. But he "refused".

Second, note *the character of his choice:* he "chose rather to suffer affliction with the people of God, than to enjoy the pleasures of sin for a season". It was not that suffering was thrust upon him, but that he voluntarily elected it. It was not that there was no escape from it but he deliberately determined to throw in his lot with a despised and persecuted people. He preferred hardship to comfort, shame and reproach rather than fame and honor, afflictions rather than pleasures, the wilderness rather than the court. A remarkable choice was this, and mark it, this was the choice not of a child, but of a full-grown man; not of a fool, but of one skilled in all the wisdom of the Egyptians.

Third, observe *the satisfaction he enjoyed:* "esteeming the reproach of Christ greater riches than the treasures in Egypt". The place Moses volunteered to occupy was a hard one, in every respect the very opposite of that in which he had been reared. Yet Moses did not repine or murmur. So far from being dissatisfied with his bargain, he valued the "reproach" which it brought him. So far from complaining at the affliction, he prized it. He not only endured suffering, but he esteemed it as of more worth than the wealth of the greatest and richest country on earth. In this he puts many of us to shame!

Fourth, mark *the motive spring of his actions:* "By faith Moses....refused....chose....esteemed". As another has said, "He must have *heard* from God that he was not to accept this high privilege. Inasmuch as 'faith cometh by hearing', Moses must have *heard!* And, inasmuch as this 'hearing cometh by the Word of God', God must have spoken or communicated His will to Moses; for Moses heard, Moses believed, Moses obeyed. God had other counsels and purposes with regard to Moses. Moses must have been told that 'God, by His hand, would deliver' Israel from Egypt's bondage. The 'things to come' had been revealed to him. The 'things of Christ' had been made known 'in part'. He knew God. He knew that Jehovah had a people, and that they were in sore bondage in Egypt. He knew that they were to be delivered. How, then, could he accept the position of heir to Egypt's throne?".

Finally, attend to *the object set before him:* "for he had respect unto the recompense of the reward". Moses must have "heard" of "the eternal weight of glory", and therefore he looked not at the "things that are seen". The pleasures of sin were of brief duration—only for "a season"; but, in view of the eternity of the glory, the "affliction" seemed brief—but "for a moment," and therefore, "light". Moses, then, walked by faith and not by sight; he had his eyes on the invisible, not the tangible; he was occupied with the future rather than the present; and, consequently, it was an easy matter to exchange the palace for the wilderness, and the pleasures of sin for the reproach of Christ. May like precious faith be vouchsafed reader and writer.

Returning to the narrative we are next told, "And it came to pass in those days, when Moses was grown, that he went out unto his brethren, and looked on their burdens: and he espied an Egyptian smiting an Hebrew, one of his brethren. And he looked this way and that way, and when he saw that there was no man, he slew the Egyptian, and hid him in the sand" (Ex. 2:11, 12). One of the features of Scripture which constantly impresses the writer is the absolute fidelity with which the lives of Bible heroes are described. Unlike so many human biographies, the characters of Scripture are painted in the colors of nature and truth. They are described as they actually were. An instance of this is before us here. Moses was truly a wonderful character, and endowed with no ordinary faith; yet, the Holy Spirit has not concealed his defects. Moses was in too big a hurry. He was running before the Lord. God's time had not yet come to deliver Israel. Another forty years must yet run their weary course. But Moses waxed impatient and acted in the energy of the flesh. Some writers have sought to vindicate him, but the words "he *looked* this way and that, and when he *saw* there was no man, he slew the Egyptian" make it evident that he was then walking by sight, rather than by faith; and the fact that we are told he "hid him in the sand" brings out his fear of being discovered. Thus we see that, like ourselves, Moses was one who offended in many things (Jas. 3:2, R.V.).

"And when he went out the second day, behold, two men of the Hebrews strove together: and he said to him that did the wrong, Wherefore smitest thou thy fellow? And he said, Who made thee a prince and a judge over us? Intendest thou to kill me, as thou killedst the Egyptian? And Moses feared, and said, Surely this thing is known. Now when Pharaoh heard this thing, he sought to slay Moses. But Moses fled from the face of Pharaoh, and dwelt in the land of Midian" (2:13-15). This confirms our interpretation of the verses immediately preceding. Moses' eye was not on God but on man, and the fear of man bringeth a snare. Apprehensive that Pharaoh might take vengeance upon him, he fled to Midian. And yet while this is true from the human side, we ought not to ignore the over-ruling Providence of God. The *Lord's* time for delivering Israel had not yet arrived; and what is more to the point, the act of Moses was not at all in accord with the methods which *He* proposed to employ. Not by insurrection on their part, nor by a system of assassination, were the Hebrews to be delivered from the house of bondage. God, therefore, caused this deed of Moses (which he believed had passed unwitnessed) to become known, both to his own brethren and to the king. Thus did He teach a salutary lesson to this one who was yet to be employed as His servant. And is there not also a needed lesson here for us? When a servant of God is not permitted to perform a certain service for Him, on which his heart is set, it does not necessarily follow that this is due to some failure in the servant himself; it may be because *God's* time for the proposed service is not ripe. Such was the case with David who, prompted only by an ardent desire for God's glory, was not permitted to build Jehovah a "house"; yet in the end this "house" was built, though not by David or in David's time.

"Now the priest of Midian had seven daughters: and they came and drew water, and filled the trough to water their father's flock. And the shepherds came and drove them away: but Moses stood up and helped them, and watered their flock. And when they came to Reuel their father, he said, How is it that ye are come so soon today? And they said, an Egyptian delivered us out of the hand of the shepherds, and also drew water enough for us, and watered the flock. And he said unto his daughters, And where is he? Why is it that ye have left the man? Call him, that he may eat bread. And Moses was content to dwell with the man: and he gave Moses Zipporah his daughter" (2:16-21). Here again we may discern *God* working behind the scenes. That Moses should have "stood up" against those shepherds, single-handed, shows plainly that the Lord was on his side; and in thus befriending the daughters of Reuel, Moses was enabled to win the esteem of their father. The sequel shows how the Providence of God thus opened to Moses a home during his long exile from Egypt. Thus did God make all things work together for his good.

Arthur W. Pink.

THE FOURTH COMMANDMENT.

"Remember the Sabbath day to keep it holy. Six days shalt thou labor, and do all thy work: but the seventh day is the Sabbath of the Lord thy God: in it thou shalt not do any work, thou, nor thy son, nor thy daughter, thy manservant, nor thy maidservant, nor thy cattle, nor thy stranger that is within thy gates: for in six days the Lord made heaven and earth, the sea, and all that in them is, and rested the seventh day: wherefore the Lord blessed the Sabbath day, and hallowed it" (Ex. 20:8-11).

There has been an awful letting-down in this country regarding the Sabbath during the last twenty-five years, and many a man has been shorn of spiritual power, like Samson, because he is not straight on this question. Can *you* say that you observe the Sabbath properly? You may be a professed Christian: are you obeying this commandment? Where were you last Sabbath? How did you spend it?

I honestly believe that this commandment is just as binding today as it ever was. I have talked with men who have said it has been abrogated, but they have never been able to point to any place in the Bible where God repealed it. When Christ was on earth, He did nothing to set it aside; He freed it from the traces under which the scribes and Pharisees had put it, and gave it its true place. "The Sabbath was made for man, not man for the Sabbath". It is just as practicable and as necessary for men today as it ever was—in fact, more than ever, because we live in such an intense age.

The Sabbath was binding in Eden, and it has been in force ever since. This fourth commandment begins with the word "Remember", showing that the Sabbath already existed when God wrote this law on the tables of stone at Sinai. How can men claim that this one commandment has been done away with when they will admit that the other nine are still binding?

I believe the Sabbath question today is a vital one to the whole country. It is the burning question of the present time. If you give up the Sabbath the church goes; if you give up the church the home goes; and if the home goes the nation goes. That is the direction in which we are travelling. The church of God is losing its power on account of so many people giving up the Sabbath, and using it to promote selfishness.

"Sabbath" means "rest", and the meaning of the word gives a hint as to the true way to observe the day. God rested at the creation, and ordained the Sabbath as a rest for man. He blessed it and hallowed it. "Remember *the rest-day* to keep it *holy*". It is the day when the body may be refreshed and strengthened after six days of labor, and the soul drawn into closer fellowship with its Maker. True observance of the Sabbath may be considered under two general heads: cessation from ordinary secular work, and religious exercises.

I. Cessation from secular work.

A man ought to turn aside from his ordinary employment one day in seven. There are many whose occupation will not permit them to observe Sunday, but they should observe some other day as a Sabbath. Saturday is my rest-day because I generally preach on Sunday. Ministers and missionaries often tell me that they take no rest-day; they do not need it because they are in the Lord's work. That is a mistake. When God was giving Moses instructions about the building of the tabernacle, He referred especially to the Sabbath, and gave injunctions for its strict observance; and later, when Moses was conveying the words of the Lord to the children of Israel, he interpreted them by saying that not even were sticks to be gathered on the Sabbath to kindle fires for smelting or other purposes. In spite of their zeal and haste to erect the tabernacle, the workmen were to have their day of rest. The command applies to ministers and others engaged in Christian work today as much as to those Israelite workmen of old.

Works of necessity and of emergency. In judging where any work may or may not be lawfully done on the Sabbath, find out the reason and object for doing it. Exceptions are to be made for works of necessity and works of emergency. By the former I mean those acts that Christ justified when He approved of leading one's ox or ass to water: watchmen, police, stokers on board steamers, and many others have engagements which necessitate their working on the Sabbath. By the latter I mean those referred to by Christ when He approved of pulling an ox or an ass out of the pit on the Sabbath day. In case of fire or sickness a man is often called on to do things that would not otherwise be justifiable. No man should make another work seven days in the week. One day is demanded for rest. Many Christians are guilty in this respect.

Sabbath travelling. Take, for instance, the question of Sabbath travelling. I believe we are breaking God's laws by using the cars on Sunday and depriving conductors and others of their Sabbath. Remember the fourth commandment expressly refers to "the stranger that is within thy gates". Does not that touch Sabbath travel? But you ask, "What are we to do? How are we to get to church?" I reply, On foot. It will be better for you. Once when I was holding meetings in London, in my ignorance I made arrangements to preach four times in different places one Sabbath. After I had made the appointments I found I had to walk sixteen miles; but I walked it, and I slept that night with a clear conscience. I have made it a rule never to use the cars, and if I have a private carriage, I insist that horse and man shall rest on Monday. I want no hackman to rise up in judgment against me.

Sabbath trading. There are many who are inclined to use the Sabbath in order to make money faster. This is no new sin. The apostle Amos hurled his invectives against transgressors and said, "When will the new moon be gone, that we may sell corn? and the Sabbath, that we may set forth wheat?" Covetous men have always chafed under the restraint, but not until the present time do we find that they have openly counted on Sabbath trade to make money.

Necessary and beneficial. The good effect of a nation's health and happiness produced by the return of the Sabbath, with its cessation from work, cannot be over estimated. It is needed to repair and restore the body after six days of work. It is proved that a man can do more work in six days than in seven. Lord Beaconsfield said; "Of all Divine institutions, the most Divine is that which secures a day of rest for man. I hold it to be the most valuable blessing to be conceded to man. It is the corner-stone of all civilization, and its removal might effect even the health of the people". Mr. Gladstone recently told a friend that the secret of his long life (he lived to be almost ninety, Ed.) is that amid all the pressure of public cares he never forgot the Sabbath, with its rest for the body and the soul. The constitution of the United States protects the President in his weekly day of rest. He has ten days, "Sunday excepted", in which to consider a bill that has been sent to him for signature. Every working man in the Republic ought to be as thoroughly protected as the President.

II. Religious Activity.

But "rest" does not mean idleness. "Satan finds some mischief still for idle hands to do". The best way to keep off bad thoughts and to avoid temptation is to engage in active religious exercises. As regards these we should avoid extremes—On the one hand we find a rigor in Sabbath obervance that is nowhere commanded in Scripture, and that reminds one of the formalism of the Pharisees more than of the spirit of the Gospel. Such strictness does more harm than good. On the other-hand we should jealously guard against a loose way of keeping the Sabbath.

Public worship. Make the Sabbath a day of religious activity. First of all, of course, is attendance at public worship. But we must not mistake the means for the end. We must not think that the Sabbath is just for the sake of being able to attend meetings. There are some people who imagine they must spend the whole day at meetings or private devotions. The result is that at night-fall they are tired out, and the day has brought them no rest. The number of church-services attended ought to be measured by the person's ability to enjoy them and get good from them, *without being wearied.* Attending meetings is not the only way to observe the Sabbath. The Israelites were commanded to keep it *in their dwellings* as well as in holy convocation. The home, that center of so great influence over the life and character of the people, ought to be made the scene of true Sabbath observance.

Home observance. Jeremiah classified godless families with the heathen: "Pour out Thy fury upon the heathen that know Thee not, *and* upon the families that call not on Thy name". Make family prayers especially attractive by having the children learn some verse or story from the Bible. Give more time to your children than you can give on week days, reading to them and perhaps taking them a walk in the afternoon. Show by your conduct that the

Sabbath is a delight, and they will soon catch your spirit. Set aside some time for religious instruction, without making this a task.

Private observance. Apart from public and family observance, the individual ought to devote a portion of the time to his own edification. Prayer, meditation, reading, ought not to be forgotten. Think of men devoting six days a week to their body, which will soon pass away, and begrudging one day for the soul, which will live on and on forever! Is it too much for God to ask for one day to be devoted to the growth and training of the spiritual senses, when the other senses are kept busy the other six days? If your circumstances permit, engage in some definite Christian work,—such as teaching in Sunday School, or visiting the sick. Do all the good you can. Sin keeps no Sabbath, and no more should good deeds. Make your Sabbaths down here a foretaste of the eternal Sabbath that is in store for believers.

The Sunday newspaper. Their contents make them unfit for reading any day, not to say Sunday. A merchant who advertises in Sunday papers is not keeping the Sabbath. They are an unnecessary evil. Can not you read enough news on week days without desecrating the Sabbath? We had no Sunday papers till the war came (the Civil War, Ed.), and we got along very well without them.

Punishment or blessing? No nation has ever prospered that has trampled the Sabbath in the dust. Show me a nation which has done this, and I will show you a nation that has got in it the seeds of ruin and decay. I believe that Sabbath desecration will carry a nation down quicker than anything else. Adam brought marriage and the Sabbath with him out of Eden, and neither can be disregarded without suffering. When the children of Israel went into the Promised Land God told them to let their land rest every seven years, and He would give them as much in six years as in seven. For four hundred and ninety years they disregarded that law. But mark you, Nebuchadnezzar came and took them off into Babylon, and kept them seventy years in captivity, and thus the land had its seventy Sabbaths of rest. So they did not gain much by breaking this law. You can give God His day, or He will take it. On the other hand, honoring the fourth commandment brings blessing: "If thou turn away thy foot from the Sabbath, from doing thy pleasure on My holy day; and call the Sabbath a delight, the holy of the Lord, honorable; and shalt honor Him, not doing thine own ways, nor finding thine own pleasures, nor speaking thine own words ('thine own' as contrasted with what God enjoins), *then* shalt thou delight thyself in the Lord; and I will cause thee to ride upon the high places of the earth, and feed thee with the heritage of Jacob thy father, for the mouth of the Lord hath spoken it" (Isa. 58:13, 14).

—D. L. Moody.

THE RIGHTEOUSNESS OF GOD.

Rom. 1:17 and 3:21.

In various parts of Scripture this phrase, "The Righteousness of God", signifies either that holiness and rectitude of character which is the attribute of God, or that distributive justice by which He maintains the authority of His law; but where it refers to man's salvation, and is not merely a personal attribute of Deity, it signifies that fulfillment of the law, or perfect conformity to it in all its demands, which, consistently with His justice, God has appointed and provided for the salvation of sinners. This implies that the infinite justice of His character requires what is provided, and also that it is approved and accepted; for if it be God's righteousness it must be required, and must be accepted by the justice of God. The righteousness of God, which is received by faith, denotes something that becomes the property of the believer. It cannot, then, be here the Divine attribute of justice, but the Divine work which God has wrought in His Son. This, therefore, determines the phrase in these places, as referring immediately not to the Divine attribute, but to the Divine work. The former can never become ours. This also is decisive against explaining the phrase as signifying a method of justification. The righteousness of God is contrasted with the righteousness of man; and as Israel's own righteousness, which they went about to establish, was the righteousness of their works, not their method of justification, so God's righteousness as opposed to this, must be a righteousness wrought by Jehovah. As in 2 Cor. 5:21 the imputation of sin to Christ is contrasted with our becoming the righteousness of God in Him, the latter cannot be a method of justification, but must intimate our becoming perfectly righteous by possessing Christ's righteousness, which is provided by God for us, and is perfectly commensurate with the Divine justice.

No explanation of the expression, "the righteousness of God", will at once suit the phrase and the situation in which it is found in the passage before us, but that which makes it that righteousness or obedience to the law, both in its penalty and requirements, which has been yielded to it by our Lord Jesus Christ. This is indeed the righteousness of God, for it has been provided by God, and from first to last has been effected by His Son Jesus Christ, who is the mighty God and the Father of eternity. Everything that draws it off from this signification tends to darken the Scriptures, to cloud the apprehension of the truth in the children of God, and to corrupt the simplicity that is in Christ. To that righteousness is the eye of the believer ever to be directed; on that righteousness must he rest; on that righteousness must he live; on that righteousness must he die; in that righteousness must he appear before the judgment-seat; in that righteousness must he stand forever in the presence of a righteous God. "I will greatly rejoice in the Lord; my soul shall be joyful in my God: for He hath clothed me with the garments of salvation, He hath covered me with the robe of righteousness" (Isa. 61:10).

The righteousness of God provided for the salvation of sinners, like that salvation itself, differs essentially from all other righteousness that ever was or can ever be performed. It differs entirely from the righteousness of men and angels, in its *Author,* for it is the righteousness not of creatures but of the Creator—"I the Lord have created it" (Isa. 45:8). It is a Divine and infinitely perfect righteousness, wrought out by Jehovah Himself, which in the salvation of man preserves all His attributes inviolate. It is the righteousness of God as of the Godhead, without respect to distinction of personality, and strictly so in that sense in which the world is the work of God. The Father created it by the Son in the same way as by the Son He created the world; and if the Father effected this righteousness because His Son effected it, then His Son must be one with Himself. Peter, in the first verse of his second epistle, according to the literal rendering of the passage, calls this righteousness the righteousness of Jesus Christ: "Simon Peter, a servant and an apostle of Jesus Christ, to them that have obtained like precious faith with us, in the righteousness of our God and Saviour Jesus Christ". Most of the places in which the righteousness of God is spoken of, refer to it as the righteousness of the Father, as in 2 Cor. 5:21, where the Father is distinguished from the Son; but in this passage of Peter it is explicitly declared to be the righteousness of the Son, where He is expressly called God.

It was during His incarnation the Son of God wrought out this righteousness. Before He came into the world He was not a member or subject of the kingdom of heaven, He was its Head. He then acted in the form of God; that is to say, as the Creator and Sovereign of the world, but afterwards in the form of a servant. Before that period He was perfectly holy, but that holiness could not be called obedience. It might rather be said that the law was conformed to Him, than that He was conformed to the law. His holiness was exercised in making the law, and by it governing the world. But in this latter condition it was that law by which He Himself was governed. His righteousness or obedience, then, was that of infinitely the most glorious person that could be subjected to the law. It was the righteousness of Immanuel, God with us,—and this obedience of the Son of God in our nature conferred more honor on the law than the obedience of all intelligent creatures. He gave to every commandment of the law, and to every duty it enjoined, more honor than it had received of dishonor from all the transgressors that have been in the world. When others obey the law, they derive from that obedience honor to themselves, but on the occasion now referred to, it was the law that was honored by the obedience of its sovereign. "The law", says the Psalmist, "is well pleased for His righteousness' sake; He will magnify the law, and make it honorable" (Isa. 42:21).

The obedience of Jesus Christ magnified the law, because it was rendered by Divine appointment, He was chosen of God and anointed for this end. He was Jehovah, whom Jehovah sent. "Lo, I come, and I will dwell in the midst of thee, saith Jehovah,—and thou shalt know that Jehovah of hosts hath sent Me unto thee" (Zech. 2:10, 11). And when it is considered that the most astonishing work of God which can be conceived, is the incarnation of His Son, and His sojourning in the world, and that these wonders were performed in order to magnify the law,—it necessarily follows, that it is impossible to entertain too exalted an idea of the regard which God has for the character of His holy law. In its *Author,* then, this righteousness is immeasurably distinguished from any other righteousness. And not only does it differ in its Author, it differs also in its *nature,* in its *extent,* in its *duration,* and in its *influence,* from all other righteousness that ever was or ever can be performed.

In its *nature,* this righteousness is twofold, fulfilling both the precepts of the law and its penalty. This, by any creature the most exalted, is absolutely impossible. The fulfillment of the law in its precepts is all that could be required of creatures in their original sinless condition. Such was at the beginning the state of all the angels, and of the first man. But the state of the Second Man, the Lord from heaven, when He came into the world, was essentially different. Christ was made under the law, but it was a *broken law,* and consequently He was made under its curse. This is not only implied when it is said He was "made of a woman", who was a transgressor, but it is also expressly asserted that He was "made a curse for us" (Gal. 3:13). Justice, therefore, required that He should fulfill not only the *precept,* but also the *penalty* of the law,—all that it threatened, as well as all that it commands.

A mere creature may obey the precept of the law, or suffer the penalty it denounces, but he cannot do both. If he be a transgressor, he may be punished with everlasting destruction from the presence of the Lord; and God, whose vengeance he is suffering, being to him an object of unmingled hatred and abhorrence, there can be no place for his repentance, his love or obedience. But Jesus Christ was capable at the same moment of suffering at the hands of God, and of obeying the precept to love God. This was made manifest during the whole period of His incarnation, as well as by the memorable words which He uttered on the Cross, "My God, My God, why hast Thou forsaken Me?". We are here taught that the prediction by the Prophet, "Awake, O sword, against the man that is My Fellow", was at that moment receiving its accomplishment. The sword of Divine justice, according to the prophetic declarations contained in the twenty-second Psalm, was then piercing His inmost soul, but still He addressed God as His God. From this it is evident, that while suffering under the full weight of His Father's wrath against the sins of His people, which He had taken upon Him, all the feelings, both of love and confidence, also expressed in the same Psalm, were at that moment in full exercise. His righteousness, therefore, or conformity to the law, was at once a conformity in two respects which could not have been exemplified but by Himself throughout the whole universe.

By the sufferings of Jesus Christ, the execution of the law was complete; while no punishment which creatures could suffer can be thus designated. The law was fully executed when all the threatenings it contained were carried into effect. Those who are consigned to everlasting punishment will never be able to say, as our blessed Lord said on the Cross, "It is finished". It is He only who could *put away sin* by the sacrifice of Himself. By enduring the threatened punishment, He fully satisfied justice. In token of having received a full discharge He came forth from the grave; and when He shall appear the second time, it shall be without sin—the sin which He had taken upon Him, and all its effects, being forever done away.

This fulfillment of the law, in its penalty, by the Son of God, is an end which cannot otherwise than through eternity be attained by the punishment of mere creatures. Sin, as committed against God, is an infinite evil, and requires an infinite punishment which cannot be borne in any limited time by those who are not capable of suffering punishment in an infinite degree. But the sufferings as well as the obedience in time of Him who is infinite, are equivalent to the eternal obedience and sufferings of those who are finite.

The death of the Son of God serves to magnify the law, by demonstrating the certainty of that eternal punishment, which, if broken, it denounces as its penalty. There are no limits to eternity; but when the Son of God bore what was equivalent to the eternal punishment of those who had sinned, He furnished a physical demonstration of the eternal punishment of sin.

But if nothing beyond the suffering of the penalty of the law had taken place, men would only have been released from the punishment due to sin. If they were to obtain the reward of obedience, its precept must also be obeyed; and this was accomplished to the utmost by Jesus Christ. Every command it enjoins, as well as every prohibition it contains, were in all respects fully honored by Him. In this manner, and by His sufferings, He fulfilled all righteousness. The righteousness, therefore, of our God and Saviour Jesus Christ is infinitely glorious. It is the righteousness of the law-giver. And, being in its character twofold, it differs entirely in its *nature* from all other righteousness, and is of an order infinitely higher than ever was or can be exemplified by any or all of the orders of intelligent creatures.

This righteousness differs from all other righteousness in its *extent*. Every creature is bound for himself to *all* that obedience to his Creator of which he is capable. He is under the obligation to love God with all his heart, with all his soul, and with all his strength, and beyond this he cannot advance. It is evident, therefore, that he can have no *superabounding* righteousness to be placed in the way of merit to the account of another. And, besides this, if he has sinned, he is bound to suffer for himself the *whole* penalty annexed to disobedience, no part of which, consequently, can be borne by him to satisfy for the transgression of others. He is not in possession of a life at his own disposal to lay down for them; and, if he had laid it down, it being in that case forfeited forever, he could not take it again. But the obedience of Jesus Christ, who is Himself infinite, as well as the punishment He suffered, being in themselves of infinite value, are capable of being transferred in their effects without any diminution in their respective values. His life, too, was His own; and, as He suffered voluntarily, His obedience and sufferings, which were infinitely meritorious, might, with the most perfect regard to justice, being imputed to as many of those whose nature He took, as to the Supreme Ruler shall seem good.

This righteousness likewise differs from all other righteousness in it *duration*. The righteousness of Adam or of angels could only be available while it continued to be performed. The law was binding on them in every instant of their existence. The moment, therefore, in which they transgressed, the advantages derived from all their previous obedience ceased. But the righteousness of God, brought in by His Son, is an "*everlasting* righteousness" (Dan. 9:24). It was performed within a limited period of time, but in its effects it can never terminate. "Lift up your eyes to heaven, and look upon the earth beneath; for the heaven shall vanish away like smoke, and the earth shall wax old like a garment, and they that dwell therein shall die in like manner: but My salvation shall be *forever*, and My righteousness shall ***not be abolished***—My righteousness shall be *forever*" (Isa. 51:6, 8). "Thy righteousness is an everlasting righteousness" (Psa. 119:142). "By His own blood He entered in *once* into the holy place, having obtained *eternal* redemption" (Heb. 9:12). In respect to its duration, then, this righteousness reaches back to the period of man's fall, and forward through the endless ages of eternity.

The paramount *influence* of this righteousness is also gloriously conspicuous. It is the sole ground of the reconciliation of sinners with God, and of their justification before Him, and also of intercession with Him before the throne. "If any man sin, we have an Advocate with the Father, Jesus Christ *the righteous*" (1 John 2:1). It is the price paid for those new heavens and that new earth, wherein dwelleth righteousness; for that kingdom prepared for those who are clothed with righteousness—a kingdom commensurate with the dignity of Him by whom it was provided. The paradise in which Adam was placed at his creation was a paradise on *earth*. It might be *corrupted*, it might be *defiled*, and it might *fade away*, all of which accordingly took place. But the paradise which, in virtue of the righteousness of God, is provided, and to the hope of which, by the resurrection of Jesus Christ from the dead, His people are begotten, is an inheritance which is *incorruptible* and *undefiled*, and that *fadeth not away*, reserved *in heaven*. This righteousness, then, is the ransom by which men are delivered from going down to the pit of everlasting destruction, and the price of heavenly and eternal glory. It is the fine linen, clean and white, in which the bride, the Lamb's wife, shall be arrayed, "for the fine linen is the righteousness of saints". Man was made lower than the angels, but this righteousness exalts him above them. The redeemed people of God stand nearest to the throne, while the angels stand "round about" them. They enter heaven clothed with a righteousness infinitely better than that which angels possess, or in which Adam was created.

The idea which some entertain, that the loss incurred by the fall is only compensated by what is obtained through the redemption which is in Christ Jesus, is so far from being just, that the superabounding of the gain is unspeakable and immense. By the disobedience of the first Adam, the righteousness with which he was originally invested was lost for himself and all his posterity, and the sin which he had committed was laid to their charge. By the obedience of the last Adam, not only the guilt of that one offense is removed, but pardon also is procured for all the personal transgressions of the children of God; while the righteousness, infinitely glorious, which He wrought, is placed to their account. By the entrance of sin and death, the inheritance on earth was forfeited. By the gift of the everlasting righteousness, their title to eternal glory in heaven is secured. "And not as it was by one that sinned, so is the gift: for the judgment was by one to condemnation; but the free gift is of many offences unto justification. For if, by one man's offence, death reigned by one; *much more* they which receive abundance of grace, and of the gift of righteousness, shall reign in life by one, Jesus Christ" (Rom. 5:16, 17).

—Extract from a most excellent commentary on Romans by Robert Haldane (1814, reprinted 1847).

AN ANSWERED PRAYER.

Judge Graham was eminent and revered in the English courts of law. Pastor Taylor received the following account of his conversion from his niece, who had been asking this boon of the Hearer of prayer for sixty years:

You may remember that before you left Long Ditton my uncle came to reside with his sister and myself at our former house. He had lately lost his wife and was then at an advanced age, too old to enter into society, and preferred the retirement of the home he had chosen with us. He seldom left the house, except to take his daily airing, in which I always accompanied him, the carriage coming to our door usually at the same hour. Every day I read the Bible to him, and this quiet and regular routine seemed to suit his declining years. He had passed his ninetieth birthday: but the freshness and energy of his mind was extraordinary; his memory still retained its powers, and his conversation was full of interest to me, enriched as it was with anecdotes of the distinguished men, his contemporaries, with whom he had associated during so many years of his long life. He and I, with the exception of one or two dear intimate friends, passed most of our time alone together; for my poor aunt was a confirmed invalid, and seldom quitted her chamber. She shared with me in my deep anxiety for the salvation of her brother's soul.

We knew that the day could not be far distant when he would be taken from us, and we had good reason to fear that, notwithstanding his uprightness and integrity, and the kindness of his disposition, and his many estimable qualities, he was yet a stranger to the saving truths of the gospel and to all vital godliness. He had a great respect for the outward observances of religion, and for those persons whom he knew to be sincerely religious; but, though he said little, he held firmly to his own opinions. His wife had been a Unitarian, and we feared that my uncle had been, perhaps unconsciously, influenced by her defective views. During her life time there had been little intercourse between him and his sister, or myself; but we had always loved and highly esteemed him. His proposal to make his home with us for the remainder of his days on earth had indeed been joyfully accepted by us. It was, therefore, with real satisfaction and thankfulness to God that, at his request, I began to read the Bible to him daily. I was reading to him one morning, at our usual hour, the ninth chapter of the book of the prophet Isaiah, when my uncle suddenly stopped me. "My dear", he said, "you must have made a mistake. Will you read that passage again to me—the verses which begin with those words, 'Unto us a child is born'?" I did so: "Unto us a child is born, unto us a son is given, and the government shall be upon his shoulder; and his name shall be called Wonderful, Councellor, The Mighty God, The Everlasting Father, The Prince of Peace. Of the increase of his government and peace there shall be no end, upon the throne of David, and upon his kingdom, to order it and to establish it with judgment and with justice from henceforth, even forever. The zeal of the Lord of Hosts will perform this." I paused. "That is the passage," said my uncle. For a while he said no more—he seemed deep in thought. Then turning to me, his voice deepened in earnestness, "My dear child", he said, "there must be some mistake. I have read the Scriptures constantly for many years; I am well acquainted with the prophecies of Isaiah; but it cannot be that I have passed over those verses. Are you sure you have made no mistake?" "I am sure, dear sir," I replied, "I have made no mistake. Judge for yourself", I added, "shall I give you the book?" "Yes", he said, "I must satisfy myself, I must read that passage, though I will not doubt your word. Strange, indeed, that I have never noticed these words!" He rose up and drew his chair to the table, and I placed the open Bible before him. The carriage came to the door—it was the hour when we took our drive. He was intently accupied with the holy volume. He did not raise his eyes. I waited a little while, and then told him that the carriage was there. "Tell me in what direction you will drive to-day", he said, "I will follow you and you can take me up. I cannot leave this book just yet". He did not leave it until he had thoroughly satisfied himself that I had made no mistake. He was convinced and when once convinced He was too just a man, and had too sincere a reverence for the Word of God, to dispute its Divine authority. When we met again I deemed it the wiser part to ask no questions, to make no remark, but to leave that Word to do its own work, while we—his sister and I—did not cease to pray that the Holy Spirit might enlighten the eyes of the understanding of him who was so tenderly beloved by us, to understand and receive into his heart those inspired words which had arrested his attention. Our prayer was heard. My uncle's simple, straight-forward character showed itself in the way in which he told me plainly, but with deep feeling, how thankful he felt, how thankful he should always feel that God had been so good as to bring him to the knowledge of the truth. "I have been like a blind man when this book was before me," he said, looking up from the Bible, which had now become his constant study. "My dear, I have been miserably blind during my long life; but **He** who leads the blind by a way that they know not has graciously led me, and whereas I was blind, now I see. It is all plain to me now—the whole glorious scheme. Strange, indeed, that I should never have seen it till now! He who was an infant of days is no other than the Mighty God. The Everlasting Father." Yes, he had learnt to know that the Lord Jesus is the true God, and eternal life.

And thus it was that the change had taken place—that change which no power on earth has ever yet wrought in the heart of man. Few persons would have observed it, many would have denied that there was any such change. His sister and his niece, from whose intense and anxious love nothing escaped, constantly noted some incident, some little word or action that was new to them, such as had never appeared before, the indication of a work going on within—a touching gentleness, a deep humility, and at the same time an earnestness and fixedness of purpose with regard to that which had become the one chief object of his existence. The Word of God had been read to him before as a formal and daily duty, which had grown into a habit, a thing to be done, and then done with for the day; but now it might almost be said it was never done with. "All the day long am I occupied with Thy statutes", said the Psalmist. The aged judge might have said the same; and not only during many hours of the day, but often when he had retired to rest, the Holy Bible lay on the table of his dressing-room, with the light of his shaded reading-lamp concentrating its full radiance upon its open pages, while the old man was bending over them far into the night. His intellect was indeed still as vigorous as in its younger days, and his whole heart was engaged with an increasing interest in the study of the wonderful book. He had learned when turning with unwearied diligence from one inspired testimony to another, declaring the divinity of the Lord Jesus, that He is the image of the invisible God, and the brightness of His Glory, and that by Him were all things created that are in heaven, and that are in earth, visible and invisible, whether they be thrones, or dominions, or principalities, or powers; that all things were created by Him and for Him; and that He is before all, and by Him all things consist. And he had marked that this full and glorious testimony is accompanied by those blessed words, "In Him we have redemption through His blood, even the forgiveness of sins"; and he had also learned that all the testimonies of the Word to the Godhead of the Lord Jesus are written, "that we might believe that Jesus is the Christ, the Son of God, and that believing we might have life through His name."

The day drew on that the aged pilgrim must depart. The summons to the better country had come, and He who had sent it had prepared His servant to receive it. It was a solemn time, and it could not be otherwise than a saddening time to those who loved him,—his sister and his niece. Tears would rise to their eyes, but they were quietly wiped away. They knew that the time could not be very long before they would follow him to the glorious mansions of their Father's house, whither the forerunner is for us entered, even Jesus. In their sorrow they could but raise their thoughts in heart-felt thankfulness to their God for the prolonged life of their beloved and revered relation, and still more for the mercy and goodness of their heavenly Father, who, after a long, long season of darkness had at eventide decreed there should be light. Not long before the last hours of the dying man, when the two medical men who had attended him were present, his niece bent down over him, and said in a gentle and distinct voice, "your whole trust, dear uncle—" she paused, waiting for him to finish the sentence. In a voice almost as clearly articulate as her own, he said, "in Jesus Christ, my Lord and my God, in Him alone". Those few distinct, adoring words were the last words of the aged Judge Graham.

It was many years after the death of her uncle and his invalid sister—it was when their niece had passed her ninetieth year —that she narrated to me the facts I have now written down. There is another fact of even deeper interest, with which she concluded her account of the marvellous change in the venerable man. For sixty years his devoted sister had prayed for him—prayed unceasingly, with one chief object always at heart. She had prayed, hoping, trusting, believing that her prayers were heard, and had waited patiently for God's good time to answer them. That time had come; her anxious prayers had been turned into joyful praises, and the outpouring of her full heart in adoring thanksgivings. "They who thus sow in tears shall reap in joy".

Sunday at Home—1873.

To New Readers: The twelve copies of 1922, and the twelve of 1923, neatly bound, may be had for $1.50 each. They contain articles by the Editor on The Blood, Eternal Punishment, Second Coming of Christ. The Sabbath, Romans 7, The Antichrist, and Expositions of John's Gospel from the first verse. We have only a limited supply.

To Foreign Subscribers: Please send **only** International Money Orders, made out to the Editor.

JUDGMENT BEGINNING AT THE HOUSE OF GOD

"For the time is come that judgment must begin at the House of God; and if it first begin at us what shall the end be of them that obey not the gospel of God?. And if the righteous scarcely be saved, where shall the ungodly and the sinner appear?" (1 Peter 4:17, 18.)

The "judgment" which the apostle says is to "begin at the House of God" has its immediate reference to the fiery trial which he intimates was, when he wrote, impending those Christians to whom the Epistle was addressed (see verse 12). That there is, however, the beginning of "judgment at the House of God" whenever Christians suffer for Christ's sake or for righteousness sake, or for well doing, is evident from verses 13-16. Thus, judgment in verse 17, is "suffering as a Christian", v. 16. (Comp. 3:14-17). Whilst the suffering according to the will of God (v. 19) may be disciplining and chastening (Heb. 12:5-13), and while the latter may be viewed as judgment from the Lord because of unfaithfulness (1 Cor. 11:30-32), it is not merely in this sense that Peter speaks of the suffering of the Christian and "judgment". No doubt it is a judgment of "purifying" to those that suffer and thus proclaims that God must be faithful to His own holiness (1 Pet. 1:7). But Peter, in the verse in question, views the afflictions, reproaches, and persecutions, of the saints rather as the indication of judgment coming upon the world by whose hands these are inflicted. Hence, "the judgment which begins at the House of God" is a matter which should occasion "rejoicing" to those who suffer under it, inasmuch as it is just the token of the glorious fact that they "are now partakers of Christ's sufferings, that, when His glory shall be revealed, they may be glad also with exceeding joy" (v. 13). The whole passage (vv. 12-19) may be profitably compared with Paul's remarks on the same subject. Peter views God's judgment of the world as beginning, and as betokened by judgment "at the House of God", or as he really writes *"from* the House of God"! Paul says that the suffering or endurance of saints is *"an evident token of the righteous judgment of God,* that they may be counted worthy of the kingdom of God for which they also suffer: seeing it is a righteous thing with God to recompense tribulation to those that trouble them, when the Lord Jesus shall be revealed from heaven" (II Thess. 1:5-7). Peter, looking at God's righteous judgment as taking its rise at the House of God, asks, *"what shall the end be of them that obey not the gospel of God?"* Paul answers the question in the passage just cited, "the Lord Jesus shall be revealed from heaven with His mighty angels, *taking vengeance* on them that obey not God, and that *obey not the gospel of our Lord Jesus Christ"* (II Thess. 1:7, 8). It is a terrible fact for the world that He is judging His saints *now.* All the *"judgment" of suffering* they shall ever endure is completed in this life (1 Cor. 11:32); for as to punitive judgment it was borne and exhausted for them by Christ (Rom. 8:3). But the Lord's long-suffering silence toward the gospel rejectors!—that is a fearful thing. And that silence will break the instant God's judgment has done its blessed work in His "house" (see Ps. 50). (Personally, I think there is, most probably, an interval between these two—A. W. P.)

When Peter repeats his question in other words—in the form of a quotation from the Greek of the book of Proverbs—"And if the righteous (one) *scarcely* be saved", etc., he certainly cannot design to raise any doubt as to the salvation of the righteous. However difficult the salvation, or however narrowly he may escape, the righteous *will* certainly be saved.

The words themselves attest this. The word *"scarcely"* has been referred by some to such as, like Lot, are "saved yet so as by fire", losing the whole fruit of their labor here (1 Cor. 3; Gen. 19). We rather believe that the word applies generally. The salvation of the righteous is absolutely certain, for he is righteous only in Christ's righteousness, and is in Him who is his righteousness; and as Christ is safe, so is he. But all who are saved "enter in at the straight gate" and reach eternal life by the "narrow way"; they all "through much tribulation enter the kingdom". This we believe to be the sense in which "the righteous one scarcely is saved", and this view seems to be most harmonious with the concluding verse of the chapter: "wherefore, let them that suffer according to the will of God"—those who through affliction are carried on to the salvation—"commit the keeping of their souls to Him in welldoing as unto a faithful Creator" (v. 19.)

C. Campbell 1873

VOL. III APRIL, 1924 NO. 4

STUDIES in the SCRIPTURES

"Search the Scriptures" John 5:39.

A PERIODICAL (MONTHLY "IF THE LORD WILL") DEVOTED TO BIBLE STUDIES and EXPOSITIONS

Arthur W. Pink, Publisher & Editor,
227 N. Creighton St., Philadelphia, Pa.

Price: 10 cents per copy; $1.00 per year. Foreign $1.00 per year.

THE CHRISTIAN'S TWO NATURES

What is a Christian? He is a person who has been born again. But what is the new birth? What is it that differentiates a man who is dead in sins from one who has passed from death unto life? Upon this point there is much ignorance and confusion. There are many who suppose that the new birth is experiencing a change of heart, and it is exceedingly difficult to convince them to the contrary. They have heard so many preachers, orthodox preachers, speak of a 'change of heart', that they have never thought of challenging the scripturalness of this expression; yet it *is* unscriptural. The Bible may be searched from Genesis to Revelation, and nowhere does this expression 'change of heart' occur on its pages.

The sad thing is that 'change of heart' is not only unscriptural, but it is anti-scriptural, untrue, and therefore utterly misleading. In the one who has been born again there is no change of heart, though there is a change of life, both inward and outward. The one who is born again now loves the things he once hated, and he hates now the things he once loved; and, in consequence, his whole line of conduct is radically affected. But, nevertheless, it remains true that his old heart (which is deceitful above all things, and desperately wicked) remains in him, unchanged, to the end.

It is because there is such confusion on this point that thousands of real Christians are unhappy in their souls. How often has one heard a young convert say, "I thought I was saved, but I begin to fear that, after all, I have been deceiving myself. Not only do I feel no better in myself, but, if anything, even worse than I used to". And when one comes to examine the condition of such a person, it is to find that, in most cases, it is not so much sins that are troubling them, as it is the heart-sickening disappointment they feel, as more and more they discover that the new birth has not only effected no improvement in their evil nature, but that the old nature seems more active than ever.

What, then, is the new birth? We answer, It is not the removal of anything from the sinner, nor the changing of anything within the sinner; instead, it is the communication of something to the sinner. The new birth is the impartation of the new nature. When I was

(Continued on page 96.)

IMPORTANT NOTICES

All new subscriptions will be dated back to January, 1924.

Set of twelve issues for **1922**, unbound, **$1.00.** Bound, **$1.50.**

Set of twelve issues for **1923**, unbound, **$1.00.** Bound **$1.50.**

Note: We cannot break a set or now supply any **single** 1923 issues.

Subscription Price: **$1.00** per year to any address in the world. Single copies **10 cents.**

Change of Address: Please notify me promptly of any change of address, and be certain to give both old and new addresses.

Non-subscribers receiving this Magazine regularly will understand their subscription has been entered by a friend.

Copies lost in the mail duplicated only if we are notified promptly.

Entered as second-class matter December 15th, 1923, at the post office at Philadelphia, Pa., under Act of March 3rd, 1879.

CONTENTS

JOHN'S GOSPEL.

28. CHRIST AND THE ADULTEROUS WOMAN: John 8:1-11.

We begin with the customary Analysis:—

1. Jesus retires to the mount of Olives: v. 1.
2. Jesus teaching in the temple: v. 2.
3. The Pharisees confront Him with an adulterous woman: vv. 3-6.
4. Christ turns the light upon them: vv. 6-8.
5. The Pharisees overcome by the light: v. 9.
6. The woman left alone with Christ: v. 10.
7. The woman dismissed with a warning: v. 11.

In this series of expositions of John's Gospel we have sedulously avoided technical matters, preferring to confine ourselves to that which would provide food for the soul. But in the present instance we deem it necessary to make an exception. The passage which is to be before us has long been the subject of controversy. Its authenticity has been questioned even by godly men. John 7:53 to 8:11 inclusive is not found in a number of the most important of the ancient manuscripts. The R. V. places a question mark against this passage. Personally we have not the slightest doubt but that it forms a part of the inspired Word of God, and that for the following reasons:

First, if our passage be a spurious one then we should have to pass straight from 7:52 to 8:12. Let the reader try this, and note the effect; and then let him go back to 7:52 and read straight through to 8:14. Which seems the more natural and reads the more smoothly?

Second, if we omit the first eleven verses of John 8, and start the chapter with v. 12, several questions will rise unavoidably and prove very difficult to answer satisfactorily. For example: *"Then* spake Jesus"—when? What simple and satisfactory answer can be found in the second part of John 7? But give John 8:1-11 its proper place, and the answer is, Immediately after the interruption recorded in v. 3. "Then spake Jesus again *unto them*" (v. 12)—unto whom? Go back to the second half of John 7 and see if it furnishes any decisive answer. But give 8:2 a place, and all is simple and plain. Again in v. 13 we read, "The *Pharisees* therefore said unto Him": this was in the temple (v. 20). But how came the Pharisees there? 7:45 shows them elsewhere. But bring in 8:1-11 and this difficulty vanishes, for 8:2 shows that this was the day following.

In the third place, the contents of John 8:1-11 are in full accord with the evident design of this section of the Gospel. The method followed in these chapters is most significant. In each instance we find the Holy Spirit records some striking incident in our Lord's life, which serves to introduce and *illustrate* the teaching which follows it. In chapter 5 Christ quickens the impotent man, and makes that miracle the text of the sermon He preached immediately after it. In John 6 He feeds the hungry multitude, and right after gives the two discourses concerning Himself as the Bread of life. In John 7 Christ's refusal to go up to the Feast publicly, and openly manifest His glory, is made the background for that wondrous word of the *future manifestation* of the Holy Spirit through believers—issuing from them as "rivers of living water". *And the same principle may be observed here in John 8.* In 8:12 Christ declares, "I am *the light* of the world", and the first eleven verses supply us with a most striking illustration and solemn demonstration of the *power* of that "light". Thus it may be seen that there is an indissoluable link between the incident recorded in John 8:1-11 and the teaching of our Lord immediately following.

Finally, as we shall examine these eleven verses and study their contents, endeavoring to sound their marvelous depths, it will be evident, we trust, to every spiritual intelligence, that no uninspired pen drew the picture therein described. The internal evidence, then, and the spiritual indications (apprehended and appreciated only by those who enter into God's thoughts) are far more weighty than external considerations. The one who is led and taught by the Spirit of God need not waste valuable time examining ancient manuscripts for the purpose of discovering whether or not this portion of the Bible is really a part of God's own Word.

Our passage emphasizes once more the abject condition of Israel. Again and again does the Holy Spirit call our attention to the fearful state that Israel were in during the days of Christ's earthly ministry. In chapter 1 we see the ignorance of the Jews as to the identity of the Lord's forerunner (1:14), and blind to the Divine Presence in their midst (1:26). In chapter 2 we have illustrated the joyless state of the Nation, and are shown their desecration of the Father's House. In chapter 3 we behold a member of the Sanhedrim dead in trespasses and sins, needing to be born again (3:7), and the Jews quibbling with John's disciples about purifying (3:25). In chapter 4 we discover the callous indifference of Israel toward their Gentile neighbors—"The Jews have no dealings with the Samaritans" (4:9). In chapter 5 we have a portrayal of God's covenant people in the great multitude of impotent folk, "blind, halt and withered". In chapter 6 they are represented as hungry, yet having no appetite for the Bread of life. In chapter 7 the leaders of the Nation send officers to arrest Christ. And now in chapter 8 Israel is contemplated as Jehovah's unfaithful wife—"adulterous."

"Jesus went unto the mount of Olives" (v. 1). This points a contrast from the closing verse of the previous chapter. There we read, "Every man went unto his own house". Here we are told, "Jesus went unto the mount of Olives". We believe that this contrast conveys a double thought, in harmony with the peculiar character of this fourth Gospel. All through John two things concerning Christ are made prominent: His essential glory and His voluntary humiliation. Here, the Holy Spirit presents Him to us as the eternal Son of God, but also as the Son come down from heaven, made flesh. Thus we are given to behold, on the one hand, His uniqueness, His peerless excellency; and on the other, the depths of shame into which He descended. Frequently these are placed almost side by side. Thus in chapter 4, we read of Him, "wearied with His journey" (v. 6); and then in the verses that follow, His Divine glories shine forth. Other examples will recur to the reader. So here in the passage before us. "Jesus went unto the *mount of Olives*" (following 7:53) suggests the *elevation* of Christ. But no doubt it also tells of the *humiliation* of the Saviour. The foxes had holes, and the birds of the air had nests, but the Son of man had not where to lay His head (Matt. 8:20): therefore, when "every man went unto *his own* house," "Jesus went unto the mount of Olives", for *He* "owned" no "house" down here. He who was rich for our sakes became poor.

"And early in the morning He came again into the temple" (v. 2). There is nothing superfluous in Scripture. Each one of these scenes has been drawn by the Heavenly Artist, so we may be fully assured that every line, no matter how small, has a meaning and value. If we keep steadily before us the *subject* of this picture we shall be the better able to appreciate its varied tints. The theme of our chapter is the outshining of the Light of Life. How appropriate then is this opening word: the *early* "morning" is the hour which introduces the daylight!

"And early in the morning He came again into the temple" (v. 2). This word also conveys an important practical lesson for us, inasmuch as Christ here leaves an example that we should follow His steps. In the first sermon of our Lord's recorded in the New Testament we find that He said, "Seek ye *first* the kingdom of God, and His righteousness" (Matt. 6:33), and *He* ever practised what He preached. The lesson which our Redeemer here exemplified is, that we need to *begin* the day by seeking the face and blessing of God! The Divine promise is, "They that seek Me *early* shall find Me" (Prov. 8:17). How different would be our lives if we *really* began each day with God! Thus only can we obtain that fresh supply of grace which will give the needed strength for the duties and conflicts of the hours that follow.

"And all the people came unto Him" (v. 2). This is another instance where the word "all" must be understood in a modified sense. Again and again is it used relatively rather than absolutely. For example, in 3:26 we read of the disciples of John coming to their master in complaint that Christ was attracting so many to Himself: "*all* come to Him", they said. Again, in 6:45 the Lord Jesus declared, "They shall be *all* taught of God". So here, "*all* the people came unto Him". These and many other passages which might be cited should prevent us from falling into the errors of Universalism. For example, "I, if I be lifted up from the earth will draw *all* unto Me" (John 12:32), does not mean all without exception. It is a very patent fact that everybody *is not* "drawn" to Christ. The "all" in John 12:32 is *all without distinction*. So here "*all* the people came unto Him" (v. 2) signifies all that were in the temple, that is, all kinds and conditions of men, men of varied age and social standing, men from the different tribes.

"And He sat down, and taught them" (v. 2). Jesus *stood;* Jesus *walked;* Jesus *sat.* Each of these expressions in John's Gospel conveys a distinctive moral truth. Jesus "stood" directs attention to the dignity and blessedness of His person, and it is very solemn to note that in no single instance (where this expression occurs) was the glory of His person recognized: cf 1:26; 7:37 and what follows; 20:14, 19, 26; 21:4. Jesus "walked" refers to the public manifestation of Himself: see our notes on 7:1. Jesus "sat" points to His condescending lowliness, meekness and grace: see 4:6; 6:3; 12:15.

"And the scribes and Pharisees brought unto Him a woman taken in adultery; and when they had set her in the midst, they say unto Him, Master, this woman was taken in adultery, in the very act. Now Moses in the law commanded us, that such should be stoned: but what sayest Thou? This they said, tempting Him, that they might have to accuse Him" (vv. 3-6). Following the miscarriage of their plans on the previous day—through the failure of the officers to arrest Christ (7:45)—the enemies of Christ hit upon a new scheme: they sought to impale Him on the horns of a dilemma. The roar of the "lion" had failed; now we are to behold the wiles of the "serpent".

The awful malignity of the Lord's enemies is evidenced on the surface. They brought this adulterous woman to Christ not because they were shocked at her conduct, still less because they were grieved that God's holy law had been broken. Their object was to use this woman to exploit her sin and further their own evil designs. With cold-blooded indelicacy they acted, employing the guilt of their captive to accomplish their evil intentions against Christ. Their motive cannot be misinterpreted. They were anxious to discredit our Lord before the people. They did not wait until they could interrogate Him in private, but, interrupting as He was teaching the people, they rudely challenged Him to solve what must have seemed to them an unsolvable enigma.

The problem by which they sought to defy Infinite Wisdom was this: A woman had been taken in the act of adultery, and the law required that she should be stoned. Of this there is no room for doubt, see Lev. 20:10 and Deut. 22:22*. "What sayest Thou?" they asked. An insidious question, indeed. Had He said, "Let her go", they could then accuse Him as being an enemy against the law of God, and His own word, "Think not that I am come to destroy the law, or the prophets: I am not come to destroy, but to fulfill" (Matt. 5:17) had been falsified. But if He answered, "Stone her", they would have ridiculed the fact that He was the "friend of publican and sinners". No doubt they were satisfied that they had Him completely cornered. On the one hand, if He ignored the charge they brought against this guilty woman, they could accuse Him of compromising with sin; on the other hand, if He passed

* Where the form of death was not specified, it was by stoning.

sentence on her, what became of His own word, "For God sent not His Son into the world to condemn the world; but that the world through Him might be saved" (John 3:17)? Here, then, was the dilemma: if Christ palliated the wickedness of this woman, where was His respect for the holiness of God and the righteousness of His law; but if He condemned her, what became of His claim that He had come here to "seek and to save that which was lost" (Luke 19:10)? And yet of what avail was their satanic subtlety in the presence of God manifest in flesh!

Ere passing on it may be well to notice how this incident furnishes an illustration of the fact that wicked men can quote the Scriptures when they imagine that it will further their evil designs: "Now Moses in the law commanded us, that such should be stoned". But what cared they for the law? They were seeking to turn the point of the Spirit's "sword" against the One they hated; soon they were to feel its sharp edge for themselves. Let us not be deceived then and conclude that every one who quotes Scripture to us must, necessarily, be a God-fearing man. Those who quote the Scriptures to condemn others are frequently the guiltiest of all. Those who are so solicitous to point to the mote in another's eye, generally have a beam in their own.

But there is far more here than meets the eye at first glance, or second too. The whole incident supplies a most striking portrayal of what is developed at length in the epistle to the Romans. It is not difficult to discern here (skulking behind the scenes) the hideous features of the great Enemy of God and His people. The hatred of these scribes and Pharisees was fanned by the inveterate enmity of the Serpent again the woman's "Seed". The subject is profoundly mysterious, but Scripture supplies more than one plain hint that Satan is permitted to *challenge* the very character of God—the book of Job, the third of Zechariah, and Rev. 12:10 are proofs of that. No doubt one reason why the Lord God suffers this is for the instruction of the unfallen angels—cf Eph. 3:10.

The problem presented to Christ by His enemies was no mere local one. So far as human reason can perceive it was the profoundest moral problem which ever could or can confront God Himself. That problem was how justice and mercy could be harmonized. The law of righteousness imperatively demands the punishment of its transgressor. To set aside that demand would be to introduce a reign of anarchy. Moreover, God is holy as well as righteous; and holiness burns against evil, and cannot allow that which is defiled to enter His presence. What, then, is to become of the poor sinner? A transgressor of the law he certainly is; and equally manifest is his moral pollution. His only hope lies in mercy; his salvation is possible only by grace. But how can mercy be exercised when the sword of justice bars her way? How can grace flow forth except by slighting holiness? Ah, human wisdom could never have found an answer to such questions. It is evident that these scribes and Pharisees thought of none. And we are fully assured that at the beginning Satan himself could see no solution to this mighty problem. But blessed be His name, God *has* "found a way" whereby His banished ones may be restored (2 Sam. 14:13, 14). What this is we shall see hinted at in the remainder of our passage.

Let us observe how each of the essential elements in this problem of all problems is presented in the passage before us. We may summarize them thus: First, we have here the person of that blessed One who had come to seek and to save that which was lost. Second, we have a sinner, a guilty sinner, one who could by no means clear herself. Third, the law was against her: that law she had broken, and the declared penalty of it was death. Fourth, the guilty sinner was brought before the Saviour Himself, and was *indicted* by His enemies. Such, then, was the problem now presented to Christ. Would grace stand helpless before law? If not, wherein lay the solution? Let us attend carefully to what follows.

"But Jesus stooped down, and with His finger wrote on the ground" (v. 6). This was the first thing that He here did. That there was a symbolical significance to His action goes without saying, and what this is we are not left to guess. Scripture is its own interpreter. This was not the first time that the Lord had written "with His finger". In Ex. 31:18 we read, "And He gave unto Moses, when He had made an end of communing with him upon mount Sinai, two tables of testimony, tables of stone, *written with the finger of God.*" When, then, our Lord wrote on *the ground* (from the ground must the' "tables of *stone"* have been taken), it was as though He had said, You remind *Me* of the *law!* Why, it was *My* finger which wrote that law! Thus did He show these Pharisees that He had come here, not to destroy the law, but to fulfill it. His writing on the ground, then, was (symbolically) a *ratification* of God's righteous law. But so blind were His would-be accusers they discerned not the significance of His act.

"So when they *continued* asking Him" (v. 7). It is evident that our Lord's enemies mistook His silence for embarassment. They no more grasped the force of His action of writing on the ground, than did Belshazzar understand the writing of that same Hand on the walls of his palace. Emboldened by His silence, and satisfied that they had Him cornered, they continued to press their question upon Him. O the persistency of evil-doers! How often they put to shame our *lack* of perseverence and importunity.

"So when they continued asking Him, He lifted up Himself, and said unto them, He that is without sin among you, let him first cast a stone at her" (v. 7). This, too, has a far deeper meaning than what appears on the surface. God's Law was a holy and a righteous one, and here we find the Lawgiver Himself turning its white light upon these men who really had so little respect for it. Christ was here intimating that *they,* His would-be *accusers,* were no fit subjects to demand the enforcement of the law's sentence. None but a holy Hand should administer the perfect law. In principle, we may see here the great Adversary and Accuser *reprimanded.* Satan may stand before the angel of the Lord to resist "the high priest" (Zech. 3:1), but, morally, *he* is the *last* one who should insist on the maintainance of righteousness. And how strikingly this reprimanding of the Pharisees by Christ adumbrated what we read of in Zech. 3:2 ("The Lord *rebuke* thee, O Satan") scarcely needs to be pointed out.

"And again He stooped down, and wrote on the ground" (v. 8). Profoundly significant was this, and unspeakably blessed. The symbolic meaning of it is plainly hinted at in the word "again": the Lord wrote on the ground *a second time.* And of what did that speak? Once more the Old Testament Scriptures supply the answer. The first "tables of stone" were dashed to the ground by Moses, and broken. A *second* set was therefore written by God. And what became of the second "tables of stone"? *They* were laid up in the ark (Ex. 40:20), and were covered by the blood-sprinkled mercy-seat! Here, then, Christ was giving more than a hint of *how* He would save those who were, by the law, condemned to death. It was not that the law would be set aside; far from it. As His first stooping down and with His finger writing on the ground intimated, the law would be *"established".* But as He stooped down and wrote the *second* time, He signified that the shed blood of an innocent substitute should come between the law and those it condemned!

"And they which heard it, being convicted by their own conscience, went out one by one, beginning at the eldest, even unto the last" (v. 9). Thus was "the strong man bound" (Matt. 12:29). Christ's enemies had thought to ensnare Him by the law of Moses; instead, they had its searching light turned upon themselves. Grace had not defied, but had upheld the law! One sentence from the lips of Holiness incarnate and they were all silenced, all convicted, and all departed. At another time, a self-righteous Pharisee might boast of his fastings, his tithes and his prayers; but when God turns the light on to a man's heart, his moral and spiritual depravity become apparent even to himself, and shame shuts his lips. So it was here. Not a word had Christ uttered against the law; in no-wise had He condoned the woman's sin. Unable to find any ground for accusation against Him, completely baffled in their evil designs, convicted by their consciences, they slunk away: "beginning at the eldest", because he had the most sin to hide and the most reputation to preserve. And in the conduct of these men we have a clear intimation of how the wicked will act in the last great Day. Now, they may proclaim their self-righteousness, and talk about the 'njustice of eternal punishment. But then, when the light of God flashes upon them, and their guilt and ruin are fully exposed, they shall, like these Pharisees, be speechless.

"And they which heard it, being convicted by their own conscience, went out" (v. 9). There is a solemn warning here for sinners who may be exercised in mind over their condition. Here were men who were "convicted by their own conscience", yet instead of this causing them to cast themselves at the feet of Christ, it resulted in them *leaving* Christ! Nothing short of the Holy Spirit's quickening will ever bring a soul into saving contact with the Lord Jesus.

"And they which heard it, being convicted by their own conscience, went out one by one, beginning at the eldest, even unto the last: and Jesus was left alone, and the woman standing in the midst" (v. 9). This is exceedingly striking. These scribes and Pharisees had challenged Christ from the law. He met them on their own ground, and vanquished them by the law. "When Jesus had lifted up Himself, and saw none but the woman, He said unto her, Woman, where are those thine accusers? hath *no man* condemned thee? She said, *No man,* Lord. And Jesus said unto her, Neither do I condemn thee" (vv. 10, 11). The law required two witnesses before its sentence could be executed (Deut. 19:15), yea, those witnesses must assist in the carrying out of the sentence (Deut. 17:7). But here not a single witness was left to testify against this woman who had merely been indicted. Thus the law was powerless to touch her. What, then, remained? Why, the way was now clear for Christ to act in "grace *and* truth."

"Neither do I condemn thee: go, and sin no more" (v. 11). No doubt the question occurs to many of our readers, Was this woman saved at the time she left Christ? Personally, we believe that she was. We believe so because *she* did not leave Christ when she had opportunity to do so; because she addressed Him as "Lord" (contrast "Master" of the Pharisees in v. 4); and because Christ said to her, "Neither do I condemn thee". But, as another has said, "In looking at these incidents of Scripture, we need not ask if the objects of the grace act in the intelligence of the story. It is enough for us that here was a sinner exposed in the presence of Him who came to meet sin and put it away. Whoever takes the place of this woman meets the word that clears of condemnation, just as the publicans and sinners with whom Christ eats in Luke 15, set forth this, that if one takes the place of the sinner and the outcast, he is at once received. So with the lost sheep and the lost piece of silver. There is no intelligence of their condition, yet they set forth that which, if one take, it is representative. To make it clear, one might ask, 'Are you as sinful as this woman, as badly lost as that sheep or piece of silver?' " (Malachi Taylor)

"And they which heard it, being convicted by their own conscience, went out one by one, beginning at the eldest, even unto the last: and Jesus was left alone, and the woman standing in the midst. When Jesus had lifted up Himself, and saw none but the woman, He said unto her, Woman, where are those thine accusers? hath no man condemned thee? She said, No man, Lord. And Jesus said unto her, Neither do I condemn thee: go, and sin no more" (vv. 9-11). How striking and how blessed is this sequel to what has been before us! When Christ wrote on the ground the *second* time (not before), the "accusers" of the guilty departed! And then, after the last accuser had disappeared, the Lord said, "Neither do I condemn thee". How perfect the picture! And to complete it, Christ added, "Go, and sin no more", which is still His word to those who have been saved by grace. And the *ground,* the *righteous* ground on which He pronounced this verdict "Neither do I condemn thee", was, that in a short time *He* was going to be "condemned" in her stead. Finally, note the *order* of these two words of Christ to this woman who owned Him as "Lord" (1 Cor. 12:3)). It was not, "Go and sin no more, *and* I will not condemn thee", for that would have been a death-knell rather than good news in her ears. Instead, the Saviour said, "Neither do I condemn thee". And to every one who takes the place this woman was brought into, the word is, "There is therefore now *no condemnation*" (Rom. 8:1). "And sin no more" placed her, as we are placed, under the *constraint* of His love.

This incident then contains far more than that which was of local and ephemeral significance. It, in fact, raises the basic question of, How can mercy and justice be harmonized? How can grace flow forth except by slighting holiness? In the scene here presented to our view we are shown, not by a closely reasoned out statement of doctrine, but in symbolic action, that this problem is *not* insoluable to Divine wisdom. Here was a concrete case of a guilty sinner leaving the presence of Christ *un*-condemned. And it was neither because the law had been slighted nor sin palliated. The requirements of the law were strictly complied with, and her sin was openly condemned—"sin *no more*". Yet, she herself, was not condemned. She was dealt with according to "grace *and* truth". Mercy flowed out to her, yet not at the expense of justice. Such, in brief, is a summary of this marvelous narrative; a narrative which, verily, no man ever invented and no uninspired pen ever recorded.

This blessed incident not only anticipated the epistle to the Romans, but it also outlines, by vivid symbols, the Gospel of the grace of God. The Gospel not only announces a Saviour for sinners, but it also *explains how* God can save them consistently with the requirements of His character. As Rom. 1:17 tells us, in the Gospel is "the *righteousness* of God revealed". And this is precisely what is set forth here in John 8.

The entire incident is a most striking amplification and exemplification of John 1:17: "For the law was given by Moses, but *grace and truth* came by Jesus Christ". The grace of God never conflicts with His law, but, on the contrary, upholds its authority. "As sin hath reigned unto death, even so might grace reign *through righteousness* unto eternal life by Jesus Christ our Lord" (Rom. 5:21). But as to *how* grace might reign "through righteousness" was a problem which God alone could solve, and *Christ's* solution of it here marks Him as none other than "God manifest in flesh". With what blessed propriety, then, is this incident placed in the fourth Gospel, the special design of which is to display the Divine glory of the Lord Jesus!

Before we consider the dispensational bearings of our passage perhaps a separate word needs to be said on v. 7, in connection with which some have experienced a difficulty; and that is, Do these words of Christ enunciate a principle which *we* are justified in using? If so, under what circumstances? It is essential to bear in mind that Christ was not here speaking as Judge, but as One in the place of the Servant. The principle involved has been well stated thus, "We have no right to say to an official who in condemning culprits or in prosecuting them is simply discharging a public duty, "See that your own hands be clean, and your own heart pure before you condemn another'; but we have a perfect right to silence a private individual who is officiously and not officially exposing another's guilt, by bidding him remember that he has a beam in his own eye which he must first be rid of" (Dr. Dods).

We must now retrace our steps and go over our passage again to note its dispensational significance as it bore upon Israel. The "scribes and Pharisees" who brought the guilty adulteress to Christ must be viewed as *representative of their Nation* (as Nicodemus in John 3 and the impotent man in John 5). What, then, was the spiritual condition of Israel at that time? It was precisely that of this guilty woman: an "evil and adulterous generation" (Matt. 12:37) Christ termed them. But they were blinded by self-righteousness: they discerned not their awful condition, and knew not that they, equally with the Gentiles, were under the curse that had descended upon all from our father, Adam. Moreover, they were under a deeper guilt than the Gentiles—they stood convicted of the additional crime of having broken their covenant with the Lord. They were, in fact, the unfaithful, the adulterous wife of Jehovah (see Ezek. 16; Hosea 2, etc.). What, then, did Jehovah's law call for in such a case? The answer to this question is furnished in Num. 5, which sets forth "the law of jealousy", and describes the Divinely-ordered procedure for establishing the guilt of an unfaithful wife.

We cannot here quote the whole of Num. 5, but would ask the reader to turn to and read vv. 11-31 of that chapter. We quote now vv. 17, 24, 27:—"And the priest shall take holy water in an earthen vessel; and of the dust that is in the floor of the tabernacle the priest shall take, and put it into the water....and he shall cause the woman to drink the bitter water that causeth the curse: and the water that causeth the curse shall enter into her, and become bitter ....and when he hath made her to drink the water, then it shall come to pass, that if she be defiled, *and have done trespass against her husband,* that the water that causeth the curse shall enter into her, and become bitter, and her belly shall swell and her thigh rot: and the woman shall be a curse among her people!"

What light these verses cast upon our Lord's dealings with the Pharisees (representatives of Israel) here in John 8. "Water" is the well-known emblem of the Word (Eph. 5:26, etc.). This water is here termed *"holy"*. It was to be in an *earthen* vessel (cf 2 Cor. 4:7). This water was to be mixed with "the dust which is in the floor of the tabernacle". Thus the water becomes *"bitter* water", and the woman was made to drink it. The result would be (in case she was guilty) that her guilt would be *outwardly evidenced* in the swelling of her belly (symbol of pride) and the rotting of her thigh—her strength turned to corruption. Now put these separate items together, and is it not precisely what we find here in John 8? The Son of God is there incarnate, "made flesh", an "earthen vessel". The "holy water" is seen in His holy words—"He that is without sin among you, let him first cast a stone at her". In stooping down and writing on the floor of the temple, He mingled "the dust" with it. As He did this it became "bitter" to the proud Pharisees. In the conviction of their consciences we see *how* "bitter", and in going out, one by one, abashed, we see the withering of their strength! And thus was the guilt of Jehovah's unfaithful wife made fully manifest!!

What has been pointed out by no means exhausts the marvelous depth and scope of this truly wonderful passage. In addition to what has been said, let us, in closing this paper, call attention to a very striking prophetic foreshadowment which this scripture also contains. John 8, like each of the preceding chapters, contains a typical picture of future events. The subject of the picture here presented to our view may be termed, The Coming Justification of Israel. This justification of Israel will occur at the beginning of the Millennium. Zech. 3 gives us a most striking forecast of it, and in its light we shall now examine the prophetic significance of John 8: 1-11.

1. John 8:1 speaks of Christ's return to this earth: see Zech. 14:4. 2. "And early in the morning He came again into the temple" (v. 2). This is the symbolical *time-mark*. The long night of Israel's apostasy and dispersion will then be over. A new day will have dawned. As the *early*-morning hour intimates, the "Sun of righteousness" will have arisen (Mal. 4: 2). 3. "And the scribes and Pharisees brought unto Him a woman taken in adultery" (v. 3). This woman accurately pictures Israel in her national condition, as the unfaithful wife of Jehovah (Hosea 2). 4. Against her stand the adversaries of Christ, accusing her unto the Lord. This is exactly parallel with what we read of in Zech. 3:1: "And he showed me Joshua the high priest standing before the angel of the Lord, and Satan standing at his right hand to resist him". The "high priest" acted as the representative of the Nation. It will be noted that Zech. 3:1 opens with the word "and," which links it with the closing verses of the previous chapter. There we read, "And the Lord shall inherit Judah His portion in the holy land, and shall choose Jerusalem again. Be silent, O all flesh, before the Lord. For He is raised up out of His holy habitation" (Zech. 2: 12, 13). How striking is the correspondency between this and what is before us, in such vivid tableau, in John 8. Zechariah's prophecy announces that Israel is about to be saved. Jehovah prepares to execute His purpose. But Satan stands there to resist: cf Rev. 12:10. 5. The condition of the "woman" is stated: "This woman was taken in adultery, in the very act" (John 8:4). Note the parallel in Zech. 3:3: "Now Joshua was clothed with filthy garments, and stood before the angel"! 6. The accusers of the woman are silenced and made to depart, John 8:9: so in Zech. 3 the adversary disappears. 7. Grace, reigning through righteousness, gains a mighty victory. The Lord says to the woman, "Neither do I condemn thee: go, and sin no more"(8:11). So in Zech. 3 the sentence goes forth, "Behold, I have caused thine iniquity to pass from thee" (v. 4)! Read the closing verses of Zech. 3 and it will be seen that that chapter treats of Israel at the beginning of the Millennium. The whole purpose of it is to show *how* Israel is to be restored to God's favor. John 8, in turn, throws its own light on the subject, by assuring us that this will be in full harmony with the righteous requirements of God's holy law.

The following questions bear upon our next lesson:—

1. What is meant by "the world" in v. 12? Do not jump to conclusions.
2. What kind of *light* does "the world" enjoy? v. 12.
3. What is "the light of life"? v. 12.
4. To *what* "witness of the Father" was Christ referring? v. 18.
5. What does "die in your sins" (v. 21) prove concerning the Atonement?
6. What is the meaning of v. 31?
7. What does the truth make free *from?* v. 32.

—Arthur W. Pink.

GLEANINGS IN EXODUS.

4. Moses at the Burning Bush: Exodus 3.

In our last article we saw how Moses' attempt to deliver Israel was inopportune, for God's time had not arrived. Moreover, the leader himself was not fully prepared, nor were the Hebrews themselves ready to leave Egypt. The impetuosity of Moses caused him to act with a zeal which was not according to knowledge and this, as is usually the case, brought him into serious trouble. The king sought his life, and to escape him, Moses fled into Midian. So much for the human side. Turning to the Divine, we are made to wonder at and worship before the infinite wisdom of Him who maketh the wrath of man to praise Him and who bringeth good out of evil.

God had an important work for Moses to do and for this he must be prepared. That work was to lead His people out of Egypt, and conduct them unto the promised inheritance. And for this work Moses was not yet equipped. It is true that this one who had become the adopted son of Pharaoh's daughter had received a thorough education, for he was "learned in *all* the wisdom of the Egyptians". Nor was he any longer a youth, but now forty years of age—in the very prime of life. Nor was he only a student or theorist—he was "mighty in words and deeds" (Acts 7:22). What, then, was lacking? Surely here was one who possessed all the necessary qualifications for leadership. Ah, how different are God's thoughts from ours! "That which is highly esteemed among men is abomination in the sight of God" (Luke 16:15). What we have enumerated above were but natural attainments and acquirements; and the natural man is set aside before God, for no *flesh* can glory in *His* presence (1 Cor. 1:29).

The "wisdom of the Egyptians", profound as men esteem it, was, after all, only "the wisdom of the world"; and that is "foolishness with God". The colleges of this world cannot equip for the Divine service; for *that* we must be taught in the school of God. And that is something which the natural man knows nothing about—"And the Jews marvelled, saying, How knoweth this man letters, having never learned?"—in *their* academies (John 7:15). To learn in the school of God, then, Moses must turn his back on the land of the Pharaoh's. It is so still. The heart must be separated, the spirit divorced from the world, if progress is to be made in spiritual things. "The hand of man can never mould a vessel 'meet for the Master's use'. The One who is to use the vessel can alone prepare it".

"Now Moses kept the flock of Jethro his father-in-law, the priest of Midian: and he led the flock to the backside of the desert, and came to the mountain of God, even to Horeb" (Ex. 3:1). From Egypt to "the backside of the desert", from the palace to the sheepfold, was a radical change for this man who was yet to fill so important a role. Tending flocks seems a strange preparation for one who was to be the liberator of a nation of slaves. And again we are reminded of how different are God's thoughts and ways from man's. And the ways of God are not only different from ours, but they are obnoxious to the flesh: as Gen. 46:31 tells us, "Every *shepherd* is an abomination to the Egyptians". Thus God leads His servants to take that very place which is hateful to worldlings.

"The 'backside of the desert' is where men and things, the world and self, present circumstances and their influences, are all valued at what they are really worth. There it is, and there alone, that you will find a Divinely-adjusted balance in which to weigh all within and all around. There are no false colors, no borrowed plumes, no empty pretensions. The enemy of your souls cannot gild the sand of that place. All is reality there. The heart that has found itself in the presence of God at 'the backside of the desert', has right thoughts about everything. It is raised far above the exciting influences of this world's schemes. The din and noise, the bustle and confusion of Egypt, do not fall upon the ear in that distant place. The crash in the monetary and commercial world is not heard there; the sigh of ambition is not heard there; this world's fading laurels do not tempt there; the thirst for gold is not felt there; the eye is never dimmed with lust, nor the heart swollen with pride there; human applause does not elate, nor human censure depress there. In a word, everything is set aside save the stillness and light of the Divine presence. God's voice alone is heard, His light enjoyed, His thoughts received. This is the place to which all must go to be educated for the ministry;

and there all must remain if they would succeed in the ministry" (C. H. M.).

What strikes us as even more strange is that Moses should have to remain *forty years* in Midian. But God is in no hurry; nor should we be—"He that believeth shall not make haste" (Isa. 28:16). There is much here which every servant of God needs to ponder, particularly the younger ones. In this day it is the common custom to pitchfork new converts into Christian activities without any serious inquiry as to their fitness for such solemn and momentous duties. If a person is "mighty in words and deeds" that is considered all that is necessary. "*Not a novice,* lest being lifted up with pride he fall into the condemnation of the Devil" (1 Tim. 3:6) might as well not be in the Bible, for all the weight it has with most of our moderns.

In a place of *retirement* Moses spent the second forty years of his life; a place where every opportunity for *communion* with God was afforded. Here he was to learn the utter vanity of human resources and the need for entire dependence on God Himself. To be much alone with God is the first requisite for every servant of His. But why is it that no details are recorded of God's dealings with His servant during this interval? Practically nothing is told us of the experiences through which he passed, the discipline of which he was the subject, the heart exercises he suffered. As in the case of the training of the prophets, John the Baptist, Paul in Arabia, this is passed over in silence. Is it because God's dealings with one of His servants are not fitted to another? Are there not some things we can learn neither by precept nor example? Certain it is that there is *no uniform curriculum* in the school of God. Each servant is dealt with according to his individual needs and disciplined with a view to the particular work which God has for *him* to do.

"And he led the flock to the backside of the desert, and came to the mountain of God, even to Horeb" (v. 1). Horeb was the name of a mountain range; Sinai, the "mount of God" (see Ex. 24:12, 13), was a particular peak in that range. It was in this same mount that, centuries later, the Lord met with and commissioned Elijah (1 Kings 19:4-11), as, perhaps, it was also at the same place He gave the Gospel of His glory to the apostle Paul (Gal. 1:17; 4:25).

"And the angel of the Lord appeared unto him in a flame of fire out of the midst of a bush: and he looked, and, behold, the bush burned with fire, and the bush was not consumed. And Moses said, I will now turn aside, and see this great sight, why the bush is not burnt" (Ex. 3:2, 3). Here was a wonder which all the magicians of Pharaoh could not produce. Here was something which must baffle all the wisdom of the Egyptians. Here was a manifestation of God Himself. The Hebrew word here for "bush" occurs in only one other passage, namely, Deut. 33:16, where we read, "And for the precious things of the earth and fulness thereof, and for the good will of Him that *dwelt* in the bush". In this verse the word for "dwelt" is "shah-chan". It was, then, the *Shekinah* glory which was now displayed before the wondering eyes of Moses. This, we take it, is the meaning of "the angel of the Lord *appeared* unto him in *a flame*" here manifested in the Shekinah-glory.

The "Angel of the Lord" was none other than the Lord Jesus in theophanic manifestation, for in v. 4 He is denominated "Lord" and "God". This sets forth a truth of vital moment to the servant of God. Before Moses can be sent forth on his important mission he must first behold the ineffable glory of the Lord. To serve acceptably we must work with an eye single to God's glory, but to do this we must first gaze upon that glory. It was so here with Moses. It was thus with Isaiah (Isa. 6). It was the same in the case of the great apostle to the Gentiles (Acts 9:3, etc.). Make no mistake fellow-laborer, a vision of the glory of God is an essential prerequisite if we are to serve Him acceptably.

Ere considering the Lord's words to Moses, let us first turn aside and view the "great sight" of the Burning Bush. We are satisfied that there is much here of deep significance; may God grant us discernment to understand and appreciate.

Spiritually the Burning Bush speaks of the Gospel of God's grace. The symbol used was unique and startling. A bush burned with fire, and yet the bush (in that arid desert a most imflammable object) was not burnt. Here was a mysterious phenomenon, but it set forth a mystery far more profound—the former natural, the latter moral. Fire in Scripture is uniformly the emblem of Divine judgment, that is, of God's holiness in active opposition against evil. The final word on the subject is, "Our God is a consuming fire" (Heb. 12:29). Here, then, is the deeper mystery: How can God, who is 'a consuming fire'—burning up all that is contrary to His holy nature—reveal Himself without consuming? Or, to put it in another form: How can He who is "of purer eyes than to behold evil and canst not look on iniquity" (Hab. 1:13) have to do with men, other than in judgment! Nothing but the Gospel contains any real solution to this problem. The Gospel tells of how grace reigns, not at the expense of righteousness, but "through righteousness, unto eternal life, through Jesus Christ our Lord" (Rom. 5:21).

And how has this been accomplished? By the Holy One of God being made a "curse" for us (Gal. 3:13). It is deeply significant that the word "seneh" means "*thorny* bush", for thorns are the lasting reminder of the curse (Gen. 3:18). Into the place of the curse entered our blessed Substitute. The fierce flames of holy wrath engulfed Him, but, being "mighty" (Psa. 89:19), they did not, and could not, consume Him. The "Root out of a dry ground" perished not. It was not possible that death should hold the Prince of life. Three days only did He remain in the tomb: on the third day He came forth triumphant, and is now alive for evermore. And it is as the God of *resurrection* He now saves. Note how this, too, comes out in our type. Said the Saviour to the Sadducees, "Now that the dead are raised, even Moses showed *at the bush,* when he called the Lord the God of Abraham, and the God of Isaac, and the God of Jacob. For He is not a God of the dead, but of the living: for all live unto Him" (Luke 20: 37, 38). And how perfect this type is: it was not until after the Deliverer (Moses) had been rejected by Israel (Ex. 2:14) that God thus revealed Himself at the bush!

But there is a *dispensational* significance as well. Equally clear it is that the Burning Bush was a figure of *the nation of Israel.* At the time the Lord appeared here to Moses, the Hebrews were suffering in "the iron *furnace* of Egypt" (Deut. 4:20), but fiercely as the flames had burned against them for fully forty years, they had not been consumed. And so also has it proven all through these many centuries since then. The fires of persecution have blazed hotly, yet have they been marvelously, miraculously sustained. And why? Ah, does not our type make answer? God Himself was in the Burning Bush; and so He has been with Israel. Just as He was there with the three Hebrews in the midst of Babylon's furnace, so has He been with the Jews all through their checkered history. In the day to come this will be fully owned, for then shall it appear, "in all their affliction *He* was afflicted, and the Angel of His presence saved them" (Isa. 63:9).

While the miraculous preservation of Israel during all their fiery trials is no doubt the prominent thought here, there are others equally significant. The symbol selected by God was most suggestive. It was not in a majestic tree of the forest that God appeared to Moses, but in a humble acacia, or thorn-bush of the desert. And how fitly this represented both the lowly origin of the Hebrew people—"A Syrian ready to perish was my father" (Deut. 26:5); and their subsequent history—a separated nation, dwelling as it were in the desert. Nor is this all. This humble bush, which possessed neither beauty nor comliness, became, temporarily, the abode of Jehovah, and from it He revealed Himself to Moses. And has it not been thus with Israel: it is from *their midst* God has manifested Himself. Finally, the fact that it was an acacia bush burning with fire, represented in a forceful figure the *spiritual* history of Israel—bearing thorns rather than fruit, and in consequence, being chastened of God. Naturalists tell us that thorns are abortive branches, which if developed would bring forth leaves and fruit.

"And when the Lord saw that he turned aside to see, God called unto him out of the midst of the bush, and said, Moses, Moses. And he said, Here am I. And He said, Draw not nigh hither: put off thy shoes from off thy feet, for the place whereon thou standest is holy ground" (vv. 4, 5). How this helps to interpret for us the moral meaning of the "flame of fire"—the activities of Divine holiness. The Shekinah-glory which abode upon the mercy-seat over the ark was not only the evidence of Jehovah's presence in Israel's midst, but was the manifest emblem of His *holiness*—abiding in the Holy of Holies. It was in holiness God was about to deal both with the Egyptians and with His own people, and of this Moses needed to be instructed. He must put off the shoes of every day walk and life, and draw near in the spirit of true worship. Another important lesson is this for the servant of God today. Each laborer in the vineyard needs to keep constantly before him the fact that the One with whom he has to do, and whom he serves, is holy, thrice holy. A realization of this would check the lightness and levity of the flesh.

"Moreover He said, I am the God of thy father, the God of Abraham, the God of Isaac, and the God of Jacob. And Moses hid his face; for he was afraid to look upon God" (v. 6). Thus the Lord stood revealed before Moses as the covenant-keeping God, the God of all grace. When God picked up Abraham, Isaac and Jacob, and made them the fathers of His chosen people, it was not because of any excellence in them, seen or foreseen; rather was it His pure sovereign benignity. So, too, now that He is about to redeem the Hebrews from the land of bondage, it is not because of any good in them or from them. It is as the God of Abraham—the sovereign Elector; the God of Isaac—the almighty Quickener; the God of Jacob—the long-suffering One; who is about to bare His arm, display His power and deliver His people. And in this *same* threefold character does He act today. The God of Abraham is our God the One who sovereignly chose us in Christ before the foundation of the world. The God of Isaac is our God—the One who by His own miraculous power made us new creatures in Christ. The God of Jacob is our God—the One who bears with us in infinite patience, who never forsakes us, and who has promised to perfect that which concerns us (Psa. 138:8).

"And the Lord said, I have surely seen the affliction of My people which are in Egypt, and have heard their cry by reason of their taskmasters; for I know their sorrows" (v. 7). Mark carefully the condition of these Hebrews: crushed by the cruel oppression of Egypt's slavery; groaning beneath the iron rod of Pharaoh. And how this pictures the condition of the natural man, the bond-slave of sin, the captive of the Devil. This is true not only of the slave of lust or the helpless victim of drugs, but of the moral and refined. They, too, are in bondage to gold, pleasure, ambition, and a dozen other things. The "affliction" which sin has brought is everywhere to be seen, not only in physical suffering, but in mental restlessness and heart discontent. The varied "lusts of the flesh" are just as merciless as the Egyptian taskmasters of old; and the "sorrows" of sin's slaves to-day just as acute as those of the Israelites midst the iron furnace of Egypt. What woe there really is behind the fair surface of society! How fearful the misery which has come on the whole race of man through sin! How great the need for the Saviour! How terrible the guilt of despising Him now that He has come!

"And the Lord said, I have surely *seen* the affliction of My people which are in Egypt, and have *heard* their cry by reason of their taskmasters; for I know their sorrows" (v. 7). The One speaking here is termed in the second verse "the Angel of the Lord". This we know from Mal. 3:1, and other scriptures, was Christ Himself, in theophanic manifestation. It is very helpful and instructive to trace Him as "the Angel of the Lord" all through the Old Testament. The first time He is thus brought before us is in Gen. 16:13: "And she called the name of the Lord (the "Angel of the Lord", see vv. 9, 10) that spake unto her, Thou God *seest* me: for she said, Have I also here looked after Him that *seeth* me?" The second occurrence is in Gen. 21:17 "And the Angel of God called to Hagar out of heaven, and said unto her, What aileth thee, Hagar? Fear not; for God hath *heard* the voice of the lad where he is". Thus, in the third reference here in Ex. 3, we have combined the "seeth" and "heard" which are the central things in the first two. Let the interested reader follow out the other references for himself. How blessed for us to know that there is One above who never slumbers nor sleeps, but "hears" and "sees" all *our* afflictions!

"For I know their sorrows" (v. 7). With this should be compared Ex. 2:23: "And it came to pass in process of time, that the king of Egypt died: and the children of Israel *sighed* by reason of the bondage, and they *cried,* and their cry came up unto God by reason of the bondage." The tenderness of the original is hidden by this rendering. The R. V. gives it: "And it came to pass in the course of *those many days,* that the king of Egypt died", etc. How these words throb with Divine compassion. There were between fourteen and fifteen thousand "days", during that forty years of Moses' sojourn in Midian; and each of them were days of anguish for them. But God had not ignored them, nor been indifferent to their hard lot—"I know their sorrows". How blessed for us, in times of stress and distress to remember that there is One above who takes notice. This was how Job consoled himself (see Job 23:10). The Call Moses received and his Responses thereto we reserve for separate consideration.

Arthur W. Pink

HIS WORKMANSHIP.

"For we are His workmanship, created in Christ Jesus unto good works, which God hath before ordained that we should walk in them." Eph. 2:10.

Those who have been quickened from the death in sins are God's "workmanship". There is a day coming when whole nations shall be the subjects of His excellent working. First, in that day, Israel shall be "the work of His hands", of which He shall say, "this people have I formed for Myself"; and in that day Israel shall sing, "Know ye that the Lord He is God: it is He that hath made us, and not we ourselves" (Isa. 29:23; 43:31; Ps. 100:3). Meanwhile, He, puts forth His mighty power, not on nations but on individuals whom He "calls by His name and creates and forms for His glory". "For *we* are His Workmanship".

And each subject of His regenerating power is a complete formation. We are His completed work. This must be distinguished from His work *in* us which goes on evermore, and which He will "perform until the day of Christ". The child of God being fed and nourished and exercised, according to God's appointment, grows, but he does not grow into a child; *that* he is *by birth,* or according to the view in our passage, by the operation of God. The believer is not in process of making. He had been the subject of creating power, and because his creation is complete, his growth begins and goes on. In this the individual believer is to be distinguished from the Church, which is the house of God," "a temple in the Lord". So long as "living stones" are being built upon the foundation, so long "all the building fitly framed together *groweth* into an holy temple in the Lord". (Eph. 2: 21, 22; 1 Pet. 2:5). But the church is not a place for making Christians, anymore than Solomon's temple was a place for hewing stone. "And the house when it was in building, was built of stone made ready before it was brought thither; so that there was neither hammer nor axe nor any tool of iron heard in the house, while it was in building" (1 Kings 6:7). How different all this from the thoughts of many. They think of the Church as a place for producing Christians; whereas it is the congregation of Christians, each one a hewn stone of God's workmanship. and so the ordinances and privileges of the house are degraded to "hammers and axes, and tools of iron" for fashioning "living stones". God quickens, raises, and saves by grace, and then adds the saved to the Church. Men go into the Church, or "join" it with a vague and superstitious hope that its ordinances may, perchance, by some mysterious process, transmute them into the precious stones of the sanctuary. Wherever this falsehood prevails Christ has become of none effect, the Holy Spirit of no account, and man's workmanship is preferred and lauded, rather than God's workmanship. But in the day when "the Headstone shall be brought forth with shoutings, crying, Grace, grace unto it", the infinite difference between the work of God and the work of man will be revealed to all the universe.

Among the many interesting points, as to God's workmanship, suggested by the allusion just made to the stones of the temple made with hands, we only touch on one—a difference between the typical and the "living stones". There is this difference, that the "living stones" can "remember" something of their former condition when they were dead stone in the quarry of nature; they can "look unto the rock whence they were hewn, and to the hole of the pit whence they were dug". They find it salutary to "remember that they were in times past in the flesh without Christ; strangers to the covenants of promise; having no hope, and without God in the world" Eph. 2:12. And the remembrance exalts the grace which brought them nigh by the blood of Christ, the grace which quickened them when they were dead. What force do such recollections give to the apostle's repeated use of the little word "for". "FOR by grace ye have been saved", "FOR we are HIS workmanship". And indeed it is the immediate design of the statement to clinch the argument of salvation by grace. The crowning demonstration of the truth that it is not of works, is that "WE ARE HIS WORKMANSHIP".

Our passage further engages our

thoughts on the nature of God's operation by which we became His workmanship. We were *"created in Christ Jesus"*. Our condition as quickened, and our position as raised up together with Christ, and seated in heavenly places in Him (vv. 5-6), were not achieved by a gradual process. If we were not made Christians by Church ordinances no more were we made Christians by process of education and gradual reform. We are God's workmanship by *creation*. As He said "Let there be light", and the light shone out of darkness, so hath He shined in our hearts. As the Lord Jesus said, "Lazarus come forth" and he that was dead came forth, so are we God's creation. In the creation of the heavens and the earth God created, by Jesus Christ, through the Spirit (Gen. 1:1; John 1:3; Job 26:13; Ps. 104:30). In like manner we, His workmanship, were created by the *will* of the Father, by the *word* of Christ the Son, through the *energy* of the Holy Spirit (James 1:18; John 5:25; Titus 3:5). True the salvation is "through faith", but the faith "cometh by hearing and hearing by the word of God". It is surely no small ingredient in the joy of God's salvation that it *is* effected by His creating Word. It seems to me one of the most blessed thoughts I ever gained from the precious gospel, that we are "His workmanship" by the same creating fiat which spake into being all things that were made. To think that, as by His word He made the heavens and all the host of them by the breath of His mouth, so He created me in Christ Jesus by His own word of grace and power. He saw me lying among the dead, myself dead, "in my blood," and He passed by and uttered the word "Live"; yea He said, "Live", and it was done. Truly blessed I am, "His workmanship, created in Christ Jesus". What is there in common between this creating, and the pretence of saving men by education, and elevation and religious observances?. Can these give life?. Do these produce "newness of life"?. Of course not. You may educate men, you may elevate them, you may instruct them in religion, you may induce their most scrupulous observance of religious forms, withal, you may repeat the decalogue in their ears, and obtain from their lips the most sincere responses; and if you could thus operate upon men for the lifetime of a Methuselah, you would never succeed in saving a single soul; the subjects of your operations would remain but dead stones in nature's darkness. "Circumcision availeth nothing, nor uncircumcision, but a *new creature*".

Moreover, the scene of our creation is Christ Jesus; we are created "IN" Christ Jesus. As the same apostle says elsewhere, "if any man be in Christ Jesus he is a new creature", or "a new creation" (II Cor. 5:17). In both these passages the connection between our creation and the death and resurrection of Christ is maintained. In the latter it is the declared result of the death of Christ, as of the ONE who died for the all and rose again (II Cor. 5:14, 15). In Ephesians our "creation" is viewed as the prolonged exercise of God's act in raising Him up from the dead; it is the display of "the exceeding greatness of His power toward us who believe, which He wrought in Christ when He raised Him from the dead, and set Him at His own right hand in the heavenly places" (1:19, 20). The death of Christ was the judicial accomplishment of our death-doom, the resurrection of Christ and His exaltation to God's right hand were the two parts of the judicial proclamation of our justification by His death (Rom. 4:25).

We use the word judicial in its proper sense, appertaining to judgment. God's act, when He made the soul of His beloved Son an offering for sin, was His act of righteous judgment against sin, and upon Him who knew no sin, but whom "HE MADE TO BE SIN, that we might become the righteousness of God in Him". God's acts, in raising Jesus up from the dead, and setting Him at His right hand, were the righteous acts of judgment which demonstrated and proclaimed that the judicial penalty had suffered to meet all the claims of justice on our behalf—and justice as it is in Him and administered by Him whose judgment is according to truth. God's exceeding greatness of power *then* wrought in Christ *"towards* us who believe, when He raised Christ from the dead and set Him at His own right hand in the heavenly places". But it was effectually put forth upon us who believe *when* He in His rich mercy "quickened us together with Christ, and raised us up together and made us sit together in the heavenly places *in Christ Jesus,* (Eph. 2:5, 6). Our "creation in Christ Jesus" is thus no mere figure of speech. It is an actually accomplished fact. We are in Him a new creation, and partake of all the blessing and benefits secured for us in and by His obedience unto death, on account of which God hath highly exalted Him. We are in Him who is true. We are in Him who is made unto us wisdom from God, both righteousness, and sanctification and redemption.

Thus, in point of fact, does creation in Christ Jesus set its subjects upon heights infinitely above the high places of human attainment. It is pretended that the softening and elevating influences brought to bear upon fallen men by a weak, and often sickly, philanthropy, can heal the deadly malady which afflicts humanity; and they dare to claim that these influences, in their successful application secure for their subjects the approbation of God, and afford them a reasonable prospect of eternal blessing. They do well indeed when they describe their processes as "humanizing"; and their manipulations of humanity are very satisfactory to all the well disposed, in so far as they succeed in making men less fierce and more kindly or otherwise moral. But alas, what will all this accomplish toward the salvation of the soul?. God is judge. He will have righteousness in order to justification; He demands truth in the inward parts. You may humanize the dangerous classes, you may elevate the respectable, you may make all men as moral and all as religious as was he who could honestly say, "I was touching the righteousness which is in the law, blameless", and "I was exceedingly zealous of the traditions of my fathers"; but if there be no new creation in Christ Jesus, there is no participation in the righteousness, sanctification, and redemption, apart from which there is no salvation. Man has for many centuries been left to make his own laws, and to break them. Man can be content with anything but what he terms even-handed justice, but God's law and justice are inflexible. God demands that His judgment against man must be met by the sinner or by a substitute; God demands that His claims upon us must be answered by positive and perfect obedience by ourselves or by a substitute. In His amazing grace He found in His own bosom One who could fulfill all for sinners; He sent Him forth, made of a woman, made under the law; He made Him to be sin for us; and the reception which men gave to the Substitute and Sin-bearer, determines whether they are created in Him or remaining in nature's death, satisfied with nature's course and with nature's attainment. Those saved by His grace are in no sense the product of nature's energies and efforts; they are wholly God's "WORKMANSHIP", *created* in Christ Jesus".

But the chief end of salvation by grace is nevertheless God's glory; His saved are His children "according to the good pleasure of His will, to the praise of the glory of His grace"; and, as the work of His hands, they are created *"unto good works*, which God hath before ordained that we should walk in them"! Of His redeemed Israel He says, "this people have I formed for myself, *they shall show forth my praise"*. So those who in the present dispensation are created in Christ Jesus are ordained to be "a kind of first fruits of His creatures". "Ye are a chosen generation, a royal priesthood, a holy nation, a peculiar people,; *that ye should show forth the praises of Him that hath called you out of darkness into His marvellous light"* (1 Pet. 2:9).

It is important to have it deeply impressed upon our hearts that the good works for which we are created are wrought not *for* salvation but *from* salvation. Works wrought with the design of obtaining or securing salvation are all excluded from the good works in which the saved are to walk. We are saved by grace, not of works, lest any man should boast; and the proof of this is that we, the saved, so far from contributing to our salvation, are ourselves *HIS* "handiwork". Our salvation was completed and placed beyond all imperilment when we were "created in Christ Jesus, unto good works". Every work then, which is performed with a view to obtain or to secure salvation is a virtual denial of salvation "by grace not of works". Believers, when they are acting according to the grace wherein they stand, do not work for mercy; they "have obtained mercy" (1 Pet. 2:10).

Furthermore, the "good works" of God's first-fruits-creatures are divinely wrought. "Work out your own salvation with fear and trembling, *for it is God that WORKETH IN YOU* both to will and to do of His good pleasure" (Phil. 2:12). The works of our natural energies are evil and dead works. Hence the very responsibility laid upon us in the last quoted passage, has its foundation in the fact that we *are* saved, and its enforcement in the great fact that "it is God that worketh" in His saved ones. It is our *"own* salvation" that we are to *"work out"* to its proper, its designed end; the designed end of the salvation bestowed being that we should walk in the "good works" for, unto which, we were created in Christ Jesus. And we can meet this responsibility only because, having salvation, our bodies have become temples of the Holy Spirit which we have of God; God dwelleth in us, and worketh in us both to will and to do. In other words, we have each of us become a habitation of God in which He operates according to His good pleasure, forming our very desires, and directing the work of our hands. So elsewhere we are taught that the persons nd members of those that are "alive from the dead" are the "servants" and "instruments" of righteousness; and that the responsibility of God's living workmanship is to *"yield"* themselves and their members *unto God* who worketh in them (Rom. 6:13, 19).

When we began this paper it was chiefly with the design of offering some remarks on the remarkable statement about the Divine fore-ordination of the good works, in which the saved should walk. It seemed unnatural and unbecoming to enter upon this without some notice of the whole sentence, but our extended remarks on the former clauses have left us but little space to consider the last clause of this most interesting verse. A few words must suffice.

We were created "unto good works which God had *"before ordained"* that "we should walk in them", or better, as Bishop Ellicott translates "for good works which God before *prepared* that we should walk in them". One of the most striking and distinctive features of this Epistle to the Ephesians is that everything of which it treats is brought into notice as having its origin in God; His eternal thoughts are revealed. Everything is referred to His electing and predestinating grace. He hath blessed us "according as He hath *chosen* us in Christ *before the foundation of the world"*; He *"predestinated* us to the sonship by Christ"; we have "obtained inheritance being *predestinated"*; the mystery of the church, the one body, which was hidden from the ages in God has been opened, that all men might see its fellowship, and that "to the principalities and powers in the heavenly places might be known the manifold wisdom of God *"according to the eternal purpose which He purposed in Christ Jesus our Lord"*. It is then in perfect harmony with all this that it should be announced that the "good works" were *"before ordained of God"*, that the created in Christ Jesus "should walk in them."

Nevertheless, the passage is unique. The passages in Scripture which testify our election and predestination, according to God's forethought and foreknowledge are very numerous; here only do we read that our very works were all pre-appointed and before prepared for our performance. There is something like this suggested by the words of Christ, "I have chosen you that ye should go and bring forth fruit, and that your fruit should remain" (John 15:16). But this saying of the Lord declares the choice of the *fruit-bearers* or workers; while that before us in our text declares that the *good works* were themselves the subject of God's fore-preparation.

Surely, beloved in the Lord, this will both interest our hearts and stimulate our zeal of the good works in which we are called to walk. Think of it! The same love which was in the eternal ages past, before the foundation of the world, busy with us, occupied in choosing and predestinating us sons and heirs, the same grace which was bestowing itself upon us for salvation in Christ, before the times of the ages, was preparing the good works in which the appointed heirs of glory should occupy themselves while waiting for that glory which they are to obtain with and in Christ. The chosen are "vessels of mercy before prepared unto glory" (Rom. 9:23), and meanwhile they are "vessels unto honor"—that is, if they are truly and purely offering themselves for the Master's use—"vessels unto honor, sanctified, and meet for the Master's use, and prepared unto every good work" (II Tim. 2:20-21).

While then we, as intelligent vessels of God's handiwork, are performing the functions for which He formed us, it cannot fail to incite us both to purification of ourselves, and devotion to the Master's use, to carry with us the blessed thought that when we were in God's counsels fore-ordained for the "good works" in which we walk, the good works themselves, were, in the same counsels, "FORE-PREPARED *that we should walk in them"*. We must surely highly esteem the works as those which He eternally anticipated to the praise of His own glory in us and by us. The joy of our own walk in the good works must surely be promoted by the thought that He made us for them, and prepared them for us. Let this thought be carried into all that we are doing in the name of Christ. Suppose that you are giving "only a cup of cold water unto one of these little ones who believe in Him", what a new joy of this privilege may spring up in your heart, as you recollect that not only will He own this as done to Himself, but that He recognizes, and would have you recognize that little action as appointed by His Father before the world began. And were it not well to carry forward the thoughts of the fore-preparation of good works for our walk into that walk, with the constant enquiry of ourselves whether what we are doing is among the works fore-ordained for us by His love. The Scripture is abundantly clear as to what the good works are, and we may easily know them. But in this period of failure we need all that God has revealed on every point, to sustain our hearts and to direct our feet in the holy way, and our hands to the performance of the good works which God before prepared that we should walk in them. Our salvation and sonship are to the praise of the glory of His grace, and we are to inherit to the praise of His glory; but our present life is to *show forth His praises,* and this we can only do as we engage in the works He before prepared that we should walk in them.

C. Campbell 1873

THE WAY OF SALVATION.

"What must I do to be saved?" Acts 16:30.

There are two things which have never changed: Man's *need,* and God's *provision* to supply that need. Men are the same the world over: they are all guilty, lost sinners. Reader, *you* may be cultured and refined, but as a descendant of Adam *you* are a sinner. You may be rich and affluant, but by nature *you* are a child of wrath. Your reputation may be excellent, you may be highly esteemed by a wide circle of friends, but if you are out of Christ you are on the Broad Road that leadeth to destruction. Or, you may be poor and uneducated, nevertheless, if you have not believed to the saving of your soul, you are "condemned already." "There is no difference: for *all* have sinned, and come short of the glory of God" (Rom. 3:22, 23). This was true in the first century of the Christian era, and it is true now in this twentieth century. Man's *need* is the same now as it was then.

The *Provision* which God has made to supply the sinner's need also remains unchanged. Medical science has discovered many new ways of treating old diseases, but it has found no new remedy for sin. The inventive faculty of man has devised many new contrivances for reducing manual labor, but it is unable to provide any rest for the soul. We have many new methods of locomotion and can now travel beneath the waters and fly above the earth, but there is no other way back to God except thro' Christ, who said, "No man cometh unto the Father but by Me" (John 14:6). There is only one remedy for sin, one Saviour for sinners, one hope for the lost, and that is the Lord Jesus Christ. "Neither is there salvation in any other: for there is none other name under heaven given among men, whereby we must be saved" (Acts 4:12).

"What must I do to be saved?" This question is almost as old as the hills, and nothing can vie with it in importance. It is *the* question of all questions because the Divine answer to it and our response thereto fixes eternal destiny. Three things are beyond dispute:—First, *Every man needs saving,* and deep down in his heart he *knows* it. He may seek to silence the still small voice within, he may attempt to drown it among the pleasures of the world, yet, in the hour when he is face to face with his soul's highest interests he *knows* that he is a lost sinner. The second great fact is: *Every man may be saved if he will*—the trouble is so many are *not willing.* The terms are easy, the way is plain, the Gospel proclamation is broad enough to include even the chief of sinners, yet many will not come to Christ that they might have life. The third great fact is: *Every man will be eternally lost if he dies unsaved.* The sinner is "condemned already," and there is no hope beyond the grave. Scripture knows nothing of any "second chance" after death. God's Word says, "He that believeth not shall be damned" (Mark 16:16).

"What must I do to be saved?" Many and varied are the answers which man has returned to this question. Before considering *God's* answer let us examine and refute the leading ones given by different schools of human thought.

I. There is no Salvation by the Elimination of sin.

Let us explain what we mean. Many imagine they must treat their lives like gardens and root up their sins as they would obnoxious weeds. They suppose they must fit themselves for God's presence, and in order to this they seek to get rid of bad habits and substitute good ones. The delusion is widespread: it is illogical, unscriptural, impossible. That there is no salvation this way is evident from three considerations:—

1 Man has too little time at his disposal. Life is far too short to deal with every sin. Many have found that it takes the best part of a life-time to even imperfectly conquer a single sin, and tho' the reader should live to be a thousand years old he would find it impossible to eradicate every sin from his life.

2 Man is unable to reach *the root* of sins. Evil habits are but the fruit of an evil nature, and just as a corrupt tree cannot bring forth good fruit; so nothing but evil can issue from a heart that is "deceitful above all things and desperately wicked" (Jer. 17:9). The sinner's attempt to *fit himself* for the presence of the thrice holy God by eliminating his sinful habits, is more useless than for a farmer to cut off the heads of thistles while leaving their *roots* still in the ground.

3 Suppose a man were to go on eliminating from his character and life *everything* that was sinful in God's sight—in the end what would be left? Nothing! Said the apostle Paul, "For I know that in me, that is, in my flesh (all that he was by his natural birth), dwelleth *no* good thing" (Rom. 7:18). And again Scripture declares, "But we are all as an unclean thing, and all our righteousnesses are as filthy rags" (Is. 64:6).

II. There is no Salvation by the Education of the mind.

We shall not here tyrade against educational agencies as such. God sets no premium on ignorance. Properly used, education may become a great blessing. But one of the great delusions of the day is that you can educate people into the kingdom of God. For all time it stands written, "The world by wisdom knew not God" (1 Cor. 1:21). Of the ancient nations the two most highly educated were the Egyptians and the Greeks: from the former God had to deliver His people Israel, to take them into the wilderness for Divine instruction; and concerning the latter we read, "We preach Christ crucified, unto the Jews a stumbling-block, and *unto the Greeks foolishness*" (1 Cor. 1:23).

There are many that tell us sin is ignorance and that education will make saints. There are not a few who believe that the best way of dealing with those in our penitentiaries is to substitute education for corporal punishment. But the more you educate a criminal the more dangerous he becomes to society. Moreover, it is a simple fact of observation that the majority of the most highly educated are sceptics and agnostics. The word of our Lord Jesus Christ pointedly exposed the delusion of salvation thro' education. Said He, "Except ye be converted, *and become as little children,* ye shall not enter into the kingdom of heaven" (Matt. 18:3).

III. There is no Salvation by Reformation of life

How many there are who think that what God requires from the sinner is that he alter the manner of his living, affect a radical change in his course, adopt new ideals and ways. How often we hear of preachers exhorting the members of their congregation to 'quit their meanness' and turn over a new leaf. But there is no salvation this way.

In the first place, to tell the sinner he must turn over a new leaf makes no provision for his failings and sins in the *past.* When a child turns over a new page in his copy-book that does not remove the blots on the earlier pages.

In the second place, reformation deals merely with the *external* life. A rusty pump is rusty still even tho' it be given a new coat of paint. A leper is a leper still even tho' he be decked out in fine garments. And a sinner is a sinner still even tho his deportment be irreproachable. Man looketh on the outward appearance, but the Lord looketh on the heart. If a man's heart is not right in the sight of God, no matter how clean his habits may be they count for nothing in the eyes of the Lord.

In the third place, the attempt to win God's approval by reformation is only another species of the false doctrine of salvation by works. Scripture is plain and pointed on this subject. Of Christians it is said, "*Not by works* of righteousness which we have done, but according to His mercy He saved us" (Titus 3:5). And again it is written, "But to him that *worketh not,* but believeth on Him that justifieth the ungodly, his faith is counted for righteousness" (Rom. 4:5). If sinners could save themselves by their own attempts at reformation, then there was no need for the Son of God to come down to this earth and die the shameful death of the Cross!

IV. There is no Salvation by the Cultivation of Character.

There are multitudes who suppose that if they are zealous in their efforts to cultivate a noble character they have done all that God can require of them. People are taught that if they will develop a spirit of self-sacrifice, and minister in love to the needy all around them, they shall assuredly go to Heaven when they die. The popular sentiment found free expression during the recent war. It was taught that those of our soldiers who gave their lives for their country would receive an everlasting reward in glory. But these sentiments are utterly false for they one and all ignore the great sacrifice of Calvary.

My reader: you may have a noble character in the estimation of your friends, you may be sweet-tempered, loving, self-sacrificing, kind in the home, honest in business, a law-abiding citizen, a regular attender at church, yet if you are out of Christ *you are a lost sinner* on the road to eternal perdition. Make no mistake upon this point: you may be a kind husband, an indulgent father, a faithful friend, a baptized member of some orthodox denomination, and a regular partaker of the Lord's Supper, but unless you have been "born again" you are *dead in trespasses and sins,* "having no hope and without God in the world."

No amount of character culture can take the place of faith in the blood of Christ. Cain was the first "cultivator." It is written that "Cain brought of the fruit of the ground an offering unto the Lord"—it was the product of his own labors, the fruitage of his own industry. On the other hand, Abel brought unto the Lord a lamb, and we are told, "The Lord had respect unto Abel and to his offering: But unto Cain and to his offering *He had not respect*" (Gen. 4:4, 5).

V. There is no Salvation by the Consecration of Self.

It is the custom of many evangelists and revivalists at the close of their addresses to urge the unsaved to come forward to the front and take their place at what is known as the "mourners bench". Those who respond are then told to "lay their all on the altar and consecrate their lives to God." But that is not the Gospel. The Gospel of God's Grace does not command the sinner to *give* anything to God, but instead, it bids him *receive*—receive salvation as *God's* gift. But, it may be asked, Do not the Scriptures say, "I beseech you therefore, brethren, by the mercies of God, that ye present your bodies a living sacrifice, holy, acceptable unto God, which is your reasonable service" (Rom. 12:1)? The answer is, Yes, but this is addressed to saints not sinners. But again it may be asked. Does not God say, "Son, give Me thine heart"? We reply, He does, but it is to one who is already a *son* that God says this! Clearly, it is the duty and privilege of every Christian to yield himself absolutely to the Lord, to remember he is not his own but bought with a price, and, out of *gratitude,* seek whole-heartedly to please his Master and promote His glory. But this is something that no sinner can do. Man says, Try to live *as* a son and God will make you a son; but God says, First become a son thro' faith in Jesus Christ and then live as a son.

VI. There is no Salvation by the Imitation of Christ.

How often Christ is held up before sinners as the perfect Pattern, the great Examplar, the Ideal to be followed. But nowhere does Scripture present the perfect life of Christ as *the ground* of our salvation: instead, it is His atoning Death that saves—"Without shedding of blood is no remission" (Heb. 9:22). When Nicodemus asked the Lord Jesus how he could be born again, instead of telling him to keep the commandments or to imitate the life of Himself, He said, "As Moses lifted up the serpent in the wilderness, even so must the Son of Man be *lifted up*: that whosoever believeth in Him should not perish, but have eternal life" (John 3:14, 15).

Attempts to be saved by following the

example of Christ must be utterly vain. Surely a moment's reflection will show this. How impossible is it for sinners to imitate the Sinless!

VII. There is no Salvation by Association in the Church.

A preacher once asked a lady to unite with his church. She said in response, "I am not good enough." He answered, "Join the church and it will help you to become good." This idea is in the minds of many. They look upon the church as an institution for helping people to become religious, to supply their lack, to save them. Many talk about joining the church very much as they do about joining some secret order. If their names are upon the church register they believe it has something to do with their salvation. But the very worst place in the world for an unconverted person is in the church, because it gives him a sense of fancied security where there is none. Oftentimes the church becomes the very cradle of Satan to rock the deluded soul into an eternal sleep. The church is *for* saved people, not *to* save people. The order is thro' Christ to the church and not thro' the church to Christ.

Make sure then, my reader, that there is no salvation by the elimination of sin, by the education of the mind, by reformation of the life, by cultivation of character, by consecration of self, by imitation of Christ, or by association in the church. All of these *cannot* save your soul.

"What must I do to be saved?" Having disposed of the erroneous replies of man to this question let us now consider,

God's Answer:

"What must I do to be saved? *Believe on the Lord Jesus Christ,* and thou shalt be saved, and thy house" (Acts 16:30, 31). Saving faith is faith in a Person. Saving faith is believing what God has told us in His Word about His own beloved Son, and resting on Him only for salvation. We are saved thro' faith alone. It is not faith plus works, faith plus baptism, faith plus sorrowing for sin, faith plus good feelings, or faith plus anything, but a simple, naked, confident *reliance upon* the person and work of Christ.

We must distinguish between faith and *its fruits.* A living faith will bring forth living fruit. A living faith will issue in good works. A living faith will seek to please God and promote His glory. A living faith will be constrained by the love of Christ and will seek to follow His steps. But all of these are the results of faith and none of them enter into *the ground* of our salvation. We repeat, salvation is thro' faith *alone*—faith in the Lord Jesus Christ.

"Believe on the Lord Jesus Christ, and thou shalt be saved, and thy house." But what is it to "believe"? To believe on the Lord Jesus Christ is to *receive* Him—"As many as *received Him,* to them gave He power to become the sons of God, even to them that believe on His name" (John 1:12). We are to receive Him as *the only-begotten Son of God* for none but God can save. We are to receive Him as *the great Propitiation,* for God hath set Him forth "to be a propitiation thro' faith in His blood" (Rom. 3:25). We are to receive Him as *the Lamb of God,* sacrificed for sin, wounded for our transgressions and bruised for our iniquities, receiving the wages for our sins. We are to receive Him as *our Substitute*: the One who took our place, suffered in our stead, endured on our behalf the whole of wrath Divine. We are to receive Him as our *Sin-Bearer,* as the One who was "made sin for us" (2 Cor. 5:21). We are to receive Him as *the Saviour* who finished the work of atonement on the Cross. We are to receive Him as *our Lord,* yielding to His dominion, submitting to His authority, obeying His commands.

Reader, you cannot complain that the way of salvation is difficult. The only difficulty is *your unwillingness.* Will you *receive Christ* as *your* Saviour? Despise Him no longer. Delay not another moment. Receive Him *now.* It is receive or refuse. Receive Him and God will receive you *just as you are.* Receive Him and your sins shall be blotted out. Receive Him and eternal life is yours as *a free gift.* Refuse Him and you reject the best Friend for this life, the only Refuge in the hour of death, and the only Hope for eternity. "Believe on the Lord Jesus Christ, and *thou* shalt be saved." Believe not, and *thou* shalt be damned, for God says "He that believeth not shall be damned" (Mark 16:16).

Arthur W. Pink.

The above article may be obtained from the Editor in neat tract form, for 60 cents per 100, or $5.00 per 1000. Long distances, postage extra.

PETER AND THE KEYS.

It was a good confession which Peter witnessed to and for his Lord: "Thou art the Christ, the Son of the living God. And Jesus answered and said unto him, Blessed art thou, Simon Barjona: for flesh and blood hath not revealed it unto thee, but My Father which is in heaven. And I say also unto thee, that thou art Peter (Petros); and upon this rock (Petra) I will build My church; and the gates of hell shall not prevail against it. And I will give unto thee the keys of the kingdom of heaven: and whatsoever thou shalt bind on earth, shall be bound in heaven; and whatsoever thou shalt loose on earth, shall be loosed in heaven" (Matt. 16:16-19).

The honest student of the Bible will take God's Word as he finds it, and receive its teachings, whether they cut across his prejudices, his predilections, his traditional teaching, or not. His only aim will be to discover what the Book says, and to cling to it at any cost. To this end he will compare scripture with scripture, until by the aid of the Holy Spirit he arrives at the truth. Now if our Lord meant that Peter would be the foundation of the church, He contradicted all of the many passages in the Old Testament, which affirm that Jehovah alone is the Rock. He contradicts what Peter himself says when he writes, "To Whom coming, (that is, to Christ), as unto a living stone ......ye also as living stones, are built up a spiritual house" (1 Pet. 2:4, 5). He contradicts what the Holy Spirit says by Paul; "Other foundation can no man lay than that is laid, which is Jesus Christ" (1 Cor. 3:11). Peter never made any such blasphemous claims of Divine power and authority, as would be implied in believing him to be the foundation of the church; but on the other hand distinctly says to the Jews concerning Christ, "This is the stone which was set at nought of you builders, which is become the head of the corner. Neither is there salvation in any other: for there is none other name under heaven given among men, whereby we must be saved" (Acts 4:11,12).

Even Roman Catholic expositors do not regard him as the foundation in any other sense than that he was the first rock laid upon the stone. For example, Archbishop Kenrick says, "The force of the figure is: I will make thee the foundation stone of My church: in a far higher sense Christ is the foundation-stone and rock of the church". But Peter was nothing more than the other apostles in this respect, for it is written, ye "are built upon the foundation of the apostles and prophets, Jesus Christ Himself being the chief corner stone" (Eph. 2:20). Peter was *petros* of *petra*, a fragment of the stone, and upon the truth revealed to him, his recognition and confession of the person of our Lord, the church was to be built, and the gates of the unseen world should not prevail against it.

This throws light upon the meaning of the next wonderful statement, "I will give unto thee the keys of the kingdom of heaven: and whatsoever thou shalt bind on earth, shall be bound in heaven", etc. Whatever authority is implied by this, it is certainly not confined to Peter, for soon afterwards we find that he addressed *all* of the apostles in almost precisely the same language: "Whatsoever ye shall bind on earth, shall be bound in heaven; and whatsoever ye shall loose on earth, shall be loosed in heaven" (Matt. 18:18). So after His resurrection, He said to all the disciples except Thomas, who was absent, "Whose soever sins ye remit, they are remitted unto them; and whose soever sins ye retain, they are retained" (John 20:23). There is no difference, therefore, between Peter and the other apostles in this respect also.

But most persons in reading the passage over-look the fact that the Lord gave to Peter the keys *of the kingdom of heaven*, not the church, which is plainly distinguished from the kingdom in the preceding verse. This phrase "the kingdom of heaven", is found nowhere out of Matthew, which is the Gospel of the King of the Jews. It refers to the kingdom of heaven, mentioned in Daniel, when dominion was taken from the unfaithful Jews, and transferred to the Gentiles. It is never spoken of in the New Testament as having come, but only as "nigh". The promised King appeared, but they would not receive Him; and hence the promised kingdom exists in mystery and patience now, to be manifested in glory and power hereafter.

The kingdom of heaven never means the church nor heaven itself. If it meant either, one might imagine a pope, though even in that case it would be impossible to imagine a successor of the apostles, because an apostle must have seen the Lord, he must have received his commission directly from the risen Christ, he must be endowed with miraculous gifts, and his words must be inspired by the Holy Spirit. The kingdom of heaven in its state of mystery answers to the present dispensation, and hence our Lord likens it to that which contains tares as well as wheat, defiling birds of the air as well as a great tree, the hidden working of false doctrine as well as the truth, bad fish as well as good, foolish virgins as well as wise, the slothful servant as well as the faithful. When the risen Jesus ascended into heaven, waiting the times and seasons which the Father hath put under His own authority for the restoration of the kingdom to Israel, (Acts 1:7), God brought in a new economy, as a preparatory stage, to that future kingdom. This is the kingdom of heaven not yet revealed, or continuing for a time in mystery.

The keys of the kingdom of heaven in this sense, and in this sense only, were committed to Peter. One of them he used on the day of Pentecost, when he opened the doors to the Jews; the other he used when he opened the doors to the Gentiles—Cornelius and his household. He also used them when he excluded Annanias and Sapphira and Simon Magus (Acts 5; 8). But after this he retires from the scene, and we hear of him no more. If a man is baptized, he enters the kingdom of heaven, even though he turns out to be a hypocrite. He will never enter heaven, of course, if he remains an unbeliever, but he is in the kingdom of heaven. Whatever Peter did, whatever the other apostles did, whatever those now do who speak for Christ, when they act in His Name, and in the power of the Holy Spirit, is ratified in heaven.

—James H. Brookes.

During his residence at Antwerp, William Tyndal, sent over a letter to Mr. Frith, (then a prisoner in the London Tower, and afterwards a martyr) exhorting him to fortitude under his sufferings for the name of Christ. And this, in part, is what this Flemish martyr wrote: "The will of God be fulfilled! and what He hath ordained to do, ere the world was made, that come, and His glory reign over all. There falleth not an hair, till God's hour be come: and when His hour is come, necessity carrieth us hence, though we be not willing. Be cheerful; and remember, that among the hard-hearted in England, there is a number reserved by grace; for whose sakes, if need be, you must be ready to suffer. —William Tyndal, 1535 A.D.

The man Christ Jesus, being formed without sin, and by the immediate agency of the Holy Ghost, was doubtless transcendently fair and augustly beautiful Hence His human nature was compared to the Temple: a structure eminently holy, and peculiarly elegant. Prior to His sufferings, He was, literally, fairer than the children of men. It was not till His blessed person had been disfigured with wounds and emaciated with grief; until His face was foul with weeping, and on His eye-lids sat the shadow of death; that He is said to have had neither form nor comeliness; but that His face was marred more than any man's, and His countenance than the sons of men.

—August Toplady, 1768. Author of "Rock of Ages".

To New Readers: The twelve copies of 1922, and the twelve of 1923, neatly bound, may be had for $1.50 each. They contain articles by the Editor on The Blood, Eternal Punishment, Second Coming of Christ, The Sabbath, Romans 7, The Antichrist, and Expositions of John's Gospel from the first verse. We have only a limited supply.

To Foreign Subscribers: Please send **only** International Money Orders, made out to the Editor.

(Continued from page 73.)

born the first time I received from my parents their nature: so, when I was born again, I received from God His nature. The Spirit of God begets within us a spiritual nature: as we read in 2 Pet. 1:4, "Whereby are given unto us exceeding great and precious promises: that by these ye might be partakers of the Divine nature".

Here, then, is the character or nature of the new birth. It is not the reformation of the outward man, it is not the education of the natural man, it is not the purification of the old man, but it is the creation of a new man. It is a Divine begetting (James 1:18). It is a birth of the Spirit (John 3:6). It is a being made a new creation (2 Cor. 5:17). It is becoming a partaker of the Divine nature (2 Pet. 1:4). It is a being born into God's family. Every born again person has, therefore, two natures within him: one which is spiritual, the other which is carnal. These two natures are contrary the one to the other (Gal. 5:17), and in consequence, there is an unceasing warfare going on within the Christian. It is only the grace of God which can subdue the old nature; and it is only the Word of God which can feed the new nature.

Above, we have referred to the discouragement found in many young believers because of the discovery made that not only did not the new birth change or improve the old nature, but that the old nature now seems worse than formerly. Really, it is not, but the believer is now far more *conscious* of its evil character. When am I the most conscious of the grime and dust in a dirty room—when the blinds are drawn, or when they are raised? Manifestly, the latter. The more the light floods that room the more evident is its uncleanness. It is the same with the believer. Before he was born again, the windows of his understanding were darkened, and to a large extent he was unaware of the deceitfulness and wickedness of his heart. But when he was born again the Spirit of God took up His abode in the believer, and the presence of the Holy Spirit illumines, and reveals the awful effects of the Fall, and the terrible depravity of the natural man.

What, then, should be the effect of this? Discouragement and despair? No, indeed. The discovery of the sinful nature within me, and the realization that I have no strength of my own to cope with it, should drive me to my knees, daily, to earnestly seek from God that grace which He declares is "sufficient".

But more. I not only need the grace of God to enable me to "keep under my body", to "resist the Devil", and to "flee youthful lusts", but I also need the Word of God to feed that new nature within me which has been born of Him: "As newborn babes, desire the sincere milk of the Word that ye may grow thereby" (1 Pet. 2:2). It is only as I feed daily on the Heavenly Manna, it is only as I diligently seek from God that portion which my soul needs, that I shall "grow in grace, and in the knowledge of our Lord and Saviour Jesus Christ", and become "strong in the Lord and in the power of His might".

Arthur W. Pink.

VOL. III MAY, 1924 No. 5

STUDIES in the SCRIPTURES

"Search the Scriptures" John 5:39.

A PERIODICAL (MONTHLY "IF THE LORD WILL") DEVOTED TO BIBLE STUDIES and EXPOSITIONS

Arthur W. Pink, Publisher & Editor,
227 N. Creighton St., Philadelphia, Pa.

Price: 10 cents per copy; $1.00 per year. Foreign $1.00 per year.

A MESSAGE OF COMFORT.

"FOR OUR LIGHT AFFLICTION, WHICH IS BUT FOR A MOMENT, WORKETH FOR US A FAR MORE EXCEEDING AND ETERNAL WEIGHT OF GLORY" (2 COR. 4:17).

These words supply us with a reason why we should not faint under trials nor be overwhelmed by misfortunes. They teach us to look at the trials of time in the light of eternity. They affirm that the present buffetings of the Christian exercise a beneficient effect on the inner man. If these truths were firmly grasped by faith they would mitigate much of the bitterness of our sorrows.

"For our light affliction, which is but for a moment, worketh for us a far more exceeding and eternal weight of glory". This verse sets forth a striking and glorious antithesis, as it contrasts our future state with our present. Here there is "affliction", there "glory". Here there is a "light affliction", there a "weight of glory". Here there is "momentary affliction", there "eternal glory". In our affliction there is both levity and brevity; it is a light affliction, and it is but for a moment; in our future glory there is solidity and eternity! To discover the preciousness of this contrast let us consider, separately, each member, but in the inverse order of mention.

1 "A far more exceeding and eternal weight of glory". It is a significant thing that the Hebrew word for "glory"—kabod—also means "weight". When weight is added to the value of gold or precious stones this increases their worth. Heaven's happiness cannot be told out in the words of earth; figurative expressions are best calculated to convey some imperfect views to us. Here in our text one term is piled up on top of another. That which awaits the believer is "glory", and when we say that a thing is *glorious* we have reached the limits of human language to express that which is excellent and perfect. But the "glory" awaiting us is weighted, yea it is "far more exceeding" weighty than anything terrestrial and temporal; its value defies computation; its transcendent excellency is beyond verbal description. Moreover, this wondrous glory awaiting us is not evanescent and temporal, but divine and eternal; for "eternal" it could not be unless it were divine. The great and blessed God is going to give us that which is worthy of Himself, yea that which is like Himself—infinite and everlasting.

2 "Our light affliction, which is but for a moment". (1) "Affliction" is the common lot of human existence; "Man is born unto trouble as the sparks fly upward" (Job 5:7). This is part of the entail of sin. It is not meet that a fallen creature should be perfectly happy in his sins. Nor are the children of God exempted; "Through *much* tribulation *we* must enter into the kingdom of God". (Acts 14:22). By a hard and rugged road does God lead us to glory and immortality.

(2) Our affliction is "light". Afflictions are not light in themselves for ofttimes they are heavy and grievous; but they are light comparatively! They are light when compared with what we really deserve. They are light when compared with the sufferings of the Lord Jesus. They are light when compared with the torments of the damned. But perhaps their real lightness is

(Continued on page 120.)

IMPORTANT NOTICES

All new subscriptions will be dated back to January, 1924.

Set of twelve issues for **1922**, unbound, **$1.00**. Bound, **$1.50**.

Set of twelve issues for **1923**, unbound, **$1.00**. Bound **$1.50**.

Note: We cannot break a set or now supply any **single** 1923 issues.

Subscription Price: **$1.00** per year to any address in the world. Single copies **10 cents.**

Change of Address: Please notify me promptly of any change of address, and be certain to give both old and new addresses.

Non-subscribers receiving this Magazine regularly will understand their subscription has been entered by a friend.

Copies lost in the mail duplicated only if we are notified promptly.

Entered as second-class matter December 15th, 1923, at the post office at Philadelphia, Pa., under Act of March 3rd, 1879.

CONTENTS

JOHN'S GOSPEL.

29. CHRIST, THE LIGHT OF THE WORLD: John 8:12-32.

The following is a Summary of the passage which is to be before us:—

1. Christ the Light of the world: v. 12.
2. The Pharisees' denial: v. 13.
3. Christ enforces His claim to absolute Deity: vv. 14-18.
4. The Pharisees' question and Christ's reply: vv. 19, 20.
5. Christ's solemn warning to the Pharisees: vv. 21-24.
6. The Pharisees' question and Christ's reply: vv. 25-29.
7. The many who "believed" and Christ's warning to them: vv. 30-32.

The first division of John 8 forms a most striking and suitable introduction to the first verse of our present lesson, which, in turn, supplies the key to what follows in the remainder of the chapter. The Holy Spirit records here one of the precious discourses of "The Wonderful Counsellor", a discourse broken by the repeated interruptions of His enemies. Christ announces Himself as "The Light of the world", but this is prefaced by an incident which gives wonderful force to that utterance.

As we saw in our last lesson, the first eleven verses of John 8 describe a venomous assault made upon the Saviour by the scribes and Pharisees. A determined effort was made to discredit Him before the people. A woman taken in adultery was brought, the penalty of the Mosaic law was defined, and then the question was put to Christ, *"but* what sayest *Thou?"*. We are not left to speculate as to their motive: the passage tells us "This they said, tempting Him, that they might have *to accuse* Him". Think of it! They imagined that they could substantiate an accusation against the Law-giver Himself! What perversity: what blindness: what depravity! Yet how effectively this serves as a *dark* back-ground on which to display, the better, "the Light"! Nor is that all that this introduction effected.

In our exposition of these verses we intimated that what was there presented to Christ was the problem—altogether too profound for creature wisdom—of how to harmonize justice and mercy. The woman was guilty; of that there could be no doubt. The sentence of the law was plainly defined. What reply, then, could Christ make to the open challenge, "What sayest Thou?". There is little need for us to repeat what was said in the previous article, though the theme is a most captivating one. By symbolic action our Lord showed that it was not the Divine intention for mercy to be exercised at the expense of justice. He intimated that the law would be enforced. But by writing on the ground the *second* time, He reminded His would-be accusers that a shelter from the exposed law was planned, and that a blood-sprinkled covering would protect the guilty one from its accusing voice. Thus did the Redeemer intimate that God's *righteousness* would be magnified in the Divine method of saving sinners, and that His *holiness* would shine forth with unsullied splendor. And *"light"* is the emblem of holiness and righteousness! Fitting introduction, then, was this for our Lord's announcement of Himself as "the *Light* of the world".

But not only did the malice of the Lord's enemies supply a dark back-ground to bring into welcome relief the outshining of the Divine Light; not only did their attack supply Christ with an opportunity for Him to manifest Himself as the Vindicator of God's holiness and righteousness; but we may also discover a further reason for the Holy Spirit describing this incident at the beginning of our chapter. Following His symbolic action of writing on the ground, the Lord uttered one brief sentence, and one only, to His tempters, but that one was quite sufficient to rout them completely. "He that is without sin among you, let him first cast a stone at her", was what He said. The effect was startling: "Being convicted by their conscience" they "went out one by one, beginning at the eldest, even unto the last: and Jesus was left alone, and the woman standing in the midst". It was the holy "light" of God which smote their sin-darkened understandings, and their departure demonstrated the *power* of that light! Observe, too, the words of Christ to the adulterous woman: "Go", He said, *not* "in peace"; but "GO, and *sin no more*". How that evidenced the spotless *purity* of "the Light"! Thus we see, once more, the great importance of studying and weighing the *context;* for here, as everywhere, it gives meaning to what follows.

"Then spake Jesus again unto them" (v. 12). *"Then"* signifies after the departure of the Pharisees and after the adulterous woman had gone. "Then spake Jesus again *unto them*". This takes us back to the second verse of our chapter, where we are told that in the early morning Christ entered the temple, and, as all the people came unto Him, He sat down and taught them. Now, after the rude interruption from certain of the scribes and Pharisees, He resumed His teaching of the people, and spake "again unto them". And herein we may discover, once more, the perfections of the God-man. The disagreeable interruption had in no wise disturbed His composure. Though fully aware of the malignant design of the Pharisees, He possessed His soul in patience. Without exhibiting the slightest perturbation, refusing to be turned aside from the task He was engaged in, He returned at once to the teaching of the people. How differently *we* act under provocation! To us disturbances are only too frequently perturbances. If only we realized that *everything* which enters our life is ordered by God, and we acted in accord with this, then should we maintain our composure and conduct ourselves with unruffled serenity. But only one perfect life has been lived on this earth; and our innumerable imperfections only serve to emphasize the *uniqueness* of that life.

"Then spake Jesus again unto them, saying, I am the light of the world" (v. 12). This is the second of the "I am" titles of Christ found in this fourth Gospel. It calls for most careful consideration. We may observe, in the first place, that this announcement by Christ was in full accord with the Old Testament prophecies concerning the Messiah. Through Isaiah God said concerning the Coming One, "I the Lord have called Thee in righteousness, and will hold Thine hand, and will keep Thee, and give Thee for a covenant of the people, for *a light* of the Gentiles" (42:6). And again, "And He said, It is a light thing that Thou shouldest be My servant to raise up the tribes of Jacob, and to restore the preserved of Israel: I will also give Thee for *a light* to the Gentiles, that Thou mayest be My salvation unto the end of the earth" (49:6). And again, He was denominated "the *Sun* of righteousness" who should arise "with healing in His wings" or "beams" (Mal. 4:2).

"I am the light of the world". We may notice, in the second place, that "light" is one of the three things which God is said to be. In John 4:24 we are told, "God is *Spirit*". In 1 John 1:5, "God is *light*"; and in 1 John 4:8, "God is *love*". These expressions relate to the *nature* of God, what He is in Himself. Hence, when Christ affirmed "I am *the light* of the world", He announced His absolute Deity. Believers are said to be "light *in the Lord* (Eph. 5:8). But Christ Himself *was* "the Light".

But what is meant by "I am the light *of the world*"? Does this mean that Christ is the Light of the whole human race, of every man and woman? If so, does this prove that Universalism is true? Certainly not. The second part of our verse disproves Universalism: it is only the one who "follows" Christ that has "the light of life". The one who does not "follow" Christ remains in darkness. The words of Christ in John 12:46 supply further repudiation of Universalism: "I am come a light into the world, that whosoever *believeth on Me* should not abide in darkness". But if "I am the light of the world" does not teach Universalism, what does it mean? We believe that its force will best be ascertained by comparing John 1:4, 5, 9. As we have given an exposition of these verses in the second article of this series, we would ask the reader to turn to it. Suffice it now to say we understand that "light" in these passages is not to be restricted to the spiritual illumination enjoyed by believers, but is to be taken in its widest signification. If John 1:4 be linked with the preceding verse (as it should be), it will be seen that the reference is to the relation sustained by the *Creator* to "men". The "light" which lightens every man that cometh into the world is that which constitutes him a rational being. Every rational creature is *morally* enlightened. Christ is the Light of the world in the widest possible sense, inasmuch as all creature intelligence and all moral perception proceed from Him.

Perhaps it may be well to ask here, Why is it that "the world" is mentioned so frequently in this fourth Gospel? The "world" occurs only fifteen times in the first three Gospels added together; whereas in John it is found seventy-seven times! Why is this? The answer is not far to seek. In this fourth Gospel we have a presentation of what Christ is *essentially* in His own person, and not what He was in *special* relation to the Jews, as in the other Gospels. John treats of the *Deity* of Christ, and as God He is the Creator of all (1:3), and therefore the life and light of His creatures (1:4). It is true that in a number of instances "the world" has a restricted meaning, but these are not difficult to determine: either the context or parallel passages show us when the term is to be understood in its narrower sense. The principle of interpretation is not an arbitrary one. When something is predicated of "the world" which is true only of the redeemed, then we know it is only *the world of believers* which is in view: for instance, Christ giving (not proffering) life—here *eternal* life as the context shows—unto the world (John 6:33). But when there is nothing that is predicated of "the world" which is true *only* of believers, then it is "the world of the ungodly" (2 Pet. 2:5) which is in view.

"He that followeth Me shall not walk in darkness, but shall have the light of life" (v. 12). At first glance this clause will seem, perhaps, to conflict with the definition we have given of "light" in the first part of the verse. "I am the light of the world" we understand to signify (in accord with John 1:4, 5, 9), I am the One who has bestowed intelligence and moral sensibility on all men. But now Christ says (by necessary implication) that unless a man "follows" Him he will "walk in *darkness*". But instead of conflicting with what we have said above, the second part of v. 12 will be found, on careful reflection, to confirm it. "He that followeth Me" said our Lord, "shall not walk in darkness (Greek, "the darkness"), but shall", shall what? "enjoy the light"? No, "shall have the light of life". These words point a contrast. In the former sentence He spoke of Himself as the *moral* light of men; in the second He refers to the *spiritual* light which is possessed by believers only. This is clear from the expression used: he "shall have" not merely "light"—which all rational creatures possess; but "he shall have the light *of life*", that is, of spiritual, Divine light, which is something possessed only by those who "follow" Christ.

"He that followeth Me shall not walk in darkness, but shall have the light of life" (v. 12). In these words, then, Christ defined the state of the natural man. The unregenerate *have* "light": they are capable of weighing moral issues; they have a conscience which either "accuses or excuses them" (Rom. 2:15); and they have the capacity to recognize the innumerable evidences which testify to the existence and natural attributes of the great Creator (Rom. 1:19); so that "they are without excuse" (Rom. 1:20). But *spiritual* light they do not have. Consequently, though they are endowed with intelligence and moral discernment, spiritually, they are "in the darkness". And it was because of this that the Saviour said, "He that followeth Me shall not walk in the darkness, but shall have the light of life". The necessary implication of these words is that the world *is in* spiritual darkness. It was so two thousand years ago. The Greeks with all their wisdom and the Romans with all their laws were spiritually in the dark. And the world is the same today. Notwithstanding all the discoveries of science and all the efforts to educate, Europe and America are in the dark. The great crowds see not the true character of God, the worth of their souls, the reality of the world to come. And *Christ* is the only hope. He has risen like the sun, to diffuse life and light, salvation and peace, in the midst of a dark world.

"He that followeth Me shall not walk in darkness, but shall have the light of life" (v. 12). What is it to "follow" Christ? It is to commit ourselves unreservedly to Him as our only Saviour and Lord in doctrine and conduct (see 1:37 and contrast 10:5). A beautiful illustration (borrowed from Bishop Ryle) of this is to be found in the history of Israel in the wilderness as they followed the "Cloud". Just as the "Cloud" led Israel from Egypt to Canaan, so the Lord Jesus leads the believer from this world to heaven. And to the one who really follows Christ the promise is, he "shall not, like those all around him, walk in darkness. "Light", in Scripture, is sometimes the emblem of true knowledge, true holiness, true happiness; while "darkness" is the figure for ignorance and error, guilt and depravity, privation and misery. Because the believer follows the One who is Light, he does not grope his way in doubt and uncertainty, but he sees where he is going, and not only so, he enjoys the light of God's countenance. But this is his experience only so far as he really "follows" Christ. Just as if it were possible to follow the sun in its complete circuit, we should always be in broad day-light, so the one who is actually following Christ shall not walk in darkness.

"The Pharisees therefore said unto Him, Thou bearest record of Thyself; Thy record is not true" (v. 13). Christ had just made the fullest claim to Deity: when He said "I am the Light of the world" the Pharisees could not understand Him to mean anything less; Jehovah-Elohim was the God of light, as numerous passages in the Old Testament plainly taught. When Jesus made this asservation the Pharisees *therefore* said, "Thou bearest record of Thyself; Thy record is not true." The force of their objection seems to be this: That *God* is the Light of the world we fully allow, but when *you* avow this of yourself we cannot accredit it; what you say is false.

"The *Pharisees* therefore said unto Him" (v. 13). Evidently these were a different company of Pharisees than those who had brought in the adulteress. Enraged by the discomforture of their brethren, their fellows insultingly said to the Lord, Thy record is not true. They shrank from the Light. They could not endure the holy purity of its beams. They desired only to extinguish it. How solemnly this illustrated John 1:5—"The Light shineth in darkness, and the darkness comprehended it not"!

"Jesus answered and said unto them, Though I bear record of Myself, yet My record is true: for I know whence I came, and whither I go; but ye cannot tell whence I come, and whither I go" (v. 13). Here the Lord tersely replies to the unbelieving denial of the Pharisees, and ratifies what He had said just previously. Though My Divine glory is now veiled, though at present I am not exercising My Divine prerogatives, though I stand before you in *servant* form, nevertheless, when I affirmed that I am the Light of the world I spoke the truth. My record *is* true because "I know whence I came and whither I go", which is a knowledge possessed absolutely by none else. He had come from the Father in heaven, and thither He would return; and therefore, as the Son, He could not give a false witness. But as to His heavenly nature and character they were in complete ignorance, and therefore altogether incompetent to form, and still less to pass, a judgment.

"Though I bear record of Myself yet My record is true" (v. 14). Some have experienced a difficulty in harmonizing this with what we read of in 5:31—"If I bear witness of Myself, My witness is not true". But if each of these statements be interpreted in strict accord with the context the difficulty vanishes. In John 5 the Lord was proving that the witness or record He bore was not in *independence* of the Father, but in perfect accord therewith. The Father Himself (5:37) and the Scriptures inspired by the Father (5:39) *also* testified to the absolute Deity of Christ. But here in John 8 the Lord Jesus is making *direct* reply to the Pharisees who had said that His witness was false. This He denies, and insists that it was true; and immediately after He appeals again to the confirmatory witness of the Father (see 8:18).

"Ye judge after the flesh; I judge no man" (v. 15). We believe that there is a double thought here. When Christ said "Ye judge after (according to) the flesh", He meant, we think, first, You are deciding

My claims according to what you see; you are judging according to outward appearances. Because I am in the likeness of sinful flesh you deem it impossible for *Me* to be "the Light of the world". But appearances are deceptive. I do not form My judgments thus: I look on the heart, and see things as they actually are. But again; when Christ said: "Ye judge after the flesh", this was to affirm that they were *incapable* of judging Him. They adopted the world's principles, and judged according to carnal reasoning. Because of this they were incapable of discerning the Divine nature of His mission and message.

"I *judge* no man" has been variously interpreted. Many understand it to signify that Christ here reminded His critics that He was not then exercising His judicial prerogatives. It is regarded as being parallel with the last clause of John 12:47. But we think it is more natural, and better suited to the context, to supply an ellipsis, and understand Christ here to mean, *I do not* judge any man after the flesh; when I judge it is according to spiritual and Divine principles. The Greek word signifies "to determine, to form an estimate, to arrive at a decision", and here it has precisely the same force in each clause. When Christ said to these Pharisees, "Ye *judge* after the flesh", He did not refer to a judicial verdict, for He was not then replying to some formal pronouncement of the Sanhedrim. Instead, He meant, You have *formed your estimate* of Me after the flesh, but not so do I form My estimates.

"And yet if I judge, My judgment is true: for I am not alone, but I and the Father that sent Me" (v. 16). This confirms what we have just said upon the last clause of the previous verse. "If I judge", or better, "*when* I judge", *My* judgment is true. *You* may determine according to carnal principles; but I do not. I act on spiritual principles. I judge not according to appearances, but according to reality. My judgment is according to truth, for it is the judgment *of God*—"I am not alone, but I and the Father that sent Me". This was a full claim to Deity. It affirmed the absolute oneness of the Son with the Father. This statement of Christ's is parallel with the one He made later: "I and Father are one" (John 10:30). He speaks here in John 8 of the Divine wisdom which is *common* to the Father and the Son. This being so, how could His judgment be anything but true?

"It is also written in your law, that the testimony of two men is true. I am one that bear witness of Myself, and the Father that sent Me beareth witness of Me" (vv. 17, 18). Here Christ repeats in another form what He had just affirmed. His testimony was not unsupported. The Mosaic law required two witnesses to establish the truth. The present case was not one where this law was strictly applicable; nevertheless, the circumstances of it were in fullest accord therewith. Christ bore personal witness to His Divine person and mission, and the Father also bore witness thereto. *How* the Father bore witness to the Son was before us in the fifth chapter of this Gospel. He bore witness to Him in the prophecies of the Old Testament, which were now so gloriously fulfilled in His character, teaching, actions, and even in His very rejection by men. The Father had borne witness to the Son through the testimony of His servant, John the Baptist (see John 1). He had borne witness to Him at the Jordan, on the occasion of His baptism. Thus by the principles of their own law these Pharisees were *condemned.* Two witnesses established the truth, but here *were* two Witnesses, the Father and the Son, and yet they rejected the truth! It was not, as several of the commentators have thought, that Christ was here *appealing to* the law in order to *vindicate* Himself. His manifest purpose was to condemn *them,* and that is why He says, "*your* law" rather than "*the* law".

"Then said they unto Him, Where is Thy Father? Jesus answered, Ye neither know Me, nor My Father: if ye had known Me, ye should have known My Father also" (v. 19). How the Light revealed the hidden things of darkness! Christ had appealed to the testimony of the Father, but so obtuse were these Pharisees, they asked, "Where is Thy Father?". In our Lord's answer to them we are shown once more how that none can know the Father save through and by the Son. As He declared on another occasion, "Neither knoweth any man the Father, save the Son, and he to whomsoever the Son will *reveal Him*" (Matt. 11:27).

"These words spake Jesus in the treasury, as He taught in the temple: and no man laid hands on Him; for His hour was not yet come" (v. 20). "The treasury was in the forecourt of the women, in which were placed thirteen bronze chests, to receive the taxes and free-will offerings of the people. The mention of the treasury here would be quite in keeping with the genuineness of the history of the woman taken in adultery. To the court of the women only could she have been brought to meet the Lord. Of these chests, nine were for legal payment of the worshippers, and four for free-will offerings" (C.E.S. from Barclay's Talmud).

"And no man laid hands on Him: for His hour was not yet come" (v. 20). This plainly intimates that the Pharisees were greatly incensed at what Christ had said, and had it been possible they would have at once subjected him to violence. But it was not possible, and never would have been unless God had withdrawn His restraining hand. It is indeed striking to note how this feature is repeated again and again in the fourth Gospel, see 7:30; 7:44; 8:59; and 10:39, etc. These passages show that men were unable to work out their evil designs until God permitted them to do so. They demonstrate that God is complete master of all; and they prove that the sufferings Christ did undergo were endured voluntarily.

"Then said Jesus again unto them, I go My way, and ye shall seek Me, and shall die in your sins" (v. 21). The word "again" looks back to 7:33, 34, where on a previous occasion Christ had made a similar statement. "I go My way" signifies I shall very shortly leave you. It was a solemn word of warning. "And ye shall seek Me, and shall die in your sins". Christ here addressed these Pharisees as the representatives of the Nation, and looked forward to the sore trials before it. In but a few years, Israel would suffer an affliction far heavier than any they had experienced before; and when that time came, they would seek the delivering help of their promised Messiah, but it would be in vain. Having refused the Light they would continue in the darkness. Having despised the Saviour, they should "die in their sins". Having rejected the Son of God, it would be impossible for them to come whither He had gone.

"Ye shall seek Me, and shall die in your sins". It is unspeakably solemn that these words have a present application. How dreadful! that the Saviour may be sought, but *sought in vain.* A man may have religious feelings about Christ, even weep at the thought of His Cross, and yet have no saving acquaintance with Him. Sickness, the fear of death, a serious financial reverse, the drying up of creature-sources of comfort—these frequently draw out much religiousness. Under a little pressure a man will say his prayers, read his Bible, become active in church work, profess to seek Christ, and become quite a different character; but only too often such an one is but reformed, and not transformed. And frequently this is made apparent in this world. Let the pressure be removed, let health return, let there be a change of circumstances, and how often we behold the zealous professor returning to his old ways. Such an one may have "sought" Christ, but because his motive was wrong, because it was not the effect of a deep conviction of being lost and undone, his seeking was in vain.

"Ye shall seek Me, and shall die in your sins". Far more solemn is the application of these words to a class of people today which we greatly fear is by no means a small one. How many there are who, under the superficial and temporary influence of the modern Evangelistic Meetings, come forward to the front seeking Christ. For the moment, many of them, no doubt, are in earnest; and yet the sequel proves that they sought in vain. Why is this? Two answers may be returned. First, with some, it is because they were not in dead earnest. Of old God said, "Ye shall seek Me, and *find* Me, when ye shall search for Me *with all* your heart" (Jer. 29:13). Second, with others, and with by far the greater number, it is because they do not seek *in the right place.* The seeker in the average Meeting is exhorted to "lay his all upon the altar", or is told that he must "pray through". But Christ is not to be found by either of these means. *"Search the Scriptures"*, was the word of the Saviour Himself, and the reason given was, "they are they which testify of Me". In the volume of the book it is written of Christ. It is in the written Word that the incarnate Word is to be found.

"Ye shall seek Me, and shall die in your sins". These words will yet have a further application to a coming day, when it will be *too late* to find Christ. Then the "door" will be shut. Then sinners will call upon God but He will not answer; they shall seek the Lord, but they shall not find Him (Prov. 1:28, etc.).

"Whither I go, ye cannot come" (v. 21). Not "ye shall not come", but "ye *cannot* come". Cannot because the *holiness* of God makes it impossible: that which is corrupt and vile cannot dwell with Him; there can be no communion between light and darkness. Cannot because the *righteousness* of God makes it impossible. Sin must be punished; the penalty of the broken law must be enforced; and for the reprobate "there remaineth no more sacrifice for sins". Cannot because they have *no character* suited to the place whither Christ has gone. In the very nature of the case every man must go to "his *own* place" (Acts 1:25), the place for which he is fitted. If, by grace, he has the nature of God, then later on he will go and dwell with Him (John 13:36); but if he passes out of this world *"dead* in sins" then, of necessity, he will yet be cast into the Lake of Fire, "which is the Second Death" (Rev. 20:14). If a man *dies* "in his sins" he *cannot* enter heaven. How completely this shatters the "Larger Hope"!

"Then said the Jews. Will He kill Himself? because He saith, Whither I go, ye cannot come?" (v. 22). The Pharisees replied with profane levity, and with an impious sneer. This is frequently the resort of a defeated opponent: when unable to refute solid argument, he will avail himself of ridicule. With what infinite grace did our Lord forbear with His enemies!

"And He said unto them, Ye are from beneath; I am from above: ye are of this world; I am not of this world" (v. 23). There seems to be a double thought conveyed by these words. First, Christ pointed out the reason or cause why they understood not His words and received not His witness. There was an infinite gulf separating Him from them: they were from beneath, He was from above. Second, Christ explained *why* it was that whither He was going they could not come. They belonged to two totally different spheres: they were of the world, He was not of the world. The friendship of the world is enmity against God, how then could they who were not only in the world, but *of it,* enter heaven, which was His home?

"I said therefore unto you, that ye shall die in your sins: for if ye believe not that I am, ye shall die in your sins" (v. 24). How terrible is the end of unbelief! The one who persists in his rejection of the Christ of God will die in his sins, unpardoned, unfit for heaven, unprepared to meet God! How unspeakably solemn is this! How little are we impressed by these fearful words, "die in your sins"—true of the vast majority of our fellows as they pass out of this world into an hopeless eternity. And how sadly mistaken are they who say that it is harsh and uncharitable to speak of the future destiny of unbelievers. The example of Christ should teach us better. *He* did not hesitate to press this awful truth, nor should we. In the light of God's Word it is criminal to remain silent. In the judgment of the writer this is the one truth which above all others needs to be pressed today. Men will not turn to Christ until they recognize their imminent danger of the wrath to come.

"Ye shall die in your sins." This is one of many verses which exposes a modern error concerning the Atonement. There are some who teach that on the Cross Christ bore all the sins of all men. They insist that the entire question of sin was dealt with and settled at Calvary. They declare that the *only* thing which will now send any man to hell, is his rejection of Christ. But such teaching is entirely unscriptural. Christ bore all the sins *of believers,* but for the sins of unbelievers *no* atonement was made. And one of the many proofs of this is furnished by John 8:24: "Ye shall die in your *sins*" could never have been said if the Lord Jesus removed *all* sins from before God*.

"Then said they unto Him, Who art Thou? And Jesus said unto them, Even the same that I said unto you from the beginning". (v. 25). We believe that this is given much more accurately in the R. V., especially the marginal rendering: "They said therefore unto Him, Who art Thou? Jesus said unto them, *Altogether that which I also speak unto you*". This was a remarkable utterance. The Pharisees had objected that Christ's witness of Himself was not true (v. 13). The Lord replied that His witness *was* true, and he proved it by an appeal to the corroborative witness of the Father. Now they ask, "Who art Thou?". And the incarnate Son of God answered, I am essentially and absolutely that which

* See the author's booklet on "The Atonement". 5 cents. From The Editor.

I have declared Myself to be. I have spoken of "light": *I am* that Light. I have spoken of "truth": *I am* that Truth. I am the very incarnation, personification, exemplification of them. Wondrous declaration is this! None but He could really say, I am Myself that of which I am speaking to you. The child of God may speak the truth and walk in the truth, but he is not the Truth itself. A Christian may let his light "shine", but he is not the Light itself. But Christ was, and therein we perceive His exalted uniqueness. As we read in 1 John 5:20, "We know that the Son of God is come, and hath given us an understanding, that we may know Him that is true," not "Him who taught the truth", but "Him that is true".

"I have many things to say and to judge of you: but He that sent Me is true; and I speak to the world those things which I have heard of Him" (v. 26). As nearly as we can gather, the force of this verse is as follows: Your incredulity is very reprehensible, and your insulting sneers deserve the severest censure, but I forbear. If Christ had dealt with these insulting opponents as they thoroughly merited, not only would He have upbraided them, but He would have passed an immediate sentence of condemnation upon them. Instead of doing so, He contented Himself by affirming once more that the witness He bore of Himself was true, because it was in the most perfect accord with what the Father Himself had said. Perfect example for us. Whenever the servant of Christ is criticized and challenged because of the message he brings, let him learn of his Master, who was meek and lowly in heart. Instead of passing sentence of condemnation on your detractors, simply press upon them the eternal veracity of Him in whose name you speak.

"They understood not that He spake to them of the Father" (v. 27). O the blinding power of prejudice; the darkness of unbelief! How solemnly this reveals the woeful condition that the natural man is in. Unable to understand even when the Son of God was preaching to them! "Except a man be born again he *cannot* see". And this is the condition of *every man* by nature. Spiritually, the unregenerate American is in precisely the same darkness that the heathen are in, for both are in *the darkness of death!* Men need something more than external light; they need *inward* illumination. One may sit all his life under the soundest Gospel ministry, and at the end, understand no more *with the heart* than those in Africa who have never heard the Gospel. Let these solemn words be duly weighed—"they *understood not*", understood not the words which none other than the Son of God was saying to them! Then let every reader who *knows* that he is saved, praise God fervently because He "hath *given us an understanding,* that we may know Him that is true" (1 John 5:20).

"Then said Jesus unto them, When ye have lifted up the Son of man, then shall ye know that I am, and that I do nothing of Myself; but as My Father has taught Me, I speak these things" (v. 28). His "lifting up" referred to His approaching death and the manner of it, see John 12:32, 33. "Then shall ye know that I am" intimated that the crucifixion would be accompanied and followed by such manifestations of His Divine glory that He would be fully vindicated, and many would be convinced that He was indeed the Messiah, and that He had done and said only what He had been commissioned by the Father to do and say. How strikingly was this word of Christ verified on the day of Pentecost! Thousands, then, of the very ones who had cried, "Crucify Him", were brought to believe on Him as "both Lord and Christ".

"And He that sent Me is with Me: the Father hath not left Me alone; for I do always those things which please Him" (v. 29). "Whatever opinion men might form of His doctrines or conduct, He knew that in all He said, and in all He did, He was the Father's elect servant upheld and delighted in by Him—His beloved Son, in whom He was well pleased" (Dr. J. Brown). Men who were blinded by Satan, might regard Him as an impostor, and as a blasphemer, but He knew that the Father approved and would yet vindicate Him fully. How could it be otherwise when He did *always* those things that pleased Him?—a claim none other could truthfully make.

"As He spake these words, many believed on Him" (v. 30). This does not mean that they believed to the saving of their souls, the verses which follow evidence they had not. Probably nothing more is here signified than that they were momentarily impressed so that their enmity against Him was, temporarily, allayed. Many were evidently struck by what they observed in the demeanor of Christ—bearing the perverseness of His enemies so patiently, speaking of so ignominious a death with such holy composure, and expressing so positively His sense of the Father's approbation. Nevertheless, the impression was but a fleeting one, and their believing on Him amounted to no more than asking, "When Christ cometh, will He do more miracles than those which this (fellow) hath done?" (see John 7:31).

"Then said Jesus to those Jews which believed on Him, If ye continue in My word, then are ye My disciples indeed" (v. 31). Our Lord here describes one of the marks of a *genuine* disciple of His. Continuance in His word is not a condition of discipleship, rather is it the *manifestation* of it. It is this, among other things, which distinguishes a true disciple from one who is merely a professor. These words of Christ supply us with a sure test. It is not how a man begins, but how he continues and ends. It is this which distinguishes the stony ground hearer from the good ground hearer—see Matt. 13:20, 21, and contrast Luke 8:15. To His apostles Christ said "He that endureth to the end shall be saved" (Matt. 10:22). Not, we repeat, that enduring to the end is a *condition* of salvation, it is an evidence or *proof* that we have already passed from death unto life. So writes the apostle John of some who had apostatized from the faith: "They went out from us, but they were not of us; for if they had been of us, they *would* have *continued* with us", etc. (1 John 2:19).

"If ye continue in My word, then are ye My disciples indeed" (v. 31). The word "indeed" signifies truly, really, genuinely so. By using this word Christ here intimated that those referred to in the previous verse, who are said to have "believed on Him", *were not* "genuine disciples". The one who has been truly saved will not fall away and be lost; the one who does fall away and is lost, was never truly saved. To "continue" in Christ's word is to "keep His word" (Rev. 3:8). It is to hold fast whatever Christ has said; it is to perseveringly follow out the faith we profess to its practical end.

"And ye shall know the truth, and the truth shall make you free" (v. 32). "To know the truth is something more definite than to know what is true; it is to understand that revelation with regard to the salvation of men, through the mediation of the incarnate Son, which is so often in the New Testament called, by way of eminence, 'the truth',—the truth of truths,—the most important of all truths,—the truth of which He is full,—the truth that came by Him, as the law came by Moses,—the truth, the reality in opposition to the shadows, the emblems, of the introductory economy,—what Paul termed, 'the word of the truth of the Gospel', Col. 1:5" (Dr. John Brown).

"The truth shall make you free". Note the striking connection between these three things: (1) "Continue in My word", v. 31; (2) "Ye shall know the truth", v. 32; (3) "The truth shall make you free", v. 32. This order cannot be changed. The truth gives spiritual liberty; it frees from the blinding power of Satan (2 Cor. 4:4). It delivers from the darkness of spiritual death (Eph. 4:18). It emancipates from the prison-house of sin (Isa. 61:1). Further enlargement upon the character and scope of spiritual freedom will be given when we come to v. 36. In the meantime let the student work on the following questions:—

1. To what extent is the sinner the "servant" *(bond-slave)* of sin, v. 34?
2. What does v. 36 teach about the will of the natural man?
3. What is the difference between Abraham's "children" (v. 39), and his "seed" (v. 33)?
4. What is the meaning of v. 43?
5. What is the force of "of God" in v. 47?
6. What is the meaning of v. 51?
7. To what was Christ referring in v. 56?

—Arthur W. Pink.

GLEANINGS IN EXODUS.

5. Moses Called and his Response: Ex. 3.

In our last article we contemplated Moses in Midian and pondered the significance of God appearing to him in the burning bush. It was there he received his call and commission to act as Jehovah's favored instrument in delivering His people from their hard bondage. As Moses turned aside to behold the amazing sight of the bush burning and yet not being consumed, the voice of God addressed him. First, God reminded Moses of His holiness (v. 5). Next, He revealed Himself in covenant-relationship (v. 6). Then, He expressed His compassion (v. 7). Then He declared His purpose: "I am come down to deliver them out of the hand of the Egyptians", etc. (v. 8). Finally, He addressed Himself to His servant: "Come now therefore, and I will send thee unto Pharaoh, that thou mayest bring forth My people the children of Israel out of Egypt" (v. 10).

Ere considering Moses' Call, let us weigh what is recorded in verses 7 and 8: "And the Lord said, I have surely seen the affliction of My people which are in Egypt, and have heard their cry by reason of their taskmasters; for I know their sorrows; And I am come down to deliver them out of the hand of the Egyptians, and to bring them up out of that land unto a good land and a large, unto a land flowing with milk and honey". Notice the *completeness* of this statement. First, the Lord said, "I have surely *seen the affliction* of My people which are in Egypt". Second, "And have *heard their cry* by reason of their taskmasters". Third, "For I *know their sorrows*". Fourth, "And *I am come down to deliver them*". Fifth, "Out of the hand of the Egyptians". Sixth, "And to bring them up out of that land *unto a good land*", etc. Seventh, "Unto a good land and a large, unto *a land flowing with milk and honey*".

Second, observe the *definiteness* and *positiveness* of Jehovah's assertions. There were no "perhaps's" or "peradventure's". It was no mere invitation or offer that was made to Israel. Instead, it was the unconditional, emphatic declaration of what the Lord would do—"I am come down *to deliver*". So it is now. The Gospel goes forth on no uncertain errand. God' Word *shall not* return unto Him void, but "it *shall* accomplish that which He pleases, and it *shall* prosper in the thing whereunto He sends it" (Isa. 55:11).

Finally, admire the blessed *typical picture* here, a prophetic picture of the Divine Incarnation. First, the Divine compassion which *prompted* the unspeakable Gift: "I have surely seen the affliction of My people which are in Egypt"—God contemplated the wretched condition of sinners and their need of deliverance. Second, the *Incarnation itself*: "I am *come down*". Thus it was fifteen hundred years later, when Jehovah-Jesus left His Father's House on high and came down to these scenes of sin and suffering. Third, the *purpose* of the Incarnation: to "deliver" His people and "bring them up out of that land", which symbolizes the world. Fourth, the *beneficent design* of the Incarnation: to "bring them into a good land and large, unto a land flowing with milk and honey"—to bring us on to resurrection ground, where there would be everything to satisfy and rejoice the heart.

"Come *now* therefore, and I will send thee unto Pharaoh, that thou mayest bring forth My people the children of Israel out of Egypt" (Ex. 3:10). Notice the little word which we have placed in italics. God is not to be rushed: our business is not (irreverently) to seek to hurry God, rather is it to *wait on Him* and *for Him*. For many long years had the groans and cries of the distressed Hebrews gone up; but the heavens were silent. Forty years previously, Moses had become impatient at the delay, and thought to take matters into his own hands, only to discover that the time for deliverance was not yet ripe. But "now". *Now* the four hundred years of servitude and affliction (Gen. 15:13) had run their ordained course. *Now* the hour for Divine intervention had struck. *Now* the time for Jehovah to deal with the haughty oppressor of His people had arrived. *Now* the children of Israel would be in a condition to appreciate the promised inheritance. The pleasant pastures of Goshen and the carnal attractions of Egypt had, no doubt, quelled all longings for Canaan, but *now* that their afflictions were fast becoming unbearable, the land flowing with milk and honey would be a pleasing prospect.

And now that the time for deliverance had arrived, what is the method of Divine procedure? A captive people is to be emancipated; a nation of slaves is to be liberated. What, then, is the first move toward this? Had God so chosen He could have sent forth His angels, and in a single night destroyed all the Egyptians. Had He so pleased He could have appeared before the Hebrews in person and brought them out of their house of bondage. But this was not His way. Instead, *He appointed a human ministry to effect a Divine salvation.* To Moses He said, "I will send *thee* . . . . .

that *thou* mayest bring forth My people . . . . out of Egypt". There is little need to apply this to ourselves. God's way then, is God's way now. Human instrumentality is the means He most commonly employes in bringing sinners from bondage to liberty, from death to life.

"Come now therefore, and *I will send* thee unto Pharaoh, that thou mayest bring forth *My people* the children of Israel out of Egypt" (v. 10). What, then, is the response of our patriarch? Surely he will bow in worship before the great I am at being thus so highly honored. Surely he will ask, in fullest submission, "Lord, *what* would'st Thou have me to do?" But how did Moses reply? "And Moses said unto God, Who am I, that I should go unto Pharaoh, and that I should bring forth the children of Israel out of Egypt?" (v. 11).

Moses at eighty was not so eager as at forty. Solitude had sobered him. Keeping sheep had tamed him. He saw difficulties in himself, in the people, and in his task. He had already tried once and failed, and now for long years he had been out of touch with his people. But while all this was true, it was *God* who now called him to this work, and *He* makes no mistakes.

"And Moses said unto God, Who am I, that I should go unto Pharaoh, and that I should bring forth the children of Israel out of Egypt?" (v. 11). This brings out a principle in connection with Divine service which is strikingly illustrated in Luke 9. In v. 57 we read, "And it came to pass, that, as they went in the way, a certain man said unto him, Lord, I will follow Thee whithersoever Thou goest". In response our Lord said, "Foxes have holes, and birds of the air have nests; but the Son of Man hath not where to lay His head". Then we read, "And He said unto another, Follow Me. But he said, Lord, suffer me first to go and bury my father. Jesus said unto Him, Let the dead bury their dead: but go thou and preach the kingdom of God. And another also said, Lord, I will follow Thee; but let me first go bid them farewell, which are at home at my house". The principle is this: When the will of man acts in self-appointed service, he does not feel the difficulties in the way; but when there is a true call from God these *are* felt. Thus it was with Moses. When he went forth in the energy of the flesh (Ex. 2:11, etc.) he was full of confidence in the success of his mission. This comes out clearly in Acts 7:25: "For he supposed his brethren would have understood how that God by his hand would deliver them: but they understood not". But now that he is called of God to this work he is very conscious of the difficulties in the way. The discipline of the "backside of the desert" had not been in vain. Shepherding had chastened him.

The Lord, therefore, graciously encourages him by promising to be with him and assuring him of the ultimate success of his mission. "And He said, Certainly I will be with thee; and this shall be a token unto thee, that I have sent thee: When thou hast brought forth the people out of Egypt, ye shall serve God upon this mountain" (v. 12). This was very comforting. God did not ask Moses to go forward alone: an all-mighty One would accompany him. And this is still the Divine promise to each Divinely-called servant. I doubt not that the apostles must have felt much like Moses when the risen Saviour commissioned them to go and preach the Gospel to every creature—Who am I that I should go? If so, their hearts were reassured with the same promise Moses received—"Lo I am with you alway". And fellow-worker, if the Lord has manifestly called *you* to some task for which you feel utterly insufficient, rest on this precious promise—"Certainly I will be with thee". This is a word that every one engaged in Christian service needs to take to heart. When we think of what is involved in bringing a soul out of darkness into light; when we encounter the fierce opposition of the devil; when we face the frowns and sneers of the world, little wonder that we hesitate, and ask, "Who is sufficient for these things?" But take courage faint-heart, and remember the unfailing promise, "Certainly I will be with thee".

"And Moses said unto God, Behold, when I come unto the children of Israel, and shall say unto them, The God of your fathers hath sent me unto you; and they shall say to me, What is His name? What shall I say unto them?" (v. 13). Let us not be too quick to condemn Moses here—the Lord did not! This was no small difficulty for Moses. No visible presence would accompany him. He was to go alone to the enslaved Hebrews and present himself as the Divinely-sent deliverer. He was to tell them that the God of their fathers had promised to free them. But, as we shall see later, this was not likely to make much impression upon a people who were, most of them at least, sunk in the idolatries of the Egyptians. He felt that they would quickly want to know, Who is this God? What is His character? Prove to us that He is worthy of our confidence. And does not a similar difficulty arise before us! We go forth to tell lost sinners of a God they have never seen. In His name we bid them trust. But cannot we anticipate the response—"Show us the Father, and it sufficeth us" is still, in substance, the demand of the doubting heart. Moses felt this difficulty; and so do we.

"And God said unto Moses, I AM THAT I AM: and He said, Thus shalt thou say unto the children of Israel, I AM hath sent me unto you" (v. 14). At first sight this may strike us as strange and mysterious, yet a little reflection should discover its profound suggestiveness to us. "I am" is the great Jehovistic name of God. Dr. Pentecost says, "It contains each tense of the verb 'to be', and might be translated, I was, I am, and I shall always continue to be". The principle contained in this word of Jehovah to Moses contains timely instruction for us. We are to go forth declaring the name and nature of God as He has been revealed. No attempts are to be made to prove His existence; no time should be wasted with men in efforts to reason about God. Our business is to *proclaim* the Being of God as He has revealed Himself in and through Jesus Christ. The "I am" of the burning bush now stands fully declared in the blessed Person of our Saviour who said, *"I am* the bread of life", *"I am* the good Shepherd", *"I am* the door". *"I am* the light of the world", *"I am* the way, the truth and the life", *"I am* the resurrection and the life", *"I am* the true vine". He is the eternal "I am"—"the Same, yesterday, and today, and forever".

"And God said unto Moses, I AM THAT I AM: and He said, Thus shalt thou say unto the children of Israel, I AM hath sent me unto you" (v. 14). There is a depth here which no finite mind can fathom. "I am that I am" announced that the great God is self-existent, beside whom there is none else. Without beginning, without ending, "from everlasting to everlasting" He *is* God. None but He can say "I am *that* I am"—always the same, eternally changeless. The apostle Paul could say "By the grace of God I am *what* I am"—what grace has made me, but he could not say "I am *that* I am".

"And God said moreover unto Moses, Thus shalt thou say unto the children of Israel, The Lord God of your fathers, the God of Abraham, the God of Isaac, and the God of Jacob, hath sent me unto you: this is My name forever, and this is My memorial unto all generations" (v. 15). This was most blessed. Here was indeed something which ought to win the hearts of the Hebrews when Moses repeated it to them. The God of Abraham, Isaac and Jacob, was the God of sovereign grace, who had singled out these men from the mass of fallen humanity, and made them His high favorites. The God of Abraham, Isaac and Jacob, was the God of unconditional promise, who had pledged to give to them and their seed the land of Canaan for their inheritance. The God of Abraham, Isaac and Jacob, was the covenant-keeping God; for with Abraham God entered into solemn covenant, and with Isaac and Jacob He confirmed it. Note, also, the *threefold* repetition of God—*"The God* of Abraham, *the God* of Isaac, and *the God* of Jacob". Was there not here something more than a hint of the Holy Trinity!

In the remaining verses of Ex. 3 we learn how God further re-assured His servant by declaring what should be the results of his mission (see vv. 16-22). And mark once more the positive terms used: *"I will* bring you up out of the affliction of Egypt . . . . And *they shall* hearken to thy voice . . . . *I am sure* that the king of Egypt will not let you go . . . . And *I will* smite Egypt with all My wonders . . . . and *I will* give this people favor in the sight of the Egyptians", etc. Everything is definitely determined. There is no possibility of the Divine purpose failing. There are no contingencies; no 'I will do my part, *if* you do yours'. The Lord has sworn, "My counsel shall stand, and I will do *all* My pleasure" (Isa. 46:10). Let this be the ground of our confidence. Though all the powers of evil array themselves against us, whatever *God* hath called us to do will issue precisely as He has appointed. It is true that these promises of God to Moses were not made good in a day. It is true that there was much in the sequel to severely test the faith of Moses, ere the children of Israel *were* delivered from Egypt. And it is also true that with two exceptions, the six hundred thousand men who left Egypt perished in the wilderness, and thus Moses died *without seeing* the complete fulfillment of Israel's actually reaching the land flowing with milk and honey—for God's promises were made to Israel *as a nation*, not to any particular generation of that nation. Nevertheless, in the end, every word of Jehovah was made good. So, too, God may commission us to a work for Him, and we may die before the determined issue appears; but notwithstanding, the Divine purpose *will be* realized.

"And they shall hearken to thy voice: and thou shalt come, thou and the elders of Israel, unto the king of Egypt, and ye shall say unto him, The Lord God of the Hebrews hath met with us: and now let us go, we beseech thee, three days' journey into the wilderness, that we may sacrifice to the Lord our God. And I am sure that the king of Egypt will not let you go, no, not by a mighty hand" (vv. 18, 19). This presented another test to Moses' faith. Had he stopped to reason about the commission God was giving him, it probably would have appeared foolishness to him. Here was he ordered to go, accompanied by the elders of Israel, unto Pharaoh, and present to Him the message of Jehovah. He was to request that the Hebrews should be allowed to go a three days' journey into the wilderness that they might worship God. And, yet, before he starts Jehovah assures him, "I am *sure* that the king of Egypt *will not* let you go". He might have asked, What, then, is the use of me wasting my breath on him? But it is not for the servant to question his master's orders: it is for him to obey. But not yet was Moses ready to respond to God's call.

"And Moses answered and said, But, behold, they will not believe me, nor hearken unto my voice: for they will say, The Lord hath not appeared unto thee" (4:1). Were it not that we were acquainted in some measure with our own desperately-wicked hearts, it would appear to us well-nigh unthinkable that Moses should continue objecting and cavilling. But the remembrance of our own repeated and humiliating failures only serves to show how sadly true to life is the picture here presented before us. The Lord had favored His servant with the awe-inspiring sight of the burning bush, He had spoken of His tender solicitude for the afflicted Hebrews, He had promised to be with Moses, He had expressly declared that He would deliver Israel from Egypt and bring them into Canaan. And yet all of this is not sufficient to silence unbelief and subdue the rebellious will. Alas! what is man that the Almighty should be mindful of him! Nothing but Divine power working within us can ever bring the human heart to abandon all creature props and trust in God.

"And Moses answered and said, But, behold, they will not believe me, nor hearken unto my voice". Awful presumption was this. The Lord had emphatically declared, "They *shall* hearken to thy voice" (3:18), and now Moses replies, They *will not*. Here was the servant daring to contradict his Lord to His face. Fearfully solemn is this; the more so, when we remember that *we* are made of precisely the same material that Moses was. There is in us the same evil, unbelieving, rebellious heart, and our only safeguard is to cast ourselves in the dust before God, beseeching Him to pity our helplessness and to keep down, subdue, overcome, the desperate and incurable wickedness which indwells us.

How what has been before us repudiates the modern sophistry that God only uses those who are fully consecrated to Him! How often Arminian teachers insist that the measure of our faith and faithfulness will determine the measure of our success in the Lord's service. It is true that every servant of Christ *ought* to be "a vessel unto honor, sanctified, and *meet* for the Master's use" (2 Tim. 2:21), nevertheless, God is *not limited* by our failure at this point, and clearly does this come out in the passage before us. Moses was timid, hesitant, fearful, unbelieving, rebellious, *and yet God used him!* Nor does he stand by any means alone in this respect. God used the mercenary Balaam to give one of the most remarkable prophecies to be found in the Old Testament. He used a Samson to deliver Israel from the Philistines. He used a Judas in the apostolate. If God were to wait until He found a human instrument that was *worthy* or *fit* to be used by *Him*, He would go on waiting until the end of time. God is sovereign in this, as in everything. The truth is that God uses whom He pleases.

Not yet was Moses ready to respond to Jehovah's Call. There were other difficulties which the fertile mind of unbelief was ready to suggest, but one by one Divine power and long-sufferance overcame them. Let us take this lesson throughly to heart, and seek that grace which will enable us to place God between us and our difficulties, instead of putting difficulties between God and us. In our next paper we shall dwell upon the three "signs" which God gave to Moses; let the interested reader give these much prayerful meditation as he studies Ex. 4, and thus be prepared to test our exposition.

—A. W. Pink

HOW MAY I KNOW THAT I AM A CHILD OF GOD.

There is a very plain answer to that question in 1 John 5:1, "Whosoever believeth that Jesus is the Christ, is born of God." This is the unqualified testimony of the Holy Spirit, and no one can have the audacity to insinuate that in such a statement there can be any hidden or indirect meaning, or any trick of words which conceals while it affects to reveal. Any one who says that he believes that Jesus is the Christ, and yet says that he is not born of God, is directly at issue with the word of God. Nor is the testimony of this passage singular or unsupported. On the contrary, it is in harmony with the whole revelation of God's grace in "the adoption of sons." We quote the word 'adoption' as being equivalent to regeneration, though presenting the same fact in another aspect. For, as pardon in the scriptural sense is not, as in the human sense, a mere formal remission of the consequences of transgression, leaving the guilt and shame of it unaffected, but is a complete removal of the guilt, so that the sin is buried in eternal oblivion and an accusing conscience is appeased; so adoption, in the evangelical sense, is not a mere formal act which confers the legal benefits of sonship, leaving the real paternity of the adopted child unchanged, but is the actual transference of a child of wrath into the family of God, by the communication of a new life derived from God, and bearing all the characteristic marks of its origin.

In showing, as briefly as possible, that the declaration, "Whosoever believeth that Jesus is the Christ, is born of God," is in harmony with the whole revelation of God's grace in the adoption of sons, we remark:

That *the Word of God* is continually represented as the means of regeneration. James says of the Father of lights: "Of His own will begat He us *by the word of truth*." Peter also speaks of those who, by Christ, believed in God, and who had purified their hearts by obeying the truth, through the Spirit: "Being born again, not of corruptible seed, but of incorruptible, *by the word of God*, which liveth and abideth for ever." In explanation of this testimony, he adds: "And this is the word which by the Gospel is preached unto you." The word, which is declared to be the means by which they are born of God, is explained to be the Gospel, the burden of which is that Jesus is the Christ; and those who are addressed as "being born again" are described as redeemed by the precious blood of Christ, by whom they believed in God; and in a preceding verse they are said to be "begotten again unto a lively hope by the resurrection of Jesus Christ from the dead;" an event which is the conclusive proof that Jesus is the Christ.

Again when Jesus startled Nicodemus with the announcement, "Except a man be born again, he cannot see the kingdom of God," which was just, in other words, to say, "Flesh and blood cannot inherit the kingdom of God, neither doth corruption inherit incorruption;" and when Nicodemus at length asked how regeneration could be affected, Jesus replied: "As Moses lifted up the serpent in the wilderness, even so must the Son of Man be lifted up; that whosoever believeth on Him should not perish, but have eternal life. For God so loved the world, that He gave His only begotten Son, that whosoever believeth on Him should not perish, but have everlasting life." To enter the kingdom of God is to enjoy eternal life; and one who is perishing, who has the sentence "dying, thou shalt die" enstamped on his nature, and on whom the wrath of God abides, can only have everlasting life by being born again, by receiving new life, by being a new creature; and the Lord expressly states that men receive this new life—that is, they are born again, by believing in Him. In other words, the Lord announces, in effect, the very proposition affirmed by His Apostle through the Spirit: "Whosoever believeth that Jesus is the Christ, is born of God."

Again, when John is bearing testimony of the Word who was with God, and was God, that "in Him was life, and the life was the light of men"—life not merely as an inherent possession, but to communicate to men—he says that "He was in the world, and the world knew Him not," "He came to His own, and His own received Him not." The mass of mankind closed their eyes to the light, and did not receive the life which He had to communicate; but "as many as received Him, to them gave He power to become sons of God, even to them that believe on His name, which were born, not of blood, nor of the will of man, but of God." In the case of the former, "This is the condemnation, that light is come into the world, and men loved darkness rather than light, because their deeds are evil;" and under that condemnation they perish. In the case of the latter, reception of the true light was the reception of everlasting life; which is, in other words, to be born of God. The destiny of men turns upon the reception or rejection of Jesus as the Christ; as the same evangelist testifies: "He that believeth on the Son hath everlasting life: and he that believeth not the Son shall not see life, but the wrath of God abideth on him."

In none of these passages is the marvelous fact explained that belief on Him is the means of regeneration; but the fact is most explicitly stated. It should be sufficient for us that it is a divine appointment; as the lifting up of the serpent in the wilderness was the divinely appointed means of restoring the perishing Israelites to life and health. It is no more necessary that we should understand how believing in Him is the means or occasion of communicating everlasting life to us, than it was necessary to the Israelites to understand how looking to the brazen serpent should be the means of restoring them to natural life. God's Word was a sufficient warrant to them, and it is a sufficient warrant to us. The result in either case is the work of God; and, accordingly, while the word of God is everywhere represented as the means, and our believing it as the occasion of being born again, the Spirit of God is everywhere spoken of as the agent. Nor could we for a moment suppose that any thing less than the power which presided over the first creation could suffice for this new creation; that any thing less than the power which at first breathed into man's nostrils the breath of life, and he became a living creature, could suffice for this second and more noble birth. While in the fullest sense it is a divine work, the word of God, the Gospel which is preached unto you, is not only a means, but *the* only means of regeneration. They, and they only, who are in Christ are new creatures; they, and they only, who believe on the Son are made sons of God. There are no exceptions on either side. Of the whole redeemed family of God, it can be said, "Ye are all the children of God by faith in Christ Jesus;" and "Whoso believeth that Jesus is the Christ, is born of God." The question whether any man is born of God is, therefore, to be determined by the question: Does he believe that Jesus is the Christ? If he does, then we have God's word for it that he is born of God; if he does not, it is equally certain that he is not born of God.

As the matter of faith is stated in 1 John 5:1, it may seem to be a bare proposition, a historical fact, namely, "that Jesus is the Christ," which, it may seem, is to be determined by a similar process by which a man would arrive at the conclusion "that Napoleon is Emperor of the French;" and it might be asked why should the belief of a historical fact be attended with such consequences? In most of the passages which we have quoted, there is a variation of the language which must not be overlooked. Thus, in one passage, it is, "he that believeth on the Son," as though it implied confidence in His veracity, rather than credence of the fact that He is the Christ. In another it is, "he that believeth in Him," implying trust reposed in Him, rather than confidence in His veracity, or credence of the fact that He is the Christ. Or, again, it is, "as many as received Him," implying the acknowledgement of Him in a given character, or in a given relationship to the recipient. But a little reflection on the character and relation in which He is presented to us in the Gospel, will lead us to the conclusion that any one of these involves the others.

A man may believe that Napoleon is Emperor of the French without having confidence in his veracity. He may be a person whom men "could not believe under oath;" for there is nothing in the character or position of an emperor which precludes the possibility of his falsehood. But to believe that Jesus is the Christ, is to acknowledge Him to be the truth itself, immaculate and incorruptible; and it is to receive whatever He teaches or testifies as unquestionably true. To believe Him is necessarily to believe that He is the Christ, for it is in that character He presents Himself to us.

We may believe that Napoleon is Emperor of the French, and, if he were a man of unquestionable veracity, there would be no intelligible sense in which we could be said to rely upon him, or put our trust in him, because in that character he sustains no relations to us in which we can confide in him. In the same way, had the office of Christ related only to the Jews as a nation, we might have acknowledged His veracity, without believing *in* Him. Indeed, in that case, it would have been absurd if any but the Jews had professed to believe in Him. But the office of Christ does not relate exclusively to the Jews; and to believe that Jesus—the lowly, suffering Man of Nazareth, the bleeding Sacrifice of Golgotha, the risen and glorified One at the right hand of God—is the Christ, is, by the very fact, to believe that God so loved the world that He gave His only-begotten Son, that whosoever believeth on Him should not perish, but have everlasting life; it is, by the very fact, to believe what God testifies of our guilt and ruin which needed such a Saviour, and to believe that He hath put away sin by the sacrifice of Himself; that, having died on account of our sins, He was raised again on account of our justification, and that He is able to save to the very uttermost all that come unto God through Him; it is, by the very fact, to know and believe that God hath given us eternal life, and this life is in His Son. It is, indeed, a very possible thing for men to form their own notions of the Christ, or accept some current or traditional notion of the Christ, as many of the Jews did, and in that sense they may believe that Jesus is the Christ without believing in Him, or finding eternal life in Him. The belief that Jesus is the Christ of which we speak rests upon the testimony of God; and it is a startling view of the guilt of unbelief that "he that believeth not God, hath made Him a liar: because he believeth not the record that God gave of His Son." To receive this testimony that Jesus is the Christ—to believe this record that God gave of His Son—is evidently, at the same time, "to receive Him," "to believe Him," and "to believe on Him." And it is in this sense, when we receive not the testimony of men, but the witness of God, which is greater, that it is affirmed, "Whosoever believeth that Jesus is the Christ, is born of God."

Millions of men have *said* in their own sense that Jesus is the Christ without being born of God; but no one ever really *believed* it, or said, "Thou art the Christ," as Peter did when the Lord pronounced him blessed, and attested, "Flesh and blood hath not revealed it unto thee, but my Father which is in heaven," without being born of God, else this assurance of the word of God, which we have so often repeated in this article, were false; for there are no exceptions, *"Whosoever believeth"*, "to *as many* as received Him", "ye *are all* the children of God by faith in Christ Jesus." The answer to the question, How may I know that I am a child of God? is therefore exceedingly plain, however it may have been involved in perplexity by the devices of Satan, or the vain speculations of men. None are the children of God, except by faith in Christ Jesus, and there is not one who believes that Jesus is the Christ who is not born of God.

It would be an endless task to follow all the devices of self-torture by which men obscure this plain truth, or by which they endeavor to settle this question on some other grounds than *the word of God*. The awakening of a sinner is frequently attended by deep and tumultuous emotion, which is often prolonged by the resistance of the proud heart to the self-denying doctrine of the Cross. These emotions and the agonizing struggle of the soul in contact with the truth, have been observed and recorded; And then men have endeavored to decide whether they have been born of God, by observing how far their own emotions, or "experience," as it is styled, correspond with those of the recorded instance. Or, again, the matter is subjected to the test of feeling, and men doubt whether they are children of God, because they do not feel they are, or they conclude that they are sons of God because they feel that they are. Or, again, certain marks and characteristics of the children of God are gathered from the Scriptures, and the self-torturing inquirer endeavors to satisfy himself that these marks and characteristics are found in him. There is not a word in the New Testament which countenances any such procedure; and we may venture to affirm that none but the self-righteous hypocrite ever got beyond the sphere of doubt and uncertainty by any such course.

For, first, as to the emotions which commonly accompany the transition of a sinner from death to life, they are as various as the character and circumstances of men, and form no part of the change itself. The life and character of John Bunyan were very peculiar; he was a man of powerful fancy and intense feelings, and when we consider what his previous life had been, and what was the character of the influences and instructions to which he was subject when he was awakened to a sense of sin and danger, we need not wonder at the experience which he has embodied in the description of the flight of Christian from the City of Destruction. But, unhappily, his 'experience' has been erected into a standard by which that of other men is tried, and in some regions a Christian would be asked, "Were you long in the Slough of Despond?" as though the slough of despond were a divine institution, and the only way of salvation lay through it. Andrew Fuller put that question to an aged saint, who replied: "I was never there at all, sir; I went straight to the Cross of Christ." That was the scriptural way, and it is to be remarked that the Scriptures place nothing between the sinner and the Cross, nor do they clog the free message with a single qualifying condition. "Believe on the Lord Jesus Christ, and thou shalt be saved." Multitudes have deceived themselves by mistaking the agony of remorse, or the terror of hell, for conversion, and have found a false and transient peace in a confidence in their own sufferings, instead of true peace in a confidence in Him who hath suffered for us, the just for the unjust.

Second. As to the test of feeling, we quote the words of George Muller, because they are plain and scriptural; "Perhaps you say I do not *feel* that I am born again, born of God, and therefore I have no enjoyment. In order that you may have the enjoyment which is the result of the knowledge that you are a child of God, you must receive God's testimony. He is a faithful witness, He speaks nothing but the truth, and His declaration is that every one who believes that Jesus is the Christ is born of God. If you receive the testimony of God, you to whom it is given to believe, that Jesus is the Christ cannot but be happy, from the fact that God Himself says that you are His child. But if you wait till you *feel* that you are a child of God, you may have to wait a long time; and even if you felt it, your feelings would be worth nothing, for either it might be a false feeling, or, though it were real, it might be lost the next hour. Feelings change, but *the word of God* remains unalterably the same. You have, then, without having had a dream about it, without having had a portion of the word in more than a usual way impressed upon your mind concerning the subject, without having heard something like a voice from heaven about it, you have to say to yourself, If I believe that Jesus is the promised Messiah, I am a child of God. And then, from the belief of what God declares in this passage concerning you who believe that Jesus is the Christ, even that you are His child, springs peace and joy in the Holy Ghost."

Third. As to the characteristics of the children of God, any believer who turns into himself to search for them will necessarily be distracted by conflicting evidence, if the inspired description of the Christian's life on earth be invariably true, "For the flesh lusteth against the Spirit, and the Spirit against the flesh, and these are contrary the one to the other, so that ye cannot do the things that ye would." You may say: "If I am a child of God, must I love Him?" Yes, for it is the necessary result of knowing and believing the love God hath to us; as an Apostle expresses it, "We love Him because He first loved us;" but it by no means follows that, as a child of God, you will be satisfied with your love to Him. There could be no more lamentable proof of spiritual deadness and fatal self-deception than a self-complacent view of our love to God, on the ground of which a man should conclude that he is a child of God; as though it had been written, "Behold the manner of love with which we have loved Him, that we should be called the sons of God." This is the history of all the love of God that ever warmed the heart of a child of God, "We love Him because He first loved us;" and if so, then, surely, even so far as the growth of our love to God is concerned, we should be occupied with His love, not with ours; and whatever casts a shade over our view of the former must necessarily chill the latter. The language that becomes a believer, and the thought that satisfies a believer, is, "We have known and believed the love that God hath to us;" and the evidence, the complete demonstration of it, is found, not in ourselves, but in Christ. "Herein is love, not that we loved God, but that He loved us, and sent His Son to be the propitiation for our sins."

In the natural relations of mankind it is not the love which a son bears to his father that constitutes him the child of that father, though filial love is the natural and proper result of the relationship. An exalted estimate of the character of a father and of the sacredness of the relationship will often render an affectionate child dissatisfied with himself. "I reproach myself daily that I love my father so little." "I can never love such a father as I ought, or repay all I owe to him." Such may be the language of filial devotedness. Now, would it be a legitimate conclusion from such a humbling conviction on the part of a son—would it be honoring to his father and worthy of himself if he should argue, "Because I do not love him as I ought, it cannot be that I am his child"? or, "because I love him so little, I question very much if he loves me at all"? Yet it is thus men are continually arguing with reference to a heavenly Father, and this, in point of fact, is precisely what the attempt to settle the question of our adoption by an estimate of our love to God amounts to.

Our love to God did not attract His love to us, nor had we any excellence or virtue which fitted us for a place in His family, on the ground of which He adopted us. On the contrary, "God commendeth His love toward us in that, while we were yet sinners, Christ died for us." Consequently, that in which alone we can find satisfaction and assurance is the manifestation of *His* love. "Behold what manner of love the Father hath bestowed upon us, that we should be called the sons of God." The love of God found a way by which sinners might be righteously received into His family, and by which, at the same time, they might really become His children. "In this was manifested the love of God toward us, because that God sent His only-begotten Son into the world that we might live through Him." The question, therefore, is not about our love to God, but His love to us; it is not about what there is in us, but what there is in Christ. This truth is perhaps obscured by a passage in 1 John 4: 17: "Herein is our love made perfect, as He is, so are we in this world. There is no fear in love; but perfect love casteth out fear: because fear hath torment. He that feareth is not made perfect in love." This language may seem to encourage the examination of our own hearts for that which shall give boldness in the day of judgment and cast out tormenting fear, and may seem to justify the disposition to settle the question, Am I a child of God? upon the evidence of our love to God, rather than His love to us; upon what we are, rather than what Christ is; upon our own experience rather than upon the word of God. But if this were a warrantable use of the passage, surely we must conclude that it is a strange connection in which we find it, where attention is concentrated on the love of God manifested in Christ, and when, in the verse immediately preceding, we read: "And we have known and believed the love that God hath to us. God is love, and he that dwelleth in love dwelleth in God and God in him." The true reading is in the margin—not our love to God, but His love to us—"love with us." It is this which casts out fear, which enables us to look forward to the day of judgment with boldness—not the boldness of conscious innocence, but the boldness of simple faith which looks up to the perfect love of God and the perfect righteousness of Christ; which, in the person of the judge, beholds the perfect proof of God's love, beholds our righteousness, our advocate, and knows that to condemn a believer would be to condemn Himself.

The more we know of the truth of God the less satisfaction will we find in looking inward for any ground of assurance before God; but then the more satisfaction will we find in looking to Christ as the ground of our assurance; the less we will have to say of our love to God, but the more we will have to say of the love of God to us. Some one has well said; "If you want to be miserable, *look within.* If you want to be distracted, *look around.* If you want to be happy, *LOOK UP.*" An objector may still demand, "But is it not said that the children of God have the witness in themselves?" and on this account may be travelling on in darkness and sorrow, searching in themselves for the evidence which shall warrant them to "rejoice, believing." It is only necessary to remind them that the testimony of the Spirit is, "He that believeth on the Son of God hath the witness in himself;" and surely no one can look for the witness in himself while he is doubting or in any way questioning the testimony of God; for it is added: "He that believeth not God hath made Him a liar, because he believeth not the record that God gave of His Son. And this is the record, that God hath given us eternal life, and this life is in His Son." God-dishonoring doubt and unbelief can never surely produce the fruits of faith; and that man must be bewildered and perplexed who reverses the order of things, and who so pitiably confounds the *warrant* of faith and its *results.* Nor can the soul ever find a solution of its perplexity till it takes God simply at His word, and rests satisfied with the simple assurance—"whosoever believeth that Jesus is the Christ, is born of God." —*James Inglis (1864).*

THE TRIAL BY FIRE.

I Cor. 3:13-15.

It was undoubtedly of the work of the ministry that these words were especially spoken. But primary application is to those who are ambassadors for Christ. But while this is their first application they are not confined to any one class of men. The principle involved is of universal application. It is a principle that holds not in the case of ministers alone, but in the case of every member of that holy body of believers, which the apostle Peter, in the fifth and ninth verses of the second chapter of his first epistle, calls a "holy" and a "royal priesthood". All, surely, are to be subject to a like review of life, to be attended with like results, dependent on the character of each.

With the unbelieving the apostle, in I Cor. 3, has nothing to do. There is no allusion to them here. It is of the results of *Christian*" life that he is speaking. It is true, indeed, that *every* man shall give account of himself to God. But this truth of universal accountability is not the truth brought out now. We have to do with that manifestation of *Christian* character, which shall yet take place, and with that award which God shall yet give to His believing people, according to the faithfulness of their service and the closeness of their walk with Him. It is only true Christians who can be represented as working at all for God, as building with anything, whether it be gold or stubble. Others are not in His vineyard at all. Only we who believe can be said to be "workers together with God".

Not only, then, is there to be "a day of judgment and perdition of *ungodly* men", but to us who are the children of God by faith in Jesus Christ there is to come a time of trial when, as it were, fire shall be applied to our life's work; and the place of rulership that we shall have in the coming kingdom shall depend on our ability to stand the test to which we shall be made subject. As Christian people, we are daily determining what the character of our future shall be, what the measure of our reward. If we are Christ's, we are at work, we are building, *of what sort* is our work, this is what one day shall be made manifest. And as has been already said, every day is determining this. Every thought of your heart, every word of your lips, every act of your life, each has its bearing thus upon your future. Every thing in you that is only dross, your unfaithfulness, your pride, your worldliness, whatever in you is un-Christlike, all this the fire of the coming day will burn. What will be left when this is done? Is there any thing in you that shall abide? any thing that that fire shall have no power to harm?. Oh! if we could have that Day always printed in our remembrance would we live the lives we do?. Would there not be a more earnest consecration to Him who bought us with His blood, if our thoughts oftener went forward to the accounts that we shall give—if we were duly alive to the fact that, for all our unfaithfulness, even though we are saved, we shall suffer loss, loss that can never be repaired?. If their lives were regulated by this thought, our Christian people would live more above the world, and would indeed be "living epistles known and read of all men". Now such a day as this *is* coming—a day to try every man's work—your work—my work. Beloved, it must be tried. Every thing about it must be manifested before God. That which is hidden shall be brought to light, and according to what we have done in the flesh shall our judgment be. What we have sown, that shall we also reap. Just what we really are, judged by God's own estimate shall we be shown to be; and according to what we are, or are not all as Christians we ought to be, shall we be saved "abundantly" or "so as by fire".

Asuming the fact that there shall be such a day of manifestation of Christian character when the fire shall try every believer's life-work, the first thing that the apostle makes plain in reference to that day is, that all who then shall be found resting on Christ the One Foundation, shall be saved. Even though his work is burned, the man is represented as himself saved. The meaning certainly is not all *professed faith* shall then stand approved, that every one bearing the Christian name shall be saved. On the contrary, we know that many will call upon the Saviour then to whom He will say, "I never knew you". But all *real* faith shall stand. All whom God discerns to be resting upon the Lord Jesus, grounded upon Him as a Rock, shall be saved. There may be different degrees in the ripeness of Christian character attained. Some will bring more fruit to perfection than others. But all in whose hearts Christ is, who in very truth have received Him, all such are children, "And if children then heirs". There is one respect in which all Christian people are alike—in which there is no difference between the babe in Christ and the perfect man. The one who today, with tremblingly extended hand, has laid his sin on the Saviour, and the one who through a long course of years has been adorning Christ's doctrine—there is one point of exact resemblance between these two. They are alike "in Christ Jesus"; alike cleansed by His precious blood, alike clothed with His perfect righteousness. Every soul which is justified at all, is perfectly justified. And every soul is justified that with any faith, even the weakest, cleaves to Jesus Christ. In forgiveness, acceptance, adoption, there are no degrees. The person who has these blessings at all, has them in their perfectness and entirety. God does not partially forgive, nor partially accept. Of all whom He receives, it may be said, "Ye are washed, ye are sanctified, ye are justified". All believers stand in the full merit of the Saviour's perfectness. The measure of their faith affects not their standing in Him. Their comfort, their happiness, the efficiency of their service, will be affected by the measure of their faith, but not their standing in the Saviour. Appreciated or not, be sure of it or be doubtful about it, be joyful in it or be full of fears, the fact itself can be affected by none of these things. If God sees that with any trust you cling to the Lord Jesus then in His sight you are as Christ is. He looks upon you, not as you are in yourself, but as you are in Him. And so, being as Christ is, you are complete in Him. And being thus, as the result of any faith, clothed upon with all the perfectness of Christ, your salvation is thereby made secure. Being found in Christ, so long as He lives you shall live also. You can never perish, nor shall any be able to pluck you out of His hand.

There is one sense in which believers shall never come into judgment. Our judgment is already past. When Christ was judged for us upon the cross, when He was there dealt with as a sinner, and made a curse for us, that was *our* judgment. We in Him then answered for sin. Our sin was then condemned. When One died for the all, then all died in Him. And never are we, as accused persons or as criminals, to be dragged before a judgment-seat, to have it determined whose we are. That is already determined when we believe, and by believing became one with Christ. It is impossible that we shall ever stand before a throne trembling lest perchance we yet be cast away. God cannot deal so with those whom in Christ He loves with an everlasting love. But resting on the one sole Foundation we are eternally secure. Merely because God sees us in Christ we are safe. And when Christ comes again, what is His first act to be?. To summon all men, the living and the dead, before Him to decide who is His and who is not?. By no means—He knows this already. And the first act of His appearing will be to gather unto Him those who *are* His. Of the living some shall be "taken" while others shall be "left". Of the dead some awaking shall have part in the first resurrection, while the rest of the dead live not until the thousand years are finished. Judgment then in this respect is not awaiting us, as to whether we are Christ's or not. Judgment has already been passed upon us, and we were executed in Christ. In Him we have already died unto sin, and been made alive unto God. Even now we have everlasting life; and all that awaits us is our own manifestation, the time when we shall shine forth as the sun in the kingdom of our Father.

All this comes as the result of any faith. They who, whether strongly or weakly, yet truly rest on Christ Jesus as their Foundation, shall be saved, for justification admits of no degrees. All who are justified are justified from all things. The question of our salvation is forever settled, by the simple fact of our resting on the Cornerstone, elect, precious.

But evidently there will be great differences among the saved in respect of the measure of their reward. We see great differences in Christian character. And can we doubt that the awards eventually given will be in proportion to the faithfulness of the service?. At the same time that our salvation is secure our *work* is to be tried, of what sort it is. And our place in the glory will be determined by what we have done in the flesh. That there is a judgment thus in respect of our faithfulness is evident. And the distinction between such a judgment as this, and a judgment whose object is to determine whether we shall be acquitted or condemned is also evident. Into such a judgment as this the believer shall never come. And between such a judgment and one that tries not our *foundation* but our *work*, there is, as has been said, all the difference that there is between a loving father taking account of the conduct of his children, and a stern judge, taking his place upon the bench to try criminals for their lives. Just this distinction is recognized by the apostle; he whose work when tried by fire abides, receives a reward. He whose work is burned and who therefore suffers loss is yet represented as himself being saved, though as out of fire, because he is building on the right Foundation.

If, then, we have the happy consciousness that we are trusting in Jesus, we may let our minds be at rest, as to our acquittal or condemnation. There is no more condemnation to them that are in Christ Jesus. And we may triumphantly ask, "Who shall lay anything to the charge of God's elect?". God hath justified! "Who is he that condemneth?". Christ hath died, yea, rather hath risen again. He is ever at the right hand of God; He also maketh intercession for us. From His love *nothing* shall separate us.

But while we rest thus peacefully in regard to our *acceptance*, what watchfulness should we exercise in regard to our *work*. That at length it may stand approved; that when the Master cometh, He may say to us, "Well done!" "Thou hast been faithful!"

Now, do we not see about us Christians who represent both these classes of builders? They rest upon the same Foundation. We have, perhaps, no reason to doubt that. But how different their work!.

Some we recognize as building with "Gold, silver, precious stones". We not only believe them to be in Christ Jesus—we see them positively adorning His doctrine. Every thing in their lives is conformable to the faith which they profess. While conscious of many deficiencies in their service, they yet have the testimony of their own consciences that they are faithful. If death were to come to them, they would not turn pale at its approach, but they could calmly say, "I am now ready to be offered". They know that they have an inner life of fellowship with the Lord Jesus. Christ abides in them and they in Him. They pray without ceasing. The Word of God is as honey to their taste. The Lord's day is above all days to them. The Lord's house is as the gate of heaven. They can say of the Church,

"Beyond my highest joy
I praise her heavenly ways,
Her sweet communion, solemn vows,
Her hymns of love and praise."

Nor is there only this inner life of joy and peace—this alone were worthless. But with this the outer life agrees. To those who are building thus with "gold, silver, precious stones", religion is not a garment for Sunday use. It does not consist merely in pleasing emotions. It is an influence hallowing all the life. It transforms the character. It goes with the man wherever he goes, regulating all his thoughts, all his words, all his actions. Such an one makes Christ his example. More than for any thing else he longs to be Christ-like. In all his dealings with men he is at once merciful and just. He seeks not by any doubtful ways his own advancement. He would rather by far be poor than have ill-gotten gain. His chief concern is not to lay up treasure here. His treasure lies within the veil, and where his treasure is there his heart is also. He cannot be corrupted by any of the meanness, treachery, or wrong that is in the world. He goes straight on in duty, swerving not for pleasure, for honor, or for gain. Touched by others' woes, even as was his Lord, he makes himself the friend of all who are in any trouble, and turns not from the cry of the poor and destitute. All the good he can do for Christ he does gladly and of a willing mind, giving freely as he has received. A watch is set upon his lips, to keep him from offending with his tongue, and his speech is with grace seasoned with salt. Of such an one others take knowledge that he has been with Jesus. His religion is not a mere outward thing. It is a part of his character. Christ is actually in him, and you see the blessed result of having an indwelling Saviour. When troubles come, how meekly they are borne, how patiently! The head is bowed to let the waves go over it, and the soul doth not complain. If it must suffer, it can suffer and not murmur.

Such Christians are unhappily too few. But surely you have seen them, those whom you could but own to be all that Christians ought to be; not, indeed, wholly free from infirmity, but yet showing wonderfully the power of faith. Such are building with "gold, silver, precious stones". And when the fire tries *their* work it shall survive. They shall stand approved. They shall be saved not merely as by fire, but as good and faithful servants. An entrance shall be ministered unto them abundantly into the everlasting kingdom of our Lord and Saviour Jesus Christ (2 Peter 1:11).

Thus it is with some—they are burning and shining lights. Thus it is not with all; there are others whom we may believe to be in Christ Jesus, who *are* in Christ Jesus, but who are not earnest in the Christian life. The life that now is has too strong a hold upon them. If really on the One Foundation, they shall be saved. But *how* saved?. "So as by fire"! Looking back upon life as its close is drawing near, they shall not be able to use such language as this, (which every Christian ought then to be able to use) "I have fought a good fight", "I have glorified Thee on the earth". Rather their dying-bed will be one of vain regrets, on which they will make the confession, "I have been unfaithful, I have not lived as I ought to have lived; could I go back and live the past over again, oh! how differently would I order my conversation!" Such shall indeed be saved, if truly Christ's. But they shall surely suffer loss —loss even through all eternity—loss that can never be made up to them. Your reward shall not be like that of those who have been faithful. Your crown shall never shine as bright, the music of your heart shall never be as sweet, the palm in your hand you shall never wave as victoriously.

Oh! what an incentive to holiness of living, to earnestness in godliness, to fullness of consecration!. "The fire shall try every man's work of what sort it is". Some are so living that the work which they have built upon the One Foundation—Christ—shall abide, and they shall receive an exceeding great reward. Others are so living that, though saved because resting upon the true Corner-stone, they yet shall suffer loss. Their worthless work shall be burned. In the review of life they shall be ashamed, and be saved "so as by fire". Surely none will be satisfied with this. You do not want merely to be saved, barely to escape Hell!. If the love of Christ is in your heart, it must constrain you to something nobler than this. So live that as a Christian man or woman you shall not have to look back upon your life with unavailing sorrow, but that in the hour of your departure you may be able to use this language of the apostle; "Our rejoicing is this, the testimony of our conscience, that in simplicity and godly sincerity, not with fleshly wisdom, but by the grace of God, we have had our conversation in the world" (2 Cor. 1-12).

James Inglis (1863)

(Continued from page 97.)
best seen by comparing them with the weight of glory which is awaiting us. As said the same apostle in another place, "For I reckon that the sufferings of this present time are not worthy to be compared with the glory which shall be revealed in us" (Rom. 8:18).

(3) "Which is but for a moment". Should our afflictions continue throughout a whole lifetime, and that life be equal in duration to Methusalah's, yet is it momentary if compared with the eternity which is before us. At most our affliction is but for this present life, which is as a vapor that appears for a little while and then vanishes away. O that God would enable us to examine our trials in their true perspective.

3 Note now the connection between the two. Our light affliction, which is but for a moment *"worketh for us"* a far more exceeding and eternal weight of glory". The present is influencing the future. It is not for us to reason and philosophize about this, but to take God at His Word and believe it. Experience, feelings, observation of others, may seem to deny this fact. Ofttimes afflictions appear only to sour us and make us more rebellious and discontented. But let it be remembered that afflictions are not sent by God for the purpose of purifying the flesh: they are designed for the benefit of the "new man". Moreover, afflictions help to prepare us for the glory hereafter. Affliction draws away our heart from the love of the world; it makes us long more for the time when we shall be translated from this scene of sin and sorrow; it will enable us to appreciate (by way of contrast) the things which God had prepared for them that love Him.

Here then is what faith is invited to do: to place in one scale the present affliction, in the other, the eternal glory. Are they worthy to be compared? No, indeed. One second of glory will more than counterbalance a whole lifetime of suffering. What are years of toil, of sickness, of battling against poverty, of persecution, yea, of a martyr's death, when weighed over against the pleasures at God's right hand, which are *for evermore!* One breath of Paradise will extinguish all the adverse winds of earth. One day in the Father's House will more than counterbalance the years we have spent in this dreary wilderness. May God grant unto us that faith which will enable us to anticipatively lay hold of the future and live in the present enjoyment of it.

Arthur W. Pink

For the benefit of those who are finding the articles on Exodus instructive and profitable, we wish to announce a two-volumed work "Gleanings in Genesis" by Arthur W. Pink. Price $2.50 postpaid. It contains forty-six articles on the first book in the Bible. Six years were spent in the preparation of them. Special attention is given to the types and prophecies. Many have pronounced these two volumes the most helpful work on Genesis.

Also we wish to say to new subscribers, Vol. 1 and Vol. 2 of "Studies in the Scriptures", nicely bound, can be had for $1:50 each. These contain the Expositions of John's Gospel from its first verse, besides many other articles by the Editor on The Antichrist, The Sabbath, Eternal Punishment, Creation, Romans 7, The Blood, Second Coming of Christ, etc., etc.

Foreign subscribers please send **International** Money Orders.

Send all orders to the Editor, 227 N. Creighton St. Philadelphia.

VOL. III JUNE, 1924 NO. 6

STUDIES in the SCRIPTURES

"Search the Scriptures" John 5:39.

A PERIODICAL (MONTHLY "IF THE LORD WILL") DEVOTED TO BIBLE STUDIES and EXPOSITIONS

Arthur W. Pink, Publisher & Editor,
227 N. Creighton St., Philadelphia, Pa.

Price: 10 cents per copy; $1.00 per year. Foreign $1.00 per year.

PRAYER

If ye abide in Me and My words abide in you, ye shall ask what ye will and it shall be done unto you. (John 15:7).

What erroneous conclusions have been drawn from these words! How often they have been appealed to in order to justify the most unworthy views of prayer! The popular interpretation of them is, that if the Christian's life is regulated by the Scriptures, he may then ask God for what he pleases and the Almighty will not —some go so far as to say *cannot*—deny him. But 1 John 5:14 plainly repudiates such a carnal conception; "If we ask anything according to His will He heareth us". Therefore, what we ask shall not be done unto us unless our will is subordinated to and is in accord with the will of God.

What, then, is the real meaning of John 15:7?. Certainly it does not give praying souls *carte blanche*. For God to grant us every thing we requested would not only be dishonoring to Him, but, ofttimes, highly injurious to ourselves. Moreover, the experience of those who frequent the Throne of Grace dissipates such a delusion. All of us have asked for many things which have *not* been "done unto" us. Some have asked in great earnestness, with full expectation, and they have been very importunate, and yet their petitions have been denied them. Does this falsify the Lord's promise?. A thousand times no! Every word He uttered was God's infallible truth. What, then?. Shall we fall back upon the hope that *God's time* to answer has not yet come, but that shortly He *will* give us the desires of our hearts?. Such a hope may be realized, or it may not. It all depends upon whether the *conditions* governing the promise in John 15:7 are being met. Let us note them carefully. They are two in number;

First, "*If* ye abide in Me". The reference is not to the believer's standing, but to his state. Every believer is "in Christ", yet not every believer "*abides*" in Him. Abiding in Christ has reference to *fellowship*. Let the reader take the concordance and make a prayerful study of those passages in John's Gospel and Epistles where this word "abide" (in its different tenses) occurs, and he will find a rich feast for his soul. "Abiding" in Christ signifies the *maintenance* of heart communion with Him who is Fairer than the children of men. To "abide" in Christ is to walk with Him as Enoch walked with God.

(Continued on page 144.)

IMPORTANT NOTICES

All new subscriptions will be dated back to January, 1924.

Set of twelve issues for **1922**, unbound, **$1.00.** Bound, **$1.50.**

Set of twelve issues for **1923**, unbound, **$1.00.** Bound **$1.50.**

Note: We cannot break a set or now supply any **single** 1923 issues.

Subscription Price: **$1.00** per year to any address in the world. Single copies **10 cents.**

Change of Address: Please notify me promptly of any change of address, and be certain to give both old and new addresses.

Non-subscribers receiving this Magazine regularly will understand their subscription has been entered by a friend.

Copies lost in the mail duplicated only if we are notified promptly.

Entered as second-class matter December 15th, 1923, at the post office at Philadelphia, Pa., under Act of March 3rd, 1879.

CONTENTS

JOHN'S GOSPEL.

30. CHRIST THE LIGHT OF THE WORLD (Concluded): John 8:33-59.

The passage which is to be before us continues and completes the portion studied in our last article. It brings before us Christ as the Light revealing the hidden things of darkness, exposing the pretensions of religious professors, and making manifest the awful depths of human depravity. We shall miss that in it which is of most importance and value if we localize it, and see in these verses nothing more than the record of a conversation between the Lord and men long since past and gone. We need to remind ourselves constantly that the Word of God is a *living* Word, depicting things as they *now* are, describing the opposition and activities of the carnal mind as they obtain today, and giving counsel which is strictly pertinent to ourselves. It is from this viewpoint we shall discuss this closing section of John 8. Below we give a Summary of our passage:—

1. Bondage and liberty: vv. 33-36.
2. Abraham's seed and Abraham's children: vv. 37-40.
3. Children of the Devil and children of God: vv. 41-47.
4. Christ dishonored by men, the Father honored by Christ: vv. 48-50.
5. Life and death: vv. 51-55.
6. Abraham and Christ: vv. 56-58.
7. The Saviour leaves the Temple: v. 59.

"They answered Him, We be Abraham's seed, and were never in bondage to any man: how sayest Thou, Ye shall be made free?" (v. 33). This was the reply made by the Jews to the words of the Lord recorded in the previous verses. There we find Him describing the fundamental characteristic of a genuine disciple of His: he is one who continues in Christ's word (v. 31, re-read our comments thereon). The one who continues in the Word shall know the truth, and the truth shall make him *free* (v. 32). But to be told about being *made* free is something the natural man does not like to hear. The plain implication is, that *before* he knows the truth he is *in bondage*. And such indeed is the case, little as men realize or recognize the fact. There are four things about themselves which are particularly hateful, because so humbling, to the unregenerate. First, that they are destitute of righteousness (Isa. 64:6) and goodness (Rom. 7:18), and therefore "unclean" (Isa. 64:6) and "vile" (Job 40:4). Second, that they are destitute of wisdom (Rom. 3:11) and therefore full of "vanity" (Psa. 39:5) and "foolishness" (Prov. 22:15). Third, that they are destitute of "strength" (Rom. 5:6) and "power" (Isa. 40:29), and therefore unable to do anything good of or from themselves (John 15:5). Fourth, that they are destitute of freedom (Isa. 61:1), and therefore in a state of bondage (2 Pet. 2:19).

The condition of the natural man is far, far worse than he imagines, and far worse than the average preacher and Sunday School teacher supposes. Man is a fallen creature, totally depraved, with no soundness in him from the sole of his foot even unto the head (Isa. 1:6). He is completely under the dominion of sin (John 8:34), a bond-slave to divers lusts (Titus 3:3), so that he *"cannot* cease from sin" (2 Pet. 2:14). Moreover, the natural man is thoroughly under the dominion of it. He is taken captive by the Devil at his will (2 Tim. 2:26). He walks according to the Prince of the power of the air, the spirit that now *worketh in* the children of disobedience (Eph. 2:2). He fulfills the lusts of his father, the Devil (John 8:44). He is completely dominated by Satan's power (Col. 1:13). And from this thraldom nothing but the truth of God can deliver.

"The truth shall make you free" (v. 32). As already stated, this signifies that the natural man is in bondage. But this is a truth that the natural man cannot tolerate. The very announcement of it stirs up the enmity within him. Tell the sinner that there is *no* good thing in him, and he will not believe you; but tell him that he is completely the slave of sin and the captive of Satan, that he *cannot* think a godly thought of himself (2 Cor. 3:5), that he *cannot* receive God's truth (1 Cor. 2:14), that he *cannot* believe (John 12:39), that he *cannot* please God (Rom. 8:8), that he *cannot* come to Christ (John 6:44), and he will indignantly deny your assertions. So it was here in the passage before us. When Christ said "the truth shall make you free", the Jews replied "We be Abraham's seed, and were *never in bondage* to any man".

The proud boast of these Jews was utterly unfounded; nothing could have been further from the truth. The very first view which Scripture gives us of Abraham's seed after they became a nation, is in bitter and cruel bondage (Ex. 2). Seven times over in the book of Judges we read of God delivering or selling Israel into the hands of the Canaanites. The seventy-years captivity in Babylon also gave the lie to the words of these Jews, and even at the time they spoke, the Romans were their masters. It was therefore the height of absurdity and a manifest departure from the truth for them to affirm that the seed of Abraham had never been in bondage. Yet no more untenable and erroneous was this than the assertions of present-day errorists who prate so loudly of the freedom of the natural man, and who so hotly deny that his will *is* enslaved by sin. "How sayest Thou, Ye shall be made free?": equally ignorant are thousands in the religious world today. Deliverance from the Law, emancipation from bad habits they have heard about, but real spiritual freedom they understand not, and cannot while they remain in ignorance about the universal bondage of sin.

"Jesus answered them, Verily, verily, I say unto you, Whosoever committeth sin is the servant (bond-slave) of sin" (v. 34). In saying *"whosoever . . . .* is the bond-slave" Christ was intimating to these Jews that *they* were no exception to the general rule, even though they belonged to the favored seed of Abraham. Christ was not speaking of a particular class of men more lawless than their fellows, but was affirming that which is true of *every* man in his natural condition. "Whosoever *committeth* sin", refers to the regular practice, the habitual course of a man's life. Here is one thing which distinguishes the Christian from the non-Christian. The Christian sins, and sins daily; but the non-Christian does nothing but sin. The Christian sins, but he also repents; moreover, he does good works, and brings forth the fruit of the Spirit. But the life of the unregenerate man is one unbroken course of sin. Sin, we say, not crime. Water cannot rise above its own level. Being a sinner by nature, man is a sinner by practise, and cannot be anything else. A corrupt tree *cannot* bring forth good fruit. A poisoned fountain *cannot* send forth sweet waters. Because the sinner has no spiritual nature within him, because he is totally depraved and in complete bondage to sin, because he does nothing for *God's* glory, every action is polluted, every deed unacceptable to the Holy One.

"Whosoever committeth sin is the bond-slave of sin". How different are God's thoughts from ours! The man of the world imagines that to become a Christian means to forego his freedom. He supposes that he would be fettered with a lot of restrictions which nullified his liberty. But these very suppositions only evidence the fact that the god of this world (Satan) has *blinded* his mind (2 Cor. 2:4). The very opposite from what he supposes is really the case. It is the one out of Christ, not the one in Christ, who is in bondage—in "the bond of iniquity" (Acts 8:33). He is impelled by the downward trend of his nature, and the very freedom which the sinner supposes he is exercising in the indulgence of his evil propensities is only additional proof that he *is* the "bond-slave of sin". The love of self, the love of the world, the love of money, the love of pleasure—these are the tyrants which rule over all who are out of Christ. Happy the one who is *conscious* of such bondage, for this is the first step towards liberty.

"And the bond-slave abideth not in the house forever: but the Son abideth ever" (v. 35). The commentators are far from being in agreement in their interpretation of this verse, though we think there is little room for differences of opinion upon it. The "bond-slave" is the same character referred to in the previous verse—the one who makes a constant practise of sinning. Such an one abideth not in the house forever—the "house" signifies *family,* as in the House of Jacob, the House of Israel, the House of God (Heb. 3:5, 6). We take it that our Lord was simply enunciating a general principle or stating a well-known fact, namely, that a slave has only a *temporary* place in a family. The application of this principle to those He was addressing is obvious. The Jews insisted that they were Abraham's seed (v. 32), that they belonged to the favored family, whose were the covenants and promises. But, says our Lord, the mere fact that you are the natural descendants of Abraham, gives you no title to the blessings which belong to his spiritual children. This was impossible while they remained the bond-slaves of sin. Unless they were "made free" they would soon be cut off even from the temporary place of external privilege.

"But the Son abideth ever". These words point a contrast. The slave's place was uncertain, and at best temporary, but the Son's place in the family is permanent—no doubt the word "abideth" here (as everywhere) suggests the additional thought of *fellowship.* The history of Abraham's family well illustrated this fact, and probably Christ has the case of Ishmael and Isaac in mind when He uttered these words. "The Son abideth ever". Though this statement enunciated a general principle—something that is true of every member of God's family—yet the direct reference was clearly to Christ Himself, as the next verse makes plain, for "the Son" of v. 36 is clearly restricted to the Lord Jesus.

"If the Son therefore shall make you free, ye shall be free indeed" (v. 36). The "therefore" here settles the application of the previous verse. "*The* Son" is none other than the Lord Jesus Christ, and He is able to make free the bond-slaves of sin because He *is* the Son. The Son is no bond-slave in the Father's family, but He is one in purpose and power with the Father; He is in perfect fellowship with Him, and *therefore* He is fully competent to liberate those under the tyranny of sin and the dominion of Satan. To make His people "free" was the central object in view in the Divine incarnation. The first ministerial utterance of Christ was to the effect that the Spirit of the Lord had anointed Him to preach "deliverance to the captives . . . . to set at liberty them that are bruised" or "bound" (Luke 4:18). And so thoroughly are men under the thraldom of sin, so truly do they love darkness rather than light, they have to be *made* free, compare "*maketh* me to lie down" (Psa. 23).

"Ye shall be free indeed". Free *from what?* This brings before us the truth of Christian freedom: a most important subject, but one too wide to discuss here at any length*. To sum up in the fewest possible words, we would say that Christian liberty, spiritual liberty, consists of this: First, deliverance from the condemnation of sin, the penalty of the law, the wrath of God—Isa. 42:7, 60:1, Rom. 8:1. Second, deliverance from the power of Satan—Acts 26:18, Col. 1:13, Heb. 2:14, 15. Third, from the bondage of sin—Rom. 6:14, 18. Fourth, from the authority of man—Gal. 4:8, 9, 5:1, Col. 2:20-22. So much for the negative side; now a word on the positive.

Christians are delivered from the things just mentioned that they may be free to *serve God.* The believer is "the Lord's freeman" (1 Cor. 7:22), not Christ's freeman, observe, but "*the Lord's*", a Divine title which ever emphasizes our submission to His authority. When a sinner is saved he is not free to follow the bent of his old nature, for that would be lawlessness. Spiritual freedom is not license to do as I please, but emancipation from the bondage of sin and Satan that I may do as I ought: "that we being delivered out of the hand of our enemies *might serve Him* without fear, in holiness and righteousness before Him, all the days of our life" (Luke 1:74, 75). Rom. 6:16-18 and 22 contains a Divine summary of the positive side of this subject: let the reader give it careful and prayerful study.

* See the author's booklet on "Christian Liberty". 7 cents, postpaid.

"I know that ye are Abraham's seed; but ye seek to kill Me, because My word hath no place in you" (v. 37). Our Lord's object in these words is evident. He was further emphasizing the fact that though these Jews were the seed of Abraham, they certainly were not the children of God. Proof of this was furnished by the awful enmity then at work in their hearts. They sought (earnestly desired) to kill Him who was the Son. Certainly then, they were not *God's* children. Moreover, His word had no place in them—the Greek word translated "no place" signifies no entrance. They received it not (contrast 1 Thess. 2:13). They were merely *wayside* hearers. It is this which distinguishes, essentially, a saved man from a lost one. The former is one who *receives* with meekness the engrafted word (James 1:21). He hides that word in his heart (Psa. 119:11). The believer gives that Word the place of trust, of honor, of rule, of love. The man of the world gives the Word no place because it is too spiritual, too holy, too searching. He is filled with his own concerns, and is too busy and crowded to give the Word of God a real place of attention. Unspeakably solemn are those awful words of Christ to all such: "He that rejecteth Me, and receiveth not My words, hath One that judgeth him: the word that I have spoken, *the same* shall judge him in the last day" (John 12:48).

"I speak that which I have seen with My Father: and ye do that which ye have seen with your father" (v. 38). Christ further emphasizes the infinite gulf which separated these Jews from Himself. In the previous verse He had furnished proof that these men who were the seed of Abraham certainly were not the children of God. Here He leads up to their real parentage. In the first part of this verse our Lord insists that the doctrine He taught was what He had received from the Father, and its very nature and tendency clearly showed *who* His Father was. Its spirituality evidenced that it proceeded from the thrice Holy One: its unworldliness testified to the fact that it came from Him who is Spirit: its benignity showed it was from Him who is Love. Such was *His* Father.

"Ye do that which ye have seen with your father". "'Your actions tell who your father is, as My doctrine tells who My Father is'. In both cases 'father' here seems to mean spiritual model—the being after whom the character is fashioned—the being, under whose influences the moral and spiritual frame is formed. The thought that lies at the bottom of this representation is, 'Men's sentiments and conduct are things that are formed, and indicate the character of him who forms them. Your actions, which are characterized by falsehood and malignity, distinctly enough prove, that, in a moral and spiritual point of view, neither Abraham, nor the God of Abraham, is your father. The former of your spiritual character is not in heaven, wherever else he may be found'" (Dr. J. Brown).

"They answered and said unto Him, Abraham is our father" (v. 39). These Jews surely had a suspicion of whither our Lord's remarks in the previous verse were pointing; but they pretended not to observe, and sought to represent Him as a calumniator of Abraham. When they said, "Abraham is our father", it was but the self-righteousness of the natural man exhibiting itself. They were contrasting themselves from the heathen. 'The heathen are in bondage we allow; but You are now talking to those who belong to the covenant people: *we* belong to the Jewish Church', was the force of their remarks. It is not difficult to perceive how well this describes what is a matter of common observation today. Let the servant of God preach in the churches of this land on the ruined and lost condition of the natural man; let him faithfully apply his message to those present; and the result will be the same as here. The great mass of religious professors, who have a form of godliness but know nothing and manifest nothing of its power, will hotly resent being classed with those on the outside. They will tell you, *We* belong to the true Church, *we* are Christians not infidels.

"Jesus saith unto them, If ye were Abraham's children, ye would do the works of Abraham" (v. 39). Very simple, yet very searching was this. The "seed" of Abraham Christ acknowledged them to be (v. 37), but the "children" of Abraham they certainly were not. Natural descent from their illustrious progenitor did not bring them into the family of God. Abraham is "the father" only of "them *that believe*" (Rom. 4:11). This distinction is specifically drawn in Rom. 9:7: "Neither because they are the seed of Abraham are they all children". "Children" of Abraham refers to a *spiritual* relationship; "seed" of Abraham is only a fleshly tie, and "the flesh profiteth nothing" (John 6:63).

"If ye *were* Abraham's children, ye would *do* the works of Abraham". Here was and still is the decisive test. Natural descent counts for nothing, it is a spiritual relationship with God which is the great desideratum. The profession of our lips amounts to nothing at all if it is not confirmed by the character of our lives. Talk is cheap; it is our works, what we *do,* which evidences what we really *are.* A tree is known by its fruits. The "works of Abraham" were works of faith and obedience—faith in God and submission to His Word. But His Word had "no place *in them*". Idle then was their boast. Equally so is that of multitudes today, who say Lord, Lord, but *do not* the things which He has commanded.

"But now ye seek to kill Me, a man that hath told you the truth, which I have heard of God: this did not Abraham" (v. 40). "Abraham acted not thus. If ye were Abraham's children in a spiritual sense—if you were conformed to his character—you would imitate his conduct. But your conduct is the very reverse of his. You are desiring and plotting the murder of a man who never injured you, whose only crime is that He has made known to you important and salutary, but unpalatable, truth. Abraham never did anything like this. He readily received every communication made from heaven. He never inflicted injury on any man, far less on a Divine messenger, who was merely doing his duty. No, no! If children are like their parents, Abraham is not your father. He whose deeds you do, he is your father" (Dr. J. Brown).

"Ye do the deeds of your father. Then said they to Him, We be not born of fornication; we have one Father, even God" (v. 41). When the Jews replied, "We be not born of fornication", we take it that they meant, 'We are not bastard Jews, whose blood has been contaminated with idolatrous alliances, as is the case with the Samaritans.' It seems likely that this word was provoked by what our Lord had said in v. 35—"the bond-slave abideth not in the house", which was an oblique reference to Ishmael. If so, their words signified, 'We are genuine descendants of Abraham; we are children not of the concubine, but of the wife'.

"We have one Father, even God". How this same claim is being made on every side today! Those in far-distant lands may be heathen; but America is a Christian country. Such is the view which is held by the great majority of church members. The universal Fatherhood of God and the universal brotherhood of man are the favorite dogmas of Christendom. "We have one Father, even God" is the belief and boast of the great religious masses. How this justifies our opening remark, that the passage before us is not to be limited to a conversation which took place nineteen hundred years ago, but also contains a representation of human nature as it exists today, manifesting the same spirit of self-righteousness, appealing to the same false ground of confidence, and displaying the same enmity against the Christ of God.

"Jesus said unto them, If God were your Father, ye would love Me: for I proceeded forth and came from God; neither came I of Myself, but He sent Me" (v. 42). This was an indirect but plain denial that God *was* their Father. If they were the children of God they would *love* Him, and if they loved Him they would most certainly love His only begotten Son, for "he that loveth him that begat, loveth him that is begotten of him" (1 John 5:1). But they did *not* love Christ. Though He was the image of the invisible God, the brightness of His glory, and the express image of His person, they despised and rejected Him. They were the bond-slaves of sin (v. 34); Christ's word had no place in them (v. 37); they sought to kill Him (v. 40). Their boast therefore was an empty one; their claim utterly unfounded.

"Why do ye not understand My speech? even because ye cannot hear My word" (v. 43). Christ was here addressing Himself to their consciences. His question—no doubt there was a pause before He answered it—ought to have exercised their hearts. *Why* do you not understand My speech? You claim to be the children of the Father, why then are My words so obscure and mysterious to you? My language *is that of the Father,* surely then there is something wrong somewhere! The same question comes with equal pertinency to every one who hears the Word of God today. If that Word comes to me as that of an unknown tongue, then this shows I am a *stranger* to God. If I understand not His speech, I cannot be one of His children. That does not mean, of course, that I shall be able to fathom the infinite depths of His wonderful Word. But, speaking characteristically, if I understand not His speech—which is addressed not to the intellect but to the heart—then there is every reason why I should gravely inquire as to the *cause* of this.

"Even because ye cannot hear My word". The word "hear" (an Hebrew idiom) signifies to receive and believe—compare John 9:27; 10:3; 12:47; Acts 3:22, 23, etc. And *why* was it that these Jews "could not hear" His Word? It was because they were children in whom was no faith (Deut. 32:20). It was because they had no ear for God; no heart for His Word, no desire to learn His will. Proof positive was this that they were dead in trespasses and sins, and therefore *not* children of God. Unspeakably solemn is this. Hearing God's Word is an attitude of heart. We speak now not of the Divine side, for true it is that the Lord Himself must prepare the heart (Prov. 16:1) and give the hearing ear (Prov. 20:12). But from the human side, man is fully responsible *to* hear. But he *cannot* hear the still small voice of God while his ears are filled with the siren songs of the world. That he has no *desire to hear* does not excuse him, rather does it the more condemn him. The Lord grant that the daily attitude of writer and reader may be that of little Samuel, "Speak, Lord, for Thy servant heareth".

"Ye are of your father the Devil, and the lusts of your father ye will do. He was a murderer from the beginning, and abode not in the truth, because there is no truth in him. When he speaketh a lie, he speaketh of his own; for he is a liar, and the father of it" (v. 44). This was the prime point our Lord had been leading up to. First, He had repudiated their claim to being the children of Abraham. Second, He had demonstrated that God was not their Father. Now He tells them in plain language who their father really was, even the Devil. Their characters had been formed not under Divine influence, but under a diabolical influence. The moral likeness of that great Enemy of God was plainly stamped upon them. 'Your inveterate opposition to the truth, shows your kinship to him who is the father of the Lie (the Antichrist), and your desire to kill Me evidences that you are controlled by that one who was a murderer from the beginning'.

"Ye are of your father the Devil" is true of every unregenerate soul. Renouncing their dependency on God, denying His proprietorship, loving darkness rather than light, they fall an easy prey to the Prince of darkness. He blinds their minds; he directs their walk, and works in them both to will and to do of his evil pleasure (Eph. 2:2). Nor can sinners turn round and cast the blame for this upon God. For as Christ here declares, the lusts of their father *they* will do, or they *desire* to do, which is the correct meaning of the word. They were cheerful servants, voluntary slaves.

"And because I tell you the truth, ye believe Me not" (v. 45). The human race is now reaping what was sown at the beginning. Our first parents rejected God's truth and believed the Devil's lie, and ever since then man has been completely under the power of falsehood and error. He will give credence to the most grotesque absurdities, but will regard with skepticism what comes to him with a thousand fully authenticated credentials. Some will believe that there are no such things as sin and death. Some will believe that instead of being the descendants of fallen Adam, they are the offspring of evolving apes. Some believe that they have no souls and that death ends all. Others imagine that they can purchase heaven with their own works. O the blindness and madness of unbelief! But let the truth be presented; let men hear that God says they are lost, dead in trespasses and sins; that eternal life is a gift, and eternal torment is the portion of all who refuse that gift; and men believe them not. They believe not God's truth because their hearts love that which is false—"They go astray as soon as they be born, speaking lies" (Psa. 58:3); they "delight in lies" (Psa. 62:4); they make lies their "refuge" (Isa. 28:15), therefore it is that they "turn away their ears from the truth" (2 Tim. 4:4); and though they are ever learning, yet are they "never able to come to the knowledge of the truth" (2 Tim. 3:7). And therefore Christ is still saying to men, "*because* I tell you *the truth,* ye believe Me not".

"Which of you convinceth Me of sin?

And if I say the truth, why do ye not believe Me?" (v. 46). We take it Christ was here anticipating an objection. The charge He had just made against them was a very severe and piercing one, yet He openly challenges them to refute it. If you deny what I have said and charge Me with falsehood, how will you prove your charge? Which of you can fairly convince Me of that or of any other sin? But, on the other hand, if it be evident that I have told you the truth, then why do ye not believe Me? Such, in brief, we take to be our Lord's meaning here.

"He that is of God heareth God's words: ye therefore hear them not, because ye are not of God" (v. 47). The force of this we understand as follows: Every member of God's family is indwelt by the Holy Spirit, and in virtue of this receives with affection, reverence, and obedient regard the words of his heavenly Father, by whomsoever they are brought; hence, the reason why you do not receive My words is because you are not His children. "He that is *of God*" carries a double thought. First, it signifies, he that belongs to God by eternal election. A parallel to this is found in John 10:26, "Ye believe not, because ye are not *of My sheep*". It is this which, in time, distinguishes the elect from the non-elect. The former, in due time, hear or receive God's words; the latter do not. Second, "He that is of God" signifies, he that has been born of God, he that is in the family of God. A parallel to this is found in John 18:37: "Every one that is *of the truth* heareth My voice".

"Then answered the Jews, and said unto Him, Say we not well that Thou art a Samaritan, and hast a demon?" (v. 48). This was a plain admission that they were unable to answer the Lord. Completely vanquished in argument, they resort to vulgar and blasphemous declamation. But why should these Jews have called Christ these *particular* names at *this* time? We believe the answer is found in what Christ had just said to them. He had declared that they were not the true children of Abraham (v. 39); and He had affirmed that the Devil was their father (v. 44). In reply, they retorted, "Thou art a Samaritan, and hast a demon". The general meaning of these epithets is clear: by "a Samaritan" they meant one who was an enemy to their national faith; by "Thou hast a demon" they intimated one obcessed by a proud and lying spirit. What frightful insults did the Lord of glory submit to!

"Jesus answered, I have not a demon; but I honour My Father, and ye do dishonour Me" (v. 49). To the first of their reproaches He made no reply. He passed it by as unworthy of notice, the irritated outburst of wanton malice. To the second He returns a blank denial, and then adds, "but I honour My Father". One who is controlled by the Devil is a liar, but Christ had told them the truth. One who is prompted by the Devil flatters men, but Christ had depicted fallen human nature in the most humbling terms. One who is moved by the Devil is inflated with pride, seeks honor and fame; but Christ sought only the honor of Another, even the Father. Divinely calm, Divinely dignified, Divinely majestic was such an answer. How the longsufferance of Christ, His patient bearing with these villifiers, His unruffled spirit and calm bearing, evidenced Him to be none other than the Son of God.

"And I seek not Mine own glory: there is One that seeketh and judgeth" (v. 50). "'If I did, I should not have told you the truth. Had My own aggrandizement been My object, I should have followed another course; and My not obtaining 'glory'—a good opinion—from you, no way disheartens Me'. There is One who seeketh, that is, who seeketh My glory. There is One who will look after My reputation. There is One who is pledged in holy covenant to make Me His firstborn, higher than the kings of the earth. And He who seeketh My glory, judgeth. He will sit in judgment on your judgment. These words seem plainly intended to intimate, in a very impressive way, the fearful responsibility they had incurred. He was doing His Father's will: they were treating Him with contumely. The Father was seeking the honor of His faithful Servant, His beloved Son; and dreadful would be the manifestation of His displeasure against those who, so far as lay in their power, had put to shame the God-man, whom He delighted to honor'" (Dr. J. Brown).

"Verily, verily, I say unto you, If a man keep My saying, he shall never see death". (v. 51). The commentators have quite missed the connection between the contents of this verse and what precedes. Christ had just pointed out the fearful consequence of rejecting Him and His word—there was One who would *judge* them. Locally this pointed to the awful visitation from God upon their nation in A. D. 70; but the ultimate reference is to eternal judgment, which is "the second death". Now in sharp and blessed contrast from the doom awaiting those in whom the Word had "no place", Christ now says, "If a man keep My saying, he shall never see death"! Blessed promise was this for His own. But mark how human responsibility is here pressed—the promise is only to the one who *keeps* Christ's word. To "keep" the Word is to hide it in the heart (Psa. 119:11). It is to retain it in the memory (1 Cor. 15:3). It is to be governed by it in our daily lives (Rev. 3:8). "He shall never see (know or experience) death" refers to penal death, the wages of sin, eternal separation from God in the torments of Hell. For the believer physical dissolution is not death (separation), but to be *present* with the Lord (2 Cor. 5:8).

"Then said the Jews unto Him, Now we know that Thou hast a devil, Abraham is dead, and the prophets; and Thou sayest, If a man keep My saying, he shall never taste of death. Art Thou greater than our father Abraham, which is dead? and the prophets are dead: whom makest Thou Thyself?" (vv. 52, 53). What a striking exemplification was this of what our Lord had said in v. 43: they understood not His speech and heard not His words. Devoid of discernment, they had no capacity to perceive the spiritual import of what He said. Such is the awful condition of the natural man: the things of God are foolishness to him (1 Cor. 2:14). What is revealed to babes in Christ is completely hidden from those who are wise and prudent in their own estimation and in the judgment of the world (Matt. 11:25). No matter how simply and plainly the truths of Scripture may be expounded, the unregenerate are unable to understand them. Unable because their interests are elsewhere. Unable because they will not humble themselves and cry unto God for light. Unable because their hearts are estranged from Him. Christian reader, what abundant reason have you to thank God for giving *you* an understanding (1 John 5:20)!

"Jesus answered, If I honour Myself, My honour is nothing: it is My Father that honoureth Me; of whom ye say, That He is your God" (v. 54). "It is My Father that honoureth Me": precious words are these and worthy of prolonged study and meditation. To "honour" is to do or speak that of a person which shall not only manifest our own esteem for him, but shall lead others to esteem him too. The Father's esteem for the Son is evidenced by His love and admiration for Him, as well as His desire to make Him the loved and admired of others. God honoured Him at His birth, by sending the angels to herald Him as Christ the Lord. He honoured Him during the days of His infancy, by directing the wise men from the east to come and worship the young King. He honoured Him at His baptism, by proclaiming Him His beloved Son. He honoured Him in death, by not suffering His body to see corruption. He honoured Him at His ascension, when He exalted Him to His own right hand. He will honour Him at His return, when He shall set Him King upon the holy hill of Zion. He will honour Him throughout the millennium, when the knowledge of the glory of the Lord shall cover the earth as the waters cover the sea. He will honour Him in the final judgment, when every knee shall be made to bow before Him and every tongue confess that He is Lord. And throughout eternity He shall be honoured by a redeemed people who shall esteem Him the Fairest among ten thousand to their souls. Infinitely worthy is the Lamb to receive honour and glory. Let then the writer and reader see to it that our daily lives honour Him who has so highly honoured us as to call us "brethren".

"Yet ye have not known Him; but I know Him: and if I should say, I know Him not, I shall be a liar like unto you: but I know Him, and keep His saying" (v. 55). The One who honoured Him they knew not, despite their profession to be His children. But on the other hand, if He were to deny the knowledge He had of the Father, then He would be as false as they were in pretending to know Him. But He would not deny Him; nay more, He would continue to give evidence of His knowledge of the Father by keeping His word. For Him that word meant to finish the work which had been given Him to do, to become obedient unto death, even the death of the Cross. A searching word is this for us. If we really know the Father it will be evidenced by our subjection to His Word!

"Your father Abraham rejoiced to see My day: and he saw it, and was glad" (v. 56). More literally the Greek reads, "Abraham, your father, was transported with an exultant desire that he should see My day, and he saw it and rejoiced". The Greek is much more expressive and emphatic than our English translation. It intimates that Abraham looked forward with joy to meet the Object of his desires, and exulted in a sight of it. But to what did our Lord refer when He said, Abraham saw "My day"? In the Greek the "day" is emphasized by putting it before the pronoun—"day, My". We believe that "day" is here to be understood in its dispensational sense, as signifying the entire Dispensation of Christ, which embraces the two advents. Probably what Abraham saw and rejoiced in was, first, the humiliation of Christ, terminating in His death, which would occasion the patriarch great joy as he knew that death would blot out all his sins; second, the vindication and glorification of Christ which would be manifested on earth during the Millennium.

But *how* did Abraham "see" Christ's "Day"? We believe that a threefold answer may be returned: First, Abraham saw the day of Christ *by faith* in the promises of God (Heb. 11:13). Heb. 11:10 and 16 intimate plainly that the Spirit of God made discoveries to Abraham which are not recorded on the pages of the Old Testament. Second, Abraham saw the day of Christ *in type*. In offering Isaac on the altar and in receiving him back in figure from the dead, he received a marvelous foreshadowing of the Saviour's death and resurrection; and in being blest by Melchizedek, the priest-king, God furnished a beautiful prefigurement of millennial times. Third, by *special revelation*. The "secret of the Lord" is with them that fear Him, and there is no doubt in our mind but that God was pleased to show the Old Testament saints much more of His covenant than is commonly supposed among us (see Psa. 25:14).

"Your father Abraham rejoiced to see My day: and he saw it, and was glad" (v. 56). The relevancy of this remark of Christ and its relation to what had gone before are easily perceived. More immediately, it was part of His answer to their last question in v. 53—"Whom makest Thou Thyself?" More remotely, it furnished the final proof that *they* were not the children of Abraham, for they did not his work (v. 39). If these Jews *rejoiced not* at the appearing of Christ before them, then in no sense were they like Abraham.

"Then said the Jews unto Him, Thou art not yet fifty years old, and hast Thou seen Abraham?" (v. 57). How blind they were! How thoroughly incompetent to understand His speech. Christ had not spoken of seeing Abraham, but of Abraham seeing His "day". There was a vast difference between these two things, but they were incapable of perceiving it.

"Jesus said unto them, Verily, verily, I say unto you, Before Abraham was, I am" (v. 58). Here was the full disclosure of His glory; the affirmation that He was none other than the Eternal One. That they so understood Him is evident from what follows.

"Then took they up stones to cast at Him: but Jesus hid Himself, and went out of the temple, going through the midst of them, and so passed by" (v. 59). "It is Immanuel: but there is no knee bent to Him, no loving homage tendered. They took up stones to stone Him, and He hiding Himself for the moment from their sacriligious violence, passes out of the temple" (Mr. F. W. Grant).

"Jesus hid Himself, and went out of the temple, going through the midst of them, and so passed by". Fearfully solemn is this in its present-day application. The chief design of the whole chapter is to present Christ as the "Light" and to show us *what* that Light revealed. Not by observation can we discover the full ruin which sin has wrought. It is only as the Light shines that man is fully exposed. And that which is particularly discovered here is the utter vanity of the religious pretensions of the natural man.

Apart from spiritual discernment, the religious professor presents before us a fair appearance. His evident sincerity, his punctiliousness, his unquestionable zeal, his warm devotion, his fidelity to the cause he has espoused, are frequently a mask which no human eye can penetrate. It is not until such professors are exposed to the searching *light of God* that their *real* characters are laid bare. It is only as *the Word* is faithfully applied to them that their awful depravity is revealed. It was not profligate outcasts, but orthodox Jews who are here seen taking up stones to cast at the Son of God, and they did this not on the public highway, but in the temple! Nor have things changed for the better. Were Christ here today in Servant-form, and were He to enter our churches and tell the great mass of religious professors that *they* were the bond-slaves of sin, and that *they* were of their father the Devil and that *his* lusts *they* delighted in doing, they would conduct themselves exactly as their fellows did eighteen centuries ago. Terribly significant then is the final word of our chapter: the Saviour "*hid* Himself" from them, and went out of the temple. It is so still. From the self-righteous and self-sufficient, but blinded religious formalists, Christ still hides Himself; those who deny that *they* need to be made free from the slavery of sin He still leaves to themselves. But thank God it is written, "I dwell in the high and holy place, with him *also* that is of a *contrite and humble spirit*" (Isa. 57:15).

The following questions are to help the interested student on the next lesson, John 9:1-7:—

1. What is the great doctrinal teaching of this passage?
2. What typical picture does it contain?
3. Why does it open with the word "And": v. 1.
4. To what was Christ referring in v. 4?
5. Why did Christ *again* say "I am the Light of the world," v. 5?
6. What was the symbolical meaning of vv. 6 and 7?
7. What force has "therefore" in v. 7?

—Arthur W. Pink.

GLEANINGS IN EXODUS.

6. The Significance of the Signs: Ex. 4.

In our last lesson we dwelt upon the response which Moses made to the call he received from God. After forty years in the backside of the desert he was visited by the Lord, who declared that it was His purpose to send him unto Pharaoh (3:16). Instead of bowing in wonderment and gratitude at the condescension of the Almighty in deigning to employ him in so important and honorous an errand, he answered, "Who am *I*, that I should go unto Pharaoh?". In response to this God assured Moses that *He* would be with him. Moses next enquired in whose name he should address Israel, and then it was that God revealed Himself as the great "I am", the God of Abraham, the God of Isaac, and the God of Jacob. The Lord promised that He would deliver His people from the affliction of Egypt and bring them unto the land of Canaan, and bade His servant appear before Pharaoh with the demand that the king allow the Hebrews to go a three days' journey into the wilderness that they might hold a feast unto the Lord their God. But the Lord informed Moses He was sure that Pharaoh would not grant this request, yet, notwithstanding, He would show forth such wonders that in the end the king *would* let them go; and not only so, but that He would give His people favor in the eyes of the Egyptians so that they would be enriched and go not out empty-handed. Yet notwithstanding these gracious re-assurances Moses continued to be occupied with difficulties and to raise objections: "Behold, they will not believe me, nor hearken unto my voice; for they will say, The Lord hath not appeared unto thee" (4:1). Our present lesson resumes the sacred narrative at this point.

In response to the third difficulty raised by Moses, the Lord endued His recalcitrant servant with the power to perform three wonders or signs, which were to be wrought before his fellow-countrymen for the purpose of convincing them that Moses was Jehovah's accredited ambassador. That there is a deep meaning to these three signs, and that they were designed to teach important lessons both to Moses, to Israel, and to us, goes without saying. At the beginning of Israel's history it was God's method to teach more by signs and symbols, than by formal and explicit instruction. The fact, too, that these three signs are the *first* recorded in Scripture denotes that they are of prime importance and worthy of our most careful study.

"And the Lord said unto him, What is that in thine hand? And he said, A rod. And He said, Cast it on the ground. And he cast it on the ground, and it became a serpent; and Moses fled from before it.

And the Lord said unto Moses, Put forth thine hand, and take it by the tail. And he put forth his hand, and caught it, and it became a rod in his hands: That they may believe that the Lord God of their fathers, the God of Abraham, the God of Isaac, and the God of Jacob hath appeared unto thee" (Ex. 4:2-5). The first of these signs was the turning of the rod into a serpent, and that back again into a rod. But three verses are devoted to the description of this wonder, but marvellously full are they in their spiritual suggestiveness and hidden riches. We purpose to study this miracle from seven different angles, considering in turn: its practical lessons, its doctrinal meaning, its evidential value, its evangelical message, its historical significance, its dispensational forecast, and its typical purport. May the Lord give us eyes to see and ears to hear.

(1) There can be no doubt that the first design of God in connection with this sign was to teach Moses himself *a practical lesson*. What this was it is not difficult to discover. The sign had to do with the rod in his hand. This rod or staff (as the Hebrew word is sometimes translated) was his *support*. It was that which gave him aid as he walked, it was that on which he leaned when weary, it was a means of defence in times of danger. Now in the light of Psa. 23:4 we learn that, spiritually considered, the "rod" speaks of the upholding, strengthening, protecting *grace of God*. Here, then, is the first lesson the Lord would teach His servant: while Moses continued dependent *(supporting* himself) on God, all would be well; but let him cast his "rod" to the ground, that is, let him renounce God's grace, let him cast away his confidence in Jehovah, let him attempt to stand alone, and he would at once find himself helpless before that old Serpent, the Devil. Here, then, we say, was the great practical lesson for Moses, and for us: the secret of overcoming Satan lies in *leaning* in simple dependency and conscious weakness on our "staff", i. e., the power of God!

(2) But this first sign was also designed to teach Moses, and us, a great *doctrinal* lesson, a doctrine which as the priority of this sign suggests is one of *fundamental* importance. Nor are we left to guess at what this may be. Just as the twenty-third Psalm enables us to interpret its practical meaning, so the second Psalm supplies the key to its doctrinal significance.

In Psa. 2:9 (cf Rev. 2:27) we learn that during the Millennium the Lord Jesus will rule the nations with a *rod* of iron. The "rod", then, speaks of *governmental power*. But what is signified by the "casting down" of the rod *to the ground?* Surely it speaks of God *delegating* governmental power to the rulers *of earth*. And what has been the uniform history of man's use of this delegated power? The answer is, Exactly what the "serpent" suggests: it has been employed in the service of Satan! Thus it proved with Adam, when his Maker gave him "dominion" over all things terrestrial. Thus it proved with the nation of Israel after they became the conquerors of Canaan. So, too, with Nebuchadnezzar, after earthly sovereignty was transferred from Jerusalem to Babylon. And so it has continued all through the Times of the Gentiles. But it is blessed to note that the "serpent" no more succeeded in *getting away* from Moses than the rod had *slipped* out of his hand. Moses—as God's *representative* before Israel—took the "serpent" by the tail (the time for its head to be "bruised" had not yet come) and it was transformed into a "rod" in his hand again. This tells us that Satan is no 'free agent' in the popular acceptation of that term, but is completely under God's control, to be used by Him in fulfillment of His inscrutable counsels as He sees fit. Thus would Jehovah assure His servant at the outset that the enemy who would rage against him was unable to withstand him!

(3) This sign was to be wrought by Moses before the Hebrews as a proof that God had called and endowed him to be their deliverer. The *evidential value* of this wonder is easily perceived. To see the rod of Moses become a serpent before their eyes would at once evidence that he was endowed with supernatural power. To take that serpent by the tail and transform it again to a rod, would prove that Moses had not performed this miracle by the help of Satan. Moses was to show that he was able to deal with the serpent at his pleasure, making the rod a serpent, and the serpent a rod as he saw fit. Thus in performing a wonder that altogether transcended the skill of man, and a wonder that plainly was not wrought by the aid of the Devil, he demonstrated that he was commissioned and empowered by God.

(4) This sign which Moses wrought before the children of Israel also carried an

evangelical message, though perhaps this is more difficult to discern than the other meanings it possessed. The rod cast to the ground became a "serpent", and we are told "Moses *fled* from before it". Clearly this speaks of the helplessness of man to cope with Satan. The sinner is completely under the Devil's power, "taken captive by him at his will" (2 Tim. 2:26). Such was the condition of Israel at this time. They were subject to a bondage far worse and more serious than any that the Egyptians could impose upon them, and what is more, they were as unable to free themselves from the one as from the other. Nothing but Divine power could emancipate them, and this is just what this sign was fitted to teach them. Moreover, this power was placed in the hands of *a mediator*—Moses, the one who stood between Israel and God. He, and he only, was qualified to deliver from the serpent. His power over the serpent was manifested by taking it by the tail and reducing it to nothing—it disappeared when it became a rod again. Beautifully does this speak to us of the Lord Jesus, the One Mediator between God and men, of whom Moses was a type. In Him is your only hope, dear reader; He alone can deliver you from the power of that old Serpent, the Devil.

(5) Let us consider next the *historical significance* of this wonder. The "sign" itself consisted of three things: a rod held in the hand of Moses (God's representative), the rod thrown down to the ground and becoming a serpent, the serpent transformed into a rod again. These three things accurately symbolized *the early history of Israel.* From the Call of Abraham to the going down of his descendants into Egypt, Israel had been held (miraculously supported) in the hand of God, until, in the person of Joseph, they had attained to the position of *rule* over Egypt. But then a king arose who "knew not Joseph", and the Hebrews were then "cast down to the ground"—humiliated by severe and cruel bondage, until at the time of Moses it seemed as though they were completely at the mercy of Satan. But the time for deliverance had now drawn nigh, and the Lord assures them by means of this "sign" that they should remain in the place of oppression no longer, but would be delivered. And not only so, the last part of the sign gave promise that they should be raised to the place of rulership again. This was realized when they reached the promised land and subjugated the Canaanites. Thus the sign prefigured the three great stages in the early history of Israel.

(6) But this sign also provided a *dispensational forecast.* Not only did it accurately prefigure the *early* history of Israel, but it also anticipated in a most striking way the whole of their *future* history. The rod held in the hand contemplated them in the position of authority in Canaan. This portion Judah (the *ruling* Tribe) retained till Shiloh came. But following their rejection of Christ the "rod" was cast down to the ground, and for nineteen centuries Israel have been the prey and sport of the Serpent. But not forever are they to continue thus. The time is coming when Israel shall be raised out of the dust of degradation and, in the hand of a greater than Moses, shall be made the head of the nations (Deut. 28:13). Thus did this marvellous sign prefigure both the past and the future fortunes of the Chosen Nation.

(7) Deeper still lies the *typical purport* of this sign. We believe that its ultimate reference was to Christ Himself, and that the great mysteries of the Divine Incarnation and Atonement were foreshadowed. In Psa. 110:2 the Lord Jesus is called the *Rod* of God: "The Lord shall send the Rod (it is the same Hebrew word as here in Ex. 4) of Thy strength out of Zion: *rule* Thou in the midst of Thine enemies". The reference in Psa. 110 is to the second advent of Christ when His governmental authority and power shall be fully displayed. But when He was on earth the first time, it was in weakness and humiliation, and to this the casting-down of the "rod" on the ground points. But, it will be objected, surely there is no possible sense in which the Rod became a "serpent"! Yes there was, and none other than the Lord Jesus is our authority for such a statement. The "serpent" is inseparably connected with the Curse (Gen. 3), and on the Cross Christ was "made a curse" for His people (Gal. 3: 10-13). Said He to Nicodemus, "*As* Moses lifted up *the serpent* in the wilderness, *even so* must the Son of Man be lifted up" (John 3:14). But blessed be God that is all past: the Lord Jesus (the Rod) is now exalted to God's right *hand,* and soon will He take to Himself His power and reign over the earth. Marvellously full then was

the meaning of this first sign. Equally striking was the second, though we cannot now treat of it at the same length.

"And the Lord said furthermore unto him, Put now thine hand into thy bosom. And he put his hand into his bosom: and when he took it out, behold, his hand was leprous as snow. And he said, Put thine hand into thy bosom again. And he put his hand into his bosom again; and plucked it out of his bosom, and behold, it was turned again as his other flesh. And it shall come to pass, if they will not believe thee, neither hearken to the voice of the first sign, that they will believe the voice of the latter sign" (vv. 6-8). The significance of this second sign is not difficult to discern. "Leprosy" is the well-known emblem of sin—its loathsomeness, its contagiousness, the terrible rapidity with which it spreads, its insidious nature (commencing with a seemingly harmless spot), and its incurability so far as the wisdom of man is concerned, all witness to the accuracy of the figure. Lev. 13 and 14 are the two chapters of the Bible where leprosy is treated of at greatest length. Here in the passage before us we read that Moses put his hand into his bosom—the abode of the heart—and when he drew it forth, behold, it was leprous. In response to God's command he replaced his hand in his bosom, and on plucking it thence the leprosy had disappeared. This second "sign" also admits of various applications.

(1) The sign of the leprous hand was, no doubt, designed first for the instruction of Moses. It was intended to teach him the marvelous *power* of his Lord: that he should be thus smitten instantaneously with leprosy, that it should be confined to his hand, and that it should be cured immediately, without the use of means, was an astounding wonder. It manifested the perfect ease with which God could suddenly inflict such a disease and as quickly cure it: and this evidenced how simple a matter it was for Him to deliver His people out of the hand of the Egyptians.

(2) The "hand" speaks of energy: it is the instrument for work. Moses was God's instrument for doing a wonderful work in Egypt. But the Lord here shows him that *the flesh is set aside;* it is not the energy of the natural man which is the mainspring of action in God's service. How can it be, when the flesh is corrupt and under God's curse?—here symbolized by the hand becoming leprous. By nature, man's "hand" is *unfit* to be used by God. But Divine grace interposes in cleansing power, and that which is weak becomes strong; yet in such a way that what, under God, is now accomplished by that hand is manifestly because of the Lord's power.

(3) But the principal effect which this sign was calculated to have on Moses himself was a *humbling* one. Lest he become puffed up by the power of the rod, he is forcibly reminded of the sink of iniquity, the corrupt heart, within him. Therefore whatever Jehovah was pleased to accomplish by him must be attributed alone to sovereign grace.

(4) Moses is also to be viewed here as *the representative of the Hebrews,* for he was one of them, and what was here enacted before his eyes, vividly portrayed the condition of his people. In themselves they differed nothing from the Egyptians. They too were defiled and needed cleansing. No mere outward reformation would avail, for the seat of the trouble lay within their bosoms. Strikingly accurate were the details of this sign. It was not the hand which affected the heart, but the heart which affected the hand! How this disposes of an error which has been popular in every age. How often we hear it said that such an one may be weak and wayward, but he has *a good heart.* Not so: "Out of the heart", said the One who alone knew it, "proceed evil thoughts, murders, adulteries, fornications, thefts, false witness, blasphemies". So too, cleansing must begin with the heart—here signified by the leprous hand being thrust into the bosom before the loathsome disease was removed. And how is this brought about? By the power of God. True, from the Divine side; but what of the human? The answer is at once to hand. The leprous heart symbolizes sin hidden, the leprous hand, sin exposed (F. W. G.) It was the hand plucked out of the bosom which made manifest what was within! And it is precisely this which God demands from the sinner. What is so hateful to Him and so fatal to us, is for the sinner to *deny* his ruined and lost condition. Whilever man seeks to conceal the iniquity within, whilever he disguises himself and pretends to be other than a guilty, undone sinner, there is no hope for him. Seeking to *hide* their shame was one

of the first acts of Adam and Eve after their fall. All the false religions of human devising have the same object in view. But to come out into the light, to own our lost condition, to confess our sins, is the first essential (from the human side) in salvation. *This* is evangelical repentance.

(5) Once more we are shown a solemn foreshadowing of that which was vital and central in the great work of Redemption. Moses here prefigures the great Deliverer of God's people. First, Moses is seen as whole, then as leprous, then whole again. Precisely such is the view which Scripture gives us of the Saviour. Ineffably holy in Himself: He had no sin (Heb. 4:15), did no sin (1 Pet. 2:22), knew no sin (2 Cor. 5:21). But in infinite grace He took our place—all praise to His peerless name—and "was made sin for us" (2 Cor. 5:21). "He bare our sins in His own body on the tree" (1 Pet. 2:24). Because of this He was, at that time, in the sight of God what the leper was—defiled, unclean; not inherently so, but by imputation. The leper's place was *outside* the Camp (Lev. 13:46), *away from* where God dwelt. And on the Cross Christ was separated for three terrible hours from the holy God. But after the awful penalty of sin had been endured and the work of atonement was *finished,* the Forsaken One is seen again in communion with God—"*Father* into *Thy* hands I commit My spirit" evidences that. And it was as "the *Holy* One" (Psa. 16:10) He was laid in the sepulchre. Thus, after Moses thrust his leprous hand into his bosom, he drew it forth again perfectly whole—every trace of defilement gone. In their foreshadowings of Christ, then, the first sign intimated that the great Deliverer would "destroy the works of the Devil" (1 John 3:8), while the second signified that He would "take away our sins" (1 John 3:5).

"And it shall come to pass, if they will not believe also these two signs, neither hearken unto thy voice, that thou shalt take of the water of the river, and pour it upon the dry land: and the water which thou takest out of the river shall become blood upon the dry land" (v. 9). Upon this verse Dr. Urquhart has some helpful comments: "The Nile was Egypt's life. Its waters, in the annual inundation, pouring over its banks and spreading the fertilizing mud over the ground, prepared the way for the harvest. But the sign shows that God could turn that blessing into a fearful scourge. Instead of life he might make the river bring forth death: instead of fruitfulness, corruption. The unusual form (in the Heb.) 'shall be and shall be', conveys the strong and solemn assurance that this means of blessing shall certainly be turned into a vehicle of judgment—a threatening which was afterwards fulfilled in the first two plagues".

"And it shall come to pass, if they will not believe also these two signs, neither hearken unto thy voice, that thou shalt take of the water of the river, and pour it upon the dry land: and the water which thou takest out of the river shall become blood upon the dry land" (v. 9). This third "sign" is unspeakably solemn. Its position in the series supplies the key to its interpretation. This third sign was to be wrought only if the testimony of the first two was refused. It therefore tells of the *consequences* of refusing to believe what the other signs so plainly bore witness to. If man rejects the testimony of God's Word that he is under the dominion of Satan and is depraved by nature, and refuses the One who alone can deliver from the one and cleanse from the other, nothing but Divine judgment awaits him. The water turned into blood speaks of life giving place to death. It anticipates "the second death", that eternal death, "The Lake of Fire", which awaits every Christ rejector. Be warned then, unsaved reader, and flee to Christ for refuge ere the storm of Divine wrath overtakes thee. "Believe on the Lord Jesus Christ and thou shalt be saved"

—Arthur W. Pink.

WHEN DID THE CHRISTIAN DISPENSATION BEGIN?

A great many people would answer this question by saying, At the birth of the Saviour. Were we to ask them *why* they believe that the Christian Dispensation began at the birth of Christ, they would reply, Because that important event marks the great dividing line in our Bibles—it is placed right at the beginning of the New Testament, Satisfied that their answer is the correct one, they trouble themselves no further about the matter. But a few, who desire something more than mere suppositions to base their beliefs upon, will turn to the contents of the New Testament in order to ascertain whether this view be right or wrong. As they do so, and begin to read the Gospels thoughtfully, they will at once be struck with the fact that there **is much in them which accords more with the old Dispensation than with the new, that there is more which resembles Judaism than** Christianity. For example, they will find that all the scenes in the Gospels are laid in Palestine. They will note that the Temple was yet standing and that its regular services were conducted. They will mark how the Feasts of Judaism were still observed, and how that circumcision was punctiliously administered. They will discover, perhaps with astonishment, that not until Christ expired upon the Cross was the veil of the Temple rent in twain, and the way opened into the holy of holies. As they meditate on these things, probably they will be made to seriously question their early and untested supposition, and ask themselves whether, after all, the Gospels present to us the introduction of Christianity. We doubt not that there are many today in just this puzzled frame of mind, and it is for this class, particularly, we now write.

When did the Christian Dispensation begin? It is much easier to say when it did not begin (and this is the principal design of this article), than to point with certainty to the precise time when it actually commenced. Canals are very different from rivers. Man cuts his canals between two straight lines, but not so does God direct the rivers—they wind in and out. It is very much so with the dispensations. Men make their charts and attempt to fix with mathematical exactitude the bounderies of each dispensation, but rarely (if ever) will they stand the test of the Scriptures. Man cannot improve on God's Word, and there are no charts there! This is not to say that God has observed no order in compiling the Scriptures nor would we go so far as to affirm that man is attempting the impossible when he essays to *accurately* present the truth of God (or any part of it) in the form of a diagram; though we certainly doubt the wisdom of it. Many excellent brethren have used this method we know, but it is our growing conviction that more harm than good has been done by it. We often wonder how far this is the product of the spirit of the day. Labor-saving-devices is one of the popular fads of the hour, and in many directions this is becoming more and more the case in the study of God's Word. Anything that will serve as a substitute for *the personal study* of the Word is hailed with delight by numbers of professing Christians. Little wonder then that they are so much pleased with a chart which affords them a 'birds-eye view' of the whole subject of the dispensations. What is most needed today is to press upon people the vital importance of searching the Scriptures for themselves. That ministry is most helpful which emphasizes the deep responsibility which rests upon each one of us to daily read what God has written, and which encourages us to make the Word of truth the **"man of our counsels". Contrari**wise, that ministry is the most harmful which becomes to those who sit under it a *substitute* for the prayerful waiting on God for light upon His Word.

When did the Christian Dispensation begin? So far as we are aware there is no one verse in the Bible which gives an explicit answer. Nor is this to be wondered at. The same is true of a hundred other questions which might be asked. And one chief reason for this is that God would have us daily *exercised* in heart before Him. As a general rule (and probably there are very few exceptions to it) God does not vouchsafe an understanding of His truth to lazy people, nor to those who turn to His Word merely out of idle curiosity to find what it says on any certain matter. It is the soul of the *diligent* (not the dilatory) that is made fat. (Prov. 13: 14). We need not only to read but to "*Search* the Scriptures". It is unto the one who *applies* his heart to understanding, who *crieth* after knowledge, who *seeketh* her as silver, and who *searchest* for her as for hid treasures, that the assurance is given, "*then* shalt thou *understand* the fear of the Lord, and *find* the knowledge of God" (Prov. 2:1-5). And it is by prayerfully and perseveringly "comparing spiritual things with spiritual" (1 Cor. 2:13) that the Scriptures will be opened up to us. These, then, are some of the things which *each* of us must do, if we would obtain *from God* an answer to our present inquiry.

We propose to turn now to the New Testament with the object of comparing passage with passage, particularly those of the earlier pages with what is found on its later ones. As we do this, we shall discover some striking contrasts. We shall find that some things which are mentioned many times in the Gospels occur not at all in the Epistles, and that things which are prominent in the Epistles have little or no place in the Gospels. These we shall ponder in the light of the question at the head of this article, in the endeavor to discover whether or not they furnish us with a clear and definite answer thereto.

1. The first thing which impresses us when we begin to compare the opening books of the New Testament with those that follow is that the four Gospels treat of the earthly life and ministry of the Lord Jesus, whereas in the Acts and Epistles He is viewed as no longer upon earth, but instead, we are directed to the heavens, and are there given to see Him seated at the right hand of the Majesty on high. The force of this is borne in upon us as we remember that *there* the Saviour has remained, bodily absent from this earth for almost nineteen centuries. Certainly, the centuries since the ascension of Christ fall within the bounds of this Christian Dispensation; are we then to conclude from this that the Christian Dispensation is characterized by a Christ *absent from this world?* It would certainly seem so. Moreover, this conclusion is strongly confirmed by the indisputable fact that when Christ returns to the earth the Christian Dispensation will have ended, for that Return will usher in the Millennium. This by itself should be quite sufficient to make us seriously doubt the correctness of the popular idea that the present Dispensation began with the birth of Christ, for if the Christian Dispensation is characterized by an *absent* Saviour, how could it have already commenced thirty-three years before He left the earth?

2. During the days of Christ's public ministry the Gospel was confined to the land of Palestine. The Lord Jesus Himself never preached to the heathen, and when He sent out the twelve He expressly forbade them going into the way of the Gentiles (Matt. 10:5). But *after* His death and resurrection we find Him commissioning these *same* apostles to make disciples of *all* nations (Matt. 28:19), and later we find the Holy Spirit poured out on believing Jews and Gentiles alike (Acts 2 and 10). Now this radical change can only be accounted for by *a change of dispensations.* But lest some should object that this is merely a plausible inference of ours we appeal to Eph. 2:14-16 which definitely declares that it was *by the Cross* that "the middle wall of partition", which separated Jews from Gentiles, was "broken down". Clearly, that breaking down of the middle wall of partition signified a change of dispensation, and equally clear is it that this occurred not when Christ was born, or when John the Baptist began crying in the wilderness, but at the crucifixion.

3. One of the distinctive and characteristic terms of that which is prominent in this dispensation is the word "church". This is seen from the fact that it is found no less than 68 times in the Epistles—not counting the 17 references to the "churches in Asia" in the Revelation. Now the force and significance of this should be apparent when we note that the word "church" is never once found in the Old Testament (A.V.) and but twice in the four Gospels, and one of these is a reference to the church as yet future (Matt. 16:18)! Here, too, is something which can only be accounted for by *a change of dispensations.* Yet once more, lest it be objected that this is merely a deduction of ours, we refer the reader to a clear proof text in support. In Eph. 2, when referring to Gentile saints, the apostle was moved to write, "Ye are no more strangers and foreigners, but fellowcitizens with the saints, and of the household of God, and are built upon *the foundation of the apostles and prophets,* Jesus Christ being the chief corner stone" (vv. 19, 20). Notice carefully the clause in italics. These Ephesians were built *not* upon the foundation of John the Baptist and the earthly ministry of Christ, but upon the post-resurrection ministry of the apostles and New Testament prophets! Had there been *no*

change of dispensation then Gentile believers *would have been* built upon the "foundation" *(the initial labors)* of John the Baptist and the Lord Jesus. But the very fact that the Holy Spirit was careful the rather to say "built upon the foundation of *the apostles and prophets*" is proof positive that a new Dispensation dawned *after* the crucifixion.

4. Another striking contrast between the Gospels and the Epistles may be observed in the Lord's title of "Son of man". This title is found no less than 82 times in the Gospels, but only once in the Epistles, and that once is but a quotation from the eighth Psalm. Never once in the twenty-one Epistles is the Saviour referred to as "the Son of Man!" Surely this is profoundly significant and conveys to us a most definite message if we have but ears to hear. Furthermore, it is to be noted that never once is Christ referred to or addressed as "the Son of man" in the Gospels *after His resurrection*—see the closing chapter of each Gospel. Even more suggestive is the fact that this title occurs not at all in the Pascal Discourse and High Priestly prayer of the Saviour's recorded in John 14 to 17, in which Christ takes a place *beyond* the Cross (see 17:4 and cf 14:2 and 17:24). This, too, can be accounted for only on the ground of a change of dispensations. Nor is this conclusion unsupported by clear Scripture testimony, for we find that *after* this Dispensation is over Christ *will again* be owned by this title—see Matt. 25:31, etc.

5. Another striking contrast between the Gospels and the Epistles is what they teach respecting the Holy Spirit and His relation to believers. This opens up a wide field for study, but we shall not attempt to do anything more here than call attention to the dominant feature in it which is most germaine to our present inquiry. One of the outstanding and characteristic features of *Christianity* is, that the Holy Spirit indwells every believer (Rom. 8:9, 11; 1 Cor. 6:19), and that each local assembly is the temple of God, indwelt by the Holy Spirit (1 Cor. 3:16). There was nothing like this in Old Testament times, and nothing like it even during the days of our Lord's earthly ministry. John 7:39 tells us "the Holy Ghost was not yet (given to believers), because that Jesus was not yet glorified". John 14:16 tells us that on the eve of His crucifixion the Lord said to the apostles, "And I will pray the Father, and He *shall give* you another Comforter, that He may abide with you forever". It was not until *after* His resurrection that the Lord Jesus breathed on His apostles and said, "Receive ye the Holy Ghost" (John 20:22). And it was not till seven weeks after that, on the day of Pentecost, the Holy Spirit came in power upon them (Acts 2). Proof is this, then, that the Christian Dispensation could not begin until *after* the crucifixion.

6. Equally distinctive is the teaching of the Gospels and of the Epistles concerning *baptism*. The Gospels have quite a little to say upon "the baptism of John", but nothing at all about Christian baptism. The differences between the two are very marked. Their *purpose* was different. The purpose of John's baptism was to make Christ manifest to Israel (see John 1:31); the purpose of Christian baptism is to make manifest the believer's union with Christ (Rom. 6:3). Their *subjects* were different. So far as the inspired record informs us, they who were baptized of John did nothing more than give evidence that they had repented of their sins (Matt. 3); but none are eligible for Christian baptism save those who have personally received Christ as their Saviour (Acts 8:12, 37; 16:31-33). Their *purport* was different. Those baptized by John confessed their sins (Mark 1:5); the proper subjects of Christian baptism have no sins to confess, for *their* sins were made an end of at the Cross.

7. All uncertainty as to precisely when the previous Dispensation ended is (for us) forever removed by Dan. 9:26. There we are expressly told that the Messiah was "cut off" (from God, from Israel, and from the land of the living) i. e. crucified, *after* the sixty-ninth "week" (see v. 24) and before the seventieth and yet future "week" began; the whole of this present Gentilish (Acts 15:14) period coming in parenthetically.

When did the present Dispensation, the Christian Dispensation, begin? All that we have attempted to do in this article is to show it did not and could not begin before the death and resurrection of the Lord Jesus. Later, perhaps, we may write a further article attempting a more specific answer. In the meantime let those interested, diligently study the book of Acts and the Epistles to find out *for themselves* what God has revealed on this controverted point.

Arthur W. Pink.

ONE WITH CHRIST.

"I am crucified with Christ: nevertheless I live; yet not I, but Christ liveth in me: and the life which I now live in the flesh I live by the faith of the Son of God, who loved me, and gave Himself for me." (Gal. 2:20).

This is the explanation of verse 19, "I through the law am dead to the law, that I might live unto God." How was he dead to the law?. By having endured its curse, in the person of his Surety; he died the victim of the righteous sentence by which the holy law is sanctioned; and, what was most surprising, he had died by the law that he might live unto God.

This verse explains the apparent contradiction. He speaks of himself as one of Christ's members. In the body prepared for His incarnation, there was an exhibition of His mystical body. The Apostle fully illustrates this subject: "For as we have many members in one body, so we, being many, are one in Christ, and every one members one of another." (Rom. 12:4, 5).

The natural body, though consisting of many members, is strictly one. There is no schism in the body; the members have the same care of each other as of themselves; the suffering of one is the suffering of all; and the gratification of one is the gratification of all. There may be different degrees in glory; but there will be no disappointment,—no envy of the station held by others. Each stone of the building of mercy—like the stones of the temple—is hewd and prepared for the place it is to occupy. All the members of the natural body are animated by one spirit; if it be withdrawn, the body moulders into dust, and all its symmetry is destroyed. Now, there is a real unity in the Church of Christ as in the natural body. This gives a striking view of Rom. 5:14. Not only were all mankind created in Adam, as all believers are in Christ, but the "body" of Adam, composed of many members, was the figure of the Church, the mystical body of Christ.

When the Church is spoken of as a body, Christ is represented as the head. (Eph. 4:15). All the senses—excepting feeling, which is spread over the whole body—are placed in the head, so that the body is entirely under its direction. Now, the Apostle, as a member of Christ's body, was crucified with and in Him; and as the cutting off of the head is the death of all the members, so was the death of Christ, the death of the Apostle and of all His people. Christ died a death pronounced accursed fifteen hundred years before. What is the curse? Being cut off from God. And when Christ exclaimed, "My God, My God why hast Thou forsaken me?" (Matt. 27: 46), He proclaimed that He was enduring the curse; He was tasting the bitterness of death. All God's waves and billows went over Him. His Father hid His face from Him, and He was troubled; He had sunk in deep waters. The Apostle represents himself as having in Christ been nailed to the cross, but adds, "nevertheless I live." It was not possible that the Holy One of God should remain under the power of death. (Acts 2:24). But He went down to the grave, that by Him eternal life might be communicated to all whom the Father had given Him. He had power over His life, both to lay it down and take it again. (John 10:17, 18). His death was an act of obedience to His Father. Adam forfeited his own life, and that of all his posterity; Christ, the last Adam, the Lord from heaven, came that His children might have life, and have it more abundantly. (John 10:10). Adam poured contempt on God's most holy law; Christ magnified and made it honourable, thus restoring what He took not away. He was in all things implicitly guided by His Father's will, and when He received commandment to lay down His life, He was not disobedient. An innumerable multitude had been chosen in, and given to Him to be redeemed from among men. They were to be taken from the lowest point of degradation; they were lying in their blood; in the pit where there was no water; but He, by His obedience unto death, hath made them kings and priests unto God. He came to do His Father's will for their deliverance, by offering the body prepared for Him; and for the joy set before Him He endured the cross, despising the shame, and is set down at the right hand of the throne of God, having a name given Him above every name which is named, not only in this world, but in that which is to come.

Had Christ remained in the grave, His Church would have continued under the power of death; but His rising again was the resurrection of all His people. Many of them had gone the way of the earth; many were yet unborn, but all, from righteous Abel to the last who shall be caught up in the clouds to meet the Lord in the air, were equally interested in the transaction which took place on Calvary. As all the members of Christ's natural body were nailed to the cross, so were all the members of His mystical body, the children whom God had given Him, spiritually present on that awful occasion; and as they all died in Him, with Him they all rose.

The Apostle says, *"nevertheless I live;"* but he corrects himself, "Yet not I, but Christ liveth in me." In Him I have received a new and endless life. There is a close analogy between the natural and spiritual life. Two things are essential to the preservation of the former,—air and nourishment. By these the life we derive from Adam is maintained, and, in exact correspondence with this, the spiritual life—imparted in the day of regeneration by God revealing His Son in us, or Christ being formed in us—is maintained by the supply of the Spirit of Christ, which is to the new life what air is to the old; so also, in correspondence with the food necessary for our support, the truth as it is in Jesus, concerning His incarnation, death, and resurrection, is the food of the soul. This is taught under the emblem of the necessity of eating Christ's flesh and drinking His blood. Till we receive the Spirit we are dead; but Christ quickens His people by manifesting Himself to them in a way He doth not unto the world, and they immediately, as new born babes, desire the sincere milk of the Word. "Thy words," says the prophet, "were found, and I did eat them; and Thy Word was unto me the joy and rejoicing of mine heart: for I am called by Thy name, O Lord God of hosts." (Jer. 15:16).

Men may sport themselves with their own deceivings, and say, We must first believe, and then we shall receive the Spirit. They might as well say, Lazarus must first arise, and then his spirit will return. At the word "Lazarus, come forth!" his spirit came again; just as, when the Lord said to Saul of Tarsus, "I am Jesus whom thou persecutest," (Acts 9:5) faith came to him by hearing, and he was at once overwhelmed with the sense of his own guilt, and the glory of the God of Israel shining in the face of Jesus. Christ is the fountain of life, and the water which He gives His people, is in them a well of water springing up into everlasting life. Were it possible for the believer to lose sight of Christ he would die, but his life is preserved by the supply of the Spirit, taking of the things of Christ, and showing them to his mind. The words of the prophet are equally applicable to the Church, and to each individual, "In that day sing ye unto her, A vineyard of red wine. I the Lord do keep it; I will water it every moment; lest any hurt it, I will keep it night and day." (Isa. 27:2, 3).

The relation between God and believers is expressed, either by God dwelling in them as His temple, or by Christ abiding in them. God dwells in them, in and by Christ, and Christ abides in them by His Spirit. But the Apostle was still in the body; and, while this is the case, this vail of flesh conceals from our view the spiritual world, so that we must either depend on the report which God has given us, or be altogether ignorant of it: hence we walk by faith, not by sight.

Well might Paul add *"who loved me, and gave Himself for me.* There were, in those days, many persecutors in Israel; but none of them had, like Paul, been arrested in their mad career; called by grace, and ordained to bear the name of Christ "before the Gentiles, and kings, and the children of Israel." The grace of the Lord had been exceeding abundant towards him; he had "received not the spirit of the world, but the Spirit which is of God, that he might know the things that are freely given to us of God." He had received Christ as his Almighty Saviour; he knew whom he had believed, and he could habitually approach the mercy-seat in the full assurance of faith. Every believer is encouraged to use this language. The Gospel is to be preached to all. To some it comes only in word, to others in power; and by it Christ manifests Himself to His people, as he doth not to the world. He is formed in them the hope of glory, and they feel their security. They walk about Sion, and go round about her,—they tell the towers thereof,—they mark her bulwarks,—consider her palaces, and exclaim, in the confidence of faith, This God is our God for ever and ever; He will be our guide even unto death: "Thou shalt guide me by thy counsel, and afterwards receive me to glory." This is the rejoicing of the hope which the believer is commanded to hold firm unto the end. Faith cometh by hearing; and what is faith? Confidence in Christ. All who under the conviction of guilt and helplessness, cast themselves on Christ, looking for His mercy unto eternal life, may confidently say, who loved *me,* and gave Himself for *me.* The Good Shepherd gave His life for the sheep; their names are not published in the Book of God, but their trusting in Christ is a conclusive proof that they are His. Flesh and blood cannot reveal the truth to the mind. It is a false humility, the fruit of a legal spirit, to say my sins are so aggravated that I cannot speak confidently. Is Christ an Almighty Saviour? Does His blood remove guilt of the deepest dye? Can you not trust Him? Then you are an unbeliever. Satan is changed into an angel of light; he endeavors to retain men in bondage by the consideration of their guilt. The Gospel gives God's people the knowledge of salvation by the remission of their sins; and in proportion to the measure of our faith in the perfection of Christ's atonement, and the glory of the everlasting righteousness which the Gospel reveals, shall we adorn the truth we profess. We love Him because He first loved us. The Apostle is anxious that believers should know that they have eternal life.

It is well to be watchful and circumspect. It is well to recollect, that if we sin that grace may abound, our damnation is just. It is well to remember that the full assurance of hope can only be maintained by walking closely with God; and that by untenderness, we grieve the Holy Spirit, and become proportionally blind, and unable to see afar off: forgetting that our sins are forgiven for His name's sake. But while, through the deceitfulness and desperate wickedness of the heart, there is danger of our being tempted to sin that grace may abound, there is also great danger of our falling into a legal spirit, and forgetting that *we* do not live; that our help is not in ourselves; but that Christ liveth in us. We are utterly bankrupt, having in us no good thing; and the air we breathe is not more essential to the continuance of our natural life, than the supply of the Spirit, received through faith, is to the maintenance of the life of God in the soul.

Let us then live out of ourselves. The more confidently we rely on Christ for pardon, the more shall we experience His power in subduing our iniquities, healing our backslidings, and promoting our sanctification. Let us diligently use every appointed means of our growth in grace and in the knowledge of our Lord Jesus Christ. Let us be much in prayer, and diligently observe all His ordinances. Let us expect much from Him, and flee from sin in every shape; but let not the believer doubt his acceptance in the Beloved. In doing so, we turn away from Christ, and return to the law, which has only power to condemn the children of fallen Adam.

The Apostle takes it for granted that even the little children whom he addressed, knew that their sins were forgiven them for His name's sake. Men are very apt to substitute faith for its object; which is like looking into water to catch the reflected image, instead of looking directly at the object which we wish to behold. The consequence of this substitution is, that when we persuade ourselves that we possess faith, we have comfort, and when we lose this persuasion, we are troubled. No doubt, faith is essential to spiritual comfort, as well as to salvation; unbelievers shall be cast into the lake of fire; and therefore we are commanded to examine ourselves whether we be in the faith. This duty is enforced, not only by direct precept but by a variety of passages which describe the character of believers, who are all delivered from the power of darkness, and translated into the kingdom of God's dear Son. The truth effectually works in all who believe; if we live in the Spirit, we shall walk in the Spirit, and prove by our conduct that we have been with Jesus. But although the righteous is more excellent than his neighbour, although the Spirit which dwelleth in believers influences their conduct; there is still in them so much corruption, that comfort arising from our conformity to Christ cannot be abiding.

Some have founded Christian comfort not on the fruit we bring forth, but on the consciousness that we believe. No doubt, we are conscious of what is passing in our minds; but many are conscious they believe, whose faith is not the faith of Christ. We may believe many things while in the gall of bitterness and bond of iniquity. Saul of Tarsus was conscious that he desired to do God service while trampling on the Divine authority. Our hearts are deceitful above all things, and, therefore, neither consciousness, nor any other feeling, lays a solid foundation for hope. We are commanded to rest on Christ Himself, the great object of faith, and in proportion to our confidence in Him, will be our assurance of salvation. To guard us against the deceitfulness of sin, we are commanded to compare our conduct with the fruit of the Spirit, as set forth in the Scriptures of truth. An Apostle says, "And hereby we do know that we know Him, if we keep His commandments." "My little children, let us not love in word, neither in tongue; but in deed and in truth. And hereby we know that we are of the truth, and shall assure our hearts before Him." (1 John 3:18, 19). It has been erroneously maintained, that it is impossible for a believer to entertain a doubt of his acceptance. Those who hold this sentiment suppose, that when we are commanded to make our calling and election sure, it means making it sure to others; but when the Apostle speaks of assuring our hearts before Him, He speaks of our own hearts, not the hearts of others. We may, through temptation, lose our consolation in Christ. We may, in a measure, let slip the truth, and grieve the Holy Spirit, thus losing the earnest of our inheritance. (Eph. 1:14). This is figured by Bunyan's pilgrim losing his roll, and being obliged to return for it. In this case, a believer is called to repent, and do his first works, to awake out of sleep, to arise from the dead, and Christ will give him light. Our election can only be made sure by ascertaining our calling. Thus the Apostle knew the election of the Thessalonians; and he encourages the Corinthians by reminding them of the faithfulness of God, who had called them into the fellowship of His dear Son, and who, he was assured, would confirm them to the end.

The sum of the matter is, that every sinner, without exception, who hears the Gospel, has the ample grounds for the fullest confidence in Christ for salvation, and when the Spirit takes of the things of Christ,—the dignity of His person, the infinite value of His atonement, and the freeness of His salvation,—and shows them to the mind, in other words, when God reveals His Son in them,—they put their trust in Him, obeying the truth, through the Spirit. The supply of the Spirit is as essential to the continuance, as to the commencement of faith; and although He who hath begun a good work, will perform it until the day of Christ; yet we are in constant danger of losing sight of the truth, which can only be kept in view by watchfulness and prayer.

We ought never to be satisfied with a peradventure we shall be saved; the question is too momentous to be left in doubt; let us then give diligence to the full assurance of hope unto the end, and never be satisfied without being able to say, "who loved *me,* and gave Himself for *me.*"

In order to this, it is not necessary for us to hold that Christ died for all mankind. In that case, His dying for *me* could afford me no satisfaction, for it must be admitted that many perish; but all who hear the Gospel are commanded to trust in Christ for salvation, with the assurance of acceptance. If then, having renounced every ground of hope, we look to Christ for salvation, calling upon the name of the Lord, we have the promise of God, confirmed by His oath, that we *shall* be saved. If we know the Lord as the Saviour of sinners, it is because we were first known of Him. (Gal. 4:9). What a proof is it of the corruption of our hearts, that we are so frequently diverted from cultivating the enjoyment of fellowship with God by the lying vanities of this evil world! What is all around us when viewed in the light of eternity? What are the days of man's vain life which he spendeth as a shadow, compared with an exceeding and eternal weight of glory, or to be cast into the lake of fire, where the smoke of their torment shall ascend for ever and ever? Let us then desire one thing of the Lord, and that let us seek after, that we may dwell in the house of the Lord for ever; while we are in this world, let us not be satisfied without the enjoyment of the light of God's countenance, and the anticipation of the rest which remaineth for the people of God. Let us guard against falling into temptation, not merely to open but to secret sin. We must "take us the foxes, the little foxes, that spoil the vines; for our vines have tender grapes." Christ says, and the message is addressed to believers, "Behold, I stand at the door, and knock: if any man hear My voice, and open the door, I will come in to him, and will sup with him, and he with Me." (Rev. 3:20). Let us plead with Him who has the key of David, who shutteth and none can open, and openeth and none can shut, that He would take entire possession of our hearts, and reign there without a rival. —*James Haldane—1848.*

DIVERSE VIEWS.

Is it not a strange thing that nearly eighteen hundred years have passed away since Christ was upon the earth, and yet good men, taught by the same Spirit, should hold such diverse views of Scripture Doctrine? Is it sectarianism only that brings this about?

That there should be such diverse views of doctrine ought not to surprise us, for the inspired Word plainly reveals their beginnings, and plainly declares that they will continue and increase unto the end (1 Cor. 1:9-12; 3:1-4 Acts 20:29, 30; II Tim. 4:1-4). These texts reveal the way in which "diverse views" are brought about and grow. They originate in carnality; some of them, doubtless, in the carnality of men who are *only* carnal; others, certainly, in the *remaining* carnality of men in Christ, but who, insofar as they err are "walking as men". They both *originate* in sectarianism and become the *occasion* of sectarianism; and sectarianism is a carnal thing; it is counted among "the works of the flesh", under the English word "Heresies" (Gal. 5:20). Paul (Acts 20) shows us that some of the diverse teachings originate in the carnal ambition of teachers, who wish to "draw away disciples after them"; while the other texts referred to show us that the things taught are received and held, to the dishonor of Christ, because of the carnal tendency to attach ourselves to leaders, or the desire to have the ear tickled. It would be very strange, indeed, that this state of things should exist and grow, if the *popular* idea of a triumphant Christianity were Scriptural. If the Word of God really taught that the course of Christianity during this age, was to be one of ever-advancing purity, spirituality, unity, and unanimity, we might well be surprised to find that every year developes the very opposite of all this. But while the Word demands of all who love the Lord that they should be of one mind in the Lord, it as plainly declares that there will be utter failure to regard His Word on the part of the many.

That "good men", as well as merely nominal Christians, differ, shows that they have not in every thing been "taught of the Spirit". Of course, so far as any one has *truth* he has been taught of the "Spirit of Truth"; but the Spirit is not the author of diverse views! The Spirit is of one mind, and it is surely becoming that we should own that our diverse views *do not* come from Him. Some men glory in these differences, and speak of them as fine characteristics of mental freedom. But the Word of God demands that we should be "perfectly joined together in the same mind and in the same judgement". (1 Cor. 1:10). Of course, if we do not see alike, we must, as men say, "agree to differ"; if by that it is meant that we should be no less cordial in our brotherly affections and ways because of our different thoughts. But we ought to abhor the very idea that kind feeling or mere external unity answers to the will of God; His will is that we should "be of *one mind* and all speak the same thing". He "desires truth in the inward parts". What we need is to learn the evil of schism, and diverse views, and to confess the evil in God's presence, counting on Him to set us right; and relying on the Spirit's promised teaching, and having Christ as our only object, we may be sure that "if in anything we be otherwise minded, God shall reveal even this unto us" (Phil. 3:15). It is always better to confess our failure and the failure and sin of the Church, than to question the faithfulness of the Spirit of Truth.

C. Campbell, 1873

To New Readers: The twelve copies of 1922, and the twelve of 1923, neatly bound, may be had for $1.50 each. They contain articles by the Editor on The Blood, Eternal Punishment, Second Coming of Christ, The Sabbath, Romans 7, The Antichrist, and Expositions of John's Gospel from the first verse. We have only a limited supply.

To Foreign Subscribers: Please send **only** International Money Orders, made out to the Editor.

(*Continued from page 121.*)

Second, "*If* (and) My words abide in you". Note it is not My Word, but My words abide in you. It is not the Word as a whole, but the Word, as it were, broken up. It is the precepts and promises of the Scriptures personally appropriated, fed upon by faith, hidden in the heart. It is the practical heeding of that injunction, "Man shall not *live* (his daily life) by bread alone, but by every word that proceedeth out of the mouth of God". And mark that it is Christ's word *abiding* in us. It is no fitful, spasmodic, occasional exercise and experience, but the constant and habitual *communion* with God through the Word, until its contents becomes the substance of our innermost being.

Third, "Ye shall ask what ye will". But *for what* would such an one ask? If he continues in fellowship *with Christ,* if *His* "words" remain in him, then his *thoughts* will be *regulated* and his *desires formed* by that Word. Such an one will be raised above the lusts (desires) of the flesh. In such an one "the mind of Christ" will dwell (Phil 2:5). Such an one will "bring into captivity every thought to the obedience of Christ" (2 Cor. 10:5), proving "what is that good, and acceptable and perfect will of God". (Rom 12:2). Consequently, such an one will ask God *only* for that *which is* "according to *His* will." (1 John 5:14); and *thereby* will He verify the Lord's promise "it *shall* be done unto you".

Such a view of prayer is glorifying to God and satisfying to the soul. For one who communes with the Saviour and in whom His Word dwelleth "richly", supplication is simply the pulsation of a heart that has been won to God. While the believer is in fellowship with the Lord and is governed from within by the Word, He will not ask anything contrary to the mind of God. Instead of praying in the energy of the flesh (which, alas, almost all our prayers are), he will pray "in the Holy Spirit" (Jude 20). Let us then seek a closer walk with Christ and a more intimate acquaintance with His words, and, in increasing measure, we shall find, "Ye shall ask what ye will and it *shall* be done unto you".

Arthur W. Pink.

For the benefit of those who are finding the articles on Exodus instructive and profitable, we wish to announce a two-volumed work "Gleanings in Genesis" by Arthur W. Pink. Price $2.50 postpaid. It contains forty-six articles on the first book in the Bible. Six years were spent in the preparation of them. Special attention is given to the types and prophecies. Many have pronounced these two volumes the most helpful work on Genesis.

Also we wish to say to new subscribers, Vol. 1 and Vol. 2 of "Studies in the Scriptures", nicely bound, can be had for $1:50 each. These contain the Expositions of John's Gospel from its first verse, besides many other articles by the Editor on The Antichrist, The Sabbath, Eternal Punishment, Creation, Romans 7, The Blood, Second Coming of Christ, etc., etc.

Foreign subscribers please send **International** Money Orders.

Send all orders to the Editor, 227 N. Creighton St. Philadelphia.

VOL. III JULY, 1924 NO. 7

STUDIES in the SCRIPTURES

"Search the Scriptures" John 5:39.

A PERIODICAL (MONTHLY "IF THE LORD WILL")
DEVOTED TO BIBLE STUDIES and EXPOSITIONS

Arthur W. Pink, Publisher & Editor,
227 N. Creighton St., Philadelphia, Pa.

Price: 10 cents per copy; $1.00 per year. Foreign $1.00 per year.

In a tract which was recently sent to the Editor, occurred the following words: "Never refuse any teaching because it is *new to you;* but never accept anything till you see it *for yourself* from the Word of God. Inability to receive it is not tantamount to rejecting. Do not judge the doctrine of an address by the man who delivers it, nor gauge the truth of an article by the initials at its close. Be *sure* though *slow* in acquiring truth. Though you may get truth through a *human channel,* get it *from God.* Learn to learn at the Master's feet, and then you will have no need to learn to unlearn." This is wise counsel, and much needed by all of us.

There are two extremes to guard against. On the one hand, readiness to receive, eagerness to swallow *everything* which is taught by our *favorite teacher.* On the other hand, refusing to accept, or even carefully ponder, *anything* which proceeds from any *but* our favorite teacher or teachers. This is an age which is characterized by superficiality. The vast majority are in too great a hurry, they have too many engagements and interests to allow them to *study* much for themselves. They prefer to receive things second-hand; they are willing for others to do their studying for them. Consequently, they are quite incompetent to *test* what they hear and read, and therefore fall easy victims to those who propagate error—not necessarily *fundamental error,* but Truth mis-interpreted, Truth mis-applied, through ignoring the context or by disproportionate emphasis. Just as certain herbs or drugs when combined in proper proportions make a healing potion, so the various doctrines of Scripture when correctly balanced, are healthful to the soul. But just as a combination of herbs or drugs *wrongly* proportioned are highly injurious, so by pressing one doctrine of Scripture to the ignoring of its balancing doctrine, by failing to preserve the *balance* of truth, souls are injured. It is just at this point that Christians who do not *search* the Scriptures *daily* for themselves, are most liable to be misled. *"All* Scripture is given by inspiration of God and is *profitable* for doctrine" etc. (2 Tim. 3:16)—the O. T. as much as the New; the precepts as much as the promises; the commandments equally with the prophecies.

It is because of this tendency to spiritual *sloth,* it is because God knew that His people would rather some Bible teacher did their searching for them, that He says *to each of us,* "PROVE all things, hold fast that which is good" (1 Thess. 5:21). No matter how orthodox may be the Magazine in which the articles you read appear, no matter how loyal to the Word the teacher you sit under seems to be, God holds each of us responsible to "Prove", that is, *verify by the Scriptures,* ALL that we read or hear. And the need for doing this should be evident. Not only are there *"many* false prophets gone out into the world" (1 John 4:1), false prophets who pose as the champions of the Truth, men whose moral lives are irreproachable, and in whose teaching the Word of God is frequently quoted (as Satan himself quoted it to Christ!); but even the true servants of God are but imperfectly instructed. *No one man knows all the truth!* Now "we know *in part"* (1 Cor. 13:9) is true of all alike. But the part one knows, may not be the part which another knows—hence the value of a multiplicity of teachers, each with different gifts. And herein we may also see the folly of those who measure one teacher by another. How many there are who listen to some servant of God proclaiming a doctrine which is new to them, and may be which strikes them as strange. Something within makes them uneasy. But the inward warning is disregarded. The doctrine may be new and queer, but does it not proceed from one who is a *sound* teacher? The hearer has implicit confidence in his instructor, he has

(Continued on page 168.)

IMPORTANT NOTICES

All new subscriptions will be dated back to January, 1924.

Set of twelve issues for 1922, unbound, $1.00. Bound, $1.50.

Set of twelve issues for 1923, unbound, $1.00. Bound $1.50.

Note: We cannot break a set or now supply any single 1923 issues.

Subscription Price: $1.00 per year to any address in the world. Single copies 10 cents.

Change of Address: Please notify me promptly of any change of address, and be certain to give both old and new addresses.

Non-subscribers receiving this Magazine regularly will understand their subscription has been entered by a friend.

Copies lost in the mail duplicated only if we are notified promptly.

Entered as second-class matter December 15th, 1923, at the post office at Philadelphia, Pa., under Act of March 3rd, 1879.

CONTENTS

JOHN'S GOSPEL

31. Christ and the Blind Beggar: John 9:1-7

Below will be found an Analysis of the passage which is to be before us:—

1. Jesus beholds the man born blind: v. 1.
2. The disciples' question: v. 2.
3. Christ's answer: vv. 3-5.
4. Christ anoints the blind man: v. 6.
5. Christ sends the man to the Pool: v. 7.
6. The man's prompt obedience: v. 7.
7. The miracle completed: v. 7.

That there is an intimate connection between John 8 and John 9 is manifest from the first word of the latter, and when the Holy Spirit has thus linked two things together it behooves us to pay close attention to the law of comparison and contrast (cf our remarks in Vol. I. pages 134, 210, etc.). The little conjunction at the opening of John 9 is very appropriate, for in the previous verse we read of Jesus *hiding* Himself from those who took up stones to cast at Him; while in 9:1 we behold a man blind from his birth, *unable to see* the passing Saviour. That these two chapters are closely related is further seen by a comparison of 8:12 and 9:5: in both Christ is revealed, specifically, as "the Light of the world". As we read carefully the opening verses of the chapter now before us and compare them with the contents of John 8 it will be found that they present to us a series of contrasts. For example, in John 8 we behold Christ as "the Light" exposing the darkness, but in John 9 He communicates sight. In John 8 the Light is despised and rejected, in John 9 He is received and worshipped. In John 8 the Jews are seen stooping down—to pick up stones; in John 9 Christ is seen stooping down—to make anointing clay. In John 8 Christ hides Himself from the Jews; in John 9 He reveals Himself to the blind beggar. In John 8 we have a company in whom the Word has no place (v. 37); in John 9 is one who responds promptly to the Word, (v. 7). In John 8 Christ, inside the Temple, is called a demoniac, (v. 48); in John 9, outside the Temple, He is owned as Lord, (v. 36). The central truth of John 8 is the Light testing human responsibility; in John 9 the central truth is God acting in sovereign grace *after* human responsibility has failed. This last and most important contrast we must ponder at length.

In John 8 a saddening and humbling scene was before us. There Christ was manifested as "the Light" and woeful were the objects that it shone upon. It reminds us very much of that which is presented right at the beginning of God's Word. Gen. 1:2 introduces us to a ruined earth, with darkness enveloping it. The very first thing God said there was, "Let there be light", and we are told, "There was light". And *upon what* did the light shine? what did its beams *reveal?* It shone upon an earth that had become "without form and void"; its beams revealed a scene of desolation and death. There was no sun shining by day nor moon by night. There was no vegetation, no moving creature, no life. A pall of death hung over the earth. The light only made manifest the awful ruin which sin (here, the sin of Satan) had wrought, and the need for the sovereign goodness and almighty power of God to intervene and produce life and fertility.

So it was in John 8. Christ as the Light *of the world* discovers not only the state of Israel, but too, the common atheism of man. He affirmed His power to make free the bondslaves of sin (8:32): but His auditors denied that they were in bondage. He spoke the words of the Father (8:38): but they neither understood nor believed Him. He told them that their characters were formed under the influence of the Devil and that they desired it to be so (8:44): in reply they blasphemously charged Him with having a demon. He declared that He was the Object who had rejoiced the heart of Abraham (8:56): and they scoffed at Him. He told them He was the great and eternal "I am" (8:58): and they picked up stones to cast at Him. All of this furnishes us with a graphic but accurate picture of the character of the natural man the world over. The mind of the sinner is enmity against God, and he hates the Christ of God. He may be very religious, and left to himself, he may appear to be quite pious. But let the light of God be turned upon him, let the bubble of his self-righteousness be punctured, let his awful depravity be exposed, let the claims of Christ be pressed upon him, and he is not only skeptical, but furious.

What, then, was Christ's response? Did He turn His back on the whole human race? Did He return at once to heaven, thoroughly disgusted at His reception in this world? What wonder if the Father had there and then called His Son back to the glory which He had left. Ah, but God is the God of all grace, and grace needed the dark background of sin so that its bright lustre might shine the more resplendently. Yet grace would be misunderstood and unappreciated were it shown to all alike, for in that case men would deem it a right to which they were entitled, a meet compensation for God allowing the race to fall into sin. O the folly of human reasoning! Grace would be no more grace if fallen men had any claims upon it. God is under *no* obligations to men: every title to His favor was forfeited forever when they, in the person of their representative, rebelled against Him. Therefore does He say, "I will have mercy on whom *I will* have mercy" (Rom. 9:15). It is *this* side of the truth which receives such striking illustration in the passage which is to be before us.

In John 8 we are shown the utter ruin of the natural man—despising God's goodness, hating His Christ. Here in John 9 we behold the Lord dealing in grace, acting according to His sovereign benignity. This, this is the central contrast pointed by these two chapters. In the former it is the Light testing human responsibility; in the latter, the Light acting in sovereign mercy after the failure of human responsibility had been demonstrated. In the one we see the sin of man exposed, in the other we behold the grace of God displayed.

"And as Jesus passed by, He saw a man which was blind from his birth" (v. 1). That which is dominant in this passage is intimated in the opening verse. The *sovereignty* of Divine grace is exemplified at once in the actions of our Lord and in the character of the one upon whom His favors were bestowed. The Saviour saw a certain man; the man did not see Him, for he had no capacity to do so, being blind. Nor did the blind man call upon Christ to have mercy upon him. The Lord was the one to take the initiative. It is ever thus when sovereign grace acts. But let us admire separately each detail in the picture here.

"And as Jesus passed by, He *saw* a man". How blessed. The Saviour was not occupied with His own sorrows to the exclusion of those of others. The absence of appreciation and the presence of hatred in almost all around Him, did not check that blessed One in His unwearied service to others, still less did He abandon it. Love "suffereth long", and "beareth all things" (1 Cor. 13). And Christ was Love incarnate, therefore did the stream of Divine goodness flow on unhindered by all man's wickedness. How this perfection of Christ rebukes our imperfections, our selfishness!

"He saw a man which was blind from his birth". What a pitiable object! To lose an arm or a leg is a serious handicap, but the loss of sight is far more so. And this man had *never* seen. From how many enjoyments was he cut off! Into what a narrow world did his affliction confine him! And blindness, like all other bodily afflictions, is one of the effects of sin. Not always so directly, but always so remotely. Had Adam never disobeyed his Maker the human family had been free from disease and suffering. Let us learn then to *hate sin* with godly hatred as the cause of all our sorrows; and let the sight of suffering ones serve to remind us of what a horrible thing sin is. But let us also remind ourselves that there is something infinitely more awful than physical blindness and temporal suffering, namely, sickness of soul and a blinded heart.

"He saw a man which was blind from his birth". Accurately did he portray the terrible condition of the natural man. The sinner is blind spiritually. His understanding is darkened and his heart is blinded (Eph. 4:18). Because of this he cannot see the awfulness of his condition: he cannot see his imminent danger: he cannot see his need of a Saviour—"Except a man be born again he *cannot see*" (John 3:3). Such an one needs more than light; he needs the capacity given him to see the light. It is not a matter of mending his glasses (reformation), or of correcting his vision (education and culture), or of eye ointment (religion). None of these reach, or can reach, the root of the trouble. The natural man is *born blind* spiritually, and a faculty missing at birth cannot be supplied by extra cultivation of the others. A "transgressor from the womb" (Isa. 48:18), shapen in iniquity and conceived in sin (Psa. 51:5), man needs a Saviour from the time he draws his very first breath. Such is the condition of God's elect in their unregenerate state—"by nature the children of wrath, even as others" (Eph. 2:3).

"He saw a man which was blind from his birth". The late Bishop Ryle called attention to the significant fact that the Gospels record more cases of blindness healed than that of any other one affliction. There was one deaf and dumb healed, one sick of the palsy, one sick of a fever, two instances of lepers being healed, three dead raised, but five of the blind! How this emphasizes the fact that man is in the dark spiritually. Moreover, the man in our lesson was a beggar (v. 8)—another line in the picture which so accurately portrays our state by nature. A beggar the poor sinner is: possessing nothing of his own, dependent on charity. A blind beggar—what an object of need and helplessness! Blind from his birth—altogether beyond the reach of man!

"And His disciples asked Him, saying, Master, who did sin, this man, or his parents, that he was born blind?" (v. 2). How little pity these disciples seem to have had for this blind beggar, and how indifferent to the outflow of the Lord's grace. Instead of humbly and trustfully waiting to see what Christ would do, they were philosophizing. The point over which they were reasoning concerned the problem of suffering and the inequalities in the lot of human existence—points which have engaged the minds of men in every clime and age, and which apart from the light of God's Word are still unsolved. There are many who drift along unexercised by much of what goes on around them. That some should be born into this world to enter an environment of comfort and luxury, while others first see the light amid squalor and poverty; that some should start the race of mortality with a healthy body and a goodly reserve of vitality, while others should be severely handicapped with an organism that is feeble or diseased, and still others should be crippled from the womb, are phenomena which affect different people in very different ways. Many are largely unconcerned. If all is well with them, they give very little thought to the troubles of their fellows. But there are others who cannot remain indifferent, and whose minds seek an explanation to these mysteries. Why is it that some are born blind?—a mere accident it cannot be. As a punishment for sin, is the most obvious explanation. But if this be the true answer, a punishment for *whose* sins?

"Master, who did sin, this man, or his parents, that he was born blind?". Three theories were current among the philosophers and theologians of that day. The first obtained in some measure among the Babylonians, and more extensively amongst the Persians and Greeks, and that was the doctrine of re-incarnation. This was the view of the Essenes and Gnostics. They held that the soul of man returned to this earth again and again, and that the law of retribution regulated its varied temporal circumstances. If in his previous earthly life a man had been guilty of grievous sins, special punishment was meted out to him in his next earthly sojourn. In this way philosophers sought to explain the glaring inequalities among men. Those who now lived in conditions of comfort and prosperity were reaping the reward of former merit; those who were born to a life of suffering and poverty were being punished for previous sins. That this theory of re-incarnation obtained in measure even among the Jews is clear from Matt. 16:13, 14. When Christ asked His disciples, "Whom do men say that I the Son of man am?", they said, "Some say that Thou art John the Baptist: some, Elijah; and others, Jeremiah, or one of the prophets" which shows that some of them thought the soul of one of the prophets was now re-incarnated in the body of Jesus of Nazareth. Further evidence that this view obtained to some extent among the Jews is supplied by the Apocrypha. In "the wisdom of Solomon"—8:19, 20—are found these words, "Now I was a goodly child, and a goodly soul fell to my lot. Nay rather, *being good,* I came into a body undefiled"!

But among the rabbins this theory held no place. It was so completely without scriptural support, yea, it so obviously clashed with the teaching of the Old Testament, they rejected it in toto. How then could *they* explain the problem of human suffering? The majority of them did so by the law of heredity. They considered that Ex. 20:5 supplied the key to the whole problem: all suffering was to be attributed to the sins of the parents. But the Old Testament ought to have warned them against such a sweeping application of Ex. 20:5. The case of Job should have at least modified their views. With some it did, and among the Pharisees a third theory, still more untenable, was formulated. Some held that a child could sin even in the womb, and Gen. 25:22 was quoted in support.

It was in view of these prevailing and conflicting theories and philosophies which then obtained that the disciples put their question to the Lord: "Master, who did sin, this man, or his parents, that he was born blind?". Evidently they desired to hear what He would say upon the matter. But what is the present-day application of this verse to us? Surely the reasoning of these disciples in the presence of the blind beggar points a solemn warning. Surely it tells of the danger there is of us theorizing and philosophizing while we remain indifferent to human needs. Let us beware of becoming so occupied with the problems of theology that we fail to preach the Gospel to lost souls!

"Jesus answered, Neither hath this man sinned, nor his parents: but that the works of God should be made manifest in him" (v. 3). The Lord returned a double answer to the disciples' inquiry: negatively, this man was not born blind because of sin. "Neither did this man sin *nor his parents*" must not be understood absolutely, but like many another sentence of Scripture has to be modified by its setting. Our Lord did not mean that this man's parents had never sinned, but that their sins was not the reason *why* their son had been born blind. All suffering is *remotely* due to sin, for if sin had not entered the world there would have been no suffering among humankind. But there is much suffering which is not due immediately to sin. Indirectly the Lord here rebukes a spirit which all of us are prone to indulge. It is so easy to assume the role of judge and pass sentence upon another. This was the sin of Job's friends, recorded for our learning and warning. The same spirit is displayed among some of the "Faith-healing" sects of our day. With them the view largely obtains that sickness is due to some sin in the life, and that where healing is withheld it is because that sin is un-confessed. But this is a very harsh and censorious judgment, and must frequently be erroneous. Moreover, it tends strongly to foster pride. If I am enjoying better health than many of my fellows, the inference would be, it is because I am not so great a sinner as they! The Lord deliver us from such reprehensible Phariseeism.

"But that the works of God should be made manifest in him" (v. 3). Here is the positive side of our Lord's answer, and it throws some light upon the problem of suffering. God has His own wise reasons for permitting sickness and disease; ofttimes it is that *He* may be glorified thereby. It was so in the case of Lazarus (John 11:4). It was so in connection with the death of Peter (John 21:19). It was so in the affliction of the apostle Paul (2 Cor. 12:9). It was so with this blind beggar: he was born blind that the power of God might be evidenced in the removal of it, and that Christ might be glorified thereby.

"But that the works of God should be made manifest in him". Let us not miss the present application of this to suffering saints today. Surely this word of the Saviour's contains a message of consolation to afflicted ones among His people now. Not that they may expect to be relieved by a miracle, but that they may comfort themselves with the assurance that God has a wise (if hidden) purpose to be served by their affliction, and that is, that in some way *He* will be glorified thereby. That way may not be manifested at once; perhaps not for long years. At least thirty years (see v. 23) passed before God made it evident *why* this man had been born blind. As to *what* God's purpose is in our affliction, as to *how* His purpose will be attained, and as to *when* it will be accomplished, these things are none of our affair. Our business is to meekly submit to His sovereign pleasure (1 Sam. 3:18), and to be duly "exercised thereby" (Heb. 12:11). Of this we may be sure, that whatever is for God's glory *in* us, will ultimately bring blessing *to* us. Then do not question God's love, but seek grace to rest in simple faith on Rom. 11:36 and 8:28.

"I must work the works of Him that sent Me" (v. 4). And what were these works? To reveal the perfections of God and to minister to the needs of His creatures. Such "works" the Son *must* do because He was *one* both in will and in nature with the Father. But no doubt there is another meaning in these words. The "works of Him" that sent Christ were not only works that were *pleasing* to God, but they were works which had been *predestinated* by God. These works *must* be done because God had eternally decreed them—cf the "must" in 4:4 and 10:16.

"The night cometh, when no man can work. As long as I am in the world, I am the light of the world" (vv. 4, 5). More specifically this statement had reference to what Christ was about to do—the giving of sight to the blind beggar. This is clear from the opening words of v. 6: "When He had *thus* spoken". The miracle Christ was about to perform gave a striking illustration of the yet greater miracle of the Divine bestowment of spiritual vision upon an elect sinner. Such an one *must* be illumined for the eternal counsels of Deity so determined—compare the "must" in Acts 4:12. The saving of a sinner is not only entirely the "work" of God, but it is, preeminently, that in which He delights. This is what these words of Christ here plainly intimate. How blessed to know, then, that the most glorious of all God's works is displayed in the saving of lost and hell-deserving sinners, and that the Persons of the Trinity co-operate in the outflow of grace.

"The night cometh, when no man can work". Christ here teaches us both by word and example the importance of making the most of our present opportunities. His earthly ministry was completed in less than four years, and these were now rapidly drawing to a close. He *must* then be about His Father's business. A Divine constraint was upon Him. May a like sense of urgency impel us to redeem the time, knowing the days are evil (Eph. 5:16). What a solemn word is this for the sinner: "the night cometh, when no man can work"! This is life's day for him; in front lies the blackness of darkness forever (Jude 13). Unsaved reader, your "night" hastens on. "*Today* if ye will hear His voice harden not your hearts". "Behold *now* is the accepted time; behold, *now* is the day of salvation".

"As long as I am in the world, I am the light of the world". Christ seems to be referring to the attempt which had just been made upon His life (8:59). Soon the appointed time would come for Him to leave the world, but until that time had arrived man could not get rid of Him. The light *would* shine despite all man's efforts to put it out. The stones of these Jews could not intimidate or hinder this One from finishing the work which has been given Him to do. "Light of the world" He had just demonstrated Himself to be by exposing their wicked hearts. "Light of the world" He would now exhibit Himself by communicating sight and salvation to this poor blind beggar.

"When He had thus spoken, He spat on the ground, and made clay of the spittle, and He anointed the eyes of the blind man with the clay" (v. 6). This was a parable in action and deserves our closest attention. Christ's mode of procedure here though extraordinarily peculiar was, nevertheless, profoundly significant. Peculiar it certainly was, for the surest way to blot out vision would be to plaster the eye with wet clay; and yet this was the only thing Christ did to this blind beggar. Equally sure is it that His mysterious action possessed some deep symbolic significance. What that was we shall now inquire.

"When He had thus spoken, He spat on the ground, and made clay of the spittle, and He anointed the eyes of the blind man with the clay". The first thing we must do is to study this carefully in the light of the context. What is before us in the context? This: the "Light of the world" (8:12), the "Sent One" (8:18), the "Son" (8:36) was despised and rejected of the Jews. And why was that? Because He appeared before them in such lowly guise. They judged Him "after the flesh" (8:15); they sought to kill Him because He was "a *man* that told them the truth" (8:40). They had no eyes to discern His Divine glory and were stumbled by the fact that He stood before them in "the likeness of men".

Now what do we have here in John 9? This: once more Christ affirms that He *was* "the light of the world" (9:5); then, immediately following, we read, "When He had *thus* spoken, He spat on the ground, and made clay of the spittle, and He anointed the eyes of the blind man with the clay". Surely the meaning of this is now apparent. "As a figure, it pointed to the *humanity* of Christ in earthly humiliation and lowliness, presented to the eyes of men, but with Divine efficacy of life in Him" (J. N.D.). Christ had presented Himself before the Jews, but devoid of spiritual perception they recognized Him not. And did the blind beggar, who accurately represented the Jews, did *he* see when Christ applied the clay to his eyes? No; he did not. He was still as blind as ever, and even though he had not been blind he could not have seen them. What, then, must he do? He must *obey* Christ. And what did Christ tell him to do? Mark carefully what follows.

"And said unto him, Go, wash in the pool of Siloam, (which is by interpretation, Sent)" (v. 7). This, too, was a sermon in action. What the blind beggar needed was *water.* And of what did *that* speak? Clearly of the written Word (see our notes on 3:5 and cf Eph. 5:26). It was just because the Jews *failed* to use the water of the Word that the eyes of their hearts remained closed. Turn to John 5, and what do we find there? We see the Jews seeking to kill Christ because He made Himself equal with God (v. 18). And what did He bid them do? This: "Search the Scriptures" (5:39). We have the same thing again in John 10. The Jews took up stones again to stone Him (v. 31). And the Lord asked them why they acted thus. Their answer was, "Because that Thou, *being a man,* makest Thyself God" (v. 33). What reply did Christ make, "Jesus answered them, Is it not *written?*". It was then, this very thing which (symbolically) the Lord commanded the blind beggar to do. He obeyed implicitly, and the result was that he obtained his sight. The difference between the Jews and the beggar was this: they thought they could see already, and so refused the testimony of the written Word; whereas the beggar knew that he was blind and therefore used the water to which Christ referred him. This supplies the key to the 39th verse of this chapter which sums up all that has gone before. "And Jesus said, For judgment I am come into this world, that they which see not might see; and that they which see might be made blind".

We turn now to consider the *doctrinal* significance of what has just been before us. The blind beggar is to be viewed as a representative character, i. e., as standing for each of God's elect. Blind from birth, and therefore beyond the help of man; a beggar and therefore having nothing, he fitly portrays our condition by nature. Sought out by Christ and ministered to without a single cry or appeal from him, we have a beautiful illustration of the activities of sovereign grace reaching out to us in our unregenerate state. Our Lord's method of dealing with him, was also, in principle, the way in which He dealt with us, when Divine mercy came to our rescue.

"He spat on the ground, and made clay of the spittle, and He anointed the eyes of the blind man with the clay". This seems to have a double meaning. *Dispensationally* it symbolized Christ presenting Himself in the flesh before the eyes of Israel. *Doctrinally* it prefigured the Lord pressing upon the sinner his lost condition and need of a Saviour. The placing of clay on his eyes *emphasizes* our *blindness.* "And said unto him, Go, wash in the pool of Siloam". This intimates our need of turning to the Word and *applying* it to ourselves, for it is the entrance of God's words which, alone, giveth light (Psa. 119:130).

The name of the Pool in which the blind beggar was commanded to wash is not without its significance, as is seen by the fact that the Holy Spirit was careful to interpret it to us. God incarnate is the Object presented to the needy sinner's view: the One who was *"anointed"* by the Holy Spirit (Acts 10:38). *How* is He presented to us? Not as pure spirit, nor in the form of an angel; but as "made flesh". *Where* is He to be thus found? In the written Word. As we turn to that Word we shall learn that the man Christ Jesus is none other than the "Sent One" of the Father. It is through the Word alone (as taught by the Holy Spirit) that we can come to know the Christ of God.

"He went his way therefore, and washed, and came seeing" (v. 7). The simple obedience of the blind beggar is very beautiful. He did not stop to reason and ask questions, but promptly did what was told him. As the old Puritan, John Trapp, (1647) quaintly puts in, "He obeyed Christ blindly. He looked not upon Siloam with Syrian eyes as Naaman did upon Jordan; but, passing by the unliklihood of a cure by such means, he believeth and doeth as he was bidden, without hesitation". The *dispensational* picture found in this chapter we reserve for our closing lesson on it; in the meantime, let the interested student go over the whole chapter carefully and prayerfully, seeking the *personal* application of this passage, and also that which so strikingly typifies God's future dealings with the Jews. Let the following questions be studied:—

1. Vv. 8,9: how do these verses apply to the history of a newly saved soul?
2. What do vv. 10 and 11 teach us concerning the young convert?
3. How does v. 12 fit in with the application of this passage to a babe in Christ?
4. Study vv. 13-16 from a similar viewpoint.
5. What does the beggar's words in v. 17 intimate?—cf our remarks on 4:19.
6. What does v. 18 teach the young believer to expect?
7. What do vv. 20-23 teach the babe in Christ he must do?

—Arthur W. Pink.

GLEANINGS IN EXODUS

7. Lessons in Service: Ex. 4.

Our present lesson deals with the concluding stage of the Lord's interview with Moses, and of the deliverer starting forth on his mighty errand. It is important to note that Moses was the *first* man that was ever formally called of God to engage in His *service,* and like the first notice of anything in Scripture this hints at all that is fundamental in connection with the subject. First, we are shown that no *training* of the natural man is of any avail in the work of God. Neither the wisdom of Egypt, in which Moses was thoroughly skilled, nor the solitude of the desert, had fitted Moses for spiritual activities. Forty years had been spent in Egypt's court, and another forty years in Midian's sheepfolds; yet, when the Lord appeared to him, Moses was full of unbelief and selfwill. How this shows that the quiëtude of monastic life is as impotent to destroy the enmity of the carnal mind as is the culture of high society or the instruction of the schools. It is true that Moses had been much sobered by his lengthy sojourn at "the backside of the desert", but in faith, in courage, in the spirit of obedience, he was greatly deficient—grace, not nature, must supply these.

In the second place, we are shown how the Lord *prepared* His servant. God dealt personally and directly with the one He was going to honor as His ambassador: there was a manifestation of His holiness, the avowal of His covenant-relationship, an assurance of His compassion for the suffering Hebrews, and the declaration of His self-sufficiency as the great "I am"; in short, there was a full revelation of His person and character. In addition, Moses received a definite call from Jehovah, the guarantee that God would be with him, an intimation of the difficulties that lay before him, and the promise that, in the end, God's purpose should be realized. These have ever been, and still are, the vital prerequisites for effectiveness in God's service. There must be a personal knowledge of God for ourselves: a knowledge obtained by direct revelation of God to the soul. There must be a definite call from God to warrant us engaging in His service. There must be a recognition of the difficulties confronting us and a confident resting on God's promise for ultimate success.

In the third place, the Lord *endowed* His servant for the work before him. This endowment was the bestowal upon him of power to work three miracles. The first two of these were designed to teach important lessons to God's servant: he was shown the secret of overcoming Satan, and he was reminded of the corruption of his own heart—things of vital moment for every servant to understand. Moreover, these miracles or signs had a voice for the Hebrews: they showed them their *need* of being delivered from the dominion of the Devil and the pollution of sin—things which every servant must continue pressing on those to whom he ministers. The third miracle or sign spoke of the *judgment* awaiting those who received not God's testimonies—another thing which the faithful servant must not shun to declare.

In the fourth place, we are made acquainted with the *response* which Moses made to God's call. Here again we have something more than what is local and transient. The difficulties felt by Moses and the objections which he raised are those which have, in principle and essence, been felt and raised by all of God's servants at some time or other—the perfect Servant alone excepted. If they have not been expressed by lip, they have had a place in the heart. The first three objections of Moses we have noticed in previous papers: they may be summed up as: self-occupation (3:11), fear (3:13), unbelief (4:1). The fourth, which savored of *pride,* will now engage our attention.

"And Moses said unto the Lord, O my Lord, I am not eloquent, neither heretofore, nor since Thou hast spoken unto Thy servant: but I am slow of speech, and of a slow tongue" (4:10). How many of the Lord's servants (and others who ought to be engaged in His service) regard this as a fatal defect. They suppose that the gift of oratory is a prime pre-requisite for effective ministry. Those who are being "trained for the ministry" must, forsooth, have a course in rhetoric and elocution: as though men dead in sins can be quickened by the enticing words of men's wisdom; as though carnal weapons could have a place in spiritual warfare. Sad it is that such elementary matters are so little understood in this twentieth century. Have we forgotten those words of the apostle Paul, "And I, brethren, when I came to you, *came not* with excellency of speech or of wisdom, declaring unto you the testimony of God" (1 Cor. 2:1)!

"And the Lord said unto him, Who hath made man's mouth? or who maketh the dumb, or deaf, or the seeing, or the blind? Have not I the Lord?" (v. 11). This was manifestly a rebuke. Even though he was not "eloquent", did Moses suppose that the Lord knew not what He was about in selecting *him* to act as His mouthpiece in Pharaoh's court? God was only demonstrating once more how radically different are His ways from man's. The wisdom of this world is foolishness with God (1 Cor. 3:19), and that which is highly esteemed among men, is abomination in His sight (Luke 16:15). The instrument through whom God did the most for Israel, and the one He used in bringing the greatest blessing to the Gentiles, was each unqualified when judged by the standards of human scholarship!—*see* 2 Cor. 10:1 and 11:6 for the apostle Paul as a speaker.

"And the Lord said unto him, Who hath made man's mouth? or who maketh the dumb, or deaf, or the seeing, or the blind? Have not I the Lord?". It seems evident from this that, in the previous verse, Moses was referring to some impediment in his speech. In reply, the Lord tells him that *He* was responsible for that. The force of what Jehovah said here seems to be this: As all the physical senses, and the perfection of them, are from the Creator, so are the imperfections of them according to His sovereign pleasure. Behind the law of heredity is the Law-giver, regulating it as He deems best.

"Now therefore go, and I will be with thy mouth, and teach thee what thou shalt say" (v. 12). What a re-assuring word was this! Better far, infinitely better, is the teaching of the Lord and *His* control of the tongue than any gift of "eloquence" or any of the artificialities of speech which human training can bestow. It is just these substitutes of human art which has degraded too many of our pulpits from places where should be heard the simple exposition of God's Word into stages on which men display their oratorical abilities. Little room for wonder that God's blessing has long since departed from the vast majority of our pulpits when we stop to examine the "training" which the men who occupy them have received. All the schooling in the world is of no avail whatever unless the Lord is "with the mouth" of the preacher, teaching him *what* he shall say; and if the Lord *is* with him, then, "eloquence" and rhetorical devices are needless and useless. Note it is *"what"* the preacher has to say, not *how* he says it, which matters most. God has used the simple language of unlettered Bunyan far more than He has the polished writings of thousands of University graduates!

"And he said, O my Lord, send, I pray Thee, by the hand of him whom Thou wilt send" (v. 13). That is, Send any one, but not me! Moses was still unwilling to act as the Lord's ambassador, in fact he now asked God to select another in his place. How fearful are the lengths to which the desperately-wicked heart of man may go! Not only distrustful, but rebellious. The faithfulness of Moses in recording his own sins, and the "anger" of the Lord against him, is a striking proof of the Divine veracity of the Scriptures: an un-inspired writer would have omitted such serious reflections upon himself as these.

"And he said, O my Lord, send, I pray Thee, by the hand of him whom Thou wilt send. And the anger of the Lord was kindled against Moses, and He said, Is not Aaron the Levite thy brother? I know that he can speak well. And also, behold, he cometh forth to meet thee: and when he seeth thee, he will be glad in his heart. And thou shalt speak unto him, and put words in his mouth: and I will be with thy mouth, and with his mouth, and will teach you what ye shall do. And he shall be thy spokesman unto the people: and he shall be, even he shall be to thee instead of a mouth, and thou shalt be to him instead of God. And thou shalt take this rod in thine hand, wherewith thou shalt do signs" (vv. 13-17). "Although there was nothing gained in the way of power, although there was no more virtue or efficacy in one mouth than in another, although it was Moses after all who was to speak unto Aaron, yet was Moses quite ready to go when assured of the presence and co-operation of a poor feeble mortal like himself; whereas he could not go when assured, again and again, that Jehovah would be with him.

"Oh! my reader, does not all this hold up before us a faithful mirror in which you and I can see our hearts reflected? Truly it does. We are more ready to trust anything than the living God. We move along with bold decision when we possess the countenance and support of a poor frail mortal like ourselves; but we falter, hesitate, and demur when we have the light of the Master's countenance to cheer us, and the strength of His omnipotent arm to support us. This should humble us deeply before the Lord, and lead us to seek a fuller acquaintance with Him, so that we might trust Him with a more unmixed confidence, and walk on with a firmer step, as having Him *alone* for our resource and portion" (C.H.M.).

Though God's anger was kindled against Moses, His wrath was tempered by mercy. To strengthen his weak faith, the Lord grants him still another sign that He would give him success. As Moses returned to Egypt he would find Aaron coming forth to *meet* him. What an illustration is this that when God works, He works at *both* ends of the line! The eunuch and Philip, Saul and Ananias, Cornelius and Peter supply us with further illustrations of the same principle.

"And Moses went and returned to Jethro his father in law, and said unto him, Let me go, I pray thee, and return unto my brethren which are in Egypt, and see whether they be yet alive. And Jethro said to Moses, Go in peace" (v. 18). This act of Moses was very commendable. Jethro had taken him in while a fugitive from Egypt, had given him his daughter to wife, and had provided him with a home for forty years. Moreover, Moses had charge of his flock (3:1). It would, then, have been grossly discourteous and the height of ingratitude had Moses gone down to Egypt without first notifying his father-in-law. This request of Moses manifested his thoughtfulness of others, and his appreciation of favors received. Let writer and reader take this to heart. Spiritual activities never absolve us from the common amenities and responsibilities of life. No believer who is not a gentleman or a lady is a true Christian in the full sense of the word. To be a Christian is to practise Christliness, and Christ ever thought *of others.*

"And Moses went and returned to Jethro his father in law, and said unto him, Let me go, I pray thee, and return unto my brethren which are in Egypt, and see whether they be yet alive". We are sorry that we cannot speak so favorably of Moses' words on this occasion. His utterance here was quite Jacob-like. Moses says nothing about the Lord's appearing to him, of the communication he had received, nor of the positive assurance from God that He would bring His people out of Egypt into

Canaan. Evidently Moses was yet far from being convinced. This is clear from the next verse: "And the Lord said unto Moses in Midian, Go, return into Egypt: *for* all the men are dead which sought thy life". The Lord repeated His command, and at the same time graciously removed the fears of His servant that he was venturing himself into that very peril from which he had fled forty years before. How long-suffering and compassionate is our God!

"And Moses took his wife and his sons, and set them upon an ass, and he returned to the land of Egypt: and Moses took the rod of God in his hand . . . . and it came to pass by the way in the inn, that the Lord met him, and sought to kill him" (vv. 20, 24). At last Moses starts out on his epoch-making mission. In obedience to God's command he goes forth rod in hand, and accompanied by his wife and his sons, returns to the land of Egypt. But one other thing needed to be attended to, an important matter long neglected, before he is ready to act as God's ambassador. Jehovah was about to fulfill His covenant engagement to Abraham, but the sign of that covenant was circumcision, and this the son of Moses had not received, apparently because of the objections of the mother. Such an ignoring of the Divine requirements could not be passed by, and Moses is forcibly reminded anew of the holiness of the One with whom he had to do.

"And it came to pass by the way in the inn, that the Lord met him, and sought to kill him. Then Zipporah took a sharp stone, and cut off the foreskin of her son, and cast it at his feet, and said, Surely a bloody husband art thou to me. So He let him go: then she said, A bloody husband thou art, because of the circumcision" (vv. 24-26). Whether it was the Lord Himself in theophanic manifestation who now appeared to Moses, or whether it was an angel of the Lord with sword in hand, as he later stood before Balaam, we are not told. Nor do we know in what way the Lord sought to kill Moses. It seems clear that he was stricken down and rendered helpless, for his wife was the one who performed the act of circumcision on their son. This is all the more striking because the inference seems unescapeable that Zipporah was the one who had resisted the ordinance of God—only thus can we explain her words to Moses, and only thus can we account for Moses here sending her back to her father (cf 18:2). Nevertheless, it was Moses, the *head* of the house (the one God ever holds primarily responsible for the training and conduct of the children), and not Zipporah, whom the Lord sought to kill. This points a most solemn warning to Christian fathers today. A man may be united to a woman who opposes him at every step as he desires to maintain a scriptural discipline in his home, but this does not absolve him from doing his duty.

Let us also observe how the above incident teaches us another most important lesson in connection with *service*. Before God suffered Moses to go and minister to Israel, He first required him to set his own house in order. Not until this had been attended to was Moses qualified for his mission. There must be faithfulness in the sphere of his own responsibility before God would make him the channel of Divine power. As another has said, "Obedience at home must precede the display of power to the world". That this same principle obtains during the Christian dispensation is clear from 1 Tim. 3, where we are told that among the various qualifications of a "bishop" (elder) is that he must be "one that ruleth his own house well, having his children in subjection with all gravity" (v. 14). As a general rule God refuses to use in public ministry one who is lax and lawless in his own home.

"And the Lord said to Aaron, Go into the wilderness to meet Moses. And he went, and met him in the mount of God, and kissed him. And Moses told Aaron all the words of the Lord who had sent him, and all the signs which He had commanded him" (vv. 27, 28). This is another example of how when God works, He works at *both* ends of the line: Moses was advancing toward Egypt, Aaron is sent to *meet* him. By comparing this verse with what is said in v. 14 it seems clear that the Lord had ordered Aaron to go into the wilderness *before* Moses actually started out for Egypt, for there we find Him saying to Moses, "Behold, he (Aaron) *cometh* forth to meet thee". What an encouragement was this for Moses. Ofttimes the Lord in His tenderness gives such encouragements to His servants, especially in their earlier days; thus did He to Eliezer (Gen. 24:14, 18, 19); to Joseph (Gen. 37:7, 8); to the disciples

(Mark 14:13); to Paul (Acts 9:11, 12); to Peter (Acts 10:17).

It is a point of interest and importance to note the *meeting-place* of these brothers: it was "in the mount of God". There it was that Jehovah had first appeared to Moses (3:1), and from it Moses and Aaron now set forth on their momentuous errand. The "mount" speaks, of course, of *elevation,* elevation of spirit through communion with the Most High. An essential prerequisite is this for all effective ministry. It is only as the servant has been in "the mount" with God that he is ready to go forth and represent Him in the plains! Again and again was this illustrated in the life of the perfect Servant. Turn to the four Gospels, and note how frequently we are told there of Christ retiring to "the mount", from which He came forth later to minister to the needy. This is indeed a lesson which every servant needs to learn. I must first commune *with* God, before I am fitted to work *for* Him. Note this order in Mark 3:14 in connection with the apostles: "He ordained twelve that they should be *with* Him, *and* that He might send them forth to preach"!

"And Moses and Aaron went and gathered together all the elders of the children of Israel: And Aaron spake all the words which the Lord had spoken unto Moses, and did the signs in the sight of the people. And the people believed: and when they heard that the Lord had visited the children of Israel, and that He had looked upon their affliction, then they bowed their heads and worshipped" (vv. 29-31). The "elders" are always to be viewed as the representatives of the people: they were the heads of the tribes and of the leading families. Unto them Aaron recited all that Jehovah had said unto Moses, and Moses performed the two signs. The result was precisely as God had fore-announced (3:18). Moses had said, "They will not believe me" (4:1); the Lord had declared they *would,* and so it came to pass. They believed that Moses was sent of God, and that he would be their deliverer. Believing this, they bowed their heads and worshipped, adoring the goodness of God, and expressing their thankfulness for the notice which He took of them in their distress.

In the favorable response which Moses received from the elders of Israel we may discern once more the tender mercy and grace of the Lord. At a later stage, the leaders came before Moses and Aaron complaining they had made the lot of the people worse rather than better. But here, on their first entrance into Egypt, the Lord inclined the hearts of the people to believe. Thus He did not put too great a strain upon their faith at first, nor lay upon them a burden greater than what they were able to bear. It is usually thus in the Lord's dealings with His servants. The real trials are kept back until we have become accustomed to the yoke. We heartily commend this fourth chapter of Exodus to every minister of God, for it abounds in important lessons which each servant of His needs to take to heart.

—Arthur W. Pink.

THE KINGDOM AND HUMAN RESPONSIBILITY

The question has been raised, "How could the Lord Jesus have offered to the Jews of His day a kingdom which it was not in the plan of God to establish at that time, and which would have falsified the prophecies concerning the sufferings, death and resurrection of Christ, those concerning His session at the right hand of God, and those concerning the coming and ministry of the Holy Spirit on earth?" In the final analysis this carries us back to the old, old problem of, How is it possible to harmonize human responsibility with Divine sovereignty? where is the meeting-place between God's eternal purpose and the accountability of men in time?

That it *was* "in the plan of God" that the Lord Jesus should be crucified and raised from the dead, that it *was* "in the plan of God" that Christ should sit down at the right hand of the Majesty on high and remain there all these many centuries, we have not the slightest doubt, for God "worketh *all* things after the counsel of His own will" (Eph. 1:11). That it *was not* "in the plan of God" for the Millennial Kingdom of Christ to have been set up on the earth nineteen hundred years ago is equally certain. This being so, how was it possible for Christ and His forerunner to do and say what they did? We believe that it is impossible to furnish a satisfactory answer to this question until it has been canvassed in the light of human responsibility as it relates to the will of God.

To help the reader appreciate the force of our last remark let us name a number of similar difficulties whose solution must be sought at the same place. How could God say to Adam, "of the tree of the knowledge of good and evil, thou shalt not eat of it" (Gen. 2:17) when it was "in His plan" that Adam *should* eat thereof? That it *was* in "the plan of God" that sin *should* enter the world is clear from 1 Pet. 1:20 and similar scriptures. This does not make God the Author of sin, for one who is "glorious in holiness" (Ex. 15:11) *could not* originate evil any more than He could lie (Titus 1:2). But that God eternally purposed to *permit* sin to enter this world cannot be gainsaid, and that He planned to *allow* Adam to fall is equally certain, though *He* in no-wise caused that fall. Still the question returns upon us. If it was in the plan of God that sin *should* enter the world through the fall of Adam, how could He consistently command Adam *not* to do that which caused sin to enter?

A similar difficulty—and a very real one it is to those who face it fairly and squarely—lies in connection with the Gospel in view of the clearly revealed truth of *election.* With no desire whatever to raise a controversy on this subject (alas, that it is made a matter of controversy!), let us endeavor to state the problem in a way least calculated to meet with objection. All Christians will allow that the Lord God knows the end from the beginning, and that He foresees who will receive Christ and who will reject Him. This being so, how can the Lord bid us preach the Gospel to *every* creature, *when He knows beforehand* that many will not listen to it? God "now commandeth *all men* everywhere to repent" (Acts 17:30), but why should He when He foreknows that multitudes of them never will?

Now the answer to these and all similar questions lies in defining correctly *the ground of human responsibility.* Human responsibility is measured by the revelation which men have received from God. The secret counsels of God are none of their business. "The secret things belong unto the Lord our God: but those things which are revealed belong unto us and to our children forever" (Deut. 29:29). This was true of Adam. He knew nothing about the eternal purpose of God. What he *did* know was that his Maker had *forbidden* him to eat of the tree of the knowledge of good and evil, and therefore he was responsible not to eat of it. It was to enforce his accountability that the Lord made this prohibition and faithfully warned him of the dire consequences that would follow his disobedience.

The same is true in connection with the Gospel. But let it be said right here that the Gospel is no mere *invitation* to be bandied around, leaving men free to use their own pleasure as to how they shall respond. The Gospel is an authoritative fiat from heaven. It issues not an invitation, but a Divine command: God "now *commandeth* all men everywhere to repent" (Acts 17:30), "And this is His *commandment,* that we should believe in the name of His Son Jesus Christ" (1 John 3:23); and men and women disobey at their imminent peril. The Gospel is for "faith—*obedience*" (Rom. 1:1, 5), and the One so long despised shall yet be revealed from heaven "in flaming fire taking vengeance on them that know not God, and that *OBEY not the Gospel* of our Lord Jesus Christ" (2 Thess. 1:8). Accompanying the command of the Gospel are gracious promises (its good news) that whosoever believeth in Christ should not perish, etc., etc.

The Gospel is addressed to human responsibility. Men, all men, are sinners, *therefore* God has the right to command *all men* to repent. Christ is "The Truth" *therefore* God commands all men to believe Him. And every man who hears the Gospel is *responsible to* repent and believe. God's foreknowledge *affects not* man's accountability in the slightest degree. Altogether apart from the fact as to whether or not God chose me in Christ before the foundation of the world, I am *responsible* to repent and believe, responsible because God has *commanded* me to do so.

Let us cite one other example where these same principles apply. Take the *return* of the Saviour. The New Testament Epistles uniformly present the second coming of the Lord as the *hope* of His people. They hold forth that glorious event as an *imminent* one. They interpose nothing whatever between the heart of the believer and the realization of His scriptural hope.

We are to wait for God's Son from heaven, and to be daily looking for that blessed hope as something which may happen at any moment. But suppose an objector should come along and say, Your attitude is an absurd one. Christ cannot come until the hour appointed in "in the plan of God", and before that hour can strike the "fulness of the Gentiles must come in" (Rom. 11:25), that people must first be completed which God is now taking out from among the Gentiles (Acts 15:14). What should be our reply? Surely this. The specific time which God has fixed in His plan has not been revealed to us, nor has He made known the exact number of this people which He is now taking out from among the Gentiles. That is none of our business. Our *responsibility* is determined by what God *has revealed;* and among the things revealed is, that from the standpoint of human responsibility, the return of Christ for His saints is an *imminent* event, therefore it is my bounden duty to be daily and hourly listening for that Shout which shall call me, together with all the saints, to meet our Lord in the air.

Now apply this same principle to the problem raised by the question at the head of this article. Were the Jews *responsible* to receive Christ as their King? Before we answer this question another must first be considered. *Was* Christ the *King* of the Jews? Upon this point there is no room for argument. *He was.* The very first chapter of the New Testament was written to prove it. The leading purpose in giving us the genealogy found in Matt. 1 was to demonstrate that, according to the flesh, the Lord Jesus was "the Son of David", the rightful heir to Israel's throne. To render ignorance on this point still more excuseless, the second chapter of the New Testament tells us that Jesus was "born King of the Jews". In full accord with this, when the Lord Jesus rode into Jerusalem on the back of an ass, the Holy Spirit was careful to tell us in this same first Gospel, that "all this was done, that it might be fulfilled which was spoken by the prophet, saying, Tell ye the daughter of Zion, Behold, *thy King* cometh unto thee" (Matt. 21:4, 5).

That the Lord Jesus was Prophet and Priest as well as King no one disputes, but the fact that He ministered to Israel as Prophet and died as the Priest, does not in any-wise negative the fact that He also presented Himself to Israel as their *King.* As then Christ *was* their King, the Jews were *responsible* to receive Him as such. It is quite beside the point to inquire what would have happened *had* Israel received the Lord Jesus as their rightful King, and it is only to confuse the issue to introduce at this point the foreknowledge and plan of God. To insist that what God *had made known* through the Old Testament prophets could not fail in its accomplishment is perfectly in order, and so far as we are aware has never been denied by Bible teachers; but to introduce that part of God's plan *which was not revealed* in the Old Testament scriptures is unfair and unwarrantable. That the Lord Jesus should be crucified, rise again, and ascend, and sit down at the right hand of God was all announced centuries beforehand; and therefore must be accomplished: but that there should be an interval of more than eighteen centuries before He returned to earth and set up His kingdom upon it was nowhere revealed in the Old Testament.

Should it be asked, Did the Lord Jesus or His forerunner specifically *offer* the Kingdom (the Messianic Kingdom of O. T. prophecy) to Israel? Our answer is, We prefer to say that the Kingdom was *announced* to the Jews. When John the Baptist cried, "Repent ye: for the kingdom of heaven is at hand" (Matt. 3:2)—a declaration repeated by Christ (Matt. 4:17) and by His apostles (Matt. 10:7 and cf Mark 6:12 for "repent")—a plain *announcement* of the Messianic Kingdom was then made. To insist that the "kingdom of heaven" in these passages signified anything else than the Messianic Kingdom is to be guilty of charging God with *mis-leading* those who heard that announcement. This announcement was made *before* the Lord Jesus began His public ministry and before a single page of the New Testament had been written. It was made to those who were in possession of the Old Testament Scriptures, and they who were familiar with the Prophets, and especially the contents of the book of Daniel, could not possibly understand the Baptist to refer to anything else than the Messianic Kingdom foretold of old.

"The kingdom of heaven is at hand" unquestionably means "the kingdom of heaven *has drawn near*"—cf Phil. 4:5 and see

Bagster's Interlinear. In what respect had the Kingdom "drawn near"? We answer, In that it was presented *to their responsibility,* presented to their responsibility because the King Himself was about to appear before them. That the Kingdom *was* presented to their responsibility is clear from the fact that the announcement or proclamation was accompanied by the command *to repent.* That God *foreknew* Israel would not repent, that He foresaw the King Himself would be rejected, no more invalidates what we have just said than the fact that God foreknew Adam would eat of the tree of the knowledge of good and evil, and foreknew it at the very moment He issued His prohibition; or that God foresees that multitudes of men will not repent, even though He now commands all men so to do. We shall never be able to see these things in their proper perspective until we contemplate them *separately,* in their respective spheres. Just as a prolonged effort to gaze at the same moment at two objects in different corners of the room would ultimately make us cross-eyed, so the attempt to view the Divine side and the human side *at the same time* will make our mental vision cross-eyed.

Whether our explanation above be the correct one or not *the fact remains* that the kingdom of heaven *was* announced to the Jews, and announced in as good faith by God as when He promises to save every sinner who believes on the Lord Jesus Christ, even though He knows beforehand that many will not and cannot (John 8:43; 12:39; 14:17; Rom. 8:8, etc.) believe. That the failure of Israel to repent did not in any-wise affect the "plan of God" is freely allowed. That the Messianic Kingdom will be established on earth at God's appointed time we fully believe. But before that Kingdom is set up Israel *must* "repent", and when they repent the Kingdom will come.

Arthur W. Pink.

CONSCIENCE

Conscience is a great difficulty with infidels. It is practically the weak point in their armour. Protect themselves with reasonings as they may, yet they cannot shield their conscience.

It would be, doubtless, a convenient thing for modern infidelity, if it could shew that conscience—instead of being a witness to evil present, and good lost—is a part of the system of human developement, but "the history of the conscience, from the evolutionist point of view, remains yet to be written," and we may safely assert, that the evolutionist will find such "history" difficult writing.

The beasts which perish possess consciousness of various kinds in common with man, but the beasts which perish possess not that which makes mortals quake. Man, alone, of the creatures upon this earth, has a conscience. However, as some beasts possess a power through which they acquire knowledge that some of their actions will receive the reward of their master's favour, and others punishment, from his hand, and because some beasts can be instructed in obedience by their masters, there are not wanting some men to assert that, consequently, a moral link exists between such consciousness in the beast and the conscience of a man!

By the aid of a stick a cow can be educated into refusing to pluck the green leaves over the fence which her tongue longs after. The memory of the beating she has more than once received for interfering with her master's wishes, teaches her to forego her inclinations. But memory is not conscience. A parrot too learns to fear the word "stick", learns to associate the sound of the word with a beating, and so will leave off screaming when "stick" is said. The parrot is unquestionably wiser than the cow, but the intelligence of the creature is not conscience. Yet we are invited to accept this kind of consciousness as a link in the chain of evolution, the end of which in ourselves is conscience!

It is remarkable how infidelity degrades man as a creature, while puffing up his pride. Yet, while asserting that the human race is but the outcome of former shapes, things, and being—that man is but a link in the long chain of unknowable beginning—that man is but a brute developed, a creature evolved out of atoms and apes, the infidel pauses, and inquires, "How did man become possessed of a conscience?"

Conscience is; it cannot be shelved. I am, and my conscience exists in me. And to him who is conscious of his sinful being, it is a terrible reality. Besides doing battle daily within the breasts of men, against their very wills, conscience spoils the pleasures of sin, renders the prosperous wicked man miserable, scares the sceptic, ruins the fine theories of no future, and forces men, against their judgment and feelings, to confess their crimes, and to yield themselves to justice and to death.

We do not deny that man may harden himself, till, despite his conscience, he becomes like the beasts, and shuns evil only because of its consequences, or, worse, till his conscience, seared as with a hot iron, is so dulled to every righteous influence, that his fellow men drive him from their midst as too brutish for their society. In such case we may, perhaps, allow the claims of modern infidelity, by accepting the affinity between the savage element in dog and man, and own that there is a doctrine of evolution—that out of evil evil is evolved.

How came man by this inward force, this mighty power within his breast, called conscience? or, first, what is conscience?

Clearly it is not the will, for conscience frequently pushes its way in opposition to the will. Neither is it reason, for while a man's reason will demonstrate to him that a given course of action will work him injury, yet his will impels him forward to do the right thing, even to the wronging of himself. It is not a conclusion arrived at in the mind upon weighing over the right or wrong of a question. Conscience is the moral sense of right and wrong which is innate to man. It is as much a part of his being as his reason or his will. We may describe conscience as the eye of man's moral being, or liken it to a voice within his breast commanding him concerning right and wrong.

Conscience is not a faculty in man, enabling him to know abstractedly what is right and wrong, but, given the law of right and wrong, conscience appeals to man according to the precepts of the law he knows. Conscience needs instructing, it does not instruct; and according as the conscience is faithfully instructed, so will its utterances be more or less just. In proportion as this eye is tutored will be the truthfulness of its perceptions.

Men say, we will act according to the dictates of our consciences. But conscience is no standard of right. The conscience of a heathen does not address him as that of a man knowing the letter of God's Word. The conscience of a Christian, instructed in the spirit of his Father's will, speaks very differently from that of him who knows merely the letter of the Scriptures. And amongst true Christians there is a vast difference in fineness and sensibility of conscience. Conscience is very like a window, which lets in much or little light, if clean or dirty. Some labour to keep the window clean, others are slovenly, and their whole body is not full of light. Some Christians exercise to keep the window clean, others are exercised because it is dirty.

Now, according to man's knowledge of right or wrong, is his responsibility. Having heard what is right, we are bound to obey, and conscience will speak upon the question. The heathen have the book of nature before their eyes. "The invisible things of Him, from the creation of the world, are clearly seen, being understood by the things that are made, even His eternal power and divinity." (Rom. 1:20, 21) And more, for "when the Gentiles, which have not the law, do by nature the things contained in the law, these, having not the law, are a law unto themselves: which shew the work of the law written upon their hearts, their consciences also bearing witness, and their thoughts the meanwhile accusing, or else excusing, one another." (Rom. 2:14-16).

The nominal Christian has heard of the character of God, he has heard of God's holiness and righteousness, his conscience bears witness, and condemns him. God has revealed a standard in His Word, and man's conscience tells him how utterly vile he is. Where the Word of God has been heard, we cannot dissociate God from conscience. Our moral instinct, our sense of right and wrong, bear witness to the unseen God; within us there is that which knows together with God.

How came man by this voice within him? When all was right, the voice warning of wrong was silent. It could not testify to right if no wrong existed. If man were not a sinner, he would not fear the holy God. God made man upright, and set him in a scene of good, where evil was not, and in those days man had not learned it. Had, then, man before the fall a conscience?

We do not say that he had a conscience

in the sense that he was not perfect. Conscience in itself is a good thing, but it was not good in a bad way. Before the fall, man's conscience was like the wings of the insect within the chrysalis, for man had not then broken out into that condition when he should be as gods. Innocence is not perfection, any more than ignorance is maturity. The lack of knowledge of evil is a lovely thing, and thus to us is childhood's simplicity so sweet; but vastly different is the state of the innocence from that "new man which after God is created in righteousness and true holiness. (Eph. 4:14).

In the creation, as at first, man lacked the knowledge of evil, and his state was beautiful, and he was happy. At present man has lost that simplicity. He is mature. He knows evil; he is acquainted with the contrast between right and wrong; but he is a fallen creature, he loves the evil, and cannot do good. When we say fallen, we mean fallen from God, and that condition in which God has set him. Man gained knowledge by his fall. "The Lord God said, Behold, the man has become as one of Us, to know good and evil." (Gen. 3: 22). The knowledge is unquestionable, but, together with the knowledge, there is a nature contrary to God which loves iniquity. What kind of development shall this be called?

To the Christian it is said, "Put off, concerning the former conversation, the old man, which is corrupt according to the deceitful lusts; and be renewed in the spirit of your mind; and that ye put on the new man, which after God is created in righteousness and true holiness." Not innocence regained, not a return to the first state, but righteousness and true holiness. For man has acquired the knowledge of good and evil, never to lose that knowledge, but in Christ he is no longer under the power of evil. And in the future the believer will possess the knowledge of good and evil, yet without a desire after evil, and rejoicing in the good. That will be perfection. Even in this scene of sin, and having the flesh in him, the man in Christ is shewn the path of perfect bliss below.

How came man by his conscience? By disobedience. He stole his knowledge, and thus his eyes were opened. Disobedience was the key wherewith the door into the world was unlocked. Paradise was not the world, but the garden of the earth, but when man's eyes were opened to the fatal knowledge of evil, he feared and fled from God; and so the world began, and so it developes. Man's knowledge condemned him, and condemns him still. The one step over the boundary-line set him where the darkness reigns.

Adam, made upright by God, and never having an idea of evil till he disobeyed, not acquainted as are we with sin from childhood, must have had, after his fall, a conscience of exceeding sensitiveness. Man now is used to evil, is well versed in sin, he learns it alas! from his childhood. It comes naturally to him without education, for he is born in sin and shapen in iniquity. It is as he is instructed in right, and taught of God, that he becomes sensitive to wrong. There is a vast moral difference between those first few hours in the world, when conscience awoke in man, and these last days, when it is a subject for infidel analysis.

But there is one thing respecting the sensitive and refined conscience which is self-evident—conscience is not strength. If it be a light within, shewing to man the right path, it is a light to feet which are paralysed—"How to perform I find not." Conscience makes men "cowards"; and miserable. To be sure, a man may pride himself upon a clear conscience, and we do not deny that many men not "in Christ" possess consciences so high-class and refined, that they put many Christians to shame. They would not do willfully an evil thing for any consideration. But this must not be mistaken for new life in Christ. Surely, if Adam, as he was just after his fall, could see the world as it now is, he would be astonished at its low order of conscience; and it is astonishing that even infidels can really believe the doctrine of the evolution of conscience, and credit the theory that man's conscience is today nearer perfection than it was six thousand years ago.

Now when the Spirit of God works within a man, He begins with the conscience. True, some are apparently moved through their emotions, others through their minds; but man is gained for God through the conscience. Man's departure from God was by disobedience, his first hidings from God were because of the fears of his conscience; and God begins with man where man left Him. Man's way of return to God is by obeying the Gospel, and his first laying bare of himself is the cry wrought in him by the pangs of his conscience—"I have sinned."

It is a horrible deceit of infidelity, which bids us believe that the cry, "I have sinned," is my development as a creature! It is the responsible creature now coming to his senses, awaking to the sense of what he has done in the sight of God. Quite true, I ought to be good, and to love God and to hate sin, but alas! *I have sinned.*

Now that kind of Gospel preaching which lets the conscience alone, or only deals softly with it, will produce either unreal or weakly converts. There is no going on for an hour with God unless the conscience is right with Him. And this is very true of the Christian, as of the unconverted. The latter may become a nominal Christian, and be apparently all that is required, but until the Spirit of God applies the living and powerful Word to the conscience, and lays all bare, a man is no nearer to God than Adam was when he was hiding from God. And with the Christian; unless his conscience be right before God, he cannot have communion with God. He has life in Christ, but so long as his conscience is not right with God, he is like a man asleep, or a ship ashore.

One word about Christian conscience. Conscience is the sense of right and wrong, and for those who have heard of God, this sense in relation to God. As the sense of the thing itself increases within us, so does our sensibility to it grow. Some heathens do not possess any consciousness that it is wrong to steal—they try not to be found out, but a monkey will learn to hide when he purloins. Now hiding the treasure lest it should be taken away, or lest punishment should ensue, is totally different from the moral consciousness that to steal is an evil thing. The Lord Jesus tells us that to look and long is like doing the very sin itself, and it is written of the effect produced by the law upon the quickened soul, "I had not known sin unless the law had said, Thou shalt not covet."

As the believer grows in grace, and in the knowledge of the Lord, he becomes more acute in his consciousness. He mourns over the sins of the soul. It is not punishment that he fears, but he grieves that he has done wrong against his God. It was this acute consciousness which made the Apostle exercise himself day and night in keeping a clear conscience before God and man. With too many there is such sloth of spirit—resulting from so little communion—that there is remarkably little exercise in keeping the conscience clear. The blood of Christ has purged our consciences. We know good and evil, but do not fear God, for we know that the blood of His Son has satisfied the righteousness of God. We do not fear a man who has nothing against us, and we do not fear God since He is entirely for us. He gave His Son for us, Who shed His blood for us. Our conscience instructed by the Spirit of God, concerning the death of Christ, know together with God, that God has not one thing whatever against us.

Such clearness of conscience in the presence of our holy and gracious God surely leads us to increased consciousness of every kind of evil thing. The window of the Christian's soul is unshuttered: he wishes the light to shine in, and his earnest desire is to keep every speck and spot off the glass of that window; therein doth he exercise himself.

The Bible Treasury—1878.

A PASSING WORD TO YOUNG DISCIPLES

If there were any period of human life, from infancy to old age, at which salvation were impossible, it would argue a defect in the Divine plan or in the work of Christ. We do not know, and practically it does not concern us to know, how the provisions of grace reach those who die in infancy; but we do know their salvation is secure; and Rachel, weeping for her children because they are not, is comforted with the assurance "they shall come again from the land of the enemy." Beyond the period of infancy the Gospel of the grace of God addresses itself to all, without distinction of years. The faith of the Gospel is not an exercise of great intellectual power, but of simple trust, which is a characteristic of childhood. Nor does it imply previous high attainments in virtue, for the Gospel exposes the emptiness of all human pretensions; and the pride of virtue, as well as of intellect, must be abased; all our gains must be counted loss, and, in the language of our Lord, "Whosoever shall not receive the kingdom of God as a little child, shall in no wise enter therein."

There is something unspeakably grand as well as unspeakably touching in the attitude of the Son of God as He stands amidst the scorn of this world, rejoicing in spirit, and saying, "I thank Thee, O Father, Lord of heaven and earth, that Thou hast hid these things from the wise and prudent, and hast revealed them unto babes." These things are hidden, not in the heights where only the most soaring intellects and the ripest erudition may search for them, but in a simplicity which the insolence of mortal pride disdains. We behold Him overlooking the paltry distinctions of a ruined race, reaching down His mighty hand to the lowest point of man's attenuated littleness, embracing little children, and taking the poor and the wretched to the shelter of His love; reaching down also to the lowest point of the sinner's abject degradation, and snatching the chief of sinners from the jaws of everlasting destruction. It is then that grace is most evidently grace, it is then that the glory of the Redeemer is most illustrious.

We have to regret that the faith of His followers comes so far short of the condescending grace of the Master, and that there is still among His disciples so much of the spirit which He rebuked when He said, "Suffer them to come unto Me." Yet His grace triumphs over all our failures and we can address ourselves to those whom He has called to Himself in early life. We rejoice to remind them of what He was on earth, and to assure them that His love is unchanged, and that He has carried up to the right hand of the Father the remembrance of His boyhood and youth in Nazareth. He looks down upon them with a tender sympathy which takes in every peculiarity of their trials, for which also He supplies the needed and appropriate aid out of His infinite store of grace.

The hoary sinner who finds redemption through His blood has his own peculiar grounds of gratitude, and we might well expect that he to whom most is forgiven should love most. But young disciples have also their peculiar ground of gratitude in the fact that He has not only called them, but called them in early life. They have thus the unimpaired vigor and warmth of youth to be employed in the service of Him who has called them. But more than this, His grace has interposed to save them from a thousand humbling recollections and heart piercing regrets, which haunt the man who has grown old in sin, though the guilt of it is all blotted out forever, and which are only solaced by the thought that it will all redound to His glory when it is seen that where sin abounded grace did much more abound.

Prominent among these humbling recollections is the remembrance of the friends and companions of those days which men are accustomed to describe as their brightest and best days, though that brightness must surely be overshadowed by the thought that they were spent to the dishonor of God. The Christian cannot but remember that the companionship of these years was a partnership in folly and ungodliness. So far as their influence over one another extended, it was a reciprocal encouragement in the rejection of Christ, accelerating each other's progress in evil, and heaping up wrath against the day of wrath. Now, it cannot be a trivial sorrow to one of these who may be snatched as a brand from the burning, to think that such an influence against Christ, against the souls of his warmest friends, and which has contributed to the everlasting destruction of some of them, can never, never be recalled. The sin may be forgiven, but the evil cannot be undone.

To the young disciples there is an occasion of unutterable gratitude in the fact that Divine grace has interposed to save them from the bitter experience of years of open sin, and from all these regrets of an evil influence exerted on their friends and associates to their eternal undoing. But it should be impressed on the minds of young Christians that the freedom of their after years from the most bitter regrets and self-reproaches depends upon their abiding in Christ in holy separation from the world. For if, with a profession of the faith, they are living in the world—if one day they are sitting with the worldly as partners of their gayeties and follies, and the next day are sitting down with the people of God at the table of the Lord their testimony is worse than valueless, and God is more dishonored than if without naming the name of Christ, they were running with the profligate to every excess of riot. Satan is never so effectively served as by those who have a name to live while they are dead, and there are none who fill up the future with more bitter self-reproaches than inconsistent Christians.

Young disciples need especially to be warned against worldly conformity in this dark day. There have always been nominal churches dependent on State support and the patronage of the world, in which the spirit of worldliness was unchecked. But then the members of these churches never professed to be born again, except in some merely ritual sense, and they commonly derided all thoughts of conversion and spiritual life. It is the sad peculiarity of our day that, in churches professing to take high ground in Christian doctrine, men who claim to be subjects of renewing grace, who call themselves children of God and speak of their Christian experience, have attempted practically to obliterate the distinction between the Church and the world. Shunning, it may be, the practices which would be disreputable among virtuous men of the world, they vie with these men in the pursuit of wealth, honors, fashions, and pleasures of the world. Thus a question sometimes arises among young disciples as to how far they may legitimately go with the world. On the lips of old or young it is an ill-boding question, for it intimates that their heart is with the world, and that they desire to go just as far as they can without forfeiting the Christian name. The short answer to it may be found in the Lord's description of His disciples, or rather the description should have hindered the question from arising, "They are not of the world, even as I am not of the world."

Young disciples sometimes complain of the difficulty with which they can throw off the worldly associates and escape from their importunities. The complaint generally indicates a lack of Christian decision in those who make it; otherwise they would never be sought after as companions in folly. If they were faithful witnesses for Christ, walking worthy of their high calling, maintaining the sobriety and dignity which become the children of God, and if their conversation and demeanor were pervaded by the spirit of Christ, instead of being courted they would be shunned by the world; according to the warning of the Lord, "If ye were of the world, the world would love his own, but because ye are not of the world, but I have chosen you out of the world, therefore the world hateth you."

The Lord has not left His people in the world for worldly ends, but for His own service and to glorify His name in a world that hates Him. The young disciple is not indeed called to lay aside the modesty which becomes his years, nor to assume a self-sufficient air in his Christian activities. But, on the other hand, the thought of youth and inexperience should not silence his testimony or discourage his activity. The blessing of God alone can crown the testimony of any Christian with success, and it is according to God's method of glorifying His name to show that the triumph of His truth is independent of the power, wisdom, and influence of those who are employed to bear the message. In one of the many seasons in which the name of Jehovah was blasphemed among the heathen through the unfaithfulness of His ancient people, a little Jewish maid was taken captive by the Assyrians. In the division of spoils she fell into the hands of Naaman, the commander of the Assyrian forces. No position could seem more desolate than that of this defenceless maiden in the house of her proud captors, and no situation could promise fewer opportunities of usefulness. But she had been brought up in the nurture and admonition of the Lord, and she remembered Him in the house of her bondage. Her testimony was the means of leading Naaman, who was a leper, to seek the aid of Jehovah in an affliction which the gods of Assyria and all the skill of physicians could not relieve him; and, in the issue, the haughty heathen was not only healed but converted, and was constrained to acknowledge that there was no God in all the earth but Jehovah—a confession such as never extorted from the lips of a heathen by all the might of Israel's arms.

In the presence of this example, what can any young Christian urge as an excuse for withholding himself from the testimony of Christ, or from labors of love in a sinful and suffering world? If he were called to make men Christians by his own power, or skill, or eloquence, he might well shrink desponding from the call; but he is no more called to do this than she was called to cure the leper by her power or skill. The youngest and feeblest believer in the midst of men perishing by the spiritual leprosy, may imitate her prayerfulness, and, like her, may tell them that there is balm in Gilead, and that there is a Physician there. Nor would it be at all a singular thing in the history of Christianity if the simple and affectionate earnestness of such testimony should be blessed when the most gifted advocacy had failed.

At the same time it must not be overlooked that the tendency of the times draws young disciples into a course of religious dissipation, and inspires them with a self-importance which is fatal to their growth in grace and in knowledge. There are many youthful professors who will boast of the number of Sunday-schools in which they teach, whose ignorance ought to be thought discreditable to the youngest scholars, and whose flippancy attracts the censure of children. There are many professing Christians, both old and young, who, in the conceit of their own activities, neglect the ordinances of the Lord, and who would rather display themselves in some public service than meet with the Lord's people to show His death till He come. The Lord can never be served by disobedience, nor honored by slighting His appointments. He who teaches must be taught; and, in view of these activities, as well as for other important reasons, the young disciple needs to remember the charge, "Let the word of Christ dwell in you richly," to seek a deeper work of grace in his own heart, and to desire the sincere milk of the Word, that he may grow thereby.

It is necessary to warn young disciples against waiting for great and imposing opportunities of usefulness, and separating their religion from the ordinary scenes and relations of life. In every-day associations, and not on rare or public occasions, they will find their best opportunities of testifying and exemplifying the truth. As followers of Him who washed His disciples' feet, they will find abundant opportunities of lowly service, which, in early life, they can occupy with peculiar grace; and they will not, if they are led by the Spirit, embrace them with less alacrity because no human eye can witness the service and no human tongue say, "Well done." Meekness, gentleness, and humility sit with peculiar grace upon the young, and as these graces find their greatest trial, so also they find their most important sphere in the relations of home. If the young disciple is not a model of filial love and obedience and of fraternal kindness at home, his profession away from home is as sounding brass and tinkling cymbal. So far as influence over a family of children is concerned, there are probably no more dangerous inmates of a house than sons and daughters who in words profess Christ, but in works deny Him.

There are peculiar reasons for addressing to young Christians in our day the charge which John addressed also to young men: "Love not the world, neither the things that are in the world. If any man love the world, The love of the Father is not in him. For all that is in the world, the lust of the flesh, and the lust of the eyes, and the pride of life, is not of the Father, but is of the world." This comprehensive and unqualified charge, if honestly applied, will be in direct opposition to the counsels of many who profess to be their friends, who, even in counselling them against the follies of youth, find their strongest argument in a regard to what they call success in life, and who commend religion because it will contribute to that success. Ah! followers of the Son of the carpenter, and what is success in life? Followers of the poor and persecuted Nazarene, do you think that His footsteps will guide to worldly honor, wealth, or fame? Is this then the preparation for success in life, "Let a man deny himself, take up his cross and follow Me?" Far different is the prospect that He holds out to you, but, following Him, you will reach an elevation where the possessions, rank, pomp, and pleasures of life, dwarfed by distance, will appear baubles almost beneath your contempt.

Waymarks in the Wilderness.

FAITH AND UNBELIEF

Let me here give the Christian reader a more particular discription of the qualities of unbelief, by opposing faith unto it, in these twenty-five particulars:

1. Faith believeth the Word of God, but unbelief questioneth the certainty of the soul.

2. Faith believeth the Word, because it is true, but unbelief doubteth thereof, because it is true.

3. Faith sees more in a promise of God to help than in all other things to hinder, but unbelief, notwithstanding God's promise saith How can these things be?

4. Faith will make thee see love in the heart of Christ when His mouth giveth reproofs, but unbelief will imagine wrath in His heart when His mouth and Word saith He loves thee.

5. Faith will help the soul to wait, though God defers to give, but unbelief will take snuff and throw up all if God makes any tarrying.

6. Faith will give comfort in the midst of fears, but unbelief causeth fears in the midst of comforts.

7. Faith will suck sweetness out of God's rod, but unbelief can find no comfort in its greatest mercies.

8. Faith maketh great burdens light, but unbelief maketh light ones intolerably heavy.

9. Faith helpeth us when we are down, but unbelief throws us down when we are up.

10. Faith bringeth us near to God when we are far from Him, but unbelief puts us far from God when we are near to Him.

11. Where faith reigns, it declareth them to be the friends of God, but where unbelief reigns, it declareth them to be His enemies.

12. Faith putteth a man under grace, but unbelief holdeth him under wrath.

13. Faith purifieth the heart, but unbelief keepeth it polluted and impure.

14. By faith the righteousness of Christ is imputed, but by unbelief we are shut up under the law to perish.

15. Faith maketh our work acceptable to God through Christ, but whatsoever is of unbelief is sin, for without faith it is impossible to please Him.

16. Faith giveth us peace, and comfort in our souls, but unbelief worketh trouble and tossings like the restless waves of the sea.

17. Faith maketh us see preciousness in Christ, but unbelief sees no form, beauty, or comeliness in Him.

18. By faith we have our life in Christ's fullness, but by unbelief we starve and pine away.

19. Faith gives us the victory over the law, sin, death, devil, and all evils, but unbelief layeth us obnoxious to them all.

20. Faith will show us more excellency in things not seen than in them that are, but unbelief sees more of things that are than in things that will be hereafter.

21. Faith makes the ways of God pleasant and admirable, but unbelief maketh them heavy and hard.

22. By faith Abraham, Isaac, and Jacob possessed the land of promise, but because of unbelief neither Aaron, nor Moses, nor Miriam could get thither.

23. By faith the Children of Israel passed through the Red Sea, but by unbelief the generality of them perished in the wilderness.

24. By faith Gideon did more with three hundred men and a few empty pitchers than all the twelve tribes could do because they believed not God.

25. By faith Peter walked on the water, but by unbelief he began to sink.

Thus might many more be added, which, for brevity's sake, I omit, beseeching every one that thinketh he hath a soul to save or be damned to take heed of unbelief, lest, seeing there is a promise left us of entering into His rest, any of us by unbelief should indeed come short of it.

John Bunyan (1666)

By the disobedience of Adam, sin entered into the world, and we were made sinners in Adam, and by Adam . . . . Christ was promised to our forefathers; who received the law, to the end that, knowing their sin by the law, and their unrighteousness and insufficiency, they might desire the coming of Christ, to satisfy for their sins, and, by Himself, to accomplish the law . . . . Christ is our life and truth, and peace and righteousness, and advocate, and master, and priest: who died for the salvation of all those who believe, and is raised again for our justification.

—Extract from the Waldensian Confession, 1120 A.D.

SINNING UNTO DEATH.

"IF ANY MAN SEE HIS BROTHER SIN A SIN WHICH IS NOT UNTO DEATH, HE SHALL ASK and he shall give him life for them that sin not unto death. There is a sin unto death: I do not say that he shall pray for it. All unrighteousness is sin: and there is a sin not unto death" 1 John 5:16, 17.

We believe the reference is, first, to sin which has brought chastening, as weakness or sickness, but which is not of such a nature as that the Lord sees fit to remove the "brother" out of the world. But "Sin unto death" is, we believe, sin which has brought sickness as a chastening from the Lord, but which must take its course even unto death —that is, of the body. This will be seen at once when we compare the passage with 1 Cor. 11:30: we may also compare it with James 5:14-18.

It may be asked, How shall we know that the case which comes before us is one "not unto death"?. We suppose this can only be known to interceding saints by "waiting on the Lord" in full confidence that since "we know not what to pray for as we ought", the Spirit "who helpeth our infirmities," will "make intercession for us according to the will of God" (Rom. 8:26-27). Many saints have had occasion to testify that they have been surprised when thus *waiting* to find their own will subdued, and that the petitions coming from their lips were just the opposite of all that they had purposed and planned to pray.

We are scarcely prepared to explain the last clause of verse 16—"there is a sin unto death. I do not say that he shall pray for it". The apostle may either mean, "I do not say this to induce him to *pray* concerning the sin unto death", or "I do not say this that he may *inquire* concerning the sin unto death". We prefer the latter view, because the word rendered "pray" is never elsewhere used by the Holy Spirit to designate any supplicatory address from a mere man to God; it is too bold from the creature to the Creator: the Lord Jesus only might use the word to designate *His* "asking". The word *"ask"* in the first part of the passage is the more suppliant word and is very often used of the prayer of saints.

C. Campbell—1873

Though neither heighth of magnificence, nor depth of abasement, can separate a saint from the love of God which is in Christ Jesus; yet, even after a work of grace has passed upon the heart in regeneration, such is the power of surviving depravity that not one perhaps in twenty of God's people can, humanly speaking, be trusted with prosperity. Let every afflicted believer therefore rejoice in that he is made low. God deals out our comforts and our sorrows with exact, unerring hand, in number, weight and measure. Hence we have not either of joy or adversity, a grain too little or too much. If less tribulation would suffice, less would be given. We are bad enough with all our troubles: what then should we be if we were exercised with none?

—Augustus Toplady, 1768. Author of "Rock of Ages".

Grace is properly God's favor, benevolence, or kind mind; which, of His own self, without our deserving, He reached to us: whereby He was moved and inclined to give Christ unto us, with all other gifts of grace. Which having told us, in his preface to the Epistle to the Romans, Paul telleth us, not long after, in the 9th, 10th, and 11th chapters of the Epistle, of God's predestination: from whence it springeth altogether; whether we shall believe, or not believe; be loosed from sin, or not be loosed. By which predestination, our justifying and salvation are clear taken out of our hands, and put into the hands of God only: which thing is most necessary of all. For we are so weak, and so uncertain, that, if it stood in us, there would of truth no man be saved. But now God is sure of His predestination; neither can any man withstand or hinder Him.

—William Tyndal, 1535 A.D.

All is of God's sovereign grace. Grace was given the Christian "in Christ Jesus before the world began" (2 Tim. 1:9). We are saved by grace (Eph. 2:8). We "believed through grace" (Acts 18:27). Our standing is in grace (Rom. 5:2). We grow in grace (2 Pet. 3:18). And in the "ages to come" God will show "the exceeding riches of His grace in His kindness toward us through Christ Jesus" (Eph. 2:7).

A. W. P.

(Continued from page 145.)

been so helpful to him on other subjects, that the conclusion is drawn that he *must* be right on this too! It would seem disrespectful and presumptuous to call in question the teaching of such a man! Ergo: the uneasy feeling is quietened, the fears are dismissed, and the strange teaching (given with much plausibility and dogmatism) is accepted.

On the other hand, there are those who refuse to receive anything except from the mouths of a certain teacher or teachers who belong to *their own* denominations or company. Such people would resent being told that this is the spirit of sectarianism. Yet in reality that is what it is. They confine themselves to their own circle, be it a wide or a narrow one. They arrogantly assume that *they* have all the Truth, and all others, if not actually in error, have far less light than they. Such an attitude meets with its own reward. Light vouchsafed *others,* is denied *them.* Such people, while having much to say about the various "gifts" of the Body, overlook the fact that not *all* of the gifts are to be found in *their own* immediate circle. God is sovereign in the instruments He uses, and the fact that He used a Balaam to give one of the most remarkable prophecies to be found in all the O. T. should correct the idea that He only uses those whom *we* think are His appointed mouthpieces. Paul had to withstand Peter (Gal. 2:11) because he was in error on a certain subject. How foolish would it have been for the admirers (should we say "followers"?) of Peter to have closed their ears against what Paul had to say, simply because it did not come through their particular favorite! The Lord deliver His people from such partizanship.

Here, then, are two evils to be guarded against: the tendency to receive *everything* which is given out by the accredited servants of God, and the spirit which *refuses* anything which does not emanate from those within our immediate circle of Christian fellowship. What, then, is the remedy?. The sentence first quoted in our opening paragraph points in the right direction: "Never refuse any teaching because it is *new to you;* but never accept anything till you see it *for yourself in the Word of God*". If you are a Baptist, do not refuse anything taught by a Presbyterian, simply because he *is* a Presbyterian. If you belong to those known as "Plymouth Brethren" do not spurn anything given out by a teacher from the Denominations, simply because he belongs to "the systems". What, then, is the wise course? This; *test* all you hear and all you read by the Holy Scriptures. *Weigh* it all in "the balances of the Sanctuary". *Try* the spirits "whether they are of God" (1 John 4:1). It was because the Bereans did this they were so highly commended: "These were *more noble* than those in Thessalonica, in that they received the Word with all readiness of mind, and searched the Scriptures daily *whether those things were so*" (Acts 17:11). Even when the Apostle Paul preached to them, they did not accept *un*-tested what he taught! Instead, they carefully compared his teaching with the written Word. And for this the Holy Spirit commended them. Here is the only safeguard. Here is the only preservative against error: "To the Law and to the Testimony" (Isa. 8:20). Bring everything to the test of Scripture—not hastily and carelessly, not with the determination to *prove* it, nor with the determination to *disprove* it; but with the earnest and prayerful desire to *examine* it, and see whether or not it is *scriptural.* If you find that what you have heard or read is *not* clearly and expressly taught in the Word of God, reject it—no matter *who* teaches it or *how many* believe it. If you discover *it is* plainly and explicitly taught in the Word of God, receive it, meekly and gladly, no matter from whom you first hear it (it may be a Balaam), and no matter if you do not know of another who believes it. Remember that truth is never found with the majority, because the *Truth of God* is not popular or even acceptable to the natural man (1 Cor. 2:14).

"Be *sure* though *slow* in acquiring truth" is also good advice. Beware of jumping to conclusions, be not hasty in forming your judgments. The Bereans not only tested the teaching of the Apostle Paul by "searching the Scriptures", but they searched these *"daily"*, that is, they *continued* to search. Remember that it is written, "He that believeth shall not make haste" (Isa. 28:16). Some things lie on the very surface of the Bible; others lie buried far below, and can only be obtained by much digging (Prov. 2:1-5). Some truths of Scripture may be discovered from a single text, others can only be discovered by diligently comparing one passage with another. Remember the words of the Lord Jesus to His apostles, "I have yet many things to say unto you, but ye cannot bear them *now*" (John 16:12). The *principle* of this Divine utterance applies to each of us. God does not reveal everything to us at once. As in nature so in grace, there is "first the blade, then the ear, then the full corn in the ear." Pray daily and earnestly for a mind and heart *open* to *all* the Truth. Ask God for grace to follow the light which you *do* have, that more may be given.

Finally, heed the counsel, "Though you may get truth through a human channel get it *from God.*" The only way to do this is to *"prove* all things" from the Word itself. What you really get from God, will stay with you. The chief reason why we retain so little of what we hear and read is because we fail to *confirm* it by the light of Scripture itself. Beware of allowing human writings, no matter how helpful, to become a substitute for *your own* daily study of the Word. May God give us senses *"exercised* to discern both good and evil" (Heb. 5:14), "senses" *developed* through regular searching of the Scriptures. Then, and only then, shall we be safeguarded against plausible error, and then shall we be open to receive Truth even though it be given out by a man who is in error on other things. May the Spirit of God guide both writer and reader into *"All* the Truth".

Yours by Sovereign grace,
Arthur W. Pink.

VOL. III AUGUST, 1924 NO. 8

STUDIES in the SCRIPTURES

Search the Scriptures" John 5:39.

Arthur W. Pink, Publisher & Editor,
227 N. Creighton St., Philadelphia, Pa.

Price: 10 cents per copy; $1.00 per year. Foreign $1.00 per year.

MEDITATION

"O how love I Thy law! it is my meditation all the day". (Psalm 119:97).

The more we love the Word of God the more shall we delight to *meditate* thereon. Not the more shall we *want to*, or purpose to meditate thereon, but the more *shall* we do so. And the more we *do* meditate upon the Scriptures the deeper will be our love for them. Said the prophet Jeremiah, "Thy words were found, and I did eat them; and Thy Word was unto me the joy and rejoicing of mine heart: for I am called by Thy name, O Lord God of hosts." (Jer. 15:16). The figure of *eating* is very suggestive. Jeremiah *masticated* the food which God has provided for the souls of His people. It was not the Word as a whole, but God's word*s*. He *found* (which implies a careful *search)* a certain rich morsel in the Divine storehouse and *chewed* it over, thereby extracting its "sweetness".

The word *"meditate"* comes from the same root as "ruminate", which signifies to chew the cud. It is here, perhaps, that all of us fail the worst. Meditation is the mental equivalent of mastication or rumination—the chewing over of what we have taken into our spiritual mouths. But most of us are in such a hurry, we pass so swiftly and carelessly over what we read, that we derive little more nourishment from our spiritual food than we receive from our material food when it is swallowed almost whole. How few today can say with the Psalmist, "I have more understanding than all my teachers: for Thy testimonies are my *meditation.*" (Psa. 119:99). And again, "When I remember upon my bed, and *meditate* on Thee in the night watches." (Psa. 63:6). Little wonder that we are so weak and sickly! Little wonder that we are so lacking in spiritual vigor!

But as soon as we press the *duty* of meditation—and surely we *owe* that to *God's* Word!—as soon as we make mention of the *value* of meditation, the cry of 'No time' is at once raised. So many Christians today are like Martha—"cumbered with *much* serving" and "careful about *many* things". So very few resemble Mary who chose "that good part" of "sitting at the feet of Jesus and hearing His Word". (Luke 10: 39-41). Yes, says the reader, but I have *duties* to perform, *responsibilities* to be discharged, *obligations* to be fulfilled, and *these* must not be neglected. Ah! fellow-believer, *God* has given you no "duties," or "responsibilities" which make it right or necessary to *crowd out* meditation upon His blessed Word. The truth is, that if you give more time to feeding on the Word of life, more attention to *meditation* upon His precepts and promises, it would be far easier for you *to* carry out your duties and fulfill your obligations! !

(Continued on page 192.)

IMPORTANT NOTICES

All new subscriptions will be dated back to January, 1924.

Set of twelve issues for **1922**, unbound, **$1.00**. Bound, **$1.50.**

Set of twelve issues for **1923**, unbound, **$1.00** Bound **$1.50.**

Note: We cannot break a set or now supply any **single 1923 issues.**

Subscription-price: **$1.00** per year to any address in the world. Single copies **10 cents.**

Change of Address: Please notify me promptly of any change of address, and be certain to give both old and new addresses.

Non-subscribers receiving this Magazine regularly will understand their subscription has been entered by a friend.

Copies lost in the mail duplicated only if we are notified promptly.

Entered as second-class matter December 15th, 1923, at the post office at Philadelphia, Pa., under Act of March 3rd, 1879.

CONTENTS

JOHN'S GOSPEL.

32. Christ and the Blind Beggar, continued: John 9:8-23.

We begin with our usual Analysis of the passage which is to be before us:—

1. The uncertainty of the neighbors: vv. 8, 9.
2. Their questioning of the beggar: v. 10.
3. The beggar's answers: vv. 11, 12.
4. The Pharisees and the Sabbath: vv. 13, 14.
5. The beggar before the Pharisees: vv. 15-17.
6. The skepticism of the Jews: v. 18.
7. The beggar's parents interrogated: vv. 19-23.

In our last article we pointed out how that the opening verses of John 9 supply us with a blessed illustration of the outflow of sovereign grace toward an elect sinner. Every detail in the picture contributes to its beauty and accuracy. Upon the dark background of the Jews' hatred of Christ (chapter 8) we are now shown the Saviour ministering to one who accurately portrays the spiritual condition of each of God's elect when the Lord begins His distinguishing work of mercy upon them. Seven things are told us about the object of the Redeemer's compassion:

First, he was found *outside* the Temple, portraying the fact that, in his natural condition, the elect sinner is alienated from God. Second, he was blind, and therefore unable to see the Saviour when He approached him. Third, he had been blind from birth: so, too, is the sinner—"estranged from the womb" (Psa. 58:3). Fourth, he was therefore quite beyond the aid of man: helpless and hopeless unless *God* intervened. Fifth, he was a beggar (v. 8), unable to purchase any remedy if remedy there was; completely dependent upon charity. Sixth, he made no appeal to the Saviour and uttered no cry for mercy: such is our condition before Divine grace begins to work within us. Seventh, the reasoning of the disciples (v. 2) illustrates the sad fact that no human eye pities the sinner in his spiritual wretchedness.

Our Lord's dealings with this poor fellow shadow forth His gracious work in us today. Note, again, seven things, in connection with Christ and the blind beggar. First, He *looked* in tender pity upon the one who so sorely needed His healing touch. Second, He declared that this man had been *created* to the end that the power and grace of God might be manifested in him (v. 3). Third, He intimated that *necessity* was laid upon Him (v. 4): the eternal counsels of grace "must" be accomplished in the one singled out by Divine favor. Fourth, He announced Himself as the One who had power to *communicate light* to those in darkness (v. 5). Fifth, He *pressed upon* the blind beggar his desperate need by emphasizing his sad condition (v. 6). Sixth, He pointed him to the *means of blessing* and put his faith to the test (v. 7). Seventh, the beggar obeyed, and in his obedience obtained evidence that *a miracle of mercy* had been wrought upon him. Each of these seven things has its counterpart in the realm of grace today.

As we follow the Divine narrative and note the experiences of the blind beggar *after* he had received his sight, we shall find that it continues to mirror forth that which has its analogy in the spiritual history of those who have been apprehended by Christ. What is before us here in John 9 is something more than an incident that happened in the long ago—it accurately depicts what is transpiring in our own day. The more the believer studies this passage in the light of his own spiritual history, the more will he see how perfectly this narrative describes *his own* experiences.

"The neighbours therefore, and they which before had seen him that he was blind, said, Is not this he that sat and begged?" (v. 8). When a genuine work of grace has been wrought in a soul it is impossible to conceal it from our neighbors and acquaintances. At first they will talk among themselves and discuss with a good deal of curiosity and speculation what has happened. The unsaved are always skeptical of God's miracles. When one of their fellows is saved, they cannot deny that a radical change has taken place, though the nature of it they are completely at a loss to explain. They know not that the manifestation of Christ in the outward life of a quickened soul is due to Christ now dwelling within. Yet, even the unbelieving world is compelled to take note and indirectly acknowledge that regeneration is a real thing. Ah, dear reader, if the Lord Jesus has lain His wondrous hand on you, then those with whom you come into daily contact will recognize the fact. "They will see that it is not with thee as it used to be—that a real change has passed upon thee—that the tempers and lusts, habits and influences which once ruled thee with despotic power, now rule thee no longer—that though evil may occasionally break out, it does not habitually bear sway—that though it dwells within it does not reign—though it plagues it does not govern".

"Some said, This is he: others said, He is like him: but he said, I am he" (v. 9). How marvellously accurate is this line in the picture! When one who is dead in trespasses and sins has been quickened into newness of life he becomes a new creature in Christ, but the old man still remains. Not yet has he been delivered from this body of death; for that he must await the return of our Lord. In the one who has been born again there are, then, *two* natures: the old is not destroyed, but a new has been imparted. This is plainly foreshadowed in the verse before us: some recognized the one they had known before his eyes were opened; others saw a different personality. It is this which is so puzzling in connection with regeneration. The individual is still the same, but a new principle and element have come into his life.

"Therefore said they unto him, How were thine eyes opened?" (v. 10). How true to life again! The one who has found mercy with the Lord is now put to the proof: his faith, his loyalty, his courage must be tested. It is not long before the quickened soul discovers that he is living in a world that is unfriendly toward him. At first God may not permit that unfriendliness to take on a very aggressive form, for He deals very tenderly with the babes in His family. But as they grow in grace and become strong in the Lord and in the power of His might, He suffers them to be tested more severely and no longer shields them from the fiercer assaults of their great enemy. Nevertheless, testing they must have from the beginning, for it is thus that faith is developed by casting us upon the Lord and perfecting our weakness in His strength.

"Therefore said they unto Him, How were thine eyes opened?" (v. 10). Here was an opportunity afforded this one who had so wondrously received his sight to bear witness to His gracious Benefactor. To *confess* Christ, to tell of what great things the Lord hath done for him, is the first duty of the newly-saved soul, and the promise is, "Whosoever shall confess Me before men, him shall the Son of man also confess before the angels of God" (Luke 12:8). But this is the last thing which the world appreciates or desires: that blessed Name which is above every name is an offence to them. It is striking to observe how the neighbors of the beggar framed their question: "How were thine eyes opened?", not *"Who* opened thine eyes?". They wished to satisfy their curiosity, but they had no desire to hear about Christ!

"He answered and said, A man that is called Jesus made clay, and anointed mine eyes, and said unto me, Go to the pool of Siloam, and wash: and I went and washed, and I received sight" (v. 11). The witness borne by this man was simple and honest. As yet he did not have much light, but he was faithful to the light which he did have; and that is the way to obtain more. He did not speculate nor philosophize, but gave a straightforward account of what the Lord had done to him. Two things in this man's confession should be noted as accurately illustrating the witness of a newly-saved soul today. First, it was the *work* of Christ rather than His *person* which had most impressed him; it was what Christ had *done,* rather than *who* He was that was emphasized in his testimony. It is so with us. The first thing we grasp is that it is the Cross-work of the Lord Jesus, His sacrificial death which put away our sins; the infinite value of His person we learn later, as the Spirit unfolds it to us through the Word. Second, in connection with the person of Christ it was His *humanity,* not His Deity that this man spoke of. And was it not so with us? "A man that is called Jesus"—was it not *that* aspect of His blessed person which first filled our vision! "A man that is called Jesus" speaks of His lowliness and humiliation. Later, as we study the Scriptures and grow in the knowledge of the Lord, we discover that the man Christ Jesus is none other than the Son of God.

"He answered and said, A man that is called Jesus made clay, and anointed mine eyes, and said unto me, Go to the pool of Siloam, and wash: and I went and washed, and I received sight" (v. 11). That precious name of "Jesus" was the most hated of all to those Jews; yet did the beggar boldly confess it. "It would manifestly have served the poor man's worldly interest to cushion the truth as to what had been done for him. He might have enjoyed the benefit of the work of Christ, and yet avoided the rough path of testimony for His name in the face of the world's hostility. He might have enjoyed his eyesight, and, at the same time, retained his place within the pale of respectable religious profession. He might have reaped the fruit of Christ's *work* and yet escaped the reproach of confessing His *name.*

"How often is this the case! Alas, how often! Thousands are very well pleased to hear of what Jesus has done; but they do not want to be identified with His outcast and rejected Name. In other words, to use a modern and very popular phrase, 'They want to make the best of both worlds'—a sentiment from which every true-hearted lover of Christ must shrink with abhorrence—an idea of which genuine faith is wholly ignorant. It is obvious that the subject of our narrative knew nothing of any such maxim. He had had his eyes opened, and he could not but speak of it, and tell who did it, and how it was done. He was an honest man. He had no mixed motives. No sinister object, no undercurrent. Happy for him!" (C.H.M.).

"He answered and said, A man that is called Jesus made clay, and anointed mine eyes, and said unto me, Go to the pool of Siloam, and wash" (v. 11). There is one detail here which strikingly evidences the truthfulness of this narrative, and that is one little *omission* in this man's description of what the Saviour had done to him. It is to be noted that the beggar made no reference to Christ spitting on the ground and making clay of the spittle. Being blind he could not *see* what the Lord *did,* though he could *feel* what He *applied!* It is in just such little undesigned coincidences, such artless touches, as this, that makes the more apparent the genuineness of these Divine narratives.

"Then said they unto him, Where is He? He said, I know not" (v. 12). Equally commendable was the modesty of this man here. He acted up to the light that he had, but he did not go beyond it. He pretended not to possess a knowledge not yet his. O that we were all as simple and honest. When the neighbors enquired, "Is not this he that sat and begged?", he answered, "I am he"—though it is most unseemly for a Christian to advertise the sins of his unregenerate days, yet it is equally wrong for him to deny what he then was when plainly asked. Next, they had asked, "How were thine eyes opened?", and he unhesitatingly told them, not forgetting to boldly confess the name of his Benefactor. Now they said, "Where is He?", and he frankly replied, "I know not". The babe in Christ is *guileless* and hesitates not to acknowledge that he is ignorant of much. But it is sad to observe how pride so often comes in and destroys this simplicity and honesty. Christian reader, and especially the babe in Christ, hesitate not to avow your ignorance; when asked a question that you cannot answer, honestly reply, "I know not".

Feign not a knowledge you do not possess, and have not recourse to speculation.

"They brought to the Pharisees him that aforetime was blind" (v. 13). "Now the former blind beggar was to become an object of special notice by the Pharisees. Very likely many of them had passed him unheeded. A blind beggar! Which of them would bestow a thought on him whose condition they regarded as an evidence that he was born in sin? But the beggar, no longer blind, was quite a different matter. Were they anxious to learn of the favor he had received in order to honor his Benefactor, or to solicit in their turn favors from Him? Quite the contrary. Their efforts were directed to discredit the miracle as being wrought by One sent from God. He who had shortly before affirmed of Himself in the Temple court, that He was God, had now opened that man's eyes. The insult to the Divine Majesty, as the Jews regarded it, in asserting His Deity, was followed by this miracle, of which the beggar in the Temple precincts was the subject. To discredit the Lord was their purpose. He was a Sabbath-breaker they declared; and therefore that miracle must be disowned as being any display of almighty power and benevolence" (C. E. Stuart).

"They brought to the Pharisees him that aforetime was blind" (v. 13). This was a much more severe trial for him than what he had just passed through at the hands of his neighbors. It was a real test of his faith. The opposition of the Pharisees against the Lord, and their desire to get rid of Him were well known; and their determination to excommunicate any one who confessed Him as the Christ was no secret (see v. 22). To face them, then, was indeed an ordeal. Alas that this part of the history is being repeated today. Repeated it certainly is, for the ones who will treat worst the young believer are not open infidels and atheists, but those who are loudest in their religious professions. These Pharisees have many successors: their tribe is far from being extinct, and their descendants will be found occupying the same position of religious leadership as did their fathers of old.

"And it was the Sabbath day when Jesus made the clay, and opened his eyes" (v. 14). There are two observations which we would make on this verse. First, our Lord here teaches us that the words of the fourth commandment "In it (the Sabbath) thou shalt not do *any* work", are not to be taken absolutely, that is, without any modification. By His own example He has shown us that works of necessity and also works of mercy are permissible. This 14th verse therefore reflects the glory of Christ. It was the Sabbath day: how was He occupied? First, (and note the order) He had gone to the Temple, there to minister God's Word; second, now He is seen ministering in mercy to one in need. Perfect example has He left us.

In the next place, we would call attention to the fact that our Lord knew full well that His performing of this miracle on the Sabbath would give offence to His enemies. He proceeded to its execution, nevertheless. We have another illustration of the same principle in Mark 7:2: "When they saw some of His disciples eat bread with defiled, that is to say, with unwashen hands, they found fault". Though rendering perfect obedience to all the laws of God, Christ paid no regard to the commandments of men. Here too He has left us a perfect example. Let not the believer be brought into bondage by heeding the mandates of religious legislators, when their rules and regulations have no support from the Holy Scriptures.

"Then again the Pharisees also asked him how he had received his sight. He said unto them, He put clay upon mine eyes, and I washed, and do see" (v. 15). This was no honest effort on the part of these Pharisees to investigate the teaching of that blessed One whose voice they had recently heard and whose power had now seen so signally displayed. They—or the influential among them at least, for in this Gospel "the Jews" ever refer to the religious leaders—had already agreed that if any did confess that Jesus was the Christ, he should be put out of the synagogue (see v. 22). Thus had they deliberately closed their eyes against the truth, and therefore it was impossible that they should now discern it, blinded by prejudice as they were. Their object here was twofold: to discredit the miracle, and to intimidate the one who had been the subject of it. Note the form of their question. They, too, asked the beggar *how* he had received his sight, not *who* was the one who had so graciously blest him.

"He said unto them, He put clay upon mine eyes, and I washed, and do see". The enlightened beggar was not to be cowed. He had returned a straightforward answer to the inquiries of his neighbors, he is equally honest and bold now before the open enemies of Christ. His faithful testimony here teaches us an important lesson. Behind his human interrogators it is not difficult to discern the great Enemy of souls. Satan it is who hurls the fiery darts, even though he employs religious professors as his instruments. But they fall powerless upon the shield of faith, and it is this which is illustrated here. One may be the veriest babe in Christ, but so long as he walks according to the measure of light which God has granted, the Devil is powerless to harm him. It is when we quench that light, or when we are unfaithful to Christ, that we become powerless, and fall an easy prey to the Enemy. But the one before us was acting up to the light that he had, therefore the lion roared in vain against him.

"Therefore said some of the Pharisees, This man is not of God, because He keepeth not the Sabbath day" (v. 16). A striking contrast is this from what has just been before us. These Pharisees had turned their backs upon the Light, and therefore was their darkness now even more profound. Devoid of spiritual discernment they were altogether incapable of determining what was a right use and lawful employment of the Sabbath and what was not. They understood not that "The Sabbath was made for man" (Mark 2:27), that is, for the benefit of his soul and the good of his body. True, the day which God blest at the beginning was to be kept holy, but it was never intended to bar out works of necessity and works of mercy, as they should have known from the Old Testament scriptures. In thus finding fault with Christ because He had opened the eyes of this blind beggar on the Sabbath day, they did but expose their ignorance and exhibit their spiritual blindness.

"Others said, How can a man that is a sinner do such miracles? And there was a division among them" (v. 16). We wonder if one of those who spoke up thus was Nicodemus! The argument used here is strictly parallel with the words of that "Master in Israel" which we find in John 3:1, 2. That we are next told, "And there was a division among them" shows that the second speakers held their ground and refused to side-in with the open enemies of our Lord. On this verse the Puritan Bullinger remarked, "All *divisions* are not necessarily evil, nor all concord and unity necessarily good"!

"They say unto the blind man again, What sayest thou of Him, that He hath opened thine eyes?" (v. 17). The Devil is powerless in his efforts to gain an advantage over the sheep of Christ. Repulsed for the moment by the unexpected friendliness toward Christ on the part of some of the Pharisees, the Enemy turned his attention once more to the beggar: "They say unto the blind man *again*": note the frequency with which this word is used in this passage—vv. 15, 17, 24, 26. The Devil's perseverance frequently puts our instability to shame.

"What sayest thou of Him, that He hath opened thine eyes?" (v. 17). A searching question was this. The faith of the beggar was openly challenged: he must now either confess or deny his Benefactor. But he did not flinch or dissemble. Boldly he answered, "He is a prophet." Divine grace did not fail him in the hour of need, but enabled him to stand firm and witness a good confession. Blessed be His name, the grace of God is as *sufficient* for the youngest and feeblest as for the most mature and established.

"He said, He is a prophet" (v. 17). There is a decided advance here. When answering his neighbors, the beggar simply referred to Christ as, "A man that is called Jesus" (v. 11); but now he owns Him as One whose word is *Divine*, for a "prophet" was a mouthpiece of God. This was most blessed. At first he had been occupied solely with the *work* of Christ, now he is beginning to discern the glory of His *person;* increased intelligence was his. Nor is God arbitrary in the bestowment of this. When the believer walks faithfully according to the light which he has, more is given to him. It was so here; it is so now. This is the meaning of that verse which has perplexed so many: "Take heed therefore how ye hear: for whosoever hath, to him shall be given; and whosoever hath not, from him shall be taken even that which he seemeth to have" (Luke 8:18): the reference here being to *light* used and unused—note the "therefore" which looks back to v. 16. In Matthew's account it reads, "For whosoever hath, to him shall be given, and he shall have more abundance". A striking illustration of this is furnished in John 9. Light the beggar now had; and that light he let shine forth, consequently *more* was given to him; later, we shall see how a "more abundance" was vouchsafed to him.

"He said, He is a *prophet*". This is not the first time we have had Christ owned as "Prophet" in this Gospel. In 4:19 we read that the woman of Samaria said to the Saviour at the well, "I perceive that Thou art a *Prophet*". In 6:14 we are told, "Then those men, when they had seen the miracle that Jesus did, said, This is of a truth that *Prophet* that should come into the world". Once more, in 7:40 we read, "Many of the people therefore, when they heard this saying, said, Of a truth this is *the Prophet*". These references are in striking accord with the character and theme of this fourth Gospel. A prophet was *the mouthpiece* of God, and the great purpose of John's Gospel, as intimated in its opening verse, is to portray the Lord Jesus as "the Word"!

"But the Jews did not believe concerning him, that he had been blind, and received his sight, until they called the parents of him that had received his sight" (v. 18). How skeptical are the unregenerate! "Children in whom is *no faith*" (Deut. 32:20) is what the Scriptures term them. A wonderful miracle had been performed, but these Jews were determined not to believe it. The simple but emphatic testimony of the one on whom it had been wrought went for nothing. What a lesson is this for the young convert. Marvelling at what the Saviour has so graciously done for and in him, anxious that others should know Him for themselves, he goes forth testifying of His grace and power. Full of zeal and hope, he expects that it will be a simple matter to convince others of the reality of what the Lord has done for him. Ah, it will not be long before his bright expectations meet with disappointment. He will soon discover something of that dreadful and inveterate unbelief which fills the hearts of his unsaved fellows. He must be shown that *he* has no power to convince them; that nothing but a miracle of mercy, the putting forth of invincible power by God Himself is sufficient to overcome the enmity of the carnal mind.

"And they asked them, saying, Is this your son, who ye say was born blind? how then doth he now see?" (v. 19). This was a desperate move. They had been unable to intimidate the one who had been dealt with so graciously by Christ. They were unable to meet the arguments which had been made by some of the more friendly Pharisees. They now decide to summon the beggar's parents. It was their last hope. If they could succeed in getting them to deny that their son had been born blind, the miracle would be discredited. With this object in view they arraign the parents. And Satan still seeks to discredit the witness of the young Christian by getting his relatives to testify against him! This is an oft-used device of his. Let us daily seek grace from God that we may so act in the home that those nearest to us will have no just ground for condemning our profession.

"His parents answered them and said, We know that this is our son, and that he was born blind: But by what means he now seeth, we know not; or who hath opened his eyes, we know not: he is of age; ask him: he shall speak for himself" (vv. 20, 21). How this serves to expose the folly of a wish we have often heard expressed. People say, "O that I had lived in Palestine during the days of Christ's public ministry; it had been so much easier to have believed in Him!" They suppose that if only they had witnessed some of the wonderful works of our Lord, unbelief had been impossible. How little such people know about the real nature and seat of unbelief; and how little acquainted must they be with the four Gospels. These plainly record the fact (making no effort at all either to conceal or excuse it) that again and again the Lord Jesus put forth His supernatural power, producing the most amazing effects, and yet the great majority of those who stood by were nothing more than temporally impressed. It was so here in the passage before us. Even the parents of this man born blind believed not on Christ.

They were evidently afraid of their inquisitors; and yet their answer non-plussed the Pharisees.

"These words spake his parents, because they feared the Jews" (v. 22). They represented a large class of religious professors who surround us on every side today—in such bondage are men and women, otherwise intelligent, to religious leaders and authorities. How true it is that "the fear of man bringeth a snare". The only ones who are fearless before men are those who truly *fear* God. This is one of our daily needs: to cry earnestly unto the Lord that He will put *His* "fear" upon us.

"These words spake his parents, because they feared the Jews: for the Jews had agreed already, that if any man did confess that he was Christ, he should be put out of the synagogue" (v. 22). Mark here the desperate lengths to which prejudice will carry men. They were determined not to believe. They had made up their minds that no evidence should change their opinions, that no testimony should have any weight with them. It reminds us very much of what we read of in Acts 7. At the close of Stephen's address we read that his enemies *"stopped their ears,* and ran upon him with one accord" (v. 57). This is just what these Pharisees did, and it is what many are doing today. And this is the most dangerous attitude a sinner can assume. So long as a man is honest and open-minded, there is hope for him, no matter how ignorant or vicious he may be. But when a man has deliberately turned his back upon the truth, and refuses to be influenced by any evidence, it is very rare indeed that such an one is ever brought into the light.

"Therefore said his parents, He is of age; ask him" (v. 23). Typically, this tells us that the young and tried believer must not look to man for help; his resources must be in God alone. This man might well have expected his parents to be filled with gratitude at their son's eyes being opened, that they would perceive how God had wrought a miracle of mercy upon him, and that they would readily stand by and corroborate his witness before this unfriendly tribunal. But little help did he receive from them. The onus was thrown back upon himself. And this line in the picture is not without its due significance. The young believer might well expect his loved ones to appreciate and rejoice over the blessed change they must see in him; but oftentimes they are quite indifferent if not openly antagonistic. So too with our fellow-Christians. If we look to *them* for help when we get in a tight place, they will generally fail us. And it is perhaps well that it should be so. Anything that really casts us *upon God Himself* is a blessing, even though it be disguised and appear to us a calamity at the time. Let us learn then to "have no confidence in the flesh" (Phil. 3:3), but let our expectation be in the Lord, who will fail us not.

We reserve for the next article our comments on the wonderful dispensational picture found in this chapter. In the meantime, let the interested student ponder the following questions:

1. What is meant by "Give God the praise" (v. 24)?—Cf Josh. 7:19.
2. Explain the first half of v. 25 so as not to conflict with v. 33.
3. What other verse in John's Gospel does the second half of v. 29 call to mind?
4. What connection is there between v. 31 and what has gone before?
5. Why did Christ wait till the beggar had been "cast out" (v. 34) before He revealed Himself as the Son of God (v. 35)?
6. Why are we told nothing more about the beggar after what is said in v. 38?
7. What is the meaning of v. 39?—contrast 3:17.

—Arthur W. Pink.

GLEANINGS IN EXODUS.

8. Moses and Aaron before Pharaoh: Ex. 5.

"And afterward Moses and Aaron went in, and told Pharaoh, Thus saith the Lord God of Israel, Let My people go, that they may hold a feast unto Me in the wilderness" (5:1). Let us endeavor to place ourselves in the position occupied by these two ambassadors of the Lord. Moses and Aaron were now required to confront Pharaoh in person. His temper toward their race was well known, his heartless cruelty had been frequently displayed; it was, therefore, no small trial of their faith and courage to beard the lion in his den. The character of the message they were to deliver to him was not calculated to pacify. They were to tell him in peremptory language that the Lord God required him to let that people whom he held in slavery go, and hold a feast unto Jehovah in the wilderness. Moreover, the Lord had already told His servants that He would harden Pharaoh's heart so that he *would not* let the people go. Notwithstanding these discouraging features, Moses and Aaron "went in and told Pharaoh". A striking example was this of God's power to overcome the opposition of the flesh, to impart grace to the trembling heart, and to demonstrate that our strength is made perfect in weakness.

"And afterward Moses and Aaron went in, and told Pharaoh, Thus saith the Lord God of Israel, Let My people go, that they may hold a feast unto Me in the wilderness". Careful attention should be paid to the *terms* of this request or demand upon Pharaoh. Jehovah had already promised Moses that he and his people should worship God on Mount Sinai (3:12), and that was much more than a three days' journey from Egypt—compare 12:37; 14:2; 15:22 and 19:1; yea, He had declared that He would bring them "unto Canaan" (3:8). Why, then, did not Moses tell Pharaoh plainly that he must relinquish *all* claim on the Hebrews, and give permission for them to leave his land for good? Mr. Urquhart has ably answered this difficult question:

"God is entering upon a controversy with Pharaoh and with Egypt. He is about to judge them; and, in order that they may be judged, they must first be revealed to themselves and to all men. Had they been asked to suffer the Israelites to depart from Egypt, so large a demand might have seemed to others, and certainly would have appeared to the Egyptians themselves, as so unreasonable as to justify their refusal. A request is made, therefore, against which no charge of the kind can be brought. A three days' journey into the wilderness need not have taken the Israelites much beyond the Egyptian frontier. It was also perfectly reasonable, even to heathen notions, that they should be permitted to worship their God after the accepted manner. The heart of Pharaoh and of his people was, therefore, revealed in their scornful refusal of a perfectly reasonable request. In this way they committed themselves to what was manifestly unjust; and in proceeding against them God was consequently justified even in their own eyes. Conscience was stirred. Egypt knew itself to be in the wrong; and a pathway was made there for return to the living God—the God of the conscience—for all who desired to be at peace with Him whom they had offended.

"Has God ever judged a people whom He has not first dealt with in that very way? National judgments have been preceded by some outstanding transgression in which the heart of the nation has been manifested. Carlyle traces the fearful blow which fell upon the clergy and the aristocracy in the French Revolution to the massacre of St. Bartholomew. France had sought to crush the Reformation as Egypt had sought to crush Israel. Spain dug the grave for her greatness and her fame in the establishment of her Inquisition, and in her relentless wars against a people who desired to remove from the Church what were glaring, and largely confessed scandals.

"But we have to go farther to find the full explanation of that request. The demand was indeed limited. It was seemingly a small matter that was asked for. But what was asked for set forth and inscribed in flaming characters Israel's mission. This conflict was to be waged on ground chosen by the Almighty. The battle was not one merely for Israel's deliverance from bitter bondage. It was not fought and won solely that Israel might be able to go forth and possess the land promised to her fathers. The one purpose, to which every other was subsidiary and contributory, was that Israel should dwell in God's Tabernacle. She was redeemed to be His people. Her one mission was and is to serve Jehovah. No other demand would have adequately stated the claim that God was now making and urging in the face of humanity. No other could have so set forth God's claim as against the claim of Pharaoh. Pharaoh said: 'The people is mine; I will not let them go.' God said: 'The people is Mine; thou must let them go; they have been created and chosen that they may serve Me'. The conflict was being waged over the destiny of a race, its place in history and in the service of humanity. Was Israel to be slave, or priest? Egypt's beast of burden, or the anointed of Jehovah? That was the question; and was it possible that God could have done other than put that question, written large and clear, in the forefront of this great controversy?

"And let me add that the demand was prophetic. Israel is in this matter also the type of God's people. When Christianity began its conflict with the Roman Empire, what was the one question over which the great debate proceeded? We all know now what God intended. The nations were to abandon their idols so that their very names, as the household words of the peoples, were to perish. But no demand was made by the Christian Church that the temples should be closed, and that the heathen priesthoods should be abolished. One thing only was asked, and that apparently one of the slightest. It was freedom to worship the living God—*the very demand made for Israel in Egypt.* Over that the battle raged for centuries. The triumph came when that was won. It was not for any claim the Christians made to direct the worship of the Roman Empire: it was not for their rights as citizens: it was for liberty to worship God in accordance with His demand. That claim kept them, and when the triumph came it consecrated them, as the people of God" (The Bible: Its Structure and Purpose: Vol. IV).

"And afterward Moses and Aaron went in, and told Pharaoh, Thus saith the Lord God of Israel, Let My people go, that they may hold a feast unto Me in the wilderness". So far as Pharaoh was concerned, this was God addressing *his* responsibility, giving him opportunity for obedience, speaking to him in grace. Not yet does He launch His judgments on the haughty king and his subjects. Before He dealt in wrath, He acted in mercy. This is ever His way. He sent forth Noah as a preacher of righteousness and Enoch as a herald of the coming storm, before the Flood descended upon the antediluvians. He sent forth one prophet after another unto Israel, before He banished them into captivity. And later, He sent forth His own Son, followed by the apostles, before His army destroyed Jerusalem in A. D. 70. So it is with the world today. God is now dealing in grace and long-sufferance, sending forth His servants far and wide, bidding men flee from the wrath to come. But this Day of Salvation is rapidly drawing to a close, and once the Lord rises from His place at God's right hand, the door of mercy will be shut, and the storm of God's righteous anger will burst.

"And Pharaoh said, Who is the Lord, that I should obey His voice to let Israel go? I know not the Lord, neither will I let Israel go" (v. 2). Here then was Pharaoh's response to the overtures of God's grace. Unacquainted with God for himself, he defiantly refuses to bow to His mandate. The character of Egypt's king stood fully revealed: "I know not the Lord, neither will I let Israel go". Precisely such is the reply made (if not in word, plainly expressed by their attitude) by many of those who hear God's authoritative fiat, "Repent! Believe!", through His servants today. First and foremost the Gospel is not an invitation, but a *declaration* of what God demands from the sinner—"God now *commandeth* all men everywhere to repent" (Acts 17:30); "And this is His *commandment*, that we should believe on the name of His Son, Jesus Christ" (1 John 3:3). But the response of the unbelieving and rebellious heart of the natural man is "Who is the Lord that I should obey His voice?". Thus speaks the pride of the man who hardens his neck against the Blessed God. "I know Him not" said Pharaoh, and "I know Him not" expresses the heart of the sinner today; and what makes it so dreadful is, he desires not to correct this ignorance. For these two things God will yet take vengeance when Christ returns. He will be revealed "in flaming fire taking vengeance on them that *know not* God, and that *obey not* the Gospel of our Lord Jesus Christ" (2 Thess. 1:8).

"And they said, The God of the Hebrews hath met with us: let us go, we pray thee, three days' journey into the desert, and sacrifice unto the Lord our God; lest He fall upon us with pestilence, or with the sword" (v. 3). By comparing these words of Moses with his first utterance to Pharaoh a number of interesting and important points will be seen the more clearly. First, the demand of Jehovah was, "Let My people go, that they may hold *a feast* unto Me in the wilderness" (v. 1). This speaks from the *Divine* side. The request of Moses was, "Let us go, we pray thee, three days' journey into the desert, and *sacrifice* unto the Lord our God". This speaks from the *human* side. The one tells of what God's heart sought, the other of what man's sin needed. The "feast" points to rejoicing, the "sacrifice" to what makes rejoicing possible. In the second place, observe the *ground* upon which Moses here bases the Hebrews' *need* of a "sacrifice"—"lest He fall upon us with pestilence, or with the sword". It is impossible to evade the plain implication of this language. Israel were confessedly guilty, and therefore deserving of punishment, and the only way of escape was through an atonement being made for them. God must be placated: blood must be shed: the Divine justice must be propitiated. Only thus could God be reconciled to them. Finally, observe a *"three days'* journey" was necessary before the Hebrews could sacrifice to Jehovah. Profoundly significant is this in its typical suggestiveness. "Three days" speaks of the interval between death and resurrection. It is only on resurrection-ground, as made alive from the dead, that we can hold a feast unto the Lord!

"And the king of Egypt said unto them, Wherefore do ye, Moses and Aaron, let (hinder) the people from their works? get you unto your burdens. And Pharaoh said, Behold, the people of the land now are many, and ye make them rest from their burdens" (vv. 4, 5). It seems clear from this that Pharaoh had already heard of the conference which Moses and Aaron had held with the "elders" of Israel, and knew of the signs which had been wrought before them. These had created, no doubt, a considerable stir among the rank and file of the Hebrews, and instead of going about their regular drudgery they had, apparently, expected the Lord to act on their behalf without delay. This, we take it, is what Pharaoh had in mind when he charged Moses and Aaron with hindering the people from their work. When he added "Get you unto your burdens" he referred to the whole of the people, the representatives of whom had accompanied God's two servants into the king's presence (cf 3:18).

"And Pharaoh commanded the same day the taskmasters of the people, and their officers, saying, Ye shall no more give the people straw to make brick, as heretofore: let them go and gather straw for themselves. And the tale of the bricks, which they did make heretofore, ye shall lay upon them; ye shall not diminish ought thereof: for they be idle; therefore they cry, saying, Let us go and sacrifice to our God. Let there more work be laid upon the men, that they may labor therein; and let them not regard vain words" (vv. 6-9). This is ever the effect of rejecting God's testimony. To resist the light means increased darkness: to turn from the truth is to become more thoroughly than ever under the power of him who is the arch-liar. The same sun which melts the wax hardens the clay. Instead of allowing the Hebrews to go and sacrifice to Jehovah, Pharaoh orders that their lot shall be made harder. So it is with the sinner who disobeys the Gospel command. The one who refuses to repent becomes more impenitent, more defiant, more lawless, until (with rare exceptions) the Lord abandons him to his own ways and leaves him to suffer the due reward of his iniquities.

The *unbelief* of Pharaoh comes out plainly here: "Let there more work be laid upon the men, that they may labor therein; and let them not regard *vain words*". Where God Himself is unknown His words are but idle tales. To talk of sacrificing unto Him is meaningless to the man of the world. Such are the Holy Scriptures to the sinner today. The Bible tells man that he is a fallen creature, unprepared to die, unfit for the presence of a holy God. The Bible tells him of the wondrous provision of God's grace, and presents a Saviour all-sufficient for his acceptance. The Bible warns him faithfully of the solemn issues at stake, and asks him how he shall escape if he neglects so great salvation. The Bible tells him plainly that he that believeth not shall be damned, and that whosoever's name is not found written in the book of life shall be cast into the Lake of Fire. But these solemn verities are but "vain words" to the skeptical heart of the natural man. He refuses to receive them as a message from the living God addressed to his own soul. But let him beware. Let him be warned by the awful case of Pharaoh. If he continues in his unbelief and obstinacy, Pharaoh's fate shall be his—God will surely bring him into judgment.

"And the taskmasters of the people went out, and their officers, and they spake to the people, saying, Thus saith Pharaoh, I will not give you straw. Go ye, get you straw where ye can find it: yet not ought of your work shall be diminished. So the people were scattered abroad throughout all the land of Egypt to gather stubble instead of straw. And the taskmasters hasted them, saying, Fulfill your works, and your daily tasks, as when there was straw. And the officers of the children of Israel which Pharaoh's taskmasters had set over them, were beaten, and demanded, Wherefore have ye not fulfilled your task in making brick both yesterday and today, as heretofore?" (vv. 10-14). The severe measures which Pharaoh ordered to be taken upon the Hebrews illustrate the malignant efforts of Satan against the soul that God's grace is dealing with. When the Devil recognizes the first advances of the Holy Spirit toward a poor sinner he at once puts forth every effort to retain his victims. At no place is the frightful malevolence of the Fiend more plainly to be seen than here. No pains are spared by him to hinder the deliverance of his slaves. Satan never gives up his prey without a fierce struggle. When a soul is convicted of sin, and brought to long after liberty and peace with God, the Devil will endeavor, just as Pharaoh did with the Israelites, by increased occupation with material things, to expel all such desires from his heart.

A solemn example of what we have in mind is recorded in Luke 9:42: "And as he was yet a coming, the demon threw him down, and tare him". This obscessed youth was coming to Christ, and while on the way, Satan's emissary sought to rend him to pieces. So long as a person has no desire after Christ the Devil will leave him alone, but once a soul is awakened to his need of a Saviour and begins to seriously seek Him, Satan will put forth every effort to hinder him. This is why so many convicted souls find that their case gets worse before it is bettered. So it was here with the Hebrews. Just as hope was awakened, the opposition against them became stronger: just when deliverance seemed nigh, their oppression was increased.

"Then the officers of the children of Israel came and cried unto Pharaoh, saying, Wherefore dealest thou thus with thy servants? There is no straw given unto thy servants, and they say to us, Make bricks: and, behold, thy servants are beaten; but the fault is in thine own people" (vv. 15, 16). How true to human nature is this! Instead of crying unto the Lord these leaders of the Israelites turned unto Pharaoh for relief. Doubtless they hoped to appeal to his pity or to his sense of justice. Surely they could show him that his demands were unreasonable and impossible of fulfillment Alas, the natural man ever prefers to lean upon an arm of flesh than be supported by Him who is invisible. Just so is it with the convicted sinner: he turns for help to the evangelist, his pastor, his Sunday School teacher, his parents, any one rather than the Lord Himself. God is generally our *last* resource! Deeply humbling is this! And amazing is the grace which bears with such waywardness. Grace not only has to begin the work of salvation, it also has to continue and complete it. It is *all* of grace from first to last.

"But he said, Ye are idle, ye are idle: therefore ye say, Let us go and do sacrifice to the Lord. Go therefore now, and work; for there shall no straw be given you, yet shall ye deliver the tale of bricks" (vv. 17, 18). Little good did it do Israel's "officers" in appealing to Pharaoh. He, like the master of the poor sinner, was absolutely pitiless and inflexible. Probably these officers supposed that the brutal "taskmasters" had acted without the king's knowledge. If so, they were quickly disillusioned. Instead of expressing indignation at the taskmasters, and relieving the officers of the people, Pharaoh insulted them, charging them with sloth and duplicity, arguing that it was not so much the honor of God they regarded, as that they might escape from their work. So, too, the awakened sinner accomplishes little good by turning to human counsellors for relief. When the prodigal son began to be in want he went and joined himself to a citizen of the far country, but being sent into the fields to feed swine was all he got for his pains (Luke 15:15). The poor woman mentioned in the Gospels "suffered many things of many physicians", and though she spent all that she had, she was "nothing bettered, but rather *grew worse*" (Mark 5:26). O unsaved reader, if a work of grace has already begun in your heart so that you realize your wretchedness and long for that peace and rest which this poor world is unable to give, fix it firmly in your mind that One only can give you what you seek. Allow no priest—either Roman Catholic or Protestant—to come in between you and Christ. Cease ye from man, and "seek ye *the Lord* while He may be found".

"And the officers of the children of Israel did see that they were in evil case, after it was said, Ye shall not minish ought from your bricks of your daily task. And they met Moses and Aaron, who stood in the way, as they came forth from Pharaoh: And they said unto them, The Lord look upon you, and judge; because ye have made our savor to be abhorred in the eyes of Pharaoh, and in the eyes of His servants, to put a sword in their hand to slay us" (vv. 19-21). Poor Moses! His troubles now were only commencing. He had been prepared for the rebuff which he had himself received from Pharaoh, for the Lord had said plainly that He would harden the king's heart. But, so far as the inspired record informs us, nothing had been told him that he would meet with discouragement and opposition from his own brethren. A real testing was this for God's servant, for it is far more trying to be criticized by our own brethren, by those whom we are anxious to help, than it is to be persecuted by the world. But sufficient for the servant to be as his master. The Lord Himself was hated by his own brethren according to the flesh, and the very ones to whom He had ministered in ceaseless grace unanimously cried "Crucify Him".

"And Moses returned unto the Lord, and said, Lord, wherefore hast Thou so evil entreated this people? why is it that Thou hast sent me? For since I came to Pharaoh to speak in Thy name, he hath done evil to this people; neither hast Thou delivered Thy people at all" (vv. 22, 23). Moses did well in turning to the Lord in the hour of trial, but it was most unseemly and irreverent of him to speak in the way that he did—alas that we, in our petulant unbelief, are so often guilty of asking similar questions. It is not for the servant to take it upon him to dictate to his master, far less is it for a worm of the earth to dispute with the Almighty. These things are recorded faithfully for "*our* admonition". There was no need for Jehovah to hurry. His delay in delivering Israel and His permitting them to endure still greater afflictions accomplished many ends. It furnished fuller opportunity for Pharaoh to manifest the desperate wickedness of the human heart. It gave occasion for the Lord to demonstrate how that He "bears with *much* long-suffering the vessels of wrath fitted to destruction". It served to show more clearly how righteous God was in visiting Pharaoh and his subjects with sore judgment. And, too, Israel needed to be humbled: they also were a stiff-necked people, as is clear from the words of their leaders to Moses and Aaron on this occasion. Moreover, the more they were afflicted the more would they appreciate the Lord's deliverance when His time came. Let, then, the writer and reader take this to heart: the Lord always has a good reason for each of His *delays*. Therefore, let us recognize the folly, yea, the wickedness of murmuring at His seeming tardiness. Let us daily seek grace to "Rest in the Lord, and *wait patiently* for Him".

We may add that what has been before us supplies a striking picture of that which awaits Israel in a coming day. The grievous afflictions which came upon the Hebrews in Egypt just before the Lord emancipated them from their hard and cruel bondage, did but foreshadow the awful experiences through which their descendants shall pass during the "time of Jacob's trouble", just prior to the coming of the Deliverer to Zion. Pharaoh's conduct as described in our chapter—his defiance of Jehovah, his rejection of the testimony of God's two witnesses, his cruel treatment of the children of Israel—accurately typifies the course which will be followed by the Man of Sin. Thus may we discern once more how that these pages of Old Testament history are also prophetic in their forecastings of coming events. May it please the Lord to open our eyes so that we may perceive both the application to ourselves and those who are to follow us.

—Arthur W. Pink.

THE ATONEMENT.

Was the Sin Question Finally Settled at the Cross?

It is unspeakably sad that the atoning death of the Lord Jesus Christ—the most wonderful event that has ever happened or will happen—should have been made the occasion of contention and controversy. That it has been so, affords an awful example of human depravity. The more so, that throughout the centuries of this Christian era, some of the hottest theological battles have been waged over the vital truth of the Atonement.

Speaking generally, only two views or interpretations of the Cross have received much favor among the people of God: the one which affirmed that the Atonement was effected to make *certain* the salvation of *all who believe;* the other which supposed that atonement was made in order to make *possible* the salvation of *all men.* The former is the strict Calvinist view; the latter, the Arminian. Even here, the difference was not merely one of terms, but of truth over against error. The one is definite and explicit; the other indefinite and intangible. The one affirms an Atonement which actually atones (i. e. fully satisfied God for those on whose behalf it was made); the other predicates an Atonement which was a sorry failure, inasmuch as the majority of those on whose behalf it was supposed to be offered, perish notwithstanding. The logical and inevitable corollary of the one is a satisfied, because triumphant Saviour; the other (if true) would lead, unavoidably, to a disappointed, because defeated Saviour. The former interpretation was taught by such men as Wickliff, Calvin, Latimer, Tyndal, Bunyan, Owens, Dodderidge, Jonathan Edwards, Toplady, Whitefield, Spurgeon, etc. The latter by men who, as theologians, were not worthy to unloose their shoes.

Of late, a new theory has been propounded to the Christian public, a theory which approximates perilously near that of the Universalists. Erroneously based upon a few texts whose scope is confined to the people of God, the view which is now rapidly gaining favor in circles which are regarded as orthodox, is to the effect that, at the Cross, the sin question was fully and finally settled. We are told, and told by men who are looked up to by many as the champions of orthodoxy, that *all* the sins of *all men* were laid upon the crucified Christ. It is boldly affirmed that at the Cross the Lamb of God did as much for unbelievers as He did for believers. It is dogmatically announced that the *only* grievance which God now has against *any* man, is his refusal to believe in the Saviour. It is said that the single issue between God and the world, *is not* the sin question, but the Son question.

We have said that this theory of the Atonement is a *new* one, and new it surely is. So far as the writer is aware, it was never propounded, at least in orthodox circles, till within the last two or three decades. It appears to be another product of this twentieth century, and like most if not all other of them, it is far inferior to what went before. Yet strange to say, an appeal is made to the Holy Scriptures in support of it. But in one way we are thankful for this, inasmuch as the Word of God supplies us with an infallible rule by which we may measure it. We shall, therefore, examine this strange and novel theory in the light of Holy Writ, and doing this, it will not be difficult to show how thoroughly untenable and fallacious it is.

1. If *all* the sins of *all* men were laid upon Christ, then the sin of *unbelief* was too. That unbelief *is* a sin is clear from the fact that in 1 John 3:23 we read, "And this is His *commandment,* That we should believe on the name of His Son Jesus Christ". Refusal to believe in Christ is, therefore, an act of flagrant disobedience, rebellion against the Most High. But if *all* the sins of *all* men were laid upon Christ (as it is now asserted), then He also endured the penalty for the Christ-rejector's unbelief. If this be so, then Universalism is true. But it is *not* so. The very advocates of the view we are now refuting would not affirm it. And therein may be seen the inconsistency and untenableness of their teaching. For if unbelief is a sin and Christ did not suffer the penalty of it, then *all* sin *was not* laid upon Christ. Thus there are only two possible alternatives: a strictly limited Atonement, availing only for believers; or an unlimited Atonement which effectually secures the salvation of the entire human race.

2. If *all* the sins of *all* men were laid

upon Christ, how could He say, "The blasphemy against the Holy Ghost *shall not be forgiven* unto men" (Matt. 12:31)? Observe that Christ here used the future tense, "shall not be". Note, too, He did not merely say to the blaspheming Jews that He was then addressing, "Shall not be forgiven unto *you*", but, in order to take in all others who should be guilty of this sin, He said, "Shall not be forgiven *unto men*". It is worse than idle to raise the cavil that the sin here spoken of was peculiar and exceptional, i. e. committed only by the Jews there addressed. The fact that this solemn utterance of Christ is found not only in Matthew, but in Mark, and also in Luke—the *Gentile* Gospel—disposes of it.

Without attempting to define here the precise nature of this sin of blasphemy against the Holy Ghost, it is sufficient now to point out that it is a sin quite distinct from unbelief. In Scripture "blasphemy" is always an act of the lips, not merely of the mind or will. For our present purpose, it is enough to call attention to the undeniable fact that none other than the Saviour Himself here tells us *there is* a sin (other than unbelief) *which "shall not* be forgiven unto men". This being so, then it is obviously a mistake, a serious error, to say that *all* sin was laid on Christ and atoned for.

3. If *all* the sins of *all* men were laid upon Christ, how could He possibly say to certain ones, "Ye shall seek Me, and shall die in your sins" (John 8:21)? Christ was here addressing the Pharisees. The time was only a short while before His death. He was speaking, therefore, of that which lay on the other side of His crucifixion and resurrection. This is seen from the fact that He first said, "I go My way, and ye shall seek Me". Most evidently was He referring to His return to the Father. And yet He expressly declared that *after* His departure from this world, these men would "seek" Him (but in vain), and they should die in their sins. Their death would be subsequent to His, and their death should be in *sins*. The striking thing is, that these awful words were uttered, on this same occasion, no less than three times. For in John 8:24 we read, "I said therefore unto you, That ye shall die in your sins: for if ye believe not that I am, ye *shall* die in your sins". Note, carefully, "die", not in your sin, but "in your sin*s*". Here, then, is another indubitable proof that Christ *did not* bear all the sins of all men.

4. If *all* the sins of *all* men were laid upon Christ, why did the apostle Paul (under the Holy Spirit) write, "For this ye know, that no whoremonger, nor unclean person, nor covetous man, who is an idolator, hath any inheritance in the kingdom of Christ and of God. Let no man deceive you with vain words: for *because of these things* cometh the wrath of God upon the children of disobedience" (Eph. 5:5, 6). The "children of disobedience" (cf Eph. 2:2) is a name for unbelievers. It views them as rebels against God. The passage now before us tells us *why* "the wrath of God" shall come upon them—"because of *these* things", looks back to what had been specified in the previous verses. God's wrath would yet descend upon them not only because of their rejection of Christ, but because they had been guilty of the sins of immorality and covetousness.

It is remarkable that v. 6 begins with the words, "Let no man *deceive you with vain words*". It certainly looks as though the Holy Spirit was here anticipating and repudiating this modern perversion of God's truth. Men *do* now tell us that *no* wrath from God will ever fall on men because of the sins of immorality and covetousness. Men now tell us that God's wrath for *all* sins came upon Christ. But when men tell us such things, none other than the Holy Spirit declares that they are "vain (empty) words". They are empty words because there is no truth in them! Then let us not be deceived by them.

5. If *all* the sins of *all* men were laid upon Christ, then Stephen wasted his dying breath when he prayed, "Lay not *this sin* to their charge" (Acts 7:60). The sin referred to was their stoning of himself, which was murder. But perhaps Stephen was not acquainted with this modern sophistry. Certainly he did not believe it. Had he believed that *all* sin had been "laid" on Christ, he would not have cried *"lay not* this sin to *their* charge", i. e., let not *them* suffer the *penalty* of it.

6. If *all* the sins of *all* men were laid upon Christ, what did the apostle mean when he said of the Jews, who forbade him to speak to the Gentiles that they

might be saved, "to fill up their *sins* alway" (1 Thess. 2:16)? If language has any meaning, these words of the apostle signify that the Jews were adding sins to sins. He did not say "to fill up their sin", but, "to fill up their sin*s*". Clearly, there was no place in *his* theology for this strange invention of the twentieth century.

7. If *all* the sins of *all* men were laid upon Christ, what did the apostle mean when he said, "Some men's sins are open beforehand, going before to judgment" (1 Tim. 5:24)? One thing he meant was that, *no atonement* had been made for them. Mark, again, he is speaking, not of sin, but "*sins*", and these, he declared, are "going before *to judgment*". Nothing could be plainer. These "sins" *had not* been "judged" at the Cross, therefore, they *must be* judged in the Day of Judgment.

8. If *all* the sins of *all* men were laid upon Christ, then why will a voice *from heaven* yet say to the godly Jews who shall be found in Babylon at the end-time, "Come out of her, My people, that ye be not partaker of her sins, and that ye receive not of her plagues. For her sins have reached unto heaven, and God hath remembered her iniquities" (Rev. 18:4, 5)? Here is proof positive that the theory we are now rebutting is not the theology of *heaven*. Here is proof positive that the "sins" of Babylon *were not* laid on Christ. Here is proof positive that Christ *was not* "bruised" for her "iniquities", for God would not punish *twice* for the *same* sins.

9. If *all* the sins of *all* men were laid upon Christ, then God would not have dealt in judicial wrath with Israel because of the sins of their forefathers. But he *did* do so; and He did so *after* the crucifixion of His Son. No less than Christ Himself is our authority for this: "Therefore also said the Wisdom of God, I will send them prophets and apostles, and some of them they shall slay and persecute: That the blood of all the prophets, which was shed from the foundation of the world, may be required of this generation; From the blood of Abel unto the blood of Zacharias, which perished between the altar and the temple: verily I say unto you, it shall be required of this generation" (Luke 11:49-51). This passage teaches plainly that the punishment for the accumulated sins of their forefathers was to fall upon a single generation of the Jews. Christ confirmed this by saying, *"It shall* be required of this generation". But if atonement was made for *all* sins at the Cross, then all of this would have been cancelled (remitted). That it was not so cancelled, we know from the fully authenticated fact that in A. D. 70 this solemn threat *was* executed, and God *did* "require" this at the hands of the Jews then living.

10. If *all* the sins of *all* men were laid upon Christ, then wherein lies the *need* for and wherein would be the *propriety* of the dead being "judged according to their *works*" (Rev. 20:12)? If the *only* issue between God and the world is their attitude toward Christ; if the *only* ground of condemnation for men be the rejection of the Divinely appointed Saviour, then it would be meaningless, or worse, to arraign them for their work*s*. The fact that Holy Writ *does* declare that the wicked shall yet be judged "according to their works" is incontestable evidence that they will have *more* to answer for, and will suffer for something *more* than their rejection of Christ.

11. If *all* the sins of *all* men were laid upon Christ, how could there possibly be any *degrees* of punishment for the lost? If the only sin which God now imputes to the wicked is their rejection of Christ, then *one common guilt* would rest upon all, and consequently *one common punishment* would be their portion. That there *will be* degrees of punishment among the lost is clearly established by the following scriptures:—"It shall be *more tolerable* for Tyre and Sidon at the day of judgment, than for you" (Matt. 11:22). "These shall receive *greater* damnation" (Mark 12:40). "And that servant, which knew his lord's will, and prepared not himself, neither did according to his will, shall be beaten with *many* stripes. But he that knew not, and did commit things worthy of stripes, shall be beaten with *few* stripes" (Luke 12:47, 48). "He that despised Moses' law died without mercy under two or three witnesses: Of how much *sorer punishment,* suppose ye, shall he be thought worthy, who hath trodden under foot the Son of God?" (Heb. 10:28, 29).

12. If *all* the sins of *all* men were laid upon Christ, and the *only* sin which God now imputes to any is the refusal to re-

ceive His Son, then it inevitably follows that, *all the heathen* who have lived since the crucifixion and who have never heard of Christ, will certainly be saved. There is no other alternative possible. Not having heard of Christ, they cannot be charged with *rejecting* Him, and if *all* their *other* sins were atoned for (as we are asked to believe) then, necessarily, they must stand *guiltless* before God. But if this were true then John 14:6 would be untrue, for there the recorded declaration of Christ is, "*No man* cometh unto the Father *but* by Me".

Having shown that this latest theory of the Atonement *cannot* be true—cannot because it manifestly clashes with the twelve scriptures quoted above and with others that might be quoted—we shall now examine the leading passages which are appealed to in support of it.

1. "The Lord hath laid on Him the iniquity of us *all*" (Isa. 53:6). Notice that this verse *does not say*, "the Lord hath laid on Him the iniquit*ies of all*", which is what some brethren twist it to mean. No, instead of so saying, the "all" is definitely and carefully *qualified* thus: "The Lord hath laid on Him the iniquity of *us* all". Who the "us" refers to is made plain in the next verse but one: "For the transgression of *My people* was He stricken" (Isa. 53:8). If further proof be required that the "all" is limited, it is furnished by another statement in the same chapter, for in v. 12 we read, "And He bare the sin of *many*". This restriction is meaningless if Christ bore the sin of everybody.

2. "Behold the Lamb of God which taketh away the sin of the world" (John 1:29). Again we ask the reader to note carefully the exact wording of this sentence: it is *not* (as so often misquoted) "The Lamb of God which taketh away the sin*s* of the world", but "the *sin* of the world". The word "sin" is used in the New Testament in several ways. Sometimes the reference is to the sinful *nature*, as in Heb. 4:15, 1 John 1:8, etc. Sometimes it is the sinful *act* which is in view, as in James 1:15, etc. At other times "sin" refers to the *guilt* or *penalty* of sin, as in Rom. 3:9; 6:10; 2 Cor. 5:21. It is in this last sense "sin" is used in John 1:29. The definite article (found in the Greek as well as in the English) makes this clear. The Lamb of God which beareth away the guilt and consequent penalty, is the thought.

But now what is meant by "taketh away the sin *of the world*"? Does it mean that the Lamb of God took away the guilt of the whole human race? If it does, then the whole human race will most certainly be saved, for unpunished sin (and its defilement) is the only thing which could keep any man out of heaven. But if "the world" *does not* mean the whole human race, what does it refer to? We answer, It is a general, an indefinite expression, used, first, contrastively with Israel. "It is not 'the Lamb of God who taketh away the sin of *Israel*', but the sin of 'the world' —*of any kind of* men" (Mr. F. W. Grant). The "world" here takes in believing sinners of the Gentiles, as well as believing Jews.

That "the world" *is* a general and indefinite expression, rather than a synonym for the whole human race, is clear from its meaning in other passages in John's Gospel. For example, in John 7:4, "Show Thyself to *the world*." Did they mean, "Show Thyself to the whole human race"? Surely not. Again; "Behold *the world* is gone after Him" (John 12:19). Did they mean, the whole human race had gone after Him? Of course not. "I came not to judge *the world*, but to save *the world*" (John 12:47). Did Christ mean that He had come *to* save the whole human race? How could He, when multitudes of men were even then in hell! !

The Greek word for "world" in John 1:29 is "kosmos", and in its application to humankind in the New Testament, we find there are *two* "worlds"—a world of believers and a world of unbelievers. In 2 Pet. 2:5 this expression is used, "Bringing in the flood upon *the world of the ungodly*". Contrariwise, there is a *world* of the *godly*. This is the meaning of John 1:29: it was the sin (penalty) of the world of believers—Jewish believers *and* Gentile believers—that the Lamb of God took away. This is no novel interpretation of ours, but one uniformly given by the Reformers and Puritans.

3. "He that believeth on Him is not condemned: but he that believeth not is condemned already, because he hath not believed in the name of the only begotten Son of God" (John 3:18). That refusal to believe in the name of God's Son is *a*

ground of condemnation is not disputed. The question at issue is whether this is now the *only* ground of condemnation. John 3:18 *does not say* it is. Nor does any other passage. If it did, the Scriptures would contradict themselves, for, as shown above, there are many passages which afford positive proof that God *does* reckon men guilty of *other* sins. The truth is, that man is "under condemnation" long before he ever hears of Christ: he is under condemnation from the hour of his birth. He is not only "shapen in iniquity and conceived in sin" (Psa. 51:5), but he is also *"estranged* from the womb" (Psa. 58:3). We not only inherit Adam's depravity, but we are also "by *nature* the children (not merely of "corruption" but) *of wrath"* (Eph. 2:3). The unregenerate are not only devoid of any spiritual nature, they are also *"alienated* from the life of God" (Eph. 4:18).

4. "God was in Christ, reconciling *the world* unto Himself, not imputing their trespasses unto them" (2 Cor. 5:19). This verse need not detain us very long. Like John 1:29, a right understanding of it turns upon apprehending the true meaning and scope of "the world". The "world" which God reconciled by Christ was *the world of believers.* That *un*believers *are not* "reconciled" is clear from Eph. 4:18 (and other scriptures) which speaks of them being *"alienated* from the life of God". Again, in Rom. 5:10 we are told, "Much more, being reconciled, we shall be saved by His life". That is plain enough: those "reconciled" *shall be* saved! Further proof that "the world" here said to be reconciled *does not* take in the whole human race, is found in the fact that we are expressly told God does not impute "their trespasses unto them". But He *does* "impute" trespasses unto the children of disobedience, as is clear from Eph. 5:6, etc. Psa. 32:1 tells us that the man is *"blessed"* unto whom the Lord "imputeth not iniquity". But the unbeliever is not "blessed", but *cursed.*

5. "And He is the propitiation for our sins: and not for ours only, but also for the sins of the whole world" (1 John 2:2). This is the passage which, apparently, most favors the view we are now rebutting, and yet if it be considered attentively it will be seen that it does so *only* in appearance, and not in reality. Below we offer a number of conclusive proofs to show that this verse *does not* teach that Christ has propitiated God on behalf of all the sins of all men.

In the first place, the fact that this verse opens with "and" necessarily links it with what has gone before. We, therefore, give a literal, word for word translation of 1 John 2:1 from Bagster's Interlinear: "Little children my, these things I write to you, that ye may not sin; and if any one should sin, a Paraclete we have with the Father, Jesus Christ (the) righteous". It will thus be seen that the apostle John is here writing *to* and *about* the *saints* of God. His immediate purpose was twofold: first, to communicate a message that would keep God's children from sinning; second, to supply comfort and assurance to those who might sin, and, in consequence, be cast down and fearful that the issue would prove fatal. He, therefore, makes known to them the provision which God has made for just such an emergency. This we find at the end of v. 1 and throughout v. 2. The ground of comfort is twofold: let the downcast and repentant believer (1 John 1:9) be assured that, first, he has an "Advocate with the Father"; second, that this Advocate is "the propitiation for our sins". Now *believers only* may take comfort *from this,* for they alone have an "Advocate", for them alone is Christ the propitiation, as is proven by *linking* the Propitiation ("and") with "the Advocate"!

In the second place, if other passages in the New Testament, which speak of "propitiation" be compared with 1 John 2:2, it will be found that it is *strictly limited* in its scope. For example, in Rom. 3:25 we read that God set forth Christ "a propitiation *through faith* in His blood". If Christ is a propitiation "through faith", then He *is not* a "propitiation" to those who have no faith! Again, in Heb. 2:17 we read, "To make propitiation for the sins of *the people"* (Heb. 2:17, R. V.).

In the third place, *who* are meant when John says, "He is the propitiation for *our* sins"? We answer, *Jewish believers.* And a part of the proof on which we base this assertion we now submit to the careful attention of the reader.

In Gal. 2:9 we are told that *John,* together with James and Cephas, were apostles "unto the circumcision" (i. e. *Israel*).

In keeping with this, the Epistle of James is addressed to "the twelve tribes, which are scattered abroad" (1:1). So, the first Epistle of Peter is addressed to "the elect who are sojourners of the Dispersion" (1 Pet. 1:1, R. V.). And John also is writing *to* saved Israelites, but *for* saved Jews *and* saved Gentiles.

Some of the evidences that John *is* writing *to* saved Jews are as follows. (a) In the opening verse he says of Christ, "Which *we* have seen with *our* eyes . . . . and *our* hands have handled". How impossible it would have been for the Apostle Paul to have commenced any of *his* epistles to *Gentile* saints with such language!

(b) "Brethren, I write no new commandment unto you, but an old commandment which *ye* had *from the beginning*" (1 John 2:7). The "beginning" here referred to is the beginning of the public manifestation of Christ—in proof compare 1:1; 2:13, etc. Now these believers the apostle tells us, *had* the "old commandment" *from the beginning.* This was true of *Jewish* believers, but it was not true of *Gentile* believers.

(c) "I write unto you, fathers, because *ye have known* Him from the beginning" (2:13). Here, again, it is evident that it is *Jewish* believers that are in view.

(d) "Little children, it is the last time: and as ye *have heard* that Antichrist shall come, even now are there many antichrists; whereby we know that it is the last time. *They* went out from *us,* but they were not of us" (2:18, 19). These brethren to whom John wrote *had* "heard" from Christ Himself that Antichrist should come (see Matt. 24). The "many antichrists" whom John declares "went out *from us*" were all *Jews,* for during the first century none but a *Jew* posed as the Messiah. Therefore, when John says "He is the propitiation for *our* sins" he can only mean for the sins of *Jewish believers**.

In the fourth place, when John added, "And not for ours only, but also for *the whole world*", he signified that Christ was the propitiation for the sins of *Gentile* believers *too,* for, as previously shown, "the world" is a term *contrasted* from Israel. This interpretation is unequivocally established by a careful comparison of 1 John 2:2 with John 11:51, 52, which is a strictly parallel passage: "And this spake he not of himself: but being high priest that year, he prophesied that Jesus should die for that nation; And not for that nation only, but that also He should gather together in one the children of God that were scattered abroad". Here Caiaphas, under inspiration, made known *for whom* Jesus should "die". Notice now the correspondency of his prophecy with this declaration of John's:

"He is the propitiation for our (believing Israelites) sins".

"He prophesied that Jesus should die for that nation".

"And not for ours only".

"And not for that nation only".

"But also for the whole world"—

That is, Gentile believers scattered throughout the earth.

"He should gather together in one the children of God that were scattered abroad".

In the fifth place, the above interpretation is confirmed by the fact that no other is consistent or intelligible. If the "whole world" signifies the whole human race, then the first clause and the "also" in the second clause are absolutely meaningless. If Christ is the propitiation for *everybody,* it would be idle tautology to say, first, "He is the propitiation for *our* sins and *also* for everybody". There could be no "also" if He is the propitiation for the entire human family. Had the apostle meant to affirm that Christ *is* a universal propitiation he would have omitted the first clause of v. 2, and simply said, "He is the propitiation for the sins of the whole world".

In the sixth place, our definition of "the whole world" is in perfect accord with other passages in the New Testament. For example: "Whereof ye heard before in the word of the truth of the Gospel; which is come unto you, as it is in *all the world*" (Col. 1:5, 6). Does "all the world" here mean, absolutely and unqualifiedly, all mankind? Had all the human family heard the Gospel? No; the apostle's obvious meaning is that, the Gospel, instead

*It is true that many things in John's Epistle apply equally to believing Jews *and* believing Gentiles. Christ is the Advocate of the one, as much as of the other. The same may be said of many things in the Epistle of James which is also a *catholic,* or *general* epistle, though expressly addressed *to* the twelve tribes scattered abroad.

of being confined to the land of Judea, had gone abroad, without restraint, *into Gentile lands.* So in Rom. 1:8: "First, I thank my God through Jesus Christ for you all, that your faith is spoken of throughout *the whole world*". The apostle is here referring to the faith of these Roman saints being spoken of in a way of *commendation.* But certainly all mankind did not so speak of their faith! It was the whole world *of believers* that he was referring to! In Rev. 12:9 we read of Satan "which deceiveth *the whole world*". But again this expression cannot be understood as a universal one, for Matt. 24:24 tells us that Satan does not and cannot "deceive" God's elect. Here it is "the whole world" *of unbelievers.*

In the seventh place, to insist that "the whole world" in 1 John 2:2 signifies the entire human race is to undermine the very foundations of our faith. If Christ is the propitiation for those that are lost equally as much as for those that are saved, then what assurance have we that believers too may not be lost? If Christ is the propitiation for those now in hell, what guarantee have I that I may not end in hell? The blood-shedding of the incarnate Son of God is the *only* thing which can keep any one out of hell, and *if* many for whom that precious blood made propitiation are now in the awful place of the damned, then may not that blood prove inefficacious for me! Away with such a God-dishonoring thought.

However men may quibble and wrest the Scriptures, one thing is certain: The Atonement is no failure. God will not allow that precious and costly sacrifice to fail in accomplishing, completely, that which it was designed to effect. Not a drop of that holy blood was shed in vain. In the last great Day there shall stand forth no disappointed and defeated Saviour, but One who *"shall* see of the travail of His soul and *be satisfied"* (Isa. 53: 11). These are not our words, but the infallible assertion of Him who declares, "My counsel shall stand, and I will do *all* My pleasure" (Isa. 64: 10). Upon this impregnable rock we take our stand. Let others rest on the sands of human speculation and twentieth-century theorizing if they wish. That is their business. But to God they will yet have to render an account. For our part we had rather be railed at as a narrow-minded, out-of-date, hyper-Calvinist, than be found repudiating God's truth by reducing the Divinely-efficacious atonement to a mere fiction.

Was the sin question finally settled at the Cross? For every believer, *Yes.* For unbelievers, *No,* as they shall yet find to their cost. Arthur W. Pink.

This may be had in tract form from the Editor: 5¢ a copy, 40¢ per dozen. We hope many will order a quantity, for handing out to others.

QUOTATIONS FROM THE O. T. IN THE N. T.

When any part of divine truth has been received, "not as the word of men, but as the Word of God", difficulties respecting other parts of Scripture will not surprise the believer who has learned that it was his own preoccupation, prejudice, and ignorance, and not any obscurity in the Word itself, which delayed his perception and reception of that which is now radiant with light and precious to his soul. And then, remembering that the Holy Spirit alone taught him what he already knows, he will at sight of each new difficulty, betake himself to Him who still graciously waits upon his need, ready to "guide him into all the truth". Nevertheless, He may condescend to use us to help each other in the understanding of the Word; and therefore we offer a brief notice of one difficulty frequently encountered by those who, through the Spirit, know somewhat of "the things to come". When such have learned to make distinction of those scriptures which belong respectively to "the Jew, the Gentile and the Church of God", they often find themselves perplexed in their study of the Word by the variety of ways in which the apostles quote the Old Testament Scriptures. Our limits permit only a few hints as to some of the principles on which these are made.

It is of first importance to recognize applications of Old Testament Scripture which are founded in typical relation. Passages which were obviously written to, or of Israel, and which can only have their proper, that is their literal, fulfillment in them, are quoted, in the New Testament, on the principle that "they were our types". See 1 Cor. 10:6, 11. A private Israelite was the type of a believer simply as such; a priest was a type of a believer in privileged nearness of communion and worship; a Levite, of a Christian in service, and so forth. It need not then surprise us that passages spoken of or to Israel, or if prophetic, yet awaiting fulfillment in Israel, should often very fitly serve for the instruction of our souls, who are ourselves their anti-types.

In illustration of this principle let us take 2 Cor. 6:16; 7:1, where Paul by way of enforcing upon believers the rejection of the unequal yoke, groups together several passages from the ancient Scriptures, all pertaining to Israel, but which he adduces as directly addressed to saints in the present dispensation, expressly affirming that the promises they contain are ours. Let us glance at the several parts of this passage. He says to the Corinthian saints, and therefore to us, "Ye are the temple of the living God; as God hath said, 'I will dwell in them and walk in them; and I will be their God and they shall be My people'". This quotation is composed of more than one text of the Old Testament; in fact, it occurs, in whole or in part, at least nine times in the law and the prophets; but it is impossible to question either its primary application to Israel, or its ultimate fulfillment to that people. Israel is the chosen people of God among whom He will dwell on the earth; He is the God of Israel as He is not the God of any other nation, and they are His people above all the peoples of the earth. He dwelt among them, and these relations were sustained, for a brief period *in the past;* but we know from hundreds of passages and particularly from those which Paul had before his mind when making his quotations, that God will dwell among His people of Israel and be their God forever. Ezek. 37:26, 27. But that earthly people was a type of a heavenly people, whom God has determinately constituted His special heavenly temple, and not to be indwelt by a shekinah glory only, as in Israel, but to be indwelt by Himself through the Spirit. 1 Cor. 3:16; Eph. 2:22. Since, then, the promise to the type is to have its most marvelous realization in us, it is very suitable that it should be addressed to us. And most surely this is done without despoiling it of its final and literal fulfillment to Israel the type.

Further, Paul continues, as still quoting: "Wherefore come out from among them, and be ye separate, saith the Lord, and touch not the unclean thing".

This, like some other passages given as citations from the Old Testament seems to be the sense of many passages, rather than one verbatim. Still the principle on which it is cited is the same. Israel, on the ground of their high privilege, (God dwelling among them) was, and yet shall be called to marked separation from the nations, and that of the most literal kind. But in the past they were the type of a people called into separateness more real, if not so palpably marked; they were typical of us, who are not to "go out of the world", and who yet are to "keep ourselves unspotted from it"; not to get away to form a carnal community, but to be "*in* the world", though "not *of* the world". And thus every demand made upon Israel our type to maintain national separation, is not only an appropriate call to us to be separate, but was so designed of God, as is now made known to us by the Spirit who uses the word originally addressed to the type in speaking to us who were in His sight, portrayed in it. And yet, when the earthly and typical people shall again take their standing before God, these words will still apply to them, and be owned of their hearts. May we own them in this day of far more difficulty than theirs shall be then.

Once more, in this passage, the apostle quotes; "And I will receive you, and will be a Father unto you, and ye shall be My sons and daughters, saith the Lord Almighty." Israel was distinguished as God's family. See Jer. 31; Amos 3:1, 2, etc. But God has another, a heavenly family; one not only set in gracious relation to Him, in which He deals with them *as* a Father, but one which is, according to *new creation,* and real birth of God, "by the resurrection of Jesus Christ", composed of those whom He calls His brethren in the most real sense. This needs no proof; it is *the* truth of John 1:12, 13; 20:17; of Rom. 8, and John's Epistles. The relationship of Israel is only a type of this, real as their family standing is. And if the language addressed to them was appropriate it is still more appropriately ours; so the Holy Spirit assures us; so may we own it. *"Having, therefore, these promises,* dearly beloved, let us cleanse ourselves from all filthiness of the flesh and spirit, perfecting holiness in the fear of God".

There is another citation of Paul's which may serve, still further, to illustrate this principle, and which it may be important to notice as one which, more than others, seems to perplex the earnest student of prophecy. "But Jerusalem which is above is free, which is the mother of us all. For it is written, Rejoice, thou barren that bearest not; break forth and cry, thou that travailest not; for the desolate hath many more children than she that hath an husband" (Gal. 4:26, 27). This passage is quoted from Isa. 54:1, and is addressed to Jerusalem on earth; but Jerusalem on earth was a type of the heavenly Jerusalem, *our* mother city. The word of promise shall be fulfilled in all its literal force to the earthly Jerusalem: she and her children shall be delivered from their legal bondage and curse, and be set in the grace and glory of the millennial age.

But, when the Holy Spirit so spake to Jerusalem below He was in the same word, uttering that which divinely expressed the fruitfulness of the apparently barren Jerusalem above, and when calling the former to joy in God-given fruitfulness He was using words which He esteemed suitable wherewith to call His Church to joy in His grace to her. It is thus that God differs from man in His Word, as in all else. One has said: "Man needs many instruments to accomplish one end; God accomplishes many ends with one instrument". So we may well say, man's word admits of but one application; God's Word admits of many and all consistently.

We have left ourselves but little space to notice other principles. It may be useful, however, just to name one or two. One is, that passages which are not yet wholly fulfilled, are frequently quoted on account of some *partial* fulfillment. One instance of this kind is that contained in Peter's sermon on the day of Pentecost. Act 2:16, 21. Whether you read only the quotation, or study its original, it is clear enough that the apostle did not and could not mean that it was then fulfilled as a whole. But so much was fulfilled in the outpouring of the Spirit as to leave his hearers without excuse. Nothing on God's part was wanting to the ushering in of His day and Israel's blessing, however Israel's unbelief might prove the occasion for His gracious postponement of these.

Other prophetic passages, are quoted, not as being fulfilled, but only as *showing* and *enforcing* the mind of God. Quite a number of passages from the Old Testament are quoted in Romans 15:8, 12, not with the purpose of saying any thing about their fulfillment but to prove that the Lord Jesus sustains a certain official relation to the Jewish people—"Minister of the Circumcision"—and that too as necessary to the accomplishment of the divine purpose of mercy to the Gentiles. And occasion is incidentally taken to show that *our* present connection with Christ, as being in Him by faith, enables *us* to antedate the final fulfillment of the Scripture quoted (v. 13). This, our entering into the joy by anticipation, through the Spirit, would have been more clear to the reader had our translators used the word "hope" (v. 12) instead "trust"; for it is the same word as that twice so translated in the following verse.

Imperfect as this notice of so great a subject is, let us hope that it may help some of those who earnestly desire to know "the mind of the Spirit", to realize what doubtless they surely believe, namely, that "Whatsoever things were written aforetime were written for our learning, that we through patience and comfort of the Scriptures might have hope"; and, at the same time only confirm and deepen their conviction that the Lord God of Israel will perform to Israel all the mercy of which "He hath spoken by the mouth of His holy prophets, which have been since the world began".

C. Campbell (1864)

KNOWING CHRIST AFTER THE FLESH.

"WHEREFORE henceforth know we no man after the flesh: yea, though we have known Christ after the flesh, yet now henceforth know we Him no more." (2 Cor. 5:16).

To "know a man after the flesh" is to recognize his claims according to nature or according to fleshly distinctions. Peter knew men after the flesh when he withdrew from his Gentile brethren, fearing his brethren of the circumcision. To "know Christ after the flesh" is to recognize Him *only as the Jewish Messiah,* and to reject or to be ignorant of His Divine nature and glory as the Son of God. Those who were disposed to claim that they were heirs of the kingdom, saying, "we have Abraham to our fathers", were in a condition of soul in which they could only "know Christ after the flesh". Thus Paul may have known Him, but thus he knew Him now no more. Christ was indeed, "made of the seed of David according to the flesh"; but He has been demonstrated to be "the Son of God with power according to the Spirit of holiness, by the resurrection from the dead (Rom. 1:3, 4; 9:5). Paul knew Him now as the risen and exalted Son of God, in whose death he himself had died to sin and to curse (2 Cor. 5:14, 15). He rejoiced now "to know Him no more (no longer) after the flesh", but as the One who, having risen again, is glorified at God's right hand. When Christ died we died, and now we live unto Him who died for us and rose again. Henceforth we, as risen men, ignore old things, old claims, old distinctions—the principle of our recognition of men and things is wholly changed (v. 17). Knowing Christ as the risen and glorified Son of God, as the Head of the new creation, "all things have become new". We know Him now in all the blessedness and glory of partnership with Him. This is to know Him as He is set forth in the Epistle to the Ephesians. The vast importance which the apostle attached to this knowing Christ as *raised* from the dead, appears from his solemn charge to Timothy; "Remember that Jesus Christ, of the seed of David was raised from the dead according to my gospel" (2 Tim. 2: 8). Endurance, and disentanglement from the world as His soldiers, faithfulness as His servants, yea, everything that can honor Him, depends upon our taking up our place with Him who was raised from the dead. His death and resurrection have separated us from the world and from men in the flesh; and it is fitting that our judgement and recognition of all things should be in agreement with the fact that we are one with Him who was raised from the dead.

C. Campbell—1873

"IF ONLY."

"If only this trial were removed, how happy in the Lord I should be." Often such a thought has crossed the mind. But the underlying confidence in circumstances, rather than in Himself, is a mistake, dear fellow believer. If we think that we could please the Lord in other surroundings, either our present surroundings are sinful, in which case we should break the chain, OR we are complaining of the Lord's will. Trials are His messengers, in perfect love and wisdom by the time they reach us. Often we set our heart on "something," and wish for a "change," but the Lord would draw us to praise Him amid difficulties. If we are depending on things, we are all the while excusing our failures, while certain problems remain. Our Loving Heavenly Father knows what is best. The believer who will do more study, "if only" something else takes place, is often quite unfit to be entrusted with more time. The child of God who wants to put things straight, "if only" he can get clear of certain present chains, is often perpetuating these chains. If I determine to "give" to the Lord, money or time, when a little more "prospered," the Lord may lovingly withhold. The important privilege is to trust Him TODAY, and to act with faith's beautiful simplicity.

P. W. Heward.

(Continued from page 169.)

Timothy had duties to perform, highly important ones, yet his first responsibility was to see that he did not neglect *himself* —"take heed *unto thyself*" was God's admonition, *"and* unto the doctrine" or teaching came second. (1 Tim. 4:15). And *how* was he to "take heed" unto himself? The previous verse tells us: *"Meditate* upon these things; give thyself wholly to them; that thy profiting may appear to all." (1 Tim. 4:15). It is failure at this very point which has spoiled many a promising life. It was through neglecting this very word "Take heed *unto thyself*" which has resulted in many a servant of God becoming a "castaway", i. e. rejected from God's service. O how many would have to lament (if they were honest), "They made me the keeper of the vineyards; but mine own vineyard have I not kept" (Song of Solomon 1:6). And the first step toward an *unkept* "vineyard" is neglect of meditation, daily meditation upon the word*s* of God.

Meditation ought not to be an occasional, a spasmodic thing; it should be a daily habit. Said the Psalmist, "Mine eyes prevent the night watches, that I might *meditate* in Thy Word." (119:148): "prevent" means "anticipate". In this the Psalmist foreshadowed the Lord Jesus, for of Him it is said, "His delight is in the law of the Lord; and in His law doth He *meditate* day and night." (Psalm 1:2). It is very clear that the One in view here is the incarnate Son of God. *He* is the "Blessed" Man who "walked not in the counsel of the ungodly, nor stood in the way of sinners, nor sat in the seat of the scornful" (Psa. 1:1)—the past tense is used throughout. *He* it is that was the "Tree planted by the rivers of water," that brought forth His fruit in His season,; whose leaf also did not wither; and whatsoever He did prospered" v. 3. Of Adam's fallen race it is said, *"We all* do *fade* as a leaf" (Isa. 64:6), but of the blessed Man it is written, *"His leaf* also shall not fade"! How evident it is then that none other than the Christ of God is before us in this opening Psalm!

Of Christ it is recorded "His delight is in the law of the Lord; and in His law doth He *meditate* day and night." (Psa. 1:2). Note that the *order* here is the same as in the opening quotation—"His *delight* was in the law of the Lord, *and* in His law did He *meditate* day and night." It was because He "delighted" in the Scriptures that He *"meditated"* therein! How this *condemns* us! How this exposes the idleness and emptiness of our excuse that we have no time for meditation! The truth is not that we lack opportunity or occasion, but *heart.* When there is a real heart for the things of God, we shall *make* time for the study of the Scriptures and for meditation thereon. Who was busier than Christ! Who ever crowded more into such a short earthly life? Read Mark 6:21. The same thing is repeated in Mark 3:20. Ah, *He* was the one, supremely, who could say, "I have esteemed the words of His mouth more than My necessary food." (Job 23:12). If we wish to know how much was crowded into the life of God's perfect Servant read John 21:25. And yet *He* not only delighted in the law of the Lord, but He also *meditated* therein "day and night". Again we say, How this reproves us! It is because we are so occupied with earthly things that our affection is so little *set* upon things above.

What a blessed promise is that in Joshua 1:8: "This book shall not depart out of thy mouth; but thou shalt *meditate* therein day and night, that thou mayest observe to do according to all that is written therein: for *then* thou shalt make thy way prosperous, and then thou shalt have good success." Mark the little word *"then".* It is only if we *meditate* in the Book of God, day and night, and observe to do according to *all* that is written therein, that God guarantees to make our way prosperous, and give us good success. There, then, is the explanation of so much of our leanness and failure.

How much we lose through *not* meditating upon God's Word day and night! It is because we meditate so infrequently that we have so little "respect" unto God's ways (Psa. 119:15). It is because God's testimonies are so seldom before us that we have so little "understanding" (Psa. 119:99). It is because of our neglect of this spiritual exercise that our hearts are so cold and joyless. Said the Psalmist, "My *meditation* of Him shall be sweet". (104:34). May God so endear His blessed Word to our souls that with increasing measure both writer and reader may be able to truthfully say, "O how love I Thy law! it is my meditation *all the day."*

Arthur W. Pink.

VOL. III SEPTEMBER, 1924 No. 9

STUDIES in the SCRIPTURES

"Search the Scriptures" John 5:39.

Arthur W. Pink, Publisher & Editor,
227 N. Creighton St., Philadelphia, Pa.

Price: 10 cents per copy; $1.00 per year. Foreign $1.00 per year.

"God is Light . . . . God is Love" (1 John 1:5; 4:8)

These expressions tell us what God is in Himself: they describe the Divine nature. Closely corresponding, though not exactly parallel, is that word about the Lord Jesus—"full of grace and truth" (1 John 1:14). It was in the incarnate Son that the light and love of Deity were manifested.

A careful study of Gen. 3 will show that when the Serpent attacked Eve he denied both of these qualities or perfections of the Divine nature. "Yea, hath God said?"—has He *refused* you something which is desirable and needful; then He cannot *love* you! "Ye shall not surely die," was the denial that God is *light:* Satan accused God of lying.

Now when God deals with a soul He acts both as light and love. There is a marvellous co-mingling of the two. The "light" searches the conscience and shows man what he is. The "love" penetrates to the heart and shows him what God is. There are many, many striking illustrations or examples of this. When the "light" shone on the prodigal he saw himself as an awful sinner, unworthy to be called a son; yet, notwithstanding, he made at once for the Father! Not only had his conscience been searched, his heart had been won.

We often speak of a work of grace in the sinner. Truly it is that, but more; really, it is **God**—as light and as love—*revealed* to that soul. Witness the case of the woman in Luke 7. The light shone upon her and showed her how dreadfully vile she was, nevertheless, "she loved much." While the *light* broke her heart, so that she washed the Saviour's feet with her tears (v. 38), *love* drew her to Him, and brought her *to* His feet!

How paradoxical is what we read of in Luke 5:8—"Depart from me; for I am a sinful man, O Lord." Yet the paradox is explained by what we have said above. That "light" revealed to Peter that he was a sinful man. Had "light" been alone he had fled in terror. But it was not alone: "love" accompanied it. Therefore Peter did not flee, but fell at Christ's feet!

The dying thief illustrates the same thing. Hear his words to his fellow-transgressor: "Dost thou not *fear* God, seeing thou art in the same condemnation, and we indeed *justly?*" (Luke 23:40). How evident that the *light* of God had penetrated and searched his conscience. But was that all? No; had it been so, he had died in abject despair. "Lord remember *me*" he cries. *Love* drew him to the Redeemer. Eternal praises be unto Him who is Light and Love.

Arthur W. Pink.

IMPORTANT NOTICES

All new subscriptions will be dated back to January, 1924.

Set of twelve issues for **1922**, unbound, **$1.00**. Bound, **$1.50**.

Set of twelve issues for **1923**, unbound, **$1.00**. Bound **$1.50**.

Note: We cannot break a set or now supply any **single** 1923 issues.

Subscription Price: **$1.00** per year to any address in the world. Single copies **10 cents.**

Change of Address: Please notify me promptly of any change of address, and be certain to give both old and new addresses.

Non-subscribers receiving this Magazine regularly will understand their subscription has been entered by a friend.

Copies lost in the mail duplicated only if we are notified promptly.

Entered as second-class matter December 15th, 1923, at the post office at Philadelphia, Pa., under Act of March 3rd, 1879.

CONTENTS

JOHN'S GOSPEL.

33. Christ and the Blind Beggar, concluded: John 9:24-41.

The following is offered as an Analysis of the passage which is to be before us:—

1. The beggar challenged and his reply: vv. 24, 25.
2. The beggar cross-examined and his response: vv. 26, 27.
3. The beggar reviled: vv. 28, 29.
4. The beggar defeats his judges: vv. 30-33.
5. The beggar cast out by the Pharisees, sought out by Christ: vv. 34, 35.
6. The beggar worships Christ as the Son of God: vv. 36-38.
7. Christ's condemnation of the Pharisees: vv. 39-41.

We arrive now at the closing scenes in this inspired narrative of the Lord's dealings with the blind beggar and the consequent hostility of the Pharisees. In it there is much that is reprehensible, but much too that is praiseworthy. The enmity of the carnal mind is again exhibited to our view; while the blessed fruit of Divine grace is presented for our admiration. The wickedness of the Pharisees finds its climax in their excommunication of the beggar; the workings of grace in his heart reaches its culmination by bringing him to the feet of the Saviour as a devoted worshipper.

The passage before us records the persistent efforts of the Pharisees to shake the testimony of this one who had received his sight. Their blindness, their refusal to be influenced by the most convincing evidence, their enmity against the beggar's Benefactor, and their unjust and cruel treatment of him, vividly forecasts the treatment which the Lord Himself was shortly to receive at their hands. On the other hand, the fidelity of the beggar, his refusal to be intimidated by those in authority, his Divinely-given power to nonplus his judges, his being cast out of Judaism, and his place as a worshipper at the feet of the Son of God *on the outside,* anticipated what was to be exemplified again and again in the history of the Lord's disciples following His own apprehension.

"Then again called they the man that was blind, and said unto him, Give God the praise: we know that this man is a sinner" (v. 24). The one to whom sight had been so marvellously imparted had been removed from the court of the Sanhedrim while the examination of his parents had been going on. But he is now brought in before his judges again. The examination of his parents had signally failed either to produce any discrepancy between the statements of the parents and that of their son, or to bring out any fact to the discredit of Christ. A final effort was therefore made now to shake the testimony of the man himself.

"Then again called they the man that was blind, and said unto him, Give God the praise: we know that this man is a sinner". These shameless inquisitors pretended that during his absence they had discovered something to the utter discredit of the Lord Jesus. Things had come to light, so they feigned, which proved Him to be more than an ordinary bad character—such is the force of the Greek word here for "sinner", compare its usage in Luke 7:34, 37, 39; 15:2; 19:7. It is evident that the Sanhedrim would lead the beggar to believe that facts regarding his Benefactor had now come to their knowledge which showed He could not be the Divinely-directed author of his healing. Therefore, they now address him in a solemn formula, identical with that used by Joshua when arraigning Achan—see Josh. 7:19. They adjured him by the living God to tell the whole truth. They demanded that he foreswear himself, and join with them in some formal statement which was dishonoring to Christ. It was a desperate and blasphemous effort at intimidation.

"He answered and said, Whether He be a sinner or no, I know not: one thing I know, that, whereas I was blind, now I see" (v. 25). It is refreshing to turn for a moment from the unbelief and enmity of the Pharisees to mark the simplicity and honesty of this babe in Christ. The Latin Vulgate renders the first clause of this verse, "If He is a sinner I know not". The force of his utterance seems to be this: I do not believe that He is a sinner; I will not charge Him with being one; I refuse to unite with you in saying that He is. Clear it is that the contents of this verse must not be explained in a way so as to clash with what we have in v. 33, where the beggar owned that Christ was "of God". The proper way is to view it in the light of the previous verse. There we find the Pharisees adjuring him to join with them in denouncing Christ as a sinner. This the beggar flatly refused to do, and refused in such a way as to show that he declined to enter into a controversy with his judges about the character of Christ.

"Whether He be a sinner or no, I know not: one thing I know, that, whereas I was blind, now I see". This was tantamount to saying, 'Your charge against the person of Christ is altogether beside the point. You are examining me in connection with what Christ has *done for* me, therefore I refuse to turn aside and discuss His *person*'. The Pharisees were trying to change the issue, but the beggar would not be side-tracked. He held them to the indisputable fact that a miracle of mercy had been wrought upon him. Thereupon he boldly declared again what the Lord had done for him. That his eyes had been opened could not be gainsaid: all the arguments and attacks of the Pharisees could not shake him. Let us not only admire his fearlessness and truthfulness, but seek grace to emulate him.

"One thing I know, that, whereas I was blind, now I see". These are words which every born-again person can apply to himself. There are many things of which the young believer has little knowledge: there are many points in theology and prophecy upon which he has no light: but "one thing" he *does* know—he knows that the eyes of his understanding have been opened. He knows this because he has seen himself as a lost sinner, seen his imminent danger, seen the Divinely-appointed refuge from the wrath to come, seen the sufficiency of Christ to save him. Can a man repent and not know it? can he believe on the Lord Jesus Christ to the saving of his soul and not know it? can he pass from death unto life, be delivered from the power of darkness and translated into the kingdom of God's dear Son, and not know it? We do not believe it. The saints of God are a people that "know". They *know* Whom they have believed (2 Tim. 1:12). They *know* that their Redeemer liveth (Job 19:26). They *know* they have passed from death unto life (1 John 3:14). They *know* that all things work together for their good (Rom. 8:28). They *know* that when the Lord Jesus shall appear we shall be like Him (1 John 3:2). Christianity treats not of theories and hypotheses, but certainties and realities. Rest not, dear reader, till you can say, "One thing *I know*, that, whereas I was blind, now I see".

"Then said they to him again, What did He to thee? how opened He thine eyes?" (v. 26). Unable to get this man to deny the miracle which had been wrought upon him, unable to bring him to entertain an evil opinion of Christ, his judges inquire once more about the *manner* in which he had been healed. This inquiry of theirs was merely a repetition of their former question—see v. 15. It is evident that their object in repeating this query was the hope that he would vary in his account and thus give them grounds for discrediting his testimony. They were seeking to "shake his evidence": they hoped he would contradict himself.

"Then said they to him again, What did He to thee? how opened He thine eyes?". This illustrates again how that unbelief is occupied with the modus operandi rather than with the result itself. *How* you were brought to Christ—the secondary causes, where you were at the time, the instrument God employed—is of little moment. The one thing that matters is whether or not the Lord opened the sin-blinded eyes of your heart. Whether you were saved in the fields or in a church, whether you were on your knees at a "mourner's bench" or upon your back in bed, is a detail of very little value. Faith is occupied not with the manner in which you held out your hand to receive God's gift, but with Christ Himself! But unbelief is occupied with the "how" rather than with the "whom".

"He answered them, I have told you already, and ye did not hear: wherefore would ye hear it again? will ye also be His disciples?" (v. 27). With honest indignation he turns upon his unscrupulous inquisitors and refuses to waste time in repeating what he had already told them so simply and plainly. It is quite useless to discuss the things of God with those whose hearts are manifestly closed against Him. When such people continue pressing their frivolous or blasphemous inquiries, only one course remains open, and that is to answer a fool according to his folly, lest he be wise in his own conceit (Prov. 26: 5). This Divine admonition has puzzled some, because in the preceding verse we are told, "*Answer not* a fool according to his folly, lest thou also be like unto him". But the seeming contradiction is easily explained. When God says, "Answer not a fool according to his folly, lest thou also be like unto him", the meaning is, I must not answer a fool *in a foolish manner*, for this would make me a sharer of his folly. But when God says, "*Answer* a fool according to his folly, lest he be wise in his own conceit," the meaning is, that I must answer him in a way *to expose his folly*, lest he imagine that he has succeeded in propounding a question which is unanswerable. This is exactly what the beggar did here in the lesson: he answered in such a way as to make evident the folly and unbelief of his judges.

"Then they reviled him, and said, Thou art His disciple; but we are Moses' disciples" (v. 28). The word "reviled" is hardly strong enough to express the original. The Greek word signifies that the Pharisees hurled their anathemas against him by pronouncing him an execrable fellow. How true to life! Unable to fairly meet his challenge, unable to justify their course, they resort to villification. To have recourse to invectives is ever the last resort of a defeated opponent. Whenever you find men calling their opponents hard names it is a sure sign that their own cause has been defeated.

"They reviled him, and said, Thou art *His* disciple". The man of the world has little difficulty in locating a genuine "disciple" of Christ. This man had not formally avowed himself as such, yet the Pharisees had no difficulty in deciding that he *was* one. His whole demeanor was so different from the cringing servility which they were accustomed to receive from their own followers, and the wisdom with which he had replied to all their questions, stamped him plainly as one who had *learned* of the God-man. So it is today. Real Christians need no placards on their backs or buttons on their coat lapels in order to inform their fellows that they belong to the Lord Jesus. If I am walking as a child of light, men will soon exclaim, "Thou art *His* disciple". The Lord enable writer and reader to give as clear and ringing a testimony in our lives as this beggar did.

"But we are Moses' disciple". A lofty boast was this, but as baseless as haughty. The Lord had already told them, "Had ye believed Moses, ye would have believed Me: for he wrote of Me" (5:46). This too has its present-day application. Multitudes are seeking shelter behind high pretensions and honored names. Many there are who term themselves Calvinists that Calvin would be ashamed to own. Many call themselves Lutherans who neither manifest the faith nor emulate the works of the great Reformer. Many go under the name of Baptists to whom our Lord's forerunner would say, "Flee from the wrath to come" were he here in the flesh. And countless numbers claim to be Protestants who scarcely know what the term itself signifies. It is one thing to say "We are —— disciples", it is quite another to make demonstration of it.

"We know that God spake unto Moses" (v. 29). Such knowledge was purely intellectual, something which they venerated as a religious tradition handed down by their forebears; but it neither moved their hearts nor affected their lives. And *that* is the real test of a man's orthodoxy. An orthodox creed, intellectually apprehended,

In keeping with this, the Epistle of James is addressed to "the twelve tribes, which are scattered abroad" (1:1). So, the first Epistle of Peter is addressed to "the elect who are sojourners of the Dispersion" (1 Pet. 1:1, R. V.). And John also is writing *to* saved Israelites, but *for* saved Jews *and* saved Gentiles.

Some of the evidences that John *is* writing *to* saved Jews are as follows. (a) In the opening verse he says of Christ, "Which *we* have seen with *our* eyes . . . . and *our* hands have handled". How impossible it would have been for the Apostle Paul to have commenced any of *his* epistles to *Gentile* saints with such language!

(b) "Brethren, I write no new commandment unto you, but an old commandment which *ye* had *from the beginning*" (1 John 2:7). The "beginning" here referred to is the beginning of the public manifestation of Christ—in proof compare 1:1; 2:13, etc. Now these believers the apostle tells us, *had* the "old commandment" *from the beginning.* This was true of *Jewish* believers, but it was not true of *Gentile* believers.

(c) "I write unto you, fathers, because *ye have known* Him from the beginning" (2:13). Here, again, it is evident that it is *Jewish* believers that are in view.

(d) "Little children, it is the last time: and as ye *have heard* that Antichrist shall come, even now are there many antichrists; whereby we know that it is the last time. *They* went out from *us,* but they were not of us" (2:18, 19). These brethren to whom John wrote *had* "heard" from Christ Himself that Antichrist should come (see Matt. 24). The "many antichrists" whom John declares "went out *from us*" were all *Jews,* for during the first century none but a *Jew* posed as the Messiah. Therefore, when John says "He is the propitiation for *our* sins" he can only mean for the sins of *Jewish believers**.

In the fourth place, when John added, "And not for ours only, but also for *the whole world*", he signified that Christ was the propitiation for the sins of *Gentile* believers *too,* for, as previously shown, "the world" is a term *contrasted* from Israel. This interpretation is unequivocally established by a careful comparison of 1 John 2:2 with John 11:51, 52, which is a strictly parallel passage: "And this spake he not of himself: but being high priest that year, he prophesied that Jesus should die for that nation; And not for that nation only, but that also He should gather together in one the children of God that were scattered abroad". Here Caiaphas, under inspiration, made known *for whom* Jesus should "die". Notice now the correspondency of his prophecy with this declaration of John's:

"He is the propitiation for our (believing Israelites) sins".

"He prophesied that Jesus should die for that nation".

"And not for ours only".

"And not for that nation only".

"But also for the whole world"—

That is, Gentile believers scattered throughout the earth.

"He should gather together in one the children of God that were scattered abroad".

In the fifth place, the above interpretation is confirmed by the fact that no other is consistent or intelligible. If the "whole world" signifies the whole human race, then the first clause and the "also" in the second clause are absolutely meaningless. If Christ is the propitiation for *everybody,* it would be idle tautology to say, first, "He is the propitiation for *our* sins and *also* for everybody". There could be no "also" if He is the propitiation for the entire human family. Had the apostle meant to affirm that Christ *is* a universal propitiation he would have omitted the first clause of v. 2, and simply said, "He is the propitiation for the sins of the whole world".

In the sixth place, our definition of "the whole world" is in perfect accord with other passages in the New Testament. For example: "Whereof ye heard before in the word of the truth of the Gospel; which is come unto you, as it is in *all the world*" (Col. 1:5, 6). Does "all the world" here mean, absolutely and unqualifiedly, all mankind? Had all the human family heard the Gospel? No; the apostle's obvious meaning is that, the Gospel, instead

*It is true that many things in John's Epistle apply equally to believing Jews *and* believing Gentiles. Christ is the Advocate of the one, as much as of the other. The same may be said of many things in the Epistle of James which is also a *catholic,* or *general* epistle, though expressly addressed *to* the twelve tribes scattered abroad.

did he give sight to a blind man, nor did any of the prophets ever open the eyes of one born blind. *That* was something that only Christ did!

"If this man were not of God, he could do nothing". This beggar was now endowed with a wisdom to which these learned Pharisees were strangers. How often is this same principle illustrated in the Scriptures. The Hebrew lad from the dungeon, not the wise men of Egypt, was the one to interpret the dream of Pharaoh. Daniel, not the wise men of Babylon, deciphered the mysterious writing on the walls of Belshazzar's palace. Unlettered fisherman, not the scribes, were taken into the confidences of the Saviour. So here, a mouth and wisdom were given to this babe in Christ which the doctors of the Sanhedrim were unable to resist.

"If this man were not of God, he could do nothing". What a beautiful illustration is this of Prov. 4:18!—"But the path of the just is as the shining light, that shineth *more and more* unto the perfect day". First, this beggar had referred to his Benefactor as "a man that is called Jesus" (v. 11). Second, he had owned Him as "a prophet" (v. 17). And now he declares that Christ was a man "of God". There is also a lesson here pointed for us: as we walk according to the light we have, God gives us more. Here is the reason why so many of God's children are in the dark concerning much of His truth—they are not faithful to the light they *do* have. May God exercise both writer and reader about this so that we may earnestly seek from Him the grace which we so sorely need to make us faithful and true to all we have received of Him.

"They answered and said unto him, Thou wast altogether born in sins, and dost thou teach us?" (v. 34). Alas, how tragically does history repeat itself. These men were too arrogant to receive anything from this poor beggar. They were graduates from honored seats of learning, therefore was it far too much beneath their dignity to be instructed by this unsophisticated disciple of Christ. And how many a preacher there is today, who in his fancied superiority, scorns the help which ofttimes a member of his congregation could give him. Glorying in their seminary education, they cannot allow that an ignorant layman has light on the Scriptures which *they* do not possess. Let a Spirit-taught layman seek to show the average preacher "the way of the Lord more perfectly", and he must not be surprised if his pastor says—if not in so many words, plainly by his bearing and actions—"Dost *thou* teach us?". How marvellously pertinent is this two-thousand year old Book to our own times!

"And they cast him out" (v. 34). "Happy man! He had followed the light, in simplicity and sincerity. He had borne an honest testimony to the truth. His eyes had been opened to see and his lips to testify. It was no matter of wrong or wicked lewdness, but simple truth, and for that they cast him out. He had never troubled them in the days of his blindness and beggary. Perhaps some of them may have proudly and ostentatiously tossed him a trifling alms as they walked past, thus getting a name amongst their fellows for benevolence; but now this blind beggar had become a powerful witness. Words of truth now flowed from his lips—truth far too powerful and piercing for them to stand, so they 'thrust him out'. Happy, thrice happy man! Again we say, This was the brightest moment in his career. These men, though they knew it not, had done him a real service. They had thrust him out into the most honored position of identification with Christ as the despised and rejected One" (C. H. M.).

"And they cast him out". How cruelly and unjustly will religious professors treat the real people of God! When these Pharisees failed to intimidate this man they excommunicated him from the Jewish church. To an Israelite the dread of excommunication was second only to the fear of death: it cut him off from all the outward privileges of the commonwealth of Israel, and made him an object of scorn and derision. But all through the ages some of the faithful witnesses of Christ have met with similar or even worse treatment. Excommunication, persecution, imprisonment, torture, death, are the favorite weapons of ecclesiastical tyrants. Thus were the Waldenses treated; so Luther, Bunyan, Ridley, the Huguenots; and so, in great probability, will it be again in the near future.

"And they cast him out". Ah, Christian reader, if *you* did as this man you would know something of his experience. If you bore faithful testimony for *Christ* by lip and life; if you refused to walk arm-in-arm with the world, and lived here as a stranger and pilgrim; if you declined to follow the customs of the great religious crowd, and regulated your walk by the Word, *you* would be very *un*popular—perhaps the very thing that you most fear! You would be cut off from your former circle of friends, as not wanted; cut off because your ways condemned theirs. Yea, if true to God's Word you might be turned out of your church as an heretic or stirrer up of strife.

"Jesus heard that they had cast him out; and when He had found him, He said unto him, Dost thou believe on the Son of God?" (v. 35). This is indeed precious. No sooner had the Sanhedrim excommunicated the beggar than the Saviour sought him out. How true it is that those who honor God are honored by Him. Faithfully had this man walked according to his measure of light, now more is to be given him. Great is the compassion of Christ. He knew full well the weight of the trial which had fallen upon this newly-born soul, and He proved Himself "a very present Help in trouble". He cheered this man with gracious words. Yea, He revealed Himself more fully to him than to any other individual, save the Samaritan adulteress. He plainly avowed His deity: He presented Himself in His highest glory as "the Son of God".

"Jesus heard that they had cast him out; and when He had found him, He said unto him, Dost thou believe on the Son of God?" (v. 35). The connection between this and the previous verse should be carefully noted: the beggar was "cast out" *before* he knew Christ as the Son of God. The Nation as such denied this truth, and only the despised few on the *outside* of organized Judaism had it revealed to them. There is a message here greatly needed by many of the Lord's people today who are inside man-made systems where much of the truth of God is denied. True, if they are the Lord's, they are saved; but not to them will Christ *reveal Himself*, while they continue in a position which is dishonoring to Him. It is the Holy Spirit's office to take of the things of Christ and to show them unto us. But while we are identified with and lend our support to that which *grieves* Him, He will not delight our souls with revelations of the excellencies of our Saviour. Nowhere in Scripture has God promised to honor those who *dis*honor Him. God is very jealous of the honor of His Son, and He withholds many spiritual blessings from those who fellowship that which is an offence to Him. On the outside *with Christ* is infinitely preferable to being on the inside with worldly professors who know Him not. The time is already arrived when many of God's people are compelled to choose between these two alternatives. Far better to be "cast out" because of faithfulness to Christ, or to "come out" (2 Cor. 6:17) because of others' unfaithfulness to Christ, than to remain in the Laodicean system which is yet to be "spued out" by Christ (Rev. 3:16). Whatever loss may be entailed by leaving unscriptural and worldly churches, it will be more than compensated by the Lord. It was so with this beggar.

He answered and said, Who is He, Lord, that I might believe on Him?" (v. 36). It is indeed beautiful to mark the spirit of this man in the presence of Christ. Before the Sanhedrim he was bold as a lion, but before the Son of God he is meek and lowly. Here he is seen addressing Him as "Lord". These graces, seemingly so conflicting, are ever found together. Wherever there is uncompromising boldness toward men, there is humility before God: it is the God-fearing man who is fearless before the Lord's enemies.

"And Jesus said unto him, Thou hast both seen Him, and it is He that talketh with thee" (v. 37). This is one of the four instances in this Gospel where the Lord Jesus expressly declared His Divine Sonship. In 5:25 He foretold that "the dead shall hear the voice of *the Son of God:* and they that hear shall live". Here He says "Dost thou believe on *the Son of God?* . . . . it is He that talketh with thee". In 10:36 He asked "Say ye of Him, whom the Father hath sanctified, and sent into the world, Thou blasphemest; because I said, I am *the Son of God?*". In 11:4 He told His disciples "This sickness is not unto death, but to the glory of God, that *the Son of God* might be glorified thereby". Nowhere in the other Gospels does He explicitly affirm that He was the Son of God. John's record of each of these four utterances of the Saviour is in beautiful accord with the special theme and design of his Gospel.

"And he said, Lord, I believe. And he worshiped Him" (v. 38). What a lovely climax is this in the spiritual history of the blind beggar! How it illustrates the fact that when God begins a good work He continues and completes it. All through the sacred narrative here the experiences of this man exemplify the history of each soul that is saved by grace. At first, seen in his wretchedness and helplessness: sought out by the Lord: pointed to that which speaks of the Word: made the subject of the supernatural operation of God: sight imparted. Then given opportunity to testify to his acquaintances of the merciful work which had been wrought upon him. Severely tested by the Lord's enemies, he, nevertheless, witnessed a good confession. Denied the support of his parents, he is cast back the more upon God. Arraigned by the religious authorities, and boldly answering them according to the light he had, more was given him. Confounding his opponents, he is reviled by them. Confessing that Christ was of God, he is cast out of the religious systems of his day. Now sought out by the Saviour, he is taught the excellency of His person which results in him taking his place at the feet of the Son of God as a devoted worshipper. And here, most suitably, the Holy Spirit leaves him, for it is *there* he will be forever—a worshipper *in the presence of* the One who did so much for him. Truly naught but Divine wisdom could have combined with this historical narrative an accurate portrayal of the representative experiences of an elect soul.

"And Jesus said, For judgment I am come into this world, that they which see not might see; and that they which see might be made blind" (v. 39). "This is deeply solemn! 'For judgment I am come into this world'. How is this? Did He not come to seek and to save that which was lost? So He Himself tells us (Luke 19:10), why then speak of 'judgment'? The meaning is simply this: the *object* of His mission was salvation; the *moral effect* of His life was judgment. He judged no one, and yet He judged every one.

"It is well to see this effect of the character and life of Christ down here. He was the light of the world, and this light acted in a double way. It convicted and converted, it judged and it saved. Furthermore it dazzled, by its heavenly brightness, all those who thought they saw; while, at the same time, it lightened all those who really felt their moral and spiritual blindness. He came not to judge, but to save; and yet when come, He judged every man, and put every man to the test. He was different from all around Him, as light in the midst of darkness; and yet He saved all who accepted the judgment and took their true place.

"The same thing is observed when we contemplate the cross of our Lord Jesus Christ. 'For the preaching of the cross is to them that perish foolishness; but unto us which are saved it is the power of God. . . . . But we preach Christ crucified, unto the Jews a stumbling-block, and unto the Greeks foolishness; but unto them which are called, both Jews and Greeks, Christ the power of God, and the wisdom of God' (1 Cor. 1:18, 23, 24). Looked at from a human point of view, the cross presented a spectacle of weakness and foolishness. But, looked at from a Divine point of view, it was the exhibition of power and wisdom. 'The Jew', looking at the cross through the hazy medium of traditionary religion stumbled over it; and 'the Greek', looking at it from the fancied heights of philosophy, despised it as a contemptible thing. But the faith of a poor sinner, looking at the cross from the depths of conscious guilt and need, found in it a Divine answer to every question, a Divine supply for every need. The death of Christ, like His life, judged every man, and yet it saves all those who accept the judgment and take their true place before God" (C. H. M.). This was all announced from the beginning: "And Simeon blessed them, and said unto Mary his mother, Behold, this child is set for the fall *and* rising again of many in Israel" (Luke 2:34).

"And some of the Pharisees which were with Him heard these words, and said unto Him, Are we blind also? Jesus said unto them, If ye were blind, ye should have no sin: but now ye say, We see; therefore your sin remaineth" (vv. 40, 41). This receives explanation in John 15:22-24: "If I had not come and spoken unto them, they had not had sin: but now they have no cloke (excuse) for their sin. He that hateth Me hateth My Father also. If I had not done among them the works which none other man did, they had not had sin: but now have they both seen and hated both Me and My Father". The simple meaning then of these words of Christ to the Pharisees is this: If you were sensible of your blindness and really desired light, if you would take this place before Me, salvation would be yours and no condemnation would rest upon you. But because of your pride and self-sufficiency, because you refuse to acknowledge your undone condition, your guilt remaineth. How strikingly this confirms our interpretation of v. 6 and the sequel. The blind man made to see illustrates those who accept God's verdict of man's lost condition; the self-righteous Pharisees who refused to bow to the Lord's decision that they were "condemned already" (3:18), continued in their blindness and sin.

In addition to the perfect picture which the contents of this chapter supply of the natural condition, the salvation, and the history of one of God's elect, we also find here a most remarkable prophetic foreshadowment of the future of Israel, and to the consideration of this we now turn.

John 8 closes with Christ passing out of the Temple, unseen by the Jews. This typifies the Lord turning away from Israel at the close of His first advent, with them unable to discern the glory of His presence, and their House left unto them desolate. In this sad condition they have remained for nineteen long centuries. John 9 portrays the Lord *resuming* His dealings with His covenant people during the Tribulation period, and brings before us *the godly Jewish Remnant.* It anticipates the time of "Jacob's trouble" when "darkness shall cover the earth and gross darkness the people". It shows us the pitiable moral condition of the Remnant when the Lord shall visit them in mercy. It tells us of His mode of procedure when He shall bring them out of darkness into His marvellous light.

1. The blind man pictures the spiritual blindness of Israel. 2. The fact that he was blind from his birth, emphasizes how blind Israel have been all through their long history. 3. The question of the disciples concerning the *cause* of his blindness (v. 2) illustrates the inability of the world to explain Israel's spiritual condition. 4. The statement of Christ—"he was born blind . . . . that the works of God should be made manifest in him" (v. 3)—signifies that God had a profound but good reason for judicially blinding Israel, see Rom. 11:7-11. 5. The words of Christ in v. 4 "the night cometh" suggest the yet greater darkness which will come upon Israel ere the Lord removes (2 Cor. 3:15) the veil from their hearts. 6. The anointing of the blind man with clay and the bidding him go wash in the Pool of Siloam, shows us it is through the written Word that the Remnant shall yet come to know the Lowly One of Nazareth as the Sent One of the Father, the Messiah of Israel (cf Matt. 24:15, Dan. 12:10). 7. The obedience of the blind beggar (v. 7) shows that the Remnant *will* turn to the written Word. 8. That he received his sight in such an unheard-of way teaches that the illumination of the Remnant will be a miracle of Divine grace. 9. That the blind man was a beggar emphasizes the *poverty* of the Remnant—cut off as they will be from buying and selling (Rev. 13:17). 10. The surprise of the neighbors and their questioning of the beggar (vv. 8-10) points to the suspicions of the unbelieving portion of Israel against the Remnant. 11. The confession and ignorance of the beggar (vv. 11, 12) foreshadow the imperfect understanding which the Remnant will have of spiritual things. 12. The arraignment of the beggar before the Sanhedrim (vv. 13-33) suggests the yet future testings of the Remnant at the hands of their ungodly brethren. 13. The excommunication (v. 34) points to the persecution of the Remnant by the Antichrist. 14. The Lord seeking him out and revealing Himself as the Son of God pictures the second advent of Christ and His gracious dealings with the faithful Remnant. 15. The words of Christ in v. 39 will receive a more literal and complete application and fulfillment at the second advent than they did at the first.

Let the interested student study carefully the following questions on John 10:1-10:—

1. What is the "sheepfold" of v. 1?
2. What is "the door" (v. 2) by which the shepherd enters the sheepfold?
3. Who is "the porter" of v. 3?
4. Leadeth the sheep "out of" *what?* (v. 3).
5. What is the meaning of "I am the door of the sheep" (v. 7)?
6. What entirely different line of thought does "I am the door" of v. 9 give us?
7. Who is "the thief" of v. 10?

—Arthur W. Pink.

N. B. These expositions on John's Gospel are being published separately in book form. The first Vol (375 pages) can now be obtained from the Editor for $1.50 postpaid. Invaluable for preachers and S. S. teachers.

GLEANINGS IN EXODUS.

9. Jehovah's Covenant: Ex. 6.

Our previous chapter closed with Moses turning unto the Lord in most unbecoming petulancy and daring to call into question the Divine dispensations. The Lord's servant had been severely tried: he had gone in unto Pharaoh and demanded him to let the Hebrews go so that they might sacrifice unto their God. But not only had the haughty king refused this most reasonable request, he had also given orders that his slaves should have additional burdens laid upon them. The officers of the children of Israel had interviewed Pharaoh, but had been mocked for their pains. They then sought out Moses and Aaron and called down a curse upon them, for this we take it is the force of their words, "The Lord look upon you, and *judge;* because ye have made our savor to be abhorred in the eyes of Pharaoh" (5:21). Moses then "returned unto the Lord" and poured out his heart before Him. The reference seems to be to the fact that he had committed his way unto the Lord before he had interviewed the king, and now after his seeming failure, he turns again to the throne of grace.

The discouragements which Moses had met with were more than flesh could stand, and he asks Jehovah, "Wherefore hast Thou so evil entreated this people? and why is it that Thou hast sent me?", ending by saying "For since I came to Pharaoh to speak in Thy name, he hath done evil to this people; neither hast Thou delivered Thy people at all." Moses was right in tracing the afflictions which had come upon the Hebrews to God Himself, for all things are "of Him and through Him" (Rom. 11:36); but He certainly did wrong in questioning the Almighty and in murmuring against the outworking of His counsels. But it is written, "He knoweth our frame; He remembereth that we are dust", and again, "The Lord is merciful and gracious, slow to anger, and plenteous in mercy" (Psa. 103:14, 8). Fully was that manifested on this occasion. Instead of chastising His servant, the Lord encouraged him; instead of setting him aside, He renewed his commission; instead of slaying him, He revealed Himself in all His grace.

"Then the Lord said unto Moses, Now shalt thou see what I will do to Pharaoh: for with a strong hand shall he let them go, and with a strong hand shall he drive them out of his land" (v. 1). The Lord made no answer to Moses' impatient queries but re-affirmed His immutable purpose. The defiant Pharaoh might insist I will *not* let Israel go (5:2), but the Most High declared that he *should,* nay, that he would even drive them out of his land. There was no need for Moses to be alarmed or even discouraged: the counsel of God *would* stand, and He would do *all* His pleasure (Isa. 46:10). This is a sure resting-place for the heart of every servant, and for every Christian too. No matter how much the Enemy may roar and rage against us, he is quite unable to thwart the Almighty—"There is *no* wisdom, nor understanding, nor counsel against the Lord" (Prov. 21:30). This is the high ground that the Lord first took in encouraging the drooping heart of His despondent servant. Said He, "With a strong hand *shall* he (Pharaoh) let them go, and with a strong hand *shall* he drive them out of the land". There were no "ifs" or "perhaps" about it. The event was absolutely certain, and therefore invincibly necessary, because Deity had eternally decreed it. Similar is the assurance God gives His servants today: "So shall My word be that goeth forth out of My mouth. It *shall not* return unto Me void, but *it shall* accomplish that which I please, and *it shall* prosper in the thing whereto I sent it" (Isa. 55:11).

It is also to be noted that in strengthening the heart of His servant the Lord pointed Moses forward *to the goal*—"Now shalt thou see what I will do to Pharaoh". There was much that was to happen in between, but the Lord passes over all that would intervene, and speaks of the last act in the great drama which was just opening. He bids Moses consider the successful outcome, when the great enemy of His people should be vanquished. There is much for us to learn in this. We defeat ourselves by being occupied with the difficulties of the way. God has made known to us the triumphant outcome of good over evil, and instead of being harassed by the fiery darts which the Evil One now hurls against us, we ought to rest on the assuring promise that "the God of peace *shall* bruise Satan under your feet shortly" (Rom. 16:20).

"And God spake unto Moses, and said unto him, I am the Lord: And I appeared unto Abraham, and unto Isaac, and unto Jacob by the name of God Almighty, but by My name JEHOVAH was I not known to them" (vv. 2, 3). These verses have been a sore puzzle to many Bible students. "Jehovah" is the very name which is translated "the Lord" scores of times in Genesis. Abraham knew "the name" of Jehovah, for we read that he "called on *the name of the Lord*" (Gen. 13:4). Of Isaac, too, we read, "And he built an altar there, and called upon *the name of the Lord*" (Gen. 26:25). And of Jacob we read of him praying, "O God of my father Abraham, and God of my father Isaac, *the Lord* which saidst unto me, Return unto thy country, and to thy kindred, and I will deal well with thee, I am not worthy of the least of all Thy mercies", etc. (Gen. 32:9, 10). It is, therefore, clear that the patriarchs *were* acquainted with God's name of Jehovah. What, then, did the Almighty mean when He said here to Moses, "by My name JEHOVAH was I *not known* to them"? It is clear that this is one of many scriptures which cannot be interpreted absolutely, but must be understood relatively. We believe that the key to the difficulty is supplied by what follows, where the Lord says, "I have also established My *covenant* with them".

The Divine-titles are a most important subject of study for they are inseparably connected with a sound interpretation of the Scriptures. Elohim and Jehovah are not employed loosely on the pages of Holy Writ. Each has a definite significance, and the distinction is carefully preserved. Elohim (God) is the name which speaks of the Creator and Governor of His creatures. Jehovah (the Lord) is His title as connected with His people by *covenant* relationship. It is this which explains the verses now before us. Abraham, Isaac, and Jacob were acquainted with the Jehovistic title, but they had no experimental acquaintance with all that it stood for. God has entered into a "covenant" with them, but, as Heb. 11:13 tells us, "These all died in faith, *not having received* the promises". But now the time had drawn nigh when the Lord was about to fulfill His covenant engagement and Israel would witness the faithfulness, the power, and the deliverance which His covenant-name implied. God was about to manifest Himself as the faithful *performer* of His word, and as such the descendants of the patriarchs would *know* Him in a way their fathers had not.

"And I have also established My covenant with them, to give them the land of Canaan, the land of your pilgrimage, wherein they were strangers" (v. 4). Here then was the next encouragement which the Lord set before His fearful servant. He reminds him how that He had *established* His covenant with the patriarchs, to whom He had pledged Himself to give them the land of Canaan. How impossible was it, then, that the Egyptians should continue to hold them as slaves. How foolish and how wicked Moses' unbelieving fears. If Jehovah had established a covenant it *must be* fulfilled, for that covenant was an unconditional one. A similar ground of assurance have we to stay our hearts upon in the midst of the trials of this scene. Says our God, "Incline your ear, and come unto Me: hear, and your soul shall live; and I will make an everlasting covenant with you, even the sure mercies of David", i. e. "the Beloved" (Isa. 55:3)—note how the apostle Paul quotes from this very verse in his sermon at Antioch (Acts 13:34). There are those who say that the saints of this dispensation are not related to God by covenant bonds, but this is a mistake. They are, as Heb. 13:20 makes abundantly clear, for there we read of "the blood of the *everlasting* covenant". Before time began the Father entered into a covenant with our glorious Head, (cf Titus 1:2) and that covenant was sealed by blood. And just as the covenant God made with Abraham guaranteed "an heritage" (Ex. 6:8), so the covenant which the Father made with the Son (cf Heb. 7:22) has an inheritance connected with it, even an inheritance which is "incorruptible and undefiled, and that fadeth not away, reserved in heaven" for us (1 Pet. 1:4). May our faith so lay hold upon it that even now we shall live in the enjoyment of it.

"And I have also heard the groaning of the children of Israel, whom the Egyptians keep in bondage; and I have remembered My covenant" (v. 5). Additional comfort was this for God's servant. Moses had told the Lord how that since he had spoken to Pharaoh he had done evil to the Hebrews (5:23). The Lord needed not to be told this. He was neither oblivious nor indifferent to their sufferings. *He* had heard the "groaning of the children of Israel". And, fellow-Christian, thou who art tried beyond endurance, the Lord has heard thy groanings; every tear has been recorded in His book (Psa. 56:8); and what is more, He *sympathizes* with thee, and is *touched* with the feeling of thine infirmities (Heb. 4:15). Though there may be much of unfathomable mystery as to *why* God permits our "groanings", nevertheless, here is much cause for comfort —*God* "hears them"!

"Wherefore say unto the children of Israel, I am the Lord, and (1) *I will bring you* out from under the burdens of the Egyptians, and (2) *I will rid you* out of their bondage, and (3) *I will redeem you* with a stretched out arm, and with great judgments: And (4) *I will take you* to Me for a people, and (5) *I will be to you* a God: and ye shall know that I am the Lord your God, which bringeth you out from under the burdens of the Egyptians. And (6) *I will bring you* in unto the land, concerning the which I did sware to give it to Abraham, to Isaac, and to Jacob; and (7) *I will give it you* for an heritage: I am the Lord" (vv. 6-8). Observe that these verses commence with the word "Therefore" which looks back to the closing words of the previous verse: "I have *remembered My covenant*". The contents of these verses, then, grow out of the covenant which the Lord made with Abraham, and confirmed to Isaac and Jacob. It will be noted that in them the Lord makes seven promises, prefacing them with the declaration "I will".

In Gen. 17 we find recorded another seven "I will's" of Jehovah: "And (1) *I will make thee* exceeding fruitful, and (2) *I will make nations of thee,* and kings shall come out of thee. And (3) *I will establish* My covenant between Me and thee and thy seed after thee in their generations for an everlasting covenant, to be a God unto thee, and to thy seed after thee. And (4) *I will give* unto thee, and to thy seed after thee, the land wherein thou art a stranger, all the land of Canaan, for an everlasting possession; and (5) *I will be their God* . . . . and (6) *I will establish* My covenant with him for an everlasting covenant, and with his seed after him. But My covenant (7) *I will establish* with Isaac" (vv. 6, 7, 8, 19, 21). With these passages should be compared the "new covenant" recorded in Jer. 31:33, 34. Here, too, we find *seven promises from the Lord:* "After those days, saith the Lord, (1) I will put My law in their inward parts, and (2) write it in their hearts; and (3) will be their God, and (4) they shall be My people. And (5) they shall teach no more every man his neighbour, and every man his brother, saying, Know the Lord: for they shall all know Me, from the least of them unto the greatest of them, saith the Lord: and (6) I will forgive their iniquity, and (7) I will remember their sin no more". Let us now consider, though briefly, each of the seven promises which God here made to Moses:

(1) "I will bring you out from under the burdens of the Egyptians. This speaks of God's gracious purpose. His people were groaning beneath the intolerable demands made by their cruel taskmasters. For many weary years they had toiled under a load which was becoming more and more unendurable. Was there then no eye to pity, no hand to deliver? There was. The covenant God of their fathers had promised that at the end of four hundred years' affliction they should be emancipated (see Gen. 15:13-16). And now the time had come for God to make good His word. He declares, therefore, that He *will* bring them out from under their burdens. So, too, this is what God does for each of His elect today. The first thing of which we are conscious in the application of salvation to our souls is deliverance from the burdens of our lost condition, of conscious guilt, of our unpreparedness to die.

(2). "And I will rid you out of their bondage". As another has said, "This was something far more than mere relief from their burdens: it was a complete severance from their previous condition. A slave may be sold to a kind master, and his burden removed, but he would remain a slave still; and Israel's burdens might have been removed, and they still remain captives in Egypt. But this was not God's way. He would rid them clean out of the land of bondage. Instead of them toiling in the kilns of Egypt, He would have them out in the wilderness, in communion with Himself. This is still God's way. The one who receives Christ as his Saviour is delivered from the bondage of sin, of Satan, of the fear of death".

(3) "I will redeem you". To redeem means to purchase and set free. Evan-

gelical redemption is by price and by power. The price is the shedding of atoning blood: the power, the putting forth of an all-mighty hand. It was thus God would deliver Israel. First the slaying of the paschal lamb and then the display of Divine omnipotence at the Red Sea. Thus it is with the Christian: we have been redeemed, not with corruptible things as silver and gold, but with the precious blood of the Lamb (1 Pet. 1:18, 19); we are not our own, but "bought with a price" (1 Cor. 6:20). Almighty power was put forth at our regeneration, for we read of "the exceeding greatness of His power to us-ward who believe" (Eph. 1:19).

(4) "And I will take you to Me for a people". For Israel this meant that henceforth they, as a nation, would occupy an unique relationship to God: they would be His peculiar treasure, the objects of His special care and favor. Marvellous indeed was it that the great Jehovah should own as *His* a down-trodden nation of slaves. But He did! And on what ground? The ground of *redemption*. He had redeemed them *unto Himself*. The same blessed truth is set forth on the pages of the New Testament. We, too, belong to God as His peculiar people. Utterly unfit and unworthy in ourselves, yet precious in the sight of God for *Christ's* sake—"Accepted in the Beloved".

(5) "And I will be to you a God". How fully was this exemplified in the sequel! Who but *God* could have made a way through the Sea so that His redeemed passed over dry shod; and who but He could have caused that Sea to turn back and drown the hosts of the Egyptians? Who but *God* could have guided His people through that trackless desert by a pillar of cloud by day and a pillar of fire by night? Who but *God* could have quenched their thirst from a rock, and fed a hungry multitude for forty years in a wilderness? Truly He was a "God" unto Israel. And such is His promise to us: "I will be *their God*, and they shall be My people" (2 Cor. 6:16). And daily does every believer receive a performance of this promise. None but *God* could preserve to the end a people so ignorant, so weak, so fickle, so sinful, as each of us is.

(6) "I will bring you in unto the land". Not only did the Lord bring His people out of the land of bondage, but He also brought them into the land which He had sworn to give unto Abraham, Isaac, and Jacob. It is true that many, many individuals fell in the wilderness, but nevertheless, the *nation* of Israel God brought into Canaan. They were not consumed by the Amalekites (Ex. 17). Sihon, king of the Amorites, and Og king of Bashan, might "gather all his people together" and go out against Israel (Num. 21), and Balak might hire Balaam to curse the people of God, but the Lord speedily brought to naught their efforts. God *did* bring Israel into the promised land. And He *will* bring each of us, His blood-bought ones, safely to Heaven. The world, the flesh, and the Devil may array themselves against us, but not a single sheep of Christ shall perish.

(7) "And I will give it you for an heritage". This was the goal toward which God was working. All was done in order that they might *enjoy* that which He had promised to their fathers. Not yet has this been completely fulfilled. It is in the Millennium that Israel shall enter fully into their covenanted portion. In like manner, the full enjoyment of our heritage is future. Already we have "the *earnest* of our inheritance" (Eph. 1:14); soon shall we have the portion itself. And note this is a *gift*. It is not by works of merit, but solely by sovereign grace.

"Note how these seven 'I will's' are enclosed in a framework of Divine assurance. They are prefaced and summed up with the words, 'I am Jehovah'. As if God would fix their eyes on Himself as the Almighty One, before He utters a single 'I will'; and then, at the close of the unfolding of His wondrous purposes, He would still keep their eye on the fact that it is He, *the Almighty*, who speaks. Every doubt and difficulty would vanish if faith but grasped the fact that it is 'I am' who has pledged His word. Faith remembers with calm and unruffled peace, in spite of circumstances, that 'With God all things are possible'" (Dr. Brookes).

"And Moses spake so unto the children of Israel; but they hearkened not unto Moses for anguish of spirit, and for cruel bondage" (v. 9). How this exposes the heart of the unregenerate! The condition of the poor sinner is vividly portrayed in these earlier chapters of Exodus. First, groaning in bondage; second, ignorant of that grace which God had in store for them; and now unable to value the precious promises of Jehovah. While we are in bondage to sin and Satan, even the promises of God fail to bring us any relief. Relief never comes until the shed blood of the "lamb" is applied! It was so with Israel; it is equally true with men today.

"And the Lord spake unto Moses, saying, Go in, speak unto Pharaoh king of Egypt, that he let the children of Israel go out of his land" (vv. 10, 11). Moses was not to be afraid of the haughty monarch, but must interview him again, and speak plainly and boldly, not in a supplicatory, but in an authoritative way, in the name of the King of kings. This was before the Lord proceeded to punish Pharaoh for his disobedience, that His judgments might appear more manifestly just and right.

"And Moses spake before the Lord, saying, Behold, the children of Israel have not hearkened unto me; how then shall Pharaoh hear me, who am of uncircumcised lips?" (v. 12). Why did Moses refer again to the impediment in his speech? Was it because that he thought the Lord ought to have removed it, and because he was dissatisfied at having Aaron to act as his mouthpiece?

"And the Lord spake unto Moses and unto Aaron and gave them a charge unto the children of Israel, and unto Pharaoh king of Egypt, to bring the children of Israel out of the land of Egypt" (v. 13). The Lord having previously answered this same objection of Moses (4:10-12) makes no further reply to it now, but instead, gives him a charge unto his own people—to comfort and direct them how they should conduct themselves in the interval before God's deliverance arrived—and unto Pharaoh.

From vv. 14-37 we have a list of genealogies brought in here to show us the ancestors of God's ambassadors, and also to demonstrate the Lord's sovereign grace. Only those genealogies of the Hebrews are here given which concern the offspring of the first three of Jacob's sons. The sons of Reuben and of Simeon are named, but not from either of them did God select the honored instrument of deliverance. The order of grace is not the order of nature. It was from the tribe of Levi which, along with Simeon, lay under *a curse* (Gen. 49:5-7) that God called Moses and Aaron. And here too we may see grace exemplified by giving Moses, the younger, the precedency over Aaron, the senior. It should also be noted that Levi was the *third* son of Jacob—the number which ever speaks of *resurrection*—that the deliverer came!

The last three verses of our chapter connect the narrative with v. 10. As another has said, "The objection of Moses in v. 30 is evidently the same as in v. 12. And yet there is a reason for its repetition. In chapters 3 and 4 Moses makes five difficulties in reply to the Lord; here in the 6th, are two, making *seven* altogether. It was therefore the *complete* exhibition of the weakness and unbelief of Moses. How it magnifies the grace and goodness of the Lord; for in His presence man is revealed; it also brings to light what *He* is in all the perfections of His grace, love, mercy and truth" (E. Dennett).

—Arthur W. Pink.

"FAITH COMETH BY HEARING, AND HEARING BY THE WORD OF GOD."

The inspired and the uninspired records of Christian experience, and the history of the Church from the day of Pentecost to the present hour, amply illustrate the tendency of the human heart, even after the Gospel has been known in its power, to obscure the grace of God, and to set up some legal claim to His favor. So that there has been no age in which the Church has not needed, and there is no believer who does not need, the exhortation: "Stand fast, therefore, in the liberty wherewith Christ has made you free, and be not entangled again with the yoke of bondage."

We do not, at present, propose to trace the almost imperceptible steps in which this tendency is developed, silent and unsuspected in its operation, till we are left to ask those who have begun in the spirit, Are you now made perfect in the flesh? or to ask, amid the unsatisfied strivings of souls that once knew the peace of God, Where is then the blessedness ye spake of? or to ask, amidst the coldness and langour of those who did run well, Who did hinder you that ye should not obey the truth? Only we would in love warn the brethren that the tendency is constant, the influences are subtle, the arguments plausible, by which emancipated souls may be entangled again. When the legal spirit has been driven from all its attempts to make good the justification of a sinner, it takes refuge in attempts to accomplish a sanctification in the flesh; when forced to yield the question of salvation by grace, it will seek to accomplish its end by raising a new question about the evidences of faith; and draw the ensnared soul into a fluctuating confidence in attainments, fruits, and experience, instead of a simple resting in Christ, and an assured belief of the testimony of God.

The operation of this tendency is most distinctly seen in the history of Christianity or of the Church at large. One who had profoundly and lovingly studied that history, says of it; "Periods of revival and decay succeed each other; iniquity abounds, and is allowed to proceed apparently unchecked, as if God had forsaken the earth. A few remain faithful and testify for Jehovah. All in vain. Then suddenly God steps in, makes bare His arm, does His own work, puts aside the instrument, manifests special grace, and reaps special glory to His name. Again barrenness prevails, and desolation covers the land. Then He opens the windows of heaven, and the swollen torrents rush along the valleys, diffusing life on every side. Such are His dealings with the children of men, and such the plan on which the kingdom of grace is administered, having, like that of nature, its seasons and fluctuations, its winters and its spring, its droughts and its floods, all to show forth more clearly God Himself as the doer of the whole, to sink the creature and exalt the Creator, that thus man may not mistake the hand by whose pressure the tide rises, from whose invisible but resistless influence every ripple takes its form and course. All is God, and God is all; man is the mere subject or spectator of the change."

There is a blessing in the recognition of the divine sovereignty and grace in the revivals, whether on a larger or smaller scale, by which, from age to age, the sad history of decay is illuminated; and doubtless, in the time, manner, and instruments of these revivals, it is most distinctly seen that God is all. But it is not the less observable that every revival is to be traced to a fresh presentation of the simple truth of the Gospel, as every succeeding decay is but the gradual obscuring of that truth under which we have described as operating so stealthily and steadily to entangle the individual believer in the yoke of bondage.

It is difficult to form an impartial and dispassionate judgment of the age in which we live. Each individual sphere of observation is limited, and so many personal and local considerations influence his view even of that, that we need to be very cautious in the expressions of our convictions regarding the religious condition of a whole country, and still more of Christendom. Of unblushing malignity, of the openly anti-evangelical party who, in our day, prostitute the name of Christianity, we need not to hesitate to speak. It is blatant, unscrupulous, and undisguised; and, sustained by the amplest resources of talent, literary culture, and worldly influences. It courts notoriety, and exults in the alarm its inroads excite among timid adherents of what it has pronounced an antiquated and obsolete creed. Its exultations is one of the many proofs of the feebleness and declension of the so-called evangelical party; and we do not fear the charge of censoriousness from that party themselves, when we express the conviction that the teaching of the pulpit and the faith of the pew are spoiled through philosophy and vain deceit, after the tradition of men, after the rudiments of the world, and not after Christ. They are a small minority who rejoice in the faith once for all delivered to the saints, who stand unqualifiedly committed to the Apostle's position, "Being justified by faith, we have peace with God through our Lord Jesus Christ, by whom also we have access by faith into this grace wherein we stand, and rejoice in hope of the glory of God."

Even if the conviction here expressed should happily be proved to be erroneous, we should find a sufficient reason in the perils of the individual believer for returning again and again to the statement and illustration of the fundamental doctrine of our most holy faith. Nor will the doctrine of the Cross and its story ever become tiresome by re-iteration to those who know them best. The attention of our readers is once more invited to the Gospel which God has given to be preached and to be believed, as it stands contrasted with the human systems and speculations which have usurped its name and its place. If, haply, among our readers there are any who have been deceiving themselves by a mere form of godliness, or by making "a fair show in the flesh;" or who are resting in a lifeless assent to an orthodox creed, and the lifeless observances of a hereditary religion, or in frames, and feelings, and a Christless experience; or who, against convictions of the truth, are striving vainly to find peace in these things, their attention is especially invited to the message of God's grace, which, while it exposes their delusion, reveals to them a salvation resting upon the immutable certainties of the Word of Jehovah.

The Scriptures contain no plainer testimony against any of the abominations of the flesh than against its religiousness. The most striking example of religiousness of the flesh may be found among the Jews, because that which they professed had the living God for its avowed object, and His law for its avowed rule and warrant. Paul, in expressing the most Christlike solicitude for their salvation bears them record "that they have a zeal of God". Even their hostility to the Gospel was in their own eyes a becoming devotion to "the church of their fathers". Paul had been conscientious in persecuting the followers of Christ, verily thinking that he did God service; and they, perhaps, like Paul, could claim, that touching the law they were blameless, while they did many things against the name of Jesus.

Many among us, who are accounted very religious, would do well to remember that the condemnation of the Jews was not their indifference to religion, for they had a zeal of God; nor reckless disregard of the law of God, for they went about to establish their own righteousness; nor was it, ultimately, their cruel persecution of the Church, for Paul, who was a blasphemer, a persecutor, and injurious, had obtained mercy; nor was it even that they had crucified the Holy and Just One, for many who had shared in the guilt of that awful crime received the remission of sins and the gift of the Holy Ghost. But it was that "they, being ignorant of God's righteousness, and going about to establish their own righteousness, have not submitted themselves to the righteousness of God."

"Ignorant!" And may it be asked, were they condemned for their ignorance? If there were but one remedy for a deadly disease, ignorance of that remedy would be fatal. But this is not precisely the condition of those among whom Jesus had taught and suffered, and to whom repentance and remission of sins had been preached in His name. Theirs was rather the position of one who, in an obstinate attachment to his own opinion, or through blind prejudice against the physician who administers the remedy, remained wilfully ignorant of its healing efficacy. Their ears were dull of hearing, and their eyes they had closed, lest at any time they should hear with their ears, and understand with their hearts, and be converted, and God should heal them. Their condemnation on account of their practical ignorance of the righteousness of God, when coupled with the admission of their zeal of God, should sound an alarm in the ears of many Christless religionists among us, whose zeal is only a more resolute rejection of the righteousness of God.

They did, as such religionists must do, go about to establish their own righteousness. Under the law of God, in all its length and breadth, they had the hardihood to present their duties and services, their religiousness, as a ground of acceptance with God, and as the basis of their peace. It would be hard to determine whether such an attempt to vindicate themselves, betrayed more clearly an insulting conception of God and His law, or an insolent conceit of their own character. It certainly revealed a most hardened insensibility, and their guilt was fearfully aggravated by the attempted self-vindication. But the damning wickedness of the attempt will be best seen in view of the righteousness of God, to which they refused submission.

"The righteousness of God," in the passages quoted, does not refer to righteousness as an attribute of the nature of God, but to that which God has set forth as the ground of justification to believers; "for Christ is the end of the law for righteousness to every one that believeth." To end the law or a commandment is a Scriptural expression for fulfilling it. Thus Paul opposes "ending the law" to "transgressing the law," and James says: "If ye end or fulfil the royal law, according to the Scriptures, ye do well." It is not said merely that Christ ends or fulfils the law, but emphatically, and to mark the completeness of His work, He is said to be *"the end* of the law." A law is fulfilled by obedience to its requirements; or, in case of disobedience, by the endurance of its penalty. After man had broken the law, it could be fulfilled only by the endurance of its curse. Left to himself, the sinner could never be aught else but condemned, and the wrath of God must abide upon him, under a sentence for ever in force, and never to be exhausted or set aside. When Christ took the sinner's place, sinless Himself, He was made sin for us. After a life of unbroken obedience, in which He fulfilled all righteousness, He came to the cross spotless, and put away sin by the sacrifice of Himself, He endured and exhausted the sentence, and satisfied every demand of justice. "He was made under the law, that He might redeem them that are under the law, that we might receive the adoption of sons." "He redeemed us from the curse of the law by being made a curse for us." All that was due to our sins He endured, that all the perfection of His obedience might be accounted to us. "He was made *sin* for us that we might be made *the righteousness of God* in Him." "Christ is the end of the law for righteousness to every one that believeth."

In all this we have limited ourselves to a simple statement of the doctrine of Scripture, restraining every expression of horror at the demerits of sin and thus expiated, of satisfaction with the work of Christ, of admiration of the love of God. But, "Behold, what manner of love the Father hath bestowed on us, that we might be called the sons of God." We are lost in wonder at that love when we consider that it is the love of God, glorious in holiness, fearful in praises, doing wonders, to whom our sin is infinitely abhorrent—whose goodness we despised, whose justice we outraged, and against whose honor we raised an insolent and puny rebellion. We are lost in wonder at that love when we think that it was bestowed on thankless worms of the dust—the vile and undone, dead in trespasses and sins. "Herein is love, not that we loved God, but that He loved us." We are lost in wonder at that love, when we think of its aims, which was not to shorten or alleviate our misery, nor merely to remove the curse, but to make us the righteousness of God in Christ—that we might be called sons of God, and if sons, then heirs, heirs of God and joint heirs with Christ. But most of all, that love is wonderful when we think of the means by which it accomplishes its object. Man is a sinner—the law is broken, and who shall fulfil it? "The curse" stands between us and the favor of God, and who can bear our sin and put it away? The most exalted creature under the curse of Almightiness would wither into eternal agony or nothingness, and who dares travel up beyond all creature existence to find a victim of insulted justice? Listen to the love of God exulting in its own triumph: "Deliver from going down to the pit, I have found a ransom." He gave His only-begotten and well-beloved, and did not spare Him; He put our cup of wrath into the hands of the Man that was His fellow, nor could it pass from Him till He could say, "IT IS FINISHED;" and now behold: *"Christ is the end of the law for righteousness to every one that believeth."*

The final ground of Israel's condemnation was not the enormous guilt of their sins, culminating in the crucifixion of the Prince of Life; for the blood which they shed could cleanse even the guilt of shedding it; and the grace of the Saviour was displayed in His charge to His apostles, that in preaching the remission of sins in His name, they should begin at Jerusalem, among those who had done the awful deed. But this is the condemnation, that, after all this, they went about to establish their own righteousness, and did not submit themselves to the righteousness of God. And it is thus also among the hearers of the Gospel now. They would regard it as sheer insanity to claim that their obedience has been sinless. But there may be many an attempt to escape submission to the righteousness of God as resolute as that of the Jews, rendered only more insulting under the stolen name of Christianity. Jewish unbelief could perpetrate no more heinous rejection of Christ, than is done every day by men who base a hope of eternal life on duties, prayers, frames, and feelings; zeal for a church, the observance of forms, an excited enthusiasm, a supercilious orthodoxy, and alleged evidences and marks of regeneration. The man who is loudest in boasting of these, may have to take his first lesson in the Gospel, and learn to count all things but dross, that he may win Christ, and be found in Him, not having his own righteousness by doing, but God's righteousness by believing.

We are shut up to one ground of acceptance, and that, the righteousness of God. And if any one asks, How may I occupy that ground? what must I do? we have an answer in the statement: "Christ is the end of the law for righteousness to *every one that believeth.*" If "to every one that believeth," then the answer to that question is, BELIEVE. But in the tenth chapter of Romans, from which we have quoted, the Apostle gives a more expanded answer.

I. HE TELLS US WHAT WE MUST NOT DO.

"Say not in thine heart, Who shall ascend into heaven? that is, to bring Christ down from above." God has already sent His Son to be a propitiation for our sin, and He is the door by which, if any man enter in, he shall have life. The proud thought must at once be abandoned that a man may climb to heaven by his own virtues, or win favor by services, ceremonies, tears, and prayers, or that he can contribute the weight of a feather to the purchase-price of redemption. It might seem that no heart could be presumptuous enough to ask, Who shall ascend into heaven? but it was what the Jews were in effect demanding, when they denied Christ. And this is what men are still doing, when they act as though they were left to persuade God by their entreaties, or bribe Him by their vows, and exhort eternal life from Him while they discredit the finished work of Christ. And yet professed churches, instead of pointing them to the Lamb of God, join their efforts, as though by tumultuous clamor they could bring down peace and pardon from on high.

"Neither say in thine heart, Who shall descend into the deep? That is to bring up Christ again from the dead." The resurrection of Christ was the final and formal declaration of God that His sacrifice is accepted, and that nothing remains to be done in order to the acceptance of the chief of sinners who believes. But men still seem to think that they must become worthy to receive grace, must prepare themselves to believe that the testimony of God is true, and must do some great work before they come to Christ. The Apostle teaches that all such attempts are vain as the attempt to scale the walls of heaven, or to unbar the portals of the tomb. Christ's work *is* finished, He is risen, and he that believeth on Him is justified from all things.

II. HE TELLS US WHAT THE GOSPEL SAYS.

"But what saith it? the Word is nigh thee even in thy mouth and in thy heart; that is, the Word of faith that we preach, that if thou wilt confess with thy mouth the Lord Jesus, and shalt believe in thine heart that God raised Him from the dead, thou shalt be saved." Here we have an explicit statement of the way of our individual salvation. It is not a great *work* to be done, but a *Word* to be believed, and that Word not a lofty and abstruse mystery but a Word nigh us, knocking in simplicity at the heart for entrance, and at the lips for utterance. All toilsome endeavors and costly sacrifices, all proud attempts to scale what is lofty and fathom what is profound, are arrested. Men are not summoned to go forth to establish their own righteousness, dragging a heavy burden of guilt, but are called in their helplessness *to submit* themselves to the righteousness of God. Before the arduousness of the former, a wretched man might groan out, "I cannot;" but the only negative that can be returned to the latter is: "I will not." There is all the difference between a gift to be received, and an impossibility to be accomplished.

The Word to be believed is that which the Apostles preached. There is a singular delusion on this point in the minds of men. In dealing with any other testimony, the only question regarding it would be, Is it true? and its credibility would be determined by the character of the witness. But in this case there is a disposition to make it depend upon the character of those to whom it is addressed; and men look into themselves for some warrant for believing it, or some proof that it is true. Let us rather ask the question, Who is the witness? Paul says it is "the Word of faith which we preach." But he was an apostle or ambassador of Christ, preaching not his own word, but the Word of Him that sent him—a point which he is everywhere careful to keep before his hearers. "And I brethren," he says to the saints at Corinth, "when I came unto you, came not with excellency of speech or wisdom, declaring unto you *the testimony of*

God." It is thus with them all. The gospel which they preached is the wisdom of God and the power of God—the same now as when they first preached it. It did not depend upon them for its authority, even among those to whom they personally addressed it; as Paul says to the Thessalonians: "When ye received *the Word of God* which ye heard of us, ye received it not as the word of men, but as it is in truth the *Word of God.*" So also in the conclusion of his argument in Rom. 10 he says: "Faith cometh by hearing, and hearing *by the Word of God.*" The truth is, that the subject of this testimony is such that could be received on no other authority but God's. In infinite condescension He becomes the witness of the grace which He has provided on the cross. The message of life is from God Himself. This is the divine certainty of our trust; "If we receive the witness of men, the witness of God is greater." But on the other hand, in what a light does this place the neglectors and rejectors of the Gospel. "He that despiseth, despiseth not man but God;" or as John places the matter in a yet more startling light: "He that believeth not, hath made God a liar."

Having, then, distinctly before us, that it is *the Word of God,* let us listen to the message: *"That if thou shalt confess with thy mouth the Lord Jesus, and shalt believe in thine heart that God raised Him from the dead, thou shalt be saved."* This is no general statement, no vague and indefinite proposition, but an emphatic address to a person, most explicit in its terms, and most positive in its conclusion. Who is the person thus addressed? Evidently, from the connection in which it stands, it had been addressed to those Israelites whose unbelief Paul laments; yet not to them collectively, but individually. But it is not limited to individuals of that race, as Paul shows in a subsequent verse: "For the Scripture saith, Whosoever believeth on Him shall not be ashamed. For there is no difference between the Jew and the Greek." And everywhere this message is represented as sent to all nations and to every creature, to men as men, or rather to men as sinners, to every sinner who hears it—to you reader! Thou art the man. Lay hold on this precious Word of God TO THEE." If *thou* shalt confess with *thy* mouth the Lord Jesus, and shalt believe in *thine* heart that God raised Him from the dead, *thou shalt be saved.*" There is no question as to what you are or might have been, only it is certain that you are a sinner needing salvation; there is no preparation to make or preliminaries to be settled, and no stipulation as to the future. But here is an assurance to you upon the Word of God, and you are this instant placed under the responsibility of receiving or denying the Word of God.

In regard to the matter of this precious message, it might seem unnecessary to say that the confession intended is but the utterance of the belief specified, and that the belief intended is such an energetic conviction as would seek utterance in such a confession. The fact that God raised Jesus from the dead is the final and formal proof that the work of Christ is complete, and His sacrifice for sin accepted; and that God hath made that same Jesus whom they crucified, both Lord and Christ. The belief of this fact, and the confession of His Lordship implies a conviction that Christ is the end of the law for righteousness to every one that believeth, and the message itself is but another form of the very Gospel which Paul preached in the prison at Philippi: "Believe on the Lord Jesus Christ, and thou shalt be saved."

The constant tendency of the human heart is to get away from the simplicity of the Gospel, and many of the professed preachers of it seem afraid to commit themselves to the unqualified grace of this word of God. They have displayed great ingenuity in forcing upon the message itself some qualification; as, for example, by laying a certain stress upon "confession" in this passage, as though that term might include some great and meritorious work, or sanction the validity of some ceremonial observance, as the ground of the sinner's acceptance with God. When these assumptions are met by the express testimony of the Spirit, "For with the heart man believeth unto righteousness," then one of the most plausible disguises of the simplicity of the Gospel, and to many earnest souls one of the most perplexing perversions of it is found in an attempted distinction between "believing with the heart" and "believing with the head", and a consequent discussion of "the kinds of faith," which throws the whole question of salvation into endless uncertainty.

Perhaps it may be proper to notice that in the language of Scripture and the usage of the Hebrews, there does not appear to be the distinction which we make between the head as the supposed seat of the understanding, and the heart as the supposed seat of the emotions and affections. The heart is spoken of as the seat of both, and every reader of the Bible must be able to recall the instances in which the word "heart" occurs, where, according to our use of language, "mind" is meant. Evidently, so far as the recognition of the truth or falsehood of testimony, or the reception or rejection of an assurance are concerned, it is an act of what we call the mind. The heart, in our sense of it, with its affections, passions, and prejudices, may indeed do much to blind the understanding to the perception of the truth; and the truth believed may indeed exercise a great influence over the affections and emotions. But after all, there is but one act of the mind which we call believing, and that is a simple assent to the truth of the testimony. When the Apostle says, "With *the heart* man believeth unto righteousness, and with *the mouth* confession is made unto salvation," he is not contrasting "belief with *the heart,*" and "belief with *the head,*" but is placing *believing* as an internal act in contrast with *confession* as an external act, and thus he places in the strongest light the precious Gospel truth that our justification rests upon no work or merit of ours. "With the heart man *believeth* unto righteousness." Even our confession is excluded from the ground of our acceptance; it is of faith that it may be by grace. Assuredly, if the truth is believed, confession will follow; but justification precedes the confession, for Christ is the end of the law for righteousness to every one that *believeth.* He that believeth is justified from all things.

Teachers of religion speak of a "belief of the head" as distinguished from a "belief of the heart", and bewilder anxious souls with their discussions of the different kinds of faith; but the truth is that what they style "belief of the head" *is no faith at all;*—the Gospel, the Word of God, the testimony of God concerning His Son; is not believed in any sense. A man educated in a so-called Christian land, may be acquainted with the facts of the mission, life, death, and resurrection of Jesus of Nazareth, and may acknowledge their credibility in the same way as he believes the facts of the life and character of any historical personage. He may acknowledge the validity of what are called the evidences of Christianity. He may have an extensive and accurate acquaintance with the doctrines and duties inculcated in the Scripture. He may have a strong attachment to some system of doctrines as held by some school or embodied in the creed of some church, and he may discuss with warmth all questions of ecclesiastical polity, ordinances, and discipline, but the Gospel is not in these, and the devils perhaps believe as much as he does. When he says that he believes on the Lord Jesus Christ, he does not and will not even pretend that he has abandoned every other claim and refuge, and simply relies on Christ as the end of the law for righteousness to him, and as able to save to the uttermost. When he professes to acknowledge that God so loved the world that He sent His only-begotten Son into the world, that whosoever believeth on Him should not perish, but have everlasting life, he would never for a moment think of saying with the Apostle "We know and believe the love God hath to us." The Gospel, the word of faith, is not a mere statement of facts or system of doctrine, but a direct personal message from God to the hearer, assuring him that believing on the Lord Jesus Christ he is saved, justified from all things, made a son of God, and a joint heir with Christ. But this Word of God such a man never for a moment pretends to believe; for while he professes to believe on Jesus Christ, if you ask him if he is saved, justified, sanctified, if he is born of God and has eternal life, he will not say, at all events, he does not believe, that he *is,* and thus he takes direct issue with God, who says in the Gospel: "Believe on the Lord Jesus Christ and thou *shalt* be saved." Such men do not receive what God says, but in the solemn language of the Apostle, they make Him a liar.

There are, alas! multitudes who deceive themselves and others regarding their standing before God, but they do not deceive themselves by a simple reliance on Christ and by taking God at His Word. One fertile source of self-deception is found in the teaching of those who are afraid to commit themselves to the bald simplicity of the Gospel, and have attempted to guard the approaches to the cross by certain preparatory exercises. They have, in the views of conversion which they propagate, virtually substituted the anguish of the sinner's remorse for the sufferings of Christ for us, penitential tears for atoning blood, and vows and promises and self-dedication for the righteousness of God which is by faith. Then they have collected certain marks and evidences of regeneration and send the distracted sinner to examine himself for these as the ground of his peace and rejoicing. It is here that men deceive themselves—when they cherish a hope of salvation on the ground of the anguish they endured, the tears they shed, the prayers they offered, the resolutions they formed, the vows they recorded, and all the varied emotions which followed, making up what they call a Christian experience.

There are other and grosser forms of self-deception, but this is the most subtle and the most ensnaring to those who are in earnest about the salvation of their souls. Past all these conceits of man, however countenanced by venerated names, we appeal to the Word of God, the Word of eternal life, and warn those whose confidence comes short of it, that whatever a man may have felt or experienced, may have vowed and done, in whatever position he is found—weeping, praying, vowing, or giving himself to God, at the confessional, the font, or the altar, in the pulpit or the pew—"he that believeth not God, hath made Him a liar, because he believeth not the record that God gave of His Son."

The Gospel meets the sinner just as he is, guilty and helpless. It sets Christ before him, and says: "Believe and live." Nothing of the sinner's own can enter at all into the grounds of his justification. With the heart man believeth unto righteousness. Righteousness involves salvation, including sonship, eternal life, glory—in short, all that the believer is, and has in Christ, just as guilt and condemnation involved all the ruin from which Christ came to deliver us. This salvation the grace of God presents in its completeness to our faith. It is certain the faith will be followed by confession. And so it is added: "With the mouth confession is made unto salvation." But confession does not enter into the grounds of salvation. When the Lord stood by the grave of Lazarus and cried with a loud voice, Lazarus, come forth, and he that was dead came forth, his issuing from the tomb was in no sense the source or cause of life, and the act by which he entered into the enjoyment of life, which he owed to the Word of Omnipotence.

Yes, and no less is the Gospel the wisdom of God and the power of God unto salvation to every one that believeth. Nothing less than the Word of God could pacify a guilty conscience, or quicken the soul dead in trespasses and sins, or give eternal life to those who by nature were children of wrath, even as others. This faith does not stand in the wisdom of men, but in the power of God. It is the belief of a Word which borrows nothing from human reason or authority, but which comes in its own inherent majesty as the Word of God. There is no difference in this respect between the faith of the poor blind lace-knitter, who knew, and knew no more, her Bible true, and that of the most learned theologian, who, beyond all systems and speculations, believes on the only-begotten Son of God. He indeed may have sifted the evidences of Christianity, and found them at every point impregnable against the assaults of infidelity. But his faith does not rest on these. It rests just where hers does, on the Word of God in its own inherent demonstration of its truth, so irresistible and absolute to the sage and the peasant alike, that you could sooner shake their confidence in their own existence than persuade them that the Gospel is not true and divine, or that they, believing it, can ever be put to shame.

If it be asked, Why then do not all hearers believe it? we ask in reply: Why does not a man see when he closes his eyes? That is no proof that the sun does not shine. Paul says: "If our gospel be hid, it is hid to them that are lost, in whom the god of this world hath blinded the minds of them that believe not, lest the light of the glorious Gospel of Christ, who is the image of God, should shine unto them." And it is thus wherever the Gospel is preached to those who reject it.

But while we would bear witness to an unbelieving world of their guilt in rejecting the testimony of God, we cannot forbear to exhort those who occupy the preacher's place to see to it that it is *the Gospel*, the Word of God, the message of God, to the sinner, that they preach. Preach it fearlessly, believingly, unqualifiedly, in all the personal directness of its address, in all the unconditional certainty of its assurance, in all the unfettered freeness of its grace; preach the Gospel itself, and not your own construction of it; preach it as God's Word, and not your own, as a message which it is your part faithfully to deliver without any control over its terms or any responsibility for its consequences. It is God's Word now, living and fresh as in its first utterance, and the Spirit of God, still present with it, gives it the living might of a present and pervading omnipotence as truly as when He spoke and all things stood fast. You are nothing; God is all. But what a privilege is yours, and what an errand to a perishing world. And of those who are really engaged in it, how well may it be said: "How beautiful are the feet of them that preach the gospel of peace and bring glad tidings of good things."

(Waymarks in the Wilderness)

WAITING UPON GOD.

"And thou shalt know that I am the Lord: for they shall not be ashamed that wait for ME" Isa. 49:23).

Thirty years ago, before "the Lord called me to wander from my father's house" and from my native place, I put my mark upon this passage in Isaiah—"I am the Lord: they shall not be ashamed that *wait* for ME". Of the many books I now possess, the Bible that bears that mark is the only one of them all that belonged to me at that time. It now lies before me; and I find that, although the hair which was then dark as night, has meanwhile become "a sable silvered", the ink which marked this text has grown into intensity of blackness as the time advanced, corresponding with and in fact recording, the growing intensity of the conviction, that "they shall not be ashamed that wait for Me". I believed it then; but I *know* it now; and I can write *probatum est,* with my whole heart, over against the symbol which that mark is to me, of my ancient faith.

"They shall not be ashamed that wait for Me". Looking back through the long period that has passed since I set my mark to these words—a period which forms the best and brightest, as well as the most trying and conflicting of all men's lives—it is a joy to be able to say: "I have waited for Thee, and have not been ashamed." Under many perilous circumstances, in many most trying scenes, amid faintings within and fears without, and under sorrows that rend the heart, and troubles that crush it down, I have waited for Thee; and, lo, I stand this day as one not ashamed.

Old scholars and divines were wont to write or paint up in their studies some favorite sentence from the sages of old, or some chosen text of Scripture. Those inclined to follow this custom could not do better than write up this one word, *"Wait"*. It is but a monosyllable; but it is fuller of meaning than any other word in the language, and it is applicable to all ages, and to all circumstances. At the first slight view, merely to "wait", seems so simple a thing, as scarcely entitled to be called a grace; and yet larger promises are made to it than to any other grace, except to faith; and hardly, indeed, with that exception, for the grace of "waiting" is part of the grace of faith,—is a form of faith, —is, as some would describe it, an effect of faith; or, more strictly, one of its most fruitful manifestations.

Great and singular is the honor which God has set upon patient waiting for Him. Man, seeing not as God sees, sets higher values upon his fellows' active works—the bright deeds of days or hours. God values these also; but He does not assign them the same pre-eminence as man does; He does not allow them any pre-eminence over that constant and long-enduring struggle with the risings of the natural mind, which is evinced in long and steady waiting under all discouragements for Him—in the assured conviction that He will come at last for deliverance and protection, although His chariot wheels are so long in moving.

It requires but little reflection to perceive that the Lord's judgment in this matter is better than man's. *Active* virtue brings present reward with it. Apart from the encouraging applause it obtains from some—more or fewer—it is attended with a pleasureable excitation of spirits, in the mere sense of action, as well as in the hopes and aspirations connected with it. There is nothing of this in mere patient waiting—day after day, through long years perhaps, and it may be in dust and ashes—until the Lord shall *manifest* toward us His love, His sympathy, His care. But to rest thus in the assured conviction that He *will* do so—to do Him the credit of believing that nothing less than this is His intention towards us—is a tribute rendered by faith to His honor, which He holds in most high esteem, and which He does most abundantly recompense; and this it needs. For it is a quality of the Christian character—much less one which God only can truly understand —which finds little encouragement but from Him, and which receives less than any other the outer sustainment of man's admiration and approval.

It is also eminently conducive to the completion of Christian character in its peculiar qualities, to nourish that habit of constant looking to the Lord, of constant dependence on Him, of vital faith in Him, of constant readiness for Him—which is far more precious in His sight than all the gold, frankincense, and myrrh, of which men could make oblation to Him. It is, therefore, no marvel, that this passive form is that chiefly, both for their soul's good and for His own honor, in which God has in all ages seen fit to exercise His servants—from ancient Abraham down to the youngest son of Abraham's faith. Let us take comfort and encouragement from these most true things.

Art thou plunged deep into troubles from which the hand of man will not or cannot save thee? or does thy soul lie in the deep waters, from which no strength of man can draw thee forth?. *"Wait* on the Lord; He will save thee" (Prov. 20:22); and cry to Him, "Thou art the God of my salvation: on Thee do I wait all the day" (Ps. 25:5).

Is thy good evil spoken of among men; and thy name cast forth as evil among those who once delighted in thee; but who now seek to lay thine honor in the dust?. Fear not. All will be right anon. Thy Vindicator lives, and will ere long bring thee forth in white robes, free from all the stains that men strove to cast upon thee. Remember that thy Lord suffered all this, and much more, for thee. Remember "The Lord is a God of judgment: blessed are all they that *wait* for Him" (Isa. 30:18).

There are two bitter enemies of man's true life—the world without him, and the world within him—the world in his heart. The conflict is sometimes terrible, and thou dost sometimes feel as one left without strength, and thy hands fail, and thy heart grows faint. What is this *but to teach thee* WHERE thy true strength lies, and to cast thee off from every other?. "Wait on the Lord: be of good courage, and He shall strengthen thine heart: *wait,* I say, on the Lord" (Ps. 27:14).

Sometimes the discouragement is deeper yet. We live under the hidings of our Master's face. He seems to have covered Himself with a thick cloud, which our sight cannot pierce, and which our prayers cannot pass through—they fall consciously short of their aim, and come back to the dull earth flat and unprofitable. But be of good cheer. This cannot last forever, nor last long! Only "rest in the Lord, and *wait patiently* for Him" (Ps. 37:7); and be assured that "the Lord is good to them that *wait for him"* (Lam. 3:25), and although it may be that now, for a little while, thou liest void of strength, and almost lifeless upon the ground, yet, amid this chilliness, *still wait;* though wounded, WAIT—holding fast the conviction which His promises give: "They that wait upon the Lord *shall* renew their strength. They *shall* mount up with wings as eagles; they *shall* run and not be weary; they *shall* walk and not faint" (Isa. 40:31).

To have waited for the Lord, He allows to constitute a claim to His tender consideration for us; "O Lord, be gracious unto us; we *have waited* for Thee" (Isa. 33:2). And no one ever yet could truly say, "I have waited patiently for the Lord" without being enabled rejoicingly to add,—*"and He heard my cry"* (Ps. 40:1). And in that day of full fruition of all we have waited for shall we not, out of the fulness of our replenished hearts, cry with exalting shouts to all that pass by,—"Lo, this is our God; we have waited for Him, and He will save us; this is the Lord; we have waited for Him, and will be glad and rejoice in His salvation" (Isa. 25:9).

Dr. Kitto, (1852)

MY GOD, MY SALVATION.

"He also shall be my salvation." (Job 13:16).

God hath as it were made Himself over to believers. Job doth not say, God will give or bestow salvation upon me, but he saith, "*He* shall be my salvation."

It is God Himself who is the salvation and the portion of His people. They would not care much for salvation if *God* were not their salvation. It more pleaseth the saints that they enjoy God than that they enjoy salvation. False and carnal spirits will express a great deal of desire after salvation. O, they like salvation, heaven, and glory very well, but they never express any longing desire after God and Jesus Christ. They love salvation but they care not for a Saviour. Now that which faith pitcheth most upon is God Himself. *He* shall be my salvation: let me have Him and there is salvation enough. *He* is my life, *He* is my comfort, *He* is my riches, *He* is my honour, and *He* is my all.

Thus David's heart acted immediately upon God (Psa. 18:1, 2). It pleaseth holy David more that God was his strength than that God gave him strength—that God was his deliverer than that he was delivered—that God was his fortress, his buckler, his horn, his high tower, than that he gave him the effect of all these. It pleased David, and it pleases all the saints more that *God* is their salvation (whether temporal or eternal) than that He saves them. The saints look more at God than at all that *is* God's.

They say, We desire not thine but Thee; or, Nothing of Thine like Thee. "Whom have I in heaven but Thee?" saith David again (Psa. 73:25). What are saints, what are angels, to a soul without God? 'Tis true of things as well as of persons. What have we in heaven but God? What is joy without God; what is glory without God; what is all the furniture and riches, all *delicates,* yea, and all the diadems of heaven, without the God of heaven?

If God should say to the saints, "Here is heaven, take it amongst you but I will withdraw Myself," how would they weep over heaven itself, and make it a Baca—a valley of tears indeed! Heaven is not heaven unless we enjoy God. 'Tis the presence of God which makes heaven. Glory is but our nearest being unto God (our being nearest to God). As Mephibosheth replied when David told him, "I have said, thou and Ziba divide the land, Let him take all, forasmuch as my lord the king is come again in peace to his own house," where I may enjoy him. So if God should say to the saints, "Take heaven amongst you," and withdraw Himself, they would soon say, "Nay; let the world take heaven if they will, let them take glory if they will; if we may not have Thee in heaven, heaven would be but an earth, or rather but a hell to us." That which saints rejoice in is that they may be in the presence of God—that they may sit at His table and eat bread with Him—that is that they may be near Him constantly, which was Mephibosheth's privilege with David. That's the thing, say they, which they desire, and which their souls thirst after—that's the wine they would drink.

"My soul (saith David) thirsteth for God, for the living God; when shall I come and appear before God?" He spake this in the greatness and heat of his zeal to enjoy God in the ordinances of His public worship. How much more was his soul on fire to enjoy God when he should be above ordinances! The usual saying of Christians is, "Come let us go to prayer," or "Let us go to church." We should rather say, "Come let us go *to God.*"

We should prize duties no farther than as we obey and enjoy God in doing them. Nor should we prize heaven itself farther than as we shall have there a more full and perfect enjoyment of God. Salvation itself were no salvation without the God of salvation. "*He* also shall be my salvation." *Anonymous 1652.*

"If any one shall affirm that man's free-will, moved and excited of God, does not, by consenting, co-operate with God the mover and exciter, so as to prepare and dispose itself for the attainment of justification; if, moreover, any one shall say, that the human will cannot refuse complying, if it pleases; but that it is unactive, and merely passive; let such an one be accursed.

"If any one shall affirm that, since the fall of Adam, man's free-will is lost and extinguished; or, that it is a thing merely titular, yea, a name without a thing, and a fiction introduced by Satan into the Church; let such an one be accursed."

—Decrees of the Council of Trent, 1545. The Standard of Popery.

VOL. III OCTOBER, 1924 NO. 10

STUDIES in the SCRIPTURES

"Search the Scriptures" John 5:39.

Arthur W. Pink, Publisher & Editor,
227 N. Creighton St., Philadelphia, Pa.

Price: 10 cents per copy; $1.00 per year. Foreign $1.00 per year.

"Neither is there salvation in any other: for there is none other name under heaven given among men, whereby we must be saved." (Acts 4:12).

The first thing we would note here is that the apostle insists Christ is the *only* Saviour. Salvation is not to be found in any other. *It is Christ or the Lake of Fire!* There is no other alternative. Salvation is not to be found in religious ordinances, in a creed, or church; nor is it to be obtained by self-sacrifice or good works. Salvation is in Christ alone. He Himself declared—"I am *the* way, the truth, and the life: no man cometh unto the Father, *but by Me*." (John 14:6). The same truth was revealed in the O. T. "There is no God else beside Me; a just God and a Saviour; there is *none beside Me*. Look unto Me and be saved, all the ends of the earth: for I am God, and there is *none else*." (Isa. 45:21, 22).

The second thing to which we would here direct attention is the restrictive pronoun: "there is none other Name under heaven given *among* men." This Name, this Saviour, is *not* "given *unto* men," but unto a selection from among them. "Among" clearly affirms a limitation. It announces the solemn but blessed truth of election, which runs all through Scripture. This qualifying preposition is found in other passages. For example, in Rom. 1:5 the apostle declares that he had received grace and apostleship for faith-obedience *among* all nations for His Name." So in Rom. 15:9 the apostle quotes a prophecy which declares, "I will confess to Thee *among* the Gentiles, and sing unto Thy Name." God is now *taking out of* the Gentiles a people for His Name. (Acts 15:14). At the beginning it was announced, "Thou shalt call His name Jesus, for He shall save *His people* from their sins." (Matt. 1:21).

In the third place, observe the last clause of Acts 4:12. It is not "there is none other Name under heaven given among men whereby we *might* be saved," but "whereby we *must* be saved". Nor is it "whereby *ye* must be saved", but "whereby *we* must be saved." There is no uncertainty about the salvation of God's elect. By nature dead in trespasses and sins, the captives of Satan, yet is their salvation sure. Born, perhaps of vicious parents, and reared in crime; or, born in a home of infidelity, and nurtured in error and idolatry; nevertheless, if one of God's elect, his salvation is positively assured. God's elect *must* be saved because God the Father *decreed* it, because God the Son *purchased* it, because God the Spirit will *effectuate* it.

Nor does this verse stand alone in affirming the absolute certainty of the salvation of God's elect. In John 10:16 we find the Saviour saying, "And other sheep I have which are not of this fold: them also I *must* bring, and they *shall* hear My voice; and there *shall be* one fold and one Shepherd." A beautiful illustration of this Divine necessity is found in Luke 19, in connection with the salvation of Zacchæus. Said the Saviour to him, "Zacchæus make haste, and come down; for today I *must* abide at thy house". (v. 5); and later Christ added, "This day is salvation come to *this* house, *forsomuch* as he also is a *son* of Abraham" (v. 9)—Abraham was the "father" of the elect people!

Summarizing, we find, then, three things in this precious verse: First, the Divinely appointed Son—*given* unto men. Second, the Divine restriction—"given *among* men . . . . . whereby *we* (not "ye") must be saved". Third, the Divine imperative—"whereby we *must* be saved". An elect people given unto the Saviour: an elect Saviour (Isa. 42:1) given unto an elect people. The Holy Spirit, in omnipotent power, bringing this elect people to Christ. Result—"He *shall* see of the travail of His soul and *be satisfied*." (Isa. 53:11). No disappointed Saviour is ours! Thank God for the absolute certainty of *His* counsels. Preachers may fail, men's wills may be obstinate, Satan may oppose, but *God's purpose* cannot fail. His own elect MUST be *saved!!* Hallelujah!

Arthur W. Pink.

IMPORTANT NOTICES

All new subscriptions will be dated back to January, 1924.
Set of twelve issues for **1922,** unbound, **$1.00.** Bound, **$1.50.**
Set of twelve issues for **1923,** unbound, **$1.00** **Bound $1.50. Abroad, $1.75 or 7/6.**
Note: We cannot break a set or now supply any **single** 1923 issues.
Subscription-price: **$1.00** per year to any address in the world. Single copies **10 cents.**
Change of Address: Please notify me promptly of any change of address, and be certain to give both old and new addresses.
Non-subscribers receiving this Magazine regularly will understand their subscription has been entered by a friend.
Copies lost in the mail duplicated only if we are notified promptly.
Entered as second-class matter December 15th, 1923, at the post office at Philadelphia, Pa., under Act of March 3rd, 1879.

CONTENTS

JOHN'S GOSPEL.

34. CHRIST, THE DOOR: John 10:1-10.

Below is an Analysis of the passage which is to be before us:

1. Entrance into the Sheepfold: lawful and unlawful: vv. 1, 2.
2. The Shepherd admitted by the porter: v. 3.
3. The Shepherd leading His sheep out of the fold: vv. 3, 4.
4. The attitude of the sheep toward strangers: v. 5.
5. Christ's proverb not understood: v. 6.
6. The true Shepherd and the false shepherds contrasted: vv. 7-9.
7. Antichrist and Christ contrasted: v. **10.**

As a personal aid to the study of this passage the writer drew up a list of questions, of which the following are samples: To whom is our Lord speaking? What was the immediate occasion of His address? Why does He make reference to a "sheepfold"? What is meant by "climbing up some other way" into it? What is signified by "the door"? *What* "sheepfold" is here in view?—note it is one into which thieves and robbers could climb; it was one entered by the shepherd; it was one out of which the shepherd led his sheep. Who does "the porter" bring before us? Such questions enable us to focalize our thoughts and approach the passage with some degree of definiteness.

Our passage begins with "Verily, verily, I say unto you". The antecedent of the *you* is found in "the Pharisees" of the previous chapter. The occasion of this word from Christ was the excommunication of the beggar by the Pharisees (9:34). The mention of "the sheepfold" at once views these Pharisees in a pastoral relationship. The reference to "thieves and robbers" climbing up some other way denounced the Pharisees as *false* shepherds, and rebuked them for their unlawful conduct. In the course of this "parable" or "proverb", the Lord contrasts Himself with the Pharisees as the true Shepherd. These things are clear on the surface, and the confusion of some of the commentators can only be attributed to their failure in attending to these simple details.

There are two chief reasons why many have experienced difficulty in apprehending the Lord's teaching in this passage: failure to consider the circumstances under which it was delivered, and failure to distinguish between the *three* "doors" here spoken of—there is the "door into the sheepfold" (v. 1); the "door of the sheep" (v. 7); and the "door" of salvation (v. 9). In the previous chapter we find our Lord had given sight to one born blind. This raised the jealousy of the Pharisees, so that when the beggar faithfully confessed it was Jesus who had opened his eyes, they cast him out of the synagogue. When Christ heard of this He at once sought him out, and revealed Himself as the Son of God. This drew forth the confession, "Lord, I believe". Thus did he evidence himself to be one of "the sheep", responding to the Shepherd's voice. Following this, our Lord announced, "For judgment I am come into this world, that they which see not might see; and that they which see might be made blind" (9:39). Some of the Pharisees heard Him, and asked, "Are *we* blind also?". To which the Saviour replied, "If ye were blind, ye should have no sin: but now ye say, We see; therefore your sin remaineth". It was the self-confidence and self-complacency of these Pharisees which proved them to be blind, and therefore in their sins. Unto them, under these circumstances, did Christ deliver this memorable and searching proverb of the shepherd and his sheep.

It will probably be of some help to the reader if we describe briefly the character of the "sheepfold" which obtains in Eastern lands. In Palestine, which in the pastoral sections was infested with wild beasts, there was in each village a large sheepfold, which was the common property of the native farmers. This sheepfold was protected by a wall some ten or twelve feet high. When night fell, a number of different shepherds would lead their flocks up to the door of the fold, through which they passed, leaving them in the care of the porter, while they went home or sought lodging. At the door, the porter lay on guard through the night, ready to protect the sheep against thieves and robbers, or against wild animals which might scale the walls. In the morning the different shepherds returned. The porter would allow each one to enter through the door, calling by name the sheep which belonged to his flock. The sheep would respond to his voice, and he would lead them out to pasture. In the lesson before us *this* is what the Lord uses as a figure or proverb.

"Verily, verily, I say unto you, he that entereth not by the door into the sheepfold, but climbeth up some other way, the same is a thief and a robber. But he that entereth in by the door is the shepherd of the sheep" (vv. 1, 2). The "sheepfold" here is not Heaven, for thieves and robbers do not climb up into it. Nor is it "The Church" as some have strangely supposed, for the Shepherd does not lead His sheep out of that, as He does from this fold (see v. 3). No, the "sheepfold" is manifestly *Judaism*—in which some of God's elect were then to be found—and the contrast pointed in these opening verses is between the true Shepherd and the false ones, between Christ and the Pharisees. The "door" here must not be confused with "the Door" of v. 9. Here in v. 1 it is simply contrasted from the "climbing up some *other* way". It signifies, then, the *lawful* "way" of entrance for the Shepherd to those of His sheep then to be found in Judaism.

"But He that entereth in by the door is the Shepherd of the sheep" (v. 2). The simple meaning of this is, that Christ presented Himself to Israel in a lawful manner, that is, in strict accord with the Holy Scriptures. "He submitted Himself to all the conditions established by Him who built the house. Christ answered to all that was written of the Messiah, and took the path of God's will in presenting Himself to the people" (J. N. D.). He had been born of a virgin, of the covenant people, of the Judaic stock, in the royal city —Bethlehem. He had conformed to everything which God required of an Israelite. He had been "born under the law" (Gal. 4:4). He was circumcised the eighth day (Luke 2:21), and subsequently, at the purification of His mother, He was presented to God in the Temple (Luke 2:22).

"To Him the porter openeth" (v. 3). The word "porter" signifies door-keeper. The only other time the word occurs in John's Gospel is in 18:16, 17, and how strikingly these two references illustrate, once more, the law of contrast! "But Peter stood at the door without. Then went out that other disciple, which was known unto the high priest, and spake unto her that *kept the door* (the porter), and brought in Peter. Then saith the damsel that kept the door unto Peter, Art not thou also one of this man's disciples? He saith, I am not". In John 10 the "porter" refers ultimately to the Holy Spirit, while the door-keeper in John 18 is a woman that evidently had no sympathy with Christ. In John 10 the porter opens the door to give the Shepherd access to the sheep, whereas in John 18 the door is opened that a sheep might gain access to the Shepherd. In John 10 the sheep run to the Shepherd, but in John 18 the sheep is seen in the midst of wolves. In John 10 the sheep follow the Shepherd: in John 18 one of the sheep denies the Shepherd!

"To Him the porter openeth". The "porter" was the one who vouched for the shepherd and presented him to the sheep. As to the identity of the "porter" in this proverb there can be no doubt. The direct reference was to John the Baptist who "prepared the *way* of the Lord". He it was who formally introduced the Shepherd to Israel: "that He should be *made manifest* to Israel, therefore am I come baptizing" (1:31) was his own confession. But, in the wider application, the "porter" here represented the Holy Spirit, who officially vouched for the credentials of the Messiah, and who now presents the Saviour to each of God's elect.

"To Him the porter openeth; and the sheep hear His voice; and He calleth His own sheep by name, and leadeth them out" (v. 3). Three things mark the genuine shepherd: first, he entered the fold by "the door", and climbed not over the walls, as thieves and robbers did. Second, he entered the door by "the porter" opening to him. Third, he proved himself by "the sheep" recognizing and responding to his voice. Mark, then, how fully and perfectly these three requirements were met by Christ in His relation to Israel, thus evidencing Him to be the true Shepherd.

As we have seen, the "door" was the legitimate and appointed entrance into the fold, and this figure meant that the Messiah came by the road which Old Testament prophecy had marked out beforehand. The "porter" presented the shepherd to the sheep. Not only had the prophets borne witness to Christ, but in addition, when He appeared, a forerunner heralded Him, introducing Him to the people. Besides this, when the true Shepherd of Israel was manifested, the sheep recognized His voice. The true sheep were known to Him, for He called them by name. The call was to follow Him, and to *follow* Him was to take their place with the despised and rejected One *outside* of Judaism. How beautifully this links up with what was before us in John 9 it is not difficult to perceive.

In John 9 Christ had shown how that He had entered the door into the sheepfold, for He had come working the works of God (9:4), and had thus shown Himself to be in the confidence of the Owner of the fold, and therefore the approved Shepherd of the flock. The Pharisees, on the contrary, were resisting Him and attacking the sheep; therefore they must needs be "thieves and robbers". The blind beggar was a sample of the flock, for, refusing to listen to the voice of strangers, he, nevertheless, knew the voice of the Shepherd, and drawn to Him, he found salvation, security, and sustenance.

All of this, strikingly illustrated in John 9, receives interpretation and amplification in chapter 10, where we have a blessed commentary on the condition of the excommunicated one. The Pharisees imagined they had cut him off from the place of safety and blessing, but the Lord had shown Him that it was only then he had really entered the true place of blessing. Had he remained inside Judaism he would have been the constant object of the assaults of the "thieves and robbers"; but now he was in the care of the true Shepherd, the good Shepherd, who instead of killing him, would die for him! It is beautiful to compare 10:3 with 9:34. The Pharisees' "casting out" of the poor beggar was, in reality, the Shepherd *leading him out* from the barren wilderness of Judaism to the green pastures of Christianity. Thus are we given to see the Lord Himself *behind* the human instruments—a marvellous example is this of how God ofttimes employs even His enemies to accomplish a good turn for His people.

"To Him the porter openeth; and the sheep hear His voice: and He calleth His own sheep by name, and leadeth them out" (v. 3). Mark carefully the qualification here: it is not He calleth the sheep by name, but "He calleth *His own* sheep by name". His "own sheep" were those who had been given to Him by the Father from all eternity; and when He calls, all of these "sheep" *must* come to Him, for it is written, "*All* that the Father giveth Me *shall come* to Me" (John 6:37). These "sheep", then, were the elect of God among Israel. Not to the Nation at large was Christ's real ministry; rather did He come unto "the lost sheep *of* the House of Israel". That these "lost sheep" were not co-extensive with the whole Nation is clear from the twenty-sixth verse of this chapter, for there we find the Shepherd saying to unbelieving Israelites, "But ye believe not, because *ye* are not *of* My sheep"! The sheep, then, whom Christ "called" during the days of His earthly ministry were the elect of God, whom He led out of Judaism. This was strikingly foreshadowed of old. Moses, while estranged from Israel, kept the flock of his father in other pastures, near "the mount of God" (Ex. 3:1).

"And when He putteth forth His own sheep, He goeth before them, and the sheep follow Him: for they know His voice" (v. 4). Christ began His ministry *inside* the fold of Judaism, for it was there His Jewish sheep were to be found, though mixed with others: from these they needed to be separated when the true Shepherd appeared. Therefore does His voice sound, calling the lost sheep *of* the House of Israel unto Himself. As they responded, they were put forth outside the fold, to follow Him.

"And the sheep follow Him: for they know His voice". Link this up with the third clause in the previous verse. "He calleth His own sheep by name . . . . and the sheep follow Him: for they know His voice". A number of blessed illustrations of this are found scattered throughout the Gospels. "And as Jesus passed forth from thence, He saw a man, named Matthew, sitting at the receipt of customs: and He saith unto Him, Follow Me, and he arose, and followed Him" (Matt. 9:9). Here was a lone sheep of Christ. The Shepherd *called* him; he recognized His voice, and promptly *followed* Him.

"And when Jesus came to the place, He looked up, and saw him, and said unto him, Zacchæus, make haste, and come down; for today I must abide at thy house". Here was one of the sheep, called *by name.* The response was prompt, for we are told, "And he made haste, *and came down,* and received Him joyfully".

"The day following Jesus would go forth into Galilee, and findeth Philip, and saith unto him, Follow Me" (John 1:43). This shows us the Shepherd *seeking* His sheep before He called him.

John 11 supplies us with a still more striking example of the drawing power of the Shepherd's voice as He calleth His own sheep. There we read of Lazarus, in the grave; but when Christ calls His sheep *by name*—"Lazarus, come forth"—the sheep at once responded.

As a touching example of the sheep *knowing* His voice we refer the reader to John 20. Mary Magdalene visited the Saviour's sepulchre in the early morning hour. She finds the stone rolled away, and the body of the Lord gone. Disconsolate, she stands there weeping. Suddenly she sees the Lord Jesus standing by her, and "knew not that it was Jesus". He speaks to her, but she supposed Him to be the gardener. A moment later she identified Him, and says, "Rabboni". What had happened in the interval? What enabled her to identify Him? Just one word from Him—"Mary"! The moment He *called His sheep by name* she *"knew* His voice"!

It has been thus with God's elect all down the ages. It is so today. There is a general "Call" which goes forth to all who hear the Gospel, for "Many are called", though few are chosen (Matt. 20:16). But to each of Christ's "sheep" there comes a particular, a special call. This call is inward and invincible, and therefore effectual. Proof of this is found in Rom. 8:30 and many other scriptures: there we read, "Whom He called *them He also* justified". But all are not justified, therefore all are *not* "called". Who then are "the called"? The previous clause of Rom. 8:30 tells us —"Whom He did *predestinate* them He *also* called". And who were the ones "predestinated"? They were those whom God did "foreknow" (8:29). And who were they? The previous verse makes answer —they who were "the called according to His purpose". Called not because of anything in them, forseen or actual, but solely by His own sovereign will or purpose.

This effectual *call* from God is heard by each of the "sheep" because they are given "ears to hear": "The hearing ear, and the seeing eye, the Lord hath made even both of them" (Prov. 20:12). This effectual call comes to none but the sheep; the "goats" hear it not—"But ye believe not, *because* ye are not of My sheep" (John 10:26).

There is, no doubt, a secondary application of these verses to the under-shepherds of Christ today, and considered thus they supply us with several important principles which enable us to identify them with certainty. First, a true under-shepherd of Christ is one who gains access to the sheep in the Divinely-appointed way: unlike the Pharisees, he does not intrude himself into this sacred office, but is called to it by God. Second, he is, in the real meaning of the word, a *shepherd* of the sheep: he has their welfare at heart, and ever concerns himself with their interests. Third, to such an one "the porter openeth": the Holy Spirit sets before him an "open door" for ministry and service. Fourth, the sheep hear his voice: the elect of God recognize him as a Divinely-appointed pastor. Fifth, he calleth his own sheep by name: that portion of the flock over which God has made him overseer, are known to him individually: with a true pastor's heart he seeks them out in the home and acquaints himself with them personally. Sixth, he "leadeth them out" into the green pastures of God's Word where they may find food and rest. Seventh, "He goeth before them": he sets before them a godly example, asking them to do nothing which he is not doing himself; he seeks to be "an example of the believers, in word, in conversation, in charity, in spirit, in faith, in purity" (1 Tim. 4:12). May the Lord in His grace increase the number of such faithful under-shepherds. Let the reader, especially the preacher, consult the following passages: Acts 20:28; 2 Thess. 3:9; 1 Peter 5:2-4.

"And a stranger will they not follow, but will flee from him: for they know not the voice of strangers" (v. 5). This is very important, for it describes a mark found on all of Christ's sheep. A strange shepherd they will not heed. This can hardly mean that they will *never* respond to the call of the false shepherds, but that the redeemed of Christ will not absolutely, unreservedly, completely give themselves over to a false teacher. Instead, speaking characteristically, they will *flee* from such. It is not possible to deceive the elect (Matt. 24:24). Let a man of the world hear two preachers, one giving out the truth and the other error, and he can discern no difference between them. But it is far otherwise with a child of God. He may be but a babe in Christ, unskilled in theological controversies, but instinctively he will detect vital heresy as soon as he hears it. And why is this? Because he is indwelt by the Holy Spirit, and has received an "unction" from the Holy One (1 John 2:20). How thankful we should be for this. How gracious of the Lord to have given us this capacity to separate the precious from the vile!

"This parable spake Jesus unto them: but they understood not what things they were which He spake unto them" (v. 6). This points a contrast, bringing out as it does the very reverse of what was before us in the previous one. There we learn of the spirit of discernment possessed by all of Christ's sheep; here we see illustrated the solemn fact that those who are not His sheep are quite unable to understand the truth even when it is plainly presented to them. Blind indeed were these Pharisees, and therefore totally incapacitated to perceive our Lord's meaning. Equally blind are all the unsaved today. Well educated they may be, and theologically trained, but unless they are born again the Word of God is a sealed book to them.

"Then said Jesus unto them again, Verily, verily, I say unto you, I am the door of the sheep" (v. 7). The "door of the sheep" is to be distinguished from the "door of the sheepfold" in v. 1. The latter was the Divinely-appointed way by which Christ had entered Judaism, in contrast from the false pastors of Israel whose conduct evidenced plainly that they had thrust themselves into office. The "door of the sheep" was Christ Himself, by which the elect of Israel passed out of Judaism. The Lord had not come to restore Judaism, but to lead out His own unto Himself. A striking illustration of this is to be found in Ex. 33. At the time viewed there Judaism was in a state of unbelief and rebellion against God. Accordingly, Moses, the shepherd of Israel, "took the tabernacle and pitched it *without* the camp, afar off from the camp, and called it the tabernacle of the congregation. And it came to pass, that every one that sought the Lord *went out unto* the tabernacle of the congregation, which was without the camp" (v. 7). Those who really sought the Lord had to *leave* "the camp", and go forth unto the shepherd on the outside. It is beautiful to note the sequel: "And it came to pass, as Moses entered into the tabernacle, the cloudy pillar descended, and stood at the door of the tabernacle, and the Lord talked with Moses" (v. 9). God was *with* His shepherd on the outside of the Camp! So here in John 10. Christ, the antitype of Moses (Deut. 18:18), tabernacles outside Judaism, and those whose hearts sought the Lord went forth unto Him. And history has repeated itself. God is no longer with the great organized systems of Christendom, and those of His people whose hearts cleave to *Him* must go forth "outside the camp" if they would commune with Him! The "door" here then speaks of *exit,* not entrance.

"All that ever came before Me are thieves and robbers: but the sheep did not hear them" (v. 8). It is abundantly clear that here we have another instance in John's Gospel where the word "all" cannot be taken absolutely. The Lord had been speaking of *shepherds,* the shepherds of Israel; but not *all* of them had been "thieves and robbers". Moses, Joshua, David, the prophets, Nehemiah, and others who might be mentioned, certainly could not be included within this classification. The "all" here, as is usually the case in Scripture, must be restricted. But restricted to whom? Surely to the scribes and Pharisees, who were here being addressed by the Lord. Bishop Ryle has a helpful note on this verse: "Let it be noted", he says, "that these strong epithets show plainly that there are times when it is right to rebuke sharply. Flattering everybody, and complimenting all teachers who are zealous and earnest, without reference to their soundness in the faith, is not according to Scripture. Nothing seems so offensive to Christ as a false teacher of religion, a false prophet, or a false shepherd. Nothing ought to be so much dreaded in the Church, and if needful, be so plainly rebuked, opposed, and exposed. The strong language of our Reformers, when writing against Romish teachers, is often blamed more than it ought to be."

It is a notable fact that the severest denunciations which are to be found in the Scriptures are reserved for false teachers. Listen to these awful words of Christ: "Woe unto you scribes and Pharisees, hypocrites! . . . . ye blind guides, which strain at a gnat, and swallow a camel . . . . ye serpents, ye generation of vipers, how can ye escape the damnation of hell?" (Matt. 23:27, 28, 33). So, too, His forerunner: "O generation of vipers, who hath warned you to flee from the wrath to come?" (Matt. 3:7). So, too, the apostle Paul: "For such are false apostles, deceitful workers, transforming themselves into the apostles of Christ" (2 Cor. 11:13). So Peter: "These are wells without water, clouds that are carried with the tempest; to whom the mist of darkness is reserved forever" (2 Pet. 2:17). So Jude: "Clouds they are without water, carried about with winds; trees whose fruit withereth, without fruit, twice dead, plucked up by the roots; raging waves of the sea, foaming out their own shame; wandering stars to whom is reserved the blackness of darkness forever" (vv. 12, 13). Unspeakably solemn are these; would that their alarm might be sounded forth today, as a warning to those who are so careless *whose* ministry they sit under.

But *why* should our Lord term the Pharisees "thieves and robbers"? Wherein lay the propriety of such appellations? We believe that light is thrown on this question by such a scripture as Luke 11:52: "Woe unto you, lawyers! for ye have *taken away* the key of knowledge: ye entered not in yourselves, and them that were entering in ye hindered". With this should be compared the parallel passage in Matt. 23:13. The Pharisees were *thieves* inasmuch as they seized positions which they had no right to occupy, exerted an authority which did not justly belong to them, and unlawfully demanded a submission and subjection to which they could establish no valid claim.

What, may be asked, is the distinction between "thieves" and "robbers"? The word for "thief" is "kleptes" and is always so rendered. It has reference to one who uses stealth. The word for "robbers" is "lestes", and is wrongly translated "thief" in Matt. 21:13; Luke 10:30, 36, etc. It has reference to one who uses violence. The distinction between these two words is closely preserved all through the New Testament with the one exception of v. 10, where it seems as though the Lord uses the word "kleptes" to *combine* the two different thoughts for there the "thief" is said not only to "steal", but also to "kill and destroy".

"I am the door: by Me if any man enter in, he shall be saved" (v. 9). Notice carefully the broader terms which Christ uses here. No longer does He say, as in v. 7, "I am the Door of the sheep", but "I am the Door", and this He follows at once with, "If *any man* enter in, he shall be saved". Why this change of language? Because up to this point the Lord had been referring solely to elect Israelites, which He was leading out of Judaism. But now His heart reaches forth to the elect among the Gentiles, for not only was He "a minister of the circumcision for the truth of God, to confirm the promises made unto the fathers", but He also came "that the Gentiles might glorify God for His mercy" (Rom. 15:8, 9). The "door" in v. 1 was God's appointed way for the shepherd *into* Judaism. The "Door" in v. 7 was the Way *out of* Judaism, by Christ leading God's elect in separation unto Himself. Here in v. 9 the "Door" has to do with salvation, for elect Jew and Gentile alike.

"I am the door: by Me if any man enter in, he shall be saved". This is the "door" into the presence of God. By nature we are separated, yea, "alienated" from God. Sin as a barrier comes in between and bars us out of His holy presence. This is one of the first things a convicted soul is made conscious of. I am defiled and condemned, how can I draw near to God? I am made to realize my guilty distance from Him who is Light, how then can I be reconciled to Him? Then, from God's Word, I learn Heaven's answer to these solemn questions. The Lord Jesus has bridged that awful gulf which separated me from God. He bridged it by taking my place and being made a curse in my stead. And as the exercised soul bows to God's sentence of condemnation, and receives by faith the marvellous provision which His grace has made, I, with all other believers, learn, "But now in Christ Jesus ye who sometimes were afar off *are made nigh* by the blood of Christ" (Eph. 2:13).

"I am the Door: by Me if any man enter in, he shall be saved". This is one of the precious words of Christ which is well worthy of prolonged meditation. A "door" speaks of easy ingress and is contrasted from the high walls in which it is set. There are no difficult walls which have to be scaled before the anxious sinner can obtain access to God. No, Christ is the "Door" into His presence. A "door" may also be contrasted from a long, dreary, circuitous passage—just one step, and those on the outside are now within. The soul that believes God's testimony to the truth of salvation by Christ *alone,* at once enters God's presence. But mark the definite article: "I am *the* Door". There was only one door into the ark in which Noah and his family found shelter from the flood. There was only one door into the Tabernacle, which was Jehovah's dwelling-place. So there is only one "Door" into the presence of the Father—"Neither is there salvation in any other: for there is *none other* name under Heaven, given among men, whereby we must be saved" (Acts 4:12). And again, "I am *the* Way", said Christ. "No man cometh unto the Father *but by Me*" (John 14:6). Have *you* entered by this "Door", dear reader? Remember that a door is not to be looked at and admired, but to be used! Nor do you need to knock: the Door is open, and open for "any man" who will enter. Soon, though, the Door will be shut (see Luke 13:25), for the present Day of Salvation (1 Cor. 6:2) will be followed by the great Day of Wrath (Rev. 6:17). Enter then while there is time.

Such are some of the simplest thoughts suggested by the figure of "The Door". What follows is an extract from an unknown writer who signed himself "J.B.Jr": —"The door suggests the thought of the dwelling-place to which it is the means of entrance. Within we find the possession or portion of those who can by right enter by the door. Thus it is as a place set apart for its possessors for all that which is outside. In this way we may say it is a sanctuary. These things are rightly connected with a door, it being the only right way of entrance".

"I am the door: by Me if any man enter in, he shall be saved". Notice Christ did not say, "I am the Door: if any man enter in, he shall be saved", but, *"by Me* if any man enter in". Man cannot enter of himself, for being by nature "dead in trespasses and sins" he is perfectly helpless. It is only by Divine aid, by the impartation to us of supernatural power, than any can enter in and be saved. Without Christ we can do *nothing* (John 15:5). Writing to the Philippians the apostle said, "For unto you *it is given* in the behalf of Christ, not only *to believe on Him,* but also to suffer for His sake" (1:29). Not only is it a fact that no one can come to Christ except the Father draw him (John 6:44), but it is also true that none can come to the Father except Christ empowers. This is very clear from the sixteenth verse of our chapter: "And other sheep I have, which are not of this fold: them also I must *bring*". The "sheep" enter through the Door into God's presence because Christ "brings" them. Beautifully is this portrayed in Luke 15: 5, 6: "And when he hath found it (the lost sheep), he *layeth it on his shoulders,* rejoicing. And when he cometh home, he calleth together his friends and neighbours, saying unto them, Rejoice with me".

"I am the door: by Me if any man enter in, he shall be saved, and shall go in and out, and find pasture." To go "in and out" is a figurative way to express perfect *freedom.* This was something vastly different from the experiences of even saved Israelites under the law of Moses. One of the chief designs of the ceremonial law was to hedge Israelites around with ordinances which kept them separate from all other nations. But this was made an end of by Christ, for through His death the "middle wall of partition" was broken down. Thus were His sheep perfectly free to "go in and out". It is indeed striking to discover in Neh. 3 that of the ten gates mentioned there, of the *sheep* gate only are *no* "locks and bars" mentioned. This chapter concerns the *remnant* after their captivity, and clearly foreshadows in a wonderful way the truth here taught by Christ. "The fulness of this freedom is intercourse with other saints, and in deliverance from the yoke of the (ceremonial) law (Acts 15:10), was only by degrees apprehended. That lesson, taught Peter on the housetop at Joppa (Acts 10), was the first real step in the *realization* of that freedom" (C.E. S.).

"And find pasture". This tells of the gracious provision made for the nourishment of the sheep. Our minds at once turn to that matchless Psalm which records the joyous testimony of the saints: "The Lord is my Shepherd; I shall not want. He maketh me to lie down in green pastures: He leadeth me beside the still waters". The "pastures", then, speak not only of food, but of *rest* as well. This too is a part of that wondrous portion which is ours in Christ. A beautiful type of this is found in Num. 10:33: "And they departed from the mount of the Lord three days' journey: and the ark of the covenant went before them in the three days' journey, to search out *a resting place* for them". All through the Old Testament the "ark of the covenant" is a lovely figure of the Saviour Himself, and here it is seen seeking out a resting place—the pastures—for Israel of old.

"I am the door: by Me if any man enter in, he shall be saved, and shall go in and out, and find pasture". Seven things are enumerated in this precious verse. First, "I am the Door": Christ the only Way to God. Second, "*By Me* if any man enter": Christ the Imparter of power *to* enter. Third, "If *any* man enter": Christ the Saviour for Jew and Gentile alike. Fourth, "If any man *enter in*": Christ *appropriated* by a single act of faith. Fifth, "He shall be saved": Christ the Deliverer from the penalty, power, and presence of sin. Sixth, "He shall go in and out": Christ the Emancipator from all bondage. Seventh, "And find pasture". Christ the Sustainer of His people.

Finally, it is blessed to see how the contents of this precious verse present Christ to us as the Fulfiller of the prophetic prayer of Moses: "And Moses spake unto the Lord, saying, Let the Lord, the God of the spirits of all flesh, set *a man* over the congregation, Which may *go out* before them, and which may *go in* before them, and which may *lead them out*, and which may *bring them in;* that the congregation of the Lord be not as sheep which have no shepherd" (Num. 27:15-17)!

"The thief cometh not, but for to steal, and to kill, and to destroy" (v. 10). It will be observed that Christ here uses the singular number. In v. 8 He had spoken of "thieves and robbers" when referring to all who had come before Him; but here in v. 10 He has some particular individual in view—"*The* thief". It should also be noted that in speaking of this particular "thief" our Lord *combines* in one the two distinct characters of thieves and robbers. As intimated in our comments on v. 8 the distinctive thought associated with the former is that of *stealth;* that of the latter, is *violence*. Here "*the* Thief" cometh to steal, and to kill, and to destroy. Who then is the Lord referring to? Surely it is to the last false shepherd of Israel, the "Idol Shepherd", the Antichrist, of whom it is written, "For lo, I will raise up a shepherd in the land, which shall not visit those that be cut off, neither shall seek the young ones, nor heal that that is broken, nor feed that that standeth still: but he shall eat the flesh of the fat, and tear their claws in pieces. Woe to the idol shepherd that leaveth the flock! The sword shall be upon his arm, and upon his right eye: his arm shall be clean dried up, and his right eye shall be utterly darkened".

If any doubt remains as to the identity of "The Thief" in John 10:10 it is removed by a reference to the only other place in John's Gospel where this term is used. In John 12:6 we are told that Judas was a "*thief*", and the Antichrist is Judas re-incarnated, as we have shown in our articles on that character. Remarkably does our Lord here sum up his future history as it relates to Israel. The Thief will come first to "steal": he will endeavor to steal the hearts of the Remnant away from the Lord, as Absalom sought to steal away the hearts of the people from his father David. Second, he will come to "kill": failing to succeed in alienating the hearts of the Remnant, he will use force, and put to death the faithful sheep of the flock. Third, he comes to "destroy", Not satisfied with slaying the godly Jews, he will attempt to completely destroy Israel and cut them off from being a nation in the earth —see Psa. 83:4.

"I am come that they might have life, and that they might have it more abundantly" (v. 10). Why say this *after* having already declared that "By Me if any man enter in, he shall *be saved*"? Mark this follows His reference to "The Thief". Here then our Lord seems to be looking forward to the Day of His second advent, as it relates to Israel. This indeed will be the time when *abundant* life will be theirs. As we read in Rom. 11:15, "If the casting away of them be the reconciling of the world, what shall the receiving of them be, but *life from the dead?*". In striking accord with this it should be noted that the Lord's title "I am the Door" (v. 9) is the *third* of His "I am" titles in this Gospel—the number which speaks of *resurrection.* Immediately following we find Christ saying here, "I am the good Shepherd" (v. 11). This is the *fourth* of His "I am" titles—the number of *the earth.* Thus, following the brief career of The Thief, Christ will be manifested to Israel as the abundant Life-giver, and then will He minister in grace as their good Shepherd. Thus do we find a reference to *four different Dispensations* in these verses. In v. 7 Christ is the Door out of *Judaism.* In v. 9 we have a description of the *Christian's* portion. In v. 10 reference is made to the Antichrist, who will run his awful course during the *Tribulation* period, while in v. 11, we have an anticipation of the "abundant" life bestowed on Israel during the *Millennium!*

As preparation for the next lesson let the interested student ponder carefully the following points:

1. Study the typical "shepherds" of the Old Testament.
2. Precisely what is the meaning of "for" in v. 11?
3. Did the Shepherd give His life for any besides "the sheep"?
4. What other adjectives besides "good" are applied to Christ as the "Shepherd"?
5. Who is referred to by "a hireling" (v. 12)?
6. Who are the "other sheep" of v. 16?
7. Look up proofs in the Gospels of the first part of v. 18.

—*Arthur W. Pink.*

GLEANINGS IN EXODUS.

10. A Hardened Heart: Exodus 7.

The seventh chapter begins the second literary division of the book of Exodus. The first six chapters are concerned more particularly with the *person of the deliverer,* the next six with an account of the *work of redemption.* In the first section we have had a brief description of the deadly persecution of Israel, then an account of Moses' birth and his miraculous preservation by God, then his identifying of himself with his people and his flight into Midian. Next, we have learned how God met him, commanded him to go down into Egypt, overcame his fears, and equipped him for his mission. Finally, we have noted how that he delivered Jehovah's message to the Hebrews and then to Pharaoh, and how that the king refused to heed the Divine demand, and how in consequence the people were thoroughly discouraged by the increased burdens laid upon them. Moses himself was deeply dejected, and chapter 6 closes with the Lord's servant bemoaning the seeming hopelessness of his task. Thus the *weakness* of the instrument was fully manifested that it might the better be seen that the *power* was of Jehovah alone, and of Jehovah acting not in response to faith but in covenant faithfulness and in sovereign grace.

From chapter 7 onwards there is a marked change: Moses is no more timid, hesitant and discouraged. The omnipotence of the Lord is displayed in every scene. The conflict from this point onwards was one not of words but of deeds. The gauntlet had been thrown down, and now it is open war between the Almighty and the Egyptians. It hardly needs to be pointed out that what is before us in these early chapters of Exodus is something more than a mere episode in ancient history, something more than what was simply of local interest. A thrilling drama is unfolded to our view, and though its movements are swift, yet is there sufficient detail and repetition in principle for us to discern clearly its great design. It spreads before us, in vivid tableau, *the great conflict between good and evil* as far as this comes within the range of human vision.

So far as Scripture informs us the Great Conflict is being fought out *in this world,* hence this historical drama, with its profound symbolic moral meaning, was staged in the land of *Egypt.* The great *mystery* in connection with the Conflict is forcibly shown us in the prosperity of the wicked and the adversity of the righteous. The Egyptians held the whip hand: the Hebrews groaned under unbearable oppression. The leading characters in the tableau are Moses as the vicegerant of *God,* and Pharaoh as the representative and emissary of *Satan.* The powerful and haughty king takes fiendish delight in persecuting the Lord's people, and openly defies the Almighty Himself. To outward sight *the issue* seemed long in doubt. The kingdom of Pharaoh was shaken again and again—as has the kingdom of Satan been during the course of the ages, in such events as the Flood, the destruction of the Canaanites the Advent of the Son of God, the day of Pentecost, the Reformation, etc., etc.—but each fresh interposition of Jehovah's power and the withdrawal of His judgments only issued in the hardening of Pharaoh's heart. The *prolongation* of the Egyptian contest gave full opportunity for the complete testing of human responsibility, the trying of the saints' faith, and the manifestation of all the perfections and attributes of Deity—apparently the three chief ends which the Creator has in view in suffering the entrance and *continuance* of evil in His domains. The great drama *closes* by showing the absolute triumph of Jehovah, the completed redemption of His people, and the utter overthrow of His and their enemies. Thus we have revealed to the eye of faith the Glorious Consummation when God's elect—through the work of the Mediator—shall be emancipated from all bondage, when every high thing that exalteth itself against the Almighty shall be cast down, and when God Himself shall be *all in all.* We shall now follow step by step the various stages by which this end was reached.

"And the Lord said unto Moses, See, I have made thee a god to Pharaoh: and Aaron thy brother shall be thy prophet" (7:1). This presents a startling contrast from what was before us at the close of Ex. 6. There we read of Moses' complaint before the Lord, "I am of uncircumcised lips, and how shall Pharaoh hearken unto me?". That was a confession of feebleness, but it sprang from unbelief. Here we find Jehovah acting according to His sovereign power and dealing in wondrous grace with His poor servant.

"I have made thee *a god* to Pharaoh", that is, Jehovah had selected Moses to act as His ambassador, had invested him with Divine authority, and was about to use him to perform prodigies which were contrary to the ordinary course of nature. But mark the qualification, "I have made thee a god *to Pharaoh*". Acting in God's stead, Moses was to *rule over* Egypt's proud king, commanding him what he should do, controlling him when he did wrong, and punishing him for his disobedience, so that Pharaoh had to apply *to him* for the removal of the plagues.

"And Aaron thy brother shall be *thy prophet*". If this be compared with 4:15, 16 we shall find a Divine definition of what constitutes a prophet. There we find the Lord promising Moses concerning Aaron that "thou shalt speak unto him, and put words in his mouth: and I will be with thy mouth, and with his mouth, and will teach you what ye shall do. And he shall be thy spokesman unto the people: and he shall be, even he shall be to thee instead of a mouth, and thou shalt be to him instead of God." God's prophet then is God's spokesman: he acts as God's mouthpiece, the Lord putting into his lips the very *words* he would utter. Thus Moses was a "god to Pharaoh" in this additional way, in that he had one who acted as *his* prophet.

"Thou shalt speak all that I command thee: and Aaron thy brother shall speak unto Pharaoh, that he send the children of Israel out of his land" (v. 2). This injunction was very definite. Moses was not free to make a selection from Jehovah's words and communicate to Aaron those which *he* deemed most advisable to say unto Pharaoh, but he was to speak *all* that had been commanded him. A similar charge is laid upon God's servant today: he is to "preach the Word" (2 Tim. 4:3) and to "hold fast *the form* of sound words" (2 Tim. 1:13), and is warned that "If any man teach otherwise, and consent not to wholesome words, even the words of our Lord Jesus Christ, and to the doctrine which is according to godliness; he is a fool, knowing nothing" (1 Tim. 6:3, 4). But alas! how few, how very few there are, who faithfully shun not to declare "the *whole* counsel of God".

"And I will harden Pharaoh's heart, and multiply My signs and My wonders in the land of Egypt" (v, 3). This verse brings before us one of the most solemn truths revealed in the Holy Scriptures—the Divine hardening of human hearts. At no point, perhaps, has the slowness of man to believe *all* that the prophets have spoken been more lamentably manifested than here. The hardening of Pharaoh's heart by God has been eagerly seized by His enemies to make an attack upon the citadel of truth. Infidels have argued that if Pharaoh's subsequent crimes were the result of his heart being hardened by Jehovah, then that makes God the author of his sins; and, furthermore, God must be very unrighteous in punishing him for them. The sad thing is that so many of the profest servants of God have, instead of faithfully maintaining the integrity of God's Word, attempted to blunt its keen edge in order to make it more acceptable to the carnal mind. Instead of acknowledging with fear and trembling that God's Word *does* teach that the Lord actually hardened the heart of Pharaoh, most of the commentators have really argued that He did nothing of the kind, that He simply *permitted* the Egyptian monarch to harden his own heart.

That Pharaoh *did* harden his own heart the Scriptures expressly affirm, but they *also* declare that THE LORD hardened his heart too, and clearly this is not one and the same thing, or the two *different* expressions would not have been employed. Our duty is to believe *both* statements, but to attempt to show the philosophy of their reconciliation is probably, as another has said, "to attempt to fathom infinity". In Psa. 105:25 it is said, "He turned their hearts to hate His people, to deal subtilly with His servants". Nothing could be stronger or plainer than this. Are we to deny it because *we* cannot explain the way in which God did it? On the same ground we might reject the doctrine of the Trinity. I may be asked how God could in any sense harden a man's heart without Him being the Author of sin. But the most assured belief of the fact does not require that an answer should be given by me to this question. If *God* has not explained the matter (and He has not), then it is not for us to feign to be wise above what is written. I believe many things recorded in Scripture not because I can *explain* their rationale, but because I know that God cannot lie. Calvin was right when he represented those as *perverting* the Scriptures who insist that no more is meant than a bare *permission* when God is said to harden the hearts of men. Is it nothing more than passive permission on His part when God *softens* men's hearts? Is it not, rather, by His active agency? Let us remember that it is no part of our business to vindicate God in justifying the grounds of His procedure; our responsibility is to believe *all* that He has revealed in His Word, on the sole ground of His written testimony. Our business is to "preach the Word" in its purity, not to tone it down or explain away its most objectionable portions in order to render it acceptable to the depraved reason of worms of the dust. The Lord will vindicate Himself in due time, silencing all His critics, and glorifying Himself before His saints.

It should be pointed out that the case of Pharaoh and the Egyptians does not by any means stand alone in the Holy Scriptures. In Deut. 2:30 Moses records the fact that "Sihon king of Heshbon would not let us pass by him: for the Lord thy God *hardened his spirit,* and *made his heart obstinate,* that He might deliver him into thy hand". The reference is to Num. 21:21-23 where we read, "And Israel sent messengers unto Sihon king of the Amorites, saying, Let me pass through thy land: we will not turn into the fields, or into the vineyards; we will not drink of the waters of the ground: but we will go along by the king's highway, until we be passed thy borders. And Sihon would not suffer Israel to pass through his borders". The verse in Deut. explains to us the reason of Sihon's obstinacy. Clearly it was no mere *judicial* hardening, instead it was a solemn illustration of what we read of in Rom. 9:18, *"whom He will* He hardens". So, too, in Joshua 11:19, 20 we are told "There was not a city that made peace with the children of Israel, save the Hivites the inhabitants of Gibeon: all other they took in battle. For it was of the Lord *to harden their hearts,* that they should come against Israel in battle, that He might destroy them utterly". Such solemn passages as these are not to be reasoned about, but must be accepted in childlike faith, knowing that the Judge of all the earth does nothing but what is *right*.

"But Pharaoh shall not hearken unto you, that I may lay My hand upon Egypt, and bring forth Mine armies, and My people the children of Israel, out of the land of Egypt by great judgments, and the Egyptians shall know that I am the Lord, when I stretch forth Mine hand upon Egypt, and bring out the children of Israel from among them" (vv. 4, 5). These verses supply us with one reason *why* the Lord hardened the hearts of Pharaoh and the Egyptians: it was in order that He might have full opportunity to display His mighty power. A dark background it was indeed, but a dark background is required to bring out the white light of Divine holiness. Similarly we find the Lord Jesus saying, "It *must needs be* that offences come, but woe to that man by whom the offence cometh" (Matt. 18:7). What Jehovah's "great judgments" were we shall see in the chapters that follow.

"And Moses and Aaron did as the Lord commanded them, so did they" (v. 6). Why are we told this here? We believe the answer is, To point a contrast from what we find at the beginning of Ex. 5. In the opening verse of that chapter we learn that Moses "went in, and told Pharaoh, Thus saith the Lord God of Israel, Let My people go". This was the Lord's peremptory *demand*. Then we read of Pharaoh's scornful refusal. Now note what follows: "And they said, The God of the Hebrews hath met with us: let us go, *we pray thee*, three days' journey into the desert, and sacrifice unto the Lord our God". It is plain that Moses and Aaron *changed* the Lord's words. They *toned down* the offensive message. Instead of occupying the high ground of God's ambassadors and *commanding* Pharaoh, they descended to the servile level of *pleading* with him and making a *request* of him. It is for this reason, we believe, that in 7:1 we find Jehovah saying to Moses, *"See* (that is, mark it well) I have made thee *a god* to Pharaoh": it is not for you to go and *beg* from him, it is for you to demand and command. And then the Lord added, "Thou shalt speak all that I *command thee*". This time the Lord's servants obeyed to the letter, hence we are now told that they "did *as* the Lord commanded them, *so* did they".

"And Moses was fourscore years old, and Aaron fourscore and three years old, when they spake unto Pharaoh" (v. 7). This reference to the ages of Moses and Aaron seems to be brought in here in order to magnify the power and grace of Jehovah. He was pleased to employ two *aged* men as His instruments. No doubt the Holy Spirit would also impress us with the *lengthiness* of Israel's afflictions, and the long-sufferance of Jehovah before He dealt in judgment. For over eighty years the Hebrews had been sorely oppressed.

"And the Lord spake unto Moses and unto Aaron, saying, When Pharaoh shall speak unto you, saying, Show a miracle for you: then thou shalt say unto Aaron, Take thy rod, and cast it before Pharaoh, and it shall become a serpent. And Moses and Aaron went in unto Pharaoh, and they did so as the Lord had commanded: and Aaron cast down his rod before Pharaoh, and before his servants, and it became a serpent. Then Pharaoh also called the wise men and the sorcerers: now the magicians of Egypt, they also did in like manner with their enchantments. For they cast down every man his rod, and they became serpents: but Aaron's rod swallowed up their rods" (vv. 8-12). The reason why Pharaoh asked Moses and Aaron to perform a miracle was to test them and prove whether or not the God of the Hebrews had really sent them. The miracle or sign selected we have already considered at length in Article 6. Its meaning and message in the present connection is not easy to determine. From an evidential viewpoint it demonstrated that Moses and Aaron were supernaturally endowed. Probably, too, the rod becoming a serpent was designed to speak to the conscience of Pharaoh, intimating that he and his people were under the dominion of Satan. This seems to be borne out by the fact that nothing was here said—either by the Lord when instructing Moses (v. 9), or in the description of the miracle (vv. 10-12)—about the serpent being turned into a rod again. It is also very significant that the second sign—the restoring of the leprous hand—which accredited Moses before the Israelites, was not performed before Pharaoh. The reason for this is obvious: the people of God, not the men of the world, are the only ones who have *revealed* to them the secret of deliverance from the defilement of sin.

The response of Pharaoh to this miracle wrought by Moses and Aaron was remarkable. The king summoned his wise men and the sorcerers—those who were in league with the powers of evil—and they duplicated the miracle. It is indeed sad to find almost all of the commentators *denying* that a real miracle was performed by the Egyptian magicians. Whatever philosophical or doctrinal difficulties may be involved, it ill becomes us to yield to the rationalism of our day. The scriptural account is very explicit and leaves no room for uncertainty. First, the Holy Spirit has told us that the magicians of Egypt "also did *in like manner* (as what Moses and Aaron had done) with their enchantments." These words are not to be explained away, but are to be received by simple faith. Second, it is added, "for they cast down every man his *rod,* (not something else which they had substituted by sleight of hand) and they (the rods) *became* serpents". If language has any meaning then these words bar out the idea that the magicians threw down serpents. They cast down their rods, and these *became* serpents. Finally, we are told, "but Aaron's rod swallowed up their rods", i. e., Aaron's rod, now turned into a serpent, swallowed up their rods, now become serpents. That the Holy Spirit has worded it in this way is evidently for the express purpose of forbidding us to conclude that anything other than "rods" were cast to the ground.

If it should be asked, How was it possible for these Egyptian sorcerers to perform this miracle? the answer must be, By the power of the Devil. This subject is admittedly mysterious, and much too large a one for us to enter into now at length. As remarked at the beginning of this paper, what is before us here in these earlier chapters of Exodus adumbrates the great conflict between good and evil. Pharaoh acts throughout as the representative of Satan, and the fact that he was able to summon magicians who could work such prodigies only serves to illustrate and exemplify the mighty powers which the Devil has at his disposal. It is both foolish and mischievous to under-estimate the strength of our great Enemy. The one that was permitted to transport our Saviour from the wilderness to the temple at Jerusalem, and the one who was able to show Him "all the kingdoms of the world *in a moment of time*" (Luke 4:5), would have no difficulty in empowering his emissaries to transform their rods into serpents.

"They cast down every man his rod, and they became serpents: but Aaron's rod swallowed up their rods" (v. 12). This is very striking. The magicians appeared in the name of their "gods" (cf Ex. 12:12 and 18:11), but this miracle made it apparent that the power of Moses was *superior* to their sorceries, and *opposed* to them too. This "sign" foreshadowed the end of the great conflict then beginning, as of every other wherein powers terrestrial and infernal contend with the Almighty. "The symbols of their authority have disappeared, and that of Jehovah's servants alone remained" (Urquhart).

"And He hardened Pharaoh's heart (literally, Pharaoh's heart was hardened) that he hearkened not unto them; as the Lord had said" (v. 13). Here again the commentators offend grievously. They insist, almost one and all, that this verse signifies that Pharaoh hardened his own heart, and that it was not until later, and *because* of Pharaoh's obduracy, that the Lord "hardened" his heart. But this very verse unequivocally repudiates their carnal reasonings. This verse emphatically declares that Pharaoh's heart was hardened, that he hearkened not unto them, *as the Lord had said"*. Now let the previous chapters be read through carefully and note *what* the Lord *had* said. He had said *nothing whatever* about Pharaoh hardening his own heart! But He *had* said, *"I will* harden his heart" (4:21), and again, *"I will* harden his heart" (7:3). This settles the matter. God had expressly declared that He *would* harden the king's heart, and now we read in 7:13 that "Pharaoh's heart *was* hardened (not, "was hard"), that he harkened not unto them, AS *the Lord had said"*. Man ever reverses the order of God. The carnal mind says, Do good in order to be saved: God says, You must be saved before you can do any good thing. The carnal mind reasons that a man must believe in order to be born again; the Scriptures teach that a man must first have spiritual life before he can manifest the activities of that life. Those who follow the theologians will conclude that God hardened Pharaoh's heart because the king had *first* hardened his heart; but those who bow to the authority of Holy Writ (and there are *very* few who *really* do so), will acknowledge that Pharaoh hardened his heart *because* God had first hardened it.

What is said here of Pharaoh affords a most solemn illustration of what we read of in Prov. 21:1: "The king's heart is in the hand of the Lord, as the rivers of water: *He* turneth it *whithersoever He will*". The hardening of Pharaoh's heart is not one whit more appalling than what we read of it Rev. 17:17: "For *God hath put in their hearts* to fulfill His will, and to agree, and give their kingdom unto the Beast". Here we find ten kings in league with the Antichrist, the Man of Sin, and that it is God Himself who puts it into their hearts to give their kingdom unto him. Again we say that such things are not to be philosophized about. Nor are we to call into question the righteousness and holiness of God's ways. Scripture plainly tells us that *His* ways are "*past* finding out" (Rom. 11:33). Let us then tremble before Him, and if in marvelous grace He has softened *our* hearts let us magnify His sovereign mercy unceasingly.

—Arthur W. Pink.

THE DIVINE INSPIRATION OF THE BIBLE.

The Divine Authorship of the Bible is a truth of basic importance, for it is the starting-place of all doctrinal discussion. Not until the question of the absolute sufficiency and authority of the Scriptures have been settled are we really prepared to own them as the final court of appeal. On the foundation of the inspiration and inerrancy of the Word of God rests the whole edifice of Christian truth. Grant that the Bible *is* what it claims to be, namely an infallible communication from the Lord Himself, and at once we have a platform upon which we can meet together to discuss the vital truths of our faith. But once let go this truth of the Divine Authorship of the Bible and we are left like a ship without a rudder, chart, or compass. It is, therefore, impossible to over-estimate or over-emphasize the importance of our present subject. The Inspiration of the Scriptures is the strategic center of theology, and the one point against which Satan is ceaselessly directing his fiercest assaults. If a preacher is unsound on *this* truth he is at once discredited and disqualified to teach God's truth at all.

Is it possible to be sure beyond all doubt that the Bible *is* the Word of God? Certainly it is. God has not left Himself without witness, rather has He been pleased to give us "many infallible proofs". If the Bible is an unique Book, we should expect to find it has unique credentials; if the Scriptures are a Divine revelation we should expect to discover the Divine autograph stamped upon them; if the Bible is the Word of God we should expect to find in it many things which men were incapable of originating. And, as we turn to the Bible and study it reverently, diligently, and prayerfully, we shall find these expectations are fully realized. The evidence is so full, the infallible proofs are so many that God Himself is the Author of the Book which bears His name, that our chief difficulty is to make a selection. In this article we shall confine ourself to one of the more simple and obvious lines of demonstrating the superhuman origin and nature of the Bible.

THE CHARACTER OF ITS CONTENTS EVIDENCES THE DIVINE AUTHORSHIP OF THE BIBLE

Summed up in a brief statement the force of this argument may be put thus: the *unique* teachings of the Scriptures imply an unique Origin. On every great subject of which the Bible treats its teaching differs radically from that of every other book. What the Scriptures have to say on all its leading themes is so contrary to the thoughts and ideas of men, that we are obliged to conclude that it is impossible that the human mind invented them.

1. Take the Teaching of the Bible about God Himself.

What does the Bible reveal concerning God? It represents Him as the One uncaused, uncreated, eternal Being in the universe, without beginning and without end —a representation to be found nowhere else in all the realm of literature. It represents Him as a Trinity in Unity: one God, and yet three Persons, Father, Son, and Holy Spirit, equally God and yet not three Gods—a conception which altogether transcends the grasp of the finite intellect, and therefore could not have had its birth there. It represents God as the Supreme Being, absolute Sovereign, doing "according to His will in the army of heaven, and among the inhabitants of the earth, so that *none* can stay His hand, or say unto Him, What doest Thou?" (Dan. 4:35). It represents Him as the Potter, and His creatures as the clay, to be moulded as pleaseth Him best. It represents Him as "The Judge of all the earth", unto Whom every one shall yet render an account (Rom. 14:12). It represents Him as inflexibly Just: so just that "He will by no means clear the guilty". It represents Him as being absolutely Holy: dwelling in light inaccessible; so Holy that He is "of purer eyes than to behold iniquity" (Hab. 1:13); so Holy that even the heavens are not clean in His sight. It represents Him as Immutable, as the One who changeth not, being without "variableness" or "shadow of turning" (Jas. 1:17). It represents Him as being Love, love which "passeth knowledge", a love which was manifested in the giving of His only begotten Son to die for a world of rebels that had forfeited every claim upon His notice. It represents Him as "the God of all Grace", providing a salvation, "without money and without price", for those who merit naught but eternal damnation.

Now we submit to the candid reader, that no man and no number of men ever invented such a God as this! Such a delineation of Deity is as far above human conception as the heavens are above the earth. Ransack the writings of the ancients, study the religions of heathendom, explore the whole realm of human literature, and nowhere is anything to be found which can compare for a moment, with the sublime and exalted description of the Divine Character which is discovered on the pages of Holy Writ.

2. Take the Teaching of the Bible about Man.

Unlike every other book in the world the Bible *condemns* man and all his doings. The Bible never eulogizes his wisdom nor praises his achievements, instead, it declares that "every man at his best estate is altogether vanity". What human mind ever invented such a declaration as that? Instead of teaching that man began at the bottom, and that he is now slowly but successfully climbing toward the top, it declares that he commenced at the top and through his own wickedness has fallen to the bottom. Instead of teaching that man is a wise, noble, god-like creature, it declares that he is foolish, corrupt, sinful, and vile. It represents him with a heart that is "deceitful above all things and desperately wicked" (Jer. 17:9). It represents him with a "mind that is enmity against God" (Rom. 8:7). It represents him as being "without strength" (Rom. 5:6). It represents men, all men, as being by nature without capacity to receive the things of God (1 Cor. 2:14). It represents them as "having the understanding darkened, being alienated from the life of God through the ignorance that is in them, because of the blindness of their heart" (Eph. 4:18). It declares that "there is none righteous, no, not one: there is none that understandeth, there is none that seeketh after God. They are *all* gone out of the way, they are together become unprofitable: there is none that doeth good, no, not one." (Rom. 3:10-12).

Now we submit to the candid reader that such a description of fallen human nature was never invented by the human mind. We submit that such a humiliating picture of man—so utterly *unlike* that which every other book in the world contains—was never drawn by man. We submit that a delineation of human depravity, such as the Bible depicts, and which is so repellant to the proud heart of the creature, could have been furnished by none other than God Himself.

3. Take the Teaching of the Bible about the World.

Using the term "world" of the world-system in contradistinction from the earth, what are man's thoughts of it? Man thinks highly of it, for he regards it as his world: it is that which his labours have produced, and he looks upon it with satisfaction and pride. His boast is that the world is growing better. Man's thoughts upon it have been well summarized by the poet thus: "God is in heaven, All's well with the world."

But what saith the Scriptures? Upon this subject also we find that God's thoughts are very different from man's. The Bible uniformly *condemns* the world and speaks of it as an "evil world". It declares that the "wisdom of this world is foolishness with God". Certainly no uninspired pen wrote that! It says, "Know ye not that the friendship of the world is enmity with God?" (Jas. 4:4). Certainly none of human kind ever invented that! It says, "Love not the world, neither the things that are in the world; if any man love the world, the love of the Father is not in him: For *all* that is in the world, the lust of the flesh, and the lust of the eyes, and the pride of life, is not of the Father" (1 John 2:15, 16). Here then we have the Divinely-inspired definition of the world: it is all that is opposed to the Father—opposed in its maxims and methods, its aims and ambitions, its trend and its end. The Scriptures declare that "the *whole* world lieth in the Evil One" (1 John 5:19 R.V.). This explains why the world hates Christ and His followers, why its wisdom is foolishness with God, why it is to be shunned by His children—it is under the dominion of that old Serpent, the Devil, who three times over is denominated "the Prince of this World."

Again we submit to our readers that the teaching of Scripture concerning the world, teaching which is so radically opposed to all the philosophies and beliefs of men, could have been given by none but God Himself.

4. Take the Teaching of the Bible about Sin.

Men regard sin as a misfortune and ever seek to minimize its enormity. In many quarters sin is simply regarded as ignorance, and the sinner as one who is more to be pitied than blamed. The different terms invented as substitutes for the word sin indicate the low and inadequate views which men have—"mistakes," "short-comings", "imperfections", youthful "follies" they term them, instead of transgressions, iniquities, wickedness, lawlessness.

Unlike all other books, the Bible strips man of every excuse and emphasizes his culpability. In Scripture, sin is never palliated or extenuated, but throughout, its enormity and heinousness are insisted upon. Proverbs 24:9 declares that "the thought of foolishness is sin"—what human mind ever invented such a standard as that? Romans 14:23 proclaims, *"Whatsoever* is not of faith is sin". Under the Old Testament economy God required that even "sins of ignorance" should have an atoning sacrifice. (Lev. 4).

The Bible teaches that sin is more than an act or a series of acts—it is an *attitude* which lies behind and produces the act. "Sin is lawlessness" (1 John 3:4 R.V.); that is to say, sin is spiritual anarchy. Sin is not merely a non-compliance with God's law, it is an attitude of rebellion against the Law-Giver. The Bible teaches that not only are we all sinners by practice, but that we are sinners by nature, and that each of us has to own, "Behold I was shapen in iniquity, and in sin did my mother conceive me" (Psa. 51:5). Ah, what mortal mind originated such a statement as that!

The Bible does not reserve its severest indictments for any particular class, but condemns all alike. It says, *"All* we like sheep have gone astray, we have turned every one to *his own way*" (Isa. 53:6). It declares that, "There is no difference: for *all* have sinned and come short of the glory of God" (Rom. 3:23).

Now we submit to the candid reader that the Book which uniformly depicts sin as a vile and hideous thing which God hates, which strips man of every excuse, which condemns all his ways, which declares that "every imagination of the thoughts of his heart is only evil continually" (Gen. 6:5), which brings in "all the world guilty before God" (Rom. 3:19), could not have been compiled by man, but *must* have issued forth from the Thrice Holy One.

5. Take the Teaching of the Bible about the Punishment of Sin.

A defective view of sin necessarily leads to an inadequate conception of what is due sin. Men look at sin and its deserts solely from the human viewpoint, but the Bible lets us know how *God* regards sin. For one single sin God banished our first parents from Eden. For one single sin He caused the posterity of Ham to lie perpetually under their father's curse. For one single sin He turned the wife of Lot into a pillar of salt. For one single sin He slew Dathan and Abiram. For one single sin He caused the earth to open her mouth so that Korah and his company went down alive into the Pit. For one single sin Moses was debarred from entering Canaan. For one single sin Achan and his family were stoned to death. For one single sin Gehazi was stricken with leprosy. For one single sin Ananias and Sapphira fell down dead. Thus has God exhibited His hatred of sin and the awful severity of His dealings with it.

The Scriptures teach that "the wages of sin is death", death which leads to and ends in the Lake of Fire, which is "the Second Death". Scripture declares that the doom of the one who dies in sin is eternal suffering in conscious torment. It pictures Hell as the place where even a drop of water is denied the agonizing sufferer. It represents the place of punishment as being that "where their worm dieth not, and the fire is not quenched". It depicts it as the sphere where reigns "the blackness of darkness forever" (Jude 13), where not a single ray ever penetrates into its awful dismal regions. In short, it pictures the portion of the lost as *unbearable* and yet as that which will *have to be borne,* and that "forever and ever".

Now my reader, what mortal mind ever conceived such a fate as this? What sinning man of men ever invented such an indescribably frightful doom as the Bible declares is awaiting every Christ-rejector? Who but the Thrice Holy God, that is alone capable of deciding what is due the sin done against Himself, could have lifted the veil and given us a glimpse of the awful character of sin's "wages"? The fact that this solemn truth is so distasteful to all of us, and is so widely denied by men, is surely proof positive that no man ever invented it. And the fact that Eternal Punishment *is* taught in the Bible, taught plainly and prominently, is another of the many evidences of its super-human origin and authorship.

6. Take the Teaching of the Bible about Salvation.

What must I do to be saved? Such is the earnest inquiry that issues from every exercised heart. That man is a sinner few will deny. That by virtue of his sin man is *unfit* for the presence of God is recognized on every hand. Even the heathen discern the need for propitiating their "gods". But who can provide an adequate sacrifice? Who can produce that which will be acceptable to the Most High? Who can manufacture the covering which is capable of hiding the shame of our depravity from the eyes of the Thrice Holy One?

By his own efforts man cannot be saved. Adam and Eve wove an apron of fig leaves, but such a device failed to satisfy even themselves, for when the One against whom they had sinned visited the garden in the cool of the day, they *hid* themselves from Him among the trees! ! Cain brought an offering of the fruits of the ground, but unto the product of his hands God had not respect. At Sinai the Law was given, not as a means of salvation, but to reveal more plainly man's need of salvation. There is no deliverance through law-keeping is evident, for once for all it stands written, "by the deeds of the law there shall *no flesh* be justified in His sight" (Rom. 3:20).

Is there no refuge from the wrath to come? Is there no escape from the fully merited anger of a sin-avenging God? Is there no way in which a poor sinner may have remitted the guilt and wages of all his sins? Blessed be God there is, but it is a way that could never have occurred to any of the sons of men. The obstacles which barred the sinner's access into the Presence of God were insuperable to human wisdom and might. God is holy and sin must be punished. God is righteous and the claims of His throne cannot be set aside. God is faithful and the sentence which has gone forth from His mouth must be carried out.

How could God be just and yet the Justifier of the ungodly? How could God be holy and yet receive into His Presence one who is by nature and practice a moral leper? How can God demand the payment of sin's wages, and yet save the one who is a rebel against His government? Such problems as these transcend the reach of man's mind. But God has found a solution, a solution which instead of casting a reflection upon His holy name, magnifies and glorifies it. *God's solution is substitution.* Another took the guilty sinner's place. The Just died for the unjust. The Lamb of God was sacrificed in our stead. On the blessed Head of God's own Son was visited 'the whole of wrath Divine'. And 'payment God cannot twice demand, first at my bleeding Surety's hand, and then again at mine'. Here is God's solution: "For He hath made Him to be sin for us, who knew no sin that we might be made the righteousness of God in Him" (2 Cor. 5:21).

Here then is the full and blessed answer. Christ has satisfied God, and Christ satisfies each and all who receive Him by faith. On the Finished Work of Christ is the needy sinner invited to rest. Nothing to do; all has been done. Nothing to pay; all has been paid. Nothing, now, but to receive eternal life as God's *gift* in Jesus Christ our Lord. What must I do to be saved? This—"Believe on the Lord Jesus Christ *and thou shalt be saved.*"

And here once more the Contents of the Scriptures reveal their super-human Origin. The teaching of the Bible concerning God's way of salvation demonstrates its Divine authorship. What mortal mind could have devised a way whereby God could be just and yet merciful, merciful and yet just? What human intellect would have conceived of a glorious and eternal salvation proffered to Hell-deserving sinners "without money and without price?" And what flight of man's imagination would ever have dreamed of the Lord of Glory taking upon Him the form of a servant and being made in the likeness of sinful flesh in order that He might die the death of the cross to procure salvation for the enemies of God!

A very brief word by way of application and we close. The Bible *is* an unique Book: by many infallible proofs it is demonstrated to be none other than the Word of God. What then is the practical conclusion which must be drawn? This:—An unique Book has unique claims upon us. An unique Book calls for unique attention and demands the first place in our lives. "Search the Scriptures" is its own call: honour them supremely, study them diligently, believe them implicitly, preach, teach and scatter them daily and universally.

Arthur W. Pink.

The above is the substance of one chapter from the Editor's book on the Divine Inspiration of the Bible. This book is much needed today to offset the infidelity of Rationalism. It contains twelve other arguments equally conclusive as the above. Valuable for believers. Price only 75 cents. Order from the Editor.

HAVE I REPENTED?

A word to the anxious.

The above enquiry is the burden of many anxious souls. Worlds, if possessed, would be gladly given for satisfactory evidence of genuine repentance. The writer will not forget the time when the words, *"Except ye repent, ye shall all likewise perish"*, haunted him day and night. To him repentance seemed the hard condition imposed upon the sinner before salvation would be bestowed. It is the belief that many souls are similarly situated which induces him to write this paper, in the hope that, with the blessing of God, it may be used for their deliverance.

The law given by Moses, though it expressed God's holiness, was no revelation of His heart. It confronted men with demands. "This do, and thou shalt live," was its most encouraging voice; and upon the slightest deviation from its precepts, curses were thundered forth upon the delinquent. Ah! let a man but measure himself by that perfect standard, and his heartfelt conviction will be, that "by the deeds of the law there shall no flesh be justified." (Rom. 3:20).

Doubtless many of our readers have come to this conclusion. Attempting to keep the law, its purity has shown them their utter incompetency, while its curses have filled their hearts with terror and dismay. Such naturally enquire, How shall we escape the wrath to come? "Repentance toward God, and faith toward our Lord Jesus Christ," is the gospel preached unto them. Strange to say, this reply, plunges them into deepest distress. Repentance seems to them only another law—a law the condition of which they are totally incapable of fulfilling. "To believe in the Lord Jesus," says one, "is very simple and blessed; but oh! this repentance toward God is what perplexes me."

Dear reader, you entirely misunderstand three things—the love of God, God's way of salvation, and your own condition.

GOD'S LOVE you do not know, or you would see that hard conditions are altogether contrary to it.

GOD'S WAY OF SALVATION you do not understand, for His salvation is suited to man's need.

YOUR OWN CONDITION you have imperfect views of, or you would at once perceive that if God were to make any kind of demand, you would never obtain salvation; for you are absolutely *without strength.* (Rom. 5:6).

God's love is shown "in that, while we were yet sinners, Christ died for us." Suppose that a man had given his only son, whom he tenderly loved, to die a death of no ordinary suffering in order that your life might be saved. Would you have any suspicions of that man's love? Would you expect him to make hard terms when dealing with you? Surely not! Hard terms would be entirely inconsistant with such a display of love. Yet this picture very poorly depicts the love of God." He that *spared not His own Son,* but freely delivered Him up for us all, how shall He not with Him also *freely give* us all things?"

God's way of salvation we have in John 3:14, 15: "And as Moses lifted up the serpent in the wilderness, even so must the Son of man be lifted up: that whosoever believeth in Him should not perish, but have eternal life."

Your condition is most graphically described in Luke 10:30: "A certain man went down from Jerusalem to Jericho, and fell among thieves, which stripped him of his raiment, and wounded him, and departed, leaving him half dead." Oh, what misery! what complete helplessness! If any demands had been advanced by the Samaritan, would the unfortunate traveller have stood the slightest chance? Not the slightest. He was penniless, naked, and half dead. It would have been better for the Samaritan to have walked on, like the priest and the Levite, than for him to have wearied the man by proposing terms which he was totally incapable of meeting. Dear friend, this narrative gives a true picture of your condition in the sight of God. You can do nothing to help yourself; but like the robbed, wounded, and dying man, you need the Good Samaritan to take your case entirely upon Himself. Perhaps you are ready to reply, "All that you have said may be quite true, but you have not yet removed my difficulty. The Scripture still remains, 'Except ye repent, ye shall all likewise perish.'

I have not forgotten your difficulty, but have first spoken of God's love, God's way of salvation, and your condition before Him; thinking that, if you were clear on these points, you would more easily see what repentance really is. And before going farther I would press upon you the fact, that God has written His Word that you may *know* the way of salvation. It is not His desire that you should find the way perplexing. Far from it. Hear His own word, "Cast ye up, prepare the way, take up the stumbling-block out of the way of My people." There are stumbling-blocks, it is true, but God is not the author of them. They are created by the reasonings of our own minds, by the teachings of men, and by the suggestions of Satan. But now we will consider your difficulty.

For a definition of repentance we will not apply to dictionaries, for they will give us only human thoughts; but we will turn to God's Word, and see in what sense the word repentance is used there. Let me try to illustrate this. Before the light shines into the conscience of man he is satisfied that although not altogether what he should be, yet he is not far wrong. God's Word comes home in power to his soul. Oh, what a change of thought and action takes place! He endorses entirely the description of man given by God in Romans 3, not necessarily because he feels himself to be so vile, but because God's Word thus describes him. What is the result? He takes his place in the dust before God, and centres all his hope for salvation, not in his own works, but in the precious blood of Christ. *This is repentance.*

Another man thinks himself able to appear before God on the ground of his own merits, and looks upon ordinary folk with contempt. He prides himself upon his righteous dealings with his neighbour, and his sedulous attention to religious duties. But he reads in God's Word, "By the deeds of the law there shall no flesh be justified." "The soul that sinneth it shall die." Like a two-edged sword God's Word pierces the man's heart, and slays his vain pretensions. What is the result? Instead of saying, like the Pharisee, "Lord, I thank Thee I am not as other men," his innermost feelings find expression in the words of the despised publican, "God be merciful to me a sinner." *This is repentance.*

Now, if you will turn to the fifteenth chapter of Luke's Gospel, you will find the simplest explanation of repentance that it is possible for us to have. I am referring, as perhaps you already judge, to the parable of the prodigal son; and as we ponder it, I want you to remember it was the Lord Jesus Himself who drew this picture. Here we get not only the father's heart and the father's provision, but we also have *the son's repentance.*

Now please take particular notice, for I believe this will be helpful to you. The son left his father's house, and in the far country wasted his substance with riotous living. That clearly was not repentance, but the very opposite. When he had spent all, there arose a mighty famine in that land, and he began to be in want. But that was not repentance. He joined himself to a citizen, and would fain have satisfied his hunger with the swine's food. But that was not repentance.

Now, however, a change takes place. He comes to himself, and thinks of the father's house and its provisions. He contrasts his state of misery, degradation, and hunger, with the happy condition of even the hired servants in his father's house, and resolves to return to his father in full confession of his guilt. But he did not merely resolve; he arose and came to his father, confessing his sin, and acknowledging his unworthiness. *Ah! this was repentance.*

And, dear reader, I tell you, upon the authority of God's Word, that God is willing to receive you just as you are. He bids you return to Him as a poor, lost, guilty sinner. Take the place of the destitute, go to God in the name of His Son, the Lord Jesus Christ, and you will find that He giveth liberally and upbraideth not. Do not, I pray you, approach God as Naaman the leper went to the prophet of Israel. He took what he considered sufficient to purchase the blessing; but he found that God bestows His inestimable blessings *without money and without price.*

"But", says some one, "is it not stated in the Bible that 'godly sorrow worketh repentance to salvation not to be repented of'? It is this scripture that troubles me; for although I am truly sorry for my position, yet I cannot, much as I have tried, feel what I suppose to be godly sorrow concerning my sins."

Dear friend, if you would properly understand God's Word, you must carefully avoid the unhappy habit of interpreting passages of scripture apart from their context. I would ask you to observe that the scripture that troubles you was written to the Corinthian saints, who already possessed the salvation of their souls. If you read the first epistle to the Corinthians you will see that they had been sanctioning evil, in that they allowed a person living in gross sin to sit with them at the Lord's table. Paul hearing of this grave state of affairs, wrote them a letter of rebuke. What was the effect of that letter? It wrought repentance.

When Paul had learnt of the effect of his letter, he wrote to them again as follows: "Now, I rejoice, not that you were made sorry, but that ye sorrowed to repentance: for ye were made sorry after a godly manner. . . . . . For godly sorrow worketh repentance to salvation not to be repented of." The result of their godly sorrow was that they cleansed themselves from the evil. But again I repeat, *this was written to persons whose souls were already saved by faith in Christ,* but who needed to repent of evil allowed in their midst, in order that they might be in a condition suited to their relationship with God.

And now we trust that the difficulties that have been in your mind in connection with this passage of Scripture are removed. God never intended that verse to perplex souls desiring salvation; although, no doubt, it has been an obstacle in your path by your not observing the connection in which it stands.

Perhaps some one is mentally saying, "Ah! you have not mentioned my difficulty." My dear friend, I am truly desirous to take up the stumbling-block out of your way. What is your trouble? Well," you reply, "I know that what God has written of me is perfectly true; but I do not *feel* myself so vile. I never could say that I *felt* myself deserving the flames of hell. I do indeed trust in Christ's precious blood, and in that alone, for safety; but is it not essential to repentance that I *feel* myself exceedingly vile, and worthy of hell?

Your trouble is not an uncommon one; but the root from which it springs is the deeply-seated and widely-spread error, that God demands something from the sinner before bestowing salvation. Listen a moment. A man is on trial for a crime that he has committed. He is convicted, and the judge sentences the criminal to a term of imprisonment. Although well knowing himself guilty, the man may have but little perception of the heinousness of the crime, and altogether fail to estimate aright the punishment that the crime deserves. Thus is it with us. We have been brought before the tribunal of God.

OUR CHARACTER has been thus described: "There is none righteous, no, not one: there is none that understandeth, there is none that seeketh after God. They are all gone out of the way, they are together become unprofitable; there is none that doeth good, no, not one. Their throat is an open sepulchre; with their tongues they have used deceit; the poison of asps is under their lips: whose mouth is full of cursing and bitterness: their feet are swift to shed blood: destruction and misery are in their ways: and the way of peace have they not known: there is no fear of God before their eyes." (Rom. 3)

THE VERDICT has been given. We have been brought in *guilty before God.*

THE SENTENCE has been passed: "The wicked shall be turned into hell, and all the nations that forget God." (Psalm 9:17). "Shall not the Judge of all the earth do right?" "Let God be true, but every man a liar." We will not trust our feelings, they are changeable. We will not take it upon ourselves to say what we deserve: we are not the judge, but the culprits. But we will simply set to our seal that *God is true,* whether it be as to our nature, our deeds, or the punishment we deserve.

One word more. I said above, that there are some who consider that faith is simple, but repentance is difficult. I would tell such, that repentance and faith go together. Wherever there is true faith, there is also true repentance. Nor can any man place his confidence in Christ's precious blood without abandoning self-confidence, and taking the low place before God; and this is repentance. The way of salvation is very simple; God meant it to be so.

Oh, dear reader, beware of the reasonings of thy own heart; beware of the suggestions of Satan! If thou hast but returned, through Christ, to God, as did the prodigal to his father, that best robe is placed upon thee. Receive God's Word in simplicity, or thou wilt not feel the comfort of the robe, nor enjoy its beauty. The table is spread by the Father's hand, and the Father's voice bids thee be seated. (Luke 15). Oh, why should a single anxious thought remain in thy breast? "Thy sins be forgiven thee" are the words that fell from the lips of the Saviour Himself. Why not receive them, and be glad, as was the prodigal when the father fell upon his neck, and kissed him?

Throw thy doubts, poor trembling one, to the winds; for it is God Himself that speaks. Receive His Word, and thou shalt indeed rejoice. Adorned in the best robe, the ring upon thy hand, and the shoes upon thy feet, thou shalt know what it is to sit at the Father's table, and feed upon the choicest provision. There shall be given unto thee "beauty for ashes, the oil of joy for mourning, the garment of praise for the spirit of heaviness."

Oh, blessed exchange! The language of thy heart shall be, "What shall I render unto the Lord for all His benefits toward me?" "Thou hast turned for me my mourning into dancing: Thou hast put off my sackcloth and girded me with gladness". Amen! and yet again, Amen!

Simple Testimony 1887.

GALATIANS 6:6.

"Let him that is taught in the Word, communicate unto him that teacheth in all good things."

Here the duty of supporting those who teach in the churches of Christ is inculcated. The labourer is worthy of his hire, and the Lord applies this proverb to those whom He sent out to preach. The situation of the elders of a church is somewhat different, but although they are not to be actuated by the love of money, they are entitled to support. "Let the elders that rule well be counted worthy of double honour, especially they who labour in the Word and doctrine. For the Scripture saith, Thou shalt not muzzle the ox that treadeth out the corn. And, The labourer is worthy of his reward." (1 Tim. 5:17, 18). The two branches of the elder's office are here described,—ruling and teaching. They are intimately connected. The rule of the elder of a church is not by force, but by persuasion and instruction; but those who labour in word and doctrine require to devote more time to study, and, therefore, they are specially pointed out as entitled to support, which is evidently intended by double honour. Our Lord interprets the honour due to parents, as having the same meaning. In writing to the Corinthians, he enforces the same duty: "Do ye not know, that they which minister about holy things, live of the things of the temple? and they which wait at the altar are partakers with the altar? Even so hath the Lord ordained, that they which preach the gospel should live by the gospel." (1 Cor. 9:13, 14). Thus the Lord has provided for the support of teachers in His churches. Like every other precept of Christ, it interferes with that selfish spirit and attachment to a present world, which is natural to us all. It is observed by Riccaltoun, who was himself a minister of an established church:—"Perhaps the neglect of this ordinance of God, for the support of a Gospel ministry, and substituting another method of provision in its room, has contributed more than any one thing to the corruptions which have in all ages disfigured and disgraced the Christian religion." This, like other corruptions, has taken its rise from going back to the weak and beggarly elements of Judaism, and is intimately connected with considering the clergy to be a distinct order, like the priests and Levites of old.

In the Epistles, believers are taught the importance of order and method. "God is not the author of confusion, but of peace, as in all churches of the saints." (1 Cor. 14:33). He has not only delivered rules for the government of His churches, but has appointed office-bearers, by whom these rules are to be carried into effect. If we turn to the history of Israel's journey through the wilderness, we see what regard was paid to the order of march, and how everything relating to their setting forward and encamping, was minutely regulated. The journey of so great a multitude required those minute directions, to prevent the disorder which would otherwise have ensued.

The object of the associations of believers is very simple. It is to observe the ordinances, and to watch over each other in love. Offences must come, and the elders of the churches are to watch, as those who must give an account. They are to rule in the fear of the Lord, enforcing His laws upon their brethren, and setting an example of cheerful obedience. The brethren are commanded to submit to their instructions, not as the commandments of men, but as the injunctions of Christ. Minute directions are given, both for the choice of proper guides or rulers, and in regard to the manner in which they are to execute their office. This simple ordinance has been made the occasion of the division of those called Christians into two classes, —clergy and laity. The former, after the model of the priests and Levites in Israel, claim a peculiarly sacred character, and in connection with this, we find in what are called Christian churches an intimation of the difference of rank which subsists in civil society.

Perhaps it was in view of this, that, while in the apostolic Epistles the importance of the elder's office, and the submission to which it is entitled, are sufficiently brought forward, less is said on these subjects than might have been expected. The Epistles are addressed to the churches; and only in one Epistle are the overseers or bishops mentioned. The Apostle Peter, at the close of his first epistle, gives particular instructions to the elders, but this is done precisely in the manner in which other classes of believers are particularized in this and other epistles. There appears indeed one exception.

No doubt, some have gone to the other extreme, either setting aside the elder's office altogether, or depriving it of all authority. This is the natural consequence of attempting to make a distinction between clergy and laity, and giving so much power to the former. It is quite natural that the bow when too much bent should break; but let believers be followers of God as dear children, and in this, as in every thing pertaining to the worship of Jesus, let them be guided by apostolic precept and example, neither adding to, nor diminishing from, what the Lord has ordained.

The Apostle teaches the elders at Ephesus to labour, as he had done, with his own hands, not only to support themselves, but to assist others. Thus we learn that the poverty of a church does not preclude their having an eldership. On the other hand, the repeated injunctions to support their teachers evidently prove that when a church of Christ is able, in whole or in part, to maintain its teachers, it is an incumbent duty, and places them in a more favourable situation for the study of the Word of God, and prayer, without being entangled with the cares of this life. The Lord has ordained that those who preach the Gospel should live by the Gospel, and that this precept includes the elders of churches, is apparent from the passage before us: *"Let him that is taught in the Word communicate unto him that teacheth, in all good things."*

J. A. Haldane, 1848.

GOD'S SUPPLY AND TRANSPORT.

A Record of "God's Faithfulness."

At a beautiful hill station in South India, where we had gone for a rest, the one dearest to me became seriously ill. After a year of intense daily suffering, during which time she had undergone two minor and three major operations, we found ourselves under order from, perhaps, the most eminent surgeon in India, to leave for a cold country as soon as possible.

There was a P. & O. Steamer due to leave Bombay well on in April, and we were urged by our friends to leave by this boat. We quite saw the wisdom of so doing, as the sooner we left the less likely should we be to run into the rough seas raised by the oncoming monsoon. But we needed Ten Pounds to make up our passage money for our long journey to New Zealand. We daily laid the matter before our Father in heaven, being well assured that He knew and cared for us. The last day came on which we could have caught that steamer; so we knew that we could not leave for another fortnight. This, of course, brought us much nearer the rough weather, to miss which meant much to one who was still far too weak to even walk. Three days after this we received a gift of Ten Pounds from the east coast of India. Here was the very sum we needed. We sent and booked our passages by the next steamer. And then on the voyage, right from Bombay to Freemantle, we never had a rough day. Further than this, on landing we learned that the preceding steamer (the one by which we had been urged to travel) had been unable to enter the harbour for several hours on account of the gale that was blowing!

We praised God that we had been Ten Pounds short, and thus were unable to travel by that boat. We believe, with all our hearts, That "All things work together for good to them that love God, to them who are the called according to His purpose." And we feel assured that God arranged all these circumstances for the comfort of His suffering child. The change, however, to a cooler climate did not effect the healing expected. After undergoing several further operations, and enduring constant suffering for two years, my dear wife was called to her eternal rest.

I want to place on record here for the glory of the Lord that all through those three years of acute suffering, not one murmur of complaint ever passed the lips of the patient; on the contrary, there was ever the sweet perfume of His grace and cheerfulness that made it easy to wait upon her and brought a blessing to those who visited her.

I wish also to record to the glory of the same gracious Lord that having "no visible means of support," simply trusting to the precious promises of God, we had, both in India and New Zealand, the best surgical help that money could have procured; and not only was every need abundantly supplied, but "the desires of the heart" were given too (Psa. 37:4).

While health is a great blessing, still it is not the greatest. The greatest blessing a child of God can have is to be IN THE WILL OF GOD. It seems to me that the Scriptures show that it is the will of God for some of His own to suffer great pain. If, as some teach, sickness is a wrong condition for a child of God to be in, why should there be any trials at all? Why trials of mind, and pocket if not of the body? When by grace the believer is triumphant in these circumstances does he not "*now* show forth unto principalities and powers in heavenly places the manifold wisdom of God"? What a wonderful sweep this gives to our lives! The witness of my faith and trust in God in the fiery furnace is reaching away out to unseen powers for the glory of God! Then, Lord, keep me, trusting in Thee, at all times, for it is written, "*All* things work together for good to them that love God, to them who are the called according to His purpose."

By "One of Little Faith".

VOL. III NOVEMBER, 1924 NO. 11

STUDIES in the SCRIPTURES

"Search the Scriptures" John 5:39.

Arthur W. Pink, Publisher & Editor,
227 N. Creighton St., Philadelphia, Pa.

Price: 10 cents per copy; $1.00 per year. Foreign $1.00 per year.

God's thoughts and ways are invariably different from ours. Forcibly has this been impressed upon the Editor again in connection with this little Magazine. When first published it was designed solely for the Lord's people in this country. Then it was felt that it was only right to take a tithe out of all receipts and use it for sending out the Magazine *free* to Missionaries. For each hundred subscriptions received it was sent, without cost, to ten Missionaries.

As time went by the Lord more and more laid on the Editor's heart the blessedness of ministering to lonely servants of His in the dark and difficult corners of the earth. Letters of appreciation which came in from them made us increasingly desirous of *extending* our free list. Through the gifts which have been sent in by subscribers this year we have been enabled to far exceed the number sent out free in the previous years. It now looks more and more that God's purpose in "Studies in the Scriptures" is *mainly* to cheer and strengthen the hands of the Missionaries. Below are quotations from a few of the letters which have recently come to hand:—

"I am a Bible student. I love your magazine". Native pastor in India.

"I feel I must thank some one for the very helpful and interesting Bible Studies. I truly appreciate them". Missionary in Japan.

"I want to thank you or the friend who makes it possible for you to send me 'Studies in the Scriptures' every month. I value them highly". Teacher in South Africa.

"I shall be very thankful and glad if your Magazine could be sent to my address" Missionary in China.

"'Studies' fills a great need out on the field where we are cut off from everything and cannot attend the Bible Classes as we did in the States. I am alone on this big Station, and have to do all the preaching and teaching; and your Magazine is the greatest blessing I receive. I only hope that every one who receives 'Studies' will be as greatly blessed as I have been". Honduras.

"Glad to know that your Magazine is being sent to over 250 Missionaries. The Lord will reward abundantly this sowing of the Seed. All the numbers of 'Studies' I am receiving regularly. Thank you so much for them". Siberia.

Surely there are many of our readers who will welcome such an opportunity of fellowship with the Lord's servants. *All* you send us shall be used in sending out the Magazine free during 1925. We do not want to reduce our free list, but extend it. Will you help? Send us in names and addresses of Missionaries whom you believe would value this Magazine.

Arthur W. Pink.

IMPORTANT NOTICES

All new subscriptions will be dated back to January, 1924.

Set of twelve issues for 1922, unbound, $1.00. Bound, $1.50.

Set of twelve issues for 1923, unbound, $1.00 Bound $1.50. Abroad, $1.75 or 7/6.

Note: We cannot break a set or now supply any single 1923 issues.

Subscription-price: $1.00 per year to any address in the world. Single copies 10 cents.

Change of Address: Please notify me promptly of any change of address, and be certain to give both old and new addresses.

Non-subscribers receiving this Magazine regularly will understand their subscription has been entered by a friend.

Copies lost in the mail duplicated only if we are notified promptly.

Entered as second-class matter December 15th, 1923, at the post office at Philadelphia, Pa., under Act of March 3rd, 1879.

CONTENTS

JOHN'S GOSPEL.

35. Christ, the Good Shepherd:
John 10:11-21.

The following is submitted as an Analysis of the passage which is to be before us:—

1. The good Shepherd dies for His sheep: v. 11.
2. The character and conduct of hirelings: vv. 12, 13.
3. The intimacy between the Shepherd and the sheep: v. 14.
4. The intimacy between the Father and the Son: v. 15.
5. Gentile sheep saved by the Shepherd: v. 16.
6. The relation of the Shepherd to the Father: vv. 17, 18.
7. The division among the Jews: vv. 19-21.

The passage before us completes our Lord's discourse with the Pharisees following their excommunication of the beggar to whom He had given sight. In this discourse, Christ does two things: first, He graphically depicts their unfaithfulness; second, He contrasts His own fidelity and goodness. They, as the religious leaders of the people, are portrayed as "strangers" (v. 5), as "thieves and robbers" (v. 8), as "hirelings" (vv. 12, 13). *He* stands revealed as "The Door" (vv. 9, 11), and as "the Good Shepherd" (v. 11).

The Pharisees were the shepherds of Israel. In casting out of the synagogue this poor sheep, the man that was born blind, for doing what was right, and for refusing to do what was wrong, they had shown what manner of spirit they were of. And this was but a sample of their accustomed oppression and violence. In them, then, did the prophecy of Ezekiel receive a fulfillment, that prophecy in which he had testified against those shepherds of his people who resembled thieves and robbers. Ezek. 34 (which like all prophecy has a *double* fulfillment) supplies a sad commentary upon the selfish and cruel conduct of the scribes and Pharisees. The whole chapter should be read: we quote but a fragment—"And the word of the Lord came unto me, saying, Son of man, prophesy against the shepherds of Israel, prophesy, and say unto them, Thus saith the Lord God unto the shepherds; Woe be to the shepherds of Israel that do feed themselves! should not the shepherds feed the flocks? Ye eat the fat, and ye clothe you with the wool, ye kill them that are fed, but ye feed not the flock. The diseased have ye not strengthened, neither have ye healed that which was sick, neither have ye bound up that which was broken, neither have ye brought again that which was driven away, neither have ye sought that which was lost; but with force and with cruelty have ye ruled them" (vv. 1-4).

The same prophecy of Ezekiel goes on to present the *true* Shepherd of Israel, the Good Shepherd: "For thus saith the Lord God; Behold, I, even I, will both search My sheep, and seek them out. As a shepherd seeketh out his flock in the day that he is among his sheep that are scattered; so will I seek out My sheep, and will deliver them out of all places where they have been scattered in the cloudy and dark day . . . . I will feed My flock, and I will cause them to lie down, saith the Lord God. I will seek that which was lost, and bring again that which was driven away, and will bind up that which was broken, and will strengthen that which was sick . . . . And I will set up one shepherd over them, and he shall feed them, even My servant David; he shall feed them, and he shall be their shepherd . . . . Thus shall they know that I the Lord their God am with them, and that they, even the house of Israel, are My people, saith the Lord God. And ye My flock, the flock of My pasture, are men, and I am your God, saith the Lord God" (vv. 11, 12, 15, 16, 23, 30, 31).

Ezekiel is not the only prophet of the Old Testament who presents the Saviour under the figure of a "shepherd". Frequently do the Old Testament Scriptures so picture Him. In his dying prediction, Jacob declared, "From thence (the mighty God of Jacob) is *the Shepherd,* the Stone of Israel" (Gen. 49:24). The Psalmist declared, "The Lord is my *Shepherd*" (23:1). Through Isaiah it was revealed, "The Lord God will come with strong hand, and His arm shall rule for Him: behold, His reward is with Him, and His work before Him. He shall feed His flock like *a shepherd:* He shall gather the lambs with His arm, and carry them in His bosom, and shall gently lead those that are with young" (40:10, 11). In Zechariah occurs that remarkable word "Awake, O sword, against *My Shepherd,* and against the man that is My Fellow, saith the Lord of hosts: smite *the Shepherd,* and the sheep shall be scattered: and I will turn Mine hand upon the little ones" (13:7).

In addition to the prophecies, the Old Testament is particularly rich in the *types* which foreshadow Christ in the character of a "shepherd". So far as we have been able to trace, there are five individual shepherds who pointed to Christ, and each of them supplies some distinctive line in the typical picture. First, *Abel,* for in Gen. 4:2 we are told that "Abel was a keeper of sheep". The distinctive aspect of typical truth which he exemplifies is *the death* of the Shepherd—slain by wicked hands, by his brother according to the flesh. The second is *Jacob,* and a prominent thing in connection with him as a shepherd is his *care* for the sheep—see Gen. 30:31; 31:38-40; and note particularly 33:13, 14. The third is *Joseph:* the very first thing recorded in Scripture about this favorite son of Jacob is that he *fed* the flock (Gen. 37:2). The fourth is *Moses.* Three things are told us about him: he *watered, protected* and *guided* the sheep: "Now the priest of Midian had seven daughters: and they came and drew water, and filled the troughs to water their father's flock. And the shepherds came and drove them away: but Moses stood up and helped them, and *watered* their flock. . . . Now Moses *kept* the flock of Jethro his father-in-law, the priest of Midian: and he *led* the flock to the backside of the desert, and came to the mountain of God, even to Horeb" (Ex. 2:17; 3:1). The fifth is *David,* and he is presented as *jeopardying his life* for the sheep—"And David said unto Saul, Thy servant kept his father's sheep, and there came a lion, and a bear, and took a lamb out of the flock: and I went out after him, and smote him, and delivered it out of his mouth: and when he arose against me, I caught him by his beard, and smote him, and slew him. Thy servant slew both the lion and the bear" (1 Sam. 17:34-36). There is one other individual "shepherd" referred to in the Old Testament and that is "The Idol Shepherd" (Zech. 11:16, 17), and he is the Antichrist—how significant that *he* is the *sixth!* The only other individual "shepherd" mentioned in Scripture is the Lord Jesus, and He is *the seventh!* Seven is the number of perfection, and we do not reach perfection till we come to Christ, the Good Shepherd!

"I am the *Good* Shepherd". The word for "good" is a very comprehensive one, and perhaps it is impossible to embrace in a brief definition all that is included within its scope. The Greek word is "kalos" and is translated "good" seventy-six times: it is also rendered "fair", "meet", "worthy" etc. In order to discover the prime elements of the word we must have recourse to the law of first mention. Whenever we are studying any word or expression in Scripture, it is very important to pay special attention to the initial mention of it. The first time this word "good" occurs in the New Testament is in Matt. 3:10, where we read, "Every tree which bringeth not forth *good* fruit is hewn down, and cast into the fire". The word "tree" is there used metaphorically. It is the unregenerate who are in view. No *un*believer is able to bring forth "good fruit". The "good fruit", then, is what is produced in and through a Christian. What *kind* of "fruit" is it which a Christian bears? It is *Divine* fruit, *spiritual* fruit: it is the product of the new nature. It is Divine as contrasted from what is human; spiritual as contrasted from what is fleshly. Thus in the light of this first occurrence of the word "good" we learn that when Christ said, "I am the *Good* Shepherd" He signified, "I am the *Divine* and *spiritual* Shepherd". All other shepherds were human; He was the Son of God. The "shepherds" from whom He is here contrasting Himself, were the Pharisees, and they were carnal; but He was *spiritual.*

It will also repay us to note carefully the *first* occurrence of this word "good" in John's Gospel. It is found in 2:10. When the Lord Jesus had miraculously turned the water into wine, the servants bore it to the governor of the feast, and when he had tasted it, he exclaimed, "Every man at the beginning doth set forth *good* wine; and when men have well drunk, then that which is worse: but thou hast kept the *good* wine until now". Here the meaning of the word "good" signifies *choice,* or *excellent,* yea, that which is preeminently excellent, for the "good wine" is here contrasted from the inferior. This usage of "kalos" helps us still further in ascertaining the force of this adjective in John 10:11. When Christ said, "I am the *Good* Shepherd", He intimated that He was the *pre-eminently excellent* Shepherd, infinitely elevated above all who had gone before Him.

"I am the Good *Shepherd*". This was clearly an affirmation of His absolute Deity. He was here addressing Israelites, and Israel's "Shepherd" was none other than Jehovah (Psa. 23:1; 80:1). When then the Saviour said, "*I am* the Good Shepherd", He thus definitely identified Himself with the Jehovah of the Old Testament.

"I am the Good Shepherd". This, like every other of our Lord's titles, views Him in a *distinctive relationship.* He was, says John Gill, "a Shepherd of His Father's appointing, calling, and sending, to whom the care of all His sheep, or chosen ones, was committed; who was set up as a Shepherd over them by Him, and was entrusted with them; and who being called, undertook to feed them". In the Greek it is more emphatic than in the English: literally it reads, "I am the Shepherd, the good".

"The good Shepherd giveth His life for the sheep" (v. 11). The word for "giveth" is usually translated "layeth down". "*For* the sheep" signifies, on their behalf. The good Shepherd gave His life freely and voluntarily, in the room and stead of His people, as a ransom for them, that they might be delivered from death and have eternal life. The Ethiopic Version reads, "The good Shepherd gives His life for *the redemption of* the sheep".

"The Good Shepherd giveth His life for the sheep". This is one of the many scriptures which clearly and definitely defines both the nature and extent of the Atonement. The Saviour "gave His life" not as a martyr for the truth, not as a moral example of self-sacrifice, but for *a people.* He died that they might live. By nature His people are dead in trespasses and sins, and had not the Divinely-appointed and Divinely-provided Substitute died for them, there had been no spiritual and eternal life for them. Equally explicit is this verse concerning those *for whom* Christ laid down His life. It was not laid down for fallen angels, but for sinful men; and not for men in general, but for His own people in particular; for "the sheep", and not for "the goats". Such was the announcement of God through the prophets, "For the transgression of *My people* was He stricken" (Isa. 53:8). As said the angel to Mary, "Thou shalt call His name Jesus: for He shall save *His people* from their sins" (Matt. 1:21); and as said the angel to the shepherds, "Behold I bring you good tidings of great joy, which shall be to all *the people*" (Luke 2:10). The same restriction is to be observed in the words of Christ at the Supper: "This is My blood of the new Testament which is shed for *many* for the remission of sins" (Matt. 26:28)—compare also Acts 20:28; Titus 2:14; Heb. 2:17, etc.

"But he that is an hireling, and not the shepherd, whose own the sheep are not, seeth the wolf coming, and leaveth the sheep, and fleeth: and the wolf catcheth them, and scattereth the sheep" (v. 12). It seems evident that our Lord is here pointing once more to the Pharisees, the unfaithful shepherds of Israel. The hireling shepherd is not the *owner* of the sheep—note "whose own the sheep *are not*"; he has neither a proprietorship over them nor affection for them. The "hireling" is *paid* to guard and watch them, and all such mind their own things, and not the things of the Lord. And yet in view of Luke 10:7—"The laborer is worthy of his *hire*" —and other scriptures, we must be careful not to interpret the use of this figure here out of harmony with its context. "It is not the bare receiving of hire which demonstrates a man to be a hireling (the Lord hath ordained that they who preach the Gospel should live of the Gospel); but the loving of hire; the loving the hire more than the work; the working for the sake of the hire. He is a hireling who would not work, were it not for the hire" (John Wesley). The "hireling" in a word, is a professing servant of God who fills a position simply for the temporal advantages which it affords. A hireling is a mercenary: he has no other impulse than the lust of lucre.

"But he that is an hireling, and not the shepherd, whose own the sheep are not, seeth the wolf coming, and leaveth the sheep, and fleeth: and the wolf catcheth them, and scattereth the sheep". We do not think that the "wolf" here has reference, directly, to Satan, for the false shepherds do not flee at his approach; rather does it seem to us that "the wolf" points to any enemy of the "sheep", who approaches to attack them. Note in passing the care of Christ here in the selection of His words: "the wolf catcheth them and *scattereth* the sheep", not *devoureth,* for no "sheep" of Christ can ever perish.

"The hireling fleeth, because he is an hireling, and careth not for the sheep" (v. 13). At first glance this saying of Christ's seems very trite, yet a little reflection will show that it enunciates a profound principle—a man does what he does because he is what he is. There is ever a rigid consistency between character and conduct. The drunkard drinks because he is a drunkard. But he is a drunkard *before* he drinks to excess. The liar lies because he is a liar; but he is a liar before he *tells* a lie. The thief steals because he is a thief. When the testing time comes each man reveals what he is by what he does. Conduct conforms to character as the stream does to the fountain. "The hireling fleeth because he is an hireling": this is a philosophical explanation of the fugitive's deed. It was the flight which demonstrated the man.

The same principle holds good on the other side. The Christian acts christianly because he is a Christian; but a man must be a Christian *before* he can live a Christian life. Christian *profession* is no adequate test, nor is an orthodox *creed.* The demons have a creed, and it causes them to tremble, but it will not deliver them from Hell! It is by our *fruit* that we are known: it is *deeds* which make manifest the heart.

"The hireling fleeth, because he is an hireling". Character is revealed by our conduct in the *crises* of life. When is it that the hireling fleeth? It is when he seeth "the wolf coming". Ah, it is the wolf that discovers the hireling! You might never have known what he was had not the wolf come. Very suggestive is this figure. It has passed into our common speech, as when poverty and starvation is represented by "the wolf is at the door". It suggests a crisis of trial or fierce testing. St. Paul made use of this simile when addressing the Ephesian elders: "For I know this, that after my departing shall grievous *wolves* enter in among you, not sparing the flock" (Acts 20:29). This is all very searching. How do *you* act when you see "the wolf" coming! Are you terror-stricken? Or, does approaching danger, temptation, or trial, cast you back the more upon the Lord?

"I am the Good Shepherd, and know My sheep, and am known of Mine" (v. 14). There seem to be three lines of thought suggested by this figure of the "shepherd" as applied to the Lord Jesus. First, it refers to His *mediatorial* office. The shepherd is not the owner of the flock, but the one to whom the care of the sheep is entrusted. So Christ as Mediator is the One appointed by the Father to act as shepherd, the One to whom He has committed the salvation of His elect —note how in the types Joseph, Moses, and David tended not their own flock, but those of their *fathers'*. Second, the figure speaks of *fellowship,* the Saviour's *presence* with His own. The shepherd never leaves his flock. There is only one exception to this, and that is when he commits them into the care of the "porter" of the sheepfold; and that is at nightfall. How suggestive is this! During the *night* of Christ's absence, the Holy Spirit has charge of God's elect! Finally; the Shepherd-character speaks of Christ's care, faithfulness, solicitude for His own.

In two other passages in the New Testament is Christ presented as "the Shepherd", and in each with a different descriptive adjective. In Heb. 13:20 we read, "Now the God of peace, that brought again from the dead our Lord Jesus, that *great* Shepherd of the sheep, through the blood of the everlasting covenant". Again in 1 Pet. 5:4, we are told, "When the *chief* Shepherd shall appear, ye shall receive a crown of glory which fadeth not away". There is a striking order to be observed in the three "Shepherd" titles of our Lord. Here in John 10, the reference is plainly to the Cross, so that He is the "Good" Shepherd *in death,* laying down His life for the sheep. In Heb. 13 the reference is to the empty sepulchre, so that He is the "Great" Shepherd *in resurrection.* While in 1 Pet. 5:4 the reference is to His glorious return, so that He will be manifested as the "Chief" Shepherd *in the Millennium.*

"I am the Good Shepherd, and know *My sheep*". Why does the Lord refer to His people under the figure of "sheep"? The figure is very suggestive and full. We shall not attempt to be exhaustive but merely suggestive. Under the Mosaic economy a sheep was one of the few *clean* animals: as such it suitably represents God's people, each of which has been cleansed from all sin. A sheep is a *harmless* animal: even children will approach them without fear. So God's people are exhorted to be "wise as serpents and *harmless* as doves" (Matt. 10:16). Sheep are *helpless:* nature has endowed them neither with weapons of attack nor defence. Equally helpless is the believer in himself: "Without Me", says Christ, ye can do *nothing*". Sheep are *gentle:* what so tame and tractable as a lamb! This is ever a grace which ought to distinguish the followers of Christ: "*Gentle,* easy to be entreated, full of mercy and good fruits" (James 3:17). The sheep are entirely *dependent* upon the shepherd. This is noticeably the case in the Orient. Not only must the sheep look to the shepherd for protection against wild animals, but *he* must lead them to the pastures. May we be cast back more and more upon God. Sheep are pre-eminently characterized by *a proneness to wander.* Even when placed in a field with a fence all around it, yet if there be a gap anywhere, they will quickly get out and stray. Alas, that this is so true of us. Urgently do we all need to heed that admonition, "Watch and pray *lest* ye enter into temptation". A sheep is a *useful* animal. Each year it supplies a crop of wool. In this too it prefigures the Christian. The daily attitude of the believer should be, "Lord, what wouldst Thou have me to do?".

"I am the Good Shepherd, and *know* My sheep" (v. 14). Very blessed is this. The Lord Jesus knows each one of those whom the Father has given to Him with a special knowledge of approbation, affection, and intimacy. Though unknown to the world—"the world *knoweth us not*" (1 John 3:1)—we are known *to Him.* And Christ only knoweth *all* His sheep. Ofttimes we are deceived. Some whom we regard as "sheep" are really "goats"; and others whom we look upon as outside the flock of Christ, belong thereto notwithstanding. Whoever would have concluded that *Lot* was a "righteous man" had not the *New* Testament told us so! And who would have imagined that *Judas* was a devil when Christ sent him forth as one of the twelve! "And know My sheep": fearfully solemn is the contrast presented by Matt. 7:23—"I *never* knew you"!

"And am *known* of Mine" (v. 14). Christ is known experimentally; known personally. Each born-again person can say with Job, "I *have* heard of Thee by the hearing of the ear, but *now* mine eye seeth Thee" (42:6). The believer knows Christ not merely as the outstanding Figure in history, but as the Saviour of his soul. He has a heart knowledge of Him. He knows Him as the Rest-giver, as the Friend who sticketh closer than a brother, as the Good Shepherd who ever ministereth to His own.

"As the Father knoweth Me, even so know I the Father" (v. 15). The word "knoweth" here, as frequently in Scripture, signifies a knowledge of approbation: it is almost the equivalent of *loveth.* The first part of this verse should be linked on to the last clause of the previous one, where Christ says, I "know My sheep, and am known of Mine". The two clauses thus make a complete sentence, and a remarkable one it is. The mutual knowledge of Christ and His sheep, is like unto that which exists between the Father and the Son: it is a knowledge, an affection, so profound, so spiritual, so heavenly, so intimate, so blessed, that no other analogy was possible to do it justice: *as* the Father knoweth the Son, and *as* the Son knoweth the Father, *so* Christ knows His sheep, and *so* the sheep know Him.

"And I lay down My life *for* the sheep" (v. 15). The precise significance of the preposition is unequivocally defined for us in Rom. 5:6-8, where the same Greek term ("huper") occurs: "For when we were yet without strength in due time Christ died *for* the ungodly. For scarcely *for* a righteous man will one die: yet peradventure *for* a good man some would even dare to die. But God commendeth His love toward us, in that while we were yet sinners, Christ died *for* us". The word "for" here means not merely on the behalf of, but *in the stead of:* "the Greek expression for 'dying for any one', never has any signification other than that of rescuing the life of another at the expense of one's own" (Parkhurst's Lexicon).

"And other sheep I have, which are not of this fold" (v. 16). It is clear that the Lord is here contemplating His elect among the Gentiles. Not only for the elect Jews would He "lay down His life", but for "the children of God that were scattered abroad" (John 11:52) as well. But note Christ does not here say, "Other sheep I *shall* have", but "Other sheep I *have.*" They were His even then; His, because given to Him by the Father from all eternity. A parallel passage is found in Acts 18. The apostle Paul had just arrived in Corinth, and the Lord spoke to him in a vision by night, and said unto him, "Be not afraid, but speak, and hold not thy peace; for I am with thee, and no man shall set on thee to hurt thee, *for I have much people* in this city" (vv. 9, 10). How positive, definite, and unequivocal these statements are! How they show that everything is to be traced back to the eternal counsels of the Godhead!

"And other sheep I have, which are not of this fold: them also *I must* bring, and they *shall* hear My voice" (v. 16). Equally positive is this. There is no uncertainty, no contingency. There is no *"if* they are *willing* to listen". How miserably man perverts the truth of God, yea, how wickedly he *denies* it! But it is not difficult to understand the cause of it: it is lack of faith to believe what the Scriptures so plainly teach. These "other sheep" Christ *must bring* because necessity was laid upon Him. He had covenanted with the Father to redeem them. And they *would be* brought, they *would* hear His voice, for there can be *no* failure with Him. The work which the Father gave His Son to do *shall be* perfectly performed and successfully accomplished. Neither man's stubbornness nor the Devil's malice can hinder *Him.* Not a single one of that favored company given to Christ by the Father shall perish. Each of these *shall* hear His voice, because they were predestinated so to do, and it is written, *"As many as* were ordained to eternal life believed" (Acts 13:48). "They *shall* hear My voice" was both a promise and a prophecy.

"And other sheep I have, which are not of this fold: them also I must bring, and they shall hear My voice". Upon this verse the Puritan Trapp has some most suggestive thoughts in his excellent commentary—a commentary which, so far as we are aware, has been out of print for over two hundred years. "Other sheep—the elect Gentiles, whose conversion to Christ was, among other types, not obscurely foretold in Lev. 19:23-25—'And when ye shall come into the land, and shall have planted all manner of trees for food, then ye shall count the fruit thereof as uncircumcised; three years shall it be as uncircumcised unto you: it shall not be eaten of. But in the fourth year all the fruit thereof shall be holy to praise the Lord withal. And in the fifth year shall ye eat of the fruit thereof, that it may yield unto you the increase thereof: I am the Lord your God'. The first three years *in Canaan,* the Israelites were to cast away the fruits of the trees as *un*-circumcised. So our Saviour planted the Gospel in that land for the first 'three years' of His public ministry: but the uncircumcision was *cast away;* that is, to the uncircumcised Gentiles, the Gospel was not preached. The fruit of the fourth year was consecrated to God: that is, Christ in the fourth year from His baptism, laid down His life for His sheep, rose again, ascended, and sent His Holy Spirit; whereby His apostles, and others were consecrated as the first-fruits of the Promised Land. But in the fifth year, the fruit of the Gospel planted by Christ began to be common, for the Gospel was no longer shut up within the narrow bounds of Judaism, but began to be preached to all nations for the obedience of faith"!*

"And there shall be one fold, and one Shepherd" (v. 16). Everywhere else in the New Testament the Greek word for "fold" is translated "flock", as it should be here, and as it is in the R.V. In the first part of this verse the Greek uses an entirely different word which is correctly rendered "fold"—"Other sheep I have which are not of this fold". *"This* fold" referred to Judaism, and the elect Gentiles were *outside* of it, as we read in Eph. 2:11, 12, "Ye being in time past Gentiles in the flesh, who are called Uncircumcision by that which is called the Circumcision in the flesh made by hands; That at that time ye were without Christ, being *aliens from* the commonwealth of Israel, and *strangers from* the covenants of promise, having no hope, and without God in the world". But now the Lord tells us, "There *shall be* one flock, and one Shepherd". This has been already accomplished, though not yet is it fully manifested—"For He is our peace, who hath made both (believing Jews and believing Gentiles) one, and hath *broken down* the middle wall of partition" (Eph. 2:14). The "one flock" comprehends, we believe, the whole *family* of God, made up of believers before the nation of Israel came into existence, of believing Israelites, of believing Gentiles, and of those who shall be saved during the Millennium. The "one flock" will have been gathered from *various* "folds".

"Therefore doth My Father love Me, because I lay down My life, that I might take it again" (v. 17). Christ is here speaking as the Mediator, as the Word who had become flesh. As one of the Godhead, the Father had loved Him from all eternity. Beautifully is this brought out in Prov. 30: "Then I was by Him, as one brought up with Him, and I was daily His *delight,* rejoicing always before Him" —the previous verses make it plain that it is the Son who is in view, personified as "Wisdom". But the Father also loved Christ in His incarnate form. At His baptism, the commencement of His mediatorial work, He declared, "This is My *beloved* Son, in whom I am well pleased". Here the Son declares, "Therefore doth My Father love Me, because I lay down My life that I might take it again", for the laying down of His life was the supreme example of His devotion to the Father as the next verse clearly shows—it was *in obedience* to the Father that He gave up His spirit.

"No man taketh it from Me, but I lay it down of Myself" (v. 18). When Christ died, He did so of His own voluntary will. This is a point of vital importance. We must never give a place to the dishonoring thought that the Lord Jesus was powerless to prevent His sufferings, that when He endured such indignities and cruel treatment at the hands of His enemies, it was because He was unable to avoid them. Nothing could be farther from the truth. The treachery of Judas, the arrest in the Garden, the arraignment before Caiaphas, the insult from the soldiers, the trial before Pilate, the submission to the unjust sentence, the journey to Calvary, the being nailed to the cruel tree—all of these were *voluntarily* endured. Without His own consent none could have harmed a hair of His head. A beautiful type of this is furnished in Gen. 22:13, where we read that the ram, which was placed on the altar as a substitute for Isaac, was "caught in a thicket by his *horns*". The "horns" speak of strength and power (see Hab. 3:4, etc.). Typically they tell us that the Saviour did not succomb to death through weakness, but that He gave up His life in the full vigor of His strength. It was not the nails, but the strength of His love to the Father and to His elect, which held Him to the Cross.

The pre-eminence of Christ was fully manifested at the Cross. In birth He was unique, in His life unique, and so in His death. Not yet have we read aright the inspired accounts of His death, if we suppose that on the Cross the Saviour was a helpless victim of His enemies. At every point He demonstrated that no man took His life from Him, but rather that He laid it down of Himself. See the very ones sent to arrest Him in the Garden, there prostrate on the ground before Him (John 18:6): how easily could He have walked away unmolested had it so pleased Him! Hear Him before Pilate, as He reminds that Roman officer, "Thou couldest have no power at all against Me, except it were given thee from above" (John 19:11). Be-

* Let the reader carefully re-read this paragraph.

hold Him on the Cross itself, so superior to His sufferings that He makes intercession for the transgressors, saves the dying robber, and provides a home for His widowed mother. Listen to Him as He cries with a *loud* voice (Matt. 27:46, 50)—no exhausted Sufferer was this! Mark how triumphantly He *"gave up* the ghost" (John 19:30). Verily "no *man"* took His life from Him. So evident was it that He triumphed in the hour of death itself that the Roman soldier was made to exclaim, "Truly *this was* the Son of God" (Matt. 27:54).

"I have power to lay it down, and I have power to take it again" (v. 18). Here our Lord ascribes His resurrection to His own power. He had done the same before when, after cleansing the temple, the Pharisees had demanded from Him a sign: "Destroy this temple, and in three days *I will* raise it up" (John 2:19) was His response. In Rom. 6:4 we are told that Christ was "raised from the dead by the glory of *the Father."* In Rom. 8:11 we read, "But if *the Spirit* of Him that raised up Jesus from the dead dwell in you, He that raised up Christ from the dead shall also quicken your mortal bodies by His Spirit that dwelleth in you". These passages are not contradictory, but complementary; they supplement one another; each contributing a separate ray of light on the glorious event of which they speak. Putting them together we learn that, the resurrection of the Saviour was an act in which each of the three Persons of the Trinity concurred and co-operated.

"This commandment have I received of My Father". This is parallel with what we read of in Phil. 2:8, "And being found in fashion as a man, He humbled Himself, and *became obedient* unto death, even the death of the Cross". It was to this our Lord referred in John 6:38, "For I came down from heaven not to do Mine own will, but the will of Him that sent Me".

"There was a division therefore again among the Jews for these sayings" (v. 19). This had been foretold of old: "He shall be for a sanctuary; for a stone *of stumbling* and for a rock *of offence* to both the houses of Israel, for *a gin* and for *a snare* to the inhabitants of Jerusalem" (Isa. 8:14). Similarly Simeon announced in the temple, when the Saviour was presented to God, "Behold, this child is set (appointed) for *the fall* and rising again of many in Israel" (Luke 2:34). So had the Saviour Himself declared. "Think not that I am come to send peace on earth: I came not to send peace, but a sword" (Matt. 10:34). From the Divine side this is a profound mystery to us. It had been an easy matter for God to have subdued the enmity in men's hearts and brought them all as worshippers to the feet of Christ. But instead of this, He permitted His Son to be despised and rejected by the great majority, and He permitted this because He Himself eternally decreed it (see Acts 2:23; 1 Pet. 2:8, etc.).

"And many of them said, He hath a devil, and is mad; why hear ye Him?" (v. 20). Terrible indeed was the condition of these men. The Son of God called a demoniac, Truth incarnate deemed insane! "Tigers rage", says a Puritan, "at the fragrancy of sweet spices: so did these monsters at the Saviour's sweet sayings". How humbling to remember that the same corrupt heart indwells each of us! O what grace we daily need to keep down the iniquity which is to be found in every Christian. Not until we reach the Glory shall we fully learn how deeply indebted we are to God's wondrous grace.

"Others said, These are not the words of Him that hath a devil. Can a devil open the eyes of the blind?" (v. 21). Notice it was the *"many"* who deemed Christ a madman. But there were *some*—"others"—even among the Pharisees who had, even then, a measure of light, and recognized that the Saviour neither spake nor acted like a demoniac. This minority-group were made up, no doubt, by such men as Nicodemus and Joseph of Arimathea. It is significant that they were impressed more with His *"words"* than they were with His miraculous works.

As a preparation for our exposition of the remainder of John 10, let the interested reader study the following points:—

1. What is the force of "it was winter" (v. 22) in the light of what follows?

2. Mark the contrasts between 10:23 and Acts 3:11 and 5:12.

3. What verses in John 8 are parallel with 10:26?

4. Enumerate the seven proofs of the believer's *security* found in vv. 27-29.
5. Trace out the seven things said about "the sheep" in John 10.
6. Trace out the seven things said about the "shepherd".
7. What is the meaning of "sanctified" in v. 36?

—Arthur W. Pink.

GLEANINGS IN EXODUS.

11. The Plagues upon Egypt; Ex. 7-11.

For over eighty years, and probably much longer, the Egyptians had oppressed the Hebrews, and patiently had God borne with their persecution of His people. But the time had arrived when He was to interpose on behalf of His "firstborn" (4:22) and take vengeance on those who had reduced Israel to the most servile bondage. The Lord is slow to anger and plenteous in mercy, but, "He will not always chide; neither will He keep His anger forever" (Ps. 103:9). A succession of terrible judgments therefore now decended upon Pharaoh and upon his land, judgments which are known as "the Plagues of Egypt". They were ten in number. First, the waters of the Nile were turned into blood (7:14-25). Second, frogs covered the land and entered the homes of the Egyptians (8:1-5). Third, lice was made to attack their persons (8:16-19). Fourth, swarms of flies invaded the houses of the Egyptians and covered the ground (8:20-24). Fifth, a grievous disease smote the cattle (9:1-7). Sixth, boils and sores were sent on man and beast (9:8-12). Seventh, thunder and hail were added to the terrors of these Divine visitations (9:18-35). Eighth, locusts consumed all vegetation (10:1-20). Ninth, thick darkness, which might be felt, overspread the land for three days (10:21-29). Tenth, the firstborn of man and beast were slain (11, 12). A frightful summary is found in Psalm 78: "He cast upon them the fierceness of His anger, wrath, and indignation, and tribulation, by sending evil angels among them. He made a way to His anger; He spared not their soul from death, but gave their life over to the pestilence, and smote all the firstborn in Egypt, the chief of their strength in the tabernacle of Ham" (vv. 49-51 and cf. Ps. 105:27-36).

That there is much for us to learn from the record of these judgments cannot be doubted. That they set forth many important lessons of a practical, typical, and prophetic nature, we are fully satisfied. Their order, their arrangement, their number, their nature, their purpose, their effects, each call for careful and separate study. Little or no attempt has been made (so far as we are aware) to supply a detailed interpretation of their significance, so that there is small help to be obtained from the commentaries. This must cast us back the more on the Lord Himself, who never fails a dependent soul that turns to Him for aid. Let the little light which has been granted the writer stir up the reader to earnestly seek, at the Throne of Grace, more for himself. In this article we shall generalize; in the next we shall enter more into detail.

1 The *purpose* of these plagues was manifold. First, they gave a public manifestation of the mighty power of the Lord God (see 9:16). This, the very magicians were made to acknowledge—"then the magicians said unto Pharaoh, This is the finger of God" (8:19).

Second, they were a Divine visitation of wrath, a punishment of Pharaoh and the Egyptians for their cruel treatment of the Hebrews. This the haughty monarch was compelled to admit—"Then Pharaoh called for Moses and Aaron in haste; and he said, I have sinned against the Lord your God, and against you" (10:16).

Third, They were a judgment from God upon the gods (demons) of Egypt. This is taught in Numbers 33:4—"For the Egyptians buried all their firstborn which the Lord had smitten among them; upon *their gods* also the Lord executed judgments".

Fourth, they demonstrated that Jehovah was high above all gods. This was confessed later by Jethro—"And Jethro said, Blessed be the Lord who hath delivered you out of the hand of the Egyptians, and out of the hand of Pharaoh, who hath delivered the people from under the hand of the Egyptians. *Now I know* that the Lord *is greater* than all gods; for in the thing wherein they dealt proudly He was above them."

Fifth, They furnished a complete testing of human responsibility. This is indicated by their *number*, for one of the leading signification of *ten*, is full responsibility—compare the *ten* Commandments, e. g.

Sixth, They were a solemn warning to other nations, that God would curse those who curse the Israelites (Gen. 12:3). This was plainly realized by Rahab of Jericho —"And she said unto the men, I know that the Lord hath given you the land, and that your terror is fallen upon us, and that all the inhabitants of the land faint because of you. *For we have heard* how the Lord dried up the water of the Red Sea for you when ye came out of Egypt" etc. (Josh. 2:8, 9). It was also felt by the Philistines—"Woe unto us! who shall deliver us out of the hand of these mighty Gods? these are the Gods that smote the Egyptians with all the plagues in the wilderness" (1 Sam. 4:8).

Finally, these miraculous plagues were evidently designed as a series of testings for Israel. This is taught in Deut. 4:33, 34, where Moses asked Israel, "Did ever people hear the voice of God speaking out of the midst of the fire, as thou hast heard, and live? or hath God assayed to go and take Him a nation from the midst of another nation, *by temptations*, by signs, and by wonders, and by war, and by a mighty hand, and by stretched out arms, and by great terrors, according to all that the Lord your God did for you in Egypt before your eyes?" The *outcome* of these testings was expressed in the following words—"who is like unto Thee, O Lord, among the gods? who is like Thee, glorious in holiness, fearful in praises, doing wonders?" (Ex. 15:11)!

2 The *arrangement* of the plagues plainly manifests Divine order and design. The tenth is separated from all the others because of its special relation to Israel and their redemption. The other nine are arranged in groups of three's. "They form three divisions, each division consisting of three plagues. That these dividing lines are drawn by the Scripture itself will be plain when we note one remarkable feature. A warning precedes, in each instance, the first and the second plagues; but with the third in each series no warning is given. Thus Moses is commanded to meet Pharaoh before the waters of Egypt are turned into blood. So again (8:1) when the frogs are to cover the land, Moses is to go in unto Pharaoh and announce what God is about to do. But when the dust is smitten and it becomes lice throughout the land of Egypt there is no command to seek Pharaoh's presence. So it is with the sixth plague, when the ashes of the furnace are used, and it becomes boils upon man and beast; and so also is it with the ninth plague, when the land was covered with darkness as with the pall of death. In none of these three cases is there any announcement to Pharaoh. It was a reminder that God would not always strive; and that warning, repeated but unheeded, will be followed by judgment sudden and terrible" (Urquhart). Murphy in his commentary on the book of Exodus has also called attention to the fact that "in the first three plagues, Aaron uses the rod; in the second and third, it is not mentioned; in the third three, Moses uses it, though in the last of them only his hand is mentioned. All these marks of order lie on the face of the narrative, and point to a deep order of nature and reason out of which they spring."

There is a striking *Introversion* to be observed in connection with the plagues. Thus, in the first, the waters of the Nile were turned into blood—the symbol of *death;* while in the tenth there was actual blood-shedding, in the death of all the firstborn. In the second plague, the frogs which are creatures of the night, that is, *of darkness,* came forth; while in the ninth plague there was actual darkness itself. In the third plague, the magicians were forced to exclaim, This is the finger of God (8:19); while in the eighth (the balancing number according to the Introversion) Pharaoh said, "I have sinned against the Lord your God" (10:16). In the fourth plague we are specifically informed that God *exempted* the land of Goshen—"no swarms of flies shall be there" (8:22); so also in connection with the seventh plague we read, "only in the land of Goshen, where the children of Israel were, was there no hail". While that which was common to both the fifth and the sixth plagues was the fact that in each of them the *cattle* of the Egyptians were attacked (see 9:3 and 9:9). Thus we see again the Divine hand in the arrangement and order of these different plagues.

3 The *progressive nature* of these plagues is easily perceived. There was a marked gradation, a steady advance in the *severity* of the Divine judgments. The first three interfered merely with the *comfort* of the Egyptians: the first, depriving them of water to drink and to wash in; the second, invading their homes with the frogs; the third, the lice attacking their persons. In the second three the Lord's hand was laid on their *possessions;* the first, the "flies" corrupting their land (8:24); the second, destroying their cattle; and the third, attacking their persons again, this time in the form of "boils" and "blains" (sores). The last three brought *desolation and death,* more plainly evidencing the direct hand of God; the hail destroyed both the herbage and the cattle; the locusts consuming what vegetation was not ruined by the hail; the darkness arresting all activity throughout the land of Egypt. All of this served to illustrate a principle which is very marked in all of the Divine dealings; as in nature, so in grace and also in judgment, there is first the blade, then the ear, then the full corn in the ear!

4 The *moral significance* of these plagues is very striking. They furnish a most solemn and complete description of the world-system (which Egypt accurately portrayed) in its dominant features. The water turned into blood tells of how death broods over this scene. The frogs, by their very inflation, suggest the pride and self-sufficiency of the children of this world. The plague of lice speaks of the uncleanness and filth which issue from the lusts of the flesh. The swarms of flies announces how that the wicked are of their father the Devil, i. e. "Beelzebub", which means "Lord of flies". The murrian of cattle (beasts of burden)—tells us that the service of the natural man is corrupted at its source. The boils and blains make us think of that awful description of the unregenerate given through the prophet Isaiah—"From the sole of the foot even unto the head there is no soundness in it; but wounds and bruises, and putrifying sores" (1:6). The hail (accompanied by fearful lightnings which ran along the ground) symbolized that the wrath of God abideth on the disobedient. The locusts which ate up all the vegetation, pictured the spiritual barrenness of this world—a desolate waste so far as the soul is concerned. The dense darkness shows how that the world is alienated from Him who is Light. The death of all the firstborn (representative of the family) foretells that Second Death which awaits all whose hearts are hardened against God.

5 The plagues were *designed to establish the faith of the Israelites.* For four hundred years they had dwelt in a land of idolatry, where Jehovah was entirely unknown. Moreover, the priests of Egypt were able to perform deeds which could not be explained apart from supernatural agency. The Lord therefore was pleased to so manifest Himself now that all impartial observers (whose minds were not blinded by Satan) must recognize the existence and omnipotence of the true God, in contradistinction from the impotency of the false gods of their heathen neighbors. In the plagues, the presence and power of Jehovah were demonstrated, so that He stood discovered to His people as the Living God. This comes out the more clearly when it is recognized that these displays of the Lord's power were so many judgments directed against the false confidences and idolatrous objects of the Egyptians (see 12:12). The sign which authenticated the mission of Moses to Pharaoh furnished more than a hint—the "serpent" was an object of worship among the Egyptians, and when Aaron's serpent-transformed rod swallowed those of the magicians, a plain warning was given that their god would be unable to save them from the forthcoming storm.

Others have described in detail the particular "gods" against which the different plagues were directed, so that it is unnecessary for us to say more than a few words upon this phase of our subject. The first plague smote the Nile, an object regarded with profound veneration by the Egyptians. Its waters were held as sacred as is the Ganges by the Hindoos. A fearful blow then was it to their system of worship when its waters were turned to blood and its dead fish made to stink. In the second plague, the Nile was made to send forth myriads of frogs, which invaded the homes of the Egyptians and became a nuisance and torment to the people. In the third plague, lice were sent upon man and beast, and, "if it be remembered", says Gleig, "that no one could approach the altars of Egypt upon which so impure an insect harbored; and, that the priests to guard against the slightest risk of contamination, wore only linen garments, and shaved their heads and bodies every third day, the severity of this miracle as a judgment upon Egyptian idolatry may be imagined. Whilst it lasted no act of worship could be performed, and so keenly was this felt that the very magicians explained, 'this is the finger of God' ".

The fourth plague was designed "to destroy the trust of the people in Beelzebub, or the Fly-god, who was reverenced as their protector from visitation of swarms of ravenous flies, which infested the land generally about the time of the dog-days, and removed only as they supposed at the will of their idol. The miracle now wrought by Moses evinced the impotence of Beelzebub and caused the people to look elsewhere for relief from the fearful visitation under which they were suffering. The fifth plague, which consumed all the cattle, excepting those of the Israelites, was aimed at the destruction of the entire system of brute worship. This system, degrading and bestial as it was, had become a monster of many heads in Egypt. They had their sacred bull, and ram, and heifer, and goat, and many others, all of which were destroyed by the agency of the God of Moses, thus, by one act of power, Jehovah manifested His own supremacy and destroyed the very existence of their brute idols" (Dr J. B. Walker). And so we might continue.

6. The *conduct of the magicians* in connection with the plagues is deserving of notice. It has already been intimated in a previous article that we have no patience with those who would reduce the miracles wrought by these men to mere slight-of-hand-deceptions. Not only is there no hint whatever in the sacred narrative of any deception practiced by them, not only does the inspired account describe what they wrought in precisely the same terms as it refers to the wonders performed by Moses and Aaron, but there are other insuperable objections against the conjuring theory. It is therefore deeply distressing to find men whose names command respect, pandering to that rationalism which seeks to deny everything supernatural. Have such men forgotten those words in Revelation 16:14—"they are the spirits of demons *working miracles*"!

If Jehovah was to make a public display of Himself before the Egyptians and the Israelites, it was necessary (in the fitness of things) that He should suffer the sorcerers of Egypt to enter into conflict against Himself. The magicians, appearing in the name of their gods, were completely routed, for not only was it evidenced that the power of God working through Moses was superior to their sorceries, but it was also shown that He was hostile to them and their idolatrous worship. Three times were the magicians allowed to display their powers—in the changing of their rods to serpents (7:12) in turning water into blood (7:22), and in bringing forth frogs (8:12). Beyond this they did not go. The three things which they *did* do were very significant; the first spoke of Satanic power, the second of death, and the third of pride and uncleanness. Concerning the fourth plague, we are told, "and the magicians did so with their enchantments to bring forth lice, but *they could not*". (8:18). Here is further proof that the wonders wrought by the magicians were no mere feats of legerdemain. If they were really exhibiting slight-of-hand tricks it would have been far simpler to substitute lice for dust, than it would be to substitute serpents for rods! The fact that they *could not* duplicate the miracle of the lice is proof positive that something more than a conjuring performance is in view here.

If we bear in mind that these earlier chapters of Exodus bring before us a symbolic tableau of the great conflict between good and evil, we shall easily perceive the reason why the Lord permitted Pharaoh's sorcerers to work these miracles. They serve to illustrate the activities of Satan, and this, not only as describing the character of his works, but also, as exposing both the methods he pursues and the limits of his success. The Devil is ever an *imitator*, as the parable of the tares following that of the wheat (Matt. 13) plainly shows. The aim of Pharaoh was to *nullify* the miracles of Moses. The Lord's servant had performed miracles—very well, the king would summon his magicians and show that they could do likewise. This exemplifies an unchanging principle in the workings of Satan. First, he seeks to oppose with force (persecution, etc.), as he had the Hebrews by means of their slavery. When he is foiled here he resorts to subtler methods, and employs his wiles to deceive. The one is the roaring of the "lion" (1 Pt. 5:8); the other the cunning of the "serpent" (Gen. 3:1).

There is a striking verse in the New Testament which throws light on the subject before us. In 2 Tim. 3:8, we read, "Now as Jannes and Jambres withstood Moses, so do these also resist the truth; men of corrupt minds, reprobate concerning the faith." Here we learn the names of two of the magicians (doubtless the principal ones) who worked miracles in Egypt. Jannes and Jambres *withstood* Moses. They did this not by having him turned out of the king's palace, not by causing him to be imprisoned or slain, but by duplicating his works. And, says the Holy Spirit, there are those now who similarly resist the servants of God—"*as* Jannes and Jambres withstood Moses, *so* do these (the ones mentioned in vv. 5 and 6) *also* resist the truth". This is one of the Divinely-delineated characteristics of the "perilous times". The reference is to men (and women) supernaturally endowed by Satan to work miracles. Such are found to-day, we believe, not only among Spiritualists and Christian Scientists, but also in some of the leaders of the Faith-healing cults. There are men and women now posing as evangelists of Christ who are attracting large crowds numbered by the thousand. Their chief appeal is not the message they bear, but their readiness to "anoint" and pray over the sick. They claim that "Jesus" (they never own Him as "the Lord Jesus"), in response to their faith, has through them removed paralysis, healed cancers, given sight to the blind. When their claims are carefully investigated it is found that most of the widely-advertised "cures" are impostures. But on the other hand, there *are* some cases which are genuine healings, and which cannot be explained apart from supernatural agency. So it was with the miracles wrought by the magicians of Pharaoh; though limited by God they *did* perform prodigies.

7 These plagues furnished a most striking *prophetic forecast* of God's future judgments upon the world. This is, to us, one of the most remarkable things connected with God's judgments upon Egypt. The analogies furnished between those visitations of Divine wrath of old and those which the Scriptures predict, and announce for the future, are many and most minute. We here call attention only to a few of the more striking ones; the diligent student may discover many more for himself if he will take the necessary trouble:—

(1) During the Time of Jacob's Trouble Israel shall again be sorely oppressed and afflicted (Isa. 60:14 and Jer. 30:5-8).

(2) They will cry unto God, and He will hear and answer (Jer. 31;18-20).

(3) God will command their oppressors to, Let them go (Isa. 43:6).

(4) God will send two witnesses to work miracles before their enemies (Rev. 11:3-6).

(5) Their enemies will also perform miracles (Rev. 13:13-15).

(6) God will execute sore judgments upon the world (Jer. 25:15, 16).

(7) God will protect His own people from them (Rev. 7:4; 12:6, 14-16).

(8) Water will again be turned into blood (Rev. 8:8; 16:4, 5).

(9) Satanic frogs will appear (Rev. 16:13).

(10) A plague of locusts shall be sent (Rev. 9:2-11).

(11) God will send boils and blains (Rev. 16:2).

(12) Terrible hail-stones shall descend from heaven (Rev. 8:7).

(13) There shall be awful darkness (Isa. 60:2; Rev. 16:10).

(14) Just as Pharaoh hardened his heart so will the wicked in the day to come (Rev. 9:20, 21).

(15) Death will consume multitudes (Rev. 9:15).

(16) Israel will be delivered (Zech. 14:3, 4; Rom. 11:26).

Thus will history repeat itself, and then will it be fully demonstrated that the plagues of Jehovah upon Egypt of old portended the yet more awful judgments by which the earth shall be visited in a day now very near at hand.

Arthur W. Pink.

THE SOVEREIGNTY OF GOD IN CREATION.

In the great expanse of eternity which stretches behind Gen. 1:1 the universe was unborn, and creation existed only in the mind of the great Creator. In His sovereign majesty God dwelt all alone. We refer to that far distant period before the heavens and the earth were created. There were then no angels to sing God's praises, no creatures to occupy His notice, no rebels to be brought into subjection. The great God was all alone amid the awful silence of His own vast universe. But even at that time, if time it could be called, God was sovereign. He might create or not create *according to His own good pleasure.* He might create this way or that way; He might create one world or one million worlds and who was there to resist His will? He might call into existence a million different creatures and place them on *absolute equality,* endowing them with the same faculties and placing them in the same environment; or, He might create a million creatures each *differing* from the others and possessing nothing in common save their creaturehood, and who was there to challenge His right? If He so pleased, He might call into existence a world so immense that its dimensions were utterly beyond finite computation; and were He so disposed He might create an organism so small that nothing but the most powerful microscope could reveal its existence to human eyes. It was His sovereign right to create, on the one hand, the exalted seraphim to burn around His throne, and on the other hand, the tiny insect which dies the same hour it is born. If the mighty God chose to have *one vast gradation* in His universe from loftiest seraph to creeping reptile, from revolving worlds to floating atoms, from macrocosm, to microcosm, *instead of making everything uniform,* who was there to question His sovereign pleasure?

Behold then the existence of Divine sovereignty long before man ever saw the light. With whom took God counsel in the creation and disposition of His creatures. See the birds as they fly through the air, the beasts as they roam the earth, the fishes as they swim in the sea, and then ask, Who was it that made them to differ? Was it not their Creator who *sovereignly* assigned their various locations and adaptations to them!

Turn your eye to the heavens and observe the mysteries of Divine sovereignty which there confront the thoughtful beholder. "There is one glory of the sun, and another glory of the moon, and another glory of the stars: for one star *differeth from* another star in glory" (1 Cor. 15:41). But why should they? Why should the sun be more glorious than all the other planets? Why should there be stars of the first magnitude and others of the tenth? Why such amazing *inequalities?* Why should some of the heavenly bodies be *more favorably placed* than others in their relation to the sun? And why should there be 'shooting stars', falling stars, 'wandering stars" (Jude 13), in a word, *ruined* stars? And the only possible answer is, "For Thy pleasure they are and were created" (Rev. 4:11).

Come now to our own planet. Why should two thirds of its surface be covered with water, and why should so much of its remaining third be unfit for human cultivation or habitation? Why should there be vast stretches of marshes, deserts and icefields? Why should one country be so inferior, topographically, from another? Why should one be rich in minerals and another own none? Why should the climate of one be congenial and healthy, and another uncongenial and unhealthy? Why should one abound in rivers and lakes, and another be almost devoid of them? Why should one be constantly troubled with earthquakes and another be almost entirely free from them? Why? Because thus it pleased the Creator and Upholder of all things.

Consider the angelic hosts. Surely we shall find uniformity here. But no; here, as elsewhere, the same sovereign pleasure of the Creator is displayed. Some are higher in rank than others; some are more powerful than others; some are nearer to God than others. Scripture reveals a definite and well defined gradation in the angelic orders. From arch-angel, past seraphim and cherubim, we come to "principalities and powers" (Eph. 3:10), and from principalities and powers to "rulers" (Eph. 6:12), and then to the angels themselves, and even among them we read of the "*elect* angels" (1 Tim. 5:21). Again we ask, Why this *inequality,* this difference in rank and order? And all we can say is, "Our God is in the heavens, He hath done whatsoever He hath pleased" (Ps. 115:3).

Look at the animal kingdom and note the wondrous variety. What comparison is possible between the lion and the lamb, the bear and the kid, the elephant and the mouse? Some, like the horse and the dog, are gifted with great intelligence; while others, like the sheep and the swine, are almost devoid of it. Why? Some are designed to be beasts of burden, while others enjoy a life of freedom. But why should the mule and the donkey be shackled to a life of drudgery, while the lion and tiger are allowed to roam the jungle at their pleasure? Some are fit for food, others are unfit; some are beautiful, others ugly; some are endowed with great strength, others are quite helpless; some are fleet of foot, others can scarcely crawl—contrast the hare and the tortoise; some are of use to man, others appear quite valueless; some live for centuries, others for a few months at most; some are tame, others fierce. But why all these variations and differences?

What is true of the animals is equally true of the birds and fishes. But consider now *the vegetable kingdom.* Why should roses have thorns, and lilies grow without them? Why should one flower emit a fragrant aroma and another have none? Why should one tree bear fruit which is wholesome and another that which is poisonous? Why should one vegetable be capable of enduring the frost and another wither under it? Why should one apple tree be loaded with fruit, and another of the same age and in the same orchard be almost barren? Why should one plant flower a dozen times in a year and another bear blossoms but once in a century? Truly "*whatsoever the Lord pleased,* that did He in heaven, and in the earth, in the seas, and all deep places". (Psa. 135:6).

If then we see the Sovereignty of God displayed throughout all creation why should it be thought a strange thing if we behold it operating in the midst of *the human family*? Why should it be thought strange if to one God is pleased to give five talents and to another only one? Why should it be thought strange if one is born with a robust constitution and another of the same parents is frail and sickly? Why should it be thought strange if Abel is cut off in his prime, while Cain is suffered to live on for many years? Why should it be thought strange that some should be born black and others white; some be born idiots and others with high intellectual endowments; some be born constitutionally lethagic and others full of energy; some be born with a temperament that is selfish, fiery, egotistical, others who are naturally self-sacrificing, submissive, and meek? Why should it be thought strange if some are qualified by nature to lead and rule, while others are only fitted to follow and serve? Heredity and environment cannot account for all these variations and inequalities. No; it is *God* who maketh one to differ from another. Why should He? "Even so, Father, for so it seemeth good in Thy sight" must be our reply.

Learn then this basic truth, that the Creator is absolute Sovereign, executing His own will, performing His own pleasure, and considering nought but His own glory. *"The Lord hath made all things FOR HIMSELF" (Prov. 16:4).*

Arthur W. Pink.

The above is an extract from the Editor's book on "The Sovereignty of God". 320 pages. $1:50 postpaid. The Lord has greatly blest it to many.

GALATIANS 6:14.

"But God forbid that I should glory, save in the cross of our Lord Jesus Christ, by whom (whereby) the world is crucified unto me, and I unto the world."

For his own part, the Apostle was determined to glory in nothing save the cross of Christ. He had gone out to Him without the camp, bearing His reproach, and like Moses, he counted the reproach of Christ greater riches than the treasures of Egypt. The cross is here put for the atoning sacrifice of the Son of God offered upon the cross. This is the foundation which God hath laid in Sion for the hope of the guilty. His own self bear the sins of His people in His own body on the tree; and upon this, and this alone, believers rest their hope. They do not glory in any real or fancied superiority over others. They behold the Lord shining in the face of Jesus Christ. Through the rent vail of the Redeemer's flesh, they draw near to their covenant God, seated on a throne of grace; and, beholding the perfection of the sacrifice offered on Calvary, and arrayed in their Redeemer's everlasting righteousness, they challenge the universe to lay any thing to their charge.

This doctrine is blasphemed by those who know not God, as leading to licentiousness; but so far from this being the case, it is the foundation of all holiness in fallen man. Christ crucified is the sanctification, as well as the righteousness of His people. This is the only doctrine which is according to godliness, and by which alone the love of sin is subdued in the heart. This is the truth by which sinners are sanctified. The Apostle ascribes our being freed from the dominion of sin to our not being under the law, but under grace. Our being dead is essential to our living to God. The greater our sense of unmerited forgiveness, the more will our love abound; and this is the love of God, that we keep His commandments; and His commandments are not grievous. (1 John 5:3). Love makes them all easy. This doctrine effectually works in all who believe. The grace of God exhibited in the cross of Christ teaches believers that, denying ungodliness and worldly lusts, they should live soberly, righteously, and godly in this world.

It is hardly necessary to observe, that by the cross of Christ is not meant the material cross on which Christ suffered. The cross has become an object of idolatrous veneration. It was not a piece of wood in the form of a cross, but the doctrine of the Son of God suffering and dying on the cross, which was to the Jews a stumbling-block, and to the Greeks foolishness; but unto them which are called, both Jews and Greeks, Christ the power of God, and the wisdom of God. (1 Cor. 1:24). We are guarded against superstitious regard of a crucifix, by the history of the brazen serpent. By looking at it, all who were bitten by the fiery serpents were healed. There might appear no harm in retaining such a memorial of the power of the God of Israel. He had commanded a pot of manna to be laid up in commemoration of the bread with which He fed His people in the wilderness, and the observance of this ordinance produced no bad effects. But no such commandment had been given in regard to the serpent; its preservation was a human device, and like every other contrivance of man in religion, however plausible, it proved a snare; the children of Israel burnt incense to it, but Hezekiah broke it in pieces, saying it was only brass.

The Apostle, in common with all mankind, loved the world, and the things of the world. He had risen to eminence by the progress he had made in his studies. In persecuting the Church of God, he at once gratified his own corrupt inclinations, and established a reputation for his zealous attachment to the law of Moses; and to crown all, he verily thought with himself that he was doing God service. Amidst all the self-complacency which he felt, a new object struck his view. It was the glory of the only-begotten of the Father. What was Saul's astonishment when the question was addressed to him by this Divine Personage, "Why persecutest thou Me?" Saul was persecuting those whom he considered as apostates from the worship of the God of Israel; whom he viewed as the filth of the world, and the offscouring of all things, who acknowledged One who had died an accursed death to be the Christ of God, to whom they alleged that all the prophets bore witness. They affirmed that He had risen from the dead, and entered into His glory; that He was invested with all power in heaven and in earth, and now Saul beheld His glory, and heard from His own lips that He was the crucified One, and that in persecuting those whom He is not ashamed to call brethren, he was persecuting the Son of God, fighting against the King of kings, and Lord of lords. The persecutor's high imaginations were in a moment cast down, his eyes were indeed blinded by the glory which shone around him, but the eyes of his understanding were enlightened, and he had the witness in himself that Jesus was the Christ. He now began to apprehend the mystery of godliness, God manifest in the flesh. The Sun of righteousness had arisen on him with healing in His wings, and the wonderful doctrine of mercy and truth meeting together, righteousness and peace embracing each other, filled him with astonishment. Perhaps he had witnessed the scene lately enacted on Calvary; perhaps he had united with those who had reviled the Saviour; but by manifesting

Himself to this daring rebel, the Lord gave him repentance unto life; and now all his hopes rested upon Him who died upon the cross. Saul was a sinner, his guilt was highly aggravated; he was a persecutor, a blasphemer, and injurious; but he was a vessel of mercy, and was therefore plucked as a brand from the burning, as a pattern of Divine longsuffering, and from that day he counted all things but loss for the excellency of the knowledge of Christ, from whom he cheerfully suffered the loss of all things.

Paul never forgot the glory in which the Son of God appeared to him; but he viewed this glory in connection with the cross, on which his sins had been expiated. In it he beheld the exceeding sinfulness of sin; in it, connected with Christ's resurrection and ascension, he saw the pledge of all his sins being forgiven. He was now begotten again to a lively hope of an unfading inheritance; but he viewed the cross as the centre from which every spiritual and heavenly blessing flowed, and it alone was henceforth the ground of his boasting. Here he saw justice fully satisfied; on the cross he had died with his glorious Lord and Master. The cross was not only the ground of all the Apostle's boasting, the foundation of all his hopes; it was the grand subject of his ministry. As an ambassador of Christ, he tells the Corinthians he determined to know nothing among them save Jesus Christ and Him crucified.

The whole of our Lord's character and conduct, His divine discourses, and the works which He did in the Father's name, abundantly testified that He was the Son of God; but few believed. He did not, however, previously to His death, publicly declare His true character; He chiefly taught in parables, of which He gave the interpretation to His disciples privately. We find only two instances in which He fully declared Himself to be the Christ, except to His disciples; and hence the demand of the Jews, "If thou be the Christ, tell us plainly;" to which the Lord did not give an explicit answer, but referred them to His miracles. The two instances in which He declared Himself to be the Son of God were, to the woman of Samaria, and to the man whose sight He had restored. In both these cases we have an example of His manifesting Himself to His people as He does not to the world, and of faith coming by hearing. After His resurrection, the Apostles proclaimed in the temple that He whom the Jews had crucified was the Lord of glory, who, having thus died for the sins of His people, according to the Scriptures, had risen from the dead on the third day. This was the crowning evidence, and till it was given, the Lord did not permit His disciples to tell that He was the Christ; although independently of this the evidence was abundant, and many actually believed.

The doctrine of a crucified Christ, so offensive to the natural man, was that in which the Apostle now gloried. He saw in this wonderful event the manifold wisdom of God. In it are hid all the treasures of wisdom and knowledge. Christ, as we have seen, came to deliver His people from this present evil world, and this He effects by unfolding to them the doctrine of the cross. They learn the union between Christ and His people, from their guilt being expiated by His death, their sins buried in His grave, so that they shall never again be remembered. He appeared as His people's Surety. The Lord laid on Him the iniquities of them all; but He left them in His grave, and shall appear the second time without sin, unto salvation. Through death, His redeemed follow their triumphant Leader to the mansions which He has gone before to prepare for them; they behold Him, as the reward of His humiliation, crowned with glory and honour; invested with all power in heaven and in earth, for the purpose of putting His bloodbought people in possession of an exceeding and eternal weight of glory. This eclipses in their view all the glory of this world, as the rising sun conceals the twinkling stars. They were formerly blinded by the god of this world; they walked in a vain show; they were in an atmosphere of shadows and delusions; but when brought to the foot of the cross, their eyes are opened—the Sun of righteousness rises on them with healing in His wings. They were sometimes darkness, but now they are light in the Lord, and this light streams from the cross where all their guilt was cancelled, as it is written, "God is the Lord, which hath showed us light: bind the sacrifice with cords, even unto the horns of the altar." (Psa. 118: 27). By the cross they are reconciled to

God, they see light in His light, and walk in the narrow way that leads to glory, honour, and immortality.

The world once appeared to the Apostle exceeding fair. Like others, he was intoxicated with its charms; but at that time, his mind was blinded; he was hurrying down the broad road that leadeth to destruction. But God revealed His Son in him. Christ was formed in him the hope of glory. His eyes were opened to the wiles of the well-favoured harlot; he saw that her guests are in the depths of Hell, and he fled from her with loathing and disgust. Thus the great object of coming to the Son of God is accomplished. The Apostle had commenced the Epistle by stating that Christ gave Himself for the sins of His people, that He might deliver them from this present evil world; and here, at the close, he shows how this was effected in his own experience, by the view of the cross. The world had formerly smiled on Saul, and appeared disposed to load him with its choicest benefits; but no sooner did he behold the cross, no sooner did He, whose glory darkened the noon day sun, reveal Himself, as the sufferer on Calvary, than the world disowned Paul, and marked him as an object of scorn and contempt. *J. A. Haldane, 1848.*

A MESSAGE OF COMFORT.

"But He knoweth the way that I take: when He hath tried me I shall come forth as gold" (Job 23:10).

Job here *corrects* himself. In the beginning of the chapter we find him saying: "Even today is my complaint bitter: my stroke is heavier than my groaning." (vv. 1 & 2). Poor Job felt that his lot was unbearable. But he recovers himself. He checks his hasty outburst and revises his impetuous decision. How often we all have to correct ourselves! Only One has ever walked this earth who *never* had occasion to do so.

Job here *comforts* himself. *He* could not fathom the mysteries of Providence but *God knew* the way he took. Job had diligently sought the calming presence of God, but, for a time, in vain. "Behold I go forward, but He is not there; and backward, but I cannot perceive Him. On the left hand, where He doth work, but I cannot behold Him: He hideth Himself on the right hand, that I cannot see Him." (vv. 8 & 9). But he consoled himself with this blessed fact—though I cannot see God, what is a thousand times better, *He can see me*—"He knoweth". One above is neither unmindful nor indifferent to our lot. If He notices the fall of a sparrow, if He counts the hairs of our heads, of course "He knows" the way that I take.

Job here *enunciates a noble view of life.* How splendidly optimistic he was! He did not allow his afflictions to turn him into a skeptic. He did not permit the sore trials and troubles through which he was passing to overwhelm him. He looked at the bright side of the dark cloud—*God's* side, hidden from sense and reason. He took a long view of life. He looked beyond the immediate "fiery trials" and saw that the outcome would be gold refined. "But He knoweth the way that I take: when He hath tried me I shall come forth as gold." Three great truths are expressed here: let us briefly consider each separately.

I. THE DIVINE KNOWLEDGE OF MY LIFE.

"He knoweth the way that I take."

The *omniscience* of God is one of the wondrous attributes of Deity. "For His eyes are upon the ways of man, and He seeth *all* his goings." (Job 34:21). "The eyes of the Lord are in *every* place, beholding the evil and the good." (Prov. 15:3). Spurgeon said, "One of the greatest tests of experimental religion is, What is my relationship to God's omniscience." What is *your* relationship to it, dear reader? How does it affect you? Does it distress or comfort you? Do you shrink from the thought of God knowing *all about* your way?—perhaps, the lying, selfish, hypocritical way! To the sinner this *is* a terrible thought. He denies it, or if not this, he seeks to forget it. But to the Christian, here is real comfort. How cheering to remember that my Father knows all about my trials, my difficulties, my sorrows, my efforts to glorify Him. Precious truth for those in Christ, harrowing thought for all out of Christ, that the way I am taking is fully known and observed by God.

"*He* knoweth the way that I take". *Men* did not know the way that Job took. He was grievously misunderstood, and for one with a sensitive temperament to be misunderstood, is a sore trial. His very friends thought he was a hypocrite. They believed he was a great sinner and being punished by God. Job knew that he was an unworthy saint, but not a hypocrite. He appealed against their censorious verdict. "He knoweth the way that I take: when He hath tried me I shall come forth as gold." Here is instruction for us when like circumstanced. Fellow-believer, your fellow-men, yes, and your fellow-christians, may misunderstand you, and misinterpret God's dealings with you,: but console yourself with the blessed fact that the omniscient One knoweth.

"*He* knoweth the way that I take." In the fullest sense of the word *Job himself* did not *know* the way that he took, nor do any of us. Life is profoundly mysterious, and the passing of the years offer no solution. Nor does philosophizing help us. Human volition is a strange enigma. Consciousness bears witness that we are more than automotons. The power of choice is exercised by us in every move we make. And yet it is plain that our freedom is not absolute. There are forces brought to bear upon us, both good and evil, which are beyond *our* power to resist. Both heredity and environment exercise powerful influences upon us. Our surroundings and circumstances are factors which cannot be ignored. And what of providence which "shapes our destinies"? Ah, how little do we *know* the way which *we* "take". Said the prophet, "O Lord I know that the way of man is not in himself: it is not in man that walketh to direct his steps" (Jer. 10:23). Here we enter the realm of mystery, and it is idle to deny it. Better far to acknowledge with the wise man, "Man's goings are of the Lord; how can a man then understand his way?" (Pro. 20:24).

In the narrower sense of the term Job *did* know the way which he took. What that "way" was he tells us in the next two verses. "My foot hath held His steps, His way have I kept, and not declined. Neither have I gone back from the commandment of His lips; I have esteemed the words of His mouth more than my necessary food." (Job 23:11, 12). The way Job chose was the *best* way, the *scriptural* way, *God's* way—"*His* way". What do you think of *that* way, dear reader? Was it not a grand selection? Ah, not only "patient", but *wise* Job! Have *you* made a similar choice? Can you say, "My foot hath held His steps, His way have I kept, and not declined"? (v. 11). If you can, praise Him for His enabling grace. If you cannot, confess with shame your failure to appropriate His all-sufficient grace. Get down on your knees at once, and unbosom yourself to God. Hide and keep back nothing. Remember it is written "If we confess our sins, He is faithful and just to forgive us our sins, and to cleanse us from all unrighteousness." (1 John 1:9). Does not v. 12 explain your *failure,* my failure, dear reader? Is it not because we have not trembled before God's commandments, and because we have *so lightly* esteemed His Word, that we have "declined" *from His way!* Then let us, even now, and daily, seek grace from on high to heed His commandments and hide His Word in our hearts.

"He knoweth *the way* that I take". *Which* way are you taking?—the narrow way which leadeth unto life, or the Broad Road that leadeth to destruction? Make certain on this point dear friend. Scripture declares, "So every one of us shall give account of himself to God" (Rom. 14:12). But you need not be deceived or uncertain. The Lord declared, "I am *The Way*" (John 14:6).

2. DIVINE TESTING.

"When He hath tried me."

"The fining pot is for silver, and the furnace for gold: but the Lord trieth the hearts." (Prov. 17:3). This was God's way with Israel of old, and it is His way with Christians now. Just before Israel entered Canaan, as Moses reviewed their history since leaving Egypt, he said, "And thou shalt remember all the way which the Lord thy God led thee these forty years in the wilderness, to humble thee, and to prove thee, and to know what was in thine heart, whether thou wouldst keep His commandments, or no" (Deut. 8:2). In the same way God tries, tests, proves, humbles us.

"When He hath *tried* me". If we realized this more, we should bear up better in the hour of affliction and be more patient under suffering. The daily irritations of life, the things which annoy so much —what is their meaning? why are they permitted? Here is the answer: God is "trying" you! That is the explanation (in part, at least) of that disappointment, that crushing of your earthly hopes, that great loss,—God was, is, *testing* you. God is trying your temper, your courage, your faith, your patience, your love, your fidelity.

"When *He* hath tried me". How frequently God's saints see only Satan as the cause of their troubles. They regard the great enemy as responsible for much of their sufferings. But there is no comfort for the heart in this. We do not deny that the Devil *does* bring about much that harasses us. But above Satan is the Lord Almighty! The Devil cannot touch a hair of your heads without God's permission, and when he is allowed to disturb and distract us, even then, it is only God *using him* to "try" us. Let us learn then, *to look beyond* all secondary causes and instruments to that One who worketh *all* things after the counsel of *His own* will (Eph. 1:11). This is what Job did.

In the opening chapter of the book which bears his name we find Satan obtaining permission to afflict God's servant. He uses the Sabeans to destroy Job's herds (v. 15): he sent the Chaldeans to slay his servants (v. 17): he caused a great army to kill his children (v. 19). And what was Job's response? This: he exclaimed "The Lord gave, and *the Lord* hath taken away; blessed be the name of the Lord." (1:21). Job looked beyond the human agents, beyond Satan who employed them, to the Lord who controlleth all. He realized that it was the Lord *trying* him. We get the same thing in the N. T. To the suffering saints at Smyrna John wrote, "Fear none of those things which thou shalt suffer; behold, the devil shall cast some of you into prison, *that ye may be tried.*" (Rev. 2:10). Their being cast into prison was simply God "trying" them.

How much we lose by forgetting this! What a stay for the trouble-tossed heart to know that no matter what form the testing may take, no matter what the agent which annoys, it is *God* who is "trying" His children. What a perfect example the Saviour sets us. When He was approached in the garden and Peter drew his sword and cut off the ear of Malcus, the Saviour said, "The cup which *My Father* hath given Me, shall I not drink it?" (John 18:11). Men were about to vent their awful rage upon Him, the Serpent would bruise His heel, but He looks above and beyond them. Dear reader, no matter how bitter its contents, (infinitely less than that which the Saviour drained) let us accept the cup as from *the Father's* hand.

In some moods we are apt to question the wisdom and right of God to try us. So often we murmur at His dispensations. *Why* should God lay such an intolerable burden upon me? *Why* should others be spared their loved ones, and mine taken? *Why* should health and strength, perhaps the gift of sight, be denied me? The first answer to all such questions is, "Who art thou O man, that repliest against *God?*"! It is wicked insubordination for any creature to call into question the dealings of the great Creator. "Shall the thing formed say to Him that formed it, Why hast Thou made me thus?" (Rom. 9:20). How earnestly each of us need to cry unto God, that His grace may silence our rebellious lips and still the tempest within our desperately wicked hearts!

But to the humble soul which bows in submission before the sovereign dispensations of the all-wise God, Scripture affords some light on the problem. This light may not satisfy reason, but it will bring comfort and strength when received in childlike faith and simplicity. In 1 Pet. 1:6 we read; "Wherein (God's salvation) ye greatly rejoice, though now for a season, if need be, ye are in heaviness through manifold temptations (or trials): That the trial of your faith, being much more precious than gold that perisheth, though it be tried with fire, might be found unto praise and honour and glory at the appearing of Jesus Christ". Note three things here. First, there is a *needs be* for the trial of faith. Since *God* says it, let us accept it. Second, this trying of faith is *precious,* far more so than gold. It is precious to God (cf. Psa. 116:15) and will yet be so to us. Third, *the present trial* has in view *the future.* Where the trial has been meekly endured and bravely borne, there will be a grand reward at the appearing of our Redeemer.

Again, in 1 Pet. 4:12, 13 we are told: "Beloved, think it not strange concerning the fiery trial which is to try you, as though some strange thing happened unto you: But rejoice, inasmuch as ye are partakers, of Christ's sufferings: that, when His glory shall be revealed, ye may be glad also with exceeding joy." The same thoughts are expressed here as in the previous passage. There is a needs-be for our "trials" and therefore we are to think them not strange—we should expect them. And, too, there is again the blessed outlook of being richly recompensed at Christ's return. Then there is the added word that not only should we meet these trials with faith's fortitude, but we should rejoice in them, inasmuch as we are permitted to have fellowship in "the sufferings of Christ". He, too, suffered; sufficient then, for the disciple to be as his Master.

"When He hath tried *me*." Dear Christian reader, there are no exceptions. God had only one Son without sin, but never one without sorrow. Sooner or later, in one form or another, *trial*—sore and heavy—will be our lot. "And sent Timotheous our brother . . . . . to establish you, and comfort you concerning your faith: that no man should be moved by these *afflictions;* for yourselves know that we are *appointed thereunto*". (1 Thess. 3:2, 3). And again it is written, "We must through *much* tribulation enter into the kingdom of God." (Acts 14:22). It has been so in every age. Abram was "tried", tried severely. So, too, were Joseph, Jacob, Moses, David, Daniel, the Apostles, etc.

3. THE ULTIMATE ISSUE.

"I shall come forth as gold."

Observe the tense here. Job did not imagine that he was pure gold already. I *shall* come forth as gold, he declared. He knew full well that there was yet much dross in him. He did not boast that he was *already* perfect. Far from it. In the final chapter of his book we find him saying, "I abhor myself" (42:6). And well he might: and well may we. As we discover that in our flesh there dwelleth "*no* good thing", as we examine ourselves and our ways in the light of God's Word and behold our innumerable failures, as we think of our countless sins, both of omission and commission, good reason have we for abhoring ourselves. Ah, Christian reader there is *much* dross about us. But it will not ever be thus.

"I shall come forth as gold." Job did not say, "When He hath tried me I *may* come forth as gold", or "I *hope* to come forth as gold", but with full confidence and positive assurance he declared, "I *shall* come forth as gold". But how did he know this? How can we be sure of the happy issue? Because the Divine purpose cannot fail. He which hath begun a good work in us "*will* finish it" (Phil. 1:6). How can we be sure of the happy issue? Because the Divine promise is sure: "The Lord *will perfect* that which concerneth me" (Psa. 138:8). Then be of good cheer, tried and troubled one. The process may be unpleasant and painful, but the issue is charming and sure.

"*I* shall come forth as gold." This was said by one who knew affliction and sorrow as few among the sons of men have known them. Yet despite his fiery trials he was optimistic. Let then this triumphant language be ours. "I shall come forth as gold" is not the language of carnal boasting, but the confidence of one whose mind was stayed upon God. There will be no credit to our account—the glory will all belong to the Divine Refiner. James 1:12.

For the *present* there remain two things: first, *Love* is the Divine thermometor while we are in the crucible of testing—"And He shall *sit* (the patience of Divine grace) as a Refiner and Purifier of silver etc.", (Mal. 3:3). Second, the Lord Himself is *with us* in the fiery furnace, as He was with the three young Hebrews. (Dan. 3:25). For the *future* this is sure: the most wonderful thing in heaven will not be the golden street or the golden harps, but *golden souls* on which is stamped the image of God—"predestinated to be conformed to the image of His Son"! Praise God for such a glorious prospect, such a victorious issue, such a marvelous goal.

Arthur W. Pink.

Stay thy soul, O troubled one, upon the exceeding great and precious promises of Scripture:—"Fear thou not; for I am with thee: be not dismayed, for I am thy God: I will strengthen thee, yea, I will help thee; yea, I will uphold thee with the right hand of My righteousness" (Is. 41:10). "When thou passest thro the waters, I will be with thee; and thro the rivers, they shall not overflow thee: when thou walkest thro the fire, thou shalt not be burned; neither shall the flame kindle upon thee" (Is. 43:2).

JOHN 1:12, 13.

"But as many as received Him, to them gave He power to become the sons of God, even to them that believe on His name: Which were born, not of blood, nor of the will of the flesh, nor of the will of man, but of God."

Here there is a reference to that change, without which we cannot see or enter the kingdom of God, and which is *contrasted with the three ways in which men partook of the privileges of the nation of Israel.* The first of these three ways was, being born of blood, being the descendants of Abraham; but Ishmael, and the six sons of Keturah, although sprung from Abraham, had no part in the covenant; and even Esau, who was not only descended from Abraham, but from Isaac, was also rejected. To partake of the privileges of Israel, it was necessary to be descended from Abraham, Isaac, and Jacob, and therefore they are said to be born of *bloods.* The second way in which men enjoyed the privileges of the kingdom of Israel was, by being circumcised. When a stranger was circumcised, he might eat the passover, and was to be under the same law as a home-born Israelite. This is termed by the Apostle, "the will of the *flesh,*"—submitting to circumcision in his flesh. The third way was by the will of man. When a stranger cast his lot with Israel, and desired to keep the passover, all his males were to be circumcised; and this is what the Apostle terms "the will of man." Not only was the master circumcised, but all his male slaves. In opposition to these three ways, stands the *one* way by which we partake of the blessings of Christ's kingdom, being born of God, being partakers of a Divine nature; or as the Apostle terms it being a new creature, or a new creation. *J. A. Haldane, 1848.*

GALATIANS 6:12.

"As many as desire to make a fair show in the flesh, they constrain you to be circumcised; only lest they should suffer persecution for the cross of Christ."

When the secrets of men's hearts are made manifest, it will apear that many of the differences of sentiment and practice among believers had their origin in carnal motives. Many compliances with what is highly esteemed among men will be found to have arisen from the love of this present world. Men are apprehensive of losing their income, or their rank in society, besides forfeiting the friendship of those with whom they associate, and therefore resist those convictions which, if listened to, would have led them to follow Christ fully. Believers are laid under very strong temptations to court the favour and friendship of men, by trifling with their convictions, which they may easily persuade themselves are unnecessary scruples. It is not uncommon to maintain, that the great doctrines of the Gospel are clearly revealed, but there is much obscurity, in regard to the ordinances which believers are to observe, and that much is left, in this respect, to our own discretion, according to the peculiar circumstances in which we are placed. The ordinances are sometimes represented as being on the same footing as meats and drinks; but they are, in reality, visible embodiments of the truth, and, consequently, any alteration in the ordinances, gives a false view of the doctrine which they were intended to illustrate. In fact, by the vain tradition that our circumstances are different from those of the first churches, and, that, therefore, our practice cannot correspond with that of the primitive believers, the disciples of Christ are left without any rule for their guidance and direction. It is true, our circumstances are different. But the kingdom of Christ cannot be moved; it is adapted to every possible state of society; it is not affected by the changes to which all sublunary things are liable; and the apostolic churches, as exhibited in the Word of God, which endureth forever, are *the model by which all believers, in all circumstances, are bound to regulate their association.* The rejection of this fundamental principle is the cause of believers being scattered; but the Lord will search His sheep, and seek them out, and will deliver them out of all places where they have been scattered in the cloudy and dark day. *J. A. Haldane, 1848.*

SPECIAL ADDRESSES BY THE EDITOR.

Seven of the Special Addresses which the Editor expects to deliver most frequently in his forthcoming Foreign Bible Conference tour (D.V.) have been printed separately, and we now announce them so that they may be available to our friends in this Country. We deem them amongst the most important of any thing we have had printed; and we sincerely trust that *many* subscribers of this Magazine will secure them. They are as follows:—

The Christian's Greatest Need:	An exposition of Luke 10:38-42:	$0:10
God's Food for His people:	" " " Exodus 16:	:10
The Prodigal Son:	" " " Luke 15:	:10
The Three Crosses: A precious Gospel message:	....	:10
A Threefold Salvation—From the penalty, power, & presence of sin	....	:07
The Sins of the Saints—Much used of God in the U. S. A.	....	:08
The New Birth—Greatly needed today:	....	:07

One each of the above sent post-paid for 60 cents. This offer will not be repeated after next month. We have been at much expense in publishing the first four, personally, and hope that our readers will order a dozen of each—*$1:00* per doz. They are very nicely got up, and will just go in an ordinary-sized envelope. One of these would be much more honouring to God than a "Christmas Card"!

BOUND VOLUMES OF "STUDIES IN THE SCRIPTURES".

Vol 1 containing the 12 issues for 1922: *$1:50.—$1:75 Foreign*
Vol 2 " " " " " 1923: *1:50.* " "
Vol 3 " " " " " 1924: *1:50.* " "

We have had these bound, strongly and attractively, so that interested readers could preserve the Magazines in *permanent* form. When our present supply is exhausted these will, most probably, *not* be re-printed. We will send the 3 Vols. for *$4:00* (*£1* to Foreign address). They cost us almost *40* cents each to bind, so that when we pay the postage this is practically *cost price!* $4:25 to those west of Chicago.

GLEANINGS IN GENESIS.

The 2 Vols. containing 46 special articles *$2:50.*

The Editor was six years compiling these. Many have been helped by them. They give special attention to the Types. Joseph a type of Christ in *one hundred* distinct points! Intensely interesting.

EXPOSITION OF JOHN'S GOSPEL.

Vol 1: covering the first five chapters 380 pages *$1:50*
" 2: " " next " " 400 " *2:00*

Send all orders to the Editor:

227 North Creighton Street,
Philadelphia, Pa.

Foreign subscribers please send *only* International Money Orders.

VOL. III DECEMBER, 1924 NO. 12

STUDIES in the SCRIPTURES

"Search the Scriptures" John 5:39.

Arthur W. Pink, Publisher & Editor,
227 N. Creighton St., Philadelphia, Pa.

Price: 10 cents per copy; $1.00 per year. Foreign $1.00 per year.

This issue completes the third Volume, for which we fervently praise our most gracious and ever-faithful God. The task of editing and publishing this Magazine singled-handed, in addition to our oral ministry, has been no light one; yet the Lord has supplied the needed health and strength. The circulation is still very much smaller than what we had hoped, but probably we ought not to be surprised at this. In these days the great majority of those who read, do so for recreation rather than edification. If they do not seek to be amused, yet they desire what is 'light' or sensational, and not that which makes a *demand* upon the mind and heart. Startling news-items on the Signs of the Times, refutations of Evolution, Christian Science etc., written in a racy style, anecdotes and poetry, are more acceptable to many professing Christians than the solid exposition of the Word itself. Alas that it should be so. A lack of appetite for solid and nourishing foods, is a sure sign of ill health. And the same is true spiritually!

Yet, *there are* still a few (and we believe *will be* to the very end of this Dispensation) who *hunger* for spiritual things, and who *value* that which serves, in any measure, to open up to them portions of the Holy Scriptures. *These* are the ones we are intensely desirous of reaching. There are ones and twos, here and there, who are willing to "*buy* the Truth", not in dollars and cents, but by diligent searching, patient study, and prayerful reading. We are unfeignedly thankful for having been brought into touch with several hundreds of such, and our daily prayer is, that it may please Him who condescends to employ feeble and despised instruments, to use our little Magazine to stir them up to a more careful, reverent, and systematic study of His own Word.

Once more, by the goodness of God, we are permitted to close the year with a slight balance on the right side. We take this opportunity of thanking each one of our friends who have helped by their gifts and prayers. We are fully confident that the Bread now cast upon the waters (the peoples) shall be found "after many days" (Eccl. 11:1). In view of our soon-coming departure for Foreign Lands, D. V., it will be a great help if our subscribers renew promptly, and if the Lord lays it on their hearts to add a gift to be used in sending out the Magazine *free* to Missionaries we shall value their fellowship.

No effort is being spared to make the Magazine increasingly helpful. The articles on Exodus for 1925 cover one of the most interesting and wonderful portions of the O. T. During 1925 we shall, D. V., enter the most precious and fragrant sections of John's Gospel, and we sincerely trust that *all* who have read the preceding articles will continue through another year. In addition, there will be short papers on various subjects, including "Messages of Comfort" for tried and sorrowing souls.

This is *not* a commercial venture, but "a work of faith and labour of love." Our earnest desire is to be *faithful* to God and *helpful* to His dear people. Each year several hundreds fail to renew, so that many *new* subscribers are needed to fill their places. We hope that those who *are* interested and being blessed by these pages, will send in subscriptions for their friends. Wishing you God's best, I remain, Yours by wondrous grace,

Arthur W. Pink.

IMPORTANT NOTICES

All new subscriptions will be dated back to January, 1924.

Set of twelve issues for **1922**, unbound, **$1.00**. Bound, **$1.50**.

Set of twelve issues for **1923**, unbound, **$1.00**. Bound **$1.50**.

Note: We cannot break a set or now supply any **single** 1923 issues.

Subscription Price: **$1.00** per year to any address in the world. Single copies **10 cents.**

Change of Address: Please notify me promptly of any change of address, and be certain to give both old and new addresses.

Non-subscribers receiving this Magazine regularly will understand their subscription has been entered by a friend.

Copies lost in the mail duplicated only if we are notified promptly.

Entered as second-class matter December 15th, 1923, at the post office at Philadelphia, Pa., under Act of March 3rd, 1879.

CONTENTS

JOHN'S GOSPEL.

36. Christ, One with the Father:

John 10:22-42.

It is by no means a simple task either to analyze or to summarize the second half of John 10. The twenty-second verse clearly begins a new section of the chapter, but it is equally clear that what follows is closely related to that which has gone before. The Lord is no longer talking to "the Pharisees", but to "the Jews". Nevertheless, it is in His Shepherd character as related to His own that He is here viewed. Yet while there is this in common between the first and second halves of John 10, there is a notable difference between them. In the former, Christ is seen in His mediatorship; in the latter, it is His essential glories which are the more prominent.

In the first part of John 10 it is Christ in "the form of a Servant" which is before us. He gains entrance to the Sheepfold by "the porter opening to Him" (v. 3). He is the "Door" into God's presence (v. 9), the *Way* unto the Father. There, He is seen as the One who was to "give His life for the sheep" (v. 11). There, we behold Him in the place of obedience, in subjection to the "commandment" of the Father (v. 18). But mark the contrast in the second half of John 10. Here, He presents Himself as the One endowed with the sovereign right to "give eternal life" to His own (v. 28); as One possessed of almighty power, so that none can pluck them out of His hand (v. 28); as *one* with the Father (v. 30); as "the Son of God" (v. 36). It seems evident then that the central design of the passage before us is to display the *essential* glories of the person of the God-man. It is not so much the Godhood of Christ which is here in view, as it is the Deity *of the One* who humbled Himself to become man.

What is recorded in the latter half of John 10 provides a most pertinent, though tragic, *conclusion* to the first section of the Gospel. It was ***winter-time*** **(v. 22)**; the season of ingathering was now over; the "Sun of Righteousness" had completed His official circuit, and the genial warmth of summer had now given place to the season of chilling frosts. The Jews were celebrating "the Feast of the Dedication", which commemorated the purification of the temple. But for the true Temple, the One to whom the temple had pointed—God tabernacling in their midst—they had no heart. The Lord Jesus is presented as walking in the temple, but it is to be carefully noted that He was "in Solomon's porch" (v. 23), which means that He was *on the outside* of the sacred enclosure. Israel's "house" was left unto them desolate (cf. Matt. 13:1)! While here in the porch, "the Jews" (the religious leaders) came to Christ with the demand that He tell them openly if He were "the Christ" (v. 24), saying, "How long dost Thou make us to doubt?" This was the language of unbelief, and uttered at that late date, showed the hopelessness of their condition. Following this interview of the Jews with Christ, and their unsuccessful attempt to apprehend Him, the Lord retires *beyond Jordan,* "unto the place where John at first baptized" (v. 40). Thus did Israel's Messiah return to that place where He had formally dedicated Himself to His mission. Further details will come before us in the course of the exposition. Below is an attempt to analyze our passage:

1. During the Feast of Dedication Jesus walks in Solomon's porch: **vv. 22, 23.**
2. The Jews demand an open proclamation of His Messiahship: v. 24.
3. The Lord explains why a granting of their request was useless: vv. 25, 26.
4. The eternal security of His sheep: vv. 27-30.
5. The Jews attempt to stone Him because of His avowal of Deity: vv. 31-33.
6. Christ's defence of His Deity: vv. 34-38.
7. Christ leaves Jerusalem and goes beyond Jordan, where many believe on Him: vv. 39-42.

"And it was at Jerusalem the Feast of Dedication, and it was winter" (v. 22). The Feast of Dedication was observed at Jerusalem in memorial of the purification of the Temple after it had been polluted by the idolatries of Antiochus Epiphanes. Proof of this is to be found in the fact that we are here told the time was "winter". Therefore the "feast" here mentioned could not be in remembrance of the dedication of Solomon's temple, for this temple had been dedicated at harvest-time (1 Kings 8:2); nor was it to celebrate the building of Nehemiah's temple, for that had been dedicated in the spring-time (Ezra 6:15, 16). The "feast" here referred to must be that which had been instituted by Judas Maccabæus, on his having purified the temple after the pollution of it by Antiochus, about 165 B. C. This "feast" was celebrated every year for eight successive days in the month of December (1 Macc. 4:52, 59), and is mentioned by Josephus (Antiq. 12:7, etc.). Thus the words, "and it was winter" enable us to identify this feast.

"And it was at Jerusalem the feast of the Dedication, and it was winter". Here, as always in Scripture, there is a deeper meaning than the mere historical. The mention of "winter" at this point is most significant and solemn. This tenth chapter of John closes the first section of the fourth Gospel. From this point onwards the Lord Jesus discourses no more before the religious leaders. His public ministry was over; henceforth, He is seen only with His own*. The Jews knew not their Day of Visitation, and henceforth the things which belonged to their peace were hidden from their eyes (Luke 21:42). So far as they were concerned the words of Jeremiah applied with direct and solemn force: "The harvest is past, *the summer is ended,* and we are not saved" (8:20). For them there was nothing but an interminable *"winter".* Significant and suitable then is this notice of the season of coldness and barrenness as an introduction to what follows.

What we have just pointed out in connection with the moral force of this reference to "winter" encourages us to look for a deeper significance in this mention here of "the Feast of the Dedication". Nowhere else in Scripture is this particular feast referred to. This makes it the more difficult to ascertain its significance here. That there *is* some definite reason for the Holy Spirit noticing it, and that there is a pertinent and profound meaning to it when contemplated in its connections, we are fully assured. What, then, is it?

As already pointed out, the last half of John 10 closes the first section of John's Gospel, a section which has to do with the *public* ministry of Christ. The second section of this Gospel records His *private* ministry, concluding with His death and resurrection. The distinctive character of these two sections correspond exactly with the two chief purposes of our Lord's incarnation, which were to present Himself to Israel as their promised Messiah, and to offer Himself as a Sacrifice for sin. At the point now reached in this Gospel, the formal presentation of Himself to Israel as their Messiah was almost over. What, then, remained? Only the still more important work which was to be accomplished by His death and resurrection. He had presented Himself to Israel, now, shortly, He would offer Himself as a Sacrifice to God. It is to this "the *Dedication*" here points.

It is in this Gospel, alone of the four, that the Lord Jesus is hailed as "the *Lamb* of God", and if the reader will turn back to Ex. 12 he will find that the "lamb" was to be *separated* from the flock some days

* John 12:12-15 can scarcely be regarded as an exception.

before it was to be killed (see vv. 3, 5, 6). In keeping with this, note how in this passage (and nowhere else) the Lord Jesus speaks of Himself as the One whom the Father had "sanctified" (v. 36), and mark how at the end of the chapter He is seen *leaving* Jerusalem and going away "beyond Jordan" (v. 40)! That the Holy Spirit has here prefaced this final conversation between the Saviour and the Jews by mentioning "the Feast of the *Dedication*" is in beautiful and striking accord with the fact that from this point onwards Christ was now dedicated to the Cross, as hitherto He had been engaged in manifesting Himself to Israel.

The interpretation suggested above is confirmed and established by two other passages in the New Testament. The Greek word rendered "dedication" occurs nowhere else in the New Testament, but it is found twice in its verbal form. In Heb. 9:18 we read, "Whereupon neither the first testament was *dedicated* without blood" (Heb. 9:18). In Heb. 10:19, 20 we are told, "Having therefore, brethren, boldness to enter into the holiest by the blood of Jesus, by a new and living way, which He hath consecrated (*dedicated*) for us, through the veil, that is to say, His flesh". In each of these instances "dedication" is connected with *blood-shedding!* And it was to this, the shedding of His precious blood, that the Lord Jesus was now (after His rejection by the Nation) dedicated! An additional item still further confirming our exposition is found in the fact that the historical reference in John 10:22 was to the dedication of the *temple,* and in John 2:19 the Saviour refers to Himself as "this Temple"—"destroy this *Temple,* and in three days I will raise it up". The antitypical *Dedication of the Temple* was the Saviour offering Himself to God!! Most fitting then was it that the Holy Spirit should here mention the typical dedication of the temple *immediately after* the Lord had thrice referred to His "laying down" His life (see vv. 15, 17, 18)!

"And Jesus walked in the temple in Solomon's porch" (v. 23). Josephus informs us (Antiq. 8:3) that Solomon, when he built the temple, filled up a part of the valley adjacent to mount Zion, and built a portico over it toward the East. This was a magnificent structure, supported by a wall four hundred cubits high, made out of stones of vast bulk. It continued to the time of Agrippa, which was several years after the death of Christ. Twice more is mention made of "Solomon's porch" in the New Testament, and what is found in these passages points a sharp contrast from the one now before us. In Acts 3:11 we are told that, following the healing of the lame beggar by Peter and John, *"all the people* ran together unto them in the porch that is called Solomon's, greatly wondering". But here in John 10:23, following our Lord's healing of the blind beggar, there is no hint of any wonderment among the people! Again, in Acts 5:12 we read, "And they were all *with one accord* in Solomon's porch". This is in evident contrast, designed contrast, from what is before us in our present passage. Here, immediately after the reference to our Lord walking in Solomon's porch, we read, "then came the Jews round about Him, and said unto Him, How long dost Thou make us to doubt?" *They* were manifestly *out of accord* with Him. They were opposed to Him, and like beasts of prey sought only His life. Thus we see once more the importance and value of comparing scripture with scripture. By thus linking together these three passages which make mention of "Solomon's porch" we discern the more clearly how that the design of our passage is to present the God-man as "despised and rejected of men".

"Then came the Jews round about Him, and said unto Him, How long dost Thou make us to doubt? if Thou be the Christ tell us plainly" (v. 24). The appropriateness of this incident at the close of John 10, and the force of this request of the Jews—obviously a disingenuous one—should now be apparent to the reader. Coming as it does right at the close of the first main section of this Gospel, a section which is concerned with the *public* ministry of Christ before Israel, this demand of the religious leaders makes it plain how useless it was for the Messiah to make any further advances toward the Nation at large, and how justly He might now abandon them to that darkness which they preferred to the light. By now, it was unmistakeably plain that the religious leaders "received Him not", and this request of theirs for Him to tell them "plainly" or "openly" if He were the Messiah, was obviously made with no other purpose than to gain evidence that they might apprehend Him as a rebel against the Roman government. But, if such was their evil design, did they not already have the needed evidence to formulate the desired charge against Him? The answer is, No, not evidence sufficiently explicit.

"How long dost Thou make us to doubt? if Thou be the Christ, tell us openly". It is a significant thing that the Lord Jesus *had not* declared, plainly and openly in public, that He *was* the Messiah. He had avowed His Messiahship to His disciples (1:41, 49, etc.); to the Samaritans (4:42), and to the blind beggar (9:37); but He had not done so before the multitudes or to the religious leaders. This designed omission accomplished a double purpose: it made it impossible for the authorities to lawfully seize Him before God's appointed time, and it enforced the *responsibility* of the Nation at large. That the Lord Jesus was the One that the prophets announced should come had been abundantly attested by His person, His life, and His works; yet the absence of any formal announcement in public served as an admirable *test* of the people. His miraculous works—ever termed "signs" in John's Gospel—were more than sufficient to prove Him to be the Messiah unto those who were open-minded; but yet they were not such as to make it impossible for the prejudiced to refuse their assent. This is ever God's way of dealing with moral agents. There are innumerable tokens for the existence of a Divine Creator, sufficient to render all men "without excuse"; yet are these tokens of such a nature as not to have banished atheism from the earth. There are a thousand evidences that the Holy Scriptures are the inspired Word of God, yet are there multitudes who believe them not. There is a great host of impeachable witnesses who testify daily to the Saviourhood of the Lord Jesus, yet the great majority of men continue in their sins.

Before we pass from this verse a word should be said upon the turpitude of these Jews. "How long dost *Thou* make us to doubt?" was inexcusable wickedness. They were seeking to transfer to Him the onus of their unbelief. They argued that *He* was responsible for their unreasonable and God-dishonoring doubting. This is ever the way with the unregenerate. When God arraigned Adam, the guilty culprit answered, "The woman whom *Thou* gavest to be with me, *she* gave me of the tree, and I did eat" (Gen. 3:12). So it is today. Instead of tracing the cause of unbelief to his own evil heart, the sinner blames God for the insufficiency of convincing evidence.

"Jesus answered them, I told you, and ye believed not: the works that I do in My Father's name, they bear witness of Me" (v. 25). The Lord had told them that He was "the Son of man", and that as such the Father had "given Him authority to execute judgment" (5:27). He had told them that He was the One of whom Moses wrote (5:46). He had told them that He was the "Living Bread" which had come down from heaven (6:51). He had told them that Abraham had rejoiced to see His day (8:56). All of these were statements which intimated plainly that He was the Promised One of the Old Testament Scriptures.

In addition to what He had taught concerning His own person, His "works" bore conclusive witness to His Messianic office. His "works" were an essential part of His credentials, as is clear from Luke 7:21-23: "And John calling unto him two of his disciples sent them unto Jesus, saying, Art Thou He that should come? or look we for another? . . . . Jesus answering said unto them, Go your way, and tell John what things ye have seen and heard; how that the blind see, the lame walk, the lepers are cleansed, the deaf hear, the dead are raised, to the poor the Gospel is preached. And blessed is he, whosoever shall not be offended in Me". These were the precise verifications as to what was to take place when the Messiah appeared—compare Isa. 35: 5, 6.

"But ye believe not, because ye are not of My sheep, as I said unto you" (v. 26). Unspeakably solemn was this word. They were reprobates, and now that their characters were fully manifested the Lord did not hesitate to tell them so. The force of this awful statement is definite and clear, though men in their unbelief have done their best to befog it. Almost all the commentators have expounded this verse as though its clauses had been reversed. They simply make Christ to say here to these

Jews that they were *un*-believers. But the truth is that the Lord said far more than that. The commentators understand "the sheep" to be nothing more than a synonym for born-again and justified persons, whereas in fact it is equivalent to God's elect, as the sixteenth verse of this chapter clearly shows. The Lord did not say "Because ye are not of My sheep ye believe not", but, "Ye believe not, because ye are not of My sheep". But man always turns the things of God upside down. When he comes to something in the Word which is peculiarly distasteful, instead of meekly submitting to it and receiving it in simple faith because *God* says it, he resorts to every imaginable device to make it mean something else. Here Christ is not only charging these Jews with unbelief, but He also explains why faith had not been granted to them—*they* were *not* "of His sheep": they were not among the favored number of God's elect. If further proof be required for the correctness of this interpretation, it is furnished below. A man does not have to believe to become one of Christ's "sheep": he "believes" *because he is* one of His sheep.

"But ye believe not, because ye are not of My sheep, *as I said unto you*" (v. 26). To what is our Lord referring? When had He previously avowed that these Jews were not of God's elect? When had He formerly classed them among the reprobates? The answer is to be found in chapter eight of this same Gospel. There we find this same company—"the Jews" (see v. 48)—antagonizing Him, and to them He says, "Why do ye not understand My speech? even because ye cannot hear My word" (v. 43). This is strictly parallel with "ye believe not" in 10:26. Then, in John 8, He explains *why* they could not "hear His word"—it was because *they* were "of their father the Devil" (v. 44). Again, in the forty-seventh verse of the same chapter He said to the Jews, "He that is of God heareth God's words: ye therefore hear them not, because ye are *not of God*". Strictly parallel is this with 10:26. They "heard not" *because* they were not *of* God: they "believed not" *because* they were not *of* His sheep. In each instance He gives as the reason why they received Him not the solemn fact that they belonged not to God's elect: they were numbered among the reprobates.

"My sheep hear My voice, and I know them, and they follow Me" (v. 27). Here the Lord contrasts the elect against the non-elect. God's elect *hear* the voice of the Son: *they* hear the voice of the Shepherd because they belong to His sheep: they "hear" because a sovereign God imparts *to them* the capacity *to hear,* for "The hearing ear and the seeing eye, the Lord hath made even both of them" (Prov. 20:12). Each of the sheep "hear" when the irresistible call comes to them, just as Lazarus in the grave heard when Christ called him.

"And I know them, and they follow Me" (v. 27). Each of the sheep are known to Christ by a *special* knowledge, a knowledge of approbation. They are valued by Him because entrusted to Him by the Father. As the Father's love-gift, He prizes them highly. The vast crowd of the non-elect He "*never* knew" (Matt. 7:23) with a knowledge of approbation; but each of the elect are known affectionately, personally, eternally. "And they follow Me". They "follow" the example He has left them; they follow in holy obedience to His commandments; they follow from love, attracted by His excellent person; they follow on to know Him better.

"And I give unto them eternal life; and they shall never perish, neither shall any pluck them out of My hand" (v. 28). The connection between this and what has gone before should not be lost sight of. Christ had been speaking about His approaching death, His laying down His life for the sheep (v. 15, etc.). Would this, then, *imperil* the sheep? No, the very reverse. He would lay down His life in order that it might be imparted *to them*. This "life", Divine and eternal, would be *given* to them, not sold or bartered. Eternal life is neither earned as a wage, merited as a prize, nor won as a crown. It is a free gift, sovereignly bestowed. But, says the carping objector, All this may be true, but there are certain *conditions* which must be fulfilled if this valuable gift is to be *retained,* and if these conditions are not complied with the gift will be forfeited, and the one who receives it will be lost. To meet this legalistic skepticism, the Lord added, "and *they* shall never perish". Not only is the life given "eternal", but the ones on whom this precious gift is bestowed shall *never* perish: backslide they may, "perish" they shall not, and cannot, while the Shepherd lives! Hypocrites and false professors make shipwreck of *the* faith (not *their* faith, for they never had any), but no real saint of God did or will. There are numerous cases recorded in Scripture where individuals backslided, but never one of a *real* saint apostatizing. A believer may fall, but he shall not be utterly cast down (Psa. 37:34). Quite impossible is it for a sheep to become a goat, for a man who has been born again to be *un*born.

"Neither shall any man (any one) pluck them out of My hand" (v. 28). Here the Lord anticipates another objection, for the fertile mind of unbelief has rarely evidenced more ingenuity than it has at this point, in opposing the blessed truth of the eternal security of God's children. When the objector has been forced to acknowledge that this passage teaches that the life given to the sheep is "eternal", and that those who receive it shall "never perish", he will next make shift by replying, True, no believer will destroy himself, but what of his many enemies, what of Satan, ever going about as a roaring lion seeking whom he may devour? Suppose a believer falls into the toils of the Devil, what then? This, assures our Lord, is equally impossible. The believer is in the hand of Christ, and none is able to pluck from thence one of His own. Tease and annoy him the Devil may, but seize the believer he cannot. Blessed, comforting, re-assuring truth is this! Weak and helpless in himself, nevertheless, the sheep is secure in the hand of the Shepherd.

"My Father, which gave them Me, is greater than all: and none is able to pluck them out of My Father's hand" (v. 29). Here the Lord anticipates one more objection. He knew full well that there would be some carping quibblers who would be foolish enough to say, True, the Devil is unable to pluck us from the hand of Christ, but we are still "free agents", and therefore could *jump out* if we chose to do so. Christ now bars out this miserable perversion. He shows us how that it is *impossible* for a sheep to perish even if it desired to—as though one ever did! The "hand of Christ" (v. 28) is beneath us, and the "hand" of the Father is above us. Thus are we secured between the clasped hands of Omnipotence!

No stronger passage in all the Word of God can be found guaranteeing the absolute security of every child of God. Note the *seven* strands in the rope which binds them to God. First, they are Christ's *sheep,* and it is the duty of the shepherd to care for each of his flock! To suggest that any of Christ's sheep may be lost is to blaspheme the Shepherd Himself. Second, it is said "They *follow*" Christ, and no exceptions are made; the Lord does not say they *ought to,* but declares they *do.* If then the sheep "follow" Christ they *must* reach Heaven, for that is where the Shepherd is gone! Third, to the sheep is imparted *"eternal life":* to speak of eternal life ending is a contradiction in terms. Fourth, this eternal life is *"given"* to them: they did nothing to merit it, consequently they can do nothing to *de*-merit it. Fifth, the Lord Himself declares that His sheep *"shall never* perish", consequently the man who declares that *it is* possible for a child of God to go to Hell makes God a liar. Sixth, from the *Shepherd's* "hand" none is able to pluck them, hence the Devil is *unable* to encompass the destruction of a single one of them. Seventh, above them is *the Father's* "hand", hence it is impossible for them to jump out of the hand of Christ even if they tried to. It has been well said that if one soul who trusted in Christ should be missing in Heaven, there would be one vacant seat there, one crown unused, one harp unstrung; and this would grieve all Heaven and proclaim a disappointed God. But such a thing is utterly impossible.

"I and My Father are one" (v. 30). The R. V. correctly renders this verse, "I and *the* Father are one". The difference between these two translations is an important one. Wherever the Lord Jesus says, "My Father", He is speaking as *the Mediator,* but whenever He refers to "the Father", He speaks from the standpoint of His *absolute Deity.* Thus, "*My* Father is greater than I" (John 14:28) contemplates Him in the *position* of inferiority. "I and *the* Father are one" affirms Their unity of nature or essence, one in every Divine perfection.

"I and the Father are one". There are those who would limit this oneness between the Father and Son to unity of will and design—the Unitarian interpretation of the passage. Dr. John Brown has refuted the error of this so ably and simply that we transcribe from his exposition: "Harmony of will and design, is not the thing spoken of here; but harmony or union of power and operation. Our Lord first says of Himself, 'I give unto My sheep eternal life, and none shall pluck them out of My hand'. He then says the same thing of the Father—'None is able to pluck them out of My Father's hand'. He plainly, then, ascribes the same thing to Himself that He does to the Father, not the same will, but the same work—the same work of power, therefore the same power. He mentions the reason *why* none can pluck them out of the Father's hands,—because He is the Almighty, and no created power is able to resist Him. The thing spoken of is *power,*—power *irresistible.* And in order to prove that none can pluck them out of HIS hand, He adds, 'I and the Father are one'. One in what? unquestionably in the work of power whereby He protects His sheep and does not suffer them to be plucked out of His hand. What the Father is, that the Son is. What the work of the Father is, that the work of the Son is. As the Father is almighty, so is the Son likewise. As nothing can resist the Father, so nothing can resist the Son. Whatsoever the Father hath, the Son hath likewise. The Father is in the Son, and the Son in the Father. These two are one —in nature, perfection and glory".

"I and the Father are one". It is most blessed to observe the *connection* between this declaration and what had preceded it. All the diligent care and tender devotion of the Shepherd for the sheep but expresses the mind and heart of the *Owner* toward the flock. The Shepherd and the Owner are *one,* one in their relation and attitude toward the flock; one both in power and in Their loving care for the sheep. Immutably secure then is the believer. It was the laying hold of these precious truths which caused our fathers to sing,

> "How firm a foundation
> Ye saints of the Lord,
> Is laid for your faith,
> In His excellent Word.
> What more can He say,
> Than to you He hath said,
> To you who to Jesus
> For refuge have fled."

"Then the Jews took up stones again to stone Him" (v. 31). This is quite sufficient to settle the meaning of the previous verse. These Jews had no difficulty in perceiving the force of what our Lord had just said to them. They instantly recognized that He had claimed absolute equality with the Father, and to their ears this was blasphemy. Instead of saying anything to correct their error, if error it was, Christ went on to say that which must have confirmed it.

"Then the Jews took up stones again to stone Him". Fearful wickedness was this! Who could imagine that any heart would have been so base, or any hand so cruel, as to have armed themselves with instruments of death, against such a Person, while speaking such words! Yet we behold these Jews doing just this thing, and that within the sacred precincts of the Temple! A frightful exhibition of human depravity was this. Christ had done these Jews no wrong. They hated Him *without a cause.* They hated Him because of His holiness; and this, because of their sinfulness. Why did Cain hate Abel? "Because his own works were evil, and his brother's righteous" (1 John 3:12). Why did the Jews hate Christ?—"But Me it hateth, because I testify of it that the works thereof are evil" (John 7:7). And in that measure which believers are like Christ, in the same proportion will they be hated by unbelievers: "If the world hate you, ye know that it hated Me before it hated you" (John 15:18).

"Jesus answered them, Many good works have I showed you from My Father; for which of those works do ye stone Me?" (v. 32). The word "works" is to be understood here in its widest sense. The Lord appeals to the whole course of His public ministry—His perfect life, His gracious deeds in ministering to the needs of others, His wondrous words, wherein He spake as never man had spoken. When He terms these works as "from the Father" He means not only that they met with the Father's full approval, but that they had been done by His authority and command—"I have finished the work *which Thou* gavest Me to do" (John 17:4).

"The Jews answered Him, saying, For a good work we stone Thee not; but for blasphemy; and because that Thou, being a man, makest Thyself God" (v. 33). It was most appropriate for this to be recorded in *John's* Gospel, the great design of which is to present the *Deity* of the Saviour. The carnal mind is "enmity against *God*", and never was this more fully evidenced than when God incarnate appeared in the midst of men. During His infancy, an organized effort was made to slay Him (Matt. 2). In one of the Messianic Psalms there is more than a hint that during the years Christ spent in seclusion at Nazareth, repeated attempts were made upon His life—"I am *afflicted* and ready to die from *My youth up*" (Psa. 88:15). The very first word spoken by Him in the Nazareth synagogue after His public ministry began, was followed by an attempt to murder Him (Luke 4:29). And from that point onwards to the Cross, His steps were dogged by implacable foes who thirsted for His blood. Wonderful beyond comprehension was that grace of God which suffered His Son to sojourn in such a world of rebels. Divine was that infinite forbearance which led Christ to endure "the contradiction of sinners against Himself". Deep, fervent, and perpetual should be our praise for that love which saved us at such a cost!

"Jesus answered them, Is it not written in your law, I said, Ye are gods? If He called them gods, unto whom the Word of God came, and the Scripture cannot be broken; Say ye of Him, whom the Father hath sanctified, and sent into the world, Thou blasphemest; because I said, I am the Son of God? If I do not the works of My Father, believe Me not. But if I do, though ye believe not Me, believe the works: that ye may know, and believe, that the Father is in Me and I in Him" (vv. 34-38). Upon these verses we cannot do better than quote again from the excellent remarks of Dr. John Brown:

"Our Lord's reply consists of two parts. In the first, He shows that the charge of blasphemy, which they founded on His calling Himself the Son of God, was a rash one, even though nothing more could have been said of Him, than that He had been 'sanctified and sent by the Father'; and secondly, that His miracles were of such a kind, as that they rendered whatever He declared of Himself, as to His intimate connection with the Father, however extraordinary, worthy of credit.

"Our Lord's argument in the first part of this answer is founded on a passage in the eighty-second Psalm, verse six; 'I have said, Ye are gods; and all of you are children of the most high'. There words are plainly addressed to the Jewish magistrates, commissioned by Jehovah to act as His vicegerants in administering justice to His people; who judged for God—in the room of God; whose sentences, when they agreed with the law, were God's sentences; whose judgment, was God's judgment; and rebels against whom, were rebels against God.

"The meaning and force of our Lord's argument is obvious. If, in a book which you admit to be of Divine authority, and all whose expressions are perfectly faultless, men which have received a Divine communication to administer justice to the people of God are called 'gods' and sons of the Highest; is it not absurd to bring against One who has a higher commission than they (One who had been sanctified and sent by the Father), and who presented far more evidence of His commission, a charge of blasphemy, because He calls Himself 'the Son of God'? You dare not charge blasphemy on the Psalmist;—why do you charge it on Me?. . . . He reasoned with the Jews on their own principles. Were the Messiah nothing more than you expect Him to be, to charge One who claims Messiahship with blasphemy, because He calls Himself the Son of God, is plainly gross inconsistency. Your magistrates are called God's sons, and may not your Messiah claim the same title?

"The second part of our Lord's reply is contained in the thirty-seventh and thirty-eighth verses. It is equivalent to—I have declared that I and the Father are one—one in power and operation. I do not call on you to believe this merely because of My testimony, but I do call on you to believe on My testimony *supported by* the miracles I have performed, works which nothing but a Divine power could accomplish. These works are the voice of God, and its utterance is distinct: it speaks plainly, it utters no dark saying. You cannot refuse to receive the doctrine that I and the Father are one, that the Father is in Me, and I in Him, without contradicting *His* testimony and calling *Him* a liar".

Let us notice one or two details in these verses before we turn to the conclusion of our chapter. The word "gods" in the eighty-second Psalm, quoted here by Christ, has occasioned difficulty to some. The magistrates of Israel were so called because of their *authority* and *power*, and as representing the Divine majesty in government.

Mark how in v. 35 the Saviour said, "The Scriptures cannot be broken". What a high honor did He here place upon the written Word! In making use of this verse from the Psalmist against His enemies, the whole point of His argument lay *in a single word*—"gods"—and the fact that it occurred in the book Divinely inspired. The Scriptures were the final court of appeal, and here the Lord insists on their absolute authority and verbal inerrancy.

Observe here *Christ's* use of the word "sanctified" in v. 36 refutes many modern heretics. There are those who teach that to be sanctified is to have the carnal nature eradicated. They insist that sanctification is moral purification. But how thoroughly untenable is such a definition in the light of what the Master says here. He declares that *He* was "sanctified". Certainly that cannot mean that He was cleansed from sin, for He was the Holy One. Here, as everywhere in Scripture, the term sanctified can only mean *set apart*. Observe the order: Christ was first sanctified and then sent into the world. The reference is to the Father's eternal appointment of the Son to be the Mediator.

"Therefore they sought again to take Him: but He escaped out of their hand" (v. 39). This signifies that these Jews sought to apprehend the Lord Jesus so that they might bring Him before the Sanhedrim, but they were unable to carry out their evil designs. Soon He would deliver Himself into their hands, but until the appointed hour arrived they might as well attempt to harness the wind as lay hands on the Almighty.

"And went away again beyond Jordan into the place where John at first baptized; and there He abode. And many resorted unto Him, and said, John did no miracle: but all things which John spake of this man were true. And many believed on Him there" (vv. 40-42). We have already pointed out the significance of this move of Christ. In leaving Jerusalem—to which He did not return until the appointed "hour" —and in going *beyond* Jordan to where His forerunner had been, the Lord gave plain intimation that His *public* ministry was now over. The Nation at large must be left to suffer the due reward of their iniquities. In what follows we have a beautiful illustration of this present dispensation: *"Outside* the Camp" Christ now was, but in this place, as the despised and rejected One, many resorted to Him. God would not allow His beloved Son to be universally unappreciated, even though organized Judaism had turned its back upon Him. Here beyond Jordan He works no public miracle (as He does not today), but many believed on Him because of what John had *spoken*. So it is now. It is the *Word* which is the means God uses in bringing sinners to believe on the Saviour. Happy for these men that they know the day of *their* visitation, and improved the brief visit of Christ.

Let the interested student study the following questions on the first part of John 11:—

1. Why did not the sisters name the sick one v. 3?
2. What is the force of the "therefore" v. 6?
3. Why did not Christ hasten to Bethany at once v. 6?
4. Why "into Judea" rather than "to Bethany" v. 7?
5. Why did Christ refer to the "twelve hours in the day" v. 9?
6. What is meant by the second half of v. 9?
7. What is meant by "walking in the night" v. 10? —Arthur W. Pink.

"Blessed be the Lord who daily loadeth us with benefits, even the God of our Salvation" (Ps. 68:18). How this reminds us that the blessings and privileges which we enjoy in a temporal way are the gifts of Divine grace from "the God of our *Salvation"!* Mark the *regularity* of His favors: He *daily* loadeth us with His benefits! As another of His saints declared, "His compassions *fail not:* they are new *every* morning; therefore did he add, "Great is Thy *faithfulness"!* (Lam. 3:22, 23). Note the *abundance* of His blessings: He *loadeth* us with His benefits. He gives with no sparing hand. Countless are His mercies. What, then, is our response? *"Blessed* be the Lord": thanksgiving and praise should be our daily return for all we receive from Him. Forget not to express your gratitude at the Throne of Grace.

GLEANINGS IN EXODUS.

12. The Plagues upon Egypt Concluded; Ex. 7-11.

In our last article we made a number of general observations upon the judgments which the Lord God sent upon Pharaoh and his people. The subject is admittedly a difficult one, and little light seems to have been given on it. This should make *us* seek more fervently for help from above, that *our* eyes may be opened to behold wondrous things in this portion of the Word. We shall now offer a few remarks upon each plague separately according to our present understanding of them.

1. The first plague is described in Exodus 7:14-25—let the reader turn to the passage and ponder it carefully. This initial judgment from the Lord consisted of the turning of the waters into blood. Blood, of course, speaks of death, and deatn is the wages of sin. It was, therefore, a most solemn warning from God to Egypt, a warning which intimated plainly the doom that awaited those who defied the Almighty. Similarly will God give warning at the beginning of the Great Tribulation, for then shall the moon "become as blood" (Rev. 6:12). The symbolic significance of this first plague is easily discerned. Water is the emblem of the Word (John 15:3; Eph. 5:26), and the water turned to blood reminds us that the Word is "a savor of death unto death" (2 Cor. 2:16) as well as "of life unto life".

The striking contrast between this first plague and the first miracle wrought by the Lord Jesus has been pointed out by others before us. The contrast strikingly illustrates the great difference there is between the two dispensations; "The law was given by Moses, but *grace* and truth came by Jesus Christ" (John 1:17). All that the Law can do to its guilty transgressor is to sentence him to death, and this is what the Water turned into blood symbolized. But by the incarnate Word the believing sinner is made to *rejoice,* and this is what the turning of the water into wine speaks of.

Before passing on to the next plague we would offer a word of explanation upon a point which may have troubled some of our readers. The Lord's command to Moses was, "Say unto Aaron, Take thy rod and stretch out thine hand upon the waters of Egypt, upon their streams, upon their rivers, and upon their ponds, and upon *all* their pools of water, that they may become blood" (Ex. 7:19). And yet after this we are told, "And the magicians of Egypt did so with their enchantments" (v. 22). Where then did they obtain *their* water? The answer is evidently supplied in verse 24; "And all the Egyptians *digged* round about the river for water to drink".

2. The second plague is described in Ex. 8:1-7. An interval of "seven days" (7:25) separated this second plague from the first. Full opportunity was thus given to Pharaoh to repent, before God acted in judgment again. In view of the fact that the Flood commenced on the *seventh* day (see Gen. 7:10 margin), that is, the holy Sabbath, the conclusion is highly probable that each of these first two plagues were sent upon Egypt on the *Sabbath* day, as a Divine judgment for the Egyptians' desecration of it.

This second plague, like the former, was Divinely directed against the idolatry of the Egyptians. The river Nile was sacred in their eyes, therefore did Jehovah turn its waters into blood. The frog was an object of worship among them, so God now caused Egypt to be plagued with frogs. Their ugly shape, their croaking noise, and their disagreeable smell, would make these frogs peculiarly obnoxious. Their abounding numbers marked the severity of this judgment. Escape from this scourge was impossible, for the frogs not only "covered the land of Egypt" but they invaded the homes of the Egyptians, entered their bed-chambers, and defiled their cooking-utensils.

The moral significance of these "frogs" is explained for us in Rev. 16:13—the only mention of these creatures in the New Testament. There we read "And I saw three *unclean* small spirits *like frogs* come out of the mouth of the Dragon, and out of the mouth of the Beast, and out of the mouth of the False Prophet". Frogs are used to symbolize the Powers of evil and stand for *uncleanness.* The turning of the waters into blood was a solemn reminder of the "wages of sin". The issuing forth of the frogs made manifest the character of the Devil's works—uncleanness.

Concerning this second plague we read, "And the magicians did so with their enchantments and brought forth frogs upon the land of Egypt" (8:7). This is most suggestive. The magicians were unable to remove the frogs, nor could they erect any barriers against their encroachments. All they could do was to bring forth more frogs. Thus it is with the Prince of this world. He is unable to exterminate the evil which he has brought into God's fair creation, and he cannot check its progress. All he can do is to multiply wickedness.

3. The third plague is described in Ex. 8:16-19. This judgment decended without any warning. The dust of the ground suddenly sprang into life, assuming the most disgusting and annoying form. This blow was aimed more directly at the persons of the Egyptians. Their bodies covered with lice, was a sore rebuke to their pride. Herodotus (2:37) refers to the cleanliness of the Egyptians: "So scrupulous were the priests on this point that they used to shave their heads and bodies every third day, for fear of harboring vermin while occupied in their sacred duties". As another has said, "This stroke would therefore humble their pride and stain their glory, rendering *themselves* objects of dislike and disgust".

The key to the moral significance of this third plague lies in the *source* from which the lice proceeded. Aaron smote the *dust* of the land "and it became lice in man and beast" (8:16). In the judgment which God pronounced upon disobedient Adam we read that He said, "*Cursed* is the *ground* for thy sake" (Gen. 3:17), and again, "for *dust* thou art, and unto dust shalt thou return" (Gen. 3:19). When Aaron *smote* the "ground", and its "dust" became lice, and the lice came upon the Egyptians, it was a graphic showing-forth of the awful fact that man by nature is *under the curse* of a holy God.

Concerning this plague we read, "and the magicians did so with their enchantments to bring forth lice, but *they could not*" (8:18). How small a matter the Lord used to bring confusion upon these magicians! As soon as God restrained them, they were helpless. Turn water into blood, and bring forth frogs, they might, by God's permission; but when He withheld permission they were impotent. Thus it is with Satan himself. His bounds are definitely prescribed by the Almighty, and beyond them he cannot go. Death he can inflict (by God's permission), and uncleanness he can bring forth freely—as the "magicians" illustrated in the first two plagues; but with the Curse (which the "dust" becoming lice so plainly speaks of) he is not allowed to tamper with.

The admission of the magicians on this occasion is noteworthy: "Then the magicians said unto Pharaoh, This is the finger of God" (8:19). These are their *last* recorded words. In the end they were obliged to acknowledge the hand of God. So will it be in the last Great Day with the Devil himself, and with all his hosts and victims. They, too, will have to bow before the Lord, and publicly confess the supremacy of the Almighty.

There is a striking correspondency between this third plague and what is recorded in the eighth chapter of John's Gospel. There we find a similar contest—between the Lord and His enemies. The Scribes and the Pharisees, using the woman taken in adultery as their bait, sought to ensnare the Saviour. His only response was to stoop down and write *on the ground*. After saying to them, "He that is without sin among you, let him first cast a stone at her", we read that "Again He stooped down and wrote on the ground". The effect was startling: "They which heard, being convicted by their conscience, went out one by one . . . . and Jesus was left alone, and the woman standing in the midst". What was this but the enemy of the Lord acknowledging that it was "*the finger of God*" as He wrote in *the dust*!

4. The next plague is described in Ex. 8:20-32. This plague marked the beginning of a new series. In the first three, the magicians had opposed, but their defeat had been openly manifested. No longer do they appear upon the stage of action. Another thing which evidences that this fourth plague begins a new series is the fact that God now made "a division" between His own people and the Egyptians. The Israelites too had suffered from the first three judgments, for they also merited the wages of sin, were subject to the debasing influences of Satan, and were under the curse. But now that the Lord was about to destroy the property of the Egyptians, He spared the Israelites.

It will be noted by the student that the words "of flies" are in italics, supplied by the translators, the word "swarms" being given for the original term. The Hebrew word signifies, literally, "mixture", being akin to the term "*mixed* multitude" in Ex. 12:38. Apparently these "swarms" were made up of not only flies, but a variety of insects. As we are told in Ps. 78:45, "He sent *divers sorts* of flies". Moreover, this verse in the Psalms informs us of their devastating effects—they "devoured them"; the Hebrew signifying "ate up". This was, therefore, worse than the plague of lice. The lice annoyed, but the "divers sorts of flies" preyed upon their flesh.

The deeper meaning of this plague may be gathered from the nature of its effects, and also from the fact that the Israelites were exempted from it. This judgment had to do with *the tormenting of the bodies* of the Egyptians, thus looking forward to the eternal judgment of the lost, when their bodies shall be tormented forever and ever in the Lake which burneth with fire and brimstone. In this the people of God will have no part.

5. The next plague is described in Ex. 9:1-7. This judgment was directed against the possessions of the Egyptians. A grievous disease smote their herds so that "all the cattle of Egypt died". But once more Jehovah exempted His own people—"of the cattle of the children of Israel died not one" (9:6). This afforded a striking demonstration of the absolute rulership of God. He completely controls every creature He has made. Disease strikes only when and where He has decreed. The herds of the Egyptians might be dying all around them, but the cattle of Israel were as secure as though there had been no epedemic at all.

The spiritual meaning and application of this judgment is not difficult to perceive. The cattle are man's servants. He harnesses them to do the hardest portion of his work. The destruction of all the "horses, asses, camels, oxen and sheep" of the Egyptians tells us that God will not accept the labors of the unregenerate—"the plowing of the wicked is sin" (Prov. 21:4). This world and all its works will yet be burned up—destroyed as completely as were the beasts of Egypt. The sparing of the cattle of the Israelites intimates that the works of the new nature in the believer *will* "abide" (I Cor. 3:14).

6. The plague of the boils is recorded in Ex. 9:8-12. Like the third plague, this one was sent without any warning. Moses was instructed to take "handfuls of ashes of the furnace, and sprinkle it toward heaven in the sight of Pharaoh" (9:8). The definite article implies that some particular "furnace" is meant, and that Pharaoh was near it, suggests it was no mere heating apparatus. The Companion Bible says of this furnace: "i.e., one of the altars on which human sacrifices were sometimes offered to propitiate their god *Typhon* (the evil Principle). These were doubtless being offered to avert the plagues, and Moses, using the ashes in the same way produced another plague instead of averting it." Just as the previous plague signified the worthlessness of all the *works* of the natural man, so this teaches the utter vanity of his *religious* exercises.

7. The next plague is described in Ex. 9:18-35. It marks the beginning of a third series. We quote from the Numerical Bible; "We are now, in the third stage, to see, man being what he is, what the attitude of Heaven must be toward him. The three plagues that follow all distinctly point to heaven as their place of origin. Here too the rod, which in the last three, had not been seen, appears again,—a thing which the typical meaning alone, as it would seem, accounts for. For it will be seen that the middle plagues, to men, seem scarcely Divine inflictions; they proceed more from man himself, although, in fact, the government of God may truly be seen in them. But now we come again, as in the first plagues, to direct, positive influences". In other words, the last three plagues brought out, emblematically, the *state* of the natural man; the swarms of flies breeding from filthiness; the murrian of the cattle and the boils on man, telling of impurities within, which, through the corruption of sin breaks out in moral diseases; reminding us of that graphic but awful picture of the sinner drawn by Isaiah—"From the sole of the foot even unto the head, there is no soundness in it; but wounds and bruises, and putrifying sores" (1:6).

The *severity* of this plague is marked by several particulars. It was "a very grievous hail" (9:18). It was "such as hath not been in Egypt since the foundation thereof even until now". The hail was accompanied by an electric storm of fierce intensity, so that "the fire ran along upon the ground". The effects were equally striking: "The hail smote throughout *all* the land of Egypt *all* that was in the field, both man and beast; and the hail smote every herb of the field and brake every tree of the field". This judgment was expressive of the *wrath* of a holy and sin-hating God. Similar expressions of His anger will be witnessed during the Great Tribulation—see Rev. 8:7; 16:21.

8. The eighth plague is recorded in Ex. 10:1-20. Locusts are one of the terrors of the East. They prey upon the crops, and consume all vegetation. This plague, coming on the top of the destruction of the cattle, seriously threatened the food-supplies of Egypt. Referring to this plague, the Psalmist says, "He spake and the locusts came, and caterpillars, and that without number and did eat up all the herbs in their land, and devoured the fruit of their ground" (Ps. 105:34, 35). They came at the bidding of God, and they departed at His bidding. So does every creature, the feeblest as well as the mightiest, fulfill the secret counsels of their Creator. In Joel 2:11, which speaks of a yet future judgment in the Day of the Lord, the locusts are termed, "*His* army".

We are not quite sure about the deeper meaning and spiritual significance of this eighth plague. It is clear, that like the previous one, it definitely manifested the *wrath* of God. But there would seem to be an additional line of thought suggested by these "locusts". The second chapter of Joel and the ninth of Revelation should be carefully studied in this connection. In these two chapters we have a species of *infernal* "locusts" brought to our view. They issue from the Bottomless Pit, and the Anti-Christ, is said to be their "king". It would seem then that the plaguing of Pharaoh and the Egyptians with the "locusts" points to the yet future punishing of the lost in the company of *infernal beings*: as the Lord said, "They shall be cast into everlasting fire, prepared for the Devil and his angels" (Matt. 25:41).

9. The plague of darkness is described in Ex. 10:21-29. "In Egypt the sun was worshipped under the title of Ra: the name came conspicuously forward in the title of the kings, Pharaoh, or rather Phra, meaning 'the sun'" (Wilkinson's "Ancient Egypt"). "Not only therefore was the source of light and heat eclipsed for the Egyptians, but the god they worshipped was obscured and his powerlessness demonstrated—a proof, had they but eyes to see, that a mightier than the sun, yea the Creator of the sun, was dealing with them in judgment." (Ed. Dennett).

This ninth plague formed a fitting climax to the third series. It is easily interpreted. God is Light: darkness is the withdrawal of light. Therefore, this judgment of darkness, gave plain intimation that Egypt was now *abandoned by God*. Nothing remained but death itself. The darkness continued for three days—*full manifestation* of God's withdrawal. So fearful was this "thick darkness" that the Egyptians "saw not one another, neither rose any from his place". Striking is the contrast presented in the next sentence: "But all the children of Israel *had* light in their dwellings." This light was as supernatural as the darkness. It emanated, most probably, from the Shekinah glory. The Egyptians had a darkness which they could not light up: Israel a light which they could not put out. Thus it is upon earth to-day. The people of God are "children of light" (Eph. 5:8), because God "who commanded the light to shine out of darkness, hath shined in our hearts to give *the light* of the knowledge of the glory of God in the face of Jesus Christ" (2 Cor. 4:6). But "the way of the wicked *is as darkness*: they know not at what they stumble" (Prov. 4:19), and this because they are "without God in the world" (Eph. 2:12).

The three days of darkness which brooded over the land of Egypt remind us of the three hours of darkness over all the earth when the Saviour hung upon the cross—outward expression of God's abandonment. There the Holy One of God was being "made sin" (2 Cor. 5:21) for His people, and He Who is "of purer eyes than to behold evil, and canst not look upon iniquity" (Hab. 1:13), turned away His face from the One who was being punished in our stead. It was this turning away of God from Him which caused the Saviour to cry, "My God, my God, why hast Thou *forsaken* Me?".

Finally, this three days of dense darkness upon Egypt utters a solemn warning for all who are now out of Christ. Unsaved reader, if you continue in your present course, if you go on slighting the mercy of God, if you refuse to heed His warning to flee from the wrath to come, you shall be finally cast into "the outer darkness" (Matt. 8:12)—the "blackness of darkness forever" (Jude 13). Neglect, then, thy soul's salvation no longer. Turn even now unto Him who is "the *Light* of the world", and in His light thou shalt see light.

10. The final plague upon Egypt is recorded in Ex. 11 and 12. Comments upon this we will reserve for our next papers. In this last plague, the Lord did that to which all the other plagues were logically and irresistibly leading up—the slaying of the first-born. Terrible climax was this. Disease, desolation, and darkness had visited Pharaoh's land; now *death* itself was to do its work.

The study of these plagues shows plainly the *character* of Him with whom we all have to do. The Lord is not indifferent to sin, nor can He be defied with impugnity. He bears with much longsuffering the vessels of wrath, but in the end His righteous judgments descend upon them. What point do these plagues give to that solemn word, "It is a *fearful thing* to fall into the hands of the living God" (Heb. 10:31)! Be warned, then, dear reader. To-day, if you will hear His voice, harden not *your* heart. Remember what befell Pharaoh for hardening his! Flee then to the Divinely-appointed Refuge. Believe on the Lord Jesus Christ and thou shalt be saved.

A. W. Pink

THE DEATH OF CHRIST.

The Death of the Lord Jesus Christ is a subject of never-failing interest to all who study prayerfully the Scripture of Truth. This is so, not only because the believer's all, both for time and eternity depends upon it, but also, because of its transcendent uniqueness. Four words appear to sum up the salient features of this Mystery of mysteries: the Death of Christ was natural, unnatural, preternatural, and supernatural. A few comments seem called for by way of definition and amplification.

First; the Death of Christ was *natural.* By this we mean that it was a *real death.* It is because we are so familiar with the fact of it that the above statement appears simple and commonplace, yet, what we here touch upon is to the spiritual mind one of the main elements of wonderment. The One who was "taken, and by wicked hands" crucified and slain was none less than Immanuel. The One who died on Calvary's Cross was none other than Jehovah's "Fellow". The blood that was shed on the accursed Tree was Divine—"The church of God which *He* purchased with *His own* blood" (Acts 20:28). As says the apostle "*God was in Christ,* reconciling the world unto Himself" (2 Cor. 5:19). But how could Jehovah's "Fellow" *suffer?* How could the eternal One *die?* Ah, He who in the beginning was the Word, who was with God, and who was God, *"became flesh"*. He who was in the form of God took upon Him the form of a servant and was made in the likeness of men; "and being found in fashion as a man, He humbled Himself, and became obedient unto death, even the death of the Cross" (Phil. 2:8). Thus having become incarnate the Lord of glory was capable of suffering death, and so it was that He "tasted" death itself. In His own words, "Father, into Thy hands I commend My spirit" we see how actual His death was, and the reality of it became still more apparent when He was laid in the tomb, where He remained three days.

Second, the Death of Christ was *un-natural.* By this we mean that it was *abnormal.* Above we have said that in becoming incarnate the Son of God became capable of suffering death, yet it must not be inferred from this that death therefore had a claim upon Him; far from this being the case, the very reverse was the truth. Death is the wages of sin, and He had none. Before His birth it was said to Mary "that *Holy Thing* which shall be born of thee shall be called the Son of God" (Luke 1:35). Not only did the Lord Jesus enter this world without contracting the defilement attaching to *fallen* human nature, but He "did no sin" (1 Peter 2:22), had "no sin" (1 John 3:5), "knew no sin" (2 Cor. 5:21). In His person and in His conduct He was the Holy One of God "without blemish and without spot" (1 Peter 1:19). As such, death *had no claim* upon Him. Even Pilate had to acknowledge that he could find in Him "no fault". Hence we say, for the Holy One of God to *die* was *un-natural.*

The Death of Christ was *preter-natural.* By this we mean that it was marked out and *determined for Him beforehand.* He was the Lamb slain from the foundation of the world. (Rev. 13:8). Before Adam was created the fall was anticipated. Before sin entered the world, salvation from it had been planned by God. In the eternal counsels of Deity it was fore-ordained that there should be a Saviour who should suffer the Just for the unjust, a Saviour who should die in order that we might live. And "because there was none other good enough to pay the price of sin" the only-Begotten of the Father offered Himself as the Ransom.

The preternatural character of the Death of Christ has been well termed the "*undergirding* of the Cross". It was in view of that approaching Death that God "justly passed over the sins done aforetime". (Rom. 3:25, R.V.). Had not Christ been, in the reckoning of God, the Lamb slain from the foundation of the world, every sinning person in the Old Testament times would have gone down to the Pit the moment they sinned!

Fourth; the Death of Christ was *supernatural.* By this we mean that it was *different from every other death.* In all things He has the pre-eminence. His birth was different from all other births, His life was different from all other lives. And His death was different from all other deaths. This was clearly intimated in His own utterances upon the subject—"Therefore doth My Father love Me, because *I lay down My life,* that I might take it again. *No man taketh it from Me,* but I lay it down of Myself. I have power to lay it down, and I have power to take it again" (John 10:17, 18). A careful study of the Gospel narratives which *describes* His death furnish a *sevenfold proof* and varification of His assertion.

(1) That our Lord "laid down His life," that He was *not* powerless in the hands of His enemies, comes out clearly in John 18, where we have the record of His arrest. A band of officers from the chief priests and Pharisees, headed by Judas, sought Him in Gethsemane. Coming forward to meet them, the Lord Jesus asks, "Whom seek ye?" The reply was, "Jesus of Nazareth," and then our Lord uttered the ineffable title of Deity, that by which Jehovah had revealed Himself of old to Moses at the burning bush—"I am". The effect was startling. We are told, "they went backward, and fell to the ground". These officers were awestruck. They were in the presence of incarnate Deity, and were overpowered by a brief consciousness of Divine majesty. How plain it is then that had He so pleased, our blessed Saviour could have walked quietly away, leaving those who had come to arrest Him prostrate on the ground! Instead, He delivers Himself up into their hands and is *led* (not driven) as a lamb to the slaughter.

(2) Let us now turn to Matt. 27:46—the most solemn verse in all the Bible—"And about the ninth hour Jesus cried *with a loud voice,* saying, Eli, Eli, lama, Sabachthani, that is to say, My God, My God, why hast Thou forsaken Me?" The words which we would ask the reader to observe carefully are here placed in italics. Why is it that the Holy Spirit tells us the Saviour uttered that terrible cry "with a loud voice"? Most certainly there is a reason for it. This becomes more apparent when we note that He has *repeated* them four verses lower down in the same chapter—"Jesus, when He had cried *again with a loud voice,* yielded up the spirit" (Matt. 27:50): What then do these words indicate? Do they not *corroborate* what has been said in the above paragraphs? Do they not tell us that the Saviour *was not exhausted* by what He had passed through? Do they not intimate that His strength had not failed Him? that He was still master of Himself, that instead of being conquered by death, He was but yielding Himself to it? Do they not show us that God *had* "laid help upon One that was *mighty*" (Psa. 89:19)!

(3) We call attention next to His fourth utterance on the Cross—"I thirst". This word, in the light of its setting, furnishes a wonderful evidence of our Lord's complete self-possession. The whole verse reads as follows: "After this, Jesus knowing that all things were now accomplished, *that the Scripture might be fulfilled,* saith, I thirst" (John 19:28). Of old it had been predicted that they should give the Saviour to drink, vinegar mingled with

gall. And in order that this prophecy might be fulfilled, He cried, "I thirst". How this evidences the fact that He was in full possession of His mental faculties, that His mind was unclouded, that His terrible sufferings had neither deranged nor disturbed it. As He hung on the Cross, at the *close* of the six hours, His mind reviewed the entire scope of the prophetic Word, and checked off one by one those predictions which had reference to His passion. Excepting the prophecies which were to be fulfilled *after* His death, but one remained *un*-fulfilled, namely, "They gave Me also gall for My meat; and *in My thirst* they gave Me vinegar to drink" (Psa. 69:21), and this was not overlooked by the blessed sufferer. "Jesus *knowing* that *all things* were now accomplished, that the scripture (not "Scriptures", the reference being to Psa. 69:21) might be fulfilled, saith, I thirst." Again, we say, what proof is here furnished that He "laid down His life *of Himself*"!

(4) The next verification the Holy Spirit has supplied of our Lord's words in John 10:18 is found in John 19:30—"When Jesus had received the vinegar He said, It it finished; and *He bowed His head,* and gave up the spirit." What are we intended to learn from these words? What is here signified by this act of the Saviour? Surely the answer is not far to seek. The implication is clear. *Previous to this* our Lord's head had been *held erect.* It was no impotent sufferer that hung there in a swoon. Had that been the case His *head* had lolled helplessly on His chest, and it would have been impossible for Him to "bow" it. And mark attentively the verb used here: it is not His head "fell", but He—consciously, calmly, reverently—*bowed* His head. How sublime was His carriage even on the Tree! What superb composure did He evidence. Was it not *His majestic* bearing on the Cross that, among other things, caused the centurion to cry "Truly this was the Son of God" (Matt. 27:54)!

(5) Look now at His last act of all: "And when Jesus had cried with a loud voice, He said, Father, into Thy hands *I commend My spirit,* and having said this, *He gave up* the spirit" (Luke 23:46). None else ever did this or died thus. How accurately these words agree with His own statement, so often quoted, "I lay down My life, that I might take it again. No man taketh it from Me, but *I lay it* down *OF MYSELF.*" (John 10:17, 18). The uniqueness of our Lord's action may be seen by comparing His words on the Cross with those of dying Stephen. As the first Christian martyr came to the brink of the river, he cried, "Lord Jesus, *receive* my spirit" (Acts 7:59). But in contrast with this, Christ said, "Father, into Thy hands *I commend* My spirit". Stephen's spirit was *taken from him.* Not so with the Saviour. None could take from Him *His* life. "He gave up" His spirit!

(6) The action of the soldiers in regard to the legs of those on the three crosses gives further evidence of the uniqueness of Christ's death. We read, "The Jews therefore, because it was the preparation, that the bodies should not remain upon the cross on the Sabbath day, (for that Sabbath day was an high day,) besought Pilate that their legs might be broken, and that they might be taken away. Then came the soldiers, and break the legs of the first, and of the other which was crucified with him. But when they came to Jesus, and saw that He was *dead already,* they break not His legs" (John 19:31-33). The Lord Jesus and the two thieves had been crucified together. They had been on their respective crosses the same length of time. And now at the close of the day the two thieves were still alive, for as is well known, death by crucifixion though exceedingly painful was usually a slow death. No vital member of the body was directly affected, and often the sufferer lingered on for two or three days before being completely overcome by exhaustion. It was not natural, therefore, that Christ should be dead after but six hours on the cross. The Jews recognized this, and requested Pilate that the legs of all three be broken and death thus be hastened. In the fact, then that the Saviour *was* "dead already" when the soldiers came to Him, though the two thieves yet lived, we have additional proof that He had voluntarily "laid down His life of Himself", that it was not "taken from Him".

(7) For the final demonstration of the *supernatural* character of Christ's death we turn to note the wonderful phenomena that accompanied it: "Behold, the veil of the temple was rent in twain from the top to the bottom; and the earth did quake, and the rocks rent: and the graves were

opened" (Matt. 27:51, 52). That was no ordinary death that had been witnessed on the summit of Golgotha's rugged heights, and it was followed by no ordinary attendants. First, the veil of the temple was rent in twain from top to bottom, to show that a Hand from Heaven had torn asunder that curtain which shut out the temple-worshipper from the earthly throne of God—thus signifying that the way into the Holiest was now made plain and that access to God Himself had been opened up through the broken body of His Son. Next, the earth did quake. Not, I believe, that there was *an* earthquake, nor even a "great earthquake", but that the earth itself was shaken to its very foundation and rocked on its axis, as though to show it was horrified at the awfulest deed that had ever been perpetrated on its surface. "And the rocks rent"—the very strength of Nature gave way before the greater power of that Death. Finally, we are told, "the graves were opened", showing that the power of Satan, which is death, was there shivered and shattered—all the outward attestations of the *value* of that atoning death.

Putting these together: the manifest yielding up of Himself into the hands of those who arrested Him; the crying with a "loud voice", denoting His retained vigor; the fact that He was in full and unimpaired possession of His mentality, evidenced by the "*knowing* that all things were now accomplished"; the "bowing" of the erect head; the deliberate "committal" of His spirit into the hands of the Father; the fact that He was "dead already" when the soldiers came to brake His legs;—all furnish proof that His life *was not* "taken from Him", but that He laid it down of Himself, and these, together with the tearing of the temple veil, the quaking of the earth, the rending of the rocks, and the opening of the graves, all bore unmistakable witness to the *supernatural* character of His death; in view of which we may well say with the wondering centurion, "Truly, this was the Son of God"!

The Death of Christ, then, was unique, miraculous, supernatural. In the chapters which follow we shall hearken to the words which fell from His lips while He hung upon the Cross—words which make known to us some of the attendant circumstances of the great Tragedy; words which reveal the excellencies of the One who suffered there; words in which are wrapt up the Gospel of our Salvation; and words which inform us of the purpose, the meaning, the sufferings, and the sufficiency of the Death Divine. *Arthur W. Pink.*

The above article is the Introduction to the Editor's book on *"The Seven Sayings of the Saviour on the Cross"* in which he has sought to deal in a helpful and original way with the last utterances of the dying Redeemer. The work will well repay a careful reading, and if you have enjoyed this Introduction we feel sure you will not be disappointed with the balance of the book. Many have been helped by it. Tastefully bound. It would make a beautiful present. Price $1.00 from the Editor.

WATCHMAN, WHAT OF THE NIGHT?

"The watchman said, The morning cometh, and also the night" (Isa. 21:12).

These words summarize the history of the world, both as a whole, and in its parts. They announce first a period of light, followed by a time of darkness. In other words they tell, morally, of Divine favours bestowed, succeeded by man's failure to improve them. First Divine blessings and then human perversion of them. This has been the sad and unchanging order all through the course of the centuries. Nor is it any otherwise now. Nor will there be any change while the earth lasts. It is only on the new earth that the eternal morning shall know *no* "night".

Let us start at the beginning of the Bible and ask the question, "Watchman, What of the night"? The reply is, "The morning cometh". In the opening verse of Scripture we read, "In the beginning God created the heaven and the earth" (Gen. 1:1). That was the "morning" of *creation*, when the "morning stars sang together, and all the sons of God shouted with joy" (Job 38:7). On what a fair scene *that* "morning" must have broke! How lovely must the earth have looked in its priestine beauty! As Isaiah informs us, "He formed it to be inhabited." (45:18), inhabited we doubt not by a race since fallen, which Scripture terms "demons"—distinguished from the fallen angels. At the head of these pre-Adamic creatures Satan, (then the "anointed cherub" Ezek. 28:14) most probably was placed. "Full of wisdom and perfect in beauty" (Ezek. 28:12) he was well equipped to act as God's vice-gerent on earth. The first mundane "morning" promised well. But the watchman continues, "and also the night"! Unfathomable are the ways of God; yet, we know He doeth *all things* well. He suffered earth's prince to fall. The "Son of the *morning*" (Isa. 14:12) became "lifted up with pride" (1 Tim. 3:6). A vivid description of his apostacy seems to be given us in Isa. 14. He became dissatisfied with his earthly princedom and aspired to the Governorship of the Universe, saying "For thou hast said in thine heart, I will ascend into heaven, I will exalt *my* throne above the stars of God: I will sit also upon the mount of the congregation, in the sides of the north: I will Ascend above the heights of the clouds; I will be like the most High" (vv. 13, 14). Yes, the "night" followed the "morning". Satan's original kingdom was destroyed: "the earth *became* a ruin and darkness was upon the face of the deep" (Gen. 1:2), or as Peter informs us, "the world that then was, being overflowed with water, perished" (2 Pet. 3:6).

As we go back to Gen. 1 and behold the "darkness", we ask again, "Watchman what of the night?" And again the same answer is returned, "the morning cometh". For we read, "And the Spirit of God moved upon the face of the waters. And God said, Let there be light: and there was light" (vv. 2, 3). Another era was begun: this was the "morning" of *restoration*. The earth was now to be fitted for a new race, the human race. "In six days the Lord *made* (out of material *previously* "created") heaven and earth, the sea, and all that in them is" (Ex. 20:11); and we read, And God saw everything that He had made, and, behold, it was very good" (Gen. 1:31). Once again the sun shone on a scene of wondrous beauty; once again had dawned a day which promised much. But once more, we have to heed the next ominent words of the eagle-eyed watchman, "and also the night". Again, it was to be demonstrated that no being can stand in mere creature strength. The shadows gathered swiftly. The "power of darkness" (Luke 22:53) was allowed to enter the habitation of our first parents. Man rejected God's truth and believed the Devil's lie. "By one man *sin* entered the world and death by sin, and so death passed upon all men, for that all sinned" (Rom. 5:12). All sinned in their representative and head. Long did the dark night continue, and few were the stars that afforded any relief. Not till the windows of heaven were opened and the fountains of the deep were broken, and the flood destroyed all save those in the ark, did it end.

At the close of Gen. 8 another "morning" breaks. The earth had been swept clean by the Divine besom of destruction. A fearful manifestation had been given of God's holy hatred of sin. Yet a notable exercise of His sovereign mercy had also been exemplified. Noah had "found *grace* (so it was *not* because of any personal superiority, otherwise it had *not* been "grace") in the eyes of the Lord." (Gen. 6:8), and therefore he and his family were sheltered from the storm of heaven's wrath. On to the sin-cleansed earth Noah and his family stepped from the ark. Surely *now* a "morning" had dawned which shall not be followed by the shadows of eventide. Alas, once more we hear the warning words of the watchman, "and also the night." And only too tragically true do his words prove. Before we finish the next chapter of Genesis we behold Noah himself in a drunken stupor. The day-light had begun to wane, and by the time we reach Gen. 11 the darkness is complete. Side by side with Gen. 11 should be read Rom. 1:21-32. *The whole human race apostatized:* "Because that when they knew God, they glorified Him not as God, neither were thankful; but became vain in their imaginations, and their foolish heart was darkened. Professing themselves to be wise, they became fools, "And changed the glory of the uncorruptible God into an image made like unto corruptible man, and to birds, and fourfooted beasts, and creeping things" (vv. 21-23). For this cause God *"gave them up"* (three times repeated)—abandoned them to their corruption.

What wonder if the great Creator had now turned away from the earth forever. What wonder if He had directed His attention elsewhere, to some other world which sin had not invaded. Ah, but His thoughts are not our thoughts, neither are His ways our ways. God now acted on the principle of sovereign grace, and discriminating election. He singled out one man no better than his fellows (see Joshua 24:2), and appeared to him in His glory (Acts 7:2). To Abraham came the call to separate himself from his corrupt people and go forth unto a land which God should show him. Once more we hear the watchman saying, "The *morning* cometh". To Abraham was the promise made, "And I will make thee a great nation, and I will bless thee, and make thy name great; and thou shalt be a blessing: And I will bless them that bless thee, and curse him that curseth thee: and in thee shall all the families of the earth be blessed" (Gen. 12:2, 3). Another day had dawned, a day of Divine favour and distinguishing blessing. But if we have better hopes for *this* day, they are quickly dashed, for again the omniscient forecast is made, "And also the night". And what a "night" it was! The descendants of favoured Abraham groaning in bitter bondage in Egypt! Strange indeed was this. Why should the seed of Abraham be found in such a state? Ah, read Lev. 17:7 and note "no more"; Joshua 24:14 and note "in Egypt"; Ezek. 20: 6-9 etc. Yes, the descendants of Israel had become like the Egyptians—gross idolaters. Jehovah admonished them but they regarded not; therefore did He chastise them severely and long.

Did then the Lord abandon His wayward and sinful people? No. The darkness passed and again we have the welcome news, "The morning cometh". The Lord heard the cries of His afflicted people and raised them up a deliverer. The power of His arm was manifested and His enemies were made to know that they who touched the covenant people touched the apple of Jehovah's eye (Zech. 2:8). Under the leadership of Moses, Israel were brought out of the house of bondage, and at the Red Sea their implacable foes were destroyed, so that they saw them no more. Conducted by day and night, across the wilderness by a pillar of cloud and fire, Israel were brought to Mt. Sinai, where Jehovah Himself expressed His will, and with His own finger wrote the Ten Commandments on the two tables of stone. Marvellously favoured were the children of Israel and God dealt with them in a way that He dealt with no people before or since. Israel promised implicit obedience to God's law, saying, "All that the Lord hath spoken we will do" (Ex. 19: 8). Surely *this* "day", the day of Israel's "espousals" (Jer. 2:2), will turn out differently from the disappointing ones that have preceded it. No, at this time also the mournful dirge is heard, "And also the night". The sunshine quickly disappeared. Yea, before Moses had come down from the Mount, the whole congregation were worshipping the golden calf. The even came on apace. Unbelief, murmuring, rebellion among the people swiftly followed each other, and of the six hundred thousand males who left Egypt, all but two died in the wilderness.

Did Jehovah now abandon Israel? No, that could not be. "If we believe not yet *He* abideth faithful, He cannot deny Himself" (2 Tim. 2:12). He had promised to bring Israel into Canaan, and He must make good His word. Accordingly, as soon as Moses is dead, Joshua becomes Israel's leader, and under him they safely cross the Jordan. Another "morning" had come. At last the covenant people entered the promised land, the land that flowed with milk and honey. Wondrously did God act for them. Jericho falls without a blow being struck, and one after another the various nations of Canaan either fell before them or were subdued. Now they were ready to enjoy their goodly heritage. But once more the saddening prediction is made, "And also the night". No sooner is Joshua dead, than Israel are conquered and made to taste the bitterness of oppression. Instead of turning to the Lord and obeying His law, "every man did that which was right in his own eyes" (Judges 21: 25).

After Israel's failure under the Judges, followed by the reign of Saul, God raised up a man "after His own heart". Once more He intervened signally on behalf of His people. Their enemies were overthrown, their territory was enlarged, and the kingdom was established. Following David, came Solomon, richly endowed with wisdom, and set over the fairest kingdom this earth has ever yet seen. "And there came of all people to hear the wisdom of Solomon, from all kingdoms of the earth, which had heard of his wisdom" (1 Kings 4:34). His fame spread far and wide. The queen of Sheba visited his land, and after beholding its wonders, exclaimed, "It was a true report that I heard in mine own land of thy acts and of thy wisdom. Howbeit I believed not the words, until I came, and mine eyes had seen it: and behold, the half was not told me: thy wisdom and prosperity exceedeth the fame which I heard. Happy are thy men, happy are these thy servants, which stand continually before thee, and that hear thy wisdom" (1 Kings 10:6-8). A glorious temple was built and dedicated and freely did the king pour out his heart to God both in prayer and supplication. The Lord answered him by saying, "I have heard thy prayer and thy supplication, that thou hast made before Me: I have hallowed this house, which thou hast built, to put My name there forever; and Mine eyes and My heart shall be there perpetually. And if thou wilt walk before Me, as David thy father walked, in integrity of heart, and in uprightness, and do according to all that I have commanded thee, and will keep My statutes and My judgments: Then will I establish the throne of thy kingdom upon Israel forever, as I promised David thy father, saying, There shall not fail thee a man upon the throne of Israel" (1 Kings 9:3-5). Ah, surely the long-hoped for will now be realized. Surely this wise king will profit by the lessons and warnings recorded so plainly on the pages of infallible history. Surely he will fulfil the Divine requirement. Alas, alas. His wisdom was turned unto folly. Jehovah was forsaken for the gods of the heathen, and the highly favoured son of David died under a cloud, so that it is difficult to determine whither his soul went. Most of his successors were no better. The kingdom was rent asunder: the ten tribes were carried away into captivity, followed later by the two tribes.

In Daniel's time a new "day" dawned. Israel had failed lamentably. Now we behold the golden scepter transferred to the Gentiles. The "Times of the Gentiles" began, and from a worldly viewpoint, most auspiciously. At the head of the Gentile kingdom was one to whom God's prophet said, "Thou, O king, art a king of kings: for the God of heaven hath given thee a kingdom, power, and strength, and glory. And wheresoever the children of men dwell, the beasts of the field and the fowls of heaven hath He given into thine hand, and hath made thee ruler over them all. Thou art this head of gold" (Dan. 2:37, 38). Invested with untrammelled power, absolute autocrat, head of the vastest kingdom this world had seen, an unique opportunity was his. But man in the flesh is the same, no matter where he is found. The Jew was no better than the Gentile, nor the Gentile any better than the Jew. Pride filled Nebuchadnezzar's heart, and God humiliated him by sending him out into the fields as a beast. His successor sinned even more grievously, until the Divine verdict was rendered, "Thou art weighed in the balances, and found wanting" (Dan. 5:27). Once more "night fell", a night which lasted five long centuries.

"When the fullness of time was come, God sent forth His Son" (Gal. 4:4). A new "day" broke, the most wondrous of all. The Word became flesh and tabernacled among men, He came not to judge but to save. Full not of wrath and anger, but of "grace and truth". In matchless mercy He presented Himself to Israel, and went about doing good. Never man spake as He spake, and never man ministered to the suffering, relieved the needy, and delivered the captive as He did. But once again history repeated itself. He came unto His own, and His own received Him not. The Beloved of the Father was "despised and rejected of men". The shadows gather swiftly. He Himself announced "The night cometh when no man can work" (John 9:4). The Lord of glory was condemned to death, and between two malefactors was nailed to the cruel tree. That *night* had fallen was vividly demonstrated by the "three hours darkness" over all the earth. Surely now God will ring down the curtain on human history. Had there not been more than sufficient to exhaust *His* patience? No; "where sin abounded, grace did much more abound". Night was again to give place to day.

"And when the day of Pentecost was fully come, they were all with one accord in one place. And suddenly there came a sound from heaven as of a rushing mighty wind, and it filled all the house where they were sitting. And there appeared unto them cloven tongues like as of fire, and it sat upon each of them. And they were all filled with the Holy Spirit, and began to speak with other tongues, as the Spirit gave them utterance" (Acts 2:1-4). Such is the Divine record of the dawning of the Day of Christianity. The gift of the ascended Christ, the Holy Spirit was manifested in mighty power. The apostles were endued with wisdom from on high. Wondrous were the firstfruits from this heavenly shower of blessing. Three thousand souls were saved in a single day, and we are told, "And they continued stedfastly in the apostles doctrine, and fellowship, and in breaking of bread, and in prayers. And fear came upon every soul: and many wonders and signs were done by the apostles. And all that believed were together, and had all things in common" (Acts 2:42-44). Shortly after Saul of Tarsus was gloriously saved and called to be the apostle unto the Gentiles. Would men now respond freely and gladly to the advances of Divine mercy? Would the world at last recognise its folly, own its sinfulness, and turn in faith to the all-sufficient Saviour? Or, would *this* "morning" also give place to the evening shadows and mid-night darkness? Not long was the issue left in doubt. Not only would the great majority of our race be unmoved by the Gospel proclamation, but even where the Name of Christ was professed should come in declension and corruption. To the elders at Ephesus Paul gave warning—"For I know this, that after my departing shall grievous wolves enter in among you, not sparing the flock. Also of your own selves shall men arise, speaking perverse things, to draw away disciples after them" (Acts 20:29, 30). There is no need to review the history of Christendom. The failure of the Christian profession is fully evident on every side. Not only is every fundamental of the faith now being denied by thousands and tens of thousands of those who profess to be the servants of Christ, not only are the colleges and seminaries flooded with infidelity, but the people of God themselves are imbued by the spirit of the world and know little of the power of Christ's resurrection. Feebleness and lukewarmness describe our sad, sad state. And what of the future?

Again we listen to the watchman saying, "The morning cometh, and also the night". Yet another fulfilment of his announcement is shortly to be witnessed. For the people of God there awaits the fairest "morning" of all; for the world the darkest "night" of its entire history. For the redeemed of Christ there is the "blessed hope" of removal from these scenes. "For the Lord Himself snall descend from heaven with a shout, with the voice of he archangel, and with the trump of God: and the dead in Christ shall rise first: Then we which are alive and remain shall be caught up together with them in the clouds, to meet the Lord in the air: and so shall we ever be with the Lord" (1 Thess. 4:16, 17). And then shall we be "like Him, for we shall see Him as He is" (1 John 3:2). Then shall the Saviour, the Lord Jesus Christ, "change our vile body that it may be fashioned like unto His glorious body, according to the working whereby He is able even to subdue all things unto Himself" (Phil. 3:21). Glad and blessed day. But what of the Christ-rejecting world? "Behold the darkness shall cover the earth and gross darkness the people" (Isa. 60:2). Then will God speak unto men in His wrath, and vex them in His sore displeasure (Psa. 2)". Then shall the fearful storm of judgment burst upon a world that has so long despised God's grace. The greater part of the last book of Scripture is devoted to a description of the terrors and judgments which shall fill that awful "night".

But once again, the "night" will end. Even in judgment God will remember mercy. Once more will be heard the welcome sound "The morning cometh". The Sun of righteousness shall arise with healing in His wings. The Son of man shall return to this earth and sit upon the throne of His glory. The Devil shall be bound and cast into the Bottomless Pit. The long-awaited Millennium will have come. Then "The wilderness and the solitary place shall be glad for them; and the desert shall rejoice, and blossom as the rose. It shall blossom abundantly, and rejoice even with joy and singing: the glory of Lebanon shall be given unto it, the excellency of Carmel and Sharon, they shall see the glory of the Lord, and the excellency of our God" (Isa. 35:1, 2). And again it is written, "The wolf also shall dwell with the lamb, and the leopard shall lie down with the kid; and the calf and the young lion and the fatling together; and a little child shall lead them. And the cow and the bear shall feed; their young ones shall lie down together: the lion shall eat straw like the ox. And the sucking child shall play on the hole of the asp, and the weaned child shall put his hand on the cockatrice' den. They shall not hurt nor destroy in all My holy mountain: for the earth shall be full of the knowledge of the Lord, as the waters cover the sea. And in that day there shall be a root of Jesse, which shall stand for an ensign of the people; to it shall the Gentiles seek: and His rest shall be glorious" (Isa. 11:6-10). Wars shall be made to cease unto the ends of the earth. A time of blessing such as this earth has never witnessed shall then ensue. And what is to be the end of the Millennial Day? Surely then shall be reversed the sin-marred record of human history. Surely good shall triumph over evil in the Golden Age. No, once more and for the last time the mournful plaint is heard, "And also the night". Yes, even the Millennium itself, shall close with darkness. In Rev. 20 we are told "And when the thousand years are expired, Satan shall be loosed out of his prison, And shall go out to deceive the nations which are in the four quarters of the earth, Gog and Magog, to gather them together to battle: the number of whom is as the sand of the sea. And they went up on the breadth of the earth, and compassed the camp of the saints about and the beloved city: and fire came down from God out of heaven, and devoured them" (vv. 7-9). The awful sequel to this is described in the closing verses of Rev. 20. The wicked shall all appear before the Great White Throne, that the *degree* of their punishment may be announced, after which they shall be cast into the Lake of Fire, there to be tormented "for ever and ever". For them there shall be "the blackness of darkness of a never-ending Night.

Thank God that Rev. 21 and 22 follow chapter 20. Here we learn that there shall be a *new* heaven and a *new* earth on which the redeemed shall be. Then shall it be said, "Behold the tabernacle of God is with men, and He will dwell with them, and they shall be His people and God Himself shall be with them, and be their God. And God shall wipe away all tears from their eyes; and there shall be no more death, neither sorrow, nor crying, neither shall there be any more pain: for the former things are passed away" (Rev. 21:3, 4). And again we read "In the midst of the street of it, and on either side of the river, was there the tree of life, which bear twelve manner of fruits, and yielded her fruit every month: and the leaves of the tree were for the healing of the nations. And there shall be no more curse: but the throne of God and the Lamb shall be in it; and His servants shall serve Him: And they shall see His face; and His name shall be written in their foreheads" (Rev. 22:2-4). Then will break for us the morning without clouds. That will be the perfect, *unending* Day, for it is written, "There shall be NO *night there*; and they need no candle, neither light of sun: for the Lord God giveth them light: and they shall reign forever and ever" (Rev. 22:5). Glorious prospect! Into that fair scene shall enter nothing that defileth. Then shall Christ see of the travail of His soul and be satisfied, and then shall the redeemed, in never-ending wonderment and praise, magnify the riches of sovereign grace which predestinated them unto such unspeakable bliss. "Now unto Him that is able to do exceedingly abundantly above all that we ask or think, according to the power that worketh in us, Unto Him be glory in the church by Christ Jesus throughout all ages, world without end" (Eph. 3:20, 21).

Arthur W. Pink.

SPECIAL ADDRESSES BY THE EDITOR.

Seven of the Special Addresses which the Editor expects to deliver most frequently in his forthcoming Foreign Bible Conference tour (D.V.) have been printed separately, and we now announce them so that they may be available to our friends in this Country. We deem them amongst the most important of any thing we have had printed; and we sincerely trust that *many* subscribers of this Magazine will secure them. They are as follows:—

The Christian's Greatest Need: An exposition of Luke 10:38-42: $0:10
God's Food for His people: " " " Exodus 16: .... :10
The Prodigal Son: " " " Luke 15: .... :10
The Three Crosses: A precious Gospel message: .... :10
A Threefold Salvation—From the penalty, power, & presence of sin .... :07
The Sins of the Saints—Much used of God in the U. S. A. .... :08
The New Birth—Greatly needed today:.................................... :07

One each of the above sent post-paid for 60 cents. This offer will not be repeated after next month. We have been at much expense in publishing the first four, personally, and hope that our readers will order a dozen of each—*$1:00* per doz. They are very nicely got up, and will just go in an ordinary-sized envelope. One of these would be much more honouring to God than a "Christmas Card"!

BOUND VOLUMES OF "STUDIES IN THE SCRIPTURES".

Vol 1 containing the 12 issues for 1922: *$1:50.—$1:75 Foreign*
Vol 2 " " " " " 1923: *1:50.* " "
Vol 3 " " " " " 1924: *1:50.* " "

We have had these bound, strongly and attractively, so that interested readers could preserve the Magazines in *permanent* form. When our present supply is exhausted these will, most probably, *not* be re-printed. We will send the 3 Vols. for *$4:00* (£1 to Foreign address). They cost us almost *40* cents each to bind, so that when we pay the postage this is practically *cost price!* $4:25 to those west of Chicago.

GLEANINGS IN GENESIS.

The 2 Vols. containing 46 special articles *$2:50.*

The Editor was six years compiling these. Many have been helped by them. They give special attention to the Types. Joseph a type of Christ in *one hundred* distinct points! Intensely interesting.

EXPOSITION OF JOHN'S GOSPEL.

Vol 1: covering the first five chapters 380 pages *$1:50*
" 2: " " next " " 400 " *2:00*

Send all orders to the Editor:
227 North Creighton Street,
Philadelphia, Pa.
Foreign subscribers please send *only* International Money Orders.

VOL. IV JANUARY, 1925 No. 1

STUDIES in the SCRIPTURES

"Search the Scriptures" John 5:39.

Arthur W. Pink, Publisher & Editor,
227 N. Creighton St., Philadelphia, Pa.

Price: 10 cents per copy; $1.00 per year. Foreign $1.00 per year.

"It is of the Lord's mercies that we are not consumed, because His compassions fail not. They are new every morning: great is Thy faithfulness" (Lam. 3:22, 23). Suitable passage is this for our meditation as we arrive at the close of one year and the beginning of another. As we review the past, we discover abundant evidence of God's unfailing "compassions". Patiently has He borne with us; graciously has He sustained us. As we face the future, full assurance ought we to have that His mercies will still be manifested anew every morning, for *great* is *His faithfulness.*

Another year has dawned. What does it hold for us—trouble? Doubtless, for Man is born unto trouble as the sparks fly upward" (Job 5:7). Affliction? Yes, for "yourselves know that we are appointed thereunto" (1 Thess. 3:3). Testings of faith? Assuredly, for "the trying of your faith worketh patience" (James 1:3). But what on the other side? The *presence* of Christ with us; "I will never leave thee, nor forsake thee" (Heb. 13:5). The "exceeding great and precious *promises*" of the Word (2 Peter 1:4) to cheer us. The *assurance* that we belong to One who is "able to do exceeding abundantly above all that we ask or think, according to the power that worketh in us" (Eph. 3:20). The prospect of our Redeemer's imminent *return:* "For yet a little while, He that shall come will come, and will not tarry" (Heb. 10:37). And in the little interval that is still before us, opportunities for *service:* "Let us not be weary in well-doing: for in due season we shall reap, if we faint not" (Gal. 6:9). Surely every child of God has abundant reason to exclaim, "O magnify the Lord with me, and let us exalt His name together" (Psa. 34:3).

The Lord willing, early in January the Editor, accompanied by his wife, expects to leave Philadelphia and journey to California, to conduct several Bible Conferences. On the 3rd of March, unless the Lord has come ere then, or we have been called Home, we plan to sail from San Francisco for Australia—literally the 'other side of the world'! It is entirely a journey by faith, neither of us know a single soul in that Country; no financial guarantee has been given. But the call of God is clear. And we go forth (by His sovereign grace) in simple dependence upon Him, and with our expectation in Him. We earnestly request the prayers of our Christian friends that God will direct all details to His own glory, that "a great and effectual door" may be opened unto us, and that we may be fitted and endued by Him for whatever He has for us to do. Brethren and sisters, please remember us *daily* at the Throne of Grace. Ask that the Lord's fear may be upon us, that we shun not to declare *"all* the counsel of God." Pray that He may be pleased to prepare the soil for the Seed, that many precious souls may be blest.

Will our friends kindly note that Mr. C. S. Pressel, assisted by his wife, of York, Pa., has kindly volunteered to act as our Honorary Agent in the U. S. A. After Jan. 15 please address *all* correspondence concerning the Magazine and **all orders for any of the Editor's writings** to Mr. Pressel, who will have a complete stock on hand. All personal matters, questions of the Scriptures etc. address to The Editor % *Mr. Pressel.*

IMPORTANT NOTICES

Set of twelve issues for **1922,** unbound, **$1.00.** Bound, **$1.50.**

Set of twelve issues for **1923,** unbound, **$1.00.** Bound **$1.50.** Abroad, **$1.75** or **7/6.**

Set of twelve issues for **1924,** unbound, **$1.00.** Bound **$1.50.** Abroad, **$1.75** or **7/6.**

Note: We cannot break a set or now supply any **single** 1923 issues.

Subscription Price: **$1.00** per year to any address in the world. Single copies **10 cents.**

Change of Address: Please notify me promptly of any change of address, and be certain to give both old and new addresses.

Non-subscribers receiving this Magazine regularly will understand their subscription has been entered by a friend.

Copies lost in the mail duplicated only if we are notified promptly.

Entered as second-class matter December 15th, 1923, at the post office at Philadelphia, Pa., under Act of March 3rd, 1879.

CONTENTS

JOHN'S GOSPEL

37. Christ raising Lazarus: John 11:1-10.

Below is an Analysis of the first ten verses of John 11:

1. Lazarus and his sisters vv. 1, 2.
2. Their appeal to the Lord v. 3.
3. God's design in Lazarus's sickness v. 4.
4. The delay of love vv. 5, 6.
5. Christ testing His disciples v. 7.
6. The disciples' trepidation v. 8.
7. The Lord re-assuring the disciples vv. 9, 10.

Before taking up the details of the passage which is to be before us a few words need to be said concerning the principal design and character of John 11 and 12. In the preceding chapters we have witnessed the increasing enmity of Christ's enemies, an enmity which culminated in His crucifixion. But before God suffered His beloved Son to be put to death, He gave a most blessed and unmistakable witness to His glory. "We have seen, all through John, that no power of Satan could hinder the manifestation of the Person of Christ. He met with incessant opposition and undying hatred, the result, however, being that glory succeeds glory in manifestation, and God was fully revealed in Jesus. That was His *purpose,* and *who* could hinder its accomplishment? 'Why do the heathen rage, and the people imagine a vain thing?' Man's rage against Christ, only served as an occasion *for* the manifestation of His glory. Here in John 11 the Son of God is glorified, the glory of God answering to the rejection of the Person of Christ in the preceding chapters" (R. Evans: Notes & Meditations on John's Gospel).

It is indeed a striking fact, and one to which we have not seen attention called, that the previous chapters show us Christ *rejected* in a threefold way, and then God answering by *glorifying* Christ in a threefold way. In 5:16 we read "Therefore did the Jews persecute Jesus, and *sought to slay Him,* because He had done these things on the Sabbath day": this was because of His *works.* In John 8:58 we are told, "Jesus said unto them, Verily, verily, I say unto you, Before Abraham was I am"; and immediately following, it is recorded, *"Then* took they up stones *to cast at Him";* this was because of His *words.* While in 10:30 the Lord affirmed, "I and my Father are one", which is at once followed by, *"Then* the Jews took up stones *again* to stone Him": this was on account of the claim which He had made concerning His *person.*

The threefold witness which God caused to be borne to the glory of Christ in John 11 and 12 corresponds exactly with the threefold rejection above, though they are met in their inverse order. In John 10:31 it was Christ in His absolute Deity, as God the Son, who was rejected. Here in John 11 His *Divine* glory shines forth most manifestly in the raising of Lazarus. In John 8 He was rejected because He declared "Before *Abraham* was, I am". There it was more in His *Messianic* character that He was despised. Corresponding to this, in John 12:12-15 we find Him in full Messianic glory entering Jerusalem as "King of Israel". In John 5 Christ is seen more in His *mediatorial* character, in incarnation as "the Son of man"—note v. 27. Corresponding to this we find in the third section of John 12 the *Gentiles* seeking the Lord Jesus, and to them He answered: "The hour is come that the *Son of man* should *be glorified*" (v. 23)!

Man had fully manifested *Himself.* The Light had shone in the darkness, and the darkness comprehended it not. The deep guilt of men had been demonstrated by their refusing the Sent One from the Father, and their deadness in trespasses and sins had been evidenced by the absence of the slightest response to the eternal Word then tabernacling in their midst. They had seen and hated both Him and His Father (15:24). The end of Christ's public ministry was, therefore, well-nigh reached. But before He goes to the cross, God gave a final testimony to the glory of His Beloved. Beautiful is it to behold the Father so jealously guarding the honor of His Son in this threefold way ere He left the stage of public action. And solemn was it for Israel to be shown so plainly and so fully WHO it was they had rejected and were about to crucify.

The darker the night, the more manifest the light which illumines it. The more the depravity and enmity of Israel were exhibited, the brighter the testimony which God caused to be borne to the glory of His Son. The end was almost reached, therefore did the Lord now perform His mightiest work of all—save only the laying down of His own life, which was *the* wonder of all wonders. Six miracles (or as John terms them, "signs") had already been wrought by Him, but at Bethany He does that which displayed His Divine power in a superlative way. Previously we have seen Him turning water into wine, healing the nobleman's son, restoring the impotent man, multiplying the loaves and fishes, walking on the sea, giving sight to the blind man; but here he raises the dead, yea, brings back to life one who had lain in the grave four days. Fitting climax was this, and most suitably is it the *seventh* "sign" in this Gospel.

It is true that Christ had raised the dead before, but even here the climax is again to be seen. Mark records the raising of Jairus's daughter, but she had only just died. Luke tells of the raising of the widow's son of Nain, but he had not been buried. But here, in the case of Lazarus, not only had the dead man been placed in the sepulchre, but corruption had already begun to consume the body. Supremely true was it of the Just One (Act 3:14) that His path was as the shining light, which shone "more and more unto the perfect day" (Prov. 4:18).

The same climactic order is to be seen in connection with *the state of the natural man* which John's "signs" typically portray. "They have no wine" (2:4), tells us that the sinner is a total stranger to Divine joy (Judges 9:13). "Sick" (4:46), announces the condition of the sinner's soul, for sin is a disease which has robbed man of his original health. The "Impotent man" (5:7), shows us that the poor sinner is "without strength" (Rom. 5:6), completely helpless, unable to do a thing to better his condition. The multitude without any food of their own (6:5), witnesses to the fact that man is destitute of that which imparts strength. The disciples on the storm-tossed sea (6:18), before the Saviour came to them, pictures the dangerous position which the sinner occupies—already on the "broad road" which leadeth to *destruction.* The man blind from his birth (9:1), demonstrates the fact that the sinner is altogether incapable of perceiving either his own wretchedness and danger, or the One who alone can deliver him. But here in John 11 we have that which is much more solemn and awful. Here we learn that the natural man is spiritually *dead,* "dead in trespasses and sins". Lower than this we cannot go. Anything more hopeless cannot be portrayed. In the presence of death, the wisest, the richest, the most mighty among men have to confess their utter helplessness. This, this is what is set before us in John 11. Most suitable background for Christ to display Himself as "The Resurrection and the Life". And most striking is this climax of the "signs" recorded in the Fourth Gospel, displaying both the power of Christ and the condition of the natural man.

"Now a certain man was sick, named Lazarus, of Bethany, the town of Mary and her sister Martha" (v. 1). The object of our Lord's resurrection-power is first presented to our notice. His name was Lazarus. At once our minds revert back to Luke 16, where another "Lazarus" is seen. But how striking the contrast, a contrast most evidently designed by the Holy Spirit. There are only two men mentioned in the New Testament which bear this name. Here again the 'law of comparison and contrast' helps us (cf. our remark in Vol. 1 Pages 134, 210, 308). The Lazarus of Luke 16 was a beggar, whereas everything goes to show that the Lazarus of John 11 (cf. 12:2, 3) was a man of means. The Lazarus of Luke 16 was uncared for, for we read of how the dogs came and licked his sores; but the one in John 11 enjoyed the loving ministrations of his sisters. The Lazarus of Luke 16 was dependent upon the "crumbs" which fell *from* another's table; whereas in John 12, after his resurrection, the Lazarus of Bethany is seen *at* "the table" where the Lord Jesus was. The one in Luke 16 died and remained in the grave, the one in John 11 was brought-again from the dead.

The Holy Spirit has been careful to identify the Lazarus of John 11 as belonging to *Bethany*—a word that seems to have a double meaning: "House of Figs," and "House of Affliction". It was the "town" (more accurately, "village") of Mary and her sister Martha. Though not mentioned previously by John, this is not the first reference to these sisters in the Gospel records. They are brought before us at the close of Luke 10, and what is there recorded about them sheds not a little light upon some of the details of John 11.

Martha was evidently the senior, for we are told "Martha received Him into *her* house" (Luke 10:38). This is most blessed. There were very few homes which were opened to the Lord Jesus. He was "despised and rejected of men". Men hid as it were their faces from Him and "esteemed Him not". Not only was He unappreciated and unwelcome, but He was "hated". But here was one who had "received Him", first into her heart and then into her home. So far so good. Of her sister, it is said, "And she had a sister called Mary, which also sat at Jesus' feet and heard His Word" (v. 39). It is indeed striking to note that each time Mary is mentioned in the Gospel, she is seen *at the feet* of Christ. She had the deeper apprehension of the glory of His person. She was the one who enjoyed the most intimacy with Him. Hers was the keener spiritual discernment. We shall yet see how this is strongly confirmed in John 11 and 12.

Next we are told, "But Martha was cumbered about much serving, and came to Him and said, Lord, Dost Thou not care that my sister hath left me to serve alone? bid her therefore that she help me" (Luke 10:40). The word "cumbered" means "weighted down". She was burdened by her "*much* serving". Alas, how many there are like her among the Lord's people today. It is largely due to the over-emphasis which has been placed upon "Christian service"—much of which is, we fear, but the feverish energy of the flesh. It is not that service is wrong, but it becomes a snare and an evil if it be allowed to crowd-out worship and the cultivation of one's own soul.

"And Jesus answered and said unto her, Martha, Martha, thou art careful and troubled about many things" (v. 41). This is very solemn. The Lord did not commend Martha for her "much serving". Instead, He reproved her. He tells her she was distracted and worried because she had given her attention to "*many* things". She was attempting more than God had called her to do. This is very evident from the previous verse. Martha felt that her load was too heavy to carry alone, hence her "bid her therefore that she help *me*". Sure sign was this that she had run without being sent. When any Christian feels as Martha here felt he may know that he has undertaken to do *more* than the Lord appointed.

"But one thing is needful: and Mary hath chosen that good part, which shall not be taken away from her" (v. 42). Though the Lord reproved Martha, He commended Mary. The "one thing needful" is "that good part" which Mary had chosen, and that is to *receive* from Christ. Mary sat at His feet "*and* heard His word". She was conscious of her deep need, and came to Him to be ministered unto. Later, we shall see how *she* ministered unto Christ, and ministered so as to receive His hearty commendation. But the great lesson for us here is that *we* must first be ministered unto before we are qualified to minister unto others. We must be *receivers,* before we can give out. The vessel must be filled, before it can overflow. The difference then between Martha and Mary is this: the one ministered *unto* Christ, the other received *from* Him, and of the latter He declared, she "hath chosen that good part which shall not be taken away from her". This brief examination of Luke 10, with the information it gives about the characters of the two sisters of Lazarus will enable us to understand the better their respective actions and words in John 11.

"It was that Mary which anointed the Lord with ointment and wiped His feet with her hair, whose brother Lazarus was sick" (v. 2). This explains why Mary is mentioned first in the previous verse—the only time that she is. The commentators have indulged in a variety of conjectures, but the reason is very obvious. John's Gospel was written years after the first three, one evidence of which is supplied in the verses before us. The opening verse of our chapter clearly supposes that the reader is acquainted with the contents of the earlier Gospels. Bethany was "the town (village) of Mary and her sister Martha". This Luke 10:38 had already intimated. But in addition, both Matthew and Mark record how that Mary had "anointed" the Lord with her costly ointment in the house of Simon the leper who also resided in Bethany. It is true her name is not given either by Matthew or Mark*, but it is very clear that her name must have been known, for how else could the Lord's word have been carried out: "Verily I say unto you, Wheresoever this gospel shall be preached throughout the whole world, this also that she hath done shall be spoken of for a memorial of her" (Mark 14:9). It is this which explains why Mary is mentioned first in John 11:1—she was the better known!

It was at Bethany that Lazarus lived with his sisters. Bethany was but a village, yet had it been marked out in the eternal counsels of God as the place which was to witness the greatest and most public miraculous attestation of the Deity of Christ. "Let it be noted that the presence of God's elect children is the one thing which makes towns and countries famous in God's sight. The village of Martha and Mary is noticed, while Memphis and Thebes are not named in the New Testament. A cottage where there is grace, is more pleasant in God's sight than a palace where there is none." (Bishop Ryle). It was at Bethany there was to be given the final and most conclusive proof that He who was on the point of surrendering *Himself* to death and the grave was none other than the Resurrection and the Life. Bethany was less than two miles from Jerusalem (v. 18), the headquarters of Judaism, so that the news of the raising of Lazarus would soon be common knowledge throughout all Judea.

"Therefore his sisters sent unto Him, saying, Lord, behold, he whom Thou lovest is sick" (v. 3). This must not be regarded as a protest; it was not that Martha and Mary were complaining against Christ because He suffered one whom He loved to fall sick. Instead, it was simply an appeal to the heart of One in whom they had implicit confidence. The more closely this brief message from the sisters be scrutinized, the more will their becoming modesty be apparent. Instead of prescribing to Christ what should be done in their brother's case, they simply acquainted Him with his desperate condition. They did not request Him to hasten at once to Bethany, nor did they ask Him to heal their brother by a word from a distance, as once He had restored to health the nobleman's son. (John 4). Instead, they left it for *Him* to decide what should be done.

"Lord, behold, he whom Thou lovest is sick". Each word in this touching message of Martha and Mary is worthy of separate consideration. "Lord" was the language of believers, for no unbeliever ever so addressed the despised Nazarene. "Lord" acknowledged His Deity, owned His authority, and expressed their humility. "Lord, behold": this is a word which arrests attention, focalizes interest, and expressed their earnestness. "He whom Thou lovest". This is highly commendable. They did not say, "he who loves Thee". Christ's fathomless love for us, and not our feeble love for Him, is what we ever need to keep steadily before our hearts. Our love varies; His knows no change. It is indeed striking to note the way in which the sisters refer to Lazarus. They did not name him! They did not even say, "our brother", or "Thy disciple", but simply "he whom Thou lovest is sick". They knew that nothing is so quick in discernment as *love;* hence their appeal to the omniscient love of Christ. "He whom Thou lovest is *sick*". There are two principal words in the Greek to express sickness: the one referring to the disease itself, the other pointing to its effects—weakness, exhaus-

*It is characteristic of John *to* give us her name, for he presents Christ as God manifest in the flesh, therefore everything comes out into the light: cf. the fact that John alone tells us the name of the priest's servant, whose ear the Saviour healed, John 18:10.

tion. It is the latter that was used here. As applied to individual cases in the N. T. the word here used implies deathly-sick—note its force in Acts 9:37 and Phil. 2:26, 27. In John 5:3 and 7 it is rendered "impotent". It is not at all likely that Martha and Mary would have sent to Christ from such a distance had not their brother's life been in danger. The force, then, of their message was, "He whom Thou lovest *is sinking.*"

The verse now before us plainly teaches that sickness in a believer is by no means incompatible with the Lord's *love* for such an one. There are some who teach that sickness in a saint is a sure evidence of the Lord's displeasure. The case of Lazarus ought forever to silence such an error. Even the chosen friends of Christ sicken and die. How utterly incompetent then are we to estimate God's love for us by our temporal condition or circumstances! "No man knoweth either love or hatred *by* all that is *before* them" (Ecc. 9:1). What then is the practical lesson for us in this? Surely this: "Therefore judge nothing before the time" (1 Cor. 4:5). The Lord loves Christians as truly when they are sick as when they are well.

It is blessed to mark how Martha and Mary acted in the hour of their need. They sought the Lord, and unburdened their hearts to Him. Do we always act thus? It is written, "God is our refuge and strength, a very *present* help in trouble" (Psl. 46:1); yet, to our shame, how little we *know* Him as such. When the people murmured against Moses, we are told that, "he cried unto the Lord" (Ex. 15:25). When Hezekiah received the threatening letter from Rabshakeh, he "spread it before the Lord" (Isa. 37:14). When John the Baptist was beheaded his disciples went and told Jesus" (Matt. 14:12). What examples for us! We have not an High Priest who cannot be touched with the feeling of our infirmities. No, He is full of compassion, for when on earth He, too, was "acquainted with grief". He sympathizes deeply with His suffering people, and invites them to pour out the anguish of their hearts before Him. What a blessed proof of this we find in John 20. When He met the tearful Mary on the morn of His resurrection, He asked her, "Woman, why weepest thou?" (v. 15). Why ask her such a question? Did He not know the cause of her sorrowing? Certainly He did. Was it a reproach? We do not deem it such. Was it not rather because He wanted her to unburden her heart before Him! "Cast thy burden upon the Lord" is ever His word. This is what Martha and Mary were doing. The Lord grant that every tried and troubled reader of these lines may go and do likewise.

The action of these sisters and the wording of their appeal afford us a striking example of *how* we should present our petitions to the Lord. Much of the present-day teaching on the subject of prayer is grossly dishonoring to God. The Most High is not our servant to be brought into subjection to *our* will. Prayer was never designed to place *us* on the Throne, but to bring us to our knees before it. It is not for the creature to dictate to the Creator. It *is* the happy privilege of the Christian to make known His requests with thanksgiving. But, "requests" are not commands. Petitioning is a very different matter from commandeering. Yet we have heard men and women talk to God not only as if they were *His* equals, but as though they had the right to order Him about. Coming to the Throne of Grace with "boldness" does not mean with impious impudence. The Greek word signifies "freedom of speech". It means that we may tell out our hearts *as* God's children, never forgetting though, that He is our *Father.*

The sisters of Lazarus acquainted the Lord with the desperate condition of their brother, appealed to His love, and then left the case in His hands, to be dealt with as *He* saw best. They were not so irreverent as to tell Him *what* to do. In this they have left all praying souls a worthy example which we do well to follow. "*Commit* thy way unto the Lord": that is our responsibility. "Trust also *in Him*"; that is our happy privilege. "*Trust* also in Him", not dictate to Him, and not demand from Him. People talk of "claiming" from God. But *grace* cannot be "claimed", and *all* is of grace. The very "Throne" we approach is one of *grace.* How utterly incongruous then to talk of "claiming" anything from the Sitter on *such* a throne. "Commit thy way unto the Lord, trust also in Him, and He shall *bring it to pass*". But it must ever be kept in mind that He will "bring it to pass" in His *own* sovereign way and in His *own* appointed time. And oftentimes, usually so in fact, *His* way and time will be different from ours.

He brought it *to pass* for Martha and Mary, though not in the time and way they probably expected. The apostle Paul longed to preach the Gospel in Rome, but how slow he was in realizing his desire and in what an altogether unlooked for manner he went there!

"When Jesus heard that, He said, This sickness is not unto death, but for the glory of God" (v. 4). We take it that this was our Lord's answer to the messenger, rather than a private word to His disciples, though probably it was spoken in their hearing. And what a mysterious answer it was! How strangely worded! How cryptic! What did He mean? One thing was evident on its surface: Martha and Mary were given the assurance that both the sickness of Lazarus and its issue were perfectly known to Christ—how appropriately was the record of this reserved for *John's Gospel;* how perfectly in accord with the whole tenor of it!

"This sickness is not unto death". This declaration is similar in kind to what was before us in 9:3, "Neither hath this man sinned nor his parents; but that the works of God should be made manifest in him"—compare our comments thereon. The sickness of Lazarus was "not unto death" in the ordinary sense of the word, that is, unto *abiding* death—death would not be the *final end* of this "sickness". But why not have told the exercised sisters plainly that their brother would die, and that He would raise him from the dead? Ah, that is not God's way; He would keep *faith* in exercise, have *patience* developed, and so order things that we are constantly driven to our knees! The Lord said sufficient on this occasion to encourage hope in Martha and Mary, but not enough to make them leave off seeking God's help! Bishop Ryle has pointed out how that we encounter the same principle and difficulty in connection with much of unfulfilled prophecy: "There is sufficient for faith to rest upon and to enkindle hope, but sufficient also to make us cry unto God for light"!

"This sickness is not unto death, *but for the glory of God*". What a word was this! How far, we wonder, had those two sisters entered into such a thought concerning the sickness of their brother. But now they were to learn that it was Divinely ordained, and from the sequel we are shown that Lazarus's sickness, his death, the absence of Christ from Bethany, and the blessed issue, were all arranged by Him who doeth *all* things well. Let us learn from this that God has a purpose in connection with *every* detail of our lives. Many are the scriptures which show this. The case of the man born blind provides a parallel to the sickness and death of Lazarus. When the disciples asked *why* he had been born blind, the Saviour answered, "That the works of God should be manifest in him". This should teach us to look behind the outward sorrows and trials of life to the Divine purpose in sending them.

"This sickness is not unto death, but for the glory of God that the Son of God might be glorified thereby" (v. 4). How this shows that the glory of God is one with the glory of the Son! The two are inseparable. This comes out plainly, again, if we compare John 2:11 with 11:40. In the former we are told, "This beginning of miracles did Jesus in Cana of Galilee and manifested forth *His* glory". In the latter we find Him saying to Martha, as He was on the point of raising Lazarus, "Said I not unto thee, that, if thou wouldest believe, thou shouldest see the glory *of God*". The same truth is taught once more in 14:13, "Whatsoever ye shall ask in My name, that will I do, that *the Father* may be glorified *in the Son*". What then is the lesson for us? This: "All men should honor the Son, *even as* they honor the Father" (5:23).

"Now Jesus loved Martha, and her sister, and Lazarus" (v. 5). Here the order of their names is reversed from what we have in verse 1. Martha is now mentioned first. Various conjectures have been made as to why this is. To us it appears the more natural to mention Mary first at the beginning of the narrative, for she would be the better known to the readers of the Gospel records. In v. 5, and so afterwards, it was suitable to name Martha first, seeing that she was the senior. But in addition to this, may it not be the Holy Spirit's design to show us that each sister was *equally* dear to the Saviour! It is true that Mary chose the better part, whilst Martha struggled with the needless unrest of her well-meaning mind. But though these sisters were of such widely dissimilar types, yet were they one in Christ! Diverse in disposition they might be, yet were they both loved with the same eternal, unchanging love!

"Now Jesus loved Martha, and her sister, and Lazarus". A precious thought will be lost here unless we mark carefully the exact place in the narrative that this statement occupies. It is recorded not at the beginning of the chapter, but immediately before what we read of in v. 6, where we are told that the Lord Jesus "abode two days still in the place where He was". Such a delay, under such circumstances strikes us as strange. But, as we shall see, the delay only brought out the perfections of Christ—His absolute *submission* to the Father's will. In addition to that, it is beautiful to behold that His delay was also in full keeping with His *love* for Martha and Mary. Among other things, Christ designed to strengthen the faith of these sisters by suffering it to endure the bitterness of death, in order to heighten its subsequent joy. "His love wittingly delays that it may more gloriously console them after their sufferings" (Stier). Let *us* learn from this that when God makes us *wait,* it is the sign that He purposes to *bless,* but in His own way—usually a way so different from what *we* desire and expect. What a word is that in Isa. 30:18, "And therefore will the Lord *wait,* that He may be *gracious* unto you, and therefore will He be exalted, that He may have mercy upon you: for the Lord is a God of judgment: blessed are all they that *wait* for Him."

"When He had heard therefore that he was sick, He abode two days still in the same place where He was." (v. 6). The Lord knows best at what time to relieve His suffering people. There was no coldness in His affection for those tried sisters (as the sequel clearly shows), but the right moment for Him to act had not then come. Things were allowed to become more grievous: the sick one died, and still the Master tarried. Things had to get worse at Bethany before He intervened. Ofttimes God brings man to the end of himself before He comes to his relief. There is much truth in the old proverb that 'Man's extremity is God's opportunity'. Frequently is this the Lord's way; but how trying to flesh and blood! How often we ask, with the disciples, "Master, carest Thou not that we perish?" How awful to question the tender compassion of such a One! And how foolish was the question of these disciples: how could they "perish" with *Christ* on board! What cause we have to hang our heads in shame! "When circumstances look dark, our hearts begin to question the love of the One who permits such to befall us. Oh, let me press upon you this important truth: *the dealings of the Father's hand must ever be looked at in the light of the Father's heart.* Grasp this. Never try to interpret love by its manifestations. How often our Father sends chastisement, sorrow, bereavement, pressure! How well He could take me out of it all—in a moment—He has the power, but He leaves me there. Oh, may He help us to rest patiently in Himself at such times, not trying to read His love by circumstances, but them, whatever they may be, through the love of His heart. This gives wondrous strength—knowing that loving heart, and not questioning the dealings of His hand". (C.H.M.).

But *why* did Christ abide two days still in the same place where He was? To test the faith of the sisters, to develope their patience, to heighten their joy in the happy sequel. All true; but there was a much deeper reason than those. Christ had taken upon Him the form of a servant, and in perfect submission to the Father He awaits His orders from *Him.* Said He, "I came down from heaven not to do Mine *own* will, but the will of Him that sent Me" (6:38). Most beautifully was this demonstrated here. Not even His love for Martha and Mary would move Him to act before the Father's time had come. Blessedly does this show us the anti-typical fulfillment of one detail in a most wondrous type found in Lev. 2. The Meal-offering plainly foreshadowed the incarnate Son of God. It displays the perfections of His Divine-human person. Two things were rigidly excluded from this offering: "No meat offering, which ye shall bring unto the Lord shall be made with leaven; for ye shall burn *no* leaven, *nor any honey,* in any offering of the Lord made by fire" (Lev. 2:11). The leaven is the emblem of evil. "Honey" stands for the sweetness of natural affections, what men term 'the milk of human kindness'. And how strikingly this comes out here. How differently Christ acted from what you and I most probably would have done. If we had received a message that a loved one was desperately sick, would we not have hastened to his side without delay? And *why* would we? Because we sought *God's glory?* or because our natural affections impelled us? Ah, in this, as in everything, we behold the uniqueness of the Lord Jesus. The Father's glory was ever dearest to the heart of the Son. Here then is the force of the "Therefore". "When *therefore* He heard that he is sick, then *indeed* He remained in which He was place two days" (Bagster's Interlinear—literal translation). The "Therefore" and the "indeed" look back to v. 4—"this sickness . . . is for the glory of God". And how what we read of in the intervening verse serves to emphasize this —Christ's love for His own never interfered with His dependence on the Father. His first recorded utterance exhibited the same principle: to Mary and Joseph He said, "Wist ye not that I must be about *My Father's* business?" The Father's claims were ever supreme.

What is the force of the "two days"? Not only did the Lord Jesus remain where He then was, but the Holy Spirit has been careful to tell us how long He tarried. We must not skip over such a detail. There is nothing superfluous in Scripture. There is an important *dispensational* lesson to be learned here. Lazarus, dead, clearly typifies the nation of Israel; but ere the Lord goes to raise Him, He remained for a time "where He was". And *where* was that? 10:40 tells us: it was *"beyond* the Jordan", and therefore *outside* of Judea. But more, it was "the place where John at first baptized", and 1:28 tells us this was "Bethabara" which means "House of Passage". It was evidently situated at one of the fords across the river. Now Jordan speaks of death, the passing across it tells of resurrection, and the "House" hints at the Father's House on high. And it is *there* the Lord Jesus now remains, during the time of His absence, and it is from there He will come to restore Israel. Hosea prophesied, "After *two days* will He revive us; in the third day He will raise us up, and we shall live in His sight". In the light of 2 Peter 3:8 who can doubt this intimates that the Lord would be (in round figures) *away from Judea* for two thousand years—cf. the "two days" He was in Samaria (4:40), and note that the "Marriage" was on "the third day" (2:1). The same thing in principle, is hinted at in Mark 5. While on His way to restore to life the daughter of Jairus, the woman with the issue of blood is made whole by the touch of faith—this comes in parenthetically, as does the present Dispensation of grace to the Gentiles: *between* His past and His yet future dealings with Israel.

"Then after that saith He to His disciples, Let us go into Judea again" (v. 7). Notice the manner in which the Lord expressed Himself. He did not say, Let us go to Lazarus, or to Bethany. Why not? We believe the key to the Lord's thought here lies in the word "again": note the disciples' use of the same word in the following verse. The Lord was *trying* the disciples: "Let *us* go into Judea again". If we refer back to the closing verses of John 10 the force of this will be more evident. In 10:39 we read that His enemies in Judea "sought again to take Him". Judea, then, was now the place of opposition and danger. When, then, the Lord said, "Let us go into *Judea* again," it was obviously a word of *testing*. And how this illustrates a common principle in the Lord's way of dealing with *us!* It is not the smooth and easy-going path which He selects for us. When we are led by Him it is usually into the place of testing and trial, the place which the flesh ever shrinks from.

"His disciples say unto Him, Master, the Jews of late sought to stone Thee; and goest Thou thither again?" (v. 8). The Greek is more definite and specific than the A. V. rendering here. What the disciples said was, "Master, the Jews *just now* sought to stone Thee; and goest Thou thither again?" The attempt of His enemies to stone Christ was still *present* before the eyes of the disciples, though they had now been some little time at Bethabara. The disciples could see neither the need nor the prudence of such a step. How strange the Lord's ways seem to His short-sighted people; how incapable is our natural intelligence to understand them! And how this manifests the folly of believer's being guided by what men term 'common sense'. How much all of us need to heed constantly that word, "Trust in the Lord with all thine heart; and *lean not unto thine own understanding.* In all thy ways acknowledge Him, and He shall direct thy paths" (Prov. 3:5, 6). God often leads His own into places which are puzzling and perplexing and where we are quite unable to perceive His purpose and object. How often are the servants of Christ today called upon to fill positions from which they naturally shrink, and which they would never have chosen for themselves. Let us ever remember that the One who is our Lord and Master knows infinitely better than we the best road for us to travel.

"Jesus answered, Are there not twelve hours in the day? If any man walk in the day, He stumbleth not, because he seeth the light of this world" (v. 9). This verse has proved a puzzle to many, yet we believe its meaning can be definitely fixed. The first thing to bear in mind is that the Lord Jesus here was answering the timidity and unbelief of the disciples. They were apprehensive: to return to Judea, they supposed, was to invite certain death (cf. v. 16). Christ's immediate design, then, was to rebuke their fears. "Are there not twelve hours to the day?" That is, Has not the "day" a definitely *allotted* time? The span of the day is *measured,* and expires not before the number of hours by which *it is* measured have completed their course. The night comes not until the clock has ticked off each of the hours assigned to the day. The application of this well-known fact to the Lord's situation at that time is obvious.

A work had been given Him to do by the Father (Luke 2:49), and that work He *would* finish (John 17:4), and it was impossible that His enemies should take His life *before* its completion. In John 10:39 we are told that His enemies "sought again to take Him", but "He *went forth* out of their hand"—not simply "escaped" as in the A. V. What the Lord here assures His disciples is, that His death *could not* take place before the time *appointed* by the Father. The Lord had expressly affirmed the same thing on a previous occasion: "The same day there came certain of the Pharisees, saying unto Him, Get Thee out, and depart hence: for Herod will kill Thee". And what was His reply? This, "Go ye and tell that fox, Behold, I cast out demons, and I do cures today and tomorrow, and the third day I shall be perfected" (Luke 13:32)! "As a traveler has twelve hours for his day's journey, so also to Me there is a space of time appointed for My business" (Hess). What we have here in John 11:9 is parallel to His statement in 9:4—"I *must* work the works of Him that sent Me, while it is day"—"must" because the Father had decreed that He *should!*

This word of Christ to His disciples had more than a local significance: it enunciated a principle of general application. There is no need for us to enlarge upon it here, for we have already treated of it in our remarks upon 7:30. God has allotted to each man a time to do his life's work, and no calamity, no so-called accident can shorten it. Can man make the sun set one hour earlier? Neither can he shorten by an hour his life's day.

In the second part of the ninth verse the Lord announced another reason why it was impossible for men to shorten His life: "If any man walk in the day, he stumbleth not, because he seeth the light of this world". To walk in the day is to walk in the light of the sun, and such an one stumbleth not, for he is able to see the obstacles in his way and so circumvent them. Spiritually, this means, It is impossible that one should fall who is walking with God. To "walk in the day" signifies to walk in the presence of Him who is Light (1 John. 1:5), to walk in communion with Him, to walk in obedience to His will. None such *can* stumble, for *His* Word is a lamp unto our feet and a light unto our path. It is beautiful to see the application of this to the Lord Jesus in the present instance. When He got word that Lazarus was sick, He did not start at once for Bethany. Instead, He tarried where He was till *the Father's* time for Him to go had come. He *waited* for the "light" to guide Him—a true Israelite watching for the moving of the Cloud!! Christ ever walked in the full light of God's known will. How impossible then for Him to "stumble".

"For if a man walk in the night, he stumbleth, because there is no light in him" (v. 10). Very solemn and searching is this in its immediate application to the disciples. It was a *warning* against them refusing to accompany Him. Christ was the true Light, and if they continued not with Him they would be in the dark, and then "stumbling" was inevitable. The thought here is different from what we get at the close of 9:4. There Christ speaks of a "night" in which no man *could* "work"; here of a "night" in which no believer *should* "walk". The great lesson for us in these two verses is this, No fear of danger (or unpleasant consequences) must deter us from doing our duty. If the will of God clearly points in a certain direction our responsibility is to move in that direction unhesitatingly, and we may go with the double assurance that no power of the Enemy can shorten our life till the Divinely appointed task is done, and that such light will be vouchsafed us that no difficulties in the way will make us "stumble". What shall we say to such a blessed assurance? What but the words of the apostle Jude, "Now unto Him that is able *to keep you from falling,* and to present you faultless before the presence of His glory with exceeding joy, to the only wise God our Saviour, be glory and majesty, dominion and power, both now and ever. Amen" (vv. 24, 25).

The following questions are designed to help the interested student for our next lesson:—

1. Death is likened to "sleeping" v. 11: what thoughts are suggested by this figure?

2. Why did the disciples misunderstand Christ v. 13?

3. Why was Christ "glad" for the disciples' sake v. 15?

4. What is signified by the "four days" v. 17?

5. Why are we told of the nearness of Jerusalem to Bethany v. 18?

6. Why "Resurrection" before "Life" in v. 25?

7. What is the force of "shall never die" v. 26?

Arthur W. Pink.

GLEANINGS IN EXODUS.

13. Pharaoh's Compromises.

Our plan in this series of papers is not to furnish a verse by verse exposition of the book of Exodus, but rather to treat its contents topically, singling out the more important incidents and concentrating our attention upon them. The most serious disadvantage of this method is, that after we have followed out one topic to its conclusion, we are obliged to retrace our steps to begin a new one. Yet, perhaps, this is more than offset by the simplicity of the present plan and by the help afforded the reader to remember, substantially, the contents of this second book of Scripture. It is much easier to fix details in the mind when they are classified and conveniently grouped. Having gone over the ten plagues, we are now to contemplate the effect which they had upon Pharaoh. This will require us to go back to the earlier chapters.

In the course of the revelation which Jehovah made to Moses at the burning bush, we find Him saying, "And thou shalt come, thou and the elders of Israel, unto the king of Egypt, and ye shall say unto him, The Lord God of the Hebrews hath met with us; and now let us go, we beseech thee, three days' journey into the wilderness, that we may sacrifice to the Lord our God" (3:18). And while Moses was responding to the Divine call, the Lord said unto him again, "When thou goest to return into Egypt, see that thou do all these wonders before Pharaoh, which I have put in thine hand; but I will harden his heart, that he shall not let the people go. And thou shalt say unto Pharaoh, Thus saith the Lord, Israel is My son, even My firstborn; And I say unto thee, Let my son go, that he may serve Me" (4:21-23). In this last-quoted scripture the Lord furnished a reason *why* He desired His people to go into the wilderness to serve Him—"Israel is My son, My firstborn". Two truths were here enunciated. To Israel pertained "the adoption" (Rom. 9:4). This adoption was not individual (as with us), but as a nation. The use of this term denoted that Israel had been singled out as the objects of God's special favors—"I am a Father to Israel, and Ephraim is My *firstborn*" (Jer. 31:9). The title of "firstborn" speaks of dignity and excellency (see Gen. 49:3; Ps. 89:27). Israel will yet occupy the *chief* place among the nations, and be no more the "tail", but the "head". The place of the "firstborn", then, is that of honor and privilege. To the firstborn belonged a double portion.

The *terms* of this demand upon Pharaoh call for careful consideration. First, God had said that His people must go a three days' journey into the wilderness that they might *"sacrifice* to the Lord their God"

(3:18). Then the Lord added, "that he (His "firstborn") may *serve* Me" (4:23). Finally, when Moses and Aaron delivered their message unto Egypt's king, we find them, saying, "Thus saith the Lord God of Israel, Let My people go that they may *hold a feast unto Me* in the wilderness" (5:1). The *order* of these three statements is very significant. The thought of "sacrifice" comes first! This is required to avert God's judgment. Only as the sinner places *blood* between himself and the thrice holy God, can he stand in His august presence. Nothing but simple faith in an accomplished atonement enables the heart to be quiet before Him. "Without shedding of blood is no remission (Heb. 9:22). Following this, comes *service*. None can serve God acceptably till they are reconciled to Him. "Whose I am, *and* whom I serve" (Acts 27:23) is the Divine order. Following this, comes "the feast", which speaks of *fellowship* and *gladness*. But this cannot be until the will is broken and the "yoke" has been received—for *this* is what true "service" implies. These three things, in the same beautiful order are strikingly illustrated in connection with the Prodigal Son. First the wayward one was reconciled, then he took his proper place—"make me as one of Thy hired *servants";* and then came the feasting, over the "fatted calf".

When God's demand was first presented to Pharaoh, the king repulsed it in most haughty fashion; "And Pharaoh said, Who is the Lord, that I should obey His voice to let Israel go? I know not the Lord, neither will I let Israel go" (5:2). How the "enmity" of the carnal mind is evidenced here! How the awful depravity of the unregenerate heart was displayed! The natural man knows not the Lord, neither does he hear or heed His voice. And, too, can we not clearly discern here the Arch-rebel, the "god of this world", whom Pharaoh so strikingly adumbrated? Surely we can; and as we shall yet see, this is by no means the only trace of the Adversary's footprints which are to be detected on the face of this record.

The answer of God to this defiant refusal of Pharaoh was to visit his land with sore judgments. As pointed out in a previous paper, the first three plagues fell upon Israel as well as the Egyptians. But in the fourth God said, "I will sever in that day the land of Goshen, in which My people dwell, that no swarms of flies shall be there" (Ex. 8:22). This seems to have deeply impressed the king, for now, for the first time, he pays attention to Jehovah's demand.

1. "And Pharaoh called for Moses and Aaron and said, Go ye, sacrifice to your God in the land" (8:25). At first sight it would appear that at last Pharaoh was amenable to reason, recognizing the futility of fighting against the Almighty. But a closer glance at his words will show that he was far from being ready to comply with Jehovah's requests. God's command was couched in no uncertain terms. It called for the *complete separation* of His people unto Himself. Three things made this clear. First, "The God of the *Hebrews"* said Moses, "hath met with us" (5:3). This title always calls attention to the separate character of His people (cf. 9:1; 9:13; 10:3). Second, "Let us go *three days' journey"*. From Genesis 1 onwards, the third day speaks of resurrection. God would have His people completely delivered from the land of darkness and death. Third, "Let My people go, that they may hold a feast unto Me *in the wilderness"*, that is, apart from Egypt, which speaks of the world. Only one sacrifice was offered to the Lord in Egypt, namely, The Passover, and that was to deliver from death in Egypt; all others were reserved for the tabernacle in the wilderness.

The original response of Pharaoh was, "Wherefore do ye, Moses and Aaron, hinder the people from their work? Get you unto your burdens" (5:4). As another has said, This is "typical of the world's attitude towards spiritual service. The 'burdens of Egypt' are far more important than the service of the Lord, and even among the Lord's people Martha finds more imitators than Mary, so much of Egypt do we all carry with us".

But now, when the fifth plague fell upon Egypt, Pharaoh said, "Go ye, sacrifice to your God *in the land* (8:25). The Lord had said, A three days' journey into the wilderness. Pharaoh temporized. He grants Israel permission to worship *their* God; he does not insist that they bow down to *his;* but he suggests there is no need for them to be extreme: "sacrifice to your God *in the land"*.

This proffer was very subtile and well calculated to deceive one who was not acquainted with the character of God. "It might with great plausibility and apparent force, be argued: Is it not uncommonly liberal on the part of the king of Egypt to offer you toleration for your peculiar mode of worship? Is it not a great stretch of liberality to offer your religion a place on the public platform? Surely you can carry on your religion here as well as other people. There is room for all. Why this demand for separation? Why not take common ground with your neighbors? There is no need, surely, for such extreme narrowness." (C.H.M.)

Writing to the Corinthians, the apostle said, "We are not ignorant of his (Satan's) devices" (2 Cor. 2:11). Nor need any Christian be with the Word of Truth in his hands. One merciful reason why God has given to us the Scriptures is to inform us of Satan's wiles, uncover his subtility and expose his methods of attack. They are to be sought not only in those verses where he is referred to by name, but also in passages where he is only to be discovered working behind the scenes. Referring to some incidents in the history of Israel, the apostle declared, "Now all these things happened unto them for types; and they are written for our admonition" (1 Cor. 10:11). In the light of these scriptures, then, we are fully justified in regarding these compromises of Pharaoh as samples of the temptations which the Devil now brings to bear upon the people of God.

"Sacrifice to your God *in the land"*, that is, Egypt. And Egypt represents the *world.* But God's people have been delivered "from this present evil world" (Gal. 1:4). Said the Lord to His apostles, "Ye are not of this world, but I have chosen you out of the world". (John 15:19). And again, "They are not of the world, even as I am not of the world". (John 17:14). "The friendship of the world is enmity with God" (James 4:4), how then can believers worship God "in the land"? They cannot. God *must be* worshipped "in spirit and in truth" (John 4:24), and to worship God "in spirit" means to worship Him through the new nature. It means to take our place, by faith, *outside* of the world which crucified the Son of God! It means "going forth without the camp, bearing His reproach" (Heb. 13:13). It means being separated, in spirit, from all that is of the flesh.

This is just what Satan hates. He aims to get the believer to *mix* the world and the church. Alas! how well he has succeeded. Professing Christians have, for the most part, so assimilated their worship to Egyptian patterns, that instead of being hated by the world, they have taught the men of the world to join in with them. Thus far has the offense of the cross ceased. Of few indeed can it now be said, "the world *knoweth us not,* because it knew Him not (1 John 3:1).

Insidious was Pharaoh's proposal. Moses was not deceived by it. His answer was prompt and uncompromising: "And Moses said, It is not meet so to do; for we shall sacrifice the abomination of the Egyptians to the Lord our God: lo, shall we sacrifice the abomination of the Egyptians before their eyes and will they not stone us?" (8:26). It is *not meet* or proper for God's people to worship Him in the midst of His enemies: "Come out from among them, and be ye separate, saith the Lord" (2 Cor. 6:17) has ever been His demand. Moreover, to worship God "in the land" would be to "sacrifice the abomination of the Egyptians". Light is thrown upon this expression by what we are told in Genesis 46:34—"For every shepherd is an abomination unto the Egyptians". If every "shepherd" was an abomination to the Egyptians, certainly to present a *lamb* in sacrifice to God would be equally abominable to them. Nor have things changed since then. Christ crucified—which condemns the flesh, and makes manifest the total depravity of man—is still a "stumbling-block". Again; "shall we sacrifice the abomination of the Egyptians before their eyes, will they not stone us?" Press upon men the Divine need of the Cross—God's judgment of sin (Rom. 8:3); announce that by the Cross of Christ believers are crucified to the world (Gal. 6:14), and the world's enmity is at once aroused. Said the Lord Jesus, "If ye were of the world, the world would love his own; but because ye are not of the world, but I have chosen you out of the world, therefore the world hateth you. Remember the word that I said unto you, The servant is not greater than his Lord. If they have persecuted Me, they will also persecute you; if they have kept My saying, they will keep yours also" (John 15:19, 20).

One more reason Moses gave why he would not accept Pharaoh's proposal; "We will go three days' journey into the wilderness and sacrifice to the Lord our God, *as He shall command us*" (8:27). Here Moses reveals the real point of the Enemy's attack—it was the Word of God which he sought to neutralize. The Lord had said "in the wilderness". To have worshipped God "in the land" would, therefore, have been rank disobedience. When God has spoken, that settles the matter. No room is left for debating or reasoning. It is vain for us to discuss and dispute. Our duty is to submit. The *Word* itself must regulate our worship and service, as well as everything else. Human opinions, human traditions, custom, convenience, have nothing to do with it. Divine revelation is our only Court of Appeal.

2. His first compromise firmly repulsed, Pharaoh resorts to another, even more subtile. "And Pharaoh said, I will let you go, that you may sacrifice to the Lord your God in the wilderness". (8:28). Ah, that sounded promising. It appeared as though the king was now ready to yield. But mark well his closing and qualifying words—"*only* ye shall not go very far away". Pharaoh was ready to lengthen the chain, but it *was* still *a chain*. Complete liberty he was not ready to grant the Israelites. The point at issue was the *complete separation* of God's people from Egypt (the world), and *this* Pharaoh (representing Satan) contested to the bitter end.

"Only ye shall not go very far away" is one of the favorite and most successful of the Devil's temptations. Avoid extremes; do not be fanatical; be sane and sensible in your religious life; beware of becoming narrow-minded, are so many different ways of expressing the same thing. If you really must be a Christian, do not let it spoil your life. There is no need to cut loose from your old friends and associations. God does not want you to be long-faced and miserable. Why then abandon pleasures and recreations innocent in themselves? With such whisperings Satan beguiles many a soul. Young believers especially need to be on the guard here.

"Not very far away" is incompatible with the first law of the Christian life. The very purpose for which the Lord sent Moses to Pharaoh was to lead His people out of Egypt, and to bring them into the land of Canaan. And in this Moses was a type of the Lord Jesus. The Son of God left heaven for earth that He might take a people from earth to heaven.—bring them there first in spirit and heart, later in person. "Set your affection upon things above (Col. 3:1) is God's call to His children. "Holy (separated) brethren, partakers of the heavenly calling" (Heb. 3:1) is one of our many titles, and Heaven *is* "very far away" from the world! Separation from this world in our interests, our affections, our ways, is the first law of the Christian life. "Love not the world, neither the things which are in the world. If any man love the world the love of the Father is not in him" (1 John 2:15).

But how can the Christian be happy if he turns his back upon all that engaged his mind and heart in the unregenerate days? The answer is very simple: By being occupied with that which imparts a deeper, fuller, more lasting and satisfying joy than anything which this poor world has to offer. By being absorbed with the infinite perfections of Christ. By meditating upon the precious promises of the Word. By serving the Lord. By ministering to the needy. God did not propose to bring His people out of Egypt and give them nothing in return. He would lead them into the wilderness in order that they might "hold a *feast* unto the Lord". True, the "feast" (fellowship) is now "in the wilderness", but the wilderness is Heaven begun when we are delighting ourselves with Christ; in *His* presence there is "fulness of joy".

After all, Pharaoh was only dissembling. As soon as the plague of flies was removed, he "hardened his heart . . . . neither would he let the people go" (8:32). But he reckoned without God. Heavier judgments were now sent upon his land, which brought the king to his knees, yet not in genuine repentance and submission.

3. "And Moses and Aaron were brought again unto Pharaoh; and he said unto them, Go, serve the Lord your God; but *who* are they that shall go? And Moses said, We will go with our young and with our old, with our sons and with our daughters, with our flocks and with our herds will we go; for we must hold a feast unto the Lord. And he said unto them, Let the Lord be so with you, as I will let you go, and your little ones; look to it; for evil is before you. *Not so;* go now ye that are *men*, and serve the Lord; for that ye did desire. And they were driven out from Pharaoh's presence" (Ex. 10:8-11).

This was surely a cunning wile of Satan—professing willingness to let the men go if they would but leave their little ones behind in Egypt! Thereby he would have falsified the testimony of the Lord's redeemed ones, and retained a most powerful hold upon them through their natural affections. For how could they have done with Egypt as long as their children were there? Satan knew this, and hence the character of this temptation. And how many Christians there are who become entangled in this snare! Professing to be the Lord's, to have left Egypt, they allow their families to remain behind. As another has said, "Parents in the wilderness, and their children in Egypt—terrible anomaly! This would only have been a half deliverance; at once useless to Israel, and dishonoring to Israel's God. This could not be. If the children remained in Egypt, the parents could not possibly be said to have left it, inasmuch as their children were part of themselves. The most that could be said in such a case was, that in part they were serving Jehovah, and in part Pharaoh. But Jehovah could have no part with Pharaoh. He should either have all or nothing. This is a weighty principle for Christian parents. . . . . It is our happy privilege to count on God for our children and to bring them up in the nurture of the Lord! These admirable words should be deeply pondered in the presence of God. For nowhere does our testimony so manifestly break down as in our families. Godly parents, whose walk is blameless, are seduced into permitting their children practices which they would not for one moment allow in themselves, and thus to flood their houses with the sounds and sights of Egypt" (Ed. Dennett).

Be a Christian, says Satan, if you really must, but do not force religion upon the members of your family, and especially do not tease your children with it. They are too young to understand such things. Let them be happy now; time enough for serious concerns when they grow up. If you press spiritual things upon them to-day, you will nauseate them, and drive them to infidelity. Thus the Devil argues, and only too many professing Christians heed his siren voice. Family discipline is relaxed, the Scriptures are not given their proper place, the children are allowed to chose their own companions, and no real effort is made to bring them out of Egypt.

The training of children is a most solemn responsibility, and in these days of laxity and lawlessness, an increasingly serious problem. No little grace is needed to defy the general trend of our day, and to take a firm stand. But the Word of God is plain and pointed. "Train up a child in the way he *should* go" (Prov. 22:6). For this the parent needs to be daily cast upon God, seeking wisdom and strength each hour from Him. The "training" cannot start too early. Just as a wise gardener begins, while the trees are young and tender to train the branches along the wall, so should we begin with our children in their most tender years. God has declared, "Them that honor Me, I will honor" (1 Sam. 2:20). The first lines the Christian's children should be taught are not nursery rhymes and fairy tales, but short and appropriate verses of Scripture. The first truths which need to be pressed upon the little one are the claims that God has upon all His creatures—that He should be revered, loved, obeyed. That the child is a lost sinner, in need of a Saviour, cannot be taught him too early. If it be objected that he is too young to understand such things, the answer is, Salvation does not come to any through *understanding,* but—through FAITH, and faith cometh by hearing, and hearing by the Word of God. And to give the children God's Word is the binding and daily duty of every parent. You cannot lawfully transfer this duty to someone else. Not the Sunday-School teacher but *the parent* is the one whom *God* holds responsible to teach the children.

"While on this subject of training children, we would, in true brotherly love, offer a suggestion to all Christian parents, as to the immense importance of inculcating a spirit of *implicit obedience.* If we mistake not, there is a very widespread failure in this respect, for which we have to judge ourselves before God. Whether through a false tenderness, or indolence, we suffer our children to walk according to their own will and pleasure, and the strides which they make along this road are alarmingly rapid. They pass from stage to stage, with more than railroad speed, until at length they reach the terrible goal of despising their parents altogether, throwing their authority entirely overboard, and trampling beneath their feet the holy order of God, and turning the domestic circle into a scene of godless misrule and confusion.

"How dreadful this is we need not say, or how utterly opposed to the mind of God, as revealed in His Holy Word. But have we not ourselves to blame for it? God has put into the parent's hands the reins of government and the rod of authority; but if parents through indolence suffer the reins to drop from their hands, and if through false tenderness or moral weakness, the rod of authority is not applied, need we marvel if the children grow up in utter lawlessness? How could it be otherwise? Children are, as a rule, very much what we make them. If they are *made* to be obedient, they *will* be so; and if they are allowed to have their own way, the result will be accordingly" (C.H.M.)

Here, then, in part at least, is what is signified by the believer leaving his children behind in Egypt. It is permitting them to have their own way. It is allowing them to be "conformed to this world". It is bringing them up without the fear of God upon them. It is neglecting their *soul's* interests. It is ignoring the command of God to "bring them up in the nurture and admonition of the Lord" (Eph. 6:4). It is failure to follow in the steps of "our father Abraham," of whom the Lord said. "For I know him, that he will command his children, and his household after him, and they shall keep the way of the Lord" (Gen. 18:19). The standard which God sets before Christian parents now is certainly not a lower one than what He placed before Israel of old, and to them He said, "And these words, which I command thee this day, shall be in thine heart; And thou shalt teach them diligently unto thy children, and shalt talk of them when thou sittest in thy house, and when thou walkest by the way, and when thou liest down, and when thou riseth up" (Deut. 6:6, 7). May Divine grace be earnestly sought and freely granted those of our readers who are fathers and mothers to enable them to turn a deaf ear to Satan who pleads that the little ones may be left behind in Egypt!

4. "And Pharaoh called unto Moses, and said, Go ye, serve the Lord; only let your flocks and your herds be stayed" (Ex. 10:24). "With what perseverance did Satan dispute every inch of Israel's way out of the land of Egypt! He first sought to keep them *in* the land, then to keep them *near* the land, next, to keep *part* of themselves in the land, and finally, when he could not succeed in any of these three, he sought to send them forth without any ability to serve the Lord. If he could not keep the servants, he would seek to keep their ability to serve, which would answer much the same end. If he could not induce them to sacrifice in the land, he would send them out of the land without sacrifices"! (C.H.M.)

"And Pharaoh called unto Moses and said, Go ye, serve the Lord, *only* let your flocks and your herds be stayed". This was Pharaoh's last compromise. Mark the word "only" again! The distraction of a divided heart, the vain effort to serve two masters, the miserable attempt to make the best of both worlds are suggested here. Demas was caught in this snare (II Tim. 4:10); so also were Ananias and Sapphira. The danger is very real. Where our treasure is, there will our hearts be also (Matt. 6:21). If our possessions remain in Egypt, so will our affections.

The application of the spiritual principle contained in this fourth compromise is not hard to discover. The flocks and herds of this pastoral people constituted the principle part of what they owned down here. They speak then of our earthly possessions. The issue raised is whether or not God has a title to all that we have. In the light of the Word the issue is decisively settled. Nothing that we have is really ours: all is committed to us as *stewards.* And it is right here that so many of us fail. "Give yourselves to God if you must; but do not consecrate your possessions to His service" is the Devil's final plea. And multitudes of professing Christians heed it. Look at the wealth of those who bear the name of Christ. How it has piled up! And where is it all? Surely in Egypt! How much of it is held as a sacred trust for Christ?. Is not the greater part of it used to gratify self! Of old, God charged His people with *robbing* Him of His tithes and offerings (Mal. 3:8). And the same charge can justly be laid against most of us to-day.

The answer made by Moses, to this temporizing of Pharaoh is very striking: "And Moses said, Thou must give us also sacrifices and burnt offerings, that we may sacrifice unto the Lord our God. Our cattle also shall go with us; there shall not an hoof be left behind; for thereof must we take to serve the Lord our God; and we know not with what we must serve the Lord until we come thither" (10:25, 26). Observe two things; "Not an hoof" must be left behind. The spiritual application of this is far reaching. We may place our money at the Lord's disposal but reserve our time for ourselves. We may be ready to pray but not to labor; or labor and not pray. "Not an hoof" means, that all that I have and am is held at the disposal of the Lord. Finally, it is striking to observe that Israel would not know the full Divine claims upon their responsibility until they reached the wilderness. The mind of God could not be discerned so long as they remained in Egypt!

We might easily have enlarged upon these compromises of Pharaoh at much greater length, but sufficient has been said, we trust, to put each Christian reader upon his guard against the specious temptations which the great Enemy of souls constantly brings to bear upon us. Let us faithfully recognize the fulness of God's claims upon us, and then seek daily grace to walk worthy of the vocation wherewith we have been called.

Arthur W. Pink.

TRUTH AND ERROR, or,

Letters to a Friend, by H. Bonar.

1 Introduction.

These letters are little more than fragments. They do not aim at a complete statement of the truth, or a systematic arrangement of it. It is only a few important points that they touch. To have extended them and embraced a wider range of doctrine would not have suited my design. I wished to warn you against some of the prevailing errors of the time, lest ye, being "led away from your steadfastness," should follow after the "diverse and strange doctrines" of these last days. Hence it was necessary to dwell upon those errors which have been most prominently advanced, and to open up those truths which have been most perverted and denied.

My appeal is to the Word of God. What are the reasonings, or opinions, or inferences of men? What is the chaff to the wheat? saith the Lord. Let the Bible decide each question. It is for this end that I have appended to each letter a selection of passages at length.

The real question of the present day is just this,—*Is man a totally and thoroughly depraved being by nature?*—Is he ruined, helpless, and blind, dead in trespasses and sins? Many other questions have arisen, but this is the centre one. According to the views we entertain regarding this, will be our views upon other points. It is upon the truth of this doctrine that the whole Bible proceeds. And hence I would at the outset warn you strongly against any attempt to modify, or abate, or dilute the statements of Scripture on this point.

Man being thoroughly depraved in nature, is it possible, I ask, to save him without a special and direct intervention of the Father, Son and Spirit, in his behalf? In other words, can he be saved in any way which does not involve personal election by the Father, particular redemption by the Son, and direct, immediate, overcoming operation of the Holy Spirit? Or, putting the question in another form, and using the language of science—given a totally depraved being, is it possible to save that being by any plan which makes the *previous* concurrence of his own will an indispensable preliminary, or which makes it necessary that he should take the first step in the matter of return to God? If you place the different errors of the day before you in this light, you will find that they all more or less directly deny or encroach upon the doctrine of man's original and actual depravity.

You will find, also, that the objections urged against God's sovereignty and man's helplessness, are just different manifestations of human pride,—the pride into which Satan tempted Adam, "Ye shall be as gods," and into which all his offspring have fallen along with him. Man will not consent to be nothing, that God alone may be ALL. And it is curious to observe that the objections urged against these truths are not passages of Scripture, but human reasonings—man's inferences and opinions. Take, as a specimen, the doctrine of God's sovereignty. We have many passages broadly declaring this, but not one setting forth the opposite. How, then, do men contrive to deny this truth? They begin to reason and speculate upon it; and by means of certain *inferences* of their own, try to make it appear inconsistent with other doctrines to which *they* attach great importance. They say, "Does not God invite the sinner to come to Christ, does He not tell us that He has no pleasure in the death of the wicked, but rather that he should turn and live: now how can this be true, if He is absolutely sovereign in His proceedings? We cannot reconcile these things together, therefore we must *explain away* the passages which assert God's sovereignty and electing will. They cannot be understood in their *plain* and *literal* sense: we must devise some other meaning for them which will accord with our ideas of God's love". Thus, pride of intellect, confidence in human reason, eagerness to establish one favorite doctrine and to make everything bend to it, supersede and overturn the Word of God. Scripture is not implicitly relied upon, unless borne out by the systems or the syllogisms of reason and the conclusions of man's poor fallen intellect.

Cleave, then, to the Word of God. Distrust your own heart, lean not to your own understanding,—but receive with meekness the ingrafted word. "The world through wisdom knew not God:" and we must stoop to "become fools, that we may be wise." "The natural man receiveth not the things of the Spirit of God; for they are foolishness unto him, neither can he know them, for they are spiritually discerned".

These letters by Dr. Bonar were published in 1857, and so far as we are aware have never been reprinted. Their author was much used of God in his day, and has memorialized himself in many precious hymns as well as a number of helpful books. The messages of these Letters are much needed Today. They show the natural heart has been the same in every age—opposed to God.

A. W. P.

CRUCIFIED AND YET ALIVE.

In the sixth chapter of the Epistle to the Romans we find the Apostle giving this exhortation to Christians: "Reckon ye also yourselves to be dead indeed unto sin, but alive unto God through Jesus Christ our Lord." (v. 11). It would at once be a more literal rendering, and would better bring out the meaning of the Apostle, if, instead of *through* Jesus Christ, we were to read *in* Jesus Christ; for the blessings he is speaking of do not merely come to us *through* another. There is a more intimate relation than that between believers and the Lord. The blessings that we have are found *in* Christ. There is an *absolute oneness* of our souls with Him.

What we are exhorted to, then, is in effect this: That *in* Jesus Christ our Lord we reckon ourselves first as "dead unto sin". And the question naturally arises, What are we to understand by this? In what sense is it that believers may regard themselves as "dead unto sin"?

Is it, we ask in the first place, by being dead unto *the power* of sin? Are Christians so "dead unto sin" that they are absolutely *sinless?* so that temptation always assails them entirely in vain, meeting with no response at all in them? In the victory that they gain, is there no conflict between duty and wrong desire? Does the way of right ever become so easy that they can walk in it without effort, and that they never, even in the least degree, stray from it? Is there anywhere, beneath the skies, the attaining of that perfectness which man had while yet unfallen? Evidently not. An appeal to the consciousness of every believer will satisfy him that there is not. No one is absolutely and entirely dead to the *power* of sin, so that even in the inmost recesses of his heart there is no trace of evil; so that he can say: From open transgressions and from secret faults alike I am free! In every character there is still some measure of defilement.

St. Paul undoubtedly attained as much as any mere man ever yet attained in holiness. But he found it out of his power to render unto God a service absolutely unmixed with evil. With intensity of longing he desired to do so; but he found an opposing force at work, thwarting him in his endeavors. He longed for the attainment of perfect righteousness; but, when he fain would reach it, found himself brought into captivity to the law of sin which was in his members. Man, before he fell, was, and might have continued to be, perfectly sinless. But since then, there has been but *One* perfect life on earth; but *One* who has been able to live sinlessly.

In the believer there are, as it were, *two* men. He is, in a certain sense, *double;* made up of the *old* man and the *new*. And these two are, and always will remain contrary the one to the other. They are irreconcilable. The *flesh* and the *spirit* are, and must be, at perpetual enmity. The one cannot be subject to the law of God, and would not, if it could. The other cannot be otherwise than subject to it. Once the believer, before faith came, was only *flesh*. There was no conflict in him. He was unborn of the Spirit. But when he was born again, then that which was born of the Spirit was *spirit;* and henceforth there was hostility between the *flesh*—his *former* self, and the *spirit,* his *new* self. These two, co-existing in one body, cannot harmonize. They can only keep up a conflict, which shall last till one or the other is vanquished. Which it shall be that shall finally have the victory, happily, there can be no doubt. The *new* man is the one who is made more than conqueror. But the conflict lasts; the flesh is not completely put down, until in death we rest in sure and certain hope of the time when the new man, created in us, shall dwell, not in flesh and blood, but in a body like Christ's glorious body.

As long, then, as there is this conflict going on between *flesh* and *spirit,* between the *old* man and the *new creation,* so long we cannot be said to be dead to the *power* of sin. As a matter of consciousness, we are made sensible of its depraving influence upon us. The *spirit* drawing us one way, *upward* we feel the flesh dragging us the other way, *downward.* And sometimes, in the sharpness of the struggle, between what we fain *would do,* and what through the weakness of our mortal nature, we yet do *not do,* we cannot help crying out with the apostle: "O, wretched man that I am!"

But, you ask, perhaps, Is there not danger in thus maintaining that man is of necessity sinful? Do you not thereby weaken in him the sense of his responsibility, and give him occasion to say that he is not accountable for the sin which, being a part of his very nature, he therefore cannot help? Are not the flood-gates open for evil-living, when men are taught that they *cannot* become entirely dead to the *power* of sin; but that they must continue to be imperfect, *even in death,* making confession of sin, and offering prayer for mercy? We answer confidently, *Not at all.* Because a person may not reach absolute perfectness, he is not thereby freed from the obligation of reaching the highest point he may. The finest painter who ever lived has probably never supposed that in any one of the pieces of workmanship which have made his name famous, he has exhausted his powers, and done the very best he is capable of doing. He expects, in his future works to make some gain upon his former ones; but does not expect *ever* to reach the very highest point of which his art is capable. Yet is he not deterred from effort, because he does not think to carry his art to that point that none can go beyond it. There is enough for him to strive for, and to call out all his energies, too, short of that. He need only ask to be making continual progress. Just so is it with the Christian life. The obligation to effort is not taken away, and sin is not licensed, because we shall never, in this life outgrow our sinful condition. If we may not ever be *completely dead* to the power of sin, we may be *less* under its power than we are today. And this diminution of evil is surely a worthy object of endeavor.

And, besides this, there is a just distinction to be made between sin as a *principle,* and sin as a *willful, overt* act. Sin, as a *principle,* is a part of my very nature. I was conceived and born in it. And from this, so long as I am in the flesh, I cannot be freed entirely. I shall always, more or less, feel the workings of it. But from sin as a *willful, overt* act, I may be freed. By the grace given unto me I need not yield to that, but may increasingly overcome it. There is help provided for me in the Gospel, whereby I may gain the victory over it I *need* not, I *shall* not, if I am truly Christ's, be under its sway.

Sin, as a principle in me, as a part of my natural constitution, inherited as my sad birthright, will keep my actions from rising to that state of perfectness in which they can endure the severity of God's judgment. It will prevent them from having the moral character that the action of unsinning Adam, or the doings of the sinless Jesus, had. It will make the best of them fall below God's standard of perfectness. And yet, while this is the effect of sin dwelling in me as a *principle,* as a part of my self, I shall more and more be kept from sin in *the overt act;* the *new man* in me will at least succeed in checking the open forms of evil into which the old corrupt nature would gladly go.

And this distinction between sin as an *inherent poisoning principle* and sin as a *deliberate action,* explains how it is that Christians can, and do, make such humble confession of their own unworthiness in the sight and in the estimate of God; while, at the same time, they would repel the charge of living in the indulgence of any known sin. It is sometimes spoken of as an inconsistency that men make the confessions they do in prayer, when they would turn with indignant denial upon any one who should accuse them of theft, or intemperance, or falsehood, or impurity, or any other acknowledged advise. But in reality, there is no inconsistancy. In the one case, I am judging myself by the standard of God's law, which demands *perfectness* in all that I do; and judged thus, I recognise myself as coming infinitely short of this perfect standard; my best doings are defective, and do not meet its high requirements; and I therefore humble myself before God on account of my deficiencies. In the other case, I know whereof I speak, when I claim my innocence of willful acts of sin, which, if I were committing, I should show myself unworthy of the christian name, without the christian character. The two things are quite incompatible. The christian claims freedom from willful, habitual acts of sin; and yet, in the sight of God, he is a miserable sinner, because sin is *in his nature,* defiling all that he does. Nothing that he does is so done that it would be acceptable, to God, were it not perfumed with the fragrance of the Blessed Name of the Lord Jesus.

From all that has thus been said concerning the sin that dwelleth in us, keeping us from rendering a *perfect* service, (although in Jesus Christ believers render an *accepted* service,) it will perhaps, be evident that when the Apostle speaks of us as "dead unto sin", he does not mean that we are dead unto the *power* of sin. Our own consciousness teaches us that sin is not thus dead in us; we know too well that it is yet alive. We are, then,. brought back again to the question, How are believers *"Dead unto sin"?*

We find the answer in the very words of the Apostle: Believers are "dead unto sin" *in* Jesus Christ our Lord, and only *in Him.* They are dead, not unto the *present power* of sin, but unto the *guilt* and *condemnation* of sin. *Judicially,* in the courts of God's government, we are "dead unto sin", as having ourselves in Christ actually met the death due to sin.

It is difficult fully to unfold the blessed meaning of these words: *"In* Jesus Christ our Lord". In them is treasured up all the richness of the grace of the Gospel. There are expressed that perfect *oneness* which there is between Christ and His people. The mystery of it we cannot comprehend. We only know that Christ has so made us *one with Him,* that what *He* did was as if *we* ourselves had done it. We were so *in Him* that *His* acts were as *our* acts, the full merit and blessing of them accruing to us as really as if they had been actually our own. So that *Christ's* death, since we were *in Him,* was, in effect, *our* death. We, *in Him* upon the Cross, bore the wages of sin. *His* bearing of the penalty there, was *our* bearing of the penalty. We could not more perfectly have borne it had we suffered it ourselves. The broken law of God has no further claim to make on those who believe. In the Person of Another they have met all its claims. And when the law now threatens death, we can claim exemption from its curse by pointing to our Surety, in whom we have already died.

It is thus, then, by our oneness with Christ in His death, that we have become "dead unto sin". We are not dead unto *the present power* of it, for the law of sin is still in our members; but we are dead unto *the guilt* of it. We are brought out from under *its condemning power.* And surely, there is blessing in knowing ourselves thus "dead unto sin"; that its condemning power over us is entirely and forever gone. It is stilling to the conscience as nothing else is; it brings a rest to the heart which nothing else can give—thus to look beyond our guilty selves, and see that when One died for all, that all died in Him and that there is therefore now *no condemnation* to them that are in Christ Jesus.

> No condemnation, O my soul!
> 'Tis God that speaks the word.
> Perfect in comeliness thou art
> In Christ, thy glorious Lord.

But evidently, a Saviour who was only crucified, dead, and buried, would not profit us. If we were in Christ only in His death, we should ourselves be left in death. His precious death and burial would have been in vain, had not His glorious resurrection followed. We needed to be joined to the Lord not alone in *death,* but as well in *resurrection.* And so the exhortation of the Apostle is, that believers should regard themselves not only as "dead unto sin" in Christ, but also, as in Him, *"alive unto God".* The Saviour, having first died under sin, came up from the grave alive unto God. The sin that had been *on Him* was on Him no more after His rising from the dead. Fully atoned for by His death, it was left behind Him in the grave. Death could have no more dominion over Him. He was now alive forever more.

Now, as Christ's *death* was ours, so is His *resurrection* also ours. As we were in Him in the *one,* so are we also in Him in the *other.* As He died for our sins, so did He also rise again for our justification. And we are now "alive unto God in Jesus Christ our Lord". We are looked upon by God as being in Christ Jesus. He sees us only as clothed upon with Christ. We are in the sight of God, as is the risen Son of God Himself, perfectly justified, spotlessly righteous. As Christ came up from the grave, leaving behind there every trace and vestige of that sin which had been on Him, and was owned as God's righteous Servant, so are we, *in the risen Christ,* entirely without sin, righteous in our Righteous Advocate. All our transgressions are buried with Jesus in His tomb, no more to be remembered against us. We cannot now come into condemnation. We have in Christ passed from death unto life. And being now "alive unto God", the life that we have is *eternal* life; and those blessed words of promise are ours, (and are they not a comfort to us in looking forward to the time of our departure?) "He that believeth in Me *though he were dead,* yet shall he live; and whoso liveth and believeth in Me *shall never die".* These, then, are our high privileges "in Jesus Christ our Lord". In Him we are "dead unto sin and alive unto God".

Do you ask, How shall I know myself to be so? This is what thousands are asking in perplexity; and, for want of a right answer, their souls are not at peace. They are looking for certain evidences of grace within themselves, which they suppose to be necessary to give them assurance of their personal acceptance. A heartier repentance, a stronger faith, a more lively hope, better success in the conflict with evil, these, or some other like things, you are looking for in yourself before you will let yourself be persuaded of your forgiveness and adoption. Self-examination, too, as *generally conducted,* leads to *darkness* in the Christian life, instead of *light.* Many are shut out from all comfort, because they are morbidly prying into their spiritual exercises, and are, as they always must be, dissatisfied with them. They do not find, as the result of their self-examination, what they think they ought to find, and so they are cast down. Did any soul, indeed, ever find *in itself* any thing to inspire confidence? Is not the effect of self-knowledge always humbling?—always depressing?

A better way than this the Apostle proposes. He does not bid us look to *ourselves,* but to *Christ.* The remedy that He offers is not the always disheartening one of looking *inwardly,* and trying to find something *within us* that may assure of acceptance. He bids us look *unto Jesus*—away from self—away from *all* but that dying, risen, ascended, interceding Lord, who, now before the Throne presents for us the offering of His own most precious blood. Fixing our eyes on Him, the living Christ, He bids us, *"Reckon ye also yourselves* to be dead indeed unto sin, but alive unto God in Jesus Christ our Lord"; that is, fully believe yourselves to be—act upon it as if you actually were *dead* unto the condemning power of sin—*alive* in the righteousness of God. In this there is no presumption. The testimony of God concerning men is, that when they trust—*nothing else but trust*—in the Saviour, then they are in His sight *"complete"* in Christ Jesus. You are not, then, to perplex yourself with ten thousand things, or to work yourself up to a morbid state of feeling. Receiving the testimony of God that, by Christ, all who believe are justified from all things, in childlike reliance on His Word, you are to *reckon yourself* "dead indeed unto sin, and alive unto God"; to believe yourself to be so, *just because God says you are so.* He tells you that there is no condemnation for you. Your own faithless heart says, "This cannot be so; there *must* be condemnation for one so unworthy as I!" Refuse to listen to what your own heart says and rest firmly on *the sure Word of God.* Reckon of yourself just what He bids you reckon of yourself. Count yourself to be just what He says you are: "dead indeed unto sin, and alive unto God in Jesus Christ our Lord". You will never be at rest until you come to trust thus simply in the promise of God. Your own *feelings,* your own *doings,* with neither the one nor the other will you ever be fully satisfied. They will always fall below the standard which they ought to reach. And so, if you rely on them, they will be always casting a doubt on your path. What you want is, *just as you are,* waiting for nothing whatever, to come to Jesus Christ, whom God hath set forth to be a propitiation, declaring His righteousness for the remission of sins, and to *reckon yourself* dead indeed unto sin, but alive unto God in Christ. *Simply in virtue of your connection with Christ by faith,* your transgression has been forgiven, your sin covered, and you accepted in the Beloved.

The firm grasp of this truth of our oneness with Christ in death and resurrection, will inevitably lead to holiness of living. They who are by faith entering into this their high privilege—whom in their inmost hearts, do as God bids them do, reckon themselves "dead indeed unto sin, and alive unto God"—not doubting at all the complete taking away of their guilt, but calmly sure of their acceptance—these are the persons who will be followers of God as dear children. The prisoner cannot be moved to happy future effort till assured of full forgiveness for the past. The child who has offended wants, before he can return to cheerful obedience, the knowledge of his restoration to your favor. It will be toilsome service to him if he is to obey in order to gain your favor. He longs, above all things, before he begins his service, for the knowledge that you have forgiven all. Then his heart is light. And so *we,* as the constraining power of *our* service, want a happy resting in the love of Christ. We want the *assurance* of our reconciliation; the *certaintly* of being no longer under condemnation; and then, having received from our merciful Lord pardon and peace, cleansed from all our sins, we shall serve Him with a quiet mind; serve Him gladly and faithfully, *because we have found* favor and pardon.

Waymarks in the Wilderness.

DAVID'S SHEEP.

It was a notable day in Bethlehem when Samuel the prophet journeyed there. All the people turned out to meet him, and Jesse's sons amongst them. Seven of them came, and only David stayed behind at his work.

Eliab, the firstborn, looked a likely man, but God refused him. Why? *The Lord had looked on his heart.* What a solemn announcement! In the narrow circle of home interests he failed to manifest the spirit becoming an elder brother (1 Samuel 17:28), and when the time came that he might have been offered Israel's crown he was set aside.

No doubt it seemed hard to Eliab that he should lose the kingdom because he could not keep his temper; but the Lord refused him. How can he govern others who fails in self-control? But, mark, it is not that his efforts at right living had been unsuccessful. He was wrong at heart. The glimpse we get at his character reveals a harsh, overbearing man, who "hath no rule over his own spirit".

One reason only accounts for Jehovah's preference—"the Lord looketh on the heart". Have you realized, dear reader, that the eternal God was concerning Himself about the hopes and desires of a youth in his teens! What a world of thought the acknowledgement suggests. Does He the same today? How momentous!

Reader, What are your day-dreams like? Many of us would hide our faces with shame if the pictures of the imagination were painted on the wall. What do you understand by "a castle in the air"? Let me tell you. It is a mental picture of a scene in which a huge capital I is to the front, and other persons and circumstances are arranged to make an effective background. The details infinitely varied. The character always the same. God looks on the heart.

What then had He found in David's heart? Psalm 132 will tell us. Listen!

"He sware unto the Lord, and vowed unto the mighty God of Jacob; surely I will not come into the tabernacle of my house, nor go up into my bed; I will not give sleep to mine eyes, or slumber to mine eyelids, until I find out a place for the Lord, an habitation for the mighty God of Jacob. *Lo, we heard of it at Ephratah; we found it in the fields of the wood.* We will go into His tabernacles; we will worship at His footstool. . . the Lord hath chosen Zion; He hath desired it for His habitation. This is *My* rest forever: here will I dwell: for I have desired it."

This was the secret of Jehovah's choice. By the sheepfold there, He could say, I see a youth whose desires are for My glory, whose sympathies are in step with My purposes, and who makes My interests his own. And the Lord said, "Arise, anoint him: for *this is he.*"

While David was busy with his work God's call came to him. Such an event was not without its precedent, and similar cases have occurred since. The incident has its lessons for ourselves. May we heed it.

We meet the sheep again in I Sam. 17:15, and this passing reference is not without instruction. "David went and returned from Saul to feed his father's sheep at Bethlehem." From the attractions of the court he returns to his appointed work, nor had the influences of an exalted position spoiled him for his humbler service.

It may be, dear reader, the Lord has allowed you to feed and care for some of His sheep down here, and, if so, I would say, Take heed unto the ministry that you have received of the Lord, that you fulfil it. There may be great attractions elsewhere, but do you go back to those sheep till your service among them is completed. You have not, like the apostle Paul, the care of all the churches, but surely you have a part of the cares of one. Would the saints suffer any loss if you were taken away from amongst them?

We are not told if these were black-sheep or white—prone to wander, or fond of the fold. One word only describes them—they were his *father's* sheep. That word measured their value, and David's care. It made him serve as a son, and not as a hireling. We may suppose that Jesse chose and purchased a little flock, and this consideration would give them an importance in David's eyes which their individual characteristics might not have claimed.

Eliab could speak in tones of contempt of "those few sheep in the wilderness," and unjustly taunt his brother with neglecting them (compare vv. 20 and 28); but David's estimate of worth was not based on numbers, and in a day of small things he was faithful in that which was least.

The last mention of the sheep is in verses 33-37:—

"And Saul said unto David, Thou art not able to go against this Philistine to fight with him: for thou art but a youth, and he a man of war from his youth. "And David said unto Saul, *Thy servant kept his father's sheep,* and there came a lion, and a bear, and took a lamb out of the flock: and I went after him, and smote him, and delivered it out of his mouth: and when he rose against me, I caught him by his beard, and smote him, and slew him. . . . David said, moreover, the Lord that delivered me out of the paw of the lion, and out of the paw of the bear, He will deliver me out of the hand of this Philistine".

Perhaps some of Saul's captains smiled at the youth's simplicity. His ideas did not seem to reach beyond the incidents of his shepherd life, and yet he wanted to accept the challenge of one who defied the armies of the living God!

Ah! but I like the way David turns to those sheep. In the unnoticed, but not uneventful, course of his daily life he had so proved God, that, when the supreme moment of his history came, he went forward to victory in the confidence of faith, with the five smooth stones of human weakness, and in the name of the Lord of hosts.

Now, my reader, has the daily task seemed a burden to you? Have those hours at the bench or the desk seemed time lost spiritually? Have you thought that God wills to occupy a third of your days to no profit beyond the interests of time? Then read again the lesson of David's sheep. Let its meaning sink deep into your soul, and influence every detail of your pathway. Understand that God makes no mistakes in planning out the time-sheet of your life, and if He keep you eight hours daily at the desk, it is because He can be served in no other way.

I cannot say what He would teach you by the discipline of work, or for what more public service He may be fitting you; but if you have not found *God your resource* in the occupations and trials of everyday life, you have failed to learn the lesson of David's sheep. *Simple Testimony.*

THIRD LIST OF BOOKS FROM THE EDITOR'S LIBRARY:

Dr. John Owen's Complete Theological Works: 16 Vols., averaging 500 pp. The Prince of the Puritans 1650 A. D. Mainly expository: rare and valuable.	$8:00
Dr. T. Goodwin's Complete Theological Works: 12 Vols, Aver. 500 pp. They contain many most excellent expositions of Scripture. 1640 A. D.	$6:00
The Attributes of God: 2 Vols. Charnock: mainly expository 1660 A. D.	2:00
Exposition of 1st. Peter: Dr. Leighton: 1748: 2 small vols, ½ leather.	2:00
Theology by Dr. J. Gill: Spurgeon's predecessor: 1800: rare and good.	0:90
Newberry Bible: New: best binding: *slightly* shelf-worn.	5:00
Bible: English Revised: cloth covers.	1:50
N. T. by Weymouth: cloth covers: soiled	0:60
Expos. of John's Gospel: Dr. Dods: 2 Vols.	1:25
do. do. do. : Dr. G. Brown: 2 Vols.	1:50
do. do. do. : Bishop Ryle: 2 Vols.	1:50
do. do. do. : Mr. C. E. Stewart: 1 Vol.	0:90
do. do. do. : Mal. Taylor: excellent	0:75
Expos. of Hebrews: J. Rotherham: helpful, almost new.	0:90
do. do. : W. Lincoln: do. do. do.	0:50
do. do. : Dr. Chadwick: do. do. do.	0:75
do. do. : Dr. Junkin: rare, worn.	0:90
God's Pilgrims (on Hebs.): P. Mauro: 1st. edition.	0:60
do. do. do. : P. Mauro: Revised edition.	0:75
After This: P. Mauro.	0:60
God's Present Kingdom: P. Mauro.	0:60
Sovereignty of God: 1st edition: Arthur W. Pink.	1:00
Handbook to the Controversy with Rome: New: 2 Vols: 400 pp. each.	1:50
Essay on Pantheism: New: 400 pp.	0:50
Alexander on Isaiah: 2 Vols. 1:00 Alexander on the Psalms: 2 Vols.	1:00
Isaac: W. Kelly: new: 0:40: Jacob: W. Kelly: new.	0:40
In the Beginning: (Gen. 1) W. Kelly: new.	0:60
Ellicott's Commentaries: (Gals to Titus) 2 Vols.	1:50
Newton on the Prophecies: 1754: 700 pp.: half leather.	1:50
The Epistles of Paul: Findley.	0:60
Missions in the Plan of the Ages: Dr. Calver.	0:60
The Ministry of the Spirit: Dr. A. J. Gordon.	0:75
The Twofold Life: Dr. A. J. Gordon.	0:75
Life of Christ: Dr. Stalker.	0:30
Typical Foreshadowings in Genesis: W. Lincoln:	0:60
I am Coming: J. H. Brooks: good:	0:60
Abundant Grace: W. P. Mackay—author of "Grace and Truth"	0:60
The Seeking Saviour do. do. do.	0:60
Vagaries and Verities: Dr. W. B. Riley: Helpful	0:60
Moses the Lawgiver: W. M. Taylor	0:75
Magee on the Atonement: (1813) half leather:	1:00
The Brides of Scripture: J. Denhem Smith	0:75
The Gospel in Hosea: do. do.	0:75
Positive preaching and the Modern mind: Forsyth	0:35
Paley's Philosophy:	0:50
Universalism False:	0:25
Preparation and Delivery of Sermons: Broadus.	0.90
The Acts of the Apostles: S. Griffith Thomas.	0:40
50 Hymn Books: "Awakening Songs" 250 selections: stiff paper.	4:00
100 copies "Studies in the Scriptures" 1922, 1923, 1924 odd issues.	4.00

Prices on the above *does not* include postage. When ordering please *do not* enclose payment: as each order is filled, a bill will follow, D. V. We have only one copy of each of the above: first come, first served! No credit can be given.

VOL. IV FEBRUARY, 1925 NO. 2

STUDIES in the SCRIPTURES

"Search the Scriptures" John 5:39.

Arthur W. Pink, Publisher & Editor,
R. F. D. 9, York, Pa.

Price: 10 cents per copy; $1.00 per year. Foreign $1.00 per year.

SPIRITUAL IGNORANCE.

"And if any man think that he knoweth anything he knoweth nothing yet as he ought to know" (1 Cor. 8:2).

How *sweeping* is this!. "If any man", be he young or old in the faith; be he a teacher or a learner; be he skilled in the Word of righteousness or unskilled. "If any man think that he *knoweth anything,* he knoweth *nothing* yet as he ought to know". No matter what the subject, no matter which the aspect of truth, whether it be evangelical, doctrinal, prophetic, or practical; no matter how elementary the theme, there are depths to it which he has not fathomed, there are phases of it he has not yet learned.

How *humbling* is this! No matter what a man may boast nor what his admirers may conclude the fact is that the wisest Christian "knoweth *nothing* yet as he ought to know". Verily, no uninspired mind composed this sentence!. It is far too humiliating to pride of intellect, yea, and of spiritual attainments too, to have originated with a fallen creature.

How *searching* is this! "If any man *think* that he knoweth anything". Not only is the *claim* to full knowledge ruled out here, but the very *imagination* of such possession is declared to be unwarrantable. How many appear to "think" the very thought which is here rebuked! Speak to some men about certain truths of Scripture, and if not by their words, their very attitude soon gives you to understand that *they* know all that is to be known on the subject. But how foolish such an attitude! They know *nothing* yet as they ought to know!

Here then is a word from God which ought to banish all intellectual pride from every one of us. If none of us yet know *anything* as we ought to know, what ground have we to be conceited about our stock of knowledge? None whatever.

Here too is a word which ought to make us cry earnestly to God for light. Even if God *has* graciously given us light on any part of His truth, we are in real need of further light thereon. It is nothing but unpardonable arrogance to assume that we know more than "in part".

Here is a word which ought to make us diligent in studying the Scriptures. It is the entrance of God's words which giveth light (Psl. 119:130). It is the Truth, and that alone, which frees us from ignorance and error. It is because we are so ill-acquainted with the Word that "we know nothing yet as we *ought* to know."

Here is a word which should cause us to *test* our "thoughts" by the Holy Scriptures. God declares that His thoughts are not our thoughts (Isa. 55:8). It is because that we are incompetent to think upon spiritual and eternal matters that God has revealed His mind to us. Let us then distrust *our* thoughts, let us scrutinize them in the light of the Word, and we shall quickly discover that we know *nothing* yet as we ought to know.

Here is a word which should make us yearn the more intensely for the coming of our Blessed Lord. For then (so far as we are concerned) that which is "in part" shall be done away, and that which is perfect shall have come. Then shall we see no longer through a glass darkly, but face to face. Then shall we know "even as we are known". The Lord hasten that glad Day Arthur W. Pink.

IMPORTANT NOTICES

Set of twelve issues for **1922**, unbound, **$1.00**. Bound, **$1.50**.
Set of twelve issues for **1923**, unbound, **$1.00**. Bound **$1.50**. Abroad, **$1.75** or **7/6**.
Set of twelve issues for **1924**, unbound, **$1.00**. Bound **$1.50**. Abroad, **$1.75** or **7/6**.
Note: We cannot break a set or now supply any **single** 1924 issues.
Subscription Price: **$1.00** per year to any address in the world. Single copies **10 cents.**
Change of Address: Please notify me promptly of any change of address, and be certain to give both old and new addresses.
Non-subscribers receiving this Magazine regularly will understand their subscription has been entered by a friend.
Copies lost in the mail duplicated only if we are notified promptly.

Entered as second-class matter December 15th, 1923, at the post office at Philadelphia, Pa., under Act of March 3rd, 1879.

CONTENTS

JOHN'S GOSPEL.

38. Christ Raising Lazarus (continued)
John 11:11-27

The following is a suggested Analysis of the passage which is to be before us:—

1. Christ announces Lazarus' death, but the disciples misunderstand Him vv. 11-13.
2. Christ rejoices for their sake that He had been absent from Bethany vv. 14, 15.
3. Thomas' melancholy devotion v. 16.
4. Lazarus in the grave four days already v. 17.
5. The nearness of Jerusalem to Bethany v. 18.
6. Many Jews come to comfort the sisters v. 19.
7. The conversation between Christ and Martha vv. 20-27.

In the previous lesson we have seen how the Lord Jesus received a touching message that Lazarus was dying; in the passage now before us we behold Him making for Bethany, Lazarus having died and been buried in the interval. The central thing in John 11 is Christ made known as the Resurrection and the Life, and everything in it only serves to bring out by way of contrast the blessedness of this revelation. Resurrection can be displayed only where death has come in, and what is so much emphasized here is the desolation which death brings and man's helplessness in the presence of it. First, Lazarus himself is dead; then Thomas speaks of the disciples accompanying the Lord to Bethany that they may die with Him (v. 16); then Martha comes before us; and though in the presence of Christ, she could think only of the death of her brother (v. 21); it was the same with Mary (v. 32); finally, the Jews who had come to comfort the bereaved sisters are seen "weeping" (v. 33), and even as the Lord stands before the grave they have no thought that He was about to release the tomb's victim (v. 37). What a background was all this for Christ to display His wondrous glory!

It is not difficult for us to discern here behind the dark shadows that which is far more solemn and tragic. Physical death is but the figure, as well as the effect, of another death infinitely more dreadful. The natural man is dead in trespasses and sins. The wages of sin is death, and when the first man sinned he received those fearful wages. In the day that Adam ate of the forbidden fruit he *died,* died spiritually, as a penal infliction. And Adam died spiritually not only as a private individual, but as the head and public representative of his race. Just as the severing of the trunk of a tree from its roots, means (in a short time) the death of each of its boughs, twigs and leaves, so the fall of Adam dragged down with him every member of the human race. It is for this reason that every one born into this world enters it *"alienated* from the life of God" (Eph. 4:18).

Yes, the natural man, the world over, is spiritually *dead.* He is alive worldwards, selfwards, sinwards, but dead Godwards. It is not that there is a spark of life within which by careful cultivation or religious exercises may be fanned into a flame; he is completely devoid of Divine Life. He needs to be born again; an altogether new life, than the one he possesses by nature, must be imparted to him, if ever he is to enter the kingdom of God. The sinner's condition, is far, far worse than he has any idea of, or than the great majority of the *doctors'* of divinity suppose. Of what use is a "remedy" to one who is *dead?* and yet the thoughts of very few rise any higher when they think and talk of the Gospel. Of what use is it to reason and argue with a corpse? and yet that is precisely what the sinner is from the standpoint of God. "Then, why preach the Word to sinners at all, if they are incapable of hearing it?" is the question which will naturally occur to the reader. Sad, sad indeed that such a question is asked at this late day—sad, because of the God-dishonoring ignorance which it displays.

No intelligent servant of God preaches the Word because he imagines that the will and mind of the sinner is capable of responding to it, any more than when God commanded Ezekiel to "Prophesy upon these *bones*, and say unto *them*, O ye dry bones, hear the Word of the Lord" (Ezek. 37:4) he supposed the objects of *his* message were capable of responding. "Well, why preach at all?" First, because God has *commanded* us to do so, and who are we to call into question *His* wisdom? Second, because the very words we are commanded to preach, "*They* are spirit, and they are life" (John 6:63). The Word we are to "hold forth" is "the Word of *life*" (Phil. 2:16). The new birth is "*not* of blood (by natural descent), *nor* of the will of the flesh (his own volition), *nor* of the will of man (the preacher's persuasion), but OF GOD" (John 1:13), and the seed which God uses to produce the new birth is His own Word (James 1:18).

Now this is what is so strikingly and so perfectly illustrated here in John 11. Lazarus was dead, and that he *had* died was unmistakably evidenced by the fact that his body was already corrupting. In like manner, the spiritual death of the natural man is plainly manifested by the corruptions of his heart and life. In the opening paragraph we have sought to bring out how that which is emphasized here in John 11 is the utter helplessness of man in the presence of death. And this is what the servant of God needs to lay hold of in its spiritual application. If it was only a matter of stupidity in the sinner, *we* might overcome *that* by clearly reasoned statements of the truth. If it was simply a stubborn will that stood in the way of the sinner's salvation, *we* could depend upon *our* powers of persuasion. If it was merely that the sinner's soul was sick, *we* could induce him to accept some "remedy". But in the presence of *death* we are impotent.

"All of this sounds very discouraging", says the reader. So much the better if it results in bringing us upon our faces before God. Nothing is more healthful than to be emptied of self-sufficiency. The sooner we reach this place the better. "For we", said Paul, "have *no confidence* in the flesh" (Phil. 3:3). The quicker we are made to realize our own helplessness, the more likely are we to seek help from God. The sooner we recognize that "the flesh profiteth *nothing*" (John 6:63), the readier shall we be to cry unto God for *His* all-sufficient grace. It is not until we cease to depend upon ourselves that we begin to depend upon God. "With men this *is* impossible; but with God all things are possible" (Matt. 19:26), and this, be it remembered, was said by Christ in answer to the disciples' query, "*Who* then can be saved?"

Here, then, is where light breaks in. Here is where the "glory of God" (John 11:4) shines forth. *Man* may be helpless before death, not so *God*. Lazarus could not raise himself, nor could his beloved sisters and sorrowing friends bring him back from the grave. Ah, but He who is, Himself, "The Resurrection and the Life" comes on the scene, and all is altered. And *what* does He do? Why, He did that which must have seemed surpassingly strange to all who beheld Him. He cried to the dead man, "Come forth". But what was the use of doing *that?* Had Lazarus the power in himself *to* come forth? Most certainly not—had Mary or Martha, or any of the apostles cried, "Lazarus, come forth" *that* would have been unmistakably evidenced. No man's voice is able to pierce the depths of the tomb. But it was One who was more than man, who now spake, and He said, "Come forth" not because Lazarus was *capable* of doing so, but because it was a *life-giving* Voice which spake. The same omnipotent lips which called a world into existence by the mere fiat of His mouth, now commanded the grave to give up its victim. It was a Word of *power* which penetrated the dark portals of that sepulchre. And here, dear reader, is the comforting, inspiring, and satisfying truth for the Christian worker. We are sent forth to preach the Word to lost and dead sinners, because, under the sovereign application of the Holy Spirit, that Word is "the Word of *life*". Our duty is to cry unto God daily and mightily that He may be pleased to make it such to some, at least, of those to whom we speak.

Before we come to the actual raising of Lazarus, our chapter records many interesting and instructive details which serve to heighten the beauty of its central feature. The Lord Jesus was in no hurry; with perfect composure He moved along in Divine dignity and yet human compassion to the grief-stricken home at Bethany. At every point two things are prominent: the imperfections of man and the perfections of Christ.

"These things said He: and after that He saith unto them, Our friend Lazarus sleepeth" (v. 11). The "these things" are the declaration that the sickness of Lazarus was for the glory of God, that the Son of God might be glorified thereby (v. 4); His expressed intention of returning to Judea (v. 7); and His avowed assurance that there could be no "stumbling" seeing that He ever walked in the unclouded light of the Father's countenance (v. 9). In these three things we learn the great principles which regulated the life of Christ—lowliness, dependence, obedience. He now announced that Lazarus was no longer in the land of the living, referring to his death under the figure of "sleep". The figure is a very beautiful one, and a number of most blessed thoughts are suggested by it. It is a figure frequently employed in the Scriptures, both in the Old and New Testaments: in the former it is applied to saved and unsaved; but in the N. T. it is used only of the Lord's people.* In the N. T. it occurs in such well-known passages as 1 Cor. 15:20, 51: "Now is Christ risen from the dead, and become the firstfruits of them that *slept* . . . Behold, I show you a mystery; We shall not all *sleep*, but we shall all be changed"; and 1 Thess. 4:14, 5:10: "For if we believe that Jesus died and rose again, even so them also which *sleep* in Jesus will God bring with Him . . . Who died for us, that, whether we wake or *sleep*, we shall live together with Him". Below we give some of the leading thoughts suggested by this figure:—

First, sleep is perfectly harmless. In sleep there is nothing to fear, but, much to be thankful for. It is a friend and not a foe. So, for the Christian, is it with death. Said David, "Yea, though I walk through the valley of the shadow of death I will fear *no* evil". Such ought to be the triumphant language of every child of God. The "sting" has gone from death (1 Cor. 15:56, 57), and has no more power to hurt one of Christ's redeemed than a hornet has after its sting has been extracted.

Second, sleep comes as a welcome relief after the sorrows and toils of the day. As the wise man declared, "The sleep of a laboring man is *sweet*" (Eccl. 5:12). Death, for the believer, is simply the portal through which he passes from this scene of sin and turmoil to the Paradise of bliss. As 1 Cor. 3:22 tells us "death" is *ours*. Sleep is a merciful provision, not appreciated nearly as much as it should be. The writer learned this lesson some years ago when he witnessed a close friend, who was suffering severely, seeking sleep in vain for over a week. Equally merciful is death for one who is prepared. Try to imagine David still alive on earth after three thousand years! Such a protracted existence in this world of sin and suffering would have driven him hopelessly crazy long ago. How thankful we ought to be that we have not the longevity of the ante-diluvians!

Third, in sleep we lie down to rise again. It is of but brief duration; a few hours snatched from our working time, then to awaken and rise to a new day. In like manner, death is but a sleep and resurrection an awakening. "And many of them that *sleep* in the dust of the earth shall *awake*, some to everlasting life, and some to shame and everlasting contempt" (Dan. 12:2). On the glorious resurrection morn the dead in Christ shall be awakened, to sleep no more, but live forever throughout the perfect Day of God.

Fourth, sleep is a time of rest. The work of the day is exchanged for sweet repose. This is what death means for the Christian: "Blessed are the dead which die in the Lord from henceforth: Yea, saith the Spirit, that they may *rest* from their labors" (Rev. 14:13). This applies only to the "Intermediate State", between death and resurrection. When we receive our

*The only apparent exception is the case of Jairus' daughter.

glorified bodies there will be new ministries for us to engage in, for it is written, "His servants shall *serve* Him" (Rev. 22:23).

Fifth, sleep shuts out the sorrows of life. In sleep we are mercifully unconscious of the things which exercise us throughout the day. The repose of night affords us welcome relief from that which troubles us by day. It is so in death. Not that the believer is unconscious, but that those in Paradise know nothing of the tears which are shed on earth. Scripture seems to indicate that there is one exception in their knowledge of what is transpiring down here: the salvation of sinners is heralded on high; (Luke 15:7, 10).

Sixth, one reason perhaps why death is likened to a sleep is to emphasize the *ease* with which the Lord will quicken us. To raise the dead (impossible as it appears to the skeptic) will be simpler to Him than arousing a sleeper. It is a singular thing that nothing so quickly awakens one as being addressed by the voice. So we are told "the hour is coming, in the which all that are in the grave shall hear His *voice* (John 5:28).

Seventh, sleep is a time when the body is fitted for the duties of the morrow. When the awakened sleeper arises he is refreshed and reinvigorated, and ready for what lies before him. In like manner, the resurrected believer will be endued with a new power. The limitations of his mortal body will no longer exist. That which was sown in weakness shall be raised in power.

But O how vastly different is it for one who dies in his sins. The very reverse of what we have said above will be his portion. Instead of death relieving him from the sorrows of this life, it shall but introduce him to that fearful place whose air is filled with weeping and wailing and gnashing of teeth. It is true that sinners too shall be raised from the dead, but it will be unto "the resurrection of damnation". It will be in order to receive bodies in which they will suffer still more acutely the eternal torments of the Lake of Fire. To all such, death will be far worse than the most frightful nightmare. And O unsaved reader, there is but *a step* between thee and death. Your life hangs by a slender thread, which may snap at any moment. Be warned then, ere it is too late. Flee, even now, from the wrath to come. Seek ye the Lord while He may be found, for there is *no* hope beyond the grave.

"After that He saith unto them, Our friend Lazarus sleepeth; but I go, that I awake him out of sleep" (v. 11). What marvelous condescension was it for the Lord of glory to call a poor worm of the earth His "friend"! But note He said, "*Our* friend". This, we believe, was a word of rebuke to His fearful and distrustful disciples; Our friend—yours, as well as Mine. He has also shown *you* kindness. You have professed to love him; will you now leave him to languish! His sisters are sorrowing, will you ignore them in their extremity! That is why he here says "I go"—contrast the "us" in vv. 7 and 13. *Our* friend—*I* go. I to whom the danger is greatest. *I* am ready to go. It was both a rebuke and an appeal. He had told them that the sickness of Lazarus was in order that the Son of God might be glorified thereby (v. 4), would they be indifferent as to *how* that glory would be displayed!

"I go that I may awaken"—go, even though to His own death. He "pleased not Himself". Thoughts of His own personal safety would no more retard Him than He had allowed personal affection to hasten Him. What was before Him was the Father's glory, and no considerations of personal consequences would keep Him from being about His Father's business. The moment had come for the Father's glory to shine forth through the Son: therefore, His "I go", sharply contrasted from the "He abode two days still" of v. 6. He was going to awaken Lazarus: "None can awaken Lazarus out of *this* sleep, but He who made Lazarus. Every mouse or gnat can raise us from that other sleep; none but an omnipotent power from this". (R. Hall).

"Then said His disciples, Lord if he sleep, he shall do well. Howbeit Jesus spake of His death: but they thought that He had spoken of taking of rest in sleep" (vv. 12, 13). It is clear from their language that the disciples had not understood the Lord: they supposed He meant that Lazarus was recovering. Yet, the figure He had used was not obscure; it was one which the O. T. scriptures should have made them thoroughly familiar with. Why then, had they failed to perceive His meaning? The answer is not hard to find. They were still timid and hesitant of returning to

Judea. But why should that have clouded their minds? Because they were occupied with temporal circumstances. It was "stoning" they were concerned about, the stoning of their beloved Lord—though if He was stoned there was not much likelihood that they would escape. And when our thoughts are centered upon temporal things, or when selfish motives control us, our spiritual vision is eclipsed. It is only as our eye is single (to God's glory) that our whole body is full of light.

"Then said Jesus unto them plainly, Lazarus is dead" (v. 14). What a proof was this of the omniscience of Christ. He *knew* that Lazarus was already dead, though the disciples supposed He was recovering from his sickness. No second message had come from Bethany to announce the decease of the brother of Martha and Mary. And none was needed. Though in the form of a servant, in the likeness of men, Christ was none other than the Mighty God, and clear proof of this did He here furnish. How blessed to know that our Saviour is none other than Immanuel!

"And I am glad for your sakes that I was not there, to the intent ye may believe; nevertheless let us go unto him" (v. 15). But *why* should Christ be glad for the disciples' sake that He was absent from Bethany at the time Lazarus was sinking? Because the disciples would now be able to witness a *higher* manifestation of His glory than what they otherwise would had He been present while Lazarus was sick. But what difference would His presence there have made? This: it is impossible to escape the inference that had the Lord Jesus been there, Lazarus had not died—impossible not only because His words to the disciples plainly implied it, but also because of what other scriptures teach us on the point. The implication is plain: What the Lord unmistakably signified here was that it was inconsistent with *His presence* that one should die in it. It is a most striking thing that there is no trace of any one having died in the presence of the Prince of Life (Acts 3:15). And furthermore, the Gospel records show that whenever Christ came into the presence of death, death at once fled before Him! As to the non-possibility of any one dying in the presence of Christ, we have an illustration in connection with what took place in Gethsemane. When the officers came to arrest the Saviour, Peter drew his sword and smote the high priest's servant, with the obvious intention of slaying him. But in vain. Instead of cleaving his head assunder he simply severed an ear! More striking still is the case of the two thieves who were crucified with Him: *They* died *after* He had given up *His* spirit!! As to death fleeing at the approach of Christ we have a most remarkable example in the case of the widow's son of Nain. Here it was different than in the instances of Jairus' daughter and the brother of Martha and Mary. Each of these had appealed to Him but here it was otherwise. A man was about to be buried, and as the funeral cortege was on the way to the cemetery, the Lord Jesus approached, and *touching the bier* He said to the young man, "Arise, and at once the dead sat up and began to speak" (Luke 7)!!

"And I am glad for your sakes that I was not there, to the intent ye may believe" (v. 15). How perfect are the ways of God! If Martha and Mary had had *their* wish granted, not only would *they* (and Lazarus too) have been denied a far greater blessing, but the disciples would have missed that which must have strengthened their faith. And too, Christ would have been deprived of this opportunity which allowed Him to give the mightiest display of His power that He ever made prior to His own death; and the whole Church as well would have been the loser! How this should show us both the wisdom and goodness of God in thwarting *our* wishes, in order that His own infinitely better will may be done.

This verse also teaches a most important lesson as to *how* the Lord develops faith in His own. The hearts of the disciples were instructed and illuminated *gradually*. There was no sudden and violent action made upon them. They did not attain to their measure of grace all at once. Their eyes were slowly opened to perceive who and what Christ was; it was by repeated manifestations of Divine power and human compassion that they came to recognize in Him a Messiah of a far higher order than what they had been taught to expect. John 2:11 illustrates the same principle: "This beginning of miracles did Jesus in Cana of Galilee, and manifested forth His glory; and His *disciples believed* on Him". And God deals with us in the same way. There is, in the development of our faith, first the blade, then the ear, then the full corn in the ear. Compare the development of Abraham's faith through the increasingly severe trials through which God caused him to pass.

"Nevertheless let us go unto him (v. 15). Lazarus was *dead,* and yet the Lord speaks of going to *him*". "O love, stronger than death! The grave cannot separate Christ and His friends. Other friends accompany us to the brink of the grave, and then they leave us. Neither life nor death can separate from the love of Christ.'" (Burkitt). Lazarus could not come to Christ, but Christ would go to Him.

Then said Thomas, which is called Didymus, unto his fellow disciples, Let us also go, that we may die with Him" (v. 16). No wonder that he said this to his fellow-disciples rather than to the Lord. Very melancholy was his utterance. Thomas was a man who looked on the dark side of things. Lazarus is dead, Christ is going to die, let *us* go and die too! And this, after the Lord had said, "I go, that I may awake him out of sleep" (v. 11)! How difficult is it for man to enter into the thoughts of God! Christ was going to Bethany to give life: Thomas speaks only of dying. Evident is it that he had quite failed to understand what Christ had said in v. 9. How much of unbelief there is even in a believer! And yet we must not overlook the spirit of devotion which Thomas' words breathed: Thomas had rather die than be separated from the Saviour! Though he was lacking in intelligence, he was deeply attached to the Person of the Lord Jesus.

"Let us also go, that we may die with Him" (v. 16). "This was the language of a despairing and despondent mind, which could see nothing but dark clouds in the picture. The very man who afterwards could not believe that his Master had risen again, and thought the news too good to be true, is just the one of the twelve who thinks that if they go back to Judea they must all die! Things such as these are deeply instructive, and are doubtless recorded for our learning. They show us that the grace of God in conversion does not so re-mold a man as to leave no trace of his natural bent of character. The sanguine do not altogether cease to be sanguine, nor the desponding to be despondent, when they pass from death to life, and become true Christians. This shows us that we must make large allowances for natural temperament in forming our estimate of individual Christians. We must not expect all God's children to be exactly one and the same. Each tree in a forest has its own peculiarities of shape and growth, and yet all at a distance look one mass of leaf and verdure. Each member of Christ's body has his own distinct bias, and yet all in the main are led by one Spirit and love one Lord. The two sisters Martha and Mary, the apostles Peter and John and Thomas, were certainly very unlike one another in many respects. But they all had one point in common: they loved Christ and were His friends" (Bishop Ryle).

"Then when Jesus came, He found that he had lain in the grave four days already" (v. 17). Christ did not correct the error of Thomas, but calmly left the truth to do, in due time, its own work. The reference here to the "four days" makes it evident that in John 11 we have something more than a prophetic foreshadowment of the yet future restoration of the then present condition of Israel nationally. From a doctrinal viewpoint the condition of Lazarus in the grave accurately portrayed the state of the natural man, dead in trespasses and sins, a mass of corruption. It is true that Lazarus was a Jew, but "as in water face answereth to face, *so* the heart of man to man" (Prov. 27:19). The third chapter of Romans shows plainly that the state of Israel was also the state of the Gentiles. The "day" here, as usually in this Gospel, signifies (in its deeper meaning) a thousand years. "Four days", had man been in the place of death—alienation from God—for there were exactly four thousand years from the fall of Adam to the coming of Christ. God allowed the awful state of man to be completely manifested before He sent Christ to this earth.

"Then when Jesus came, He found that he had lain in the grave four days already". Note that this verse does not say "When Jesus came *to Bethany,* He found that *Lazarus* had lain in the grave four days already", but instead, "When Jesus came, He found that he had lain in the grave four days already". The Holy Spirit had a reason for putting it so indefinitely, and that reason we have sought to show above. When "Jesus came" to this earth, "he" fallen man, had been "in the grave"—the place of death—"four days already"—four thousand years. O the minute and marvelous accuracy of Scripture!

"Now Bethany was nigh unto Jerusalem, about fifteen furlongs off" (v. 18). There seems to be a double reason why this topographical reference is made here. First, it explains why the "many Jews" had come to Bethany to comfort Martha and Mary (v. 19). Second, it shows how very near to Jerusalem the raising of Lazarus occurred. It was less than two miles from the headquarters of Judaism, within walking distance, almost within sight of the Temple. All room for excuse was thereby removed for any ignorance in the leaders of the Nation as to the identity of the Person of Christ. His last and greatest "sign" was given before many eye-witnesses almost at the very doors of the Sanhedrim. Thus in this seemingly unimportant detail the Holy Spirit has emphasized the deep guilt of those who were most responsible for rejecting Christ. As we shall yet see, there is also a dispensational significance to the "fifteen furlongs", supplying as it does one line in the prophetic picture which this chapter presents.

"And many of the Jews came to Martha and Mary, to comfort them concerning their brother" (v. 19). And poor comforters they must have made. They are in view again in v. 37. When they witnessed the tears of the Lord Jesus by the graveside of Lazarus, they said, "Could not this man, which opened the eyes of the blind, have caused that even this man should not have died?" While no doubt they looked upon Christ as a miracle-worker, it is clear they had no apprehension of the glory of His person—"this man" shows that. Furthermore, it never seems to have entered their minds that He was capable of raising the dead. How then could *they* "comfort" the sorrowing sisters? It is impossible for an unbeliever to minister real comfort to a child of God. God alone can bind up the broken-hearted. Only the Divine Comforter can speak peace to the troubled soul, and not knowing Him, an unsaved person is incapable of pointing another to the one Source of consolation and rest.

"And *many* of the Jews came to Martha and Mary, to comfort them concerning their brother". Mark here the over-ruling wisdom of God. By waiting four days before raising Lazarus, a much greater number witnessed his resurrection, and thus the miracle of Christ was more decisively authenticated, for it would be given greater publicity. The Hand which controls all things so shaped events that it was impossible for the Sanhedrin to discredit this last great "sign" of Israel's Messiah. Here then was a further reason for the "therefore" in v. 6. God not only has a good reason for each of His delays, but generally a manifold reason. Many various ends are accomplished by each of *His* actions. Not only wicked but utterly senseless are our criticisms of His ways.

"Then Martha, as soon as she heard that Jesus was coming, went and met Him" (v. 20). This action was thoroughly characteristic of Martha. Even though the Lord Jesus was not yet come into the village (v. 30), she advances to meet Him. The verses that follow show us something of the condition of her mind at this time. "But Mary sat still in the house". "It is impossible not to see the characteristic temperament of each sister coming out here. Martha—active, stirring, busy, demonstrative—cannot wait, but runs impulsively to meet Jesus. Mary—quiet, gentle, pensive, meditative, meek—sits passively at home" (Bishop Ryle). What marks of truth are these minor details! How evident that the same One who inspired Luke 10 moved John to record these little marks of character here!

"Then said Martha unto Jesus, Lord, if Thou hadst been here, my brother had not died". (v. 21). There are some who think that Martha spoke in a spirit of petulency, that she was reproaching the Lord for not having responded more promptly to the message sent Him while He was in Bethabara. But we think this is a mistake. Rather do we regard Martha's words as a sorrowful lament, the telling out the grief of her heart. Martha's words show plainly what had been uppermost in the minds of the sisters during those trying four days,—note that Mary says almost the same thing when she met Christ (v. 32). There was a strange mingling of the natural and the spiritual, of faith and unbelief in this statement of Martha's. She had confidence in Christ, yet she limited His power. She believed that her brother had not died, no matter how low he was, had Christ only been present; yet the thought never seems to have entered her mind that He was able to raise Lazarus now that He was dead. "Lord, I *believe;* help thou mine *unbelief*" would well have suited her condition at that time. And how often it is appropriate for us! Alas, that it should be so. The Christian is a strange paradox; a dual personality indeed.

"Then said Martha unto Jesus, Lord, if Thou hadst been here, my brother had not died". That which is reprehensible in this utterance of Martha is that she was making distance a limitation of Christ's power. And have not *we* often been guilty of the same thing. Have not we often envied those who were in Palestine during the time that the Word tabernacled among men? But now, alas, He is absent; and Heaven seems so far away! But it is not: it was not too far distant for Stephen to see right into it! But suppose it were; what then? Do we not have the precious promise of the Saviour, "Lo, I am *with you* alway, even unto the end of the age"! But, says the reader, Christ is *bodily* absent. True, and that was what had exercised Martha. Yet it ought not; had not the Lord healed both the centurion's servant and the nobleman's son *at a distance* by His word! He had; but memory failed Martha in the hour of trial and suffering. Alas, that this is so often the case with us.

"But I know, that even now, whatsoever Thou wilt ask of God, God will give it Thee" (v. 22). It is this additional word which indicates that there was a different meaning in Martha's words of v. 21 from Mary's in v. 32. Surely Martha must have said what she did here without any deliberation. With characteristic impulsiveness she most probably uttered the first thoughts which came into her mind. And yet we can hardly conceive of one making such a statement if she knew Christ as God the Son. The word she used for *"ask* God" indicates that she did not recognize that Christ was the One in whom dwelt all the fulness of the Godhead bodily. In N. T. Greek there are two words for "ask". The first "aiteo" signifies a familiar asking. The second "eroteo" means a supplicatory petitioning. The one is suited to express the favor asked of the Creator by the creature, the other for a son's asking of the Father. The former is never used of Christ with the Father except here on the lips of Martha! It was a dragging down of Christ to the level of the prophets. It was the inevitable outcome of having sat so little at His feet listening to His words.

"Jesus saith unto her, Thy brother shall rise again". (v. 23). These were the first words of the Lord Jesus now that He had arrived at the confines of Bethany. He was about to give "beauty for ashes, the oil of joy for mourning, the garment of praise for the spirit of heaviness" (Isa. 61:3); but not yet did He specifically announce His gracious purpose. Instead, He first gave the broad and general promise, "Thy brother shall rise again", without announcing when or how. It is the Lord's way to draw out by degrees His grace in the hearts of His own. He said enough to encourage hope and strengthen faith, but not sufficient to exclude exercise of heart. Light is given us upon the great mysteries of life gradually. "Here a *little* and there a *little*". Faith has to be disciplined, and knowledge is imparted only as the heart is able to receive it. "I have yet many things to say unto you, but ye cannot bear them *now* (John 16:12) still holds good. Unto the Corinthians Paul had to say, "And I, brethren, could not speak unto you as unto spiritual, but as unto carnal, even as unto babes in Christ. I have fed you with milk, and not with meat: for hitherto ye *were not able* to bear it, neither yet now are ye able" (1 Cor. 3:1, 2). Alas that *we* are so dull and make such slow progress in the things of God.

"Martha saith unto Him, I know that he shall rise again in the resurrection at the last day" (v. 24). Martha supposed that He was gently setting aside her implied request that He would "ask of God" and that He was pointing her forward to a future and far-distant hope. Poor Martha! As yet she had learned little from the Lord Jesus. She had nothing better than the common hope of Jews—the resurrection of the dead "at the last day". Does not this suggest another reason why the Holy Spirit tells us in v. 18 that "Bethany was *nigh* unto Jerusalem"—less than two miles away. Martha was still under the influence of Judaism! But these words of hers also contain a warning for us. Martha, like the woman at the well, understood not the *nearness* of the benefit. In each case, half despondingly, they put it into the future. To the Samaritan woman Christ said, "The hour cometh, *and now is,* when the true worshippers shall worship the Father in spirit and in truth: for the Father seeketh such to worship Him". To this she replied,

"I know that Messiah cometh, which is called Christ: *when He is come,* He will tell us all things." To Martha He had said, "Thy brother shall rise again, and she replied: "I know that he shall rise again in the resurrection *at the last day*". Each had only the vague, inoperative idea of a future and final good; whereas He spoke to each of a *present* blessing. It is easier to believe things which are in the far off (which occasion us no exercise of heart!) than it is to appropriate now that which ministers comfort and strength for the present trial. It makes less demand upon faith to believe that in a future day we shall receive glorified bodies, than to rest now on the heartening assurance that, "They that wait upon the Lord shall renew their strength".

"Jesus saith unto her, I am the Resurrection and the Life" (v. 25). This was like what the Lord said to the woman at the well. When she had, by her word, *postponed* the blessing, He answered at once, "I am that speaketh unto you"; so now He says to Mary, "I am the Resurrection and the Life". Here is something of vital importance for our souls. It is not simply that He corrected the vision of these women by turning them from the distant future to the immediate present, but that He fixes their eye upon Himself! It is not future *events* but the *Person* of the Lord, ever present with us, that we need most to be occupied with. Strength, blessing, comfort, are imparted just so far as we are taken up with Christ Himself.

"I am the Resurrection and the Life". "See how the Lord proceeds to instruct and to elevate her mind; how graciously He bears with her passing fretfulness; how tenderly He touches the still open wounds; how He leads her from grieving over her brother to believe yet more fully in her Saviour; how He raises her from dwelling on Lazarus dead, to repose implicitly in Him who is the Lord of life; how He diverts her from thinking only of a remote and general resurrection to confide in Him who is even at this present, the Resurrection and the Life" (Dr. G. Brown). So too does He remove our ignorance, helps our unbelief, and bears with our peevishness. Wondrous condescension, matchless patience, fathomless grace! And how the realization of these should humble us, and cause us to blush for very shame! "Lord, increase our faith" in Thyself.

"I am the Resurrection and the Life". This is what He *is,* in His own peerless Person. What He would here press upon Martha was that all power resided in Himself. Soon she would witness a display of this, but in the meantime the Lord would occupy her with what, or rather *who* He was in Himself. Blessed, thrice blessed is it for the soul to lay hold of this sustaining and satisfying truth. Infinitely better is it for us to be occupied with the Giver than His gifts.

But why this order: the Resurrection *and* the Life? For at least a three-fold reason. First, this is the *doctrinal* order. In *spiritual* experience Christ is to us the Resurrection *before* He is the Life. The sinner is dead in trespasses and sins, in the grave of guilt, separated from God. He has his dwelling "among the tombs" (Mark 5:3). His first need is to be brought out of this awful place, and this occurs at his regeneration. The new birth is a passing from death unto life (John 5:24); it is the being brought on to resurrection ground. The same double thought of leaving the place of death and receiving resurrection life is found again in 5:25: "The hour is coming, and now is, when *the dead* shall hear the voice of the Son of God; and they that hear shall *live*". Lazarus in the grave, raised to life by the word of Christ, gives us a perfect illustration of God's mighty work of grace in the hearts of His elect.

Second, This was the *dispensational* order. The O. T. saints were all in the grave when He who is "The Life" came down to this earth. Therefore it is in *resurrection* power that *they* will know the Christ of God. But believers in Palestine at the time when the eternal Word tabernacled among men knew Him as the Living One, God manifest in the flesh. And yet it was not until after the Cross that they knew Him as such in the fullest sense of the word. It was not until the day of His own resurrection that He breathed on the disciples and said, "Receive ye the Holy Spirit" (20:22). It is the life of a risen and never-dying Saviour which the believer now has as an inalienable and eternal possession. Christ *is* the Resurrection *because* He is the Life, and He *is* the Life *because* He is the Resurrection.

Third, This will be the *prophetic* order. When the Lord Jesus leaves His Father's throne and descends into the air, His people will be found in two great companies; by far the greater part will be (as to their bodies) asleep in the grave; the others will be alive on the earth. But "flesh and blood" cannot inherit the kingdom of God. The living saints will need to be "changed", just as much as the sleeping saints will need raising. Therefore to the one Christ will be the Resurrection, to the other the Life. The two companies of believers are clearly distinguished in 1 Thess. 4:17, "The dead in Christ shall rise first; then we which are alive and remain shall be caught up together with them in the clouds, to meet the Lord in the air". The "changing" of the living believers is mentioned 1 Cor. 15:51. It is to this "change" of believers who have not entered the grave that Rom. 11:8 refers: "But if the Spirit of Him that raised up Jesus from the dead dwell in you, He that raised up Christ from the dead shall also quicken (give life to) your *mortal bodies* by His Spirit that dwelleth in you". Marvellously full were these words of Christ, "I am the Resurrection and the Life".

"He that believeth in Me, though he were dead, yet shall he live" (v. 25). This was brought in to show that what Christ had just spoken of was eclective and not common to all men as such. He was referring to something peculiar to His own: "he that believeth" *limits* the first part of the verse to God's elect. The resurrection of unbelievers, not to "life" but to the Second Death, where, however they shall *exist* in conscious torment forever and ever, is mentioned in other scriptures such as Dan. 12:2, John 5:23, Rev. 20 etc.

"He that believeth in Me, though He were dead yet shall He live". The Greek here is very explicit and impressive. The verb, "though he *were dead*" is in the past tense, and with it is coupled a *present* participle, "yet shall he *live*", i. e. continue to live; but this, be it noted, is predicated of one who believes. How this word of Christ tells of the indestructibility of faith—its ever-living, never-dying character! Primarily; this was a message of comfort to Martha, it went beyond what He had said to her in v. 23. First He said, "Thy brother shall rise again"; next He directed attention to Himself as "the Resurrection and the Life"; now He intimates that though Lazarus had died, yet, because he was a believer, he should live. "Because I live, ye shall live also" (14:19) we regard as a parallel promise.

"And whosoever liveth and believeth in Me shall never die" (v. 26). At the close of the previous verse Christ had referred to physical resurrection, bodily life; here, He speaks of death in its ultimate sense. Rev. 20:6 repeats the same blessed truth: "Blessed and holy is he that hath part in the first resurrection; on such the Second Death *hath no power*". At the close of the previous verse the Lord Jesus had spoken of believers who had fallen asleep—they shall live. But here He speaks of living believers—they shall never die. The Lord had made the same assertion on a previous occasion: "If a man keep My saying, he shall *never* see death".

"Believest thou this?" (v. 26). Every Divine communication challenges the heart to which it is made. We understand Christ's "this" to include all that He had said in vv. 25, 26. "*Believest* thou this?" Have you really laid hold of it? How little we grasp that which has been presented to us. How little we enter into what we believe in a half-*hearted* and general way! The sequel (v. 39) clearly shows that Martha had not *really* "believed" what Christ here said to her—a most searching warning for us. Much of what we *thought* we held is found to have made no impression upon us when the hour of testing comes.

"She saith unto Him, Yea, Lord, I believe that Thou art the Christ, the Son of God, which should come into the world" (v. 27). Most of the commentators are quite astray here. They look upon this utterance of Martha as an evidence that the mists of doubt had now disappeared and that at last her faith had come out into the full sunlight. But what we read of in v. 39 clearly refutes such a view, and what is before us here must be interpreted in harmony with her final words at the grave itself. How then are we to understand her utterance in v. 27? Pressed as she was by the searching question in the previous verse, it seems to us that she fell back on a general answer, which affirmed her belief that the Lord Jesus was the promised Messiah. Having confessed Him as such, she at once went her way. She felt there was a depth to the Lord's words which she was quite incapable of fathoming. And here we must stop.

Let the interested reader ponder the following questions to prepare him for the next lesson:—

1. Why did Martha leave Christ and seek out her sister v. 28?
2. What does v. 30 reveal to us about Christ?
3. Why did Jesus weep v. 35?
4. What is the meaning of the "therefore" v. 38?
5. Why were *they* bidden to remove the stone v. 39?
6. What is the spiritual significance of v. 44?.
7. Trace out the lines of the Dispensational picture in this chapter.

Arthur W. Pink.

GLEANINGS IN EXODUS.

14. *The Death of the Firstborn; Ex. 11.*

The contest between Pharaoh and Jehovah was almost ended. Abundant opportunity had been given the king to repent him of his wicked defiance. Warning after warning and plague after plague had been sent. But Egypt's ruler still "hardened his heart". One more judgment was appointed, the heaviest of them all, and then not only *would* Pharaoh "let" the people go, but he would *thrust* them out. Then would be clearly shown the folly of fighting against God. Then would be fully demonstrated the uselessness of resisting Jehovah. Then would be made manifest the impotence of the creature and the omnipotence of The Most High. "There are many devices in a man's heart; nevertheless the counsel of the Lord, that *shall* stand. (Prov. 19:21.)

"For the Lord of hosts hath purposed, and who shall disannul it? and His hand is stretched out, and who shall turn it back?" (Isa. 14:27). No matter though it be the king of the most powerful empire upon earth, "Those that walk in pride God is able to abase" (Dan. 4:21.) Pharaoh might ask in haughty defiance, "Who is the Lord, that I should obey His voice to let Israel go?" He might blatantly declare, "I know not the Lord, neither will I let Israel go" (5:2). But now the time had almost arrived when he would be *glad* to get rid of that people whose God had so sorely troubled him and his land. As well might a worm seek to resist the tread of an elephant as for the creature to successfully defy the Almighty. God can grind to powder the hardest heart, and bring down to the dust the haughtiest spirit.

"And the Lord said unto Moses, Yet will I bring one plague more upon Pharaoh, and upon Egypt; afterwards he will let you go hence; when he shall let you go, he shall surely thrust you out hence altogether" (11:1). "One plague more". The severest of them all was this, directed as it was against "the chief of their strength" (Psl. 78:51). A mightier king than Pharaoh would visit the land of Egypt that night. The "king of terrors" would lay his unsparing hand upon the firstborn. And with all their wisdom and learning Pharaoh and his people would be helpless. The magicians were of no avail in such an emergency. There was no withstanding the Angel of Death! Neither wealth nor science could provide deliverance. Those in the palace were not one whit more secure than the occupants of the humblest cottage. Longsuffering God had surely shown Himself, but now His holy anger was to burst forth with irresistable might, and bitter and widespread would be the resulting lamentations.

"Speak now in the ears of the people, and let every man borrow of his neighbor, and every woman of her neighbor, jewels of silver, and jewels of gold" (11:2). This and the verse that follows are to be regarded as a parenthesis. The night on which the first-born were slain came between the fourteenth and fifteenth days of the month Nisan. And yet in 12:3 we find the Lord telling Moses to instruct Israel to take them every man a lamb on the *tenth* day of the month. Similarly, here in Ex. 11, the body of the chapter is concerned with what took place on the Passover night, verses 2 and 3 coming in parenthetically as a brief notice of what had happened previously.

That which is recorded in verse 2 has been seized upon by enemies of God's truth and made the ground of an ethical objection. The word "borrow" implies that the article should later be returned. But there was no thought of the Israelites giving back these "jewels" to the Egyptians. From this it is argued that God was teaching His people to practice deception and dishonesty. But all ground for such an objection is at once swept away if the Hebrew word here translated "borrow" be rendered correctly. The Hebrew word is "Sha'al". It occurs 168 times in the Old Testament, and 162 times it is translated "ask, beg or require". The Septuagint (the Greek translation of the O. T.) gives "aites" (ask). Jeromes' Latin version renders it by "postulabit" (ask, request). The German translation by Luther reads "Fordern" (demand). The mistake has been corrected by the English Revisers, who give "ask" rather than "borrow".

While the substitution of "ask" for "borrow" removes all ground for the infidel's objection that Israel were guilty of a fraudulent transaction, there is still a difficulty remaining—felt by many a devout mind. Why should the Lord bid His people "ask" for anything from their enemies? In receiving from the Egyptians, they were but taking what was their own. For long years had the Hebrews toiled in the brick-kilns. Fully, then, had they earned what they now asked for. Lawfully were they entitled to these jewels. Yet we believe that the real, more satisfactory answer, lies deeper than this. Every thing here has a profound typical meaning. The world is greatly indebted to the presence of God's people in it. Much, very much, of the benevolence practiced by the unregenerate is the outcome of this. Our charitable institutions, our agencies for relieving suffering, are really biproducts of Christianity: hospitals, and poor-houses are unknown in lands where the light of the Gospel has not shone! When, then, God took His people out of Egypt He made its inhabitants *feel* the resultant loss. In like manner when the saints are all raptured at the descent of Christ into the air, the world will probably be made to feel that all true blessing and enlightenment has departed from it.

"And the Lord gave the people favor in the sight of the Egyptians" (11:3). This was the fulfillment of the promise made by the Lord to Moses at the burning bush: "And *I will* give this people favor in the sight of the Egyptians: and it shall come to pass, that, when ye go, ye shall not go empty" (3:21). And it was also the fulfillment of one of the promises which Jehovah made to Abraham four hundred years earlier: "And also that nation, whom they shall serve will I judge: and afterward *shall* they come out *with great substance*" (Gen. 15:14). This is very blessed. No word of God can fail. For many long years the Hebrews had been a nation of slaves, and as they toiled in the brick-kilns there were no *outward* signs that they were likely to leave Egypt "with great substance". But the people of God are not to walk by sight, but by faith. How this fulfillment of God's ancient promise to Abraham should show the *certainty* of Him making good all His promises *to us!*

"And the Lord gave the people favor in the sight of the Egyptians" (11:3). Herein Jehovah manifested His absolute sovereignty. From the natural standpoint there was every reason why the Egyptians should *hate* the Israelites more than ever. Not only were they, as a pastoral people, an "abomination unto the Egyptians" (Gen. 46:34), but it was the God of the Hebrews who had so severely plagued them and their land. It was therefore due alone to God's all-mighty power, moving upon the hearts of the Egyptians which caused them to now regard His people with *favor.* Similar examples are furnished by the cases of Joseph and Potiphar (Gen. 39:3), Joseph and the prison-keeper (Gen. 39:21) Daniel and his master (Dan. 1:9) etc. Let us learn from these passages that when we receive kindness from the hands of the unregenerate it is because *God* has given us favor in their sight.

"And Moses said, Thus saith the Lord, About midnight will I go out into the midst of Egypt", (11:4). Moses was still in the Court. 11:1, 4 should be read straight on from 10:28, 29. The seeming interval between the two chapters disappears if we read 11:1 (as the Hebrew fully warrants) "the Lord *had* said unto Moses." God's servant, then, was still in Pharaoh palace, though the king and his courtiers were unable to see him because of the "thick darkness" which enveloped the land of Egypt. If further proof be required for this the 8th verse of our chapter supplies it, for there we read, "And all these thy servants shall come down unto me, and bow down themselves unto me, saying, Get thee out, and all the people that follow me: and after that I will go out. And he *went out from* Pharaoh in a great anger". The fourteenth day of Nisan had arrived, and after delivering the Divine ultimatum, Moses left forever the palace of the Pharaohs'.

"And Moses said, Thus saith the Lord, About midnight will I go out into the midst of Egypt: And all the firstborn in the land of Egypt shall die, from the firstborn of Pharaoh that sitteth upon his throne, even unto the firstborn of the maidservant that is behind the mill; and all the firstborn of beasts. And there shall be a great cry throughout all the land of Egypt, such as there was none like it, nor shall be like it anymore". (11:4-6). How this reminds us of that solemn word in Rom. 11:22, "Behold therefore the goodness and severity of God: on them which fell, severity; but toward thee, goodness!" In exempting His own people from this heavy stroke of judgment we behold the "goodness" of the Lord; in the slaying of all the firstborn of the Egyptians we see His "severity". But why, it may be asked, should the *"firstborn"* be destroyed? At least a twofold answer may be returned to this. It commonly happens that in the governmental dealings of God the sins of the fathers are visited upon the children. In the second place, Rom. 9:22 teaches us that the "vessels of wrath" are made by God for the express purpose of showing His wrath and making known His power. The slaying of the children rather than their parents served to accomplish this the more *manifestly*. Again, the death of the *first born* was a *representative* judicial infliction. It spoke of the judgment of God coming upon *all* that is of the natural man; the firstborn like "the firstfruits" being *a sample* of all the rest. But why slay the firstborn of *all* the Egyptians, when Pharaoh only was rebellious and defiant? Answer: It is clear from Ex. 14:17 that the rank and file of the Egyptians were far from being guiltless.

"But against any of the children of Israel shall not a dog move his tongue against man or beast: that ye may know how that the Lord *doth put a difference* between the Egyptians and Israel (11:7). Marvelous example was this of the absolute sovereignty of Divine grace. As we shall yet see, the Israelites, equally with the Egyptians, fully merited the wrath of God. It was not because of any virtue or excellence in them that the Hebrews were spared. They, too, had sinned and come short of the glory of God. It was simply according to His own good pleasure that God made this difference: "For He saith to Moses I will have mercy *on whom I will* have mercy, and I will have compassion *on whom I will* have compassion" (Rom. 9:15). And this was no isolated instance. It was characteristic of the ways of God in every age. It is the same to-day. Some are in Christ; many are out of Christ: *sovereign grace* alone has made the difference. There can be only one answer to the apostle's question" who maketh thee to differ from another?" (1 Cor. 4:7)—it is *God*. It is not because *our* hearts (by nature) are more tender, more responsive to the Holy Spirit, than the hearts of unbelievers; it is not that *our* wills are more pliable and less stubborn. Nor is it because of any superior mental acumen which enabled us to see *our* need of a Saviour. No; grace, distinguishing grace, sovereign grace, is the discriminating cause. Then let us see to it that we give God *all* the glory for it!

"But against any of the children of Israel shall not a dog move his tongue". Striking proof was this that every creature is beneath the *direct control* of the great Creator! It was nighttime when the Angel of death executed God's sentence. Moreover, "thick darkness" shrouded the land. On every side was the weeping and howling of the Egyptians, as they discovered that their firstborn had been smitten down. Moreover, there was the movement of the Israelites, as by their hundreds of thousands they proceeded to leave the land of bondage. There was, then, every reason why the "dogs" *should* bark and howl, yea, why they should rush upon the Hebrews. But not a single dog moved his tongue! An invisible Hand locked their jaws. Just as Babylon's lions were rendered harmless by God, when Daniel was cast into their den, so Egypt's dogs were stricken dumb when Jehovah's people set out for the promised land. What comfort and assurance is there here for the believer to-day. Not so much as a fly can settle upon you without the Creator's bidding, any more than the demons could enter the herd of swine until Christ gave them permission.

It now remains for us to say something about the spiritual condition of this people here so signally favored of God. Comparatively little is told us in the earlier chapters of Exodus concerning the relations which

Abraham's descendants sustained toward Jehovah, but one or two details of information are supplied in the later scriptures. We propose, then, to bring these together that we may contemplate, briefly, the picture which they furnish us of the moral state of the Children of Israel at the time that the Lord delivered them from the House of Bondage.

In Lev. 17:7 we read, "And they shall no more offer their sacrifices unto demons unto whom they have gone a whoring". Mark the words "no more": the implication is plain that *previously* to coming out into the wilderness, Israel *had* practiced idolatry. Plainer still is Joshua 24:14, "Now therefore fear the Lord and serve Him in sincerity and in truth: and put away the gods which your fathers served on the other side of the flood, *and in Egypt;* and serve ye the Lord". Here we learn that the patriarchs served false gods before Jehovah called them, and that their descendants did the same thing in Egypt.

"In the day that I lifted up my hand unto them, to bring them forth of the land of Egypt into a land that I had espied for them, flowing with milk and honey, which is the glory of all lands; Then said I unto them, Cast ye away every man the abominations of his eyes, and defile not yourselves with *the idols of Egypt;* I am the Lord your God. But they rebelled against Me, and *would not hearken unto Me;* they did not every man cast away the abominations of their eyes, neither did they forsake the idols of Egypt; then I said, I will pour out My fury upon them, to accomplish My anger against them, in the midst of the land of Egypt. But I wrought for My name's sake that it should not be polluted before the heathen, among whom they were, in whose sight I made Myself known unto them, in bringing them forth out of the land of Egypt" (Eze. 20:6-9). Very pointed is this, supplying us with information that is not furnished in the book of Exodus. First, this passage tells us that Israel worshiped the idols of Egypt. Second, it shows how God expostulated with them. Third, it informs us that Israel heeded not God's reproval, but instead, blatantly defied Him. Fourth, it intimates how that the earlier plagues were also visitations of judgment upon the Hebrews, as well as the Egyptians. Fifth, it shows that the Lord delivered Israel, not because of any worthiness or fitness He found in them, but simply for His name's sake.

As we turn to the book of Exodus—everything in it being typical in its significance—we find how accurately the physical condition of the Israelites symbolized their spiritual state. First, they are seen in bondage, at the mercy of a cruel king,—apt portrayal of the condition of the natural man, the "captive" of the Devil (2 Tim. 2:26). Second, we read that they "sighed by reason of their bondage, and they cried" (2:23). But nothing is said about them crying *unto God!* They were conscious of their hard lot, but not yet did they know the Source from which their deliverance must proceed. How like the natural man, when he is first awakened by the Holy Spirit! His spiritual wretchedness, his lost condition, make him to sigh and groan, but as yet he is unacquainted with the Deliverer. Beautiful is it to mark what follows in 2:23: "And their cry *came up unto God* by reason of the bondage". Yes, God *heard* their cry, even though it was not addressed to Himself. And God "remembered His covenant". Ah, *that* was the ground of His action. Not their faith, for they had none. Nor was it pity for their wretchedness, for there were many others in different parts of the earth equally wretched, whom God ignored. God had respect to them for His *covenant's* sake. And it was precisely thus with us, Christian readers. God made a covenant with Christ before the foundation of the world and it was *this,* which made Him have "respect" unto us!

And what do we next read of in Exodus? This: that all unknown to the enslaved and groaning Israelites, God had raised up for them a saviour. Ex. 3 records the appearing of Jehovah to Moses at the burning bush, and the appointing of him to be the deliverer of God's people. But at that time Israel knew it not; they were in total ignorance of the wondrous grace which God had in store for them. How truly accurate the picture!. When we were first made conscious of our woeful condition, when our consciences groaned beneath the intolerable load of guilt, at that time we knew nothing of God's appointed Deliverer.

Next we are told of the Lord sending Aaron into the wilderness to meet his brother, and together they entered Egypt, gather the elders of Israel, and tell them of God's promised deliverance. We are told,

"And the people believed; and when they heard that the Lord had visited the children of Israel, and that He had looked upon their affliction, then they bowed their heads and worshipped" (4:31). But it is clear from what follows that this was not a genuine *heart* believing, and their worship was evidently very superficial. Nor does the analogy fail us here. How many of us became very religious when the Deliverer was first presented to our view! But, alas, how superficial was our response!

The sequel is very striking! As soon as Pharaoh learned of God's intentions toward Israel he at once increases their burdens and says, "Let more work be laid upon the men" (5:9). How clearly Pharaoh forshadows Satan here! As soon as the great Enemy of souls discerns the spirit of God commencing His operations of grace within the sinner, he makes the spiritual lot of that one more miserable than ever. He sets the poor soul *to work* the harder. He tells such an one that he must labor with increased zeal if ever he is to find favor with God. "They were in evil case" says the record (5:19), and so is the poor guilt-burdened, conscience-smitten, convicted sinner.

Next, we read that the people came to Moses complaining of their increased misery. Even now they did not put their trust in the Lord, but instead, leaned upon the arm of flesh. So, too, the convicted sinner—with very rare exceptions—instead of turning at once to Christ for relief, seeks out the sunday-school teacher, the evangelist, or the pastor. Similarly did the "prodigal son" act. When he "began to be in want", he did not return at once to the Father, but "went and joined himself to a citizen of that country". How slow, how pathetically slow, is man to learn the great truth that God alone is able to meet his deep, deep need!

Moses sought the Lord, and the Lord in tender patience bade His servant to go unto the Israelites and say, "I am the Lord and *I will* bring you out from under the burdens of the Egyptians, and *I will* rid you of their bondage, and *I will* redeem you with stretched out arm, and with great judgments; And *I will* take you to Me for a people, and I will be to you a God: and ye shall know that I am the Lord your God. which bringeth you out from under the burdens of the Egyptians, and *I will* bring you in unto the land, concerning the which I did swear to give it to Abraham, to Isaac, and to Jacob; and *I will* give it you for an heritage: I am the Lord" (6:6-8). Wondrous grace was this! Sad indeed is what follows: "And Moses spake so unto the children of Israel, *but they hearkened not* unto Moses for anguish of spirit, and for cruel bondage" (v. 9). How this goes to show that their earlier bowing down and "worshipping" (4:31) was merely an evanescent thing of the moment. And again we say, How true to life is the picture presented here! While Israel groaned under the burdens of the brick-kilns of Egypt, even *the promises of God* failed to give relief. So it was with each of us. While we continued to justify ourselves by our own works, while we sought to weave a robe of righteousness by our own hands, even the promises of the Gospel failed to comfort us. Ah, it is not until the soul turns away from everything of self and puts his trust alone in the Finished Work of Christ, that peace will be obtained. "To him that *worketh not,* but believeth on Him that justifieth the ungodly, his faith is counted for righteousness" (Rom. 4:5).

"And Moses spake so unto the children of Israel: but they *hearkened not* unto Moses for anguish of spirit and for cruel bondage". This is the *last* thing which we are told about the Israelites before the Angel of Death visited the land of Egypt. How clear it is then, that when the Lord "put a difference between the Egyptians and the Israelites" it was not because of any merit which He discovered in the latter. They, too, were idolaters, rebellious and unbelieving. The more clearly we perceive the spiritual wretchedness of Israel at this time, the more shall we recognize the absolute *sovereignty* of that grace which redeemed them. So, too, the more fully we are acquainted with the teaching of Scripture concerning the utter corruption and total depravity of the natural man, the more shall we be made to marvel at the infinite mercy of God toward such worthless creatures, and the more highly shall we value that wondrous love that wrought salvation for us. May the Holy Spirit impart to us an ever-deepening realization of the terrible extent to which sin has "abounded", and make us perceive with ever-increasing gratitude and joy the "super-abounding" of grace.

Arthur W. Pink.

TRUTH AND ERROR.

2. General Principles.

"Be not carried about with divers and strange doctrines. For it is a good thing that the heart be established with grace".—Heb. 13:9.

You seem bewildered amid the opinions of the day, almost as much as you would be in the midst of a company where each spoke in a different tongue. The difficulty of judging what is truth seems to be increasing, instead of disappearing. You know not what to think, nor which way to turn, in order to discover who is right, or where certainty is to be found; so many novelties stagger and amaze you. There seem to be good men on both sides, and that perplexes you still more. You long for peace amid the jar of these unruly elements, and for stability amid these shifting sands. Yet rest comes not. There is no end of change. One novelty begets another, and that, in its turn, becomes equally productive. One error requires another to maintain it, this second must have a third or fourth to lean upon. One false step leads to twenty, or perhaps a hundred more. Who knows where all this is to end?

The changes are numerous. Every month produces some new doctrine, or at least some modification of the old. Fickle minds lie in wait for something new. As the edge of one novelty wears down, another must be provided in its place to keep up the unhealthy excitement. This fickleness becomes doubly fickle by being gratified; novelties multiply and the sore evil spreads. Men do not tremble at the thought of falling into error. To change opinions upon some casual impulse, or some shallow catch of an argument, is thought but a light thing; as if falling into error were no great matter, instead of being a fearful calamity; or as if the entrance upon truth were an indifferent occurrence, instead of being the occasion of deep and solemn joy. Many who but lately were high Calvinists are now Arminians of the lowest grade, passing through the different levels with the most singular facility and flippancy, as easily and airily as the musician runs up and down the scale with the finger or the voice.

How is all this? you will ask. It might be enough to answer that it is written, "There shall come in the last days perilous times, when men shall be heady, high-minded, ever learning, and never able to come to the knowledge of the truth; when they shall not endure sound doctrine, but after their own lusts shall they heap to themselves teachers, having itching ears, and shall turn away their ears from the truth". But let us inquire a little further. There seem to be chiefly three reasons for this; first, the soul is not at rest; secondly, the conscience is not at work; thirdly, there is little "trembling at the Word". I might refer to others, but these are the prominent ones.

1. *The soul is not at rest.*—There is a resting-place for the weary,—deep and broad, immovable and sure,—Jesus, the sin-bearing Lamb of God. But these unstable ones have not reached it. They speak much of it, talk as if they alone knew anything about it, as if none could state the gospel so freely as they; yet it is manifest that they have not yet realized that stable peace which comes from the knowledge of the living Jesus. They are not at rest; and till the *soul* be at rest, the *mind* cannot. It will always be making vain fetches after new opinions, in the hope that this or that new doctrine may perchance bring the peace which it has hitherto sought in vain. Be assured of this, that a *mind* not at rest bespeaks a *soul* not at rest; and whatever men may affirm to you about their assurance or their peace, if you see them ever on the watch, ever on the wing for some new opinion, you may be sure there is little rest within. In many cases it may be vanity, attachment to a sect, desire for proselytizing others, or simply self-will; but in most cases I have no doubt it is really in quest of peace that these poor souls are stretching out their weary hands, ready to embrace anything that will fill the dreary void, and pour over their souls that settled calm, and sunshine, to which in spite of all their profession, they are really strangers. They are not fastened to the anchor cast within the veil, or else they have let go their hold; and hence, they are drifting from place to place in quest of anchorage, but unable to find it. They try, by means of change, to allay the fever and fretfulness of an unsettled spirit, yet all the while they boast of their assurance, and perhaps censure you sorely if you cannot speak their language and assume their tone.

2. *The conscience is not at work.*—The conscience has far more to do in receiving

or rejecting opinions than many suppose. It should stand like a sentinel at the door of the mind, to try all truth before it enters. A tender conscience is cautious, and oftentimes very slow in admitting truth, and, on this very account, most tenacious in holding it fast. Hence, a child of God, with a tender conscience, is often slower in receiving truth than others. For it has to do with conscience in his case; it has to pass into the mind under a watchful eye, which fears to be rash and hasty, and trembles at the thought of giving entrance to error. A conscience asleep, or seared, or secure, makes quick work. A specious objection is presented to some old truth, or a plausible argument in favour of some new opinion, and, forthwith, the former is thrust out, the latter taken in, without any resistance, or delay, or trembling on the part of conscience, or any light and guidance from God, sought and obtained upon the matter.

Nothing is more needed in our inquiries after truth, than a watchful jealousy of a tender conscience. Yet how little there is of conscience at all in these last days! There is what is called independence of mind, or thinking for one's self; but there is no conscience. It is not waiting upon God for teaching. It is trusting in our own heart, and taking the guidance of our own eyes. It is not "ceasing from man," but the mere pretence of it. It is ceasing from one man in order to trust in another, from one age to trust in another, from one book to trust in another, and that other perhaps the most deceitful of all,—our own. Hence there is such running after novelty, such readiness to receive any plausible error, such instability of opinion and fickleness of spirit; such self-willedness and headstrong precipitance of judgment; such high-mindedness, pride, censoriousness of others; so little thought of our own foolishness and fallibility; so slender a sense of the awful responsibility we are under to God, for what we believe for ourselves, and propagate among others, as His precious and eternal truth.

3. There is little trembling at the Word.— It is a solemn thing for a man to be spoken to by God, the God of heaven and earth. Each word coming from His lips should be listened to and received with profoundest reverence. "The Lord has spoken" is enough for us. There is no room for question or cavil where His voice is heard. Each word in the Bible is to be dealt with as a sacred thing, a vessel of the sanctuary, not to be lightly handled or profanely mutilated, but to be received just as it stands. There may be passages difficult to reconcile, doctrines which apparently conflict with each other. But let us beware of smoothing down, of hammering in pieces, one class of passages, in order to bring about a reconciliation. Let us be content to take them as they are. We shall gain nothing by explaining them away. God has spoken them. God has placed them there. They cannot really be at variance with each other. The day is coming when we shall fully understand their harmony. Let us wait till then, and meanwhile tremble at the thought of misinterpreting or distorting so much as one jot or tittle. Most assuredly we shall not bring about the agreement in any such way. We are only widening the breach, and opening but new difficulties.

If I am asked, how can you preach a free gospel, and yet believe in election? I answer, I believe in both, and preach both, because I find both in the Bible. I have no authority for preaching an unconditional gospel but what I find in the Bible; and I have the same authority for preaching an unconditional personal election. God has told me that both are true; and woe be to me if I profanely attempt to mutilate either the one or the other. If one man refuses to take the simple meaning of "election", another may refuse to take the simple meaning of "gospel". And were I called upon to say which is the worse, the more profane of the two, I should say the former. I should, indeed, tremble at the thought of denying either election or the gospel; but I confess that I think the denial of the latter a less direct, and less daring insult to the sovereign majesty of Jehovah. It would be a shutting out of His grace, a closing up of all the manifestations of His character which have come to us since Adam sinned; and it would be drawing a dark cloud over our eternal prospects,—but it would not be taking the reins of government out of His hands,—it would not be the usurpation of His throne,—it would not be giving the right hand of fellowship to atheism.

But there is no need of any such comparison. Perhaps it was wrong to make it. I have done so, however, in order that you may be led to see that *election* belongs to the highest and most sacred order of truths —that it is not a doctrine to be concealed and muffled as if we were either ashamed or afraid of it, but to be firmly held, and faithfully preached, whether men will hear or forebear. Mere philosophy might tell men that, if there be a God, He must be absolutely sovereign in all things. Mere philosophy might expose the shallowness and selfishness of those who trample on God's free will, in order to establish man's —even if theology and Scripture were silent on the matter.

Why do I preach a free gospel? Is it because reason has revealed it? Is it because I find it suits me best? No. It is because God has declared it; that is my sole authority. Why do I believe in election? Just because God has made it known. I may find that reason confirms this. I may see that there can be no really free gospel without election; but still my ground for believing it is because I find it most plainly revealed.

You can only get rid of election by getting rid of the Bible. And hence you will find, among others who deny election and the work of Christ for His church, a great dislike at those passages of Scripture which allude to these topics. They pass them by, they turn away from them, they are angry if another even quotes them, though without a comment. Now I ask, would they do and feel thus, if they believed that these passages really contain the meaning which they put upon them? If these passages are quite in harmony with their views, why do they shrink from quoting them, or hearing them quoted? Is not this the plainest of all proofs, that they feel that theirs is not the honest interpretation? Does it not show that they themselves are secretly persuaded that these passages *do* teach unconditional election, and the absolute sovereignty of Jehovah? They feel that they have twisted them from their plain sense, and that the mere reading of them is enough to expose their distortions. They feel that they have not dealt fairly with the Word of God, and that their one-sided dealings cannot bear the light of day.

Let us learn to "tremble at the Word". Let us take it plainly and honestly in its simple sense. Let us not be afraid of its apparent contradictions. Let us not think ourselves capable of reconciling and harmonizing all its declarations. We see here but through a glass darkly. The day of light and harmony is coming. All shall then be plain. God will solve our difficulties. Meanwhile, let us reverence every jot and tittle of His holy Word. Let us trust our own hearts and reasonings less, and God's Word more. Let us not be so anxiously asking, *how* can this be? how can we reconcile God's sovereignty with man's responsibility? how can we harmonize the Spirit's free agency with man's free agency? Let us leave difficulties in the hands of God; and let us beware of making those difficulties greater by our miserable attempts to reach at things too high for us, or our miserable efforts to pervert and mutilate the Word of the God who cannot lie.

I do not mean, by any of these remarks, to imply that there is not the most perfect harmony between all the different doctrines taught us in the Bible. Nor do I mean to say that this harmony is incapable of being discerned here. I believe, on the one hand, that all is harmony in the truths of God, and that that harmony is discernible and demonstrable even now. But still there is an *apparent* jar. To a certain extent we can reconcile every one of the supposed discordances. Yet there are difficulties connected with them which no theory can solve, and which will remain difficulties till the great day. To attempt to reconcile or remove these by denying the plain and natural sense of Scripture is sinful and pernicious. It accomplishes nothing. It only takes away one difficulty to replace it with a greater.

There are doubtless other causes of the evil over which we mourn; but these are the three chief roots of bitterness. To these may be traced more of the manifold errors of our day than many may be willing to allow. Till these are removed, I have little hope that the instability of the times will die out, or cease to operate for the injury and subversion of the truth. Till the soul gets *rest*—not the name, but the reality—and till the conscience is awake and sensitive, and till the Word of God is reverenced and honestly interpreted, I see small prospect of an end of these changes, if, indeed, we may venture to hope that such can be until the Lord shall come.

Yet be not amazed. Jehovah changes not; neither does His Word. It abideth forever, firm as the rocks of the earth, undimmed as the azure of the heavens. Seek unto God for light, and to His Word for wisdom. Take His Holy Spirit as your teacher. Heed not the jar of man's warring opinions. Let God be true, and every man a liar. The Bible is the Bible still. If any man lack wisdom, let him ask of God. Ye have an unction from the Holy One, and ye know all things.

Do not be alarmed, as if this were some new thing in the earth. Many speak as if the truth had never arisen among men till they arose to it. But the errors of the day are those of former times. They have shot up once and again, and been so often silenced and put to shame. They are old and worn out errors though, perhaps, more daringly set forth now than heretofore; for the time seems at hand in which "the earth shall reel to and fro like a drunkard," and when false teachers and prophets shall deceive, if it were possible, the very elect. Yet do not suppose the attainment of the truth to be a hopeless thing. "The Son of God hath come, and hath given us an understanding that we may know Him that is true". It was He who taught the multitudes in the days of His flesh; and it is He who teacheth the multitude still. If He teaches not, all is vain and false; if He teaches, all is true, all is blessed. Light and knowledge are with Him; and how willing He is that all the light and knowledge should be yours. Learn of Me, He says, for I am meek and lowly; and to what teacher can a foolish erring soul betake himself, like this meek and lowly One, who can have compassion on the ignorant, and on them that are out of the way? He received gifts for men, when He ascended on high, even for the rebellious; and to whom can you go, save to Him who has the Holy Spirit, with all His gifts and graces so freely to bestow?

H. Bonar—1851.

Note carefully the sentences which begin the last paragraph above. With how much greater pertinency do they apply to our own times! Proud reason has ever rebelled against that which is so humbling, namely, that we are nothing more than clay in the hands of the Heavenly Potter. A. W. P.

SIMPLE YET PROFOUND,

or

The Search after Knowledge.

"And an highway shall be there, and a way, and it shall be called the way of holiness; the unclean shall not pass over it; but it shall be for those: the *wayfaring* men, though fools, shall not err therein." (Isa. 35:8). "If thou criest after knowledge, and liftest up thy voice for understanding; if thou seekest her as silver, and searchest for her as for *hid treasures,* then shalt thou understand the fear of the Lord, and find the knowledge of God" (Prov. 2:3-5).

The above verses contain principles at first sight involving contradiction, in reality in perfect harmony, and of the deepest importance to harmonize in practice. The passage in Isaiah gives us the simplicity of truth for souls that are in the way. This is a principle of sweetest assurance to those conscious of the folly which is inherent in us all. How precious the plainness of the "way of holiness"! Clearly it is not the subtlety of the wise of this world that is needed for a path to which "not many wise" are called. Nay, it is the first requisite for receiving the Word of God, that if any one be "wise in this world", he should "become a fool, that he may be wise". "Wherefore, laying aside all malice, and all guile, and hypocrisies, and envies, and all evil speakings, *as new-born babes,* desire the sincere milk of the Word, that ye may grow thereby". A powerful intellect is not that what is needed to receive God's thoughts. Nay, the multiplicity of *human* thoughts are apt to be entertained by those who have this, and this is often the most effectual hindrance to their doing so. "Where is the wise? where is the scribe? where is the disputer?"—the reasoner—"of this world". Hath not God made foolish the wisdom of this world?"

We have but to receive God's thoughts, not think our own. Nor does He communicate His thoughts in other than plain words. It is at least the distinctive style of the N. T., as the apostle puts it—"Seeing then that we have such hope, we use great plainness of speech" (2 Cor. 3:12). God is speaking to us face to face, with the most earnest desire that we understand Him.

How impossible for Him to use hard words and mystification then! Surely it is. "Hidden things", for us in the light of Christianity now, are "hidden things of *dishonesty*" (2 Cor. 4:2).

But while this is all true, it is not the *whole* truth. This does not mean that Scripture truth lies all upon the surface. It does not mean that there are not "things hard to be understood". Such there are, and things "which they that are unlearned and unstable *wrest*"—alas, it may even be "to their own destruction" (2 Peter 3:16). Scripture is simple—not necessarily so *to us.* God's "ways are not as our ways, nor His thoughts as our thoughts"; hence the difficulty to our minds of receiving them. They *cross* nature. They require that we be not "natural" nor yet "carnal", but "spiritual" men. For "the *spiritual* man", and he alone, "discerneth all things" (1 Cor. 2:15).

We may perceive thus how often the apostle has to labour to make his hearers (saints though they might be) to understand what he was saying. "And I brethren, could not speak unto you, as unto spiritual, but as unto carnal, even as unto babes in Christ. I have fed you with milk, and not with meat: for hitherto ye were not able to bear it, neither yet now are ye able" (1 Cor. 3:1, 2). "Of whom we have many things to say, and hard to be uttered, seeing ye are dull of hearing" (Heb. 5:11). Thus we see the plainness of the Word of God does not by any means necessarily imply *that we shall find it so.* For *that* a spiritual condition is needed. Hence the "laying aside all malice, and all guile, and hypocrisies, and envies, and all evil speaking" is in strictest connection with "as newborn babes, desire the sincere milk of the Word". *If the soul is not self-judged before God,* no searching after knowledge will at all avail.

Now look more closely at our first text. Folly shall not cause the wayfarer to err. True, for he has not to think out a path for himself; he has only to receive God's thoughts. No we must not overlook the very plain fact, that this applies to the "wayfarer", and ONLY to the wayfarer. It is not the man not upon the road, but it is the man upon it. Like Israel's pillar of fire which marked out their path, it was not hard for the least intelligent of these to know the way that pillar led, but he must be with the camp and on the march, to know it. There was no "king's highway" along which it moved; no mere chart could reveal the path it travelled; you must *move with it,* and it would be simple work to know. Are you a "wayfarer", dear reader? not a mere learner of the geography of the "way of holiness", but a traveller on it? Happy are you! Yea, "blessed is the man in whose heart are *the ways;* who, passing through the valley of Baca, make it a well, the rain also filleth the pools: they go from strength to strength, every one of them in Zion appeareth before God" (Psa. 84:5-7). Yes, there is no failure there.

This then makes way for our second text, so contradictory at first sight, so simply consistent and harmonious in reality. "If thou criest after knowledge and liftest up thy voice for understanding: if thou seekest her as silver and searchest for her as for *hid treasures*"—if there were such a hidden hoard in your garden, reader, *how* you would search!—"*then* shalt thou understand the fear of the Lord, and find the knowledge of God".

Answer to your own soul, believer: did you ever really apprehend that you were to search the Word of God like that? Alas, the carelessness, the lightness, the superficiality everywhere, do readily answer for most—it is *not* their thought. The characteristics of the day is at least not earnest devoted attention to the words of God. There is much stir and activity in other ways, doubtless. And God is giving out to us, with a clearness and fullness which has no counterpart short of apostolic times, the blessed truths of His Word. This is His grace—rich and precious it is: but what responsibility does it correspondingly lay upon us? How are we answering to it? Is it by a whole-hearted "giving ourselves" to the apprehension and enjoyment of them? Is it not, on the other hand, rather the case, that souls are found lingering upon the very threshold of wisdom—(Prov. 9:1-6),—content, if they know forgiveness, to rest there,—or at least making the acquisition of God's treasure-store a thing by the way, the employment of unoccupied moments merely? Where is the "cry"? where is the "lifting up the voice"? where is the "seeking as silver", the search as for hid treasures?—in a word, the energy of soul in persuit of things which are all our own, and our only portion—energy to which God has attached the assurance of understanding, of finding knowledge? Is this a light thing? Does it not rather reveal how little the heart is really engaged with God? Surely it does. Indolence here, whatever excuses we make, is spiritual torpor and indifference everyway.

With a multitude, and in very different degrees of actual enlightenment, it will be found at bottom, the thought of God's Word is at best but of a creed which they have got to live; and he is most acceptable who can give that to them in the simplest way, with the least exercise of soul about it. They learn it as such. Every fresh truth added to the former stock is so much gain to their theological knowledge. It is catalogued as known, and takes its place as a new plant does in the botanist's herbarium; alas, transformed from a living growth into a thing of little beauty and manifestly dead. But God has not written a creed; His words are spirit and they are life: given us in such a way, that by the very searching into them which we are called to, occupation with them should give them practical power over us. Just as occupation with the world, the *having to* employ our minds in the way we have from day to day, tends to absorb us and assimilate us to it,—so is it designed that similar needed employment with the Word, and its eternal truths should counteract this constant tendency, and faith fed by it be the overcoming of the world. The mere creed is powerless for this. The soul *unexercised* by the Word, while it may learn many truths, is proportionately a stranger to their power.

I would press then the consideration of our two texts upon the reader. The Lord give us such an earnest "search after knowledge" as may put us in possession of the "hid treasures" of God's blessed Word! Things which "eye hath not seen, nor ear heard, neither have entered into the heart of man", but which "God hath revealed to us by His Spirit; for the Spirit searcheth all things, yea the deep things of God".

Helps for Wayfarers.

THE STORM ON THE LAKE.

The record of our Lord's sail over the sea of Galilee, accompanied by His disciples, as given in Luke 8:22-26, is exceedingly interesting. It contains a lesson rich in instruction, and of deep practical value for the children of God. It pictures very vividly our passage across the sea of this turbulent world. It is a reflection of our journey through a scene of incessant though ever-varying activity, on to the haven of rest eternal.

The proposal to go to the other side was the Lord's: it was no rash undertaking of the disciples. It was the Lord who said, "Let us go." One has come to us from the bright "over there." The Father has sent to us His Son from His own house, and He has told us of the Father—of the Father's house—of heavenly things. We have heard His voice, we have received His words, we have bowed in our souls to His heavenly communications. Owned now as His brethren and companions, He shows us that His blessed home over the other side is ours, and He says, "Let us go."

His saying to His disciples "Let us go over to the other side of the lake" was the expression of His will, the authority for the journey, and the sure pledge or promise of its successful end. Beside this, He was Himself present with them—present to share their lot, whatever that might be.

Beloved, what these disciples had we have. We have His Word and His presence. We know His will is, that where He is, there we may be also. He has said so. "It is written" it is faith's answer to the question, "What reasonable ground or authority is there for denying ourselves and following a despised and rejected Christ?" Through His Word the eye of faith looks upon things "unseen and eternal," and all is assured. Possessing in His Word these three things of such incalculable value for faith—His Word being all this to the heart, how free are we to enjoy the blessing of His presence along the journey. But if His Word is not thus dwelling in our hearts, we shall not be keeping Him company, though He be with us. He was asleep on this ship as they were gliding along toward the land over the other side. He was oblivious to all around before the storm came and during the storm. A smooth sea, a balmy breeze, the beauties around, occupied neither His eye nor His heart. His disciples did not keep Him company in this obliviousness to the things of sight and sense. So when their circumstances changed,—when the smooth sea became rough, and the gentle breeze turned into a terrific gale,—the joy and pleasure of a beautiful sail was superseded by distress and fear. Now they think of Him, but they cannot bear to gaze upon His peaceful face. How descriptive this of ourselves! So long as the scene through which we pass contributes to our comfort, how we enjoy the journey! but when trouble comes,—opposition, persecution for the Word's sake, such things as the path necessitates,—not troubles our own failures and sins bring upon us, but troubles which are the necessary result of following after a rejected Christ,—when such trials come, what unhappiness, what discontent and murmuring! how much fear and trembling! How impossible to be quiet! How unbearable the quietness of the Lord! Like the disciples here, we must invoke His activity. They went to Him and said, "Master! Master! we perish." He heard their cry. He answered their prayer. He arose, spoke to the winds and commanded the waves, and there was a great calm; but He said to them, "Where is your faith?" Oh, what a rebuke!

Beloved, are the days evil and difficult? do the winds blow fiercely? are the waves rising higher and higher? He is with us. We have His Word and His presence. Is that sufficient? Are we desirous of an easier path? Is this heaving and tossing unbearable? Is His peacefulness, His mastery, His undisturbed supremacy unbearable? Well, if we cannot endure, He may respond to our desire—gracious One that He is; (have we not known Him to do so?) but if so, be assured it is a rebuke. It is to ask us, "Where is your faith?"

The disciples here were ill at ease in the calm. The solemn quiet and stillness of the calm was dreadful, too. They were not free and happy in the presence of Him who had produced for them a thorough change. They knew little of the personal glory of their Master. "What manner of Man is this?"—who is He, to do such a wondrous thing? We, too, often say, What a wonderful providence! what a remarkable interposition! while yet our hearts are ill at ease in His presence; so slow are we to learn Himself and the glories of His wondrous person. What losers we are through our lack of faith, forgetfulness of the Word and indifference to the presence of our ever-calm and restful Lord! What we would gain by allowing His Word its full place in our hearts, who can tell? Let us cultivate His company, and never weary of gazing upon His peaceful face. *(Help and Food, 1884)*

A DIVINE MIRACLE.

"As the lightning cometh out of the east, and shineth even unto the west; so shall also the coming of the Son of Man be . . . then shall appear the sign of the Son of Man in heaven; and then shall *all* the tribes of the earth mourn, and they shall *see* the Son of Man coming in the clouds of heaven with power and great glory" (Matt. 24:27, 30).

It may be asked, how can He be seen by all nations at the same time? At the instant He is described in any one part of the earth, must He not be invisible to every other? Especially, when He appears to the nations on this side of the globe, how can He be seen on the other? Let His descent be ever so rapid, must He not either make a circuit round the globe, or have all the inhabitants of the earth gather in one place, before He can be visible to them all? To those who make these objections, I reply, in the words of our Lord, on another subject—"Ye do err not knowing the Scriptures, neither the power of God". Upon this subject, and, in general, upon everything that relates to the things of God, men have found a great many difficulties; and have invented a great many solutions, which are founded on the notion that the operation of God must be conducted in some way analogous to those of men, and that the present laws that regulate the phenomena of nature, must always exist. The laws of vision, for instance, that now regulate and limit our powers of sight, are supposed to continue forever. But, in reality, there would be nothing more wonderful in our seeing round the globe or to its center, through all the dense materials of which it is com-

posed, or in our seeing the minutest objects in the fixed stars, than in our seeing an object within a few yards' distance. The greatest philosopher on earth cannot give a reason *why* we see at all. He may trace the laws of vision, he may tell us of the rays of light coming from the object to the eye—entering the eye in such a direction, and forming a picture on the bottom of it; he may tell us of the impression communicated to the brain by the optic nerve; but here he must stop. *Why* this would make the object perceivable to the mind is beyond his skill. Here he is as ignorant as the savage, or as the beast. If you ask him why he sees with his eye, rather than with his mouth, he can give no reason, but that it is the will of God. If, then, it altogether depends on the will of God, that we see with our eyes at the proper distance, could not God as easily make objects visible to us without eyes, or make us, with the eyes which we have, behold objects most perfectly all around the globe? Might we not read a volume placed at the remotest of the fixed stars or perceive what is going on in heaven itself? Stephen saw the heavens open, and the Son of Man standing on the right hand of God!

We can in no instance, judge of the extent of the powers of perception in our future state of existence, from the present laws by which they are regulated and limited. Let us, then, in ascertaining from the Scriptures the mind of God on this subject, beware of limiting the power of God, by our weak conceptions of possibility. Let us not avoid the obvious meaning of His Word on account of any inconsistency between this and the established laws of nature. Nature is but the order of His operations; and though it is unchangeable by us, it is not so to Him. Let us not make any bold conjectures, to reconcile our own views of possibility with His authoritative declarations. That all will see Christ at His descent is clear from several passages of Scripture, and, therefore, not to be questioned on account of any difficulties from the laws of Nature. Dr. Alex. Carson, (1853).

ABILITY AND INABILITY.

Some pretend that whatever is required of us or prescribed unto us in a way of duty, we have a power in and of ourselves to perform. If by this power they intend no more but that our minds, and the other rational faculties of our souls, are fit and meet, as to their *natural capacity,* for and unto such acts as wherein those duties do consist, it is freely granted; for god requires nothing of us but what must be acted in our minds and wills, and which they are naturally meet and suited for. But if they intend such an *active* power and ability as, being excited by the motives proposed unto us, can of its self answer the commands of God in a due manner, they deny the corruption of our nature by the interference of sin, and render the grace of Christ useless.

There is, or may be, a *power* in the mind to discern spiritual things, whereby it is so able to do it as that it can immediately *exercise* that power in the spiritual discernment of them upon their due proposal to it, that is, spiritually; as a man that hath the visive faculty sound and entire upon the due proposal of visible objects unto him can discern and see them. This power must be spiritual and supernatural; for whereas to receive spiritual things spiritually is so to receive them as really to believe them with faith divine and supernatural, to love them with divine love, to conform the whole soul and affections unto them, Rom. 6:17, 2 Cor. 3:18; no natural man hath power so to do. Wherefore, between the natural capacity of the mind and the act of spiritual discerning there must be an *interposition* of an effectual work of the Holy Spirit *enabling* it thereunto, 1 John 5:20, 2 Cor. 4:6. *Dr. John Owen (1650)*

God sends the Gospel to men in pursuit of His *decree of election* and in order unto its effectual accomplishment. I dispute not what other end it hath or may have, in its indefinite proposal unto all; but this is the first, regulating, principal end of it. Wherefore, in the preaching of it, the apostle Paul affirms that he "endured all things for *the elect's* sakes, that they might obtain the salvation which is in Christ Jesus with eternal glory" (2 Tim. 2:10). So God beforehand commanded him to stay and preach the Gospel at Corinth, because, "He had much people in that city",—namely, in His purpose of grace (Acts 18:10). *Dr. John Owen (1650)*

VOL. IV MARCH, 1925 NO. 3

STUDIES in the SCRIPTURES

"Search the Scriptures" John 5:39.

Arthur W. Pink, Publisher & Editor,
R. F. D. 9, York, Pa.

Price: 10 cents per copy; $1.00 per year. Foreign $1.00 per year.

And the Syrians had gone out by companies and had brought away captive out of the land of Israel a little maid, and she waited on Naaman's wife" (2 Kings 5:2).

What a strange verse on which to write an Editorial! Whatever is there in it which can minister help to us? Wherein lies its instructing and comforting message? First of all, remember, my reader, this forms part of the Word of God, and not only is there nothing in *it* which is meaningless, but there is nothing trivial. The deep significance and value of many a verse of Scripture is not apparent at first sight; sometimes the context needs to be studied diligently, sometimes passages in other parts of the Word have to be compared, at others there must be a prolonged and prayerful meditation, before its meaning is discerned and its message discovered.

"And had brought away captive out of the land of Israel a little maid". Picture the scene. Visualize the incident. One fair morning the peace of Palestine was rudely broken. The tramp of an hostile army was heard. A cruel foe was at hand. The Syrians had invaded the land of Israel, and Heaven was silent. No scourge from God smote the enemy, instead he was suffered to carry away some of the covenant people. Among the captives was "A little maid". Ah, that may mean *little to us* to-day, but it meant much to some people at that day. *A home was rendered desolate.* Picture the sorrow of her parents as their young daughter was ruthlessly snatched from them. Picture the anguish of her poor mother, wondering what would become of her. Picture her grief-stricken father, *unable* to rescue her. And endeavor to enter into the feelings of the little girl herself as she was carried away by heathen to a strange country!

Do you not suppose, dear reader, that both the maid and her parents were greatly perplexed? Must they not have been sorely troubled at this mysterious providence? Why, oh why? must have been asked by them a hundred times. *Why* had God allowed the joy of their home to be shattered? Strange, if the maiden reflected at all, must she have thought her lot. Why was *she*—a favored daughter of Abraham—now a servant in Naaman's household? *Why* this enforced isolation from her parents? Why this captivity? Such questions she might have asked at first, and *asked in vain.*

Does the reader now perceive the point we are leading up to? the lesson to be learned here? *God had a good reason for this trial.* The Lord was shaping things in His own unfathomable way for the outworking of His good and wise purpose. Nothing happens in this world by mere chance. It was *God* who directed that this "little maid" of Israel should become a member of Naaman's household. And why? That she might be a link in the chain which ended not only in the healing of her master of his leprosy but (we doubt not) in the salvation of his soul. Read the remainder of 2 Kings 5 for the happy sequel.

What are the lessons to be learned from this incident? One of them certainly is this: God has a wise and good reason for permitting each of the perplexing and heart-exercising trials in our lives. The particular reason for each trial is oft-times concealed from us—if it were not, there would be no room for the exercise of faith and patience in it. But just as surely as God had a good reason for allowing the joy of that Israelitish household to be darkened, so has He in permitting whatever sorrow has entered *your* life. *Read* Rom. 15:4.

One other lesson we would briefly notice: God delights to use the little and despised things! A "*little* maid" in captivity. Who would expect *her* to do service for God? Who would be inclined to listen to *her* voice? Her age was against her, and so was her position. Yet she told her mistress of God's prophet in Samaria, and her simple message reached the ears of the *King* of Syria! The Lord grant us like faithfulness in the place where He has put us.

Arthur W. Pink.

IMPORTANT NOTICES

Set of twelve issues for **1922**, unbound, **$1.00.** Bound, **$1.50.**

Set of twelve issues for **1923**, unbound, **$1.00.** Bound **$1.50.** Abroad, **$1.75** or **7/6.**

Set of twelve issues for **1924**, unbound, **$1.00.** Bound **$1.50.** Abroad, **$1.75** or **7/6.**

Note: We cannot break a set or now supply any **single** 1924 issues.

Subscription Price: **$1.00** per year to any address in the world. Single copies **10 cents.**

Change of Address: Please notify me promptly of any change of address, and be certain to give both old and new addresses.

Non-subscribers receiving this Magazine regularly will understand their subscription has been entered by a friend.

Copies lost in the mail duplicated only if we are notified promptly.

Entered as second-class matter January 15th, 1923, at the post office at York, Pa., under Act of March 3rd, 1879.

CONTENTS

JOHN'S GOSPEL.

39. *Christ raising Lazarus (concluded): John 11:28-44.*

The following is submitted as an Analysis of the passage which is to be before us:—

1. Mary goes to meet Jesus vv. 28-30, 32.
2. The Jews follow her v. 31.
3. Jesus groaning and weeping vv. 33-35.
4. The comments of the Jews vv. 36-38.
5. Martha's unbelief and Christ's rebuke vv. 39, 40.
6. Jesus praying and praising vv. 41, 42.
7. The raising of Lazarus vv. 43, 44.

The central design of John's Gospel is to present Christ to us as the Eternal Word become flesh, the Lord of glory in the likeness of men. Two things are made prominent throughout: His Divine dignity and His human perfections. Wonderfully perfect is the blending of these in the God-man: everything is there in Him to draw out our hearts in adoring love and reverent worship. Here we are shown His mighty power, and also His blessed tenderness. Here we behold not only His absolute authority, but also His entire dependency. It is not only that we gaze upon one of the Persons of the Holy Trinity, come down from heaven to earth, but also on One who entered fully into the conditions and circumstances of men, sin only excepted. Strikingly do these two lines of truth meet in John 11. The very chapter which chronicles His mightiest "sign" reveals the principles by which He walked—submission, dependence, obedience. Side by side with the record of His omnipotent voice calling the dead to life again, do we read of Him groaning and weeping. Absolutely unique is this wondrous Person.

The blending of Christ's *divine* glories and *human* perfections meet us at every turn in this fourth Gospel. If John is the only one of the four Evangelists who enters into the pre-incarnate dignities of Christ, showing Him to us as the One who subsisted in the beginning, both being with God, and God Himself; the Creator of all things; if John is the only one who contemplates Him as the great "I Am", equal with the Father; he also brings before us details concerning His humanity which are not to be met with in the Synoptists. John is the only one who tells us of Christ being "*wearied* with His journey" (4:6), *groaning* as He beheld the tears of His own, and *thirsting* as He hung upon the cross. Christ became Man in the fullest sense of the word, and nowhere do we behold His human sympathies and perfections more blessedly displayed than in this very Gospel which portrays Him as God manifest in flesh.

It is in John's Gospel, pre-eminently that we see the antitype of the veil, which speaks so plainly of the Son of God *incarnate*. "And thou shalt make a veil of blue, and purple, and scarlet, and fine twined linen of cunning work" (Ex. 26:31). This order "blue, purple and scarlet" is repeated over twenty times in Exodus, and is never varied. The blue and scarlet are never placed in juxtaposition in any of the fabrics in the Tabernacle. This of itself is sufficient to show that the Holy Spirit intimates there is an important truth here in connection with the person of Christ. The "blue" is the color of heaven, and speaks of Christ as the Son of God. The "scarlet" is both the color of sacrifice and human glory. The "purple" is a color produced by the mixing together of blue and scarlet. Without the purple, the blue and the scarlet would have presented too vivid a contrast to the eye; the purple coming in between them shaded off the one extreme from the other.

Now the antitype of these colors is found in the incarnate Christ. He was both God and man, and yet these two vastly dissimilar natures unite in one perfect Person. The "purple", then, coming in between the "blue" and the "scarlet" tell of the perfect *blending* or union of His two natures. The great marvel (as well as mystery) of His unique person is that in Him were *combined* all the fulness of the Godhead with all the sinless feelings and affections of man. And it is just this which is so beautifully brought out in John's Gospel, and nowhere more strikingly than in John 11. When the sisters sent to Christ telling Him that their brother was sinking, instead of hastening at once to Him, He remained two days where He was. Did this show that He was devoid of human feelings? No; His purpose was to manifest the Divine glory. But mark the sequel. When He arrives at Bethany, His heart is profoundly moved as He beholds the sorrowing sisters. And who but the God-man would have shed tears by the grave of Lazarus when He was on the very point of restoring the dead to life! Each of the three colors of the veil are clearly seen. The "blue" in the Divine power which raised the dead; the "scarlet" in the groans and tears. Now behold the "purple". When Lazarus came forth from the sepulchre he was still bound with the grave-clothes. The spectators were so amazed, so awed, so bewildered, *they* made no effort to remove them. "Loose him" were the words which proceeded from *Christ.* And who but the God-man would have been occupied with such a detail? We witness the same thing again at the Cross; "It is finished" exhibits the "blue"; "I thirst", the "scarlet"; and the "purple" is evidenced in His tender thought for His widowed mother, commending her to His beloved John!

In our previous articles upon the first sections of John 11 we have seen the Lord at Bethabara with His disciples, and then on the confines of Bethany, whither Martha, unbidden, with characteristic impatience rushed to meet Him. We sought to weigh her utterances as she gave expression to the first thoughts that entered her mind. We saw how that the responses made by Christ were quite beyond her depth, and how that in answer to His searching "believest thou this?", she replied, "yea, Lord: I believe that Thou art the Christ the Son of God, which should come into the world". Immediately following this we read, "And when she had *so* said, she went her way, and called Mary her sister secretly, saying, The Master is come, and calleth for thee" (v. 28).

In her impulsive hurry to meet the Lord (v. 20) Martha, for the time, forgot all about her sister; but now she goes to call Mary. There is nothing in the narrative to show that Christ had *asked* for Mary—if He had, John would surely have told us so. Was it then a fabrication on Martha's part? We do not so regard it: rather do we think she concluded that the profound words of Christ were more suited to her sister than herself. When Christ said, "I am the Resurrection and the Life: he that believeth in Me, though he were dead, yet shall he live; and whosoever liveth and believeth in Me shall never die", she felt that *Mary* must hear this; *she* will be able to understand.

"And when she had so said, she went her way, and called Mary her sister secretly, saying, The Master is come, and calleth *for thee*". The cryptic utterances of Christ Martha considered as a "Call" for the more spiritual Mary. What a tribute this was to the discernment of the one whom she had formerly criticised! She called her "secretly" so as not to attract the attention of the many Jews who were with her in the house (v. 19). These Jews had come from Jerusalem, and Martha knew that most of the people there were antagonistic to the Saviour. "Christianity doth not bid us abate anything of our wariness and honest policy; yea, it requires us to have no less the wisdom of the serpent as the harmlessness of the dove" (R. Hall). And, too, she probably felt that it was more fitting that Mary should enjoy an interview with Christ in undisturbed privacy. Mark that Martha terms Christ "Master" (the Teacher), not Lord!

"As soon as she heard that she arose quickly, and came unto Him". With characteristic quietness and calm Mary had remained seated in the house, but now she hears that the One at whose feet she had loved to sit was here at hand, she rises and goes forth to meet Him at once, "quickly". The knowledge that *He* was "calling" her lent wings to her feet. She needed not to tarry and inquire *who* was meant by "the Master"—she had none other! and that one word was sufficient to identify the One who was the Fairest among ten thousand to her soul.

"Now Jesus was not yet come into the town, but was in that place where Martha met Him" (v. 30). Very striking indeed is this. He was still in the same place where Martha had talked with Him. In the interval she had returned to Bethany, entered the house and spoken to her sister, and Mary had herself traveled the same distance to meet Him in whom her soul delighted. And when she completed the journey—how long a one it was we do not know—she found her Beloved awaiting her. How this brings out the calmness of Christ: there was no undue haste to perform the miracle! And how blessedly it illustrates the fact that He never hides Himself from a seeking soul. He would not disappoint this one who so valued His presence. If she "arose quickly" to go to Him, He waited patiently for her arrival!

"The Jews then which were with her in the house, and comforted her, when they saw Mary, that she rose up hastily and went out, followed her, saying, She goeth unto the grave to weep there" (v. 31). This too is striking. Man proposes but God disposes. Martha's secrecy came to nothing. God had purposed that the last great "sign" of Israel's Messiah should be given before many eye-witnesses. The Jews followed Mary because they supposed she had gone to the grave to weep *in private,* but He who doeth all things according to the counsel of His own will drew them there, that the miracle of the raising of Lazarus should be done *in public.* Doubtless their intention was to "comfort" her, and for their kindliness God would not let them be the losers. Has He not said, "Whosoever shall give to drink unto one of these little ones a cup of cold water only in the name of a disciple, verily I say unto you, he shall in no wise lose his reward" (Matt. 10:42)? Beautifully was that verified on this occasion.

The Jews who had journeyed from Jerusalem to Bethany had felt for Martha and Mary in their heavy bereavement, and came to offer what comfort they could. By so doing they reaped a rich and unexpected reward. They beheld the greatest miracle which Christ ever wrought, and as the result many believed on Him. (v. 45). "We need not doubt that these things were written for our learning. To show sympathy and kindness to the sorrowful is good for our souls. To visit the fatherless and widows in their affliction, to weep with them that weep, to try and bear one another's burdens and lighten one another's cares,—all of this will make no atonement for sin and will not take us to Heaven. Yet it is healthy employment for our hearts, and employment which we ought not to despise. Few persons are aware that one secret of being miserable is to live only for ourselves, and one secret of being happy is to try to make others happy. In an age of peculiar selfishness and self-indulgence it would be well that we took this to heart" (Bishop Ryle). It is significant that these Jews did not leave the house when Martha left it!

"Then when Mary was come where Jesus was, and saw Him, she fell down at His feet, saying unto Him, Lord, if Thou hadst been here, my brother had not died" (v. 32). This was the language of perplexity and grief. Like Martha, Mary was thinking of what *might* have happened. How often we look back on the past with an "if" on our minds! How often in our sore trials we lash ourselves with an "if". And small comfort does it bring! How often we complain "it might have been" (Mark 14:5). As Whittier says, "Of all sad words of tongue and pen, the saddest are these, 'It might have been'". Only too often these words express the inveterate sadness of one who is swallowed up with sorrow. Ofttimes it issues from forgetfulness of the Lord: He *permitted* it, so it must be for the best. It may not appear so to our dim vision; but so *it is.* It was so with Martha and Mary, as they were soon to behold.

"Then when Mary was come where Jesus was, and saw Him, she fell down at His feet, saying unto Him, Lord if Thou hadst been here, my brother had not died". While this was the language of grief and perplexity, it certainly was not a reproachful murmur, as her casting herself at the feet of Christ clearly shows. Nor does Mary here add an apologetic reflection as had her sister (v. 22). Her words had quite a different meaning from the very similar language of Martha. We say very similar, for their utterances were not identical, as a reference to the Greek will show. They each used the same words, but the *order* of them varied, and in this may be seen what was uppermost in each of their minds. The A. V. gives a literal rendering of the original language of Martha (v. 21); but what Mary said was, "Lord, if Thou hadst been here, had not died my brother". That which was uppermost in the thoughts of Martha, was her brother's death; that which was discerned by Mary was that none *could* die in the presence of Christ. *Her* words then were an expression of worship, as the casting of herself at Christ's feet was an act of adoring homage.

"Then when Mary was come where Jesus was, and saw Him, she fell down at His feet". This was ever *her* place; but, so far as is recorded, never so Martha's. It is beautiful to observe that each time the New Testament presents Mary to us, she is seen "at the feet of Jesus"—expressive of her worshipful spirit. But there is no mere repetition. In Luke 10, at Christ's feet she owned Him as *Prophet,* hearing His word (v. 39). Here in John 11 she approaches Christ as *Priest*—that great High Priest that can be "touched with the feeling of our infirmities", who shares our sorrows, and ministers grace in every time of need. In John 12:3 Mary, at His feet acknowledged Him as *"King"*—this will appear if we compare Matt. 26:7, from which we learn that she *also* anointed "the head" of the rejected King of the Jews!

"When Jesus therefore saw her weeping, and the Jews also weeping which came with her, He groaned in the spirit, and was troubled" (v. 33). The Greek word here for "groaned" is expressive of deep feeling, sometimes of sorrow, more often of indignation. In this instance the Holy Spirit has recorded the cause of Christ's groaning—it was the sight of Mary and her comforters weeping. He was here in the midst of a groaning creation, which sighed and travailed over that which *sin* had brought in. And this He felt acutely. The original suggests that He was distressed to the extremest degree: moved to a holy indignation and sorrow at the terrific brood which sin had borne. Agitated by a righteous detestation of what evil had wrought in the world. "And was troubled" is, more, literally, "He troubled Himself": he caused Himself to be troubled by what made others weep and wail. And how this "groaning" and "troubling of Himself" brings out the perfections of the incarnate Son! He would not raise Lazarus until He had entered in spirit into the solemnity and awfulness of death. Mark 8:12 intimates that the miracles which He performed *cost Him something.* Plainer still is the testimony of Matt. 8:17: "Himself took our infirmities, and bare our sicknesses"—He felt the *burden* of sickness before He removed it.

"And said, Where have ye laid him? They said unto Him, Lord come and see" (v. 34). What a mark of genuineness is this line in the picture! Who that was inventing a fictitious story would have introduced such a detail in a scene like this! But how thoroughly in keeping with everything else which the Gospels record about Christ. There was no ostentation about Him. He never used His omniscience for the mere sake of display. He wished to be invited to the sepulchre.

"Jesus wept" (v. 35). The shortest verse in the Bible, and yet what volumes it contains. The Son of God weeping, and weeping on the very eve of raising the dead man! Who can fathom it? Three times in the New Testament we read of the Lord Jesus weeping: here, over Jerusalem, (Luke 19:41), and in Gethsemane (Heb. 5:7). Each time His tears were connected with the effects or consequences of sin. By the graveside of Lazarus these tears expressed the fulness of the grief which His heart felt. They manifested the perfectness of His love and the strength of His sympathy. He was the Man of sorrows and "acquainted with grief". Yet, here too was more than an expression of human sympathy. Here were souls upon which rested the weight of the dark shadow of death, and they were souls which He loved, and He *felt* it.

"Jesus wept": "The consciousness that He carried resurrection-virtue in Him, and was about to fill the house at Bethany with the joy of restored life, did not stay the current of natural affections. 'Jesus wept'. His heart was still alive to the sorrow, as to the degradation of death. His calmness throughout this exquisite scene was not *indifference,* but elevation. His soul was in the sunshine of those deathless regions which lay far away and beyond the tomb of Lazarus, but He could visit that valley of tears, and weep with those that wept." (J. G. Bellett).

"Then said the Jews, Behold how He loved him!" (v. 36). How these tears demonstrated "the profound sympathy of the heart of Jesus with us in all the sorrows and trials through which we pass. Had those sisters for a moment questioned the love of Jesus for them and His sympathy with them in their sorrow, how they would be rebuked by these groans and tears! 'Jesus wept'. What tender sympathy and grace! And He is the same to-day. It is true the surroundings are different, but His heart is the same: "Jesus Christ, *the same yesterday and to-day and forever.*" He 'wept'. How we see the reality of His human nature! Yes; it was a perfect human heart. He wept for the sorrow and desolation which sin had brought into the world; and He entered into it as no other could. Oh! what groans and tears! How they tell out the heart of our precious Lord Jesus! He truly loved these tried ones, and they proved it. So shall we if we rest in the same tender, gracious, sympathizing Lord" (C. H. M.).

"And some of them said, "Could not this Man, which opened the eyes of the blind, have caused that even this man should not have died?" (v. 37). This sounds very much like the language of men determined to believe nothing good of our Lord, insistent on picking a hole or finding a fault, if possible, in any thing that He did. Their words have a sarcastic ring about them. Some have wondered why these carping critics did not mention the raising of Jairus' daughter or the widow's son. But it should be remembered that both of these miracles had been performed in Galilee. Moreover, the healing of the blind man in Jerusalem was much more recent. It is clear that they had no thought of help being available now that Lazarus was dead, and so they openly reproach Christ for allowing him *to* die. And men in their petulance and unbelief, especially at funerals, still ask much the same questions: Why should the Almighty have permitted this? They forget that "He giveth not account of any of His matters" (Job 33:13). "What I do thou knowest not now; but thou shalt know hereafter" (John 13:7) is sufficient for faith.

"Jesus therefore again groaning in Himself cometh to the grave. It was a cave, and a stone lay upon it (v. 38). This time, as the "therefore" indicates, the *groaning* was occasioned by the carping unbelief of those mentioned in the previous verse. Here it was a matter of Christ "enduring the contradiction of sinners against Himself" (Heb. 12:3). It shows how He *felt* the antagonism of those who knew Him not. It was not as a stoic that He passed through these scenes. Everything that was contrary to His holy nature moved Him deeply. How blessed it is for us to remember this as we, who have the firstfruits of the Spirit, "groan within ourselves, waiting for the adoption, the redemption of our body" (Rom. 8:23). How comforting to know that our Redeemer felt the same thing which the new nature within us feels; only felt it a thousand times more acutely. Not for nothing was He termed "The Man of sorrows". In us there is ever a conflict; one nature feeding on the other repelled by the things of this world. But with the Holy One of God there was nothing to neutralize, nothing to modify, the anguish which His spirit felt from His daily contact with evil and corruption. As Hebrews tells us, "He *suffered* being tempted". It is true there was nothing in Him to which Satan could appeal, and therefore there was no possibility of Him yielding. But nevertheless the temptation was a fearful reality. His holy nature recoiled from the very presence of the Evil One, as his "get thee hence, Satan" plainly intimates. His spotless purity was sickened by the vile solicitations of the Tempter. Yes, He *suffered* to a degree we do not and cannot. Suffered not only from the temptation of Satan, but from the evil which surrounded Him on every side. The "groaning" which the Holy Spirit has here recorded gives us a glimpse of what must have gone on constantly in the spirit of that blessed One so deeply "acquainted with grief."

"Jesus said, Take ye away the stone" (v. 39). "What majestic *composure* in the midst of this mighty emotion!" (Stier). Though weeping outwardly and groaning inwardly, the Lord Jesus was complete master of Himself. He acts and speaks with quiet dignity. The miracles of God avoid with the supremest propriety all that is superfluous. So often in the mighty works of God we may observe an economy of Divine power. What man *could* do, He is required to do. We have little use for the hackneyed saying that "God helps those who help themselves", for God very often helps those who are *unable* to help themselves. Yet, on the other hand, it remains true that it is not God's general way to do for us what we are responsible and capable of doing for ourselves. God is pleased to bless our use of the means which are to hand. If I am a farmer, I shall harvest no crops unless I plow and sow and care for my fields. Just as in the first miracle of this Gospel Christ ordered men to fill the jars with water, so here He ordered men to roll away the stone.

"Jesus said, Take ye away the stone". There is another lesson for us to learn here. He might have commanded the stone to roll itself away, or He might have bidden Lazarus to come forth through the impediment of the stone. Instead, He bade the bystanders remove it. Christ modestly avoided all pomp and parade and mingled the utmost simplicity with the most amazing displays of power. What an example He thus set *us* to avoid all ostentation.

"Martha, the sister of him that was dead, saith unto Him, Lord, by this time he sleepeth: for he hath been dead four days" (v. 39). What a characteristic word was this from one who was "careful about many things", ever anxious about circumstances. Did Martha suppose that Christ only desired to view the body? It would seem so. And yet how sad is the unbelief which her utterance expressed. Lazarus' own sister would put an obstacle in the way of the manifestation of Christ's glory! She supposed it was useless to remove the stone. How solemnly this warns us that natural affections can never rise to the thoughts of God, and that only too frequently we are opposed to His workings even where it is for *the blessing* of those whom we love most tenderly! How often has a husband, a wife, a parent, sought to resist the Word or providences of God, as they were operating in or on the object of our affection! Let us take to heart this lamentable resistance of Martha.

"Jesus saith unto her, Said I not unto thee, that, if thou wouldest believe, thou shouldest see the glory of God?" (v. 40). There is considerable difference of opinion as to what our Lord referred to when He declared, "Said I not unto thee? etc." Many suppose He was reminding her of some word of His spoken just before, when she had met Him alone, and which is not recorded in the context. This is mere supposition, and an unlikely one at that. It seems more natural to regard it as pointing back to the answer Christ had sent her from Bethabara: "This sickness is not unto death, but for the glory of God, that the Son of God may be glorified thereby" (v. 4). Others think it was as though He said, "Martha, thou art forgetting the great doctrine of faith which I have ever taught thee. How often you have heard Me say, All things are possible to him that believeth". There may be a measure of truth in this as well.

"Jesus saith unto her, Said I not unto thee, that, if thou wouldest believe, thou shouldest see the glory of God?" Profound word was this. "The glory of God"! That which rejoices the soul when seen and known; that, without which we must forever remain unsatisfied and unblest; that, in comparison with which all sights are as nothing,—is "the glory of God". This was what Moses prayed to see: "Show me, I beseech Thee, Thy glory". The glory of God is the revelation of His excellencies, the visible display of His invisible perfections. It was the glory of God which Christ came here to make manifest, for He is the outshining of God's glory (Heb. 1:3). But the one special point to which our Lord here referred, was His own glory as the Bringer of life out of death. It was this which He came to reveal, both in His own person, by dying and rising again, and in the works of His hands—here in the raising of Lazarus. To remove the wages of death, to undo the work which sin had wrought, to conquer him that the power of death, to swallow up death in victory—this was indeed a special manifestation of glory.

"God, who commanded the light to shine out of darkness, hath shined in our hearts, to give the light of the knowledge of the glory of God in the face of Jesus Christ" (2 Cor. 4:6). Now it is unbelief which hinders our seeing the glory of God. It is not our unworthiness, our ignorance, nor our feebleness, that stand in the way, but our unbelief, for there is far more of unbelief than faith in us, as well as in Martha. Those searching words, "Said I not unto *thee*" apply to writer and reader. He was reminding Martha of a word given her before, but which had not been "mixed with faith". Alas, how often His words to us have fallen on unresponsive hearts. Mark the order of the two verbs here: "Believe" comes before "see", and compare our remarks on 6:69.

"Then they took away the stone from the place where the dead was laid" (v. 41). As pointed out previously, two things stand out conspicuously all through this chapter: the glory of Christ and the failure of men; His perfections and their imperfections confront us at every point. Christ had bidden the bystanders "Take ye away the stone"—doubtless a heavy one (cf. Matt.

27:60) which would require several men to move. But they had not responded. They paused to listen to Martha's objection. It was not until He had replied to her, not until He had spoken of the glory of God being seen, that they obeyed—"*Then* they took away the stone". How slow is man to obey the Word of God! What trifles are allowed to hinder!

"And Jesus lifted up His eyes, and said, Father, I thank Thee that Thou hast heard Me" (v. 41). Very beautiful is this. It manifested Christ as the dependent One. Perfectly did He fulfil Prov. 3:5, 6: "Trust in the Lord with all thine heart, and lean not unto thine own understanding. In *all* thy ways *acknowledge Him.*" But more: it was the Son giving the Father the honor for the miracle which was about to be performed. He directed attention away from Himself, to One in heaven. Well might He say, "Learn of Me, for I am *meek* and *lowly* in heart" (Matt. 11:29). And too, there is another thing here. In view of His words in the next verse it seems clear that He also lifted up His eyes for the sake of those standing around. His miracles had been blasphemously attributed to Satan and Hell; He would here show the true Source from which they proceeded—"Jesus *lifted up* His eyes". Note also His, "Father *I thank* Thee". He *began* with this. Christ has left us a perfect example, not only of prayerfulness but of thankfulness as well. We are always more ready to ask than thank: but see Phil. 4:6.

"And Jesus lifted up His eyes, and said, Father, I thank Thee that Thou hast heard Me". "We now reach a point of thrilling and breathless interest. The stone had been removed from the mouth of the cave. Our Lord stands before the open grave, and the crowd stands around, awaiting anxiously to see what would happen next. Nothing appears from the tomb. There is no sign of life at present; but while all are eagerly looking and listening, our Lord addresses His Father in heaven in a most solemn manner, lifting up His eyes, and speaking audibly to Him in the hearing of all the crowd. The reason He explains in the next verse. Now, for the last time, about to work His mightiest miracle, He once more makes a public declaration that He did nothing separate from His Father in heaven, and that in this and all His work there is a mysterious and intimate union between Himself and the Father" (Bishop Ryle).

"And I knew that Thou hearest Me always" (v. 42). What perfect confidence in the Father had this One here in servant form. And what was the ground of His confidence? Has He not Himself told us in John 8:29?—"He that sent Me is with Me; the Father hath not left Me alone; *For* I do *always* those things that *please* Him"! "The Lord Jesus never had a thought which was out of harmony with the Father's will, and never did a thing which in the slightest degree deviated from His Father's word. He *always* did those things which pleased Him (Psl. 16:8); therefore did the Father always hear Him. What light this throws on our *un*-answered prayers! There is an intimate relation between our conduct and the response which we receive to our supplications: "If I regard iniquity in my heart, the Lord will not hear me" (Psl. 66:18). Equally clear is the N. T.: "And whatsoever we ask, we receive of Him, *because* we keep His commandments, and do those things that are *pleasing* in His sight" (1 John 3:22). Very searching is this. It is not what men term "legalism" but the Father maintaining the demands of His holiness. For God to answer the prayers of one who had no concern for His glory and no respect to His commandments, would be to place a premium upon sin.

"And I knew that Thou hearest Me always". Very, very blessed is this. Unspeakable comfort does it minister to the heart that rests upon it. Christ did not cease to pray when He left this earth: He still prays, prays for us, His people: "Wherefore He is able also to save them to the uttermost that come unto God by Him, seeing He ever liveth to make intercession for them" (Heb. 7:25). How much we *owe to* His intercession eternity will reveal—far, far more than we now realize. Read through John 17 and note the different things He has asked (and possibly, still asks) the Father for us. He asks that His joy may be fulfilled in us (v. 13), that we may be kept from evil in the world (v. 15), that we may be sanctified through the truth (v. 17), that we may be one (21), that we may be made perfect in one (v. 23), that we may be with Him where He is (v. 24), that we may behold His glory (v. 24). None of these things are yet ours in their fulness; but how unspeakably blessed to *know* that the time is coming when *all* of them *will* be! The Father hears Christ "always", therefore these things *must* be made good to us!

"But because of the people which stand by I said it, that they may believe that Thou hast sent Me" (v. 42). How this reminds us of Elijah on mount Carmel! "Elijah the prophet came near and said, Lord God of Abraham, Isaac, and of Israel, let it be known this day that Thou art God in Israel, and *that I am Thy servant*, and that I have done all these things at Thy word. Hear me, O Lord, hear me, that *this people may know* that Thou art the Lord God" (1 Kings 18:36, 37)! This scripture supplies the key to the meaning of the Lord's words beside the tomb of Lazarus. Like Elijah's, Christ's mission was unto Israel, and like Elijah, He here prayed that God would authenticate His mission. If *the Father* had not sent Him, He would not have heard Him in anything; the Father hearing Him here at the graveside of Lazarus was therefore a clear proof and full evidence of His *Divine* mission.

"And when He had thus spoken, He cried with a loud voice, Lazarus, come forth" (v. 43). This "loud voice" was also for the people's sake, that all might hear. Lazarus was addressed personally for, as it has been well remarked, had Christ simply cried "Come forth" Hades would have been emptied and every tenant of the grave would have been raised from the dead. We have here, in miniature, what will take place on the Resurrection-morn. "The Lord Himself shall descend from heaven *with a shout*. . . and the dead in Christ shall rise" (1 Thess. 4:16, 17). So, too, will it be a thousand years later, when the wicked dead shall be resurrected: "Marvel not at this: for the hour is coming, in the which *all* that are in the graves shall *hear his voice*" (John 5:28). It is striking to note that Christ here did nothing, except to say, "Lazarus, come forth". It was the last great public witness to Christ as the incarnate *Word*. And, too, it perfectly illustrated the means which God employs in regeneration. Men are raised spiritually, pass from death unto life, by means of the written Word, and by that alone. Providences, personal testimonies, loss of loved ones, deeply as these sometimes may stir the natural man, they *never* "quicken" a soul into newness of life. We are born again, "not of corruptible seed, but of incorruptible by *the Word of God*, which liveth and abideth forever" (1 Pet. 1:23).

"Lazarus, come forth. And he that was dead came forth" (v. 44). At the sound of that Voice the king of terrors at once yielded up his lawful captive, and the insatiable grave gave up its prey. Captivity was led captive and Christ stood forth as the Conqueror of sin, death and Satan. There it was demonstrated that He who was in the form of a Servant, nevertheless, held in His own hand "the keys of death and Hades". Here was public proof that the Lord Jesus had absolute power over the material world and over the realm of spirits. At His bidding a soul that had left its earthly tenement was called back from the unseen to dwell once more in the body. What a demonstration was this that He who could work such astounding miracles must be none other than "God over all blessed forever" (Rom. 9:5). Thank God for an all-mighty Saviour. How can any sheep of *His* ever perish when held in *such* a Hand!

"And he that was dead came forth" (v. 44). "This shows us what the energy, the utmost energy, of evil can do over those who are the beloved of the Lord; but it also shows us how the Lord Jesus sets it altogether aside in the energy and in the strength of His own power. We have here the full result of Satan's power, and the perfect triumphing of the Lord over that power. Death is the result of the power of Satan. By bringing in sin, he brought in death: 'the wages of sin'; this is the utmost of Satan's power. He brought in this at the commencement, he brought it in by deceit; for 'he was a murderer from the beginning, and abode not in the truth'. Such has he been ever since; he is called the old Serpent and the Deceiver; and having deceived, he became the murderer of the first Adam, and in one sense, of the last Adam. He was and is a liar; that is his character, as exactly opposed to Christ, who is the truth. In like manner all the variations of his character are set in opposition to that of Christ. He is the Destroyer, and Christ is the Giver of life; He is the Accuser of the brethren, and Christ the Mediator for them; Christ the Truth of God, and Satan the father of lies. In this character he is first brought before us. By misrepresenting the truth and character of God, he became the murderer of the souls of men, and brought in death—this was his power. Christ came to destroy him that had the power of death, that is, the Devil. The Son of God came to destroy the works of the Devil by bringing souls from the power of Satan to the power of the living God. This is what is so strikingly illustrated here in John 11" (Mr. Darby).

There are two ways in which the Lord Jesus has become the Resurrection and the Life of His people: First, in purchasing their redemption from the wages of sin, by paying Himself the full price which Divine justice demanded for their transgressions. This He did by His own voluntary and vicarious sufferings; being made a curse for us. Second, by making us one with Himself who is the very life of all being: "he that is joined unto the Lord is one spirit" (1 Cor. 6:17). It was this He prayed for in John 17: "That they all may be *one;* as Thou, Father, art in Me, and I in Thee, that they also may be *one in Us*" (v. 21). This is made good by the Holy Spirit: "If any man be in Christ he is a new creation" (2 Cor. 5:17). The believer is "in Christ" not only by the eternal choice of the Father (Eph. 1:4), not only by Him being constituted our federal Head (1 Cor. 15:22), but also by *vital union.* In this double way then is Christ unto us "the Resurrection and the Life", and thus has He completely triumphed over him (the Devil) who *had* (no longer "has") the power of death. A most striking figure of this was Lazarus. Dead, in the grave, his body already gone to corruption. At the allmighty word of Christ "he that was dead came forth". The children of God are the children of the resurrection. Where Christ is made the Life of the soul, there is the certainty of a resurrection to life eternal *in Christ's life:* when *His* life is communicated to us, we have that within us over which the power of Satan is unable to prevail. Dimly, but beautifully, was this foreshadowed of old in the case of Job. Afflict him Satan might, destroy his possessions he was permitted to do, but touch his *life* he could not!

The picture presented here in John 11 is Divinely perfect. It was during the bodily absence of Christ from Bethany that death exercised its power over Lazarus. It is so with us now. What we have in John 11 is not merely an individual, but a *family*—a family beloved of the Lord. How clearly this prefigured the Family of God now upon earth! While Christ was bodily absent, the power of death was felt, and sorrow and grief came in. But tears gave place to rejoicing. After abiding "two days" where He was, Christ came to that afflicted family, and His very presence manifested the power of life. So, when Christ returns for His people, it will be in this same twofold character: as the Resurrection and the Life. Then will He put away not only the grief of His people, but that which has *caused* it. In the interval His "tears" (*before* He raised Lazarus) assure us of His deep sympathy!

"And He that was dead came forth, bound hand and foot with graveclothes: and his face was bound about with a napkin" (v. 44). This line in the picture in nowise mars its accuracy, rather does it intensify it. Whether we view the raising of Lazarus as a figure of the regeneration of a sinner, the glorification of the believer, or the yet future restoration of Israel, the "graveclothes" here and the *removal* of them, are equally significant. When a sinner is born again, God's work of grace in his soul is not perfected, rather has it just commenced. The old nature still remains and the marks of the grave are still upon him. There is much to impede the movements of the "new man", much from which he needs to be "loosed", and which his spiritual resurrection did not of itself effect. The language of such a soul was expressed by the apostle Paul when he said, "To will is present with me, but how to perform that which is good I find not. . . for I delight in the law of God after the inward man; but I see another law in my members, warring against the law of my mind, and bringing me into captivity to the law of sin which is in my members" (Rom. 7:18, 22, 23). It was so here with Lazarus when the Lord called him from the tomb; he did not leave the hampering graveclothes behind him, but came forth "bound hand and foot".

"Jesus saith unto them, Loose him, and let him go" (v. 44). How this brings out the moral glory of Christ. The fact that He had to *ask* the bystanders to liberate the risen man shows that the spectators were all overcome with amazement and awe. The Lord alone remained serene and collected. That the Lord invited *them* to "loose him" (rather than, by a miracle, cause the clothes to fall from him,) points a beautiful lesson. In gracious condescension the Lord of glory links human instruments with Himself in the work which He is now doing in the world. Again and again is this seen in John's Gospel. He used the servants at the wedding-feast, when He turned the water into wine. He fed the hungry multitude through the hands of His disciples. He bade the spectators of this last public miracle roll the stone away from the grave; and now He asks them to free Lazarus from the graveclothes. And this is still His blessed way. He alone can speak the word which quickens dead sinners; but He permits us to *carry* that word to them. What an inestimable privilege—an honor not given even to the angels! O that we might esteem it more highly. There is no higher privilege this side of Heaven than for us to be used of the Lord in rolling away gravestones and removing graveclothes.

"Jesus saith unto them, Loose him, and let him go". But there is a yet deeper and even more blessed truth taught us here. In its ultimate application the raising of Lazarus points, as we have seen, to the full manifestation of Christ as the Resurrection and the Life at the time when He returns to His sorrowing "family". Then will God's wondrous work of sovereign grace be perfected. No longer shall we be left in a groaning creation, but removed to His own place on high. No longer shall we be imprisoned in these tabernacles of clay, for we shall be "delivered from the bondage of corruption" and enter into "the glorious *liberty* of the children of God". No more shall our face be "bound about with a napkin", which now causes us to see "through a glass darkly", but in that glad Day we shall see "face to face" (1 Cor. 13:12). Then shall this corruptible put on incorruption and mortality shall be "swallowed up of life" (2 Cor. 5:4). It is of *this* that the "Loose him" speaks. No more shall we wear the habiliments of death, but then shall we rejoice in that One who has forever set us free that we might walk with Him in newness of life. Then, ah, then, shall we obtain joy and gladness, and sorrow and sighing shall flee away.

"Loose him". This was to satisfy the onlookers that they had not been deceived by any optical delusion. With their own hands they were permitted to handle his body. It is very striking to observe that in this final "sign" of Christ, conclusive evidence was offered to three of their senses—nostrils, eyes, and hands: the "stink", must have been apparent when the stone was removed from the cave; they *saw* Lazarus come forth a living man; they were suffered to *touch* and handle him. All possible deception was therefore out of question.

"And let him go". The spectators were not allowed to satisfy an idle curiosity. Lazarus was to retire to the privacy of home. Those who had witnessed the miracle of his resurrection, were not suffered to pry into the secrets of the grave or ask him curious questions. "Let him go" was the authoritative word of Christ, and there the curtain falls. And fitly so. When the Lord Jesus leaves His Father's throne on high and descends into the air, we too shall *go*—go from these scenes of sin and suffering, go to be "forever with the Lord". Glorious prospect! Blessed climax! Blissful goal! May our eyes be steadily fixed upon it, running with perseverance the race set before us, looking off unto Him who "for *the joy that was set before Him,* endured the cross, despising the shame, and is set down at the right hand of the throne of God" (Heb. 12:2).

The following questions are to prepare the student for the closing section of John 11:—

1. How explain the different actions of the spectators vv. 45, 46?
2. What important truth is illustrated in v. 50?
3. What is meant by "this spake he not of Himself" v. 51?
4. What do vv. 51, 52 teach about the Atonement?
5. "Gather together" in *one* what v. 52?
6. Why did Jesus "walk *no more* openly among the Jews" v. 54?
7. What is meant by "to purify themselves" v. 55?

Arthur W. Pink.

GLEANINGS IN EXODUS.

15. The Passover: Ex. 12.

In Exodus 11:4-7 we read, "Thus saith the Lord, About midnight will I go out into the midst of Egypt: And all the firstborn in the land of Egypt shall die, from the firstborn of Pharaoh that sitteth upon his throne, even unto the firstborn of the maidservant that is behind the mill; and all the firstborn of beasts. And there shall be a great cry throughout all the land of Egypt, such as there was none like it, nor shall be like it anymore. But against any of the children of Israel shall not a dog move his tongue against man or beast, that ye may know how that the Lord doth put a difference between the Egyptians and Israel". Notice carefully the exact wording of v. 5: it was not "all the firstborn *of* the land of Egypt shall die, but "all the firstborn *in* the land of Egypt". This Divine sentence of judgment included the Israelites equally with the Egyptians. Yet in the seventh verse we are told "not a dog shall move his tongue against any of the children of Israel, for the Lord "put *a difference* between the Egyptians and Israel". Here is what the infidel would call 'a flat contradiction!' But as we are fully assured that there can be *no* contradictions in "the Word of *Truth*", so we know there must be an interpretation which brings out the harmony of this passage. *What that is,* no mere human wisdom could have devised. The sentence of universal condemnation proceeded from the *righteousness* of God; the "difference" which He put between the Egyptians and Israel was the outflow of His *grace.* But how can justice and mercy be reconciled? How can justice exact its full due without excluding mercy? How can mercy be manifested except at the expense of justice? This is really the problem that is raised here. The solution of it is found in Ex. 12. *All* the firstborn *in* the land of Egypt *did die,* and yet the firstborn of Israel were *delivered* from the Angel of Death! But how could this be? Surely both could not be true. Yes they were, and therein we may discover a blessed illustration and type of the contents of the Gospel.

Ex. 12 records the last of the ten plagues. This was the death of the firstborn, and inasmuch as death is "the wages of sin", we have no difficulty in perceiving that it is the question of SIN which is here raised and dealt with by God. This being the case, both the Egyptians and the Israelites alike were abnoxious to His righteous judgment, for both were sinners before Him. This was dealt with at some length in our last paper. In this respect the Egyptians and the Israelites were alike: both in nature and in practice they were sinners. "There is no difference: for *all* have sinned and come short of the glory of God (Rom. 3:22, 23). It is true that God had purposed to redeem Israel out of Egypt, but He would do so only on a *righteous basis.* Holiness can never ignore sin, no matter where it is found. When the angels sinned God "spared them not" (2 Pt. 2:4). The elect are "children of *wrath* even as others" (Eph. 2:3). God made no exception of His own blessed Son: when He was "made sin for us" (2 Cor. 5:21)—He spared Him not (Rom. 8:32).

But all of this only seems to make the problem more impossible of solution. The Israelites were sinners: their guilt was irrefutably established: a just God can "by no means clear the guilty" (Ex. 34:7): sentence of death was passed upon them (Ex. 11:5). Nothing remained but the carrying out of the sentence. A reprieve was out of the question. Justice *must* be satisfied; sin *must* be paid its wages. What, then? Shall Israel perish after all? It would seem so. Human wisdom could furnish no solution. No; but man's extremity is God's opportunity, and He did find a solution. "Where sin abounded, grace did much more abound" (Rom. 5:20), and yet grace was not shown at the expense of righteousness. Every demand of justice *was* satisfied, every claim of holiness *was* fully met. But how? By means of *a substitute.* Sentence of death *was* executed, but it fell upon an innocent victim. That which was *"without* blemish" died in the stead of those who had *"no* soundness" (Isa. 1:6) in them. The "difference" between the Egyptians and Israel was not a moral one, but was made solely by the blood of the pascal lamb! It was in the blood of the Lamb that mercy and truth met together and righteousness and peace kissed each other (Psl. 85:10).

The whole value of the blood of the pascal lamb lay in its being a type of the Lord Jesus—"Christ our Passover is sacrificed for us: therefore let us keep the feast" (1 Cor. 5:7, 8). Here is Divine authority for our regarding the contents of Ex. 12 as typical of the Cross-work of our blessed Saviour. And it is this which invests every detail of our chapter with such deep interest. May our eyes be anointed so that we shall be able to perceive some, at least, of the precious unfoldings of the truth which are typically set forth in our chapter.

The first great truth to lay hold of here is what we are told in the 11th verse: "It is *the Lord's* passover". This emphasizes a side of the truth which is much neglected to-day in evangelical preaching. Gospellers have much to say about what Christ's death accomplished for those who believe in Him, but very little is said about what that Death accomplished *Godwards.* The fact is that the death of Christ glorified God if never a single sinner had been saved by virtue of it. Nor is this simply a matter of theology. The more we study the teaching of Scripture on this subject, and the more we lay hold by simple faith of what the Cross meant to God, the more stable will be our peace and the deeper our joy and praise.

The particular aspect of truth which we now desire to press upon the reader is plainly taught in many a passage. Take the very first (direct) reference to the "Lamb" in Scripture. In Gen. 22:8 we read that Abraham said to his son, "God will provide Himself a lamb for a burnt offering". It was not simply God would "provide" a lamb, but that He would "provide *Himself* a lamb". The Lamb was "provided" to glorify God's character, to vindicate His throne, to satisfy His justice, to magnify His holiness. So, too, in the ritual on the annual Day of Atonement, we read of the two goats. Why *two?* To foreshadow the two great aspects of Christ's atoning work —Godwards and usward. "And he shall take the two goats and present them before the Lord at the door of the Tabernacle of the congregation. And Aaron shall cast lots upon the two goats; one lot *for the Lord*, and the other for the scapegoat" (Lev. 16:7, 8). It is *this* aspect of truth which is before us in Rom. 3:24-26, "Being justified freely by His grace through the redemption that is in Christ Jesus. Whom God hath set forth to be *a propitiation* through faith in His blood to declare *His righteousness* . . . that He might be *just*, and the justifier of him which believeth in Jesus". In 1 Cor. 5:7 we read, "Christ *our* Passover". He is now *our* Passover, because He was first *the Lord's* Passover (Ex. 12:11).

If further confirmation of what we have said above be needed it is supplied by another term which is used in Ex. 12:27. Here we are expressly told that the Passover was a "sacrifice"—"It is *the sacrifice* of the Lord's passover". Nor is this the only verse in the Scriptures where the Passover is called a sacrifice. In Ex. 34:25 we read that God said unto Israel, "Thou shalt not offer the blood of My sacrifice with leaven; neither shall *the sacrifice* of the feast of the Passover be left unto the morning". Again, in Deut. 16:2 we read, "Thou shalt therefore *sacrifice the Passover* unto the Lord thy God". So also in the New Testament, it is said, "Christ our Passover is *sacrificed* for us" (1 Cor. 5:7). We emphasize this point because it has been *denied* by many that the Passover *was* a "sacrifice". Objectors have pointed out that the pascal lamb was not slain by the priest, nor was it offered upon the altar, for there was no altar which God could own in Egypt. But such an objection is quickly removed if reference be made to the later Scriptures on the subject. *After the Exodus* the "passover" was never allowed to be killed anywhere except in the place which God had chosen. This is abundantly clear from Deut. 16:4, 5, "And there shall be no leavened bread seen with thee in all thy coasts seven days, neither shall there any thing of the flesh, which thou sacrificedst the first day at even, remain all night until the morning. Thou mayest not sacrifice the passover within any of *thy* gates, which the Lord thy God giveth thee; but *at the place* which the Lord thy God shall choose to place His name in, *there* thou shalt sacrifice the passover at even, at the going down of the sun, at the season that thou camest forth out of Egypt". The Israelites were here expressly forbidden to kill the passover in their own homes, and were commanded to sacrifice it *only* "at the place which the Lord Thy God shall choose to place His name in". What *that* "place" was we may learn from Deut. 12:5, 6 and similar passages—it was the Tabernacle, afterwards the Temple.

That the Passover was a *"sacrifice"*, a priestly offering, is further proven by the fact that in Numbers 9:6, 7, 13, it is specifically designated a "corban", and it is certain that nothing was ever so called except what was brought and offered to God in the Tabernacle or the Temple. Furthermore, there is definite scripture to show that the blood of the pascal sacrifice was poured out, sprinkled, offered at the altar by *the priests*. "Thou shalt not *offer* the blood of My sacrifice with leavened bread; neither shall the fat of My sacrifice remain until the morning" (Ex. 23:18)—only *the priests* "offered" the blood. Plainer still is the testimony of 2 Chron. 30:15, 16, "Then they killed the passover on the fourteenth day of the second month and *the priests and the Levites* were ashamed, and sanctified themselves, and brought in the burnt offerings into the house of the Lord. And they stood in their place after their manner according to the Law of Moses the man of God; *the priests* sprinkled the blood". And 2 Chron. 35:11, "And they killed the passover and *the priests* sprinkled the blood". So again Ezra 6:20, "For the priests and the Levites were purified together, all of them were pure, and killed the passover for all the children of the captivity and for their brethren the priests, and for themselves". Note "the priests and Levites" killed the passover *for* all the children of the captivity!

Now there are two lines of thought associated with *sacrifices* in Scripture. First, a sacrifice is a propitiatory satisfaction rendered unto God. It is to placate His holy wrath. It is to appease His righteous hatred of sin. It is to pacify the claims of His justice. It is to settle the demands of His law. God is "light" as well as "love". He is of "purer eyes than to behold evil, and canst not look on iniquity" (Hab. 1:13). This truth is denied on every side today. Yet this should not surprise us; it is exactly what prophecy foretold (2 Tim. 4:3, 4). Plain and pointed is the teaching of Scripture on this subject. Following the rebellion and destruction of Korah, we read that all the Congregation murmured against Moses and Aaron saying, "Ye have killed the people". What was God's response? This: "The Lord spake unto Moses saying, "Get you up from among this congregation, that I may consume them as in a moment" (Num. 16:45). How was the consuming anger of God averted? Thus: "And Moses said unto Aaron, Take a censer and put fire therein off the altar, and put on incense and go quickly unto the congregation and make an *atonement* for them; *for* there is *wrath* gone out from the Lord; the plague is begun. And Aaron took as Moses commanded and ran into the midst of the congregation; and, behold, the plague was begun among the people; and he put on incense, and made an atonement for the people. And he stood between the dead and the living; and *the plague* was stayed" (Num. 16:46-48)! A similar passage is found in the last chapter of Job. There we read, "The Lord said to Eliphaz the Temanite, My *wrath* is kindled against thee and against thy two friends; for ye have not spoken of Me the thing that is right, as My servant Job hath. *Therefore* take unto you now seven bullocks and seven rams and go to My servant Job, and offer up for yourselves a *burnt offering;* and My servant Job shall pray for you: for him will I accept; lest I deal with you after your folly."

Here, then, is the primary thought connected with "sacrifice". It is a bloody offering to appease the holy wrath of a sin-hating and sin-punishing God. And *this* is the very word which is used again and again in connection with the Lord Jesus the Great Sacrifice. Thus, Eph. 5:2: "Christ also hath loved us, and hath given Himself for us an offering and *a sacrifice to God* for a sweet-smelling savor." Again, "Once in the end of the world hath He appeared to put away sin *by the sacrifice* of Himself", (Heb. 9:26). And again, "This man, after He had offered one *sacrifice* for sins forever sat down on the right hand of God (Heb. 10:12). The meaning of these passages is explained by Rom. 3:25, 26,: Christ was unto God a "propitiation", an appeasement, a pacification, a legal satisfaction. Therefore could the forerunner of the Redeemer say, "Behold the Lamb of God which taketh away the sin of the world" (John 1:29).

The second thought associated with "sacrifice" in the Scriptures is that of *thanksgiving and praise* unto God; this being the effect of the former. It is because Christ has propitiated God on their behalf that believers can now offer "a sacrifice of praise" (Heb. 13:15). Said one of old, "And now shall mine head be lifted up above mine enemies round about me; therefore will I offer in His tabernacle *sacrifices of joy*" (Psl. 27:6). Said another, "I will sacrifice unto Thee with a voice of thanksgiving" (Jonah 2:9). This is why, after being told that "Christ our Passover hath been sacrificed for us", the exhortation follows "therefore let us keep *the feast*" (1 Cor. 5:7). The pascal lamb was first a sacrifice unto God; second, it then became the food of those sheltered beneath its blood.

The ritual in connection with the Passover in Egypt was very striking. The lamb was to be *killed* (Ex. 12:6). Death must be inflicted either upon the guilty transgressor or upon an innocent substitute. Then its *blood* was to be taken and sprinkled upon the door-posts and lintel of the house wherein the Israelites sheltered that night. "Without *shedding* of blood is no remission" (Heb. 9:22), and without *sprinkling* of blood is no salvation. The two words are by no means synonymous. The former is for *propitiation;* the latter is faith's *appropriation*. It is not until the converted sinner *applies* the blood that it avails *for him*. An Israelite might have selected a proper lamb, he might have slain it, but unless he had *applied* its blood to the outside of the door, the Angel of Death would have entered his house and slain his first-born. In like manner to-day, it is not enough for me to know that the precious blood of the Lamb of God was shed for the remission of sins. A Saviour *provided* is not sufficient: he must be *received.* There must be "*faith* in His blood" (Rom. 3:25), and faith is a *personal* thing. *I* must exercise faith. I must by faith take the blood and shelter beneath it. I must place it between my sins and the thrice Holy God. I must rely upon it as the sole ground of my acceptance with Him.

"For I will pass through the land of Egypt this night and will smite all the first-born in the land of Egypt, both man and beast; and against all the gods of Egypt I will execute judgment; I am the Lord. And the blood shall be to you for a token upon the houses where ye are; and when I see the blood I will pass over you, and the plague shall not be upon you to destroy you, when I smite the land of Egypt" (Ex. 12:12, 13). When the executioner of God's judgment saw the blood upon the houses of the Israelites, he entered not, and why? Because death had already done its work there! The innocent *had died* in the place of the guilty. And thus justice was satisfied. To punish twice for the same crime would be unjust. To exact payment twice for the same debt is unlawful. Even so those within the blood-sprinkled house were secure. Blessed, blessed truth is this. It is not merely God's mercy but His *righteousness* which is now on the side of His people. Justice itself *demands* the acquittal of every believer in Christ. Herein lies the glory of the Gospel. Said the apostle Paul, "I am not ashamed of the Gospel of Christ; for it is the power of God unto salvation to every one that believeth; to the Jew first, and also to the Greek (Rom. 1:16). And *why* was he not "ashamed" of the Gospel? Hear his next words, "*For* therein is *the righteousness of God* revealed from faith to faith".

"And when I see the blood I will pass over you". God's eye was not upon the house, but on the blood. It might have been a lofty house, a strong house, a beautiful house; this made no difference; if there was no blood there judgment entered and did its deadly work. Its height, its strength, its magnificence availed nothing, if the blood was lacking. On the other hand, the house might be a miserable hovel, falling to pieces with age and decay; but no matter; if *blood* was upon its door, those within were perfectly safe.

Nor was God's eye upon those within the house. They might be lineal descendants of Abraham, they might have been circumcised on the eighth day, and in their outward life they might be walking blamelessly so far as the Law was concerned. But it was neither their genealogy, nor their ceremonial observances, nor their works, which secured deliverance from God's judgments. It was their personal application of the shed blood, and of that alone.

"And the blood shall be to you for a token upon the houses where ye are; and when I see the blood, I will pass over you" (v. 13). To the mind of the natural man this was consummate folly. What difference will it make, proud reason might ask, if *blood* be smeared upon the door? Ah! "The natural man receiveth not the things of the Spirit of God: for they are *foolishness* unto him (1 Cor. 2:14). Supremely true is this in connection with God's way of salvation—"For the preaching of the cross is to them that perish *foolishness;* but unto us which are saved it is the power of God . . . But we preach Christ crucified, unto the Jews a stumbling-block, and unto the Greeks foolishness" (1 Cor. 1:18, 23). It is faith, not reasoning, which God requires; and it was faith which rendered the Passover-sacrifice effective; "Through *faith* he kept the passover, and the sprinkling of blood lest he that destroyed the first-born should touch them" (Heb. 11:28).

"To realize what this faith must have been, we have to go back to 'that night', and note the special circumstances, which can alone explain the meaning of the words 'by faith'. God's judgments had been poured out on Egypt and its king, and its people. A crisis had arrived; for, after nine plagues had been sent, Pharaoh and the Egyptians still remained obdurate. Indeed, Moses had been threatened with death if he ever came again into Pharaoh's presence (Ex. 10:28, 29). On the other hand, the Hebrews were in more evil case than ever; and Moses, who was to have delivered them, had not made good his promises.

"It was at such a moment that Moses heard from God what he was to do. To sense and sight it must have seemed most inadequate, and quite unlikely to accomplish the desired result. Why should this last plague be expected to accomplish what the nine had failed to do with all their accumulating terrors? Why should the mere sprinkling of the blood have such a marvelous effect? And if they were indeed to leave Egypt 'that same night' why should the People be burdened with all those minute ceremonial observances at the moment when they ought to be making preparation for their departure? Nothing but 'faith' could be of any avail here. Everything was opposed to human understanding and human reasoning.

"With all the consciousness of ill-success upon him, nothing but unfeigned faith in the living God and what he had heard from Him, could have enabled Moses to go to the people and rehearse all the intricacies of the Pascal observances, and tell them to exercise the greatest care in the selection of a lamb on the tenth day of the month, to be slain on the fourteenth day, and eaten with (to them) an unmeaning ceremony. It called for no ordinary confidence in what Moses had *heard* from God to enable him to go to his brethren who, in their deep distress, must have been ill-disposed to listen; for, hitherto, his efforts had only increased the hatred of their oppressors, and their own miseries as bondmen. It would to human sight be a difficult if not impossible task to persuade the people, and convince them of the absolute necessity of complying with all the minute details of the observance of the Passover ordinance.

"But this is just where *faith* came in. This was just the field on which it could obtain its greatest victory. Hence we read that, "*through faith* he kept the passover, and the sprinkling of blood" (Heb. 11:28), and thus every difficulty was overcome, and the Exodus accomplished. All was based on 'the hearing of faith'. The words of Jehovah *produced* the faith, and were at once the cause and effect of all the blessing" (Dr. Bullinger)

"And the blood shall be to you for a token upon the houses where ye are: and when I see the blood, I will pass over you, and the plague shall not be upon you to destroy, when I smite the land of Egypt" (v. 13). In connection with this it is deeply important that we should distinguish between two things; the *foundation* of *security* and the proof *basis* of *peace.* That which provided a safe refuge from judgment was the *death* of the lamb and *sprinkling* of the blood. That which offered a stay to the heart was the *promise* of Him who cannot lie. So many err on this second point. They want to make their experience, their feelings, something within themselves, the basis of their assurance. This is a favorite device of Satan, to turn the eye downwards upon ourselves. The Holy Spirit ever directs the eye *away from ourselves* to God and His Word.

Let us suppose a case. Here are two households on that Passover night. At the head of the one is an unbelieving father who has refused to heed the Divine warning and avail himself of the Divine provision. Early that evening his firstborn says, "Father I am very uneasy. Moses has declared that at midnight an Angel is to visit this land and slay all the firstborn, except in those houses which are protected by the blood of a lamb". To still the fears of his son, the father lies, and assures him that there is no cause for alarm seeing that he *has* killed the lamb and applied its blood to the door. Hearing this, the son is at rest, all fear is gone, and in its place he is filled with peace. *But it is a false peace!*

In the second home the situation is reversed. At the head of this house is a God-fearing man. He has heard Jehovah's warning message through Moses, and hearing, has believed and acted accordingly; the lamb has been slain, its blood placed upon the lintel and posts of the door. That evening the firstborn says, "Father, I feel very uneasy. An Angel is to smite all the firstborn to-night and how shall I escape?" His father answers, "Son, your alarm is groundless; yea, it is dishonoring to God. The Lord has said, 'when I see the blood, *I will* pass over you'". "But", continues the son, "while I know that you have killed the lamb and applied its blood, I cannot be but terrified. Even now I hear the cries of terror and anguish going up from the houses of the Egyptians. O that morning would come! I shall not feel safe 'till then". *But his fears were groundless.*

Now observe. In the first case supposed above we have a man full of happy feelings, yet he perished. In the second case, we have one full of fears yet was he preserved. Examine the *ground* of each. The oldest son in the first house was happy because he made *the word of man* the ground of his peace. The oldest son in the second house was miserable because he *failed* to rest on the sure Word *of God.* Here, then, are two distinct things. *Security* is by the applied blood of the Lamb. *Assurance and peace* are to be found by resting on the Word of God. The *ground* of both is *outside* of ourselves. Feelings have nothing to do with either. Deliverance from judgment is by the Finished Work of Christ, *and by that alone.* Nothing else will avail. Religious experiences, ordinances, self-sacrifice,

Church-membership, works of mercy, cultivation of character, avail *nothing*. The first thing for me, as a poor lost sinner, to make sure of is, Am I *relying* upon what Christ did *for* sinners? Am I *personally* trusting in His shed blood? If I am not, if instead, under the eloquence and moving appeals of some evangelist, I have decided to turn over a new leaf, and endeavor to live a better life, and I have "gone forward" and taken the preacher's hand, and if *he* has told me that I am now saved and ready to "join the church," and doing so I feel happy and contented—*my peace is a false one*, and I shall end in the Lake of Fire, unless God in His grace disillusions me.

On the other hand, if the Holy Spirit has shown me my lost condition, my deep need of the Saviour, and if I have cast myself upon Christ as a drowning man clutches at a floating spar; if I have really *believed* on the Lord Jesus Christ (Acts 16:31), and *received* Him as my own personal Saviour (John 1:12), and yet, nevertheless, I am still lacking in assurance of *my acceptance* by God, and have no *settled peace* of heart; it is because I am failing to rest in simple faith on the *written Word*. GOD SAYS, "Believe on the Lord Jesus Christ and thou *shalt be saved*". That is enough. That is the Word of Him who cannot lie. Nothing more is needed. "Verily, verily, I say unto you, He that heareth My Word, and believeth on Him that sent Me, hath everlasting life, *and shall not come into condemnation;* but is passed from death unto life" (John 5:24). Never mind about your feelings; do not stop to examine your repentance to see if it be deep enough. It is CHRIST that saves; not your tears, or prayers, or resolutions. If you *have* received Christ, then you *are saved*. Saved now, saved forever.—"For by one offering He hath perfected *forever* them that are set apart" (Heb. 10:14). How may you *know* that you are saved? In the same way that the firstborn Israelite could know that *he* was secure from the avenging Angel—by *the Word* of God. "When I see the blood *I will* pass over you". God is saying the same to-day. If you are under the blood, then you are eternally secure. Neither the Law, nor the Devil, can harm you. "It is God that justifieth, who is he that condemneth?" (Rom. 8:33, 34). Receive Christ for salvation. Rest on God's Word for assurance and peace!

Nor are we to be occupied with our *faith*, any more than with our feelings. It is not the *act* of faith which (instrumentally) saves us, but *the TRUTH itself*, which faith lays hold of. If no blood had been placed on the door, no believing it *was* there would have delivered from the avenger. On the other hand, if the blood *had been* placed on the door, and those within doubted its efficacy, peace would have been destroyed but not their security. It is faith in God's promise which brings assurance. For *salvation*, faith is simply the hand that receives the gift. For *assurance*, faith is "setting to our seal that God is true" (John 3:33). And this is simply receiving *"His* testimony".

In this paper we have only sought to develop that which is central and vital in connection with our salvation and peace. In our next we shall, God willing, take up some of the many interesting details of Exodus 12. May the Lord be pleased to use what we have written to establish His own.

Arthur W. Pink.

TRUTH AND ERROR.

3. General Principles, Continued.

Shall the clay say unto Him that fashioned it, What makest Thou? or Thy work, He hath no hands?" (Isa. 45:9).

Having stated what appears to me to be the origin of the theological opinions that are now trying to make way amongst us, I would briefly advert to some of the principles out of which they spring. I might at once have gone on to discuss the different points or opinions themselves; but I think it may be useful to notice some of the principles which they involve, or what may be called the general aspect and essence of these opinions. We have already seen the *soil* in which they flourish,—we shall forthwith proceed to advert to the branches and fruit; but, before doing so, it may be well to call attention to the *roots* of the tree. Speaking generally of the new doctrines, and the movement which has taken place in connection with them, we may affirm several things.

Man has too much to do with all this, —God too little. We hear much of what man does, and can do, and ought to do, but by no means so much of what God is doing, and has purposed to do. Man's agency stands very prominently out to view,—God's arm and power are hidden. It seems almost as if man would thrust aside God, take the reins of government out of His hands, and be to himself a god. Man gets much credit for doing and saying great things,—God gets little glory. The position of the sinner, *as a mere receiver of salvation*, and every blessing connected with it in this life or the next, is denied; and he is exalted to be a co-operator with God in the matter of salvation. He begins the work by becoming willing, and God ends it. He does what he can, and God does all the rest. He is represented as helping God to save him; or rather, we should say, God is represented as helping man to save himself! In the old creation, God did it all; but in the new creation, as being a far more stupendous work, He requires the assistance of man,—nay, He commits half the work, at least the most difficult and momentous part of it, to man himself! If some of the new theories be true, God is not all in all, but is, on the contrary, considerably indebted to man; and man, in like manner, is not a little indebted to himself. In all this, we hear still the whisperings of the old serpent. "Ye shall be as gods;" and we see man, like his first father, aspiring to the Divine prerogative.

Man's way, not God's, is taken as the guide of action. God has a way, a plan, a purpose, well and wisely ordered. This plan, which He acts by, He has revealed, and He expects us to take it as our guide in all our schemes. This plan touches and rules things both great and small,—nations, communities, churches, with all their movements. Man's wisdom would be to search out this plan, and shape all his movements accordingly. Inattention to this must not only lead to fruitless efforts and unscriptural schemes, but to much false religion, self-will, formality, excitement, and sectarianism. God's design is *to glorify Himself*,—to show the whole universe what an infinitely glorious Being He is. This is His mighty end in all He does and says,—to manifest Himself and show forth His glory. For this, sin is allowed to enter the world; for this, the "Word was made flesh;" for this, the Son of God shed His blood and died; for this, He is taking out of this world a people for Himself; to this all things are tending, and in this shall they be consummated ere long. Nothing less than this does God propose to Himself in His doings; and nothing less than this should we ever make our aim and end. All things are but means to this one end. Even the incarnation of His own Son is but means toward an end, but not the end itself. The ingathering of His chosen ones is the means, not the end. The salvation of Israel, the conversion of the world, and the restitution of all things in the day of the coming kingdom, shall be the means, but not the end. "For of Him, and through Him, and to Him are all things; to whom be glory forever."

Whenever we overlook this, we go wrong, and our efforts are but the beating of the air. When we make an end of anything lower than this, we are sure to fall into error; because, when we fix on *ends* of our own, we are certain to adopt *means* of our own. Take the case of the conversion of the soul. We cannot be too much in earnest about the saving even of one lost one. I believe we know almost nothing of that deep compassion and yearning love for a dying world, as saints, we ought ever to feel. Yet still it is quite possible to err in this matter,—not in being too earnest, but in being so intent on having men converted as to lose sight of the mighty *end* for which this is to be sought. Hence the glory of God is hidden from view; I do not say denied, but hidden from view. And what is the consequence? We cease to look at conversion in the light in which God regards it, as the way in which He is to be glorified. We think if we can but get men converted, it does not so much matter how. Our whole anxiety is, not how shall we secure the glory of Jehovah, but how shall we multiply conversions? The whole current of our thoughts and anxieties takes this direction. We cease to look at both things together; we think it enough to keep the one of them alone in our eye; and the issue is, that we soon find ourselves pursuing ways of our own. Bent upon compassing a particular object, we run recklessly forward, thinking that, as the object is right, anything that can contribute towards the securing of it cannot be wrong. We thus come to measure the correctness of our plans, simply by their seeming to contribute to our favorite aim. We estimate the soundness of our doctrine, not from its tendency to exalt and glorify, Jehovah, but entirely by the apparent facility with which it enables us to get sinners to turn from their ways. The question is not asked concerning any doctrine, *Is it in itself* a God-honoring truth, but will it afford us facilities for converting souls? Will it make conversion a more easy thing,—a thing which a man may accomplish for himself and by himself. Will it make conversion less dependent upon God, and more dependent upon man? Will it make man's salvation to hinge less purely and solely upon the will of Jehovah, and more entirely upon the will of the sinner himself? Will it enable us to meet such a text as—"No man can come unto Me unless the Father draw him;" "Ye have not chosen Me, but I have chosen you;" "Can the Ethiopian change his skin or the leopard his spots?"

The man who thinks of nothing but how he may (as he calls it) get sinners converted, is continually apt to take these devious courses. Impelled but by one force, in one direction, from one motive, he soon errs and loses himself in mazy thickets, which, as he plunges on, thicken into deeper intricacy and darkness. Such texts as these present themselves and cross his path. Intent on but one thing, he either shuns them or treads them down. They are incompatible with his *one* idea,—they seem to impede him in the pursuit of his one end. And therefore they must be got quit of. It does not occur to ask, Am I not looking at objects in a partial light, from too low a position, and with a false bias which unfits me for coming to a right judgment? Were such a question but asked and answered as it ought, there would be less of one-sided doctrines, mis-shapen systems, got up to accomplish a favorite and engrossing object. Were the glory of the infinite Jehovah seen in its true light, as the mightiest and most majestic of all objects and ends, not to the exclusion of other matters, but simply to their regulation and subordination,—then should we be saved the pain of seeing men rushing headlong over Scriptures and reason, striking out strange by-paths of their own, in their eager pursuit of an object on which they have fixed an exclusive and partial eye.

I do wonder at men, who have either lost sight of the glory of Jehovah or have made it a subordinate object, or who think that if they can only get men converted, God will look after His own glory,—I do not wonder at them being fretted when such texts as those I have referred to, confront them in their schemes for facilitating conversion, and making man the converter of himself. A man with only one object in view, and that not the highest, must be stumbled at such declarations, and feel at a loss to reconcile them with others. But the man who has set his heart upon the glory of God, and views every thing in relation to that, feels no such difficulty. He has no need to explain away even one verse or clause of the Book of Truth. He enters into the purpose of God; He looks at things in the light in which God looks at them. He tries to see them as they might have appeared in the long past eternity,—or as they will yet appear in the eternity to come. And he finds all harmony. There is no conflict, no discord at all. One class of passages show him the yearnings of God's heart over sinful man. They show him that God is in earnest in beseeching men to come to Him. They show him that the sinner's unbelief is the cause of his damnation. They show him that the water of life is *free;* free to every man; free to every sinner as he stands; and that he is invited to partake, without price or preparation, not only *although* he is a sinner, but just *because* he is a sinner. They show him these things, and in them he greatly rejoices. He does not wish to abate one jot of the blessed freeness, or cloud by one restriction the joy of the glad tidings. No. He takes these passages just as he finds them. He sees how suitable they are to one of the objects on which his heart is set,—I mean the conversion of souls. But then he finds another class of passages which follow out another line of truth. They will run him up at once into the purpose and will of Jehovah as the fount and cause of everything great or small. They are quite explicit; just as much so as the other. He cannot explain them away. They are so plain and simple, that a child may see what they mean. He has no wish to take them in any other than their obvious sense. He sees in them that which exactly meets his own feelings, and coincides with his view of God's glory as being the paramount and all-regulating end in all the movements of the universe. He sees in them not a restriction upon the gospel, but the simple statement of an infinite truth—a truth not arbitrarily thrown across the sinner's path as a stumbling-block, but a truth necessarily arising from the fact that God is God, the Creator, and that man is man, the creature, the sinner. The truth is just this, that God's will is the law of the universe,—His glory the object and end both in creation and in redemption—His everlasting purpose the mighty and all-perfect mould in which all things are cast, and from which they take their shape and fashion from first to last. In such passages he sees God pointing out to men the true end which they ought to have in view, and by which all their movements are to be regulated. In them he sees God setting a fence and guard around His own majesty, lest men should imagine that their will is everything, their salvation God's only end, and that in the gospel He has thrown the reins of this fallen earth into the sinner's hands, telling him that everything depends upon his own will and power, and that he has to put forth that will and power in order to save himself, and restore a ruined world to the perfection of its former beauty.

Whenever we lose sight of God's great end in all things—His own glory—we fall into a wrong track. We go wrong in judging of doctrine; we go wrong in the formation of our plans; we go wrong in the bent of our efforts: we miscalculate the relative importance of different truths. Thus our whole tone of feeling, judging, and working is lowered and contracted. Zeal for our own ways and opinions takes the place of higher aims. A revival is got up to propagate these opinions, or to prop up a sect. Sectarianism and selfish exclusiveness steal in. Egotism, boasting, censoriousness are introduced. Religion becomes an instrument for working out our own views and ends. The most solemn and spiritual things are spoken of with levity and irreverence. Conversion soon becomes the same as the holding of certain opinions, and the mark of an unconverted man is, that he rejects these opinions. Being loosened from their anchorage, men drift without a guide. One doctrine after another is embraced, and change succeeds change, as month follows month. To make conversion easy is the great object; and accomplish this particular end, favorite passages are dwelt upon incessantly, doctrine after doctrine smoothed over, and text after text pared away.

And after all this toil and change, what is the issue? Is anything gained? Nothing. Scripture has been perverted, man all but deified, and God all but dethroned,—but has any difficulty been cleared off, have contradiction been harmonized? No. One class of difficulties has been substituted for another that is all. The new system gets quit of the alleged contradictions of the old, only to substitute others of its own of a more serious kind. If for instance, I deny that Christ is truly God, I certainly get quit of the mystery of the incarnation, for the passages which declare His Divinity are numerous and explicit. In like manner, by denying the *direct* operation of the Holy Spirit upon the soul of the sinner, I get quit of certain apparent difficulties about man's responsibility, but I substitute for these most serious difficulties as to man's utter depravity, and as to the personal agency and operation of the Spirit. But the *old* difficulties are to some minds so stale and threadbare as not to be endurable. *New* difficulties recommend themselves by their freshness and novelty. To get quit of a single old one, some would welcome a hundred new ones.

From such roots many other evils spring, which I cannot here enumerate. There is often manifested a narrow-mindedness, a contraction of the spiritual eye, and a limitation of the spiritual horizon, which is apt to end in engrossing selfishness. Hence, we often see greater zeal to proselytize to a sect than to win men to Christ. We see great activity displayed in making known and forcing upon others the points on which the difference exists, and much less concern about propagating those in which all believers are agreed. We hear much talking about doctrines and peculiarities, little about Christ Himself. We find conversation turning too much upon the spiritual state of others, and that often in flippance or censoriousness,—this one being pronounced unconverted, that other converted, —this one being mentioned as having joined the sect, or that other as being inclined to join it, or that other as standing aloof. We find discussions arising as to whom this one was awakened under, or whom this other, as if this were a matter of any importance, provided the soul be saved, and Jesus glorified. We find people extolling the exploits of their ministers, or the doings of their sect, numbering up the conversions that took place at this or that revival, under this or that minister, in this or that village or town.

How much is there in all this of selfishness and sectarianism! how little of simple zeal for the glory of the name of Jesus! A taste for religious gossip, in which the spiritual state of others is freely canvassed, criticised, and decided on, is a very different thing from that relish for the things of God and Christ, which shows itself in the saint by the delight which he takes in spiritual converse on things pertaining to God and His glory, to Jesus and His love.

THUS SAITH THE LORD:

"Vain man would be wise, though man be born like a wild ass's colt"—Job 11:12.

"The Lord hath made all things for Himself, yea, even the wicked for the day of evil"—Prov. 16:4.

"Cannot I do with you as this potter? saith the Lord. Behold as the clay in the potter's hand, so are ye in My hand, O house of Israel"—Jer. 18:6.

"Nay, but O man, who art thou that repliest against God? Shall the thing formed say to Him that formed it, Why hast Thou made me thus"—Rom. 9:20.

Dr. H. Bonar 1851.

How markedly have things gone from bad to worse during the last 75 years! To what a fearful extent are the evils Dr. Bonar mentions now found among us! How *very* little of present-day Evangelistic work evidences any concern for *God's* glory—the presence of so much that is dishonoring to Him being the proof. A. W. P.

ISHMAEL AND ISAAC
or
Law and Grace

The history of Hagar and Ishmael is but an episode in the life of Abraham, and yet it is brought into prominence by the use which St. Paul makes of it in his Epistle to the Galatians. There we are taught that it is a typical history—a history which contains, beneath its surface, spiritual truths of great significance and value. We purpose, very briefly, to examine the details of this history in their Divinely established connection, higher truths, partly for the sake of bringing into clear relief the truths themselves, and partly for the purpose of illustrating the use which should be made of apparently unimportant portions of the Divine Word.

Did we rightly apprehend the nature of the Scriptures; did we ever remember, as we ought that each word of them has been written by the Holy Spirit we would never treat any portion of them as in any sense unimportant. We should then feel that truth is everywhere; that spiritual truth is couched in every sentence, and imbedded in every line. Surely, if St. Paul found the mystery of the Church foreshadowed in the history of our first parents; and if the Saviour heard the doctrine of the resurrection declared by Moses at the bush; then in the obscurest portions of the Bible may we search for more than lies upon the surface; then, with Augustine, may we truly say, "the N. T. in the Old is latent, the O. T. in the New is patent". What, then, let us ask, are the details of the history before us, and what their spiritual import?

"Now Sarai, Abram's wife, bare him no children: and she had an handmaid an Egyptian, whose name was Hagar. And Sarai said unto Abram, Behold now, The Lord hath restrained me from bearing: I pray thee, go in unto my maid; it may be that I may obtain children by her" (Gen. 16:1,2). The thought of introducing Hagar into the family of Abram, it is to be observed, was suggested by Sarai, who, at this period, had not become a sharer of Abram's faith. Though she was the beloved wife of Abram, and his constant companion; though she had accompanied him from Chaldea to Canaan; though she had lived with him in his tent, and worshipped with him at his altar; though she had witnessed the workings of Abram's faith, and heard promises on which it fastened, yet, up to this period, she herself believed not. She was one of God's chosen and was brought soon afterward into the consciousness and liberty of adoption, but her hour had not yet come.

How beautifully this portion of the history illustrates the "due season" of the old confession of faith! How it illustrates, also, the various ways by which souls are led to an apprehension of the truth! Some with Abram, yield their assent at once to the Divine testimony; while others, through years of instruction and discipline, are gradually enlightened. How often we see this difference, as here, in the same household—the husband taking precedence of the wife, or the wife of the husband; the parent of the child, or, it may be, the child of the parent. God's ways are not as our ways. They are sure to bring out, in some manner, the sovereignty of God's purpose, and our entire dependence on His grace.

The suggestion concerning Hagar came, not from Abram, but from Sarai; and, to understand its nature, we must revert for a moment to the preceding history. Ten years before this time, God had appeared to Abram, and promised him a son; and a few years later He had renewed the promise. Abram's faith fastened upon it. He believed in the Lord, we read, and it was imputed to him for righteousness. But, as years rolled away, and the fulfilment of the promise was delayed, Sarai became restless and impatient. No son was given to her and she would secure the promised blessing through the intervention of Hagar. But this was falling back on nature. Had a son been given to Sarai herself, under the circumstances, he would have been purely a gift of grace—a child of promise. But for this, in her unbelief, Sarai could not wait.

Now, salvation is of *grace*. We can no more attain to it by our own efforts than Sarai could bring forth a son. We are as powerless as she was. If we receive it, it must be as Isaac was subsequently received—as a free gift from the hand of God. To attempt to save ourselves by law is to fall back, as Sarai did, on nature; for the law does not save, as the Gospel does, by bestowing forgiveness and imparting life. It can only save through our own perfect compliance with its demands.

We see, then, how the two sons of Abram represent the two covenants, or salvation by law and salvation by grace. He that is of the bond-woman was born after the flesh—the fruit of nature. He that was of the free-woman was by promise—the fruit of grace. Flesh, which here represents the power of man, is contrasted with promise, which represents the power of God. The power of man, through obedience to law, cannot save. God's power alone can rescue; through Him whom Isaac typified, our Lord and Saviour Jesus Christ. The power of man, of the law, is relied upon only by those who, like Sarai, *are unbelieving*. The power of God, or the promise of the Gospel, is waited for, as by Abram, *in faith*.

"And Abram hearkened to the voice of Sarai". How it pains us to read these words! It was a real Galatian act—a sad fall on the part of the patriarch. In faith he had left Chaldea, and pitched his tent in Canaan. In faith he had fastened on the promise of a seed. In faith for ten long years had he waited, and yet now was he overcome. Like Adam, he hearkened to the voice of his wife, and through unbelief he sinned.

How sad these falls of believers are! They show how difficult a thing it is to depend habitually *on God;* how almost impossible it is for the Christian to learn that salvation from first to last is *of grace*—a receiving, not a giving—a life in Christ, consequent upon the crucifixion and burial of all that Adam gave us. Like Abram and the Galatians, we begin in the spirit, but attempt to make ourselves perfect in the flesh, forgetting that in the flesh there dwelleth no good thing. But the result is always the same. Our old nature is powerless, save for evil, and we only stumble and sin till we get back again to Christ. Our sure inheritance is disappointment and sorrow, so long as we yield to a single prompting of the fleshly mind.

And, how forcibly this fall of Abram's reminds us of the danger of unbelieving companionships! Thrice watchful must that man be whose nearest friends are of the world. A worldly wife, a circle of worldly relatives, how they drag the believer down, and tempt him from the narrow path, in which faith would always guide him! The danger is greater, because the temptation comes through those we love—through the well-meant suggestions, perhaps, of those whom it is our joy to gratify and please. From such temptations the Word alone can save us—that Word which cannot be broken; no promise of which can fail.

"And when Hagar saw that she had conceived, her mistress was despised in her eyes" (Gen. 16:4). "And Abraham made a great feast the day that Isaac was weaned. And Sarah saw the son of Hagar the Egyptian, which she had borne unto Abraham, mocking" (21:8, 9). How truthfully these words represent the conflict between the flesh and the Spirit! As soon as the flesh asserts and exercises its power it becomes proud. When the believer walks in the flesh, as sometimes he unfortunately does, he begins at once to think well of himself, and to be ashamed of the fruit of the Spirit. Meekness, gentleness, humility, charity, seem contemptible in his eyes; and in perfect helplessness to cast himself on God, seems weakness and folly. And to those whose minds are wholly fleshly, who have never been made partakers of the Divine nature, how mean appear the fruits of grace! How the Ishmaels of the world mock the Isaacs who cross their path! How proudly and scornfully they pass them by! "Now we brethren, as Isaac was, are the children of promise. But as then he that was born after the flesh persecuted him after the Spirit, even so it is now" (Gal. 4: 28, 29). Man hates the Grace of God more than he does His Holiness. In the pride of

his heart, he flatters himself that he can meet the holiness of God; but Grace humbles and provokes him. It ever reminds him that he needs Divine help, and is constantly lifting up above him those whom he thinks unworthy. He cannot bear the thought that God should pass him by, and prefer others to himself; nay, pronounce against him a sentence of banishment and condemnation. Nothing irritates him more than the grace of the Gospel. He sometimes feels that he would rather be lost than saved in such a humiliating way.

"Wherefore Sarah said unto Abraham, Cast out this bond-woman and her son. . . And God said unto Abraham. . . in all that Sarah hath said unto thee, hearken unto her voice; for in Isaac shall thy seed be called" (Gen. 21:10-12). The sentence is imperative and unalterable. As the seed from which Christ was to spring was not of nature, but by promise, so is it with salvation. It is of grace through faith, not of works; otherwise, grace is no more grace. How harsh the sentence sounded in the ears of Abraham! The thing was grievous in his sight, as the preference of Ephraim to Manasseh was grievous to Joseph afterward. But God must have His way. He must teach us that He is the only Saviour, and that if salvation flow to us, it must be through the channels which Mercy alone has made.

Though Isaac was born, yet Abraham still clung to Ishmael, just as we cling to the law, even after we are made partakers of grace. What! we say, is there no good in us? Must all that is fleshly be crucified; all that is natural be repressed and overcome? Must every good thought come from God? Must every right desire and feeling be of the Spirit's inspiration? "That which is born of the flesh is flesh, and that which is born of the Spirit is spirit". "A good tree cannot bring forth evil fruit; neither can a corrupt tree bring forth good fruit". "Mortify, therefore, your affections which are upon earth". All within us that is natural is sinful, and therefore to be crucified. All that is pure and holy comes from above —comes from the inspiration of that gracious Spirit who dwells in the new creation which He both originates and sustains.

"Cast out the bond-woman and her son". Have you obeyed this commandment? Have you learned to lay the cross on every earthly lust and longing? on every fleshly thought and imagination, looking for blessing only through that which cometh from above? Realizing that your old man has been crucified, do you live as risen with Christ, in the power of the Holy Spirit? This is at once your privilege and duty. It will cost you inward pain, and outward opposition; it will subject you to the world's reproach and mockery; but it will keep you in the presence and assure you of the favor, of your Lord. It will shut you out from earthly associations which would gratify your pride and vanity; but it will bring saints and angels near, and multiply your attachments to the skies. Blessed, thrice blessed, is a life thus lived in the freedom of the Spirit. It is a life which is heavenly in its nature—a pledge and an ante-past of that within the veil.

Waymarks in the Wilderness.

CREATURE STANDING.

No creature can be capable of immutability by nature. Mutability is so essential to a creature, that a creature cannot be supposed without it; you must suppose it a Creator, not a creature, if you allow it to be of an immutable nature. Immutability is the property of a Supreme Being. "God only hath immortality" (1 Tim. 6:16); immortality, as opposed not only to a natural, but to a sinful death; the word *only* appropriates every sort of immortality to God, and excludes every creature, whether angel or man, from a partnership with God in this by nature. Every creature, therefore, is *capable of* a death in sin. "None is good but God," and none is naturally free from change but God, which excludes every creature from the same prerogative; and certainly, if one angel sinned, all *might* have sinned, because there was the same root of mutability in one as in another. It is as possible for a creature to be a Creator, as for a creature to have naturally an incommunicable property of the Creator. All things, whether angels or men, are made of nothing, and therefore, capable of defection; because a creature being made of nothing, cannot be good, *per essentiam,* or essentially good, but by participation from another. Again, every rational creature, being made of nothing, hath a superior which created him and governs him, and is capable of a precept; and, consequently, capable of disobedience as well as obedience to the precept, to transgress it, as well as obey it. A rational creature, with a liberty of will and power of choice, cannot be made by nature of such a mould and temper, but he must be as well capable of choosing right; and, therefore, the standing angels, and glorified saints, though they are immutable, it is not by nature that they are so, but by grace, and the good pleasure of God; for though they are in heaven, they have still in their nature a remote power of sinning, but it shall never be brought into act, because God will always incline their wills to love Him, and never concur with their wills to any evil act. Since, therefore, mutability is essential to a creature as a creature, this changeableness cannot properly be charged upon God as the author of it; for it was not the term of God's creating act, but did necessarily result from the essence of God. The brittleness of glass is no blame to the act of him that blew up the glass into such a fashion; that imperfection of brittleness is not from the workman, but the matter; so, though changeableness be an imperfection, yet it is so necessary a one, and men were mutable by creation and capable to exercise their wills, yet they were not necessitated to evil, and this mutability did not infer a necessity that they should fall, because some angels, which had the same root of changeableness, in their natures with those that fell, did not fall, which they would have done, if capableness of changing and necessity of changing, were one and the same thing".

(Dr. S. Charnock, 1670).

GOD BLESSES OBEDIENCE.

In his "The Miracles of Missions", third series, the late Dr. Pierson vouches for the following:—Dr. James Evans who laboured among the wild Indian tribes away up in the heart of the British territories, a thousand miles north of St. Paul, induced a large number of Indians to become Christians, teaching them, "Remember the Sabbath day to keep it holy". In that country is the greatest fur trading company in the world, the Hudson Bay Company. They have been there since the reign of Charles the first. All the goods are taken through that part of the country by brigades of boats. Until lately they carried all their goods from distant places by Indian brigades, who bring out as the exchange cargo boat-loads of furs, which are shipped to London. Before these Indians became Christians, they traveled every day alike. When our mission was established, all the missionaries went in for the observance of the Sabbath day. At once there was opposition from the Hudson Bay Company. They argued, "Our summer is short, the people have to work in a hurry, and to lose one day in seven will be a terrible loss to us, and you missionaries must get out of the country if you are going to interfere with our business". There was downright persecution for years,—but there is none now, for it was found that the brigades of Indians who traveled only six days, and quietly rested on the Sabbath, made the journey of perhaps fifteen hundred miles, without a single exception, in less time, and came back in better health, than those who traveled without observing the Sabbath. So the Hudson Bay Company opposes no more. Thus the Lord honors those who honor Him.

Journeying mercies were granted to the Editor and his wife. First, the Lord brought us safely to Denver, where, for a week, we enjoyed a wonderful season of blessing in Dr. Gravett's church. Next, we reached Oakland, Calif., and had a royal welcome from our Christian friends there. God willing, we sail for Australia March 3: due at Sydney March 25. Continue praying for us. A. W. P.

VOL. IV APRIL, 1925 No. 4

STUDIES in the SCRIPTURES

"Search the Scriptures" John 5:39.

Arthur W. Pink, Publisher & Editor,
R. F. D. 9, York, Pa.

Price: 10 cents per copy; $1.00 per year. Foreign $1.00 per year.

THE POWER OF THE EYES.

"Mine eye affecteth mine heart"—Lam. 3:51.

These are the words of Jeremiah. Their immediate reference was to the sad condition which the prophet beheld in Israel. His people had come to a sorry pass. They had transgressed and rebelled (v. 42). Desolation and destruction had come upon them (v. 47). God's servant was deeply moved. His tears tell fast and thick—"mine eye trickleth down and ceaseth not without any intermission" (v. 49). Then he adds, "Mine eye affecteth mine heart because of all the daughters of my city." (v. 51). What he beheld—the wickedness of his people and the sore chastisement of the Lord—stirred him deeply. That which he *saw* chastened and saddened his *heart*.

But this word of the prophet, like every other sentence of Holy Writ, has more than a merely local significance. It enunciates a principle of wide application. It expresses a truth of profound significance and importance. It explains a fact of far-reaching influence. It sets forth a law of life which we do well to heed. John Bunyan wrote with all his striking impressiveness of "eye-gate". And what a part it plays in admitting enemies into Mansoul! The heart has no more influential gate than the eye.

Blessed are they use who use their eyes to noble purpose, but cursed are they who prostrate such a blessed gift. Sight is the most precious of our physical senses, yet is it the most easily turned to evil account. It was because of this that David cried—"Turn away mine eyes from beholding vanity; and quicken Thou me in Thy way" (Psa. 119: 37). by "vanity" is here intended things carnal, temporal, worldly pleasures, worldly honors, worldly riches. These things are called "vanity" or *emptiness* because they have no solid happiness in them, and because they so quickly fade and perish. Favor is deceitful, and beauty is vain, (Prov. 31:30). Yea, all beneath the sun "is vanities of vanities" (Eccl. 1:2). There may also be a reference to false worship and superstition, which are made attractive to the eye, by their pomp and pagentry.

What need each of us have to cry with David- "turn away mine eyes from beholding vanity"! He that would be conducted along God's way in vigor, must first "mortify his members which are upon the earth" (Col. 3:5). One chief means of mortification is guarding the senses. That which is specific here looks toward the general: the one so solicitous about his eyes will not be careless about his ears and other senses. The eye is singled out not only because it is the noblest of the five senses but because it is the one most easily enticed by sin. It is by lookin that we come to desiring. Through the unlawful use of the eye impure flames are kindled in the heart (see Matt. 5:28). Covetousness enters via the eye.

"Mine eye affecteth mine heart". Satan understands the deep philosophy of this full well. It was so in the first temptation.—"When the woman *saw*" is the Divine record—the record so disastrously significant for us all. It was through "eye-gate" the enemy first entered the soul. "And when the woman *saw* that the tree was good for food, and that it was pleasant to the eyes, and a tree to be desired to make one wise, she took of the fruit thereof, and did eat, and gave also unto her husband with her; and he did eat." This is the Divine account of the primitive tragedy of history: and how pitifully has it recurred and is daily recurring! Beware of the sights you see. Guard your vision and thus safeguard your heart. Say with David, "I will set no wicked thing before mine eye." (Psa. 101:3)

Many are the warning which Scripture supplies of the eye being the inlet of sin. It was thus with Lot's wife (Gen. 19:26). It was thus with Jacob's daughter: "And

(Continued on page 96.)

IMPORTANT NOTICES

Set of twelve issues for **1922**, unbound, **$1.00.** Bound, **$1.50.**

Set of twelve issues for **1923**, unbound, **$1.00.** Bound **$1.50.** Abroad, **$1.75** or **7/6.**

Set of twelve issues for **1924**, unbound, **$1.00.** Bound **$1.50.** Abroad, **$1.75** or **7/6.**

Note: We cannot break a set or now supply any single 1924 issues.

Subscription Price: **$1.00** per year to any address in the world. Single copies **10 cents.**

Change of Address: Please notify me promptly of any change of address, and be certain to give both old and new addresses.

Non-subscribers receiving this Magazine regularly will understand their subscription has been entered by a friend.

Copies lost in the mail duplicated only if we are notified promptly.

Entered as second-class matter January 15th, 1923, at the post office at York, Pa., under Act of March 3rd, 1879.

CONTENTS

JOHN'S GOSPEL.

40. *Christ feared by the Sanhedrin: John 11:45-57.*

The following is submitted as an Analysis of the passage which is to be before us:—

1. The effects of Christ's great miracle vv. 45, 46.
2. The Council and their predicament vv. 47, 48.
3. Caiaphas and his counsel vv. 49, 50.
4. The Holy Spirit's interpretation vv. 51, 52.
5. The Councils' decision and Christ's response vv. 53, 54.
6. The Feast of the Passover and the purification of the Jews vv. 55, 56.
7. The commandment of the Council. v. 57.

Before we turn to these verses this will be the best place, perhaps, to consider the typical teaching of our chapter. We have seen already that the resurrection of Lazarus provides us with a striking illustration of regeneration, as well as foreshadows the rising of the dead in Christ at the return of the Lord Jesus. But these by no means exhaust what lies behind the record of that historical event. Without a doubt John 11 contains a prophetic foreshadowment of the restoration of Israel.

There are at least four passages in the Old Testament where the future restoration of Israel is announced under the figure of *resurrection*—we say the "figure", though we doubt not that there will also be a literal resurrection of all *saved* Israelites at the beginning of the Millennium. The first is found in Isa. 26:19. The whole context here is deeply interesting. It records Israel's "song" in the Millennium. At the close of it they review the bitter experiences through which they passed in the Tribulation period. They say "we have been with child, we have been in pain, we have as it were brought forth wind; we have not wrought any deliverance from the earth". And then follows that with which they had re-assured themselves in those dark days: "Thy dead *shall live,* my dead bodies (Heb.) they *shall arise.* Awake and sing, ye that dwell in dust; for thy dew is as the dew of herbs, and the earth shall cast out the dead".

In Ezek. 37 the prophet is "carried out in the spirit of the Lord (i. e. projected forward, prophetically, in spirit), and set down in the midst of the valley which was full of bones" (v. 1). In v. 11 the prophet is told, "These bones are the whole house of Israel". Then Ezekiel is bidden to prophesy, "Thus saith the Lord God: Behold, O My people, I will open your graves, and cause you to come up out of your graves, and bring you into the land of Israel. And ye shall know that I am the Lord, when I have opened your graves, O My people, and brought you up out of your graves; and shall put My Spirit in you, and ye shall live, and I shall place you in your own land; then shall ye know that I the Lord have spoken it and have performed it, saith the Lord" (vv. 12-14).

In Daniel 12:1 we read, "At that time shall Michael stand up, the great prince which standeth for the children of thy people; and there shall be a time of trouble such as never was since there was a nation even to that same time". This refers to the unparalleled afflictions through which Israel shall pass in the Great Tribulation. Immediately following this we read, "And *at that time* thy people shall be delivered, every one that shall be found written in the book. And many of them that sleep in the dust of the earth *shall awake*, some to everlasting life, and some to shame and everlasting contempt." As we learn from Rev. 20. there will be a thousand years between the rising again of the two classes here mentioned.

In Hosea 6:1 we read, "Come, and let us return unto the Lord; for He hath torn and He will heal us; He hath smitten, and He will bind us up". This will be the language of the godly remnant of Israel at the close of the Great Tribulation. This, again, is followed by the heartening assurance: "After two days will He revive us; in the third day He will *raise us up*, and we shall live in His sight".

With these four O. T. passages should be linked Rom. 11:13-15: "For I speak to you Gentiles, inasmuch as I am the apostle of the Gentiles, I magnify mine office. If by any means I may provoke to emulation them which are my flesh, and might save some of them. For if the casting away of them be the reconciling of the world, what shall the receiving of them be, but *life from the dead?*"!

Now in the light of the above passages who can doubt that the raising of Lazarus foreshadowed the future restoration and re-establishment of Israel in the land of Palestine? But before we notice the details of the typical picture here, it is pertinent to ask, Who are suggested by Mary and Martha? The sisters occupy quite a prominent place in John 11, and the connection in which they are mentioned cannot be without deep significance. Without being dogmatic, we would suggest that they represent the exercises of soul which *the faithful Remnant* will pass through ere the Nation is raised. A number of things have led us to this conclusion. First, in v. 1 "Bethany" is said to be "the village *of* Mary and her sister Martha". Now Bethany signifies "House of Affliction", which is precisely the place which the Remnant will occupy. In the second place, the meaning of their names is most suggestive. Martha signifies "lady" which is a most appropriate designation for the holy Remnant, in contrast from the apostate section of the Nation, which is viewed under the figure of an adulterous woman! Mary means "bitter" which tells of the price the Remnant will have to pay for preserving their purity. "Martha" then speaks of the *outward* deportment of the Remnant; "Mary" of their inward experiences. Finally, the two sisters' *appeal* to the Lord on behalf of Lazarus (the Nation as a whole) who was sinking, points to the supplications of the Remnant on behalf of the Nation, predicted by Isaiah in the very chapter which announces their resurrection! Let the reader ponder carefully Isa. 26:9-16. Concerning Lazarus himself as a figure of the Nation consider the following points:—

1. Lazarus was "sick" v. 1. This was his condition *before* the Lord "abode two days" in Bethabara (v. 6). The sickness of Lazarus therefore pointed to the state of that Nation when Christ was in their midst. For long centuries this had been the condition of Israel. Isaiah had declared, "The whole head is sick, and the whole heart faint; from the sole of the foot even unto the head there is no soundness in it" (1:5, 6). Desperate indeed was their plight. 2. Lazarus was the beloved of the Lord (v. 3). So, too, was Israel. The chosen Nation had been loved with an everlasting love (Jer. 31:3). It was love which elected them (Deut. 7:7, 8). It was love which bore so patiently with their waywardness (Mal. 1:1, 2). And it was as His beloved they were delivered into the hands of their enemies. There is a remarkable verse in Jeremiah which brings this out: "I have given the *dearly beloved* of My soul into the hands of their enemies" (12:7). And Israel is still beloved of the Lord; love shall yet regather them. 3. Lazarus died (v. 14). So now Israel are "Lo-ammi" (Hos. 1:9). Their sins have alienated them from the Lord: "Your iniquities have separated between you and your God, (Isa. 59:2). 4. Lazarus' death was not the final thing. Nor shall Israel always be separated from God. In the very next verse after the one where Israel is called Lo-ammi, it is said, "Yet the number of the children of Israel shall be as the sands of the sea, which cannot be measured nor numbered; and it shall come to pass, that in the place where it was said unto them, Ye are not My people, there it shall be said unto them, Ye are the sons of the *living* God (Hos. 1:19). 5. The death of Lazarus was for "the glory of God, that the Son of God might be glorified thereby" (v. 4). So in the restoration of Israel the Lord shall be "glorified," yea, this will be the very thing which they shall

acknowledge—"O Lord, Thou hast increased the Nation: *Thou art glorified* (Isa. 26:5)!

6. Christ did not go to raise Lazarus until an interval of "two days" had passed (v. 6). So, in round figures, there will be an interval of two thousand years between Israel's separation from God and their reconciliation to God. 7. Most remarkable is it that Martha (v. 20) and Mary (29) went forth to meet Christ *"secretly"* (v. 28) *before* He came and raised Lazarus. In like manner shall the living saints on earth be secretly removed from this scene of sorrow (1 Thess. 4:17) *before* the Lord returns to the earth and restores Israel! 8. The raising of Lazarus turned upon the coming of Christ into Judea *again* (vv. 7, 11). So the restoration of Israel awaits the return of the Lord Jesus to this earth: "And so all Israel shall be saved: as it is written, There shall come out of Sion the Deliverer, and shall turn away ungodliness from Jacob" (Rom. 11:26). 9. The meaning of Lazarus' name is highly suggestive. Lazarus means "God my Helper". It is the exact equivalent of "Eliezer" in the O. T. Eliezer was the son of Moses, and his reason for so naming him is stated as follows:—"And the name of the other was Eliezer; *for* the God of my father, said he, was *mine help,* and *delivered me* from the sword of Pharaoh" (Ex. 18:4). Israel's *only* help lies in God. Unable to help themselves as Lazarus was in the grave, they are entirely shut up to the delivering power of the Almighty. 10. Most significant in *this* connection, is Christ's reference to the "twelve hours in the day" (v. 9). Twelve is the number of Divine Government, and it will be at the beginning of the Millennium that the *governmental* power of God is fully *manifested* on earth.

11. Christ was accompanied by His disciples as He went to raise Lazarus: "Let *us* go unto him" (v. 15). So "when He who is our Life shall appear, then shall we also appear *with Him* in glory" (Col. 3:4). 12. Lazarus belonged to Bethany, which signifies both "House of Affliction and "House of Figs". Each of these meanings applies most appropriately to Israel. 13. When Christ arrived at Bethany He found that Lazarus had been in the grave "four days already" (v. 17). This seems to have a double significance. Looking at Lazarus as a picture of the sinner it shows that the natural man had been in the place of death four thousand years when the Lord came down to this earth. But as it applies to Israel its dispensational significance looks in another direction: "Israel through the four days of the *four* great World-powers of Daniel 2 and 7 (Babylon, Medo-Persia, Greece, and Rome) has been in the quietness of the grave awaiting the voice of power and of life" (Malachi Taylor). 14. Instrumental agency was employed in connection with the raising of Lazarus (it *was not* in the cases of Jairus' daughter or the widow's son): "Take *ye* away the stone". It should be carefully noted that this instrumental agency was *not* for the *quickening* of Lazarus, but that he might come forth *from* the place of death. In like manner, instrumental agency will be used in connection with the bringing of Israel out of the place of death (i.e. the Dispersion in Gentile lands), though it will *not* in connection with the Rapture of the Church! In Matt. 24:31 we read, "He shall send His angels with a great sound of a trumpet, and *they* shall gather together His elect (Israelites) from the four winds, from one end of heaven to the other. 15. Most suggestive is what we read of in v. 18: "Now Bethany was nigh unto Jerusalem, about *fifteen* furlongs off". The factors of 15 are 3 and 5. Three has to do with "manifestation", and five with "grace". *From* Jerusalem shall go forth *the full manifestation of grace* when Israel is restored to God !!! Again we are bowed in wonderment and praise before this, another, typical picture in John's Gospel. None but He whose wisdom is infinite could have given us a portrayal so vivid and so complete. And how blessed to mark that before Christ hid Himself from Israel, He gave them, in the raising of Lazarus, such a marvelous pledge of their final life and glory.

In the closing section of John 11 we are shown the *effects* of the awe-inspiring miracle recorded in the earlier part of the chapter. And we are at once struck with what is here *omitted.* The Holy Spirit has told us of the varying impressions made upon the "many Jews" who witnessed the raising of Lazarus, but nothing whatever is said of the feelings of either Lazarus or his sisters! Several reasons may be suggested for this. In the first place, the Bible is not written to satisfy an idle curiosity. It would not have suited the ways of God for us to know now what was retained by the memory of Lazarus as he returned from the Unseen to this world. It is not God who moves Spiritualists to pry into that which lies behind the veil. In the second place, there is a beautiful *delicacy* in concealing from us the emotions of Martha and Mary. We are not allowed to obtrude into the privacy of their home after their loved one had been restored to them! In the third place, may we not reverently say, the joy of the sisters was *too great for utterance.* An impostor inventing this story would have made *this* item very prominent, supposing that it would furnish a suitable and appropriate climax to the narrative. But the spiritual mind discerns that its very omission is an evidence of the Divine perfections of this inspired record.

"Then many of the Jews which came to Mary, and had seen the things which Jesus did, believed on Him" (v. 45). Though John says nothing about the effects which the raising of Lazarus had upon any of the members of the Bethany family, it is striking to observe how the Holy Spirit here adheres to His unity of purpose. All through this Gospel He has shown us the growing enmity of the "Jews", an enmity which was now so swiftly to culminate in the crucifixion of the Lord of glory. So now, without stopping to draw any moral from the great "sign" which the Messiah had just given, without so much as making a single comment upon it He at once tells us how it was regarded by the *Jews!* They, as ever, were *divided* about the Lord Jesus (cf. 7:43; 9:16; 10:19,). A goodly number of those who had witnessed the coming forth of Lazarus from the tomb "believed on Him". Without attempting to analyze their faith, this we may safely say: *their* enmity was subdued, *their* hostility was discarded, temporarily at least.

"Then many of the Jews which came to Mary, and had seen the things which Jesus did, believed on Him". "It is remarkable that our Evangelist speaks of them as those who had come to *Mary.* Their regard for *her* led them to have regard to *Him* whom she so deeply loved. Perhaps too they had conversed with her about Him, and she had borne testimony unto Him, and impressed them favorably concerning Him, and prepared them for their faith in Him" (Dr. G. Brown). The wording of this 45th verse is most significant. It does not say, "Then many of the Jews came to Mary, *who,* seeing the things which Jesus did, believed on Him", but "Then many of the Jews which came to Mary, *and* had seen the things which Jesus did, believed on Him. The *two* things are linked together—the coming to Mary *and* the seeing the things which He did—as explaining *why* they "believed on Him". It reminds us of what we read of in 4:39, 41, 42: "And many of the Samaritans believed on Him for *the saying of the woman,* which testified, He told me all that ever I did. . . *And* many more believed because *of His own word;* And said unto the woman, Now we believe, not because of thy saying; for we have heard Him ourselves, and know that this is indeed the Christ, the Saviour of the world."

"But some of them went their ways to the Pharisees, and told them what things Jesus had done" (v. 46). "But": ominous word is this. Solemn is the contrast now presented. Some of those who had witnessed the miracle went at once to the Pharisees and told them of what Christ had done. Most probably they were their spies. Their motive in reporting to these inveterate enemies of our Lord cannot be misunderstood; they went not to modify but to inflame their wrath. What an example of incorrigible hardness of heart! Alas, What is man! Even *miracles* were to some "a savor of death unto death"!

"Then gathered the chief priests and the Pharisees a council. The "chief priests" were, in all probability, Sadducees; we know that the high priest was, see Acts 5:17. The "Pharisees" were their theological opponents. These two rival sects hated each other most bitterly, yet, in this evil work of persecuting the Lord Jesus, they buried their differences, and eagerly joined together in the common crime. The same thing is witnessed in connection with Herod and Pilate: "And Herod with his men of war set Him at nought, and mocked Him, and arrayed Him in a gorgeous robe, and sent Him again to Pilate. And *the same day* Pilate and Herod were made friends together: for *before* they were at enmity between themselves" (Luke 23:11, 12)! Each of these cases was a fulfillment of the prophecy which the Holy Spirit had given through David long before: "The kings of the earth set themselves, and the rulers take counsel *together,* against the Lord, and against His Christ" (Psl. 2:2).

"Then gathered the chief priests and the Pharisees a council and said, "What do we? for this Man doeth many miracles" (v. 47). The "Council" was deeply stirred by the evidence before them. Jesus had clearly demonstrated that He was the Christ, and they ought forthwith to have acknowledged Him. Instead of doing so they chided themselves for their delay at not having apprehended and silenced Him before. "What do we?" they asked. Why are we so dilitary? On a previous occasion these same men had sent officers to arrest Christ (7:32), but instead of doing so they returned to their masters saying, "Never man spake like this Man", and then, in the providence of God, Nicodemus objected, "Doth our law judge any man before it hear him, and know what he doeth?" (7:51), and this broke up their conference. But now things had come to a head. They *did* know what He was doing. "For this man doeth many miracles". This they could not deny. Very solemn was it. They *owned* the genuineness of His miracles, yet were their consciences unmoved. How this exposes the uselessness of much that is being done today. Some think they have accomplished much if they demonstrate to the intellect the *truth* of Christ's miracles. We often wonder if such men really believe in the *total* depravity of human nature. Souls are not brought into the presence of God, or saved, by such means. The *wisdom* of this world is foolishness with God. Nothing but omnipotent and sovereign grace is of any avail for those who are lost. And the *only* thing God uses to quicken the dead is His own Word. One who has really passed from death unto life has *no need* for so-called "Christian Evidences" to buttress his faith: one who is yet dead in trespasses and sins has *no capacity* of heart to appreciate them. Preach the Word, not argue and reason about the miracles of the Bible is our business!

"If we let Him thus alone, all men will believe on Him (v. 48). How these words reveal the awful enmity of their hearts: no matter what others did, they were determined not to believe. In our first article on John 11 we called attention to the link between this chapter and Luke 16. In each instance there was a "Lazarus". The very *name,* then, of the one whom Christ had just raised at Bethany, should have served to remind them of His warning words at the close of Luke 16. Well did Christ say of them, "If they hear not Moses and the prophets, *neither* will they *be persuaded,* though one rose from the dead" (v. 31). What a proof that witnessing miracles will not bring dead sinners to the feet of Christ! "We must never wonder if we see abounding unbelief in our own times, and around our own homes. It may seem at first inexplicable to us, how men cannot see the truth which seems so clear to ourselves, and do not receive the Gospel which appears so worthy of acceptation. But the plain truth is, that man's unbelief is a far more deeply-seated disease than is generally reckoned. It is proof against the logic of facts, against reasoning, against moral suasion. Nothing can melt it down but the grace of God. If we ourselves believe, we can never be too thankful. But we must never count it a strange thing, if we see many of our fellow men as hardened and unbelieving as the Jews" (Bishop Ryle).

"If we let Him thus alone, all men will believe on him; and the Romans will come and take away both our Place and Nation" (v. 48). It was only to be expected that the resurrection of Lazarus would raise a wave of popular excitement. Any stir among the common people the leaders considered would be dangerous, especially at passover time, then nigh at hand, when Jerusalem would be filled with crowds of Israelites, ready to take fire from any spark which might fall among them (cf. 12:12, 13). The Council therefore deemed it wisest to concert measures at once for repressing the nascent enthusiasm. Something must be done, but *what* they hardly knew. They feared that a disturbance would bring Rome's heavy hand down upon them and lead to the loss of what national life still remained to them. But their fears were not from any concern which they had for God's glory, nor were they even moved by patriotic instinct. It was sordid self interest. "They will take away *our* place", the Temple (Greek "topos" used in Acts 6:13, 14; 21:28, 29, where, plainly, the Temple is in view), which was the center and source of all their influence and power. They claimed for themselves what belonged to God. The holy things were, in their eyes, their special property.

Palestine had been annexed as a province to the Roman Empire, and as was customary with that people, they allowed those whom they conquered a considerable measure of self government. The Jews were permitted to continue the Temple services and to hold their Ecclesiastical Court. It was those who were in position of power who here took the lead against Christ. They imagined that if they continued to leave Him alone, His following would increase, and the people set Him up as their King. It mattered not that He had taught, "My Kingdom is *not* of this world" (18:36); it mattered not that He retired when the people *had* desired to take Him by force and make Him their King (6:15). Enough that they supposed His claims threatened to interfere with their schemes of worldly prosperity and self-aggrandisement.

It is indeed striking to see the utter blindness of these men. They imagined that if they stopped short the career of Christ they would protect themselves from the Romans. But the very things they feared came to pass. They crucified Christ. And what was the sequel? Less than 40 years afterward the Roman army *did* come, destroyed Jerusalem, burned the Temple and carried away the whole nation into captivity. A thoughtful writer has remarked on this point: "The well-read Christian need hardly be reminded of many like things in the history of Christ's Church. The Roman emperors' persecuted the Christians in the first three centuries, and thought it a positive duty not to let them alone. But the more they persecuted them the more they increased. The blood of the martyr's became the seed of the Church. So, too, the English Papists, in the days of Queen Mary persecuted the Protestants and thought that truth was in danger if they left them alone. But the more they burned our forefathers, the more they confirmed men's minds in steadfast attachment to the doctrines of the Reformation. In short, the words of the second Psalm are continually verified in this world. The kings of the earth set themselves and the rulers take counsel against the Lord. But 'He that sitteth in the heavens shall laugh; the Lord shall have them in derision'. God can make the designs of His enemies work together for the good of His people, and cause the wrath of men to praise Him. In days of trouble, and rebuke, and blasphemy, believers may rest patiently in the Lord. The very things that at one time seem likely to hurt them, shall prove in the end to be for their gain".

"And one of them named Caiaphas, being the high priest that same year, said unto them, Ye know nothing at all. Nor consider that it is expedient for us, that one man should die for the people and that the whole nation perish not" (vv. 49, 50). The Council was puzzled. They saw in Christ, as they thought, a menace to their interests, but what course to follow they scarcely knew. Up to this point they had simply asked one another questions. Impatient at the vacillations of the priests and Pharisees, the high priest brusquely and contemptuously swept aside their deliberations with, "Ye know nothing at all". 'The one point to keep before us is our own interests. Let that be clearly understood. When we once ask, What is expedient for *us*, there can be no doubt about the answer. This Man must die! Never mind about His miracles, or His teachings, or the beauty of His character, His life is a perpetual danger to *our* prerogatives. I vote for death'. As v. 53 shows us, the evil motion of Caiaphas was carried. The Council regarded it as a brilliant solution to their difficulty. If this popular Nazarene be slain not only will suspicion be removed from us, but our loyalty to the Roman Empire will be unmistakably established. The execution of Jesus will not only show that we have no intention of revolting, but rather will the slaying of this Man, who is seeking to establish an independent Kingdom, plainly show it is our desire and purpose to remain the faithful subjects of Cæsar. Thus our watchful zeal for the integrity of the Empire will not only establish confidence but win the applause of the jealous power of Rome! Caiaphas spoke as an unscrupulous politician who sacrifices righteousness and truth for party interests. So too in accepting his policy, the Council persuaded themselves that political prudence required the carrying out of his counsel rather than that the Romans should be provoked.

"Our place" was what *they* considered. It was precisely what the Lord had foretold: "But when the husbandmen saw Him, they reasoned among themselves, saying This is the Heir: come, let us kill Him that the inheritance may be *ours*" (Luke 20:14). Favor from Cæsar rather than from God, was what their hearts desired. "Unlike Abraham they took riches from the king of Sodom instead of blessings from the hands of Melchizedek. They chose the patronage of Rome rather than know the resurrection-power of the Son of God" (Mr. Bellet). Solemn warning is this for us to be governed by higher principles than "expediency".

"And this spake he not of himself: but being high priest that year, he prophesied that Jesus should die for that nation" (v. 51). "There are many devices in a man's heart nevertheless the counsel of the Lord that shall stand" (Prov. 19:21). Strikingly was this illustrated here. Caiaphas was actuated by political expediency: the Lord Jesus was to be a State victim. Little did he know of the deep meaning of the words that he uttered, "It is expedient that one man die for the people": little did he realize that he had been moved of God to utter a prophecy to the honor of Him whom he despised. What we have in this verse and in the one following is the Holy Spirit's parenthetical explanation and amplification upon this saying of the high priest. Altogether unconscious of the fact, Caiaphas had "prophesied", and as 2 Peter 1:20, 21 tells us, "No prophecy of the Scripture is of private interpretation (i. e. human origination), for the prophecy came not at any time by the will of man". The instance before us is closely parallel with the case of Balaam in the O. T., who also "prophesied" *against* his will.

The subject is indeed a profound one, and one which human wisdom has stumbled over in every age, nevertheless the teaching of Scripture is very clear upon the point: *all things,* in the final analysis, are of God. Nowhere is this more evident than in connection with the treatment which the Lord Jesus received at the hands of wicked men. Referring to this very decision of the Council (among other things) Acts 4:26-28 tells us, "The kings of the earth stood up, and the rulers were gathered together against the Lord, and against His Christ. For of a truth against Thy holy servant Jesus, whom Thou hast anointed, both Herod and Pontius Pilate, with the Gentiles, and the people of Israel were gathered together, for to do *whatsoever Thy hand and Thy counsel determined before to be done*". It had been decreed in the eternal counsels of the Godhead that Christ should die, and die for Israel, and when Caiaphas advanced his proposal he was but a link in the chain which brought that decree to pass. This was not *his* intention, of course. *His* motive was evil only, and therein was he justly guilty. What we have here is the antitype of that which had been foreshadowed long centuries before. The brethren of Joseph by their cruel counsels thought to defeat the purpose of God, who had made it known that they should yet pay homage to their younger brother. Yet in delivering him up to the Ishmaelites, though their intention was evil only, nevertheless, they did but bring to pass the purpose of God. So Caiaphas fulfilled the very counsel of God concerning Christ, which he meant to bring to nothing by prophesying that He should die for the people. Well may Christ have said to Caiaphas, as Joseph later said to his brethren, "But as for you, *ye* thought *evil* against me; but *God* meant it unto *good,* to bring to pass, as it is this day, to *save* much people alive" (Gen. 50:20)!

"And this spake he not of himself: but being high priest that year, he prophesied that Jesus should die for that nation" (v. 51). What light this throws on the *nature* of Christ's death! It brings out its twofold aspect. From the human side it was a brutal murder for political ends: Caiaphas and the priests slaying Him to avoid unpopular tumult that might threaten their prerogatives; Pilate consenting to His death to avoid the unpopularity which might follow a refusal. But from the Divine side, the death of Christ was a vicarious sacrifice for sinners. It was God making the wrath of man to praise Him. "The greatest crime ever done in the world is the greatest blessing ever given to the world. Man's sin works out the loftiest Divine purpose, even as the coral insects blindly building up the reef that keeps back the waters or, as the sea in its wild, impotent rage, seeking to overwhelm the land, only throws upon the beach a barrier that confines its waves and curbs its fury" (Dr. MacLaren).

"And not for that Nation only, but that also He should gather together in one the children of God that were scattered abroad" (v. 52). As the previous verse gives us the Holy Spirit's explanation of the words of Caiaphas, this one contains His amplification: as v. 51 informs us of the *nature* of Christ's death, v. 52 tells us of the *power* and *scope* of it. The great Sacrifice was not offered to God at random. The redemption-price which was paid at the Cross was not offered without definite design Christ died not simply to make salvation *possible,* but to make it *certain.* Nowhere in Scripture is there a more emphatic and explicit statement concerning the objects for which the Atonement was made. No excuse whatever is there for the vague (we should say, *un*scriptural) views, now so sadly prevalent in Christendom, concerning the ones for whom Christ died. To say that He died for the human race is not only to fly in the face of this plain scripture, but it is grossly dishonoring to the Sacrifice of Christ. A large portion of the human race die *un-saved,* and if Christ died for *them,* then was His death largely in vain. This means that the *greatest* of all the works of God is comparatively a failure. How horrible! What a reflection upon the Divine character! Surely men do not stop to examine whither their premises lead them. But how blessed to turn away from man's perversions to the Truth itself. Scripture tells us that Christ *"shall* see of the travail of His soul and be *satisfied"*. No sophistry can evade the fact that these words give positive assurance that every one for whom Christ died will, most certainly, be saved.

Christ died for sinners. But everything turns on the significance of the preposition. What is meant by 'Christ died *for* sinners'? To answer that Christ died in order to made it possible for God to righteously receive sinners who come to Him through Christ, is only saying what many a Socinian has affirmed. The testing of a man's orthodoxy on this vital truth of the Atonement requires something far more definite than this. The saving efficacy of the Atonement lies in the *vicarious* nature of Christ's death, in His representing *certain persons,* in His bearing *their* sins, in His being made a curse for *them,* in His *purchasing* them, spirit and soul and body. It will not do to evade this by saying, "There is such a fulness in the satisfaction of Christ, as is *sufficient* for the salvation of the whole world, were the whole world to believe in Him". Scripture always ascribes the salvation of a sinner, not to any *abstract* "sufficiency", but to the *vicarious nature,* the *substitutional* character of the death of Christ. The Atonement, therefore, is in no sense sufficient for a man, unless the Lord Jesus died *for* that man: "For God hath not appointed *us* to wrath, but to obtain salvation by our Lord Jesus Christ, *Who died for us"* (1 Thes. 5:9, 10). "If the nature of this 'sufficiency' for all men be sifted, it will appear to be nothing more than a *conditional* 'sufficiency', such as the Arminians attribute to their universal redemption—the condition is: were the whole world *to* believe on Him. The condition, however, is not so easily performed. Many professors speak of faith in Christ as comparatively an easy matter, as though it were within the sinner's power; but the Scriptures teach a different thing. They represent men by nature as spiritually bound with chains, shut up in darkness, in a prison-house. So then all their boasting 'sufficiency' of the Atonement is only an *empty offer* of salvation on certain terms and conditions; and such an Atonement is much too weak to meet the desperate case of a lost sinner" (Wm. Rushton).

Whenever the Holy Scriptures speak of the sufficiency of redemption, they always place it in the *certain efficacy* of redemption. The Atonement of Christ is sufficient because it is absolutely efficacious, and because it effects the salvation of *all for whom* it was made. Its sufficiency lies not in affording man a *possibility* of salvation, but in *accomplishing* their salvation with invincible power. Hence the Word of God never represents the *sufficiency* of the Atonement as wider than the *design* of the Atonement. How different is the salvation of God from the ideas now popularly entertained of it! "As for *Thee* also, by the blood of *Thy* covenant I have sent forth *Thy prisoners* out of the pit wherein is no water" (Zech. 9:11). Christ, by His death paid the ransom, and made sin's captives His own. He has a *legal right* to all of the persons for whom He paid that ransom price, and therefore with God's own right arm they are brought forth.

For whom did Christ die? "For the transgression of *My people* was He stricken" (Isa. 53:8). "Thou shalt call His name JESUS: *for* He shall save *His people* from their sins" (Matt. 1:21). "The Son of Man came not to be ministered unto but to minister, and to give His life a ransom *for many"* (Matt. 20:28). "The Good Shepherd giveth his life *for the sheep"* (John 10:11). "Christ also loved *the Church* and gave Himself *for it"* (Eph. 5:25). "Who gave Himself for us, that He might *redeem us* for all iniquity, and purify unto Himself *a peculiar people"* (Titus 2:14). "To make propitiation for the sins of *the people"* (Heb. 2:17). Here are seven passages which give a clear and simple answer to our question, and their testimony, both singly and collectively, declare plainly that the death of Christ was not an atonement for sin abstractedly, nor a mere expression of the Divine displeasure against iniquity, nor an indefinite satisfaction of Divine justice, but instead, a ransom-price paid for the eternal redemption of a certain number of sinners, and a plenary satisfaction for *their* particular sins. It is the glory of redemption that it does not merely render God *placable* and man *pardonable,* but that it *has* reconciled sinners to God, put away their sins, and forever perfected His set apart ones.

"He prophesied that Jesus should die for that nation" (v. 51). The *nature* of Christ's death is here intimated in the word "for": it was *in the stead* of others. Christ died for *"that* nation". (i. e, the Nation of Israel). Mark here the striking accuracy of Scripture. Caiaphas did not say that Christ should die for "*this* nation", (namely, the Jewish nation then in existence); but for "*that* nation", that is, a *future* Israel, *millennial* Israel, the Nation which shall be "born at once" (Isa. 66:6). Isa. 53 will be the confession of millennial Israel, as the beginning of Isa. 54 plainly shows. Then shall it be said, "Thy people also shall be *all* righteous: they shall inherit the land forever, the branch of My planting, the work of My hands, that I may be glorified" (Isa. 60:21).

"And not for that nation only, but that also He should gather together in one the children of God that were scattered abroad" (v. 52). Here the Holy Spirit tells us that the *scope* of Christ's death also includes God's elect from among *the Gentiles.* As the Saviour had announced on a former occasion, "I lay down My life for *the* sheep. And *other* sheep I have, which are not of *this* fold: them also I must bring and they shall hear My voice; and there shall be *one* flock and one Shepherd" (John 10:15, 16). Here then are the "other sheep", namely, God's elect scattered throughout the world. They are here called "the children of God" because they *were* such in His eternal purpose. Just as Christ said "other sheep I *have*", and just as God said to the Apostle, "I *have* much people in this city" (Acts 18:10), so in the mind of God these were *children*, though "scattered abroad", when Christ died. There is a most striking correspondency between John 11:51, 52 and 1 John 2:2: the one explains the other. Note carefully the threefold parallelism between them. Christ died with a definite end in view, and the Father had an express purpose before Him in giving up His Son to death. That end and that purpose was that Millennial Israel should be redeemed, and that "the children of God", scattered abroad, should be gathered together in one —*not* "one body", for the Church is nowhere contemplated (corporeately) in John's writings; but *one family.* In the Millennium it shall be fully demonstrated that Christ did not die in vain. The prayer of our great High Priest will then be fully answered: "Neither pray I for these alone, but for them also which shall believe on Me through their word; that they all may be *one*" (John 17:20, 21). Then shall He "see of the travail of His soul and be *satisfied*" (Isa. 53:11).

"Then from that day forth they took counsel together for to put Him to death" (v. 53). What a fearful climax was this to all that had gone before! Again and again we have noted the incorrigible wickedness of the Jews. Not only was He not "received" by His own, but they cast Him out. Not only was He despised and rejected by men, but they thirsted for His blood. The religious head of the Nation, the high priest, moved for His death, and the Council passed and ratified his motion. Nothing now remained but the actual execution of their awful decision. Their only consideration now was *how* and *when* His death could best be accomplished without creating a tumult among the people. No doubt they concluded that the raising of Lazarus would result in a considerable increase to the number of the Lord's followers, hence they deemed it wise to use caution in carrying out their murderous plan.

"Jesus therefore walked no more openly among the Jews" (v. 54). How quietly, with what an entire absence of parade, does the Holy Spirit introduce some of the most striking points in Scripture! How much there is in this word "therefore". It shows plainly that God would have us *meditate* on every jot and tittle of His matchless Word. The force of the "therefore" here is this: the Lord Jesus *knew* of the decision at which the Council had arrived. He *knew* they had decreed that He should die. It is another of the many inconspicuous proofs of His Deity, which are scattered throughout this Gospel. It witnessed to His omniscience. The Holy Spirit has shown us that *He* knew what took place in that Council, for He has recorded the very words that were uttered there. And now Christ shows us by His action here that *He* also knew. We may add that the word for "no more" signifies "not yet", or "no more at present"; "openly" signifies "publicly".

"Jesus therefore walked no more openly among the Jews"; but went thence unto a country near to the wilderness, into a city called Ephraim, and there continued with His disciples" (v. 54). Though near at hand, His "hour" had not yet come: Christ therefore retired into a place about which nothing is now known, there to enjoy quiet fellowship with His disciples. "Like the former cases of retirement, this place is significant. Ephraim means 'fruitfulness': it is the name given to the tribes in apostacy, in the Prophets, *forecasting* thus what was in God's heart about them, even though they were in rebellion and ruin. Can anything exceed the grace of God, or anything but man's depravity and obduracy bring it into action and display, and be a fitting cause and occasion for all its riches and wonders! Ah they who have been met by God in that grace, are yet to meet Him in the glory of it, to know as all through the history of their sad failures they have been known. Thus we have in chapter ten the Church gathered to the Son of God, here (anticipatively) Israel; but He must die for this" (Malachi Taylor).

"And the Jews' passover was nigh at hand: and many went out of the country up to Jerusalem before the passover "to purify themselves" (v. 55). Here was man's religiousness, punctillious about ceremonial ablutions, but with no heart for inward purity. The very ones who were so careful about ordinances, were, in a few days, willing to shed innocent blood! What a commentary upon human nature! According to the Mosaic law no Israelite who was ceremonially defiled could keep the Passover at the regular time, though he was allowed to keep it one month later (Num. 9:10, 11). It was to avoid this delay, that many Jews here came up to Jerusalem *before* the Passover that they might be "purified," and hence entitled to keep it in the month Nisan.

"Then sought they for Jesus, and spake among themselves, as they stood in the temple, What think ye, that He will not come to the feast?" (v. 56). Two things gave rise to this questioning among those who had come up to Jerusalem from all sections of Palestine. Each of the two previous years Christ *had* been present at the Feast. In 2:13 we read, "And the Jews' Passover was at hand, and *Jesus went up* to Jerusalem". It was at this season the Lord had manifested Himself as the Vindicator of the honour of His Father's House, and a deep impression had been made on those who had witnessed it. A year later, during the course of the Feast He had fed the hungry multitude on the Mount. This so stirred the people that they wanted, by force, to make Him their King (John 6:4, 15). But now the leaders of the Nation were incensed against Him. They had decreed that Jesus must die, and their decree was now public knowledge. Hence the one topic of interest among the crowds of Jews in Jerusalem was, would this Miracle-worker who claimed to be not only the Messiah but the Son of God, enter the danger zone, or would He be afraid to expose Himself?

"Now both the chief priests and the Pharisees had given a commandment, that, if any man knew where He were, he should show it that they might take Him" (v. 57). Behind the edict of the Council we may discover the enmity of the Serpent working against the woman's Seed. This verse supplies the climax to the chapter, showing the full effect of the Divine testimony which had been borne in the raising of Lazarus. The resurrection-power of the Son of God had brought to a head the hatred of him who had the power of death. It is true that Christ had raised the dead on other occasions, but here He had given a public display of His mighty power on the very outskirts of Jerusalem, and *this* was an open affront to Satan and his earthly instruments. The glory of the Lord Jesus shone out so brightly that it seriously threatened the dominion of "the Prince of this world", and consequently there was no longer a concealment of the resolution which he had moved the religious world to make—Jesus must die. But how blessed to know that the very enmity of the Devil himself is overruled by God to the outworking of His eternal purpose!

Let the student give careful attention to the following questions on our next section, John 12:1-11:—

1. In whose house was the "supper" made v. 2?
2. What do vv. 2 & 3 hint at about the Eternal State?
3. What is intimated by Mary wiping Christ's feet with her "hair" v. 3?
4. What spiritual truth is suggested by the last clause of v. 3?
5. How many contrasts are there here between Mary and Judas?
6. What blessed truth is suggested by "Let her alone" v. 7?
7. Why were the "chief priests" so anxious to get rid of Lazarus v. 10?

Arthur W. Pink.

GLEANINGS IN EXODUS.

16. *The Passover (continued) Ex. 12.*

The institution and ritual of the Passover supply us with one of the most striking and blessed foreshadowments of the cross-work of Christ to be found anywhere in the Old Testament. Its importance may be gathered from the frequency with which the title of "Lamb" is afterwards applied to the Saviour, a title which looks back to what is before us in Exodus 12. Messianic prediction contemplated the suffering Messiah "brought as a Lamb to the slaughter" (Isa. 53:6). John the Baptist hailed Him as "Behold the Lamb of God which taketh away the sin of the world" (John 1:29). The apostle speaks of Him as "a Lamb without blemish and without spot" (1 Pt. 1:19). While the one who leaned on the Master's bosom employs this title no less than twenty-eight times in the closing book of Scripture. Thus, an Old Testament prophet, the Lord's forerunner, an apostle, and the Apocalyptic seer unite in employing this term of the Redeemer.

There are many typical pictures of the sacrificial work of Christ scattered throughout the Old Testament, yet it is to be doubted if any single one of them supplies so complete, so many-sided a portrayal of the person and work of the Saviour as does the one before us. The Passover sets forth both the Godward and the manward aspects of the Atonement. It prefigures Christ satisfying the demands of Deity, and it views Him as a substitute for elect sinners. Hardly a single vital phase of the Cross, either in its nature or its blessed results, but what is typified here. That which is central and basic we contemplated in our last paper; here we shall confine our attention to details.

1. Following the order of the contents of Ex. 12, the first thing to be noted is that the institution of the Passover changed Israel's calendar: "*This* month shall be unto you the beginning of months; *it* shall be the first month of the year to you" (12:2). Deeply significant is this. Passover-month was to *begin* Israel's year; only from this point was their national existence to be counted. The type is accurate down to the minutest detail. The new year did not begin exactly with the Passover-night itself, for that fell between the fourteenth and fifteenth of Nisan. Now the pascal lamb was a type of the Lord Jesus, and the chronology of the civilized world is dated back to the birth of Christ. Anno Mundi (the year of the world) has given place to Anno Domini (the year of our Lord). The coming of Christ to this earth changed the calendar, and the striking thing is that the calendar is now dated not from His death, but from His birth. By common consent men on three Continents reckon time from the Babe of Bethlehem; thus, the Lord of Time has written His signature upon time itself!

But there is another application of what has just been before us. The Passover speaks not only of Christ offering Himself as a sacrifice, a sin-offering to God, but it also views the believing sinner's appropriation of this unto himself. The slaying of the "lamb" looks at the Godward side of the Cross; the sprinkling of the blood tells of faith's application. And it is *this* which changes our relationship to God. But *our* appropriation of Christ's atoning sacrifice is not the first thing. Preceding this is a Divine work of grace *within* us. While we remain dead in trespasses and sins, there is no turning to Christ; nay, there is no discernment, and no capacity *to* discern, our *need* of Him. Except a man be born again he "cannot *see* the kingdom (things) of God" (John 3:3). Regeneration is the cause, faith's application of the sacrifice of Christ, the effect. The new birth is the beginning of the new life. Hence, Israel's new calendar dated not from the Passover itself, but from the *beginning* of the month in which it occurred. The truth here typified is both blessed and solemn. All the years we lived before we became new creatures in Christ are not reckoned to our account. The past is blotted out. Our unregenerate days were so much lost time. Our past lives in the service of sin and Satan, were *wasted*. But when we became new creatures in Christ "*old* things passed away" and all things became *new*.

2. "Speak ye unto all the congregation of Israel, saying, In the tenth day of this month they shall take to them every man a lamb, according to the house of their fathers, a lamb for an house" (v. 3). This is the first thing in connection with the "lamb": it was singled out from the flock, separated, appointed unto death four days before it was actually slain. We believe that two things were here foreshadowed. In the antitype, Christ was marked out for death *before* He was actually slain: "Redeemed with the precious blood of Christ,

as of a lamb without blemish and without spot, who verily was *foreordained* before the foundation of the world" (1 Pet. 1:19, 20). It is to this that the singling out of the lamb *four* days before its slaying points, for four is the number of *the world.*

The second application of this detail, which has also been pointed out by others before us, has reference to the fact that *four years* before His crucifixion the Lord Jesus was singled out for death. At the beginning of His public ministry (which lasted between three and four years—cf. Num. 14:34; Ezek. 4:6, a year for a day) John the Baptist cried, "Behold *the Lamb of God* which taketh away the sin of the world." It was then that the Lamb was singled out from the flock—"the lost sheep of the House of Israel"! In the Numerical Bible Mr. Grant has called attention to the fact that Christ was about thirty years old at that time, and 30 is 10 x 3: 3 being the number of manifestation and 10 of human responsibility. This shows us *why* God commanded the Israelites to single out the lamb on the *tenth* day. Not until He had reached the age which, according to its numerical significance, spoke of human responsibility fully manifested, did the Lord Jesus enter upon His appointed work which terminated at Calvary.

3. "Your lamb shall be without blemish" (v. 5). With this should be compared Lev. 22:21, 22. "And whosoever offereth a sacrifice of peace offerings unto the Lord to accomplish his vow, or a freewill offering in beeves or sheep, it shall be *perfect* to be accepted; there shall be *no* blemish therein. Blind, or broken or maimed, or having a wren or scurvy, or scabbed, ye shall not offer these unto the Lord". The moral significance of this is obvious. Nothing but a *perfect* sacrifice could satisfy the requirements of God, who Himself is perfect. One who had sin in himself could not make an atonement for sinners. One who did not himself keep the Law in thought and word and deed, could not magnify and make it honorable. God could only be *satisfied* with that which *glorified* Him. And where was such a sacrifice to be found? Certainly not among the sons of men. None but the Son of God incarnate, "made under the law" (Gal. 4:4) could offer an acceptable sacrifice. And before He presented Himself as an offering to God, the Father testified, "This is My beloved Son, in whom I am well pleased". He was the antitype of the "perfect" lamb. As Peter tells us, Christ was "a lamb *without* blemish and *without* spot" (1:19).

4. "Your lamb shall be without blemish, *a male of the first year*" (v. 5). "The age of the sacrifice is prescribed. It is to be a male of the first year. The Hebrew phrase is 'a male, the son of a year'; that is, it is to be one year old. The lamb was not to be too young or too old. It was to die in *the fulness* of its strength. If we ask how that might apply to Christ, we note that this particular may be fully sustained as a description of Him. For He died for us, not in old age, nor in childhood, or boyhood, or in youth, but in the fulness of His opening manhood" (Urquhart). In the language of Messianic prediction, Christ was cut off "in the midst" of His days (Psl. 102:24).

Before passing on to the next verse we would call attention to a striking gradation here. In v. 3 it is "*a* lamb"; in v. 4 "*the* lamb"; in v. 5. "*your* lamb". This order is most instructive, corresponding to the enlarged apprehension of faith. While in our unregenerate state, Christ appeared to us as nothing more than *a* Lamb; we saw in Him no beauty that we should desire Him. But when the Holy Spirit awakened us from the sleep of death, when He made us see our sinful and lost condition, and turned our gaze toward Christ, then we behold Him as *the* Lamb. We perceived His uniqueness, His unrivaled perfections. We learned that "neither is there salvation in any other; for there is none other Name under heaven given among men whereby we must be saved, (Acts 4:12). Finally, when God in His sovereign grace gave us faith whereby to receive Christ as our own personal Saviour, then could He be said to be *your* Lamb, *our* Lamb. Each elect and believing sinner can say with the apostle Paul, "Who loved *me* and gave Himself for *me*" (Gal. 2:20).

5. "And ye shall keep it up until the fourteenth day of the same month; and *the whole assembly* of the congregation of Israel shall kill it in the evening (v. 6). This is very solemn. The *whole* congregation of Israel was to slay the "lamb". Not that every particular individual, man, woman and child, shared in the act itself, but they did so *representatively*. The head of the household stood for and acted on the behalf of each member of his family. It was not simply Moses and Aaron or the Levites who slew the Lamb, but the entire people, as represented by the heads of each house-

hold. The fulfillment of this aspect of our type is plainly brought out in the Gospels. It was not simply the chief priests and elders, nor the scribes and Pharisees only, who put the Lord Jesus to death. When Pilate decided the issue as to whether Barabbas or Christ should be released, he did so by the popular vote of the common people, who *all* cried "crucify Him" (see Mark 15:6-15). In like manner it is equally true that it was the sins of each individual believer which caused our Saviour to be put to death: He bare *our* sins in His own body on the tree.

6. "And ye shall keep it up until the *fourteenth* day of the same month; and the whole assembly of the congregation of Israel shall kill it *in the evening*" (v. 6). Here we have defined the exact time at which the pascal lamb was to die. It was to be "kept up" or tethered until the fourteenth day of Nisan, and then killed in the evening, or more literally, "between the evenings", that is between the fourteenth and fifteenth days of the month. To point out precisely the antitypical fulfillment of this would necessitate an examination of quite a number of N. T. passages. Only by a most minute comparison of the statements in each of the four Gospels can we discover the fact that the Lord Jesus died "between the evenings" of the fourteenth and fifteenth of Nisan. Others before us have performed this task, the best of which, perhaps, is to be found in vol. 5 of the Companion Bible. But if the reader will prayerfully study the closing chapters of each of the Gospels it will be seen that the Lamb of God died at the very time that the pascal lambs were being slain in the temple.

7. "And the whole assembly of the congregation of Israel shall kill *it* in the evening". (v. 6). Here the type passes to the Antitype. This point is very striking indeed. Many thousands of lambs were to be slain on that memorable night in Egypt, yet the Lord here designedly used the singular number when giving these instructions to Moses—Israel shall kill *it*, not "them"! It is indeed remarkable that never once is the plural "lambs" used throughout the 12th chapter of Exodus. "There was only one before God's mind—The Lamb of Calvary" (Urquhart).

8. "And they shall eat the flesh in that night, roast with fire, and unleavened bread; and with bitter herbs they shall eat it" (v. 8). Not only was the lamb to be killed, but its flesh was to be eaten. This was God's provision for those *inside* the house, as the blood secured protection from the judgment *outside*. A journey lay before Israel, and food was needed to strengthen them first. "Eating" signifies two things in Scripture: appropriation and fellowship. The "lamb" spoke of the *person* of Christ, and *He* is God's *food* for His people—"The *Bread* of Life". Christ is to be the object before our hearts. As we feed upon Him our souls are sustained and He is honored.

"It is *death* here which God ordains as the food of life. We are so familiar with this we are apt by the very fact to miss its significance. How we see nature thus everywhere instructing us, if we have but learned to read her lessons in the deepest lesson of God's wisdom! The laying down of life becomes the sustenance of life. For men this did not begin until after the Deluge; at least it is only after this we read of Divine permission for it. And when we see in that Deluge with its central figure, the ark of salvation, bearing within it the neucleus of the new world, the pregnant figure of how God has saved us and brought us in Christ into a new creation, how its similitude in what we have here bursts upon us! It is only as sheltered and saved from death—from what is alone truly such—that we can feed upon death; that Samson's riddle is fulfilled, and 'out of the eater comes forth meat, and out of the strong sweetness! Death is not merely vanquished and set aside; it is in the Cross the sweet and wonderful display of Divine love and power in our behalf accomplished in the mystery of human weakness. Death is become the food of life—yea, of a life which is eternal." (F. W. Grant).

But mark carefully the lamb is to be eaten with "unleavened bread and bitter herbs". In Scripture "leaven" uniformly symbolizes *evil*. The lesson taught here is of vital importance. It is only as we are *separated* from what is repugnant to Divine holiness that we can really feed upon Christ. While we are indulging known sin there can be no communion with Him. It is only as we "walk in the light as He is in the light" that the blood of God's Son cleanseth us from all sin and "we have *fellowship* one with another" (1 John 1:7). The "*bitter* herbs" speak of the remorse of conscience in the Christian. We cannot have "fellowship with His sufferings" (Phil. 3:10) without remembering *what* it was that made those sufferings needful, namely, *our sins;* and the remembrance of these cannot but produce a chastened spirit.

9. "Eat not of it raw, nor sodden at all with water, but roast with fire" (v. 9). How very explicit—rather, how carefully God preserved the accuracy of the type! In the previous verse we read, "eat the flesh in that night, roast with fire", here, "eat not of it raw". The Israelites were to feed not only upon that where *death* had done its work, but upon that which had been subjected to the *fire*. Solemn indeed is this. "It is appointed unto men once to die, and after this the judgment" (Heb. 9:27). These are two separate things. For the lost, *death* is not all, nor even the worst that awaits them. *After* death is "judgment," the judgment of a sin-hating God. Therefore if Christ was to take the place of His sinful people and suffer what was righteously due them, He must not only die, but pass under and through the *judgment* of God. "Fire" here, as ever, speaks of the *wrath* of a holy God. It tells of Christ being "made sin for us" (2 Cor. 5:21), and consequently being "made a curse for us" (Gal. 3:13) and as such, enduring the judgment of God. Speaking anticipatively by the Spirit, through the prophet Jeremiah, the Saviour said, "Is it nothing to you, all ye that pass by? behold, and see if there be any sorrow like unto My sorrow, which is done unto Me, wherewith the Lord hath afflicted Me in the day of His fierce anger. From above hath He sent *fire* into My bones". It was this which caused Him to also say through the Psalmist, "My moisture is turned into the *drought* of summer" (Psl. 32:4). And this it is which, in its deepest meaning, explains His cry from the Cross—"I thirst". His "thirst" was *the effect* of the agony of His soul in the fierce heat of God's wrath. It told of the *drought* of the land where the living God is not. "Not sodden (boiled) at all with water", because water would have *hindered* the direct action of the fire.

"His head with his legs, and with the purtenance (inwards) thereof" (v. 9). "The head, no doubt, expresses the thoughts and counsels with which the walk (the legs) keep perfect company. The inwards are those affections of His heart which were the motive-power impelling Him upon the path He trod. In all, the fire brought forth nothing but sweet savor; for men, it prepared the food of their true life; all is absolutely perfect; and all is ours to appropriate. Occupation with the person of Christ is thus impressed upon us; we need this. Not the knowledge of salvation alone will suffice us; it is the One who saves whom we need. Christ for our hearts alone keeps and sanctifies them, (Mr. Grant).

10. "And ye shall let nothing of it remain until the morning." (v. 10). The lamb must be eaten the same night as it was slain. Communion must not be separated from the sacrifice on which that communion was founded. Communion is based upon redemption accomplished. We find the same truth brought before us again at the close of Christ's parable of the prodigal son. As soon as the lost son enters the Father's house and is suitably attired, the word goes forth "Bring hither the fatted calf, and kill; and let us *eat* and be merry" (Luke 15:23).

Another thought is also suggested here by the words "ye shall let nothing of it remain until the morning". "The sacrifice in all its ceremonial was to be completed within a single night. The rising sun was thus to see no trace of the slain lamb. In like manner the atoning work of Christ is not a progressive but a completed thing. It is not in process of being accomplished; it has been accomplished definitely and eternally. As a fragrant and hallowed *memory* Calvary's costly sacrifice abides with God and the redeemed forever; but the sacrifice *itself* is past and completed. For God's suffering Lamb the dark night of judgment is no more, and He lives on high in the eternal sunshine of Divine favor and love" (Mr. W. W. Fereday).

11. "And *thus* shall ye eat it; with your loins girded, your shoes on your feet, and your staff in your hand; and ye shall eat it in haste; it is the Lord's Passover" (v. 11). The little word "thus" is very emphatic. It defines for us the accessories, what should accompany feeding upon Christ; four things are mentioned. First, their dress; "loins girded". "Having your loins girt about with *truth*", says the apostle. "The garments are spiritually what we may designate by the old word for them—'*habits*'. They are the moral guise in which we appear before men,—what they identify with us at least, if they are not, after all, *ourselves*. And if not just 'ourselves' we may be in many ways *read in them;* pride or lowliness, boldness or unobtrusiveness, sloth or diligence, and many another thing.

"The long robes of the East, as we are all aware, required the girdle in order that there might be no hindrance in the way of a march such as Israel now had before them. If they were allowed to flow loose, they would get entangled with the feet and overthrow the wearers; and the dust of the road would get upon them and defile them. The *truth* it is which is to be our girdle, keeping us from the loose and negligent contact with ever-ready defilement in a world which the lust of the flesh, the lust of the eyes, and the pride of life characterizes, and from the entanglement to our feet which lax habits prove.

"Garments *un*-girded are thus practically near akin to the 'weights' (Heb. 12:2) which the apostle bids us 'lay aside', and which are not things in themselves sinful, and yet nevertheless betray us into sin. Have you noticed *the connection* in that exhortation of his 'lay aside every weight and the sin which doth so easily beset us'? If you had a pack of wolves following you, you would understand very quickly why if carrying a weight you would be indeed 'easily beset'. And herein, many a soul may discern, if he will, why he has so great and so little successful conflict. The 'weight' shows, like the flowing garment that whatever else we may be, we are not *racers*. . . . Fit companions then with unleavened bread and bitter herbs are these girt loins. We must arise and depart for this is not our rest" (Mr. Grant).

"Your shoes on your feet". This, again, was in view of the journey which lay before them. It tells of preparation for their walk. There is a most interesting reference to these "shoes" in Deut. 29:5, where at the close of his life, Moses said, "I have led your forty years in the wilderness; your clothes are not waxen old upon you, and thy *shoe* is not waxen old upon thy foot", And again he reminded them, "Neither did thy foot swell these forty years" (Deut. 8:4). Remarkable was this. For forty years Israel had wandered up and down the wilderness, yet their shoes were neither torn to pieces nor did their feet suffer. How this tells of the *sufficiency* of that provision which God has graciously provided for the walk of His saints! When the prodigal son came to His Father, there was not only the best robe for his body, and the ring for his hand, but there were also "shoes for his feet" (Luke 15:22)! The significance of these "shoes" is explained for us in Eph. 6:15—"Your *feet shod* with the preparation of the Gospel of peace".

"Your staff in your hand". The staff is the sign of *pilgrimage*. As they journeyed to the Promised Land, Israel were to pass through a wilderness in which they would be strangers and pilgrims. So it is with Christians as they pass through this world. Their *home* is not here: "Our citizenship is in heaven" (Phil. 3:20). Therefore does God say, "I beseech you *as* strangers and pilgrims" (1 Pet. 2:11). Staff in hand signifies that as Israel journeyed they were to *lean* on something *outside* of themselves. Clearly this is the written Word, given us for a stay and support. The dependent soul who leans hard upon it can say with the Psalmist, "Thy rod and *Thy staff* they comfort me" (23:4).

"And ye shall eat it in haste". "They were to eat it in haste because they expected that any moment the Lord might come and pass over them; any moment they might be called to arise and go out of the land of bondage. They expected the imminent Coming of the Lord. That is to say, because the Coming of the Lord *was* imminent they expected it". (Dr. Haldeman).

12. "When I see the blood, I will pass over you" v. 13. Upon this Mr. Urquhart has made some illuminating remarks. "The term rendered Passover *'pesach'* does not seem to have that meaning. It is entirely different from the Hebrew verb, *a-bhar,* or *ga-bhar,* so frequently used in the sense of 'to pass over'. *Pasach* (the verb) and *pesach* (the noun) have no connection with any other Hebrew word. They closely resemble, however, the Egyptian word *pesh,* which means 'to spread the wings over,' 'to protect'. The word is used—we may say explained—in this sense in Isa. 31:5: "As birds flying, so will the Lord of Hosts *defend* Jerusalem; defending also He will deliver it; and passing over (pasoach, participle of pasach) He will *preserve* it'. The word has, consequently, the very meaning of the Egyptian term for 'spreading the wings over', and 'protecting'; and *pesach,* the Lord's Passover, means such sheltering and protection as is found under the outstretched wings of the Almighty. Does not this give a new fulness to those words of our Saviour, 'O Jerusalem! Jerusalem! . . . . how often would I have gathered thy children together, as a hen does gather her brood under her wings, and ye would not' (Luke 13:34)? Jesus of Nazareth was her PESACH, her *shelter* from the coming judgment; and she knew it not! Quite in keeping with this sense of protecting with outstretched wings is the fact that this term *pesach* is applied (1) to the ceremony, 'It

is the Lord's Passover' (Ex. 12:11), and (2) to the lamb (v. 21); 'draw out and take you a lamb according to your families and kill the Passover'. The slain lamb, the sheltering behind its blood and the eating of its flesh, constituted the *pesach,* the protection of God's chosen people beneath the sheltering wings of the Almighty". This interpretation is clearly established by what we read in verse 23: "For the Lord will pass through to smite the Egyptians; and when He seeth the blood upon the lintel and upon the two side posts, the Lord will pass over the door, *and will not suffer the Destroyer to come in unto your houses to smite you*". It was not merely that the Lord passed by the houses of the Israelites, but that He stood on guard *protecting* each blood-sprinkled door!

13. "And this day shall be unto you for a memorial; and ye shall keep it a feast to the Lord throughout your generations; ye shall keep it a feast by an ordinance forever" (v. 14). It is interesting to trace Israel's subsequent response to this command. Scripture records just *seven* times when this Feast was kept. The first in Egypt, here in Ex. 12. The second in the Wilderness (Num. 9). The third when they entered Canaan (Joshua 5). The fourth in the days of Hezekiah (2 Chron. 30). The fifth under Josiah (2 Chron. 35). The sixth after the return from the Captivity (Ezra 6). Just six in the O. T. The *seventh* was celebrated by the Lord Jesus and His apostles immediately before the institution of "the Lord's Supper, (Luke 22:15, etc.). In that last Passover the true Lamb of God is seen, who had been prefigured by the preceding pascal lambs. "It should also be observed, that Jesus Christ, who celebrated the last Passover, had been Himself in Egypt, where the first had been observed. As the passover came from Egypt, so Jesus Christ, who is the true Passover was called out of Egypt (Matt. 2:15)" (Robert Haldane: Evidence and Authority of Divine Revelation).

14. "And ye shall take a bunch of hyssop and dip it in the blood that is in the basin, and strike the lintel and the two side posts with the blood that is in the basin" (v. 22). This gives us a marvelous typical picture of the sufferings of our blessed Lord upon the Cross, though the picture is marred by translating here, the original word, "basin". Once more we avail ourselves of the scholarly help of Dr. Urquhart. The word rendered 'basin' is *sap,* which is an old Egyptian word for the step before a door, or the threshold of a house. The word *is* translated 'threshold' in Judges 19:27 and 'door' in 2 Kings 12:9—apparently for the sole reason that the sense 'basin', favored by lexicographers and translaters could not possibly be given to the word in these passages. . . .No direction was given about putting the blood upon the threshold, for the reason that the blood *was already there.* The lamb was evidently slain at the door of the house which was protected by its blood". We may add that the Septuagint gives "para ten thuran", which means along the door-way! While the Vulgate reads, "in sanguine qui est limine"—in the blood which is on the threshold. This point is not simply one of academic interest, but concerns the accuracy of the type. The door of the house wherein the Israelite was protected had blood on the lintel (the cross piece), on the side posts and on the step.* How marvelously this pictured Christ on the Cross; blood above, where the thorns pierced His brow; blood at the sides, from His nail-pierced hands; blood below, from His nail-pierced feet!!

15. The blood was to be applied with "a bunch of hyssop" (v. 22). Nothing in the Word is meaningless: the smallest detail has its due significance. Nor are we ever left to guess at anything; Scripture is ever its own interpreter. The "hyssop" was not connected with the "lamb", but with the application of its blood. It speaks, then, not of Christ but of the sinner's appropriation of His sacrifice. The "hyssop" is never found in connection with any of the offerings which foreshadowed the Lord Jesus Himself. It is beheld, uniformly, in the hands of the sinner. Thus in connection with the cleansing of the leper, Lev. 14; and the restoration of the unclean, Num. 19. From Psl. 51:7 we may learn that "hyssop" speaks of *humiliation of soul,* contrition, repentance. Note that in 1 Kings 4:33 "hyssop" is contrasted with "the cedars", showing that "hyssop" speaks of *lowliness.*

Perhaps a word should be added concerning the Feast of Unleavened Bread which followed the Passover: "And ye shall observe the Feast of Unleavened Bread; for in this selfsame day have I brought your armies out of the land of Egypt; therefore shall ye observe this day

*The objection that blood on the step would cause the Israelite to walk upon it, is obviated by Jehovah's instructions. *"And none of you shall go out at the door* until the morning" (v. 22)!

in your generations by an ordinance forever. In the first month, on the fourteenth day of the month, at even, ye shall eat unleavened bread, until the one and twentieth day of the month at even. Seven days shall there be no leaven found in your houses; for whosoever eateth that which is leavened, even that soul shall be cut off from the congregation of Israel, whether he be a stranger or born in the land. Ye shall eat nothing leavened; in all your habitations shall ye eat unleavened bread" (vv. 17-20). The interpretation of this for us is supplied in 1 Cor. 5:7, 8: "Purge out *therefore* the old leaven, that ye may be a new lump, as ye are unleavened. For even Christ our passover is sacrificed for us; *therefore* let us keep the feast not with old leaven, neither with the leaven of malice and wickedness; but with the unleavened bread of sincerity and truth".

Upon the above we cannot do better than quote from Mr. C. H. MacIntosh: the Feast spoken of in this passage is that which, in the life and conduct of the Church, corresponds with the Feast of unleavened bread. This lasted seven days (a complete circle of time A. W. P.); and the Church collectively, and the believer individually, are called to walk *in practical holiness,* during their days, or the entire period of their course here below; and this, moreover, as the direct *result* of being washed in the blood, and having communion with the sufferings of Christ.

"The Israelite did not put away leaven in order to be saved, but because he was saved; and if he failed to put away leaven it did not raise the question of security through the blood, but simply of fellowship with the assembly. The cutting off of an Israelite from the Congregation answers precisely to the suspension of Christian fellowship, and if he be indulging in that which is contrary to the holiness of the Divine presence. God cannot tolerate evil. A single unholy thought (entertained: A. W. P.) will interrupt the soul's communion; and until the soil contracted by any such thought is got rid of by confession, founded on the advocacy of Christ, the communion cannot possibly be restored (see 1 John 1:5-10)".

May the Lord stir us up to a more diligent and prayerful study of His wonderful Word.

Arthur W. Pink.

TRUTH AND ERROR,

or

Letters to a Friend

4. God's Will and Man's Will.

"Cannot I do with you as this potter? saith the Lord. Behold, as the clay is in the potter's hand, so are ye in My hand, O house of Israel".—Jer. 18:6.

Much of the present controversy is concerning the *will of God.* On this point many questions have arisen. The chief one is that which touches on the connection between the will of God and the will of man. What is the relation between these? What is the order in which they stand to each other? Which is the first? There is no dispute as to the existence of these two separate wills. There is a will in God, and there is also a will in man. Both of these are in continual exercise;—God willeth; and man willeth. Nothing in the universe takes place without the will of God. This is admitted. But it is asked, Is this will *first* in everything?

I answer, yes. Nothing that is good can exist which God did not will to be, and nothing that is evil can exist which God did not will to allow. The will of God goes before all other wills. It does not depend on them, but they depend on it. Its movements regulate them. The "I will" of Jehovah, is that which sets in motion everything in heaven and in earth. The "I will" of Jehovah, is the spring and origin of all that is done throughout the universe, great and small, among things animate and inanimate. It was this "I will" that brought angels in to being, and still sustains them. It was this "I will' that was the origin of salvation to a lost world. It was this "I will" that provided a Redeemer, and accomplished redemption. It was this "I will" that begins, and carries on, and ends salvation in each soul that is redeemed. It is this "I will" that opens the blind eye, and unstops the deaf ear. It was this "I will" that awakens the slumberer, and raises the dead. I do not mean that, merely generally speaking, God has declared His will concerning these things: but each individual conversion, nay, and each movement that forms part of it, originates in this supreme "I will". When Jesus healed the leper, He said, "I will", be thou clean"; so when a soul is converted, there is the same distinct and special forthputting of the Divine will,

"I will, be thou converted". Everything that can be called good in man, or in the universe, originates in the "I will" of Jehovah.

I do not deny that in conversion man himself wills. In everything that he does, thinks, feels, he of necessity wills. In believing he wills; in repenting he wills; in turning from his evil ways he wills. All this is true. The opposite is both untrue and absurd. But while fully admitting this, there is another question behind it of great interest and moment. Are these movements of man's will towards good the effects of the forthputting of God's will? Is man willing, because he has made himself so, or because God has made him so? Does he become willing entirely by an act of his own will, or by chance, or by moral suasion, or because acted on by created causes and influences from without?

I answer unhesitatingly, he becomes willing, because another and a superior will, even that of God, has come into contact with his, altering its nature and its bent. This new bent is the result of a change produced upon it by Him who alone, of all beings, has the right, without control, to say, in regard to all events and changes, "I will". The man's will has followed the movement of the Divine will. God has made him willing. God's will is *first* in the movement, not second. Even a holy and perfect will depends for guidance upon the will of God. Even when renewed it still *follows,* it does not *lead.* Much more an unholy will, for its bent must be first changed; and how can this be, if God is not to interpose His hand and power?

But is not this to make God the *author* of sin? No. It does not follow that because God's will originates what is *good* in man, that it must therefore *originate* what is *evil.* The existence of a holy, happy world, proves that God had created it with His own hand. The existence of an unholy, unhappy world, proves that God *allowed it to fall into that state:*—but it proves nothing more. We are told that Jesus was delivered by "the determinate counsel and foreknowledge of God." God's will was there. God permitted that deed of darkness to be done; nay, it was the result of His "determinate counsel". But does that prove that God was the *author* of the sin of either Judas or Herod? Had it not been for the eternal "I will" of Jehovah, Christ would not have been delivered up; but does this prove that God compelled either Judas to betray, or Herod to mock, or Pilate to condemn, the Lord of Glory? Still further, it is added in another place, "Of a truth against Thy holy child Jesus, whom Thou hast anointed, both Herod and Pontius Pilate, with the Gentiles and people of Israel, were gathered together *for to do whatsoever Thy hand and Thy counsel determined before to be done*". Is it possible to pervert this passage so as to prove that it has no reference to predestination? Does it make God the author of the deed referred to? Must God be the author of sin, because it is said that Israel and the Gentiles "were gathered together to do what His counsel had determined"? Let our opponents attempt an explanation of such a passage, and tell us how it can be made to harmonize with their theory.

It may be argued that God works *by means,* in changing the will. "There is no need, it will be said, that there should be these special and direct forth-putting of His will and strength. He has ordained the means, He has given His Word, He had proclaimed His Gospel, and by these means He effects the change. His will does not come directly into contact with ours. He leaves it to these instruments to effect the change". Well, let us see what amount of truth there may be in this. I suppose no one will say that the Gospel *can* produce the alteration in the will *so long as the will rejects it.* No medicine, however excellent, can operate unless it be taken. The will of man then rejects the Gospel; it is set against the truth of God. How then is it made to receive it? Granting that in receiving it there is a change, yet the question is, How was it so far changed already as to be willing to receive it? The worst feature of the malady is the determination *not* to touch or taste the medicine; and how is this to be overcome? Oh! It will be said, this resistance is to be overcome with arguments. Arguments! Is not the Gospel itself the great argument? and it is rejected. What arguments can you expect to prevail with a man that refuses the Gospel? Admit that there are other arguments, yet the man is set against them all. There is not one argument that can be used which he does not hate. His will resists and rejects every persuasive and motive. How then is this resistance to be overcome,—this opposition to be made to give way? How is the bent of the will to be so altered as to receive that which it rejected? Plainly by his will coming into contact with a superior one,—a will that can remove the resistance,—a will such as that which said, "Let there be light, and there was light". The will itself must undergo a change before it can choose that which it rejected. And what *can* change it but the finger of God?

Were man's rejection of the Gospel simply occasioned by his misunderstanding it, then I can see how, upon its being made plain, resistance would cease. But I do not believe that such is the case; for what does it amount to but just that the sinner never rejects the *truth,* it is only error which he rejects, and were his mistake rectified, he would at once embrace the truth! The unrenewed man, then, so far from having enmity to the truth, has the very opposite! So little of depravity is there in his heart, and so little perversity in his will—such instinctive love of truth and abhorrence of error is there in him, that as soon as the truth is made plain to him, he embraces it! All his previous hesitation arose from the errors which had been mingled with the truth presented! One would think that this was anything but depravity. It might be ignorance, but it could not be called enmity to the truth, it is rather enmity to error. It would thus appear that the chief feature of the sinner's heart and will is not enmity to truth, but hatred to error and love of truth!

Man's heart is enmity to God,—*to God as revealed in the Gospel,*—to God as the God of grace. What truth can there be in the assertion that all the sinner's distrust of God and darkness of spirit arise from his not seeing God as the God of grace? I grant that oftentimes this is the case. I know that it is very frequently misapprehension of God's merciful character, as seen and pledged in the cross of Christ, that is the cause of darkness to the anxious soul, and that a simple sight of the exceeding riches of the grace of God would dispel these clouds; but that is very different from saying that such a sight, apart from the renewing energy of the Spirit upon the soul, would change man's enmity into confidence and love. For we know that the unrenewed will is set against the *Gospel;* it is enmity to God and His truth. The more closely and clearly truth is set before it, and pressed home upon it, its hatred swells and rises. The presentation of truth, however forcible and clear, even though that truth were the grace of God, will only exasperate the unconverted man. It is the Gospel that he hates; and the more clearly it is set before him he hates it the more. It is God that he hates; and the more closely God approaches him, the more vividly that God is set before him, the more does his enmity awaken and augment. Surely, then, that which stirs up enmity cannot of itself remove it. Of what avail, then, are the most energetic means *by themselves?* The will itself must be directly operated upon by the Spirit of God: He who made it must remake it. Its making was the work of Omnipotence: its re-making must be the same. In no other way can its evil bent be rectified. God's will must come into contact with man's will, and then the work is done. Must not God's will then be first in every such movement? Man's will follows; it cannot lead.

Is this a hard saying? So some in these days would have us to believe. Let us ask *wherein* consists its hardness. Is it hard that God's will should take the precedence of man's? Is it hard that God's will should be the leader and man's the follower in all things great and small? Is it hard that we should be obliged to trace the origin of every movement of man towards good to the will of a sovereign Jehovah?

If it be hard, it must be that it strips man of very fragment of what is good, or of the slightest tendency to good. And this we believe to be the secret origin of the complaint against the doctrine. It is a thorough leveller and emptier of man. It makes him not only nothing, but worse than nothing,—a sinner all over,—nothing but a sinner, with a heart full of enmity to God, set against Him as the God of righteousness, and still more set against Him as the God of grace, with a will so bent away from the will of God, and so rebellious against it, as not to have one remaining inclination to what is good and holy, and spiritual. This he cannot tolerate. Admit that a man is totally worthless and helpless, and where is the hard saying? Is it hard that God's blessed and holy will should go before our miserable and unholy wills, to lead them in the way? Is it hard that those who have nothing should be indebted to God for everything? Is it hard, seeing that every movement of my will is downwards, earthwards, that God's mighty will should come in and lift it omnipotently upwards, heavenwards?

If I admit that God's will regulates the great movements of the universe I must admit that it equally regulates the small. It *must* do this, for the great depend upon the small. The minutest movement of my will is regulated by the will of God. And in this I rejoice. Woe is me if it be not so. If I shrink from so unlimited control and guidance, it is plain that I dislike the idea of being wholly at the disposal of God. I am wishing to be in part at my own disposal. I am ambitious of regulating the lesser movements of my will, while I give up the greater to His control. And thus it comes out that I wish to be a god to myself. I do not like the thought of God having *all* the disposal of my destiny. If He gets His will, I am afraid that I shall not get mine. It comes out, moreover, that the God about whose love I was so fond of speaking, is a God to whom I cannot trust myself implicitly for eternity. Yes, this is the real truth. *Man's dislike at God's sovereignty arises from his suspicion of God's heart.* And yet the men in our day, who deny this absolute sovereignty, are the very men who profess to rejoice in the love of God,—who speak of that love as if there were nothing else in God but love. The more I understand of the character of God, as revealed in Scripture, the more shall I see that He *must* be sovereign, and the more shall I rejoice from my inmost heart that He is so.

It was God's sovereign will that fixed the time of my birth. It is the same will that has fixed the day of my death. And was not the day of my conversion fixed as certainly by that same will? Or will any but "the fool" say that God has fixed by His will the day of our birth and death, but leaves us to fix the day of our conversion by our own will; that is, leave us to decide whether we shall be converted or not, whether we shall believe or not? If the day of conversion be fixed, then it cannot be left to be determined by our own will. God determined, where and when, and how we should be born; and so He has determined where, and when, and how we shall be born again. If so, His will must go before ours in believing; and it is just because His will goes before ours that we become willing to believe. Were it not for this, we should never have believed at all. If man's will precedes God's will in everything relating to himself, then I do not see how any of God's plans can be carried into effect. Man would be left to manage the world in his own way. God must not fix the time of his conversion, for that would be an interference with man's responsibility. Nay, He must not fix that he shall be converted at all, for *that* must be left to himself and to his own will. He must not fix how many are to be converted, for that would be making His own invitation a mere mockery, and man's responsibility a pretence! He may turn a stray star into its course again by a direct forth-putting of power, and be unchallenged for interference with the laws of nature. But to stretch out His arm and arrest a human will in its devious course, so as to turn it back again to holiness, is an unwarrantable exercise of His power, and an encroachment upon man's liberty! What a world! where man gets all his own way, where God is not allowed to interfere, except in the way that *man* calls lawful! What a world! where everything turns upon man's will;—where the whole current of events in the world or in the church is regulated, shaped, impelled by man's will alone. God's will is but a secondary thing. Its part is to watch events, and follow in the track of man's! Man wills, and God must say—Amen!

In all this opposition to the absolute will of God, we see the self-will of the last days manifesting itself. Men wanted to be a god at the first, and he continues the struggle to the last. He is resolved that his will shall take the precedence of God's. In the last Antichrist, this self-will shall be summed up and exhibited. He is the king that is to do "according to his will". And in the free-will controversy of the day, we see the same spirit displayed. It is Antichrist that is speaking to us, and exhorting us to proud independence. Self-will is the essence of anti-christian religion. Self-will is the root of bitterness, that is springing up in the churches in these days. And it is not from above, it is from beneath. It is earthly, sensual, devilish.

THUS SAITH THE LORD:

"I will be gracious to whom I will be gracious, and will show mercy on whom I will show mercy"—Exodus 33:19.

"I, even I, am He, and there is no God with Me. I kill and I make alive; I wound and I heal; neither is there any that can deliver out of My hand"—Deut. 32:39.

"Behold He breaketh down, and it cannot be built again; He shutteth up a man, and there can be no opening"—Job 12:14.

"He doeth according to His will in the army of heaven, and among the inhabitants of the earth, and none can stay His hand, or say unto Him, What doest Thou?"—Dan. 4:35.

"Who hath saved us and called us with an holy calling, not according to our works, but according to *His own purpose* and grace, given us in Christ Jesus before the world began"—2 Tim. 1:9.

H. Bonar, 1851.

THE NAMING OF JOHN THE BAPTIST.

With Thoughts on Godliness in the Home.

It is a privilege to read the Scriptures for enjoyment of the Lord, *and* for food, *and* for definite guidance in the varied circumstances of our own daily home life. The "little" things there, are not little if they are opportunities to please our Heavenly Father. Our relationship to one another in the home, and to the little ones, and to relatives, are *all* set forth in the Scriptures. There are no circumstances which are "unprovided for". God delights that His people should "know" what to do.

Zacharias and Elizabeth received a wondrous testimony in Luke 1:5, 6. As Job was humbled to see his failure, and Paul acknowledged he required a thorn in the flesh to prevent him from being "lifted up", so Zacharias needed the painful chastening of months for a few words of unbelief. The question of Luke 1:18 implied: "I do not know". We remember 1 Kings 13, and would pray that we also may be guarded.

When John was born, neighbours and relatives arrived. Dealing with *such* to God's glory is always a problem. How many children of God have become "broader" because of what relatives "say", or "may think", or because of their gifts, e.g., decorations for the home, and worldly clothing for the children. "Naturally" on this occasion "the relatives" began to act. "They called him (or "were calling him") Zacharias": (59). Let Christian parents be determined, from the *outset*, to maintain their own responsibility *to God's glory* in their own homes. Unsaved uncles and aunts, and even those who profess the Lord's Name, will *want* to arrange for the children, and will speak in a worldly way before them. Do not welcome any to the home, unless you can exalt the Lord. Guard the door: it belongs to Him. Do not ruin your children, beloved friends, for the sake of courtesy. On this occasion, there was a problem. The father should act at all times, with the wife as a "help", but *he* was dumb, and, doubtless, "felt" the reproof of *his unbelief.* A tenderhearted saint *feels* chastisement, and is thus often held back.

But in the emergency the godly character of Elizabeth is manifested. She does not work independently of her husband, as Eve. There is, in accord with God's will, a beautiful *harmony* between husband and wife. 1 Peter 3:1-7 is deeply impressive. In like manner the Book of Proverbs presents the father and mother as *of one mind.* Whenever they differ, and even differ before their children, is it a surprise that home-order is wrecked? Elizabeth is firm, *"No,* but (on the contrary) he *shall* be called John". Happy is the child of God who can say "No" at the right time, and who does not waste the gift of time by argument and parleying. How definitely we see that Zacharias and his wife had *talked together* (v. 13). If believing women allow relatives to "interfere" they grieve God's Holy Spirit. The objection of verse 61 is quite "natural": but customs and habits are not to decide. Shall we fall in with the "fashion", or obey God?

Zacharias is *still* dumb—how painful this seems. *Yet God has not forgotten.* Some beckon to him, and he seeks a writing tablet, and shows the *"Obedient faith"* the lack of which had brought months of trial:—"John IS his name". The *exact* testimony of Elizabeth, but *expressed* more strongly: how befitting as to "manner" for a godly husband and wife alike. And at once his mouth is opened, and opened to praise! And graciously the Lord removed the chastisement and the *first* words are thanksgiving.

Surely, beloved brethren, we need to pray for such an attitude in the home to the praise of God's glory. And are we willing to put Himself, and His glory, *first from today?* Tomorrow is too late. The Lord is ready to refresh His people who are willing to believe that His arrangements (e.g. in Eph. 5) are meant for homes in the twentieth century as well as the first.

Percy W. Heward.

Let the reader ponder prayerfully Gen. 18:19—"For I know that he will command his children and his household after him, and they shall keep the way of the Lord, to do justice and judgment; that the Lord may bring upon Abraham that which He hath spoken of him", A. W. P.

FUTURE OF ISRAEL.

Take His chosen people, the Jews; they were the only nation, His darling; Theirs were the oracles of God, the promises, the covenant, and they were all in all with Him for many thousand years. Why? He scatters them, breaks them all in pieces; the ten tribes He carrieth away captive long before the two tribes and then the two tribes. And when He had thus scattered them all, what was His promise? Isa. 9:11, 12, "It shall come to pass," saith the text, "that the Lord shall set His hand again the second time to recover the remnant of His people. And He shall gather together the dispersed of Judah from the four corners of the earth." He will gather them together in one again. What saith the Apostle, Rom. 9:11? "Have they stumbled," saith He, "that they shall fall?" Or as the prophet Jeremiah expresseth it,—we may allude to it, if it be not the meaning of the place,—chapter 8:4, "Shall they fall, and not rise?" He compareth the casting off of the Jews but to a stumbling, it was no more; yet it was the greatest stumble that ever was, for they stumbled upon the Rock, Christ: they crucified Him, and yet God calls it but a stumbling; but it was a stumbling of a long-stride, for it was sixteen hundred years. But, shall they stumble, saith He, that they shall fall? No, He will recover them again. Shall they fall, and not rise? Yes, and their rising shall be "Life from the dead," as it followeth v. 15. In Ezek. 37:3, God compareth them to dry bones: "Can these dry bones live saith He? Their hope was gone, all was gone. "Behold," saith He, "I will cause breath to enter into these bones, and they shall live." v. 5. He comes over them the second time, and makes all these bones come together, and flesh comes upon them, and they shall live, and He will never cast them off again. Compare but Rom. 9:26, the apostle quoteth but one Scripture to prove the calling of the Jews there; it is out of Isa. 59:20. Read but that chapter, and you shall find that when they are once called, He will never cast them off again; but their seed's seed shall remain forever. And, Isa. 65:17, He saith that the former heaven and earth shall no more be remembered, nor come to mind.

(Dr. T. Goodwin, 1640).

REPENTANCE AND FAITH.

It is well and commonly said that the simplicity of the Gospel is its difficulty with souls. God's ways are not our ways, nor His thoughts our thoughts. We do not know ourselves even, until the Word of God reveals us to ourselves, and we resist the revelation as long as it is possible at all to do so. Hence, repentance, i. e., the bowing in heart to the judgment which the Word has pronounced concerning us, is in God's order absolutely necessary to the reception of the Gospel. It is not, and cannot be, as some in the present day would have it, "Believe the Gospel and repent", but as we find the Lord Himself preaching it (Mark 1:15)—"Repent ye, and believe the Gospel".

Faith in the Word must thus, however, precede repentance, for only from faith can repentance flow; and as soon as faith is in the soul, its fruits begin to manifest themselves. Conversion is the turning of the man to God. Naturally his dependence is upon himself and not upon God; and it is as his face is turned Godward his back is turned upon himself. Thus repentance, the soul's judgment of itself according to the Word, is never absent where faith is—comes as it were with it, and yet is the fruit of it.*

But it is as the soul is thus turned from its self-confidence,—as it receives and bows to the judgment of God upon itself,—that the Gospel becomes clear, suitable, necessary, and how precious! None could have *imagined* it ever. The greatness of our necessity is no argument in itself that God could come so far to meet it,—no revelation of the way by which it could be met; but the way being revealed, and the love of God declared in the gift of His Son, the knowledge of our necessity prepares us to apprehend and receive the joyful news of salvation otherwise unintelligible and untrusted. It is then and thus it becomes simple. John the Baptist in this way comes with the baptism of repentance to prepare the way of the Lord, and the Lord Himself begins His ministry with a John-Baptist strain; and while Pharisees murmured at His grace, all the publicans and sinners drew near to hear Him". (Mr. F. W. Grant.

*The above distinctions are important. Faith precedes repentance, but repentance precedes salvation. The order is: first, faith *in the written Word*, then repentance (judgment of self), and then believing the Gospel, i.e., *saving* faith. (A. W. P.).

(*Continued from page 73.*)

Dinah . . . . went out *to see* the daughters of the land" (Gen. 34:1)—read what follows for the tragic sequel. It was so with Potiphar's wife (Gen. 39:7). It was so with the ten "spies" (Num. 13:32, 33). It was so with Achan (Josh. 7:21)—mark the order: "I saw" . . . . I coveted . . . . took . . . . hid"! It was so with Samson (Judges 16:1). It was so with David (2 Sam. 11:2). What point do these solemn warnings convey! How urgently we need to cry unto God daily—"Turn away mine eyes from beholding vanity" (Psa. 119:37).

Scripture speaks of the "lust of the eyes" (1 John 2:16) as one of the chief marks of worldliness, and warns us again and again against the unlawful use of sight. "Look not upon the wine when it is red" (Prov. 23:31). Again we are told, "He that winketh with the eye causeth sorrow" (Prov. 10:10). Our Lord declares that "whosoever *looketh* upon a woman to lust after her hath committed adultery with her already in his heart" (Matt. 5:28). The eye, then, needs to be disciplined. "Let thine eyes look right on, and let thine eyelids look straight before thee." (Prov. 4:25). That is, Let us attend to the business before us, which is to tread the Narrow Way that leadeth unto life. Let us not allow our gaze to wander so that our heart becomes enchanted with earthly things.

"Wisdom is before him that hath understanding; but the eyes of a fool are in the ends of the earth." (Prov. 17:24). One cause of much distraction is curiosity of the senses. Our eyes run to and fro, and then our hearts wander from the Lord and His interests. History records how that when a Spartan youth who held the censor while Alexander offered sacrifice, and a red-hot cinder fell upon his bare arm, suffered it to burn, rather than cry out, and disturb the worship. How this puts *us* to shame that our hearts are not more fixed in the service of God!

Let us learn from Job—"I made a covenant with mine eyes" (31:1). Eyes be faithful to my soul, that there be nothing to stir up carnal and impure thoughts, that there be no unclean object to fire my heart. Nearly three hundred years ago a Puritan wrote upon this verse: "Oh the foolishness of this age. Some will smile at the self-discipline of Job, and ask, Why be so strict and precise? But why should they? Has sin grown less dangerous? or is man's nature wiser or stronger? or are we better fortified against temptation? Are our hearts purer than God's saints of old? I trow not. Therefore set a watch upon your eyes, that sin enter not your heart."

Let us not forget that it is written, that one of the characteristics of those who shall "dwell on High" (Isa. 33:16) is he that "shutteth his eyes from seeing evil" (v. 15). Let each of us pray from the heart *"Turn away* mine eyes from beholding vanity." The assistance of Divine grace must be sought. He that inclineth the heart *to* desire spiritual things, must bridle the senses *against* sinful things. Therefore let us beg this mercy from Him. Finally "Look off *unto Jesus* the Author and Finisher of faith". Be occupied with Him, and the things of the world will no longer allure.

"Mine eye affecteth mine heart". Thus far we have dealt mainly with the negative side of our subject; let our final word be upon the positive. Following His exhortations to Christian's to "run with patience the race" set before them, the Holy Spirit adds, *"Looking (off) unto Jesus"* (Heb. 12:2, 3). It is only as our eyes are fixed steadfastly upon the Saviour that our hearts will be kept right. By faith Abraham "sojourned in the land of promise as in a strange country". Why? How? "For he *looked* for a city which hath foundations, whose builder and maker is God" (Heb. 11:9, 10). By faith Moses "forsook Egypt, not fearing the wrath of the king". Why? "For he endured as *seeing* Him who is invisible" (Heb. 11:27). His eye affected his heart!

Arthur W. Pink.

VOL. IV MAY, 1925 NO. 5

STUDIES in the SCRIPTURES

"Search the Scriptures" John 5:39.

Arthur W. Pink, Publisher & Editor,
R. F. D. 9, York, Pa.

Price: 10 cents per copy; $1.00 per year. Foreign $1.00 per year.

LEPROSY A TYPE OF SIN.

One reason why God gave us the Bible was to show man how *His* holy eyes regard sin. The world thinks and speaks lightly of sin, and even Christians have low views of it—that is why we are so puffed up. Scripture speaks of "the exceeding sinfulness of sin" (Rom. 7:13), and the more we perceive the infinite evil of sin, the more shall we abhor ourselves. Nothing humbles us like a view of our corrupt hearts.

Now the Holy Spirit has used a great variety of means in exposing and exhibiting the heinousness of sin. He has shown us what it did to Adam in innocency. He has shown us the terrible judgment of God upon it in the drowning of the antediluvians, the burning of Sodom and Gomorrah, the plagues upon Egypt. He has shown us the *eternal* punishment which awaits those who die in their sins. And last, but not least, he has shown us that God's elect could not be saved from their sins unless His own Beloved Son was made *a curse* for them. But it is not of these things we would now enlarge upon. The Holy Spirit has also given us a vivid portrayal of the character of sin in the most fearful disease that can possibly affect the human body. Leprosy is God's type of sin. Mark the following analogies:—

1. To the outward eye leprosy has *an insignificant beginning.* It starts as a "rising, a scab, or bright spot" (Lev. 13:2). It is so trivial that usually no attention is paid to it. Little or no warning is given of the fearful havoc it will work. So with the entrance of sin into this world. To the natural man the eating of the forbidden fruit appears a very small matter, altogether uncommensurate with the awful effects it has produced.

2. Leprosy is *inherited.* It is a communicable disease. It poisons the blood, and is readily transmitted from parents to child. It is so with sin. "By one man sin entered into the world, and death by sin; and so death passed upon all men for that all sinned" (Rom. 5:12). None escaped. "Behold, I was shapen in iniquity; and in sin did my mother conceive me" (Psl. 51:5), is equally true of every member of Adam's race.

3. Leprosy *spreads* with deadly rapidity. Beginning as a small spot in the skin, like a locust on the twig of a tree, it eats its way through the flesh till nothing but the skeleton is left. This is what sin has done to man. It has corrupted every part of his being until he is totally depraved. Heart, mind, will, conscience, spirit, soul and body,—none has escaped: "from the sole of the foot even unto the head there is *no* soundness" (Isa. 1:6).

4. Leprosy is highly *infectious.* Inherited inwardly, contagious outwardly. The leper communicates his terrible disease to others wherever he goes. So it is with sin. It is not only inherited as a nature, but it is developed by association with the wicked. "Evil communications *corrupt* good manners" (1 Cor. 15:33). "But shun profane and vain babblings; for they will *increase* unto more ungodliness. And their word *will eat as doth a canker*" (2 Tim. 2:16, 17).

5. Leprosy is peculiarly *loathsome.* There is nothing more repellent to the eye than to look upon one stricken with this disease. Despite our pity we are obliged to turn away from such a nauseating sight with a shudder. But sin is infinitely more repellent to the thrice Holy One who is "of purer eyes than to behold evil, and canst not look on iniquity" (Hab. 1:13).

6. Leprosy is *a state of living death.* "An eye falls out, a hand or a foot drops off; it is a state of daily and progressive death. Sin is a state of spiritual death—a living on the natural side of existence, but dead to all things spiritual. The apostle speaks of

(Continued on page 120.)

IMPORTANT NOTICES

Set of twelve issues for **1922**, unbound, **$1.00.** Bound, **$1.50.**

Set of twelve issues for **1923**, unbound, **$1.00.** Bound **$1.50.** Abroad, **$1.75** or **7/6.**

Set of twelve issues for **1924**, unbound, **$1.00.** Bound **$1.50.** Abroad, **$1.75** or **7/6.**

Note: We cannot break a set or now supply any **single** 1924 issues.

Subscription Price: **$1.00** per year to any address in the world. Single copies **10 cents.**

Change of Address: Please notify me promptly of any change of address, and be certain to give both old and new addresses.

Non-subscribers receiving this Magazine regularly will understand their subscription has been entered by a friend.

Copies lost in the mail duplicated only if we are notified promptly.

Entered as second-class matter January 15th, 1923, at the post office at York, Pa., under Act of March 3rd, 1879.

CONTENTS

THE GOSPEL OF JOHN.

41. Christ Anointed at Bethany:
John 12:1-11.

Below is an Analysis of the passage which we are about to study:—

1. Jesus at Bethany again v. 1.
2. The supper v. 2.
3. Mary's devotion v. 3.
4. Judas' criticism v. 4-6.
5. Christ's vindication of Mary v. 7, 8.
6. The curiosity of the crowd v. 9.
7. The enmity of the priests vv. 10, 11.

What is recorded in John 12 occurred during the last week before our Lord's death. In it are gathered up what men would term the "results" of His public ministry. For three years the unvarying and manifold perfections of His blessed Person had been manifested both in public and in private. Two things are here emphasized: there was a deepening appreciation on the part of His own; but a steady hardening of unbelief and increasing hostility in His enemies. Three most striking incidents in the chapter illustrate the former: First, Christ is seen in the midst of a circle of His most intimate friends, in whose love He was permanently embalmed; second, we behold how that a striking, if transient, effect, had been made on the popular mind: the multitude hailed Him as "King"; third, a hint is given of the wider influence He was yet to yield, even then at work, beyond the bounds of Judaism: illustrated by the "Greeks" coming and saying, "*We* would see Jesus". But on the other hand, we also behold in this same chapter the workings of that awful enmity which would not be appeased until He had been put to death. The hatred of Christ's enemies had even penetrated the inner circle of His chosen apostles, for one of them was so utterly lacking in appreciation for His person that he openly expressed his resentment against the tribute of love which Mary paid to his Master. And at the close of the first section of this chapter we are told, "But the chief priests consulted that they might put Lazarus also to death". "In this hour there meet a ripeness of love which Jesus has won for Himself in the hearts of men, and a maturity of alienation which forbodes that His end cannot be far distant" (Dr. Dods).

In a most remarkable way and in numerous details John 12 abounds in contrasts. What could be more exquisitely blessed than its opening scene: Love preparing a feast for its Beloved; Martha serving, now in His presence; Lazarus seated with perfect composure and in joyous fellowship with the One who had called him out of the grave; Mary freely pouring out her affection by anointing with costly spikenard Him at whose feet she had learned so much. And yet what can be more solemn than the death-shades which fall across this very scene: the Lord Himself saying, "Against the day *of My burying* hath she kept this", so soon to be followed by those heart-moving words, "Now is My soul troubled" (v. 27). His own death was now in full view, present, no doubt, to His heart as He had walked with Mary to the tomb of Lazarus. As we have seen in John 11, He felt deeply the groaning and travailing of that creation which once had come so fair from His own hands. It was sin which had brought in desolation and death, and soon He was to be "made sin" and endure in infinite depths of anguish the judgment of God which was due it. He was about to yield Himself up to death for the glory of God (vv. 27, 28), for only in the Cross could be laid that foundation for the accomplishment of God's eternal counsels.

Christ had ever been the Object of the Father's complacency. "When He appointed the foundations of the earth: *then* I was by Him, as one brought up with Him and I was daily His delight" (Prov. 8:29, 30). So too at the beginning of His public ministry, the Father had declared, "This is My beloved Son, in whom I am well pleased" (Matt. 3:17). But now He was about to give the Father *new* ground for delight: *"Therefore* doth My Father love Me, *because* I lay down My life, that I might take it again" (John 10:17). Here then was the deepest character of His glory, and the Father saw to it that a fitting testimony should be borne to this very fact. His grace prepared one to enter, in some measure at least, into what was on the eve of transpiring. Mary's heart anticipated what lay deepest in His, even before it found expression in words (13:31). She not only knew that He would die, but she apprehended the infinite preciousness and value of that death. And how more fittingly could she have expressed this than by anointing His body "to the burying" (Mark 14:8)!

The link between John 11 and 12 is very precious. There we have, in figure, one of God's elect passing from death unto life; here we are shown that into which the new birth introduces us: Lazarus sitting at meat with the Lord Jesus. "But now in Christ Jesus ye who sometimes were far off *are made nigh* by the blood of Christ" (Eph. 2:13). This is the marvel of grace. Redemption brings the sinner into the presence of the Lord, not as a trembling culprit, but as one who is at perfect ease in that Presence, yea, as a joyful worshipper. It is this which Lazarus *sitting* at "the table" with Christ so sweetly speaks of. And yet the opening scene of John 12 looks forward to that which is still more blessed.

The opening verses of John 12 give us *the sequel* to what is central in the preceding chapter. *Here* we are upon resurrection ground. That which is foreshadowed in this happy gathering at Bethany is what awaits believers in the Glory. It is that which shall follow the complete manifestation of Christ as the Resurrection and the Life. Three aspects of our glorified state and our future activities in Heaven are here made known. First, in Lazarus seated at the table with Christ we learn of both our future position and portion. To be where Christ is, will be the place we shall occupy: "That where *I* am, there *ye* may be also" (John 14:3). To share with Christ His inherited reward will be our portion. And how blessedly this comes out here: "They made *Him* a supper. . . Lazarus was one of them that sat *at the table with Him"*. This will find its realization when Christ shall say, "The glory which Thou gavest *Me* I have given *them"* (John 17:22)! "And Martha *served"*. As to our future occupation in the endless ages yet to come Scripture says very little, yet this we do know, "His servants shall *serve* Him" (Rev. 22:4). Finally, in Mary's loving devotion, we behold the unstinted worship which we shall then render unto Him who sought and bought and brought us to Himself.

"Then Jesus six days before the Passover came to Bethany, where Lazarus was which had been dead, whom He raised from the dead" (v. 1). This verse has long presented a difficulty to the commentators. A few have demurred, but by far the greater number in each age have considered that Matthew (chap. 26) and Mark (chap. 14) record the same incident that is found in John 12. But both Matthew and Mark introduce the anointing at Bethany by a brief mention of that which occurred only *"two* days" before the Passover; whereas John tells us it transpired *"six* days" before the Passover (see Matt. 26:2; Mark 14:1; John 12:1). But the difficulty is *self* created, and there is no need whatever to imagine as a few have done, that Christ was anointed *twice* at Bethany, with costly ointment, by a different woman, during His last week. The fact is, that, excepting the *order* of events, there is nothing whatever in the Synoptists which in any wise conflicts with what John tells us. How could there be when the Holy Spirit inspired every *word* in each narrative? Both Matthew and Mark begin by telling us of the decision of the Sanhedrin to have Christ put to death, and then follows the account of His anointing at Bethany. But it is to be carefully noted that after recording the decision of the Council "two days" before the Passover, Matthew *does not* use his characteristic term and say *"Then* when Jesus was in Bethany, He was anointed"; nor does Mark employ his customary word and say, "And ***immediately"*** or "*straightway* Jesus was anointed". But how are we to explain Matthew's and Mark's description of the "anointing" *out of its chronological order?*

We believe the answer is as follows: The conspiracy of Israel's leaders to seize the Lord Jesus is followed by a *retrospective* glance at the "anointing" because what happened at Bethany *provided them with an instrument* which thus enabled them to carry out their vile desires. The plot of the priests was successful through the instrumentality of *Judas,* and that which followed Mary's expression of love shows us *what immediately occasioned* the treachery of the betrayer. Judas protested against Mary's extravagance, and the Lord *rebuked* him and it was immediately afterward that the traitor went and made his awful pact with the priests. Both Matthew and Mark are very definite on this point. The one tells us that immediately following the Lord's reply "*Then* one of the twelve called Judas Iscariot, went unto the chief priests" (26:14); Mark linking together without a break, the rebuke of Christ and the betrayer's act by the word "and" (14:10). John mentions the "supper" at Bethany in its historical order, Matthew and Mark treat of the events *rising out of* the supper, bringing it in to show us that the rebuke of Christ rankled in the mind of Judas and caused him to go at once and bargain with the priests.

But how are we to explain the discrepancies in the different accounts? We answer, There are none. Variations there are, but nothing is inconsistent. The one supplements the other, not contradicts. When John discribes any event recorded in the Synoptists, he rarely repeats all the circumstances and details specified by his predecessors, rather does he dwell upon other features not mentioned by them. Much has been made of the fact that both Matthew and Mark tell us that the anointing took place in the house of Simon the leper, whereas John is silent on the point. To this it is sufficient to reply, the fact that the supper was in Simon's house explains why John tells us Lazarus "sat at the table with Him": if the supper had been in Lazarus' house, such a notice would have been superfluous. Admire then the silent harmony of the Gospel narratives.*

"Then Jesus six days before the Passover came to Bethany" (v. 1). The R. V. more correctly renders this, "Jesus *therefore* six days before the Passover came to Bethany". But what is the force of the "therefore"? with what in the context is it connected? We believe the answer is found in 11:51: Caiaphas "prophesied that Jesus should *die* for that nation" etc.—"Jesus *therefore* six days before *the Passover* came to Bethany". He was the true paschal Lamb that was to be *sacrificed for* His people, *therefore* did He come to Bethany, which was within easy walking distance of Jerusalem, where He was to be slain. It is very striking to note that the very ones who thirsted so greedily for His blood said, "*Not* on the Feast lest there be an uproar among the people" (Matt. 26:5)—repeated by Mark 14:2). But God's counsels could not be thwarted, and at the very hour the lambs were being slain, the true Passover was sacrificed. But why "*six* days before the Passover"? Perhaps God designed that in this interval *man* should fully show forth what he was.

"Then Jesus six days before the Passover *came to Bethany*". The memories of Bethany cannot fail to touch a chord in the heart of any one who loves the Lord Jesus. His blood-bought people delight to dwell upon anything which is associated with *His* blessed name. But what makes Bethany so attractive is that He seemed to find in the little company there a resting-place in His toilsome path. It is blessed to know that there was one oasis in the desert, one little spot where He who "endured the contradiction of sinners against Himself" could retire from the hatred and antagonism of His enemies. There was one sheltered nook where He could find those who, although they knew but little, were truly attracted to Him. It was to this "Elim" in the wilderness (Ex. 15:27) that the Saviour now turned on His last journey to Jerusalem.

"Where Lazarus was which had been dead, whom He raised from the dead", this is very blessed as an introduction to what follows. The Lord Jesus interpreted the devotion of Mary as "against the day of *My burying* hath she kept this" (v. 7). The Father ordered it that His beloved Son should be "anointed" here in this home at Bethany in the presence of Lazarus whom Christ had raised from the dead: it attested the power of *His* own resurrection!

"There they made Him a supper" (v. 2). This evening meal took place not at the home of Martha, but, as we learn from the

*Other points which have occasioned difficulty to some will be dealt with in the course of this exposition.

other Evangelists, in the house of Simon, who also dwelt at Bethany. He is called "the leper" (as Matthew is still named the "tax-gatherer" *after* Christ had called him) in remembrance of that fearful disease from which the Lord, most probably, had healed him. It is quite likely that he was a relative, or an intimate friend of Martha and Mary, for the elder sister is here seen ministering to his guests as her own, superintending the entertainment, doing the honors, for so the original word may here imply—compare the conduct of the mother of Jesus at the marriage in Cana: John 2. It is blessed to observe that this "supper" was made *for Christ,* not in honor of Lazarus!

"There they made Him a supper". Note the use of the plural pronoun. Though this supper was held in the house of "Simon the leper" it is evident that Martha and Mary had no small part in the arranging of it. This, together with the whole context, leads us to the conclusion that a feast was here made as an expression of deep gratitude and praise for the raising of Lazarus. Christ was there to share their happiness. In the previous chapter we have seen Him weeping with those who wept, here we behold Him rejoicing with those who rejoice! When He restored to life the daughter of Jairus, He gave the child to her parents and then withdrew. When He raised the widow's son at Nain, He restored him to his mother and then retired. And why? because, so far as the record informs us He was a *Stranger* to them. But here, after He had raised Lazarus, He *returned* to Bethany and partook of their loving hospitality. It was *His* joy to behold *their* joy and share in the delight which His restoration of the link which death had severed had naturally produced. *That* is His "recompense": to rejoice in the joy of His people. Mark another contrast: when He raised Jairus' daughter He said "Give *her to eat*"; here after the raising of Lazarus, they *gave Him* to eat!

"There they made Him a supper". This points another of the numerous contrasts in which our passage abounds. Almost at the very beginning of His ministry, just before He performed His *first* public "sign", we see the Lord Jesus invited to a marriage-feast; here, almost at the very close of His public ministry, just after His *last* public "sign", a supper is made for Him. But how marked the antithesis! At Cana He turned the water into wine—emblem of the joy of life; here at Bethany He is anointed in view of His own burial!

"And Martha *served.*" This is most blessed. This was *her* characteristic method of showing her affection. On a former occasion the Lord had gently reproved her for being "cumbered with much serving", and because she was anxious and troubled about many things. But she did not peevishly leave off serving altogether. No; she still served: served not the less attentively, but more wisely. Love is unselfish. We are not to feast on our *own* blessings in the midst of a groaning creation, rather are we to be channels of blessing to those around: John 7:38, 39. But mark here that Martha's service is connected *with the Lord:* "They made *Him* a supper *and* Martha served". This alone is true service. We must not seek to imitate others, still less, work for the sake of building up a reputation for zeal. It must be done to and for Christ: "Always abounding in the work *of the Lord*" (1 Cor. 15:58).

"And Martha served:" no longer *outside* the presence of Christ, as on a former occasion—note her "serve *alone*" in Luke 10:40. "In Martha's 'serving' now we do not find her being 'cumbered', but something that is acceptible, as in the joy of resurrection, the new life, unto Him who has given it. Service is in its true place when we have first *received* all from Him, and the joy of it as begotten by Himself sweetly ministers to Him". (Malachi Taylor).

"But Lazarus was one of them that sat at the table with Him" (v. 2). This illustrated the true Christian *position.* Lazarus had been dead, but now alive from the dead, he is *seated* in the company of the Saviour. So it is *(positionally)* with the believer: "When we were dead in sins hath quickened us together with Christ, and hath raised us up together and made us *sit* together in the heavenlies in Christ Jesus" (Eph. 2:5, 6). We have been "made meet to be partakers of the inheritance of the saints in light" (Col. 1:12). Such is our perfect standing before God, and there can be no lasting peace of heart until it be apprehended by faith.

"But Lazarus was one of them that sat at the table with Him". This supplies more than a vague hint of our condition in the resurrected state. In this age of rationalism the vaguest views are entertained on this subject. Many seem to imagine that Christians will be little better than disembodied ghosts throughout eternity. Much is made of the fact that Scripture tells us "flesh and blood shall not inherit the kingdom of God", and the expression "spiritual body" is regarded as little more than a phantasm. While no doubt the Scriptures leave much *un*said on the subject, yet they reveal not a little about the nature of our future bodies. The body of the saint will be "fashioned like unto" the glorious body of the resurrected Christ (Phil. 3:21). It will therefore be a *glorified* body, yet *not* a *non*-material one. There was no blood in Christ's body after He rose from the dead, but He *had* "flesh and bones" (Luke 24:39). True, our bodies will not be subject to their present limitations: sown in weakness, they shall be "raised in *power*". A "spiritual body" we understand (in part) to signify a body *controlled by* the spirit—the highest part of our beings. In our glorified bodies we shall *eat*. The daughter of Jairus needed food after she was restored to life. Lazarus is here seen at the table. The Lord Jesus ate food after He had risen from the dead.

"But Lazarus was one of them that sat at the table "with Him". "A happy company it must have been. For if Simon was healed by the Lord at some previous time, as has been supposed, full to overflowing must his heart have been for the mercy vouchsafed. And Lazarus, there raised from the dead, what proofs were two of that company of the Lord's power and goodness! God only could heal the leper; God only could raise the dead. A leper healed, a dead man raised, and the Son of God who had healed the one, and had raised the other, here also at the table—never before we may say without fear of contradiction had a supper taken place under such circumstances" (C. E. Stuart).

"Then took Mary a pound of ointment of spikenard, very costly, and anointed the feet of Jesus" (v. 3). Mary had often heard the gracious words which proceeded out of His mouth: the Lord of glory had sat at their humble board in Bethany, and she had sat at His feet to be instructed. In the hour of her deep sorrow He had wept with her, and then had He delivered her brother from the dead, crowning them with lovingkindness and tender mercy. And how could she show some token of her love to Him who had first loved her? She had by her a cruse of precious ointment, too costly for her own use, but not too costly for Him. She took and broke it and poured it on Him as a testimony of her deep affection, her unutterable attachment, her worshipful devotion. We learn from v. 5 that the value of her ointment was the equivalent of *a whole year's wages* of a labouring man (Cf. Matt. 20:2)! And let it be carefully noted, this devotion of Mary was prompted by no sudden impulse: "against the day of My burying hath she *kept* this" (v. 7)—the word means "diligently preserved", used in John 17:12, 15!

"Then took Mary a pound of ointment of spikenard, very costly, and anointed the feet of Jesus". Mary's act occupies the central place in this happy scene. The ointment was "very costly", but not too costly to lavish upon the Son of God. Not only did Mary here express her own love, but she bore witness to the inestimable value of the person of Christ. She entered into what was about to be done to and by Him: she anointed Him for burial. He was despised and rejected of men, and they were about to put Him to a most ignominious death. But before any enemy's hand is laid upon Him, love's hands first anoint Him! Thus another striking and beautiful contrast is here suggested.

"Then took Mary a pound of ointment of spikenard, very costly, and anointed the feet of Jesus". Mark tells us she "broke the box" before she poured it on the Saviour. This, in figure, spoke of the breaking of His body, of which the broken bread in the Lord's Supper is the lasting memorial. Both Matthew and Mark tell us that she anointed the *head* of Christ. This is no discrepancy. Evidently, Mary anointed *both* His head and feet, but most appropriately was John led to notice only the latter, for as the Son of God it was fitting that this disciple should take her place in the dust before Him!

"And wiped His feet with her hair" (v. 3). How the Holy Spirit delights in recording that which is done out of love to and for the glory of Christ! How many little details has He preserved for us in connection with Mary's devotion. He has told us of the kind of ointment it was, the box in which it was contained, the weight of it, and its value; and now He tells us something which brings out, most blessedly, Mary's discernment of the glory of Christ. *She* recognized something of what was due Him, therefore after anointing Him she wiped His feet with her "hair"—*her* "glory" (1 Cor. 11:15)! Her silent act spread around the savour of Christ as One infinitely precious. Before the *treachery* of Judas,

Christ receives the testimony of Mary's *affection.* It was the Father putting this seal of deepest devotion upon the One who was about to be betrayed.

"And the house was filled with the odor of the ointment" (v. 3). This is most significant, a detail not supplied in the Synoptics, but most appropriate here. Matthew and Mark tell us how Christ gave orders that "Wheresoever this gospel shall be preached throughout the whole world, this also that she hath done shall be spoken of for a memorial of her" (Mark 14:9). This John omits. In its place he tells us, "And the house was filled with the odour of the ointment". In the other Gospels the "memorial" goes forth: here the fragrance of Christ's person abides in "the *house*". There is much suggested here: not simply the "room" but "the house" was filled with the sweet fragrance of the person of Christ anointed by the spikenard. Sooner or later, all would know what had been done to the Lord. The people on the housetop would perceive that something sweet had been offered below. And do not the angels above know what we below are now rendering unto Christ (cf. 1 Cor. 11:10 etc.)!

"Mary came not to hear a sermon, although the first of Teacher's was there; to sit at His feet and hear His word, was not now her purpose, blessed as that was in its proper place. She came not to make known her requests to Him. Time was when in deepest submission to His will she had fallen at His feet, saying, 'Lord if Thou hadst been here, my brother had not died'; but to pour out her supplications to Him as her only resource was not now her thought, for her brother was seated at the table. She came not to meet the saints, though precious saints were there, for it says 'Jesus loved Martha and Mary and Lazarus'. Fellowship with them was blessed likewise and doubtless of frequent occurrence; but fellowship was not her object now. She came not after the weariness and toil of a week's battling with the world, to be refreshed from Him, though surely she, like every saint, had learned the trials of the wilderness; and none more than she, probably, knew the blessed springs of refreshment that were in Him. But she came, and that too at the moment when the world was expressing its deepest hatred of Him, to pour out what she had long treasured up (v. 7), that which was most valuable to her, all she had upon earth, upon the person of the One who had made her heart captive, and absorbed her affections. She thought not of Simon the leper—she passed the disciples by—her brother and her sister in the flesh and in the Lord engaged not her attention then—'Jesus only' filled her soul—her eyes were upon Him. Adoration, homage, worship, blessing, was her one thought, and that in honor of the One who was 'all in all' to her, and surely such worship was most refreshing to Him" (Simple Testimony).

"Then saith one of His disciples, Judas Iscariot, Simon's son, which should betray Him, Why was not this ointment sold for three hundred pence, and given to the poor?" (vv. 4, 5). What a contrast was this from the affectionate homage of Mary! But how could he who had no heart for Christ appreciate her devotion! There is a most striking series of contrasts here between these two characters. She *gave* freely what was worth *three hundred* pence; right afterwards Judas *sold* Christ for *thirty* pieces of silver. She was in a "Simon's" house; He was a "Simon's son". Her "box" (Mark 14:3); his "bag" (John 12:6). She a worshipper; he a thief. Mary drew the attention of all *to* the Lord; Judas would turn away the thoughts of all *from* Christ to "the poor". At the very time Satan was goading on the heart of Judas to do the worst *against* Christ, the Holy Spirit mightily moved the heart of Mary to pour out her love *for* Him. Mary's devotion has given her a place in the hearts of all who have received the Gospel; Judas by his act of perfidy went to "his own place"—the Pit!

Everything is traced to its source in this Gospel. Matthew tells us that "When His disciples saw it (Mary's tribute of love) they had indignation, saying What purpose is this waste?" But John shows us who was the one that had injected the poison into their minds. *Judas* was the original protester, and his evil example affected the other apostles. What a solemn case is this of evil communications corrupting good manners (1 Cor. 15:33)! Every thing comes out into the light here. Just as John is the only one who gives us the name of the woman who anointed the Lord, so he alone tells us who it was that started the criticising of Mary.

In v. 3 we have witnessed a devotedness of faith and love never surpassed in a believer. But behind the rose-bush lurked the serpent. It reminds us very much of Psa. 23:5: "Thou preparest *a table* before Me in *the presence of Mine* enemies: **Thou** *anointest* My head with oil"! The murmuring of Judas right after the worship of Mary is most solemnly significant. True valuation of Christ always brings out the hatred of those who are of Satan. No sooner was He worshiped as an infant by the wise men from the East, then Herod sought to slay Him. Immediately after the Father proclaimed Him as His "Beloved Son", the Devil assailed Him for forty days. The apostles were seized and thrown into prison because the Leaders of Israel were incensed that they "taught the people and preached *through Jesus* the resurrection from the dead" (Acts 4:2, 3). So in a coming day many of the godly Jews will be beheaded "for the testimony *of Jesus*" (Rev. 20:4).

"Why was not this ointment sold for three hundred pence, and given to the poor?" (v. 5). This was the criticism of a covetous soul. How petty his range of vision! How sordid his conception! He argued that the precious ungent which had been lavished upon Christ ought to have been *sold*. He considered it had been wasted (Mark 14:4). His notion of "waste" was crude and material in the extreme. Love is never "wasted". Generosity is never "wasted". Sacrifice is never "wasted". Love grudges nothing to the Lord of love! Love esteems its costliest nard all inferior to *His* worth. Love cannot give Him too much. And where it is given out of love to Christ we cannot give too much for His servants and His people. How beautifully this is expressed in Phil. 4:18: "Having received of Epaphroditus the things which were sent from you *an odour of a sweet smell*, a sacrifice acceptable, wellpleasing to God".

Judas had no love for Christ, hence it was impossible that he should appreciate what had been done for Him. Very solemn is this: he had been in the closest contact with the Redeemer for three years, and yet the love of money still ruled his heart. Coldheartedness toward Christ and stinginess toward His cause always go together. "To whom little is forgiven, the same loveth little" (Luke 7:47). There are many professing Christians today infested with a Judas-like spirit. They are quite unable to understand true zeal and devotedness to the Lord. They look upon it all as fanaticism. Worst of all, such people seek to cloke their miserliness in giving to Christian objects by a pretended love for the poor: 'charity begins at home' expresses the same spirit. The truth is, and it had been abundantly demonstrated all through these centuries that those who do the most for the poor, are the very ones who are most liberal in supporting the cause of Christ. Let not Christians be moved from a patient continuance in well doing by harsh criticisms from those who understand not. We must not expect professors to do anything *for* Christ when they have no sense of indebtedness *to* Christ.

"Why was not this ointment sold for three hundred pence and given to the poor?" These are the *first* words of Judas recorded in the Gospels; and how they revealed his heart! He sought to conceal his base covetousness under the guise of benevolence. He posed as a friend of the poor, when in reality his soul was dominated by cupidity. It reminds us of his hypocritical "kiss". It is solemn to contrast his *last* words, "I have betrayed innocent blood" (Matt. 27:4).

"This he said, not that he cared for the poor; but because he was a thief and had the bag, and bare what was put therein" (v. 6). It is good to care for the poor, but at that moment the whole mind of God was centered on the person and work of His Son, evidenced by Him moving Mary to anoint the Saviour for His burial. Opportunities for relieving the poor they always had, and it was right to do so. But to put them in comparison with the Lord Jesus at such a time, was to put them out of their place, and to lose sight of Him who was supremely precious to God.

Judas evidently acted as treasurer for the apostolic company (cf. 13:29), having charge of the gifts which the Lord and His disciples received: Luke 8:2, 3. But the Holy Spirit here tells us that he was a "thief". We believe this intimates that the "field" (or "estate") which he purchased (Acts 1:18) "with the reward of iniquity" (or, "price of wrong doing") had been obtained by the money which he pilfered from the same "bag". Usually this "field" is confounded with the "field" that was bought with the thirty pieces of silver which he received for the betrayal of his Master. But *that* money he *returned* to the chief priests and elders (Matt. 27:3, 5), and with it *they* bought "the potter's field to bury strangers in" (Matt. 27:30).

"Then said Jesus, Let her alone" (v. 7). How blessed! Christ is ever ready to defend His own! It was the Good Shepherd protecting His sheep from the wolf. Judas condemned Mary, and others of the apostles echoed his criticism. But the Lord approved of her gift. Probably others of the guests misunderstood her action: it would seem an extravagance, and a neglect of duty towards the needy. But Christ knew her motive and commended her deed. So in a coming day He will reward even a cup of water which has been given in His name. "Let her alone": did not this foreshadow His work on high as our Advocate repelling the attacks of the Enemy, who accuses the brethren before God day and night (Rev. 12:10)!

"Against the day of My burying hath she kept this" (v. 7). This points still another contrast. Other women "bought sweet spices, that they might come and *anoint* Him" (Mark 16:1), *after* He was dead; Mary anointed Him *"for* His burial" (Matt. 26:12) six days before He died! Her faith had laid hold of the fact that He *was* going to die—the apostles did not believe this (see Luke 24:21 etc.). She had learned much at His feet! How much we miss through our failure at this point!

Matthew and Mark add a word here which is appropriately omitted by John. "Verily I say unto you Wheresoever this gospel shall be preached throughout the whole world this also that she hath done shall be spoken of for a memorial of her" (Mark 14:9). He whose Name is "as ointment poured forth" (S. of S. 1:3), commended her who, all unconsciously, fulfilled the prophecy, "While the King sitteth at His table my spikenard sendeth forth the sweet smell thereof" (S. of S. 1:12). In embalming Him, she embalmed herself: her love being the marble on which her name and deed were sculptered. Note another contrast: Mary gave Christ a momentery embalming; He embalmed her memory forever in the sweet incense of His praise. What a witness is this that Christ will never forget that deed, however small, which is done wholeheartedly to His name and for Himself!

"Hereupon we would further remark that while this can not diminish the sin of Judas, by making his covetousness any thing but covetousness, yet but for his mean remonstrance, we might not have known the prodigality of her love. But for the objection of Judas, we might not have had the commendation of Mary. But for his evil eye, we should have been without the full instruction of her lavish hand. Surely 'The wrath of man shall praise Thee'!" (Dr. J. Brown).

"For the poor always ye have with you: but Me ye have not always" (v. 8). There is a little point here in the Greek which is most significant, bringing out, as it does, the minute accuracy of Scripture. In the previous verse "Let alone (aphes) her" is in the singular number, whereas, "The poor always *ye* have (exete) with you", is in the plural number. Let her alone was Christ's rebuke to Judas, who was the first to condemn Mary; here in v. 8 the Lord addresses Himself to the Twelve, a number of whom had been influenced by the traitor's words. Remarkably does this show the entire consistency and supplementary character of the several narratives of this incident. Let us admire the *silent harmonies* of Scripture!

"For the poor always ye have with you: but Me ye have not always" (v. 8). There is a very searching message for *our* hearts in these words. Mary had *fellowship* with His sufferings, and her *opportunity* for this was brief and soon passed. If Mary had failed to sieze her chance to render love's adoring testimony to the preciousness of Christ's person at that time, she could never have recalled it throughout eternity. How exquisitely suited to the moment was her witness to the fragrance of Christ's death before God, when men deemed Him worthy only of a malefactor's cross. She came beforehand to anoint Him "for His burial". But how soon would such an opportunity pass! In like manner we are privileged today to render a testimony to Him in this scene of His rejection. We too are permitted to have *fellowship* with His *sufferings.* But soon this opportunity will pass from us forever! There is a real sense in which these words of Christ to Mary apply to us, "Me ye have not always". Soon shall we enter into the fellowship of His *glory.* O that we may be constrained by His love to deeper devotedness, a more faithful testimony to His infinite worth, and a deeper entering into His sufferings in the present hour of His rejection by the world.

"For the poor ye have always with you: but Me ye have not always". One other thought on this verse before we leave it. These words of our Lord's "Me ye *have not* always" completely overthrow the Papist figment of transubstantiation. If language means anything, this explicit statement of Christ's positively repudiates the dogma of His "real presence", under the forms of bread and wine at the Lord's Supper. It is impossible to harmonise that blasphemous Romish doctrine with this clear-cut utterance of the Saviour. The "poor have ye *always* with you" in like manner disposes of the idle dream of Socialism.

"Much people of the Jews therefore knew that He was there; and they came not for Jesus' sake only, but that they might see Lazarus also, whom He had raised from the dead" (v. 9). "This sentence is a genuine exhibition of human nature. Curiosity is one of the most common and powerful motives in man. The love of seeing something sensational and out of the ordinary is almost universal. When people could see at once both the subject of the miracle and Him that worked the miracle we need not wonder that they resorted in crowds to Bethany" (Bishop Ryle).

"But the chief priests consulted that they might put Lazarus also to death; because that by reason of him many of the Jews went away, and believed on Jesus" (vv. 10, 11). "Lazarus is mentioned throughout this incident as forming an element in the unfolding of the hatred of the Jews which issued in the Lord's death: notice the climax, from the mere connecting mention in v. 1, then nearer connection in v. 2,—to his being the cause of the Jews flocking to Bethany in v. 9,—and the joint object with Jesus of the enmity of the chief priests in v. 10" (Alford). Mark it was not the Pharisees but the "chief priests", who were Sadducees, (cf. Acts 5:17), that "consulted that they might also put *Lazarus* to death": They would, if possible, kill him, because he was a striking witness *against* them, denying as they did the truth of resurrection. But how fearful the state of their hearts: they had rather commit murder, than acknowledge they were wrong.

In the passage which has been before us we behold another of the striking typical pictures which meet us at every turn in this Gospel. This time, we have portrayed most beautifully, *the spiritual state of the godly Remnant* during the Tribulation period. Its dispensational place is plainly indicated by what we read of in the passage which immediately follows—the "Triumphal Entry" of the Lord Jesus into Jerusalem, which is plainly an anticipation of the Millennium. Verse 12 begins with "On the *next day*". The Millennium is the *seventh* of earth's great "Day's". What we have here in John 12:1-11 pictures conditions just before the Millennium dawns. Mark how every detail here bears this out:—

1 What we have in the first section of John 12 is a *sixth* "day" scene, and the Tribulation period *closes* the Sixth Day! Hence the opening sentence, "Then Jesus *six* days before the Passover came to Bethany"! 2. But more: this is the *close* of the "sixth" day. It was *eventide* "supper" time (v. 2)! 3. The scene is laid at *Bethany* (v. 1), which means "House of Affliction". Such will be the place occupied by God's earthly witnesses in that day. 4. The spiritual state of the Remnant is here revealed in a fourfold way: they are quickened (Lazarus), serving Christ (Martha) in fellowship with the Lord (the "supper"), and worshipping Him (Mary)! 5. They are *opposed*. This is seen first in the evil criticism of Judas, who stands for the *apostate* section of the Nation; then in v. 10 we learn how the Leaders purposed to slay them. So the persecution of the Remnant will increase in severity as the end draws near. 6. But the Lord Jesus is there with them: *He* "came to *Bethany*" (v. 1). His presence will sustain them in the very place of affliction. Of old He promised, "When thou passest through the waters *I will be with thee;* and through the rivers they shall not overflow thee" (Isa. 43:2). 7. Finally it is most blessed to behold the Shepherd *defending* His sheep: "Let her alone" (v. 7). So the Lord Jesus will take the part of His severely-tried people in that dark night, meeting the attacks of the Adversary, and preserving them in the midst of a hostile scene (See Rev. 12:12, 14)! How precious to know that even at the time when the Anti-christ is here in power, the Lord will still maintain a witness to Himself upon earth!

Let the thoughtful student ponder carefully the following questions:—

1. What does v. 13 teach us about Prophecy?
2. Why a "young ass" v. 14?
3. V. 15 cf. Zech. 9:9; why are some of its words omitted here?
4. In what sense did Christ then "come" as *King* v. 15?
5. Why did not the disciples "understand" v. 16?
6. Why does v. 17 come in just here?
7. Trace out the Dispensational picture.

Arthur W. Pink.

GLEANINGS IN EXODUS.

17. The Accompaniments of the Passover: Ex. 12, 13.

Though we have entitled this paper "the Accompaniments of the Passover", other things will come before us. The instructions which Jehovah gave to Israel concerning the observance of the Feast of Unleavened Bread are found part in Ex. 12 and part in Ex. 13. Therefore as these two chapters are to be the portion for our study, we must not pass by other incidents recorded in them. First, then, a brief word upon the carrying out of the death-sentence upon the Egyptians.

"And it came to pass, that at midnight the Lord smote all the firstborn in the land of Egypt, from the firstborn of Pharaoh that sat on his throne unto the firstborn of the captives that was in the dungeon; and all the firstborn of cattle. And Pharaoh rose up in the night, he, and all his servants, and all the Egyptians; and there was a great cry in Egypt; for there was not a house where there was not one dead" (12:29, 30). The very first message which the Lord commanded Moses to deliver to Egypt's ruler was, "Thus saith the Lord, Israel is My son, even my firstborn; And I say unto thee, Let My son go, that he may serve Me; and if thou refuse to let him go, behold, *I will slay thy son, even thy firstborn"* (4:22, 23). It is evident from the sequel that Pharaoh did not believe this message. In this he accurately represented the men of this world. All through this Christian dispensation the solemn word has been going forth, "Except ye repent ye shall all likewise perish" (Luke 13:3): "He that believeth not shall be damned" (Mark 16: 16). But, for the most part, the Divine warning has fallen on deaf ears. The vast majority do not believe that God means what He says. Nevertheless, though oftentimes men's threats are mere idle words and empty bombast, not so is it with the threatenings of Him who cannot lie. It is true that God is "slow to anger" and long does He leave open the door of mercy, but even *His* long-sufferance has its limits. It was thus with Pharaoh and his people. Pharaoh received plain and faithful warning and this was followed by many appeals and preliminary judgments. But the haughty king and his no less defiant subjects only hardened their hearts. And now the threatened judgment from heaven fell upon them, and neither wealth nor poverty provided any exemption—"there was not a house where there was not one dead". A most solemn proof is this unto rebels against God to-day, that in a short while at most, unless they truly repent, Divine wrath *shall* smite *them.*

"Now the sojourning of the children of Israel, who dwelt in Egypt, was four hundred and thirty years. And it came to pass at the end of the four hundred and thirty years, even the selfsame day it came to pass, that all the hosts of the Lord went out from the land of Egypt" (12:40, 41). It is very striking to observe the accuracy of the type here. It was not until the day following the Passover-night that Israel was delivered from Egypt. As we have gone over the first twelve chapters of Exodus we have witnessed the tender compassion of God (2: 23-25); we have seen the appointment of a leader (3:10); we have listened to the Divine promises (6:6-8); and we have beheld remarkable displays of Divine power (in the plagues), and yet not a single Israelite was delivered from the house of bondage. It was not until the blood of the "lamb" was shed that redemption was effected, and as soon as it *was* shed, even the very next morning, Israel marched forth a free people—remarkable is the expression here used: "All the hosts *of the Lord* (not "of Israel") went out from the land of Egypt" (12:41). They were the Lord's by purchase—"bought with a price", and that price "not corruptible things as silver and gold, but with the precious blood of a Lamb"!

The same thing is to be seen in the Gospels. Notwithstanding all the blessed display of grace and power in the life and ministry of the Lord Jesus, at the close of His wonderful works of mercy among men, had there been nothing more, He must have remained alone. Listen to His own words; "Verily, verily, I say unto you, Except a corn of wheat fall into the ground and die, it abideth *alone;* but if it die, it bringeth forth much fruit (John 12:24). As another has well said, "Blessed as was that ministry, great as were His miracles, heavenly as was His teaching, holy as was His life, yet had He not died, the Just for the unjust, not one of all the sons of Adam could possibly have been saved. What a place this gives to redemption!" (Mr. C. Stanley). How sadly true. Though Christ *"spake* as never man spake" (John 7:46), and though men confessed "He hath *done* all things well;

He maketh both the deaf to hear and the dumb to speak (Mark 7:37), yet at the close we read, even of His apostles, "they *all* forsook Him and fled". But how different after His precious blood had been shed! Then He is no longer "alone". Then, for the first time, He speaks of the disciples as His "brethren" (John 20:17)!

The *order* of truth in Ex. 12, like every other chapter in the Bible, is according to *Divine* wisdom, yet the writer has to confess dimness of vision in *perceiving* the purpose and beauty of the arrangements of its contents. One thing is very clear, it evidences plainly that it was not of Moses' own design. Here, as ever, God's thought and ways are different from ours. A trained mind, accustomed to think in logical sequence, would certainly have reversed the order found here. Yet we have not the slightest doubt that *God's* order is infinitely superior to that of the most brilliant human intellect. These remarks are occasioned by what is found in verses 43-50. After telling us in verse 41 that "The selfsame day it came to pass, that all the hosts of the Lord went out from the land of Egypt", vv. 43 to 50 give us the "*ordinance* of the Passover", and then in v. 51 it is repeated that "The Lord did bring the children of Israel out of the land of Egypt". The strange thing is that this ordinance was for Israel's guidance in the *future*, hence one would naturally have expected to find these instructions given at a later date, as a part of the ceremonial law. But though, at present, we can offer no satisfactory explanation of this, several points of interest in the "ordinance" itself are clear, and these we will briefly consider.

"And the Lord said unto Moses and Aaron, This is the ordinance of the Passover; There shall no stranger eat thereof; but every man's servant that is bought for money, when thou hast circumcised him, then shall he eat thereof. A foreigner and an hired servant shall not eat thereof" (vv. 43-45). Here we learn that three classes of people were debarred from eating the Passover. First, no *stranger* was to eat thereof. This Feast was for Israel alone, and therefore no foreigner must participate. The reason is obvious. It was only the children of Abraham, the family of faith, who had participated in God's gracious deliverance, and they alone could commemorate it. Second, no *hired servant* should eat the Passover. This too is easily interpreted. An "hired" servant is an outsider; he is actuated by self-interest. He works for pay. But no such principle can find a place in that which speaks of redemption: "To him *that worketh not* but believeth on Him that justifieth the ungodly, his faith is counted for righteousness" (Rom. 4:5). Third, *no uncircumcised person* should eat thereof. (v. 48). This applies to Israel equally as much as to Gentiles. "Circumcision" was the sign of the Covenant, and only those who belonged to the Covenant of Grace can feed upon Christ. Circumcision was God's sentence of death written upon nature. Circumcision has its antitype in the Cross. (Col. 2:11, 12).

"But every man's servant that is bought for money when thou hast circumcised him, then shall he eat thereof. . . . and when a stranger shall sojourn with thee, and will keep the Passover to the Lord, let all his males be circumcised, and then let him come near and keep it; and he shall be as one that is born in the land: for no uncircumcised person shall eat thereof" (vv. 44, 48). A wall was erected to shut out enemies, but the door was open to receive friends. No hired servant could participate in the Feast, but a *bond*-servant who had been purchased and circumcised, and who was now one of the household, could. So, too, the foreigner who *sojourned* with Israel, provided he would submit to the rite of circumcision. In this we have a blessed foreshadowing of Grace reaching out to the Gentiles, who though by nature were "aliens from the commonwealth of Israel and strangers to the covenants of promise", are now, by grace "no more strangers and foreigners, but fellow-citizens with the saints and of the household of God" (Eph. 2:12, 19).—a statement which manifestly looks back to Ex. 12.

"In one house shall it be eaten; thou shalt not carry forth ought of the flesh abroad out of the house; neither shall ye break a bone thereof (v. 46). "The lamb was to be eaten under the shelter of the atoning blood, and there alone. Men may admire Christ, as it is the fashion very much to do, while denying the whole reality of His atoning work, but the Lamb can only be eaten really where its virtue is owned! Apart from this, He cannot be understood or appreciated. Thus the denial of His *work* leads to the denial of His *person*. Universalists and Annihilationists slip naturally into some kind of Unitarian doctrines as is evidenced on every hand.

"Thus this unites naturally with the commandment 'Neither shall ye break a bone thereof'. God will not have the perfection of Christ disfigured as it would be in type by a broken bone. With the bones perfect a naturalist can show the construction of the whole animal. Upon the perfection of the bones depends the symmetry of form. God will have this preserved with regard to Christ. Reverent, not rash handling, becomes us as we seek to apprehend the wondrous Christ of God. And looking back to what is in connection with this, how suited a place to preserve reverence, the place 'in the house' under the shelter which the precious blood has provided for us! With such a one, so sheltered, how could rationalism or irreverence, we might ask, be found? And yet, alas, the injunction, we know too well is not unneedful" (Mr. Grant).

It is indeed blessed to mark how God guarded the fulfillment of this particular aspect of the type. That there might be no uncertainty that Christ Himself, the Lamb of God, was in view here, the Spirit of prophecy also caused it to be written (in one of the Messianic Psalms), "He keepeth all His bones; not one of them is broken" (34:20). And in John 19 we behold the antitype of Ex. 12 and the fulfillment of Psl. 34. "The Jews therefore, because it was the preparation that the bodies should not remain upon the Cross on the Sabbath day (for that Sabbath day was an high day), besought Pilate that their legs *might be broken,* and that they might be taken away" (v. 31). Here was Satan, in his malignant enmity attempting to falsify and nullify the written Word. Vain effort was it. "Then came the soldiers and brake the legs of the first, and of the other which was crucified with Him" (v. 32). Thus far might the agents of the Roman empire go, but no farther—"But when they came to Jesus and saw that He was dead already, *they brake not His legs,"* (John 19:33). Here we are given to see the Father *"keeping"* (preserving) all the bones of His blessed Son. Pierce His side with a spear a soldier might, and this, only that prophecy might be fulfilled, for it was written, "They shall look on Him whom they *pierced,* (Zech. 12:10). But brake His legs they could not, for "a bone of Him *shall not* be broken", and *it was not!*

"And the Lord spake unto Moses saying, Sanctify unto Me all the firstborn, whatsoever openeth the womb among the children of Israel both of man and of beast it is Mine" (13:1, 2). "The narrative of the Exodus from Egypt is suspended to bring in certain consequences,—responsible consequences for the children of Israel—consequences which flowed from their redemption out of the land of bondage. For, although, they are still in the land, the teaching of the chapter is founded upon their having been brought out, and it is indeed anticipative of their being in Canaan. If God acts in grace toward His people, He thereby establishes claims upon them, and it is these claims that are here unfolded" (Ed. Dennett).

A redeemed people become the property of the Redeemer. To His New Testament saints God says, "Ye are not your own; for ye are bought with a price" (1 Cor. 6:19, 20). It is on this same principle that Jehovah here says unto Moses, "Sanctify unto Me all the firstborn". The reference to the "firstborn" here should be carefully noted. It was the *firstborn* of Israel who had been redeemed from the death-judgment which fell upon the Egyptians, and now the Lord claims these for Himself. Typically this speaks of practical holiness, setting apart unto God. Thus the first exhortation in Romans which follows the doctrinal exposition in chapters 1 to 11 is, "I beseech you therefore, brethren, by the mercies of God, that ye present your bodies a living sacrifice, holy, acceptable unto God, which is your reasonable service" (12:1). Personal devotedness is the first thing which God has a right to look for from His blood-bought people.

"Seven days thou shalt eat unleavened bread, and in the seventh day shall be a feast to the Lord. Unleavened bread shall be eaten seven days; and there shall no leavened bread be seen with thee, neither shall there be leaven seen with thee in all thy quarters" (13:6, 7). Typically this shows the nature of sanctification. Throughout Scripture "leaven" is the symbol of evil, evil which spreads and corrupts everything with which it comes into contact, for "a little leaven leaveneth the whole lump" (1 Cor. 5:6). To eat "unleavened bread" signifies separation from all evil, in order that we may feed upon Christ. That this Feast lasted "seven days", which is a *complete* period, tells us that this is to last throughout our whole sojourn on earth. It is to this that 1 Cor. 5:7, 8 refers. "Purge out therefore the old leaven, that ye may be a new lump, as ye are unleavened. For even Christ our Passover is sacrificed for us;

Therefore let us keep the feast not with old leaven, neither with the leaven of malice and wickedness; but with the unleavened bread of sincerity and truth." Because we are saved by *grace,* through the sprinkled blood of Christ, it is not that we may now indulge in sin without fear of its consequences, or that grace may abound. Not so. Redemption by the precious blood of Christ imposes an additional responsibility to separate ourselves from all evil, that we may now show forth the praises of Him who has called us out of darkness into His marvelous light. Carelessness of walk, evil associations, worldliness, fleshly indulgences are the things which hinder us from keeping this Feast of *un*leavened Bread.

But much more is included by this figure of "leaven" than the grosser things of the flesh. We read in the N. T. of "the *leaven* of the *Pharisees,* (Matt. 16:6). This is superstition, the making void of the Word of God by the *traditions* of men. Formalism, and legality are included too. Sectarianism and ritualism as well are the very essence of Phariseeism. Then we read of "the *leaven* of the Sadducees" (Matt. 16:6). The Sadducees were materialists, denying a spirit within man, and rejecting the truth of resurrection, (Acts 23:8). In its present-day form, Higher Criticism, Rationalism, Modernism answers to Sadduceeism. We also read of "the *leaven* of *Herod* (Mark 8:15). This is worldliness, or more specifically, the friendship of the world, as the various statements made about Herod in the Gospels will bear out. All of these things must be rigidly excluded. The allowance of any of them makes it impossible to feed upon Christ. Is it not because of our failure *to* "purge out the old leaven" that so few of the Lord's people enter upon "the *feast* of unleavened bread"!

"And thou shall show thy son in that day, saying, this is done because of that which the Lord did unto me when I came forth out of Egypt" (13:8). Striking indeed is this. The basis of this Feast was what the Lord had done for Israel in delivering them from the land of bondage. In other words, its foundation was redemption accomplished, entered into, known, enjoyed. No soul can really *feast* upon Christ while he is in doubt about his own salvation. "Fear hath torment" (1 John 4:18) and this is the opposite of joy and salvation, of which *"feasting"* speaks. Little wonder then that there are so many joyless professing Christians. How could it be otherwise? "Rejoice" said Christ to the disciples, "that your names *are* written in heaven" (Luke 10:20). Until this joy of assurance is ours there cannot be, we say again, any *feasting* upon Christ.

"And it shall be for a sign unto thee upon thine hand, and for a memorial between thine eyes, that the Lord's law may be in thy mouth; for with a strong hand hath the Lord brought thee out of Egypt". (13:9). The Feast was a "sign" upon the *hand,* that is, it signified that their *service* was consecrated to God. It was also a "memorial between the eyes", that is, upon the forehead, where all could see; which being interpreted, signifies, *an open manifestation* of separation unto God. Finally, it was to be accompanied with "the Lord's law in their mouth". The correlative of "law" is obedience. God's redeemed are not a lawless people. Said the Lord Jesus, "If ye love Me, keep My *commandments*" (John 14:15); and as John tells us, "His commandments are not grievous" (1 John 5:3). Those who insist so urgently that in no sense are Christians under Law evidence a sad spirit of insubordination; it shows how much they are affected and infected, with the spirit of *lawlessness* which now, alas, is so prevalent on every side and in every realm.

"And it shall be when the Lord shall bring thee into the land of the Canaanites, as He sware unto thee and to thy fathers, and shall give it thee, That thou shalt set apart unto the Lord all that openeth the matrix and every firstling that cometh of a beast which thou hast; the males shall be the Lord's. And every firstling of an ass thou shalt redeem with a lamb; and if thou wilt not redeem it, then thou shalt break his neck; and all the firstborn of man among thy children shalt thou redeem". (13:11-13). The deep significance of this cannot be missed if we observe the connection—that which precedes. In Ex. 12 we have had the redemption of the "firstborn" of *Israel,* here it is the redemption of the "firstling" of an *ass.* In the second verse of chapter 13 the two are definitely joined together—"Sanctify unto Me all the firstborn, whatsoever openeth the womb of the children of Israel, both of man *and* of beast; it is Mine". That there may be no mistaking what is in view here, the Lord gave orders that the firstling of the ass was to be redeemed with a lamb, just as the firstborn of Israel were redeemed with a lamb on the passover night. Furthermore, the ass was to have its neck broken, that is it was to be destroyed, unless redeemed; just as the Israelites would most certainly have been smitten by the avenging Angel unless they had slain the lamb and sprinkled its blood. The conclusion is therefore irresistible: God here compares the natural man with the ass! Deeply humbling is this!

The "ass" is an *unclean* animal. Such is man by nature; shapen in iniquity conceived in sin. The "ass" is a most *stupid and senseless* creature. So also is the natural man. Proudly as he may boast of his powers of reason, conceited as he may be over his intellectual achievements, the truth is, that he is utterly devoid of any *spiritual intelligence.* What saith the Scriptures? This: "Walk not as other Gentiles walk in the vanity of their mind, having the understanding darkened, being alienated from the life of God through the ignorance that is in them" (Eph. 4:17, 18). Again; "If our Gospel be hid, it is hid to them that are lost; in whom the god of this world (Satan) has *blinded* the minds of them which believe not" (2 Cor. 4:3, 4). How accurately, then, does the "ass" picture the natural man! Again; the "ass" is *stubborn and intractable,* often as hard to move as a mule. So also is the natural man. The sinner is rebellious and defiant. He *will not* come to Christ that he might have life (John 5:40). It is in view of these things that Scripture declares, "For vain man would be wise, though *man be born like a wild ass's colt*" (Job 11:12).

It is instructive to trace the various references to the "ass" in Scripture. The first mention of the "ass" is in Gen. 22; from it we learn two things. "Abraham rose up early in the morning and *saddled* his "ass". (v. 3). The "ass" is not a free animal. It is a beast of burden, *saddled.* So, too, is the sinner—"serving divers lusts". Second, "And Abraham said unto his young men, *Abide ye here with the ass;* and I and the lad will go yonder and worship" (Gen. 22:5). The "ass" did not accompany Abraham and Isaac to the place of worship. Nor can the sinner worship God. Third, in Gen. 49:14 we read, "Issachar is a strong ass, couching down *between two burdens*". So, too, is the sinner—*heavily* "laden" (Matt. 11-28). Fourth, God forbade His people to plow with an ox and ass together (Deut. 22:10). The sinner is shut out from the service of God. Fifth, in 1 Sam. 9:3 we are told, "And the asses of Kish Saul's father were *lost*", and though Saul and his servant sought long for them they recovered them not. The sinner, too, is lost, away from God, and no human power can restore him. Sixth, In Jer. 22:19 we read, "He shall be buried with the burial of an ass, drawn and *cast forth beyond* the gates of Jerusalem". Fearfully solemn is this. The carcass of the ass was cast forth *outside* the gates of the holy city. So shall it be with every sinner who dies outside of Christ; he shall not enter the New Jerusalem, but be *"cast* into the Lake of Fire". The final reference to the "ass" is found in Zech. 9:9 "Rejoice greatly O daughter of Zion; shout, O daughter of Jerusalem, behold, thy King cometh unto thee, He is just, and having salvation; lowly, and *riding upon an ass*". Most blessed contrast is this. Here we see the "ass" *entering Jerusalem,* but only so as it was beneath the controlling hand of the Lord Jesus! Here is the sinner's only hope—to submit to Christ!

In Gen. 16:12 we have a statement which is very pertinent in this connection, though its particular force is lost in the A. V. rendering; we quote therefore from the R. V., "And he shall be a *wild-ass* man among men; his hand shall be against every man, and every man's hand against him". Those were the words of the Lord to Sarah. They were a prophecy concerning Ishmael. From Gal. 4 we learn that Ishmael stands for *the natural man,* as Isaac for the believer, the seed of promise. In full accord, then, with all that we have said above is this striking description of Sarah's *"firstborn";* he was a *wild-ass* man. The Bedowin Arabs are his descendants, and fully do they witness to the truth of this ancient prophecy. But solemn is it to find that here we have *God's* description of the natural man. And more solemn still is what we read of Ishmael in Gal. 4; he *"persecuted* him that was born after the Spirit" (v. 29), and in consequence had to be "cast out" (v. 30).

In view of what has been said above, how marvelous the *grace* which provided *redemption for* "the firstling of an ass"! "But God commendeth His love toward us, in that, *while we were yet sinners,* Christ died for us" (Rom. 5:8). Ah, dear reader, have you taken *this place* before God? Do you own that the "ass" is an accurate portrayal of all that you are in yourself—unclean, senseless, intractable, fit only to have your neck broken? Do the words of the apostle suitably express the real sentiments of your heart—"Christ Jesus came into the world to save sinners; *of whom I am chief*" (1

Tim. 1:15)? Or, are you like the self-righteous Pharisee, who said, "God, I thank Thee, that *I am not* as other men are, extortioners, unjust, adulterers" (Luke 18:11)? Christ came not to call the righteous but *sinners* to repentance, (Luke 5:32). He came "To seek and to save *that which was lost*" (Luke 19:10). Again, we ask, Have you taken this place before God? Have you come to Him with all your wretchedness—undone, corrupt, guilty, lost? Have you abandoned all pretentions of worthiness and merit, and cast yourself upon His undeserved mercy? Have you seen your own need of the *sinner's* Saviour, and thankfully received Him? If you *have,* then will you gladly "set to your seal that God is true", and acknowledge that the "ass" *is* a suitable figure to express what you were and still are by nature. And, then, too, will you praise God for the matchless grace which redeemed you, not with corruptible things as silver and gold, "but with the precious blood of Christ, as of a Lamb without blemish and without spot" (1 Peter 1:19). Thank God for the *Lamb* provided for the *ass.* The more fully we realize the accuracy of this figure, the more completely we are given to see how *ass-like* we are in ourselves, the deeper will be our gratitude and the more fervent our praise for the redemptive and perfect Lamb. *Arthur W. Pink.*

TRUTH AND ERROR,

or

Letters to a Friend.

5. Election.

"Many are called, but few are chosen"—Matt. 22:14.

"As many as were ordained to eternal life believed".—Acts 13:48.

You know what a very prominent place in Scripture the doctrine of election holds. It meets us everywhere, both in the Old and New Testament. Whatever may be the meaning of the word, one cannot help feeling that the truth which it expresses must, in God's sight, be a vitally important one.

But how can this be the case, if it mean no more than God's choosing those that choose Him? If it mean no more than God's choosing those whom He foresaw would believe of their own accord and by their own power, it is not worthy of the prominent place it holds in Scripture; nay, it is not worthy of a separate name, least of all of such a name as election. If there be any election at all in such a case, it is plainly not God's election of man, but man's election of God. So that the question comes to be simply this, Does election mean God's choosing man, or man's choosing God? It cannot mean both; it must be either the one or the other. Which of the two can any reasonable being suppose it to mean?

As the right understanding of this word is of great importance, I think it well to note down a few passages, which will help to shed light upon the meaning of the word.

"The man's rod, whom *I shall choose,* shall blossom".—Num. 17:5.

"Thou shalt set him King over thee, whom the Lord thy God *shall choose*" Deut. 17:15.

"Did I *choose him out* of all the tribes of Israel."—1 Sam. 2:28.

"The place which the Lord *hath chosen,* to put His name there".—Deut. 12:21.

"Them the Lord thy God *hath chosen* to minister unto Him".—Deut. 21:5.

"Jerusalem the city which I have *chosen out of* all the tribes of Israel".—I Kings 9:32.

"The Lord *chose* me, before all the house of my father, to be king over Israel".—1 Chron. 28:4.

"For His elect's sake whom He *hath chosen*".—Mark 13:20.

"He is a *chosen* vessel unto Me."—Acts 9:15.

"I know whom I have *chosen*".—John 13:18.

"Ye have not *chosen* Me, but I have *chosen* you".—John 15:16.

"According as He hath *chosen us* in Him before the foundation of the world".—Eph. 1:4.

"God hath from the beginning *chosen* you unto salvation".—2 Thess. 2:13.

These are but a few out of the many passages that might have been selected. But they are quite enough to show the meaning of the word. No one who wishes to take words plainly as he finds them, can find any difficulty in understanding what choosing or election means, after reading such passages as these.

I would just ask, What does the word in common speech mean? When we speak of the election of a member of parliament, does that mean that the member first chose himself, and then the people chose him, because he had chosen himself? Or when we speak of the election of a minister, do we mean that he first chose himself, then the people chose himself, because he had chosen himself? No such theory of election would be listened to for a moment in such matters. Election has but one meaning there. It means the people's choosing their representative by a distinct act of their own will, or the congregation choosing their minister by an equally distinct act of their own will. And shall man have his will, and shall not God have His? Shall man have his choice, and shall not God have His?

But let us take an instance from the Bible. What does God's choosing Abraham mean? He is a specimen of a sinner saved by grace; a sinner called out of the world by God. Well, how did this choosing take place? Did not God think of him long before he ever thought of God? Did not God choose him long before he ever thought of choosing God? Were there not thousands more in Chaldea that God might have chosen, and called, and saved, had He pleased? Yet He chose Abraham alone. And what does the Bible call this procedure on the part of God? It calls it *election.* "Thou art the Lord, the God who didst *choose* Abraham, and broughtest him forth out of Ur of the Chaldees."—Neh. 9:7. Does any one say, O, but God chose Abraham, because He foresaw that Abraham would choose Him. I answer, the case is precisely the reverse of this. He chose Abraham just because He saw that otherwise Abraham would *not* choose Him. It was God's foreseeing that Abraham would *not* choose Him, that made election necessary. And so it is with us. God chooses us, not because He foresees that we would choose Him, or that we would believe, but for the very opposite reason. He chooses us just because He foresees that we would neither choose Him nor believe of ourselves at all. Election proceeds not upon foreseen *faith* in us, but upon foreseen *unbelief.*

The truth is, that election has no meaning, if it be not the expression of God's will in reference to particular persons and things,—saying to each, thus and thus shalt thou be, not because thou choosest to be so, but because I, the infinite Jehovah, see fit that thou shouldest be so. To one creature He says, thou shalt be an angel, to another thou shalt be a man. To one order of beings, thou shalt dwell in heaven, to another, thou shalt dwell upon earth. To one man, thou shalt be born in Judea, where My name is named and My temple stands; to another, thou shalt be born in Egypt, or Babylon, where utter darkness reigns. To one He says, thou shalt be born in Britain, and hear the glad tidings; to another, thou shalt be born in Africa, where no gospel has ever come. Thus He expresses His will, and who can resist it? Who can find fault, or say to Him, what doest Thou? Men may object at being placed thus entirely at the disposal of God, but the apostle's answer to such is, "Nay but, O man, who art thou, that repliest against God?" Election, then, is the distinct forthputting of God's sovereign will, for the purpose of bringing a thing to pass, which, but for the explicit forthgoing of that will, would not have come to pass.

But does this not lead to the conclusion that *sin* is the direct result of God's decree? Does it not teach us that it is God and not man that produces sin? No. God does not foreordain sin, But He decrees to *allow* man to sin. God is holy, and hates sin. He does not lead men into it; neither does He decree to lead men into it. But He decrees that, for infinitely wise ends, the creature should be permitted to fall, and sin to be perpetuated.

1. God forces no man to sin, either by what He decrees or what He does, either by commanding or constraining or alluring.

2. It is absurd to say, that if we hold that God is the author of good, He must be the author of evil; that if He, from eternity, purposed to create what is good in man, He must therefore have purposed to create that which is evil. It is absurd to say, that if I hold that it is God who sets my will *right* I must hold that it was God who set it *wrong.*

3. God frequently gave predictions of evil long before the time. Of course, then, if evil be predicted regarding either nations or individuals, it must be fixed and sure. He predicted the curse on Canaan and his descendants. But does that prove that He delighted in the curse, or that He was the author of it, or that those who were the instruments of inflicting it, and so fulfilling the prophecy, were guiltless?

4. Even our opponents admit that there are some events decreed beforehand, such as the birth and death of Christ, the judgment-day, etc. If, then, they admit that He has decreed a single event, they are in precisely the same difficulty in which they seek to fix us. If one event is decreed, why not all? Who is to draw the line and say, these are decreed, but those are not? God's will

has already fixed one or two, and is man's will, or chance, to settle the rest?

In farther explanation of this point, let me quote a few paragraphs from a tract which I published some years ago. It was written before the "new light" dawned; and the present controversies have only tended to deepen the sense I then had of the importance of the truth contained in it.

I know that the sinner must have a *will* in the matter too. It is absurdity to speak of a sinner loving, believing, etc., against his will, or by compulsion. The sinner must doubtless *will.* He must will to refuse, and he must will to receive Christ. He must will to take the broad way, and he must will to take the narrow way. His will is essential to all these movements of his soul. But in what state do we find his will at present? We find it is wholly set against the truth. Every will since the fall, is wholly opposed to God and His Word. Man needs not foreign influence, no external power, to make him reject the truth. That he does by nature. He hates it with his whole heart. When a sinner then comes to receive the truth, how is this accomplished? Does he renew himself? Does he change the enmity of his will by the unaided act of his will? Does he of himself bend back his own will into the opposite direction? Does he, by a word of his own power, cause the current that had been flowing down hill to change its course and flow upward? Does his own will originate the change in itself, and carry the change into effect? Impossible. The current would have flowed forever downward had it not been arrested in its course by something stronger than itself. The sinner's will would have remained forever in depravity and bondage, had not another will, mightier far than itself, come into contact with it, and altered both its *nature* and *course,* working in the sinner "both to will and to do". Was the sinner willing *before* this other will met his? No. Was he willing after? Yes. Then, is it not plain that it was God's will, meeting and changing his, that made the difference? God's will was *first.* It was God's will that began the work, and made the sinner willing. *He never would have willed had not God made him willing.* "Thy people shall be willing in the day of Thy power". It is the power of Jehovah applied to us that makes us willing. Till that is applied, we are unwilling. It is His hand, operating directly upon the soul, that changes its nature and its bent. Were it not for that, our unwillingness would never be removed. No outward means or motives would be sufficient to effect the change; for all these means and motives are rejected by the sinner; nor does he become willing even to allow the approach or application of these means and motives till God makes him willing. To speak of his being changed by that which he rejects is as absurd as to speak of a man's being healed by a medicine which he persists in refusing. "Can the Ethiopian change his skin, or the leopard his spots?"

Are all, then, willing? Does not the depraved will remain in most, while the new will appears in few? What makes the difference? God's choice. "Even so, Father, for so it seemed good in Thy sight". "Hath not the potter power over the clay, of the same lump to make one vessel unto honor, and another unto dishonor?" "Except the LORD OF HOSTS HAD LEFT unto us a very small remnant, we should have been as Sodom, and we should have been like unto Gomorrah".

Does God then hinder sinners from believing and willing? No,—by no means. He hinders none. They are their own hinderance. "Ye will not come to Me that ye might have life." Not one soul would be saved if left to his own will. But, in His infinite mercy, God does not leave them to their own wills. He puts forth His mighty power on some to make them willing. Were it not for this, all would be lost, for all would reject the Saviour.

But is not this unjust? Is God dealing fairly with His creatures in making some willing, and leaving the rest to their unwillingness? What! Are we to prohibit God from saving any, unless He saves all? Are we to accuse Him of injustice, because He leaves some to reap the fruits of their unbelief, and delivers others from them? Is God unjust in saving whom He will, when all were lost?

Some are given to accusing us of making God guilty of partiality. As if they were singular in their zeal for God's honor, they exclaim, "We cannot bear a *partial* God!" Partiality means of course injustice; it means also that the sinner has a *right* to favor from God. They must show, then, that for God to save some when all were lost is *unjust.* They must show that all sinners had a *right* to His favor, for if none had any right, there can be no partiality. But if this theory be true, then God was partial in not providing a Saviour for fallen angels. He was partial in choosing

Israel, and not choosing Babylon or Egypt, as the nation to whom He made Himself known. He was partial in sending prophets to Israel, and not to Tyre and Sidon. He was partial in doing His mighty works in the land of Judea. And Jesus was partial in commanding His disciples not to go to either Gentiles or Samaritans. In short, if *sovereignty* be partiality, then the Bible is full of it. And it would be just as well for these men to say at once what their theory implies,—That God is not at liberty to act as He pleases, but only as man may dictate!

But why does God save some, and not all? Because such is "the good pleasure of His will." He has infinitely wise reasons for this, though we understand them not. Might we not with equal propriety ask, Why did He keep some angels from falling? and why did He allow others to fall? Or, may we not ask, Why did He not think of saving angels, why think of saving men alone? Is Jehovah not at liberty to do what He will with His own? Is He not at liberty to create as many worlds and as many beings as He pleases? And when these are ruined, is He not at liberty to redeem as many or as few as He pleases?

The real question in all this is just, "Are all men so depraved that they will not be saved unless God puts forth His mighty power?" If so, then, it is plain that God must put forth His power to save every one that is saved; and surely He is at liberty to choose whom He is to save. If indeed men are not totally depraved, then there is no need for the interposition of God's hand either in choosing or in saving. But admit man's total ruin and depravity, and you must admit the direct forth-putting of the arm of Jehovah. And hence it is that many in our day are beginning to deny man's total depravity of nature. They are smoothing down the expressions refering to it in Scripture, and claiming for man as much remaining power and goodness as will enable him in part to save himself, and do without the interposition of God.

The following remarks of Calvin will show, that in his day none but "Papist theologians" held the doctrine, that God elects men because He foresaw they will believe. "The Papist theologians have a distinction current among themselves, that God does not elect men according to the works which are in them but that *He chooses those who He foresees will be believers.* And therein they contradict what we have already alleged from St. Paul, for he says that we are chosen and elected in Him, 'that we might be holy and without blame'. Paul must needs have spoken otherwise, if God elected us having foreseen that we should be holy. But he has not used such language: he says, He hath elected us that we might be holy.' He infers, therefore, that the latter (faith) depends upon the former (election). Those who think otherwise, know not what man and human nature is". Such is the testimony of Calvin against the Papist theologians of his day. Since that time many have joined the ranks of these theologians, and glory in their heresies.

Oh, but it is said, we do not deny election. We merely maintain that God elected those who He foresaw would believe. I answer, this is a total denial of election; and it is either dishonesty or ignorance to call this by such a name. God elected those who He foresaw would believe! And who were they? None,—absolutely none. *He foresaw that none would believe, not one.* And because He foresaw this, He elected some to believe. Otherwise not one would ever have believed at all.

With regard to the foreseeing who would believe, I have some difficulties to state. According to the Arminian theory, I may believe to-day and disbelieve to-morrow, according to my own will. I may thus go on believing and disbelieving alternately till the day of my death. God then one day foresees that I will believe, and He decrees to save me. But the next day He foresees me not believing, and He decrees that I should perish. How in such a case is the matter to be finally settled? Is it according to the state in which God foresees the sinner will be just at the last moment of his life? Or when? Let our opponents solve the difficulty if they are able.

Oh, but some profane objector says, "Does God make men to be damned?" Let me in a few words answer the miserable atheism of such an objection; and I do it not out of regard for the pride of the objector, but for the sake of those who may be perplexed by this poor catch of an argument which is so freely and flippantly about,—an argument which befits the scoffer only,—an argument whose father is the father of lies. It is somewhat remarkable that this is precisely the argument of Socinians, Universalists, and Deists, against the existence of such a place as hell. If you speak of hell or everlasting fire to such, the answer is, "Did God make men to damn them?" And however abominable and unscriptural their notion is, it is at least consistent with their own theory. Making God to be all love and nothing else, they think it inconsistent with His love that He should allow such a place as hell in the universe. They believe in no hell, and ask scornfully, "Did God make men to damn them?"

But let me answer the question, however profane it may be. God did *not* make men to damn them. He did *not* make the angels "who kept not their first estate," to damn them. He did *not* make Lucifer for the purpose of casting him out of heaven. He did *not* make Adam for the purpose of driving him out of Paradise. He did *not* make Judas for the purpose of sending him to his own place. God made man,—every man, and everything to GLORIFY Himself. This every creature, man and angel, must do, either actively or passively, either willingly or unwillingly,—actively and willingly in heaven, or passively and unwillingly in hell. This is God's purpose; and it shall stand. God may have many other ends in creation; but this is the chief one, the ultimate one,—the one which is above all the rest, and to which all the rest are subordinate.

In this sense then plainly, God did not make men either to destroy them or to save them. He made them for His own glory. If the question is asked, Did God make the devil and his angels only to damn them? I answer, He made them for His own glory. They are lost forever; but does that prove that He made them only to destroy them? He kept their companions from falling, and hence they are called the "elect angels,"—while He did not keep *them.* He *could* have kept them all by His power, yet He did not. But does this prove that He made them to destroy them? They fell, and were in a moment consigned to everlasting chains; He made no effort to save them—He sent no redemption to them. But does this prove that He made them only to destroy them? If ever such an accusation *could* be preferred against God, it must be in the case of angels, to whom no salvation was sent. It cannot be said of *man,* to whom a salvation has come.

Whatever is right for God to *do,* it is right for Him to *decree.* If God's casting sinners into hell be not wrong or unjust, then His purposing to do so from all eternity cannot be wrong or unjust. So that you must either deny that there is a hell, or admit God's right to predetermine who are to dwell there forever. There is no middle way between Calvinism and Universalism.

With these remarks I leave this point; and in doing so I would merely call your attention to one or two passages of Scripture, which it would be well for those to ponder who put such a question as that to which I have been adverting. "The Lord hath made all things for Himself; yea, even the wicked for the day of evil,"—Prov. 16:4. "As many as were ordained to eternal life believed,"—Acts 13:48. "The Scripture saith unto Pharaoh, even for this same purpose have I raised thee up, that I might show My power in thee, and that My name might be declared throughout all the earth. . . what if God willing to show His wrath and to make His power known, endured with much longsuffering the vessels of wrath fitted to destruction,"—Rom. 9:17, 22.

Texts like these are not to be explained away or overlooked. They are part of God's holy Word, just as much as "God is love". And if one class of texts is to be twisted or turned away from, why not another? Let us fearlessly look both in the face; and let us believe them both, whatever difficulty we may find in reconciling them. Our first duty is to *believe,* not to *reconcile.* There are many things which in this life we shall not be able to reconcile; but there is nothing in the Bible which we need to shrink from believing.

H. Bonar.

SANCTIFICATION.

As a good deal of confusion exists in the minds of many of the Lord's people as to the meaning of sanctification, it is proposed in this little paper to look into the teaching of Scripture on this most important subject.

A Christian said to the writer, not so very long ago, "It is three years since I was justified, but only about four months since I was sanctified". The reply given her was, "According to the teaching of Scripture, you were sanctified *before* you were justified." But this is not what many think. They look upon sanctification as a growing in holiness, and thus a growing in meetness for heaven. The more holy or sanctified they are, the more fit they suppose themselves to be for the presence of the Lord. Thus the true basis of peace for the soul is lost sight of; so that instead of depending alone upon the finished work of Christ on the cross *for* the sinner, the work of the Holy Spirit *in* the soul is looked to as that which is to give perfect fitness for glory.

This, however, is not only far from the teaching of the Word, but is in direct antagonism to it. In Col. 1:12 we find these words: "Giving thanks unto the Father, *which hath made us meet* to be partakers of the inheritance of the saints in light"; and this is founded upon the fact of Christ's "*having made peace* through the blood of His cross" (v. 20).

The work of redemption is accomplished; nothing can be added to it, nor can anything be taken from it. The measure of the believer's acceptance before God is Christ risen from the dead. This is very simple and most blessed. Pardon, peace, acceptance in present favour, all depend upon what Christ has accomplished for us. This has to be carefully and jealously guarded; for if anything is allowed to intermix with this, we not only suffer great loss in our own souls, but the Lord is dishonoured, inasmuch as the integrity and everlasting worth of His all-sufficient work are called into question. Again, let it be said, nothing must be allowed to touch or add to our perfect justification through Him who was "delivered for our offences, and raised again for our justification" (See Rom. 4:24, 25; and chap. 5:1).

Now first of all let us ask, What is sanctification? The answer is, It is *a setting apart* or *separating*. In proof of this see John 10:36, where the Lord Jesus speaks of *Himself* as having been "sanctified", and sent into the world by the Father. Again, in chap. 17:19 He speaks of *sanctifying Himself* for the sake of "His own" who were in the world. These passages plainly show that it is not of the blessed Lord's being made more holy that they speak. To affirm that such was the case would be blasphemy; for He was ever the Holy One of God. It is, however, easy to understand that He was set apart by the Father for all that was before Him, and sent into the world. There is no difficulty either in seeing that He set Himself apart; i.e., went on high for the sake of His people. We therefore find Him spoken of in Hebrews 7:26, as He is now, "holy, harmless, undefiled, *separate*" (really separat*ed*) "from sinners, and made higher than the heavens". Again, we learn from 1 Tim. 4:5 that the very food Christians eat is sanctified (or set apart for their use) by the word of God and prayer. In Isaiah 66:17 there were those who "sanctified" (or separated) "themselves" to do evil and their end was to be consumed.

We shall now turn to some passages of Scripture in order that we may see the truth as to the subject we are considering. In 1 Cor. 6:11 the answer given to the Christian already referred to is confirmed; viz., that she was sanctified before she was justified. The verse reads, "And such were some of you: but ye are washed, but ye are sanctified, but ye are justified in the name of the Lord Jesus and by the Spirit of our God". They had been washed. This was the moral purifying effect of the Word of God. "Now ye are clean through the word which I have spoken unto you" (John 15:3). That which was involved and included in their being thus cleansed was that they were sanctified and justified. It is important to notice that *sanctification* comes first; that is to say, God, sets the soul apart for blessing. In 1 Peter 1:2 we find the same order adhered to. The saints* there are addressed as being "elect. . . *through sanctification of the Spirit*, unto . . . the sprinkling of the blood of Jesus Christ." They are set apart *unto* the sprinkling of blood. Sanctification is *first*, then the blood in all its value is apprehended. So in 2 Thess. 2:13. "We are bound to give thanks alway to God for you, brethren beloved of the Lord, because God hath from the beginning chosen you to salvation through sanctification of the Spirit and belief of the truth." *Before salvation* there had been the sanctification of the Spirit and belief of the truth. This is to be much observed.

From these passages, as well as from others that might be adduced, we learn that sanctification is an *absolute* thing. It is an accomplished fact already and true of every believer.

There is, however, another way in which sanctification is spoken of; namely, as a progressive (growing), *practical* thing. The measure of our actual, absolute sanctification—our separation *from* the world, our separation *to* God—is Christ where He is. As we read in 1 Cor. 1:30, "But of Him are ye in Christ Jesus, who of God is made unto us wisdom, and righteousness, and *sanctification*, and redemption". Christ *now* is our sanctification, and therefore the measure of our being set apart. Twice over He says in John 17 (vv. 14, 16), of His people,

*We are "saints" by calling ("called saints," see Rom. 1:7). But the meaning of "saint" is simply a separated person.

"They are not of the world, even as I am not of the world". We are separated ones —no more of the world than Christ was of it.

Now it is one thing to *know* this blessed truth as a matter of fact and doctrine, and quite another thing to *carry it into effect* by putting it into practice day by day. We shall now look at some of the passages in which it is thus brought before us. In turning to 2 Cor. 6:14 to the end, we find *practical* separation called for, and then the blessed promises to those who responded to such a call. The Lord Almighty would be a Father to them, and they would be to Him for sons and daughters. There would be the *enjoyment* of the relationship. Stimulated by such promises, they were to cleanse themselves from every pollution of the flesh and spirit (without and within), perfecting holiness (or sanctification) in the fear of God. God had said He would dwell in them and walk in them; they were *absolutely* separated to Him. But now they were to put this into practice in their daily life. Their practical separation was to correspond with what was already true of them. Moses in his day (Exodus 33:16) knew something of this truth when he said, "Wherein shall it be known that I and Thy people have found grace in Thy sight? *is it not in that Thou goest with us? so shall we be separated*, I and Thy people, from all the people that are upon the face of the earth".

In Hebrews 12, where we find the educational process going on—God dealing with us as with sons—the object in view is, that we may be partakers of His holiness (v. 10); that is, that there may be more distinct, practical separation to Himself. In addition to this, the peaceable fruit of righteousness is yielded to Him that is *exercised* as to the dealings of the Father with him. "This is the will of God, even your sanctification" (1 Thess. 4:3).

There is one verse that often causes difficulty to honest and earnest souls. It seems to them that the verse warrants their looking for a better state of things in themselves. It is 1 Thess. 5:23, and it reads thus: "And the very God of peace sanctify you wholly; and I pray God your whole spirit and soul and body be preserved blameless unto the coming of our Lord Jesus Christ".

Now there really is no difficulty in this passage. It does not teach that sanctification—a process of becoming more holy—goes on until *perfection in the flesh* is attained. Such a thought is contrary to the whole teaching and tenor of the word of God.

When God made man in innocency, His component parts were spirit and soul and body. They are still; but through man's departure from God, he has got what Scripture calls *the flesh* in him as well. This evil thing called the flesh is unimprovably bad. It remains flesh to the end of the chapter. No amount of care, culture, education, or anything else will ever make it other than it is. It is flesh. It may be refined flesh, educated flesh, or it may be openly bad and evil flesh. It matters not how it may be treated. It is never changed by any process it may be put through. "The flesh profiteth nothing" (John 6:63) are the emphatic words of the Lord Jesus Himself. The mind of the flesh is enmity against God, as we read in Romans 8:7. It is not, nor can it be, subject to the law of God. This "flesh", then, never becomes holy or separated to God. "That which is born of flesh is flesh" (John 3:6). It remains as it ever was—a corrupt and thoroughly bad thing.

But there is no difficulty in seeing that it is the will of God, and what the apostle earnestly desired, that the saints should be wholly separated to God and that not in an outward way only, but in *spirit*, and in soul, and in body, and in view of the coming of our Lord Jesus Christ.

Now this is what we have found in looking into the Word of God. First, that sanctification means setting apart; secondly, that all believers are sanctified or set apart *absolutely* by the Spirit unto the sprinkling of the blood of Jesus Christ; that is, before they are justified; thirdly, inasmuch as Christians are to be so *practically* and growingly, as they know more of Him to whom they are set apart. The Lord grant blessing through what we have found in His own blessed Word on this subject.

(Simple Testimony 1887).

PRAYER.

Prayer is the expression of desire for benefit, by one who needs it, to one who, in his estimation, is able and disposed to confer it. Request of petition is therefore its leading element; but, in the expression of desire by one intelligent being to another, it is natural that the reasons why the desire is cherished, and the request presented, should be stated, and the grounds unfolded, on which the hope is founded that the desire shall be gratified by the request being granted. Petition and pleading are thus connected in prayer from man to man; and they are so, likewise, in prayer from man to God. Whoever reads carefully the prayers uttered by holy men, guided and influenced by the Spirit of God, recorded in Scripture, will be struck with the union of petition and pleading, by which they are distinguished. When they are brought "near God,"—when they, as Job says, "find Him, and come even to His seat," how do "they order their cause before Him, and fill their mouths with arguments!" (Job 23:3, 4). They "plead" with Him, as Jeremiah expresses it (Jer. 12:1). Every consideration arising from the character, promise, law, and administration of God, from the relations in which the petitioner stands to God, and the circumstances in which he is placed, which can be made to bear upon the subject, which is calculated to show that it is becoming the Divine greatness and goodness, righteousness and faithfulness, condescension and grace, to grant the petition, is brought forward, and earnestly, though humbly, urged.

The wise men of this world profess to wonder at this. They seem to find it somewhat difficult to see the fitness or usefulness of even presenting requests to such a being as the Divinity; but as to pleading with Him to grant these requests, it appears to them the very consummation of fanatical folly. Does He stand in need of information, either as to our desires or the reasons of them, as to the effects which are likely to result from His granting or refusing our requests? Does He need any additional impulse towards what is right; or can we, in the slightest degree, influence Him towards what is wrong? Does He want either information or motive? Can anything that man can say or do make Him change His mind or alter His plans? He who thinks that man's petitions and pleadings are needed to gain some of these ends, or capable of gaining any of them, must have very unworthy ideas of the Divine character and administration—very different from those presented in Scripture, or entertained by the persons who are most in the habit of petitioning and pleading with God. None ever placed the truth that God is previously acquainted with our wants, and disposed to supply them, in a clearer light than Jesus Christ in His Sermon on the Mount; but He urges the truth as a preventive of anxiety, not as a dissuasive from prayer. On the contrary, the thought that our Father in heaven knows what we need, is in Scripture represented as equally the reason why we should be "anxious about nothing," and why, "in everything, with prayer and supplication, we should make our requests known unto God" (Phil. 4:6, 7).

It is supposable that an economy might have been established, in conformity with the ideas of our philosophical objectors, against the reasonableness of prayer; and that the communication of the blessings which men need, and God is able and disposed to give, should have been suspended on man's never expressing any desire, but silently waiting for, and acquiescing in, whatever God is pleased to give,—making prayer, what these men's principles seem to make it, foolish and sinful, instead of wise and dutiful. But not only is it quite plain that such an economy is not that which, according to the Scriptures,—a well-accredited divine revelation,—has in fact been established, but it is equally plain, that such an economy would require, as its foundation, that God should have given to man a totally different—in some points a directly opposite—kind of mental constitution from that which He has given him.

It is of the very nature of the constitution God has given man, that when he has a desire, he uses means to have it granted; that, when he wants something which he knows another is able and disposed to supply him with, he expresses his wants, he requests their supply. It is of man's nature to "ask, that he may receive; to seek that he may find; to knock, that it may be opened to him". Unless you proceed on the atheistical principle, that there is no such thing as, what in any adequate sense of the word can be called, intercourse between God and man, it seems very strange that man should be called on to do constant violence to his nature in reference to those desires which God only can gratify—those wants which He only can supply. He must not express desire, however fervent—he must not solicit supply, however needed—because God knows this desire, and is disposed to furnish this supply.

I am really so little of a modern philosopher, as, with my Master in heaven, to find in the reasons against prayer arguments for it. I will tell God my desire, for He knows it already, and will not be offended at my following the impulse of the nature He has given me, which bids me express it to Him, who alone can gratify it; and I will ask Him to give me what I want, because I know He is disposed to supply all my need, according to His glorious riches. It would be painful restraint to me, to desire without being allowed to express my desires, and the reasons on which they are grounded; to feel my want, and know that He is able and willing to supply all my necessities, without giving utterance to this feeling and conviction, and to all that seems to me to warrant this utterance; and the form of this utterance of desire, this request of blessing with the reasons of my desire, and of my hope, naturally takes, is addressed to Him who alone can gratify my desire and supply my want,—that is, prayer, consisting both of petition and of pleading. I find in this the best preparation for obtaining what, from my confidence in God, I hope for. As to spiritual blessings, in asking them, pleading for them, I find I have obtained them. I am sure that, without those exercises which *prayer* implies, I should be less holy and less happy than I am; and while I will not puzzle myself to find out how God has so arranged His infinitely wise, unalterable plan of procedure, that blessings are secured by believing prayer which could not otherwise have been obtained,—as that restraint of prayer is punished by the withholding of blessings and believing, persevering prayer rewarded by the bestowal of blessing as its answer,—I find no difficulty in believing that it is so,—I cannot believe that it is otherwise,—and I bless His wisdom and kindness, in so arranging matters, as that I can innocently and safely follow the impulses of that nature He has given me, in the utterance of my desire of good, and of the reasons why I entertain them, and of the hopes which I cherish of having them gratified, to Him from whom I expect every blessing; that I can pour out all my mind and heart before Him, and expect that He will show He is pleased at this by giving me what I need, though it may not be exactly what I anticipate,—while believing that His plans are unaltered, unalterable, and "His eternal thoughts move on His undisturbed affairs". *(Dr. John Brown).*

(Continued from page 97.)

those who are dead while they live." (Dr. Haldeman). Scripture also declares the sinner is "dead in trespasses and sins" (Eph. 2:1).

7. Leprosy is dealt with not by quarantine, but by *banishment*. No leper was allowed to remain in the congregation of Israel. The terms of the Mosaic law were explicit: "He shall dwell alone; without the camp shall his habitation be" (Lev. 13:46). In the center of the camp was Jehovah's abode, and around the tabernacle were grouped His covenant people. From them the leper was excluded. In like manner, sin shuts out the sinner from God's presence: "Having the understanding darkened *being alienated* from the life of God" (Eph. 4:18).

8. The leper was *an object of shame*. The law required that, "his clothes shall be rent, and his head bare, and he shall put a covering upon his upper lip, and shall cry, Unclean, unclean." (Lev. 13:45). What a spectacle! What a picture of isolation! What a solemn portrayal of the natural man.

9. Leprosy is *incurable* so far as man is concerned. One really stricken with this disease is beyond human aid. The outcome is inevitably fatal. Medical science is helpless before its advance. In like manner, sin is beyond human cure. It can neither be eradicated nor ameliorated. No power of will nor effort of mind can cope with it. Neither legislation nor reformation is of any avail. Education and culture are equally impotent. Sooner can the Ethiopian change his skin or the leopard his spots than those do good who are accustomed to do evil (Jer. 13:23).

10. *But God can heal the leper.* What is beyond the power of man *is* possible with God. Where the science of the ages stands helpless, the Saviour manifests His sufficiency. It is written, "Behold, there came a leper and worshipped Him saying, "Lord, if Thou wilt, Thou canst make me clean" (Matt. 8:2). And we are told, "Jesus put forth His hand and touched him, saying, I will; be thou clean. and immediately his leprosy was cleansed". Blessed, thrice blessed, is this. So also we read, "Wherefore He is able also to save them to *the uttermost* that come unto God by Him". (Heb. 7:25).

In view of the first nine points above, how profoundly thankful ought every Christian to be that "the blood of Jesus Christ, God's Son *cleanseth* us from *all sin.* (1 John 1:7)!

Arthur W. Pink.

VOL. IV JUNE, 1925 NO. 6

STUDIES IN THE SCRIPTURES

"Search the Scriptures" John 5:39.

Arthur W. Pink, Publisher and Editor,
R. F. D. 9. York, Pa.

Price: 10 cents per copy; $1.00 or 5/- per year.

"In Journeyings Often."

"My times are in Thy hand" (Psa. 31:15). This has been the comforting assurance of the Editor and his wife as we have travelled far by land and sea during the past three months. Our "Times" have not been in the hands of the engine-driver nor the sea-captain, but in those of the living God. Most graciously has our faithful God supplied our every need as we have journeyed to the other side of the world. "My presence shall go with thee," was the precious promise which the Lord gave us through one of His saints just before we "moved our tent," and most blessedly has it been made good as we have travelled three thousand miles across land and six thousand five hundred miles across the ocean. It is with fervent praise that we here acknowledge our deep indebtedness to Him whose angel has encamped round about us, delivering from dangers known and unknown.

Leaving Philadelphia on January 5, we arrived safely in Denver three days later. There we were privileged to take part in the Rocky Mountain Bible Conference, speaking two and three times each day to appreciative congregations, the Lord granting us much liberty of utterance. The meetings were held in the Galilee Baptist Church, and we greatly enjoyed a week of Christian fellowship with Brother Gravett and his people. While there we were permitted to address the Baptist Pastors of the city and suburbs, emphasising the need and value of expository preaching. We had a good hearing, and are confident that the Lord honored His Own Word.

From Denver we journeyed to Oakland, where, for six weeks, we had the joy of ministering the Bread of Life to many hungry souls. The first Meeting in the Swedish Mission Church greatly encouraged us; the earnestness, eagerness and joy of the congregations evidenced, once more the satisfying power of the Word. The two weeks spent in the First Presbyterian Church will be long remembered. Its Pastor, Dr. Silsley, was in hearty accord, and his prayerful co-operation was a great help. We commend him to the prayers of our readers, that God will strengthen his hands and mightily use him to His glory. The three Sunday-night services in his Church were most blessed and solemn occasions. Well over a thousand people were present each time, and there was a holy hush over the congregation which could be felt. At the closing service, when we spoke on our Lord's Return, extra seats had to be carried in. Only Eternity will reveal the fruitage.

In addition to the above Meetings, we also spoke in San Francisco, and gave a series of Bible expositions in the Friends' Meeting-house in Berkeley. While there we had the joy of meeting an ex-medium, who, three years ago, was delivered from the power of Satan and translated into the kingdom of God's dear Son through reading our pamphlet, "The Philosophy of Spiritualism"; also a sister who was brought to Christ through the tract "Not saved." Thus we left California with hearts full of praise to Him who deigned to use one so feeble and unworthy. We take this opportunity of thanking our many friends for their intercessions. God certainly answered prayer.

(*Continued on page 144*).

IMPORTANT NOTICES

Set of twelve issues for **1922**, unbound, **$1.00** or **5/-**. Bound **$1.50** or **7/-**.

Set of twelve issues for **1923**, unbound, **$1.00** or **5/-**. Bound **$1.50** or **7/-**.

Set of twelve issues for **1924**, unbound, **$1.00** or **5/-**. Bound **$1.50** or **7/-**.

Note: We cannot break a set or now supply any **single** 1924 issues.

Subscription Price: **$1.00** or **5/-** per year to any address in the world.

Change of Address: Please notify me promptly of any change of address, and be certain to give both old and new address.

Non-subscribers receiving this Magazine regularly will understand their subscription has been entered by a friend.

Copies lost in the mail duplicated only if we are notified promptly.

Entered as second-class matter January 15th, 1923 at the post office at York, Pa., under Act of March 3rd, 1879.

CONTENTS

THE GOSPEL OF JOHN

42. *Christ's Entry into Jerusalem*: *John*, 12:12-20.

The following is an Analysis of the passage which is to be before us:—

1. The crowd going forth to meet Jesus, v. 12.
2. The joyous acclamations of the people, v. 13.
3. The Saviour mounted on an ass, v. 14.
4. The King's presentation of Himself to Israel, v. 15.
5. The dullness of the disciples, v. 16.
6. The cause why the people sought Jesus, vv. 17, 18.
7. The chagrin of the Pharisees, v. 19.

The passage which is to be before us brings to our notice one of the most remarkable events in our Lord's earthly career. The very fact that it is recorded by all the four Evangelists at once indicates something of uncommon moment. The incident here treated of is remarkable because of its *unusual* character. It is quite unlike anything else recorded of the Lord Jesus in the Gospels. Hitherto we have seen Him withdrawing Himself as much as possible from public notice, retiring into the wilderness, avoiding anything that savoured of display. He did not court attraction: He did not "cry or strive, or cause His voice to be heard in the streets" (Matt. 12:19). He charged His disciples they should "tell no man that He was Jesus the Christ" (Matt. 16:20). When He raised the daughter of Jairus, He "straightly charged them that no man should know of it" (Mark 5:43). When He came down from the Mount of Transfiguration He gave orders to His disciples that "they should tell no man what things they had seen, till the Son of Man was risen from the dead" (Mark 9:9).

We wish to press upon the reader the *uniqueness* of this action of Christ entering Jerusalem in the way that He did, for the more this arrests us the more shall we appreciate the motive which prompted Him. "When Jesus perceived, therefore, that they (the multitude which He had fed), would come and take Him by force, to make Him *a king*, He *departed* again into a mount Himself alone" (John 6:15). When His brethren urged "show Thyself to the world" (John 7:4), He answered, "My time is not yet come." Here, on the contrary, we see Him making a public entry into Jerusalem, attended by an immense crowd of people, causing even the Pharisees to say, "Behold, the world has gone after Him." And let it be carefully noted that Christ Himself *took the initiative* here at every point. It was not the multitude who brought to Him an animal richly caparisoned, nor did the disciples furnish the colt and ask Him to mount it. It was the Lord who *sent* two of the disciples to the entrance of Bethphage to get it, and the Lord *moved* the owner of the ass to give it up (Luke 19:33). And when some of the Pharisees asked Him to rebuke His disciples He replied, "I tell you that, if these should hold their peace, these stones would immediately cry out" (Luke 19:40).

How, then, are we to account for this startling change of policy on the part of Christ? What is the true explanation of His conduct? In seeking an answer to this question, men have indulged in the wildest conjectures, most of which have been grossly dishonouring to our Lord. The best of the commentators see in the joyous acclamations of the crowds an evidence of the *power* of Christ. He *moved* them to own Him as their "King," though as to *why* He should here do so they are not at all clear, nor do they explain why His moving their hearts produced such a *transcient* effect, for four days later the same crowds shouted "Crucify Him." We are therefore obliged to look elsewhere for the key to this incident.

We need hardly say that here, as everywhere, the perfections of the Lord Jesus are blessedly displayed. Two things are incontrovertible: the Lord Jesus ever acted with the Father's *glory* before Him, and ever walked in full accord with His Father's *Word.* "In the volume of the book" it was written of Him, and when He became incarnate He declared "I come to do *Thy* will, O God." These important considerations must be kept in mind as we seek a solution to the difficulty before us. Furthermore, we need to remember that the counsels of the Father always had in view *the glory of the Son.* It is by the application of these fundamental principles to the remarkable Entry into Jerusalem that light will be shed upon its interpretation.

Why, then, did the Lord Jesus send for the ass, mount it, and ride into the royal city? Why did He suffer the crowds, unrebuked, to hail Him with their "Hosannas"? Why did He permit them to proclaim Him their King, when in less than a week He was to lay down His life as a sacrifice for sin? The answer, in a word, is, because *the Scriptures so required!* Here, as ever, it was submission to His Father's Word that prompted Him. Loving obedience to the One who sent Him was always the spring of His actions. His cleansing of the Temple was the fulfilment of Psa. 69:9. The testimony which He bore to Himself was the same as the O.T. scriptures announced (John 5:39). When on the cruel cross He cried, "I thirst," it was not in order for His sufferings to be alleviated, but "that the scripture might be fulfilled" (John 19:29). So here, He entered Jerusalem in the way that He did in order that the Scriptures might be fulfilled.

What scriptures? The answer to this question takes us back, first of all, to the prophecy which dying Jacob made, a prophecy which related what was to befall his descendants in "the last days"—an O.T. expression referring to the times of the Messiah: begun at His first advent, completed at His second. In the course of his Divine pronouncement, the aged patriarch declared, "the scepter shall not depart from Judah, nor a lawgiver from between his feet until Shiloh come; and unto Him shall the *gathering* of the people be. Binding His foal unto the vine and His ass's colt unto the choice vine" (Gen. 49:9, 10). The word "scepter" here signifies *tribal rod.* Judah was to preserve the separate independency of his Tribe until the Messiah came. The fulfilment of this is seen in the Gospels. Though the Ten Tribes had long before been carried into captivity, from which they never returned, Judah (the "Jews"), were still in Palestine when the Son of God became incarnate and tabernacled among men. Continuing his prophecy, Jacob announced, "And unto Him (Shiloh—the *Peacemaker*—c.f. 'thy peace' in Luke 19:42), shall the *gathering* of *the* people (Israel) be." This received its first fulfilment at Christ's official entry into Jerusalem. But mark the next words, "Binding His foal unto the vine, and His ass's colt unto the choice vine."—the "vine" was Israel (Isa 5, etc.); the "*Choice* Vine" was Christ Himself (John 15:1). Here, then, was *the fact itself* prophetically announced. But this by no means exhausts the scriptural answer to our question.

We turn next to that remarkable prophecy given through Daniel respecting the "seventy weeks." This prophecy is found in Dan. 9:24-27. We cannot now attempt an exposition of it, though it is needful to make reference to it. This prophecy was given while Israel were captives in Babylon. In it God made known the length of time which was to elapse from then till the day when Israel's transgressions should be finished, and everlasting righteousness be brought in. "Seventy weeks" were to span this interval. The Hebrew word for "weeks" is "hebdomads," and simply means *septenaries*; "Seventy sevens" gives the true meaning. Each of the "hebdomads" equals seven years. The "seventy sevens," therefore, stood for four hundred and ninety years.

The "seventy sevens" are divided into three unequal parts. Seven "sevens" were to be spent in the rebuilding of Jerusalem: the book of Ezra and Nehemiah record the fulfilment of this. After Jerusalem *had been* restored, sixty-two more "sevens" were to run their course "unto the Messiah the Prince." And then we are told, "After threescore and two sevens (added to the previous seven 'sevens', making sixty-nine in all), shall Messiah be cut off." Here, then, is a definite computation, and a remarkable and most important Messianic prophecy. "Messiah *the Prince*" (cf. Rev. 1:5), was to present Himself to Jerusalem (note "Thy holy city" in Dan 9:24), at the expiration of the sixty-ninth "seven," or more specifically, precisely four hundred and eighty three years after God gave this prophecy to His beloved servant.

Now, it is *this* prophecy which received its fulfilment and supplies the needed key to what is before us in John 12. The entry of the Lord Jesus into Jerusalem in such an auspicious manner, was the Messiah *formally and officially presenting Himself to Israel as their "Prince."* In his most excellent book "The Coming Prince," the late Sir R. Anderson marshalled conclusive proofs to show that our Saviour entered Jerusalem *on the very day* which marked the completion of the sixty-ninth "hebdomad" of Dan 9. We make here a brief quotation from his masterly work:—

"No student of the Gospel-narrative can fail to see that the Lord's last visit to Jerusalem was not only in fact, but in the purpose of it, the crisis of His ministry, the goal towards which it had been directed. After the first tokens had been given that the Nation would *reject* His Messianic claims, He had shunned all public recognition of them. But now the twofold testimony of His words and works had been fully tendered. His entrance into the Holy City was to proclaim His Messiahship, and to receive His doom. Again and again His apostles even had been charged that they *should not* make Him known. But now He accepted the acclamations of 'the whole multitude of the disciples,' and silenced the remonstrance of the Pharisees with indignation.

"The full significance of the words which follow in the gospel of Luke is concealed by a slight interpolation in the text. As the shouts broke forth from His disciples, 'Hosanna to the Son of David, blessed is the King of Israel that cometh in the name of the Lord,' He looked off toward the Holy City and exclaimed, 'If *thou* also hadst known, even *on this day*, the things which belong to thy peace but now they are hid from thine eyes' (Luke 19:42). The time of Jerusalem's visit had come, and she knew it not. Long ere this, the Nation had rejected Him, but this was the predestined day when their choice must be irrevocable."

One other prophecy remains to be considered, in some respects the most wonderful of the three. If God announced through Jacob the simple fact of the gathering of the people unto the Peacemaker, if by Daniel He made known the very year and day when Israel's Messiah should officially present himself as their Prince, through Zechariah He also made known the very *manner* of His entry into Jerusalem. In Zech. 9:9 we read: "Rejoice greatly, O daughter of Zion, shout, O daughter of Jerusalem; behold, thy King cometh unto thee; He is just, and having salvation; lowly, and riding upon an ass, and upon a colt, the foal of an ass." As we shall see, several words in this prophecy are not quoted in the Gospels, therefore this prediction (like all prophecy) will receive *another* fulfilment; it will be completely realised when the Lord Jesus returns to this earth.

Before we come to the detailed exposition, let us offer a brief comment upon what has just been before us. At least three prophecies were fulfilled by Christ on His official entry into Jerusalem, prophecies which had been given hundreds of years before, prophecies which entered into such minute details that only one explanation of them is possible, and that is *God Himself* must have given them. This is the most incontrovertible and conclusive of all the proofs for *the Divine inspiration* of the Scriptures. Only He who knows the end from the beginning is capable of making accurate forecasts of what shall happen many generations afterwards. How the recorded accomplishment of these (and many other) prophecies *guarantees* the fulfilment of those which are still future! And how the fulfilment of prophecy in the past provides us with a sure key to the interpretation of unfulfilled prophecy! Just as those prophecies were *literally* fulfilled to the very letter, *so* those which will yet be fulfilled must not be spiritualised or generalised, but taken at their simple face value.

"On the next day much people that were to come to the feast, when they heard that Jesus was coming to Jerusalem, took branches of palm trees, and went forth to meet Him, and cried: 'Hosanna, blessed is the King of Israel that cometh in the Name of the Lord'" (vv. 12, 13). It is important to note the opening words of this quotation. What we have here is the sequel to the first verse of our chapter, "Then Jesus six days before the Passover came to Bethany." During the week preceding the Passover Jerusalem was crowded with Jews, who came in companies from every section of Palestine. They came early in order that they might be ceremonially qualified to partake of the feast (11:55). Already we have learned that the main topic of conversation among those who thronged the Temple at this time was whether or not *Jesus* would come up to the feast (11:56). Now, when the tidings reached them that He *was* on the way to Jerusalem, they at once set out to meet Him.

In view of what we read of in 11:57, some have experiencbed a difficulty here. "Both the chief priests and the Pharisees had given a commandment that if any man knew where He were, he should show it, that they might take Him." How came it then that we now read of "*much* people . . . took palm branches and went forth to meet

Him?" The difficulty is quickly removed if only close attention be paid to what the Holy Spirit has said. First, note that in 11:57 the past tense is used, "*had* given commandment;" this was before the Lord Jesus retired to Ephraim (11:54). Second, observe that 11:55 tells us "many went *out of the country* up to Jerusalem (11:55). It is evident therefore that many (if not all) of those who now sallied forth with palm branches to greet the Lord were men of *Galilee,* pilgrims, who had come up to the metropolis from the places where most of His mighty works were done. It was the *Galileans* who on a previous occasion sought to make Him "a King" (John 6:15 c.f. v. 1). They were not only far less prejudiced against Him than were those of Judea, but they were also much less under the influence of the chief priests and Pharisees of Jerusalem. Marvellously accurate is Scripture. The more minutely it is examined the more will its flawless perfections be uncovered to us. How this instance shows us, once more, that our "difficulties" in the Word are due to our negligence in carefully noting exactly what it says, and *all* it says on any given subject!

"Took branches of palm trees, and went forth to meet Him" (v. 13). This was a sign of joy, a festival token. In connection with the Feast of Tabernacles (which points to the Millennium) God instructed Moses to tell Israel, "And ye shall take ye on the first day the boughs of goodly trees, *branches* of palm trees . . . and ye shall *rejoice* before the Lord your God" (Lev. 23:40). In Rev. 7:9, where we behold the "innumerable multitude before the Throne and before the Lamb," they have "*palms* in their hands."

"And cried, Hosanna, blessed is He who comes in the Name of the Lord, the King." The word Hosanna means "Save now!" It is a cry of triumph, not of petition. As to how far these people entered into the meaning of the words which they here uttered, perhaps it is not for us to say. The sequel would indicate they were only said under the excitement of the moment. But looking beyond their intelligent design, to Him whose overruling Hand directs everything, we see here the Father causing a public testimony to be borne to the glory of His Son. At His birth He sent the angels to say to the Bethlehem shepherds, "Unto you is born this day in the city of David, a Saviour, which is Christ the Lord," and now He suffered this multitude to hail Him as the Blessed One come in the Name of the Lord. Again; before the public ministry of Christ commenced the wise men from the East were led to Jerusalem to announce that the *King* of the Jews had been born; and now that His public ministry was over, it is again testified to that He is "the *King* of Israel." But note in passing, for it is most significant, that only here is He denominated the King of *Israel.* It is speaking from the *Divine* viewpoint (most appropriate in *this* Gospel), for the Ten Tribes were not then in the land.

"And Jesus when He had found a young ass sat thereon; as it is written (v. 14). This is simply a comprehensive statement, gathering up in a word the results of the details supplied by the other Evangelists, and which John takes for granted we are familiar with. The fullest account of the *obtaining* of the young ass is furnished by Luke, and very striking is it to note what occurred—*see* Luke 19:29-35. There is nothing in his account which conflicts with the shorter statement which John has given us. "And Jesus, when He had found a young ass, sat thereon." *He* "found" it because He directed the disciples *where* to find it! It is another of those incidental allusions to the *Diety* of Christ, for in an unmistakable way it evidenced His omniscience; He knew the precise spot where the ass was tethered!

"Fear not, daughter of Sion; behold thy King cometh, sitting on an ass's colt" (v. 15). Emphasis is here laid on the age of the animal which Christ rode. It was a "young" one; Luke tells us that it was one "whereon yet never man sat" (19:30). This is not without deep significance. Under the Mosaic economy only those beasts which had never been worked were to be used for sacrificial purposes (see Num. 19:2; Deut. 21:3). Very striking is this. Like His birth of a *virgin,* like His burial in a *new* sepuchre, "wherein was never man yet laid" (John 19:41); so here, on the only occasion when He assumed anything like majesty, He selected a colt which had never previously been ridden. How blessedly this points to the dignity, yea, the uniqueness of His person hardly needs to be dwelt upon.

"Sat thereon, *as it is written.*" How this confirms what we said at the beginning. It was in order to fulfil the prophetic Word that the Lord Jesus here acted as He did. That which was "written" was what ever controlled Him. He lived by *every* word which procedeth out of the mouth of the Lord. The incarnate Word and the written Word never conflicted. What ground then had He to say, "I do *always* those things that please Him!" O that *we* might have more of *His* spirit!

"Fear not, daughter of Sion, behold thy King cometh, sitting on an ass's colt." Momentous hour was this. Israel's true King, David's Son and Lord, now officially presented Himself to the Nation. Various have been the attempts made to interpret this. In recent years the view which has had most prominence among students of prophetic and dispensational truth is, that Christ was here *offering* the Kingdom to Israel, and that had Israel received Him the millennial reign would have been speedily inaugurated. It is worse than idle to speculate about what would have happened *if* the Nation had acted differently from what they did; idle, because "secret things belong unto the Lord." Our duty is to search diligently and study prayerfully" those things which *are* revealed" (Deut. 29:29), knowing that whatever difficulties may be presented, Israel's rejection and crucifixion of the Lord Jesus were according to what *God's* hand and counsel *"determined before* to be done" (Acts 4:28).

What then was Christ's purpose in presenting himself to Israel as their King? The immediate answer is, to meet the requirements of God's prophetic Word. But this only takes the inquiry back another step. What was *God's purpose* in requiring Israel's Messiah to so act on this occasion? In seeking an answer to this, careful attention must be paid to the setting. As we turn to the context we are at once impressed by the fact that one thing there is made unmistakably prominent—the *death* of Christ looms forward with tragic vividness. At the close of John 11 we find the Leaders of the Nation "took counsel together for to put Him to death," and the Council issued a decree that "If any man knew where He was, he should show it, that they might take Him" (11:53, 57). The 12th chapter opens with the solemn intimation that it now lacked but six days to the Passover. The all-important "hour" for the slaying of the true Lamb drew on apace. Then we have the anointing of Christ by Mary, and the Saviour interpreted her act by saying, "Against the day of My *burying* hath she kept this."

Here, then, is the key, hanging, as usual, right on the door. The Lord of Glory was about to lay down His life, but before doing so the dignity of His person must first be publicly manifested. Moreover, wicked hands were about to be laid on Him, therefore the guilt of Israel must be rendered the more inexcusable by them now learning *Who* it was they would shortly crucify. The Lord therefore purposely drew the attention of the great crowds to Himself by placing Himself prominently before the eyes of the nation. What we have here is, Christ pressing Himself upon *the responsibility* of the Jews. None could now complain that they knew not who He was. On a former occasion they had said to Him, "How long dost Thou make us to doubt? If Thou be the Christ, tell us plainly" (10:24). But now all ground for ignorance was removed; by fulfilling the prophecies of Jacob, of Daniel, and of Zechariah, the Lord Jesus demonstrated that *He* was none other than Israel's true King. It was His last public testimony to the nation! He *was* their "King," and in fulfilment of the plain declarations of their own Scriptures He here presented Himself before them.

The prophecy of Zechariah is not quoted in its entirety by any of the Evangelists, and it is most significant to mark the different words in it which they omit. First of all, none record the opening words, "Rejoice greatly, O daughter of Zion; shout, O daughter of Jerusalem." The reason for this is obvious: Israel could not be called upon to "rejoice" while she was *rejecting* her King! That part of the prophecy awaits its realisation in a future day. Not until she has first *"mourned"* as one mourneth for his only son (Zech. 12:10), not until Israel "acknowledge their offence" (Hosea 5:15), not until they "repent" (Acts 3:19), not until they say, "Come, and let us *return* unto the Lord, for He hath torn, and He will heal us; He hath smitten, and He will bind us up" (Hosea 6:1); in short, not until their sins are put away, will the spirit of joy and gladness be given unto them.

In the second place, the words "Just and having salvation" are omitted from each of the Gospels. This also is noteworthy, and a striking proof of the *verbal* inspiration of the Scriptures. It was not in *justice,* but in *grace,* that the Lord Jesus came to Israel the first time. He came "to seek and to save that which was lost." He appeared "to put away sin by the sacrifice of Himself." But when He comes the second time, God's word through Jeremiah shall receive its fulfilment—"Behold, the days come, saith the Lord, that I will raise unto David a *righteous* Branch, and a King shall reign and prosper, and shall execute *judgment and justice* in the earth." But why the omission of "having salvation?" Because Israel as a nation would not have salvation. Oftimes would He have gathered her children together, but they "would not."

One other omission remains to be noticed: the smallest, but by no means the least significant. Zechariah foretold that Israel's King should come "*lowly,* and riding upon an ass." Matthew mentions the lowliness of Christ, though in the A.V. it is rendered "meek" (21:5). But this word is *left out by John.* And why? Because it is the central design of the fourth Gospel to emphasise the *glory* of Christ. (See 1:14; 2:11; 11:4, etc.)

"Fear not, daughter of Sion; behold, thy King cometh, sitting on an ass's colt" (v. 15). The fact that the Lord Jesus was seated upon "an ass" brings out His moral glory. As the Son of David according to the flesh, He was "made under the law" (Gal. 1:1), and perfectly did He fulfil it at every point. Now, one thing that marked out Israel as God's peculiar people was the absence of the *horse* in their midst. The "ox" was used in plowing, and the "ass" for riding upon, or carrying burdens. An express decree was made forbidding the king to multiply horses to himself: "But he *shall not* multiply horses to himself, nor cause the people to return to Egypt, to the end that he should multiply *horses*" (Deut. 17:16). Thus the king of God's separated people was to be sharply distinguished from the monarchs of the Gentiles—note how Pharaoh (Ex. 14:23; 15:1), the kings of Canaan (Josh. 11:4), Naaman (2 Kings 5:9), the king of Assyria (Isa. 37:8), are each mentioned as the possessors of many horses and chariots. But the true Israelites could say, "Some trust in chariots, and some in horses: *but we* will remember the name of the Lord our God" (Psa. 20:7). It is remarkable that the first recorded sin of Solomon was concerning this very thing: "And Solomon had forty thousand stalls of horses for his chariots, and twelve thousand horsemen" (1 Kings 4:26). It was, therefore, as One *obedient* to the Law, that Christ purposely selected an "ass"!

"Fear not, daughter of Sion: behold thy King cometh, sitting on an ass's colt." How evident it is that Christ *had* laid aside His glory (John 17:5). He Who was in the form of God, and thought it not robbery to be equal with God, made Himself of "no reputation," and took upon Him the form of a *servant.* Not only does this action of our wonderful Saviour mark His perfect subjection to the law of Moses, but it also brings out His gracious lowliness. When He formally presented Himself to Israel as their King, He rode not in a golden chariot, drawn by powerful stallions, but instead He came seated upon the colt of an ass. Neither was the beast harnessed with any goodlier trappings than the garments which His disciples had spread thereon. And even the ass was not His own, but borrowed! Truly the things which are highly esteemed among men are abomination in the sight of God (Luke 16:15). "No Roman soldier in the garrison of Jerusalem, who, standing at his post or sitting in his barrock-window, saw our Lord riding on an ass, could report to his centurion that He looked like one who came to wrest the kingdom of Judea out of the hands of the Romans, drive out Pontius Pilate and his legions from the tower of Antonia, and achieve independence for the Jews with the sword" (Bishop Ryle). How evident it was that *His* kingdom was "not of this world!" What an example for us to "Be not conformed to this world" (Rom. 12:2)!

Perhaps some may be inclined to object: But does not Rev. 19:11 *conflict* with what has just been said? In no wise. It is true that there we read, "And I saw heaven open, and behold a white *horse;* and He that *sat upon him* was called Faithful and True." There is no room to doubt that the Rider of this "white horse" is any other than the Lord Jesus Christ. But He will appear thus at His *second* advent. Then everything shall be changed. He Who came before in humiliation and shame shall return in power and majesty. He Who once had not where to lay His head shall then sit on the Throne of His *glory* (Matt. 25:31). He Who was nailed to a malefactor's cross shall, in that day, wield the scepior of imperial dominion. Just as the "ass" was well suited to the One Who had laid aside His glory, so the white "war-horse" of Rev. 19 is in perfect keeping with the fact that He is now "crowned with glory and honour."

"These things understood not His disciples" (v. 16). How ingenuous such a confession by one of their number! No impostor would have deprecated himself like this. How confidently may we depend upon the veracity of such honest chroniclers! Like us, the apostles apprehended Divine things but slowly. Like us, they had to "*grow* in grace and in the knowledge of our Lord and Saviour Jesus Christ." But mark, it does not say "these things *believed not* His disciples." It is our privilege, as well as our bounden duty, to believe *all* God has said, whether we "understand" it or no. The more implicitly we believe, the more likely will

God be pleased to honour our faith by giving us understanding (Heb. 11:3).

"But when Jesus was glorified, then remembered they that these things were written of Him, and that they had done these things unto Him" (v. 16). From the fact that the plural number is twice used here—"these things"—and from the very similar statement in John 2:22 we believe that the entire incident of our Lord's entry into Jerusalem, with all its various accompaniments, are here included. Probably that which most puzzled the disciples is what Luke has recorded: "And when He was come near, He beheld the city, and *wept over it*" (19:41). In view of this verse it would be more accurate to speak of our Lord's *tearful* entry into Jerusalem, rather than His *triumphant entry.* Christ was not misled by the excited cries of the people. He knew that the hour of His crucifixion, rather than His coronation, was near at hand. He knew that in only a few days' time the "Hosannas" of the multitudes would give place to their "Away With Him!" He knew that the nation would shortly consummate its guilt by giving Him a convict's gibbet instead of David's throne.

But *why* should the disciples have been so puzzled and unable to understand "these things?" It was because they were so reluctant to think that this One Who had power to work such mighty miracles should be put to a shameful death. To the very end they had hoped He would restore the kingdom and establish His throne at Jerusalem. The honours of the kingdom attracted, the shame of the cross repelled them. It was because of this that on the resurrection-morning He said to the two disciples, "O fools, and slow of heart to believe all that the prophets have spoken: ought not Christ to have suffered these things and to enter into His glory?" (Luke 24:25, 26). Yes, there had to be the sufferings *before* the glory, the Cross before the Crown (c.f. 1 Pet. 1:11). But when Jesus was "glorified," that is, when He had ascended to heaven and the Holy Spirit had been given to guide them into all truth, *then* "remembered they that these things *were* written of Him."

"The people, therefore, that were with Him when He called Lazarus out of his grave, and raised him from the dead, bear record. For this cause the people also met Him, for that they heard that He had done this miracle" (vv. 17, 18). This line in the picture is supplied only by John, and suitably so, for it was in the raising of Lazarus that the glory of *the Son of God* had been manifested (11:4). They who had witnessed that notable miracle had reported it in Jerusalem, and now it was known that He who had power to restore the dead to life was nearing the Capital, many came forth to meet Him. Doubtless one reason why this is brought in here is to emphasise the deep guilt of the nation for rejecting Him whose credentials were so unimpeachable.

"The Pharisees therefore said among themselves, perceive ye how ye prevail nothing? behold the world is gone after Him" (v. 19). Here is one of the many evidences of the truthful consistency of the independent accounts which the different Evangelists have given us of this incident. Luke tells us: "And some of the Pharisees from among the multitude said unto Him, Master, rebuke Thy disciples (19:39), and the Lord had answered them, I tell you that, if these should hold their peace, the stones would immediately cry out." Here we are shown their chagrin. They were envious of His popularity; they feared for their own hold over the people.

But here a difficulty confronts us, and one which we have seen no real effort to solve. The majority of the commentators suppose that the joyous greetings which the Lord Jesus received from the crowds on this occasion were the result of a secret putting forth of His Divine power, attracting their hearts to Himself. But how shall we explain the *evanescent* effect which it had upon them? how account for the fact that less than a week later the same crowds cried, "Crucify Him?" To affirm that this only illustrates the *fickleness* of human nature is no doubt to say what is sadly too true. But if *both* of their cries were simply expressions of 'human nature," where does the influencing in their heart by *Divine* power come in? We believe the difficulty is self-created, made by attributing the first cry to a wrong cause.

Two things are very conspicuous in God's dealings with men: His *constraining* power and His *restraining* power. As illustrations of the former, take the following examples. It was *God* who gave Joseph favour in the sight of the keeper of the prison (Gen. 39:22), who moved Balaam to bless Israel when he was hired to curse them (Num. 23:30), who stirred up the spirit of Cyrus to make a proclamation giving the Jews the right to return to Palestine (Ezra. 1, 1, 2). As illustrations of the latter, mark the following cases. It was *God* who "withheld" Abimelech from sinning (Gen. 20:6); the brethren of Joseph "conspired against him to *slay* him" (Gen. 37:18), but God did allow them to carry out their evil intentions.

Now, these same two things are given a prominent place in the Gospels in connection with the Lord Jesus. At His bidding the leper was cleansed, the blind saw, the dead were raised. At His word the disciples forsook their nets, Matthew left the seat of custom, Zaccheus came down from his leafy perch and received Him into his house. At His command the apostles went forth without bread or money (Luke 9:3); made the hungry multitudes sit down for a meal, when all that was in sight were five small loaves and two little fishes. Yes, a mighty *constraining* power did He wield. But equally mighty, if not so evident, was the *restraining* power that He exerted. At Nazareth His rejectors "led Him into the brow of the hill . . . that they might cast Him down headlong. But He, *passing through the midst of them,* went His way" (Luke 4:29:30). In John 10:39 we are told "They sought again to take Him, but *He went forth out of their hands.*" When the officers came to arrest Him in the Garden, and He said, "I am," they "went backward and fell to the ground" (18:6)!

But the *restraining* power of Christ was exercised in another way than in the above instances. He also *checked* the fleshly enthusiasm of those who were ready to welcome Him as an Emancipator from the Roman yoke. When they would "come and take Him by force, to make Him a king, He *departed* (6:15). All through His ministry He discouraged all public tokens of honour from the people, lest (humanly speaking) the envy of His enemies should bring His preaching to an untimely end. But His public ministry was over, so He now *removes the restraint* and allows the multitudes to hail Him with their glad Hosannas, and this, not that He now craved pomp, but in order that the Scriptures might be fulfilled. These transports of joy from the Galileans were raised because they imagined that He would there and then set up His temporal kingdom. Hence, when *their* hopes were disappointed, their transports were turned into rage, and therefore did *they* join in the cry of "crucify Him!"

In what has been just before us we have a most blessed foreshadowment of the future. Our Lord will not always be rejected and "by the world disowned." A day is coming when the kingdom of this world shall become the kingdom of our Lord and of His Christ, when He shall sit upon the throne of His father David, and of His kingdom there shall be no end. Then will that blessed prophecy of Zephaniah 3:13-20 be made good unto Israel.

The real *Triumphant* Entry of Christ into Jerusalem is yet to be. The complete fulfilment of Zech. 9:9 has not yet taken place. But His entry into Jerusalem on the eve of His crucifixion strikingly foreshadowed His yet future entrance. Mark the following points:—

1. The *time* when this occurred: the Holy Spirit has emphasised this here in John 12: "On the next day" (v. 12). We would refer the reader back to the close of the last article, where we dwelt upon the dispensational significance of what is recorded at the beginning of John 12. The anointing at Bethany and the criticism it evoked foreshadowed the godly Remnant and their experiences in the Great Tribulation. What *follows* this will be *the Millennium;* hence, the "*next day*" here. 2. The *place* where this occurred is equally significant. Matthew tells us (21:1) it was when the Lord reached "the Mount of *Olives*" that He sent for and mounted the ass. From this same Mount He will descend to inaugurate His Millennial reign —see Zech. 14:4, 3. Mark how the people went forth to *meet* Christ *before* He entered the royal city (12:13). So, it is not until the hearts of Israel truly go out unto their rejected Messiah that He shall come unto them. 4. Behold how they went forth with *palms* in their hands (v. 13). These are associated with the Feasts of Tabernacles (Lev. 23:40), and *this* is the Feast which points forward so strikingly to the Millennium (See vol. 2. chap. 25). 5. Note the *cry* with which they greeted Him: "Blessed is He that cometh in the name of the Lord, the King of Israel" (v. 13. Greek). So Christ announced, "Ye shall not see Me henceforth, till ye shall say Blessed is He that cometh in the name of the Lord" (Matt. 23:39)! 6. Christ presented Himself as their *King* (v. 15). It is in *this* character that He shall return to the earth. 7. The *animal* on which He rode had a symbolical significance, in full accord with the typical picture here. It was an animal which had never been broken in, yet did it respond freely to His hand! How strikingly this indicated that Christ will not rule over a people who have to be *forced* into subjection; but, instead, over a newly-born nation who shall yield a *free* obedience! "Thy people shall be willing in the day of Thy power" (Psa. 110:3). The mother-ass following (as Matthew's account suggests) *gives the link*

between the new Israel and the Israel of the past!

Ponder the following questions as a preparation for our next article:—

1. Why did the Greeks seek out "Philip," v. 20?
2. Why did Philip first tell Andrew, not Christ, v. 22?
3. What is meant by "glorified" in v. 23?
4. Why did Christ say v. 24 at this time?
5. What is meant by v. 31 ?
6. What is meant by "draw," v. 32?
7. Why did Jesus "hide" Himself, v. 36?

—ARTHUR W. PINK.

GLEANINGS IN EXODUS

18. Israel's Exodus from Egypt: Ex. 12-14.

"And the Egyptians were urgent upon the people, that they might send them out of the land in haste; for they said, We be all dead men. And the people took their dough before it was leavened, their kneading-troughs being bound up in their clothes upon their shoulders. And the children of Israel did according to the word of Moses; and they borrowed of the Egyptians jewels of silver, and jewels of gold, and raiment. And the Lord gave the people favour in the sight of the Egyptians so that they lent unto them such things as they required. And they spoiled the Egyptians" (Ex. 12: 33-36). At last was fulfilled the promise made by Jehovah to Abraham more than four hundred years before. He had said, "Know of a surety that thy seed shall be a stranger in a land that is not theirs, and shall serve them; and they shall afflict them four hundred years" (Gen. 15:13). Literally had this been fulfilled. The experiences of Abraham's seed in Egypt was precisely as God had said. But He had also declared to Abraham, "And also that nation, whom they shall serve, will I judge; and afterward shall they come out with great substance" (Gen 15:14). This, too, was now made good. There were no provisos, no ifs or peradventures. "Afterward *shall* they come out with great substance." So God had decreed, so it came to pass. So had God promised, so He now made good His word.

"And it came to pass at the end of the four hundred and thirty years, even the self-same day it came to pass that all the hosts of the Lord went out from the land of Egypt" (12:41). Upon this verse we commented briefly in our last paper. Those who went forth from the land of bondage are here termed "the hosts *of the Lord.*" Israel were the Lord's hosts in a threefold way: first, by covenant purpose, by the eternal choice of a predestinating God; second, by creation, who had made them for Himself; third, by purchase, for He had redeemed them by precious blood.

"And it came to pass the selfsame day, that the Lord did bring the children of Israel out of the land of Egypt by their armies" (12:51). The last three words in this quotation show that Israel did not issue from Egypt as a disorderly mob. How could they, seeing that it was *the Lord* who "brought them out!" God is not the author of confusion. There is a supplementary word in 13:18 which brings this out in further detail: "The children of Israel went up *by five in a rank* (margin) out of the land of Egypt." A similar example of Divine *orderliness* is to be observed in connection with our Lord feeding the hungry multitude. In Mark 6:29 we are told that Christ commanded the disciples to "make all sit down *by companies* upon the green grass." And we are told "they sat down *in ranks,* by hundreds, and by fifties." The fact that Israel went forth by "*five* in a rank" exemplified and expressed God's *grace,* for five in Scripture ever speaks of grace or favour.

There is another word in Psalm 105:37 which adds a beautiful touch to the picture here before us. There we are told, "He brought them forth also with silver and gold; and *there was not one feeble person* among their tribes." How this illustrates the need of diligently *comparing* Scripture with Scripture if we would obtain the *full* teaching of the Word on any subject! Nothing is said of this in the historical narratives of Exodus; it was reserved for the Psalmist to tell us of this Divine miracle, for miracle it certainly was, that not a single one in all that vast host was sickly or infirm.

"And Moses took the bones of Joseph with him; for he had straitly sworn the children of Israel, saying, God will surely visit you; and ye shall carry up my bones away hence with you" (13:19). This was no ancestor or relic worship, but an act of faith, the declaration of Joseph's belief that the destination of Israel was to be the land which God had promised to give to Abraham and his seed, which promise the faith of Joseph had firmly laid hold of. During their long bondage in Egypt this commandment which Joseph gave concerning "his bones" must have often been the theme of converse in many of the Hebrew households; and now, by taking with him the embalmed remains, Moses showed his sure confidence that a grave would be found for them in the land of promise. Nor was his confidence misplaced, as Joshua 24:33 shows: "And the bones of Joseph, which the children of Israel brought up out of Egypt, buried they in Shechem."

Hebrews 11:22 tells us that this commandment which Joseph gave was "by *faith*," and here, hundreds of years after, we behold God's *response* to the faith of His servant. Moses had much to occupy him at this time. An immense responsibility and undertaking was his—to organise the "armies of Israel" and lead them forth in orderly array. But in simple dependence Joseph had put his dying trust in the living God, and it was impossible that he should be disappointed. Therefore did Jehovah bring to the mind of Moses this command of Joseph, and caused him to carry it out. Blessed demonstration was it of the *faithfulness* of God.

But what, we may ask, is the *typical* lesson in this for *us?* Every other detail in the exodus of Israel from Egypt, as well as all that preceded and followed it, has a profound significance and spiritual application to us. What, then, is foreshadowed in Israel carrying the bones of Joseph with them as they commenced their journey across the wilderness toward the promised land? If we bear in mind that Joseph is a type of Christ the answer will not be difficult to discover. 2 Cor., 4:10 gives us the N.T. interpretation: "Always bearing about in the body *the dying of* the Lord Jesus, that the life also of Jesus might be made manifest in our bodies." It is the power of the cross applied to the mortal body which ever craves present ease and enjoyment. It is only by "keeping under" the body that the *life* of Jesus (the new nature) is manifested by us.

"And the children of Israel journeyed from Rameses to Succoth, about six hundred thousand on foot that were men, beside children" (12:37). "Rameses means 'child of the sun.' It was a fortress the Israelites, as slaves, had helped to build for the Egyptians. It was named after one of their great kings, whose remains, as a mummy, are now in the British Museum. He was the Pharaoh who oppressed Israel so cruelly, and the father of the Pharaoh who pursued the Israelites and was drowned in the Red Sea. He was a great warrior; he conquered Ethiopia and other lands." Typically, Rameses speaks of that system: 'This present evil world,' from which the grace and power of God delivers His elect, that system over which the mighty fallen angel, Satan, presides as Prince.

"So here, on the very threshold of their journey, we have a strange and wonderful parable—a picture that everyone who knows the rudiments of astronomy can appreciate. As the literal Israel was called out of the domains of the 'child of the sun' to journey to a land unknown to them, so is the spiritual Israel—the Church—called out from the realm described in the book of Ecclesiastes as 'under the sun'—all this kingdom in which the planets ('wanderers') move in their never-ceasing revolutions around the sun—to go to that undiscovered realm, in which, because what of it is visible to the eye is at such an inconceivable distance from us that their movements can hardly be detected at all, we call them fixed stars—that calm, immovable heaven of heavens that we see gazing at us every night, unperturbed and untouched by anything that can occur in our solar system of wanderers, where our earth, like the rest, is a poor restless wanderer in a path that never arrives anywhere. How graphically Solomon describes all our life 'under the sun', its mirths, its cares, its toils, its joys, and its sorrows, as unceasing 'vanity and vexation of spirit'! . . . . 'The thing that hath been is that which shall be, and that which *is* done is that which *shall be* done; and there is no new thing under the sun' (Ecc. 1:9).

"To that 'third heaven,' as Paul calls it (2 Cor., 12), that Paradise altogether beyond and free from any of the influences of our planatary system, the believer is going. We belong not to the world. Chosen in Christ before this world's foundation, we belong to an eternal realm beyond and apart from all men's ambitions, schemes, philosophies, religions (Eph. 1:4-10).

"Such a calling *is* mysterious. No wonder Paul, even when in the very act of trying to explain it to us, lifts up an earnest prayer that a spirit of wisdom and revelation might be given us, so that we might be able to *"know* what is the hope of His calling' (Eph. 1:18). It is all so new; it is all so *un*-earthly; its doctrines, its maxims, its hopes and fears, its rules of conduct, are all so different to what is *'under* the sun'" (C. H. Bright).

"And the children of Israel journeyed from Rameses to Succoth." "Succoth" means "booths" or "tents." This spoke plainly of the *pilgrim* character of the journey which lay before them. This was one of the great lessons learned by the first pilgrim: "*Here* have we no *continuing city*" (Heb. 13:14); for "by faith he sojourned in the land of promise, as in a strange country, dwelling in *tents* with Isaac and Jacob, the heirs with him of the same promise." (Heb. 11:3). *Booths* are all that we have down here, for "our citizenship is in heaven" (Phil. 3:20). But, blessed be God, the day is now near at hand when we shall exchange our temporary "tents" for the eternal "mansions" of the Father's House.

"And a mixed multitude went up also with them" (12.38). Very solemn is this; it was a wily move of the Enemy. Scripture presents him in two chief characters—as the roaring lion and as the cunning serpent. The former was exemplified by the cruel oppressions of Pharaoh; the latter, in what is here before us. Satan tried hard to keep some, at least, of the Israelites in Egypt; failing in this, he now sends some of the Egyptians to accompany Israel to Canaan! This "mixed multitude" would doubtless be made up of Egyptians and others of different nations who resided in Egypt. A variety of causes and motives might prompt them. Some, through intermarriages with the Israelites (Lev. 24:10), and now loth to part with their relatives; others, because afraid to remain any longer in a land so sorely afflicted with Divine judgments, and now rendered desolate and untenable; others, because quick to perceive that such wonders wrought on behalf of the Hebrews plainly marked them out as a people who were the favourites of Heaven, and therefore deemed it good policy to throw in their lot with them (c.f. 9:20). But it was not long before this "mixed multitude" proved a thorn in the side of Israel. It was this same "mixed multitude" who first became dissatisfied with the manna and influenced Israel to murmur. (See Num. 11:4.)

It has been well said that "when a movement of God takes place men are wrought upon by other motives than those by which the Holy Spirit stirs the renewed heart, and a mass attach themselves to those who are led forth." Witness the fact that when God "called Abraham *alone*" (Isa. 51:2), Terah (his father) and Lot (his nephew) accompanied him (Gen. 11:31). Witness the Gibeonites making a league with Joshua (Jos. 9). So, too, we find that after the Jewish remnant returned from the captivity "a mixed multitude" joined themselves to Israel (Neh. 5:17), though later "they *separated* from Israel all the mixed multitudes" (Neh. 13:3). So, too, we read of the Pharisees and Sadducees coming to John the Baptist (Matt. 3:7)! And these things are recorded for *our* "learning." This fellowshiping of believers with unbelievers, this sufferance of the ungodly among the congregation of the Lord, has been the great bane of God's saints in every age, the source of their weakness, and the occasion of much of their failure. It is because of this the Spirit of God says, "wherefore come out from among them and *be ye separate*" (2 Cor. 6:17).

"And it came to pass when Pharaoh had let the people go that God led them not through the way of the land of the Philistines, although that was near; for God said, Lest peradventure the people repent when they see war and they return to Egypt" (13:17). How this reminds us of Psl. 103: 13, 14: "Like as a father pitieth his children, so that Lord pitieth them that fear Him. For He knoweth our frame; He remembereth that we are dust." This people who had spent many long years in slavery were now starting out for the promised land, and it is beautiful to see this tender concern for them. It exemplifies a principle of general application in connection with the Lord's dealings with His people. The Lord is not only very compassionate, but His mercies are "tender" (James 5:11). The Lord does not suffer His "babes" to be tested as severely as those who are more mature; witness the various trials to which He subjected Abraham—the command for him to offer Isaac was not the first but the *last* great test which he received. It was so here with Israel. Later, there would be much *fighting* when Canaan was reached, but at the beginning He led them not the way of the land of the Philistines, for that would have involved warfare. He had respect unto their weakness and timidity. "The Lord, in His condescending grace, so orders things for His people that they do not, at their first setting out, encounter heavy trials, which might have the effect of discouraging their hearts and driving them back." (C.H.M.)

"God *led* them not through the way of the land of the Philistines." This is the *first* thing noticed by the Holy Spirit after Israel left the land of Egypt—*God* chose the way for His people through the wilderness. Unspeakably blessed is this. "The *steps* of a good man are ordered by the Lord, and He delighteth in his way (Psl. 37:23). We are not left alone to choose our own path. "As many as are *led* by the Spirit of God they are the sons of God" (Rom. 8:14). And what is it that the Spirit uses in His leading of us to-day? In this, as in everything, it is the written

Word—"Thy Word is a lamp unto my feet," to reveal the pitfalls and obstacles of the way, "and a light unto my path"—to make clear the by-paths to be avoided (Psl. 119:105). What a full provision has been made for us! Nothing is left to chance, nothing to our own poor reasoning—"we are His workmanship, created in Christ Jesus unto good works, which God hath before ordained *that we should walk in them*" (Eph. 2:10).

"But God led the people about through the way of the wilderness of the Red Sea (13:8). It is often said that the "wilderness" had no place in the *purpose* of God for Israel. But this is certainly erroneous. It was *God* Himself who led the people round about "the way of the wilderness of the Red Sea." It was God's original intention that Israel *should* take exactly the route which they actually followed. Not only is this evident from the fact that the Pillar of Cloud *led* them each step of their journey to Canaan, but it was plainly intimated by the Lord to Moses *before* the exodus took place. At the very first appearing of Jehovah to His servant at Horeb (Ex. 3:1—see our note on this in Article 4), He declared, "When thou has brought forth the people out of Egypt ye shall serve God upon *this mountain.*" God's purpose in leading Israel to Canaan through the wilderness, instead of via the land of the Philistines, was manifested in the sequel. In the first place, it was in order that His marvellous power might be signally displayed on their behalf in bringing them safely through the Red Sea. In the second place, it was in order that Pharaoh and his hosts might there be destroyed. In the third place, it was in order that they might receive Jehovah's laws in the undisturbed solitude of the desert. In the fourth place, it was in order that they might be properly organised into a Commonwealth and Church-state (Acts 7:53) prior to their entrance into and occupation of the land of Canaan. Finally, it was in order that they might be humbled, tried, and proved (Deut. 8:2, 3), and the sufficiency of their God in every emergency might be fully demonstrated.

"And they took their journey from Succoth, and encamped in Etham, on the edge of the wilderness. And the Lord went before them by day in a pillar of a cloud, to lead them the way; and by night in a pillar of fire, to give them light; to go by day and night" (13:20, 21). Very precious is this. Just as Jehovah—the *covenant* God, the *promising* God, the One who heard the groanings of Israel, the One who raised up a deliverer for them—reminds us of *God the Father,* just as the Lamb—without spot and blemish, slain and its blood sprinkled, securing protection and deliverance from the avenging angel—typifies *God the Son;* so this Pillar of Cloud—given to Israel for their guidance across the wilderness—speaks to us of *God the Holy Spirit.* Amazingly full, Divinely perfect, are these O.T. foreshadowings. At every point the teaching of the N.T. is anticipated. But the anointed eye is needed to perceive the hidden meaning of these primitive pictures. Much prayerful searching is necessary if we are to discern their spiritual signification.

This "pillar" was the visible sign of the Lord's presence with Israel. It is called "a pillar of cloud" and "a pillar of fire." Apparently its upper portion rose up to heaven in the form of a column; its lower being spread out cloudwise, over Israel's camp. Note how in Ex. 14:24 the two descriptive terms are combined, showing that the "pillar" did not change its form, as a "cloud" by day and a "fire" by night as is popularly supposed; but, as stated above, it was *one*—a "pillar of fire" in its upper portion, a "cloud" below." It is clear, though, from subsequent scriptures (Num. 14:14, etc.), that the whole "cloud" was illuminative by night-time "to give them light in the way wherein they should go" (Neh. 9:12). Let us now consider some of the points in which the Cloud typified the Holy Spirit.

1. The "Cloud" was not given to Israel until they had been delivered from Egypt. First, the slaying of the Pascal Lamb, then the giving of the Cloud. This is the order of the N.T. First, the death of God's Lamb, followed by His resurrection and ascension, and then the public descent of the Holy Spirit on the day of Pentecost. So, also, is it in Christian experience. There is first the sinner appropriating by faith the death of Christ, and then the coming of the Holy Spirit to indwell that soul. It is on the ground of Christ's shed blood—not because of *any* moral fitness in us—that the Spirit of God seals us unto the day of redemption. Strikingly is this order observed in the epistle to the Romans—the great doctrinal treatise of the N.T. There, as nowhere else so fully, is unfolded God's method of salvation. But it is not until *after* the believing sinner is "justified" (5:1) that we read of the Spirit of God. In 2:4-10 we get repentance; in 3:22-28, faith; and then in 5:5 we read, "the love of God is shed abroad in our hearts by *the Holy Spirit which is given unto us!*"

2. The "Cloud" was God's gracious *gift* to Israel. No word is said about the people *asking* for this Guide. It came to them quite unsought, as a tender provision of God's mercy. Do we not find the same thing in the Gospels? At the close of His mission the Lord Jesus told the disciples of His departure, of His return to the Father. And though we read of them being troubled and sorrowful, yet there is no hint that any of the apostles *requested* Him to send them another Comforter. The purpose to do this proceeded alone from Himself—"*I* will pray the Father, and He shall give you another Comforter" (John 4:16).

3. The Cloud was given to *guide* Israel through their wilderness journey. What a merciful provision was this—an infallible Guide to conduct them through the tractless desert! "The Lord went before them by day in a pillar of cloud, *to lead* them the way" (Ex. 13:21). In like manner, the Holy Spirit has been given to Christians to direct their steps along the Narrow Way which leadeth unto life. "As many as are *led* by the Spirit of God, they are the sons of God" (Rom. 8:14).

4. The Cloud gave *light*. "And by night in a pillar of fire to *give them light*" (Ex. 13:21). Beautifully does Nehemiah remind their descendants of this hundreds of years later: "Thou leadest them in the day by a cloudy pillar and in the night by a pillar of fire, *to give them light* in the way wherein they should go" (Neh. 9:12). By day or by night Israel was "thoroughly furnished." For a similar purpose is the Holy Spirit given to Christians. He is "the Spirit of wisdom and understanding, the Spirit of counsel and might, the Spirit of knowledge and of the fear of the Lord" (Isa. 11:2). Said the Lord to His apostles, "When He, the Spirit of truth, is come, He will *guide* you into all the truth" (John 16:13).

5. The Cloud was given *for a covering*: "He spread a cloud for a covering" (Psl. 105:39). This Cloud was for Israel's protection from the scorching heat of the sun in the sandy desert where there was no screen. Beautifully has this been commented upon by one who knew from an experience of contrast the blessedness of this merciful provision of God for Israel: "To appreciate what the cloud was to Israel, we must transport ourselves in imagination to a rainless country like Egypt. We lived many years on the coast of Peru—hundreds of miles as rainless as Egypt. We recalled with horror that some English hymn writer had sung the glories of a "cloudless sky, a waveless sea." In a small schooner, becalmed under a tropical sun off the coast of Equador, we tasted the awfulness of a waveless sea, and in Peru for half the year we had a cloudless sky, and rainless always. How beautiful the distant clouds looked, away off there on the peaks of the lofty Andes. We could not but feel, 'What must be the soothingness of being under a cloud like those Indians who lived up there in that happy fertile region of clouds amid the valleys and mountains!' Therefore, that cloud must have been a welcome sight to those ex-slaves, accustomed to labour in the fields under the sun of Egypt. It was a proof to them of the *all*-mighty power of Jehovah. He could give them a cloud where there was nothing in Nature to form clouds. He could furnish a shelter to *His* people when no other people had a shelter (C. H. Bright). So, too, is the Holy Spirit our Protector—we are "*sealed* unto the day of redemption" (Eph. 4:30).

6. God *spake* from the Cloud: "He spake unto them *in the cloudy pillar* (Psl. 99:7). The Psalmist is here referring back to such passages as Ex. 33:9—"And it came to pass, as Moses entered into the tabernacle, the cloudy pillar descended, and stood at the door of the tabernacle, and the Lord *talked* with Moses" (Num. 12:5). In like manner the Holy Spirit is to-day the Spokesman for the Holy Trinity. "He that hath an ear, let him hear what *the Spirit* saith unto the churches" (Rev. 2, 3).

7. This Cloud was *darkness to the Egyptians*: "And it came between the camp of the Egyptians and the camp of Israel, and it was a cloud *and darkness to them*" (14:20). Fearfully solemn is this. God not only reveals, but He also conceals: "At that time Jesus answered and said, I thank Thee, O Father, Lord of Heaven and Earth, because *Thou hast hid* these things from the wise and prudent" (Matt. 11:25). It is so with the Holy Spirit—"The Spirit of truth whom the world *cannot* receive" (John 14:17).

8. This Cloud rested upon the Tabernacle as soon as it was erected. "So Moses finished the work. *Then* a cloud covered the tent of the congregation, and the glory of the Lord filled the Tabernacle, and Moses was not able to enter into the tent of the congregation because the cloud abode thereon, and *the glory* of the Lord filled the Tabernacle" (Ex. 40:33-35). How strikingly this foreshadowed the coming of the Holy Spirit upon that Blessed One who tabernacled among men, of Whom it is written, "We beheld His *glory* (John 1:14). So, too, the Holy Spirit came upon the twelve apostles on the day of Pentecost

and they were all *filled* with the Holy Spirit" (Acts 2:4).

9. All through Israel's wilderness wanderings this Cloud *was never taken away from them*: "Yet Thou in Thy manifold mercies forsookest them not in the wilderness; the pillar of the cloud *departed not* from them" (Neh. 9:19). Despite all Israel's failures—their murmurings, their unbelief, their rebellion—God never withdrew the Cloudy Pillar! So, too, of the Holy Spirit given to believers the sure promise is, "He shall give you another Comforter, that He may (should) abide with you *forever*" (John 14:16).

10. It is blessed to learn that the Cloud shall once more descend upon and dwell among Israel. When God regathers His scattered people, when He resumes His covenant relationship with them, and brings them to a saving knowledge of their Messiah-Redeemer, then shall be fulfilled the ancient promise, "When the Lord shall have washed away the filth of the daughters of Zion, and shall have purged the blood of Jerusalem from the midst thereof by the spirit of judgment, and by the spirit of burning. And the Lord will create upon every dwelling-place of mount Zion, and upon her assemblies, a Cloud and smoke by day and a shining of *a flaming fire* by night; for upon all the Glory shall be a defence" (Isa. 4:6). What a truly marvellous type of the person and ministry of the Holy Spirit was the fiery and cloudy "pillar!"

—ARTHUR W. PINK.

TRUTH AND ERROR,

or

Letters to a Friend.

6. *Predestination and Foreknowledge.*

"Being predestinated according to the purpose of Him Who worketh all things after the counsel of His own will" (Eph. 1:11).

It is of some importane that we should settle the real nature of these two things, predestination and foreknowledge, and ascertain which of the two is first. The question is, does God fix a thing, simply because He foreknows it, or does He foreknow it because He has fixed it? There are vague ideas in men's minds of those points, and it is well to know the truth with distinctness. I answer then, unhesitatingly, that predestination must be the foundation of foreknowledge. God foreknows everything that takes place, because He has fixed it. In proof of this I remark,

1. *The opposite of this is an impossibility.*

To fix a thing is to make that thing certain to come to pass, which, but for that fixing, would not have come to pass. If, then, there be any kind of foreknowledge before predestination, it is simply the foreknowledge that the thing which He desires would not come to pass, unless He sees fit to fix it. God knew all that might *possibly* have come to pass had He let the world alone to act out its iniquity. In all the infinity of possibles, He saw that the thing He wanted was not to be found. Seeing the end from the beginning, He saw that the thing He desired would never come to pass unless brought into being by a direct act of His own will. No other will would desire or could effect that which He saw to be best, either in regard to persons or events. The thing He wanted was not to be found among the *possibles,* but among the *impossibles,* if matters were left to themselves, and to the operation of the usual laws. How, then, shall that which is impossible be rendered not only possible, but certain? Evidently by the direct interference of God. God having thus interfered and *arranged* everything according to His wisdom, of necessity must *know* them as to come to pass. In other words, He foreknows everything, because He has arranged everything. Everything is certain in His foreknowledge, because everything is certain in His arrangements.

Take the case of a saved sinner, such as Saul of Tarsus. In looking forward from eternity, God saw that sinner. He saw him in his guilt and sin. He saw him hastening away from Himself. He saw that if left to himself, or to the usual laws of things, he would only go deeper into sin, and farther from Himself. He saw that in such a case his salvation was impossible —that he never would believe, and never repent, and never turn. This was all that mere foreknowledge could tell. Foreknowledge alone can do nothing as to salvation. But here predestination comes in. God forms a design to bring man to glory; he is a "chosen vessel." And having this design regarding him, He resolves to put forth His power, He pre-arranges all His plans concerning him, He fixes the day and hour of his conversion, and thus He *foreknows* its certainty, because He has *forearranged it.* Otherwise it could not have been known; nay, it would have been an impossibility.

2. *The opposite of this is an absurdity.* What can be more absurd than to *fix* a thing which I already know will come to pass, whether I fix it or not? This is truly imputing foolishness to God. It represents Him as giving a solemn decree, to fix a thing which is already certain. As if the queen of this realm were giving forth a statue, decreeing that the sun should rise to-morrow, because she knew that it would be the case from the laws of Nature. Is it not a mockery of God? It makes Him thus to speak:—"I foreordain that a sinner shall be saved, because I foresee that he will be saved." Unless, then, we impute folly to God, and affirm that there is nothing in the word predestinaion, we must admit that God must foreordain before He foreknows, and that He knows everything just because He has forearranged everything according to His own infinite wisdom and grace.

These are two arguments which appear to me quite conclusive. But let us turn to Scripture. I need not again direct your attention to the passages which were quoted in the previous letters. I shall rather notice one or two on which I have not yet dwelt. Acts 2:23: "Him being delivered by the DETERMINATE COUNSEL and foreknowledge of God, ye have taken, and by wicked hands have crucified and slain." Acts 4:27: "Of a truth against Thy holy child Jesus, both Herod and Pontius Pilate, with the Gentiles and the people of Israel, were gathered together for to do whatsoever THY HAND AND THY COUNSEL DETERMINED BEFORE to be done." On these passages I offer a few remarks:—

1. The language is very explicit and plain. It is the strongest that could possibly have been used to denote foreordination. There is nothing about it ambiguous or hard to be understood. To take it in any other sense would be absurd. The doctrine may be inscrutable, but the words are plain. And is the nature of the doctrine a reason for our refusing to take the words of God in their natural and simple sense?

2. Admitting *our* views of foreordination to be true, could they have been expressed in language different from this, or from that employed in the Epistle to the Romans and Ephesians? Had we been left to choose our words for setting forth our views, we could not have desired any other than these. Can our opponents say the same? Are these words the most natural and appropriate for expressing *their* views?

3. This determinate counsel is said to have fixed certain events in Christ's history. Now, if some were fixed, we have reason to conclude that all others also were. Yet in the life and death of Christ we see nothing, but what seemed outwardly to occur in the natural order of events. It will certainly be conceded that the will of the Son of God was *free* from first to last. Yet we learn that what He *voluntarily* did and suffered was also pre-determined by God. In His case there was entire free-will, yet entire pre-ordination. What, then, becomes of the objection to predestination, arising from its supposed interference with the free-will of moral agents? In Christ's life and death we have a series of pre-ordained events, and at the same time a series of free actions. And this is a sufficient answer to the current objection. We may not be able to reconcile these things, yet there they stand palpably before us.

4. This determinate counsel is said to have delivered up Christ into the hands of men. Pilate and Herod, etc., are said to have done what God's hand and counsel had pre-determined. Here is something still more striking. The deeds of these wicked men are said to have come to pass according to this counsel, yet these deeds are not less wicked, and those men are not less responsible. Here, again, we have another objection answered, or at least silenced. To reconcile these things may be difficult, yet the statement in this passage is plain. What pride and folly, then, are there in the questions and cavils which we so often hear in connection with this doctrine. "If God has arranged everything, man's will is not free. How can the sinner be responsible? How can he be plied with motives and arguments? Of what use is it to do anything towards an end, if all be arranged beforehand by another? How unjust is it in God to warn and invite sinners, when He has fixed everything already?" All these cavils have their answer in the passages quoted above. It is vain to think of putting questions such as these, till those strong and explicit declarations have been explained away or denied. They teach us plainly that our world's history, in all things great and small, is a history of events pre-ordained by God from eternity, yet at the same time coming to pass by the free agency of man. This preordination is the effect and the expression of God's will, yet it does not in the least interfere with man's responsibility; nor does it suppose any violence done to the will of man.

It was *certain* that the ten tribes were to revolt, for it was predicted long before; but did that make their revolt less voluntary? It was *certain* that Israel was to apostatise, and to be carried away into Babylon, but did that make their apostasy less voluntary or less sinful, or Nebuchadnezzar's act of carrying them captive less free? It was *certain* that Christ was to be born at Bethlehem, but did that make the coming of His parents to that town less voluntary? It was *certain* that Judas was to betray Christ, for it had been predicted by David in the Psalms long before, but did that lessen the sin of Judas, or make his act less free? In the same way I might go over every prophecy in Scripture, and ask the same question. And I wonder greatly what the answer of our opponents would be. How can *they* reconcile with *their* ideas of free agency the fact that the sin of Judas was predicted by the Holy Spirit, as certain, one thousand years before it came to pass? Was Judas a mere machine, or was God the author of his sin?

But it will be said, Are we not told that this election or pre-destination is according to foreknowledge? (1 Peter 1:2; Rom. 8:29). In reference to the first two of these passages, I would remark that the word "foreknowledge," in the second verse in the original, is the same as that rendered "fore-ordained" in the twentieth. Now, in the latter of these (20th), there can be no doubt that it means pre-ordination, for it refers to Christ as the appointed Lamb; and if so, then it is impossible to suppose that the word foreknowledge, in the 2nd, refers simply to foreseeing, and nothing more.

But then we are asked to look at Rom. 8:29, "Whom He did foreknow He also did predestinate to be conformed to the image of His Son." The word "foreknow" means not simply to know beforehand, but to "fix the choice upon." The meaning of the passage is then evidently, whom God set His choice upon, them He predestinated to be conformed to the image of His Son. These saints were the objects of His eternal choice, and being so, they were appointed by Him to the honour of being made in the image of His own Son.

But on this I shall not dwell farther. I wish to notice some concessions of our adversaries which appear to me to overthrow their whole system. They admit that in certain things there is a real election. They admit, for instance, that there was a real election of the tribe of Levi to the priesthood, and a real election of David to the throne. They admit also that there is a real election of particular nations to particular privileges and favours.

This admission is fatal to their theory. Their main prop was, that the election of individuals was just another word for favouritism and injustice. Now, if the election of persons be unjust, that of nations must be more unjust. If the one be inconsistent with man's responsibility, so must be the other. If the election of persons shows an undue partiality, much more must the election of nations. For God to reveal Himself to the Jews and not to the Egyptians, is as much favouritism as for Him to convert one soul, and not to convert another. He did far more for Israel than He did for any other nation. He brought them near Him. He gave them His Word. He taught them the way of forgiveness through the blood of the sacrifice. He placed them in circumstances of peculiar advantage. He did not do this for Babylon or Nineveh, to Assyria or Egypt. Can it be wrong, then, to choose individuals, and right to choose nations? Can it be wrong *not* to choose an individual to salvation, and yet not to choose a nation to those privileges through which alone salvation comes? Can it be right to pass by some nations, and yet wrong to pass by individuals? Nations are composed of individuals, and to choose a nation is *to give individuals in that nation a peculiar advantage which is denied to others,* an advantage which issues in the eternal life of thousands. And hence, if there be any injustice in the matter, there is more injustice in a national election than in a personal one. It will be said, God knew what nations would reject His message, and therefore He did not send it to them. On this I offer the following remarks:—

1. A nation being composed of individuals, our opponents must maintain that God foresaw that *every soul* in these would reject the truth. If not, would it not be hard, upon their theory, for God to withhold the Gospel from the whole nations, if He knew that *some* in these nations would have believed and been saved?

2. If these nations were denied the Gospel, because God foreknew they would reject it, then they are condemned for a thing which they never did, but which God merely foresaw they would do. Whole nations are treated as criminals, rejecters of the Gospel, when the opportunity was never given them either to receive or reject it. I am not aware of anything in Calvinism so hard or unjust as this. We teach that God punishes men and nations on account of what they *actually do,* not on account of what He foresees they would do if He allowed them the means. This theory, on the other hand, teaches that

whole nations are condemned to that most fearful of all curses, a deprivation of the Gospel, not on account of their actual sins, but because certain things were foreseen which they would have done! Now, if God can justly condemn nations on account of sin *not committed,* but merely foreseen as likely to be committed, why may He not condemn sinners to eternal death for sins never committed, but only foreseen? Would this be just? Strange that men should maintain the justice of depriving nations of the Gospel for sins which they never committed, yet affirm the injustice of God choosing a soul to everlasting life, according to His sovereign will. But this is just one of the paradoxes of Arminianism. God chooses some to life, it is said, because He foresees they will believe, and He does not choose others because He foresees they will not believe. So that it is not faith that saves us, but God's foresight of our faith; nor is it actually unbelief that ruins us, but God's foresight of our unbelief.

3. God speaks of sending His messages to some who would reject, and of not sending it to others who were more likely to have received it. Ezek. 3:5, 6. "Son of man, go get thee unto the house of Israel, and speak with My words unto them. For thou art not sent to a people of a strange speech, and of an hard language, but to the house of Israel; not to many people of a strange speech, and of an hard language, whose words thou canst not understand. *Surely had I sent thee to them they would have harkened unto thee."* This surely settles the matter. It is not a nation's foreseen willingness to hear that leads God to send His messengers, nor a nation's foreseen unwillingness that prevents Him from sending these. It is all according to His own sovereign will and purpose.

It is affirmed that there is a work *equally* in the hearts of all men alike: that God has done, and is doing, the very utmost that can be done for every individual of our race; and that to maintain anything else is to charge God with partiality and injustice, as well as to deny the responsibility of man. The proof adduced in support of these statements is a passage in the fifth chapter of Isaiah, "What could have been done more to My vineyard that I have not done to it?" But it is remarkable that this is one of the strongest proofs that God did a great deal more for Israel than He did for any other nation. He allowed the whole world to remain a wilderness, but He made them His vineyard. He fenced this vineyard, He gathered out the stones thereof, and planted it with the choicest vine. "He dealt not so with any other nation." Was this partiality or injustice? Or was this doing the same thing for all?

Besides, it is evident that this passage is perverted. It does not mean that God at that time had done all He could for Israel. For He went on to do much more for them. Not only did He not cease to bless them, but He multiplied His blessings, and increased His strivings with them, long after He had uttered the words referred to. So that the passage cannot mean that He had done *all* He could; for He proceeded to do a great deal more, raising up prophet after prohpet, giving them line upon line. Nay, many of the most gracious words that Israel ever heard were spoken after this time. If, then, the verse does really mean that God had actually done His utmost, the inference which is founded upon it falls to pieces.

It is plain, then, that God does more for some nations than for others. He did more for Israel than He did for Egypt or Babylon. He did more for Israel at one time than at another, for one generation than another—nay, for one district of Judea than another—nay, for one individual than another. What else is the meaning of the words of Jesus? "I tell you of a truth, many widows were in Israel in the days of Elias; but unto none of them was Elias sent, save unto Sarepta, a city of Sidon, unto a woman that was a widow. And many lepers were in Israel in the time of Eliseus the prophet, and none of them was cleansed saving Naaman the Syrian" (Luke 4:25). Will any of the deniers of God's sovereignty furnish a solution of this passage in accordance with their views? On their principles, what can the Lord mean?

It is not true, then, that God does more for one nation, or for one individual, than another. The opposite of this is, and has always been, the *fact*—a fact frequently referred to in Scripture, as a proof of God's right to do according to His will in the armies of heaven and among the inhabitants of the earth. No reasonings of men can alter the fact; nor can any ingenuity deprive that fact of its deep and solemn meaning. I may perhaps be told that the cause of this inequality is in the Church of Christ, which has not done its duty. Had Christians, it is said, acted aright, the world would have been converted long ere this. As this is a common way of attempting to solve the difficulty, it may be well to answer it fully.

1. Who told them that the cause is wholly in the church? Who told them that the

world would have been converted before this had Christians been what they professed? Give me one single passage of Scripture that states this. Surely it is a bold and hazardous assertion to make, without one verse of Scripture to support it.

2. It is not true. What! Is such a mighty and majestic event as the salvation of the world to be dependent upon a creature's will? Is it to depend upon *man* whether the world is to be converted or not? Has God no purpose to be carried out? Has He nothing at all to say in the matter? Is He to stand by looking on, wondering whether it may please His people to put forth their energies and convert the world?

3. It is unscriptural. There are passages of Scripture which explicity contradict it. What, for instance, does God mean, when, speaking of Corinth, and giving a reason why He enjoined Paul to remain and labour there, He said, "I have much people in this city?" Again, what is meant by that similar passage, "As many as were ordained to eternal life believed?" Again, what did our Lord mean, when, as if explaining the reason why so many rejected Him, He said, "Many are called, but few are chosen?" Or what did He mean when He said, "This Gospel of the Kingdom must be preached among all nations FOR A WITNESS, and then shall the end come?" And, lastly, what did the Holy Spirit mean, first by forbidding the apostles to preach the Word in Asia, and then by prohibiting Paul from passing over and preaching the Gospel in Bithynia? (Acts 16:6, 7).

4. It is profane. It is saying that the wickedness of the world cannot be remedied by God, but only by the church; that God has no power to convert the world; that it is the church which has all the power; and that unless she pleases to put forth her might and zeal, God can do nothing for the world. Poor world! This is sad news indeed! Thy destiny hangs upon the power and love of thy fellow-sinners! The strength and love of thy God are nothing, and can do nothing for thee! Miserable comfort, and miserable comforters, indeed! Yet these are the men who speak so much of the love of God, and accuse others of hiding or denying it!

Yet I am far from saying that Christians are not much to blame. How little do the most zealous amongst us do for souls! How much more might we do by prayer, by labour, and by holy living! Still, I deny that the inactivity or unbelief of saints will account for the darkness that overspreads the nations. Failure in duty on the part of the people of God may account for many things, but not for all. Did the prophets of old fail in their duty, and was their failure the reason why so few in Israel believed the report, or the reason why Nineveh, or Tyre, or Sidon, were not converted? Was it their fault that they were not sent to these cities, and received no message for them? Why were there so many prophets raised up within that small territory, and not one commissioned to bear tidings to a dark and dying world? Could none be spared? Could no more be raised up? Did they refuse to go? Had God no message of grace to give them for the dark millions of Europe in the west, or Asia in the east, or Ethiopia in the south?

Did the Son of God fail in His duty, in that He did not preach the Gospel save to the lost sheep of the house of Israel? Why did He make this distinction? Why did He never travel beyond the narrow Judean circle? Why did He command His disciples at first to make the same difference, prohibiting them from preaching the Gospel in that city, either of the Gentiles or Samaritans? Might not the Samaritans have said, you tell us that the utmost has been done for us that can be done, and that all are equally dealt with? Why, then, are we passed by? And why are the messengers of peace prohibited from entering our territory? What answer could be given, save that such was the will and purpose of the God only wise?

Did the apostles afterwards fail in their duty, when, after Pentecost, they went abroad to proclaim the everlasting Gospel? Was their failure the reason why the world was not then converted? Are we not plainly taught that such was not the case? Why was it, for instance, that when Paul wished to go to Bithynia to preach the Gospel there, the Spirit suffered him not? Was this doing the utmost for Bithynia that God could do? Nay, it was not even doing the utmost that Paul could have done, and wanted to do. If the Spirit work in all, then it is plain that the reason why He succeeds in some and fails in others must either be the one or the other of the following:—

1. It might be because some have naturally better hearts than others, more inclined towards what is good, made of less rebellious, and more *believing, materials.* This better class of sinners, less stout-hearted than others, yield and obey, and so are saved! The rest, being more stubborn and ungodly, hold out and are lost! What hope does this give to the chief of sinners? Where in all this is there the plucking of brands from the burning?

2. Because the Spirit has attempted a work beyond His power. He fails in His efforts. The sinner has overpowered Him, and proved stronger than He. The sinner is able to overcome the Spirit; but the Spirit is not able to overcome the sinner. The Spirit has done His utmost, and failed.

But, finally, to say that the Spirit is doing all He can possibly do for the sinner is either a mere quibble, a play upon words, or else is most melancholy profanity. If it means that literally and truly OMNIPOTENCE *has* been tasked to its utmost, and failed in the attempt to convert a sinner, it is profanity; for it is saying that the creature is mightier than the Creator, and able to withstand, nay, to overcome, Omnipotence. If, however, this is not what is meant, then what else can be the meaning, but that God is doing *all that He sees fit to do* for each individual? He is putting forth in each the utmost degree of power that His infinite wisdom sees fit. And if this be all that is intended, then there is no dispute between us. We are at one. For what is this but merely another way of stating Jehovah's absolute and all-wise sovereignty in giving or withholding His blessings?

"What shall we say then? Is there unrighteousness with God? God forbid. For He saith to Moses, I will have mercy on whom I will have mercy, and I will have compassion on whom I will have compassion. So then it is not of him that willeth, not of him that runneth, but of God that showeth mercy. For the Scripture saith unto Pharoah, even for this same purpose have I raised thee up, that I might show My power in thee, and that My name might be declared in all the earth. Therefore hath He mercy on whom He will have mercy, and whom He will He hardeneth. Thou wilt say then unto Me, why doeth he yet find fault? For who hath resisted His will? Nay, but, O man, who art thou that repliest against God? Shall the thing formed say to Him that formed it, why hast Thou made me thus? Hath not the potter power over the clay, of the same lump, to make one vessel unto honour, and another unto dishonour? What if God, willing to show His wrath, and to make His power known, endured with much long-suffering the vessels of wrath fitted to destruction; and that He might make known the riches of His glory on the vessels of mercy, which He hath afore prepared unto glory, even us, whom He hath called, not of the Jew only, but also of the Gentiles?" (Rom. 9:16-24).

—H. BONAR, 1850.

GALATIANS 5: 16.

"This I say then, walk in the Spirit, and ye shall not fulfil the lusts of the flesh."

This is the only effectual remedy against living in malice and envy, and against the indulgence of all other lusts of the flesh and of the mind, to which we are naturally so prone. Walk in the Spirit, under the influence of the Spirit, which all believers have of God. The Spirit is to the Christian what air is to the natural man. Mankind are born of corruptible seed, and the moment they are born they begin to breathe the air, a constant supply of which is essential to the continuance of natural life. Believers are begotten with the Word of truth and the supply of the Spirit communicated by the Great Head of the Church to all members of His mystical body, is not less essential for the preservation of spiritual life. There is, however, a material point of difference; breathing the air is a process which constantly goes forward without any attention on our part. We may by exertion stop our breath for a moment, but no exertion is necessary in order to breathe. However we are occupied, however out attention is engrossed, the process of breathing is uninterrupted. But the supply of the Spirit is received by looking to Jesus, and although the attention of the believer is often diverted from the stedfast contemplation of His glory, we are commanded to set the Lord always before us; whether we eat or drink, or whatsoever we do, to do all in the name of the Lord Jesus, and to be on our guard against at any time losing sight of this our guiding star. We are enjoined to maintain habitual communion with the Father, and with His Son Jesus Christ. This is walking in the Spirit, and is the only security against believers fulfilling the lusts of the flesh. We have observed that Adam and Christ, the old and new man, still live in the believer. They are directly opposed to each other; the one exciting us to love the world and the things of the world, the other leading us to seek those things which are above, where Christ sitteth at the right hand of God. The Christian life resembles the contest of Israel and Amalek. When Moses held up his hands Israel prevailed, and when he let them down Amalek prevailed. The hands of our Great Intercessor are never heavy, like those of Moses, but we are apt to lose sight of our entire dependence on Him through Whom alone we are able to hold our ground against the devil, the world, and the flesh.

Herein is love, not that we loved God, but that He loved us, and He did so for the same reason that He loved Israel of old; because, says Moses, "the Lord loved you" (Deut. 7:8). God loved the true Israel with an everlasting love. He made a covenant with His chosen; He swore unto David His servant, "Thy seed will I establish forever, and build up thy throne to all generations." His children are blessed with all spiritual blessings in heavenly places in Christ, according as He hath chosen them in Him before the foundation of the world, that they might be holy and without blame before Him in love. In this covenant of peace between the Father and the Son, which stands immovable, provision is made for the counteraction of the natural perverseness of believers. "If His children forsake My law, and walk not in My judgments; if they break My statutes, and keep not My commandments; then will I visit their transgression with the rod, and their iniquity with stripes. Nevertheless, My loving-kindness will I not utterly take from him, nor suffer My faithfulness to fail. My covenant will I not break, nor alter the thing that is gone out of My lips. Once have I sworn by My holiness, that I will not lie unto David. His seed shall endure forever, and his throne as the sun before Me" (Psa. 89:30-36).

In the Word of God, and more especially in the apostolic epistles, in which revelation is completed, the privileges of the people of God, their security and duty, are all exhibited in the fullest and clearest manner. In human writings, we too often find an undue attachment to particular parts of truth. Some delight to dwell on the eternal and irrevocable determination of God to bestow on His people the kingdom prepared for them before the foundation of the world; and to avoid whatever may have the remotest appearance of interfering with this, and rendering its accomplishment problematical, they slur over the solemn warnings and exhortations so frequently given to believers to steadfastness and perseverance. While a still greater number, under the conviction of our proneness to sloth and worldly mindedness, and turning the grace of God into lasciviousness, are ever urging the cautious and precepts against drawing back, and frequently endeavour to dilute and weaken those passages which so clearly make known the security of the people of God. The former method of treating Divine truth tends to Antinomianism, the latter, to a legal and self-righteous spirit, and it is hard to say which is the more pernicious. Both are denounced in the Scriptures of truth; we read of some who promise their followers liberty, while themselves are the servants of corruption. Against this error our natural conscience testifies, and, unless we are given up to a reprobate mind, we feel that it proceeds from the prince of darkness. But while here he appears in his own shape, he is hardly less dangerous when, transformed into an angel of light, he urges us to self-confidence, to trust in our watchfulness and helplessness, and that all our springs are not in Christ. Although fallen man is without strength, he is ever disposed to recur to the works of the law for acceptance with God: and although he may acknowledge that he has no hope of obtaining the favour of God by his own works, yet he frequently appears to expect the help of Christ through his own diligence and attention, or, as the Apostle says, "as it were by the works of the law."

Not a few seem to halt between two opinions. When discoursing from a passage which treats of the grace of God, they appear to understand the truth, and ascribe all to the distinguishing favour of God. If, on the other hand, they are illustrating what is termed a practical subject, they appear in a great measure to lose sight of the Gospel. Their object seems to be to lead men to expect salvation by their diligence and attention to duty. Hence a practical subject is a better criterion of a preacher's acquaintance with the truth than what is commonly called a doctrinal subject. From the imperfection of our knowledge, we are in danger of leaning either to the one side or the other, and hence the necessity of believers, and more especially preachers, looking to Him Who said, "My grace is sufficient for thee, My strength is made perfect in weakness," that the words of their mouth, and the meditation of their heart, may be acceptable in the Lord's sight, and may minister grace to the hearers. Even an inspired Apostle exclaims, "Who is sufficient for these things?" This question is unanswerable; there was One, and *but* One, Who could say, "We speak what we know, and testify what we have seen." *He* was fully acquainted with truth in all its bearings and relations, but every one who is called to show to his fellow-men the way of salvation may say, "Our sufficiency is of God."

As there is no schism in the human body, and the most perfect harmony exists in every part, so it is with every part of truth in its doctrines and precepts. The latter spring from the former, as the fruit from the tree; every tree produces its own peculiar fruit. Were the nature of the tree changed, there would be a corresponding change in the quality of the fruit; and not less certainly do erroneous views of the Gospel affect our practice. Hence the importance of contending earnestly for the faith once delivered to the saints, and holding fast to the truth in its purity. It is, indeed, certain that holiness and circumspection of conduct do not always correspond with the apparent accuracy of our views of the Gospel, but the truth is the great means of sanctification, it is the mould into which the believer is cast; and, therefore, we may rest assured that the man who is most conformed to the perfect example of our Lord Jesus has the clearest perception of the truth, although, from inferiority of intellect or utterance, he may express himself in a less clear and perspicious manner than another who is really his inferior.

Here we may advert to the difference between legal or moral, and evangelical preaching. It does not consist in one denying and the other maintaining that salvation is through Christ. Both admit that it is so; nor does it consist in the one dwelling on the importance of good works, while the other makes light of them; both insist that they are essential to the Christian character. The difference consists in the moral preacher representing good works as the *cause,* while the evangelical preacher affirms they are the *effect* of salvation. As it is written, "He shall save His people from their sins." He blesses them by turning away every one of them from their iniquities.

—J. A. HALDANE, 1848.

THE LAW AND THE SAINT

"And Moses made an end of speaking all these words to all Israel: And he said unto them, Set your hearts unto all the words which I testify among you this day: which ye shall command your children to observe to do, all the words of this law. For it is not a vain thing for you; because it is *your life*: and through this thing ye shall prolong your days in the land, whither ye go over Jordan to possess it" (Deut. 32:45-47).

In the Word of God the common law has two great principles which characterise and regulate it: first, what is *right in itself,* and secondly, what is *good for man.* Those are the two great principles of common law. They are recognised, both of them, in the Holy Scriptures. For instance, when Moses spoke to the people and gave them God's statutes and commandments, what did he say when he bade them obey? What was the great motive which he put before them? He said, "For it is *your life*": that is to say, "This body of commandments is based upon a deeper principle. It is not simply an expression of God's will, but back of God's will is God's love, God's benevolence, God's kindness to men. He wants to promote man's true life; to make every man like a tree planted by the rivers of water, rooting itself down where the sources of moisture lie, reaching up and spreading itself out towards the heavens, the sunshine, the atmosphere, the dew, and the rain, and bearing abundant fruit. And so He gave this law, not to satisfy the arbitrary will of a great tyranical Governor, but to satisfy the loving and the longing heart of a father toward his children—it is for your life. It is the best thing for you to keep the commandments of almighty God."

And then Paul says, in the 6th chapter of Ephesians, "Children, obey your parents in the Lord, for *this is right.*" There you have the other principle of common law—what is *right* in itself, as well as what is *best* for the subject. Those are the principles on which all common law is based; and if there be any statute law in any truly great nation which can be shown to interfere with common law, any statute law that can be proven to be not right in itself, or not best for the interest of the people, the intelligence and virtue of the nation would be prompt to abolish that statute.

Now, what about the *sanctions* of law? We need these sanctions, as appears so soon as we understand their purpose and object. What are sanctions? They are what sustain law. They are twofold: the reward of righteousness, and the punishment of disobedience. Both are equally necessary law and government; and they are equally beautiful and lovely and desirable in themselves, and both of them reflect equal glory upon God as Governor.

This should be said with emphasis, because most people do not see matters in this light. They turn toward the *love* of God, but turn away from His *wrath.* Men justify His rewards, but feel an aversion as to His penalties. They seem to think that rewards make God attractive, but that punishments make Him repulsive! We like to talk about His mercy, but we do not like to talk about His judgments. But mercy and judgment are *equally beautiful* in God, equally necessary to God, equally essential to His law. Suppose you build an arch. You put under it two massive pillars. Each pillar is equally necessary to support the arch. If you take away the right-hand pillar, the arch comes down, as surely as when you take away the left-hand pillar. Now, reward for righteousness and punishment for sin are the two colossal pillars which the arch of God's law spans, and upon which His government rests; and both are necessary to support that arch, upon which is built the whole structure of the government of God without His moral universe; and, if you take away the retribution of evil you as surely break down that government, and overthrow the arch, as though you took away the rewards of righteousness. Christian disciples ought, therefore, to learn to magnify the sanctions of almighty God.

It is sometimes said that the Old Testament is vindictive, but the New Testament is merciful. *I utterly deny the distinction.* The Old Testament is full of mercy and full of wrath, and the New Testament is full of mercy and full of wrath; and when God said to His ancient people that, if they would obey, they should be prosperous even in temporal things, He simply meant to make temporal prosperity the type or the prophecy of spiritual prosperity, as much as to say, "It is impossible to serve God without getting the smile and the favour of God; and it is impossible to sin against Him without receiving punishment and retribution for sin." What would be thought of a Judge who, having the power of life and death, should show himself favourable, lenient, indulgent, to offenders who resisted the whole power and authority of the law? No such Judge would be allowed to disgrace, on the Bench, any enlightened, law-abiding community. We all know perfectly well that it is the man who, in the execution of law, will show absolutely no favour, who will acquit the innocent and condemn the guilty, who helps to preserve the whole fabric of society from overthrow and ruin. And it is the glory of God that He is not insipidly and irresolutely amiable. His love is not at the expense of His justice. His mercy is not in conflict with His judgments. The sanctions of reward and penalty unite to hold up His throne, and those sanctions are equally sacred in His eyes, and equally to be maintained. As surely as you obey He will smile upon you; as surely as you disobey He will frown upon you. If you conform to the law of God prosperity will attend you, and if you disobey the law of God adversity will be your portion. God's abhorrence of wrongdoing is as certain as His complaisance toward goodness.—(A. T. Pierson, from a sermon preached in Spurgeon's Tabernacle in 1896.)

PRIDE

Of all the evils of our corrupt nature there is none more connatural and universal than pride: it is the grand wickedness, self-exalting in our own and other's opinion. Though I will not contest what was the first step in that complicated first sin, yet certainly this of pride was one, and a main ingredient in it, that which the unbelief conceived going before, and the disobedience following after, were both servants to; and ever since it sticks still deep in our nature. Augustine says truly, "That which first overcame man is the last thing he overcomes." Some sins, comparatively, may die before us, but this hath life in it, as long as we. It is as the heart of all, the first living, and the last dying; and whereas other sins are fomented by one another this feeds even on virtues and graces as a moth breeds in beautiful garments: it will secretly cleave to the best actions and prey upon them. And, therefore, is there so much need that we continually watch, and fight, and pray against it, and be restless in the pursuit of real and deep humiliation.

—Dr. LEIGHTON, 1748.

JUSTIFICATION.

We are justified by God, the author of it (Rom. 3:26).

We are justified by grace, the spring of it (Rom. 3:24).

We are justified by blood, the ground of it (Rom. 5:9).

We are justified by resurrection, the acknowledgment of it (Rom. 4:25).

We are justified by faith, the principle of it (Rom. 5:1).—(Sound Words, 1877.)

(*Continued from page 121.*)

On March 3 we sailed from San Francisco, making our first stop at Honolulu six days later. Though we suffered a little physical discomfort during the first two days, the Lord mercifully gave us a calm passage to the Hawaiian Islands. We were there eight hours, during which time we had an opportunity to go on shore and get some needed exercise. Honolulu is full of Japanese and Chinese, and from what we saw, very little seems to be done there to give them the Gospel of Christ.

From Honolulu we next sailed to the Samoan Islands, a journey which lasted exactly a week; this took us through the Tropics, but the fresh "trade winds" supplied a refreshing breeze, which made the voyage comfortable and pleasant. One thing which impressed us deeply was the heavens by night. In the Southern Hemisphere the stars appear to be much closer and brighter, and more numerous, too. It made us think of the Psalmist's words, "The heavens declare the glory of God, and the firmament showeth His handiwork." The "southern cross," which is not visible in the Northern Hemisphere, is very beautiful, composed of four stars all by themselves—each of the first magnitude—they are so placed as to give a perfect outline of a cross.

The approach to the Samoan Islands is very pleasant, and we wound in and out between the smaller ones for a couple of hours before docking at Pango Pango. Here is a small U.S.A. Naval Station, where some twenty or thirty American families are located: the rest of the population being made up of natives that are descended from cannibals. Two Mormon Missionaries landed here to propagate their pernicious teachings. The scenery is indescribably grand. From a narrow beach, cliffs rise precipitously to a height of from seven hundred to a thousand feet. They are literally covered with luxuriant vegetation from base to summit: as showers of rain descend there almost daily, everything is beautifully fresh and green. The night before we landed a heathen chief had died, and we witnessed the natives marching to the funeral with palms in their hands, and chanting their weird lamentations as they passed along. While standing by, we wondered how many of them had ever heard "The Word of Life." How thankful we were that it had pleased our gracious God for us to be born in Christian homes.

Leaving Pango Pango on March 16, we began the last stage of our journey, sighting, four hours out, the Isle of Apia, where Robert Louis Stevenson lies buried. The weather was warm, though not unduly hot, as we crossed the equator. There we lost one whole day, jumping from Wednesday to Friday. On the Friday evening a sad incident happened which reminded us that "in the midst of life we are in death"; a fellow-passenger being washed overboard that evening through a sudden lurch of the vessel. She was an ardent "Christian Scientist," and without a moment's warning was swept out of time into eternity. Oh, the vital importance of being prepared!

As we neared Australia the sea was rougher than at any other part of the voyage, due to the vernal equinox. The last two days we encountered high winds, the vessel pitched and tossed badly, it being so rough that the doctors and customs officers were unable to come on board until we were almost at the dock; but He who rules the waves and has given to the sea His decree brought us safely to Sydney on the morning of March twenty-four, after being on the ocean twenty-one days. Thus did our faithful God richly supply us with journeying mercies and bring us to our desired haven. May He here use us to His glory in the edifying of His saints. "Brethren, pray for us!"

ARTHUR W. PINK,
5 Norton Street,
Ashfield, N.S.W.
Australia.

P.S. April 22.

Most graciously has God wrought for us here, in giving us favour in the eyes of His people and in opening many doors of ministry. We are already reluctantly obliged to refuse numbers of invitations, being booked up for several months ahead. There has been very little Bible teaching here in Australia, but there has been much prayer on the part of numbers that the Lord would supply this felt need. Everywhere we have been there are many really hungry for spiritual food. We fully expect a joyous season of Heaven-sent blessing.

VOL. IV JULY, 1925 NO. 7.

STUDIES IN THE SCRIPTURES

"Search the Scriptures" John 5:39.

Arthur W. Pink, Publisher and Editor,
5 Norton Street, Ashfield, N.S.W., Australia.

Price: 10 cents per copy; $1.00 or 5/- per year.

The Guarded Lips.

"Set a watch, O Lord, before my mouth; keep the door of my lips."—*Psa.* 141:3.

Though we are provided with two eyes and two ears we have only one tongue, as if to show that we ought to see and hear twice as much as we say. It is also significant that the tongue is protected by the teeth, and these in turn by the lips, as an indication to us that this loose and unruly member needs to be held in by bit and reins. Well for us if we heeded these physiological hints which nature supplies. But sad to say, we do not. "The tongue can no man tame; it is an unruly evil, full of deadly poison" (Jas. 3:8).

The Holy Spirit has warned us that, "In the multitude of words there wanteth not sin; but he that refraineth his lips is wise" (Pro. 10:19). Again, "The tongue of the wise useth words aright; but the mouth of fools poureth out foolishness" (Pro. 15:2). Once more, "In all labour there is profit; but the talk of the lips tendeth only to penury" (Pro. 14:23). Hence, one of the New Testament admonitions is, "Wherefore, my beloved brethren, let every man be swift to hear, slow to speak, slow to wrath" (James 1:19).

In view of the above scriptures, what need has each of us to make David's prayer his own, and cry unto God, "Set a watch, O Lord, before my mouth: Keep the door of my lips"! Upon this Dr. Pierson said, "Our tongues hang loosely, and swing easily: without our knowledge of it. We are betrayed into hasty and wicked words. Hence the need of a Divine sentinal to keep watch, to demand of each word that would go forth the countersign of its right to leave us, the proof that it is not an enemy to betray, but a servant of God and man to fulfil some holy mission. It is also to be remembered that while warriors, and others, who go out from a gate return through the same gate, no words ever go back into the city of Mansoul. When once they leave those gates it is forever, whether to exercise some good work, or to wander hither and thither as messengers of evil.

"The question now arises, What is God's sentinel, stationed at the lips to challenge our words? It is *conscience*, especially illuminated by the Word of God, and taught by the Holy Spirit. Conscience may demand the evidence of a Divine sanction whether words go forth as traitors to our own good and conspirators against others. How quick is their passage to the ears of others, and how soon they prove hostile. and lead others to evil doing, reacting also upon our purity and peace!"

The power of speech is a noble gift and a merciful privilege. It is one of the things which sets man high above the animals. There is no comparison between the chatter of the ape and the prattle of the parrot and the articulated language of man. By means of speech we express our thoughts and make known our wants. By means of speech we may tell sinners of the Saviour and edify and comfort saints of God. Speech is a Divine gift, and as such ought to be consecrated to God's glory. But how few have thought of dedicating their tongues to God?

But while it is a blessed gift, it is also a grave responsibility, for it is not only capable of producing much good, but also of working incalculable harm. It

(*Continued on page 168*).

IMPORTANT NOTICES

Set of twelve issues for **1922**, unbound, **$1.00** or **5/-**. Bound **$1.50** or **7/-**.

Set of twelve issues for **1923**, unbound, **$1.00** or **5/-**. Bound **$1.50** or **7/-**.

Set of twelve issues for **1924**, unbound, **$1.00** or **5/-**. Bound **$1.50** or **7/-**.

Note: We cannot break a set or now supply any single 1924 issues.

Subscription Price: **$1.00** or **5/-** per year to any address in the world.

Change of Address: Please notify me promptly of any change of address, and be certain to give both old and new address.

Non-subscribers receiving this Magazine regularly will understand their subscription has been entered by a friend.

Copies lost in the mail duplicated only if we are notified promptly.

Entered as second-class matter January 15th, 1923 at the post office at York, Pa., under Act of March 3rd, 1879.

CONTENTS

THE GOSPEL OF JOHN

43. *Christ sought by Gentiles*: *John* 12:20-36.

The following is a suggested analysis of the passage which is to be before us:—

1. The desire of the Greeks to see Jesus, vv. 20-23.
2. Christ's response, vv. 24-26.
3. Christ's prayer and the Father's answer, vv. 27, 28.
4. The peoples' dulness, vv. 29, 30.
5. Christ's prediction, vv. 31-33.
6. The peoples' query, v. 34.
7. Christ's warning, vv. 35, 36.

The end of our Lord's public ministry had almost been reached. Less than a week remained till He should be crucified. But before He lays down His life, His varied glories must be witnessed to. In John 11 we have seen a remarkable proof that He was the *Son of God*: evidenced by Him raising Lazarus. Next, we beheld a signal acknowledgement of Him as *the Son of David*: testified to by the jubilant Hozanna's of the multitudes as the King of Israel rode into Jerusalem. What is before us now concerns Him more especially as *the Son of Man*. As the Son of David He is related only to Israel, but His Son-of-Man title brings in a wider connection. It is as "the Son of Man" He comes to the Ancient of days, and as such there is "given Him dominion and glory, and a kingdom, that *all* people, nations, and languages, should serve Him" (Dan. 7:14). In perfect keeping with this, our present passage shows us Gentiles seeking Him, saying, "We would see," not "the Christ," but *"Jesus."* Thus the Father saw to it that His blessed Son should receive this threefold witness ere He suffered the ignominy of the cross.

It is both instructive and blessed to trace the *links* which unite passage to passage. There is an intimate connection between this third section of John 12 and what has preceded it. Again and again in the course of these expositions we have called attention to the *progressive unfolding* of truth in this Gospel, and here, too, we would observe, briefly, the striking *order* followed by Christ in His several references to His own death and resurrection. In John 10 the Lord Jesus is before us as the Shepherd, leading God's elect out of Jerusalem and bringing them into the place of liberty, and in order to this He *lays down His life* that He may possess these sheep (vv. 11, 15, 17, 18). In John 11 He is seen as the Resurrection and the Life, as *the Conqueror of death*, with power in Himself to raise His own—a decided advance on the subject of the previous chapter. But in John 12 He speaks of Himself as "The Corn of wheat" that falls into the ground and dies, that it may bear "much fruit." This speaks both of *union and communion*, blessedly illustrated in the first section of the chapter, where we have the happy gathering at Bethany *supping* with him.

If the Lord Jesus is to be to others the "Resurrection" and the "Life," we now learn what this involved *for Him*. He should be glorified by being the Firstborn among many brethren. But how? Through death: "Except a Corn of wheat fall into the ground and *die*, it abideth *alone*: but if it die, it bringeth forth much fruit" (v. 24). Life could not come to us but through His death; resurrection-life out of death accomplished. *Except* a man be born again he cannot enter the Kingdom of God; and *except* Christ had died none could be born again. The new birth is the impartation of a new life, and that life none other than the life of a resurrected Saviour, a life which has passed through death, and, therefore, for ever *beyond* the reach of judgment. "The gift of God is eternal life *in* Jesus Christ our Lord" (Rom. 6:23 Greek).

Some have experienced a difficulty here: If the Divine life in the believer is the life of the *risen* Christ, then what of the Old Testament saints? But the difficulty is more fanciful than real. It is equally true that there could be *no salvation* for any one, no putting away of sins, until the great Sacrifice had been offered to God. But surely none will infer from this that no one *was* saved before the Cross. The fact is that both life and salvation flowed *backwards* as well as forwards from the cross and the empty sepulchre. It is a significant thing, however, that nowhere in the O.T. are we expressly told of believers then possessing "eternal life," and no doubt the reason for this is stated in 2 Tim. 1:10, "But is now made manifest by the appearing of our Saviour Jesus Christ, Who hath abolished death, and *hath brought* life and immortality *to light* through the Gospel."

It is very striking to observe that our Lord did not speak of the union and communion of believers with Himself until the *Gentiles* here sought him. It is a higher truth altogether than any which He ever addressed to Israel. His Messiahship resulted from a fleshly relationship, the being "Son of David," and it is on *this* ground that He will yet sit upon the throne of His father David and "reign over the house of Jacob" (Luke 1:32, 33). But this was not the goal before Him when He came to earth the first time: to bring a people to His own place in the glory was the set purpose of His heart (John, 14:2, 3). But a heavenly people must be related to Him by something higher than fleshly ties: they must be joined to Him in spirit, and this is possible only on the resurrection side of death. Hence that word, "Wherefore henceforth know we no man after the flesh: yea, though we have known Christ *after the flesh,* yet now henceforth know we Him no more (2 Cor. 5:16). It is the One Who has been "lifted up" (*above* this earth) who now draws *all*—elect Gentiles as well as Jews—unto Himself.

"And there were certain Greeks among them that came up to worship at the feast: The same came therefore to Phillip, which was of Bethsaida of Galilee, and desired him, saying, Sir, we would see Jesus" (vv. 20, 21). This is very striking. The rejection of Christ by Israel was soon to be publicly evidenced by them delivering Him up to the Romans. As Daniel had announced centuries before, after sixty-nine weeks "shall Messiah be cut off" (9:26). Following His rejection by the Jews, God would visit the Gentiles to take out of them a people for His name" (Acts 15:14). This is what was here foreshadowed by "the Greeks" supplicating Him. The *connection* is very striking: in v. 19 we find the envious Pharisees saying, "The *world* is gone after Him," here, "*And* . . . . . certain *Greeks* . . . . saying, We would see Jesus." It was a "first-fruit," as it were, of a coming harvest. It was the pledge of the "gathering together into one the children of God that were scattered abroad" (11:52). It was another evidence of the fields being "white already to harvest" (4:35). These "Greeks" pointed in the direction of those other "sheep" which the Good Shepherd must also bring. It is also significant to note that just as Gentiles (the wise men from the East) had sought Him soon after His birth, so now these "Greeks" came to Him shortly before His death.

Exactly who these "Greeks" were we cannot say for certain. But there are two things which incline us to think that very likely they were Syro-Phenicians. First, in Mark 7:26, we are told that the woman who came to Christ on behalf of her obscessed daughter, was "a *Greek,* a Syro-Phenician by nation." Second, the fact that these men sought out *Phillip,* of whom it is expressly said that he "was of Bethsaida of Galilee," a city on the borders of Syro-Phenicia. The fact that Phillip sought the counsel of *Andrew,* who also came from Bethsaida in Galilee (see 1:44), and who would therefore be the one most likely to know most about these neighbouring people, provides further confirmation. That these "Greeks" were not idolatrous heathen is evidenced by the fact that they "came up to *worship* at the feast," the verb showing they were in the habit of so doing!

These "Greeks" took a lowly place. They "desired" Philip: the Greek word is variously rendered "asked," "besought," "prayed." They supplicated Philip, making known their wish and asking it if were possible to have it granted; saying, "Sir, we would see Jesus," or more literally, "Jesus, we desire to see." At the very time the leaders of Israel sought to *kill*

Him, the Greeks desired to *see* Him. This was the first voice from the outside world which gave a hint of the awakening consciousness that Jesus was about to be the Saviour of the Gentiles as well as the Jews. Of old it had been said, "And the *Desire* of all nations shall come" (Hag. 2:7). That it was more than an idle curiosity which prompted these Greeks we cannot doubt, for if it were only a physical sight of Him which they desired, that could have been easily obtained as He passed in and out of the Temple or along the streets of Jerusalem, without them interviewing Philip. It was a *personal* and *intimate* acquaintance with Him that their souls craved. The form in which they stated their request was prophetically significant. It was not "We would *hear* Him," or "We desire to witness one of His mighty works," but "We would *see Jesus.*" It is so to-day. He is no longer here in the flesh: He can no longer be handled or heard. But He *can* be *seen,* seen by the eye of faith!

"Philip cometh and telleth Andrew" (v. 22). At first sight this may strike us as strange. Why did not Philip go at once and present this request of the Greeks to the Saviour? Is his tardiness to be attributed to a lack of love for souls? We do not think so. The first reference to him in this Gospel pictures a man of true evangelical zeal. No sooner did Philip become a follower of Christ than he "*Findeth* Nathanael, and saith unto him, We have found Him, of Whom Moses in the law, and the prophets, did write, Jesus of Nazareth" (1:45). How, then, shall we account for his now seeking out Andrew instead of the Lord? Does not Matt. 10:5 help us? When Christ had sent forth the Twelve on their first preaching tour, He expressly commanded them, "*Go not into* the way of the *Gentiles,* and into any city of the Samaritans enter ye not." Furthermore, the disciples had heard Him say to the Canaanitish woman, "I am not sent but unto the lost sheep of the house of Israel" (Matt. 15:24). Most probably it was because these definite statements were in Phillip's mind that he now sought out Andrew and asked his advice.

"And again, Andrew and Philip tell Jesus" (v. 22). In the light of what has just been before us, how are we to explain this action of the two disciples? Why did they not go to the "Greeks" and politely tell them that it was impossible to grant their request? Why not have said plainly to them, Jesus is the Messiah of Israel, and has no dealings with the Gentiles? We believe that what had happened just before had made a deep impression upon the apostles. The Saviour mounting the ass, the acclamations of the multitudes which He had accepted without a protest, His auspicious entrance into Jerusalem, His cleansing of the Temple immediately afterwards (Matt. 21:12, 13), no doubt raised their hopes to the highest point. Was the hour of His ardently desired exaltation really at hand? *Would* "the *world*" now go after Him (John 12:19) in very truth? Was this request of the "Greeks" a further indication that He was about to take the Kingdom and be "a light to lighten the Gentiles" as well as "the Glory of His people Israel." In all probability *these* were the very thoughts which filled the minds of Andrew and Philip as they came and told Jesus.

"And Jesus answered them, saying, the hour is come, that the Son of Man should be glorified" (v. 23). Now, for the first time, the Lord declared that His "hour" had come. At Cana He had said to His Mother, "Mine hour is not yet come" (2:5), and about the midst His public ministry we read, "No man laid hands on Him because His hour was not yet come" (7:30). But here He announced that His hour *had* arrived. the hour when He, as Son of Man, could be "glorified." But what is here meant by Him being "glorified?" We believe there is a double reference. In view of the connection here. the occasion when the Lord Jesus uttered these words, their first meaning evidently was: the time has arrived when the Son of Man should be glorified by receiving the worshipful homage of the Gentiles. He intimated that the hour was ripe for the blessing of all the families of the earth through Abraham's seed. But, linking this verse with the one that immediately follows, it is equally clear that He referred to His approaching death. To His followers, the Cross must appear as the lowest depths of humiliation, but the Saviour regarded it (also) as His glorification. John 13:30, 31 fully bears this out: "He then having received the sop, went immediately out: and it was night, *therefore,* when he was gone out, Jesus said, *Now* is the Son of Man *glorified, and God is glorified in Him.*" The two things are intimately related: salvation could not come to the Gentiles except through His death.

It is by no means easy to determine to whom Christ uttered these words. We strongly incline to the view that they were said to the disciples. The record is silent as to whether or not the Lord here granted these "Greeks" an interview; that is, whether He left the Temple enclosure where He then was and went into the outer court, beyond which Gentiles were not permitted to pass. Personally, we think, everything considered, it is most unlikely that He suffered them to enter His presence. If the wish of these "Greeks" was not granted, it would teach them that salvation was not through His perfect life or His wondrous works, but by faith in Him as the *crucified* One. They must be taught to look upon Him not as the Messiah of Israel, but as "the Lamb of God which taketh away the sin of *the world*."

"Verily, verily, I say unto you, except a corn of wheat fall into the ground and die, it abideth alone: but if it die, it bringeth forth much fruit" (v. 24). Very different were the thoughts of Christ from those which, most probably, filled the minds of His disciples on this occasion. He looked, no doubt, to the distant future, but He also contemplated the near future. Death lay in His path, and this engaged His attention at the very time when His disciples were most jubilant and hopeful. There must be the suffering before the glory: the Cross before the Crown. Outwardly all was ready for His earthly glory. The multitudes had proclaimed Him King; the Romans were silent, offering no opposition (a thing most remarkable); the Greeks sought Him. But the Saviour knew that before He could set up His royal kingdom He must first accomplish the work of God. None could be with Him in glory except He died.

"Except a corn of wheat fall into the ground and die, it abideth alone, but if it die, it bringeth forth much fruit." "Nature is summoned here to show the law of increase which is stamped upon her; and that creative law is made an argument for the necessity of the death that is before Him. What an exaltation of the analogies in Nature to exhibit and use them in such a way as this! And what a means of interpreting Nature itself is here given us! How it shows that Christ, ignored by the so-called "natural" theology, is the true key to the interpretation of Nature, and that the Cross is stamped ineffacably upon it! Nature is thus invested with the robe of a primeval prophet, and that the Word, Who is God, is the Creator of all things, becomes not merely the announcement of Scripture, but a plainly demonstrated fact before our eyes to-day.

"The grain of wheat falls into the ground and dies: it has life in it, and carries it with it through death itself. The death which it undergoes is in the interest even of the life, which it sets free from its encasement—from the limitations which hedge it in—to lay hold of and assimilate the surrounding material, by which it expands into the plant which is its resurrection, and thus at last into the many grains which are its resurrection-fruit. How plain it is that this is no accidental likeness which the Lord here seizes for illustration of His point. It is as real a prediction as ever came from the lips of an Old Testament prophet: every seed sown in the ground to produce a harvest is a positive prediction that the Giver of life must die. The union of Christ with men is not in incarnation, though that, of course, was a necessary step towards it. But the blessed man, so come into the world, was a new, a Second Man, who could not unite with the old race, and the life was the light of men; but if that were all, the history would be summed up in the words that follow: 'And the light shineth in darkness and the darkness comprehend it not. He was in the world . . . . and the world knew Him not.' To the dead life must be communicated that there may be eyes to see. Men can only be born again into the family of God, of which the Son of God as Man is the beginning.

"Yet the life cannot simply communicate the life. Around Him are the bands of eternal righteousness, which has pronounced condemnation upon the guilty, and only by the satisfaction of righteousness in the penalty incurred can these bands be removed. Death—death as He endured it—alone can set Him free from these limitations: He is '*straitened* till it be accomplished.' In resurrection He is enlarged and becomes the Head of a new creation; and 'if any man be in Christ, it is new creation' (2 Cor. 5:17). In those redeemed by His blood the tree of life has come to its precious fruitage" (Numerical Bible).

"He that loveth his life shall lose it; and he that hateth his life in this world shall keep it unto life eternal" (v. 25). First of all, this was a word of warning for the beloved disciples. They had just witnessed the palms of victory waving in His path: soon they should see Him numbered with the transgressors. The echoes of the people's "Hozanna's" were still sounding in their ears: in four days' time they should hear them cry, "Crucify Him." Then they would enter into the fellowship of His sufferings. But these things must not move them. They must not, any more than He, count their life dear unto them. He warns them against selfishness, against cowardice, against shrinking from a martyr's cross. But the principle here is of wider application.

There is no link of connection between the natural man and God. In the Man Christ Jesus there *was* a life which was in perfect harmony with God, but because of the condition of those He came to save. He must lay it down. And He has left us an example that we should follow His steps. If we would save our natural life, we must lay it down: the one who loves his life in this world must necessarily lose it, for it is *"alienated"* from God; but if by the grace of God a man *separates himself in heart* from that which is at enmity with God (James 4:4), and devotes all his energies to God, then shall he have it again in the eternal state.

"If any man serve Me, let him follow Me; and where I am there shall also My servant be: if any man shall serve Me, him shall My Father honour (v. 26). If the previous verse was a *warning* to the disciples, this was spoken for their *encouragement.* "Each grain of wheat that is found on the parent stem follows of necessity by the law of its own nature the pattern of the grain from which it came. His people, too, must be prepared to follow Him upon the road on which He was going. Here is the rule, here is the reward of service: to be with Christ where He is, is such reward as love itself would seek, crowned with the honour which the Father puts upon such loving service. The way of attainment is by the path which He has trodden, and what that was, in its general character at least, is unmistakably plain" (Mr. F. W. Grant).

"Now is My soul troubled; and what shall I say?" (v. 27). That was the beginning of the Saviour's travail ere the new creation could be born. He was siezed by an affrighting apprehension of that dying of which He had just spoken. His holy soul was moved to its very depths by the horror of that coming "hour." It was the prelude to Gethsemane. It reveals to us something of His inward sufferings. His anguish was extreme; His heart was suffering torture—horror, grief, dejection, are all included in the word "troubled." And what occasioned this? The insults and sufferings which He was to receive at the hands of men? The wounding of His heel by the Serpent? No, indeed. It was the prospect of being "made a *curse* for us," of suffering the righteous wrath of a sin-hating God. "What shall I say?" he asks, *not* "What shall I *choose?"* There was no wavering in purpose, no indecision of will. Though His holy nature shrank from being "made sin," it only marked His perfections to ask that *such* a cup might pass from him. Nevertheless, He bowed, unhesitatingly, to the Father's will, saying, "But for this cause came I unto this hour." The bitter cup was accepted.

"Father, glorify Thy Name" (v. 28). Christ had just looked death, in all its awfulness, as the wages of sin, fully in the face, and He had bowed to it, and that, that the Father might be glorified. This it was which was ever before Him. Prompt was the Father's response. *"Then* came there a voice from heaven, saying, I have both glorified, and will glorify again" (v. 28). The Son of God had been glorified at the grave of Lazarus as Quickener of the dead, and now He is glorified as Son of man by this voice from heaven. But there is more than this here: the Father uses the future tense—"I *will* glorify again." This He would do in bringing again from the dead our Lord Jesus, that great Shepherd of the sheep: "raised up from the dead by *the glory* of the Father" (Rom. 6:4).

The people, therefore, that stood by and heard, said that it thundered: others said, an angel spake to Him" (v. 29). What a proof was this that the natural man is incapable of entering into Divine things. A similiar instance is furnished in the Lord speaking from heaven to Saul of Tarsus at the time of his conversion. In Acts 9:4 we read that a voice spoke unto him, saying, "Saul, Saul, why persecutest thou Me?" In 22:9 we are told by Paul, "They that were with me saw indeed the light, and were afraid; but they heard not the voice of Him that spake to me." They perceived not what He said. As the Saviour had declared on a former occasion, "Why do ye not understand My speech? Even because you cannot hear My word" (John 8:43). How the failure of these Jews to recognise the Father's voice emphasised the absolute necessity of the Cross!

"Jesus answered, and said, This voice came not because of Me, but for your sakes" (v. 30). Three times the Father spoke audibly unto the Son: at the beginning, in the middle, and at the end of His Messianic career, and in each case it was in view of His *death.* At the Jordan Christ went down, symbolically, into the place of death; on the Holy Mount Moses and Elijah had talked with Him "of His decease" (Luke 9:31); and here, Christ had just announced that His "hour" was at hand. It is also to be observed that the first time the Father's voice was heard was at Christ's consecration to His *prophetic* office; the second time it was in connection with His forthcoming decease, His *priestly* work, the offering Himself as a

Sacrifice for sin; here, it followed right on His being hailed as *King,* and who was about to be invested (though in mockery) with all the insignia of royalty, and wear His title, "The *King* of the Jews," even upon the Cross itself. Mark also the *increasing publicity* of these three audible speakings of the Father. The first was heard, we believe, only by John the Baptist; the second by three of His disciples; but the third by those who thronged the Temple. "For your sakes": to strengthen the faith of the disciples; to remove all excuse from unbelievers.

"Now is the judgment of this world" (v. 31). How this brings out the importance and the value of the great work which He was about to do! In this and the following verse three consequences of His death are stated. First, the world was "judged": its crises had come: its probation was over: its doom was sealed by the casting forth of the Son of God. Henceforth, God would save His people *from* the world. Second, the world's Prince here received his sentence, though its complete execution is yet future. Third, God's elect would be drawn by irrisistible power to the One whom the world rejected.

"Now shall the Prince of this world be cast out" (v. 31). The tense of the verb here denotes that the "casting out" of Satan would be as *gradual* as the "drawing in the next verse (Alford). The Lord here anticipates His victory, and points out the way in which it should be accomplished: a way that would have never entered into the heart of men to conceive, for it should be by shame and pain and death; a way that *seemed* an actual triumph for the Enemy. Not only was life to come out of death, but victory out of apparent defeat. The Saviour crucified is, *in fact,* the Saviour glorified!

"Now shall the Prince of this world be *cast out.*" As pointed out above, the casting out of Satan was to be a gradual process. In the light of this verse, and other passages (e.g., Heb. 2:14, 15), we believe that Satan's hold over this world was broken at the Cross. The apostle tells us that Christ "spoiled principalities and powers, having made a show of them openly; triumphing over them" (Col. 2:15), and this statement, be it noted, is linked with His Cross! We believe, then, the first stage in the "casting out" of Satan occurred at the Cross, the next will be when he is *"cast out"* of heaven into the earth (Rev. 12:10); the next, when he is *"cast into* the Bottomless Pit" (Rev. 20:3); the final when he is *"cast into* the lake of Fire and Brimstone (Rev. 20:10).

"And I, if I be lifted up from the earth, will draw all unto Me. This He said, signifying what death He should die" (vv. 32, 33). A truly wonderful and precious word is this. It is Christ's own declaration concerning His death and resurrection. "I, if I be lifted up from the earth" referred to His crucification; but *"will* draw all unto Me" look to the resurrection-side of the Cross, for a *dead* Saviour could "draw" nobody. Yet the two things are most intimately connected. It is not simply that Christ is the magnet; it is the crucified Christ. "It is crucifixion which has imparted to Him His attractive power; just as it is death which has given Him His life-giving power. It is not Christ without the Cross; nor is it the Cross without Christ; it is both of them together" (H. Bonar). And wherein lies the attraction? *"Because of the love which it embodies.* Herein is love—the love that passeth knowledge! What so magnetic as love? *Because of the righteousness which it exhibits.* It is the cross of righteousness. It is righteousness combining with love taking the sinner's side against law and judgment. How attractive is righteousness like this! *Because of the truth which it proclaims.* All God's truth is connected with the Cross. Divine wisdom is concentrated there. How can it but be magnetic? *Because of the reconciliation which it publishes.* It proclaims peace to the sinner, for it has made peace. Here is the meeting-place between men and God" (Ibid).

But what is meant by "I will draw?" Ah, notice the sentence does not end there! "I will draw all *unto Me."* The word "men" is not in the original. The "all' plainly refers to all of *God's elect.* The scope of the word "all" here is precisely the same as in 6:45—"And they shall be *all* taught of God." It is the same "all" as that which the Father has given to Christ (6:37). "The promise, 'I will draw all unto Me,' must, I think, mean that our Lord after His crucifixion would draw men of all nations and kindreds and tongues to Himself, to believe in Him and be His disciples. Once crucified, He would become a great centre of attraction, and draw to Himself; releasing from the Devil's usurped power, vast multitudes of all peoples and countries, to be His servants and followers. Up to this time all the world had blindly hastened after Satan and followed him. After Christ's crucifixion great numbers would turn away from the power of Satan and become Christians (Bishop Rule). Christ's design was to show that His grace would not be confined to Israel.

The Greek word here used for "draw" is a very striking one. Its first occurrence is in John 6:44, "No man can come to Me, except the Father which hath sent Me *draw* him." Here it is the power of God overcomnig the enmity of the carnal mind. It occurs again in 18:10, "Then Simon Peter having a sword *drew* it, and smote the high priest's servant." Here the term signifies that Peter *laid firm hold of* his sword and *pulled it out* of its sheath. It is found again in 21:6, 11, "Simon Peter went up and *drew* the net to land full of great fishes." Here it signifies the putting forth of strength so as to *drag* an inanimate and heavy object. It is used (in a slightly different form) in James 2:6, "Do not rich men oppress you and *draw* you before the judgment seats?" Here it has reference to the *impelling* of *unwilling* subjects. From its usage in the New Testament we are therefore obliged to understand Christ here intimated that, following His crucifixion, He would put forth an invincible power so as to effectually draw unto Himself all of God's elect, which His omniscient foresight then saw scattered among the Gentiles A very striking example of the Divine drawing-power is found in Judges, 4:7, "And *I will draw* unto thee to the river Kishon, Sisera, the captain of Jabin's army, with his chariots and his multitude; and I will deliver him into thine hands." In like manner Christ draws us unto Himself.

"Thus it is His heart relieves itself. The glory of God, the overthrow of evil, the redemption and reconciliation of men is to be accomplished by that, the cost of which is to be for Him so much. He weighs the gain against the purchase-price for him, and is content" (Mr. Grant).

"The people answered Him, We have heard out of the Law that Christ abideth for ever: and how sayest Thou, the Son of man must be lifted up? Who is this Son of man?" (v. 34). It seems exceedingly strange that men acquainted with the Old Testament should have been stumbled when their Messiah announced that He must die. Isaiah 53, Daniel's prophecy that He should be "cut off" (9:26), and that solemn word through Zechariah, "Awake, O sword, against My Shepherd, and against the Man that is My Fellow, saith the Lord of hosts: smite the Shepherd" (13:7), should have shown them that His exaltation could be only after His sufferings.

"Then Jesus said unto them, Yet a little while is the Light with you. Walk while ye have the light, lest darkness come upon you: for he that walketh in darkness knoweth not wither he goeth" (v. 35). His questioners, most probably, in their malignant self-conceit, flattered themselves that they had completely puzzled Him. But He next spoke as though He had not heard their cavil. They were not seeking the truth, and He knew it. Instead of answering directly, He therefore gave them a solemn warning, reminding them that only for a short space longer would they enjoy the great privilege then theirs, and stating what would be the inevitable consequence if they continued to despise it.

"While ye have light, believe in the Light, that ye may be the children of Light. These things spake Jesus and departed, and did hide Himself from them" (v. 36). "Christ had spoken. Introduced at the commencement of the Gospel as the Light of men (1:4), He had proclaimed Himself to be the Light of the world, that whosoever should follow Him should not walk in darkness, but have the light of life (8:12). He had also said that, as long as He was in the world, He was the light of it (9:5). Soon would the Light be withdrawn, His death being near at hand. Is there not, then, something awfully solemn in these few words of our chapter (vv. 35, 36). He had preached among them. He had wrought miracles among them. He had kept, too, in His ministry to the land which God had promised to Abraham. He had never ministered outside of it. The people in it had enjoyed opportunities granted to none others. What, now, was the result, as His public ministry was thus terminating? 'He departed, and did hide Himself from them.' Who of them all mourned over His departure? or sought where to find Him" (Mr. C. E. Stuart).

In closing, let us admire the typical picture which is sketched for us here. The first section of John 12 views, dispensationally, the godly Remnant in the Tribulation period. The second anticipates the beginning of the Millennium. Our present passage foreshadows that which shall be a common occurrence during the Millennium, namely, the Gentiles seeking Israel's Messiah. Note the following particulars:—

1. The connecting link: v. 20 opens with the word "And," joining it to what we are told in v. 19—"The *world* is gone after Him!" 2. Those who now sought Christ: "Greeks"—Gentiles (v. 20). How striking to note that it was when Christ had presented Himself as *King* to Israel that the Gentiles sought Him! 3. Their business: They came to Jerusalem "to worship at the Feast—" And it shall come to pass, that every one that is left of *all the nations* which came against Jerusalem shall

even go up from year to year *to worship the King,* the Lord of hosts, and to keep *the Feast* of Tabernacles" (Zech. 14:16). The time when these Greeks sought Christ was the Feast of the Passover. But mark how the Holy Spirit here simply says that they "came up to worship at *the Feast,*" and striking is it to note here the "*palm* branches" which are especially associated with the Feast *of Tabernacles* (see Lev. 23:40). 4. Behold their mode of procedure: these Greeks did not go direct to Christ, but first sought His disciples. So will it be in the Millennium: "In those days it shall come to pass, that ten men shall take hold out of all languages of the nations, even shall take hold of the skirt of Him that is *a Jew,* saying, *We* will go with *you*: for we have heard that God is with you" (Zech. 8:23). 5. Consider their desire: it was to *"see Jesus."* This will be the magnet which will draw Gentiles to Jerusalem during the Millennium, as Zech. 8:23 shows us—"We have heard that *God* is with you." 6. How striking are Christ's words here: "The hour is come, that the Son of man should be *glorified"* (v. 23). In the Millennium the Son of man will sit upon the throne of His *glory* (Matt. 25:31). 7. Mark the prophecy Christ uttered on this occasion: "Except a corm of wheat fall into the ground and die, it abideth alone: but if it die, it bringeth forth *much* fruit" (v. 4). The ultimate fulfilment of this will appear during the Millennium!

Study the following questions on our next lesson:—

1. What is the central design of this passage, 12:36-50?
2. Why is Isa. 53 quoted here, v. 38?
3. Why was it "they could not believe" v. 39?
4. Whose "glory" is referred to in v. 41?
5. Had those mentioned in v. 42 *saving* faith?
6. When and where did Jesus say what is found in vv. 44-50?
7. What is the "commandment" of vv. 49, 50?

—*Arthur W. Pink.*

GLEANINGS IN EXODUS

19. Israel crossing the Red Sea: Ex. 14.

In this lesson we are to have for our consideration one of the most remarkable miracles recorded in the O.T., certainly the most remarkable in connection with the history of Israel. From this point onwards, whenever the servants of God would remind the people of the Lord's power and greatness, reference is almost always made to what He wrought for them at the Red Sea. Eight hundred years afterwards the Lord says through Isaiah, "I am the Lord thy God, that divided the sea, whose waves roared; the Lord of hosts in His name" (Isa. 51:15). Nahum announced, "The Lord hath His way in the whirlwind and in the storm, and the clouds are the dust of His feet. He rebuketh the sea, and *maketh it dry."* (Nahum 1:3, 4). When the Lord renewed His promise to Israel, He takes them back to this time and says, "According to the days of thy coming *out of the land of Egypt* will I show unto him marvellous things" (Mich. 7:15 and cf. Joshua 24:6, 7: Neh. 9:9; Psl. 106:7, 8; Jer. 31:35, etc.). It was *this* notable event which made such a great impression upon the enemies of the Lord: "For we have *heard* how the Lord dried up the water of the Red Sea for you, when ye came out of Egypt; and what ye did unto the two kings of the Amorites, that were on the other side Jordan, Sihon and Og, whom ye utterly destroyed, and as soon as we have heard these things, *our hearts did melt,* neither did there remain any more courage in any man because of you; for the Lord your God, He is God in heaven above, and in earth beneath" (Josh. 2:10, 11).

The miracle of the Red Sea occupies a similar place in the O.T. scriptures as the *resurrection* of the Lord Jesus does in the New; it is appealed to as a standard of measurement, as the supreme demonstration of God's power (cf. Eph. 1:19, etc.). Little wonder, then, that each generation of infidels has directed special attacks against *this* miracle. But to the Christian, miracles occasion no difficulty. The great difference between faith and unbelief is that one brings in God, the other shuts Him out. With *God* all things are possible. Bring in God and supernatural displays of power are to be expected.

Before we consider the miracle of the parting of the Red Sea, we must first give a brief notice to what preceded it. Exodus 14 opens by telling us, "And the Lord spake unto Moses, saying, Speak unto the children of Israel that they turn and encamp before Pi-hahiroth, between Migdol and the sea, over against Baalzephon; before it shall ye encamp by the sea" (vv. 1, 2). In this word God commanded Israel to turn off from the route they were following, and encamp before the Red Sea. Many attempts have been made to ascertain the precise location, but after such a lapse of time and the changes incident upon the passing of the centuries it seems a futile effort. The third verse tells us all that it is necessary for us to know, and the information it supplies is far more accurate and reliable than any human geographies Israel were "shut in by the wilderness," and the Red Sea stretched before them. Thus Israel were so placed that there was no human way of escape. In the mountain fastnesses they might have had a chance; but surrounded by the wilderness, it was useless to flee before the cavalry and chariots of Egypt.

"Speak unto the children of Israel, that they turn and encamp before Pihahiroth, between Migdol and the sea, over against Baal-zephon; before it shall ye encamp by the sea" (14:2). Here, as everywhere in Scripture, these names are full of meaning. They are in striking accord with what follows. "Pi-hahiroth" is rendered by Ritchie "Place of Liberty." Such indeed it proved to be, for it was here that Israel were finally delivered from those who had long held them in cruel bondage. "Migdol" signifies "a tower" or "fortress." Such did Jehovah demonstrate Himself to be unto His helpless and attacked people. Newberry gives "Lord of the North" as the meaning of "Baal-zephon," and in Scripture the "north" is frequently associated with *judgment* (cf. Joshua 8:11, 13; Isa. 14:31; Jer. 1:14, 4:6; 6:1; Eze. 1:4, etc.). It was as the Lord of Judgment that Jehovah was here seen at the Red Sea.

"For Pharaoh will say of the children of Israel, They are entangled in the land, the wilderness hath shut them in" (14:3). How this brings out the inveteracy of unbeleif! How it demonstrates the folly of human reasoning! Granting that Israel *were* "entangled in the land," that they *were* "shut in" by the wilderness, that they *were* trapped before the Red Sea, did Pharaoh suppose that they would fall easy victims before his onslaught? What of Israel's God? Had He not already shown Himself strong on their behalf? Had He not already shown Egypt that those who persecuted His covenant people "touched the apple of His eye" (Zech. 2:8)! What a fool man is? How he disregards every warning? How determined he is to destroy himself? So it was here with Pharaoh and his army. Notwithstanding the ten plagues which had swept his land, he now marches out against Jehovah's redeemed to consume them in the wilderness.

"And I will harden Pharaoh's heart, that he shall follow after them; and I will be honoured upon Pharaoh, and upon all his hosts; that the Egyptians may know that I am the Lord. And they did so" (14:4). Here was God's reason for commanding Israel to "encamp by the sea." "Terrible as Egypt's chastisements had been, something more was still needed to humble her proud king and his arrogant subjects under the felt hand of God, and to remove from Israel all further fear of molestation. There was one part of Egypt's strength, their chief glory, which had so far escaped. Their triumphant army had not been touched. Moses is told that, when Pharaoh's spies carried the tidings to him that the Israelites had gone down by the Egyptian shore, it would seem to the king that his hour for vengeance had come. A force advancing rapidly upon the rear of the Israelites would block their only way of escape, and so the helpless multitude would be at his mercy" (Urquhart).

"And it was told the king of Egypt that the people fled; and the heart of Pharaoh and of his servants was turned against the people, and they said, Why have we done this, that we have left Israel go from serving us? And he made ready his chariot, and took his people with him; and he took six hundred chosen chariots, and all the chariots of Egypt, and captains over every one of them. And the Lord hardened the heart of Pharaoh, king of Egypt, and he pursued after the children of Israel; and the children of Israel went out with an high hand But the Egyptians pursued after them, all the horses and chariots of Pharaoh and his horsemen and his army, and overtook them encamping by the sea, beside Pi-hahiroth, before Baal-Zephon" (vv. 5-9). All happened as God had foretold. Pharaoh and his courtiers became suddenly alive to their folly in having permitted Israel to go, and now a splendid opportunity seems to be afforded them to retrieve their error. The army is summoned in hot haste, Pharaoh and his nobles arm and mount their chariots. The famous cavalry of Egypt sally forth with all their glory. Not only the king, but his servants also, the very ones who had entreated him to let Israel go (10:7), are urgent that Israel should be pursued and captured. The judgments of God being no more upon their land, and recollecting the great service the Hebrews had rendered them, the advantages of having them for slaves, and the loss sustained by parting with them, they are now anxious to recover them as speedily as possible.

"And when Pharaoh drew nigh, the children of Israel lifted up their eyes and behold the Egyptians marched after them; and they were sore afraid; and the children of Israel cried out unto the Lord. And they said unto Moses, because there were no graves in Egypt hast thou taken us away to die in the wilderness? Wherefore hast thou dealt with us, to carry us forth out of Egypt? Is not this the word that we did tell thee in Egypt, saying, Let us alone, that we may serve the Egyptians? For it had been better for us to serve the Egyptians, than that we should die in the wilderness" (vv. 10-12). This was a sore trial of faith, and sadly did Israel fail in the hour of testing. Alas! that this should so often be the case with us. After all God had done on their behalf in Egypt, they surely had good reason to trust in Him now. After such wondrous displays of Divine power, and after their own gracious deliverance from the Angel of Death, their present fear and despair were inexcusable. But how like ourselves! Our memories are so short. No matter how many times the Lord has delivered us in the past, no matter how signally His power has been exerted on our behalf, when some new trial comes upon us we forget God's previous interventions, and are swallowed up by the greatness of our present emergency.

"And when Pharaoh drew nigh, the children of Israel lifted up their eyes, and, behold, the Egyptians marched after them. (v. 10). Their eyes were upon the Egyptians, and in consequence they were 'sore afraid.' It is always thus. The only cure for fear is for the eye to remain steadfastly fixed on the Lord. To be occupied with our circumstances and surroundings is fatal to our peace. It was so in the case of Peter as he started to walk on the waters to Christ. While he kept his gaze upon the Lord he was safe; but as soon as he became occupied with the winds and the waves, he began to sink.

"And they were sore afraid; and the children of Israel cried out unto the Lord" (v. 10). Had they prayed unto God in this their distress for help and assistance, protection and preservation, with a holy yet humble confidence in Him, their crying had been right and laudable; but it is clear from the next two verses that theirs was the cry of complaint and despair, rather than of faith and hope. It closely resembles the attitude and action of the disciples in the storm-tossed ship as they awoke the Master and said, "Carest Thou not that we perish?" How solemn it is to see that such unbelief, such despair, such murmuring, can proceed from the people of God! How the realisation that *we* have the same evil hearts within us should humble us before Him.

"And they said unto Moses, Because there were no graves in Egypt, hast thou taken us away to die in the wilderness? wherefore hast thou dealt thus with us to carry us out of Egypt?" (v. 11). How absurd are the reasonings of unbelief! If death at the hands of the Egyptians was to be their lot, why had Jehovah delivered them from the land of bondage? The fact that He had led them out of Egypt was evidence enough that He was not going to allow them to fall before their enemies. Besides, the Lord had promised they should worship Him in Mount Horeb (3:12). How, then, could they now perish in the wilderness? But where faith is not in exercise, the promises of God bring no comfort and afford no stay to the heart.

Israel had been brought into their present predicament by God Himself. It was the Pillar of Cloud which had led them to where they were now encamped. Important truth for *us* to lay hold of. We must not expect the path of faith to be an easy and smooth one. Faith must be tested, tested severely. But, why? That we may learn the *sufficiency* of our God! That we may prove from experience that He *is* able to supply our every need (Phil. 4:19), make a way of escape from every temptation (1 Cor. 10:13), and do for us exceedingly abundantly above all that we ask or think.

"Is not this the word that we did tell thee in Egypt, saying, Let us alone that we may serve the Egyptians? For it had been better for us to serve the Egyptians than that we should die in the wilderness" (v. 12). Behind the rage of Pharaoh and his hosts who were pursuing the Israelites, we are to see the enmity of Satan against those whom Divine grace has delivered from his toils. It is not until a sinner is saved that the spite of the Devil is directed against him who till recently was his captive. It is now that he goes forth as a roaring lion seeing to devour Christ's lamb. Beautiful it is to see here the utter failure of the enemy's efforts. Now that the Divine righteousness had been satisfied by the blood of the Lamb, it was solely a question between God and the Enemy. Israel had to do no fighting —*God* fought *for* them, and the enemy was utterly defeated. This is one of the outstanding lessons of Ex. 14—"If God be for us who can be against us?"

Vitally important it is for the believer to lay firm hold on this soul-sustaining truth. How often it occurs (exceptions must surely be few in number) that as soon as a sinner has fled to Christ for refuge, Satan at once lets fly his fiery darts. The young believer is tempted now as he never was in his unregenerate days; his mind is filled with evil thoughts and doubts, and he is terrified by the roaring of the "lion," until he wonders who is really going to gain possession of his soul—God or Satan. This was precisely the issue raised here at the Red Sea. It *looked* as though Jehovah had deserted His people. It *seemed* as though they must fall victims to their powerful and merciless foes. But how deceptive are appearances? How quickly and how easily the Lord Almighty reversed the situation? The sequel shows us *all* Israel *safe* on the other side of the

Red Sea, and *all* the Egyptians *drowned* therein! But how was this brought about? Of deep moment is every word that follows.

"And Moses said unto the people, Fear ye not, stand still, and see the salvation of the Lord, which He will show to you to-day; for the Egyptians whom ye have seen to-day, ye shall see them again no more forever" (v. 13). The first word was, "Fear not." The servant of God would quieten their hearts and set them in perfect peace before Him. "Fear not" is one of the great words recurring all through the Scriptures. "Fear not" was what God said to Abraham (Gen. 15:1). "Fear not, neither be thou dismayed" was His message to Joshua (8:1). "Fear not" was His command to Gideon (Judges 16:23). "Fear not" was David's counsel to Solomon (1 Chron. 28:20). This will be the word of the Jewish remnant in a day to come: "Be strong, fear not, behold, your God will come" (Isa. 35:4). "Fear not" was the angel's counsel to Daniel (10:12). "Fear not little flock" is the Lord's message to us (Luke 12:32). "I will fear no evil" said the Psalmist (23:4), "for Thou art with me." But how is this to be attained? *How* is the heart to be established in peace? Does not Isa. 26:3 sum it all up—"Thou wilt keep him in perfect peace whose *mind is stayed in Thee* because He trusteth in Thee."

"Stand still" was the next word of Moses to Israel. All attempts at self-help must end. All activities of the flesh must cease. The workings of nature must be subdued. Here is the right attitude of faith in the presence of a trial—*"stand still."* This is impossible to flesh and blood. All who know, in any measure, the restlessness of the human heart under anticipated trial and difficulty, will be able to form some conception of what is involved in standing still. Nature must be *doing* something. It will rush hither and thither. It would feign have some hand in the matter. And although it may attempt to justify and sanctify its worthless doings, by bestowing upon them the imposing and popular title of " a legtimate use of means," yet are they the plain and positive fruits of unbelief, which always shut out God, and sees nought save every dark cloud of its own creation. Unbelief creates or magnifies difficulties, and then sets us about removing them by our own bustling and fruitless actions, which, in reality, do but raise a dust around us which prevents our seeing God's salvation.

"Faith, on the contrary, raises the soul above the difficulty, straight to God Himself, and enables one to 'stand still.' We gain nothing by our restless and anxious efforts. We cannot make one hair white or black, nor add one cubit to our stature. What could Israel do at the Red Sea! Could they dry it up? Could they level the mountains? Could they annihilate the hosts of Egypt? Impossible! There they were, enclosed within an impenetrable wall of difficulties, in view of which nature could but tremble and feel its own impotency. But this was just the time for God to act. When unbelief is driven from the scene, then God can enter; and in order to get a proper view of His actings, we must 'stand still.' Every movement of nature is, so far as it goes, a positive hindrance to our perception and enjoyment of Divine interference on our behalf" (C.H.M.).

"And see the salvation of the Lord." It is surprising how many have missed the point here. Most of the commentators regard this word as signifying that Israel were to remain passive until the waters of the Red Sea should be cleft asunder. But this is clearly erroneous. Heb. 11:29 tells us that it was "by *faith* they passed through the Red Sea," and faith is the opposite of sight. The mistake arises from jumping to the conclusion that *"see* the salvation of the Lord" refers to *physical* sight. It was *spiritual sight* that Moses referred to, the exercising of the eyes of the heart. Faith is a looking not at the things which are seen, but a *looking* "at the things which are not seen" (2 Cor. 4:18)—strange paradox to the natural man! As we read in Heb. 11:13, "These all died *in faith*, not having received the promises, but having *seen* them afar off." And of Moses we read, "he endured *as seeing* Him who is invisible" (Heb. 11:13)—that is, seeing Him with the eyes of faith. To *"see* the salvation of the Lord" we must first "stand still"—all fleshly activity must cease. We have to be *still* if we would *know* that God *is* God (Psl. 46:10).

"For the Egyptians whom ye have seen to-day, ye shall see them again no more forever. The Lord shall fight for you, and ye shall hold your peace" (vv. 13, 14). Notice the repeated use of the future tense here: "He *will* show you . . . . ye *shall* see them again no more . . . . the Lord *shall* fight for you." How this confirms what we have just said. Jehovah's "salvation" had first to be seen by the eye of faith before it would be seen with the eye of sense. *That* "salvation" must first be revealed to and received by "the hearing of faith." "Which *He will* show you to-day" was the *ground* of their faith. Striking are the closing words of v. 14: "and ye shall hold your peace," or, as some render it, "ye shall keep silence." Six hundred thousand men, besides women and children, were to remain motionless in the profound silence which befitted them in a scene where so unparalleled a drama was to be enacted, moving neither hand, foot, nor tongue! How well calculated was such an order to draw the trembling heart of Israel away from a fatal occupation with its own exigencies to faith in the Lord of hosts!

"And the Lord said unto Moses, Wherefore criest thou unto Me? Speak unto the children of Israel that they go forward" (v. 15). "Go forward" does not contradict, but complements the "stand still." This is ever the spiritual order. We are not ready to "go forward" until we have first "stood still" and *seen* the salvation of the Lord. Moreover, before the *command* was given to "Go forward" there was first the *promise*, "see the salvation of the Lord which *He will* show you today." Faith must be based on the Divine promise, and obedience to the command must spring from the faith thus produced. Before we are ready to "go forward" faith must *see* that which is invisible, namely, the "salvation of the Lord," and this, *before* it is *actually* wrought for us. Thus "by *faith* Abraham went out, not knowing whither he went" (Heb. 11:8).

"But lift thou up thy rod and stretch out thine hand over the sea, and divide it: and the children of Israel shall go on dry ground through the midst of the sea . . . And Moses stretched out his hand over the sea: and the Lord caused the sea to go back by a strong east wind all that night, and made the sea dry land, and the waters were divided. And the children of Israel went into the midst of the sea upon the dry ground; and the waters were a wall unto them on their right hand and on their left hand" (vv. 16:21, 22). The best commentary upon this is Heb. 11:29: "*By faith* they passed through the Red Sea as by dry land." From this it is very clear that the waters of the Red Sea did not begin to divide until the feet of the Israelites came to their very brink, otherwise they would have crossed by sight, and not "by faith." Equally clear is it that the sea was not divided throughout at once. As another has said, "It does not require faith to begin a journey when I can see all the way through; but to begin when I can merely see the first step, this is faith. The sea opened as Israel moved forward, so that every fresh step they needed to be cast upon God. Such was the path along which the redeemed of the Lord moved, under His own directing hand." So it was then; such is the true path of faith now. It is beautiful to observe another word in Hebrews 11:29—"The children of Israel *walked* upon dry land in the midst of the sea." They did not rush through at top speed. There was no confusion. With absolute confidence in the Lord they crossed in orderly procession.

"And the Egyptians pursued, and went in after them to the midst of the sea, even all Pharaoh's horses, his chariots, and his horsemen. And it came to pass, that in the morning watch the Lord looked unto the host of the Egyptians through the pillar of fire and of the cloud, and troubled the host of the Egyptians, and took off their chariot wheels, that they drove them heavily: so that the Egyptians said, Let us flee from the face of Israel; for the Lord fighteth for them against the Egyptians. And the Lord said unto Moses, Stretch out thine hand over the sea, that the waters may come again upon the Egyptians, upon their chariots, and upon their horsemen. And Moses stretched forth his hand over the sea, and the sea returned to his strength when the morning appeared; and the Egyptians fled against it; and the Lord overthrew the Egyptians in the midst of the sea. And the waters returned, and covered the chariots, and the horsemen, and all the host of Pharaoh that came into the sea after them; there remained not so much as one of them" (vv. 23:28). The practical lesson to be learned from this is very plain: Those who attempt to do without faith, what believers succeed to do by faith—those who seek to obtain by their own efforts, what believers obtain by faith—will assuredly fail. By faith, the believer obtains peace with God; but all of the unbeliever's efforts to obtain peace by good works, are doomed to disappointment. Believers are sanctified by the truth (John 17:19); those who aim to arrive at holiness without believing are following a will o' the wisp. In the little space that remains let us summarise some of the many lessons our passage sets forth.

Typically the crossing of the Red Sea speaks of Christ making a way through death for His people. "The Red Sea is the figure of death—the boundary-line of Satan's power" (Ritchie). Note the words of God to Moses: "Lift thou up *thy rod*, and stretch out thine hand over the sea, and divide it; and the children of Israel shall go on dry ground through the midst of the sea" (v. 16). Moses is plainly a type of Christ, the "rod" a symbol of His power and authority. The Red Sea completely destroyed the power of Pharaoh (Satan) over God's people. Heb. 2:14 gives us the antitype—"That *through death* He might destroy him that had the power of death, that is, the Devil." The *effect* of Moses lifting up his rod and stretching forth his hand is blessed to behold—"And the children of Israel went into the midst of the sea upon the dry ground; and *the waters were a wall unto them* on their right hand, and on their left" (v. 22). Not only had that which symbolised *death* no power over Israel, but it was now *a defence* to them! This very sea, which at first they so much feared, became the means of their deliverance from the Egyptians; and instead of proving their enemy became their friend. So if death overtakes the believer before the Lord's return it only serves to bring him into the presence of Christ—"Whether Paul or Apollos, or Cephas, or the world, or life, *or death*, or things present, or things to come; *all are yours*" (1 Cor. 3:22). But deeply solemn is the other side of the picture: "By faith they passed through the Red Sea as by dry land: *which the Egyptians assaying to do, were drowned*," for the natural man to meet death in the power of human confidence is certain destruction.

"Evangelically the crossing of the Red Sea tells of the completeness of our salvation. It is the sequel to the Passover-night, and *both* are needed to give us a full view of what Christ has wrought for us. In Heb. 9:27 we read, "It is appointed unto men once to die, but after this the judgment." For the believer this order is reversed, as it was with his Substitute. It was during the three awful hours of darkness, while He hung on the cross, that the Lord Jesus endured the "judgment" of God against our sins. Having passed through the fires of God's wrath, He then "yielded up the spirit." So in our type. On the Passover-night, we see Israel sheltered by blood from the judgment of God—the avenging angel; here at the Red Sea, we behold them brought safely through the place of death. The order is reversed for the unbeliever. "After death, the judgment" for him.

"Doctrinally the passage through the Red Sea sets forth the believer's union with Christ in His death and resurrection. "I am crucified *with Christ*" (Gal. 2:20), refers to our judicial identification with our Substitute, not to experience. That Israel passed *through* the Red Sea, and emerged safely on the far side, tells of resurrection. So we read in Rom. 6:5, "If we have been planted together in the likeness of His death, we shall be also in the likeness of His resurrection." And again, "When we were dead in sins, hath quickened us together with Christ, and raised us up together" (Eph. 2:5 6).

Practically the deliverance of Israel from the Red Sea illustrates the absolute sufficiency of our God. The believer to-day may be hemmed in on every side. A Red Sea of trial and trouble may confront him. But let him remember that Israel's God is *his* God. When His time comes, it will be an easy matter for Him to cleave a way through for you. Take comfort from His promise: "When thou passeth through the waters, *I will be with thee;* and through the rivers, they shall not overflow thee" (Isa. 43:2). God can protect His people in the greatest difficulties and dangers and make a way of deliverance for them out of the most desperate situations.

Dispensationally the passing of Israel through the Red Sea foreshadows the yet future deliverance and restoration of the Jews. The "sea" is a well-known figure of *the Gentiles* (Psalm 65:7; Daniel 7:2; Revelation 17:15). Among the Gentiles the seed of Abraham have long been scattered, and to the eye of sense it has seemed that they would be utterly swallowed up. But marvellously has God preserved the Jews all through these many centuries. The "sea" *has not* consumed them. They still dwell as "a people apart" (Num. 23:9), and the time is coming when Jehovah will fulfil the promises made to their fathers (Ezek. 20:34; 37:21, etc.). When these promises are fulfilled our type will receive its final accomplishment. Israel shall be brought safely *out of* the "sea" of the Gentiles, into their own land.

—Arthur W. Pink.

TRUTH AND ERROR,

or

Letters to a Friend.

7. The Work of Christ.

"The Church of God which He hath purchased with His own blood."—Acts 20:28.

I do not intend to enter fully upon the subject of Christ's work. This would require a much fuller discussion than I am able at present to bestow upon it. It would in truth require a volume of itself.

I set out with asserting that Christ is said in Scripture to have given Himself as a ransom and substitute for His church, and to have done so in a way such as He has not done for any other beings. This seems implied in the very first promise—the promise regarding the woman's seed. Here we have at the very outset the identifying work of Christ and His people—the setting them before us as entirely *one* with Him. For while it is especially Christ Himself that is the woman's seed, it is doubtless also His church as one with Him. His destinies and theirs are thus from the beginning represented as entirely one. We recognise here not only the Redeemer, but the chosen people, the people given Him of the Father, with whom He identifies Himself, and in whose behalf He is to do and to suffer—to bruise the serpent's head, and to submit to the bruising of His own heel.

It is not merely Christ Who is said to have died. His people are spoken of as dying with Him. Very frequently does the Apostle Paul dwell upon this idea—representing the church as crucified with Christ, dying with Him, rising with Him, ascending up with Him, and sitting with Him in heavenly places. In Jehovah's eye His people were with Him all the time, from His coming into the world. He stood in their stead, and they were viewed as one with Him from His cradle to His cross, and from His cross to His throne. They were taken up to the cross with Him. They died there with Him. They went down to the grave with Him. They came up again along with Him. They ascended up along with Him. Now, I confess I cannot understand these expressions unless I believe in a definite number, for whom all this was specially done. I cannot see how it is possible for the atonement to be *indefinite,* so long as I read that in all its parts the church *was associated with Christ.* This renders *definiteness* an essential element in the idea of redemption.

But how can there be any truth in all this, if Christ had no special object in view in dying, save merely to render salvation possible to all, but certain to none? In that case He could only die as a man for His fellow-men—not as a substitute, not as a representative, not as a surety, not as a shepherd at all. I put it to you, my friend, which of these is most in accordance with the Word of God. Being myself what is called a millennarian, I confess this seems an important view, and weighs very strongly with me; but I am sure that even with others it cannot fail to have its weight.

It is the view which would present itself to the eye looking from the past eternity into the future, contemplating the glorious issue. And it is the view which we hereafter shall, I doubt not, more fully realise when we get into that eternity, and begin to look back upon the whole finished scheme. Viewed from either of these points, the far past or the far future, the thing seems striking and vivid. I confess that, standing as we do in the present in the very midst of the scenes, with the smoke of the world all around us, seeing but through a glass darkly, we may find it more difficult to realise this. But faith can rise out of these dark elements below. It can transport itself to either of these eternal eminences of which I speak; and, looking at things as God looks upon them, contemplating *results* as He does, it will be able to realise God's purpose regarding the church in all the different stages of its progress now, as if it had actually been represented in visible brightness, and the other parts which confuse us hidden from view. The moment when the statuary is hewing out his statue is not the best time to ascertain what he means. You must look at his designs, or you must wait till he has finished his work.

In connection with this, I may appropriately introduce here some of the many passages which present Christ's work as a peculiar one on behalf of His church.

"I am the good shepherd; the good shepherd giveth His life for the sheep."—John 10:11.

"I am the good shepherd, and know My sheep, and am known of Mine."—John 10:14.

"I lay down My life for the sheep."—John 10:15.

"Ye believe not, because ye are not of My sheep."—John 10:26.

"Thou hast given Him power over all flesh, that He should give eternal life to as many as Thou hast given Him."—John 17:2.

"I pray for them, I pray not for the world, but for them whom Thou hast given Me."—John 17:9.

"Husbands, love your wives, even as Christ also loved the church and gave Himself for it.—Eph. 5:25.

In these passages we hear Christ repeatedly speaking of those whom He calls *sheep,* and telling us He gave His life for them—for them in a peculiar sense, as He did for no other. It is as *a shepherd* that He dies with a shepherd's love and a shepherd's care—for His sheep as such. Again, He prays for His own, for those whom the Father has given Him, NOT FOR THE WORLD. Can words be plainer? Here is certainly a distinction made, "I pray not for the world." Here at least is something peculiar for His church alone. And *one* such peculiarity is enough, at least, to answer the objections of adversaries. Is not the way in which He prayed, an illustration of the way in which He died? Are not those for whom He prayed the same as them for whom He died?

But over against all this are set those many passages in which the word *all* occurs, and in which we read, "Christ died for all." Now, with reference to this, I ask your attention to a few remarks. The passages I have already quoted are more explicit, and cannot be overthrown. They are too plain to be mistaken. And if our opponents would take them in their simplicity, I confess I should have less fear with regard to others. But this they refuse to do.

I admit there are difficulties with regard to some of the passages in whcih the word *all* occurs. But I would rather confess the difficulty, and wait for further light, than at once proceed to do violence to the passage itself, or make its difficulty a reason for doing violence to others.

With regard to the meaning of the word "all" in the Bible, especially in the New Testament, a few remarks will be necessary. It occurs there upwards of 1200 times, as any scholar will find by consulting his Greek concordance. These 1200 texts may be subdivided into four classes.

Class I. consists of a very large number of passages, several hundreds, I am sure, in which it is undeniable that the word *cannot* mean literally *all*. I give one or two specimens. We are told in one place (Mark 1:5), "There went out unto Him *all* the land of Judea and they of Jerusalem, and were *all* baptised of Him," etc. This we know was not literally the case. Every individual in the whole land did not come; for we are expressly told in another place (Luke 8:30) that "the Pharisees and lawyers were not baptised of Him." Again we read (Mark 1:37), "All men seek Thee." Literally this was not true. Every individual in the human race, or even every individual in Judea, did not seek Him. Again, we have such passages as these:—"He told me all that ever I did"; "all things are lawful to me"; "all our fathers were under the cloud"; "all they who are in Asia are turned away from me"; "ye know all things."

Class II. consists of passages in which it is very doubtful whether *all* be literally universal. It may or it may not be. There is nothing positively to determine it. "*Every* nation under heaven," Acts 2:5. "*All* they which dwelt in Asia," Acts 19:10. "The care of *all* the churches," 2 Cor. 2:28. "*All* that dwell upon the earth shall worship Him," Rev. 13:8. These are specimens of a very large class of doubtful passages, which, of course, can prove nothing as to the literal meaning of *all*.

Class III. consists of passages which are only determined by the context, not by the expressions themselves. The whole passage, taken together, fixes the literal universality. But were it not for that, the literal meaning would have been doubtful. "All ye are brethren" (Matt. 23:8). "All these things shall come to pass" (Matt. 25:5). "They all slumbered and slept" (Matt. 25:5). "When Jesus had finished all these sayings" (Matt. 26:1). In all these passages, and many similar ones, it is not the word *all* itself that points out the strict universality; it is some other word that occurs along with it, such as "all *these* things"—"all *these* sayings." In these cases, while in one sense the word has a universal sense, in another it has a limited one—limited by the words with which it is connected. It means all of a certain class, all of a certain number. So that we gather from these, that when *all* is to be understood literally, we must learn from the context what "all" it is that is to be understood—whether all of one nation, or all of another—whether all of one class, or all of another. And this consideration answers at once the oft-repeated argument, which consists merely in vociferating the word "all," as if the loudness or the frequency of the outcry were enough to demonstrate the meaning of the word. That meaning must be determined in each separate case by the other words, or parts of the passage.

Class IV. are the passages in question, which are supposed to imply a universal atonement. On these I cannot enter here. They are, in point of numbers, the fewest of all the four classes. Our opponents say that they must be interpreted literally. Let us see how the proof stands.

There are upwards of 1200 passages, in which the word "all" occurs in the New Testament. Of these a very large number cannot possibly mean literally *all*. Another large number are exceedingly doubtful. Another large number are only proved to mean literally "all" by the context. The fewest in number of these four classes are those which are claimed by our opponents! You may judge of the strength of their argument.

The result of this statement is simply this, that the mere occurrence of the word "all" does not determine the question at all. Nothing but a careful examination of the whole passage can settle it. Do not then, I beseech you, be deceived by the loud repetitions of the words *all* and *every* which you hear, and which are intended to supply the place of more solid proof.

I should like to have entered into an examination of some of the passages often rested on. But this is impossible. I select one, as being one of the strongest, and also one that affords an admirable illustration of the necessity of looking at the context to determine the meaning of the word. It is Heb. 2:9. "He tasted death for every man." It is literally "for each"; there is nothing about *men* in the original. The question then arises, what does the apostle mean by "each?" The context must settle it. It either carries us back to the "heirs of salvation," or forward to the "many sons." For obviously it must refer to some of whom the apostle was speaking. Now, he was only speaking of the angels and of the many sons, the heirs of salvation, and of no other. It cannot be meant of the former, and, therefore, it must be of the latter. They may be said to be the peculiar theme of the whole chapter, and anyone following the apostle's reasonings would *naturally* understand this expression to refer to them. It is straining it to refer to any others. If it does refer to others, it might as well refer to angels; more naturally so than to the *world,* for he is speaking of them, but not of the world at all. The fifteenth chapter of 1st Corinthians is an illustration of this. The apostle is treating of the resurrection of the *saints,* and not of the wicked. It is only by keeping this in view that his statements there regarding the "all" can be fully understood. So the *each* here referred to must be the *each* of those he was speaking of. And very strikingly is the singular used here—not simply as individualising the saints, but as doing so in connection with the *whole* work of Christ. *All* that Christ did, He did for each. His *whole* work, His *whole* propitiation, His *whole* tasting of death, belongs to each, just as much as if only one had been saved. The *whole* of what Christ did is the property of each saint. His work is not made up of so many parts, or extending to certain dimensions, greater or smaller according to the number of the saved; so that each of them only gets a *part* of Himself, and a part of His work. No. His work is such that each gets the whole of it—the whole of His glorious self, and the whole of His glorious work. Each gets the benefit of His tasting death, as if endured for himself singly and alone.

But I cannot dwell longer upon this topic. I have merely thrown out a few hints, which may lead to establish you in the faith, and may assist you in repelling the objections of opponents. The real question before us is, was the atonement of Christ a definite or indefinite thing? That is the essence and marrow of the controversy. It is upon this that the case of things hinges. There is a mighty difference between a definite and an indefinite work. Search the Scriptures, and see if the language in which they speak does not necessarily imply something definite and certain—*something which infallibly secured the object for which the Son of God took flesh and died.* That was, you know, "to bring many sons into glory."

THUS SAITH THE LORD.

"For the transgression of My people was He stricken."—Isa. 53:8.

"I am the good Shepherd; the good Shepherd giveth His life for the sheep." —John 10:11.

"As the Father knoweth Me, even so I know the Father; and I lay down My life for the sheep."—John 10:15.

"Ye believe not because ye are not of My sheep."—John 10:26.

"Thou hast given Him power over all flesh, that He might give eternal life to as many as Thou hast given Him."—John 17:3.

"I have manifested Thy name unto the men which Thou gavest Me out of the world."—John 17:9.

"Those that Thou gavest Me have I kept."—John 17:12.

"For their sakes I sanctify Myself."—John 17:19.

"Feed the church of God, which He hath purchased with His own blood."—Acts 20:29.

"Husbands, love your wives, even as Christ also loved the church, and gave Himself for it."—Eph. 5:25.

—*Mr. H. Bonar, 1851.*

FORBIDDEN DIVERSITY.

"Thou shalt not sow thy vineyard with divers seeds: lest the fruit of thy seed which thou hast sown, and the fruit of thy vineyard, be defiled. Thou shalt not plow with an ox and an ass together. Thou shalt not wear a garment of divers sorts, as of woollen and linen together." (Deut. 22:9-11).

God is not the author of confusion. In Him is unmixed good, and His ways are the display of that goodness. In His people He seeks the formation of that which is according to His own nature and character without any admixture of that which is evil.

With Satan is unmixed evil. He whose testimony cannot be questioned said of him, "He was a murderer from the beginning, and abode not in the truth, because there is no truth in him; when he speaketh a lie he speaketh of his own: for he is a liar, and the father of it" (John 8:44). It would be his delight to establish on the earth unmixed evil in defiance of all that is Divine. But God has not abandoned the earth, though His acting, in permission of evil, may be to us mysterious. He allows Satan to make full proof of his wickedness, and He is willing that all man's weakness and sinfulness should be clearly manifested; yet amidst all this He is working out the accomplishment of His own gracious purposes. In due time all that God has wrought shall be triumphantly displayed and the power of evil for ever set aside. The God of peace shall bruise Satan under our feet shortly. In the meantime He would have us wise unto that which is good and simple concerning evil (Rom. 16:19, 20).

We have, then, in this present world, the evil workings of Satan amidst the gracious working of that which is good by the blessed God. Hence the scene of confusion which it presents. Further than this we need to understand that the evil workings of Satan are often of the most subtle nature, so that the unwary are deceived. And in his subtlety he takes advantage of the deceitfulness of our own hearts, presenting things which suit our natural tastes, and easily persuading us that such things are not evil. How deeply important it is, then, that the children of God should have exercised senses to discern both good and evil (Heb. 5:14), and should be so kept in communion with God as to that which is good, in the power of the Holy Spirit, that they may be enabled to refuse that which is evil.

In these days there is constant temptation to mingle good and evil. As Satan cannot overthrow the work of God, either in the world or in the experience of the individual, he works insidiously to corrupt it, and often the believer unsuspectingly falls into the snare. With a master-hand Satan seeks to blend the human with the Divine, the principles of the flesh with those of the Spirit, and the elements of the world with those of Christianity. In this way he cheats the children of God out of the present enjoyment of their true blessings, and dishonours the name of Him to whom they belong.

The Word of God comes in to help us, for it is profitable for doctrine, for reproof, for correction, for instruction in righteousness. It plainly prohibits the mischievous mingling which Satan would bring about. Both in the principles of the Old Testament and in the doctrine of the New Testament it is forbidden alike. Further than this the true character of the evil principles is exposed to us that we may be on our guard against them. And still better, the preciousness of that which is Divine is unfolded to captivate and hold the heart so that nothing beside shall be desired.

With all this in view let us consider the portion quoted at the head of this paper. It is an Old Testament ordinance for the earthly people of God, but its principles are unmistakable and deeply important in their spiritual bearing.

Our first question may be:—

What do we cultivate?

The ordinance related to the cultivation of an Israelite's vineyard, producing the wine which, it is said, "cheereth God and man." It must not be sown with divers seeds, or the end would be defilement.

All own that there is cultivation in a moral sense, and all are cultivating something morally, even if it be, alas! the proverbial "wild oats." Whatever it be that man is cultivating he expects to find joy in it, even as the Israelite expected cheering wine from the cultivation of his vineyard.

There is a large variety of things which man cultivates, but all may be divided into two classes, for there are two sources of what may be called joy—the flesh and the Spirit. It is evident that if anyone cultivates the flesh in a wicked way he will in the end have nothing but corruption and sorrow. Drunkenness, immorality, and every form of open wickedness bring their own solemn end; but the fruit of the cultivation of the flesh in all its refined taste is not so openly manifest. The book of Ecclesiastes, written by the wise king of Israel, whom none excelled, shows us that the end of all his pursuits was "vanity and vexation of spirit." Again, we have in Saul of Tarsus the most beautiful cultivation of religious flesh the world has ever seen. Yet he was not happy in it. The One who spoke to him from the glory, knowing the inmost secrets of his heart, said, "It is hard for thee to kick against the pricks." And when his eyes were opened, even at the very topmost pinnacle of religious success, he found himself a high-handed rebel against God, His Christ, and His church. Surely "the flesh profiteth nothing," and those who cultivate it, even in its most refined pursuits or in its most religious ways, reap only sorrow and dissatisfaction.

Let us now recall the well-known words of the Lord Jesus: "Whosoever drinketh of this water shall thirst again: but whosoever drinketh of the water that I shall give him shall never thirst; but the water that I shall give him shall be in him a well of water springing up into everlasting life" (John 4:13, 14). He proposed to give to man here upon earth present, perfect, absolute satisfaction in the power of the Holy Spirit whom believers receive. Further than this He made known the precious communications He brought from a Father's heart, saying, "These things have I spoken unto you, that My joy might remain in you, and that your joy might be full" (John 15:11). What wondrous words are these! And how precious the reality to which they testify! He delights to bring His loved ones into the very depth of the Father's affections, that in that heavenly circle they may have Divine fulness of joy.

This, then, is the present portion of the believer in the Lord Jesus. He has been taught the vanity of the world and the profitlessness of the flesh, but the grace of God has opened to him, through the death of Jesus and in His resurrection, a scene of cloudless and eternal joy, in which it is his privilege even now to live by faith and in the power of the Spirit. The believer, instructed by the Scripture, thankfully accepts this as truth. Yet how many are grieving because of the realisation of it in their soul is so dim, and some, recalling the blessedness they had when first they knew the Lord, are mourning over a growing coldness which they seem powerless to overcome.

Let us be permitted, then, to turn to a most solemn passage of Scripture (Gal. 6:7, 8), "Be not deceived; God is not mocked; for whatsoever a man soweth, that shall he also reap. For he that soweth to his flesh shall of the flesh reap corruption; but he that soweth to the Spirit shall of the Spirit reap life everlasting." Does not this expose to us the sad secret of our joylessness? Is it not that we have in some way been cultivating the flesh and neglecting the Spirit? and when we have expected a harvest of joy we have only reaped one of sorrows? Do not think we speak of open wickedness. The reaping in that case is so evident that we need not to say anything. But let us consider our ways. Have we been kept conscious at all times of the presence of the blessed Spirit of God within us? and have we, through grace, been cultivating that which is of Himself? Has the Word of God been our food, prayer, our daily breath of dependence upon God, everything touched and handled for Him alone? Alas! how sadly we have to confess that we have sown with divers seeds! Our Bibles have not been wholly neglected, and we have not altogether refused prayer, yet in how many things found cultivating the flesh? It would be mischievous to think that when the apostle spoke of sowing to the flesh he had only open wickedness in view. The Galatians were sowing to their flesh in seeking to adopt circumcision and to put themselves under law, but they could not revive the flesh doctrinally, in whatever fair ways they would do it, without reaping of all its corruption in practice. Oh, how needful, then, is this solemn warning! It is as we sow to the Spirit that we shall reap all the joy and blessedness of eternal life, which is our own blessed portion through the grace of our God.

But there may be two practical difficulties which we will name. Some may say, Is it not legality? Will it not be grievous bondage to be afraid of touching anything that would minister to our flesh? May we not glance at a newspaper nor read ordinary books, nor be sociable with our friends? Our reply is that it is in the Epistle foremost against legality that this solemn warning is written for us. Man fosters the flesh in submission to legal ordinances, but as we walk in the Spirit we delight to be obedient to God's will. We are never free for a moment, nor in the slightest matters to do our own will; we are ever free to do the will of God, which is the only true liberty. And again, if poisoned dishes were set before you of the daintiest morsels, would you think yourself legal in abstaining from them? Or if you meddled with them in the smallest degree would you be surprised if you were unwell as the consequence? It is God's will, and our true health and happiness, that we abstain from everything that would minister to the flesh, but that we diligently cultivate that which is of the Spirit.

There is another true difficulty, however, on the other hand. Some may say, We have businesses or professions which necessitate our having to do with newspapers and books of various kinds. What shall we do? To such we say, It is your privilege to do God's will. It has been said that the path of duty is the path of safety, and certainly we count upon Him whom we serve to preserve us in the way He has ordained for us. But let us see to it that all things we do form links of practical intercourse with God, instead of being means of severing our souls from communion with Him. Thus, even in the path of our ordinary duties in prayerful intercourse with God about them, the sowing goes on which results in a harvest of joy and blessing.

The second question we must consider a little is,

With whom do we associate?

Ploughing is a means to an end. Man is often careless as to means if he but reaches his end. Some even go so far as to say that the end justifies the means. But God is careful about the means as well as the end. So in the matter of ploughing. An Israelite might have viewed it as a matter of indifference whether animals yoked together in his plough were diverse or otherwise, if he could only have his field ploughed and cultivated. But God would not have it so. "Thou shalt not plough with an ox and an ass together."

Nor was it with Him a merely arbitrary decision. He ever has perfectly wise reasons for that which He denies His people. In this case it is easy to see the comliness of His ordinance, for, turning to Lev. 11 we find that ceremonially the ox was a clean animal, chewing the cud and dividing the hoof, whereas the ass, doing neither, was esteemed unclean. God would not, therefore, have the clean and the unclean yoked together.

To this ordinance the apostle evidently referred when to the Corinthians (2 Co., 6:14-18) he wrote these solemn words: "Be ye not unequally yoked together with unbelievers: for what fellowship hath righteousness with unrighteousness? and what communion hath light with darkness? and what concord hath Christ with Belial? or what part hath he that believeth with an unbeliever? (literally) and what agreement hath the temple of God with idols? for ye are the temple of the living God; as God hath said, "I will dwell in them, and walk in them; and I will be their God, and they shall be My people. Wherefore come out from among them, and be ye separate, saith the Lord, and touch not the unclean thing; and I will receive you, and will be a Father unto you, and ye shall be My sons and daughters, saith the Lord Almighty.'

It has been asked, "Can two walk together, except they be agreed?" (Amos 3:3). The ox and the ass are not so diverse as are the believer and the unbeliever in God's thoughts of them. To express that diversity He puts in contrast righteousness and unrighteousness, light and darkness, Christ and Belial, the temple of God and idols: so widely diverse are believers and unbelievers.

Yet Satan has various schemes for yoking them together, and often blinds the eyes of believers by bidding them heed the good end which is to be attained. To take one of the commonest forms, What is a greater snare to a young believer than worldly companions? Perhaps they were his companions before conversion, or they may be employed in the same place of business, or there is some other link which serves to put them together. They cannot go together without the believer feeling the diversity which exists between them; for if he desires to walk with God, to feed upon His Word, to live in the enjoyment of heavenly things, he must feel that the bent of his companions is quite different. Then, perhaps, when his conscience becomes uneasy about it he seeks to silence it by saying, Who knows but my companionship may prove their salvation? Yet lower and lower he sinks, losing relish for the Word of God and Divine things; for as the worldling cannot rise to the level of the believer, the believer must sink to the level of the worldling. Oh, we would most earnestly warn the young believer against worldly companions! Let the word which God in His love and wisdom has written for us be obeyed. Let us beware of any seductive influence which would set it aside. We may not be, for any reason whatever, the associates of the world.

Yet some may say, We have to work amongst the unsaved. So it may be, but there is an immense difference between encountering them in the path of duty and choosing them as our companions. A traveller in a foreign country may need to pass along a path which is infested by poisonous serpents, and he does it carefully, ever on the look-out. But he would never think of taking one of the serpents he dreads, to fondle it and make it his companion. We may count upon grace to keep us in our duties, but let us diligently see to it that we walk with God and his beloved people in holy separation from the world.

We need not now stay to dwell upon the various associations of many kinds and for many purposes for which the believer is continually sought. Once the principle is firmly established in our souls the application of it is easy, although it may demand self-sacrifice. Yet what is that sacrifice when we compare it with the irreparable loss of communication with God, which we must suffer if walking in disobedience to His Word and in neglect of Divine principles?

Our third question is:—

What is the formation of our own character?

God was careful of His earthly people, even to the appearance which they should present to others. He arranged even their dress. So here we have it, "Thou shalt not wear a garment of divers sorts, as of woollen and linen together." In the case of God's priests their dress when ministering to Him was wholly linen. As it is said respecting the priests of the time to come, "They shall be clothed with linen garments; and no wool shall come upon them while they minister in the gates of the inner court, and within. . . . They shall not gird themselves with anything that causeth sweat" (Ezekiel 44:17, 18). That which was connected with the mere exuberance of nature would not suit the presence and the service of God.

We are also reminded of the clothing of the Lamb's wife, as she is spoken of in Rev. 19:8. "To her was granted that she should be arrayed in fine linen, clean and white, for the fine linen is the righteousness of the saints." Thus is seen the suited companion for Christ in glory. There is not one woollen thread mingled with the fabric of her dress; it is of fine linen, clean and white. It is explained to us also that by this is set forth the righteous acts of the saints. Not the product of a natural heart wrought out in fleshly energy, but the precious fruit of the Spirit wrought out in His beloved saints, and now manifested in glory as divine in its character and suited to Christ. What can be more sweet to the one who realises his place and portion with Christ than thus to look forward and see the fashion of that heavenly dress? To suit him everything must *now* partake of that order of things, He rejects the woollen, even to a thread of it, for he must have the fine linen, clean and white.

We find it in the apostle Paul and his companions: "Our rejoicing is this, the testimony of our conscience, that in simplicity and godly sincerity, not with fleshly wisdom, but by the grace of God, we have had our conversation in the world, and more abundantly to you-ward" (2 Cor., 1:12). He was continually seen, as one might say, in the priestly linen, the fabric which alone will suit the bride in the day of her supreme joy. Again, we hear him saying, "Ye are witnesses, and God also, how holily and justly and unblameably we had behaved ourselves among you that believe" (1 Thess., 2:10). The formation of his outward character was, through grace, such as man and God approve.

We commend these things to your earnest consideration, beloved reader, convinced of their deep importance. In our cultivation let us not mingle the flesh with the Spirit; in our association let us not connect the world and the children of God; and in the formation of our character let us not introduce that which is human to mar that which is divine. May our God, in His infinite grace, keep us in the enjoyment of that which is good, that we may be enabled to refuse that which is evil.

Simple Testimony.

THE CHRISTIAN SABBATH.

John 9:13-16.

These verses show us *how little the Jews of our Lord's time understood the right use of the Sabbath day.* We read that some of the Pharisees found fault because a blind man was miraculously healed on the Sabbath. They said, "This man is not of God, because He keepeth not the Sabbath day." A good work had manifestly been done to a helpless fellow-creature. A heavy bodily infirmity had been removed. A mighty act of mercy had been performed. But the blind-hearted enemies of Christ could see no beauty in the act. They called it a breach of the Fourth Commandment!

These would-be wise men completely mistook the intention of the Sabbath. They did not see that it was "made for man," and meant for the good of man's body, mind, and soul. It was a day to be set apart from others, no doubt, and to be carefully sanctified and kept holy. But its sanctification was never intended to prevent works of necessity and acts of mercy. To heal a sick man was no breach of the Sabbath day. In finding fault with our Lord for so doing the Jews only exposed their ignorance of their own law. They had forgotten that it is as great a sin to add to a commandment as to take it away.

Here, as in other places, we must take care that we do not put a wrong meaning on our Lord's conduct. We must not for a moment suppose that the Sabbath is no longer binding on Christians, and that they have nothing to do with the Fourth Commandment. This is a great mistake, and the root of great evil. Not one of the Ten Commandments has ever been repealed or put aside. Our Lord never meant the Sabbath to become a day of pleasure, or a day of business or a day of travelling and idle dissipation. He meant it to be "kept holy" as long as the world stands. It is one thing to employ the Sabbath in works of mercy, in ministering to the sick, and doing good to the distressed. It is quite another thing to spend the day in visiting, feasting, and self-indulgence. Whatever men may please to say, the way in which we use the Sabbath is a sure test of the state of our religion. By the Sabbath may be found out whether we are in communion with God. By the Sabbath may be found out whether we are in tune for heaven. By the Sabbath, in short, the secrets of many hearts are revealed. There are only too many of whom we may say with sorrow, "These men are not of God, because they keep not the Sabbath day."

—Bishop Ryle.

A REAL BLESSING.

"Blessed is he, whosoever shall not be offended in Me" (Matt. 11:6).

In proclaiming this blessing, the Lord Jesus took a word pertaining to this world, but He purified it like as silver is tried in the fire, i.e., He used the word "offended" in a sense in which man had never used it before. Man had always used it in a physical or natural sense of being caught or taken in a trap, of being tripped up or snared: and had never used it in a moral sense. But the Lord never uses it in a physical sense, but always with a new moral and spiritual signification—meaning, "Blessed is he whosoever shall see nothing to stumble at in Me."

And when we think of how many, when the words were spoken, and ever since, have stumbled at the person or the work of Christ, it is a blessing indeed when we see nothing which causes us to stumble.

1. *His Person.* How many have stumbled at that, and how many do so to-day! The Jews cast Him out as a blasphemer. His own family, His mother and His brethren (Mark 3:21, 31) thought Him "beside Himself." The Pharisees hated Him. The Scribes and Lawyers thought evil of Him. The Priests loathed Him, as they always do loathe true prophets—men who are God's spokesmen—and regard them as their natural enemies. Even His disciples stumbled because He was not exactly what they wished Him to be. It is remarkable that in the Gospel of John there are three attempts on His life recorded; and they are all connected with his person. Namely: John 5:17, 18; 8:58, 59; 10:30, 31. To this day men stumble at this stumbling-stone. Their proud intellect will not submit to or admit this claim to Deity; though in their folly they can believe He was "a good man," in spite of what they hold to be a false claim. And yet if He be not God, how can He be our Saviour?

2. *His Words,* also, many stumble at. It was so in the synagogue at Nazareth At first they "wondered at the gracious words which proceeded out of His mouth" (Luke 4:22), but when it came to *distinguishing* grace which sent Elijah to one widow, and she a Gentile, while there were "many widows in Israel"; and which cleansed Naaman, and he a Syrian, though there were "many lepers in Israel" (Luke 4:25-27), they could not understand such grace as that, and would not receive it; for "all they in the synagogue when they heard these things were filled with wrath," and sought to take His life (vv. 28, 29). Yes! man will hear the Gospel, and admire it, and wonder at it; but when it comes to *distinguishing* grace, which distinguishes Jew from Gentile and one sinner from another, then his enmity is aroused, and he will, like Cain before him, do anything rather than submit to God's truth.

Herod, we are told (Mark 6:20), could listen to John the Baptist, and admire him as a preacher, for he "heard him gladly" and "did many things"; but when matters came to the point he "did" one thing—and that was to send and "behead John in prison!" Oh, how solemn that man may hear the Word and listen to the Gospel, but will give it up rather than give himself up!

So again in John 6:65, 66, when the Lord Jesus said, "No man can come to Me, except it were given unto him of My Father. FROM THAT TIME many of His disciples went back, and walked no more with Him." And that is exactly what they have done to this day. They stumble at such words as these. They prate about "the preaching of Jesus," but *this* teaching they unanimously agree to reject! Churches and Chapels where this is done and the opposite is preached, viz., that man *can* come without the power being given of the Father, these will be thronged, because it flatters the pride of the old nature to be told that they can do this and must do that (not that they ever think of doing it!) while those places, where Christ's words are faithfully believed and reverently stated and taught, will be shunned until the gracious gift of the Father is experienced! But the voice of the Lord comes to us to-day, and asks, "Will ye also go away?" We trust that all our readers can answer with Peter, "Lord, to whom should we go?" and can thus enjoy the blessing, the real blessedness of which we are speaking.

3. And then *the work of Christ* is a cause of stumbling to some, and counted foolishness by others (1 Cor. 1:23, 24). The Righteousness of Christ is also stumbled at (Rom. 9:30-32). Yes, and man always will stumble at this, for it is too humbling for him to be told that we have no righteousness of our own; that we are poor, empty, sinful, unworthy, guilty, and undone. And to have to realise this to the end, and even more than we did at the beginning! Oh, it is a hard lesson: and no wonder that even the saint stumbles often at the whole truth involved in Christ our Righteousness.

"Blessed is he, whosoever shall not be offended in Me." And why? Ah! because no one was ever yet brought into that blessing without being deeply offended with himself. And not only does he find none occasion of stumbling in Christ, but the *Person* of Christ is that which meets his need, as He is the Saviour Whom God has provided, and hence is "God our Saviour." The *Word* of Christ is just that which suits him: nothing imputed to him, but Christ in all that He is and all that He has. "Accepted in the Beloved," "Complete in Him," "Perfect in Christ Jesus," "Made the Righteousness of God in Him." Oh, how "blessed" is such an one! And the freeness of God's distinguishing grace is just what he wants. When we hear the words, "Therefor it is of faith, that it might be by grace," *that* is just what our souls require and desire. And as the years pass by we feel that if it were less free and less for the unworthy we could never be saved.

And further, how full of that very grace are these words of our Lord! How condescending, how tender, to mention the very lowest negative evidence! He does not say, Blessed is he whose faith is great, whose hope is strong, or whose love is fervent, but "blessed is he whosoever shall not be offended in Me." Surely we can say this. And if so, be sure of this, that the less offence we find in the Lord, the more we shall be offended with ourselves. We shall see sin where we never saw it before. We shall detect evil where we never expected it. This will be the necessary result of occupation with Him. The more we learn of His perfections, the more we shall see our own deformity, our infirmities, and our sins. We shall never discover them while we are occupied with them and are looking for *them.* Only as we come in contact with God's plumb-line, shall we see our own crookedness; only as we are tested by His "spirit-level" or "straight-edge" shall we discover our own unevenness; only in the balances of the sanctuary shall we learn how we come utterly short of anything that we can be, or do, or bring for God's acceptance.

Finally, the less we are offended at anything in Christ, the more will the world be offended with us. Let us not be cast down at this. Marvel not if the world hate us. Let us not be ashamed of the "offence of the cross," and let us esteem "the reproach of Christ" as greater riches than all the world could offer us.

Things to Come, 1898.

TO OUR FELLOW-CHRISTIANS IN AMERICA.

May 27, 1925.

Numbers of our friends in the U.S.A. are probably wondering why they have not received a few lines from us ere this. We take this opportunity of saying that it is *not* a case of "out of sight, out of mind." The truth is that we are now speaking ten times a week, and preparation for these services and the interviewing of different ones who are anxious to be shown the way of the Lord more perfectly is consuming almost all of our available time. But though it is well-nigh impossible to write letters to many whom we love in the Lord, it is our daily privilege to remember them at the Throne of Grace, and to look forward to that joyous Day—near at hand —when we shall meet around the Lamb, to be *"forever* with the Lord."

The meetings here afford *much* ground for praise to our most gracious God. The attendances are steadily increasing, the interest is most manifest, and goodly numbers are being blest. Many here have been earnestly praying for months past that the Lord would send a teacher to open up to them some of the inexhaustible treasures of the Scriptures. Hundreds of eager souls are coming out five and six nights a week, with Bibles and notebooks. God is granting most blessed liberty of utterance and joy of heart in ministering His precious Word. We are receiving more invitations than we can accept. There is every indication that "a great and effectual door is opened unto us. Join us in continued prayer, dear friends, that the sheep of Christ may be fed, that He may become increasingly real and precious to His own, and that His unprofitable servant may be made and kept humble before Him Who deigns to place His treasure in earthen vessels.

With affectionate greetings to all from us both.

Yours by Sovereign Grace,

The Editor and his Wife.

Psa. 37:4—*"Delight thyself also in the Lord; and He shall give thee the desires of thine heart."*

(*Continued from page 145.*)

is striking to observe how much is said in the Word about the *tongue;* how many exhortations there are to guard its utterances. Even human prudence has drawn up the maxim, "Think twice before you speak." But more than thinking is needed to guard against the unlawful use of the tongue: a careful study of Scripture upon it and earnest prayer unto God about it are still more necessary.

First of all, we need to be much on our guard against *gossiping*—a habit formed by many before they are even aware of it. The Lord Jesus told us that "Every idle word that men shall speak, they shall give account thereof in the Day of Judgment" (Matt. 12:36). Solemn indeed is this. Life is too short, and far too solemn, to waste valuable time in gossiping—the retailing of news which profits not the hearer. Yet how much time *is* wasted in this, even by many Christians! If the hours, or even minutes, which are daily used by some for idle talking, were spent in secret prayer, in quiet mediation, ,in the reverent searching of Scripture, or in *profitable* conversation, how much better for ourselves and those who listen to us!

Worse than gossiping is *tale-bearing* and *backbiting.* How many of us must shamefully confess our guilt in this. Scripture is very plain upon the point, "The words of a talebearer are as wounds, and they go down into the innermost parts of the belly" (Prov. 18:8). "Where no wood is there, the fire goeth out: so where there is no talebearer the strife ceaseth" (Prov. 26:20).

Another thing forbidden by Scripture is *foolish talking* and *jesting.* Says the Holy Spirit, "But fornication, and all uncleanness, or covetousness, let it not be once named among you, as becometh saints; neither filthiness, nor foolish talking, nor jesting, which are not convenient: but rather of giving of thanks" (Eph. 5:3, 4). How much is this exhortation needed to-day? Even those who occupy the pulpit are frequently guilty of "foolish talking and jesting," and in some instances of that which is much worse.

We also need to watch and pray against such times as we may be under great provocation to *angry words.* Someone has said, "If our house was on fire our first impulse would be to run for a bucket of water; but when our temper catches fire, our first impulse is to throw on more fuel." The best water-bucket for an aroused temper is resolute silence: silence will cool both ourselves and our provokers. "A fool is full of words" (Eccl. 10:13), but "he that hath knowledge spareth his words" (Prov. 17:27). Let us ever remember the Perfect One "Who did no sin, neither was guile found in His mouth. Who when He was reviled, *reviled not again;* when He suffered He threatened not, but committed Himself to Him that judgeth righteously" (1 Peter 2:22, 23). It is remarkable that these words are immediately prefaced by the statement that "Christ also suffered for us, *leaving us an example,* that we should follow His steps."

Solemn, too, and very condemning, are the words of Ecc. 5:1, 2, concerning our speech when we enter the House of God, "Keep thy foot when thou goest to the House of God, and be more ready to hear than to give the sacrifice of fools; for they consider not that they do evil. Be not rash with thy mouth, and let not thine heart be hasty to utter anything before God: for God is in heaven, and thou upon earth: therefore let thy words be few." If it be objected that there is no "House of God" to-day, our reply is that the *principle* most certainly obtains in all our public gatherings. "God is greatly to be feared in the assembly of saints, and to be had in reverence of all them that are about Him" (Psa. 89:7), verifies this.

What has been said above is more along the negative side—what we should *avoid.* Scripture is equally explicit about the positive side. Two more passages must suffice—Eph. 4:29: "Let no corrupt communication proceed out of your mouth, but that which is good to the use of *edifying,* that it may minister grace unto the hearers." Col. 4:6, "Let your speech be always with *grace,* seasoned with salt, that ye may know how ye ought to answer every man."

Finally, how the above Scriptures (which condemn every one of us) serve to point us, by way of *contrast* to the Lord Jesus Christ! Of Him it is written, "Thou art fairer than the children of men; *grace is poured into Thy lips* (Psa. 45:2). *He* never uttered a word which needed to be recalled, or a word that had to be repented of before God. His very enemies acknowledged, "Never man *spake* like this Man" (John 7:46). Let us then learn of Him and earnestly seek closer conformity to Him.

VOL. IV AUGUST, 1925 NO. 8

STUDIES IN THE SCRIPTURES

"Search the Scriptures" John 5:39.

Arthur W. Pink, Publisher and Editor,
5 Norton Street, Ashfield, N.S.W., Australia.

Price: 10 cents per copy; $1.00 or 5/- per year.

Contentment.

"I have learned, in whatsoever state I am, therewith to be content" (*Phil.* 4:11).

Discontent! Was there ever a time when there was so much restlessness in the world as there is to-day? We very much doubt it. Despite our boasted progress, the vast increase of wealth, the time and money expended daily in pleasure, discontent is everywhere. No class is exempt. Everything is in a state of flux, and almost everybody is dissatisfied. Many even among God's own people are affected with the evil spirit of this age.

Contentment! Is such a thing realisable, or is it nothing more than a beautiful ideal, a mere dream of the poet? Is it attainable on earth, or is it restricted to the inhabitants of heaven? If practicable here and now, may it be retained, or are a few brief moments or hours of contentment the most that we may expect in this life? Such questions as these find answer, an answer at least, in the words of the apostle Paul: "Not that I speak in respect of want: for I have learned, in whatsoever state I am, therewith to be content" (Phil. 4:11).

The force of the apostle's statement will be better appreciated if his condition and circumstances at the time he made it be kept in mind. When the apostle wrote (or most probably dictated) the words, he was not luxuriating in a special suite in the Emperor's palace, nor was he being entertained in some exceptional Christian household, the members of which were marked by unusual piety. Instead, he was "in bonds" (cf. Phil. 1:13, 14); "a prisoner" (Eph. 4:1), as he says in another Epistle. And yet, notwithstanding, he declared he was *content!*

Now, there is a vast difference between precept and practice, between the ideal and the realisation. But in the case of the apostle Paul contentment was an *actual* experience, and one that must have been continuous, for he says, "in *whatsoever* state I am." How then did Paul enter into this experience, and of what did the experience consist? The reply to the first question is to be found in the word, "I have *learned*. . . . to be content." The apostle did not say, "I have received the baptism of the Spirit, and therefore contentment is mine." Nor did he attribute this blessing to his perfect "consecration." Equally plain is it that it was not the outcome of natural disposition or temperament. It is something he had *learned* in the school of Christian experience. It should be noted, too, that this statement is found in an Epistle which the apostle wrote near the *close* of his earthly career!

From what has been pointed out it should be apparent that the contentment which Paul enjoyed was *not* the result of congenial and comfortable surroundings. And this at once dissipates the vulgar conception. Most people suppose that contentment is impossible unless one can have gratified the desires of the carnal heart. A prison is the last place to which they would go if they were seeking a contented man. This much, then, is clear: contentment comes from within not without; it must be sought from God, not in creature comforts.

But let us endeavour to go a little deeper. *What is* "contentment"? It is the being satisfied with the sovereign dispensations of God's providence. It is the opposite of murmuring, which is the spirit of rebellion—the clay saying to the Potter,

(*Continued on page 192*).

IMPORTANT NOTICES

Set of twelve issues for **1922**, unbound, **$1.00** or **5/-**. Bound **$1.50** or **7/-**.

Set of twelve issues for **1923**, unbound, **$1.00** or **5/-**. Bound **$1.50** or **7/-**.

Set of twelve issues for **1924**, unbound, **$1.00** or **5/-**. Bound **$1.50** or **7/-**.

Note: We cannot break a set or now supply any **single** 1924 issues.

Subscription—price: **$1.00** or **5/-** per year to any address in the world.

Change of Address: Please notify me promptly of any change of address, and be certain to give both old and new address.

Non-subscribers receiving this Magazine regularly will understand their subscription has been entered by a friend.
Copies lost in the mail duplicated only if we are notified promptly.

CONTENTS

THE GOSPEL OF JOHN

44. *Christ's Ministry Reviewed: John* 12:37-50.

The following is an Analysis of the closing section of John 12:—

1. The Nation's response to Christ's ministry, v. 37.
2. The forecast of Israel's unbelief by Isaiah, vv. 38-41.
3. The condition of those who had been impressed by Christ, vv. 42, 43.
4. Christ's teaching about His relation to the Father, vv. 45, 45.
5. Christ's teaching concerning the design of His ministry, vv. 46, 47.
6. Christ's teaching concerning the doom of all who despised Him, vv. 48, 49.
7. Christ's teaching concerning the way of life, v. 50.

The passage before us is by no means an easy one to understand. The previous section closes as follows: "These things spake Jesus, and *departed*, and did *hide* Himself from them" (v. 36). Many have thought, and we believe rightly so, that this statement brings the *public* ministry of Christ to a close in this Gospel. When we enter the thirteenth chapter it is very evident that a new section there begins, for from the beginning of 13 to the end of 17 the Lord is *alone* with His apostles; while in the 18th He is arrested and led to judgment. But if 12:36 marks the ending of Christ's public ministry, how are we to understand the verses which follow to the end of the chapter? especially in view of what is said in v. 44: "Jesus cried and said," etc.

Now, we believe the answer to this question has been well stated by Dr. J. Brown: "The paragraph itself (12:37-50) is of a peculiar, I had almost said unique, structure and character. The history of our Lord's public ministry is closed. It terminates in the verse immediately preceding. The account of His private interview with His friends, previous to His passion, is about to commence. It begins with the first verse of the following chapter. One scene in the eventful history is closed; another is about to open. The curtain is, as it were, falling upon the theatre in which the public acts of Jesus were performed, and the Evangelist is about to conduct us into the sacred circle of His disciples, and communicate to us the sublime and consoling conversations which the Redeemer, full of love, had with them before His final departure. But before He does this he makes a pause in the narrative, and, as it were, looks back and around; and, in the paragraph before us, presents us in a few sentences with a brief but comprehensive view of all the Lord had taught and done during the course of His public ministry, and of the effects which His discourses and miracles had produced on the great body of His countrymen."

John here gives us a resumé of Christ's public ministry, mentioning His miracles and recapitulating His teaching. The closing section of John 12 forms an epilogue to that chapter of our Lord's life which had just been brought to a close in v. 36. Four vital truths which had occupied a prominent place in Christ's oral ministry are here singled out: His appeal to the Father which sent Him (vv. 44, 45, 49); Himself the Light of the world (v. 46); the danger of unbelief (vv. 47-49); the end of faith (v. 50). The Holy Spirit's design in moving John to pen this section was, we believe, at least twofold: to explain the seeming failure of Christ's public ministry, and to show that the guilt of unbelief rested inexcusably upon Israel.

"The rejection of Jesus Christ by the great body of His fellow-countrymen, the Jews, is a fact which, at first view, may seem to throw suspicion on the greatness of His claims to a Divine mission, as indicating the evidence adduced in their support did not serve its purpose with those to whom it was originally presented, and who, in some points of view, were placed in circumstances peculiarly favourable for forming a correct estimate of its validity. It may be supposed that had the proofs of His Divine mission and Messiahship been as strong and striking as the friends of Christianity represent them, the prejudices of the Jews, powerful as they unquestionably were, must have given way before them; and the believers of His doctrine must have been as numerous as the witnesses of His miracles. Such a supposition, though plausible, argues on the part of its supporters, imperfect and incorrect views of the human constitution, intellectually and morally" (Ibid). In other words, it ignores the *total depravity* of man!

Now, in the closing section of John 12 the Holy Spirit has most effectively disposed of the above objection. He has done so by directing our attention to Old Testament predicitions which accurately forecast the very reception which the Messiah met with from the Jews. First, Isa. 53 is referred to, for in this chapter it was plainly foretold that He should be "despised and rejected of men." And then Isa. 6 is quoted, a passage which tells of God judicially blinding His people because of their inveterate unbelief. Thus, the very objection made against Christianity is turned into a most conclusive argument in its favour. The very fact that the Lord Jesus was put to death by His countrymen demonstrates that He *is* their Messiah! Thus has God, once more, made "the wrath of man to praise Him."

"But though He had done so many miracles before them, yet they believed not on Him" (v. 37). Fearful proof was this of the depravity of the human heart. The miracles of Christ were neither few in number nor unimpressive in nature. The Lord Jesus performed prodigies of power of almost every conceivable kind. He healed the sick, expelled demons, controlled the winds, walked on the sea, turned water into wine, revealed to men their secret thoughts, raised the dead. His miracles were wrought openly, in the light of day, before numerous witnesses. Nevertheless "they"—the Nation at large—"believed not on Him." Altogether inexcusable was their hardness of heart. All who heard His teaching and witnessed His works, ought, without doubt, to have received Him as their Divinely-accredited Messiah and Saviour. But the great majority of His countrymen refused to acknowledge His claims.

"The prevalence of unbelief and indifference in the present day ought not to surprise us. It is just one of the evidences of that mighty foundation-doctrine, the total corruption and fall of man. How feebly we grasp and realise that doctrine is proved by our surprise at human incredulity. We only half believe the heart's deceitfulness. Let us read our Bibles more attentively, and search their contents more carefully. Even when Christ wrought miracles and preached sermons there were numbers of His hearers who remained utterly unmoved. What right have we to wonder if the hearers of modern sermons in countless instances remain unbelieving? 'The disciple is not greater than His Master.' If even the hearers of Christ did not believe, how much more should we expect to find unbelief among the hearers of His ministers? Let the truth be spoken and confessed: man's obstinate unbelief is one among many of the indirect proofs that the Bible is true" (Bishop Ryle).

"That the saying of Isaiah the prophet might be fulfilled, which he spake, Lord, who hath believed our report? and to whom hath the arm of the Lord been revealed?" (v. 38). This does not mean that the Jews continued in unbelief with the conscious design of fulfilling O.T. prophecy. Nor does the Holy Spirit here teach that God exercised a secret influence upon the hearts of the Jews, which prevented them from believing, in order that the prophecy of Isaiah might not fail of accomplishment. The Jews *did* fulfil the predictions of Isaiah, but it was ignorantly and unwittingly. As one able expositor has well said, "The true interpretation here depends on the fact, that the participle rendered *that,* in the sense of *in order that* sometimes signifies *so that,* pointing out, not the connection of cause and effect, but that of antecedent and consequence, prediction and accomplishment. For example, in the question of the disciples, 'Who did sin, this man or his parents, *that* he was born blind?' the meaning plainly is, 'Is this man's blindness *the consequence* of his parent's sin, or of his own in some preexistent state?'" We believe it had been better to render it thus: "They believed not, *consequently* the saying of Isaiah was fulfilled." God does not have to put forth any power to cause any sinner *not* to believe: if He leaves him to himself, he never will believe.

It is highly significant that Isa. 53 opens in the way it does. That remarkable chapter tells of the treatment which the Saviour met with from Israel when He was here the first time. As is well known, the Jews will not own it as a prophecy concerning the Messiah: some of them have attempted to apply it to Jeremiah, others to the Nation. How striking then that the Triune-God has opened it with the question, "Who hath *believed* Our report?"! Most suitably does John apply it to the unbelieving Nation in his day. "And to whom is the arm of the Lord revealed?" The "arm of the Lord" signifies the *power* of God as it had been manifested by the Messiah. There are therefore two things here: Who hath believed our *report?"* points to Christ's *oral* ministry; "to whom is the *arm* of the Lord revealed?" to His *miracles.*

"Therefore they could not believe, because that Isaiah said again" (v. 39). This is exceedingly solemn. It is explained in the next verse. In consequence of their rejection of Christ the Nation as a whole was judicially blinded of God, that is, they were *left* to the darkness and hardness of their own evil hearts. But it is most important to mark the *order* of these two statements: in v. 37 they *did not* believe; here in v. 39, they *could not* believe. The most attractive appeals had been made: the most indubitable evidence had been presented: yet they despised and rejected the Redeemer. They *would not* believe; in consequence, God gave them up, and now they *could not* believe. The harvest was past, the summer was ended, and they were not saved. But the fault was entirely theirs, and now they must suffer the just consequences of their wickedness.

"He hath blinded their eyes, and hardened their heart; that they should not see with their eyes, nor understand with their heart, and be converted, and I should heal them" (v. 40). This was God's response to the wicked treatment which Israel had meted out to His beloved Son. They had refused the Light, now darkness shall be their dreadful portion. They had rejected the Truth, now a heart which loved error should be the terrible harvest. Blinded eyes and a hardened heart have belonged to Israel ever since; only thus can we account for their continued unbelief all through these nineteen centuries; only thus can we explain Israel's attitude toward Christ to-day.

"All through His Divine ministry in this Gospel, the Lord had been acting in grace, as 'the Son of the Father' and as 'the Light of the world.' His presence was *day-time* in the land of Israel. He had been shining there, if haply the darkness might comprehend Him. And here, at the close of His ministry (vv. 35, 36) we see Him still as the light casting forth His last beams upon the land and the people. He can but shine, whether they will comprehend Him or not. While His presence is there it is still day-time. The night cannot come till He is gone. 'As long as I am in the world, I am the Light of the world!' But here, He *'departed* and did *hide* Himself from them' (v. 36); and then God, by His prophet, brings the *night* upon the land: v. 40" (Mr. J. G. Bellett).

Fearfully solemn is it to remember that what God did here unto Israel He will shortly do with the whole of unbelieving Christendom: "And for this cause *God shall send them* strong delusion, that they should believe a lie: that they all might be damned who believe not the truth, but had pleasure in unrighteousness" (2 Thess. 2:11, 12). Just as in the days of Nimrod God "gave up" the entire Gentile world because they despised and rejected the revelation which He had given them (Rom. 1); just as He abandoned Israel to their unbelief, through the rejection of His Son; so in a soon-coming day He will cause unfaithful Christendom to receive the Antichrist because "they received not the love of the truth, that they might be saved" (2 Thess. 2:10). Oh, dear reader, be warned by this. It is an unspeakably solemn thing to trifle with the overtures of God's grace. It is written, "How shall *we escape* if we neglect so great salvation?" (Heb. 2:3). Then "Seek ye the Lord *while He may be found,* call ye upon Him *while He is near"* (Isa. 55:6).

"These things said Isaiah, when he saw His glory, and spake of Him" (v. 41). A striking testimony is this to the absolute Deity of Christ. The prediction quoted in the previous verse is found in Isa. 6. At the beginning of that chapter the prophet sees "Jehovah sitting upon a throne, high and lifted up, and His train filled the Temple. Above the throne stood the seraphim, with veiled face, crying, "Holy, Holy, Holy, is the Lord of hosts." The sight was too much for Isaiah, and he cried, "Woe is me! for I am undone." Then a live coal was taken from off the altar and laid upon his mouth, and thus cleansed, he is commissioned to go forth as God's messenger. And here the Holy Spirit tells us in John 12, "These things said Isaiah, when he saw *His* glory, and spake of Him" —the context makes it unmistakably plain that the reference is to the Lord Jesus. One of the sublimest descriptions of the manifested Deity found in all the Old Testament is here applied to Christ. That One born in Bethlehem's manger was none other than the Throne-Sitter before Whom the seraphim worship.

"Nevertheless among the chief rulers also many believed on Him; but because of the Pharisees they did not confess Him, lest they should be put out of the synagogue" (v. 42). Here is a statement which affords help on such verses as John 2:23; 7:31; 8:30; 10:42; 11:45; 12:11. In each of these passages we read of *many* "believing" on the Lord Jesus, concerning whom there is nothing to show that they had saving faith. In the light of the verse now before us it would seem that John, all through his Gospel, divides the unbelieving into *two* classes: the hardened mass who were altogether unmoved by the wondrous works of Christ, and a company, evidently by no means small, upon whom a temporary impression was made, but yet who failed to yield their hearts captive to the Saviour—the fear of man, and loving the praise of man, holding them back. And do we not find the same two classes in Christendom to-day? By far the greater number of those who come under the sound of the Gospel remain unmoved, heeding neither its imperative authority nor being touched by its winsome tidings. They are impervious to every appeal. But there is another class, and its representatives are to be found, perhaps, in every congregation; a class who *are* affected in some measure by the Word of the Cross. They do not despise its contents, yet, neither are their *hearts* won by it. On the one hand, they are not openly antagonistic; on the other, they are not out and out Christians.

"Nevertheless among the chief rulers also many believed on Him; but because of the Pharisees they did not confess Him, lest they should be put out of the synagogue" (v. 42). This points a most solemn warning to the class we have just mentioned above. A faith which does not *confess* Christ is not a *saving* faith. The New Testament is very explicit on this. Said the Lord Jesus, "Whosoever shall *confess Me* before men, him shall the Son of Man also confess before the angels of God: But he that *denieth Me* before men shall be denied before the angels of God" (Luke 12:8, 9). And in the Epistle to the Romans we are told, "If thou shalt *confess* with thy mouth the Lord Jesus, and shalt believe in thine heart that God hath raised Him from the dead, thou shalt be saved" (10:9). These Jews referred to in our text were satisfied that Christ was neither an impostor nor a fanatic, yet were they not prepared to forsake all and follow Him. They feared the consequences of such a course, for the Jews had agreed already "That if any man did *confess* that He was Christ, he should be put out of the synagogue" (9:22). These men then deemed it wisest to conceal their convictions and wait until the Messiah should place Himself in such a position that it would be safe and advantageous for them to avow themselves His disciples. They were governed by *self-interest,* and they have had many successors. If any should read these lines who are attempting to be *secret* disciples of the Lord Jesus, fearing to come out into the open and acknowledge by lip and life that He is their Saviour and Lord, let them beware. Remember that the *first* of the eight classes mentioned in Rev. 21:8 who are cast into the Lake of Fire are the *"fearful"!*

"For they loved the praise of men more than the praise of God" (v. 43). These men, whose minds were convinced but whose hearts remained unmoved, not only *feared* the religious authorities, but they also *desired* the approbation of their fellows. They were determined to retain their good opinion, even though at the expense of an uneasy conscience. They preferred the good will of other sinners above the approval of God. O the short-sighted folly of these wretched men! O the madness of their miserable choice! Of what avail would the good opinion of the Pharisees be when the hour of death overtook them? In what stead will it stand them when they appear before the Judgment-throne of God? "What shall it profit a man if he shall gain the whole world, and lose his own soul?" How we are reminded of our Saviour's words, "How can ye believe which receive honour *one of another,* and seek not the honour that cometh from God only?" (John 5:44). Let us remember that we cannot have both the good-will of sinners and the good-will of God: "Know ye not that the friendship of the world is enmity with God? whosoever therefore will be a friend of the world is the enemy of God" (James 4:4).

"Jesus cried and said, He that believeth on Me, believeth not on Me, but on Him that sent Me" (v. 44). Notice that nothing whatever is said about either the time or the place where the Saviour made this utterance. We believe that John still contines his epilogue, giving us in vv. 44 to 50 a summary of Christ's teaching. The substance of what he here says plainly indicates this. "How strange that this supposed discourse of Jesus should to an extent of which there is no previous example, consist of *repetitions* alone, and, moreover, of only such words as are already found in John's Gospel. Did the Lord ever *recapitulate* in this style, uttering connectedly so long a discourse without any new thoughts and distinct sayings? but, when for once St. John racapitulates, seeming (though only seeming) to put *his* words into the Lord's lips, what an instructive example he gives us, not venturing to add anything of his own! Yea, verily, all this the Lord *had said*, each saying in its season; but St. John unites them all retrospectively together" (Stier). The tense of the verbs here, "Jesus *cried* and *said*," signify, as Stier and Alford have pointed out, that Christ was *wont* to, that it was His customary course of repeated action.

"And he that seeth Me seeth Him that sent Me" (v. 45). That John *is* giving us in these verses a summary of the teachings of Christ is evidenced by a comparison of them with earlier statements in this Gospel. For example: compare "He that believeth *on Me*, believeth not on Me, *but on Him that sent Me*" (v. 44) with 5:24—"He that heareth *My word* and *believeth on Him that sent Me*." So here: "He that seeth Me seeth Him that sent Me." Compare with this 8:19, "If ye had known *Me*, ye should have known *My Father also;*" and 10:38, "That ye may know and believe that the Father is in Me, an *I in Him*." This was one of the vital truths which occupied a prominent place in our Lord's teachings. No man had seen God at any time, but the only begotten Son had come here to "declare" *Him* (1:18). What we have here in v. 45 is a reference to the frequent mention made by Christ to that mysterious and Divine union which existed between Himself and the Father.

"I am come a light into the world, that whosoever believeth on Me should not abide in darkness" (v. 46). Clearly this is parallel with 8:12 and 9:5: "I am the Light of the world: he that followeth Me shall not walk in darkness. . . As long as I am in the world, I am the Light of the world." "I am come a light into the world": upon this verse Dr. G. Brown has the following helpful comments: "This proves, first, that Christ existed *before* His incarnation, even as the sun exists before it appears above the eastern hills; second, it is implied that He is the *one* Saviour of the world, as there is but *one* sun; third, that He came, not for one nation only, but for *all;* even as the sun's going forth is from the end of the heaven, and his circuit unto the ends of it; and there is nothing hid from the heat thereof." This verse continues John's reference to the general teaching of Christ concerning the character and tendency of His mission. He had come here into this world as a *light*—revealing God and exposing man—and this, in order that all who believed on Him should be delivered from the *darkness*, that is, from the power of Satan (Col. 1:13) and the ruin of sin (Eph. 4:18).

"And if any man hear My words, and believe not, I judge him not: for I came not to judge the world but to save the world" (v. 47). Here the Evangelist calls attention to another truth which had held a prominent place in our Lord's teachings. It respected His repeated announcement concerning the character and design of His mission and ministry. It tells of the lowly place which He had taken, and of the patient grace which marked Him during the time that He tabernacled among men. It brings into sharp contrast the purpose and nature of His two advents. When He returns to this earth it will be in another character and with a different object from what was true of Him when He was here the first time. Before, He was here as the lowly servant; then, He shall appear as the exalted Sovereign. Before, He came to woo and win men; then, He shall rule over them with a rod of iron.

"And if any man hear My words, and believe not, I judge him not," with this compare 5:45, "Do not think that *I* will accuse you to the Father. For I came not to judge the world, but to save the world," compare with this John 3:17, "For God sent not His Son into the world to condemn the world; but that the world through Him might be saved," and note our original comments upon John 3:17.

"He that rejecteth Me, and receiveth not My words, hath One that judgeth him" (v. 48). The first part of this verse is almost identical with what we read of in 3:18: "But he that believeth not is condemned already, because he hath not believed in the name of the only begotten Son of God." "The words that I have spoken, the same shall judge him in the Last Day." This takes us back to Deut 18:19, where, of the great Prophet God promised to raise up unto Israel He declared, "And it shall come to pass, that whosoever will not harken unto My words which He shall speak in My name, I will *require it of him*."

"The word that I have spoken, the same shall judge him in the Last Day" (v. 48). Very solemn indeed is this, for its application is to *all* who have heard the Gospel. It tells us three things.

First, there is to be a "last day." This world will not remain forever. The bounds of its history, the length of its existence are Divinely determined, and when the appointed limit is reached, "The Day of the Lord will come as a thief in the night; in the which the heavens shall pass away with a great noise, and the elements shall melt with fervent heat, the earth also and the works that are therein shall be burned up" (2 Peter 3:10).

Second, this Last Day will be one of *judgment:* "Because He hath appointed a day, in the which He will judge the world in righteousness by that Man whom He hath ordained" (Acts 17:31). Then shall hidden things be brought to light: the righteous vindicated, and the unrighteous sentenced. Then shall God's broken law be magnified, and His holy justice honored. Then shall all His enemies be subjugated and God shall demonstrate that He *is* GOD. Then shall every proud rebel be made to bow in subjection before that Name which is above every name, and confess that Jesus is Lord to the glory of God the Father.

Third, *Christ's Word* will judge sinners in that Day. His Word was a *true* Word, a *Divine* Word, a Word *suited* to men. Yet men have slighted it, attacked it, denied it, made its holy contents the subject of blasphemous jesting. But in the last great Day it shall *judge* them. First and foremost among the "books" which shall be opened and out of which sinners shall be "judged" (Rev. 20:12) will be, we believe, the written word of God—"In the day when God shall judge the secrets of men by Jesus Christ *according to my Gospel*" (Rom. 2:16).

"For I have not spoken of Myself; but the Father which sent Me, He gave Me a commandment, what I should say, and what I should speak" (v. 49). This was something which Christ had affirmed repeatedly, see John 5:30; 7:16; 8:26-28, etc. It expressed that intimate and mysterious union which existed between the Father and Himself. His purpose was to impress upon the Jews the awfulness of their sin in refusing *His* words: in so doing, they affronted *the Father Himself,* for *His* were the very words which the Son had spoken to them. In like manner, to-day, "he that believeth not God hath made Him a liar; because he believeth not the record that God gave *of His Son*" (1 John 5:10). How terrible then is the sin of despising the testimony of Christ!

"And I know that His commandment is life everlasting: whatsoever I speak therefore, even as the Father said unto Me, so I speak" (v. 50). This is an abstract of what we read of in 3:11; 5:32; 8:55. It brings out once more the perfections of the incarnate Son. He acted not in independency, but in perfect oneness of heart, mind, and will, with the Father. Whether the Jews believed them or not, the messages which Christ had delivered were Divinely true, and therefore were they words of life to all who receive them by simple faith. This closing sentence in John's summary of Christ's teachings is very comprehensive: *"Whatsoever"* He had spoken, was that He had received of the Father. Therefore in refusing to heed the teaching of Christ, the Jews had despised the God of their fathers, the God of Abraham, the God of Isaac, and the God of Jacob.

"And I know that His commandment is life everlasting: whatsoever I speak therefore, even as the Father said unto Me, so I speak" (v. 50). Once more we have a declaration which is not confined to its local application. This verse speaks in clarion tones to all who come under the sound of the Gospel to-day. God has given not an "invitation" for men to act on at *their* pleasure, but a *"commandment"* which they disobey at their imminent peril. That commandment is "That we should believe on the name of His Son Jesus Christ" (1 John 3:23), hence at the beginning of the Epistle of the Romans, where Paul refers to the Gospel of God, he says, "By whom we have received grace and apostleship, for faith-*obedience* among all nations" (1:5). This commandment is "life everlasting" to all who receive it by the obedience of faith. Adam brought death upon him by disobeying God's commandment: we receive life by obeying God's commandment. Then "see that ye *refuse not* Him that speaketh. For if they escaped not who refused Him that spake on earth, much more shall not we escape, if we turn away from Him that speaketh from heaven" (Heb. 12:25).

Studv the following questions in view of our next lesson:—

1. What is meant by the last clause of v. 1?
2. What "supper" is referred to in v. 2?
3. What is the symbolic significance of Christ's actions in v. 4?
4. What is signified by the washing of the disciples' feet, v. 5?
5. Why is Peter so prominent in vv. 6-9?
6. What is meant by "no part with Me?" v. 8.
7. What is the meaning of v. 10?

—*ARTHUR W. PINK.*

GLEANINGS IN EXODUS

20. *Israel's Song:* Ex. 15.

Exodus 15 contains the first song recorded in Scripture. Well has it been said, "It is presumably the oldest poem in the world, and in sublimity of conception and grandeur of expression, it is unsurpassed by anything that has been written since. It might almost be said that poetry here sprang full-grown from the heart of Moses, even as heathen mythology fables Minerva come full-armed from the brain of Jupiter. Long before the ballads of Homer were sung through the streets of the Grecian cities, or the foundation of the Seven-hilled metropolis of the ancient world was laid by the banks of the Tiber, this matchless ode, in comparison with which Pindar is tame, was chanted by the leader of the emancipated Hebrews on the Red Sea shore; and yet we have in it no polytheism, no foolish mythological story concerning gods and goddesses, no gilding of immorality, no glorification of mere force; but, instead, the firmest recognition of the personality, the supremacy, the holiness, the retributive rectitude of God. How shall we account for all of this? If we admit the Divine legation and inspiration of Moses, all is plain; if we deny that, we have in the very existence of this Song, a hopeless and insoluble egnima. Here is a literary miracle, as great as the physical sign of the parting of the Sea. When you see a boulder of immense size, and of a different sort of stone from those surrounding it, lying in a valley, you immediately conclude that it has been brought hither by glacier action many, many ages ago. But here is a boulder-stone of poetry, standing all alone in the Egyptian age, and differing entirely in its character from the sacred hymns either of Egypt or of India. Where did it come from? Let the rationalist furnish his reply; for me it is a boulder from the Horeb height whereon Moses communed with the great I AM—when he saw the bush that burned but yet was not consumed—and left here as at once a witness to his inspiration, and the nations' gratitude" (W. M. Taylor, Moses the Law-giver).

This first Song of Scripture has been rightly designated the Song of Redemption, for it proceeded from the hearts of a redeemed people. Now there are two great elements in redemption, two parts to it, we may say: redemption is by *purchase* and by *power*. Redemption therefore differs from ransoming, though they are frequently confounded. Ransoming is but a part of redemption. The two are clearly distinguished in Scripture. Thus in Hosea 13:14 the Lord Jesus by the Spirit of Prophecy declares, "I will *ransom* them from the power of the grave; I will *redeem* them from death." And again we read, "For the Lord hath redeemed Jacob *and* ransomed him from the hand of him that was stronger than he" (Jer. 31:11). So in Eph. 1:14 we read, "which is the earnest of our inheritance until *the redemption* of *the purchased* possession."

Ransoming is the payment of the price; redemption, in the full sense, is the *deliverance* of the persons for whom the price was paid. It is the latter which is the all-important item. Of what use is the ransom if the captive be not released? Without actual emancipation there will be no song of praise. Who would ever thank a ransomer that left him in bondage? The Greek word for "Redemption" is rendered "*deliverance*" in Heb. 11:35—"And others were tortured not accepting deliverance." "Not accepting *deliverance*" means release from their affliction, i.e., not accepting it on the terms of their persecutors, namely, upon condition of apostacy. The two-fold nature of Redemption is the key to that wondrous and glorious vision described in Rev. 5. The "book" there, is the Redeemer's title-deeds to the earth. Hence his dual character; "Lamb"—the Purchaser; "Lion"—the powerful Emancipator.

On the Passover-night Israel were secured from the *doom* of the Egyptians; at the Red Sea they were delivered from the *power* of the Egyptians. Thus delivered—"redeemed"—they sang. It is only a redeemed people, conscious of their deliverance, that can really praise Jehovah, the Deliverer. Not only is worship impossible for those yet dead in trespasses and sins, but intelligent worship cannot be rendered by professing Christians who are in doubt as to their standing before God. And necessarily so. Praise and joy are essential elements of worship; but how can those who question their acceptance in the Beloved, who are not *certain* whether they would go to Heaven or Hell should they die this moment,—how could such be joyful and thankful? Impossible! Uncertainty and doubt beget fear and distrust, and not gladness and adoration. There is a very striking word in Psalm 106:12 which throws light on Ex. 15:1—"*Then believed* they His words; they sang *His praise.*"

"*Then* sang Moses and the children of Israel this song unto the Lord" (15:1). "Then." When? When "the Lord saved Israel that day out of the hand of the Egyptians; and Israel saw the Egyptians dead upon the sea shore" (14:30). A close parallel is met with in the book of Judges. At the close of the 4th chapter we read, "So God subdued on that day Jabin the King of Canaan before the children of Israel. And the hand of the children of Israel prospered, and prevailed against Jabin the king of Canaan, until they had destroyed Jabin king of Canaan" (vv. 23, 24). What is the immediate sequel to this deliverance of Israel from Jabin? This: "*then* sang Deborah and Barak the son of Abinoam on that day, saying, Praise ye the Lord for the avenging of Israel" (5:1). An even more blessed example is furnished in Isaiah. The 53rd chapter of this prophecy (in its *dispensational* application) contains the confession of the Jewish remnant at the close of the Tribulation period. Then will their eyes be opened to see that the One whom their nation "despised and rejected" was, in truth, the Sin-Bearer, the Saviour. Once their *faith* lays hold of this, once they have come under the virtue of Christ's atoning sacrifice, everything is altered. The very first word of Isa. 54 is, "*Sing* O barren thou that didst not bear; break forth into singing."

"Then *sang* Moses and the children of Israel." What a contrast is this from what was before us in the earlier chapters! While in the house of bondage no joyful strains were upon the lips of the Hebrews. Instead, we read that they "*sighed* by reason of the bondage, and they *cried* . . . . and God heard their *groaning.*" But now their sighing gives place to singing; their groans to praising. They are occupied no longer with themselves, but with the Lord. And what had produced this startling change? Two things: the blood of the Lamb, and the power of the Lord. It is highly significant, and in full accord with what we have said above, that we never read in Scripture of *angels* "singing." In Job 38:7 they are presented as "shouting," and in Luke 2:13 they are seen "praising" God, while in Rev. 5:11, 12 we hear them "saying," Worthy is the Lamb. Only the redeemed "sing!"

"Then sang Moses and the children of Israel this song unto the Lord." And what did they sing about? Their song was entirely about Jehovah. They not only sang *unto* the Lord, but they sang *about* Him! It was all concerning Himself, and nothing about themselves. The word "Lord" occurs no less than twelve times within eighteen verses! The pronouns "He," "Him," "Thy," "Thou," and "Thee" are found thirty-three times!! How significant and how searching is this! How entirely different from modern hymnology! So many hymns to-day (if "hymns" they deserve to be called) are full of maudlin sentimentality, instead of Divine adoration. They announce *our* love to God instead of *His* for us. They recount our experiences, instead of His mercies. They tell more of human attainments, instead of Christ's Atonement. Sad index of our low state of spirituality! Different far was this Song of Moses and Israel: "I will exalt *Him*" (v. 3), sums it all up.

"I will sing unto the Lord, for He hath triumphed gloriously: the horse and his rider hath He thrown into the sea" (v. 1). How many there are who imagine that the first thing for which we should praise God is our *own* blessing, what He has done for *us!* But while that is indeed the *natural* order, it is not the *supernatural.* Where the Spirit of God is fully in control He always draws out the heart unto God. It was so here. So much was self forgotten, the Deliverer *alone* was seen. "Out of the abundance of the heart the mouth speaketh," and where the heart is really occupied with the Lord, the mouth will tell forth *His* praises. "*The Lord* is my strength and song." Beautiful and blessed was this first note struck by God's redeemed. O that *our* hearts were so set upon things above that *He* might be the constant theme of our praise—"singing and making melody in your hearts *unto the Lord*" (Eph. 5:19).

"I will sing unto the Lord, *for* He hath triumphed gloriously; the horse and his rider hath He thrown into the sea." The *theme* of this song is what the Lord had done: He had delivered His people and destroyed their enemies. Israel began by magnifying the Lord because in overthrowing the strength of Egypt He had glorified Himself. This is repeated in various forms: "Thy right hand O Lord, is become glorious in power: Thy right hand, O Lord, hath dashed in pieces the enemy. And in the *greatness of Thine excellency* Thou hast overthrown them that rose up against Thee" (vv. 6, 7). Joy is the spontaneous overflowing of a heart which is occupied with the person and work of the Lord. It ought to be a *continuous* thing—"Rejoice in the Lord *alway*"—in the Lord, not in your experiences nor circumstances; "and again I say, Rejoice" (Phil. 4:4).

"The Lord is my strength *and* song" (v. 2). The connecting of these two things is significant. Divine strength and spiritual song are inseparable. Said Nehemiah, "The joy of the Lord is your strength" (8:10). Just as assurance leads to rejoicing, so rejoicing is essential for practical holiness. Just in proportion as we are rejoicing in the Lord shall we have power for our walk.

"And He is become my salvation" (v. 2). Not until now could Israel, really, say this. Not until they had been brought right out of the Enemy's land and their foes had been rendered powerless by death, could Israel sing of salvation. It is a very striking thing that never once is a believer found saying this in the book of Genesis. Not that Abel, Enoch, Noah, Abraham, were not saved; truly they were; but the Holy Spirit designedly reserved this confession for the book which treats of "Redemption." And even here we do not find it until the Red Sea is reached. In 14.13 Moses said, "Fear ye not, stand still and see the salvation of the Lord, which He *will* show to you to-day." And now Jehovah *had* "shown" it to them, and they can exclaim, "The Lord *is become* my salvation."

"He is my God, and I will prepare Him an habitation" (v. 2). Beautiful is this. A spirit of true devotion is here expressed. An "habitation" is a dwelling-place. It was Jehovah's *presence* in their midst that their hearts desired. And is it not ever thus with the Lord's redeemed—to enjoy *fellowship* with the One who has saved us! True, it is our happy privilege to enjoy communion with the Lord even now, but nevertheless the soul pants for the time when everything that hinders and spoils our fellowship will be forever removed—"Having a desire to depart, and *to be with Christ;* which is far bettter" (Phil. 1:23). Blessed beyond words will be the full realisation of our hope. Then shall it be said, "Behold *the Tabernacle of God* is with men, and He will *dwell with* them, and they shall be His people, and God Himself shall be with them and be their God. And God shall wipe away all tears from their eyes; and there shall be no more death, neither sorrow, nor crying, neither shall there be any more pain; for the former things are passed away" (Rev. 21:3, 4).

"The Lord is a man of war: The Lord is His name" (v. 3). This brings before us an aspect of the Divine character which is very largely ignored to-day. God is "light" (1 John 1:5) as well as "love;" holy and righteous, as well as longsuffering and merciful. And because He *is* holy, He hates sin; because He *is* righteous, He must punish it. This is something for which the believer should *rejoice;* if he does not, something is wrong with him. It is only the sickly sentimentality of the flesh which shrinks from believing and meditating upon these Divine perfections. Far different was it here with Israel at the Red Sea. They praised God *because* He had dealt in judgment with those who so stoutly defied Him. They looked at things from the Divine viewpoint. They referred to Pharaoh and his hosts as *God's* enemies, not as *their's*. "In the greatness of Thine excellency Thou hast overthrown them that rose up *against Thee*" (v. 7). The same thing is seen in Rev. 18 and 19. Immediately after the destruction of Babylon by the fearful plagues of God, we read, "And after these things I heard a great voice of much people in heaven, saying, Alleluia; Salvation, and glory, and honor, and power, unto the Lord our God; for true and righteous are His judgments; for He hath judged the great whore which did corrupt the earth with her fornication, and hath avenged the blood of His servants at her hand. And *again* they said, *Alleluia*" (Rev. 19:1-3).

Far different were the sentiments of Israel here than those which govern most our moderns. When they magnified Jehovah as a Man of War their meaning is clearly expressed in the next words of their song: "Pharaoh's chariots and his hosts hath *He* cast into the sea; his chosen captains also are drowned in the Red Sea. The depths have covered them; they sank into the bottom as a stone." They did not regard this Divine judgment as a reflection upon God's character; instead, they saw in it a display of His perfections. "He hath triumphed *gloriously* . . . Thy right hand, O Lord, is become *glorious* in power . . . in the greatness of Thine *excellency* Thou hadst overthrown them (vv. 6, 7) was their confession. The "modernists" have not hesitated to criticise Israel severely, yea, to condemn them in unmeasured terms, for their "vindictive glee." Such a conception of the Lord as Israel here expressed was worthy, we are told, of none but the most ferocious of the Barbarians. But that Israel were not here *mis*-representing God, that they were not giving utterance to their own carnal feelings, is abundantly clear from Rev. 15:3, where we read of saints *in Heaven* singing "The *Song of Moses* the servant of God, and the Song of the Lamb." Certainly there will be no manifestations of the flesh in Heaven!

Strikingly does the Song of Exodus 15 set forth the *perfect ease* with which the Almighty overthrew His enemies: "The Enemy said, I will pursue you, I will overtake, I will divide the spoil; my lust shall be satisfied upon them; I will draw my sword, my hand shall destroy them. Thou didst *blow* with Thy wind, the sea covered them; they sank as lead in the mighty waters" (vv. 9, 10). The Lord had promised to bring His redeemed into Canaan, the haughty Egyptians thought to resist the purpose of the Most High. With loud boastings of what *they* would do, they followed Israel into the parted waves of the Red Sea. With one breath of His mouth the Lord overthrew the marshalled forces of the enemy, in their mightiest array, as nothing more than a cob-web which stood in the pathway of the onward march of His eternal counsels.

Well might Israel cry, "Who is like unto Thee, O Lord, among the gods? who is like Thee, glorious in holiness, fearful in praises, doing wonders?" (v. 11). And well may we ask to-day, "Who is like Thee, O God of the Holy Scriptures, among the 'gods' of Christendom?" How entirely different is *the Lord*—omnipotent, immutable, sovereign, triumphant—from the feeble, changeable, disappointed and defeated "god" which is the object of "worship" in thousands of the churches! How few to-day *glory* in God's "holiness!" How few *praise* Him for His "fearfulness!" How few are acquainted with His "wonders!"

"Thou in Thy mercy hast led forth the people which Thou hast redeemed. Thou hast guided them in Thy strength unto Thy holy habitation" (v. 13). This was a *new standing*—brought nigh to God, into His very presence. This is what redemption effects. This is the *position* of all believers in the Lord Jesus Christ. "For Christ also hath once suffered for sins, the just for the unjust, that He might *bring us to God*" (1 Peter 3:18). God's redeemed are a people whom He has purchased for Himself, to be with Himself forever—"that where *I am,* there *ye* may be also." "Thou hast guided them in Thy strength unto Thy holy habitation." "This is our place as His redeemed. That is, we are brought to God according to all that He is. His whole moral nature having been completely satisfied in the death of Christ, He can now rest in us in perfect complacency. The hymn therefore does but express a Scriptural thought which says—'So near, so very near to God, I nearer cannot be, For in the person of His Son, I am as near as He.' The place indeed is accorded to us in grace, but none the less in righteousness; so that not only are all the attributes of God's character concerned in bringing us there, but He Himself is also glorified by it. It is an immense thought, and one which, when held in power, imparts both strength and energy to our souls—that we are even now *brought to God.* The whole distance—measured by the death of Christ on the cross, when He was made sin for us—has been bridged over, and *our* position of nearness is marked by the place *He* now occupies as glorified by the right hand of God. In Heaven itself we shall not be nearer, as to our position, because it is *in Christ.* It will not be forgotten that our *enjoyment* of this truth, indeed our apprehension of it, will depend upon our *present* condition. God looks for a state corresponding with our standing, i.e., our responsibility is measured by our privilege. But until we know our place there cannot be an answering condition. We must first learn that we are brought to God if we would in any measure walk in accordance with the position. State and walk must ever flow from a *known relationship.* Unless therefore we are taught the truth of our standing before God, we shall never answer to it in our souls, or in our walk and conversation" (Ed. Dennett).

"The people shall hear, and be afraid; sorrow shall take hold on the inhabitants of Palestina. Then the dukes of Edom shall be amazed; the mighty men of Moab, trembling shall take hold upon them; all the inhabitants of Canaan shall melt away. Fear and dread shall fall upon them; by the greatness of Thine arm they shall be as still as a stone; till Thy people pass over, O Lord, till the people pass over, which Thou hast purchased. Thou shalt bring them in, and plant them in the mountain of Thine inheritance, in the place, O Lord, which Thou hast made for Thee to dwell in, in the Sanctuary, O Lord, which Thy hands have established" (vv. 14-17). What firm confidence do these words breathe! What God had wrought at the Red Sea was the guaranty to Israel that He who had begun a work for them, would finish it. They were not counting on their own strength—"By the greatness of *Thine* arm they (their enemies) shall be as still as a stone." Their trust was solely in the Lord—"*Thou* shalt bring them in," blessed illustration of the first outflowings of simple but confident faith! Alas, that this early simplicity is usually so quickly lost. Alas, that so often it is displaced by the workings of an evil heart of unbelief. Oh, that we might ever *reason* as did Israel here, and as the apostle Paul—"Who *delivered* us from so great a death, and *doth* deliver; in whom we trust that He *will yet* deliver (2 Cor. 1:10)."

"Fear and dread shall fall upon them; by the greatness of Thine arm they shall be as still as a stone" (v. 16). Opposition there would be, enemies to be encountered. But utterly futile would be their puny efforts. Impossible for them to resist successfully the execution of God's eternal counsels. Equally impossible is it for *our* enemies, be they human or demoniac, to keep us out of the promised inheritance.

"Who shall separate us from the love of God in Christ Jesus?" Who, indeed! "For I am persuaded, that neither death, nor life, nor angels, nor principalities, nor powers, nor things present, nor things to come, nor height, nor depth, nor any other creature, shall be able to separate *us*" (Rom. 8:38, 39). Thus the end is sure from the beginning, and we may, like Israel, sing the Song of Victory *before* the first step is taken in the wilderness pathway!

Israel's confidence was not misplaced. A number of examples are furnished in later Scriptures of how tidings of Jehovah's judgments on Israel's behalf became known far and wide, and were used by him to humble and alarm. Jethro, the Midianite, comes to Moses and says, "Blessed be the Lord, who hath delivered you out of the hand of the Egyptians and out of the hand of Pharaoh . . . now I *know* that the Lord is greater than all gods" (Ex. 18, 10, 11). Rahab of Jerico declared to the two spies, "I know that the Lord hath given you the land and that *your terror* is fallen upon us, and that all the inhabitants of the land faint because of you. For *we* have *heard* how the Lord dried up the water of the Red Sea for you," etc. (Jos. 2:9, 10). Said the Gibeonites to Joshua, "From a very far country thy servants are come because of the name of the Lord thy God; for *we have heard* the fame of Him and all that He did in Egypt" (Josh. 9:9). Hundreds of years later the Philistines said, "Who shall deliver us out of the hand of these mighty Gods? these are the Gods that smote the Egyptians with all the plagues in the wilderness" (1 Sam. 4:8)!

"The Lord shall reign forever and ever" (v. 18). And here the Song ends—the next verse is simply the inspired record of the historian, giving us the cause and the occasion of the Song. The Song ends as it began—with "The Lord." Faith views the eternal future without a tremor. Fully assured that God is *sovereign*, sovereign because omnipotent, immutable, and eternal, the conclusion is irresistible and certain that, "The Lord *shall* reign *forever and ever*."

"And Miriam the prophetess, the sister of Aaron, took a timbral in her hand; and all the women went out after her with timbrals and with dances. And Miriam answered them, Sing ye to the Lord, for He hath triumphed gloriously; the horse and his rider hath He thrown into the sea" (vv. 20, 21). "The women's voices, with their musical accompaniments, take up the refrain. It is the seal of *completeness*. Sin had come in through the women; now her heart is lifted up in praise, which testifies in itself of victory over it. The mute inanimate things also become responsive in the timbrals in her hand. The joy is full and universal in the redeemed creation" (Numerical Bible). Blessed witness to the final fruits of Redemption.

Some persons have experienced a difficulty here in that Miriam also *led* in this Song of Victory. It seems to clash with the teaching of the New Testament, which enjoins the subordination of women to the men in the assembly. But the difficulty is self-created. There is nothing here which in anywise conflicts with 1 Cor. 14-34. Observe two things: it was *only* the "women" (v. 20) whom Miriam led in song! Second, this was *not* in the presence of the men—"*all* the women *went out* after her!" Thus Divine order was preserved. May the Lord grant a like spirit of subordination to His daughters to-day.

—*ARTHUR W. PINK.*

TRUTH AND ERROR,

or

Letters to a Friend.

8. *Faith and the Gospel.*

"By grace are ye saved, through faith, and that not of yourselves, it is the gift of God."—Eph. 2:8, 9.

"Being justified by faith, we have peace with God."—Rom. 5:1.

I find Scripture presenting *faith* to us in more aspects than one. It is sometimes called *hearing*, sometimes *knowing*, sometimes *believing*, sometimes *receiving*, and sometimes *trusting*. Strictly speaking, it is simply *the belief of the truth*, yet it is referred to throughout in Scripture under these different names. These may be said to be its different stages; and it is useful oftentimes to lay hold of it at each of these, and contemplate it under each of these views. They are not in reality the same thing, yet they are all *illustrative* of the same thing, and they all point to one object. The things which we *hear;* the truth which we *know;* the tidings which we *believe;* the gift which we *receive;* the Being whom we *trust*, may be different in one sense, yet in another they are the same.

Some adopt so exclusively one aspect and others another, that the object itself is lost sight of. Some particular definition is fastened on and elevated into such prominence as to become little better than a party watchword, furnishing much matter for self-righteousness and self-confidence, no less than for condemnation of others who may chance in somewhat to differ.

I see, for instance, a person glorying in what he calls his simple views of faith, and spurning every other idea of it but what he calls "the bare belief of the bare truth." I ask such an one, "where is your child-like *confidence in God,* where is the *resting* of the soul upon Jesus HIMSELF as to the resting-place? You are making a saviour of your faith, an idol of the truth. You are just as self-righteous and proud in your 'simple views of faith' as is the mystic whose religion you profess to shun. Your God seems to be a mere bundle of abstract propositions; your Saviour a mere collection of evangelical phrases, which you use as the *shibboleth* of a sect."

Again, I see another individual going into the opposite extreme. He overlooks the simplicity of faith. He undervalues the TRUTH. He is wholly occupied with some mystical actings of his own mind, and trying to exert himself to put forth some indescribable efforts which he calls receiving and resting on Christ. I say to such an one, "You are on the road to mysticism, if you be not already enveloped in its mists. You are occupied with your own self, with your own actings, and feelings; and you are making a Saviour of these. You certainly need more simple views of true faith. You need to be called from your self-righteous perplexities about your own acts, to the precious Word of Truth, which you are despising, as if it contained no comfort for you unless you can be conscious of putting forth certain acts of your own in connection with it."

From this you will see how it is quite possible to admit the full meaning of those words in Scripture which speak of confidence, and trust, and rest, etc.; while, at the same time, we rejoice in those other expressions which represent faith as an "acknowledgment of the truth," and the salvation of the sinner as the result of his "coming to the knowledge of the truth." It is quite consistent with Scripture to represent peace as flowing from confidence in God through Christ, and yet as rising from "believing the record which God hath given to His Son."

I shall not, however, attempt a definition of faith. This only let me say in a few words, that that faith which goes no farther than the intellect, can neither save nor sanctify. It is no faith at all. It is unbelief. No faith is saving, but that which links us to the PERSON of a living Saviour. Whatever falls short of this is not faith in Christ. Hence, while salvation is described sometimes in Scripture as a "coming to the knowledge of the truth," it is more commonly represented as a "coming to Christ Himself." "Ye will not come to ME that ye might have life." "Him that cometh to ME I will in no wise cast out."

But whatever view of faith we take, one thing is obvious, that it is from first to last "the gift of God." Make it as simple as you please, still it is the result of the Holy Spirit's direct, immediate, all-quickening power. *Never attempt, I beseech you, my dear friend, to make faith simple, with the view of getting rid of the Spirit to produce it.* This, I believe, is one of the wretched devices of Satan in the present evil day. By all means correct every mistake in regard to faith, by which hindrances are thrown in the sinner's way, or darkness thrown around the soul. Show him that it is with the object of faith, even with Christ and His cross, that he has to do, not with his own actings of faith; that it is not the virtue of merit that is in his faith that saves him, but the virtue and merit that are in Christ Jesus alone. Tell him to look outward not inward for his peace. Beat him off from his self-righteous efforts to get up a peculiar kind of faith or peculiar acts of faith in order to obtain something in himself—something short of Christ, to rest upon. Simplify, explain, and illustrate faith to such an one, but never imagine that thereby you are to make the Spirit's help less *absolutely necessary.*

This, I believe, is the aim of the propagators of the new theology. Their object in simplifying faith is to bring it within the reach of the *un*renewed man, so that by performing this *very simple* act he may become a renewed man. In other words, their object is to make man the beginner of his own salvation. He takes the first step, and God does the rest! He believes, and then God comes in and saves him!

This is nothing short of a flat and bold denial of the Spirit's work altogether. If at any time more than another the sinner needs the Spirit's power, it is *at the beginning.* And he who denies the need of the Spirit at the *beginning* cannot believe in it at the after stages—nay, cannot believe in the need of the Spirit's work at all. The mightiest and most insuperable difficulty lies at the beginning. If the sinner can get over *that* without the Spirit, he will easily get over the rest. If he does not need the Spirit to enable him to *believe* he will not need Him to enable him to *love.*

If when a *true object* is presented to me, I can believe without the Spirit; then when a *lovable* object is presented, I can love without the Spirit. In short, what is there in the whole Christian life, which I cannot do of myself, if I can *begin* this career without help from God? *The denial of the Spirit's direct agency in faith and conversion is the denial of His whole work in the soul both of the saint and the sinner.*

But is it not said, "Faith cometh by hearing?" Certainly it is. And who doubts the blessed truth? How can there be faith where there is not something to be believed. "There is an inseparable relation between faith and the Word, and these can be no more torn asunder from each other than rays of light from the sun" (Calvin). But does this mean that hearing alone is necessary to the production of faith? The words in the original explain this. They are these, "faith arises out of what we hear, and what we hear comes to us through means of the Word of God." Who then would say anything but what the apostle does here? viz.: that the foundation of faith is what we hear—(lit., a hearing or report). But does this exclude the Spirit from His work in preparing the soul for the believing what it hears?

And now, having said this much as to *faith* itself, let me add a few words as to what it receives, "the glorious gospel of that blessed God." That which we preach, and which faith believes, "is the glad tidings of great joy." It is God's testimony of His own character, His declaration of His gracious mind towards the sinner, the utterance of His manifold yearnings over His lost and long-wandered offspring. That which we make known is the story of Divine love. We tell man that there is such a thing as love in God towards the sinful; that this love hath found vent to itself in a righteous way, and that to the participation and enjoyment of this love ALL are welcome. We show them how God has opened up His *heart,* to let them see what riches of grace are there; and how He has done a work upon the earth by which we may measure the infinite dimensions of that gracious heart. These are the NEWS we bring. These are the tidings which we present to the sinner, to be believed, and to be rejoiced in with joy unspeakable and full of glory. These tidings are *free;* truly, absolutely, unconditionally, free. They are without money and without price. They make known the exceeding riches of God's grace. They show us how these riches are pouring themselves freely upon all this fallen world. They tell us that not only is there *grace* in God for sinners, but also that that grace has found vent to itself, and is flowing down in a *righteous* channel to *unrighteous* men. They tell us that the darkness is past, and the true light has risen upon the world. They tell us that the veil is rent from top to bottom, and that ever sinner may go freely in. They tell us that there is forgiving love in the bosom of the Father, of which every sinner, without exception, is invited to avail himself. They point each wandering eye to the cross, that it may read there the Divine compassion, the yearning tenderness of Him who made us, towards the lost, the rebellious, the unholy. They come up to every man, and invite him to partake of all the fulness of God: they make no exception, but address themselves, in all their gladness and amplitude, to each man as he stands. Hear the words of Trail: "Shall we tell men that unless they be holy they must not believe on Jesus Christ; that they must not venture on Christ for salvation till they be qualified and fit to be received and welcomed by Him? This were to forbear preaching the Gospel at all, or to forbid all men to come to Christ. For never was any sinner qualified for Christ. *He* is well qualified for us; but a sinner out of Christ has no qualifications for Christ but sin and misery. . . . Shall we warn people that they should not believe on Christ too soon? It is impossible that they should do it too soon. Can a man obey the command of the Gospel too soon; or do the great work of God too soon? . . . If he should say, what is it to believe on Jesus Christ? As to this, I find no question in the Word, but that all did some way understand the notion of it. They all, both Christ's enemies and disciples, knew that faith in Him was believing that the Man, Jesus of Nazareth, was the Son of God, the Messiah and the Saviour of the world, so as to receive and look for salvation in His name. If he yet ask *what* he is to believe, you tell him that he is not called to believe that he is in Christ, but that his sins are pardoned, and that he is a justified man; but that he is to believe God's record concerning Christ; and that this record is, that God giveth to us eternal life in His Son, Jesus Christ, and that all who with the heart believe this report, and rest their souls on these glad tidings, shall be saved. If he still say that believing is hard, ask what it is he finds makes believing difficult to him? Is it unwillingness to be saved? Is it a distrust of the truth of the Gospel record? This he dare not own. Is it a doubt of Christ's ability or goodwill to save? This is to contradict the testimony of God in the Gospel. . . . If he say that he cannot believe on Christ, and that a Divine power is needful to draw it forth, which he finds not, you tell him that believing in Jesus Christ is no work, but a resting on Jesus Christ, and that this pretence is as miserable as if a man wearied of his journey, and who is not able to go one step farther should argue, I am so tired that I am not able to lie down, when, indeed, he can neither stand nor go."

But I may be asked, how is all this freeness consistent with Christ's substitution for His church alone? I answer, that the Gospel is not "Christ died for the elect;" neither is it, "Christ died for all." But it is, "Christ died for *sinners.*" It was thus that the apostles preached and that men believed. Any reader of the Acts of the Apostles may see this. They preached the glad tidings in such terms as these: "To Him gave all the prophets witness, that through His name whosoever believeth in Him shall receive remission of sins" (Acts 10:43). Or again, "Be it known unto you, men and brethren, that through this man is preached unto you the forgiveness of sins; and by Him all that believe are justified from all things from which ye could not be justified by the law of Moses" (Acts 13:38).

The passage in 1 Corinthians 15:3 is often appealed to as a proof that the apostles preached everywhere that Christ died for all. I have already remarked that in the only book in which we have a full account of their preaching (Acts) there is nothing of this kind stated. And, in regard to this passage, I would just ask anyone how it is possible to extort such a declaration out of it? The apostle went to Corinth. He stood up in a city of heathens. He cried out, "Christ died for *our* sins." He did not say, "for all and every one;" nay, he did not say "for *your* sins;" he simply said, "for *our* sins." Now, I have no wish to restrict the Gospel, or to make it appear as if not literally and actually for all. But it is plain that the words here are *restrictive.* So much so that had there been some cavilling hearer in the way he might have said like some modern objectors, "Oh! he does not preach the Gospel; he says Christ died for *our* sins;" he should have said, "Christ died not for our sins only but for the sins of *all.*"

The man who lays stress on what he calls the Gospel upon *all,* the *me,* or on the other hand, upon the *elect* or the *church,* plainly does not preach the Gospel as the apostles did. And the man, who, in believing, is turning his whole thoughts to these words, is going aside from the glad tidings themselves. He is thinking of nothing but *himself,* and the bearing of the Gospel upon *himself* alone. He is losing sight of the glorious revelation of HIMSELF which God has made in the Gospel, and is only concerned about that part of it which he thinks includes his own salvation.

But how is this, you will ask? For this obvious reason, that it is not with the work of Christ as a work done specially for myself that I have in the first place to do. in believing, but as a work which opens up to me the grace of God. It shows me that there is such a thing as *grace,* or free love to sinners. It is the pledge of its reality and the measure of its extent and dimensions. Whether we suppose it to be work done for many or few, still it is the declaration of God's free love, and it is that free love that is the sinner's resting-place. The real question that troubles an anxious soul is in substance this: "Is there free love in God, free love reaching even to the vilest, free love which no amount of sin can either repel or quench? Is there enough of free love to reach even to me and remedy a case like mine?" The work of Christ settles all these perplexities, and yet in settling them it does not raise the question, "was that work done especially for me," any more than it raises the question, "am I elected or not?" It is the *meaning* of that work to which an inquirer has to look in the first place, not to its ultimate and particular destination. He who understands the character of God as the Lord God merciful and gracious will not be disquieted by the subtle suggestion of the evil one, Am I elected? So he who understands the work of Christ, which is the grand exposition and opening up of that character, will never think of putting the question, Was that work specially intended for me? Apart from such a question, that work contains enough to remove all his fears.

H. Bonar, 1851.

N.B.—

The above article is an important one, especially for those who do the work of an evangelist. No servant of God is warranted in saying to an unsaved man, "Christ bore *your* sins," for the truth of substitution is for believers only. To an exercised soul I may say, "The Son of Man is come to seek and to save that which was lost," and then ask him, "Have you taken the place of a *lost sinner* before God? If so, there is a Saviour *for you.*" "Christ died for the *ungodly*" (Rom. 5:6)—will *you* own yourself before God to be *such* an one?

—*A.W.P.*

NAAMAN: 2 KINGS 5.

Who was Naaman? The first verse of our chapter tells us: "Now Naaman, captain of the hosts of the king of Syria, was a great man with his master, and honourable, because by him the Lord had given deliverance unto Syria: he was also a mighty man in valour, but he was a leper." Naaman was a successful leader of Syria's army, honoured by his sovereign, high in favour at court. Position, fame, riches, were his; all that the world could give, short of a throne, he had. According to human estimation he was one of fortune's most highly favoured sons. But one thing he lacked which the world could not supply, and that was health. "He was a leper." All his possessions, if sold at the highest price which man would put upon them, could not purchase this much-coveted boon. Here was the one bitter ingredient in his cup of happiness.

Naaman was an honourable and a mighty man, but he was a leper, and as such he illustrates the condition of the sinner, portraying the utter ruin of the creature. Man has much to make him happy. It is true that he is born into a world where the marks of the "Curse" are visible on all sides, yet the evidences of the Creator's handiwork far out-number these. The tokens of God's goodness surround us on every hand: "He maketh His sun to rise on the evil and on the good, and sendeth rain on the just and on the unjust" (Matt. 5:45). As said the apostle concerning the benevolent Maker of heaven and earth, "He left not Himself without witness, in that He did good, and gave us rain from heaven, and fruitful seasons, filling our hearts with food and gladness" (Acts 14:17). In view of this, every regenerate heart is constrained to cry, "Oh, that man would praise the Lord for His goodness, and for His wonderful works to the children of men!" (Psl. 107:8).

Yes, man has very much to be thankful for, and much to make him happy. And yet we must not ignore the other side, the dark side. The natural man has much to make him miserable. Shapen in iniquity and conceived in sin, he enters the world "alienated from the life of God." Conscience within and Scripture without witness to his fallen condition. A noble creature he may be, higher than any other on earth. Made, originally, in the image and likeness of God. *But he is a leper*—defiled, unclean, unfit for the presence of the thrice Holy One.

Leprosy is the Divinely-chosen type of *sin*. Its nature—working from within outwards. Its contagiousness—infecting all with whom it comes into direct contact. Its consuming effects—spreading with deadly rapidity from one member of the body to another. Its entail—poisoning the blood and being transmitted from parent to child. Its loathsomeness — nauseating and repelling those who gaze upon its unhappy victim. Its incurability—baffling the efforts of the ages to discover a cure and still defying medical science. These, and other characteristics which might be mentioned, all stamp it as a tragically accurate figure of *sin*.

And Naaman, the honoured commander of Syria's army, was a *leper*. "Alas! this was a sad drawback—a grievous blight upon all his dignities—a heavy cloud upon all his glory. The foul disease which covered his person not only prevented his enjoyment of the honours which fortune had heaped upon him, but actually changed them into so many sources of humiliation and chagrin. His very elevation made his malady conspicuous, and the sunshine of prosperity made his personal vileness apparent. His military costume enwrapped the person of the leper, and his laurel of victory crowned a leper's brow. In short, the lowest menial in Naaman's establishment would not have felt the humiliation of leprosy so keenly as the noble captain himself. The higher he was in position the more intensely must he have felt the degradation and depression of his loathesome disease. What would he not have given to anyone to take his leprosy?" (C.H.M.)

Thus we see how Naaman pictures the sinner in his natural state. No matter how favoured his outward circumstances, no matter how honourable his position in the world, he is an outcast from God. It matters not though he be born of respectable parents and has been reared in an environment of refinement, he is a lost creature. Highly educated he may be, surrounded by all the comforts which wealth can purchase, admired by a wide circle of friends, yet is he a sinner, in dire need of a Saviour. "There is *no difference*, for all have sinned and come short of the glory of God." Happy the man who has discovered the wretchedness of his condition. Happy the one who has seen that, spiritually, he is a leper. Happy the one who longs to have his guilt cancelled, his sins removed, his conscience cleansed. But *how* is that to be?

"Naaman was a leper." The physicians of Damascus could not cure him. The priests of Rimmon could not take away the dreadful disease, which, if unchecked, would speedily sap his vitality and terminate in a horrible death. The waters of Abana and Pharpar could not heal him. All the wealth and influence he commanded could not purchase one day's respite. What, then? Was he doomed to end his days in a lazar-house? No; God had marked him out for healing, but before this should be bestowed he must first be brought down to supplicate for this blessing, in that very land over which he had triumphed, and from the servant of that God whose people he had overcome in battle.

The second verse of our chapter presents to us a most striking contrast: "And the Syrians had gone out by companies, and had brought away captive out of the land of Israel a little maid; and she waited on Naaman's wife." First we are shown "A *great* man," now "A *little maid.*" The one is named, the other unnamed. The one was a "captain," the other a "captive." The one was "honourable," the other a "servant-girl." But notwithstanding the disparity between them she knew that of which he was ignorant, and was used of God as an instrument toward his salvation.

"And she said unto her mistress, Would God my lord were with the prophet that is in Samaria! for he would recover him of his leprosy" (v. 3). There is much for us to learn from this little maid, for she puts all of us to shame. Hers was a trying situation. She had been rudely snatched from her home and carried away by an heathen. But there was no bitterness toward her captors nor murmuring against God for His mysterious providences. Instead, on the one hand, she was moved with compassion toward her leprous master; and on the other, with a desire to bear faithful witness to the God of Israel. Her opportunities were limited, but she made the most of them. She just told out the good news that there was salvation even for lepers, and she referred her mistress to Elisha the prophet, whose name, most significantly means, "The *salvation of God.*" By bearing this simple testimony, she was used in bringing Naaman, at last, to Elisha. "Look at this little girl, a grand preacher of the Gospel; she could preach while in the kitchen, where she was; she did not require to go on a platform to do it—no, she could do it in the kitchen. We need more *kitchen preaching!"* (W. P. Mackay).

"And one went in, and told his Lord saying, Thus and thus said the maid that is of the land of Israel. And the king of Syria said, Go to, go, and I will send a letter unto the king of Israel" (vv. 4, 5). Poor Naaman, he was misdirected through heeding the word of the king of Syria, The Hebrew maid had said nothing about "the *king* of Israel;" she had spoken of "The *prophet* that is in Samaria." Well if he had paid careful attention to her words. How often the poor sinner, awakened in measure to his desperate condition and deep need, turns aside to empty cisterns. It is rare that the exercised soul finds relief at once. More frequently he is like the poor woman of the Gospels who "suffered many things of *many* physicians, and had spent all she had, and was nothing bettered, but rather grew worse" (Mark 5:26)! Or, like the "prodigal son" who, when he *"began* to be in want, went and joined himself to a citizen of *that* (the 'far') country" (Luke 15:15), and got nothing better than "the husks that the swine did eat" for his pains.

"And he departed, and took with him ten talents of silver, and six thousand pieces of gold, and ten changes of raiment" (v. 5). The value of these metals was upward of 70,000 dollars, or £14,000. What a commentary on the human heart, which, by nature, is a total stranger to the *grace* of God! The thought of being cleansed for nothing never entered Namman's mind. He was ready to pay handsomely for his healing. The idea of being recovered from his leprosy *"without* money and *without* price" never occurred to him. Ah, how many think that the gift of God can be purchased with money (Acts 8:20). This is the error of the human heart in every age and in every clime. As though the Possessor of heaven and earth could be induced to *sell* anything! Equally foolish is it for any one to suppose that he can purchase a place in Heaven by his own morality or religiousness. Neither reformation, good works, tears, penance, prayers or feelings are demanded as the price, or any part thereof. God is not a *receiver* but a GIVER. Said Christ to the woman at the well, "If thou knewest the *gift of God,* and who it is that saith to thee, Give me to drink; thou wouldest have *asked* of Him, and He would have *given* thee living water" (John 4:10). It was *this* which Naaman had yet to learn.

"And he brought the letter to the king of Israel, saying, Now when this letter is come unto thee, behold, I have therewith sent Naaman my servant to thee, that thou mayest recover him of his leprosy" (v. 6). A characteristic letter was this from one who was a stranger to the Lord. His mind did not reach beyond the realm of the things of sight. Certainly God was not in the thoughts of the king of Syria as he wrote his letter to Jehoram.

There was some excuse, perhaps, for Naaman's royal master writing in the strain he did: nothing better could be expected from a heathen. But it is sad to see the effect which it had upon the king of Israel: "And it came to pass, when the king of Israel had read the letter, that he rent his clothes, and said, Am I God, to kill and to make alive, that this man doth send unto me to recover a man of his leprosy? wherefore consider, I pray you and see how he seeketh a quarrel against me" (v. 7). He knew much *about* God, but it is very evident he did not *know* God. Instead of getting down on his knees and supplicating Jehovah, he rent his clothes. Instead of seeing in this appeal an opportunity for the God of Israel to display His grace and glory, he was filled with alarm. His thoughts were upon himself; it was his own well-being that he was concerned about—"he seeketh a quarrel against *me.*" How this manifested the apostate condition of Israel at that time—the reason why the Lord had suffered the Syrians to conquer them. We cannot but contrast the conduct of Hezekiah when he received a letter from another Gentile sovereign (Isa. 37:14). He "spread it before the Lord," and received an answer. But Jehoram had no refuge in the time of trouble.

"And it was so, when Elisha the man of God had heard that the king of Israel had rent his clothes, that he sent to the king, saying, Wherefore hast thou rent thy clothes? let him come now to me, and he shall know that there is a prophet in Israel" (v. 8). Very blessed is this. The counsels of God's grace toward His elect cannot fail. Naaman might have been mis-directed, his royal master might be ignorant of the Almighty, the king of Israel might be unbelieving, but nevertheless Naaman *shall* discover that there is a prophet in Israel, and that Elisha's God was able and willing to heal him. *How* Elisha learned of the appeal to Jehoram and of the king's fear we are not told. Sufficient for us to know that he *had* learned—"the secret of the Lord is with them that fear Him," and such an one was the prophet.

"So Naaman came with his horses and with his chariots, and stood at the door at the house of Elisha" (v. 9). One can readily picture the scene. The humble dwelling-place of God's servant which, we doubt not, had no attraction for the outward eye. The very reverse was the pompous train of Naaman. Most important and imposing to a worldling must this poor-rich leper have looked—sitting in his chariot, accompanied by his liveried attendants, and guard of honor. There, too, was the silver and gold and rich apparel as a handsome doctor's fee. No doubt Naaman expected that the prophet would be duly impressed, and that he would fawn upon him with servile deference. But he was greatly mistaken. Such things make no impression upon "a man of God." The spiritual eye at once recognises that the millionaire in his mansion or the king on his throne is, by nature, nothing more than a depraved lost sinner, bound for Hell, unless sovereign mercy snatch him as a brand from the burning.

As Naaman stood before the door of Elisha's house, with his fine equipage and the wherewithal for a handsome remuneration to the one who should heal him, he provides us with a strikingly accurate picture of the sinner resting upon his own self-righteousness, his good works, his diligent efforts to merit the notice of God. According to the standard of human judgment, Naaman was provided with everything that could reasonably be expected. In reality, all his preparations were but a useless encumbrance, and the servant of God quickly made that plain to him.

"And Elisha sent a messenger unto him, saying, Go and wash in Jordan seven times, and thy flesh shall come again to thee. And thou shalt be clean" (v. 10). Here was no servile obeisance, nor recognition of the mightiness of Naaman. The captain of Syria's army must be humbled; pride must be removed far from him. The prophet did not even greet him; he did not so much as go out of his house to meet him. Instead, he sent him a message by a servant. Ah, God is no respector of persons; nor should His servants be. Before Naaman could be healed, he had to be brought low; and before any sinner is saved his pride must be abased. God will not tolerate any parading of fleshly distinctions before him—"*no* flesh shall glory in *His* presence" (1 Cor. 1:29). The Son of Man came to seek and to save that which was *lost,* and there are no distinctions here. "By one man sin entered into the world, and death by sin; and so death passed upon all men, for that all sinned" (Rom. 5:12). There are no degrees in death! Ah, my reader, *that* is what God requires of thee; that you take *this* place before Him—own yourself as guilty, undone, lost.

But there is another way in which to view the prophet's action. He was not indifferent to Naaman's welfare; the fact that he sent out his servant proved that. But Elisha knew full well that the all-important thing was not the *messenger,* but the *message.* It mattered nothing *who* delivered the message—himself or his servant—but it mattered everything that the God-given word should be faithfully communicated. Elisha knew full well that Naaman's expectation lay *in him,* so like a true "man of God" he diverted attention *away from himself.* What a needed lesson for us! How much better should we serve souls, if, thus hidden, we occupied them with the Word of God, instead of ourselves.

"But Naaman was wroth, and went away" (v. 11). How accurate the picture! How true to life. The flesh resents the humbling truth of God. Man hates to be abased. Naaman was angry, and so will some of the hearers of every servant of God be if he faithfully ministers the Word in its unadulterated purity. "The brief, pointed, simple message, '*go wash,*' swept away all confidence in gold, silver, raiment, retinue, the king's letter. It stripped Naaman of everything, and reduced him to his true condition of a poor defiled leper needing to be washed. It put no difference between the illustrious commander-in-chief of the hosts of Syria, and the poorest and meanest leper in all the coasts of Israel. The former could do nothing less; the latter needed nothing more. Wealth cannot remedy man's ruin, and poverty cannot interfere with God's remedy. Nothing that a man has done need keep him out of Heaven; nothing that he can do will ever get him in. 'Go wash,' is the word in every case. Naaman evidently felt the prophet's message to be deeply humbling. He was not prepared for such a total setting aside of human pretentions. He would have liked to be called upon to tell out *his* pieces of gold, *his* talents of silver, *his* changes of raiment; but to be told, 'go *wash,*' without the slightest allusion to any of these things, was quite too humiliating" (C.H.M.).

"But Naaman was wroth, and went away, and said, Behold, I thought, He will surely come out to me, and stand and call on the name of the Lord his God, and strike his hand over the place, and recover the leper" (v. 11). "In Naaman's mind all was arranged. He pictured the scene to himself, and made himself the foremost figure in the group—the Gentile idolator waited on by the prophet of God. The incongruity of this he did not then see. We see it. God would visit him in grace, but as one who had no ground of his own to stand on. As a sinner He could meet him. As a leper He could heal him. As the captain of the hosts of the king of Syria He would not receive him. What place has a sinner before God save that of one to whom *mercy* can be shown? What place is suited to the leper save that *outside* the camp? Naaman has to learn his place. He may be wroth with the prophet, but he cannot move him. Before him he is only a leper, whatever he may appear before others. Learning his place he has to learn his vileness. He imagined Elisha would have struck his hand over the place. A sign—a scene he expected—not a mere word. He did not know what a defiling object he was. The priest looked on the leper to judge whether he was leprous or not. He touched him only when he was clean (Lev. 14). Of Naaman's leprosy there is no doubt, for he had come to be healed of it. To touch him ere he was clean would only have defiled the prophet! But further, if he had been able to touch him, and so have healed him, would not man have thought there was virtue in the prophet? By sendnig him to the Jordan to wash, it would be clearly seen the cure was direct from *God.* Man has no virtue in himself—he can only be the channel of God's grace to others. *God* must have *all* the glory of the cure, and Naaman must be taught his own condition and vileness" (Mr. C. E. Stuart).

"And Naaman was wroth and went away, and said, Behold, *I thought,* He will surely come out to me, and stand, and call on the name of the Lord his God, and strike his hand over the place, and recover the leper. Are not Abana and Pharpar rivers of Damascus, better than all the waters of Israel? may I not wash in them and be clean? So he turned and went away in a rage" (vv. 11, 12). What right had he, *a leper,* to either argue or prescribe? Far, far less has any sinner any right to make terms with God. It is for Him to say *how* a sinner shall be saved. For this reason, God not only says, "Let the wicked *forsake* his ways," but also "and the unrighteous man his *thoughts*" (Isa. 55:7). Man must abandon his own opinions, turn away from his own schemes, reject his prejudices and preconceptions. It is spiritual anarchy for me to put an "I thought" over against a "Thus saith the Lord." And yet there are still multitudes in the religious world following their own sin-darkened reason: "For they being ignorant of God's righteousness and going about to establish their own righteousness, have not submitted themselves to the righteousness of God" (Rom. 10:23).

"I thought he would surely come out to *me.*" He was willing to be restored to health, but he wanted to be restored in his own way. He was ready to be healed provided he should be honored. He had come all the way from Syria to be rid of his leprosy, but he did not want it God's way. How foolish! He had received now what the king had failed to give him—full directions for his cure. There was no uncertainty about the prescription: "Go, wash in Jordan seven times, and thou *shalt* be clean." But he was humiliated, made nothing of, and he departed from the prophet's house in a towering rage.

"And his servants came near, and spake unto him, and said, My father, if the prophet had bid thee to do some great thing, wouldst thou not have done it? How much rather then, when he saith to thee, Wash, and be clean?" (v. 13). When God begins a work of grace within a soul, He does not cease it until His own eternal purpose is accomplished. The flesh may resist, and the Devil may oppose, but all in vain. Better might a worm resist the tread of an elephant than man withstand the drawing-power of Omnipotent Love. Is it not written, "Thy people *shall be willing* in the day of Thy power" (Psl. 110:3)? The day of God's power had now arrived for Naaman, and he shall speedily realise its transforming effects. It is remarkable to see the instruments which God here employed. Truly, His ways and thoughts are vastly different from ours. The "little maid" was not present to speak to her august master; the prophet of Samaria had been despised. What, then, shall Naaman return home *un*healed? No, that could not be. He was to learn that there was a *God* in Israel, and that He had thoughts of mercy toward him. But he must first be humbled. God now moves his own followers to admonish Naaman and to show him the folly of his proud reasoning. Deeply significant is it to mark that it was first a *servant* maid that God employed to acquaint Naaman with the one who told him how to be healed; then the prophet employed *his* "servant" to communicate with Naaman; and now his own *servants* are the final link in the chain. All of this was designed for Naaman's humbling.

"Then went he down, and dipped himself seven times in Jordan" (v. 14). "Go wash" was a simple test of *obedience.* Everything was narrowed down to this one thing: would he bow before the authoritative Word of God! In like manner, the Gospel tests the sinner to-day. The Gospel proclamation is no mere "Invitation" to be heeded or not as man pleases. Grossly dishonoring to God is it for us to term it such. God "now *commandeth* all men everywhere to repent" (Act. 17:30). And again we are told, "And this is His *commandment,* That we should believe on the name of His Son Jesus Christ" (1 John 3:23). The Gospel is "for faith-*obedience*" (Rom. 1:5). Christ is "The Author of eternal salvation unto all them that *obey* Him" (Heb. 5:9). And to those "that *obey not* the Gospel" He will yet come in flaming fire, taking vengeance (2 Thess. 1:7).

"Then went he down, and dipped himself seven times in Jordan" (v. 14). But why should Naaman have to wash in the *Jordan?* If bathing in a river was all that was necessary for his healing, why should not "Abana and Pharpar" suffice? Ah, the grace of God could be extended to sinners of the Gentiles, but they must first be taught that this grace proceeds from the God of *Israel,* therefore must he wash in one of Israel's rivers. This truth is writ large across the pages of Holy Scripture. The harlot of Jericho was to be spared when her city was destroyed, but only because she heeded the word given her by two sons of Abraham. The widow of Sarepta was preserved through the famine, but only by receiving Elijah in her house. The Ninevites were spared from impending wrath, but it was at the preaching of Jonah. The king of Babylon received a dream from God, but for its interpretation he had to turn to Daniel. To the Samaritan adultress our Lord declared, "Salvation is of *the Jews*" (John 4:22). Let us heed the warning of Rom. 11:—"Boast not against the branches. But if thou boast, *thou* bearest not the root, but *the root thee.* . . . For I would not, brethren, that ye should be ignorant of this mystery, lest ye should be wise in your own conceits" (vv. 18, 25).

If then Naaman must wash in the waters of Palestine. why could he not go to the river Kishon or the pool of Bethesda? Why was it necessary for him to journey to the uninviting *Jordan?* The answer to this question reveals the striking accuracy of our type. As leprosy (sin) was in question, the *curse* must be witnessed to. Sin has called down the curse of Him against whom it has raised its defiant head (see Gen. 3). The Curse is God's *judgment* upon sin, and that judgment is *death.* It is this of which the "Jordan" ever speaks. It was not because the waters of Jordan possessed any magical properties or healing virtues, but because it is the lasting symbol of Divine judgment upon sin. The New Testament leaves us in no doubt upon this point. Those who heeded the message of our Lord's forerunner on earth, "were all baptised of him in the river Jordan, *confessing their* SINS" (Mark 1:5). The Jordan speaks of death, and by death alone (the death of Christ) can any soul be delivered from the dominion and guilt of sin.

Here then was the great lesson that Naaman had to learn. His costly treasures could not purchase him healing. His high social standing availed him nothing. All he needed to bring to God was his leprosy! The sinner would feign bring his good works to Christ. But they are worthless. He must come bringing nought but his deep guilt. Naaman must stoop to *own his vileness.* No less than *seven* times must he be submerged in the dark waters —he had to confess his *total* uncleanness. A person slightly soiled may be cleansed by a single washing. But Naaman must be washed "Seven times" to show *how great* his defilement was! The *seven* times also indicates to us that God requires *complete* submission to His will.

"Then went he down, and dipped himself seven times in Jordan, *according to the saying of the man of God:* and his flesh came again like unto the flesh of a little child, and he was clean" (v. 14). God's word through His servant (v. 10) was faithfully and literally fulfilled. His defilement was gone. In place of disease and emaciation was the flesh of a little child—beautiful type of "the *babe*" in Christ. "And he was clean": "The blood of Jesus Christ, God's Son, *cleanseth* us (believers) from *all* sin" (1 John 1:7). Naaman might have washed in the waters of "Abana and Pharpar" a thousand times over, and remained just as he was; but the moment he believed and obeyed God, he was made whole, immediately and perfectly.

"And he returned to the man of God, he and all his company, and came, and stood before him" (v. 15). This is very blessed. Naaman quickly gave evidence that a real work of grace had been wrought upon him. He at once seeks out "the man of God," whom previously he had turned away from in a rage. All was changed now. No longer does the prophet decline to see him. How beautifully does this set forth the truth that when a sinner has been saved he desires fellowship with the people of God.

"And he said, "Behold, *now* I *know* that there is no God in all the earth but in Israel" (v. 15). Naaman was the first to speak, and he at once confessed God. He had heard no lectures on the evidences for the Divine existence; nor did he need them; effectively is a soul taught when it partakes of sovereign grace. Naaman was as sure now as Elisha that Jehovah is God, and He alone.

"Now therefore, I pray thee take a blessing of thy servant. But he said, as the Lord liveth, before whom I stand I will receive none. And he urged him to take it; but he refused" (vv. 15, 16). Naaman is now taught the *freeness* of God's grace. When God gives to sinners, He gives freely. "Why did Elisha refuse to take a blessing from Naaman's hand? For a truly noble reason. He would have Naaman return to Syria with this testimony, that *the God of Israel had taken nothing from him but his leprosy.* He would have him go back and declare that his gold and silver were useless in dealing with One Who gave *all* for *nothing.* Elisha would not tarnish the lustre of Divine grace by accepting a shekel of the stranger's money" (C.H.M.). Have we, Christian readers, ever entertained the thought of trying to pay the Saviour back in instalments for all that He has done for us? That is not possible: nor is it necessary. Yea, such a thought is dishonoring to His grace. God delights in being *the Giver.* If you wish to please Him, *continue* to come before Him as a *receiver.* Listen to David: "What shall I render unto the Lord for all His benefits? I will *take* the cup of salvation and *call* upon His name" (Psl. 116:12, 13). In other words, he will "render" to Him *by receiving more!*

"And Naaman said, Shall there not then, I pray thee, *be given* to thy *servant* two mules' burden of earth? for thy servant will henceforth offer neither burnt offering nor sacrifice unto other gods, but unto the Lord" (v. 17). Note he does not offer to purchase this soil. Grace had taught him to take the place of a *receiver* and a *servant.* Beautiful is it to mark *the purpose* for which he wanted this "two mules' burden of earth." It was not superstitious veneration of the soil, but that he might erect an altar and sacrifice unto the Lord. The healed man had now the spirit of *worship.* But were there not "altars" in Syria? Yes, plenty of them. But not from them could he present his offerings to the only true God.

"But here a difficulty arises. Naaman will worship Jehovah alone, but can he refuse to attend his master the king in the house of Rimmon? 'In this thing the Lord pardon thy servant that when my master goeth into the house of Rimmon to worship there and he leaneth on my hand, and I bow myself in the house of Rimmon; when I bow down myself in the house of Rimmon, the Lord pardon thy servant in this thing (v. 18).' Here again we surely see the spiritual instincts of a new-born soul. Fresh from the Jordan he learned how incompatible is all other worship with that of the true God. God cannot admit of a rival. He sees something of this; and learns that there cannot be the blending of the false with the true. He cannot worship Jehovah and Rimmon. As a heathen, he might have introduced the worship of Jehovah to his countrymen, as a fresh rite to be practised side by side with the old one. As a new-born soul, this he sees cannot be. What is he to do? Elisha answers 'go in peace' —a strange reply at first sight it appears. Is God willing to share His glory with another? Could Elisha have bowed himself in the house of Rimmon, if honored by being the support of the king of Syria? A wise answer it was, if we reflect on it. *He leaves Naaman to be taught of God,* as he is able to receive it. He could not sanction what Naaman speaks of. He did not excuse it, nor make light of it. He refused to direct him about it. *Could Naaman have walked by Elisha's faith?* Naaman's words show he saw it was wrong to act as he speaks of, but he did not see how wrong. Could one who saw it clearly have said, 'the Lord pardon thy servant in this thing?' When it was a question of teaching Naaman the freeness of God's grace, Elisha is plain and decided; when it is a question of how Naaman should act, his eyes as yet *half* opened, Elisha *leaves him with God!* Should we not do well to follow the prophet sometimes in this?" (Mr. C. E. Stewart).

"Go in peace" was the parting message of Elisha to Naaman—the identical words of the Lord Jesus in Luke 7, see v. 50. The one whose condition, typically, sets forth so strikingly the depth of man's ruin, the pride of his heart, the worthlessness of self-righteous efforts, and whose healing portrays so vividly the freeness of God's sovereign grace, the power of Christ's death, and the regenerating work of the Holy Spirit, now departs in the consciousness of a known salvation. He left Syria a defiled, but haughty, leper; he returns a humble, but joyful, worshipper. May the Lord be pleased to bless this rich portion of His blessed Word to many souls.

—*ARTHUR W. PINK.*

THE GUILTY BY NO MEANS CLEARED.

This is the assertion of Jehovah in Ex. 34:7, in proclaiming His name and His attributes. Moses had asked, in Ex. 33:18, "Show me Thy glory." Jehovah had replied in the next verse, "I will make all My goodness pass before thee." And the promise is fulfilled in 34:5-7, when He descended in the cloud. . . . and proclaimed the name of Jehovah. So that in these words, "and will by no means clear the guilty," we have part of the very glory and goodness of God. It is as much God's *goodness* as it is His *glory* to "not clear the guilty."

Jehovah tells us not only *what* He will not do, but *why* He will not do it. This does not mean that there is any unwillingness on His part to show mercy. On the contrary, it is declared (Psa. 86:5), "Thou Lord, art good and ready to forgive." Nothing that we can do can make Him more ready than He is to do all His will. It is, however, here, not a mere question of *forgiveness,* but of atonement. The word is (*nakee*), and its clear meaning may be traced from Gen. 24:8: "Then their name shall be *clear* from this Mine oath"; 44:10: "Ye shall be *blameless";* Ex. 21:7: *"guiltless";* Ex. 21:28: "the owner of the ox shall be *quit"; 23:7: "innocent".*

It means, therefore, that God will not forgive without satisfaction made to justice. He will be "faithful and just" in the forgiveness of sins (1 John 1:9). There can be no display of mercy at the expense of justice. A penalty has been fixed upon sin, and Jehovah will never pronounce the sentence of acquital except in full accordance with justice in the payment of that penalty.

And yet the world's religion is based upon the very opposite of this fundamental truth of the Gospel. The world believes that God will clear the guilty! that God is love, and God is merciful. This is the source of the delusion that the sinner can, by his own meritorious conduct and repentance and "works," obtain this mercy. This is the cause of all the deceptive resting in ordinances that we see around us. It is only a half-gospel, leading to a false peace, to declare to sinners and the world at large that "God is love." To begin God's gospel here is to begin building from the top. It is not so begun in Romans 1, when God lays the true foundation. He does not separate the two great truths. He does not reveal His "righteousness" apart from His "wrath." See Rom. 1:16, 17, 18.

It is our place, therefore, to proclaim that *God is just,* "and that He will by no means clear the guilty"; because on this foundation we can at once proceed to build. It is the very foundation of the truth that "God is love." For if there were the clearing of the guilty, if there were acquital, apart from the law, if there were any such conniving at sin, it would be treating it as a light thing and putting a premium on sin, and we should lose the very ground of the manifestation of God's holy love, which is not manifested to us apart from Christ.

Apart from Christ "the Lord is a man of war," revealing His wrath against all ungodliness and unrighteousness. But it is in Christ that He is seen as the God of peace, revealing His love, by imputing the sins of His people to Christ. What a wondrous truth! Sin imputed to Him who "knew no sin," who "did no sin," who was "holy, harmless, and undefiled." Yes, the sins of His people were indeed laid to His charge, and He was dealt with as guilty. And when even He was dealt with as guilty, He was by no means cleared! He drank the bitter cup to the dregs! He paid the utmost farthing! He endured the full penalty of the guilt of all His people. Not some of the penalty for all men, but all the penalty for some, yea, many, even all His people.

That holy and blessed One was not cleared! And if any now are determined to bear their own guilt, it is perfectly certain that they will never be cleared. What blessedness, then, there is in these words in Ex. 34:7, when we read them in connection with the revelation of God's gospel as declared in the Epistle to the Romans. How full of encouragement for us. Do we sometimes say when we see ourselves in the light which He shines upon us and in us—"How can He clear me? I am all guilt. When I think of all His goodness, which has been leading me and following me, how can He clear me?"

Ah! The answer of God's gospel comes to us and answers all our questions, removes all our doubts, calms all our fears. Jehovah transferred all my sins to Christ! and when they were laid upon Him *He was not cleared!* Therefore the penalty has been borne, the heavy debt has been paid. He bore the wrath, He endured the curse, and the blessed consequences is that I (and all such) stand before God *without a spot,* righteous in Christ's righteousness; accepted in all His acceptableness; perfect in Christ Jesus, complete in Him; yea, holy in His holiness, and only waiting to be glorified with His glory. It is almost beyond belief. When we realise it only in part it seems almost too good to be true.

What! Will He never condemn me? "No condemnation"? Not, though I see in myself every day and every hour I am deserving of all condemnation? What! Does He stoop to my infirmities, and bear with my frailties? Yes! It is true! He will by no means break His word. He laid all my sins upon my Substitute, and when He bore them *He was not cleared.*

Oh, what a blessed truth. Every sin, every iniquity, every transgression, every backsliding, every thought, word, and deed, all foreknown and laid on Him, who, though He knew the awful burden He had to bear, did not withdraw His neck from the yoke, but drank the cup of wrath to the dregs that He might give now to His church and people the cup of blessing for all eternity.

In Him we were not cleared: for in Him we died, and in Him we are risen again. Neither the law nor death has any further claim upon us or power over us. Though "it is appointed unto all men once to die," there is really, now, no reason why we should ever die at all. All we who are "in Christ" have already died in Him, and in Him they are risen again, and only wait for Ascension, and not death. If they are called to fall asleep, it will only be sleep: they will soon wake again when He comes forth in the air and sounds forth His great assembling shout, and then they will be caught up to meet Him in the air, and so to be ever with the Lord.

How blessed the thought, yea, the fact, that we are not merely pardoned for having got into debt, but that the debt has been paid, and our liability cleared, and that a Risen Christ is our receipt for payment in full! Not merely pardoned, but justified; not merely justified, but accepted; and accepted, too, in Christ, as He is accepted with the Father, and have Him, not merely *substituted* for us, but ourselves identified with Him.

What a precious truth for us to dwell upon in the trials of life, in our seasons of depression, in a sick room or on a dying bed. To know that I am cleared because the Lord Jesus was not; that I am acquitted because He was dealt with as guilty. May the Lord carry home His own word and truth with power to our hearts and He shall have all the praise.

Things to Come, 1899.

There is not an Arminian in the world who ever once prayed for grace, or gracious assistance against sin and temptation, with a real sense of his want of it, but that his prayers contradicted his profession. To think that by all these petitions, with others innumerable dictated to us in the Scripture, and which a spiritual sense of our wants will engage unto, we desire nothing but only that God would persuade, excite, and stir us up to put forth a power and ability *of our own* in the performance of what we desire, is contrary unto all Christian experience. Yea, for a man to pray with earnestness and importunity for that which *is* in his own power, and can never be effected but *by* his own power, is ridiculous; and they do but mock God who pray unto Him to do that for them which they can do for themselves, and which God cannot do for them but only *when* and *as* they do it themselves. Suppose a man to have a power in himself to believe and repent; suppose these to be such acts of his will as God doth not, indeed cannot, by His grace work in him, but only persuade him thereunto, and show him sufficient reason *why* he should so do—to what purpose should this man, or with what propriety could he, pray that God would *give him* faith and repentance? Dr. John Owen (1650).

(*Continued from page 169.*)

"*Why* hast Thou made me *thus?*" Instead of complaining at his lot, a contented man is thankful that his condition and circumstances are no worse than they are. Instead of greedily desiring something more than the supply of his present *need*, he rejoices that God still cares for him. Such an one is "content with such as" he has (Heb. 13:5).

One of the fatal hindrances to contentment is covetousness, which is a canker eating into and destroying present satisfaction. It was not, therefore, without good reason, that our Lord gave the solemn commandment to His followers—"*Take heed, and beware of covetousness*" (Luke 12:15). Few things are more insidious. Often it poses under the fair name of thrift, or the wise safeguarding of the future—present economy so as to lay up for "a rainy day." The Scripture says, "covetousness which is *idolatry*" (Col. 3:5)—the affections of the heart being set upon material things rather than upon God. The language of a covetous heart is that of the horseleache's daughter, Give! Give! The covetous man is always desirous of *more*, whether he has little or much. How vastly different the words of the apostle—"And having food and raiment let us be therewith content" (1 Tim. 6:8). A much needed word is that of Luke 3:14: "Be content with your wages!"

"Godliness with contentment *is great gain*" (1 Tim. 6:6). Negatively, it delivers from worry and fretfulness, from avarice and selfishness. Positively, it leaves us free to *enjoy* what God *has* given us. What a contrast is found in the word which follows—"But they that will be (desire to be) rich fall into temptation and a snare, and into many foolish and hurtful lusts, which drown men in destruction and perdition. For the love of money is the root of all evil: which while some coveted after, they have erred from the faith, and pierced themselves through with many sorrows" (1 Tim. 6:9, 10). May the Lord in His grace deliver us from the spirit of this world, and make us to be "content with such things as we have."

Contentment, then, is the product of a heart resting in God. It is the soul's enjoyment of that peace which passeth all understanding. It is the outcome of my will being brought into subjection to the Divine will. It is the blessed assurance that God doeth *all* things well, and is, even now, making *all* things work together for my ultimate good. This experience has to be "learned" by "*proving* what is that good, and acceptable, and perfect, will of God" (Rom. 12:2). Contentment is possible only as we cultivate and maintain that attitude of accepting everything which enters our lives as coming from the Hand of Him who is too wise to err, and too loving to cause one of His children a needless tear.

Let our final word be this: real contentment is only possible by being much in the presence of the Lord Jesus. This comes out clearly in the verses which follow our opening text: "I know both how to be abased, and I know how to abound: everywhere and in all things I am instructed both to be full and to be hungry, both to abound and suffer need. I can do all things *through Christ* which strengthens me" (Phil. 4:12, 13). It is only by cultivating intimacy with that One who was never discontent that we shall be delivered from the sin of complaining. It is only by daily fellowship with Him who ever delighted in the Father's will that we shall learn the secret of contentment. May both writer and reader so behold in the mirror of the Word the glory of the Lord that we shall be "changed into the same image from glory to glory, even as by the Spirit of the Lord" (2 Cor. 3:18).

Arthur W. Pink.

P.S.—

The meetings here are still affording much ground for praise. In the hearts of many God is deepening an interest for and delight in His wondrous Word. Many open doors are before us, and we are booked up for months to come. Invitations are to hand from Melbourne, but it will be some time yet before we can leave Sydney and its suburbs. Of course, there is opposition from those who object to man being laid in the dust. It is ever thus: when the *absoluteness* of God and the *nothingness* of man are pressed, the pride of the human heart and the enmity of the carnal mind are soon manifested. But "if I yet pleased man I should not be the servant of Christ" (Gal. 1:10) still holds good. Let our fellow-Christians continue praying that we may be kept in that place where neither the *frowns* nor the *flatteries* of men will either move or affect us. May Divine grace enable us to say in truth, "In God will I praise His Word: in the Lord will I praise His Word." In God have I put my trust; I will not be afraid what man can do unto me" (Ps. 56:10, 11).

VOL. IV SEPT., 1925 NO. 9

STUDIES IN THE SCRIPTURES

"Search the Scriptures" John 5:39.

Arthur W. Pink, Publisher and Editor,
5 Norton Street, Ashfield, N.S.W., Australia.

Price: 10 cents per copy; $1.00 or 5/- per year.

Our Thoughts.

"Casting down imaginations and every high thing that exalteth itself against the knowledge of God, *and bringing into captivity every thought* to the obedience of Christ" (2 Cor. 10:5).

In his attempt at self-improvement man aims to cultivate good morals and manners, and rests satisfied with the absence of open misconduct. Only too often the ambition of the Lord's people rise little above this level. While it is allowed on all sides that the mind needs to be educated and disciplined, yet who is exercised about his *thoughts?* Thoughts seem to come unasked and to depart unbidden. It is commonly assumed that our thoughts are *beyond* our control. But our thought-life is a very important element, and to deny that we are accountable for its regulation is to deny a vital part of human responsibility. Yet how many of us have *confessed* to God our sins of thought? How many of us have asked His forgiveness for the exercise of evil thoughts, or of wandering thoughts, when engaged in prayer?

The power to think is one of the noblest faculties of our being. By it character is shaped and conduct is formed. Thought has a marvellous assimilating power; its subjects and objects mould our personalities. What is first an idea becomes an image, and that an ideal, which, whether good or evil, regulates our actions. Hence the vital importance of *meditating* on the Word of God, for it is only as His Word is hidden in the heart that we are kept from sinning against Him.

As we turn to the Holy Scripture we find they have not a little to say about our "thoughts." First, we find that no allowance is made for evil thoughts. "Beware that there *be not a thought* in thy wicked heart, saying, The seventh year, the year of release, is at hand" (Deut 15:9). "Curse not the king, *no not in thy thought*" (Eccl. 10:2). Second, we find that they are condemned. "The *thought of foolishness* is sin" (Prov. 24:9). What a proof of the Divine inspiration of the Scriptures is this—no uninspired mind would ever have invented such a statement. "The *thoughts of* the wicked are an abomination to the Lord" (Prov. 15:26). That is why we not only read, "Let the wicked forsake his way:"; but also, "and the unrighteous man *his thoughts*" (Isa. 55:7). How solemn are the words of Peter to Simon the sorcerer—"Repent therefore of this thy wickedness, and pray God, if perhaps *the thought of thine heart* may be forgiven thee" (Acts 8.22).

God is not indifferent to our thoughts. "The Lord knoweth the *thoughts of man*" (Psa. 94:11). And again, the Psalmist declared, "Thou knowest my downsitting and mine uprising, Thou understandest *my thought* afar off" (Psa. 139:2). Equally pointed is what we read of in Heb. 4:12—"For the Word of God is quick, and powerful, and sharper than any two-edged sword, piercing even to the dividing asunder of soul and spirit, and of the joints and marrow, *and is a discerner of the thoughts and intents of the heart*" (Heb. 4:12). How dishonoring to God, then, if we entertain the idea that He is indifferent about our thoughts, and how contrary to His Word for us to seek to evade our responsibility by declaring we cannot control our thoughts!

If, then, our thoughts exert such a powerful influence upon our lives if God takes notice of them, if we are responsible for the exercising of them, how shall we

(*Continued on page 216*).

IMPORTANT NOTICES

Set of twelve issues for **1922**, unbound, **$1.00** or **5/-**. Bound **$1.50** or **7/-**.

Set of twelve issues for **1923**, unbound, **$1.00** or **5/-**. Bound **$1.50** or **7/-**.

Set of twelve issues for **1924**, unbound, **$1.00** or **5/-**. Bound **$1.50** or **7/-**.

Note: We cannot break a set or now supply any **single** 1924 issues.

Subscription—price: **$1.00** or **5/-** per year to any address in the world.

Change of Address: Please notify me promptly of any change of address, and be certain to give both old and new address.

Non-subscribers receiving this Magazine regularly will understand their subscription has been entered by a friend.
Copies lost in the mail duplicated only if we are notified promptly.

CONTENTS

THE GOSPEL OF JOHN

45. *Christ washing His disciples' feet: John* 13:1-11.

Below is an Analysis of the passage which is to be before us:—

1. Christ's unchanging love, v. 1.
2. Judas' inveterate hatred, v. 2.
3. Christ's return to the Father, v. 3.
4. Christ performing a slave's work, vv. 4, 5.
5. Peter's blundering ignorance, vv. 6-9.
6. Bathing and cleansing, v. 10.
7. The Traitor excepted, v. 11.

We are now to enter upon what many believers in each age have regarded as the most precious portion of this Gospel, yea, as one of the most blessed passages in all the Word of God. John 13 begins a new section, a section clearly distinguished and separated from what has gone before. At the beginning of the Gospel two things were stated in connection with the *outcome* of Christ's mission and ministry: the Nation, as such, "received Him *not*": this has been fully demonstrated, especially in chapters 5-12; second, those who *did* "receive Him" were to be brought into the place of children of God. In 13-17 we see Christ alone with His own, separated from the world, telling them of their peculiar portion and privileges.

At the close of Christ's public ministry, we are told "He departed and did *hide* Himself from them"; that is, from the Nation (12:36). In 13-17 we find the Saviour, in most intimate fellowship with His disciples, *revealing* to them the wondrous place which they had in His love, and how that love would be continually exercised on their behalf now that He was about to leave them and go to the Father. He had told them that, "The Son of Man came not to be ministered unto, but *to minister,* and to give His life a ransom for many" (Matt. 20:28). All through His career Christ *had* "ministered" to His own, but now, His public ministry was over and He was on the eve of giving His life a ransom for them, to be followed by Him taking His place on high. It would, therefore, be natural for the disciples to conclude that His "ministry" unto them was *also ended.* But not so. It would continue, and *that* is what *this* blessed section of John's Gospel is primarily designed to show us. He loved these disciples (and us) not only unto the Cross, but "unto *the end.*" His return to the Father would neither terminate nor diminish the activities of His love for His own: in Heaven He is still occupied with the interest of His people.

The central design of the "Paschal Discourse" of Christ was to lead His own into a spiritual understanding of their *new* place before the Father, and their *new* position in the world, as distinguished from the portion and place which they had had in Judaism. What we have in John 13 to 17 takes the place of the long Olivet discourse recorded by each of the Synoptists. Here, instead of taking His seat upon the Mount and speaking of Jewish matters, He brings the disciples, in spirit, into Heaven, and reveals the glories, blessedness, and holiness of the Sanctuary there. Instead of treating of the horrors of the Tribulation, He discloses to the family of God the activities of their great High Priest, as well as their own sorrows and joys during the time of their journey through this wilderness.

While there is a marked contrast between what we have at the close of John 12 and the beginning of 13, there is also a close link of connection between them, a link which further develops the progressive unfolding of truth in this wondrous Gospel. In chapter 12 Christ had spoken of Himself as "the Corn of wheat" which had to die in order that it might bring forth "much fruit." As we have seen, this speaks of *union and communion*—blessedly illustrated in the opening scene, the "supper" in Bethany. But here in chapters 13 and onwards, He makes known His own most gracious work for *maintaining* believers in fellowship with Himself. Two things, each most blessed and evidencing His perfections, are to be noted. First, His eye is on the Heavenly Sanctuary (v. 1); second, His eye is upon His own (v. 4). He *guards* the holy requirements of God, and He *cares* for and *ministers* to His people. We are left here in this world, and its dust is defiling, unfitting us for entrance into the Holiest. Here in John 13 we see Christ fitting us *for* that place. It is important for us to recognise, though, that it is *God's* interests which He has at heart in washing our feet! Christ is here seen as the *Laver* which stood between the brazen altar and the sanctuary, and which was approached only after the brazen altar had done its work.

There is a further link between John 12 and 13 which brings out a most blessed contrast—let the student be constantly on the look-out for these. At the beginning of John 12 we behold the *feet* of the Lord; in John 13 we see the *feet* of the disciples. The "feet" of Christ were *anointed*, those of the disciples were *washed*. As the Saviour passed through this sinful world He contracted no defilement. He left it as He came: "holy, harmless, and undefiled." The "feet" speak of the *walk*, and the fact that Christ's feet were *anointed* with the fragrant spikenard tells of the sweet savor which ever ascended from Him to the Father, perfectly glorifying Him as He did in every step of His path. But in sharp contrast from Him, the walk of the disciples *was* defiled, and the grime of the way must be removed. Note, also, that the anointing of the Saviour's feet is given *before* the washing of the disciples' feet—in all things *He* must have "the preeminence" (Col. 1:18)!

That which opens this section and introduces the "Pascal Discourse" is the Lord washing the feet of His disciples. The first thing to observe, particularly, is that it was *water* and not blood which was used for their cleansing. It is deeply important to note this, for many of the Lord's own people seem to be entirely ignorant about the distinction. Their speaking of a *re*-application of the blood, of coming anew to "the fountain" which has been opened for sin and uncleanness when they have transgressed, proves that this is only too sadly true. The New Testament knows nothing whatever of a *re*-application of the blood, or of sinning Christians needing to be washed in it again. To speak of such things is to grossly *dishonor* the all-efficacious sacrifice of the Cross. The blood of Jesus Christ God's Son cleanseth us from *all* sin (1 John 1:7). By "one offering He hath *perfected forever* them that are set apart" (Heb. 10:14). This being so, what provision, we may ask, has been made for the removal of the defilements which the Christian contracts by the way? The answer is *"water."*

A careful study will show that in the Old and New Testaments alike the "blood" is *Godward*, the "water" is *saintward*, to remove impurity in practice: the one affects our standing, the other our state; the former is for *judicial* cleansing, the latter is for *practical* purification. In the types, Lev. 16 makes known God's requirements for the making of atonement; Num. 19 tells of God's provision for the defilements of the way, as Israel journeyed through the wilderness. This latter was met not by blood, but by "the *water* of purification." Judicial cleansing from the guilt of *all sin* is the inalienable portion of every believer in the Lord Jesus Christ. Moral cleansing, the practical purification of the heart and ways from all that defiles and hinders our communion with God is by *water*, that is, *the Word*, applied to us in power by the Holy Spirit.

"Now, before the feast of the Passover, when Jesus knew that His hour was come that He should depart out of this world unto the Father, having loved His own which were in the world, He loved them unto the end" (v. 1). This opening verse supplies us with the first key to what follows. What we have here *anticipates* that which was in view in Christ's *return* to the Father. He graciously affords us a symbolic representation of His *present* service for us in Heaven. He is seated at the right hand of the Majesty of High, but He is there in *our interests,* ever living to make intercession for us, ever there as our Advocate with the Father, ever maintaining and succouring us by the way.

"Now before the Feast of the Passover," immediately before, for on the morrow Christ was to die as the true Lamb. The "passover" itself was eaten at the close of the *fourteenth* day of Nisan (Ex. 12:6, 8); but "the feast," which lasted seven days, began on the *fifteenth* (Num. 28:17). What we have here, then, transpired on the eve before our Lord's death.

"When Jesus knew that his hour was come." Christ is the only One Who has ever trod this earth that was never taken by surprise. All was known and felt in the Father's presence. "That He should depart out of this world": note *"this* world," not "the world." It is striking to see how frequently this term occurs at the close of His life: "And Jesus said, For judgment I am come into *this world"* (9:39); "He that hateth his life in *this world* shall keep it into life eternal" (12:25); "Now is the judgment of *this world*: now shall the Prince of *this world* be cast out" (12:31). *"This world"* was evidently a terrible place in the Lord's mind! He could not stay here. *He* had made *the* world (1:10), but *sin* has made *this* world what it is. Note "that He should depart out of this world *unto the Father,"* not unto *heaven!* How blessed! It was *the Father's* presence His heart desired!

"Having loved His own which were in the world, He loved them unto the end." *"His own!"* After all the previous conflicts with an unbelieving world, after all His unavailing appeals to Israel, Christ now comforts His heart by lavishing His love upon the few who despised Him not. What a blessed expression—"His own!" "Ye are *not your own"* (1 Cor. 6:19); we belong to Christ. We all know the delight which comes from being able to call something *our own.* It is not so much the value of what is possessed which constitutes this satisfaction, as it is the simple consciousness that it is *mine.* It is the Holy Spirit here declaring the heart of the Saviour in the terms of love. It is not with our poor estimate of Him, still less with our wretched selves, that He would occupy us. He would have us taken up with *Christ's* thoughts about us! We belong to the Lord Jesus in a threefold way. First, by *the Father's eternal election.* We are the Father's love-gift to the Son: "chosen in Christ before the foundation of the world." Second, we are His by *His own redemptive rights.* He paid the purchase price. He bought us for Himself: "Christ also loved the church, and gave Himself *for* it." Third, we are His by *the effectual call of the Holy Spirit.* If any one be in Christ, he is a new creation, and we are created anew by the Third Person of the Holy Trinity "born of the Spirit."

"He loved them unto the end." Here is the care of the Good Shepherd for the sheep. Unto "the end" *of what?* Who can define it? First, unto the end of our earthly pilgrimage. We *need* the assurance of His love as we pass through this wilderness. We shall *not* need it when we see Him face to face and know as we are known. But we *do* need the full *assurance* of it now. And what a resting-place for the poor heart amid all the buffetings of this life—the bosom of the Saviour! It is here that John turned (v. 23), and it is blessedly accessible to us, in spirit. Yea, it is to maintain us in the unending enjoyment of our place there, that the Lord Jesus is here seen washing the disciples' feet *before He* begins the long discourse which follows to the end of chapter 16. The love of Christ must be *occupied about its objects,* and this is what we see here. God is "light" (1 John 1:5), and God is "love" (1 John 4:16). In the first twelve chapters of this Gospel Christ is seen as *light,* revealing the Father, exposing men (1:17; 3:19; 8:12; 9:5). But now we behold Him (with "His *own";*) as *love* (Compare 13:34; 14:12; 15:9; 17:26, etc.). But mark it, it is a *holy* love. Divine love cannot allow that which is unclean. Therefore does the holy love of Christ *begin* by removing defilement from the feet of His disciples! Most blessed is this. We delight to contemplate the love which caused Him to lay down His life for us, but let us never lose sight of the *present* activities of it.

"He loved them unto the end"! Not only unto the last, but to the *farthest extent* of their need and of His grace. He knew that Philip would misunderstand Him, that three of them would sleep while He prayed and agonised, that Peter would deny Him, that Thomas would doubt Him, that *all* would "forsake Him"—yet He "loved *them* unto the end"! And so it is with us, dear Christian reader. "His own" are the *objects* of His love; "unto the end" is the *extent* of His love. He loves us unto "the end" of our miserable failures, unto the "end" of our wanderings and backslidings, unto the "end" of our unworthiness, unto the "end" of our deep need.

"*His* love *no* end or measure knows,
No change can turn its course;
Eternally the same it flows
From one eternal Source."

The first part of our verse intimates two things about the Lord Jesus at this time: the Cross was before Him with all its horrors; the joy of returning to the Father was before Him with all its bliss; yet neither the fearful prospect of woe nor the hope of unspeakable rest and gladness shook His love for His own. He is the *same* yesterday and to-day and forever, therefore His love never varies. *He* is *eternal,* therefore has He loved us with an *everlasting* love. He is *Divine,* therefore is His love different from all others, passing human knowledge.

"And supper being ended, the Devil having now put into the heart of Judas Iscariot, Simon's son, to betray Him" (v. 2). What a fearful contrast! From love to hate; from the Saviour to Satan; from "His own" to the Traitor! The mention of Judas here seems to be for the purpose of enhancing the beauty of what follows. The Devil had full mastery over the heart of the Betrayer: thus *in figure* the Cross was passed—Satan had accomplished his design.

"Jesus, knowing that the Father had given all things into His hands, and that He was come from God, and went to God" (v. 3). "These statements of Christ's Divine origin, authority, and coming glory are made so as to emphasise the amazing condescension of the service to which He humbled Himself to do the office of a bond-slave" (Companion Bible).

"Jesus, knowing that the Father had given all things into His hands, and that He was come from God, and went to God; He riseth from supper, and laid aside His garments; and took a towel and girded Himself (vv. 3, 4). It was not in forgetfulness of His Divine origin, but in full consciousness of it, He discharged this menial function. As He had divested Himself of the 'form of God' at the first, stripping Himself of the outward glory attendent on recognised Deity; and had taken upon Himself 'the form of a servant,' so now He laid aside His garment and girded Himself; assuming the guise of a household slave. For a fisherman to pour water over a fisherman's feet was no great condescension; but that He, in Whose hands are all human affairs and Whose nearest relation is the Father, should thus condescend, is of unparalleled significance. It is this kind of action that is *suitable* to One whose consciousness is Divine. Not only does the dignity of Jesus vastly augment the beauty of the action, but it also sheds new light on the Divine character" (Dr. Dods).

Three things are to be carefully noted here as *reasons* why He washed His disciples' feet on this occasion. First, He knew that His hour was come when He should depart out of this world (v. 1); second, He loved His own unto the end (v. 1); third, because all things had been given into His hands, and He that had come from God was returning to God—for these reasons He arose from the table and girded Himself with a towel. As we shall see, all of this finds its explanation in the Lord's words to Peter, "If I wash thee not, thou hast *no part with Me*" (v. 8). For three years the disciples *had* had "a part" with Him. But now He was about to leave them; but before doing so He would assure them (and us) that His wondrous love continues undiminished and unchanged after His return to the Father. Christ began a service in the Glory which, in another manner, He will continue forever. The service in which He is now engaged is to *maintain* our "part" with Him.

There has been much controversy as to *what* "supper" is referred to here in John 13. Most assuredly it was *not* the "Lord's Supper," for in v. 26 we find Christ giving the "sop" to Judas, and the Synoptists make it unmistakably plain that this was at the *Pascal* supper. The Lord's Supper receives no mention in the Fourth Gospel. On this fact Bishop Ryle strikingly says, "I think it was specially intended to be a witness forever against the growing tendency of Christians to make an idol out of the sacraments. Even from the beginning there seems to have been a disposition in the Church to make a religion of forms and ceremonies rather than of heart, and to exalt outward ordinances to a place which God never meant them to fill. Against this teaching St. John was raised up to testify. The mere fact that in his Gospel he leaves out the Lord's Supper altogether, and does not even name it, is strong proof that the Lord's Supper cannot be, as many tell us, the first, chief, and principal thing in Christianity. His perfect silence about it can never be reconciled with this favourite theory. It is a most conspicuous silence, which the modern advocates of the so-called sacramental system can never get over, or explain away. If the sacrament of the Lord's Supper really is the first and chief thing in Christianity, why does St. John tell us nothing about it? To that question I can only see one answer: it is because it is not a primary, but a secondary thing in Christ's religion."

"He riseth from supper." In the order of events this comes right after what we read of in v. 1: the time-mark there being connected with Christ's action here. Evidently it was just before the beginning of the meal that the Lord Jesus rose from the table—the meal being the Pascal one. It is important to note that John's narrative carries everything on in strict connection from this point to 14:31, and then on to 18:1: therefore this "supper" and Christ's discourse to His disciples was at once followed by the going forth to Gethsemane. The question of Peter in 13:24 is inexplicable if the Pascal supper had already taken place (as quite a number have insisted), for the Synoptists are explicit that our Lord named the Betrayer during this meal. Most of the difficulty has been created by the first clause of v. 2, which should be rendered, "when the supper arrived," i.e., was ready. Mark how that 13:12 shows us Christ *resuming* His place at the table.

"He riseth from supper, and laid aside His garments; and took a towel, and girded Himself" (v. 4). Everything here, we doubt not, has a deep symbolical meaning. The "supper" was the Pascal one, and clearly spoke of Christ's death. The *rising* from supper and the *laying aside* of His garments (cf 20:6) pictured our Lord on the resurrection-side of the grave. The girding Himself speaks of *service,* the *heavenly* service in which He is now engaged on behalf of His people. It is a wonderful thing that the Lord never relinquished His *servant* character. Even after His return to the Glory He still ministers to us. Beautifully was this typified of old in connection with the Hebrew servant in Exodus 21. "If thou buy an Hebrew servant, six years he shall serve: and in the seventh, he shall go out free. . . . If the servant shall plainly say I love my master, my wife, and my children; I will *not* go out free, then his master shall bring him unto the judges; he shall also bring him to the door, and unto the door-post; and his master shall bore his ear through with an aul; and he shall *serve* him forever" (vv. 2-5, 6). This will be expounded at length, D.V., in our "Gleanings in Exodus." Suffice it now to say that it affords us a most blessed foreshadowment of the perfect Servant. *Christ* will "serve forever." To-day He is serving us, applying the Word (by His Spirit) to our practical state, dealing with what unfits us for fellowship with Himself on high. Luke 12:37 gives us a precious word upon His *future* service: "Blessed are those servants, whom the Lord when He cometh shall find watching: verily I say unto you, that He shall *gird* Himself and make them to sit down to meat, and will come forth and *serve* them." And *how* will He "serve" us then? By ministering to our happiness and enjoyment as "His guests!"

"After that, He poureth water into a basin," etc. (v. 5). Everything here is Divinely perfect. *Seven* distinct actions are attributed to the Saviour: "He (1) riseth from supper, and (2) laid aside His garments, and (3) took a towel, and (4) girded Himself. After that He (5) poureth water into a basin, and (6) began to wash the disciples' feet, and (7) to wipe them with the towel wherewith He was girded." It was *their feet* which He here proceeded to wash. Their *persons* were already cleansed. They had been brought out of Judaism, and a heavenly portion was now theirs—a place in the Father's House. But their conduct must be suited to that House. Their *walk* must be in accord with their heavenly calling. They must be kept clean in their ways.

The water with which the Saviour here cleansed the soiled feet of His disciples was an emblem of the Word: "Wherewithal shall a young man *cleanse* his *way?* by taking heed thereto according to Thy *Word"* (Psa. 119:9). Fully and blessedly is this brought out in Eph. 5:25, 26: "Christ also loved the Church, and gave Himself for it; that He might sanctify and cleanse it with the washing of water by the Word." "Every clause of this passage is found here in John 13. He 'loved' them, the Church. He 'gave Himself' for them, the 'supper' setting forth that: that He might 'sanctify,' separate to Himself, thus they were 'His own'; and 'cleanse' it with the washing of water by the Word. It is complete; His constant, perfect provision for our being kept clean" (Mr. Malachi Taylor). It is to be particularly observed that the Lord did not leave this work unfinished or half done: like a perfect servant, our Lord not only "washed" their feet, but He "wiped" them as well!

"Then cometh He to Simon Peter: and Peter saith unto Him, Lord, dost Thou wash my feet?" (v. 6). Simon was ever blundering, and his sad faults and failings are recorded for our learning. "In Divine things the wisdom of the believer is subjection to Christ and confidence in Him. What He does we are called on to accept with thankfulness of heart, and as Mary said to the servants at the marriage-feast, 'Whatsoever He saith unto you, do it.' This Simon Peter did not, for when the Lord approached him in the form of a servant or bond-man, he demurred. Was there not faith 'working by love' in Peter's heart? Both, undoubtedly, yet not then in action, but buried under superabundant feeling of a human order, else he had not allowed his mind to question what the Lord saw fit to do. He had rather bowed to Christ's love and sought to learn, as He might teach, what deep need must be in him and his fellows to draw forth such a lowly yet requisite service from his Master. . . . Too self-confident and indeed ignorant not only of himself and the defiling scene around, but of the depths and constancy of Christ's love, Peter says to Him, 'Lord, dost Thou wash my feet?' Granting that he could not know what was not yet revealed, but was it comely of him, was it reverent, to question what the Lord was doing? He may have thought it humility in himself, and honour to the Lord, to decline a service so menial at His hands. But Peter should never have forgotten that as Jesus never said a word, so He never did an act save worthy of God and demonstrative of the Father; and now more than ever were His words and ways an exhibition of Divine grace, as human evil set on by Satan, not only in those outside, but within the innermost circle of His own, called for increased distinctness and intensity.

"The truth is we need to learn from God *how* to honour Him, and learn to love *according to His mind.* And if any man think that he knoweth anything, he knoweth nothing yet as he ought to know; this, too, was Peter's mistake. He should have suspected his thoughts, and waited in all submissiveness on Him who, as many confessed that knew far less than he did, 'hath done all things well,' and was absolutely what He was saying, truth and love in the same blessed Person. The thoughts of God are never as ours; and saints slip into those of man, unless they are taught of God, by faith, in detail, too, as well as in the main; for we cannot, ought not, to trust ourselves in anything. God the Father will have the Son honoured; and He is honoured most when believed in and followed in His humiliation. Peter therefore was equally astray when he once ventured to rebuke the Lord for speaking of His suffering and death, as now when he asks, 'Dost Thou wash my feet?'" (Bible Treasury).

"Jesus answered and said unto him, What I do thou knowest not now; but thou shalt know hereafter" (v. 7). We take it that the force of this is, briefly, as follows: Peter, this gives a picture, a sample, of the work which I shall perform for My people when I return to the Father. You do not see the significance of it now, but you *will* do later, when the Holy Spirit has come. This was really a rebuke; but given tenderly. Peter ought to have known that in his Lord's mysterious action there must be a purpose and a meaning in it worthy of His subjection to the Father and expressive of His love for His own. But like us, Peter was dull of discernment, slow to learn. Instead of gladly submitting to the most high Sovereign now performing the service of a slave, he plunges still further into worse error: "Peter saith unto Him, Thou shalt never wash my feet" (v. 8). It was ignorance, yea, affection, which prompted him; but that did not excuse him. But how blessed that he had, and that we have, to do with One who bears with us in our dulness, and whose grace corrects our faults!

"Peter saith unto Him, Thou shalt never wash my feet" (v. 8). We are all ready to censure Peter for not complying immediately with the Lord's will when he knew it. But let us beware lest *we* be guilty of something more inexcusable than what we condemn in the apostle. Peter said he would not submit, yet he *did,* and that very quickly. Is it not sadly true of us that we often *say* we will submit, and yet remain obstinately disobedient? As another has said, "We do not *use* Peter's words, but we *act* them, which he durst not do. What, then, is the difference between us and him? Is it not just the difference between the two sons in the parable—the one of whom said, 'I go, and went not,' the other of whom said, 'I will not go, and afterwards repented and went?' Which of these did the will of the father?' Whether do you think Peter's refractory expression, or our disobedient conduct, most deserving of censure?"

"Jesus answered him, if I wash thee not, thou hast no part with Me" (v. 8). "If *I* wash thee not": we cannot wash our own feet; we are totally incompetent, not only for the saving of our souls, but also for the cleansing of our defiled walk. Nor has even the Word *apart from His living presense* any efficacy. Our feet must be in *His* hands, that is to say, we must completely *yield* to Him. It is not simply that we are to judge our ways according to *our* apprehension of the Word, and its requirements, but *He* must interpret and apply it, and for this we *must* be in His presence.

But what is meant by "no part with Me?" Ah, here is the key that unlocks the chamber that conducts us to the very centre of this incident. The word "part" has reference to *fellowship*. This is seen from our Lord's words concerning the sister of Martha: "Mary hath chosen *that good part*" (Luke 10:42). The meaning of this word "part" is clearly defined again in 2 Cor. 6:15, "What concord hath Christ with Belial? or what *part* hath he that believeth with an infidel?"

What is the "washing?" "If I *wash* thee not, thou hast no part with Me." It is something which is needed by *all* believers. We say "believers," for though all such have a portion *in* Christ, how often they fail to enjoy their "part" *with* Him? This "washing" is something more than confession of sin and the consequent forgiveness. It is the searching out by the Word, in the *presence* of God, of that which led me into evil; it is judging the *root*, of which sins are the fruit. Yet this "washing" must not be *limited* to God's remedy for our declension and failure, rather should we view it as His gracious provision for our daily need, as a *preservative* and *preventative* against outward failures. We need to get alone with our Lord each day, opening our hearts to the light as the flower does its petals to the sun. Alas! that we have so little consciousness of our deep need for this, and that there is so little retirement and examination of our ways before God. To really place our feet for washing in the blessed hands of Christ is to come before Him in the attitude of the Psalmist: "*Search me*, O God, and *know* my heart: *try* me, and know my thoughts: And see if there be any wicked way in me and lead me in the way everlasting" (139:23, 24). This is imperatively necessary if, while in such a defiling place as this world, we *are* to have a "part" *with Him*.

"Simon Peter saith unto Him, Lord, not my feet only, but also my hands and my head" (v. 9). Here, with characteristic impulsiveness, Peter rushes to the opposite extreme. As he hears that he could have no part with Christ *except* the Lord wash him, he is ready now to be washed all over. It was the passionate outburst of a warm-hearted if dull-minded disciple. Nevertheless, his ignorance voiced another error. He needed not now to be washed all over. The sinner does, but the saint does not. It is only our *walk* which needs cleansing.

"Jesus saith to him: He that is washed needeth not save to wash his feet, but is clean every whit" (v. 10). The distinction which our Lord here drew is of vital importance. "He that is washed," better, "He who has been *bathed*," that is, his whole person cleansed: "Needeth not only to wash his *feet*," then is he completely fit for communion with the Lord. There is a washing which believers have in Christ that needs not to be ever repeated. In Him there is to be found a cleansing which is never lost. "By one offering He hath *perfected forever* them that are set apart" (Heb. 10:14). The believer has been purged from *all* sin, and *made meet* to be a partaker of the inheritance of the saints in light (Col. 1:12). *This* purging needs no repetition. It is of first moment that the Christian should be clear upon this basic truth. The benefits which Christ confers upon the believer are never recalled; the efficacy of His precious blood abides upon him eternally. The moment a sinner, drawn by the Holy Spirit, comes to Christ, he is completely and finally cleansed. It is the apprehension of this which gives a firm rock for my feet to rest upon. It assures me that my hope is a stable one; that my standing before God is immutable. It banishes doubt and uncertainty. It gives the heart and mind abiding peace to know that the benefits I have found in Christ are never to be recalled. I am brought out from under condemnation and placed in a state of everlasting acceptance. All this, and more, is included in the "bathing" which Christ has declared needs not to be repeated. I stand resplendent in the sight of God in all the Saviour's beauty and perfections. God looks upon believers not merely as forgiven, but as *righteous*: as truly as Christ was "made sin" for us, so have we been "made" the righteousness of God in Him."

But side by side with this blessed truth of a *bathing* in Christ which needs not, and cannot be, repeated, stands another truth of great practical importance: "He that is bathed needeth not save to *wash his feet,* but is clean every whit." There is a *partial cleansing* which the believer still needs, a daily washing to counteract the defiling effects of this world. Our daily contact with the evil all around causes the dust of defilement to settle upon us so that the mirror of our conscience is dimmed and the spiritual affections of our heart are dulled. We need to come afresh into the presence of Christ in order to learn what things really are, surrendering ourselves to His judgment in everything, and submitting to His purging Word. And who is there that, even for a single day, lives *without* sin? Who is there that does not need to daily pray, "Forgive us our trespasses"? Only One has ever walked here and been unsoiled by the dust of earth. He went as He came, unstained, uncontaminated. But who is there among His people that does not find much in his daily walk that makes him blush for shame! How much unfaithfulness we all have to deplore! Let me but compare my walk with *Christ's,* and, unless I am blinded by conceit or deceived by Satan, I shall at once see that I come infinitely short of Him, and though "following His steps" (not "*in* His steps" as so often is misquoted), it is but "afar off." So often my acts are *un*-Christlike in character, so often my disposition and ways have "the flesh" stamped upon them. Even when evil does not break out in open forms, we are conscious of much *hidden* wrong, of sins of thought, of vile desires. How real, then, how deep, is our daily need of putting our feet in the hands of Christ for cleansing, that everything which hinders communion with Him may be removed, and that He can then say of us, "Ye are *clean!*"

"And ye are clean, but not all. For He knew who should betray Him; therefore said He, Ye are not *all* clean" (v. 11). Christ here referred to Judas, though He did not name the Traitor. Judas must have known what He meant, but his conscience was seared as with a red-hot iron, and his heart was harder than the nether mill-stone. Even this touching exhibition of the condescending love and grace of Christ toward His disciples made no impression upon him. In less than one hour he went forth to sell his Master. In his case it was not a matter of *losing* spiritual life, but of *manifesting* the fact that he never had it. It was not a sheep of Christ becoming unclean, but of a dog returning to his vomit. Unspeakably solemn warning is this for those who, for a time, maintain an *outward* form of godliness, but are strangers to its inward power.

The following questions are to help the student prepare for the next lesson:—

1. What is the typical teaching of v. 12?
2. What is the important lesson on reverence in v. 13?
3. How are *we* to obey vv. 14, 15?
4. What is the thought suggested by v. 16 coming right after vv. 14, 15?
5. What lessons are to be learned from v. 17?
6. What is the meaning of v. 19?
7. What blessed truth is expressed in v. 20?

—*Arthur W. Pink.*

GLEANINGS IN EXODUS

21. *Israel in the Wilderness.* *Ex.* 15.

"So Moses brought Israel from the Red Sea, and they went out into the wilderness of Shur" (15:22). When God separates a people unto Himself, it is not only needful that that people should be redeemed with "precious blood," and then brought near as purged worshippers, but it is also part of God's wise purpose that they should pass through the wilderness ere they enter into the promised inheritance. Two chief designs are accomplished thereby. First, the trials and testings of the wilderness make manifest the evil of our hearts, and the incurable corruption of the flesh, and this in order that we may be humbled—"to hide pride" from us; and that we may prove by experience that entrance into the inheritance itself is also and solely a matter of sovereign grace, seeing that there is *no worthiness,* yea, *no* "good thing" in us. Second, inasmuch as when Jehovah leads His people into the wilderness He goes with them and makes His presence and His love manifest among them. Inasmuch as it is His purpose to display His power in saving His redeemed from the consequences of their failures, and thus make their need the opportunity of lavishing upon them the riches of His grace, we are made to see not only Israel, but God *with* them and *for* them in the waste howling desert.

Trial and humiliation are not "the end of the Lord" (James 5:11), but are rather the occasions for fresh displays of the Father's long-sufferance and goodness. The wilderness may and will make manifest the weakness of His saints, and, alas! their failures, but this is only to magnify the power and mercy of Him who brought them into the place of testing. Further: God has in view our ultimate wellbeing—that He may "do thee good at thy *latter* end" (Deut. 6:18); and when the trials are over, when our faithful God has supplied our *"every* need," *all,* all shall be found to be to *His* honour, praise, and glory. Thus God's purpose in leading His people through the wilderness was (and is) not only that He might try and prove *them* (Deut. 8:2-5), but that in the trial He might exhibit what *He* was for them in bearing with their failures and in supplying their need. The "wilderness," then, gives us not only a revelation of *ourselves,* but it also makes manifest the *ways* of God.

"So Moses brought Israel from the Red Sea, and they went out into the wilderness of Shur." This is the first time that we read of them being *in* "the wilderness." In 13:18 we are told that "God led the people about *the way of* the wilderness," but that they had not then actually entered it is clear from v. 20—"And they took their journey from Succoth, and encamped in Etham, in *the edge of* the wilderness." But now they "went out *into* the wilderness." The *connection is very striking and instructive.* It was their passage through the Red Sea which introduced God's redeemed to the wilderness. Israel's journey through the Red Sea speaks of the believer's union with Christ in His death and resurrection (Rom. 6:3, 4): Typically, Israel were now upon resurrection-ground. That we may not miss the force of this, the Holy Spirit has been careful to tell us that "Moses brought Israel from the Red Sea, and they went out into the wilderness of Shur; and they went *three days* in the wilderness." Here, as in many other passages, the "three days" speaks of *resurrection* (1 Cor. 15:4).

It is only when the Christian's faith lays hold of his oneness with Christ in His death and resurrection, recognising that he is a "new creature" in Him, that he becomes conscious of "the wilderness." Just in proportion as we apprehend our new standing before God and our portion in His Son, so will this world become to us a dreary and desolate *wilderness.* To the natural man the world offers much that is attractive and alluring; but to the spiritual man all in it is only "vanity and vexation of spirit." To the eye of sense there is much in the world that is pleasant and pleasing; but the eye of faith sees nothing but death written across the whole scene —"change and decay in *all* around I see." It has much which ministers to "the lust of the flesh, the lust of the eye, and the pride of life," but nothing whatever for the new nature. So far as the spiritual life is concerned, the world is simply a *wilderness*—barren and desolate.

The wilderness is the place of *travellers,* journeying from one country to another; none but a madman would think of making his *home* there. Precisely such is this world. It is the place through which man journeys from time to eternity. And *faith* it is which makes the difference between the way in which men regard this world. The unbeliever, for the most part, is content to *remain* here. He settles down as though he is to stay here for ever. "Their inward thought is, their houses shall continue *forever,* and their dwelling-places to all generations; they call their land after their names" (Pel. 49:11). Every effort is made to prolong his earthly sojourn, and when at last death claims him, he is loath to leave. Far different is it with the believer, the *real* believer. *His* home is not here. He looks *"for* a city which hath foundations whose builder and maker is God" (Heb. 11:10). Consequently, he is a stranger and pilgrim here (Heb. 11:13). It is of *this* the "wilderness" speaks. Canaan was the country which God gave to Abraham and his seed, and the wilderness was simply a strange land through which they passed on their way to their inheritance.

"And they went three days in the wilderness, *and found no water"* (v. 22). This is the first lesson which our wilderness-life is designed to teach us. There is nothing down here which can in anywise minister to that life which we have received from Christ. The pleasures of sin, the attractions of the world, no longer satisfy. The things which formerly charmed, now repel us. The companionships we used to find so pleasing have become distasteful. The things which delight the ungodly only cause us to groan. The Christian who is in communion with his Lord finds absolutely nothing around him which will or can *refresh his thirsty soul.*

For him the shallow cisterns of this world have run dry. His cry will be that of the Psalmist: "O God, Thou art my God; early will I seek Thee; my soul thirsteth for Thee, my flesh longeth for Thee, *in a dry* and *thirsty* land, where no water is" (Psl. 63:1). Ah, here is the believer's Resource: *God* alone can satisfy the longings of his heart. Just as he first heeded the gracious words of the Saviour, "If any man thirst, let him come unto *Me,* and *drink*" (John 7:37), so must he *continue to go* to Him who alone has the Water of Life.

"And when they came to Marah they could not drink of the waters of Marah, for they were bitter; therefore the name of it was called Marah" (v. 23). A sore trial, a real test, was this. Three days' journey in the hot and sandy wilderness without finding any water; and now that water *is* reached, behold, it is *"bitter!"* "How often this is the case with the young believer, aye, and with the old one, too. We grasp at that which we think will satisfy, and only find bitter disappointment. Has it not proved so? Have you tried the pleasures, or the riches, or the honours of the world, and only found them *bitter?* You are invited to a gay party. Once this would have been very delightful; but now, how bitter to the taste of the *new nature!* How utterly disappointed you return home. Have you set your heart on some earthly object? You are permitted to obtain it; but how empty! Yea, what you expected to yield such satisfaction only brings sorrow and emptiness" (C. Stanley).

Israel were now made to feel the bareness and bitterness of the wilderness. With what light hearts did they begin their journey across it? Little prepared were they for what lay before them. To go three days and find no water, and when they reached some to find it bitter! How differently had they expected from God! How natural for them, after experiencing the great work of deliverance which He had wrought for them, to count on Him providing a smooth and easy path for them. So, too, is it with young Christians. They have peace with God and rejoice in the knowledge of sins forgiven. Little do they (or did we) anticipate the tribulations which lay before them. Did not we expect things would be agreeable here? Have we not sought to make ourselves happy in this world? And have we not been disappointed and discouraged, when we found "no water," and that what there is was "bitter?" Ah, we enter the wilderness without understanding what it is! We thought, if we thought at all, that our gracious God would screen us from sorrow. Ah, dear reader, it is at *God's right hand,* and not in this world, that there are "pleasures for evermore."

As we have said, the "wilderness" accurately symbolises and portrays this world, and the *first* stage of the journey forecasts the whole! Drought and bitterness are all that we can expect in the place that owns not Christ. How could it be otherwise? Does God mean for us to settle down and be content in a world which hates Him and which cast out His beloved Son? Never! Here, then, is something of vital importance for the young Christian. I ought to start my wilderness journey *expecting* nothing but dearth. If we expect peace instead of persecution, that which will make us merry rather than cause us to groan, disappointment and disheartenment at not having our expectations realised, will be our portion. Many an experienced Christian would bear witness that most of his failings in the wilderness are to be attributed to his starting out with a wrong view of what the wilderness is. Ease and rest are not to be found in it, and the more we look for these, the keener will be our disappointment. The first stage in our journey must proclaim to us, as to Israel, what the true nature of the journey is. *It is Marah.*

"And the people *murmured* against Moses, saying, What shall we drink?" (v. 24). Very solemn is this. Three days ago this people had been singing, now they are murmuring. Praising before the Red Sea gives place to complaining at Marah! A real trial was this experience, but how sadly Israel failed under it. Just as before, when they saw the Egyptians bearing down upon them at Pihahiroth, so now once more they upbraid Moses for bringing them into trouble. They appeared to have overlooked entirely the fact that they had been *led* to Marah by the Pillar of Cloud (13:22)! Their murmuring against Moses was, in reality, murmuring against the Lord. And so it is with us. Every complaint against our circumstances, every grumble about the weather, about the way people treat us, about the daily trials of life, is directed *against* that One Who "worketh *all* things after the counsel of *His Own* will (Eph. 1:11). Remember, dear reader, that what is here recorded of

Israel's history is "written for *our admonition*" (1 Cor. 10:11). There is the same evil heart of unbelief and the same rebellious will within us as were in the Israelites. Therefore do we need to earnestly seek grace that the one may be subdued and the other broken.

And what was the *cause* of their "murmuring?" There can be only one answer: their eye was no longer upon God. After the wonders of Jehovah's power which they had witnessed in Egypt, and their glorious deliverance at the Red Sea, it ought to have been unmistakably evident to them that *He* was *for* and *with* them in very truth. But so far from recognising this, they do not seem to have given *Him* a single thought. They speak as if they had to do with Moses only. And is it not frequently so with us? When we reach Marah, do we not charge some fellow-creature with being responsible for *our* hard lot? Some friend in whom we trusted, some counsellor whose advice we respected, some arm of flesh on which we leaned has failed us, and we *blame them* because of the "bitter waters!"

"And he cried unto the Lord" (v. 25). Moses did what Israel ought to have done—he took the matter to God in prayer. This is what our "Marah's" are for—to drive us to the Lord. I say *"drive,"* for the tragic thing is that most of the time we are so under the influence of the flesh that we become absorbed with His blessings, rather than with the Blesser Himself. Not, perhaps, that we are entirely prayerless, but rather that there is so little *heart* in our prayers. It is sad and solemn, yet nevertheless true, that it takes a "Marah" to make us cry unto God *in earnest.* "They wandered in the wilderness in a solitary way; they found no city to dwell in. Hungry and thirsty their soul fainted in them. *THEN they cried unto the Lord in* their trouble, and He delivered them out of their distresses. . . . Therefore He brought down their heart with labour; they fell down, and there was none to help. *THEN they cried unto the Lord* in their trouble, and He saved them out of their distresses. . . . Their soul abhorreth all manner of meat; and they drew near unto the gates of death, *THEN they cry unto the Lord* in their trouble, and He saveth them out of their distresses. . . . They reel to and fro, and stagger like a drunken man, and are at their wits' end. *THEN they cry unto the Lord* in their trouble, and He bringeth them out of their distresses" (Psl. 107:4, 5, 12, 13, 18, 19, 27, 28). Alas that this is so often true of writer and reader.

"And he cried unto the Lord; and the Lord showed him a tree, which, when he had cast into the waters, the waters were made sweet" (v. 25). Moses did not cry unto God in vain. The One who has provided redemption for His people is the God of all grace, and with infinite long-sufferance does He bear with them. The faith of Israel might fail, and instead of trusting the Lord for the supply of their need, give way to murmuring; nevertheless, He came to their relief. So with us. How true it is that "He hath not dealt with us *after* our sins, nor rewarded us *according to* our iniquities" (Psl. 103:10). But *on what ground* does the thrice Holy One deal so tenderly with His erring people? Ah, is it not beautiful to see that at this point, too, our type is perfect—it was in response to the cries of an *interceding mediator* that God acted. In His official character Moses is seen all through as the one who came between God and Israel. It was in response to *his* cry that the Lord came to Israel's relief! And blessed be God there is also One who "ever liveth to make intercession for us" (Heb. 7:25), and on *this* ground God deals tenderly with us as we pass through the wilderness: "If any man sin we have an *Advocate* with the Father, Jesus Christ the Righteous" (I. John 2:1).

The form which God's response took on this occasion is also deeply significant and instructive. He showed Moses "a tree." The "tree" had evidently been there all the time, but Moses *saw* it not, or at least knew not its sweetening properties. It was not until the Lord *"showed* him" the tree that he learned of the provision of God's grace. This shows how *dependent* we are upon the Lord, and how blind we are in ourselves. Of Hagar we read, "And God *opened her eyes,* and she saw a well of water" (Gen. 21:19). So in 2 Kings 6:17 we are told, "And the Lord *opened the eyes* of the young man, and he saw; and, behold, the mountain was full of horses and chariots of fire round about Elisha." Clearly "the hearing ear, and *seeing eye,* the Lord hath made even both of them" (Prov. 20:12).

And *what* was it that the Lord "showed" Moses? It was "a tree." And what did this "tree" which sweetened the bitter waters, typify? Surely it is the person and work of our Blessed Saviour—the two are inseparably connected. There are several Scriptures which present Him under the figure of a "tree." In the 1st Psalm it is said, "He shall be *like a tree* planted by the rivers of water, that bringeth forth His fruit in His season, His leaf also shall not wither; and whatsoever He doeth shall prosper" (v. 3). Again, in Song of Solomon 2:3 we read, *"As the apple tree* among the trees of the wood, *so* is my Beloved among the sons. I sat down under His shadow with great delight, and His fruit was sweet to my taste." Here is the second great lesson of our wilderness-life—nothing can sweeten the bitter cup of our earthly experiences except reposing under the shadow of Christ! Sit down at *His* feet, dear reader, and *you* shall find His fruit "sweet" unto your taste, and His words sweeter than the honey or the honey-comb.

But the "tree" also speaks of the *cross* of Christ: "Who His own self bare our sins in His own body *on the Tree"* (I. Pt. 2:24), "The cross of Christ is that which makes what is naturally bitter sweet to us. It is *the fellowship of His sufferings* (Phil. 3:10), and the knowledge of its being that, what suffering can it not sweeten! . . . . Let us remember here that these sufferings of which we speak are therefore sufferings which are peculiar to us *as Christians.* This 'bitterness' of death in the wilderness is not simply the experience of what falls to the common lot of man to experience. It is not the bitterness simply of being in the body—of enduring the ills which, they say, flesh is heir to. It is the bitterness which results from being linked with Christ in His own path of suffering here. 'If we suffer with Him we shall also reign with Him.' Marah then is sweetened by this 'tree'; the cross, the cross of shame; the cross which was the mark of the world's verdict as to Him—the cross it is that sweetens the struggles. If we endure shame and rejection for Him, as His, we can endure it, and the sweet reality of being linked with Him makes Marah itself drinkable" (Mr. Grant). A beautiful illustration is furnished in Acts 16. There we see Paul and Silas in the prison of Philippi; they were cruelly scourged, and then thrown into the innermost dungeon. Behold them in the darkness, feet fast in the stocks, and backs bleeding. That was *"Marah"* for them indeed. But how were they employed? They *"sang praises,"* and sang so lustily that the other prisoners heard them (Acts 16:25). There we see the "tree" sweetening the bitter waters. How was it possible for them to sing under such circumstances? Because they rejoiced that they were "counted worthy to suffer shame for *"His name"* (Act 5:41)! This, then, is *how we are to use* the Cross in our daily lives—to regard our Christian trials and afflictions as opportunities for having fellowship with the sufferings of the Saviour.

"There He made for them a statute and an ordinance, and there he proved them and said, If thou wilt diligently hearken to the voice of the Lord thy God and wilt do that which is right in His sight, and wilt give ear to His commandments, and keep all His statutes, I will put none of these diseases upon thee, which I have brought upon the Egyptians" (vv. 25, 26). It is very important to mark the context here. Nothing had been said to Israel about Jehovah's "statutes and commandments" while they were in Egypt. But now that they were redeemed, now that they had been purchased for Himself, God's governmental claims are pressed upon them. The Lord was dealing with them in wondrous grace. But grace is not lawlessness. Grace only makes us the more indebted to God. Our obligations are increased not cancelled thereby. Grace reigns "through righteousness," not at the expense of it (Rom. 5:21). The obligation of obedience can never be liquidated so long as God *is* God. Grace only establishes *on a higher basis* what we most emphatically and fully OWE to Him as His redeemed creatures.

This principle runs throughout the Scriptures and applies to every dispensation: blessing is dependent upon obedience. Israel were to be immune from the diseases of Egypt only so long as they hearkened diligently to the voice of the Lord their God and did that which was right in His sight! But let us be clear on the point. The keeping of God's commandments has *nothing* to do with our salvation. Israel here were *already* under the blood and had been, typically, brought through death on to resurrection-ground. Yet *now* the Lord reminds them of His commandments and statutes. How far wrong, then, are they who contend that *the law* has *nothing* to do with Christians? True, it has nothing to do with their salvation. But it *is* needful for the regulation of their walk. Believers, equally with unbelievers, are subject to God's government. Failure to recognise this, failure to conform our daily lives to God's statutes, failure to obey His commandments, will not forfeit our salvation, but it *will* bring down upon us the chastening "plagues" of our *righteous* Father (John 17:25).

A separate word is called for upon the closing sentence of verse 26: "For I am the Lord that *healeth* thee." This has been seized upon by certain well-meaning people whose zeal is "not according to knowledge." They have detached this sentence of Scripture and "claimed" the Lord as their *Healer.* By this they mean that in response to their appropriating faith God recovers them from sickness *without* the use of herbs or drugs. From it they deduce the principle that it is *wrong* for a believer to have recourse to any doctor or medical aid. The Lord is *their* Physician, and it is distrust of Him to consult an earthly physician. But if this scripture be examined in its context, it will be found that instead of teaching that God *disdains* the use of means in the healing of His people, *He employs them.* The bitter waters of Marah were healed not by a peremptory fiat from Jehovah, but by a "tree" being cast into them! Thus, in the *first* reference to "healing" in the Bible we find God deliberately choosing to *employ means* for the healing and health of His people. Similarly, did He bless Elisha in the use of means (salt) in healing the waters at Jericho (2 Kings 2:19-22). Similarly did God instruct His servant Isaiah to use means (a fig-poultice) in the healing of Hezekiah. So also in Psl. 104:14 we read, "He causeth the grass to grow for the cattle and *here* for the service of *man;* that he may bring forth good out of the earth." So we find the apostle Paul exhorting Timothy to take a little wine for his stomach's sake (1 Tim. 5:23). Even on the new earth God will use *means* for healing the bodies of the nations which have lived through the millenium without dying and being raised in glorified bodies: "The leaves of the tree were for *the healing* of the nations" (Rev. 22:2).

"And they came to Elim, where were twelve wells of water, and three-score and ten palm trees, and they encamped there by the waters" (v. 27). This does not conflict with our remarks upon the previous verses. Elim is the complement to Marah, and this will be the more evident if we observe their order. First, the bitter waters of Marah sweetened by the tree, and then the wells of pure water and the palm trees for shade and refreshment. Surely the interpretation is obvious: when we are walking in fellowship with Christ and the principle of His cross is faithfully applied to our daily life, not only is the bitterness of suffering for His sake sweetened, but we enter into the pure joys which God has provided for His own, even down here. "Elim" speaks, then, of the satisfaction which God gives to those who are walking with Him in obedience. This joy of heart, this satisfaction of soul, comes to us through *the ministry of the Word*—hence the significance of the *twelve* "wells" and the *seventy* "palm trees"; the very numbers selected by Christ in the sending forth of His apostles. (See Luke 9:1-10:1!) May the Lord grant that we shall so heed the lesson of Marah that Elim will be our happy lot.

—*Arthur W. Pink.*

THE SOVEREIGNTY OF GOD

In the 36th chapter of Job and the 2nd verse we read these words: "Suffer me a little, and I will show thee that I have yet to speak on God's behalf." How many hundreds of preachers there are to-day who are speaking on *man's* behalf!—extolling his greatness, magnifying his achievements, praising his virtues and almost deifying him; and those who do not go quite thus far, most of them, at least, insist loudly on man's free will, and that he is the architect of his own fortunes and the determiner of his own destiny. But how very few there are to-day who are speaking on *God's* behalf! emphasising *His* greatness, magnifying *His* sovereignty, insisting that *God* has a free will! How rarely do you hear a series of sermons to-day on the attributes of God, His being, His character, His perfections, His mighty power, His holiness, His majesty, His faithfulness, His exalted excellency. When a preacher now comes along who says very little about man's responsibility, who seems to rob man of a little of his glory, there is a loud outcry at once; but when a preacher is silent about God's sovereignty, when the preacher robs God of some of the glory that belongs alone to Him, there is very rarely any outcry: it passes without a protest. What is needed to-day, and what we need to pray for to-day, is that it may please God to raise up men who will speak on *His* behalf as Elihu did here.

Now, with that preliminary word, turn to the 97th Psalm and the 2nd verse. I will read the first verse to give the context: "The Lord reigneth; let the earth rejoice; let the multitude of isles be glad"—not that the Lord *is going* to reign when the millenium comes, but the Lord *reigneth* even now; and because the Lord reigneth let the earth rejoice, "let the multitude of isles be glad thereof. Clouds and darkness are round about Him: righteousness and judgment are the habitation of His throne." Now, all true religion starts with the Being of God: that is why the Bible opens in the way that it does, "In the beginning *God,*" and all true religion starts with the Being of God.

The Being of God is a fact that is universally recognised. There is not a nation on earth to-day but which in some form recognises the existence of God. It is a remarkable fact, which perhaps is not known to many, that in all the world's history there are not recorded the names of fifty avowed atheists, and there is not a single atheist mentioned in all Scripture. Even Satan himself acknowledged the existence of God in the presence of Christ. So the demons said, "We know Thee Who Thou art, the Holy One of God." We can no more question the existence of God than we can the sunshine.

Now then, since there is a God, in His Being He must outweigh the entire universe which He has created by the breath of His mouth. Take all the suns and the moons and the stars and the worlds and the angels and human beings and inanimate matter, roll them all together and then what will they weigh? Nothing, nothing, and less than nothing in comparison with the infinite greatness of God, the immensity of deity. Turn to the 40th chapter of Isaiah, beginning at the 12th verse. I want you to see here how God speaks of Himself:—

"Who hath measured the waters in the hollow of His hand, and meted out heaven with the span, and comprehended the dust of the earth in a measure, and weighed the mountains in scales, and the hills in a balance? Who hath directed the Spirit of the Lord, or being His counsellor hath taught Him? With whom took He counsel, and who instructed Him, and taught Him in the path of judgment, and taught Him knowledge, and showed to Him the way of understanding? Behold, the nations are as a drop of a bucket, and are counted as the small dust of the balance: behold, He taketh up the isles as a very little thing." Verse 17: "To whom, then, will ye liken God? or with what likeness will ye compare unto Him?" God only is great, and God alone is to be exalted and magnified. Because God is great He is to be regarded with awe. Because God is great He is to be feared. His name is not to be taken lightly upon our lips. His truth is not to be the subject of impious argument. The word that is needed for this hour above all others is, "Be *still* and know that I *am* God." And my friends, I make so bold as to say, there will never be any real revival in the true sense of the word that does not have GOD as its centre, God as its inspirer, God as the end in view—*His* glory as that around which everything centres. My friends the main thing in conversion is not one man being reconciled to another; it is not the sinner being brought into the congregation of the Lord's people; the main thing in conversion is man being reconciled to God, being brought into right relationship with Him. Look at that verse again, if you please, in Psalm 97, "Clouds and darkness are round about Him." That is only a figurative way of saying that God is incomprehensible to us. It is the Divine affirmation that His very Being is shrouded in mystery. "Clouds and darkness are round about Him," and if God were not a mystery to us He would not be God. That mystery is the inevitable outcome of the vast chasm which separates the Infinite from the finite, the Creator from the creature; and that chasm itself necessarily and inevitably involves the mystery that He is as far above our comprehension and understanding as the sun is above the earth.

Now look at the text again, if you please: "Clouds and darkness are round about Him, righteousness and judgment are the habitation of His throne." I want you to mark it carefully that God has *a throne,* and if God has a throne He must be sovereign, and if God is sovereign He must be an *absolute* sovereign. A God who is swayed by His creatures, a God who is influenced by His creatures, is no God at all. It narrows itself down to this: There is no other possible alternative—either God sways or He *is* swayed; either God rules or He *is* ruled; either God *does* His will or His will is thwarted. God is either supreme in fact or there is no God. Therefore, when we say that God *is* God we affirm that He has the absolute right to rule and to dispose of the whole universe and everything in it (which He has created for His Own glory); that He has the right to dispose of it just as He pleases. God did not make us for our glory; He made us for His glory; and glorified in us and by us He *will* be, if not in one way, in another. Either His grace will be magnified by us in heaven as redeemed sinners, as the monuments of His *mercy,* or His *justice* and *holiness* will be magnified in our very torments in hell. Those in hell will glorify God, for they will magnify His justice and His holiness in putting them there. O make no mistake, dear friends, God has created us for *His Own* glory, and glorified He *shall* be—if not in one way, in another. Proverbs 16.4 says "The Lord hath made all things *for Himself;*" and Revelation 4.11 says, "for *Thy* pleasure they are and were created."

Now, then, we are ready to define our terms "The Sovereignty of God." When we say that God is sovereign we affirm that God always has been and always will be the Supreme Being. When we say that God is Sovereign, we affirm that the helm of the universe is in His hand, and that He is controlling and directing all things for the outworking of His eternal purpose. When we say that God is Sovereign we affirm that it is utterly impossible for any creature or all creatures combined to prevent the execution of His counsels. When we say that God is Sovereign, we affirm that He is ruling and reigning in every sphere and doing according to His Own pleasure. When we say that God is Sovereign, we affirm that He is the heavenly Potter and that we are nothing more than a lump of clay to be shaped and moulded as He pleases. When we say that God is Sovereign, we affirm—I measure my words, and I say this next sentence fully conscious of the fact that I shall yet have to render an account to God for it at the judgment-seat of Christ, and yet I calmly, but deliberately, say—that it is just as impossible for God to *fail* in the execution of His purpose as it is for God to *sin*. One is just as much impossible as the other. God would cease to be *holy* if He sinned. God would cease to be *God* if His purpose failed. Now, then, my friends, such is the God of the Bible—a God Who is all-mighty in fact as well as in name; a God who is Most Holy, ruling over heaven and ruling over earth. And I also say this calmly, that the man who does not believe in *such* a God is an *atheist*. All the standard dictionaries define an atheist as "one who does not believe in a *Supreme* Being." Now, I want you to mark carefully what I just said. I did not say that the man who does not believe in *election* is an atheist. I did not say that. I did not say that the man who refuses to believe in predestination is an atheist. But I do say, and I repeat it, that the man who does not believe that God *is God in fact* as well as in Name, that He is on the Throne directing all things for His Own glory, that God is Lord Supreme and cannot be hindered, let alone thwarted; the man who does not believe in *such* a God is an atheist; and he is an atheist for this reason: There is *only one* God (revealed in three Persons), and that God, the God of the Bible, is Supreme. My friends, there is no possible alternative between an *absolutely sovereign* God and *no* God at all!

Now, then, having given those definitions, I am going to present the proofs, and proofs from Scripture alone. I am not going to read from any theology or from any of man's writings to-night, but I am going to ask you to turn with me to no less than 20 passages—not one or two, or three, but twenty—which back up, and which confirm, plainly and positively, what I have just been saying. And every one of these passages is just like a cannon ball, a live shell that utterly demolishes all the vain and proud reasonings of man against God.

Turn with me first of all to the first book of Chronicles, and the 29th chapter, verses 11 and 12: "Thine, O Lord, is the greatness, and the power, and the glory, and the victory, and the majesty: for all that is in the heaven and the earth is Thine; Thine is the kingdom, O Lord, and Thou art exalted as head above all"—not simply exalted as head over His own people: there are no exceptions made: "Thou art exalted as head above all, both riches and honour come of Thee, and Thou reignest over all"—not *will* do, in the millenium, but *does* so *now,* and *has been* doing all the time—"and in Thine hand is power and might; and in Thine hand it is to make great, and to give strength unto all." Ah, my friends, God is no mere figurehead. The title of God is no empty one: God is God in fact as well as in Name.

Turn next to II. Chronicles, chapter 20, verses 5 and 6. I am going slowly because I want you to follow me. I want you to see that I am not reading out of a Bible of my own composition, but a Bible that is like yours. "And Jehoshaphat stood in the congregation of Judah and Jerusalem, in the house of the Lord, before the new court, and said, O Lord God of our fathers, art not Thou God in heaven? and rulest not Thou over all the kingdom of Israel? Certainly He ruled over the kingdom of *Israel,* and there are a lot of people to-day that are willing to admit that God *does* rule over His own people now, but they say He does *not* rule over the wicked because they won't let Him. Then, if that is true, poor God! I say that in all reverence: If God is *defeated,* then He is to be sympathised with! How different is the language of Scripture from the theories and views and opinions of man, any man, none excepted! "O Lord God of our fathers, art not Thou God in heaven? and in Thine hand is not there power and might, so that *none* is able to withstand Thee?" None, not even the devil himself! *That* is the God of the Bible: a God who is worthy of our respect, a God who is worthy of our worship, a God who is something more than a pasteboard monarch. Listen, God is the great Autocrat of the universe. Before

Him, Caesar and Charlemagne and Napoleon and the Kaiser are less than grasshoppers in comparison. I repeat that deliberately—God is *the Great Autocrat* of the universe. Before Him the greatest and mightiest of men are nothing more than grasshoppers in comparison. "*None* is able to withstand Thee." I wonder how many of us really believe that! I really wonder how many here to-night (I am not going to ask for any show of hands, because that does not mean anything, and it is not worth anything: you can get a dummy to stick its hand up if you charge it with electricity). But I wonder how many here to-night in their hearts *really* and *truly* believe that fact, that *none* is able to withstand God—I do not mean the God of modern Christendom, but I mean the God of the Bible. Do you know I believe with all my heart that if the Apostle Paul were here on earth to-day he would tell us that over many of our churches we ought to have inscribed on the entrance, "To *the unknown* God;" and I believe if Paul were here to-day he would stand in many a pulpit and say: "Him Whom ye *ignorantly* worship, Him declare I unto you." You talk about ignorance and the darkness in heathendom, it is almost as bad as Christendom. The great difference is that in heathendom they manufacture gods out of wood and stone. In Christendom we manufacture gods out of our sentiments and our imaginations; that is the difference—a God who is nothing more than love and mercy and compassion. That is *not* the God of the Bible. The God of the Bible is a God to be feared, a God to be trembled at, and we *would* tremble before Him, every one of us here to-night, if we only had a vision of His greatness and exalted majesty. We need what Isaiah had when he saw God holy and mighty and lifted up, seated on the throne; and when Isaiah saw Him, what did he do? He says, "Woe is me, for I am undone." *That* is what some of us would say if only God in His sovereignty granted us a view *of Himself.* The God that is preached in most places in Christendom to-day would not cause anybody to cry that! You can preach God's love until you are as old as Methuselah and you will never get anyone to say "Woe is me for I am undone," under that preaching.

Now turn to the 23rd chapter of Job and the 13th verse. "But He is in one mind, and who can turn Him, and what His soul desireth"—*a few* of those things He doeth? Oh, I beg your pardon—"and *some* of those things He doeth." No, it is even stronger than that. "What His soul desireth *even that* He doeth." Ah, my friends, the God of Scripture is no fictitious sovereign, He is in reality the Invincible Potentate, the King of kings, and Lord of lords.

Turn now to Psalm 115, verse 3. "But our God is in the heavens" (Our God, mind you!): "But our God is in the heavens: He hath done *a few* of the things which He hath pleased, and the others men would not let Him do." *That* is how it ought to read to harmonise with modern theology! That is precisely how it ought to read to fit in with twentieth-century ideas! "Our God is in the heavens": He hath done *whatsoever* He hath pleased." I wonder how many of us believe that? I wonder! That God has done *everything* that He pleased, that *every* purpose of His will *has been* accomplished. "He hath done *whatsoever* He pleased." There is no qualification, so *you* had better not make any. God says, "Add thou not to His Word, lest He reprove thee, and thou be found a liar." (Prob. 30:6.) That is Scripture, so don't you dare to add anything to this verse. "He hath done *whatsoever* He pleased," no exceptions, no qualifications. Ah, my friends, the God of the Bible is not a Being who is filled with amiable intentions which He is *unable to* carry out.

Now turn to the 19th chapter of Proverbs, verse 21: "There are many devices in a man's heart." Yes, there *are* in every man's heart. "There are many devices in a man's heart: nevertheless the counsel of the Lord, that shall stand." No matter how much men may plan and scheme, no matter how much they rebel and resist, God's cousel (that is, what He has purposed in Himself) is immutable and irresistible. "Nevertheless the counsel of the Lord, that shall stand." You need not turn to it, you all remember it, I hope—the 2nd Psalm; how does it open? "The kings of the earth set themselves, and the rulers take counsel together, against the Lord, and against His anointed." Yes, and what is heaven's response? "He that sitteth in the heavens shall laugh." That is what *God* does when man thinks of defying Him. I wonder if any of you ever heard a sermon in all your lives on a *laughing* God! I am pretty sure you did not. It is there in the Bible all the same. "He that sitteth in the heavens shall laugh: He shall hold them in derision." *Why* does He? Because of the extreme folly of it; as though all the kings of the earth and all their armies united together could do one single thing to thwart *Him!* He laughs at the very idea of it, and so does everybody else who believes in God's sovereignity. My friends, a worm of the ground might just as well attempt to resist the tread of an elephant, or a little child in its ignorance might just as well go down to the beach and attempt to stop the ocean from rolling, as for any creature (the devil included) to attempt nullify the purpose of the Almighty, eternal God. That is the God I believe in, and if you do not. I am sorry for you. That is the God of Scripture!

Turn to the 21st chapter of Proverbs, the 1st verse: "The king's heart is in the hand of the Lord, as the rivers of water: He turneth it whithersoever He will." And if the *king's* heart is in the hand of the Lord, and God turns it which ever way *He* wants to, that is certainly true of the *subjects.* If it is true of the king, much more is it true of the subjects—or equally so rather—there cannot be any "much more" where God is concerned. "The king's heart is in the hand of the Lord and He turneth it whithersoever He will." That does not give much place to *the king's* "will"! Well, it is there in Scripture. Be very careful how you murmur against Scripture, for you are fighting against God if you do. You cannot manage God, but He can manage you; so be careful. You cannot injure God, but He can grind you to powder if He wants to; and He *will* do if you fight against Him. On whomsoever that Stone shall fall He shall be ground to powder, says Scripture.

Now notice in the 30th verse of that same chapter (Proverbs 21). "There is no wisdom nor understanding nor counsel against the Lord." You notice there is no qualification. It is not modified or restricted at any point. There is *no* wisdom nor understanding nor counsel against the Lord. The devil may be wise, and the devil may plot against God and he may scheme for all he is worth, but he is absolutely unable to defeat the counsel of God at any point.

Now turn to the book of Isaiah, chapter 14, verses 26 and 27. "This is the purpose that is purposed upon the whole earth"—not some parts of it, but *every* part—"and this is the hand that is stretched out upon all the nations"—not simply the so-called Christian nations, but all the nations, none excepted. "For the Lord of hosts hath purposed, and who shall turn it back?" My friends, the God of the Bible is *the great Despot,* the great Despot of heaven and earth. If any of you will consult the Greek in the 4th chapter of Acts, and the That is one of His titles: Acts 4:24. It is translated "Lord" into English: it ought not to have been. Any Greek scholar knows that "despotes" is Despot. The Greek word in Acts 4:24 is not "Kurios" at all: it is "despotes," from which we get our English word "despot." God is the great Despot of heaven and earth. If the translators had done their duty with that verse they would have translated it "Despot." I guess they thought it a little too harsh, but the Holy Spirit did not think so.

Turn now to the 46th chapter of Isaiah, verses 8 and 10: "Remember this, and show yourselves men: bring it again to mind, O ye transgressors. Remember the former things of old: for I am God, and there is none else"—none else in comparison. "I am God, and there is none like Me." In what respects? First, "declaring the end from the beginning and from ancient times the things that are not yet done;" second, "saying, My counsel shall stand and I will do all My pleasure. That is what God says: "My counsel shall stand and I will do all My pleasure." *all,* A-L-L! My friends, the God of the Bible is the great Autocrat of the universe. He panders to none. He consults none. He refuses to give any account of His matters to anybody. And God declares that no mere creature has any more right to call into question His ways than a clay-vessel has to criticise the potter that made it.

Now turn to the 4th chapter of Daniel, verses 34 and 35: "And at the end of the days I, Nebuchadnezzar, lifted up mine eyes unto heaven, and mine understanding returned unto me" Yes, and he proved that in his next words: "And I blessed the most High, and I praised and honoured Him that liveth for ever, whose dominion is an everlasting dominion, and His kingdom is from generation to generation: and all the inhabitants of the earth are reputed as nothing." That is not very palatable; is it? Those of you who are in the habit of puffing out your chests and strutting around like peacocks, and have such a sense of your own importance (O you can call this satire if you like: you deserve something worse than satire, some of you. You are going to get something worse later on). But those who are in the habit of strutting around in their own self-importance and imagine the work of God would come to an end if *they* dropped out, here is what God thinks of you, my friend: God says you are just a cypher, that is all, just a cypher, just a mere nought, a *"nothing."* That is how the Almighty God looks down at you right now. You are just a *"nothing."* That is how He looks down on me, too, every last one of us. "All the inhabitants of the earth are reputed as "nothing." Mind you, I am speaking of us now as creatures, not as believers in Christ; our position in Him. I am speaking of us as mere creatures, and as human creatures we are just *nothings* in God's sight, and that throws light on an expression that has probably puzzled some of you in the first chapter of Corinthians, where it says: "God hath chosen the things which *are not,* to bring to nought the things that are. Now, in the Greek "the things that are not" is all one word, and it just means "nonentities." God hath chosen nonentities, mere nothings, cyphers, to bring to nought the things that are. Well, now, let us go on. Daniel 4.35: "And all the inhabitants of the earth are reputed as nothing: and *He* doeth according to *His* will in the army of heaven." Oh, yes, we all believe that; no difficulty there. We are quite satisfied that God does according to His will *in heaven,* but it does not stop there. "He doeth according to His will in the army of heaven and among the inhabitants of the earth: and none can stay His hand, or say unto Him, "What doest Thou?" My friend, God is *the Almighty* in truth as well as in name.

Now, so far, I have given you ten Scriptures, and perhaps some of you say, "Well, but they are all from the Old Testament." What of that? Is the God of the Old Testament a *different* God from the God of the New? What sort of theology do you believe in? The God of the Old Testament and the God of the New Testament are one and the same. Whatever the Old Testament says about God remains true of God for all time and eternity so far as His character and Person is concerned. But now, in order to shut every mouth and silence every objection, we will have ten from the New Testament. There will not be time for me to comment on each one—at any length, at any rate. John 17, verse 2. I will read you the first verse to give the context. John 17.1: "These words spake Jesus, and lifted up His eyes to heaven, and said, Father the hour is come; glorify Thy Son, that They Son also may glorify Thee." John 17.2:"As Thou hast given Him power"—*exousia,* not "dunamis." "As Thou hast given Him power" (it means authority) "As Thou hast given Him authority over all flesh." The authority of the Lord Christ is not limited to the Church. His authority extends and reaches out to all flesh. Christ has authority over the wicked as well as over believers, and, my friends, that truth and fact will shortly be made manifest when He makes His enemies His footstool. It is true to-day, but it is not *manifest* before us: in the millenium it *will* be. The great difference between the millenium and this present dispensation is this, that the Throne of God will then be on the earth instead of in heaven, and His rule will be *manifested* outwardly before men's eyes instead of being secret and invisible as it is now. But even now Christ has authority over all flesh, unbelievers as well as believers, and in the millenium it will be made manifest when He makes His foes His footstool.

And now turn to John 19, verses 10 and 11. I will read you the 9th verse: "And went again into the judgment hall, and saith unto Jesus, Whence art Thou? But Jesus gave him no answer. Then saith Pilate unto him, Speakest thou not unto *me?* Knowest thou not that I have power to crucify thee, and have power to release thee." That was what Pilate thought. The man was honest enough, but he was ignorant. Pilate *did not* have power to release Christ, for God would not allow him to. That was the boast of man. Pilate there was giving expression to the universal pride of the human heart that says, "I have power." Yes, that is what the poor fool thinks today. Oh, you say, please modify your language a little. I won't. That is the language of Scripture. There was a certain man who had much goods laid up for many days, and he said, I will say unto my soul, thou hast much goods laid up for many days, and he says, I will do so and so. And God says, "Thou *fool!*" And that is what God says to any man and every man who stands up prating against Him and boasting of *his* will and what *he* can do. Pilate was giving expression to his ignorance. "Knowest Thou not that I have power to crucify Thee, and have power to release Thee?" That is what he thought. The man was sincere, but he was ignorant. "Jesus answered, Thou couldest have no power at all against Me, except it were given thee from above: therefore, he that delivered Me unto thee hath the greater sin." *No power at all,* even though you are a high official in the Roman Empire. Yes, a high official in the Roman Empire; and Pilate, you have got *no power,* except what is given you from above! That puts man down into the dust, doesn't it? That is exactly why this truth is so unpopular and so unpalatable. Men hate it because it makes nothings out of them. Well, that it what God says you are. The whole crowd of us put together, we are just *nothings.* You must not quarrel against me. I am not giving you my theories and views and opinions to-night; I am giving you what God says. I am not telling you what Calvin taught. The thing that matters is, *what do the Holy Scriptures say?*

Now turn over to the 4th chapter of Acts, verses 27 and 28: "For of a truth against Thy Holy Child Jesus, whom Thou hast anointed, both Herod, and Pontius Pilate, with the Gentiles, and the people of Israel were gathered together." A very powerful company, weren't they, a very influential crowd? Pilate, Herod, the Gentiles, people of Israel, all gathered together, and what did they do? The next verse tells us: "For to do whatsoever Thy hand and Thy cousel *determined* before to *be* done." That is all they did. They just did what God had predestinated they should do, for that is what the word "determined" there means.

Turn now to Acts 17, verses 24, 25, 26: "God that made the world and all things therein, seeing that He is Lord of heaven and earth, dwelleth not in temples made with hands; neither is He worshipped with men's hands, as though He needed anything, seeing He giveth to all life, and breath, and all things, and hath made of one blood all nations of men for to dwell on all the face of the earth, and hath determined the times before appointed, and the bounds of their habitation." What I want you to notice particularly in that passage is in the 24th verse, that God is not only Lord of heaven (that is, over the angels), but He is *Lord of earth* as well!

Now turn to Romans 8, verse 28. Now, here is a verse we are all very familiar with, I doubt not. "And we know that all things work together for good to them that love God, to them who are the called according to His purpose." But, now listen. How can we *know this?* How is it possible for us *to* know that *all* things work together for our good, unless all things are in the hand of God, being directed by Him? I challenge any man to answer that question in any other way. How could we know, how could we be sure that all things *did* work together for good unless God has absolute control over *all* things? If God does not have control over some things, then those some things mav work together for our ill, and we could not be sure beforehand that they would turn out for our good. The only way we we *can* be sure, and that we *can* know, that *all* things work together for our good is, because God is over all, directing all.

Now turn to Romans 11.36, and I want you to notice this carefully. The last verse of Romans 11. "For of Him (as the Originating Cause) and through Him (as the Providential Director), and to Him (as the great End in view), are all things." Of Him, through Him, to Him are all things—no exceptions. That is what the Bible says, and if you do not believe that, you do not believe God's Word, that is all. "Of Him, and through Him, and to Him are *all* things." I am not going to offer any explanation, I will just let it be. I won't darken counsel by words. I believe that God there says what He means and means what He says.

I. Corinthians 8, verse 6: "But to us there is but one God, the Father, of whom are all things." "One God, the Father, of whom are all things": not *some* things, but *all* things. "And one Lord Jesus Christ, by whom are all things, and we of Him." If you doubt that, you take issue with God's Word, and you will yet have to answer to Him for it.

1 Corinthians, 11tht chapter and the 12th verse: "For as the woman is of the man, even so is the man also by the woman; but *all things* of God." All is according to His eternal purpose which He purposed in Himself before the foundation of the world. My friends, it was predestined by God before this world began that I should occupy this pulpit to-night, and that you should sit in those chairs to-night, and that I should speak on the subject that I am speaking on to-night, and that you should hear it. It was all fixed by God before this world began, and if any of you question that, I bring you back to these Scriptures, *"All* things are of God"!

Now to-night I am only introducing the subject. I recognise at once that there are a hundred difficulties cropping up in your minds, and a thousand questions; but never mind your difficulties and never mind your questions: the first thing you have to ask is this, Is this truth in God's Word, or is it not? If it *is* in God's Word it *must* be true, whether I understand it or not, and whether I can harmonise it with other things or not, and whether I like it or whether it appeals to my heart or not. *Is it in God's Word?* That is the only question for you to consider right now. And if you are not going to believe in this doctrine until all your difficulties are disposed of and all your questions are answered, then your faith is not worth a snap of the fingers. Your faith would then only stand in the wisdom of man, instead of in the power of God, and none of you need waste your time by writing any questions for me to answer to-morrow night because I am not going to attempt to answer any. You had better go direct to the Lord. He can answer them far better than I can. He can give you wisdom if you will seek it. If you are going to come to me with your difficulties and wait to have them solved and then believe this truth afterwards, your faith would stand in the wisdom of man.

Now, two other Scriptures. Ephesians 1, verse 11: "In whom also we have obtained an inheritance, being predestinated according to the purpose of Him Who worketh all things after the counsel of His own will." According to the purpose of Him Who worketh *all* things after the counsel of His own will! That does not need any explanation; it just means what it says. Now turn to the 4th chapter of Revelation and the 11th verse: "Thou art worthy, O Lord, to receive glory and honour and power; for thou hast created all things." Yes, why? *Why* did God create and for what did God create us? "Thou hast created all things and *for Thy pleasure* they are and were created."

Now, my friends, I have been speaking almost an hour and a half and I have only just got started, but let me wind up with this one point. What ought our attitude be toward *such* a God? Let me give you four answers and I won't enlarge at all. One ought to *fear* Him and *tremble* in His presence. The God of the Bible is a God to be feared and regarded with the utmost awe. Second, what ought our attitude be towards such a God as this? One of *implicit obedience,* for He is sovereign and we are simply His servants. He is sovereign and we are simply His subjects to do what *He* says and to obey *His* commands, however unreasonable they may seem to be to us. Third, what ought our attitude be towards such a God as this? One of *abounding praise,* that He is able to make all things work together for our eternal good; and He is able to, *because* He is sovereign, supreme, and none can hinder Him. He is a God to be praised. Finally, what ought our attitude be towards such a God as this? One of *devout worship.* He is the Almighty King of kings and Lord of lords, and our only suitable place is in the dust at His feet in adoration and in thanksgiving unto Him.

———— : o : ————

N.B.—The above is a verbatim report of an Address delivered by the Editor on June 18 at the Baptist Tabernacle, Ashfield—one of the strongest Churches in Sydney. We have only corrected a word here and there. We earnestly solicit the prayers of God's saints for its loyal and faithful Pastor—L. Sale-Harrison, B.D.—that the Lord will use him increasingly to His glory.—*A.W.P.*

OUR GREATEST ENCOURAGEMENT.

"Now all these happened unto them for ensamples (lit., for types), and they were written for our admonition" (1 Cor. 10:11).

There is a blessed *application* of Num., 16:8 for the Lord's people to-day, because we have the truth revealed and proclaimed to us in the epistles, and a powerful illustration of it in this episode, in the history of Israel. *"If the Lord delight in us, then will He bring us into this land, and give it us."*

The first thought of the religious old nature is, "Then I must try and behave so that I may enable Him to delight in me"! But this does not come up even to the Old Testament standard, still less to the New. Those under the old covenant had truer views of God and the promise of God. They saw the "giants," but not the right hand of God which could subdue them. They saw the "walled cities." But not the strength of Jehovah which could crumble them to dust. They said, "They are stronger than we," because they forgot the Strong One in their midst. They were in their enemies' sight as grasshoppers, but did not think of what their enemies were in God's sight. They wept because of the giants and walls, and forgot God's covenant which He made with Abraham, Isaac, and Jacob.

What a difference there is between Numbers 16 and Exodus 15! In Num. 16 it was all "we": "we came," and "we saw," and "we were," etc. Whereas in Exodus 15 it was "Who is like unto Thee?" "Thou hast led forth," "Thou hast redeemed," "Thou hast guided," "Thou shalt bring in." Thereore it is no wonder we read, "Then sang Moses and the children of Israel this song." And it is no wonder likewise that we read in Num. 16:1, "the people wept that night."

And what is the answer of faith to all this weeping? It is given in the words of Joshua and Caleb (verse 8), *"If the Lord delight in us, He will bring us into this land, and give it us."* This was the ground of faith in Exodus. It was the fact that "God remembered His covenant with Abraham, with Isaac, and with Jacob" (Exodus 2:24). No other ground can give true cause for singing of Jehovah's praise. And any other ground will give cause for weeping instead of singing.

Notice the three verbs: "delight," "bring," and "give"! They all refer to Jehovah's action, and not to ours. What is there in us to call forth, still less to merit, one or the other? What is there to call forth the notice, the esteem, or respect of a holy God? Why should He delight in sinful worms of the earth—miserable, rebellious creatures? What is there in us? Everything that would cause Him to abhor us.

God's delight in us is wholly in virtue of His *covenant!* It is to this that He always has "respect." And the covenant which He has made with us in Christ is on resurrection-ground. It is as having died and risen in Christ that the Father can delight in His people. He looked on Christ and said, "This is My Beloved Son, in whom I am well pleased," and He looks on each one who is in Christ, and says the same. Hence it is written in Psa. 16:2, "O my soul, thou hast said unto Jehovah, Thou art my Lord, my goodness extendeth not to Thee, but to the saints that are in the earth, and to the excellent, *in whom is all My delight.*" These are the words of the great surety of the covenant speaking in this Resurrection-Psalm on behalf of His people.

This is our greatest encouragement in times of doubt and difficulty and depression. This has always been the encouragement of God's saints even under the old covenant. David, when suffering under chastisement for an open sin, held on to this, like a ship to its anchor. He said to Zadok, Carry back the ark of God into the city: *if I shall find favour in the eyes of Jehovah,* He will bring me again and show me both it and His habitation. But if He thus say, *"I have no delight in thee*: Behold, here I am, let Him do as seemeth Him good" (2 Sam. 15:25, 26). This is the language of faith in time of chastening, but it is the same in time of praise. In 2 Sam. 22:20, "He brought me forth also into a large place; He delivered me *because He delighted in me.*"

Here is all our security. But to be a true encouragement we must be certain of the grounds on which God's delight in His people is based. It is nothing in themselves, but wholly in Himself. He delights in us simply because He has respect to His covenant in Christ: Because He has redeemed us by his Son through "the blood of the covenant": and because He has made it known to us in regeneration by the Holy Spirit as the witness to the covenant. The Father delights in the people of His choice. The Son delights in the fruits of the travail of His soul. The Spirit delights in His own workmanship.

It is the Father's delight to will to draw them to Himself. It is the Son's delight to do the will of God, and it is the Spirit's delight to witness to that will in their heart's experience. But there is more than delight in these words; there is *determination.* "Then He will bring us in." There may be doubts and misgivings and fears, but we rest in this: *"He will bring us in."* The Giants of Distrust and Dismay and Despair may defy us, but *"He will bring us in."* The walled cities of Ignorance, Indifference, and Infidelity may withstand us, but in spite of all, *"He will bring us in."* And why? Because our walk is correct? Because our life is worthy? No! but because—look at the words as written in Psalm 44:3—"Because *Thou hast a favour unto them.*" That is the reason, and the only reason that God gives, and that precious faith thankfully confesses.

No. Israel was carefully reminded that "Not for thy righteousness, or for the uprightness of thy heart, dost thou go to possess their land . . . . but that He may perform the word which the Lord sware unto thy fathers" (Deut. 9:1-6). And so with His people now. It is because He loved and chose them in Christ, because Christ, "having loved His own, loved them unto the end" (John 13:1), that *"He will bring us in."* Yes, "in," to the eternal relationship with Himself, "in" to the blessedness of all the truth which He has revealed for them, and "in" to the possession and enjoyment of all spiritual blessings in Christ, treasured up in Christ for them.

"He will bring us in." Where? Into the possession and enjoyment of all that He has promised. For Israel, that was "the land." For us, it is "all spiritual blessings in Christ." Like that land to Israel, ours is a matter of Divine revelation (Gen. 12:2). It is a possession that is *inalienable,* for it is written, "The land shall not be sold forever: for the land is Mine: for ye are strangers and sojourners with Me"; or, as in the margin, "the land shall not be sold *to be quite cut off.*" It often appears to be nearly cut off in our experience in times of doubt and difficulty. But we may be certain of this, that, however nearly it may seem to be "cut off," it is never "quite." "Being confident of this very thing that He which hath begun a good work in you, will perfect (i.e., finish) it until the day of Jesus Christ" (Phil. 1:6).

Like Israel's inheritance, ours is one of *covenant favour.* Psa. 85:1, "Lord, Thou hast been favourable unto Thy land"! Yes, and all that we have is by His favour

(Psa. 5:12). We are exalted by His favour (Psa. 89:7). We shall be victorious through His favour (Psa. 41:11), and we shall be "satisfied with favour and full with the blessings of the Lord" (Deut. 33:23).

Like Israel's inheritance, ours is characterised by precious *fruit*: "The land shall yield her increase, and the trees of the field shall yield their fruit" (Lev. 26:4). Yes, "fruit," not "fruits." For "the fruit of the Spirit is love, joy, peace, long-suffering, gentleness, goodness, faith, meekness, temperance" (Gal. 5:22, 23). And all is the gift of God, for "He will give it us." Not sell it, but give it. We cannot earn it, work for it or deserve it. No! God loves; and God gives. We believe; and we have (John 3:16). He gave His Son, He gives His Spirit; He gives a new nature; He gives precious faith; He gives all things. "He that spared not His own Son, but delivered Him up for us all, how shall He not with Him also freely give us all things" (Rom. 8:32). This is why the Holy Spirit Himself is given, *"That we might know the things that are freely given to us* of God" (1 Cor. 2:12). All blessings flows forth from His free, spontaneous, uninfluenced grace, enjoyed with Christ, and communicated to the hearts of His people by the power of the Holy Spirit. He has proved that He does delight in the work of His own hands; therefore "He will bring us in." He has given grace: therefore He will give us the glory.

Things to Come, 1899.

PRACTICAL HOLINESS.

We may here divert a little to consider what ought to be the frame of our minds in the pursuit of practical holiness with respect unto these things, namely, what regard we ought to have unto the *command* on the one hand, and to the *promise* on the other—to our own *duty*, and to the *grace* of God. Some would separate these things as inconsistent. A command, they suppose, leaves no room for a promise, at least, not such a promise as wherein God should take on Himself *to work in us* what the command *requires of us;* and a promise, they think, takes off all the influencing authority of the command. "If practical holiness be our *duty,* there is no room for *grace* in this matter; and if it be an effect of *grace,* there is no place for *duty."* But all these arguings are a fruit of the wisdom of the flesh; but "the wisdom that is from above" teaches us far otherwise. It is true our works and God's grace *are* opposed in the matter of justification, as utterly inconsistent: if it be of works it is not of grace, and if it be of grace it is not of works (Rom. 11:6). But our duty and God's grace are nowhere opposed in the matter of sanctification, yea, the one absolutely supposes the other. We cannot perform our duty therein without the grace of God, but God gives us this grace only unto the end that we may rightly perform our duty. He that shall deny either that God commands us to be holy in a way of duty or promiseth to work holiness in us in a way of grace, may with as much modesty reject the whole Bible.

Our regard unto the *command* consisteth in three things: (1) That we get our consciences always affected with the *authority* of it, as it is the command of God. Where this is not, there is no holiness. Our practical holiness is our obedience; and the formal nature of obedience ariseth from its respect unto the authority of the command. (2) That we perceive the *reasonableness,* the equity, the advantage of the command. Our service is a reasonable service, and in keeping God's commands there is great reward. If we judge not thus, if we rest not herein, and are thence filled with indignation against everything within us or without us that opposeth it or riseth up against it, whatever we do in compliance with it in a way of duty, we are not holy. (3) That hereon we *love* and delight in it, because it is holy, just, and good; because the things it requires are upright, easy, and pleasant to the new nature.

We have a due regard unto the *promise* to the same end only. (1) When we walk in a constant sense of our own *inability* to comply with the command in any one instance from any power in ourselves; for we have no sufficiency of ourselves, our sufficiency is of God. (2) When we *adore that grace* which hath provided help and relief for us. Seeing that without the grace promised we could never have attained unto the least degree of holiness, and seeing we could never deserve the least dram of that grace, how ought we to continually praise that infinite bounty which hath freely provided us of this supply? (3) When we put forth *faith* in prayer and *expectation* of the promise *for* supplies of grace enabling us unto holy obedience, and when we have *especial regard* thereunto with respect unto especial temptations and particular duties. Dr. John Owen (1650).

(*Continued from page 193.*)

set about their regulation? What help does Scripture afford us here? Real help, we may be assured, for the Word is given us "that the man of God may be *complete*, thoroughly furnished unto *all* good works" (2 Tim 3:17).

First, we need to cry with David—"Search me, O God, and know my heart: try me and know my thoughts: And see if there be any wicked way in me, and lead me in the way everlasting" (Psa. 139:23, 24). Ask God to turn His holy searchlight upon us, that the hidden evils within may be made manifest. This will reveal to us our need of confessing to Him our hitherto *unjudged thoughts*, and humility of heart and godly sorrow for sin are ever the first conditions for any growth in grace and conformity to Christ.

Second, diligently heed the counsel of Prov. 16:3—"Commit thy works unto the Lord, and thy *thoughts* shall be established." A remarkable word is this. It is not to be reasoned or philosophised about, but received by simple child-like faith. *Here* is God's antedote for wandering thoughts! The word "commit" here signifies *"roll."* The "works should not be restricted: thy plans and undertakings, whether temporal or spiritual. Devolve all upon Him, cast *all* care upon Him, count upon Him for support and supply, and "thy thoughts *shall be* established." When the believer has, by faith and prayer, committed himself, his ways and his works, into the hands of the Lord, his mind is made easy, his thoughts are composed, and he quietly waits the issue of things, knowing that *all* things are working together for his good and God's glory.

Third, by occupying the mind with high and holy objects and occupations. "Finally, brethren, whatsoever things are true, whatsoever things are honest, whatsoever things are just, whatsoever things are pure, whatsoever things are lovely, whatsoever things are of good report; if there be any virtue, and if there be any praise, *think on these things*" (Phil. 4:8). Emulate the Psalmist who he said, "According to Thy name, O God, so is Thy praise unto the ends of the earth" (Psa. 48:10). Heed the admonition of the Holy Spirit—"Consider the Apostle and High Priest of our profession" (Heb. 3:1).

Finally, call to mind the words of 2 Co. 10.5, "bringing into captivity every thought to the obedience of Christ." *Pray* to God for an exercised conscience about this! Ask Him to take charge of your mind and heart. Trust *Him to* do this! Count on His mighty power to do for you what you cannot achieve by your own resolutions and efforts. Nothing is too hard for Him. The one Who formed the heart and endowed us with the power of thought, is well able to control them. May it not be that much of our past failures in this respect is due to our unbelief! Frank and faithful confession, committing all concerns and intents to the Lord, the mind occupied with the things of God, the prayer of faith—these are God's gracious provisions for "bringing into captivity ever thought to the obedience of Christ."

———:o:———

P.S.—During the months of June and July, the Lord has favoured us with a most gracious season of blessing. At the close of the second Campaign in Ashfield we delivered a series of Addresses on the much-neglected but most important truths of God's Sovereignty and Divine Election. The weather was wet and cold, yet from four to five hundred came out, Mondays to Fridays inclusive, and on Sundays the Tabernacle was packed, many extra seats having to be brought in. The Lord most signally honoured His Word, saints being edified and sinners saved. We are therefore publishing herein, one each month, these Addresses, practically verbatim. Of course there has been opposition and bitter persecution, as there always has when these man-humbling but God-honouring truths have been preached. But this moves us not. "If the world hate *you*, ye know that it hated *Me* before it hated *you*" (John 15:18). Sufficient for the disciple to be as his Master.

We were obliged to close the second meeting at Ashfield to keep an appointment at Auburn. There we spent two very happy weeks in the Baptist's Church, enjoying the most hearty co-operation of its widely loved Pastor, Cleugh Black. Will our many praying friends in other lands please remember this faithful preacher of the Gospel each Lord's Day at the Throne of Grace, that God may be pleased to use him still more extensively in his important fields of labour. We praise God fervently for such devoted, humble, and zealous souls as Pastors Sale-Harrison and Cleugh Black. We are unfeignedly thankful to God for bringing us to Australia. The fields here are white unto harvest, and the labourers, especially teachers, are few.

—*A.W.P.*, July 30.

VOL. IV OCT. 1925 NO. 10

STUDIES IN THE SCRIPTURES

"Search the Scriptures" John 5:39.

Arthur W. Pink, Publisher and Editor,
5 Norton Street, Ashfield, N.S.W., Australia.

Price: 10 cents per copy; $1.00 or 5/- per year.

"Who can utter the mighty acts of the Lord? Who can show forth all His praise?" (Psa. 106:2). These are the words which come before us as we look back and review the last five months. During this time our gracious God has permitted us to conduct six Bible-teaching Campaigns. The attendances have been most encouraging and the interest is deepening. Fully half of the congregation bring Bibles with them and look up the references: many have testified that God's Word is now a new book to them.

The Lord willing, to-morrow we begin a month's Campaign at Crow's Nest. What a privilege it is to spread the riches of Divine grace before hungry souls! How wondrous that God should place His treasure in earthen vessels. "Feed My sheep" are the words which are constantly ringing in our ears. Nothing on this earth is so precious to the Good Shepherd as those for whom He laid down His life, and nothing is more blessed to a servant of His than to lead them into the green pastures of the Word.

We have no plans: our times are in *His* hands. "There are many devices in a man's heart, nevertheless the counsel of the Lord that shall stand" (Prov. 19:21). Our daily prayer ought to be that the Holy Spirit will so guide our feet that we may ever walk in those good works "which God hath before ordained that we should walk in them" (Eph. 2:10). Graciously is our Master blessing us with health and strength, supplying our every need, and filling our hearts with joy as we minister His Word. What more can we ask?

In His infinite condescension, God is still pleased to own these pages. Many letters are coming in telling of help and blessing received. Several hundreds of new subscriptions have been taken in this Country. Another year will soon be ended, therefore we shall much appreciate it if our American friends (U.S.A. and Canada) will kindly remit their dollar at once to Mr. C. S. Pressel, 559 Dupont Ave., York, Pennsylvania. Prompt attention to this will help us. The 1925 issues will be bound, D.V., and we hope to make an announcement in the December issue stating the date when they can be procured. Let those who are receiving help from "Studies" pray daily that this publication may reach other hungry souls. We do no advertising, but count on the Lord bringing it into the hands of those for whom He has designed it.

With hearty Christian greetings to all our friends,

Yours in His glad service,

—*ARTHUR W. PINK.*

August 21.

"What Thou shalt to-day provide,
Let me as a child receive
What to-morrow may betide.
Calmly to Thy wisdom leave.
'Tis enough that Thou wilt care,
Why should I the burden bear?"

IMPORTANT NOTICES

Set of twelve issues for **1922**, unbound, **$1.00** or **5/-**. Bound **$1.50** or **7/-**.

Set of twelve issues for **1923**, unbound, **$1.00** or **5/-**. Bound **$1.50** or **7/-**.

Set of twelve issues for **1924**, unbound, **$1.00** or **5/-**. Bound **$1.50** or **7/-**.

Note: We cannot break a set or now supply any **single** 1924 issues.

Subscription—price: **$1.00** or **5/-** per year to any address in the world.

Change of Address: Please notify me promptly of any change of address, and be certain to give both old and new address.

Non-subscribers receiving this Magazine regularly will understand their subscription has been entered by a friend.

Copies lost in the mail duplicated only if we are notified promptly.

CONTENTS

THE GOSPEL OF JOHN

46. *Christ's Example for us*: John 13: 12-20.

The following is given as an Analysis of the second section of John 13:—

1. Christ's searching question, v. 12.
2. Christ's dignity and authority, v. 13.
3. Christ's example for us to follow, vv. 14, 15.
4. Christ's warning against pride, v. 16.
5. Christ's approval of practical godliness, v. 17.
6. Christ's word about the Traitor, vv. 18, 19.
7. Christ's encouragement to His servants, v. 20.

The opening portion of John 13 makes known the provision which Divine love has made for failure in our walk as we journey through this world-wilderness, and the means which are used to maintain us in fellowship with Christ. Its central design is stated by the Lord when He said to Peter, "If I wash thee not, thou hast no part with Me." The washing of our feet is imperative if we are to enjoy fellowship with the Holy One of God. "Grace" has given us a place *in Christ*, now "truth" operates to maintain our place *with Christ*. The effect of this ministry is stated in v. 10: "He that is bathed needeth not save to wash his feet, but is clean *every whit*."

There is a *double* washing for the believer: the one of his entire person, the other of his feet; the former is once for all, the latter needs repeating daily. In both instances the "washing" is by *the Word*. Of the former we read, "Thieves nor coveteous, nor drunkards, nor revilers, nor extortioners, shall inherit the kingdom of God. And such were some of you: but ye are *washed*, but ye are sanctified, but ye are justified in the name of the Lord Jesus, and by the Spirit of our God" (1 Cor. 6:10, 11). And again, "Not by works of righteousness which we have done, but according to His mercy He saved us, by *the washing* of regeneration, and renewing of the Holy Spirit" (Titus 3:5). The "washing of regeneration" is not by blood, though it is inseparable from redemption by blood; and neither the one nor the other is ever repeated. Of the latter we read, "Christ also loved the Church, and gave Himself for it: That He might sanctify and cleanse it *with the washing of water* BY THE WORD. That He might present it to Himself a glorious Church, not having spot, or wrinkle, or any such thing; but that it should be holy and without blemish" (Eph. 5:25-27). This same distinction was plainly marked in the Old Testament. When Aaron and his sons were consecrated, they were bathed all over (Exodus 29:4; Lev. 8:6); but at the "lavar" it was only their hands and feet which were daily cleansed (Exodus 30:19, 21).

In our last article we pointed out how that the "blood" is *Godward*, the "water" *saintwards*. The one is for legal expiation, the other for moral purification. Now, while both the "bathing" (Titus 3:5) and the "washing" of the saints' feet is by the "water of the Word," there *is* a "cleansing" by blood—"the blood of Jesus Christ His Son cleanseth us from all sin" (1 John 1:7). But *this* "cleansing" is *judicial*, not experimental. The precious blood has *not* been applied to my *heart*, but it *has* cancelled my *guilt*. It has *washed out* the heavy and black account which was once against me on High. A "book of remembrance" is written before God (Mal. 3:16), but in it there is not left on record a single sin against any believer. Just as a damp sponge passed over a slate removes every chalk mark upon it, so the blood of Christ has *blotted out* every transgression which once was marked up against me. How deeply significant, then, to read that when the Roman soldier pierced the side of the dead Saviour that *"forthwith* came there out blood *and* water" (John 19:34)! The blood for penal expiation, the water for moral purification. But mark the *order*: first, the "blood" to satisfy the demands of a holy *God*, then the "water" to meet the needs of His defiled *people!*

The distinction between the bathing of the entire body and the washing of the feet was aptly illustrated by the ancient custom of bathers. A person returning from the public baths was, of course, clean, and needed not to be re-bathed. But wearing only sandals, which covered but part of the feet, he quickly needed the foot-bath to cleanse himself from the dust of travel encountered on his way from the baths to his home. Even to-day bathers in the sea are often seen going to their dressing-room with a pail of water to cleanse their soiled feet. This may be regarded as a parable of the spiritual life. Believers were bathed, completely cleansed, at the new birth. The "dressing-room" is Heaven, where we shall be robed in white raiment and garments of glory. But the pail of water is needed for our present use in connection with the daily walk.

In the second section of John 13 the Lord Jesus makes a practical application to the disciples of what He had just done for them. He intimates very plainly that there was a spiritual meaning in His washing of their feet: "Know ye not what I have done to you?" He tells them expressly that *they* ought to wash one another's feet. If they shrank from such lowly service, He reminds them that none other than He, their Master and Lord, had done as much for them. He warns them that a theoretical knowledge of these things was of no value, unless it resulted in an actual carrying out of them: "If ye know these things, happy are ye *if* ye *do* them." Then He recurs again to the fact that one of their number must be excepted. The presence of the Traitor seems to have cast a shadow upon Him, but He tells them beforehand that the Scriptures had predicted his defection, so that when the Betrayer delivered up their Master into the hands of His enemies the faith of the other disciples might not falter. Finally, He encourages them with the assurance that whosoever received His servants received Himself, yea, received the One who had sent Him. What dignity that gave to their calling!

"So after He had washed their feet, and had taken His garments, and was set down again, He said unto them, Know ye what I have done to you?" (v. 12). It is important to note that it was from the "supper" that the Lord arose when He girded Himself for the washing of His disciples' feet; to it He now returns. Typically, it was Christ's "leaving the place of communion, as if this were interrupted, until His necessary work for them should renew it once more. He rises, therefore, from supper, and girded Himself for a fresh service. His sacrificial work is over, the shedding of blood is no more needed, but only the washing of water; and here also not the 'bath of regeneration' (Titus 3:5 Gk.), but simply as He pointed out to Peter, the washing of the feet. It is defilement contracted in the walk that is in question; and He puts Himself at their feet to wash them. As of old, Jehovah could say to Israel, 'Thou hast made Me to *serve* with thy sins' (Isa. 43:24), so may He still say to us; but His unchanging love is equal to all possible demands upon it. Notice here that *all* the disciples need it, and that thus He invites us all to-day to put *our* feet into His hands continually, that they may be cleansed according to *His* thought of what is cleanness, Who alone is capable of judging according to the perfect standard of the Sanctuary of which He is indeed Himself the Light" (Numerical Bible).

"So after He had washed their feet, and had taken His garments, and was set down again, He said unto them, Know ye what I have done to you?" This is the sequel to what we read of in v. 4. There He had *laid aside* His outer garments, here He *resumes* them. We believe that the former act had a *double* symbolical meaning. First, we are told, "He riseth from supper": *what* supper is not here specified. Now, "supping" speaks of *communion*, therefore when we are told "He riseth *from* supper *and* laid aside His garments and took a towel and girded Himself," the first and deepest meaning would be, He left His place on High, where from all eternity He had been the Father's delight, and with whom He had enjoyed perfect communion as the Son, but now divested Himself of His outward glory and took upon Him the *form* of a servant. But the "supper" is also the memorial of

His death, hence the *rising* from it and the laying aside of His garments would suggest the additional thought of His resurrection. Now, we believe that the Lord's action here in v. 12 connects with and is the sequel to the *first* thing pointed out above. The *putting on* of His garments and the *sitting down again* would typify His return to the Father's presence, the resumption of His original glory (John 17:5), and His resting on High.

The Lord was about to explain (in part) and enforce what He had done unto the disciples. Before pondering what He had to say, let us first admire the calmness and deliberation which marked His actions. He quietly resumed His garments (there is no hint of the apostles offering to assist Him!) ere He seated Himself upon the couch or cushion, in His character of Teacher and Lord, thus giving His disciples time to recover from their surprise, collect their thoughts, and prepare themselves for what He was about to say. This gives additional meaning to His posture. Note that ere He began the "Sermon on the Mount" He first *seated* Himself (Matt. 5:1); so it was while *seated* in a ship (Matt. 13:2) He delivered the seven parables of the Kingdom; so while He *"sat* upon the Mount of Olives" (Matt. 24:3), He gave his longest prophetic announcement; so here He *seated* Himself before giving the great Pascal Discourse. The force of these notices is seen by comparing them with Luke 5:3: "He *sat down* and *taught* the people."

"So after He had washed their feet," that is, the feet of each of the twelve. "We may learn an important lesson here as to dealing with offenders in the assembly. The Lord knew all about Judas, and all he was doing, but treated him as one of the apostles, till he displayed himself. There may be suspicion about some individual, that all is not right with him; but mere suspicion will not suffice to act on. The matter must come clearly out, ere it can be rightly dealt with. Were this remembered, cases of discipline, instead of causing trouble in the assembly through lack of common judgment, would be clear to all unprejudiced persons, and the judgments of the assembly be accepted as correct. Has it not at times been the reverse?" (Mr. C. E. Stuart).

"He said unto them, Know ye what I have done to you?" Very searching was this. In washing the feet of His disciples He had not only displayed a marvellous humility, which He would have them take to heart, but He had cared for them in holy love. Not only had He saved them, but He was concerned about their fellowship with Himself, and for this, strict attention must be paid to the walk. For when the feet are soiled, the dust of this world must be removed. In His question the Lord illustrates how that it is His way to teach us *afterwards* the good which He has *already* done for us; as we grow up in Him in the truth, we are enabled to enter into and appreciate more deeply what at first we understood but slightly. The same grace which brought salvation *teaches us,* that "denying ungodliness and worldly lusts, we should live soberly, righteously, and godly, in this present world; looking for that Blessed Hope" (Titus 2:11, 12). Deeply humbling is it to discover how little we understood the love and the grace which *had been* acting on our behalf.

"Know ye what I have done to you?" "This is a question which we should often put to ourselves respecting what our Lord says, and what He does to us. None of His works are 'the unfruitful works of darkness.' They are all full of meaning. They are all intended to serve a purpose, and a good one; and it is of importance, in most cases, that we should be aware of it. If we look at His work in the light of His Word, and seek the guidance of His good Spirit, we shall generally be able to discern His wise and benign purpose, even in dispensations at first sight very strange and mysterious. He only can explain His intentions, and He will not suffer His humble, enquiring disciples to remain ignorant of them, if it be for their real benefit to know them" (Dr. J. Brown).

"Ye call Me Master and Lord: and ye say well; for so I am" (v. 13). Beautifully does this bring out the fact that the Lord Jesus *is* "full of grace *and* truth." Though He had just fulfilled for His disciples the most menial office of a slave, yet He had not abandoned the place of authority and supremacy. He reminds them that He is still their "Master and Lord," and that, by their own confession, for the word "call" here signifies *address* —"Ye address Me as Master and Lord." In *thus* owning the incarnate Son of God they "did well." Alas! that so many of His professing followers now treat Him with so much *less* respect than that which He here commended in the Twelve. Alas! that so many who owe their all for time and eternity to that peerless One who was "*God* manifest in flesh," speak of Him simply as "Jesus." Jesus is the Lord of glory, and surely it is due the dignity and majesty of His person that this should be *recognised* and *owned*, even in our very references to Him. We do not expect that those who despise and reject Him should speak of Him in any more exalting terms than "The Nazarene," or "Jesus"; but those who have been, by amazing grace, given "an understanding, that we may know Him that is true" (1 John 5:20) ought gladly to confess Him as *"The Lord* Jesus Christ!"

"Ye call Me Master and Lord: and ye say well; for so I am." Surely this is sufficient for any humble-minded Christian. If our blessed Redeemer says we *"say well"* when we address Him as "Master and Lord," how can we afford to speak of Him in terms upon which His approval is *not* stamped? Never once do we find the apostles addressing Him as "Jesus" while He was with them on earth. When He exhorted them to make request of Him for an increase of labourers He bade them, "Pray ye therefore *the Lord* of the harvest" (Matt. 9:28). When He sent forth the disciples to secure the ass on which He was to ride into Jerusalem, He ordered them to say, *"The Lord* hath need of him" (Luke 19:31). When He required the use of the upper room, it was *"The Lord* saith My time is at hand; I will therefore keep the passover at thy house" (Matt. 26:18).

Above, we have said that the apostles never once addressed our Lord simply as "Jesus." Mark, now, *how they did* refer to the Blessed One. "And Peter answered Him, and said, *Lord* if it be Thou, bid me come unto Thee on the water" (Matt. 14:28). "And when His disciples James and John saw this they said, *Lord,* wilt Thou that we command fire to come down from Heaven and consume them?" (Luke 9:54). "And they were exceeding sorrowful, and began every one of them to say unto Him, *Lord,* is it I?" (Matt. 26:22). "And they rose up the same hour, and returned to Jerusalem, and found the eleven gathered together, and them that were with them, saying, *The Lord* is risen indeed" (Luke 24:33, 34). "Thomas saith unto Him, *Lord* we know not whither Thou goest" (John 14:5). "That disciple whom Jesus loved saith unto Peter, It is *The Lord*" (John 21:7).

It may be objected that the Gospel narratives commonly refer to the Lord as "Jesus." It was *Jesus* who was led of the Spirit into the wilderness to be tempted of the Devil. It was *Jesus* who was moved with compassion as He beheld the sufferings and sorrows of humanity. It was *Jesus* who taught the people, etc. This is true, and the explanation is not far to seek. It was the *Holy Spirit of God* who, through the pens of the Evangelists, *thus* referred to Him, and this makes all the difference. What would be thought of one of the subjects of King George referring to the reigning Monarch of Great Britain and saying, "I saw *George* pass through the city this morning?" If, then, it would be utterly incongruous for one of *his* subjects to speak thus of the King of England, how much more so is it to refer to the *King of kings* simply as Jesus! But now, King George's *wife* might refer to and speak of her husband as "George" with perfect propriety. Thus it is that the *Holy Spirit* refers to our Lord by His personal name in the Gospel narratives.

Our modern hymns are largely responsible for the dishonour that is now so generally cast upon that "Worthy Name" (James 2:7), and we cannot but raise our voice in indignant protest against much of the trash (for such it is) that masquerades under the name of "hymns" and religious "songs." It is sad and shocking to hear Christians sing "There's not a friend like the lowly Jesus." There is *no* "lowly Jesus" to-day. The One who once passed through unparalleled humiliation has been "made both Lord and Christ" (Acts 2:36). and is now seated at the right hand of the Majesty on High. If the earnest student will turn to the four Gospels and note *how* different ones addressed the Son of God he will be well repaid. The *enemies* of Christ constantly referred to Him as *Jesus* (Matt. 26:71, etc.), and so did the *demons* (Mark 1:23, 24). Let us pray God to deliver us from this flippant, careless, and irreverent manner of speaking of His Blessed Son. Let us gladly own our Saviour as "Lord" during the time of His rejection by the world. Let us remember His own words: "All should honour the Son, *even as* they honour the Father. He that honoureth not the Son honoureth not the Father which hath sent Him" (John 5:23). This is no trivial or trifling matter, for it stands written, "By thy *words* thou shalt be *justified,* and by thy *words* thou shalt be *condemned*" (Matt. 12:37).

"If I, then, your Lord and Master, have washed your feet" (v. 14). "Master" means *Teacher.* The "Teacher" is *believed;* the "Lord" is *obeyed.* Here Christ proceeded to enforce and apply what He had just done unto them. The connection is obvious, not only with what precedes, but also with that which follows. If the Greatest could minister to the least, how much more should the less minister to his equal! If the Superior waited upon His admitted inferiors, much less should that inferior wait upon his fellows. And mark the premise from which He draws this conclusion. He did not say, "I *am* your Teacher and Lord," but "*Ye call* Me Teacher and Lord." It was from the confession of their own lips that He now proceeds to instruct them. The order in which these titles occur is significant. First, these disciples had heard Christ as "Teacher," and later they had come to know Him as their "Lord." But now Christ *reverses* the order: "If I, then, your Lord and Teacher." Why is this? Because *this* is the experimental order now. We must surrender to Him as "Lord," bowing to His authority, submitting to His yoke, *before* He will *teach us!*

"Ye also ought to wash one another's feet" (v. 14). So they ought, and why had they not already done so? The supper-room here was already supplied with water, pail, and towel. Why had not *they used* them? Luke 22:24 tells us, "And there was also strife among them, which of them should be accounted *the greater.*" This occurred, be it noted, at this very time. It was then that the Saviour shamed them by saying, "For whether is greater, he that sitteth at meat, or he that serveth? is not he that sitteth at meat? but *I* am among you as He that *serveth*" (Luke 22:27).

"Ye also ought to wash one another's feet." Let us consider the application of these words to ourselves: "In discovering any stain that may be resting on the feet of our brethren, we are not to blind ourselves to its presence, or to hide from ourselves its character by calling evil good. If we are to be honest and faithful in respect of ourselves, we shall be equally honest and truthful in respect of others. On the other hand, we have to beware of looking on the sins and failures of our brethren with Pharisaic complacency and cold indifference. What condition is more awful than that one who finds his joy in searching out iniquities, and exulting in exposing and magnifying them when discovered? Such, indeed, has reason to remember that with whatsoever judgment they judge, they shall be judged; and that the measure they mete out to others shall be meted out to themselves again. How continually, should we remind ourselves that the love of the same gracious Lord that is toward us is toward our brethren likewise, and that one of our chief privileges is the title to appeal to it and intercede on their behalf, asking that sins, even of deepest dye, may be removed; and that the deserved results of chastisement and sorrow might be averted. So we should not be as those who 'bite and devour one another,' but be as those who 'wash one another's feet'" (Mr. B. W. Newton).

Yes, a most needful word is this for us all, ever ready as we are to lift up the skirts of a brother and say, "See how soiled his feet are!" But much exercise of soul, much judging of ourselves, is needed for such lowly work as this. I have to *get down* to my brother's feet if I am to wash them! That means that "the flesh" in me must be subdued. Let us not forget that searching word in Gal. 6:1: "Brethren, if a man be overtaken in a fault, ye which are spiritual, restore such an one in the *spirit of meekness;* considering thyself, lest thou also be tempted. Bear ye one another's burdens, and *so* fulfil the law of Christ." I must be emptied of *all* sense of self-superiority before I can restore one who is "out of the way." It is the *love of Christ* which must constrain me as I seek to be of help to one of those for whom He died. It is as "*dear children*" (Eph. 5:1) that we are called upon to be "imitators of God!" Very wonderful and blessed is what is here before us: when the Lord appoints on earth a witness of *His* ways in Heaven, He tells us to wash one another's feet, and to love one another (v. 34). There must be a patient forebearing with our brother's faults, a faithful but tender applying of the Word to his particular case, and an earnest and daily intercession for him: these are the main things included in this figure of "washing." But let us not stop short at the "washing": there must be the "drying," too! The service when done must be regarded as a service *of the past.* The failure which called for it, is now removed, and therefore is to be buried in the depths of oblivion. It ought never to be cast against the individual in the future.

"For I have given you an example, that ye should do as I have done to you" (v. 15). It is well known that not a few have regarded this as a command from Christ for His followers now to practice *literal* foot-washing, yea, some have exalted it into a "Church ordinance." While we cannot but respect and admire their desire to *obey* Christ, especially in a day when laxity and self-pleasing is so rife, yet we are fully satisfied that they have mistaken our Lord's meaning here. Surely to insist upon literal foot-washing from this verse is to miss the meaning as well as the spirit of the whole passage. It is *not* with literal water (any more than the "water" is literal in John 3:5; 4:14; 7:38) that the Lord would have us wash one another. It is the Word (of which "water" is the emblem) He would have us apply to our fellow-disciples' walk. This should not need arguing, but for the benefit of those who think that the Lord here instituted an ordinance which He would have practised to-day, we would ask them to please weigh carefully the following points:—

That that which the Lord Jesus here did to His disciples looked beyond the literal act to its deep symbolic significance is clear from these facts: First, the Lord's word to Peter, "What I do thou *knowest not* now" (v. 7): certainly Peter knew that his feet had been literally washed! Second, the further words of Christ to Peter, "If I wash thee not, thou hast *no part* with Me" (v. 8): certainly there are multitudes of believers that *have* a part with Christ who have never practised foot-washing as a religious ordinance. Third, His words, "Ye are clean, but not all" (v. 10): Judas could never have been *thus* excepted if only literal foot-washing was here in view. Fourth, His question, "Know ye what I have done to you?" clearly intimates that the Lord's act in washing the feet of the disciples had a profound *spiritual* meaning. Fifth, note that here in v. 15 the Lord *does not* say "Ye should do *what* I have done unto you," but "*as* I have done to you!" Add to these considerations the fact that this incident is found in *John's* Gospel, which is, pre-eminently, the one which treats of *spiritual* relationships under various *figures*—bread, water, Shepherd and sheep, Vine and the branches, etc., and surely all difficulty disappears.

"For I have given you an example that ye should do as I have done to you" (v. 15). We take it that the force of these words of Christ is this: I have just shown you how spiritual love *operates*: it ever seeks the good of its objects, and esteems no service too lowly to secure that good. It reminds us very much of the Lord's words following His matchless picture of the Good Samaritan who had compassion on the wounded traveller, dismounting, binding up his wounds, pouring in oil and wine, setting him on *His own* beast, bringing him to the inn and taking care of him—"Go, and do thou likewise" (Luke 10:33-37). When real love is in exercise it will perform with readiness difficult, despised, and even loathsome offices. There are some services which are even more menial and repulsive than the washing of feet, yet, on occasion, the service of *love* may call for them. It should hardly be necessary to add, that Christians living in Oriental lands, where sandals are worn, *should* be ready to wash *literally* the feet of a weary brother, not simply as an act of courtesy, but as a service of love.

"For I have given you an example, that ye should do *as* I have done to you." We believe that one thing included in this comparative "as" is that it looks back to a detail in v. 4 which is usually overlooked: it was *as girded with a towel* that Christ washed the feet of His disciples, and that which was *signified* by the "towel" *applies to us*. The "towel" was that with which Christ was *girded*: it bespoke the *servant's* attitude. Then the Lord *used* that with which He was girded upon their feet: emblematically, there was *applying to them* the *humility* which marked Him. Mr. Darby tells us that it was a *linen* towel which was employed, and in the N.T. "linen" signifies "the *righteousness* of saints" (Rev. 19:8, R.V.). It was His own spotless love which fitted Him to approach His disciples and apply the Word to them. How searching is all of this for us! If we would imitate Him in this labour of love we must ourselves be clothed with humility, we must employ nothing but the Word, and we must have on the linen towel of practical righteousness to dry with.

"Verily, verily I say unto you, The servant is not greater than his Lord; neither he that is sent greater than He that sent him" (v. 16). The Lord acts as His own interpreter. He here gives plain intimation of the meaning of His symbolic action. He draws an important lesson from what He had just done, the more needful because He was about to withdraw from them. It would fare ill with His people if their leaders were found disputing among themselves, devouring one another. Surrounded as they were by Judaism and Paganism, lambs in the midst of wolves, much depended upon their humility and mutual helpfulness. Much needed by every Christian, and especially by those engaged in Christian service, is that word of Christs', "Take My yoke upon you, and learn of Me; for I am meek and lowly in heart."

"Verily, verily I say unto you, The servant is not greater than his Lord, neither he that is sent greater than He that sent him." That this is of more than ordinary importance is evidenced by the solemn and emphatic "Verily, verily" with which the

Lord prefaced it. Moreover, the fact that at a later point in this same discourse the Lord said to His apostles, *"Remember* the word that I said unto you, The servant is not greater than his Lord" (v. 15:20), shows that it is one which is specially needed by His ambassadors. How many a dark page of "Church history" had never been written if the ministers of Christ had heeded this admonition! How vain the pretensions of those who have lorded it over God's heritage in the light of this searching word! Sad indeed have been the manifestations of Nicolaitanism in every age. Even before the last of the apostles left this world he had to say, "I wrote unto the church: but Diotrephes, who loveth to have the pre-eminence among them, receiveth us not" (3 John 9); and the same spirit is far from being dead today.

"If ye know these things, happy are ye if ye do them" (v. 17). If ye know *what* "things?" First, the vital need of placing *our* feet in the hands of Christ for cleansing (v. 8). Second, the owning of Christ as "Master and Lord" (v. 13). Third, the need of washing one another's feet (v. 14). Fourth, the performing of this ministry *as* Christ performed it—in lowly love (v. 15). Now, said our Saviour, If ye *know* "these things," happy or blessed are ye if ye *do* them. A mere speculative knowledge of such things is of no value. An intellectual apprehension, without the embodiment of them in our daily lives, is worse than useless. It is both significant and solemn to note that the one Christ termed a wise man that built his house upon the rock is, "Whoso heareth these sayings of Mine and *doeth* them" (Matt. 7:24). No one *knows* more truth than the Devil, and yet none works more evil!

"If ye know these things, happy are ye if ye do them." "It has been well remarked that our Lord does not say, 'Happy are ye if these things be *done to* you,' but 'Happy are ye if *ye* do them.' We are apt to suppose that we should be happy if men loved *us,* and were ready on every occasion to serve *us.* But, in the judgment of Christ, it would more conduce to our happiness that our hearts were like His, full of love to all our brethren, and our hands like His, ever ready to perform to them even the humblest offices of kindness. We often make ourselves unhappy by thinking that we are not treated with the deference and kindness to which we consider ourselves entitled. If we would be really happy, we must think more of others and less of ourselves. True happiness dwells within; and one of its leading elements is the disinterested self-sacrificing love which made the bosom of Jesus its constant dwelling-place" (Dr. J. Brown).

"I speak not of you all: I know whom I have chosen" (v. 18). The immediate reference is to what the Lord had said in the previous verse. Just as in v. 10 He had said to the twelve, "Ye are clean," and then added, "but not all," so after saying, "Happy are ye if ye do them," He at once says, "I speak not of you all." Faithfulness required Him to make an exception. There was no happiness for Judas; before him lay "the blackness of darkness for ever." When Christ said, "I know whom I have chosen" it is evident that He was not speaking of election to salvation, but to the apostolate. Where *eternal election* is in view the Scriptures uniformally ascribe it to God the Father. But where it is a question of ministry or service, in the N.T., the choice and the call usually proceed from the Lord Jesus—see Matt. 9:30; 20:1; 28:18-20; Acts 1:24; 26:16; Eph. 4:11, etc. His words here in v. 18 are parallel with those in 6:70: "Have not I chosen you twelve? and one of you is a devil."

"But that the Scripture may be fulfilled, He that eated bread with Me hath lifted up his heel against Me" (v. 18). As to *why* the Lord Jesus chose Judas to be one of the twelve, see our remarks on 6:70, 71. Very remarkable is this statement here in the light of the context. Christ had washed the feet of the very one whose heel was raised against Himself! Into what depths of humiliation did the Son of God deign to descend! He now foretells the defection of Judas, and announces that this was but the fulfilment of the prophetic Word. The reference is to the 41st Psalm, which exposes the awful character of the Betrayer; the 109th Psalm makes known the outcome of his treachery. Christ then had suffered the Traitor to remain with Him that the Scriptures might be fulfilled; but as soon as the "sop" had been given to him, Christ would say, "That thou doest, do quickly" (13:27). "How wondrous the patience which, knowing all from the beginning, bore all to the end, without a frown or sign of shrinking from the Traitor! But so much the more withering must be the sentence of judgment when it comes from His lips, the Lord of glory, the hated and despised of men" (Mr. W. Kelly).

"He that eateth bread with Me hath lifted up his heel against Me." The local reference in Psa. 41 is to what David suffered at the hands of Ahithophel, but that was but a foreshadowment and type of what the Saviour suffered from Judas. In now quoting from this prophetic Psalm the Lord Jesus evidenced His Divine knowledge of what lay before Him, and testified to the inestimable value of the Scriptures. Nothing proves more conclusively their Divine origin than the accurate and literal fulfilment of their prophecies. Predictions were made of events which were not to transpire till hundreds, and in some cases thousands, of years afterwards; minute details are furnished, and the specific accomplishment of them can only be accounted for on the one ground that He who knows the end from the beginning was their Author.

The wording of this prophecy about Judas is very striking. "*His* heel! the most contemptible rejection possible: was it not such to sell the Lord of glory for the price of a slave? It was as if *he* would inflict upon Christ the Serpent's predicted wound (Gen. 3:15)!" (Mr. Grant.)

"Now I tell you before it come, that, when it is come to pass, ye may believe that I am" (v. 19). What care did He evince for His own! What blessed proof was this of His loving them "unto the end!" Christ would here assure the disciples that *everything* which befel Him, even that which was most staggering to faith, was but the strict fulfilment of what had long ago been recorded. He was the great One typified and prophesied throughout the Old Testament, and He now assures the apostles of Judas' perfidy *before* he went forth to bargain with the priests, that they might know *He had not* trusted in him, nor had He been deceived by him, as had David by Ahithophel! Thus, instead of the apostles being stumbled by the apostasy of one of their number, it should strengthen their faith in every written word of God to know that that very Word had long before announced what they were on the eve of witnessing. Moreover, their faith in Christ should be strengthened, too. By calling their attention to the fulfilment of Psalm 41 He showed them that *He* was the Person there marked out; that *He* was a true Prophet, announcing the certain accomplishment of David's prediction before it came to pass; and that *He* was the great "I am" who "searcheth the hearts and trieth the reins of the children of men," being fully acquainted with their secret thoughts and most carefully concealed designs.

"Verily, verily I say unto you, He that receiveth whomsoever I send receiveth Me; and he that receiveth Me receiveth Him that sent Me" (v. 20). At first sight there appears to be no connection between this verse and the ones preceding, yet a little thought will soon discover the link between them. The Lord had been exhorting His disciples to follow the example which He had given, assuring them they would be happy if they did so. Then He announced the apostasy of Judas. Now He informs them that *their* vocation was by no means affected by the defection of the Betrayer. "The whole circle of the apostles seemed to be disorganised by the treachery of Judas; and therefore the Lord *confirms* the faithful in their election, and that very fittingly by a repetition of that earlier promise (Matt. 10:42) on which all depended" (Stier). It was the Lord *comforting* His own and most graciously *establishing* their hearts by turning their attention away from the Traitor to their Master, who abides forever the same, as does the Father.

Judas had been one of the twelve whom the Lord had sent forth to preach the Gospel and to work miraculous signs in His name (Matt. 10). Would then all that *he* had done as an apostle be discredited, when his real character became known? This important question here receives answer from our Lord: "He that receiveth *whomsoever* I send receiveth Me." The Lord knew how apt His people are despise the work done if the worker proves to be unworthy; therefore does He teach us to look beyond the instrument to the One who sent him. The Lord has the right to appoint whom He pleases. If, then, the *message* is from God's Word, reject it not because the messenger proves a fraud. What matters it to me whether the postman be black or white, pleasant or unpleasant, so long as he hands me the right letter?

"He that receiveth whomsoever I send receiveth Me; and he that receiveth Me receiveth Him that sent Me." There is another important principle here. The apostles were the *ambassadors* of the Lord, and in the person of an ambassador the sovereign himself is received or set at naught. As *His* ambassadors, how circumspectly ought each of His servants to walk! And as *His* ambassadors, how dutiful and respectful in its reception should the Church be of them! As *He* was sent from the *Father*, so *they* were sent from *Him*. By this gracious analogy He arms them with authority and inspires them with courage. Thus the Lord fully *identifies* them with Himself.

The following questions need studying to prepare for our next lesson:—

1. What three things are clearly implied in v. 22?
2. Why did not Peter ask the Lord directly, v. 24?
3. Why did Jesus say to Judas, v. 27?
4. In how many respects was the Son of Man glorified at the Cross, v. 31?
5. What attributes of God were glorified at the Cross, v. 31?
6. In what sense was it a "new commandment," v. 34?
7. What is the meaning of v. 36?

—*Arthur W. Pink.*

GLEANINGS IN EXODUS

22. *The Manna: Ex.* 16.

Not for long were Israel permitted to enjoy the grateful refreshment and shade of the wells and palm trees of Elim (15:27). The first verses of our chapter tell us, "And they took their journey from Elim, and all the congregation of the children of Israel came unto the wilderness of Sin." If we compare Num. 33, which records the various stages or stopping-places in Israel's journeys, we find that "they removed from Elim, and encamped by the Red Sea" (v. 10). Most probably this was some bay or creek of the Sea, where for a short time their camp was now pitched, perhaps with the design of them looking once more at those waters through which they had passed dry-shod, but which had overwhelmed their enemies. Evidently their stay there was a short one, and as nothing of importance happened, it is omitted in Ex. 16.

The leading of Israel into the Wilderness of Sin brings out the strength of Moses' *faith.* Here, for the first time, the full privation of desert life stared the people fully in the face. Every step they took was now leading them farther away from the inhabited countries and conducting them deeper into the land of desolation and death. The isolation of the wilderness was complete, and the courage and faith of their leader in bringing a multitude of at least two million people into such a howling waste, demonstrates his firm confidence in the Lord God. Moses was not ignorant of the character of the desert. He had lived for forty years in its immediate vicinity (3:1), and, therefore, he knew full well that only a miracle, yea, a series of daily miracles, could meet the vast needs of such a multitude. In this his faith was superior to Abraham's (Gen. 12:10).

"And they took their journey from Elim, and all the congregation of the children of Israel came unto the Wilderness of Sin, which is between Elim and Sinai, on the fifteenth day of the second month after their departing out of the land of Egypt" (v. 1). Why, we may ask, such particularity in noting the *time-mark* here? As a matter of mere history it seems of little interest or importance. What difference does it make to us to-day *which* month and *what* day of the month it was when Israel entered the Wilderness of Sin? It was on "the fifteenth day of the second month" after their leaving Egypt that Israel came unto this wilderness. The very fact that the Holy Spirit *has* recorded this detail is sufficient proof it is not meaningless. There is nothing trivial in the Word *of God.* Even the numerals are there used with Divine purpose and significance. And herein we may discover the answer to our question. It was the "second month," and in Scripture "two" speaks of *witness* or *testimony* (cf. Rev. 11:3, etc.). It was the "fifteenth day" of the month, and the factors of 15 are five and three. In Scripture "five" signifies *grace or favour* (Gen. 43:34, etc.), and "three" is the number of *manifestations*—hence the number of resurrection, when life is fully manifested. By combining these definitions we learn that God was now to give unto Israel a witness and manifestation of His grace. How fully the sequel bears this out is most apparent.

In order for grace to shine forth there must first be the dark background of sin. Grace is unmerited favour, and to enhance its glory the demerits of man must be exhibited. It is where *sin* abounded that *grace* did much more abound (Rom. 5:21). It was so here. The very next thing that we read of is, "And the whole congregation of the children of Israel *murmured* against Moses and Aaron in the Wilderness: And the children of Israel said unto them, Would to God we had died by the hand of the Lord in the land of Egypt, when we sat by the flesh-pots, and when we did eat bread to the full; for ye have brought us forth into this wilderness to kill this whole assembly with hunger" (vv. 2, 3). A darker background could scarcely be imagined.

Here was the self-same people who had been divinely spared from the ten plagues on Egypt, who had been brought forth from the land of bondage, miracuously delivered at the Red Sea, Divinely guided by a Pillar of Cloud and Fire, day and night, —now "murmuring," complaining, rebelling! And it was not a few of the people who did so; the "*whole* congregation" were guilty. It was not simply that they muttered among themselves, but they murmured *against* their Divinely-chosen leader. Their sin, too, was aggravated by an oath; they took the Divine name "in vain"—"would *to God* we had died by the hand of the Lord in the land of Egypt." It is also evident that in their hot-headed insubordination they *lied,* for as slaves of the merciless Egyptians there is no ground whatever for us to suppose that they "sat by the flesh-pots" or "ate bread to the full." Finally, their wicked unbelief comes out in the words, "for *ye* have brought us forth into this wilderness to *kill* this whole assembly with hunger." It was *Jehovah,* not simply Moses and Aaron, who had brought them forth; and He had promised they should worship Him at Sinai (Ex. 3:12). It was not possible, then, for them to die with hunger in the wilderness.

What, then, was the Lord's response to this awful outbreak of rebellious unbelief? Verse 4 tells us: "Behold, I will rain"—what: "fire and brimstone that ye may be consumed"? No; "Behold, I will rain *bread from heaven for you.*" Marvellous grace was this; sovereign, unmerited favour! The very first word here is designed to arrest our attention. In Scripture, "behold" is the Holy Spirit's exclamation mark. "Behold"—mark with worshipful wonder. Here, then, is the blessed force of the *time-mark* in verse 1. The raining (which speaks of a *plentiful* supply) of bread from Heaven for these murmuring Israelites was indeed a *witness* to the *grace* of God *fully manifested!*

That which follows here in Exodus 16 is deeply important. Every detail in it speaks loudly *to us,* if only we have ears to hear. The manna which Jehovah provided for Israel is a beautiful type of *the food which God has provided for our souls.* This food is His own Word. This food is both His written Word and His incarnate Word. We propose to consider these separately. In the remainder of this article we shall trace some of the many points of analogy between the manna and the Scriptures as the heavenly food for God's people. In our next paper we shall view the manna as a type of the Lord Jesus, the Heavenly One come down to earth.

1. *The manna was a supernatural gift.* "Then said the Lord unto Moses, Behold, I will rain *bread from heaven* for you" (v. 4). This is the first great lesson which the manna is designed to teach us. The manna was not a product of the earth; it was not manufactured by man; it was not something which Israel brought with them out of Egypt—there was no manna there. Instead, it came down from heaven. It was a gift from God.

Various attempts have been made to explain away the supernatural in connection with the manna. Some have declared that it grew on a certain tree found in the wilderness; but they fail to explain how it grew in winter as well as summer; how that it was obtainable in every part of the wilderness, no matter where Israel's camp was pitched; or, how that sufficient was to hand to feed upwards of two million souls for almost forty years! How foolish is man's infidelity. The only possible explanation of the manna is to see in its continued supply *a miracle.* It was furnished by God Himself. So it is with that which the manna prefigured—the written Word. The Scriptures are the spiritual manna for our souls, and at every point they manifest their supernatural origin. Many efforts have been made to account for the Bible, but on this point man's reasonings are as ridiculous as when he attempts to explain the manna on natural lines. The Bible is a miraculous production. It was given by Divine Inspiration. It has come from heaven. It is the gift of God.

It is striking to note how the supernatural is evidenced in connection with the giving of the manna. In Ex. 16:16 we read, "This is the thing which the Lord hath commanded; gather of it every man according to his eating, *an omer for every man,* according to the number of your persons; take ye every man for them which are in his tents." Now, a conservative estimate of the total number of Israelites who came out of Egypt would be two million, for they had six hundred thousand men able to go forth to war" (See Num. 1:45, 46). An "omer" was to be gathered for every one of these two million souls, and an "omer" is the equivalent of six pints. There would be twelve million pints, or nine million pounds gathered daily, which was four thousand five hundred tons. Hence, ten trains, each having thirty cars, and each car having in it fifteen tons, would be needed for a *single* day's supply. Over a *million tons* of manna were gathered annually by Israel. And let it be remembered this continued for forty years! Equally wonderful, equally miraculous, equally Divine is the Bible.

2. *The manna came right to where the people were.*

"And in the morning the dew lay *round about the host;* and when the dew that lay was gone up, behold, upon the face of the wilderness there lay a small round thing" (vv. 13, 14). No long journey had to be taken in order to secure the manna. The Israelites did not have to cross the wilderness before they could secure their needed food. It was right to hand; before their eyes. There, just outside their tent door, lay the manna on the ground. So it is with the Word of God. It is blessedly accessible to all of us. I often think that if it were harder to procure a Bible than it is some of us would prize it more than we do. If we had to cross the ocean and journey to the other side of the world to obtain a copy of the Holy Scriptures we would value them far more than we do now!

But the very accessibility of the manna only added to the responsibility of Israel. Its very nearness measured their obligation. By virtue of the fact that it lay on the ground just outside their tents they *had to* do something with it. They *must* either gather it or trample it beneath their feet! And my reader, this is equally true of God's Word. The very fact that it *is* right here to your hand determines your responsibility. You are *obliged* to do one of two things with it: show your appreciation by gathering it unto your soul, or despise and trample it beneath your feet by a criminal neglect.

3. *The manna was small in size.*

"And when the dew that lay was gone up, behold, upon the face of the wilderness there lay a *small* round thing, as *small* as the hoar frost on the ground" (v. 14). Who would have imagined that a complete and perfect revelation *from* God and *of* God could be comprised within the compass of a comparatively small volume? Think of it—the sum total of God's revealed Truth in a book which can be carried in your pocket! All that is needed to make us wise unto salvation; all that is needed to sustain our souls throughout our earthly pilgrimage; all that is needed to make the man of God "perfect" (complete), within the compass of the Bible!

Observe that not only is the size but also the shape of the manna is given. It was "a small *round thing.*" It had no angles, and no rough edges. Continuing to regard the manna as a symbol and a type of the Word of God, what does this teach us? Why, surely, it prefigured the beautiful symmetry of Scripture. It tells us that the Bible is a perfect whole, complete and entire.

4. *The manna was white in colour.*

"And the house of Israel called the name thereof manna: and it was like coriander seed, *white*" (v. 31). Everything here has a spiritual significance. The Holy Spirit had a good reason for telling us the particular colour of the manna. There is nothing meaningless in Scripture anywhere. Everything in God's Word has a value and message for us.

Now "white" is the emblem of *purity.* Thus we have emphasised the absolute purity of the Word of God. Let us link together three Scriptures. "The words of the Lord are *pure words;* as silver tried in a furnace of earth, purified seven times" (Psl. 12:6): they are pure morally and they are pure spiritually. They are like the "pure river of the water of life" which proceedeth out of the throne of God and of the Lamb—they are "clear as crystal" (Rev. 22:1). Again, we read in Psl. 119: 140, "Thy Word is *very pure*: therefore Thy servant loveth it." The Scriptures are termed the *"Holy* Scriptures" because they are separated off from all other writings by virtue of their exalted spirituality and Divine purity. Once more, in Prov. 30:5, we read, *"Every word* of God *is pure."* There is *no* admixture of error in God's Word. In it there are no mistakes, no contradictions, no blemishes.

5. *The manna was to be eaten.*

This brings us to the central and most important point in connection with our type. The manna was not given simply to look at, or admire; but to be eaten. It was for food. It was God's provision to meet the bodily need of His people Israel. It is thus with the spiritual manna. God's Word is to be turned to practical account. It is given to provide food for our souls. But in order to derive from it the nutriment we require we need to learn *how* to feed on the Bread of Life. Just as a neglect of suitable diet or proper feeding in the natural sphere results in a low condition of bodily health, so to neglect our spiritual food or to ignore the laws of spiritual dietetics results in a sickly state of soul. In all correct eating there are three things: appropriation, mastication, assimilation. Let us consider each one separately.

Appropriation. This is a point so obvious that many may think it is unnecessary to develop it. And yet it is just here that so many of God's children fail. When I sit down to a well-spread table it is apparent that I cannot begin to eat everything before me. Nor is that required. The first thing necessary is to appropriate to myself *a portion* of the food before me. No matter how excellent the quality of the food may be, or how tastily prepared, it will avail me nothing to sit and admire it. I need to have a certain portion of it placed upon my own plate, and then to eat it.

It is so with the spiritual manna. The Word of God is exhaustless in its contents. In it is stored sufficient for the people of God in all ages. There is far more in it than ever I can possibly assimilate. What I must do is make an appropriation to my own soul's needs. And this must be done just as definitely as the eating of my material food. We are anxious to be of real help here to all our readers, so let us be very simple.

Our first need is to *appropriate*. To appropriate means to take unto ourselves, to *make our own*. This was the initial lesson in connection with our salvation. The difference between an unbeliever and a believer is in the employment of the personal pronoun. An unbeliever may speak of *the Saviour*, but only the believer can truthfully say "*my* Saviour." Faith appropriates unto ourselves. Faith personalises. When I read in Isa. 53 concerning Christ that "He was wounded for *our* transgression," faith individualises it and says, "He was wounded for *my* transgressions." This is what we mean by appropriation. We appropriated Christ when we *took Him as our own* personal Saviour.

Now, just as we appropriated the Saviour, so we need to appropriate the *promises* and the *precepts* of God's Word. For example, when I read in Matt. 7:7, "Ask, and it shall be given you; speak, and ye shall find; knock, and it shall be opened unto you," faith makes it personal, and applying to myself what I read there, I say—"Ask, and it shall be given *me*; seek, and *I* shall find; knock, and it shall be opened unto *me*." And again, I read in Rom. 8:32, "He that spared not His own Son, but delivered Him up for us all, how shall He not with Him also freely give *us* all things," and faith takes this to myself. I apply it to my *own* case, and read, "How shall He not with Him also freely give *me* all things?"

A Scottish pastor once called on an aged saint of God. At once she handed the minister the Bible and asked him to read some portion to her—would that we had more like her to-day; many a pastor's heart would be rejoiced if, when he called on his members, they desired him to read and pray with them instead of wanting him to discuss the gossip and scandal of the town. As the minister turned the pages he noticed that in the margins had been written the letters T. and T.P. He asked the old lady what these letters signified. She answered, Observe that they are always placed opposite some *promise* of God. T. means "tried," and T.P., "tried and proven." She had learned to *feed* on God's Word. She had appropriated the promises unto *herself*. Have you learned this lesson yet, dear reader? God's promises will afford *you* no comfort, and minister no strength to you until you make them *your own*. For example, I read in Phil. 4:19, "My God shall supply all *your* need according to His riches in glory by Christ Jesus," and when I really *appropriate* this to myself I shall say, "My God shall supply all Arthur Pink's need."

It must be the same with the *precepts* of Scripture. The commands, the exhortations, the admonitions of the Bible, are not so many abstractions. No; they are a revelation of Gods will *for me*. I must read the Scriptures as addressed to me *personally*. When I come to some word of God which condemns my ways, I must not pass it over, but be honest and take it unto myself. May God give all of us grace to daily appropriate *both* His promises *and* precepts.

Mastication. After a certain portion of the food spread before me had been placed on my own plate and in my mouth, the next thing is to *chew* it, to chew it slowly and thoroughly. But in this matter most of us are serious offenders. We bolt our food. We swallow it *before* it has been properly masticated. We eat too hurriedly. That is the chief reason why so many suffer from dyspepsia—they give their stomachs the work to do which the teeth were intended to perform. A little food thoroughly masticated will supply far more nutrition to the system than a lot of food swallowed almost whole, and our general health would be much better, too.

This is equally true spiritually. Thousands of God's children are grievous offenders here. They have never learned to use their *spiritual teeth*. The Bread of Life must be *chewed* if we are to derive from it the sustenance we so much need. What do I mean? This: *meditation stands to reading as mastication does to eating*. Re-read, and ponder this last sentence. Dear reader, you will derive far more benefit from a single verse of Scripture read slowly and prayerfully, and duly meditated upon, than you will from ten chapters read through hurriedly!

Meditation is well-nigh a lost art. And it is at the root of most of our troubles.

How many complain that they find it so difficult to *remember* passages of Scripture, passages which they have read perhaps many times. But this is easily explained. It is because the passage was not turned over in the mind; it was not duly "pondered" (Luke 2:19). Did you ever notice that the "Blessed Man" of Psl. 1 *"meditated"* in God's Law day and night? Meditation is a wonderful aid to fixing in our minds verses and passages of Scripture.

Let us give an illustration of what we mean by *meditation.* We select one of the most familiar verses in all the Bible (Psl. 23:4), "Yea, though I walk through the valley of the shadow of death I will fear no evil, for Thou art with me; Thy rod and Thy staff they comfort me." Now, as I begin to meditate upon this I take *each* word or expression *separately* and then *ask* them questions. The first thing that strikes my attention is the way in which the verse opens. It does not say *"When I shall* walk through the valley," but *"Yea, though* I walk." I ponder this over. I ask it a question; I say, *why* this indefinite language? Is it not certain that one day I *shall* be called on to walk through the valley of shadows? And then I remember that blessed word in 1 Cor., 15:51, "We shall *not all* sleep, but we shall all be changed." Then I see *why* the Holy Spirit caused this Psalm to open thus.

Next I turn to the central thing in this verse—"the valley of the shadow of death," through which the believer, who *does* die, passes. I ask, *Why* is dying likened to walking through a "valley"? What are the thoughts suggested by *this* figure? As I turn this question over in my mind it soon occurs to me (as it should to anyone who gives it a little thought). Why, a "valley" suggests peacefulness, fertility, beauty, and particularly, *easy travel.* A "valley" is the antithesis of a "mountain," which is *difficult and dangerous* to climb. In contradistinction, then, from climbing a mountain which is arduous and hazardous, death is likened to walking through a valley which is *delightful and safe!*

Then I go back to the beginning of the verse, and note thoughtfully each single word. As the believer comes to the end of his earthly pilgrimage he learns that death is simply like passing through a valley. Note he *walks,* not runs, as though afraid. Then, observe, "though I walk *through."* He does not *stay in* the "valley," but walks through it. Death is only *a door* through which the believer passes from these scenes of sin and sorrow to the realm of glory and bliss.

Next I observe that this "valley" is called the "*shadow* of death." Why is this? I must not hurry, or I shall be the loser. Let me continue pondering each word separately, so that I may extract its own peculiar sweetness. What is a "shadow"? Ah, how often it terrifies! How many of us, especially during childhood, were *frightened* by shadows! But if we had only walked right up to them we should have quickly discovered they were powerless to injure us. And how many a believer has filled the valley of death with terrifying phantoms! How fearfully has he contemplated these images of his own unbelief! O fellow-believer there is nothing, absolutely nothing, for thee to *fear* in death should it overtake you before the Lord Jesus returns. This valley is called "the valley of the *shadow* of death" because a "shadow" is the most *harmless* thing there is!

And now, as though at last the believer has fully grasped the blessedness of these beautiful figures, having discovered that Death is not a difficult and dangerous mountain to climb, but a "valley"—peaceful and easy-going—to pass through; having learned that in this valley there is nothing more terrifying than a "shadow" he now cries with exulting confidence, "I will fear *no evil,* for Thou art with me."

Here, then, is an example of what we mean by *feeding* on God's Word. *Meditation stands to reading as mastication does to eating.* Take a single verse of Scripture at the eginning of the day; write it out on a slip of paper, and carry it with you wherever you go. Refresh your memory as opportunity occurs by re-reading it. Pray over it, and ask God to give *you* a blessing out of this verse; to reveal to you its beauty and preciousness. Then ponder each word separately. Ask the verse questions and seek to discover its deeper meaning. Suppose you are meditating on Psl. 34:7, "The angel of the Lord encampeth round about them that fear Him, and delivereth them." Ask such questions as these: Why *"the* angel"? *who* is it? "Encampeth"; note the perfect tense (continuous)—*what* is suggested by this figure? "Round about"—what is meant by this? "Them that fear Him"—am I one of them? "And *delivereth* them"—*from what?*—find answer from other Scriptures which speak of "deliver" and "deliverance."

Assimilation. This is the result of appropriation and mastication, and the chief end in view. The food which I eat is to supply the waste of the body. The food which I have masticated and digested is now taken up into my system, and is transmuted into blood and tissue, thereby affording health and strength. The food thus assimilated appears in the vigour of my step, the strength of my arm, the glow on my face. And now equipped, my system is able to ward off the disease germs which attack my body. All of this has its counterpart in the spiritual man. The food which I have taken into my soul, if properly digested, will build up the new nature. It will nourish faith, and supply the needed strength for my daily walk and service. Moreover, it will be a safeguard against the germs of temptation which assail me—"Thy Word have I hid in mine heart, *that I might not* sin against Thee" (Psl. 119: 11).

Here, then, is the grand end in view. God's Word is given us to feed upon, and this feeding is for the purpose of translating the Scriptures into the terms of daily living. The principles and precepts of the Bible must be incorporated into my life. The Word has not been assimilated until it has become the regulator of my walk and the dynamo of my service.

6. *The manna was gathered daily.*

Then said the Lord unto Moses, "Behold I will rain bread from Heaven for you; and the people shall go out and gather a certain rate *every day*" (v. 4). The manna which Israel gathered to-day would not suffice them for to-morrow. A new supply must be secured each day. The spiritual application of this is very evident. The soul requires the same systematic attention as does the body, and if this be neglected and our spiritual meals are taken irregularly, the results will be equally disastrous. But how many fail at this very point! What would you think of a man who sat down to his Sunday dinner and tried to eat sufficient then, at one meal, to last him for the whole week? And yet that is precisely the method followed by multitudes of people with their spiritual food. The only time they get an adequate spiritual meal is on Sunday, and they make *that* last them for the remainder of the week. Is there any wonder that so many Christians are weak and sickly! O let us face the fact that our souls are in urgent need of a *daily* supply of the Bread of Life. Whatever else be left undone let us see to it that we *regularly* feed on the spiritual manna. Remember, it is not the amount of time spent, but the amount of *heart* which is put into the time which counts.

7. *The manna was gathered in the morning.*

"And *in the morning* the dew lay round about the host. And when the dew that lay was gone up, behold, upon the face of the wilderness there lay a small round thing" (vv. 13, 14). Here is a lesson which all of us need to seriously take to heart. It was in the early morning, *before other things had time to occupy their attention*, that God's people of old gathered their daily supply of the manna. And this is recorded "for our learning." The Divine Word must not be given a secondary place if we would have *God's* blessing upon us. What a difference it would make in many a Christian life if *each* day was BEGUN in God's presence! How many, now weak and sickly, would become strong in the Lord and in the power of His might if they formed the *habit* of feeding each *morning* on the Bread of Life! If the soul was fed at the time of "the dew," strength would be obtained and we should be equipped for the duties that lay before us and girded for the temptations which confronted us throughout the day!

Let no reader complain that he has not the time. You may not have time for the careful study of a *whole* chapter each morning, though even that is to be seriously questioned, but certain it is that you *have* time to prayerfully select one verse of Scripture and write it out on a piece of paper and attempt to commit it to memory, consulting it during your spare minutes through the day, on the train, or the street-car, if needs be—the writer memorised the whole epistle of Ephesians on the street-car, a verse at a time. Certain it is that you *do* have time to meditate on this one verse throughout the day, and to ponder each word separately. And after the labours of the day are over you may sit down (if only for five minutes) and look up the parallel passages, given in the marginal references. If you will do this daily you will be surprised and delighted at the incalcuable blessing it will bring to your soul. "Seek ye *first* the kingdom of God and His righteousness" (Matt. 6:33).

8. *The manna was obtained by labour.*

"We are reminded by the gathering of it, of the Lord's words, '*Labour* for the meat.' They did not indeed labour to bring it from Heaven; their labour was to gather it when rained down to them from thence. And here we find that they had to use diligence. It would not keep; they could not lay up a stock for the future: every day they had afresh to be employed with it. If they were not out early and the sun rose upon it, it melted. And here is where *diligence* on our part is so much needed. Would that we understood this, beloved brethren, better! Manna *did not fall into their mouths,* but around their tent. They had to use diligence to gather it. Do we understand the necessity of diligence in the apprehension of Divine things? Do we understand that the character of the Word of God is such, as that however plain in a sense it may be, yet it ministers in fact its fulness only to those who have *earnestness* of heart to seek it. Only 'if thou criest after knowledge' says the wise man, 'and lifted up thy voice for understanding; if thou *seekest* her as silver, and *searchest* for her as for hid treasures; then shalt thou understand the fear of the Lord and find the knowledge of God.' And yet He adds 'for the Lord giveth wisdom.' But He gives it according to the rules of His own holy government.

"*Labour* is here, therefore, very specially needed; not that the labour simply by itself is anything; not that man's efforts only can ever here procure for himself what God alone supplies, but still God seeks from us that *diligence* which shows our apprehension of the treasure that His Word is. He does not give to carelessness or indolence of soul, nor is faith simply a receiver here, but a *worker with God.*" (Mr. Grant.) Before "an omer" could be gathered *much* labour was entailed, for them manna was "a *small* round thing."

9. *The manna was gathered by stooping*

It grew not upon the trees, but fell upon the ground. In order to obtain it the Israelites had to go down on their knees. How significant, and how accurate the type! Diligence on our part is required if we are to appropriate from the Word that which our souls need. But something more than diligence is necessary. There must be *dependence* upon God, the Author of the Word. There must be a *seeking from Him.* We must get down on our knees and cry, "Open Thou mine eyes, that I may behold wondrous things out of Thy Law."

10. *Some gathered more, some less.*

"And the children of Israel did so, and gathered some *more,* some *less*" (v. 17). How like what we find around us to-day! Some Christians confine themselves to the Psalms and the Gospels, rarely referring to any other section of the Bible. Others study the Church Epistles, but neglect the prophetical portions. A few study the Old Testament, as well as the New, and derive immeasurable delight in the wonderful types to be found there on almost every page. It is also true with the spiritual manna that some "gather more, some less."

11. *What was gathered must be used.*

"Let no man leave of it till the morning" (v. 19). Divine truth is not to be hoarded up, but turned to present profit. We are to use what God has given us. We are first to walk in the truth ourselves, and then to recommend it to others.

As the Lord gives us opportunities it is our happy privilege to pass on to others what He has given to us. It is in this way that Christian fellowship becomes most helpful—when we spend an hour, or even a few minutes, with a fellow-believer and discuss together the things of God, instead of the things of the world.

12. *The manna was incomprehensible to the natural man.*

"And when the children of Israel saw it they said one to another it is manna: *for they wist* (knew) *not* what it was" (v. 15). There was something about this manna which the Israelites could not understand. It was different from anything else they had ever seen. They possessed no knowledge of it. The very word "manna" means "What is it"? "They wist not what it was." Thus it is also with that which the manna prefigured. The unregenerate are unable to comprehend the Scriptures: "The natural man receiveth not the things of the Spirit of God for they are foolishness unto him; neither can he know them because they are spiritually discerned" (1 Cor., 2:14).

13. *The manna was despised by the mixed multitude.*

"And the mixed multitude that was among them fell a lusting and the children of Israel also wept again, and said, Who shall give us flesh to eat? We remember the fish which we did eat in Egypt freely: the cucumbers, and the melons, and the leeks, and the onions, and the garlic: But now our soul is dried away: there is nothing at all, besides this manna before our eyes" (Num. 11:4-6). Israel were not alone as they came forth from Egypt. They were accompanied by "A mixed multitude" which had, doubtless, been deeply impressed by Jehovah's plagues and interventions on Israel's behalf, but who had no knowledge of God for themselves. Just so it is to-day; side by side with the wheat grows the tares. There is a "mixed multitude" in the Christian profession, and these like their ancient forefathers, despise the manna. They have no relish for spiritual things. They may own a Bible, perhaps one with an expensive binding and beautifully gilded; but its contents are dry and incipid to them.

13. *The manna was preserved in the Ark.*

"And Moses said unto Aaron, 'Take a pot, and put an omer full of manna therein, and lay it up before the Lord to be kept for your generations.' (v. 33). Heb. 9:4 tells us that it was a 'golden pot.' This is very striking. The manna was not to be stored up in the tents of the Israelites for a single day; yet here we see it preserved for almost forty years in the Tabernacle. It was to be kept for the land of Canaan. And so with the antitype: while we cannot feed on yesterday's experience and make that satisfy the need of to-day, nevertheless, our experiences from day to day in the wilderness will be found again with rich and blessed fruitage. The 'golden pot' in which the manna was stored tells of what a *high value* God sets upon that which it typified. The fact that the manna was kept in the ark till Canaan was reached, tells of how God has *preserved* the Scriptures all through the ages.

15. *The manna lasted until Canaan was reached.*

"And the children of Israel did eat manna forty years until they came to a land inhabited: they did eat manna until they came unto the borders of the land of Canaan" (v. 35). This tells of what an *inexhaustible supply* God has for His people. To the end of the wilderness journey the manna continued. And thank God this is true of the spiritual manna. The grass withereth and the flower fadeth, but the Word of the Lord endureth forever. We may be in the "last days" of this age; the "perilous times" may be upon us; but we still have God's blessed word. May we prize it more highly, read it more carefully, study it more diligently.

Here is the grand secret of a healthy and vigorous spiritual life. It is by earnestly desiring the sincere (pure) milk of the Word, that we grow thereby. It is by daily feeding on the Bread of Life that we obtain the strength which we need. It is through having God's Word in our hearts that we are kept from sinning against Him. And it is in this way that we should be able to say with Jeremiah, "Thy words were found *and I did eat them;* and Thy Word was unto me the joy and rejoicing of mine heart." (15:16).

Arthur W. Pink.

At considerable expense we have had this article (slightly changed in form) printed separately in a booklet, on good quality paper, and in a size that will just go into an ordinary envelope. We felt its message was deeply needed by God's children to-day. We are hoping that *many* of our readers will order a quantity. Price, 10 cents. (5d.) each, or $1.00 (4/6) a dozen. Five dollars (£1) for six dozen, post paid.

THE SOVEREIGNTY OF GOD

We will turn first of all to the 11th chapter of the Epistle to the Romans and the last verse (Romans 11-36). "For of Him and through Him and to Him are all things, to whom be glory forever, Amen." "Of Him and through Him and to Him are *all* things." Now, that is almost universally denied to-day. It is denied in two dierent ways, by two different classes. In the first place, there are those who shut God out of His own creation—those known as Evolutionists, who deny that every separate thing was created by a separate fiat of God. There are others who do not go thus far—who do not deny God's *creation,* but who, if they do not deny that, question and seriously modify His *administration.* The one denies that God *made* all things, the other—the Arminian—denies that God *directs* and *controls* all things. Each of them is a flat repudiation of the Scriptures which pointedly and plainly insist that "Of Him and through Him and to Him are all things."

Now that is one of the twenty Scriptures which were before us last night, in which I endeavoured to show that the Word of God plainly and dogmatically affirms that He is Sovereign over all, that all creatures are under His control, that all creatures are the subjects of His invincible government, that all are the servants of His will. Now to-night I want to enter into detail and show that God is Sovereign in every realm.

I am going to begin at the lowest, and show God's government of, and perfect control over, *inanimate matter.* That truth is plainly revealed on the very frontispiece of Divine revelation; that is, in the opening chapter of Scripture we find that God has complete control even over inanimate matter. God said, "Let there be light and there was light." God said, "Let the waters be gathered together into one place and let the dry land appear and it was so." God said, "Let the earth bring forth and it brought forth." He spoke and it was done, He commanded and it stood fast; and what you have revealed there in the first chapter of Scripture is illustrated and demonstrated throughout the remainder of the Bible.

Now, take for example the plagues which God sent on Egypt. How definitely and how clearly they manifested His perfect control over inanimate matter. At God's bidding the light was turned into darkness and the waters into blood. At God's bidding the hail descended when He would, where He would, and as He would.

Now, those were no exceptional cases—they were no isolated instances, but the same thing is repeated in various forms and illustrated in a hundred different ways throughout the Scriptures. At God's word the fire and brimstone descended from heaven and destroyed the Cities of the Plain. At God's word the waters of the Red Sea were rent asunder and stood up in walls; at His word they came together again and overwhelmed Israel's enemies. The same God who *created* inanimate matter has absolute *control* over it. It obeys His will, it performs His bidding, and carries out His counsels. At His command the earth opened its mouth and Korah and his rebellious company went down into the pit. At His word the fires of Babylon's furnace were rendered impotent so that they could not harm His servants. Even the very elements are controlled by God. I want you to turn to one very striking passage among many which proves that fact.

In the book of Amos—I want you to find this in your own Bibles; I want you to see that I am not reading it from some special Bible, but from *God's* Word. Book of Amos, 4th chapter. Perhaps I had better read from the 5th verse to show who the Speaker is: "And offer a sacrifice of thanksgiving with leaven, and proclaim and publish the free offerings; for this liketh you, O ye children of Israel, *saith the Lord God*. And *I also* have given you cleanness of teeth in your cities, and want of bread in all your places; yet have ye not returned unto Me, saith the Lord. And also *I have* withholden the rain from you, when there were yet three months to the harvest, and *I caused it* to rain upon one city and caused it not to rain upon another city; one piece was rained upon, and the piece whereupon it rained not withered." Therefore, every time we complain about the weather we are murmuring against God Most High. Every time we joke about the weather we are blaspheming God, for God and God only is the regulator of the weather! "*I* have caused it to rain and *I* have withheld the rain." The elements are in *His* hands. He is the One who directs them. He is the One who gives the commandment where the rain is to fall, and how often it is to fall, and when it shall not fall. The rain does not please itself, nor does it please us, or rather it does not ask our pleasure—it is subject only to the will of the Creator.

My friends, God is God in fact as well as in name. He is no mere figurehead. God is no pasteboard monarch. God is the great Autocrat of the universe. He does as He pleases, only and always as He pleases, and just because He pleases. God *is God!*

We will turn now to the 105th Psalm, verse 16. This is very striking, and it is very solemn. Psalm 105:16: "Moreover, *He* called for a famine upon the land." The success and the measure of the harvest is determined alone by the will of God Most High. When He says there shall be abundance there *is* abundance. When He calls for a famine there *is* a famine.

Now, then, in the second place, let us rise a stage, let us come one step higher. God has absolute control over all *irrational creatures*. Turn now to the 2nd chapter of Genesis, verse 19: "And out of the ground the Lord God formed every beast of the field and every fowl of the air and brought them unto Adam." The same God who had *made* them had *control over* them. Every beast of the field—everyone without an exception—and every fowl of the air, He brought to Adam. That proves that they were subject to His bidding, that they were under His control, that they were subservient to His will. Oh, you say that was *before* the Fall; that was in Paradise, before God's curse had descended upon creation. Yes, but the same thing that was true then is equally true now. The curse that has come upon creation has not abolished God's control, has not in any-wise limited His government over the creatures of His own hands.

Turn now to the 6th chapter of Genesis, verses 19, 20. These were the words of God to Noah 1600 years after the creation: "And of every living thing of all flesh two of every sort shalt thou bring into the ark to keep them alive with thee, they shall be male and female. Of the fowls after their kind, and of cattle after their kind, of every creeping thing of the earth after his kind, two of every sort shall come unto thee to keep them alive." Now look at it closer. "Two of every sort *shall* come unto thee." The lion of the jungle, the elephant of the forest, the untamable wolf, the ferocious tiger, the eagle of the mountain-cliff! "Two of every sort *shall* come unto thee." The One who made the beasts of the field here manifested His perfect control over them by directing two—no more! They did not come in multitudes promiscuously, but God singled out the two —there is Sovereignty for you! God singled out the male and female, and they came meekly like a flock of little lambs—the lions, the tigers, the elephants, and wolves—at *His* bidding!

You see the same thing manifested again in the plagues of Egypt, which demonstrate God's control over inanimate matter, and equally so over irrational creatures. At God's bidding swarms of flies came over Egypt, but there were none in the Israelites' dwellings! At God's bidding the frogs came up out of the waters, and, contrary to their nature, they invaded the houses and homes of the Egyptians. At God's bidding swarms and clouds of locusts came just when He said they would, just where He said they would, and as long as He pleased. Ah, my friends, angels are not the only ones who do His bidding, that hearken to the words of His mouth—even irrational creatures are subject to the will of their Almighty Maker.

Turn now to 1st Samuel, 6th chapter. I will begin reading at the first verse that you may get the setting: "And the Ark of the Lord was in the country of the Philistines seven months." (The Ark of the Lord—it brought a lot of trouble on them and they wanted to get rid of it, and they did not know how!) "And the Philistines called for the priests and diviners, saying, What shall we do to the Ark of the Lord? Tell us wherewith we shall send it to his place. And they said, If ye send away the Ark of the God of Israel, send it not empty; but in any-wise return Him a trespass offering, then ye shall be healed, and it shall be known to you why His hand is not removed from you. Then said they, What shall be the trespass offering which we shall return to Him? They answered, Five golden emerods and five golden mice, according to the number of the lords of the Philistines; for one plague was on you all and on your lords. Wherefore ye shall make images of your emerods, and images of your mice that mar the land, and ye shall give glory unto the God of Israel: peradventure He will lighten His hand from off you, and from off your gods, and from off your land. Wherefore, then, do ye harden your hearts as the Egyptians and Pharaoh hardened their hearts? When He had wrought wonderfully among them did they not let the people go, and they departed? Now, therefore, make a new cart and take two milch kine on which there hath come no yoke and tie the kine to the cart and bring their calves home from them; and take the Ark of the Lord, and lay it upon the cart, and put the jewels of gold which ye return Him for a trespass offering, in a coffer in the side thereof; and send it away that it may go. And see if it goeth up by the way of his own coast to Beth-shemesh, then He hath done us this great evil; but if not, then we shall know that it is not His hand that smote us; it was *a chance* that happened to us." (Very suitable language for the heathen! We have a whole lot of heathen in Christendom to-day who think that things happen by "chance," and they are just as much heathen as the Philistines were, who thought that things happen by chance!) "And the men did so: and took two milch kine and tied them to the cart and shut up their calves at home. And they laid the Ark of the Lord upon the cart and the coffer with the mice of gold and the images of their emerods." (And the kine stampeded and ran round and round in a circle and did not know where to turn. Well, why not? They had no *driver;* that is to say, they had no *human* driver. There were those kine with no reins to drive them, no human hand guiding them. Now look at what it says.) "And the kine took *the straight way* to the way of Bethshemesh and went along the highway lowing as they went, and *turned not aside* to the right hand or the left hand, and the lords of the Philistines went after them." You could not have a clearer case and a more positive demonstration of the invisible Hand of God, controlling even irrational creatures. *His* Hand was guiding that cart and His Will was directing those kine, so that they took the "straight way" to Beth-shemesh and "turned not aside" from one side to the other!

Oh, my friends, God has perfect control even over irrational beasts. God opened the mouth of the ass to rebuke the madness of the prophet. Daniel was thrown into the lions' den, and if there had been no God the next morning there would have been no Daniel! But there *was* a God, and the same God who had created those lions had shut their mouths! I do not know if any of you are silly enough to believe that a lion has a "free will," but they certainly *did not* have any free will that night! It did not matter how hungry they were, they were not allowed to make a meal of God's servant!

God has perfect control over every irrational creature. He demonstrated that in the case of Jonah. He caused the beast of the ocean to swallow him and vomit him on dry land—note that it was not in the middle of the ocean! I presume that Jonah could not swim, and so the Lord directed the whale to the edge of the ocean, to vomit him out on dry land! Why did it? Because God made it, *that* is precisely the reason why, and the *only* reason why. There was another creature without a "free will"; the whale *had to do* what *God* wanted it to! Ah, if we only had eyes to see, we might discern the controlling hand of God Almighty over inanimate matter and over irrational creatures.

At God's will the cock crowed thrice just when He said it should. Ah, yes, no cockerel can crow without God permits. The cockerel crows when He pleases, and when He pleases it will remain silent! "Oh," you say, "I do not believe *that.*" No, the heathens in China do not, and if *you* do not you are no better than they are on that point. I am not excited; I am speaking very calmly, weighing my words, and each one of these addresses will be taken down and published in black and white, God willing.

Now, let us ascend one step higher. God has absolute control over inanimate matter, over irrational creatures, the whole kingdom of the beasts—but what about *man?* Is man such a mighty creature that God has *no* control over him, or is man so rebellious and intractable that God *cannot* control him? There are many who say. "No, certainly he is not; God *can* control man—every man, but God has created man a free-will being, a moral agent, and God *must not* interfere with him; God must not infringe upon his liberty and must not *make* him do anything, or he would just be a machine and no longer an accountable creature." My friends, those who speak thus *do err,* not knowing the Scriptures or the power of God, and I care not who they are; Scripture teaches plainly, clearly, and dogmatically, that God *has* absolute control of and perfect government over *every human being.* Not that He *will have* in the millennium, but that He *does have now!*

Now, I am going to ask you to turn to fourteen scriptures. I only gave you two on inanimate matter and three on the beasts, but we shall have fourteen on man, and we will just see what *God's Word* teaches us thereon. Never mind what we have been brought up to believe, never mind what we have been taught by any man, speaker included, but let us just come humbly to the Word of God and see what it teaches about God's relationship to man and His government over him.

Let us turn first of all to Psalm 76:10: "Surely the wrath of man shall praise Thee, the remainder of wrath shalt Thou restrain." Now *there* is an infringement of man's liberty! God exerts upon the wicked *restraining* power. He will not allow them to do all they want to do. God has said to the wicked, just like the sea, "Thus far shalt thou go and no farther"! He maketh the wrath of man to praise Him, and the remainder of wrath *He restraineth.* He puts a curb on him, or, to change the expression, He puts the brake on man; holds him in. The remainder of wrath He "restraineth." *That* is an infringement on man's liberty. Man has not the power to do all he *wants* to do, and none of you here to-night ought to have any difficulty in seeing what I mean. There is not a person in this church who has done half what he *intended* doing. We have all of us made plans and schemes to do a whole lot of things, but *have not* done them, and that shows that our liberty is not absolute.

Now turn back to Genesis 20:6: "And God said unto him (that is king Abimelch mentioned in verse 2) in a dream, Yea, I know that thou didst this in the integrity of thy heart for I also withheld thee from sinning against Me, therefore suffered I thee not to touch her." I *also withheld thee* from sinning against Me! How often you have heard man say that God created Adam in Eden a moral responsible free-will agent, and having created Adam such, God was *unable* to restrain or prevent Adam from sinning, or otherwise it would have reduced him to an irresponsible machine. My friends, that philosophy *will not* stand the test of Scripture. Here we have in the 20th chapter of Genesis, verse 6, a Divine statement made by God Himself that *He* "withheld" a man *from* sinning, and if God can withhold a fallen creature from sinning, why was it impossible for God to withhold an unfallen creature from sinning? This man was a fallen creature, a corrupt sinner, and yet God *withheld* him from sinning, and if God withheld Abimelch from sinning you may depend upon it He *could* have withheld Adam from sinning had He so pleased! "Do you mean to say then, preacher, that God *made* Adam sin?" No, certainly not. I say God *could* have *prevented* Adam from sinning if He had pleased, as He prevented Abimelch from sinning; so if you take issue with that you take issue with *God's Word,* not with me!

Now let us turn to Exodus 34:23,

These were God's instructions to the people of Israel concerning the national feasts. "Thrice in the year shall all your men children appear before the Lord God, the God of Israel, for I will cast out the nations before thee and enlarge the borders, neither shall any man desire thy land when thou shall go up to appear before the Lord thy God thrice in the year." Now, then, here is the point: three times every year God appointed that all the male Israelites should *leave* their farms and their homes, and all of them go up to Jerusalem (or to Shiloh it was at first, and later on to Jerusalem), and there worship Him; and they were surrounded by heathens who hated them, who resented their very presence as occupants of the land of Canaan. Now consider the circumstances. Here were their farms, their homes deserted by all their *men*, who had gone up to Jerusalem; and the women and children were left behind in the farms and homes surrounded by heathen! Now, then, look at verse 24 again: "For I will cast out the nations before thee and enlarge thy borders; neither shall any man *desire* thy land when thou shall go up to appear before the Lord thy God." God has such perfect control over men that they cannot even "desire" a thing *unless He allows it;* can never do a thing, not even desire a thing unless He permits it! These people were not believers, not seekers after God, not anxious to do His will; but *heathen,* yet God had such perfect control over them that He said, "When your men go up to Jerusalem to worship, and your farms and your homes are left without male to defend them. I will see that none of the heathen even desire your land while you are gone." What proof was that; what a marvellous demonstration was that, of God's absolute control over men, and heathen men at that —He controlled even their desires!

Now turn to Numbers 23:19, 20. I will read you the 18th verse to give you the setting: they were the words of Balaam the prophet—"And he took up this parable and said, Rise up, Balak, and hear; hearken unto me thou son of Zippor. God is not the son of man that He should lie, neither the son of man that He should repent; hath he said and shall He not do it? or hath He spoken and shall He not make it good? Behold (now notice carefully what follows) I have received commandment to bless and He hath blessed, and I *cannot* reverse it." There is God's control over man! Here is Balaam, a heathen soothsayer, and he is hired by king Balak to go and curse Israel, and king Balak offered to Balaam a huge sum of money as a big reward if he *would* curse Israel; and Balaam was anxious to get that reward, and God made Balaam do something *he* did not *want* to do. It was not a question of *being willing* or "allowing Him" to do anything. But God *made* him do it *against* his will! Balaam wanted to curse them and get his reward. God had perfect control over Balaam, even though he was a heathen sooth-sayer!

Now turn to the book of Ezra, 1st verse: "Now in the first year of Cyrus, king of Persia, that the word of the Lord by the mouth of Jeremiah might be fulfilled, the Lord stirred up the spirit of Cyrus, king of Persia, that he made a proclamation. (Now, then, how does that harmonise with this miserable philosophy and false theology which says that God *must not* "interfere" with man: that God *must* leave man alone or He will reduce him to a *machine?*) God "stirred up" the spirit of Cyrus to make the proclamation, and if there had been no God there would have been no proclamation! God stirred him up to do this very thing. God interferes with man whenever He wishes and exactly as He pleases and He does not ask his approval. God is *Lord,* doing as *He* pleases; *that* is the God of the Bible! I know He is not the God of most of our twentieth-century pulpits. My friends, there is no wonder that Evolutionism is sweeping over this land to-day like a tidal wave; no wonder when so many preachers get right away from the teaching of the Bilbe, and do not believe that God really and truly *governs* this world; bowing Him out of this world as some helpless spectator, looking on from some far distance, wringing His hands in despair, wanting to do things, and men won't let Him ! If they rule Him out of the world, why not go one step further and rule Him out of creation! As cause stands to effect, so the getting away from the sovereignty of God has been responsible for the popularisation of Darwin's theory of Evolution! It was a very short step to "evolution" when they ceased to believe that God was *God* over every creature that He made! If they no longer believe that God *rules* His creatures why should they believe God *made* them? One is just as absurd as the other. If God *made* us He *rules* us. If He does *not* rule us He did *not* make us! The two stand or fall together! When man *gets away from* a Sovereign God, Who is God *in fact* as well as in Name, and who reigns supreme over all His creatures, it is a short step into the bogs of evolutionism. There is one still shorter step left—into black Atheism!

Now let us turn to the book of Proverbs, chapter 16, verse 7. Before I read it, let me intersperse this remark. If any one present to-night will give me the name of one real Calvinistic preacher who has gone over to Evolutionism I will give £10 next Monday to the British and Foreign Bible Society. I mean what I say. If any of you will give me the name of one man who was once a firm believer in the absolute sovereignity of God, and has now gone over to evolutionism, I will give £10 to the British and Foreign Bible Society. You will find that every last one of these preachers who have gone over to preaching "evolution" were originally *Arminians* and *freewillers* to a man! You won't find an exception. There is a reason *why* God is *allowing* evolutionism to sweep over this and all the other lands in Christendom. The reason is because they no longer believe in the God of the Bible—a God who is *absolutely supreme* over all! Now, in the 7th verse of Proverbs 16: "When a man's ways please the Lord He maketh (He *maketh*) even his enemies to be at peace with him." What a proof that is of God's absolute control over man. No matter *who* these "enemies" are; no matter what *their* will in the matter may be, God *maketh* them—He does not *ask* them *to be* peaceful, He *maketh* them—to be at peace! *That* is the God of the Bible, the God who has absolute control over every human being. "He maketh them to be at peace with those whose ways please Him!"

Now, there is the 9th verse of the same chapter: "A man's heart deviseth his way." True. A man's heart "deviseth." It has all manner of plans and schemes and designs. "A man's heart deviseth his way, *but* the Lord directeth his steps." God not only directs the steps of His own people, but He directs the steps of *all* men. This verse here is not speaking about the *saints* at all. "A *man's* heart deviseth his way, but the Lord directeth *his* steps." The Bible says so, and I believe it! And, my friends, I would go on believing it if there were no other person in Australia who believed it! I am not going to take my theology from any human majority, and I am not going to ask myself *what* do *other* Christians believe? That has *nothing* to do with it. The *only* question for everyone is, "What does *God's Word* say?" And by His grace, I will believe His Word even should no other man on earth believe what He says. I say by His grace. That is by His sovereign grace alone; because I have a wicked heart, a foolish heart, by nature; I have a mind at enmity against Him, and it is only by His sovereign grace and by His Almighty power that He has made *me* bow before His Word like a little child, and believe that God says what He means and means what He says! A man's heart deviseth his way, but the Lord directeth his steps, and it was the Lord who directed *your* steps to this Church to-night, and it is the Lord who directs them when you leave. There is nothing in this universe that happens by chance. There is nothing that happens by blind fate. *Whatsoever* cometh to pass is by the eternal decree of the living God. "Of Him, through Him, and to Him are *all* things." The Book *says* so, and if you do *not* believe it, then you take issue with God Himself! I am not here to propagate any human theory. I am not here to expound Calvinism—I have a great respect for John Calvin, and under God am greatly indebted to his writings, but I call no man master. If Calvinism does not harmonise perfectly with this Book, then away with his teachings, or any other man's. We are bound by no human creed or catechism. Our creed is, What saith the Lord? May God in His grace make us all more simple, more childlike, that we may crucify our reason (our proud rebellious reason, that ever raises its head like a serpent against God!), to bring us into the dust, to believe just what *He* says, *all* that He says.

Now notice Proverbs 19.21: "There are many devices in a man's heart." And there surely *are!* God alone knows how many. All kinds of reasonings and devices going on in our hearts, some of them, even *now*, perhaps. "There are many devices in a man's heart, nevertheless (it is) the counsel of the Lord that shall stand." It is only *God's* eternal purpose that is going to be accomplished. Whatever He has counselled, no matter what the devices of our hearts may be, that counsel *shall* stand.

Now, notice Proverbs, 20th chapter, 24th verse: "Man's goings are of the Lord." Not only the *believer's,* but *man's* goings are. There is no qualification, no limitation, no reservation. "Man's goings are of the Lord, how can a man then understand his own way?" He cannot, God says so, and, my friends, this is a sledge-hammer blow against the theory of man's "free will." Man tried to invent a philosophy that will *explain* "man's goings." Man says, "I will do this, and not do that, and because I *willed* it is the reason why I act. I came out here to Church because I *willed* to come; if I had willed to stop at home I *should* have stayed at home." Man has invented that theory to get rid of a difficulty. God said, "Man's ways are of the Lord. *How,* then, can a man *under-*

stand his own *ways*." He can't, and God does not ask him to either. "Man's goings are of the Lord!"

Now, turn to Proverbs, 21, 1st verse: "The king's heart is in the hands of the Lord as the rivers of water, He turneth it whithersoever He will." Ah, yes, *God* has a will, my friend,*God* has a "free will," you do not often hear *that,* do you?

You have heard about *man's* freewill all your lives. I wonder if you have ever heard of God's freewill, God *has* a "freewill," and God's will is *always* done. "He turneth it whithersoever He will." Turneth *what?* The "heart of the king." If that is true, then the heart of the king is not free. If the king's heart is turned in whichever direction God wants it, then the king has not absolute control over it! There is not much "free-will" in that verse, nor in any other.

Now turn to the book of Isaiah, 44th chapter, 28th verse. The speaker here is Jehovah: "That saith of Cyrus He is My shepherd and shall perform all My pleasure." Who was *Cyrus?* Why, Cyrus was one of the godly kings of Israel. *Was* he? He was nothing of the kind. Cyrus was a *heathen,* and if any of you want to find out what sort of a creature he was, wade through Josephus and you will not find much there recorded to his credit. And yet God says of this wicked Cyrus, he is "My shepherd," and "shall perform all My pleasure." Not much "free agency" there! *Why* did God call Cyrus His "shepherd?" Because he was responsible for leading out His *sheep,* who were in captivity. That is why. The flock of Israel was yonder in captivity, and God stirred up the spirit of Cyrus to issue an edict that should lead that flock out of the land of captivity, that they might go back to their own land. Therefore God calls him "His shepherd."

First chapter Daniel, verse 9: "Now, God had brought Daniel into favour and tender love with the prince of the eunuchs." *God* brought Daniel into "favour" with another *heathen!* God not only moves upon the hearts of the righteous, but when He so pleases to do so, He moves upon the hearts of *the wicked* and softens them towards His people. He *did so* here! God touched the heart of this heathen Babylonian, Daniel's jailor—that is about all he was, and Daniel found favour in his eyes.

Now turn to Matthew 22, 2nd verse. I want you to put on your spectacles and read this verse closely: "The kingdom of heaven is like unto a certain King which made a marriage for His Son." There is one of the few verses that affirms that God is King. "A certain King made a marriage for His Son." Christ is going to exercise his Kingship in the Millenium. *God's* Kingship is now. "A certain King made a marriage for His Son." That is God the Father made a marriage for His Son, the Lord Jesus Christ. Verse 7: "But when the King heard thereof He was wroth and sent forth His armies and destroyed those murderers and burned up their city." I think I will have to read the intervening verses to let you get hold of that. Verse 2: "The kingdom of heaven is like unto a certain King which made a marriage for His Son, and sent forth His servants to call them that were bidden to the wedding, and they would not come. Again He sent forth other servants, saying, Tell them which are bidden, Behold I have prepared My dinner; My oxen and My fatlings are killed, and all things are ready, come unto the marriage. But they made light of it and went their ways, one to his farm, another to his merchandise. And the remnant took His servants and entreated them spitefully and slew them. But when the King heard thereof He was wroth, and He sent forth His armies and destroyed those murderers and burned up their city." *Whose* city? What city? The city of Jerusalem. The Jew's city. *When* was it burnt up? A.D. 70. *Who* was it that destroyed it? Titus and his army. Now read the verse with your glasses on. "But when the King heard thereof He was wroth and He sent forth *His* armies." *That* army was a *Roman* army, a *heathen* army under Titus, yet God Himself calls it HIS army! *Why* did He call it "His army?" Because it was doing *His* bidding, fulfilling *His* pleasure, carrying out *His will!* That Roman army, composed of heathen, was called God's army because God had complete control over it! There is another proof of God's absolute control *even over the wicked!* Yes, we need to read our Bibles afresh, don't we? We don't need a new Bible. We need new spectacles. We find we have been reading through coloured eyeglasses and mighty smoky ones they were, covered with man's false theories! That is why we know so little of the God of the Bible, who called the Roman army *His* army because He had complete control over it!

Now turn to the last book of the Bible. Revelation, 17th chapter, 17th verse. I will read the previous verse. Verse 16: "And the ten horns which thou sawest upon the beast, these shall hate the whore and shall make her desolate and naked, and shall eat her flesh and burn her with fire. For God hath put in their hearts to fulfil His will and to agree and give their kingdom unto the beast, until the words of God shall be fulfilled." Not much free-agency there, is there? *God* hath put in their hearts. *Whose* hearts? Godless men, Christless men, yet God hath put in *their* hearts, speaking of the coming "leagues of nations" in the tribulation period. God hath put in *their* hearts to fulfil *His* will. What is that? That they should preach the Gospel? The very opposite. "And to agree and give their kingdom unto the Beast. God's absolute control over them! Ten kings, and when God's time comes for the Antichrist to obtain full supremacy over the earth. God will put it into their hearts to give *him* their kingdoms!

You say, "well, I don't know how to harmonise all this!" God doesn't ask you to, my friend." "Well, I don't see how to reconcile it with the fact that man is a responsible being? What are you driving at preacher? Do you mean to say that man is *not* a responsible being?" No, I have not said that. This Book teaches from cover to cover that man *is* a responsible being, that *every* man shall render an "account unto God." But the same Book also teaches Divine Sovereignty, and it teaches Sovereignty that is absolutely *universal;* just as human responsibility is universal, the world over; God's Sovereignty is universal.

I am about two-thirds through, and have spoken an hour and a half; I have just shown, first of all, that God has absolute control over inanimate matter, over irrational creatures, over the children of men and this same Book teaches that God has absolute control over *the devil himself* Even Satan cannot do one single thing without the Almighty permits. If he could, I would not be speaking here to-night, for there is nothing the Devil hates worse than the truth about *God*. My friends, this is a gloriously comforting doctrine. I can come here night by night in absolute confidence that the Devil himself cannot touch one hair of my head unless Almighty God permits it, and I tell you if I did not believe that God had full control over Satan I would quit preaching; it would be a waste of time! What is the use of preach ing if the Devil can overthrow it all? The Devil cannot do one thing unless he gets God's permission! Satan could not sift Peter until the Lord allowed him to. When he came and tempted Christ at the end of the temptation the Lord Jesus said, "Get thee *hence,* Satan." What are we to learn from that? At that moment the Devil *departed* from Him. He *had* to! He could not do anything else! When Christ comes back again He will manifest openly to the eyes of all His absolute control over Satan, by laying hold of him, binding him and casting him into the Bottomless Pit.

Now, then, what is the *value* of this doctrine? In the first place, it maintains God's creatorial *rights,* it gives Him His true place. It shows that the same God who has made us, *rules* us.

Secondly, it is a great *comfort* to the heart that believes it. The heart that believes this truth, knows that our lives are not a product of chance, or of blind fate, but that everything in them is ordered by God! If you cannot get any comfort out of that, I pity you sincerely, no matter who you are. If you cannot get any comfort out of the fact that God is the moulder and director, the architect and potter over your life, that nothing can enter it without His permission, then you are to be pitied!

Thirdly, this truth is an absolute guarantee of the ultimate triumph of good over evil. God is on the Throne, the Devil is in His hand, therefore the final issue is sure. It could not be otherwise. If God has lost control over any of His creatures, and any to-day is successful in defying Him and thwarting Him, then there is absolutely no certainty left as to what the final issue will be. There is not a man on earth to-night who can refute the logic of that statement. If God is being defeated *now,* why may He not *always* be defeated? If God's purpose is being thwarted now, why may it not be thwarted a thousand years hence? The only absolute guarantee of the ultimate triumph of good over evil is the fact that God has *not* lost control, that the helm is in *His* hand, that He is directing *everything* to the out-working of His eternal will! "For of Him, and to Him, and through Him, are *all* things." Amen

---

N.B.—The above is a verbatim report of an Address delivered by the Editor on June 19 at the Baptist Tabernacle, Ashfield one of the strongest Churches in Sydney. Between four and five hundred people were present. The substance of it was (alas) entirely new to most of them. "Some believed the things which were spoken, and some believed not" (Acts 28:24)!

Wholly set up and Printed by the W.H.B. Printing Co. Ltd. 416-8 Elizabeth Street, Sydney

VOL. IV NOV., 1925 NO. 11

STUDIES IN THE SCRIPTURES

"Search the Scriptures" John 5:39.

Arthur W. Pink, Publisher and Editor,
5 Norton Street, Ashfield, N.S.W., Australia.

Price: 10 cents per copy; $1.00 or 5/- per year.

Romans 8: 18.

"For I reckon that the sufferings of this present time are not worthy to be compared with the glory which shall be revealed in us" (*Rom.* 8:18).

Ah, says someone, that must have been written by a man who was a stranger to suffering, or by one acquainted with nothing more trying than the milder irritations of life. Not so. These words were penned under the direction of the Holy Spirit, and by one who drank deeply of sorrow's cup, yea, by one who suffered afflictions in their acutest forms. Hear his own testimony: "Of the Jews five times received I forty stripes save one. Thrice was I beaten with rods, once was I stoned, thrice I suffered shipwreck, a night and a day I have been in the deep; in journeyings often, in perils of waters, in perils of robbers, in perils by mine own countrymen, in perils by the heathen, in perils in the city, in perils in the wilderness, in perils in the sea, in perils among false brethren; in weariness and painfulness, in watchings often, in hunger and thirst, in fastings often, in cold and nakedness" (2 Cor. 11:24-27).

"For I reckon that the sufferings of this present time are not worthy to be compared with the glory which shall be revealed in us." This, then, was the settled conviction not of one of "fortune's favourites," not of one who found life's journey a carpeted pathway, bordered with roses, but, instead, by one who was hated by his kinsmen, who was oft-times beaten black and blue, who knew what it was to be deprived not only of the comforts but the bare necessities of life. How, then, shall we account for his cheery optimism? What was the secret of his elevation over his troubles and trials?

The first thing with which the sorely-tried apostle comforted himself was that the sufferings of the Christian are but of *brief* duration—they are limited to "this present time." This is in sharp and solemn contrast from the sufferings of the Christ-rejector. *His* sufferings will be eternal: forever tormented in the Lake of Fire. But far different is it for the believer. His sufferings are restricted to this life on earth, which is compared to a flower that cometh forth and is cut down, to a shadow that fleeth and continueth not. A few short years at most, and we shall pass from this vale of tears, into that blissful country where groans and sighs are never heard.

Second, the apostle looked forward with the eye of faith to "the glory." To Paul the "glory" was something more than a beautiful dream. It was a practical reality, exerting a powerful influence upon him, consoling him in the darkest and most trying hours of adversity. This is one of the real tests of faith. The Christian has a *real* support in the time of affliction, which the unbeliever has not. The child of God knows that in his Father's presence there is "fulness of joy," and that at *His* right hand there are "pleasures forever more." *And faith lays hold of them,* appropriates them, and lives in the comforting cheer of them even now. Just as Israel in the wilderness were encouraged by a sight of what awaited them in the promised land (Num. 13:23, 26), so, the one who to-day walks by faith, and not by sight, contemplates that which eye hath not seen, nor ear heard, but which God by His Holy Spirit *hath* revealed unto *us* (1 Cor. 2:9, 10).

(*Continued on page 264*)

CONTENTS

THE GOSPEL OF JOHN

47. *Christ's Warnings*: *John* 13:21-38:

Below is an analysis of the passage which is to be before us:—

1. The Betrayer and his identification vv 21-26.
2. The departure of Judas and the thoughts of the Eleven vv 27-30.
3. A threefold glorification vv 31-32.
4. The new commandment v 34.
5. The badge of Christian discipleship v 35.
6. Peter's questions vv 36-37.
7. Christ's warning prediction v 38.

We have entitled this article Christ's Warnings: it scarcely covers everything in the passage, yet it emphasises that which is most prominent in it. At the beginning of our present section Christ warns Judas; at the close, He warns Peter. In between, there are some gracious and tender instructions for the beloved disciples, and these too partake very large of the nature of *warnings.* He warns them against misinterpreting the nature of His death vv 31-32. He warns them of His approaching departure v 33. He warns them of their need of a *commandment* that they should "love one another" v 34. He warns them that only by the exercise of *love* toward each other would it be made manifest that they were *His* disciples v 35.

Our passage opens with a plain announcement of the Saviour's Betrayer. This Betrayer had been plainly announced in Old Testament prophecy: "He that eateth bread with Me hath lifted up his heel against Me" (Psa. 41:9). "A man's *foes,*" said the Lord, "are they of his own household" (Matt. 10:36), and fearfully was this verified in His own case. A "familiar friend" became a *familiar fiend.* How this exposes the error of those who suppose that all which fallen man needs is *example* and *instruction.* Judas enjoyed both, yet was not his evil heart moved. For three years had he been not only in the closest possible contact, but in the nearest intimacy with the Saviour. His had been a favoured place in the innermost circle of the Twelve. Not only had he listened to the daily preaching of Christ as He taught the people, not only had he witnessed most, at least, of His wondrous miracles, but he had also gazed upon the perfections of Christ in His private life. And yet, after all this, Judas was unmoved and unchanged. Nothing could more forceably demonstrate our Lord's utterance, "Except a man *be born again* he *cannot* see the kingdom of God!" So near to Christ, yet unsaved! What a challenge for every heart!

The case of Peter points a most solemn warning of quite another character. Outwardly Judas *posed* as a disciple of Christ; inwardly Simon *was* a believer in Him. The one exhibits the sin and madness of hypocrisy; the other the danger and sad results of self-confidence. It was to Peter that the Lord said, "The spirit (the new nature) indeed is willing, but the flesh (the natural man) is weak." But this utterance was never intended as an *excuse,* behind which we might take refuge when we fail and fall; but was given as a lasting warning to have "*no* confidence in the flesh" (Phil. 3:3). The Holy Spirit has faithfully recorded the sad defection of one who was especially dear to the heart of the Saviour, that all Christians who follow Him might seek grace from God to avoid the snare into which he fell.

From a human view, Peter failed at his *strongest* point. By nature he was bold and courageous. Probably there was not a stouter heart among the apostles. He quailed not before the marvellous scene on the Mount of Transfiguration. He it was who stepped out of the ship and started to walk across the waves to Christ. And he it was who drew his sword in the Garden, and smote the high priest's servant as the officers arrested his beloved Master. No coward was Peter. And yet *he* trembled in the presence of a maid, and when taxed with being a disciple of Christ, denied it with an oath! How is this to be explained? Only on the ground that in order to teach him and us the all-important lesson, that if left to ourselves, the strongest is as weak as water. It is in conscious weakness that our *strength* lies (2 Cor. 12:10). Peter was fully assured that though *all* should be offended, yet would not *he* (Mark 14:29). And, without a doubt, he fully meant what he said. But he did not *know himself;* he had not learned, experimentally, the exceeding deceitfulness of the human heart; he knew not as yet that without the upholding power and sustaining grace of the Lord he could do *nothing* (John 15:5). O that we might learn from him.

"We fancy sometimes, like Peter, that there are some things *we* could not possibly do. We look pityingly upon others who fall, and plume ourselves in the thought that at any rate *we* should not have done so. We know nothing at all. The seeds of *every* sin are latent in our hearts, even when renewed, and they only need occasion, or carelessness, or the withdrawal of God's grace for a season, to put forth an abundant crop. Like Peter, we think we can do wonders for Christ, and like Peter, we learn by bitter experience that *we* have no might and power at all. A humble sense of our own innate weakness, a constant dependency on the Strong for strength, a daily prayer to be held up, because we cannot hold up ourselves—these are the true secrets of safety" (Bishop Ryle). Surely the outstanding lesson for us in connection with the fall of Peter is this: "Let him that thinketh he standeth take heed lest he fall" (1 Cor. 10:12).

"When Jesus had thus said, He was troubled in spirit, and testified, and said, Verily, verily, I say unto you, that one of you shall betray Me" (v. 21). The Lord had been ministering to His disciples, teaching and comforting them. He had spoken of their future, but in the midst of these anticipations a dark shadow falls upon Him, troubling Him. Already had He hinted at it, now He proceeds to testify more plainly to the Traitor who was among the Twelve. The Lord was "troubled in spirit." It is remarkable that this is mentioned most frequently by the very Evangelist whose special design it was to portray the Lord Jesus as God manifest in flesh —cf. 11:33, 38; 12:27. These statements prove the reality of His humanity, showing that He had a real human soul as well as body. They also prove that it is no infirmity or imperfection to be *troubled* by the presence of evil. Christ was no stoic: He felt keenly all that was contrary to God. Really, none was so truly and so completely sensitive as He. He was the Man of sorrows, and it is just because He has Himself passed through this scene, suffering within at every step of the way, that He is able to be touched with "the feeling of *our* infirmities."

"When Jesus had thus said, He was troubled in spirit, and testified, and said, Verily, verily, I say unto you, that one of you shall betray Me." It is well to remind ourselves that what the Lord Jesus endured upon the cross was but the climax and completion of His sufferings. Throughout His life He suffered at the hands of Satan, His enemies, and His friends. He felt acutely the unbelief and hostility of the Scribes and Pharisees. His tearful lament over Jerusalem evidences the depths of His anguish over Israel's rejection. Here it was the bitter sorrow of seeing one of the apostles deliberately becoming an apostate. Nothing wounds more deeply than ingratitude, and that one, who had been a constant companion with Him for three years, should now raise his heel against Him, was a sore trial. If Judas was unmoved, the Lord was not. Seeing no beauty in Christ after all he had heard and witnessed during years of closest contact with Him, unaffected by His marvellous grace to sinners, caring only for paltry gain, dominated by self, and the rebuke he had received in Simon's house rankling within, he turned against his Master and arranged to sell Him to His enemies. No wonder the Lord was "troubled" as He thought of such deceit, treachery, and cupidity. He had said "Ye are clean, but *not* all," and still Judas retained his place, and gave no sign of retiring.

"Verily, verily, I say unto you, that one of you shall betray Me." There is a melancholy emphasis on the pronoun here: one of *you* at the table with Me; one of *you* whose feet I have just washed; one of *you* who have had the high honour of being My first ambassadors, shall take advantage of your intimacy with Me and knowledge of My ways, to guide the enemy to My place of retirement, and deliver Me into the hands of those who seek My life. He was "troubled" by the enormity of the crime, and no doubt, too, over the awful doom which lay before Judas.

How deeply "troubled" the Saviour was we may learn from His words in Psa. 55: "Wickedness is in the midst thereof: deceit and guile depart not from her streets. For it was not an enemy that reproached Me; then I could have borne it: neither was it he that hated Me that did magnify himself against Me; then I would have hid Myself from him: But it was thou, a man Mine equal, My guide, and Mine acquaintance. We took sweet counsel together, and walked unto the house of God in company" (vv. 11-14). How vividly this brings out before us the *grief* with which the Man of sorrows was "acquainted"! How deeply His holy soul was stirred, we may learn from the solemn but righteous imprecations which He called down upon the base ingrate in Psa. 109: "Let his days be few; and let another take his office; let his children be fatherless, and his wife a widow" (vv. 8, 9), etc.

"Then the disciples looked one on another, doubting of whom He spake" (v. 22). Three things are made very evident by this verse: one thing about the disciples, one about Judas, and one about the Lord Himself. First, it is plain that what Christ had said in v. 18 had made no impression upon the Eleven. And this was most natural. No doubt their minds were so occupied with what the Saviour had just done for them that they had scarcely recovered from their surprise. They were so impressed by His amazing condescension that His statement "He that eateth bread with Me hath lifted up his heel against Me" fell upon ears that heeded Him not. But now He speaks more plainly and directly, and they exchanged puzzled glances with each other, wondering which of them it was to whom He had referred.

Second, the fact that "The disciples looked one on another, doubting of whom He spake" is proof positive that Judas had succeeded in concealing his turpitude from his fellows. His outward conduct had given the other apostles no occasion to suspect him. To what lengths cannot hypocrisy go! Matthew tells us that when Christ announced to the Twelve that one of them should betray Him, "They were exceedingly sorrowful, and began every one of them to say, Lord, is it I?" (26:22), upon which Matthew Henry says: "They are to be commended for their charity, in that they are more jealous of themselves than of each other. It is the law of charity to hope the best; because we assuredly know, therefore we may justly expect, more evil of ourselves than of our brethren. They are also to be commended for their acquiescence in what Christ said. They trusted, as we would well to do, more to His words, than to their own hearts, and therefore do not say, "It is not—it cannot be—I'; but 'Lord, is it I'? See if there be such a way of wickedness, such a root of bitterness in me, and discover it to us, that I may pluck up the root, and stop up that way." Boldly playing his role of duplicity to the last, Judas dares to ask, "*Master*, is it I?" (Matt. 26:25)—a clear proof, though, that *he* was unsaved, for no man can say *Lord* Jesus but by the Holy Spirit (1 Cor. 12:3).

Third, the fact that the apostles were perplexed, wondering to whom the Lord had referred, brings out most blessedly the infinite patience with which Christ had borne with the Son of Perdition. Throughout His ministerial life He must have treated Judas with the same condescending grace, gentleness, kindness, as the Eleven. He could not have exhibited any aversion against him, or the others would have noticed it, and known now of whom He spake. How this tells of the perfections of our Saviour! His kindness ill-requited, His favours unappreciated, His holy soul loathing such a sink of iniquity so near to Him—yet He bowed to the sovereign will and authoritative word of the Father, and patiently bore this trial.

"Now there was leaning on Jesus' bosom one of His disciples, whom Jesus loved" (v. 23). Here is one of those striking contrasts in which this Gospel abounds, and a most blessed one it is. Our attention is diverted for a moment from the base treachery and horrible hatred of Judas to one whom Christ had attracted, whose heart had been won by His beauty, and who now affectionately reposed on the Saviour's breast. It is blessed, and an evident mark of the Holy Spirit's guidance to see how John here refers to himself. It was not "one who loved Jesus," though truly he did; but "one of His disciples whom Jesus loved." Nor does he mention his own name—love never advertises itself.

"Simon Peter therefore beckoned to him, that he should ask who it should be of whom He spake" (v. 24). This is one of many statements in the New Testament which effectually disposes of the Roman Catholic figment that Peter was the pope of the apostolate. As one of the older Protestant writers well said, "So far from Peter having any primacy among the apostles, he here uses the intercession of John." There was no doubt a moral reason why Peter put his question through John, instead of asking it direct. Is it not clear from vv. 6, 8, 37 that Peter's state of soul was not altogether right before God? And, does not his fearful fall, that very evening, supply still further proof? Matthew tells us that after the arrest of the Saviour, Peter "followed Him *afar off* unto the high priest's palace" (26:38), and a sense of *distance* began to make itself felt in Peter's soul even here —there was a measure of reserve between himself and the Lord.

"He then, lying on Jesus' breast, saith unto Him, Lord, who is it?" (v. 25). The contrast here between John and Peter is very noticeable. John was close to the Lord: affection had drawn him there. He was so near to Christ and his spirit so unclouded, he could look up into the face of the Saviour and ask Him any question. This is the blessed portion and privilege of every Christian. Alas! that so many are like Peter on this occasion—ready to turn to a *brother,* rather than to the Lord Himself. Why is it that when the average Christian meets with some difficulty in His reading of the Word, or some problem in his spiritual life, he says, "I will ask or write Brother So-and-so?" Why not enjoy the blessed privilege of referring *directly* to the Lord Jesus? It is a question of *intimacy* with Him, and that is very searching. While there is any self-confidence, as in Peter's case, or any known hindrance in my spiritual life, that at once places me at a moral distance from Christ. But is it not blessed to see that, at the end, Peter came to the same place which John is seen occupying here? 'And he said unto Him, Lord, Thou knowest all things; Thou knowest that I love Thee" (21:17). He threw open his heart. What was it but saying, Lord, there was a time when I would not ask You questions, but now I can invite You to look into my heart! Let us then come before Him now, asking Him to search our hearts and put His finger on anything that hinders us from having direct access to Him in everything. Let us ever be on the watch that we do not enjoy a greater intimacy with some brother than with the Lord Himself.

"Jesus answered, He it is, to whom I shall give a sop, when I have dipped it" (v. 26). It seems clear from what follows that these words of Christ must have been whispered to John, or spoken in such a low tone that the other disciples were unable to catch them. At last the Lord Jesus identified the Betrayer. The mask of hypocrisy which he had worn had thoroughly deceived the apostles, but He with whom "all things are naked and open" cannot be imposed upon. While man looketh on the outward appearance, He looks upon the heart; so He now unmasks the false disciple, and shows him to be—what *He* always knew, though none else suspected that he was—a traitor.

"And when He had dipped the sop, He gave it to Judas Iscariot the son of Simon" (v. 26). The sign given by Christ to identify the Betrayer was suggestive and solemn. "It was a mark of honour for the host to give a portion to one of the guests. The Lord had appealed to the *conscience* of Judas in v. 21, now He appeals to His *heart*" (Companion Bible). The "sop" was, most probably, a piece of unleavened bread, now dipped in the sauce prepared for the eating of the pascal lamb. That Judas accepted it shows the unthinkable lengths to which he carried his hypocrisy. Determined as he was to perpetrate the foulest treachery, yet he hereby renews his pledge of friendship. It makes us think of the "Hail Master" and the "kiss" when he was in the act of delivering Him to His enemies. But how wonderful, how blessed, the meekness of our Lord, surely none but He *could* have acted thus. In complete command of Himself, no sign of ill-will toward the one who had already taken counsel with the chief priests, He gives him the sop. Closely did this correspond with the prophetic declaration already referred to, "He that *eateth* with Me hath lifted up his heel against Me."

"And after the sop Satan entered into him" (v. 27). The receiving of the sop, expressive of friendship, ought to have broken him down in an agony of repentance; but it did not. He was like those mentioned in Heb. 6:8: ground on which the rain came oft, but which instead of bringing forth herbs, bore only thorns and briars, whose end is to be burned. It is remarkable to note that not until now are we told of Satan's entrance into him. Equally striking is it to observe that as soon as he *had* received the "sop" the Enemy took full possession of his only too willing victim.

"Then said Jesus unto him, That thou doest, do quickly" (v. 27). Fearful words were these. Space for repentance had now passed forever. His doom was sealed. But what else lay behind these words of Christ? We believe it was the formal announcement of the Saviour surrendering Himself to the Father's will. It was as though He said, *I am ready* to be led as a lamb to the slaughter; go, Judas, and do that which you are so anxious to do; *I* will not withstand thee! But again; may we not regard this word of Christ as in one sense parallel with the one He had addressed to the Devil at the close of the great temptation. There was a needs be for Him to be tempted of the Devil for forty days; but when that needs be had been fully met, He said, "Get thee *hence*, Satan" (Matt. 4:10). So, in order that Scripture might be fulfilled, it was necessary for there to be a Judas in the apostolate, so that he could eat with Christ. But now that prophcey had been accomplished, now that the Traitor's heel had been lifted against his Master, Christ says, "Depart"! Moreover, was not this the formal dismissal of Judas from the Lord's service? Christ had *called* Him to a place in the apostolate: for three years He had used him: now He announces his discharge, later, another shall "take *his bishoprick*." Finally, we believe it can be established from the other Gospels that it was right after this that the Lord instituted His own "supper" as a lasting memorial of Himself; but before doing so He first banishes the Traitor, for *that* "supper" is for His own only.

"Now no man at the table knew for what intent He spake this unto him" (v. 28). At this point John, at least, and most probably Peter also, knew who it was who should betray their beloved Master, yet in the light of this verse it is evident that none of them suspected that the act of treachery was so soon to be perpetrated. None of them perceived the awfulness of the issues then pending.

"For some of them thought, because Judas had the bag, that Jesus had said unto him. Buy those things that we have need of against the feast; or, that he should give something to the poor" (v. 29). "These thoughts of the disciples were mistaken ones, but they do them no discredit. They are excuseable and even praiseworthy. They indicate the operation of the charity which thinketh no evil, but is ever disposed to put on words and actions the most favourable construction they will reasonably admit. The mistakes of charity are wiser and better than the surmises of censoriousness, even when they turn out to be according to the truth. Judas had all along been a bad man; but hitherto he had given no such evidence of his unprincipled character as would have warned his fellow-disciples to entertain suspicions of him. Knowing that he was the treasurer and steward of this little society, they supposed that the words of the Master might refer to his speedily obtaining something which would be requisite for the feast of the passover, which lasted for a week; or that he should immediately give some alms to the poor.

"It is plain from these words that our Lord and His disciples were in the habit of giving, especially at the time of the great festivals, out of their scanty pittance, something to those more destitute than themselves. Their 'deep poverty abounded unto the riches of their liberality': and by His example He has taught us not merely that it is the duty of those who may have but little to spare to give of that little to those who have still less, but that religious observances are gracefully connected with deeds of mercy and alms-giving. He joined humility with piety in His practice as well as in His doctrine; and in this He hath left us an example that we should follow His steps" (Dr. J. Brown). To these remarks we may add that the fact the disciples had supposed Judas had gone to *purchase* things for "the feast" is clear proof that the Lord did not work miracles in order to procure the food needed by Himself and His apostles. It also shows that they did not *beg*, but managed their temporal affairs with prudence and economy (cf. 4:8).

But far different were the base designs of Judas from what the apostles had charitably supposed. "It was not to buy things needful, but to *sell* the Lord and Master; it was no preparation for the feast, but that to which it, not they, had ever looked onward—the fulfilment of God's mind and purpose in it, though it were the Jews crucifying their own Messiah, by the hands of lawless men; it was not that *Judas* should *give* to the poor, but that *He should* who was rich yet for our sakes became poor, that we through His poverty might be made rich" (Bible Treasury).

"He then having received the sop went immediately out: and it was night" (v. 30). There is something more here, something deeper, than a mere reference to the time of the day. As Judas went forth on his dastardly errand, there then began that "hour" of the Power of *darkness* (Luke 22:53), when God suffered His enemies to put out the Light of life. So, too, it was "night" in the soul of Judas, for he had turned his back on "The *Light*." Like Cain he went out from the "presence of the Lord"; like Baalam he loved "the wages of unrighteousness"; like Ahitophel he went to betray his "familiar Friend." It was *night*: "Men love darkness rather than light, because their deeds are *evil*": fitting time was it, then, for the Son of Perdition to perpetrate his dark deed! "*Immedi-*

ately" he went: *his* feet were "swift to shed blood"!

"Therefore, when he was gone out, Jesus said, Now is The Son of man glorified" (v. 31). A most remarkable word was this. The Lord Jesus spoke of His *death,* but He regarded it neither as a martyrdom nor as a disgrace. There is nothing quite like this in the other Gospels. Here, as ever, John gives us the highest, the *Divine* viewpoint of things. The Saviour contemplates His death on the shameful tree as His *glorification.* "It seems very strange that, in these circumstances, Jesus should say, 'Now—now is the Son of man glorified.' It would not have been wonderful if, on the banks of Jordan after His baptism, with the mystic love descending and abiding on Him, and the voice of the Eternal pealing from the open heaven, 'This is my beloved Son, in whom I am well pleased'; or, on the summit of the Mount of Transfiguration, when His face did shine as the sun, and His garments became white as the light,' and Moses and Elijah appeared to Him in glory, and a voice came forth from the cloud of glory. 'This is My beloved Son, hear Him,' our Lord had said, in holy exaltation, '*Now* is the Son of man glorified'! But, when these words were spoken, what was before the Redeemer but the deepest abasement, and the severest sufferings—heavy accusations—a condemnatory sentence—insults—infamy—the fellowship of thieves—the agonies of death—the lonely sepulchre! How does He, in these circumstances, say, 'Now is the Son of man glorified'" (Dr. J. Brown).

But *wherein was* Christ's death on the cross His *glorification?* Notice, first, that He said, "Now is the *Son of man* glorified." It was the Son of God *as incarnate* who was "glorified" on the cross. But how? Wherein? First, in that He there performed the greatest work which the whole history of the entire universe ever witnessed, or ever will witness. For it the centuries waited; to it the centuries look back. Second, because there He reversed the conduct of the first man. The first Adam was *disobedient* unto death, the last Adam was *obedient* unto death, even the death of the Cross. The glory of man is to glorify God; and never was God more glorified than when His own incarnate Son laid down His life in submission to His command (10:18); and never was human nature so glorified as when the Son of man thus glorified God. Third, because through death He destroyed him who had the power of death, that is the devil (Heb. 2:14). What a notable achievement was this, that one made in the likeness of sin's flesh should accomplish the utter defeat of the arch-enemy of God and man! Fourth, because at the cross was paid the ransom-price which purchased for Himself all the elect of God. What glory for the Son of man was this, that He should do what none other in all the realm of creation could do (through immeasurable suffering and shame)—"bring many sons unto glory." The manner in which He wrought this work also glorified Him: He was a willing sufferer; the price was cheerfully paid; He was led, not driven, as a lamb to the slaughter; He endured the cross despising the shame; and not until offended justice and a broken law were fully satisfied did He cry, "It is finished." Finally, by virtue of His cross-work, He acquired a glory which He never had before (John 17:22). "*Wherefore* God also hath highly exalted Him, and given Him the name which is above every name" (Phil. 2.10).

"And God is glorified in Him" (v. 31). What a theme! One which no human pen can begin to do justice to. The cross-work of Christ was not only the basis of our salvation, and the glorification of the Son of man Himself, but it was also the brightest manifestation of the glory *of God.* Every attribute of Deity was superlatively magnified at Calvary.

The *power* of God was exceedingly glorified at the cross. There the kings of the earth and the rulers took counsel together against God and against His Christ; there the terrible enmity of the carnal mind and the desperate wickedness of the human heart did their worst; there the fiendish malignity of Satan was put forth to its fullest extent. But God had laid help upon One that is *mighty* (Psa. 89:19). None was able to take His life from the Saviour (John 10:18). After man and Satan had done their worst, the Lord Jesus remained complete master of Himself and not until *He* saw fit did He *lay down* His life of Himself: Never was the power of God more illustriously displayed. Christ was crucified "through weakness" (2 Cor. 11:4), offering no resistance to His enemies: but it is written, "The weakness of God is *stronger* than men" (1 Cor. 1:25), and gloriously was that demonstrated at the cross, when the power of God sustained the humanity of Christ as He endured His outpoured wrath.

The *justice* of God was exceedingly glorified at the cross. Of old He declared that He "will by no means clear the guilty" (Exodus 34:7), and when the Lord laid on our blessed Substitute "the iniquities of us all" He hung there as *the* Guilty

One. And God is so strictly and immutably just that He would not spare His own Son when He had made Him to be sin for us. He would not abate the least mite of that debt which righteousness demanded. The penalty of the broken law must be enforced, even though it meant the slaying of His well Beloved. Therefore did the cry go forth, "Awake, O sword, against My Shepherd, and against the man that is My Fellow, saith the Lord of hosts: *smite* the Shepherd" (Zech. 13:7). The justice of God was more illustriously glorified by the propitiation which was made by the Lord Jesus than if every member of the human race were to suffer in Hell forever.

The *holiness* of God was exceedingly glorified at the cross. He is "of purer eyes than to behold evil, and canst not look on iniquity" (Heb. 1:13), and when Christ was "made a curse for us" (Gal. 3:13) the thrice Holy One turned away from Him. It was this which caused the agonising Saviour to cry, "My God, My God, why hast Thou *forsaken* Me?" Never did God so manifest His hatred of sin as in the sufferings and death of His Only-begotten. There He showed it was impossible for Him to be at peace with that which had raised its defiant head against Him. All the honour due to the holiness of God by all the holy angels, and all the cheerful obedience and patient suffering of all the holy men who have ever existed, or ever will exist, are nothing in comparison with the offering of Christ Himself in order that every demand of God's holiness, which sin had outraged, might be fully met.

The *faithfulness* of God was exceedingly glorified at the cross. God had sworn, "The soul that sinneth it shall die," and when the Sinless One offered to receive the full and fearful wages of sin, God showed to all heaven and earth that He had rather that the blood of His Fellow be spilt than that one tittle of the Word should fail. In the Scriptures He had made it known that His Son should be led as a lamb to the slaughter, that His hands and His feet should be pierced, that He should be numbered with transgressors, that He should be wounded for our transgressions and bruised for our iniquities. These and many other predictions received their exact fulfilment at Calvary, and their accomplishment there supplied the greatest proof of all that God cannot lie.

The *love* of God was exceedingly glorified at the cross. "God so loved the world that He gave His only begotten Son" (John 3:16). "Herein is love, not that we loved God, but that He loved us, and sent His Son to be the propitiation for our sins" (1 John 4:10). "The light of the sun is always the same, but it shines brightest at noon. The cross of Christ was the noontide of everlasting love—the miridian-splendour of eternal mercy. There were many bright manifestations of the same love before; but they were like the light of the morning that shines more and more unto the perfect day; and that perfect day was when Christ was on the cross, and darkness covered all the land" (McLaurin).

"O when we view God's grand design,
To save rebellious worms,
How vengeance and compassion join
In their sublimest forms!

Our thoughts are lost in rev'rent awe—
We love and we adore;
The first archangel never saw
So much of God before!

Here each Divine perfection joins,
And thought can never trace,
Which of the glories brightest shines—
The justice or the grace."

"If God be glorified in Him, God shall also glorify Him in Himself, and shall straightway glorify Him" (v. 32). "This verse may be paraphrased as follows: 'If God The Father be specially glorified in all His attributes by My death, He shall proceed at once to place special glory on Me, for My personal work, and shall do it without delay, by raising Me from the dead, and placing Me at His right hand.' It is the same idea that we have in the seventeenth chapter more fully. 'I have glorified Thee on the earth; now, O Father, glorify Thou Me with Thine own self'" (Bishop Ryle).

"Little children, yet a little while I am with you. Ye shall seek Me: and as I said unto the Jews, Whither I go, ye cannot come; so now I say to you" (v. 33). Here for the first time the Lord Jesus addressed His disciples by this special term of endearment, "little children." It is striking to observe that the Lord waited until *after* Judas had gone out before using it: teaching us that *un*believers must not be addressed as *God's* "children"! "Ye shall seek Me" tells of their love for Him, as the "little children" had expressed His for them. "Whither I go ye cannot come" seems to have a different force from what it signified when addressed to the unbelieving Jews in 7:33. He declared to them, "I go unto Him that sent Me. . . and where I am, thither ye cannot come." The reference is the same in 8:21. But here the Saviour was not speaking of His return to the Father, but of His going to the

Cross—*thither* "they" could not come. In His great work of redemption He was alone. Just as in the type, "There shall be *no man* in the tabernacle of the congregation when he (the high priest) goeth in to make an atonement" (Lev. 16:17), so in the anti-type.

"A new commandment I give unto you, That ye love one another; as I have loved you, that ye also love one another" (v. 34). "The immense importance of Christian love cannot possibly be shown more strikingly than the way that it is urged on the disciples in this place. Here is our Lord leaving the world, speaking for the last time, and giving His last charge to the disciples. The very *first* subject He takes up and presses on them is the great duty of loving one another, and that with no common love; but after the same patient, tender, unwearied manner that He had loved them. Love must needs be a very rare and important grace to be so spoken of! The want of it must needs be plain proof that a man is no true disciple of Christ. How vast the extent of Christian love ought to be" (Bishop Ryle).

"A new commandment I give unto you, That ye love one another; as I have loved you, that ye also now love one another." The Nation now disappears. It is no question of loving one's neighbour, but of Christ's disciples, and their mutual love according to His love. Nor is it here activity of zeal in quest of sinners, blessed as that is; but the unselfish seeking of the good of saints, as such, in lowliness of mind. The Law required love of one's neighbour, which was a *fleshly* relationship; Christ enjoins love *to our brethren*, which is a *spiritual* relationship. Here, then, is the first sense in which this "commandment" was a *new* one. But there is a further sense brought out by John in his Epistle: "A new commandment I write unto you, which thing is true *in Him* and in you" (1 John 2:8). *Love* had now been manifested, yea, personified, as never before. Christ had displayed a love superior to the faults of its objects a love which never varied, a love which deemed no sacrifice too great. Scott has well observed on this new commandment, "Love was now to be explained with new clearness, enforced by new motives and obligations, illustrated by a new example, and obeyed in a new manner."

"By this shall all know that ye are My disciples, if ye have love one to another" (v. 35). Love is the *badge* of Christian discipleship. It is not knowledge, nor orthodoxy, nor spiritualistic activities, but (supremely) *love* which indentifies a follower of the Lord Jesus. As the disciples of the Pharisees were known by their phylacteries, as the disciples of John were known by their baptism, and every school by its particular shibboleth, so the mark of a true Christian is *love;* and that, a genuine, active love, not in words but in deeds. 1 Cor. 13 gives a full exposition of this verse.

"Simon Peter said unto Him, Lord, whither goest Thou? Jesus answered him, Whither I go, thou canst not follow Me now; but thou shalt follow Me afterwards" (v. 36). How evident it is that even the Eleven had not grasped the fact that their beloved Master was going to be taken from them! Often as He had spoken to them of His death, it seems to have made no lasting impression upon them. This illustrates the fact that men may receive much religious instruction, and yet take in very little of it, the more so when it clashes with their preconceptions. The Christian teacher needs much patience, and the less he expects from his work, the less will he be disappointed. Christ's words here, "Whither I go" had a different meaning than in v. 33. There He had spoken of taking His place alone in death: here He refers to His return to the Father, therefore is He careful to add, "Thou *shalt* follow Me afterwards."

"Peter said unto Him, Lord, why cannot I follow Thee now? I will lay down my life for Thy sake" (v. 37). Peter knew and really loved the Lord, but how little he as yet knew himself! It was right to feel the Lord's absence; but he should have heeded better the mild, but grave, admonition that where Christ was going he was not able to follow Him now; he should have valued the comforting assurance that he should follow Him later. Alas! how much we lose now, how much we suffer afterwards, through *not* laying to heart the deep truth of Christ's words! We soon see the bitter consequences in Peter's history; but we know, from the future words of our Lord in the close of this Gospel, how grace would ensure in the end the favour, compromised by that self-confidence at the beginning, which He here warned against.

"But we are apt to think most highly of ourselves, of our love, wisdom, moral courage, and every other good quality, when we least know and judge ourselves in God's presence, as here we see in Peter; who, impatient of the hint already given, breaks forth into the self-confident question, 'Lord, why cannot I follow Thee now? I will lay down my life for Thy sake.' Peter therefore must learn, as we also, by painful experience, what he might have understood even better by subjection of heart, in faith, to the Lord's words. When He warns, it is rash and wrong for us to question; and rashness of spirit is but the precursor of a fall in fact, whereby we must be taught, if we refuse otherwise" (Bible Treasury)

"Jesus answered him, Wilt thou lay down thy life for My sake? Verily, verily, I say unto thee, The cock shall not crow, till thou hast denied Me thrice" (v. 38). Once more the Lord manifests His omniscience, this time by foretelling the fall of one of His own. Utterly unlikely did it seem that a real believer would deny his Lord, and not only so, but at once follow it up with further denials. Little likelihood did there appear that one who was so devoted to Christ, who had enjoyed such unspeakable privileges, and who was expressly warned that he should "watch and pray *lest* ye enter into temptation," should prove so unworthy. Yet incredible as it might appear to the Eleven the Lord foresaw it all, and here definitely announces the fearful sin of Peter. He knew that so far from Peter laying down his life for His sake, he would that very night try to save his own life, by a cowardly denial that he was His disciple. And yet the Lord did not cast him off. He loved even Peter "unto the end," and after His resurrection sought him out and restored him to fellowship again. Truly such love passeth knowledge. O that we were so fully absorbed with it that, for very shame, we might be withheld from doing anything that would grieve it.

The following questions are to help the students to prepare for the lesson on the first section of John 14:—

1. What is meant by *"Believe* also in Me" v. 1?
2. What is meant by the "Father's House" v. 2?
3. How is Christ "preparing a place for us" v. 3?
4. What is meant by "the way" v. 4?
5. What did Philip mean v. 8?
6. How did the disciples see the Father in Christ v. 9?
7. What "works' sake" did Christ refer to in v. 11?

—*Arthur W. Pink.*

GLEANINGS IN EXODUS

23. *The Manna a type of Christ. Ex.* 16.

In our last paper we considered the "manna" with which Jehovah supplied the bodily need of Israel in the wilderness as a type of the Food which God had so graciously provided for the sustenance of our souls. That Food is His own blessed Word. But "the Word" is used both of the Scriptures and of the Lord Jesus Christ. The two are most intimately related. "In the volume of the Book," said Christ, "it is written of *Me*" (Psl. 40:7); and again, "Search the Scriptures . . . they are they which testify *of Me*" (John 5:39). Almost everything that can be postulated of the one can be predicted of the other. But the chief value of the written Word is to set forth the perfections and bring us into communion with the incarnate Word. It is only as we feed upon *Christ Himself* that we truly feed upon the written Word. Therefore in this article we shall confine our attention to the manna typifying the person and perfections of the Lord Jesus Christ.

Beneath many a figure and behind innumerable shadows and symbols the anointed eye may discern the glories of our blessed Lord. It should be our chief delight as we read the O.T. Scriptures to prayerfully search for that which foreshadows Him of whom "Moses and the prophets" did write. All doubt is removed as to whether or not the manna pointed to the incarnate Son by His own words in John 6:32, 33. There we find the Saviour saying, "Verily, verily, I say unto you, Moses gave you not that bread from Heaven; but My Father giveth you the true Bread from Heaven. For the Bread of God is He which cometh down from Heaven and giveth life unto the world." May the Spirit of God now condescend to open our sin-blinded eyes as we earnestly desire to behold "wondrous things" out of His perfect Law.

1. *The Occasion of the giving of the Manna* is both striking and solemn. After being the recipients of wondrous mercies from the Lord, Israel arrived in the Wilderness of Sin. But no sooner had they come thither than we find that the whole congregation of the children of Israel *murmured* against Moses and Aaron, saying, "Would to God we had died by the hand of the Lord in the land of Egypt, when we sat by the flesh-pots, and when we did eat bread to the full; for ye have brought us forth into this wilderness, to kill this whole assembly with hunger" (v. 3). A more fearful exhibition of unbelief, ingratitude, and rebellion could scarcely be imagined. The marvel is that the fiery judgments of God did not consume them there and then. But instead of pouring upon them His wrath, He dealt with them in marvellous grace by raining bread from Heaven for them.

Strikingly does this picture the condition of that world into which the Lord of Glory descended. For four thousand years the temporal and governmental mercies of God had been showered upon the human race, making His sun to rise on the evil and on the good, sending His rain on the just and the unjust (Matt. 5:45). And what had been man's response? "When they knew God, they glorified Him not as God, neither were they thankful; but became vain in their imaginations, and their foolish heart was darkened. Professing themselves to be wise, they became fools, and changed the glory of the uncorruptible God into an image made like to corruptible man, and to birds, and to four-footed beasts, and creeping things" (Rom. 1:21-23). Little better was it with Israel, as a glance at their O.T. history will show. What wonder, then, if God had abandoned the whole race! But no; in matchless, wondrous grace, He sent forth His own beloved Son to a world wherein every human creature had forfeited every possible claim upon His goodness and mercy.

2. *The Place where the Manna fell* is also deeply significant. It was in the "Wilderness of Sin" (16:1) that the "bread from Heaven" first fell. Surely it were impossible to select a more fitting title to accurately describe the character of that world into which the Son of God descended. Verily, a *wilderness of sin* was this world to the Holy One of God! A *wilderness!* What is a "wilderness"? It is a *homeless* place. No one would think of building a house there. And a homeless place was this world to the Son of God. No room in the inn at His birth; not where to lay His head during the days of His public ministry; a borrowed grave for His crucified body, sums it all up. A wilderness *of sin!* Never was that more apparent than when the Sinless One was here. How the Light exposed the hidden things of darkness! How the murder of the Saviour demonstrated the sinfulness of Jew and Gentile alike!

3. *The Glory of the Lord was linked with the giving of the Manna.* "And it came to pass as Aaron spake unto the whole congregation of the children of Israel that they looked toward the wilderness, and, behold, *the glory* of the Lord appeared in the Cloud" (v. 10). This is very striking indeed. It is the *first time* we read of the appearing of "the glory of the Lord," not only in connection with Israel, but in Scripture. Marvellously accurate is this detail of our type. Not until the Son of God became incarnate was "the glory of the Lord" fully revealed. But when the eternal Word became flesh and tabernacled among men, then, as the beloved apostle declares, "We beheld His *glory, the glory* as of the Only-begotten of the Father" (John 1:14). The "glory of God" is seen *"in the face of Jesus Christ"* (2 Cor. 4:6).

4. *The Manna came down from Heaven.* "Then said the Lord unto Moses, Behold I will rain bread from Heaven for you." The manna was not a product of this earth. It grew neither in the wilderness nor in Egypt. It was neither produced by human efforts nor manufactured by human skill. It descended from God. It was a gift from Heaven come down to earth. So our Lord Jesus was no native product of this earth. As we read in Eph. 4:10, "He that *descended* is the same also that ascended up far above all heavens." The first man (Adam) was of the earth, earthy; but the second Man (Jesus Christ) was "The Lord from Heaven" (1 Cor. 15:48).

5. *The Manna was a free gift from God.* "And Moses said unto them, This is the bread which the Lord hath *given* you to eat" (v. 15). No charge was made for this manna. It was neither a wage to be earned nor a prize to be won, but was a token of God's grace and love. No payment was demanded for it. It was without money and without price. "For God so loved the world that He *gave His only begotten Son,* that whosoever believeth in Him should not perish, but have everlasting life" (John 3:16). Let us join with the apostle in saying, "Thanks be unto God for His unspeakable Gift" (2 Cor. 9:15).

6. *The Manna was sent to the Israelites.* "Behold I will rain bread from Heaven *for you;* and *the people* shall go out and gather a certain rate every day" (v. 4). Two truths are here illustrated. First, the Manna was God's provision for His elect people, and for none others. We do not read of God raining manna upon Egypt nor upon Canaan. It was given to Israel in the wilderness and to them alone, just as the Pascal lamb was for them and not for the Egyptians. So, too, Christ is God's Provision for those whom He "ordained unto eternal life." Listen to His own words in John 17:19: "For *their sakes* I sanctify Myself"—set Myself apart unto death. It was for "the sheep," not the goats, that He gave His life (John 10:11).

But second, this manna was also sent to a needy and foodless people. Whatever food Israel had brought with them out of Egypt was, by this time, all consumed. From the human side, they seemed in imminent danger of starving to death. Had not God met their need they *would* have perished in the wilderness. But from the Divine side everything was sure. God had purposed to bring Israel to Sinai (3.12), and His counsel cannot fail. A complete provision did He make for His needy people. It is the same now. By nature, the elect of God are "children of wrath, even as others" (Eph. 2.3). Shapen in iniquity and conceived in sin, their lot is indeed a desperate one. But praise be to God, full provision is made for them. The Bread of Life is their all-sufficient supply. Even before His birth it was announced, "Thou shalt call His name Jesus, *for* He shall *His people* from their sins" (Matt. 1:21).

7. *The Manna came right down to where the Israelites were.* The Israelites were in immediate danger of starving to death, but as we have seen, God graciously made provision to supply their need and now we would notice that no long journey had to be taken in order to secure that which would satisfy their hunger—the manna fell all around the camp. "And in the morning the dew lay *round about the host*; and when the dew that lay was gone up, behold, upon the face of the wilderness there lay a small round thing" (vv. 13, 14). Here we have foreshadowed the blessed fact that, to the sinner conscious of his need and anxious to meet with the Saviour, God says, "Say not in thine heart Who shall ascend into Heaven? (that is to bring Christ down from above) or, Who shall descend into the deep? (that is, to bring Christ again from the dead). But what saith it? *The Word is nigh thee.*" And out of this very nearness springs the sinner's responsibility. All around each tent door lay the manna. Something had to be done with it. It must either be gathered or trodden under foot! Sinner, what are you doing with the Christ of God? Remember His searching words, "He that is not with Me is against Me."

8. *The Manna must be gathered by each individual.* "This is the thing which the Lord hath commanded, Gather of it *every man* according to his eating" (v. 16). It is so spiritually. Receiving Christ (John 1:12) is a personal matter. No one can believe for another. There is no salvation by proxy. The gospel of Christ is, "the power of God unto salvation to *every one that believeth*" (Rom. 1:16), and "he that believeth not shall be damned" (Mark 16:16). Saving faith is that act whereby each awakened sinner appropriates Christ unto himself. It is true that Christ loved the Church as a whole, and gave Himself for *it* (Eph. 5:25), but it is also the happy privilege of each member of that Church to say with the Apostle Paul, "Who loved *me* and gave Himself for *me*" (Gal. 2:20). Have *you*, dear reader, believed on the Lord Jesus Christ?

9. *The Manna met a daily need.* "Then said the Lord unto Moses, Behold, I will rain bread from heaven for you; and the people shall go out and gather a certain rate *every day*" (v. 4). The manna which they gathered to-day would not suffice them for to-morrow. They needed to obtain a fresh supply each day. It is just here that so many of the Lord's people fail. We, too, need to feed upon Christ "*every* day." Just as in the physical realm the food which I ate yesterday will not nourish me to-day, so my past experiences and attainments will not meet the exigencies of the present. Christ must be kept constantly before the heart. "Give us day by day our *daily bread,*" should be the prayer of every child of God.

10. *Appetite determined the amount gathered.* "This is the thing which the Lord hath commanded. Gather of it every man according to his eating, an omer for every man, according to the number of your persons take ye every man for them which are in his tents. And the children of Israel did so and gathered, some *more*, some *less*" (vv. 16, 17). Thus we see that the appetite governed the amount gathered. How strikingly and how solemnly true is this of the believer, "We all have as much of Christ as we desire, no more, no less. If our desires are large, if we open our mouth wide, He will fill it. We cannot desire too much, nor be disappointed when we desire. On the other hand, if we are but feebly conscious of our need, a little only of Christ will be supplied. The measure, therefore, in which we feed upon Christ as our wilderness food, depends entirely upon our felt spiritual need—upon our affections" (Ed. Dennett).

11. *The Manna was despised by those who were not the Lord's people.* "And the mixt multitude that was among them fell a lusting, and the children of Israel also went again, and said, Who shall give us flesh to eat? We remember the fish, which we did eat in Egypt freely; the cucumbers, and the melons, and the leeks, and the onions, and the garlic. But now our soul is dried away; there is nothing left at all, beside this manna, before our eyes" (Num. 11:4-6). How these words remind us of the language of Isa. 53—"And when we shall see Him there is no beauty that we should desire of Him. He is despised and rejected of men." The sin-blinded eyes of the natural man are incapable of perceiving the attractiveness of the Lord Jesus; His wondrous perfections

he is unable to discern. So, too, he sees not his deep need, and how Christ alone is able to meet that need. Hence he neither comes to Christ nor desires Him.

12. *The Manna fell upon the dew, not upon the dust of the ground.* "And when the dew fell upon the camp in the night, the manna fell *upon it*" (Num. 11:9). Everything in the Scriptures has a spiritual meaning and application. What, then, is the significance of the above? Gen. 3:19 throws light on this passage—"dust thou art and unto dust thou shalt return." These words were spoken to fallen man and called attention to the corruption which sin had worked in him. "Dust," here, and onwards, speaks of *fallen humanity.* Now the manna *fell* not upon "the dust," but upon the dew. How clearly this foreshadowed the uniqueness and incorruptibility of our Lord's humanity! The Word became flesh, but in His humanity the Lord Jesus shared not our corrupt nature. He took upon Him the form of a servant, but the body which was prepared for Him (Heb. 10:5) belonged not to the "dust" of this earth. Before He was born the angel announced unto His mother, "The Holy Spirit shall come upon thee and the power of the Highest shall overshadow thee: therefore also that *holy thing* which shall be born of thee shall be called the Son of God" (Luke 1:35).

13. *The Manna was white in colour.* We read in Ex. 16:31, "And the house of Israel called the name thereof manna; and it was like coriander seed, *white.*" This speaks of the spotless purity of our Lord as manifested outwardly in His daily walk. He "knew no sin" (2 Cor. 5:21). "He was without sin" (Heb. 4:15). "He did no sin" (1 Pt. 2:22). He was "holy, harmless, undefiled, *separate from sinners*" (Heb. 7:26). In 1 Peter 1:19 we are told that He was a lamb "without spot and without blemish." The former expression referring to the absence of outward pollution, the latter to the absence of inward defect. In His walk through this scene of corrupiton He contracted no defilement. He only could touch the leper without becoming contaminated. He was "without spot," pure, white.

14. *The Manna was sweet to the taste.* "And the taste of it was like wafers of honey" (v. 31). We need to go to the Song of Solomon for the interpretation of this. There we read, "As the apple tree among the trees of the wood, so is my Beloved among the sons. I sat down under His shadow with great delight, and His fruit was *sweet* to my taste" (2:3). And again, "His cheeks are as a bed of spices, as *sweet* flowers; His lips like lillies, dropping *sweet* smelling myrrh . . . . His mouth is *most sweet;* yea, He is altogether lovely" (5:13, 16). The Lord grant that *our* "meditation of Him shall be sweet" (Psl. 104:34).

15. *The Manna was ground and baked.* "And the people went about and gathered it, and *ground it* in mills, or *beat* it in a mortar, and *baked* it in pans, and made cakes of it" (Num. 11:8). How this speaks to us of the *sufferings* of our blessed Lord! Such expressions as "He groaned for their hardness of heart," He "sighed" because of their unbelief, He "wept" over Jerusalem, and many others, tell of the *grinding* of the manna. His treatment at the hands of the Jews and the brutal soldiers in Herod's judgment-hall show us the *beating* of the manna. On the Cross we behold Him subjected to the fierce *fires* of God's wrath. Thus we learn that the manna, ground and beaten, speaks to us of Him who "was *bruised* for our iniquities."

16. *The Manna was preserved on the Sabbath.* "And he said unto them, This is that which the Lord hath said, to-morrow is the rest of the holy Sabbath unto the Lord, bake that which ye will bake, and seeth that ye will seeth, and that which remaineth over, lay up for you *to be kept until the morning.* And they laid it up till the morning, as Moses bade; and it did not stink, neither was there any worm therein" (vv. 23, 24). On the Sabbath day the manna was preserved, and in this, too, it speaks to us of our blessed Lord. He is the only one who was preserved through death. He lay in the tomb on the Sabbath day and was "kept," for God had said, "Neither wilt Thou suffer Thine Holy One *to see corruption*" (Psl. 16:10).

17. *The Manna was laid up before the Lord.* "And Moses said unto Aaron, Take a pot and put an omer full of manna therein, and lay it up before the Lord (v. 33). Concerning the anti-type, we read, "For Christ is not entered into the holy place made with hands which are the figures of the true; but into Heaven itself, now to appear in the presence of God for us" (Heb. 9:24). The golden pot in which the manna was preserved tells of how God is glorified in Him whom it foreshadowed. "Although the Son of Man it is that gives it to us; although it is humanity here that we know, and humanity in the form in which we shall not find it when we shall reach Him above, yet it *is* humanity in which God is glorified now, and so He will be glorified in it forever. We shall find in the One upon the Throne of Glory, though no longer 'with a face marred more than any man's,' and a form more than the sons of men—the very One whose face

was marred—the very One whose heart put Him into the sorrow in which we, of necessity there, learned to know Him thus" (Mr. Grant).

18. *The Manna is called angel's food.* We read in Psl. 78:25, man did eat *angel's* food; He gave them meat to the full"; the reference here is to the giving of the manna to Israel in the wilderness. The anti-type of this is brought before us in several passages in the last book of Scripture. Christ not only feeds the souls of those of His people who are upon earth, but He also satisfies the hearts of celestial beings. The unfallen angels find their chief delight in feeding upon Christ. They worship Him, they serve Him, and they tell forth His praises.

19. *The Manna was given in the night.* It was during the hours of darkness that the manna was sent to the Israelites. It is while they were asleep (picture of man's helplessness, for we are never so helpless as when we are asleep) that the bread was given from Heaven. So, too, it was when we were in darkness and unbelie. impotent, "without strength," that Christ came to us. Moreover, it will be at the close of this world's night, when "the darkness shall cover the earth, and gross darkness the people," that the Bread of God shall return and give Life to the world.

20. *The Manna is now hidden.* In Rev. 2:17 we read, "To him that overcometh will I give to eat of the hidden manna." So, too, Christ, of whom the manna continually speaks, is now "hidden." Unseen by the eye of sense, He remains in Heaven till that day when He shall be manifested before all the world. "We shall not only 'see' the Heavenly manna, but we shall 'eat' of it again. Fresher than ever will be our realisation of His love and the perfection of the grace which is manifested toward us. It is then in fact, when we come to be there, that we shall have the full enjoyment; knowing as we are known, of all the experiences, which though they be experiences of the wilderness, yet, wait for the land to which we are hastening to find their full interpretation and blessing. The meat *endures* to everlasting life. The meat itself endures. We are enjoying that which shall be our joy for eternity. We are feeding on that which shall be our food for eternity" (Mr. Grant).

We are conscious that our treatment of this wonderful and precious type is most inadequate and unworthy. But if it leads our fellow-believers to a more careful study of the written Word, and to a deeper longing to become better acquainted with the incarnate Word, our feeble efforts will be well repaid.

—*Arthur W. Pink.*

AN EXPOSITION OF LUKE 15

The fifteenth of Luke is comparatively well known to those who attend church and to those who read the Bible. Probably it is preached from more frequently than any other chapter in that Gospel. It contains the parable of the lost sheep, the lost coin, and the lost son. Yet, familiar as are its contents, there are quite a few details in it which puzzle many of the Lord's people. Who are pictured by the ninety and nine sheep that went not astray? Who is represented by the woman that searched for the lost piece of silver? Whom does the prodigal son stand for, a lost sinner or a backsliding believer? And what character is pictured by the elder son? Few can give definite and satisfactory answers to these questions.

Before we begin our exposition of this truly wondrous chapter, perhaps we had better first anticipate and remove an objection. What is before us in Luke 15 is one of the *parables* of Christ. Now there are not a few who entertain very inadequate and erroneous conceptions of the parables. They say, "O that is *only* a parable!" They argue that we must not build anything on "a *mere* parable." Thus they imply that the parables are less reliable, less authoritative, or less explicit than the other teachings of Christ. But several considerations should at once show how dishonouring is such a view.

First, the fact that *so much* of the recorded teaching of Christ is in the form of parables should at once warm us against adopting a principle that would lead us to set aside or treat as of secondary importance such a large part of the Gospels.

Second, what are many of the Old Testament *types* but parables in action? Yet no one with spiritual discernment disparages *their* importance and value. While it is true that the types are only to be understood in the light of New Testament teaching, yet how often they amplify and magnify that teaching!

Third, the value of His parables was forever established in the *interpretation* which Christ Himself gave of the "Sower" and of the "Tares" (see Matt. 13). In His exposition of these two parables the Lord showed that *every detail* had a meaning, thus warning us that we should be the losers if we imagined that the minor points were without definite significance. It is with the settled conviction that everything in Luke 15 has a Divine meaning and message that we now approach it.

In order to obtain the correct interpretation of any parable due attention must be paid to the same laws which determine the sound exposition of any other portion of Scripture. There are certain principles—elementary yet fundamental—which *must* be observed if we are to intelligently approach the study of any passage in God's Word. We cannot expect to understand the *details* of any verses until we ask and answer the following questions: *To whom* was this passage addressed—Jews or Gentiles, unsaved, or saved people? Under what *circumstances* was it uttered, what was the *occasion?* What was the *central design* or purpose of the utterance? What are its main *divisions?* Careful attention must be paid to the context and setting of the passage about to be studied, and especially close heed given to the opening verses.

If the reader will examine the first four verses of Luke 15 he will there find the answers to these preliminary questions. What is recorded in Luke 15 was not spoken by Christ to His disciples, but was *addressed to His enemies.* The *occasion* when Christ uttered these words was the "murmuring" of the Pharasees and Scribes because He received sinners: the parable Which follows being His reply to their unfriendly criticism. The purpose of His discourse was twofold: A expose the condition of their hearts, and to manifest the grace of God's heart. The main *divisions* of the chapter are indicated in verses 4, 8, II.

In what followed, Christ did two things. First he showed the true spiritual state of His carping critics; second, He made known the *ground* on which He received sinners into fellowship with Himself. His object was a double one: to disclose the unsaved condition of His self-righteous opponents, and to reveal the Divine operations which issue in the salvation of the sinner. The first object is accomplished by drawing a picture of those who condemned Him; the second was achieved by giving us a blessed portrayal of the activities of Divine grace. The important thing to note is that in v.\3 we are told, "He spake this parable unto *them,"* i.e., the Pharisees and Scribes.

Here, then, is the solution to the details in this chapter which have puzzled so many—Who are represented by the ninety-nine sheep that went not astray (v. 4), and whom Christ interprets as "just persons who need no repentance" (v. 7)? Who is pictured by the "elder son"—who was "angry" and who refused to "go in" (v. 28) when he learned of the cordial welcome his dissolute brother had received—of whom the father said, "Son, thou art ever with me, and all that I have is thine" (v. 31). Wild are the conjectures which have been indulged and varied are the interpretations which have been given, due to the failure of the commentators to heed the context and observe the scope of the passage.

In the ninety-nine sheep Christ portrays the *self-righteous* Pharisees. He terms them "sheep," not because they were really so, but because this was what they claimed to be: He designated them according to their own *profession,* just as the wise *and* the foolish are *all* termed "virgins" in Matt. 25, and just as those who deserted Him (John 6:66) are called "disciples." The important point to note is the *place* occupied by these ninety-nine "sheep." Mark carefully *where* Christ represented them as dwelling—"in the wilderness." A certain hymn which has been popular for years past reads, "There were ninety and nine that safely lay in the shelter of the fold," but, like many another popular hymn, this one will not stand the test of Holy Scripture. The deplorable thing is that to-day so many church-goers derive their theology from the hymn-book instead of from God's Word. No, these ninety-nine sheep instead of being safe in the fold of God, were out yonder in the *wilderness*—the place of desolation and death. This was precisely the place occupied by the self-righteous Pharisees. *Externally* considered they might dwell in Jerusalem and be regular attenders at the Temple, but *spiritually* their lives were barren, accurately represented by "the wilderness."

In the second section of our chapter the hypocritical Pharisees and Scribes are looked at under the figure of coins—*inanimate* objects - which fitly described their spiritual deadness, "alienated from the life of God' (Eph 4:18). It is significant to notice the repeated nines-ninetynine sheep and nine pieces of silver-for in Scripture nine is the number which stands for Divine *judgment.* but it is "in the elder son" that we have the fullest description of the Pharisee. Seven details are given, each of which clearly *identifies* the one who is there depicted.

First, his *position*: "now his elder son

was *in the field*" (v. 25), he was *outside* the "father's house." This is parallel with "the wilderness" in v. 4. More especially, the "field" stands for the *world*—"the field is the world" (Matt. 13:38).

Second, his *ignorance* is exposed: "he heard music and dancing, and he called one of the servants, and *asked* what these things meant" (v. 26). He was a stranger to the joy of the Father's House! Such is the heart-condition of the modern Pharisees: theirs is a joyless religion—the performance of irksome duty, going the weary round of their self-imposed pious performances.

Third, the *enmity* of his carnal mind is displayed: "he was angry and would not go in" (v. 28). Not only was he a stranger to spiritual merriment, but he was incensed against the happiness of the returned prodigal. How clearly this indicated *who is* in view here: it is just what we have at the beginning of the chapter—the Pharisees and Scribes *murmuring* because Christ *received* sinners and *ate* with them! Further, the elder son *refused* to enter—"he would not go in." This was the very attitude of Christ's critics: they scorned the bounties of the Gospel-feast which was spread by Him. And how like the formalists and ritualists of to-day—serving God with their hands, but their hearts far from Him!

Fourth, his *legality* was evidenced: "Lo, these many years do I serve thee" (v 29). Surely this is sufficient to remove all doubt as to who is in view here. The cold-heartedness of the legalist is at once apparent. There is no devotion to the "Father" expressed, no gratitude, no love, nothing but the "I *serve* thee" of the merit-monger. Working for a wage was all that he knew.

Fifth, his *self-righteousness* was displayed: "neither transgressed I at any time Thy commandment" (v. 29). This proud boast at once calls to mind the language of another *Pharisee*—"God, I thank Thee, that I am not as other men, extortioners, unjust, adulterers," etc. (Luke 18:11). The same spirit of self-complacency is found in the sacerdotalists and sacramentarians to-day.

Sixth, his lack of *communion* was pointed out: "and yet thou never gavest me a kid, that I might merry with my friends" (v. 29). How his language betrayed him! The "kid" for feasting on, speaks of communion. Note, he did not say, "that I might make merry with *Thee*." He was a stranger to the Father! To have fellowship with his "friends" was his highest thought.

Seventh, his *hatred of free grace* comes out in his complaint against the "father" for the welcome accorded the prodigal: "But as soon as this thy son was come, which hath devoured they living with harlots, thou hast killed for him the fatted calf" (v. 30). He was indignant that he, with his punctillious service and flawless deportment, should have no place at the feast, whilst the profligate wanderer from the far-country should be treated so royally. Ah, the self-righteous religionist is still ignorant of the marvellous and measureless grace of God: not feeling his need of it, he is quite unable to appreciate its blessedness; yea, he rants against it.

The closing words of the chapter are to be interpreted in the light of all that has gone before. Just as in the earlier part of the parable the Lord referred to the Pharisees and Scribes as "sheep," so here He speaks of them according to their own haughty but vain pretentions. *"Thou* art ever with me, and all that I have is *thine,"* is parallel with "just persons who need no repentance." Such was *their* estimate of themselves. How false this was is seen from the fact that, in truth, they were, "in the wilderness," *outside* of the "father's" house!

The second great object of Christ in this discourse was to answer the charge which His detractors had brought against Him (v. 2), and to make known the *ground* on which sinners *were* received. This is developed in His teaching upon the lost sheep, the lost coin, and the lost son putting the three together we have a marvellously comprehensive portrayal the salvation of the sinner.

It is important to note that Luke 15 does not contain three parables, as is commonly supposed, but instead, one parable in three parts. In v.3 we are told, "And He spake *this parable* unto them." This parable as, a whole, and in its several parts, describes both the Divine and the human sides of salvation, and much is lost by failing to discern its unbroken unity. The parable give us a most blessed portrayal of the concern and actions of each of the three Persons of the Godhead, and just as God is *One*, one God revealed in three Persons, so Luke 15 contains one parable, but in three parts.

In the third part of the parable we see a lost sinner reconciled, *coming* into the presence of the Father, given a loving welcome, and accorded a place at His table. But it is to be carefully noted that *this* comes in the *last* section of the parable. In the first two sections we are shown what takes place *before* the sinner becomes conscious of his need, what it is that *causes* him to say, "I will arise and go unto my Father, and say unto Him, Father, I have sinned," etc. In other words, the opening parts of Luke 15 set forth the *Divine* side—the activities of God's grace—whilst the last section shows us the human side—the *effects* and *results* of those Divine operations.

"What man of you, having an hundred sheep, if he lose one of them, doth not leave the ninety and nine in the wilderness and go after that which is lost, until he find it?" (v. 4). How blessed it is to note the point at which Christ commenced this parable. He *began* by presenting to us the Person and Work of the Good Shepherd! Here is the Divine foundation on which our salvation rests. Here is the basis of our reconciliation with God. Here is what made possible a place at the Father's table. Here is the resting-place for our guilt-burdened conscience—the work of Christ for poor lost sinners. As we study vv. 4 to 7 we discover seven different points about the Good Shepherd in relation to His sheep.

First, Christ is presented as the *Owner* of the sheep: "What man of you *having* an hundred sheep?" Even the ninety-nine belong to Christ by virtue of the fact that He *created* them (John 1:3, Col. 1:16). But the one sheep that is "lost," which He seeks and finds, is His in a double sense: His not only by creation, but His also by donation, His by the Father's gift before the foundation of the world. It is *this* which makes the lost sheep so precious in His eyes, this which causes Him to *"leave* the ninety and nine in the wilderness" and go after the one. Very striking and most blessed is this: the sheep which He secured was His even *before* it was "lost"!

The same precious truth is expressed in those words of Christ in John 10:16. At the end of v. 15 He said, "I lay down My life for the sheep," i.e., God's elect among the Jews (contrast v. 26), and then He went on to say, "And other sheep I have." These *"other* sheep" were God's elect scattered among the Gentiles. And mark it well, the Lord Jesus did not here say, "and other sheep I *shall* have," but "other sheep I *have*"—they were His even then, His because given to Him by the Father before the foundation of the world. Many are the scriptures which speak of this: "That He should give eternal life to as many as Thou hast *given Him*" (John 17:2). "I have manifested Thy Name unto the men which *Thou gavest Me* out of the world" (John 17:6). "I pray not for the world, but for *them which Thou hast given Me*" (John 17:9). Comforting truth is this to the saint of God. Hated doctrine by present-day Pharisees!

Second, Christ *seeks* His sheep: "and go after that which is lost." How much is covered by this one short sentence? It speaks of that wondrous condescension of the Son of God when He laid aside His outward majesty (John 17:5), and took upon Him the form of a servant (Phil. 2:6). It involved that marvellous stoop from Heaven's glory to Bethlehem's manger. It covered the whole of His blessed earth-life of humiliation, when He had not where to lay His head. How these words, "And *go after* that which is lost," remind us of another of His precious utterances: "The Son of Man is come to *seek* and to save that which was lost" (Luke 19:10). Blessed quest! Gracious search! The sheep did not return to the Shepherd so the Shepherd seeks out His sheep. So it was God who sought out Abraham (Acts 7:2), and not Abraham who sought God. It was God who sought Jacob (Gen. 28:13), not Jacob who sought God. It was God who sought Moses (Ex. 3:2), and not Moses who sought God. Equally so, Christian reader, it was God who sought thee, and not you that sought God (Rom. 3:11).

Third, the *patient grace* and *success* of the Shepherd is announced: "until He find it." Nothing could deter or dishearten the Shepherd. His descent from Heaven to earth might be unappreciated; despised and rejected of men though He were, yet this did not cause Him to abandon His mission of grace. Very blessed, yet unspeakably solemn are these words, "until He find it." To find His sheep the Shepherd had to go to where they were. And where was that? It was the place of condemnation, the place of alienation, the place of death. To find His sheep our blessed Saviour had to go to Calvary, and there be made a curse for us. It is the *Cross* which is in view then in this third point. How Christ must have valued those sheep to have gone *there* to find them! And *why* did He thus value the sheep? Not because of any excellency in them, but because they were His Father's love-gift to Him! It is not the intrinsic worth of the present which makes us prize it so highly, but the love we have for the One who made it. So with Christ and those given to Him by the Father.

Fourth, next we are told of the *tender care* of the Saviour for His own: "When He hath found it, He layeth it on His shoulders" (v. 5). When Christ finds His sheep, He does not *drive* it before Him, nor does He *entrust* it to the care of someone else. He lays it upon His own shoulders. I suppose that one of the first pictures we recall, as we look back to the days of our childhood, is that of Christ as the Good Shepherd carrying a lamb in His arms. But observe how it is put in our parable: "He layeth it on His shoulders": mark the plural number. In Isaiah 9:6 we are told that when He comes back to earth "the government shall be upon His shoulder." One shoulder is sufficient to sustain the government of the world, but both shoulders are engaged when He finds His sheep! The "shoulder" is the place of strength, and "shoulders" here indicates the *security* of the sheep.

Fifth, next we are told of the Shepherd's *satisfaction*: "He layeth it on His shoulders, *rejoicing*." Very wonderful is this, that He, the Self-sufficient One, should "rejoice" over *us!* This is one of the blessed truths of Divine revelation which none of us had ever discovered for himself. A rejoicing saint who learns to know the Saviour is readily comprehended, but that Christ should find cause of rejoicing in me "passeth knowledge." Yet thus it is. The "pearl" was of "great price" in the estimation of Him who sought and bought it! The same truth is expressed in Heb. 12:2, "Who for *the joy* that was set before Him endured the Cross." Was not that "joy" the Saviour's anticipation of the success of His mission, His looking forward to the time when His redeemed shall be with Him forever! Yes, He shall yet "see of the travail of His soul and be *satisfied*."

Sixth, "And when He cometh Home." This tells of the happy *issue*, the triumphant conclusion of the Saviour's gracious quest. He not only seeks and finds the sheep, He not only lays it upon His shoulders, but He conducts it safely Home. Thank God for *bringing* grace: "other sheep I have . . . . them also I must bring" (John 10:16). The Jewish "Bride" will yet say (and by application the members of Christ's body may now say), "He *brought* me to the banqueting-house, and His banner over me was love (S. of S. 2:4). It is blessed to see how Christ here speaks of heaven as Home. "Home" is the place of separation from the world, the place of seclusion, of rest, of joy, of companionship, of fellowship with those we love best.

Seventh, "And when He cometh Home He calleth together His friends and neighbours, saying unto them, Rejoice with Me, for I have found my sheep which was lost" (v. 6). Very blessed is this. How it reveals the Saviour's heart—He *shares* His own joy with others! And who is represented by His "friends and neighbours?" His "friends" are His own people (John 15:15), now in the Home above. Those who have been taken to Heaven are blissfully ignorant of what transpires in this world of sin and sorrow. But there is one blessed exception to this: Every time a sheep of Christ is saved on earth the glad tidings of this is communicated to those who have gone on before. The "neighbours," a term pointing to a less intimate relation than "friends," are the angels of God. They, too, rejoice as they see filled the vacancies in Heaven left by the angels which sinned—filled with redeemed sinners from among men.

In the second division of the parable (vv. 8-10), we have depicted *the work of the Holy Spirit* in our salvation. Before we take this up in detail, let it be pointed out that the *place* occupied by the "woman" seeking and finding the lost coin, at once fixes the interpretation. What we have here *follows* the gracious activities of the Shepherd, and *precedes* the prodigal's turning unto the Father. Thus, it is clearly the operations of the Spirit which are in view: *His* ministry is based upon the work of Christ, and is *the cause* which produces convertion. That which is before us here is deeply important and calls for some general observations ere we turn to the exposition of our passage.

Even where preachers are more or less sound on the atoning-death of Christ as the alone ground of acceptance before God, the utmost confusion prevails concerning *the work of the Holy Spirit*. How few there are who recognise the fact that if God had done nothing more than give His beloved Son to die for sinners, not one had ever been saved: that if He did nothing more than send the Gospel to us, all would be in vain: that if He simply proposed to us, every man would spurn His offer: that if He merely invited us to be saved, all would reject. How few perceive that God Himself must commence, continue and complete—that "salvation is *of the Lord*" (Jonah 2:9) from start to finish.

Three things were absolutely essential for the salvation of any sinner. First, God the Father had to *purpose* his salvation, for nothing ever comes to pass without His foreordination. Second, God the Son had to *purchase* his salvation, for none is ever delivered apart from His redemption. Third, God the Spirit had to *effect* his salvation, for no one ever passes from death unto life apart from His quickening operation. The Spirit *applies* the value and virtue of the atoning-sacrifice of Christ in His regenerating activities. The Holy Spirit is here to glorify an absent Saviour, and this He does by making alive spiritually those for whom Christ died.

But where does "believing" come in? Rather let us ask, *When* is it that the sinner believes? We answer, *After* he has been *awakened* from the sleep of death, *after* he has been *convicted* of his lost condition, *after* he has been enabled to *see* his need of the Saviour. And when is this? After the Holy Spirit has "begun a good work *in*" him (Phil. 1:6), after he has been "born of the Spirit." It is not till the *third* part of the parable in Luke 15 that we are shown a sinner saying "I will arise and go to my Father, and will say unto Him, Father, I have sinned." *Before* this, is the second part of the parable, which depicts the Work of the Holy Spirit, showing us—as cause stands to effect—*what* it is which *produces* this happy issue. Many are the Scriptures which teach that regeneration *precedes* a sinner's believing in Christ.

Take first the parable of the Sower. In it Christ portrays the results of the sowing of the Seed, which is the Word. He likens the *hearts* of the different ones to whom the Word comes to various types of soil. He divides them into four classes: the wayside-hearers, where the ground is so hard that the Seed finds no lodging-place; the stony-ground-hearers, where the soil is so shallow the Seed takes no root; the thorny-ground-hearers where the Seed is choked; the good-ground-hearers where fruit *is produced*. The first three yielded no harvest; the fourth did. Why? Not because a different Seed was sown in this last case, but because a different soil received it. Those who bore fruit are termed "good-ground" hearers. And who are they? Which among the sons of men have "good" hearts? None by nature! Only those who have been *given* "a new heart" by God: in other words, only those who have been regenerated. "The preparations of the heart in man, and the answer of the tongue, is from the Lord" (Prov. 16:1). Here, then, is the Divine order: first, the impartation of a new heart (resulting in the "*good* ground"), and then "*receiving*" the Seed, "understanding" it, and "bearing fruit" (see Matt. 13:23).

Take the teaching of the New Testament concerning "eternal life." This is presented in two ways, according as it is approached from the standpoint of human responsibility or of God's sovereign grace. In John 3:15, 16, it is "whosoever believeth in Him (Christ) should not perish, but have eternal life." Here is the Gospel order, the addressing of man's accountability—it is his *duty* to "believe" in order to obtain "eternal life." But in this he utterly fails. So, again, in John 5:40, we find Christ saying, "Ye will not come to Me that ye *might have* life." Had they "come" life had been given them. But they did not, and would not. The fact is they *could not*, and yet they *ought* to have done so. Man's inability does not destroy his responsibility. Through Isaiah God said, "Hear ye deaf; and look, ye blind, that ye may see" (Isa. 42:18). Here God bids the "deaf" to *hear*, and the "blind" to *see*, which is the one thing they are *unable* to do. In like manner, He bids the unregenerate to "believe" that they may have "life," and this, because they are responsible so to do. God has not lost His right to demand because man has lost his power to perform. But there is another class of passages where "eternal" life" is presented not as something which all *need*, but as something which some actually *possess*. And these passages explicitly teach that eternal life is imparted *before* we believe. "He that believeth on the Son *hath* life" (John 3:36). The fact that he believes in Christ is the *proof* that he *has* eternal life: it is not that he has eternal life *because* he "believed." The very opposite is the case: He now "believes" because he *has* (by God's gift) eternal life. So, again, in John 5:24, "Verily, verily, I say unto you, He that heareth My Word, and believeth on Him that sent Me, *hath* (not "shall have") everlasting life," and shall not come into condemnation, but *is passed* from death unto life." The very fact that I have "heard" and "believed" is the *evidence* that I have *previously* passed from death unto life. Such, once more, is the teaching of 1 John 5:1, "whosoever believeth that Jesus is the Christ *is* (Greek 'has been') born of God." There cannot be the manifestation of life apart from the *presence* of life. Life must be imparted *before* there can be any activities of that life.

"You hath *He* quickened who were dead in trespasses and sins" (Eph. 2:1). Quickening, making alive, is the work *of God*. The sinner can no more quicken himself spiritually than a corpse can sit up in its coffin. Nor does the sinner *co-operate* with God in the work of regeneration, any more than he will in connection with his physical resurrection. To say that God regenerates in response to our faith is an absurdity, for if the natural man has repented and believed, wherein would lie the *need* for him to be born again? If the sinner has already perceived his deep need and has received Christ as his Saviour, then of what use is it to now "quicken" him? Why regenerate a *believer?* The truth is that God must first quicken him in order for him *to be* capable of believing.

Much confusion has been caused by failing to distinguish between regeneration and salvation . A sinner is not actually saved until he personally repents and believes. To the woman of Luke 7 Christ said, *"Thy faith* hath saved thee" (v. 50). To Bartimaeus, the erstwhile blind beggar, the Lord declared, "*thy* faith hath saved thee" (Luke 18:4). To the one who asked, "What must I do to be *saved?*" the apostles answered, "*Believe* on the Lord Jesus Christ, and thou shalt be saved (Acts 16:31). But a *dead* man cannot believe, and every descendent of fallen Adam is born into this world, "*alienated* from the *life* of God" (Eph. 4:18). Therefore, apart from the quickening operations of the Holy Spirit none would ever believe. A man must be born again *before* he can ever discern spiritual things: "Except a man be born again he *cannot see* the kingdom of God" (John 3:3). That is final.

The trouble with so many to-day is that their theology is derived from their *experiences* instead of from the Scriptures. They prefer to follow the testimony of their own hearts instead of the teaching of God's Word. The first thing of which the Christian became *conscious* was *his* sense of need, *his* realisation that he was a lost sinner, *his* crying unto God for mercy, *his* turning to Christ. And because he was *not conscious* of the quickening-work of the Spirit within him *before* he was ever awakened and convicted, he is very slow to allow the reality of it. But this ought not to be: to the Law and to the Testimony (Isa. 7:18) is the final court of appeal. Were we not alive physically (in the antenatal state) long before we had any consciousness of our existence! So it is spiritually: there must be life before there can be consciousness of that life.

The second part of this wondrous parable (vv. 8 to 10) of Luke 15 is still dealing with the Divine side of the sinner's salvation. Now, concerning God's operations, it needs to be said that none can know anything about them save what has been revealed in the Scriptures; and what is said there is addressed not to our senses, but to *faith.* Whenever we come to the Divine side of things we at once enter the realm of mystery, and therefore our urgent need is a Divine Interpreter. And who are the ones that *He* instructs? Psalm 25:9 tells us: "The *meek* will He guide in judgment: and the *meek* will He teach His way." A childlike spirit of simplicity and submission, which humbly bows before the Word, is what we all need to pray for daily.

When Christ Himself was speaking of the Divine side of things to Nicodemus, He insisted on the *mystery* element: "The wind bloweth where it listeth, and thou hearest the sound thereof, but *canst not tell* whence it cometh, and whither it goeth: *so* is every one that is born of the Spirit" (John 3:8). In the light of this verse we may say unhesitatingly that whenever a preacher sets forth the doctrine of the new birth in such a way that all *difficulty* vanishes and no mystery remains, it is sure proof that his treatment of the subject is inadequate and faulty. For example, if he insists that the new birth is the *result* of my believing, *that* may commend itself to my intellect, but it *denies* the mystery-element: it may appear very reasonable, but it contradicts the Scriptures! The issue is clear-cut: Christ says, "Thou *canst not* tell," Arminians say, "You *can* tell, for it comes through my believing." If, on the other hand, the preacher says, "Regeneration is a *sovereign* act of God (James 1:18), due to nothing whatever in us or from us," then the mystery element is preserved.

Another Scripture which plainly and categorically sets forth the Divine *order* in connection with regeneration and believing is 2 Thess. 2:13: "God hath from the beginning chosen you to salvation through sanctification of the Spirit and belief of the truth." Here we have a declaration concerning God's *purpose* of grace and the manner in which that purpose is *accomplished.* His purpose of grace is expressed in the words, "God hath from the beginning chosen you to salvation." This is an act of pure sovereignty, uninfluenced by anything in the creature, whereby God singled out from Adam's fallen and guilty race certain ones and appointed them unto salvation. The words "through sanctification of the Spirit and belief of the truth" state *how* God's purpose is made good. God has not only predestined the end, but also the *means* by which that end is attained. The same God who chose certain ones unto salvation also determined the manner and means whereby salvation should become theirs in actual experience. This manner and means is twofold, having both a Divine and a human side. Let us consider each in turn.

"Through sanctification of the Spirit." The word "through" here signifies by *means of.* "*Unto* salvation" is the end in view: "Through sanctification of the Spirit" is the first step in the direction of that goal. Now, "sanctification" always means "setting apart," and the reference in 2 Thess. 2:13 is to the *new birth.* Here is a congregation of a hundred unregenerate souls: the Word of God is preached to them: In His sovereign operations the Holy Spirit takes that Word and applies it to one individual in that company, and by it quickens him into newness of life. The moment He does so, that individual is *separated* from the other ninety-nine who are "*dead* in trespasses and sins." *This* is "sanctification of the Spirit"—the bringing of God's elect out of the realm of death and setting them apart on resurrection-ground.

"And belief of the truth." Notice carefully the order. This comes *after* the "sanctification of the Spirit!" No one can "believe the truth" until after he has been made a "new creature" in Christ, made so by the regeneration-power of the Spirit. But, not until he *has* "believed the truth" can he rejoice in God's salvation, not until he has personally exercised faith in the Lord Jesus Christ is he actually saved. Regeneration does not save him: it simply supplies him with the capacity *to* believe *unto* salvation. God hath chosen us unto salvation, but it is only by the *Spirit's* sanctification and *our own* belief of the truth that God's purpose is made good.

This same order is set forth again in 1 Peter 1:2: "Elect according to the foreknowledge of God the Father, through sanctification of the Spirit, unto obedience and sprinkling of the blood of Jesus Christ." "Elect according to" corresponds with "God hath from the beginning chosen you to salvation." "Sanctification of the Spirit" is the empowering cause which makes good that election. "Unto obedience and sprinkling of the blood" is parallel with "belief of the truth." The "obedience" here is the "obedience *of faith*" (Rom. 1:5), the "obedience of the heart" (Rom. 6:17); the "sprinkling" is faith's *appropriation* of the blood shed once for all. But what we would here direct attention to is the fact that "sanctification of the truth" *precedes* this "obedience and sprinkling!"

"It is the Spirit that quickeneth; the flesh profiteth nothing" (John 6:63). What could be plainer than this? The "flesh"—all that man is by nature—profiteth *nothing.*" The intellect, the affections, the will of the natural man, do not contribute a single thing to the new birth. But if it be true that the unregenerate sinner must believe in *order to be* born again, then the flesh *would* profit much, so much that the decision of man would be the determining factor. But this declaration of Christ is final:—"The flesh profiteth *nothing.*" "It is the *Spirit* that quickeneth," not the preacher's persuasion, not my decision, not even my co-operation with God.

Take again John 1:13: "Which were born, not of blood, nor of the will of the flesh, nor of the will of man, but of God." The context here is very striking. In v. 10 we read, "The world knew Him not." In v. 11 we are told, "His own received Him not." Then in v. 10 it is said, "But as many as received Him, to them gave He power to become the sons of God." But *why* did these "receive" Christ? Was it because *their* wills were less stubborn than those mentioned in the previous verses? Not at all. V. 13 is brought in for the express purpose of repudiating self-righteousness, brought in to correct our false notions, brought in to show the real Agent in regeneration, that we should ascribe *all* the glory of *God.* Note the past tense: "Which (the ones mentioned in v. 12) *were* born (*that is why* they "believed") not of blood (through a pious ancestry), nor of the will of the flesh (man's will has nothing to do with it—*God* here says so), nor of the will of man (through the persuasive power of the preacher), but OF GOD!" Thus, we are here explicitly taught that those who "receive" Christ (v. 12) were, had been, born of God!

Finally, it is written, "The natural man receiveth not the things of the Spirit of God: for they are foolishness unto Him: neither can He know them: because they are spiritually discerned" (1 Cor. 2:14). Now, *what* are the "things of the Spirit of God"? Did not the Lord answer this in John 16:14, "He shall receive of Mine, and shall show it unto you"? But these the natural man "receiveth not." Therefore to affirm that a sinner *can* believe in Christ *before* he be regenerated is to fly in the face of this Scripture which so positively affirms that no one in his *natural* (i.e., unregenerate state) can either receive or know. This same passage adds the reason for this: "because they are spiritually discerned." Before spiritual things can be spiritually discerned there must be a *faculty* of discernment, and this, in turn, requires a spiritual *nature,* and this necessitates the new birth! If, then, the reader *has seen* his or her need of Christ and *has* "come to Him," it is because God "gave" you "an understanding that we may know Him" (1 John 5:20).

After these lengthy observations on the *nature* of the Spirit's work and the *need* for Him to quicken the unregenerate so as to enable them to turn to God—developed by us so fully because of the pathetic ignorance that obtains to-day—we now take up the details of Luke 15:8-10. "Either what woman having ten pieces of silver, if she lose one piece, doth not light a candle and sweep the house, and seek diligently till she find it?"

First, we note how that the Holy Spirit is here represented by a "woman." Many have been puzzled by this, but the figure was most suitably chosen. The Spirit's work on the *inside of the house,* the *tenderness* of His operations, and the fact that *regeneration* is His distinctive work—"born of the Spirit"—all go to show the striking appropriateness of Him being thus portrayed.

Second, mark the *sphere* of the Spirit's operations. This is on the *inside,* in sharp contrast from the activities of the Shepherd on the outside. It is most important that the Christian should clearly distinguish between the work of Christ *for* him and the work of the Spirit *in* him. The former is the basis of the latter. Just as in the types it was the "oil" (emblem of the Spirit) that was placed *on* the blood—see Lev. 8:24, 31; 14:14, 17—so the Spirit works within the hearts of those for whom Christ died.

Third, the figure here selected to represent *the object* of the Holy Spirit's gracious operations is also most suggestive and significant. A "piece of silver." Now, "silver" is the symbol of *redemption,* as "brass" is of *judgment* (Numbers 21:9; Rev. 1:15), and "gold" is of *glory* (Heb. 9:5 cf., Ex. 25:18). Proof that silver has to do with redemption is found in Numbers 18:16: "And those that are to be *redeemed* from a month old shalt thou redeem, according to thine estimation, for the money of five shekels, after the shekel of the sanctuary"—cf. Lev. 5:15), "shekels of *silver,* after the shekel of the sanctuary." Note how the "sockets" of the Tabernacle were made of *silver* (Ex. 26:19), because *redemption* is the basis of our communion with God. Thus the fact that the Spirit's search for a lost piece of "silver" tells us that it is only in those whom Christ redeemed that His gracious work is done!

Fourth, notice next that the woman "lights a candle," and observe that this is done *before* she sweeps the house and recovers the lost coin. How accurate the figure! How clearly this serves to identify the gracious One who is here in view! The first work of the Spirit is to illuminate the sin-darkened heart: it is only in His light that we see light. And *what* is it that the Spirit uses to illuminate, what but that Divine Word which is given as a lamp unto our feet and a light unto our path! It is written, "The entrance of Thy words giveth light" (Psa. 119:130), and it is by the action of the Holy Spirit that these "words" obtain entrance into our hearts.

Fifth, "and sweep the house." Clearly it is the work of *conviction* which is here in view. It is the Word of God applied by the Spirit to our conscience, bringing to light the hidden things of darkness, revealing our depravity, discovering our uncleanness, making manifest our need of the Saviour. This sweeping of the house corresponds to the Sword of the Spirit "piercing even to the dividing asunder of soul and spirit and of the joints and marrow," discerning the thoughts and intents of the heart (Heb. 4:12).

Sixth, "and seek diligently." This is very solemn, yet unspeakably blessed. It tells of the gracious patience and perseverance of the Spirit. O how *long,* Christian reader, did the Spirit of God "seek" *you?* What resistence He met with! How marvellous His long-suffering! In Luke 19:10 we learn of the Son's "seeking." In John 4:23 we read of the Father "seeking." Here in Luke 15:8 we are told of the Spirit "seeking." Thus we learn of the oneness of the Triune God.

Seventh, "till she find it." This tells of the Spirit's triumph. No unsuccessful Worker is He. He is here to glorify an absent Christ, and being omnipotent, He cannot fail. "Ye do always resist the Holy Spirit (Acts 7:51), refers simply to His *external* testimony to men through God's servants. But in His *internal* operations He is ever victorious. Whenever He begins a "good work' *in* any soul, it is always brought to a successful conclusion (see Phil. 1:6). Note the parallel between vv. 6 and 9: like Christ, the Spirit shares His joy with others.

(To be continned.)

SEVEN "SURE" THINGS.

1. Sure Promise: Rom. 4:16.
2. Sure Word: 2 Peter 1:19.
3. Sure Hope: Heb. 6:19.
4. Sure Covenant: 2 Sam. 23:5.
5. Sure Testimony: Psa. 19:7.
6. Sure Election: 2 Peter 1:10.
7. Sure Foundation: Isa. 28:16.

—ARTHUR W. PINK.

"THE MOTHER OF JESUS."

The touching incident of our Lord on The Cross, commending His mother to the care of John, has often been the subject of comment, and always with the object of pointing out His tender filial care for her, and His wish that she should not be desolate. Doubtless such was His purpose; but was it all or nearly all? Had this been all, would He be likely to have chosen almost His last moment, and the most public occasion possible, for the fulfilment of a private family duty, besides using a most strange and peculiar form of expression? Surely not. There seems to be a far deeper purpose, which may appear if we trace the Lord's treatment of His earthly parent from the beginning. The first recorded words uttered by the Lord to His mother were a gentle remonstrance: "How was it that ye sought Me? wist ye not that I must be about *My Father's* business?" *"Thy father* and I," said Mary. She seems to have been leaving the Heavenly Father for a moment out of sight, and a reminder was necessary, and though the Child Jesus returned and was "subject unto them," and eighteen quiet years of loving intercourse followed, the first strand of the tie which had united mother and Son had been parted, and their relation to one another can never have been quite the same as before.

The next recorded conversation was at the marriage at Cana: *"Woman, what have I to do with thee?"* The words sound strangely stern; doubtless they were softened by the tenderest tone and manner, but they were, for all that, a sharp reminder that Mary's maternal authority was now at an end, and another strand was parted, this one the opening of His public ministry, as the first was at the opening of His life of Manhood.

A little later on His mother and His brethren stood without desiring to speak with Him, seeking to lay hands on Him, for they said, "He is beside Himself" (Mark 3:21, 31). The Lord's reply was startling, for it placed His mother on an absolute level with the humblest believers. "Who is My mother and who are My brethren?" "Whosoever shall do the will of My Father which is in Heaven, the same is My brother and sister and mother!" (Matt. 12:48-50). Another strand was gone! The last mention of Mary in the Gospels is one with which we started, and which is now seen in a stronger light.

One by one we have seen the ties which bound together Divine Son and human mother severed by His own hand, now the last is cut, and she is His no longer. "Woman, behold *thy son,"* said the dying Saviour. "Then said He unto the disciple, hold *thy mother."* A remarkable form of expression it seems. *We* should have expected Him to say, "I commend unto thee My mother;" but never once is it recorded that the Lord either addressed Mary or spoke of her as *My mother,* and now as He is about to lay down His earthly life and afterwards assume His resurrection glory, He sets the human relationship aside forever. And Mary, who was wont to ponder things in her heart, seems to have meekly acquiesced, though doubtless this was one of the sharpest thrusts of the sword which pierced through her soul. "From that hour," apparently an early hour, "that disciple took her unto his own home." Perhaps she did not see Him die. Certainly her name is not among those present at the empty grave; indeed, it is not *recorded* that she ever saw Him in His resurrection body.

Once more does Mary appear in Holy Writ: Acts 1:14, where she is seen among a little company of humble believers who continued in prayer and supplication, waiting for the promise of the Father; and then we altogether lost sight of her.

Each of the occasions on which our Lord repudiated Mary's interference were public occasions, as if to emphasise and provide ample testimony to His action, and the last was the most public of all, when He finally relinquished the filial relationship and transferred it to another man.

Preachers have taken much pains to minimise and explain away the apparent distance of our Lord towards Mary; but that it existed there can be no doubt, and *we* can see the "needs be" of it. The time was coming when the humble human instrument of His incarnation would be styled "The Mother of God," and "The Queen of Heaven," and would be accorded idolatrous reverence, and the Lord foreseeing it took strong measures to discountenance such misplaced devotion; and hard as it may have seemed to Mary at the time, she will understand it all, and "magnify the Lord" for it, in that day when she shall "awake" with His "likeness" and be "satisfied."—Mr. P. H.

(*Continued from page 241.*)

Third, the apostle rejoiced in "the glory which should be revealed *in us.*" All that this means we are not yet capable of understanding. But more than a hint has been vouchsafed us. There will be:—

(a) The "glory" of a *perfect body.* In that day this corruption shall have put on incorruption, and this mortal, immortality. That which was sown in dishonour shall be raised in glory, and that which was sown in weakness shall be raised in power. As we *have* borne the image of the earthly, we *shall* also bear the image of the heavenly (1 Cor. 15:49). The content of these expressions is summarised and amplified in Phil. 3:20, 21: "For our conversation is in heaven; from whence also we look for the Saviour, the Lord Jesus Christ: Who shall change our vile body, that it may be fashioned *like unto His glorious body,* according to the working whereby He is able even to subdue all things unto Himself."

(b) There will be the glory of a *transformed mind.* "For now we see through a glass darkly; but then face to face: now I know in part; but then shall I know even as also I am known" (1 Cor. 13:12). O what an orb of intellectual light will be each glorified mind! What range of light will it encompass! What capability of understanding will it enjoy! Then will all mysteries be unravelled, all problems solved, all discrepencies reconciled. Then shall each truth of God's revelation, each event of His providence, each decision of His government, stand yet more transparently clear and resplendent than the sun itself. Do you, in your present quest for spiritual knowledge, mourn the darkness of your mind, the weakness of your memory, the limitations of your intellectual faculties? Then rejoice in hope of the glory that is to be revealed in you—when all your intellectual powers shall be renewed, developed, perfected, so that you shall know even as you are known.

(c) Best of all, there will be the glory of *perfect holiness.* God's work of grace in us will then be completed. He has promised to "perfect that which concerneth us" (Ps. 138:8). Then will be the consummation of purity. We have been predestinated to be "conformed to the image of His Son" (Rom. 8:29), and when we shall see Him, "we *shall* be *like Him*" (1 John 3:2). Then our minds will be no more defiled by evil imaginations, our consciences no more sullied by a sense of guilt, our affections no more ensnared by unworthy objects.

What a marvellous prospect is this! A "glory" to be revealed *in me* who now can scarcely reflect a solitary ray of light! In me—so wayward, so unworthy, so sinful; living so little in communion with Him who is the Father of lights! Can it be that *in me* this glory shall be revealed? So affirms the infallible Word of God. If I *am* a child of light—through being "in Him" who is the effulgence of the Father's glory—even though now dwelling amid the world's dark shades, one day I shall outshine the brightness of the firmament. And when the Lord Jesus returns to this earth He shall "be admired *in* all them that believe" (2 Thess. 1:10).

Finally, the apostle here weighed the "sufferings" of this present time over against the "glory" which shall be revealed in us, and as he did so he declared that the one is "not worthy to be compared" with the other. The one is earthly, the other is heavenly. The one is transient, the other is eternal. As, then, there is no proportion between the finite and the infinite, so there is no comparison between the sufferings of earth and the glory of heaven.

One second of glory will outweigh a lifetime of suffering. What were years of toil, of sickness, of battling with poverty, of sorrow in any or every form, when compared with the glory of Immanuel's land! One draught of the river of pleasure at God's right hand, one breath of Paradise, one hour amid the blood-washed around the throne, shall more than compensate for all the tears and groans of earth. "For I reckon that the sufferings of this present time are not worthy to be compared with the glory which shall be revealed in us."* May the Holy Spirit enable both writer and reader to lay hold of this with appropriating faith and live in the present possession and enjoyment of it to the praise of the glory of Divine grace.

—*Arthur W. Pink.*

*It is interesting to know that with *this verse* on his lips, John Calvin became "absent from the body, present with the Lord," in 1564.

VOL. IV DEC., 1925 NO. 12

STUDIES IN THE SCRIPTURES

"Search the Scriptures" John 5:39.

Arthur W. Pink, Publisher and Editor,
5 Norton Street, Ashfield, N.S.W., Australia.

Price : 10 cents per copy ; $1.00 or 5/- per year.

This issue completes Vol. 4. By the abundant mercies of God we have been enabled to continue publishing "Studies in the Scriptures" month by month. This has been no light task during the present year. The breaking up of our home in Philadelphia; crossing the American continent; conducting Conventions in Denver, Oakland, and Berkeley; journeying across the Pacific; and holding seven successive Bible-teaching Campaigns in Australia, each averaging three weeks, has made it difficult to snatch the necessary time for composing articles, correcting proofs, and answering correspondence. Yet, thank God, we have proved afresh the veracity and blessedness of His promise "My grace is sufficient for thee." During the year, the Editor has spoken over three hundred times, but "as thy days so shall thy strength be" is our Divinely-given guarantee. The untiring efforts of the Editor's wife in typing the articles, looking after subscriptions, keeping the books, and mailing out the magazines, fills him with praise for such a capable and loving "help-mate."

The current year, like the previous ones, has been one of testing. The publication of the magazine, from the start, has been a venture of faith, and faith must be tried to prove its reality. But the same One who imparts faith sustains it. God never disappoints those whose expectation is truly in Him. Both the cost of printing and of mailing is higher in Australia than in the U.S.A., but the Lord has graciously provided. Within a few days of our arrival in Sydney He brought us into touch with a Christian printer who is out and out for the Lord. The extra expenses have been met by the increased number of subscriptions received in Australia.

We regretted breaking in on the series of articles "Truth and Error," but we felt it urgently needful to publish the Addresses delivered in Ashfield on the sadly-neglected truths of God's Sovereignty and Divine Election; and these, in turn, were necessarily interrupted in the last two numbers by our Exposition of Luke 15. God willing, we shall resume the series on God's Sovereignty in the January issue following these with the remaining articles by Dr. Bonar. The Expositions of John's Gospel and the Gleanings in Exodus will also be continued, D.V.

The Addresses on Divine Election were markedly owned of God, hundreds of those who attended hearing this blessed truth expounded for the first time. Scores of Christians had their faith strengthened and their gratitude to God deepened. Of course there has been opposition, which has ever been the case where this doctrine has been scipturally presented; and, as in our Lord's day, the fiercest persecution comes from those who make the most pretentions. But "the foundation of God standeth sure:" all the raging of Jehovah's enemies is but like the angry waves spending their force in vain as they break upon the rocky shore. Some have been shaken by the winds of opposition, for it is written "Every plant, which My heavenly Father *hath not* planted, shall be rooted up." Some who stood by us while the crowds were in attendence have now deserted, but we read that when the Lord Jesus declared "No man can come unto Me except it were given unto him of My Father," that "from that time many of His disciples went back, and walked *no more* with Him." (John 6:65-66)—sufficient for the disciple to be as his Master. Others have been made to search the

(*Continued on page 288*)

IMPORTANT NOTICES

Set of twelve issues for **1922**, unbound, **$1.00** or **5/-**. Bound **$1.50** or **7/-**.

Set of twelve issues for **1923**, unbound, **$1.00** or **5/-**. Bound **$1.50** or **7/-**.

Set of twelve issues for **1924**, unbound, **$1.00** or **5/-**. Bound **$1.50** or **7/-**.

Note: We cannot break a set or now supply any **single 1924** issues.

Subscription—price: **$1.00** or **5/-** per year to any address in the world.

Change of Address: Please notify me promptly of any change of address, and be certain to give both old and new address.

Non-subscribers receiving this Magazine regularly will understand their subscription has been entered by a friend.

Copies lost in the mail duplicated only if we are notified promptly.

CONTENTS

THE GOSPEL OF JOHN

48. *Christ Comforting His Disciples* (John 14:1-11).

Below is an analysis of the passage which is to be before us:—

1. Christ's call to faith in Himself, v. 1.
2. Christ's teaching about Heaven, v. 2.
3. Christ's precious promises, vv. 3, 4.
4. Thomas' question, v. 5.
5. Christ perfectly suited to us, vv. 6, 7.
6. Philip's ignorance, v. 8.
7. Christ's reproof, vv. 9-11.

It is in the fourteenth chapter of John that the Lord Jesus really begins the Pascal Discourse, a discourse which for tenderness, depth, and comprehensiveness is unsurpassed in all the Scriptures. The circumstances under which it was delivered need to be steadily borne in mind. This heart-melting Address of Christ was given to the Eleven on the last night before He died, affording a manifestation of Him which has been strikingly likened to the "glorious radiance of the setting sun, surrounded with dark clouds, and about to plunge into darker, which, frought with lightning, thunder, and tempest, wait on the horizon to receive Him." Most blessedly do His words here bring out the perfections of the God-man. Any other man, even a man of superior strength of mind and kindliness of heart placed, so far as he could be placed in our Lord's circumstances, would have had his mind thrown into such a state of uncontrollable agitation, and most certainly would have been too entirely occupied with his own sufferings and anxieties to have any power or disposition to enter into and sooth the sorrows of others. But though completely aware of all that awaited Him, though feeling the weight of the awful load laid upon Him, though tasting the bitter cup which He must drain, He not only retained full self-possession, but took as deep an interest in the fears and sorrows of the apostles as if He Himself had not been a sufferer. Instead of being occupied with what lay before Himself, He spent the time in comforting His disciples: He "loved them unto the end."

During His public ministry and in His private intercourse with them, the apostles had heard repeated statements from His lips concerning His approaching sufferings and death, statements which appear to us simple and plain, but which perplexed and amazed them. It is most charitable, and perhaps most reasonable, to conclude that His disciples regarded His references to His coming passion as *parables*, which were not to be understood literally; and that, at any rate, He could not mean anything inconsistent with His immediately restoring the kingdom to Israel. They were fully convinced that *He* was the Messiah, and their only idea in connection with the Messiah was that of an illustrious Conqueror, a prosperous King; therefore, whatever was obscure in their Master's sayings, must be understood in the light of these principles. And it is probable that their hopes had never risen higher than when they had seen Him ride into Jerusalem amid the joyous acclamations of the multitudes, hailing Him as the Son of David.

But right after His entry into Jerusalem they had heard Him speak of Himself as the Corn of wheat which must fall into the ground and die, and this, at least, must have awakened dark forebodings. And, too, His conduct and sayings during the passover-supper, and what followed, must have deeply perplexed and distressed them. "Now is My soul troubled, and what shall I say? Father, save Me from this hour?" must have filled them with painful misgivings. He had said, "Yet a *little* while I am with you. Ye shall seek Me: and as I said unto the Jews, Whither I go, *ye* cannot come; so now I say to you." This was, indeed, sufficient to fill them with anxiety and sorrow. They dearly loved Him. The thought of Him dying, and of their parting with Him, was unbearable. Moreover, they must have asked themselves, How can *this* be reconciled with His Messiahship? Are we, after all, to give up our hope that this is He who would redeem Israel? And what is to become of us! We have forsaken all to follow Him, will He now forsake us, leaving us amid enemies, as sheep in the midst of wolves, to suffer the fierce malignity of His triumphant foes!

"Our Lord, who knew what was in man, was well aware of what was passing in the minds of His disciples. He knew how they were troubled, and what anxious, desponding, and despairing thoughts were arising in their hearts, and He could not but be touched with the feeling of their infirmities. There lay on His own mind a weight of anguish which no being in the universe could bear along with Him. *He* could not have the alleviation of sympathy, He must tread the winepress alone. They could not enter into *His* feelings; but He, the magnanimous One, could enter into theirs. There was room in His large heart for *their* sorrows, as well as His own. He feels their griefs, as if they were His own; and kindly comforts those whom He knew were soon to desert Him in the hour of *His* deepest sorrows! 'In all their afflictions, He was afflicted;' and He shows in the address which He made to them that 'the Lord who anointed Him to comfort those who morn, and to bind up the broken-hearted,' had indeed 'given to Him the tongue of the learned that He might speak a word in season to them who were weary.' Isa. 61:1; 50:4" (Dr. J. Brown).

"Let not your heart be troubled" (v. 1). It was the sorrows of their hearts which now occupied the great Heart of Love. "Troubled" they were; deeply so. They were troubled at hearing that one of their number should betray Him (13:21). They were troubled at seeing their Master "troubled in spirit" (13:21); troubled because He would remain with them only a "little while" (13:33); troubled over the warning He had given to Peter, that he would deny His Lord thrice. Thus this little company of believers were disquieted and cast down. Wherefore the Saviour proceeded to comfort them.

"Ye believe in God, believe also in Me" (v. 1). Commentators have differed widely as to the precise meaning of these words. The difficulty arises from the Greek. Both verbs are exactly the same, and may be translated (with equal accuracy) either in the imperative or the indicative mood Either will make good sense, and possibly each is to be kept in mind. The R.V. reads: "Believe in God, believe also in Me." Thus translated, it is a *double exhortation*. The force of it would then be: Your purturbation of spirit arises from *not* believing in what God has spoken by His prophets concerning My sufferings and the glory which is to follow. God has announced in plain terms that I *was to be* despised and rejected of men, that I am to be wounded for your transgressions and bruised for your iniquities. These are the words of Jehovah Himself; then doubt them not. "Believe also in Me." I too have warned you what to expect. I have told you that I am to suffer many things at the hands of the chief priests and scribes and be killed. These things *must* be. Then hold fast the beginning of your confidence steadfast unto the end: be not "offended" in Me, even though I go to a criminal's cross.

But it should be remembered that the Lord was speaking not only to the Eleven, but to *us* as well. Even so, the above interpretation supplies an exhortation which we constantly need. "Believe in God" O Christian. Let not your heart be troubled *for* thy Father is possessed of infinite power, wisdom, and goodness. He knows what is best for thee, and He makes all things work together for thy good. *He* is on the Throne, ruling amid the army of heaven and among the inhabitants of the earth, so that none can stay His hand. Why, then, art thou cast down, O my soul? God is our refuge and strength, a very present help in trouble; therefore will we not fear, though the earth be removed, and though the mountains be carried into the midst of the sea; though the waters thereof roar and be troubled, though the mountains shake with the swellings thereof. What though trials come thick and fast, what though I am misunderstood and unappreciated, what though Satan roar and rage against me? "If God be for us who can be against us?" *Believe in God.* Believe in His absolute sovereignty, His infinite wisdom, His unchanging faithfulness, His wondrous love. "Believe also in Me." I am the One who died for thy sins and rose again for thy justification; I am the One who ever liveth to make intercession for thee. I am the *same,* yesterday, and to-day, and forever. I am the One who shall come again to receive you unto Myself, and ye shall be forever with Me. Yes, "*Believe also in Me!*"

While the above interpretation is fully justified by the Greek, while the double exhortation was truly needed both by the Eleven and by us to-day, and while many able expositors have advanced it, yet we cannot but think that the A.V. gives the truer force of our Lord's words here, rendering the first verb in the indicative and the second in the imperative. "Believe also in Me." What, then, did Christ mean? The apostles *had* already, by Divine illumination, recognised Him as the Christ, the Son of the living God. It is clear, then, that He was not here challenging their faith. We take it that what the Lord had in view was this: the apostles already believed in Him as the Messiah, and as the Saviour, but their confidence reposed in One who dwelt in their midst, who went in and out among them in the sensible relationship of daily companionship. But He was about to be *removed* from them, and He whom they had seen with their eyes and had handled with their hands (1 John 1:1) was to be *invisible* to the outward eye. Now, says He, "Ye believe in God," *who is invisible;* you believe in His love, though you have never seen His form; you are conscious of His care, though you have never touched the Hand that guides and protects you. "Believe, also, in *Me*"; that is to say, In like manner you must have full confidence in My existence, love, and care, even though I am no longer present to sight. *This* comfort remains for *us;* this is the faith in which we are now to live: "Whom having not seen, ye love; in whom, though now ye see Him not, yet believing, ye rejoice with joy unspeakable and full of glory" (1 Peter 1:8).

"Believe also in Me." The "also" here brings out the absolute Deity of Christ in a most unmistakable manner. "Here thou seest plainly that Christ Himself testifies that He is equal with God Almighty; because we must believe in Him even as we believe in God. If He were not true God with the Father, this faith would be false and idolatrous" (Dr. Martin Luther).

"In My Father's House are many mansions" (v. 2). The Father's "House" is His dwelling-place. It is noteworthy that the Lord Jesus is the only one who ever referred to the "Father's House," and He did so on three occasions. First, He had said of the Temple in Jerusalem, "Make not My Father's *House* a house of merchandise" (John 2:16). Then He had mentioned it in connection with the "prodigal son" and his elder brother: "As he came and drew nigh to the *house* (the 'father's) he heard music and dancing"; here it is presented as the place of joy and gladness. In John 14 Christ mentions it as the final abode of the saints.

The glories and blessedness of Heaven are brought before us in the New Testament under a variety of representations. Heaven is called a "Country" (Luke 19:12, Heb. 11:16); this tells of its vastness. It is called a "City" (Heb. 11:10, Rev. 21); this intimates the large number of its inhabitants. It is called a "Kingdom" (2 Peter 1:11); this suggests its orderliness. It is called "Paradise" (Luke 23:43; Rev. 2:7); this emphasises its delights. It is called the "Father's House," which bespeaks its permanency.

The Temple at Jerusalem had been called the Father's "House" because it was there that the symbol of His presence abode, because it was there He was worshipped, and because it was there His people communed with Him. But before the Lord Jesus closed His public ministry He disowned the Temple, saying, "Behold *your* House is left unto you desolate" (Matt. 23:38). Therefore does the Saviour now transfer this term to the Father's dwelling-place on High, where He will grant to His redeemed a more glorious revelation of Himself, and where they shall worship Him, uninterruptedly, in the beauty of holiness.

The "Father's House" has been the favourite term for Heaven with most Christians. It speaks of *Home,* the Home of God and His people. Sad it is that in this present evil age one of the most precious words in the English language has lost much of its fragrance. Our fathers used to sing, "There is no place like home." To-day the average "home" is little more than a boarding-house—a place to eat and sleep in. But "home" used to mean, and still means to a few, the place where we are loved for our own sakes; the place where we are always welcome; the place whither we can retire from the strife of the world and enjoy rest and peace; the place where loved ones are together. Such will Heaven be. Believers are now in a strange country, yea, in an enemy's land; in the life to come, they will be at *Home!*

"In My Father's House are *many mansions.*" The many rooms in the Temple prefigured these (see 1 Kings 6:5, 6; Jer. 35:1-4, etc., and see Ezek. 40:7, 10; 41:5-7 for the millennial Temple). The word for "mansions" signifies "abiding-places"—a most comforting term, assuring us of the *permanency* of our future home in contrast from the "tents" of our present pilgrimage. Blessed, too, is the word "many;' there will be ample room for the redeemed of the past, present, and future ages; and for the unfallen angels as well.

"If it were not so I would have told you" (v. 2). Had there been no room for believers in the many mansions of the Father's House, Christ would have said so. He had never deceived them; truth was His only object—"To this end was I born, and for this cause came I into the world, that I should bear witness unto the truth" (John 18:37). It was because full provision had been made for their complete and eternal happiness that He encouraged them to entertain such high hopes. He would never have brought them into such an intimacy with Himself if that was now to end forever.

"I go to prepare a place for you" (v. 2). "He does not explain *how* the place in the Father's House should be prepared for them; nor were they yet, perhaps, able to understand. The Epistle to the Hebrews will show us, if we turn to it, that the heavenly places had to be purified by the better sacrifices which He was to offer, in which all the sacrifices of the law would find their fulfilment. Ephesians speaks similarly of the 'redemption of the purchased possession'; and Colossians of the 'reconciliation of things in heaven' (Heb. 9:23, Eph. 1:14, Col. 1.20). Such thoughts are even now strange to many Christians; for we are slow to realise the extent of the injury that sin has inflicted, and equally, therefore, the breadth of the application of the work of Christ. This is not the place to enlarge upon it; but it is not difficult to understand that wherever sin has raised question of God—and it has done so, as we know, in Heaven itself—the work of Christ as bringing out in full His whole character in love and righteousness regarding that which had raised the question, has enabled Him to come in and restore, consistently with all that He is, what had been defiled with evil. Thus our High Priest, to use as the apostle does, the figure of Israel's day of atonement, has entered into the Sanctuary to reconcile with the virtues of His sacrifice the holy places themselves, and make them accessible to us" (Numerical Bible).

"I go to prepare a place for you." We also understand this to mean that the Lord Jesus has procured *the right*—by His death on the cross—for every believing sinner to enter Heaven. He has "prepared" for us a place there by entering Heaven as our Representative and taking possession of it on behalf of His people. As our Forerunner He marched in, leading captivity captive, and there planted His banner in the land of glory. He has "prepared" for us a place there by entering the "holy of holies" on High as our great High Priest, carrying our names in with Him. Christ would do all that was necessary to secure for His people a welcome and a permanent place in Heaven. Beyond this we cannot go with any degree of certainty. The fact that Christ has promised to "prepare *a place*" for us—which repudiates the vague and visionary ideas of those who would reduce Heaven to an intangible nebula—guarantee that it will far surpass anything down here.

"I go to prepare a place for you." God never has, and never will, take His people into a place *un*-prepared for them. In Eden God first "planted a garden," and then placed Adam in it. It was the same with Israel when they entered Canaan: "And it shall be, when the Lord thy God shall have brought thee into the land which He swear unto thy fathers, to Abraham, to Isaac, and to Jacob, to give them great and goodly cities, which *thou* buildest not, and houses full of all good things, which *thou* filledst not, and wells digged which *thou* diggedst not, vineyards and olive trees which *thou* plantedst not" (Deut. 6:10, 11). So, too, of Palestine in the future, when God is ready for Israel to occupy it again, He will renew it: "The wilderness and the solitary place shall be glad for them; and the desert shall rejoice and blossom as the rose" (Isa. 35:1). And what can we say of the grace manifested by the Lord of glory going to prepare a place for us? He will not entrust such a task to the angels. Proof, indeed, is this that He loves us "unto the end."

And if I go and prepare a place for you" (v. 3). "A special people taken from the earth in a risen Christ must have a special place. A new thing was to take place, *men brought into Heaven!* Man was not made for Heaven, but for the earth, and so placed here to till the earth and live upon it. By sinning he lost the earth and the earth shared his ruin. But by sinning he brought down the Son of God from Heaven, who by His descent opened Heaven as the normal place for those believing on Christ, and so in Him" (Mr. Mal. Taylor).

"I will come again, and receive you unto Myself" (v. 3). This was the *first time* that the Lord Jesus had mentioned the Rapture, nor had it ever been referred to by any of the prophets. The second coming of the Lord Jesus is to be in two stages. In the first He comes as Son of God; in the second He comes as Son of man: the one will be secret, the other public. In the first stage He comes into the air to catch up sleeping and living saints unto Himself; in the second He descends to the earth, bringing His saints with Him. The first stage was typified by the translation of Enoch to Heaven (Heb. 11:5); the second was foreshadowed by Elijah, who has yet to return to this earth to herald the judgments of the great and terrible day of the Lord (Mal. 4:5). First the Lord comes as our *Saviour* (Heb. 9:28), later He returns to the earth as its *King* (Rev. 19:11, 16). There will be an interval of at least seven years, probably much longer, between the two stages of the Second Advent, during which God will be sweeping the earth with the besom of destruction, preparatory to the establishment of Christ's Throne in Jerusalem.

"I will come again." The Lord will not *send* for us, but come in person, to conduct us into the Father's House. How precious we must be to Him! "The Lord *Himself* shall descend from Heaven with a shout, with the voice of the arch-angel, and with the trump of God; and the dead in Christ shall rise first: Then we which are alive and remain shall be caught up together with them in the clouds, to meet the Lord in the air" (1 Thess. 4:16, 17).

"And receive you unto Myself." Notice, not "take" but *receive*. The Holy Spirit has charge of us during the time of our absence from the Saviour; but when the mystical body of Christ is complete then is *His* work here done, and He hands us over to the One who died to save us. "And receive you *unto Myself*." To have us with Himself is His heart's desire. To the dying thief He said, "To-day shalt thou be *with Me* in Paradise." To the Church it is promised that we shall "ever be *with the Lord*" (1 Thess. 4:17).

"That where I am, there ye may be also" (v. 3). The place which was due the *Son* is the place which grace has given to the *sons*. This is the blessed sequel to what was before us in John 13. There Christ said, "If I wash thee not, thou hast not part with Me." There, it is the Saviour maintaining His own on earth in communion with Himself. Here, in due time, we shall be with Him, to enjoy unbroken fellowship forever. This had been *promised* before: "If any man serve Me, let him follow Me; and *where I am* there shall *also* My servant be" (John 12:26). Here it is formally *declared*. In John 17:24 it is *prayed for*: "Father, I will that they also, whom Thou hast given Me, be *with Me* where I am."

Here, then, is the Divine specific for heart trouble; here, indeed, is precious consolation for one groaning in a world of sin. First, faith in the Lord Jesus Christ. Second, the assurance that the Father's House on high will be our eternal Home. Third, the realisation that the Saviour has done and is doing everything necessary to secure us a welcome there and fit that Home for our reception. Fourth, the blessed hope that He is coming in person to receive us unto Himself. Finally, the precious promise that we are to be with Him forever. But, and mark it well, it is only in proportion as *we* are "troubled" by our absence from Him, that we shall be comforted and cheered by these precious words! Here is solid ground for consolation, conclusive arguments against despondency and disquietude in the present path of service and suffering, the Saviour lives and loves and cares for us! He is active, promoting our interests, and when God's time arrives He shall come and receive us unto Himself.

"And whither I go ye know, and the way ye know" (v. 4). To understand this verse it is necessary to keep in mind the connection. Only a very short time before, Peter had asked, "Lord, *whither* goest Thou?" (13:33), and when He replied, "Whither I go, thou canst not follow Me now; but thou shalt follow Me afterwards," he rejoined, "Why cannot I follow Thee now?" Both of these questions of Peter, and they probably expressed the thoughts of all the apostles, were answered by our Lord in the verses which have just been before us. "It is as if He had said, 'You are troubled in spirit because you know not whither I go; and because I have said, ye cannot follow Me now. I am going to My Father; to His House of many mansions; let not, therefore, these fears about Me distress you; and as to your following Me—as to the reason why you cannot follow Me now—and as to the way in which you are to follow Me hereafter, know that arrangements must be made for your coming to where I am going. I go to make these arrangements, and when they are completed I will come and take you to Myself, that where I am, there ye may be also. That is whither I am going—that is the reason why you do not go with Me, or follow Me now—that is the way in which you *are* afterwards to come where I am going; and, i.e., *thus* 'ye know,' for I have plainly told you 'whither I go' and the 'way' in which you are to come whither I shall have gone" (Dr. J. Brown). The "whither" was *unto the Father;* the "way" was the *process* by which *they* would arrive there. It was not simply the *goal*, but the *path* to it; not simply the *whither* but the *how* which Christ had just revealed to them.

"Thomas saith unto Him, Lord, we know not whither Thou goest; and how can we know the way?" (v. 5). Our Lord had spoken very simply and plainly, yet was

He misunderstood. The Father, His House, its many mansions, Christ going there to prepare a place, and His promise to come and receive His people unto Himself and share His place with us—these things were dim and unreal to the materialistic and rationalistic Thomas. His mind was on earthly things. Did the "Father's House" mean some palace situated outside Palestine, and did Christ's "going away" signify His removing to that palace? He was not sure, and tells the Lord so. Well, if we brought *our* difficulties unto Him. But let us not forget that the Spirit of truth had not yet been given to the disciples to *show* them "things to come" (John 16:13). He *has* been given to us, therefore is our ignorance the more excuseless.

"Jesus saith unto Him, I am the Way, the Truth, and the Life" (v. 6). Before sin entered the world Adam enjoyed a threefold privilege in relation to God; he was in communion with his Maker; he knew Him, and he possessed spiritual life. But when he disobeyed and fell, this threefold relationship was severed. He became alienated from God, as the *hiding* of himself painfully demonstrated; having believed the Devil's lie, he was no longer capable of perceiving the truth, as the making of fig-leaf aprons clearly evidenced; and he no longer had spiritual life, for God's threat *"In the day* thou eatest thereof thou shalt *surely die"* was strictly enforced. In this same awful condition has each of Adam's descendants entered this world, for "that which is born of the flesh is flesh"—a fallen parent can begat nought but a fallen child. Every sinner, therefore, has a three-fold need—reconciliation, illumination, regeneration. This three-fold need is perfectly met by the Saviour. He is the Way to the Father; He is the Truth incarnate; He is the Life to all who believe in Him. Let us briefly consider each of these separately.

"I am the Way." Christ spans the distance between God and the sinner. Man would fain manufacture a ladder of his own, and by means of his resolutions and reformations, his prayers and his tears, climb up to God. But that is impossible. *That* is the way which *seemeth right* unto a man, but the end thereof are the ways of death (Pro. 14:12). *It is Satan* who would keep the exercised sinner on his self-imposed journey to God. What faith needs to lay hold of is the glorious truth that Christ has come all the way down to sinners. The sinner could not come in to God, but God in the person of His Son has come out to sinners. He is *the Way,* the Way to the Father, the Way to Heaven, the Way to eternal blessedness.

"I am the Truth." Christ is the full and final revelation of God. Adam believed the Devil's lie, and ever since then man has been groping amid ignorance and error. "The way of the wicked is as *darkness;* they know not at what they stumble" (Pro. 4:19). "Having the understanding darkened, being alienated from the life of God through the *ignorance* that is in them, because of the *blindness* of their heart" (Eph. 4:18). A thousand systems has the mind devised. "God hath made man upright; but they have sought out *many* inventions" (Eccl. 7:29). "There is none that understandeth" (Rom. 3:11). Pilate voiced the perplexity of multitudes when he asked, "*What is* truth?" (John 18:38). Truth is not to be found in a system of philosophy, but in a Person—Christ is "The Truth": He reveals God and exposes man. In Him are hid "All the treasures of wisdom and knowledge" (Col. 2:3). What tremendous folly to ignore Him! What will it avail you in Hell, dear reader, even though you have mastered all the sciences of men, were acquainted with all the events of history, were versed in all the languages of mankind, were thoroughly acquainted with the politics of your day? O, how you will wish then that you had read your newspapers less and your Bible more; that with all your getting you had got understanding; that with all your learning you had bowed before Him who is *the Truth!*

"I am the Life." Christ is the Emancipator from death. The whole Bible bears solemn witness to the fact that the natural man is spiritually lifeless. He walks according to the course of this world; he has no love for the things of God. The fear of God is not upon him, nor has he any concern for His glory. *Self* is the centre and circumference of his existence. He is alive to the things of the world, but he is *dead* to heavenly things. The one who is out of Christ exists, but he has no spiritual life. When the prodigal son returned from the *far* country the father said, "This, my son, was *dead,* and is alive again; he was lost, and is found" (Luke 15:24). The one who believes in Christ has passed out of death into life (John 5:24). "He that believeth on the Son hath everlasting life (John 3.36). Then turn to Him who is *the Life.*

"I am the Way." Without Christ men are Cains—*wanderers.* "They are all gone out of the way" (Rom. 3:12). Christ is not merely a Guide who came to show man the path in which they ought to walk: He is Himself *the Way* to the Father. "I am the Truth." Without Christ men are *under the power of the Devil,* the father of lies. Christ is not merely a Teacher who came to reveal to men a doctrine regarding God: He is Himself *the Truth* about God. "He that hath seen Me hath seen the Father." "I am the Life." Without Christ men are *dead* in trespasses and sins. Christ is not merely a Physician who came to invigorate the old nature, to refine its grossness, or repair its defects. "I am come," said He, "that they might have *life*, and that they might have it more abundantly" (John 10:10).

"No man cometh unto the Father but by Me" (v. 6). Christ is the *only* way to God. It is utterly impossible to win God's favour by any efforts of our own. "Other foundation can no man lay than that is laid, which is Jesus Christ" (1 Cor. 3:11). "Neither is there salvation in any other; for there is none other name under Heaven given among men, whereby we must be saved" (Acts 4:12). "There is one God, and one Mediator between God and men, the man Christ Jesus" (1 Tim. 2:6). Let every Christian reader praise God for His unspeakable Gift, and "Having, therefore brethren, boldness to enter into the holiest by the blood of Jesus, by a new and living *way*, which He hath newly made for us, through the veil; that is to say, His flesh; and having an High Priest over the house of God. Let us draw near with a true heart in full assurance of faith" (Heb. 9:19-22).

"If ye had known Me, ye should have known My Father also and from henceforth ye know Him, and have seen Him" (v. 7). This is intimately connected with the whole of the immediate context. The reason why the apostles found it so hard to understand the Lord's references to the Father, the Father's House, and His and their way there, was because their views respecting Himself were so defective and deficient. The true knowledge of the Father cannot be obtained but by the true knowledge of the Son; and if the Son be really known, the Father is known also. The Father is known just so far as the Son is known; no farther. Christ was more than a manifestation *of* God; He *was* "God manifest in flesh." He was the Only-begotten, who fully declared Him.

"From henceforth ye know Him, and have seen Him." "These words of our Lord are a prediction, which, like many predictions, is uttered in the past tense—the event not only being as certain as if it had already taken place, but appearing as accomplished to the mind of the prophet, rapt into the future by the inspiring impulse. It is equivalent to, 'Yet a very little while and ye shall know Him—know Him so clearly that it may be said you *see* Him! The prediction was accomplished on the day of Pentecost. From the time these words were uttered, a series of events took place, in close succession, in which through the atoning sufferings, and death, and glorious resurrection of our Lord Jesus, the character of God the Father, was gloriously illustrated. But, till after the resurrection, the disciples saw only the dark side of the cloud in which Jehovah was; and even till 'the Spirit was poured out from on High,' they but indistinctly discerned the true meaning of these events. Then, indeed, 'the darkness was passed, and the true light shone.' The Holy Spirit took of the things of Christ and showed them unto them" (Dr. J. Brown).

"Philip saith unto Him, Lord, show us the Father, and it sufficeth us" (v. 8). What the Lord had just said to Thomas, Philip was unable to thoroughly grasp. With that, strange faculty of the human mind to pass over the most prominent and important points of a subject and to seize only on that on which our own mind had been running, this disciple can think only of "seeing" the Father, not *how* He is *to be* seen. Possibly Philip's mind *reverted* to the experience of Moses on the Mount, when, in answer to earnest prayer, he was placed in a cleft of the rock and permitted to see the retiring glory of Jehovah as He passed by; or, he may have remembered what Moses, Aaron, Nadab and Ahihu and the seventy elders of Israel were permitted to witness when "they saw the God of Israel, and under His feet, as it were, a paved work of a sapphire stone, and, as it were the body of heaven in his clearness" (Exodus 35:5-8). He may have recalled that prophecy, "The glory of the Lord shall be revealed, and all flesh shall *see it* together" (Isa. 40:5).

"Jesus saith unto him, Have I been so long time with you, and yet hast thou not known Me, Philip? He that hath seen Me hath seen the Father; and how sayeth thou then, Show us the Father?" (v. 9). This was a rebuke, the more forceful by being addressed to Philip individually. He had said, "Show *us* the Father." Christ replied, "Hast *thou* not known Me, Philip?" The force of this was: Have you never yet apprehended *who* I am? The corporeal representation of God, such as Philip desired, was unnecessary; unnecessary because a far more glorious revelation of Deity was there right before him. The Word, made flesh, was tabernacling among men, and *His* glory was "the glory of the Only-begotten of the Father." He was the visible Image of the invisible God. He was the "Brightness of His glory, and the express image of His person." In Him dwelt all the fulness of the Godhead bodily.

"Believest thou not that I am in the Father, and the Father in Me? The words that I speak unto you I speak not of Myself: but the Father that dwelleth in Me He doeth the works" (v. 10). Christ was in the Father and the Father was in Him. There was the most perfect and intimate union between Them. Both His words and His works were a perfect revelation of Deity. It is very striking to note here that the Son refers to *His* "words" as *the Father's* "works." *His* words were works, for they were words of power. "He *spake* and it was *done;* He commanded, and it stood fast!" He *said* "Lazarus, come forth;" and he that was dead came forth.

"Believe Me that I am in the Father, and the Father in Me: or else believe Me for the very works' sake" (v. 11). This is solemn. The Lord has to descend to the level that He took when speaking to His enemies—"Though ye believe not Me *believe the works* that ye may know, and believe that the Father is in Me and I in Him" (John 10:38). So now He says to Philip, if ye will not, on My bare word, believe that I am One with the Father, at least acknowledge the proof of it in My works. How thankful we should be that the Holy Spirit has been given to us, to make clear what was so dark to the disciples. Let us praise God that "we know that the Son of God is come, and hath given us an understanding, that we may know Him that is true" (1 John, 5:20).

Let the interested student carefully ponder the following questions:—

1. For whom are the promises in v. 12 intended?
2. Who has ever done anything "greater" than Christ did, v. 12?
3. What does it mean to ask "in the name of" Christ, v. 13?
4. How is v. 14 to be qualified?
5. Is obeying God's commandments "legalism," v. 15?
6. Why cannot "the world" receive the Holy Spirit, v. 17?
7. What is the meaning of v. 20?

Arthur W. Pink.

GLEANINGS IN EXODUS

24. The Smitten Rock; Ex. 17.

"And all the congregation of the children of Israel journed from the Wilderness of Sin" (v. 1). Mark that this chapter opens with the word "And," connecting it with the one preceding. So, too, chapter 16 begins with "And," linking it on to the closing verses of 15. "And" is a little word, but we often miss that which is of much importance and value through failing to weigh it carefully. There is nothing trivial in *God's* Word, and each word and syllable has its own meaning and worth. At the close of Ex. 15 (v. 23) Israel came to Marah, and they could not drink of the waters there because they were bitter. At once we find the people *murmuring* against Moses, saying, "What shall we drink?" (v. 24). Sad, sad was this, after all that the Lord had done for them. Moses cried unto God, and in long-suffering grace He at once came to the relief of the people. The Lord showed him a tree, which when cast into the bitter waters, at once sweetened them. After this experience they reached Elim, where were twelve wells of water. There Ex. 15 closes.

Ex. 16 opens with "And." Why? To connect with what has just preceded. But for what purpose? To show us the inexcusableness and to emphasise the enormity of the conduct of Israel immediate following; as well as to magnify the marvellous patience and infinite mercy of Him who bore so graciously with them. Israel had now entered the wilderness, the Wilderness of Sin, and it furnished no food for them. How, then, do they meet this test of faith? After their recent experience at Marah, one would suppose they promptly and confidently turned unto their Divine Benefactor and looked to Him for their daily bread. But instead of doing this we read, once more, "The whole congregation of the children of Israel *murmured* against Moses and Aaron" (16:3), and not only so, they "spake against God; they said, Can God furnish a table in the wilderness?" (Psl. 78:19). Yet, notwithstanding their petulency and unbelief, the Lord again came to their relief and rained down bread from Heaven. The remainder of the chapter is occupied with details concerning the manna.

Now, once more, the chapter before us for our present study, begins with "And." The opening verse presents to us a scene very similar to that which is found at the beginning of the previous chapter. Israel are once again face to face with a trial of faith. Their dependency upon God is tested. This time it is not lack of food, but absence of water. How this illustrates the fact that the path of faith is a path of trial. Those who are led by God must expect to encounter that which is displeasing to the flesh, and also a constant and real testing of faith itself. God's design is to wean us from everything down here, to bring us to the place where we have no reliance upon material and human resources, to cast us completely upon Himself. O how slow, how painfully slow we are to learn this lesson! How miserably and how repeatedly we fail! How *long*-suffering the Lord is with us. It is *this* which the introductory "And" is designed to point. Here in Exodus 17 it is but a tragic repetition of what it signifies at the beginning of chapter 16.

"And there was no water for the people to drink." What of that? This presented no difficulty to Him who could part the sea asunder and then make its waves return and overwhelm their enemies. It was no harder for Jehovah to provide water than it was for Him to supply them with food. Was not He their Shepherd? If so, shall they want? Moreover, had not the Lord Himself *led* Israel *to* Rephidim? Yes, for we are here expressly told, "The children of Israel journeyed according to *the commandment of the Lord,* and pitched in Rephedim." *He* knew there was *no* water there, and yet He directed them to this very place! Well for *us* to remember this. Ofttimes when we reach some particularly hard place, when the streams of creature-comfort are dried up, we blame ourselves, our friends, our brethren, or the Devil perhaps. But the first thing to realise in *every* circumstance and situation where faith is tested, is, that the Lord Himself has *brought us* there! If this be apprehended, it will not be so difficult for us to trust Him to *sustain* us while we remain there.

"Wherefore the people did chide with Moses, and said, Give us water that we may drink" (v. 2). The word "chide" signifies that the people expostulated with Moses in an angry manner for bringing them hither, reproaching and condemning him as the cause of their trouble. When they said to him, "Give us water that we may drink," it was either that they petulantly demanded *he* should give what God only could provide, signifying that he was under obligations to do so, seeing that he was the one who had brought them out of Egypt into the wilderness; or, because they had seen him work so many wonders, they concluded it was in *his* power to miraculously obtain water for them, and hence, insisted that he now do this.

"And Moses said unto them, Why chide ye with *me?* Wherefore do ye tempt *the Lord?*" (v. 2). Moses at once reminded the Israelites that in criticising him they arraigned the Lord. The word "tempt" in this verse seems to signify try or test. They tried His patience, by once more chiding His servant. They called into question both His goodness and faithfulness. Moses was their appointed leader, God's representative to the people; and therefore to murmur against him was to murmer against the Lord Himself.

"And the people thirsted there for water; and the people murmured against Moses, and said, Wherefore is this that thou hast brought us up out of Egypt, to kill us and our children and our cattle with thirst?" (v. 3). As their thirst increased they grew more impatient and enraged, and threw out their invectives against Moses. "Had Israel been transported from Egypt to Canaan they would not have made such sad exhibitions of what the human heart is, and, as a consequence, they would not have proved such admirable ensamples or types for us; but their forty years' wandering in the desert furnish us with a volume of warning, admonition, and instruction, fruitful beyond conception. From it we learn, amongst many other things, the unvarying tendency of the heart to distrust God. Anything, in short, for it but God. It would rather lean upon a cobweb of human resources than upon the arm of an omnipotent, all-wise, and infinitely gracious God; and the smallest cloud is more than sufficient to hide from its view the light of His blessed countenance. Well, therefore, may it be termed 'an evil heart of unbelief,' which will ever show itself ready to 'depart from the living God'" (C.H.M.).

"And Moses cried unto the Lord, saying, What shall I do unto this people? they be almost ready to stone me" (v. 14). It is beautiful to see that Moses made no reply to the cruel reproaches which were cast upon him. Like that Blessed One whom he in so many respects typified, "When He was reviled, He reviled not again; when He suffered, He threatened not; but committed Himself to Him that judgeth righteously" (I Peter, 2:23). This is what we see Moses doing here. Instead of returning an angry and bitter rejoinder to those who falsely accused him, he sought the Lord. Blessed example for us. This was ever his refuge in times of trouble (cf. 15:25, etc.). The fact that we are told Moses "*cried* unto the Lord" indicates the earnestness and vehemance of his prayer. "What shall I do?" expressed a consciousness of his own inability to cope with the situation, and also showed his confidence that the Lord would come to his and their relief. How often should we be spared much sorrowful regret later, if, instead of replying on the spur of the moment to those who malign us, we first sought the Lord and asked, "What shall I do?"

"And the Lord said unto Moses, Go on before the people, and take with thee of the elders of Israel; and thy rod, wherewith thou smotest the river, take in thine hand, and go. Behold, I will stand before thee there upon the rock in Horeb; and thou shalt smite the rock, and there shall come water out of it, that the people may drink. And Moses did so in the sight of the elders of Israel" (v. 5, 6). This brings before us one of the many Old Testament types of the Lord Jesus, one for which we have New Testament authority for regarding it as such. In 1 Cor. 10:1-4 we read, "Moreover, brethren, I would not that ye should be ignorant, how that all our fathers were under the cloud, and all passed through the sea; And were all baptised unto Moses in the cloud and in the sea; And did all eat the same spiritual meat; And did all drink the same spiritual drink; for they drank of that spiritual Rock that followed them: And *that Rock was Christ.*"

The "Rock" is one of the titles of Jehovah, found frequently on the pages of the O.T. In his "song," Moses laments that Israel forsook God and "lightly esteemed the *Rock* of his salvation" (Deut. 32:15). In his song, we also hear the sweet singer of Israel saying, "The Lord is my *Rock,* and my Fortress, and my Deliverer" (2 Sam. 22:2). The Psalmist bids us make a "joyful noise to the *Rock* of our salvation" (95:1). While the prophet Isaiah tells us "And a Man shall be as an hiding place from the wind, and a covert from the tempest as rivers of water in a dry place, as the shadow of *a Great Rock* in a weary land" (32:2). In the N.T. we get that memorable and precious word, "Upon *this Rock* (pointing to Himself, not referring to Peter's confession) I will build My church" (Matt. 16:18).

The first thing that impresses one when we see a rock is its *strength and stability,* a characteristic noted in Scripture in the question of Bildad to Job, "Shall the rock be removed out of his place?" (Job. 18:4). This is a most comforting thought to the believer. The Rock upon which he is built cannot be shaken: the floods may come, and the winds may beat upon it, but it will "stand" (Matt. 7:25).

Another prominent characteristic of rocks is their *durability.* They outlast the storms of time. Waters will not wash them away, nor winds remove them, from their foundations. Many a vessel has been dashed to pieces on a rock, but the rock stands unchanged; and it is a deeply solemn thought that those who are not *built* upon The Rock, will be *shattered* by it—"And whosoever shall fall on this Stone shall be broken," said Christ, pointing to Himself, "but on whomsoever it shall fall, it will grind him to powder" (Matt. 21:24).

A third feature that may be mentioned about a rock is its *elevation.* It towers high above man and is a landmark throughout that part of the country where it is situated. Some rocks are so high and so steep that they cannot be scaled. Each of these characteristics find their application to and realisation in the Lord Jesus. He is the strong and powerful One—"The *mighty* God" (Isa. 9:6). He is the durable One—"the *Same* yesterday and to-day and forever." He is the elevated One, exalted to the Throne of Heaven, seated at the right hand of the Majesty on high.

The first thing to be noted here in our type is that the rock was to be *smitten.* This, of course, speaks of the death of the Lord Jesus. It is striking to note the *order* of the typical teaching of Ex. 16 and 17. In the former we have that which speaks of the incarnation of Christ; in the latter, that which foreshadowed the crucifixion of Christ. Ex. 17 is supplementary to chapter 16. Christ must descend from Heaven to earth (as the manna did) if He was to become the Bread of life to His people; but He must be smitten by Divine judgment if He was to be the Water of life to them! Here is another reason for the opening "And."

There are three details here which enable us to fix the interpretation of the smiting of the rock as a type of *the death* of the Lord Jesus. First, it was to be smitten by the *rod* of Moses. The "rod" in the hand of Moses had been the symbol of *judgment.* The *first* reference to it definitely determines that. When he cast it on to the ground it became a "serpent" (4:3)—reminder of the *curse.* With his rod the waters of the Nile were smitten and turned into blood (7:17), and so on. Second, only the "elders of Israel" witnessed the smiting of the rock. This emphasises the *governmental* character of what was here foreshadowed. Third, Jehovah Himself stood upon the rock while it was smitten. "*Behold,* I will stand before thee *there* upon the rock in Horeb" (v. 6)—marvellous line in the picture was this. Putting these things together what spiritual eye can fail to see here a portrayal of our Substitute being smitten by the rod of Divine justice, held in the hand of the Governor of the Universe. Doubtless that word in Isa. 53:4, 5 looks back to this very type—"*Smitten* of God . . . . by His *stripes* we are healed." How solemn to behold that it was the people's *sin* which led to the smiting of the rock!

Out from the smitten rock flowed the water. Beautiful type was this of the *Holy*

Spirit—gift of the crucified, now glorified, Saviour. May not this be one reason why the Holy Spirit is said to be *"poured out"* (Act. 2:18)?—speaking in the language of this very type. The gift of the Holy Spirit was consequent upon the crucifixion and exaltation of the Lord Jesus. This is clear from His own words from John 7:37, 38: "Jesus stood and cried, saying, If any man thirst, let him come unto Me, and drink. He that believeth on Me, as the Scripture hath said, out of his belly shall flow rivers of living water." Now mark the interpretation which is given us in the very next verse: "But this spake He *of the Spirit,* which they that believe on Him should receive: for the Holy Spirit was not yet given because that Jesus was not yet glorified."

The Holy Spirit has given us a supplementary word through the Psalmist which enhances the beauty of the picture found in Exodus 17. There we are told, "He opened the rock, and the waters gushed out; they ran in the dry places like a river. *For He remembered* His holy promise (to) Abraham His servant" (105:41, 42). It was because of His covenant to Abraham that God gave the water to Israel. So, too, we read of God *promising* to give eternal life to His elect *"before* the world began" (Titus 1:1, 2), and this, on the basis of "the everlasting covenant" (Heb. 13:20).

1 Cor., 10, also supplements Ex. 17. In the historical narrative we read of Moses striking the rock in the presence of "the elders" of Israel, but nothing is there said about the people drinking of the streams of water that flowed from it. But in 1 Cor., 10:4, we are told, "And did *all* drink the same spiritual drink." This is an important word. It affirms, in type, that *all* of God's people have received the Holy Spirit. There are some who deny this. There are those who teach that receiving the Holy Spirit is a *second* work of grace. This is a serious error. Just as *all* the children of Israel (God's covenant people) drank of the water from the smitten rock, so, in the anti-type, *all* of God's children are made partakers of the Holy Spirit, gift of the ascended Christ—"And because ye are sons, God had sent forth the Spirit of His Son into your hearts, crying, Abba, Father" (Gal. 4:6). There is no such thing as a believer in Christ who has not received the Holy Spirit: "If any man have not the Spirit of Christ, he is none of Him" (Rom. 8:9).

Much of the blessedness of our type will pass unappreciated unless we note carefully *the occasion* when the stream of living water gushed from the smitten rock. It was not when Israel were bowed in worship before the Lord, it was not when they were praising Him for all His abundant mercies toward them. No such happy scene do the opening verses of Ex. 17 present to our view. The very reverse is what is there described. Israel were murmuring (v. 3); they were almost ready to stone God's servant (v. 4); they were filled with unbelief, saying, "Is the Lord among us, or not?" v. 7). The giving of the water, then, was God acting according to His marvellous grace. Where sin abounded, grace did much more abound. But, be it well noted, it was grace acting on a *righteous* basis. Not till the rock was *smitten* did the waters flow forth. And not till the Saviour had been bruised by God was the Gospel of His grace sent forth to "every creature." What, my reader, is the response of your heart to this amazing and rich mercy of God? Surely you say, out of deepest gratitude, "thanks be unto God for His unspeakable Gift" (2 Cor. 9:15).

This paper would not be complete were we to close without a brief word upon Num. 20, where we again find Moses smiting the rock. "And the Lord spake unto Moses, saying, Take the rod, and gather thou the assembly together, thou, and Aaron, thy brother, and speak ye unto the rock before their eyes, and it shall give forth His water, and thou shall bring forth to them water out of the rock; *so* thou shalt give the congregation and their beasts drink" (vv. 7, 8).

What is recorded in Num. 20 occurred forty years later than what has been before us in Ex. 17. Almost everything here is in sharp contrast. The rock in Ex. 17 foreshadowed Christ on the cross; the rock in Num. 20 pictured Him on high. The Hebrew word for "rock" is not the same. The word used here in Num. 20 means an *elevated* rock, pointing plainly to the Saviour in His exaltation. Next, we notice that Moses was *not* now bidden to "strike" the rock, but simply to *speak* to it. In Ex. 17 the rock was smitten before the "elders" of Israel; here Moses was bidden to "gather the assembly together." And while Jehovah bade him take a rod, it was not the rod used in Ex. 17. On the former occasion Moses was to use his *own* rod—"Thy *rod,* wherewith thou smotest the river." That was the rod of judgment. But here he was to take *"The* rod" (Num. 20:8), namely, the rod of Aaron. This is clear from verse 9, "And Moses took the rod *from before the Lord,* as He commanded him" if we compare it with Num. 17:10—"And the Lord saith unto Moses, Bring *Aaron's* rod again *before the testimony* (viz., the Ark in the Holy of Holies), to be kept for a token against the rebels." This, then, was the *priestly* rod. Mark also how this aspect of truth was further emphasised in the type by the Lord bidding Moses, on this second occasion, to take *Aaron* along with him—Aaron is *not* referred to at the first smiting of the rock!

The interpretation of the typical meaning of Num. 20:8 is therefore abundantly clear. The rock must not be *smitten* a second time, for that would spoil the type. "Knowing that Christ being raised from the dead *dieth no more;* death hath no more dominion over Him. For in that He died, He died unto sin *once; but in that He liveth, He liveth unto God.*" (Rom. 6:9, 10). "But now *once* in the end of the world hath He appeared to put away sin by the sacrifice of Himself . . . . So Christ was *once* offered to bear the sins of many" (Heb. 9:26, 28). Streams of spiritual refreshment flow to us on the ground of *accomplished* redemption and in connection with Christ's *priestly ministry.*

How solemn the sequel here. The servant of the Lord failed—there has been but one *perfect* "Servant" (Isa. 42:1). The meekest man upon earth became angry at the repeated murmurings of Israel. He addressed the covenant people of God as "Ye rebels." He asked them, "Must *we* fetch you water out of the rock?" He "*smote* the rock *twice*"—indicating the heat of his temper. And because of this God suffered him not to lead Israel into Canaan. He is very jealous of the types—more than one man was slain because his conduct marred them.

It is striking to note that though Moses smote the rock instead of speaking to it, nevertheless, the refreshing waters gushed forth from it. How this should warn us against the conclusion that a man's *methods* must be right if the Lord is pleased to *use* him. Many there are who imagine that the methods used in service *must* be pleasing to God if His blessing attends them. But this incident shows plainly that it is not safe to argue thus. Moses' methods were *wrong;* notwithstanding, God gave the blessing! But how this incident also manifests, once more, the wondrous grace of God. In spite of (not because of) Israel's murmuring, and in spite of Moses' failure, water *was* given to them, their every need was supplied. Truly, our God *is* the "God of *all* grace." May the realisation of this draw out our hearts in adoring worship, and may our lives rebound more and more unto His glory.

Arthur W. Pink.

AN EXPOSITION OF LUKE 15.

We now reach the third part of this wondrous and lovely parable. In the light of what has already been before us, there should be no difficulty whatever in identifying the one that is here in view. The Prodigal son does not represent a backslidden believer, but a sinner needing salvation. Let us first briefly present the proofs that it is *not* a backslider which is here pictured.

First, the whole context shows plainly the class that is portrayed throughout the entire chapter. In the second verse of Luke 15 we are told, "Then drew near unto Him all the publicans and sinners for to hear Him. And the Pharisees and Scribes murmured, saying, This man receiveth *sinners,* and eateth with them." Here then, Christ is seen in connection with the lost. It was in answer to this criticism of the Pharisees and Scribes that our Saviour proceeded to utter the parable which has brought life and peace to countless souls since then. And in this parable the Lord is not warning His disciples against the danger of backsliding, but is vindicating Himself for "receiving sinners."

That part of the parable which treats of what has been termed "the prodigal son" begins at the eleventh verse, but what we have here and in the verses that follow is only a continuation of what the Lord said as recorded in the preceding verses. In these previous verses He depicts a man going after a lost sheep until he finds it: and also a woman who loses one piece of silver, and who sweeps the house and seeks diligently until she finds it. Surely there can be no doubt whatever as to who is figured by the "*lost* sheep," and the "*lost* piece of silver." Is it not obvious that these picture an unsaved sinner and not a backslidden believer?

In the third place, the words which the "father" spoke when the wandering son returned, furnish another proof that it is a sinner and not an erring saint who is before us. Said he, "Bring forth the best robe, and put it on him" (v. 22). The "best robe" here speaks of the Robe of Righteousness which each sinner receives when he first comes to Christ (see Isa. 61:10). Had it been a backslidden believer, his need would be to have his feet "washed" (John 13).

Finally, the "father's" statement concerning his son is proof positive that it is no erring Christian that is here in view. The father said, "This my son *was dead,* and is alive again; he *was lost,* and is found" (v. 24). This is conclusive to all who believe that "the gifts and calling of God are without repentance" (Rom. 11:29). Every believer is in present possession of *eternal life,* which he has received from God as his "gift" (Rom. 6:23); and this "gift" is never recalled. If, then, the believer is in present possession of eternal life he can *never die* (see John 8:51). That the father spoke of the returning prodigal son as one who "was dead," and who "was lost," is proof positive that an unsaved sinner is here in view. Note how emphatic Christ makes this by *repeating* these words (vv. 24. 32)!

There is only one argument that is of any force against what we have said above, and that we will briefly consider. We are asked to explain how Christ could speak of this wanderer as a "son" if he represented an unsaved sinner. Insuperable as the difficulty appears at first sight, it is, nevertheless, capable of simple solution. We answer in a word that this wanderer who came to the "father" was *a son by election.* He was a son *in the purpose* of God. If we should be asked to point to a scripture which justifies such an assertion, where those of God's elect are termed "sons" *before* they are actually saved, we would at once refer to John 11:51, 52: "He prophesied that Jesus should die for that nation; and not for that nation only, but that also He should gather in one *the children of God* that were scattered abroad." Here we are told that the ones who were to definitely benefit from the death of Christ, and who should be "gathered together in one" (that is, into *one Family*), were, at that time, "scattered abroad," nevertheless, they were denominated "the children of God"! Another scripture which enunciates the same principle is John 10:16, where we find the Saviour declaring "Other *sheep* I have which are not of this fold: them also I must bring": even before they were brought to Himself the Good Shepherd terms them His *sheep.* So also the Lord said to the apostle Paul when he first went to Corinth, "I *have* much people in this city" (Acts 18:10).

In the first part of the parable we are shown what God the Son has done *for* lost sinners: in the second section we have pictured the work of God the Spirit *in* the sinner: in the closing section we learn the *result* of this—the sinner coming into the presence of the Father! This parable, then, tells us three things about the Godhead: the Shepherd's *toil,* the Spirit's *search,* and the *hearty welcome* which the Father gives to the sinner who repents and comes to Him.

This parable then tells us three things about the Godhead: the Shepherd's *toil,* the Spirit's *search,* and the *hearty welcome* which the Father gives to the sinner that comes back to Himself.

We are also taught three outstanding things in connection with *the sinner.* In the first part of the parable he is seen under the figure of a *sheep* that is *lost:* this intimates the stupidity of the sinner who, like a lost sheep, is *unable* to find his way back home, and who, if he is to be restored, must be *sought.* In the second part of the parable he is seen under the figure of a *coin* that is *lost:* here we have an *inanimate* object, in other words, that which accurately portrays the solemn fact that the sinner is spiritually *dead.* In the third part of the parable he is seen under the figure of a dissolute son, away in the *far country:* this gives us a representation of the natural man's moral condition: alienated from God and wayward at heart.

It is the third part of this parable which is now to engage our attention, that part of the parable which views the sinner coming into the presence of God. It is the *human side* that is now made prominent. Here we are shown the sinner's consciousness of his need: he "began to be in want." Here we are shown the sinner exercising his will: "I will arise." Here we are shown the sinner repenting: "I will say unto Him, Father, I have sinned against heaven, and before Thee, and am no more worthy to be called Thy son." But let it be borne in mind that *before* the sinner does any of these three things *God* has *previously* been at work upon and within him. Let us not forget that in this wonderful and blessed parable the Lord Jesus gives us *the Divine side first,* before He makes mention of the human side. Therefore, let those who desire to "follow His steps" give careful heed to this principle. We shall now consider

I. The Prodigal Himself.

1. He had a "substance" or "portion."

"A certain man had two sons: and the younger of them said to his father, Father, give me *the portion* of goods that falleth to me. And he divided unto them (his) *living"* (vv. 11. 12). In addition to our natural endowments or talents, and our time and strength, God has given to every one of His creatures a *soul.* This soul may be regarded as capital in hand with which to do our trading both for time and eternity. It is a most valuable portion, for it is worth more than "the whole world": it is worth more than the whole world because it will endure after the world and all its works have been *burnt* up.

The parable begins by bringing into view the sinner *before* he goes out into the "far country," or to use the language of the parable, before he "*took his journey* into a far country." It was while in the father's house that he received his "portion of goods," and that "he (the father) divided unto them (his) *living*," so that the portion received was a *living portion*. This can only refer to the creature, prior to his birth into this world, receiving from "the Father of Spirits" (Heb. 12:9) a "living soul." That he is here represented as *asking* for this "portion" emphasises his responsibility in connection with his soul.

2. He "took his journey into a far country," v. 13.

The "far country" is the world which is away from God, so far away that "the whole world lieth in the wicked one" (1 John 5:19). As the result of Adam's sin man was separated from God, and all of Adam's descendants enter this world "*alienated* from the life of God" (Eph. 4:18). There is a great gulf between the thrice holy God and the sinful creature which none but Christ can bridge. The sinner is away from God in his heart, in his thoughts, in his ways. How much this explains!

It explains Atheism. Atheism is simply man's attempt to hide from the discomforture of God's acknowledged presence. Men will give you many reasons as to why they are infidels, agnostics, and atheists, but these reasons are, in reality, only so many "excuses" (Luke 14:18): the real reason is that men are determined to get away from the avowed acknowledgement of God.

This explains the general neglect among men of the Bible. They will give you many reasons as to why they do not read it—they cannot find the time, there is much in it they cannot understand, and there are so many conflicting interpretations of its contents, and so they leave it alone. Men esteem the holy Word of God less highly than they do the writings of their fellow-sinners. And yet the Scriptures treat of many subjects of profound importance and vital moment: they furnish the *only* reliable information concerning the origin of man, the nature of man, the purpose of man's existence, and the life beyond the grave, etc., etc. Impelled by an uneasy conscience many will read a chapter in the Bible now and again, but that is all, and the real reason for this is because the Bible brings man into the presence of God, and *that* is the very last thing the natural man desires. What a proof is this, then, that he *is* in "the far country;" that at heart he is away from the Father!

This explains why it is that sinners, as such, have no delight in Prayer. Real prayer is a direct speaking to God through the mediation of Christ. It is that which brings us into contact and communion with the Great Invisible. But the sinner has no heart for this. He finds no enjoyment in pouring out his soul to God. If he prays at all, prayer is an irksome task and a mere repetition of words. He had rather do almost anything than pray, and the reason for this is because he wants to keep away from God.

This explains why it is that the sinner has no real delight in the public worship of God. It is true that he may go to church: a vague sense of duty may take him there, or it may be from force of habit acquired through a Christian upbringing, or it may be an uneasy conscience which renders him a punctual attendant. Nor is he always an uninterested hearer. When the preacher delivers his message with oratorical fire and with rhetorical embellishments that are pleasing to the ear, he is not only interested, but gratified. But let the preacher forget his rhetoric, let him leave his generalisations, let him address himself directly to the sinner's conscience, and say, "Thou art the man;" let him be brought into *the presence of God*, and the poor unsaved listener will at once be rendered uneasy, and it is more than doubtful whether he will return any more to hear *that* preacher.

3. He "wasted his substance with riotous living," v. 13.

As pointed out above, "the substance" is the *living soul* which every man receives from his Creator, and which is to be regarded as capital in hand with which to do his trading both for time and for eternity. And here is how the sinner, every sinner, uses the "portion" that he has received from the Father of spirits. He *squanders* it.

Let it be said emphatically that this "prodigal son" is not merely a representation of some particular class of sinners who are more wicked than their fellows, whose offences against God are more flagrant than the general run of sinners; but, instead, the "prodigal son" pictures the course that is followed by *every* descendant of Adam.

"And there wasted his substance with riotous living." From the hour of his birth the natural man has never cherished a single feeling, exercised a single thought, or performed a single deed that is acceptable to God. So far as eternity is concerned, he is spiritually barren: his life is *fruitless*. But not only has he ignored the claims of God, not only has he neglected the things of God, not only has he failed to love the Lord his God with all his heart, but he has squandered his time, misused his talents, and *lived entirely for himself*.

4. He encountered "a mighy famine."

"And when he had spent all, there arose a mighty famine in that land" (v. 14). "That land" is the "far country." It is the world, that world which is away from God, and which, in consequence, "lieth in the wicked one." And in that land there is *"a mighty famine"* all the while. It is to be noted, however, that we are told "there *arose* a mighty famine in that land." It was not so there, always. The famine "arose" when man became separated from God, i.e., at the Fall. The "famine" has reference to the fact that there is nothing whatever in this world that can minister to man's *soul*.

5. He "began to be in want," v. 14.

Here, in the history of a sinner who is saved eventually, is where hope begins. There are many living in this "far country" to-day where there is "a mighty famine," but the tragic thing is that they are *unconscious* of it. They are satisfied with what they find here. They are sensible of no need which this world fails to meet. It is only after *God* begins His work upon the soul that the sinner discovers that everything here is only "vanity and vexation of spirit." Happy the one who has reached this point. Happy the one who has begun "to be in want." Happy the one who is conscious of an aching void in his heart, of a yearning in his soul, of a need in his spirit, which the things of this world and the pleasures of sin have failed to satisfy. Such an one is "not far from the kingdom." Nevertheless, this beginning to be "in want" is but the initial experience. There are other experiences, painful ones, to be passed through *before* the sinner actually comes to God. Let us follow further the history of "the prodigal son," which so accurately traces the course pursued by each Christian before he was saved.

6. He "went and joined himself to a citizen of that country," v. 15.

How true to life! Notice he did not decide at once to return to his father—that he did not come until later. Instead of returning to the father, he *turned to man* for relief, and *went to work,* for as we read, "he (the citizen of that country) sent him into his field *to feed swine.*" Does the Christian reader need an interpreter here? Does not his own past experience supply the key to the meaning of v. 15? The beginning to be "in want" finds its counterpart in the first *awakening of the soul,* or to use other terms, it corresponds to *conviction of sin*. And when a soul has been awakened, when it has been convicted of sin, when it has been made conscious of a "want" not yet supplied, what does such an one invariably do? Did you, dear reader, turn *at once* to the Saviour? Not if your experience was anything like that of the writer and the vast majority of other Christians he has talked with. If your experience corresponds in anywise with his or theirs, after you were first awakened you began to attempt to work out a righteousness of your own, you betook yourself to the task of reformation, and to aid you in this you turned to man for counsel and help. And unless the sovereign grace of God overruled it, instead of seeking help from a real Christian who (if he had intelligence in the things of God) would at once have urged you to "search the Scriptures" to discover *God's remedy,* you turned to some professing Christian, who in reality was only a "citizen of *that* country"—the world. And if you turned to such an one he did for you precisely what we read here in the parable—he sent you "to feed swine." Allowing Scripture to interpret Scripture, the "swine" here represent professing Christians, who ultimately apostatize (see 2 Pet. 2:20-22). The one to whom you went for advice told you that what *you* needed to do was to engage in Christian service, "work for the Lord," "get busy in helping others"—and this, while you were still *dead* in trespasses and sins! Perhaps you were asked to teach a class of unsaved children in the Sunday School, or to be an officer of a young people's society (the majority of whom were, probably, like yourself—unsaved), and thus *"feed* the swine"!

7. He "came to himself."

"And he would fain have filled his belly with the husks that the swine did eat: and no man gave unto him. And when he came to himself, he said," etc. (vv. 16, 17). And again we say, How true to life! What did this joining of himself to a citizen of that country, and this working in the fields amount to? What relief did it bring to his hungry soul? Just nothing. All there was for him there were *"the husks* that the swine did eat." And what did all your labours as an awakened but unsaved sinner amount to? What relief did they afford your poor heart? None whatever. All your zeal and sacrifices in your so-called "Christian service" provided you with nothing but "husks," the same husks that the *swine* "did eat." And how pathetic are the words that follow next—"And *no man* gave unto him"! Ah, the need of the awakened sinner lies deeper than any "man" can reach unto. It is this lesson that the sinner must next be taught. He must learn to turn away from *man* and look unto Christ Himself. It is not until he does this that there will be any relief.

"And when he *came to himself."* This means that he had recovered his sanity, for previously he was "beside himself"—out of his mind. The Scriptures represent the sinner as suffering from *spiritual insanity,* and regeneration as the bestowment of a right mind. In Eph. 4:17, 18, the saints of God are exhorted to "walk not *as other Gentiles walk* in the vanity of their mind, having the understanding darkened, being alienated from the life of God, through the ignorance that is in them, because of the blindness of their heart." Again, in Mark 5, we have in the demoniac a type of the sinner in bondage to Satan, who, when delivered by our Lord, is seen "sitting, and clothed, and *in his right mind."* Finally, in 2 Tim. 1:7, the change which the new birth produces is described in the following terms: "For God has not given us the spirit of fear, but of power, and of love, and *of a sound mind."*

Insanity is the lack of capacity to think correctly, and to form proper estimates of ourselves and others. It is a suffering from various forms of hallucination. An unmistakable evidence of insanity is, that the one whose mind is deranged is quite *ignorant of the fact,* and suppose himself to be all right. What is true in the natural realm has its counterpart in the spiritual. The sinner's understanding is darkened; his mind is full of strange delusions; he is unable to arrive at correct conclusions; and what is the saddest part of it all is, that he is totally unconscious of his spiritual disease. But when the Holy Spirit of God has worked upon a man, these hallucinations are removed, the darkness is taken away from his understanding and, like the "prodigal," he "comes to himself."

8. He said, "I will arise and go to my father," v. 18.

It is not until after the sinner has been made to feel "the mighty famine" that exists in the far country, it is not until he has discovered that "no man" can give unto him, and it is not until he has "come to himself," that he begins to reason aright and remind himself that in his father's house there is "bread enough and to spare." And it is only then that he declares, "I will arise and go to my father," which means, it is only then that the will *begins* to move Godwards. And what is the next thing that we read? Why, that the prodigal not only determines to arise and go to his father, but he announces that he will "say unto him, Father, I have sinned against heaven and before Thee." In other words, he is now willing *to take the place* of a lost sinner before God. This is what repentance is.

9. He is still legalistic.

"I will say I have sinned against heaven, and before Thee, and am no more worthy to be called Thy son; make me as one of Thy hired servants" (vv. 18, 19). Applying the language of this to the history of the sinner coming to God, we here reach the point where, though the Holy Spirit has done much for the awakened one—discovering his need, enlightening his mind, directing his will, and producing conviction—the work of grace is not yet complete. The sinner is now deeply conscious of his own utter unworthiness, but not yet has he learned of the marvellous *grace* of God which more than meets his deep need. This comes out in the fact that the highest conception that the mind of the returning "prodigal" rose to was that of being made one of the *"hired* servants." How legalistic the mind of man is! How tenaciously he clings to his own performances! How strenuously he will contend for the need of bringing in his own doings! A "hired" servant" is one who has to *work* for all he gets.

10. He "arose and came to his father," v. 20.

Blessed be His Name, God does not cease His patient work within us until this point has been reached. Dull of comprehension though we are, our minds at enmity against Him, our wills essentially opposed to Him, He graciously perseveres with us until our understandings have been enlightened, our enmity has been removed, and our will so subdued that we arise and come to Him.

And what was the reception the prodigal met with? Do you know what portion was meted out to a "prodigal son" *under the Law?* Read with me the following passage: "If a man have a stubborn and rebellious son, which will not obey the voice of his father, or the voice of his mother, and that, when they have chastened him, will not hearken unto them: Then shall his father and mother lay hold on him and bring him out unto the elders of his city, and unto the gate of his place; And they shall say unto the elders of his city, This, our son, is stubborn and rebellious, he will not obey our voice; he is a glutton, and a drunkard. And all the men of his city shall *stone him with stones, that he die"* (Deut. 21:18-21). How then did the father receive *this* "prodigal?" And this brings us to consider:

II. The Prodigal's Reception.

How many an exercised heart has wondered what sort of a reception he would meet with if *he* came to God. Blessed it is to ponder the closing portion of the third part of this matchless parable. In expounding the significance of what is recorded of this "prodigal son" as he departed from the "father," we have seen portrayed the *representative* experiences of the sinner. As we turn now to the happy sequel, we shall see that what happened to him as he returned to the "father," also picture the representative experiences of the believer.

1. The Hearty Welcome he received.

"And he arose, and came to his father. But when he was yet a great way off his father saw him, and had compassion, and ran and fell on his neck, and kissed him" (v. 20). How inexpressibly blessed this is! Five things (the number of *grace*) are here predicated of "his father." First, when he was yet a great way off his father *"saw* him." And what does this tell us? Why, that the father was *looking out for him!* The father was eagerly waiting for him. And how keen are *love's* eyes! Even while he was yet a "great way off" his father saw him. But how solemnly this brings out the *distance* in which by nature we were from God! Even after the sinner has "come to himself," and turned his back upon the "far country," and has set his face homewards, he is "yet a *great way* off!" Nevertheless, all praise to His sovereign grace, "But in Christ Jesus ye who sometimes *were far off are made nigh* by the blood of Christ" (Eph. 2:13).

Second, his father *"had compassion."* The "prodigal" must have presented a miserable appearance: he had devoured his living with harlots, v. 30 (the *illicit love* for the things of the world, instead of loving God with *"all* our hearts"), he had suffered the effects of the "mighty famine," v. 14, and he had gone out into the fields to "feed swine," v. 15. What a pitiable object he must have been! Yet did his father have "compassion" on him! And, O dear Christian reader, how did you and I look just before the Father received us? Understandings darkened, hearts desperately wicked, wills rebellious, minds at enmity against Him, with *"no* good thing" in us! Nevertheless "God, who is rich in mercy, for His great love wherewith He loved us, *even when we were dead in sins,* hath quickened us together with Christ" (Eph. 2:4, 5).

Third, his father *"ran"* to meet him. We do not read of the "prodigal" *running* as he set out to return to his "father." All that is said of him is that "he arose, and came to his father." But of the "father" it is said that *he* "ran"! Do you know dear reader, that this is the only verse in all the Bible which represents God *as being in a hurry!* In the restoration of the ruined earth He acted orderly, we might say leisurely. In everything else but this, God is viewed as acting with calmness and deliberation, as befits One who has all eternity at His disposal. But here is what we may term the *impatience* of Divine Love.

Fourth, his father *"fell on his neck."* He not only "saw him" while a great way off, he not only had "compassion" on this woe-begone prodigal, he not only "ran" to meet him, but "fell on his neck;" he *embraced* him: he flung around him the welcoming arms of love.

Fifth, his father *"kissed* him." Once more we would point out that nothing is said here of the *son* kissing the father. It is the "father" who takes the lead at every stage! He "kissed" him, not rebuffed him. He "kissed" him, not bade him depart. He "kissed" him, not chided him for his wanderings. What marvellous grace! How all this *reveals the Father's heart!* The "kiss" speaks of love, of reconciliation, of intimate relationship.

2. The Prodigal's Response.

Notice now the "prodigal's" response. "And the son said unto him, Father, I have sinned against heaven, and in Thy sight, and am no more worthy to be called Thy son." Notice three things. First, he is deeply conscious of his *sinful condition,* and he hesitates not to confess it. And the nearer we approach the thrice holy God the clearer shall *we* perceive our vileness. Second, he was profoundly convinced of his *unworthiness,* and delayed not to own it. It is a discovery of the marvellous grace of God which brings us to a deeper realisation of how thoroughly undeserving we are, for grace and merit are as much opposed to each other as light and darkness. Third, observe that he says nothing now about being made a "*hired* servant!" No; the wondrous grace of the "father" had taught him better.

3. The Robe which was put upon him.

"But the father said to his servants, bring forth the best robe, and put it on him" (v. 22). There are four things to be noted here. First, the *position* the "son" yet occupied. We cannot but admire the marvellous accuracy and beauty of every line in this Divinely-drawn picture. The previous verses have shown us the happy meeting between the father and the son, the father's hearty welcome, and the son's broken-hearted confession. And this, be it remembered, is viewed as occurring *some distance away* from the father's house, for he "ran" out to meet him. Now, as the father and son draw near to the house, the father calls to his servants, and says, "*bring forth* the best robe." Ah, the "father" could not have the prodigal at *his* table in his filthy rags. No; that would be setting aside the righteous requirements of His House: "*Grace* reigns *through righteousness*" (Rom. 5:21), and never at the expense of it. Beautiful it is, then, to behold the *grace* which ran out to meet the "prodigal," and now the *righteousness* which makes provision for the covering of his filthy rags!

Second, we behold with thankful hearts the provision that is made for the poor wanderer. Note it carefully that the prodigal did not bring his "robe" with hi. out of the far country, nor did he procure it on his homeward journey. No, indeed; i' was provided *for* him. It was furnished by the "father." It was there *ready* for him, *waiting* for him!

Third, admire the *quality* of the clothing provided for him. Said the father, "Bring forth the *best* robe." What marvellous grace was this! The "best robe" in the father's house was reserved for the prodigal! And what can this signify but that the sinner saved by grace shall be robed in a garment *more glorious* than that worn by the unfallen angels! But, we exclaim, can such a thing be? Is that possible? Ah, dear reader, *what* is this "best robe?" Why, it is the *imputed righteousness of Christ Himself* which shall cover the filthy rags of our unrighteousness—that "imputed righteousness" which was wrought out for us in the perfect obedience and vicarious death of our Saviour. Read with me Isa. 61:10: "I will greatly rejoice in the Lord, my soul shall be joyful in my God; for He hath *clothed me* with *the garments of salvation,* He hath *covered me* with *the robe of righteousness.*" How remarkable it is to notice that this "best robe" was the *first* thing which the "prodigal" received at the hands of his Father! Right here is the answer to the objection made by those who reject the evangelical interpretation of this parable, for in the "best robe" we have that which speaks of the life and death of Christ.

Fourth, notice that the best robe was *placed upon him*—"Bring forth the best robe, and *put it on him*" (v. 22). *Everything was done FOR him.* Not only was the "best robe" *provided for* him, it was also *placed upon* him. How this reminds us of what we read in Gen. 3:21: "Unto Adam also and to his wife did the Lord God *make* coats of skins, *and clothed them.*" The Lord God not only Himself supplied those "coats of skins," but He "clothed" our first parents! We find the same thing again in Zech. 3—"Take away the filthy garments from him, and unto him he said, Behold, I have caused thine iniquity to pass from thee, and *I will clothe thee* with change of raiment" (Zech. 3:4). "O to grace *how great* a debtor!"

4. The Ring placed upon his hand.

"And put a ring on his hand" (v. 22). Again we notice that the ring was not supplied *by* him, but provided *for* him. And, too, it was not *handed to* him, but *put on* him! Not a thing did he do for himself. And of what does the "ring," put "on his hand," speak? The "ring" is the *seal* of love, of plighted troth. Later, it becomes the symbol of wedded *union.* And, is it not true that the returning sinner receives not only the "best robe" of Christ's imputed righteousness, but also God's *seal,* which "seal" is the Holy Spirit Himself—"Who hath *also sealed us,* and given the earnest of the Spirit in our hearts" (2 Cor. 1:22). Yes, the Holy Spirit is the seal of God's love, the evidence of a plighted troth, for, "grieve not the Holy Spirit, whereby ye are sealed *unto* the day of redemption" (Eph. 4:30). And, again, it is the Holy Spirit who *unites* us to Christ—"But he that is *joined* unto the Lord is one spirit" (1 Cor. 6:17). The "ring" also speaks of *ownership*—the woman who wears my ring does so as a sign that she is mine—my wife. So, too, the Holy Spirit in us tells that we *belong* to Christ—"If any man have not the Spirit of Christ, he is *none of His*" (Rom. 8:9). And once more, in Scripture the "ring" is given as a mark of *high* honour and esteem—"And Pharaoh took off his ring from his hand, and put it upon Joseph's hand, and arrayed him in vestures of fine linen, and put a gold chain about his neck . . . . and they cried before him, Bow the knee" (Gen. 41:42, 43). This "ring" which the "father" gave to the "prodigal" was *put on his hand*. Now, the hand speaks of labour. As, then, the "ring" is here the emblem of the Holy Spirit, does not this signify that, henceforth, all our works should be performed in the power of that same Spirit?

5. THE SHOES PROVIDED FOR HIS FEET.

"And shoes on his feet" (v. 22). Once more we are constrained to say, How marvellously complete is this lovely parabolic picture. Here we see *every* need of the believer met. The "kiss" of reconciliation to assure him of a hearty welcome; the "best robe" to cover his filthy rags; the "ring" put on his hand to show that he belongs to God, and to denote that his labours henceforth must be in the power of the Spirit. And now the "shoes" for his "feet" speak of God's provision for the *daily walk!*

In giving instructions to Moses concerning the observance of the Passover, the Lord said, "And thus shall ye eat it; with your loins girded, *your shoes on your feet*, and your staff in your hand" (Ex. 12:11). They were not prepared to go forth on their pilgrimage until "shoes" were on their feet. And how blessed is the sequel: forty years later Moses reminded them that though the Lord had led them for forty years in the wilderness—"Your clothes are not waxen upon you, and thy shoe is not waxen old upon thy foot!" So, again; when the Lord sent forth the twelve, He said to them, *be shod with sandals* (Mark 6:9). And in Eph. 6, where believers are exhorted to "put on the whole armour of God," one of the specifications is, "And your *feet shod* with the preparation of the Gospel of peace." Not until our feet are thus shod are we prepared to go forth with the Gospel of God's grace to a perishing world. It is exceedingly blessed to contrast these two passages: "Their feet (the wicked) *run to evil*, and they make hasfe to shed innocent blood" (Isa. 59:7); "How beautiful upon the mountains are the feet of him that *bringeth good tidings*, that publisheth peace; that bringeth good tidings of good, that publisheth salvation!" (Isa. 52:7).

6. THE FATTED CALF KILLED AND EATEN.

"And bring hither the fatted calf, and kill it: and let us eat, and be merry" (v. 23). First, note the contrast between the words of the "father" in connection with the "best robe," and here with the "fatted calf." In the former it was "bring forth," which indicated that the "prodigal" was then on the *outside*. But now that he has been clothed, now that he has had put on him the "best robe," now that he has been suitably adorned for the father's presence—"made us *meet* to be partakers of the inheritance of the saints in light" (Col. 1:12)—he is now *inside* the "father's" house, hence the "bring *hither*." How marvellously and minutely accurate!

The "*fatted* calf" speaks of Christ Himself in all His excellency, provided, too, by the Father. The *killing* of the "calf" tells of the Saviour's death for us, thus making it possible for sinners to be reconciled to a holy God. But the "fatted calf" was not only killed, it was like the Passover "lamb," to be *eaten*, and eating here speaks of *communion*. And observe the word of the "father" here: it was not "and let *him* eat," but "let *us* eat." It is the Father with the now reconciled sinner coming together, and they communing together over that which speaks of *Christ*. It is the sacrifice of Christ which is the *ground* of our fellowship with the Father.

7. THE RESULTANT JOY.

"And let us eat, *and be merry*: for this my son was dead, and is alive again; he was lost, and is found. And they began to be merry" (vv. 23, 24). How inexpressably blessed is this! What a glorious climax. Here is the prodigal, now a son at the Father's table, a place—not among the "hired servants," but in the Father's family is now his. Together they commune over that which tells of Christ, the perfect One, slain for us. And what is the *fruit* of "communion"? Is it not *joy*, such merriment of heart of which this poor world knows nothing. And note again the plural number: it is not only that "he," the son, was "merry," but "*they* began to be merry." The Father finds *His* delight, together with His children, feeding upon Christ the Son.

It is indeed striking to contrast what is before us here in Luke 15 with another scene presented in the Old Testament Scriptures. In 1 Sam. 28 we have brought before us the apostate Saul and the Witch of Endor—a greater contrast could not be imagined! And here, too, we read of a fatted calf being killed, *but how great the difference!* "And the woman had a fat calf in the house; and she hasted, and killed it, and took flour, and kneaded it, and did bake unleavened bread thereof. And she brought it before Saul, and before his servants; and they did eat. Then they rose up, and went away that night" (1 Sam. 28:24, 25). Yes, they did "eat," but notice that nothing was said of *them* being "merry." No, indeed. They represented that large company found among the profest people of God, who take the name of Christ on their lips, and even go through the form of communing with Him as they come to His "table." But after all, it is only a pretence, a mechanical performance. Their hearts are not in it. Their *souls* do not feed upon Christ.

And note, too, another striking contrast. Of Saul and his servants it is said, "They did eat. Then they rose up and *went away* that NIGHT" (1 Sam. 28:25). Ah, solemn thought, unspeakably solemn. The formal professor rises from the "table" and goes *away—leaves* that which speaks of Christ; goes away as joyless and empty as he came; goes away into that dark "night" which shall never end.

But how entirely different is what we read of concerning the reconciled "prodigal"! He, together with his father, sits down to eat of the fatted calf and "they began to be merry." And *there* the picture leaves them! Nothing is said about going "away," still less is there any reference to the "night." And "they *began* to be merry," and that merriment is only just begun. Blessed be God it shall know no ending. Together with the Father, finding our joy in Christ, we shall be "merry" *for ever and ever.*

By comparing carefully six clauses it will be found they are arranged in couplets, and each couplet points a striking contrast. First, we read "There *arose* a mighty famine in the land" (v. 14): now contrast what we read in v. 20, "And HE *arose,* and came to his father." Second, "He *came to himself*" (v. 17): now contrast what is said in v. 20, he *"Came to his Father."* Third, "He *began to be in want*" (v. 14): now contrast what we have in v. 24, "And they *began to be merry.*" And how striking is the order of these.

Now, dear reader, is this intelligible to you, or have we been speaking in an unknown tongue? Have *you* felt the "famine" of this world? Have you been "in want"—your soul crying out for a satisfying portion? Have you "come to yourself," come to your senses, and discovered the "exceeding sinfulness of sin"? If so, have you come to God and taken the place of a lost sinner before Him? Have you cast yourself upon His sovereign grace and received as your own this wondrous Provision He has made for hell-deserving sinners? If you have, then you know the blessedness of belonging to God's family. If you have not, and will come to God now, just as you are, confessing your utter sinfulness and unworthiness, and casting yourself on His free grace, you, too, shall receive a hearty welcome, the kiss of reconciliation, the robe of righteousness, and a place in communion with God Himself. "Come, for all things are now ready."

N.B.—We have had this Exposition of Luke 15 printed in a booklet so that those who wished to do so may obtain it in separate form and send it to their friends. Its message is much needed to-day. We can supply it for 9d. a copy post paid, or 6/- per dozen. We trust that many will avail themselves of this opportunity to scatter the good Seed. Australian subscribers, please order from the Editor.

American subscribers, kindly note that our Honorary Agent, Mr. C. S. Pressel, 559 Dupont Avenue, York, PA., can fill their orders. He has this booklet in two sizes. The whole of the Exposition of Luke 15 at 20 cents a copy; the latter half on "The Prodigal Son" at 10 cents.

He who loved us from before the foundation of the world has immutably determined all the steps of our pilgrimage. Wherefore then disturb thyself? There is a hand upon the helm, which shall steer thy vessel safely enough between the rocks and by the quicksands and away from the shoals and headlands, through the mists and through the darkness, safely to the desired haven. Our Pilot never sleeps, and His hand never relaxes its grasp.—Adopted from "Scripture Truth."

RENEW! IT'S DUE!! THANK YOU!!!

THE LAW AND THE SAINT.

The third use of the law, which is the principal one, and which is more nearly connected with the proper end of it, relates to the faithful, in whose hearts the Spirit of God already lives and reigns. For although the law is inscribed and engravened on their heart by the finger of God—that is, although they are so excited and animated by the direction of the Spirit, that they desire to obey God—yet they derive a twofold advantage from the law. For they find it an excellent instrument to give them, from day to day, a better and more certain understandign of the Divine will to which they aspire, and to confirm them in the knowledge of it. As, though a servant be already influenced by the strongest desire of gaining the approbation of his master, yet it is necessary for him carefully to inquire and observe the orders of his master, in order to conform to them. Nor let any one of us exempt himself from this necessity; for no man has already acquired so much wisdom, that he could not by the daily instruction of the law make new advances into a purer knowledge of the Divine will.

In the next place, as we need not only instruction, but also *exhortation*, the servant of God will derive this further advantage from the law; by frequent meditation on it he will be excited to obedience, he will be confirmed in it, and restrained from the slippery path of transgression. For in this manner should the saints stimulate themselves, because, with whatever alacrity they labor for the righteousness of God according to the Spirit, yet they are always burdened with the indolence of the flesh, which prevents their proceeding with due promptitude. To this flesh the law serves as a whip, urging it, like a dull and tardy animal, forwards to its work; and even to the spiritual man, who is not yet delivered from the burden of the flesh, it will be a perpetual spur, that will not permit him to loiter. To this use of the law David referred, when he celebrated it in such remarkable encomiums as these: "The law of the Lord is perfect, converting the soul: the statutes of the Lord are right, rejoicing the heart: the commandment of the Lord is pure, enlightening the eyes" (Psa. 19:7, 8). Nor are these assertions repugnant to those of Paul, in which he shows, not what service the law renders to the regenerate, but what it can bestow upon man merely of itself; whereas the Psalmist in these passages celebrates the great advantage derived through the Divine teaching, from the reading of the law, by those whom God inspires with an inward promtitude to obedience. And he adverts not only to the precepts, but to the promise of grace annexed to their performance, which alone causes that which is bitter to become sweet. For what would be less amiable than the law, if by demands and threats it only distressed the mind with fear, and harassed it with terror? But David particularly shows, that in the law he discovered the Mediator, without whom there is nothing pleasant or delightful.

Some unskilled men, being unable to discern this distinction, rashly explode Moses altogether, and discard the two tables of the law; because they consider it improper for Christians to adhere to a doctrine which contains the administration of death. Far from us be this profane opinion; for Moses has abundantly taught us that the law, which in sinners can only produce death, ought to have a better and more excellent use in the saints. For just before his death he thus addressed the people: "Set your hearts unto all the words that I testify among you this day, which ye shall command your children to observe, to do all the words of this law. For it is not a vain thing for you; because it is your life" (Deut. 32:46, 47). But if no one can deny that the law exhibits a perfect model of righteousness, either we ought to have no rule for an upright and just life, or it is criminal for us to deviate from it. For there are not many rules of life, but one, which is perpetually and immutably the same. Wherefore, when David represents the life of a righteous man as spent in continual meditations on the law (Psa. 1:2), we must not refer it to one period of time only, because it is very suitable for all ages, even to the end of the world. Let us neither be deterred, therefore, nor fly from its instructions, because it prescribes a holiness far more complete than we shall attain, so long as we remain in the prison of the body. For it no longer exercises towards us the part of a rigorous exactor, only to be satisfied by the perfect performance of every injunction; but in this perfection, to which it exhorts us, it shows us a goal, to aim at which, during the whole of our lives, would be equally conducive to our interest and consistent with our duty; in which attempt it is happy for us if we fail not. For the whole of this life is a course, which, when we have completed, the Lord will grant us to reach that goal, towards which at so great a distance our efforts are now vigorously directed.

Now, because the law, in regard to the faithful, has the force of an exhortation, not to bind their consciences with a curse, but by its frequent admonitions to arouse their indolence, and reprove their imperfection—many persons, when they design to express this liberation from its curse, say that the law (I still speak of the moral law) is abrogated to the faithful; not that it no longer enjoins upon them that which is right, but only that it ceases to be to them what it was before—no longer terrifying and confounding their consciences, condemning and destroying them. And *such* an abrogation of the law is clearly taught by Paul. It appears also to have been preached by our Lord, since He would not have refuted the opinion concerning His abolishing the law, unless it had prevailed among the Jews. Now, as this opinion could not prevail without any pretext, it is probable that it proceeded from a false interpretation of his doctrine; in the same manner as almost all errors have usually taken some colour from the truth. But lest we ourselves fall into the same error, let us accurately distinguish *what* is abrogated in the law, and what *still remains* in force. When the Lord declares that He came "not to destroy the law, but to fulfill it," and that "till heaven and earth shall pass, one jot or one tittle shall in no wise pass from the law, till all be fulfilled" (Matt. 5:17, 18) He sufficiently proves that His advent would detract nothing from the observance of the law. And with sufficient reason, since the express end of His advent was to heal the transgressions of it. The doctrine of the law remains, therefore, through Christ, inviolable; which by tuition, admonition, reproof, and correction, forms and prepares us for every good work.

The assertions of Paul respecting the abrogation of the law evidently relates, not to the instruction itself, but to the power of binding the conscience. For the law not only teaches, but authoritatively requires, obedience to its commands. If this obedience be not yielded, and even if there be any partial deficiency of duty, it hurls the thunderbolt of its curse. For this reason the apostle says, that "As many as are of the works of the law are under the curse; for it is written, cursed is every one that continueth not in all things" (Gal. 3:10). Now, he affirms those to be "of the works of the law," who place not their righteousness in the remission of sins, by which we are released from the rigor of the law. He teaches us, therefore, that we must be released from the bondage of the law, unless we would perish in misery under it. But what bondage? The bondage of that austere and rigid exaction, which remits nothing from its strictest requirements, and permits no transgression to pass with impugnity; I say, Christ, in order to redeem us from *this* curse, was "made a curse for us. For it is written, Cursed is every one that hangeth on a tree" (Gal. 3:13). In the following chapter, indeed, he tells us that Christ was "made under the law, to redeem them that were under the law"; but in the same sense; for he immediately adds, "that we might receive the adoption of sons" (Gal. 4:4, 5). What is this? That we might not be oppressed with a perpetual servitude, which would keep our consciences in continual distress with the dread of death. At the same time this truth remains for ever unshaken, that the law has sustained no diminution of its authority, but ought always to receive from us the same veneration and obedience.

—John Calvin (Institutes), 1536.

THE TWO NATURES.

The more excellent a mere natural man is, the less of evil is he conscious of possessing. Not so the child of God; for the more spiritually-minded he becomes, the more conscious he is of his imperfections, and of his utter inability of himself for anything good before God. This is the only feature in the child of God which has no natural imitation. There may be a natural faith in Christ, a natural love for Christ, a natural following of Christ, and a natural conviction of utter inability for anything good before God. This is entirely and always the result of a spiritual nature previously given. The more a mere natural man has of natural religious regard for the Lord Jesus, the more satisfied he is with himself; whereas, the more there is of spiritual regard for the Lord Jesus, the more there is of increased dissatisfaction with self. . . . The natural man has no new spiritual nature, with its spiritual principles, whereby to judge the natural, and therefore the natural judging the natural, he is right well pleased. The child of God, however, posesses a new spiritual nature, whereby, with its spiritual principles, he can judge the natural that is in him. He only is able to have a right understanding of the natural; and the more healthy the manifestation of the spiritual nature, the more deep and vivid is the consciousness of the evil of the mere natural.

—Things to Come, 1899.

(*Continued from page 265.*)

Scriptures more diligently for themselves; may they continue doing so, that their faith may not stand "in the wisdom of men, but in the power of God" (1 Cor. 2:5).

Mr. G. E. Ardill, Hon. Director of the Evangelisation Society of N.S.W., has been a staunch friend. Through his influence and by his kind efforts we have held Bible campaigns in seven different churches. He has gone to much trouble in making these known, and we wish to record here our deep appreciation for his generous and continued co-operation and help. When others have turned from us, he has stood by us. Mr. Ardill was the first to interest himself in connection with our proposed visit to this country, and, humanly speaking, it was through his paving the way that we ever came to Australia. We are deeply indebted to him: may the Lord Himself reward for all he has done on our behalf.

As the outcome of the various campaigns we have been brought into touch with many hungry souls who are getting little spiritual food in most of the churches. A letter to hand this morning—a sample of many we have received– contains this pathetic sentence: "It seems terrible that hungry hearts are sent away empty from most churches." O what an account will many an unfaithful pastor yet have to render to the One whom he now professes to serve! How solemn to think that each of those men who *say* they believe in God's Sovereignty and Divine Election, but who *have not courage* to preach these fundamental truths, will yet have to stand before Him who has said, "Ye shall not *add* unto the Word which I command you, neither shall ye *diminish ought* from it" (Deut. 4:2)!

To feed the needy and starved sheep of Christ is our fondest desire. In order for this we organised, the beginning of October, Bible-study Classes in three different centres, one night each week, where we are taking up the Gospel of John and going through it verse by verse. We covet the prayers of all our Christian readers for God's rich blessing on these meetings. In addition, we are supplying the pulpit of the Strict and Particular Baptist Church, Sydney, each Lord's day. Here there is a company of God's people who yearn for "*all* the counsel of God" to be delivered unto them; a company whom, though despised by the modern Pharisees, plainly bear the marks of God's favoured ones.

We have no plans for the future. How long the Lord will have us go on in our present path we know not—our times are in His hands. God willing, "Studies in the Scriptures" will be published during 1926. As soon as we have sufficient subscribers to justify it we shall reduce the price. We desire no financial gain, it being published as a labour of love. But we do long to see this magazine reach a greater number of needy souls, especially those in rural and isolated places. Do *you* not know of lonely Christians who would value it? If so, "Go your way, eat the fat, and drink the sweet, and *send portions* unto them for whom nothing is prepared" (Neh. 8:10)! We trust that all who have received help from this magazine will at least speak of it to their fellow-Christians.

All subscriptions expire with the December issue. It will be a great help to us if our subscribers will renew *promptly*—delay makes it very difficult to know how many copies to order in advance from the printer, so please do not put it off to another day. If you wait too long we may not be able to supply the January number. American friends please remit to Mr. C. S. Pressel, 559 Dupont Street, York, Pennsylvania. Early in the new year, D.V., Mr. Pressel will be able to supply all except in Australia with bound volumes of the 1925 issues at $1.65 post paid. Australian subscribers can obtain same from the Editor for 7/6 post paid. If subscribers here desire to have their 1925 copies bound, please forward to us not later than December 12, with their name written on the front page of each number, and we will have them bound and mailed back for 2/6—cost price.

This Magazine is being sent out free to over 300 Missionaries who, in their loneliness, value its monthly visits and messages. Those desiring to have fellowship in this work may forward their gifts to the Editor. If our friends know of any other Missionaries whom they feel sure would appreciate and read "Studies in Scriptures," kindly send us their name and address, and we will add them to our free list.

Wishing all our friends a Merry Christmas and a Prosperous New Year.

Yours by Divine grace, *Arthur W. Pink.*

9 781589 602144

www.ingramcontent.com/pod-product-compliance
Lightning Source LLC
LaVergne TN
LVHW020514100826
845148LV00010B/1233

* 9 7 8 1 5 8 9 6 0 2 3 1 1 *